The
BIRDS of
AFRICA
Volume I

The BIRDS of AFRICA
Volume I

LESLIE H. BROWN
Karen, Kenya

EMIL K. URBAN
Department of Biology, Augusta College,
Augusta, Georgia, USA

KENNETH NEWMAN
Benmore, Transvaal, South Africa

Illustrated by
Martin Woodcock and Peter Hayman

1982

ACADEMIC PRESS
A Subsidiary of Harcourt Brace Jovanovich, Publishers
London · New York
Paris · San Diego · San Francisco · São Paulo · Sydney · Tokyo · Toronto

ACADEMIC PRESS INC. (LONDON) LTD.
24/28 Oval Road, London NW1

United States Edition published by
ACADEMIC PRESS INC.
111 Fifth Avenue
New York, New York 10003

Brown, Leslie, *1917–1980*
The birds of Africa.
Vol. 1
1. Birds—Africa
I. Title   II. Urban, Emil K.
III. Newman, Kenneth
598.296   QL692.A1

ISBN: 0–12–137301–0
LCCCN: 81–69594

Text filmset by Northumberland Press Ltd, Gateshead, Tyne and Wear and printed by Fletcher and Son Ltd, Norwich.
Colour originated and printed by W. S. Cowell Ltd, Ipswich.

FOREWORD

In 1969 I was fortunate enough to be able to visit the Rift Valley lakes of Ethiopia and to watch and photograph some of the very large number of species of birds that are either resident in that area or pass through it on their migrations. Our creature comforts were assured by the kindness of the Emperor Haile Sellassie who generously arranged the camp facilities.

The organizer, guide and mentor on that expedition was Leslie Brown and also present was Emil Urban. Their knowledge of the birds of Africa and their infectious enthusiasm was so remarkable at the time that I was not in the least surprised to hear of their plan to produce a comprehensive and authoritative book on the birds of Africa. Sadly Leslie Brown did not live to see the completion of the first volume, but I am sure that it was his inexhaustible energy and driving spirit that inspired his co-authors and all the collaborators to go on with the task.

This is to be the first of four volumes and when the series is complete some 1850 species of African birds will be beautifully and accurately described and recorded in word and picture. The series will be a monument to Leslie Brown and I have no doubt that it will take its place among the classic ornithological publications of the world.

H.R.H. THE DUKE OF EDINBURGH

PREFACE

Information about African birds is at present scattered through a large, expensive, often unobtainable and now largely out-of-date quantity of books; through the ornithological journals of British, American, French, German, South African and many other societies; and in such unpublished material as nest record card schemes, collections of migration data and postgraduate theses. Much unpublished information has also existed up until now in our personal notes and those of many others.

It has therefore been our aim in compiling this work to gather together the available material from all these sources and to produce therefrom a definitive handbook of the birds of the continent of Africa and its off-shore islands. In order to cover the some 1850 species concerned in four volumes, it has inevitably been necessary to cut wordage to a minimum and thus some well-known and much-studied species have had to be treated in far less detail than would have been ideal. Nevertheless, we believe that we have always included the most important information on each species and have produced not a leisurely, discursive piece of ornithological literature but a compressed compendium of essential facts. Every species occurring in the continent of Africa, whether resident, migrant or vagrant, is to be covered and nearly all of these will be illustrated in colour.

Our competence to prepare this work stems primarily from our practical field experience (over 80 years between us) in many parts of Africa. We have each been individually responsible for writing texts on specific families, aided by comments from each other and, in addition, by much advice from recognized experts on different groups. We are deeply grateful to those who have given help and information in this and other ways and have (we sincerely hope) cited them all in the Acknowledgements (p. ix).

We hope that this work will fill the very definite need which exists for a comprehensive handbook on the birds of Africa. We also hope that its publication will pinpoint subjects and species worthy of further study and that it will thus stimulate much-needed research on the avifauna of this fascinating continent.

April 1980

Leslie H. Brown
Emil K. Urban
Kenneth Newman

For years Leslie Brown had a very special goal—to write *the* book on the birds of Africa. I became involved in this during one of Leslie's visits to Ethiopia when we agreed that I would write part of the envisioned work with him. The project became a reality in September 1978 when we, with Ken Newman and Academic Press, began work on it. Sadly Leslie never saw the book in final form, for he died suddenly of a heart attack in his home in Karen, Kenya, on 6 August 1980. To ensure that the project would continue, I assumed his responsibilities as senior author.

Before his death, Leslie had organized the plates for Volumes I and II and had written much of the Introduction and the species accounts on the Ostrich, grebes, tropicbirds, frigatebirds, storks, Hamerkop, Shoebill, flamingoes and diurnal birds of prey. All three of us commented on all the species accounts, except those for geese, swans and ducks which were prepared after Leslie's death. The remainder of the work to be done on his sections (some writing but mainly the compilation of references, preparation of maps and checking of proofs and illustrations) was carried out by myself for the Introduction and Ostrich through flamingoes, and by Alan Kemp for the birds of prey. David Snow, Stuart Keith, Hilary Fry, Gerard Morel and Kai Curry-Lindahl have been helpful in many ways, especially in checking proofs and finalizing the Introduction. It is my sincere hope that all the people who assisted Leslie Brown have been recognized; I apologize to those I may have missed.

The literature has been covered, as far as possible, up to July 1980. A few significant references from the remaining part of 1980 and from 1981 have also been included. We were able to determine Leslie's key references which appear in the text and at the end of the species accounts. We were not, however, able to determine any other of his references that were to appear in Part 2 of the Bibliography at the end of this volume.

Leslie's untimely death has necessitated a reorganization of the structure of Volumes II–IV. These volumes are being written by a wide range of ornithologists under the editorship of myself, Hilary Fry and Stuart Keith. The format for these volumes will remain unchanged from that devised for Volume I, and a fifth volume on the Malagasy region is under active discussion.

I am very grateful to all who have helped in the preparation and publication of this volume.

October 1981
Augusta, Georgia

Emil K. Urban

ACKNOWLEDGEMENTS

We are extremely grateful for the considerable co-operation given to us in reviewing our texts, in providing unpublished records, and in proffering the help and encouragement so necessary in seeing this volume through to publication. All of our accounts were read and critically commented on by many experts. It was not possible, however, to determine with much accuracy who had read which of Leslie Brown's drafts and we apologize to those who may have helped but whose contributions we have not been able to ascertain. We know that they were read at least by the following: B. C. R. Bertram, R. K. Brooke, J. F. Colebrook-Robjent, J. Cooper, T. M. Crowe, K. Curry-Lindahl, A. W. Diamond, R. J. Dowsett, S. K. Eltringham, L. M. Hurxthal, A. C. Kemp, M. P. Kahl, J. A. Ledger, G. L. Maclean, J. M. Mendelsohn, G. J. Morel, P. J. Mundy, D. E. Pomeroy, W. R. Siegfried, P. R. B. Steyn, W. R. Tarboton, J.-M. Thiollay and R. T. Wilson. In addition, C. W. Benson, P. L. Britton, K. Curry-Lindahl, A. W. Diamond, H. Elliott, S. K. Eltringham, C. H. Fry, A. Guillet, D. N. Johnson, A. C. Kemp, G. S. Keith, G. J. Morel, D. E. Pomeroy, K. E. L. Simmons, D. W. Snow, J.-M. Thiollay and G. E. Watson helped in the preparation of his maps, in determining the references to his species accounts and Introduction, and in providing measurements. Also, R. W. Storer assisted in grebe classification. Leslie had often mentioned how grateful he was to D. W. Snow at the Sub-department of Ornithology, British Museum (Natural History), Tring, UK, and W. R. Siegfried at the Percy Fitzpatrick Institute for African Ornithology, Cape Town, South Africa, for their co-operation and the use of their facilities; to R. D. Chancellor, H. Elliott and D. Amadon for their companionship and hours spent talking about the birds of Africa; and to Charles, his late son, and Barbara, his wife, for their assistance, encouragement and support.

Emil Urban's maps and texts were critically examined in draft form by the following: H. H. Berry, J. Cooper and G. S. Keith (*Phalacrocorax*), A. Brosset (*Bostrychia, Tigriornis*), H. Elliott (*Ardea, Ardeola, Egretta*), R. de Naurois and D. Whitelaw (*Platalea*), U. Hirsch and D. E. Manry (*Geronticus*), M. P. S. Irwin (*Egretta*), M. P. Kahl (Threskiornithidae), D. H. Mock (*Ardea, Egretta*), O. T. Owre (*Anhinga*), A. Prigogine (*Ardeola*), W. R. Siegfried (Ardeidae, especially *Bubulcus*), W. R. Tarboton (*Ardeola, Botaurus, Butorides, Egretta, Gorsachius, Ixobrychus, Nycticorax*) and D. N. S. Tomlinson (*Ardea, Egretta*).

Ken Newman's maps and texts were critically examined in draft form by the following: R. K. Brooke (*Diomedea, Macronectes*), A. Clark (Anatidae), J. Cooper (Sphenisciformes), I. N. Geldenhuys (*Tadorna, Alopochen*), M. J. F. Jarvis (*Sula capensis*), G. S. Keith (Procellariiformes, Sulidae), J. B. Nelson (Sulidae), P. Palmes (Anseriformes), R. Randall (*Spheniscus demersus*), M. K. Rowan (*Anas undulata*), W. R. Siegfried (*Anas*), J. C. Sinclair (Procellariiformes), D. M. Skead (*Anas*), W. R. Tarboton (*Nettapus auritus*), J. M. Winterbottom (*Anas capensis*) and E. A. Zaloumis (*Nettapus, Plectropterus, Sarkidiornis*).

The late Charles Brown, W. R. Siegfried, R. K. Brooke and many others extracted data from the South African Ornithological Society nest record cards; we are very grateful to them and also to the Society for its co-operation in this and other ways. M. S. Irwin allowed us to photocopy his bibliography card index on the birds of Africa, while P. W. P. Browne kindly supplied a list of the birds of Mauritania specifically for our use. The Reese Library of Augusta College, Augusta, Georgia, USA obtained much of the inter-library loan material and provided office space to Leslie Brown during his annual visits. Augusta College Foundation provided financial assistance in obtaining this material, and P. Allen, J. S. Ash, I. L. Brisbin, R. K. Brooke, N. A. Bryant, P. R. Colston, I. L. Gibson, R. Hilton, J. Hinshaw, A. Howe, E. D. H. Johnson, P. Kinghorn, I. Marshall, M. Minot, U. Newman, R. B. Payne, R. W. Schreiber, G. Underhill, L. L. Urban, C. J. Vernon and G. E. Watson helped in many ways.

We are delighted to have worked with Martin Woodcock and Peter Hayman on this volume who have produced the excellent colour plates and also some of the black and white illustrations for the book. Thanks are also due to all those who kindly gave permission for us to reproduce drawings from other publications. Both artists were greatly helped by the wealth of material, especially skins, made available to them by the British Museum at Tring, UK.

We would like to acknowledge the efforts of the board of advisers, and all at Academic Press, London, but especially Jennie Morley there for her very major part in making this volume a reality.

To all above we are most grateful.

Emil K. Urban
Kenneth Newman

CONTENTS

BIBLIOGRAPHY

INDEXES

LIST OF PLATES

Plates 1–17 painted by Peter Hayman and Plates 18–32 by Martin Woodcock

INTRODUCTION

1. The Main Features of African Bird Faunas

1.1 The Geological Past

It may be considered curious to begin a discussion of present-day African bird faunas with a note on the geological past. However, available information indicates that what happened long ago, especially perhaps within the last million years or so, had a profound effect on the distribution of various habitats in Africa, and accordingly on the evolution and distribution of the bird faunas associated with these habitats. In particular, alternating periods of aridity and moister climates caused deserts and forests to expand or contract. These changes had far-reaching effects on the bird fauna of Africa and still affect its character and composition today. Some idea of past events is therefore desirable as a background to present-day conditions.

Africa has been approximately the same shape for at least the last 100 million years, but has had overland connections with other land masses only within the last 20 million years. About 12 million years ago, vast areas of southern and eastern Africa were uplifted by some 1300 m, and extensive volcanic activity created the high peaks of Ethiopia and East Africa. Much of what is now the Congo Forest in Zaïre was then submerged by an enormous lake. About 10–11 million years ago, this lake was drained by the river, which 'captured' it by erosion from the west. Within the last million years or so the development of the Rift Valley in Northeast and Central Africa produced the huge troughs now occupied by Lake Tanganyika, Lake Malawi and others. Lake Victoria was formed between its two arms. Large new volcanoes arose in the neighbourhood of the Rift Valley, and also in the Central Sahara, in Tibesti. This period was one of violent tectonic activity; in which most of the more spectacular topographic features of present-day Africa were formed.

At the same time, a succession of glaciations in the Northern Hemisphere was accompanied by widespread changes of climate within Africa. The precise nature of these changes is still a matter for investigation, but it seems certain that they caused certain habitats to expand and contract according to the prevailing climate at the time. According to one view, expounded by Moreau (1966) in 'The Bird Faunas of Africa and its Islands', periods of glaciation ('ice ages') in the temperate and subtropical zones of Europe and Asia would have coincided with expansion of glaciers on high mountains in Africa (a few still existing as remnants today). The climate now experienced in highland areas above 1500 m would then have been experienced at *c.* 500 m. Moreau considered that this would have resulted in a huge montane area connecting what are now isolated mountain massifs, for instance Mt Kilimanjaro and the Mt Kenya–Aberdare–Elgon–Ruwenzori massifs. With higher rainfall, forests and swamplands would have expanded, and forest would have stretched right across Africa to the east coast, dividing northern and southern areas of grasslands and more arid habitats from one another for long enough to permit speciation to occur.

In between glaciations, temperatures would gradually have increased with the retreat of the glaciers and more arid conditions would have been general. The montane or highland conditions of today would then have been experienced only above 1900 m. Forests and swamplands would have retreated, the former to comparatively small refugia. The Sahara Desert would then have extended very much further south than at present, and the Upper and Lower Guinea forests would have been separated by a very much wider gap than they are today. Likewise, the Kalahari desert would have extended very much further north.

Moreau's interpretation of possible events has been considered incorrect as a result of more recent findings, which suggest that at the time of glaciations in the temperate zone and on the East African heights the climate at lower altitudes was not wetter than at present, but in fact more arid (Livingstone 1975). In other words, ice ages in the north perhaps corresponded with periods when deserts and savannas in Africa expanded, and forests were reduced to comparatively small refugia in which a limited number of forest species could survive. In the interglacial periods wetter climates would have prevailed at lower altitudes, and forests would then have expanded while savannas and deserts contracted.

The precise timing of these recurrent events may be of less importance than the fact that they occurred. According to Livingstone (1975) the water level in Lake Victoria, for instance, fell at least 75 m, reducing what is now the second largest freshwater lake in the world to a relatively small puddle, with no outlets, and only 13 m above a level that would have meant that it dried up completely. The existence of vast areas of Kalahari sand within what is now *Brachystegia* woodland and even forest shows that at that time the great Congo Basin forests must have been reduced to comparatively small areas. These examples will indicate the magnitude of the changes that occurred. In particular, it seems clear that savannas and deserts covered very much larger areas of Africa than they do at present, and this helps to explain why the bird faunas of Africa are particularly rich in some families adapted to desert or savanna conditions, for instance larks and weaver birds, and relatively poor in some typically forest families such as trogons or broadbills. In Africa there are none of the very highly specialized forest passerines which perform lek displays, such as the cotingas of South America and the birds of paradise and bower-birds of Australasia, though whether this is entirely due to the small size of African forest refugia is as yet conjectural (Snow 1980).

Repeated expansion and contraction of major habitats

1

in response to climatic changes would have forced their avian and other inhabitants either to adapt to new habitats, or to reduce their total populations in accordance with the available habitat, and perhaps become extinct if certain habitats disappeared altogether. At periods when the forests and swamplands were more extensive, populations of northern and southern species would have been separated. In some cases they only evolved to subspecific level; in others they evolved to become full species, subsequently unable to interbreed with their nearest relations in the other hemisphere. A good example among birds is the two species of ground hornbills, the Abyssinian Ground Hornbill *Bucorvus abyssinicus* found in the western and northern tropics, and the Southern Ground Hornbill *B. leadbeateri* in East and South Africa. Today, the species occur within 50 km of one another in the Baringo Rift Valley and adjacent plateaus of Kenya and North Uganda.

For a fuller exposition of the arguments concerning past events the reader is referred to Moreau (1966), Livingstone (1975), Diamond and Hamilton (1980), and references quoted by them. Whatever did happen, the broad and local distribution of birds today is largely controlled by the interacting conditions, especially through variations of temperature and rainfall. Geological erosion, arising from varied topography, has also brought about the distribution of different types of soils, with characteristic associated vegetation, in any particular set of climatic conditions. Finally, probably beginning with the regular use of fire (at least 350,000 years ago), man has affected the existing habitats to a marked degree. Today his handiwork, either directly or through the effects of grazing and browsing by domestic stock, is a dominant and usually catastrophic influence.

1.2 Climate

The climate of Africa is mainly tropical. As the earth orbits the sun, with its axis tilted in relation to the plane of its orbit, the sun's changing position in the sky determines earth's changing seasons. In effect, the sun's position moves north and south across the equator twice a year, reaching the zenith on 23 June at the Tropic of Cancer and on 22 December at the Tropic of Capricorn. Summer in the north is roughly from May to August, and in the south from October to February. The terms 'winter' and 'summer', commonly used in temperate latitudes to describe cold or warm seasons respectively, are meaningless unless related to the northern or southern hemisphere. At and near the equator within the tropics there is no winter or summer, only alternate wet and dry seasons. Really cold conditions are encountered only at high altitudes, and even there only at night, or in cloudy weather.

While the general circulation of the atmosphere is not yet fully understood, sufficient is known to suggest a simple climatic model (Fig. 1). The atmosphere over most of Africa can be represented as two cells rotating in mesh astride the equator. Descending air masses on the outside correspond to belts of high pressure, with a belt of low pressure between them over which air

ascends. The ascending air is cooled by expansion resulting from reduced pressure, causing saturation, condensation, cloud formation and rainfall. Descending air on the other hand is warmed by compression, reducing its relative humidity, which may earlier have been reduced by condensation and rainfall. These conditions, very broadly, result in arid belts in the northern tropics and subtropics, and smaller arid belts at similar latitudes in the south, typified in Africa by the enormous Sahara Desert and the smaller Kalahari and Namib Deserts respectively (Brown and Cochemé 1969).

Winds from the northern and southern high pressure belts blow towards each other over the zone of intervening low pressure, which is also the zone of greatest solar heating since, on average, it is nearest to the equator. This zone of low pressure is often known as the Intertropical Convergence Zone (ITCZ). The three parallel zones, the two high pressure belts and the ITCZ, oscillate north and south annually, the ITCZ following the sun's position with a time lag of about five weeks.

Thus, at the time of the vernal or autumnal equinoxes, the ITCZ lies over the equator. Anticyclonic circulation of the high pressure belts in both hemispheres causes converging winds known as trade winds to blow from the east (always from the east because of the direction of the earth's spin). At the height of summer, in the northern or southern hemisphere, the ITCZ approaches the tropic line, resulting in cyclonic conditions, with rainfall in those latitudes. Real 'winter', involving cold conditions and frost, is unknown in the northern and southern tropics; but dry seasons correspond to the winter months at higher latitudes, and wet seasons to summer. Near the equator, the biannual movement of the ITCZ results in two short rainy seasons and two dry seasons each year. Temperatures at and near the equator, though generally higher on average, seldom reach the extremes experienced late in the dry seasons in the northern or southern tropics.

There are no hard and fast lines of division between one main climatic regime and another; nevertheless one may discern the following main rainfall patterns in Africa:

(i) 'Mediterranean' winter rainfall regimes, in which most of the rainfall occurs during the cold (or cooler) winter months, from November to March in the Mediterranean basin itself, and from April to September at the southern tip of Africa. On high mountains, such as the Atlas or the Zwartberg Mts, much of the precipitation occurs as snow. Cool or cold wet winters are separated from hot dry summers by a short spring in which the vegetation, both in the north and south, is typified by a profusion of beautiful flowers.

(ii) The northern tropical rainfall regime, in which rain falls in one long wet season from April to October, usually with a somewhat drier break in June–July, and a long dry season from November to March in which little or no rain falls. In the moister parts of this zone, with rainfall exceeding 1200 mm/year, the rainy season extends from March to October, with showers or storms in other months. In the drier parts, with annual rain-

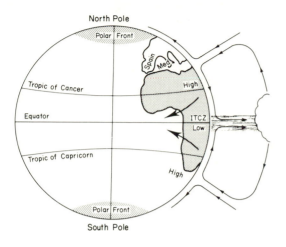

I At vernal and autumnal equinox: rain near equator to
about 4° N-S; spring in Mediterranean; autumn at Cape

←— Winds converging at ITCZ

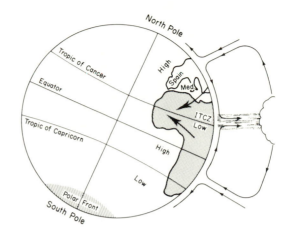

II Northern summer June-August: earth has altered position till
sun position is over Tropic of Cancer; rain in northern
tropics; dry in southern tropics and at equator;
wet cold winter at Cape

←— Winds at ITCZ

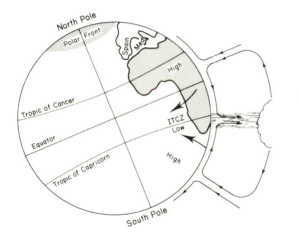

III Southern summer November-February:
earth has swung to bring sun over Tropic of Capricorn;
rain in southern tropics; dry hot summer at Cape;
wet cold winter in Mediterranean

←— Winds at ITCZ

Fig. 1. Movements of the Intertropical Convergence Zone (ITCZ) in response to the
earth's oscillation relative to the position of the sun.

fall of less than 500 mm, the rainy season is short, from
June to September, with the intervening eight months
extremely dry. Great variations may occur over comparatively short distances.

This regime affects the whole of West Africa south of
the Sahara, Sudan, much of Ethiopia, and parts of North
Uganda, Zaïre and Kenya. It has profound effects on
the biology of intra-African migrant species, resulting in
more or less regular north-south movements by many
species over a wide belt at least from Senegal to northern
Zaïre. For those Palearctic migrants (probably the
majority) which do not pass the equator to winter
further south, it means that they encounter dry conditions in most of their winter range.

(iii) The equatorial bimodal rainfall regime, with
peaks of rainfall following the vernal and autumnal equinoxes, from late March to mid-June, and from late
October to mid-December. These short rainy seasons
are separated by short (three months) dry seasons, never
quite so long or severe as in areas of equivalent rainfall
in the northern or southern tropical rainfall regimes.
This zone extends for about 4° N and S of the equator.
In those parts with more than 1200 mm annual rainfall
the rainy seasons tend to merge, and the vegetation is
typically forest, as in parts of Uganda, Zaïre or Gabon.
In the drier parts, such as eastern Kenya and Somalia,
both rainy seasons are short and unreliable, separated
by three- to four-month dry seasons of varying severity,

with June through to September usually cool and overcast, and January through to April normally hot and sunny. North or south of the equator one of the rainy seasons tends to be longer and more reliable (the 'Long Rains'), and the other shorter and less reliable (the 'Short Rains').

(iv) The southern tropical rainfall regime, which is the opposite of (ii) above. Rain falls mainly from November to April, with May to September dry, and some rain in October. This rainfall pattern affects all those Palearctic winter migrants which pass on south of the equator and thus encounter wet conditions in most of their winter range. It also affects some intra-African transequatorial migrants such as Abdim's Stork *Ciconia abdimii*, which breeds just before or in the rains in the northern part of its range, and 'winters' in the southern tropics, enjoying warm wet conditions for most of its life.

In all these main rainfall regimes the rains tend to be more unreliable in areas of lower mean annual rainfall. While such changes occur in West Africa over distances of several hundred km, in some mountainous parts of East and Northeast Africa (for instance eastern Ethiopia or on the northern slopes of Mt Kenya) one may pass from a copious and reliable rainfall to a low and unreliable rainfall within 50–100 km; and consequently from a regularly productive environment, where birds may be sedentary and breed at regular seasons, to areas only sporadically productive when unreliable rain falls, and where birds must opportunistically take advantage of good conditions as and when they occur.

These main rainfall regimes gradually merge into one another, with marginal areas where the season may be confused and more erratic, and they do not always occur in nicely arranged parallel belts related to latitude. In some areas, notably in and near the East African Rift Valley and adjacent high plateaux, the main rainfall systems may be quite sharply divided from each other over comparatively short distances. For instance, within 100 km of Nakuru, Kenya, there are areas typical of three of these main rainfall systems, (ii), (iii) and (iv) (Brown and Britton 1980). Climate and vegetation can vary in a bewildering way in quite a small area, especially if mountainous. Broad generalizations must often be modified in the light of local variations.

In most of tropical Africa temperature does not critically limit vegetative growth as it does in temperate Europe or North America. Accordingly, it has relatively minor effects on food supplies and the behaviour of birds. However, the average air temperature falls by *c*. 0·6°C per 100 m increase in altitude (= 3·3°F per 1000 ft). Thus, there is a real temperature difference between the top and bottom of a large mountain; and a soaring eagle, vulture or stork, reaching only 500 m (1500 ft) above ground, encounters air at least 3°C (or 5°F) cooler than on the ground. They may soar for thermoregulation as well as to locate possible food, or to travel.

In the tropics large mountain massifs, such as the highlands of Ethiopia, Mts Cameroon, Kilimanjaro, Kenya and the Ruwenzori range, create small isolated areas of low temperature. On some, for instance Kili-manjaro, Kenya and the Ruwenzoris, there are permanent glaciers, frequent snow and hail, and cold rock peaks devoid of vegetation. Somewhat lower down, at *c*. 3800–4500 m (11,500–14,000 ft), nightly frosts occur throughout the year, with warm sunshine in the dry season by day, so that such climates are aptly described as 'summer all day and winter all night'. These climatic conditions are associated with extraordinary 'Afro-alpine' vegetation, and such mountain tops or high massifs often harbour endemic bird species, or local races or populations of more widespread species. For instance, the Cape Grass Owl *Tyto capensis* is found in South Africa, Kenya and in Cameroon; this (and other evidence) suggests that at some colder and wetter period in the past these now isolated areas were connected to one another by tracts of similar vegetation, no longer in existence.

Further south, on the great eastern escarpment or 'Berg' of South Africa, the high mountains of Lesotho and the Natal Drakensberg up to 3500 m experience a severe winter. Here there are well-marked altitudinal migrations; for instance, many species of birds are winter visitors to the Kruger National Park, breeding in summer in the montane forests at the top of the escarpment. Equally, some altitudinal migration may be observed on the slopes of Mts Kenya or Kilimanjaro. For example, both Grey and Red-billed Hornbills *Tockus nasutus* and *T. erythrorhynchus* normally move uphill on the eastern slopes of Mt Kenya in the dry season and return to lower altitudes in the wet season.

Even on quite small mountains rising from otherwise gently undulating or flat plains (usually called 'inselbergs', or island mountains), climatic effects related to altitude are strikingly evident. The summit of such a mountain is invariably cooler than its foot; and since decrease in temperature is often accompanied by an increase in rainfall or cloud, and a decrease in evaporation by solar heat, the top of such a mountain is relatively wetter than its lower slopes. Such local effects, over only a few kilometres, may result in a patch of luxuriant forest near or on the top of a small inselberg whose footslopes are in semi-desert. This particular feature results in the local isolation, comparable to the situation on an oceanic island, of many Central and East African species, which are confined to one or a few such isolated mountain tops. Of 25 endemic species now described from Ethiopia all but four are essentially montane; and many East and Central African species are confined to mountain ranges of no great elevation, but with isolated forests on their summits. Here are found some of the rarest and most acutely threatened species, such as the Dappled Mountain Robin *Modulatrix orostruthus* and the Black-cap Bush-Shrike *Malaconotus alius*.

1.3 Vegetation

The natural vegetation is, broadly speaking, the result of the local climate, not the cause of it. This is not to say that the widespread destruction of vegetation may not have far-reaching deleterious effects. Destruction of

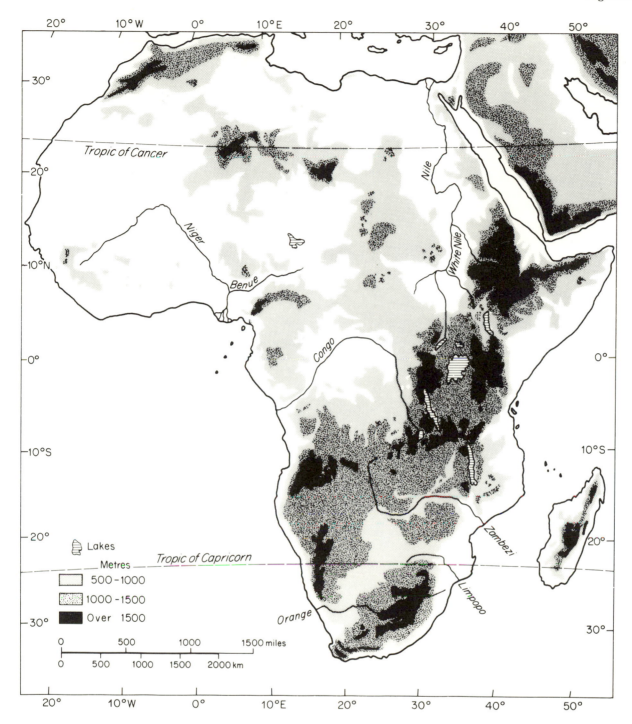

Fig. 2. Topographical map of Africa.

forest, for instance, may result in the loss of 60% or more of incident rainfall, and in much higher ground temperatures, while soil loss may be multiplied by a factor of 50–200. In effect, such a process converts a once luxuriant wooded countryside into semi-desert, as for instance over vast tracts of northern Ethiopia.

The topographical features of Africa are shown in Fig. 2, and the main vegetation types in Fig. 3, simplified from Keay (1959), an arrangement used by many recent authors (e.g. Moreau 1966). However, mapping on such a scale does not permit an understanding of the local variations in vegetation and associated bird com-

munities that can occur over very short distances. Any detailed vegetation map of a small area will demarcate pockets of vegetation not characteristic of that broad vegetation zone, as shown on a continental vegetation map. Such small variations result from orographic effects or from drainage patterns, modifying the local climate and the amount of soil water available.

There is a direct relationship between available soil moisture (not necessarily total annual rainfall) and the vegetation in any tropical area. If the soil were absolutely flat and free-draining (a condition found nowhere in the world) there would be a gradual increase in the

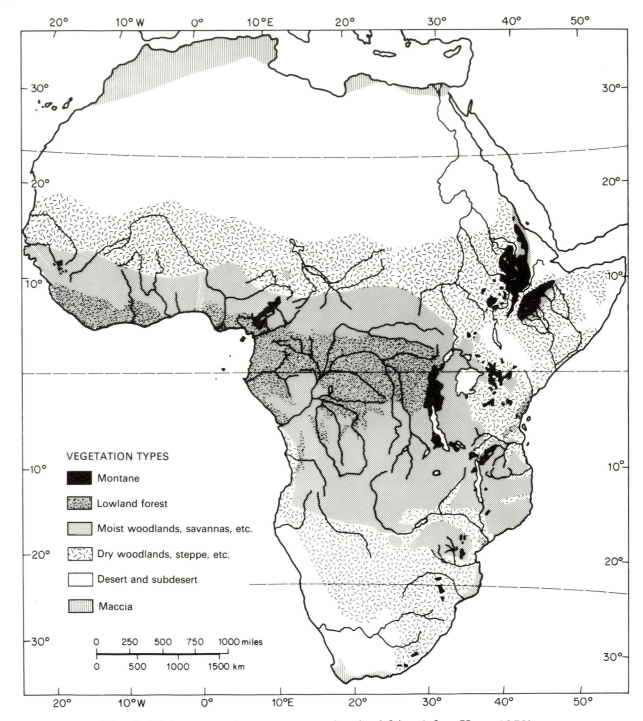

Fig. 3. Main vegetation types occuring in Africa (after Keay 1959).

height, bulk, and annual productivity of the vegetation from very low to very high rainfall, as shown in Fig. 4. In an annual rainfall of 200 mm, fluctuating greatly from year to year and failing altogether in some years, only a few specialized perennials, usually with extensive root systems and small, often succulent upper parts, can survive. Much of the total productivity consists of swift-growing annuals able to take advantage of occasional years of relatively high rainfall. Such plants typically have small root systems and thin stemmy upper parts, but produce abundant flowers and seed very quickly.

This seed then lies dormant until another year of high rainfall causes the desert to 'blossom like the rose'. In such a climatic regime many birds tend to be nomadic and are opportunistic breeders, reproducing in large numbers when conditions are good but in other years not breeding at all.

At the other extreme, with an annual rainfall of 2000 mm or over and some rain in every month, the natural vegetation will be luxuriant tropical forest. In such conditions bird communities tend to be stable, composed mainly of permanent residents, and with some

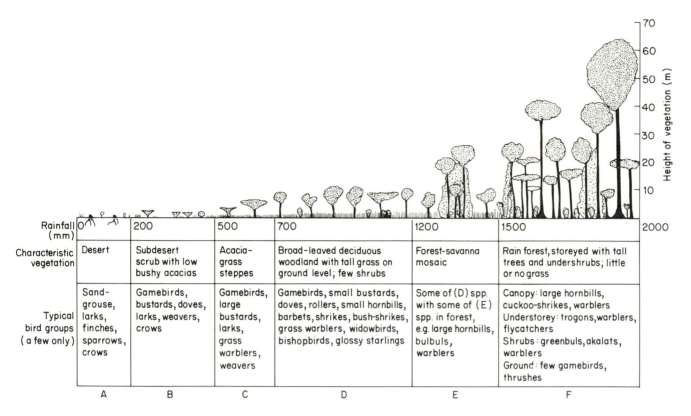

Fig. 4. Idealized relationship between available soil moisture and vegetation in rainfall of 0–2000 mm/year.

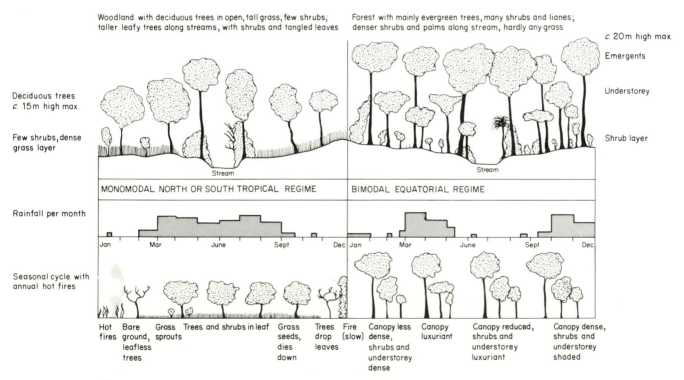

Fig. 5. Effect of seasonality of rainfall of 1200 mm/year on vegetation.

species breeding in almost every month of the year, though forest insectivores and fruit-eaters may breed at different seasons (Brown and Britton 1980).

The direct relationship which would occur in uniform rainfall conditions is affected by (i) seasonality of rainfall, and (ii) topography and drainage resulting in non-uniform conditions over quite small areas. Figure 5 shows the effect of seasonality when the annual rainfall is 1200 mm. Where the whole annual rainfall falls in one six-month wet season, followed by a severe dry season of similar length, woodland or savanna occurs, typified by relatively small fire-resistant deciduous trees usually not more than 10–12 m tall, and long coarse tufted grasses which in the dry season are burned in fierce fires, killing any perennial shrubs down to their rootstocks. Suppression of annual fires results in an increase in tree cover, reducing the heat of any fires that occur, and in time creating a closed-canopy woodland; but the tree species remain relatively small, and are deciduous in the dry season. In an equatorial bimodal rainfall regime, with two short rainy seasons alternating with two short, less severe dry seasons and some rain in any month, a total rainfall of 1200 mm will produce forest up to 40 m tall, with some shrubby undergrowth but little or no grass, and consequently no fierce annual fires. The bird communities of these habitats are quite different, although the total annual rainfall is similar.

Such broad effects are further varied by local topography, drainage and soil type. Rainfall is rapidly absorbed in sandy or free-draining loamy soils, but on heavy clays the soil surface is quickly sealed, preventing further penetration, so that more of the total rainfall escapes as runoff, even under luxuriant grass cover. This results in an apparently paradoxical situation where what seems to be a wet swampy valley or vlei in the rains, may actually absorb less total moisture than relatively dry adjacent ridges of free-draining soil.

Soil transported over geological ages of erosion, even for quite a short distance (a few hundred metres), where the total rainfall and temperature cannot vary greatly, may result in extremely striking local variations in vegetation and in the associated bird communities. Such variations of soil type and drainage result in a mosaic of vegetation types and bird communities, stable, under natural conditions at least, over several centuries. For instance (Fig. 6) the top of a small mountain rising only a few hundred metres from a plain may be bare rock, from which all water runs off, so that it supports only a few succulents similar to those of desert environments. The base of the rock may support tall trees on the abundant runoff, with poor grassland nearby. On the sides of the mountain, in deep transported top soil, there may be a patch of luxuriant forest; and at its foot there may be swampy grasslands with heavy clay soil allowing runoff in the rains, which remains wet with seepage even in the dry season.

Regular variations may occur in succession on gently undulating country, with relatively free-draining soil on the tops of the ridges and heavy clay in the bottoms of the valleys. The ridges may support woodland or forest; the valleys may be open grassland, or a more xerophilous type of woodland, or swamp. Such conditions (Fig. 7), often termed catenary formations, may be repeated more or less regularly over vast areas according to the drainage pattern.

Man originated in Africa about three million years ago. The vegetation was probably little affected by him until the use of fire was established at least 350,000

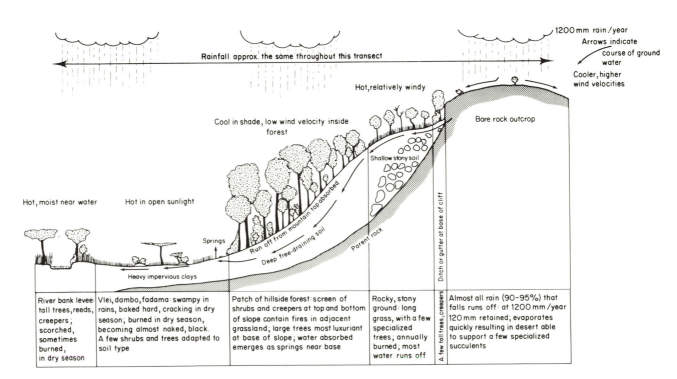

Fig. 6. Flow of ground water, associated soils and vegetation on a small mountain with rainfall of 1200 mm/year.

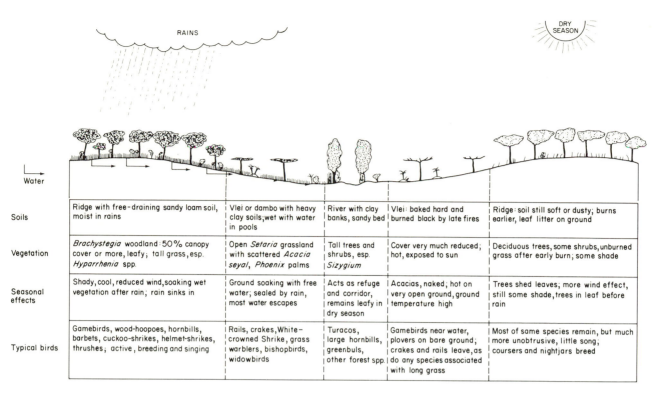

Soils	Ridge with free-draining sandy loam soil, moist in rains	Vlei or dambo with heavy clay soils; wet with water in pools	River with clay banks, sandy bed	Vlei: baked hard and burned black by late fires	Ridge: soil still soft or dusty; burns earlier, leaf litter on ground
Vegetation	*Brachystegia* woodland: 50% canopy cover or more, leafy; tall grass, esp. *Hyparrhenia* spp.	Open *Setaria* grassland with scattered *Acacia seyal*, *Phoenix* palms	Tall trees and shrubs, esp. *Sizygium*	Cover very much reduced; hot, exposed to sun	Deciduous trees, some shrubs, unburned grass after early burn; some shade
Seasonal effects	Shady, cool, reduced wind, soaking wet vegetation after rain; rain sinks in	Ground soaking with free water; sealed by rain, most water escapes	Acts as refuge and corridor, remains leafy in dry season	Acacias, naked; hot on very open ground, ground temperature high	Trees shed leaves; more wind effect, still some shade, trees in leaf before rain
Typical birds	Gamebirds, wood-hoopoes, hornbills, barbets, cuckoo-shrikes, helmet-shrikes, thrushes; active, breeding and singing	Rails, crakes, White-crowned Shrike, grass warblers, bishopbirds, widowbirds	Turacos, large hornbills, greenbuls, other forest spp.	Gamebirds near water, plovers on bare ground; crakes and rails leave, as do any species associated with long grass	Most of same species remain, but much more unobtrusive, little song; coursers and nightjars breed

Fig. 7a. Catenary formation in area of *Brachystegia* woodland with rainfall of 1200 mm/year and severe dry seasons.

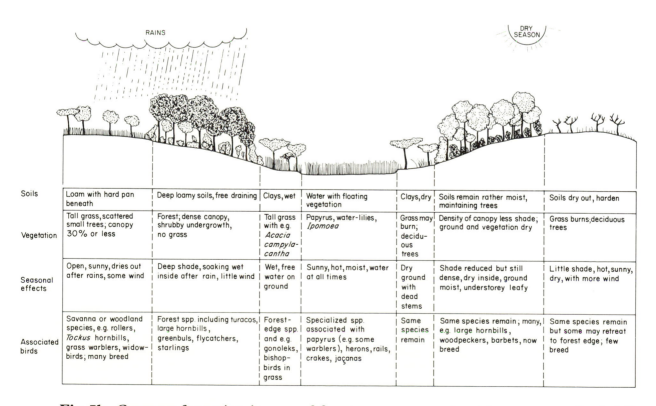

Soils	Loam with hard pan beneath	Deep loamy soils, free draining	Clays, wet	Water with floating vegetation	Clays, dry	Soils remain rather moist, maintaining trees	Soils dry out, harden
Vegetation	Tall grass, scattered small trees; canopy 30% or less	Forest; dense canopy, shrubby undergrowth, no grass	Tall grass with e.g. *Acacia campylacantha*	Papyrus, water-lilies, *Ipomoea*	Grass may burn; deciduous trees	Density of canopy less shade; ground and vegetation dry	Grass burns; deciduous trees
Seasonal effects	Open, sunny, dries out after rains, some wind	Deep shade, soaking wet inside after rain, little wind	Wet, free water on ground	Sunny, hot, moist, water at all times	Dry ground with dead stems	Shade reduced but still dense, dry inside, ground moist, understorey leafy	Little shade, hot, sunny, dry, with more wind
Associated birds	Savanna or woodland species, e.g. rollers, *Tockus* hornbills, grass warblers, widowbirds; many breed	Forest spp. including turacos, large hornbills, greenbuls, flycatchers, starlings	Forest-edge spp. and e.g. gonoleks, bishopbirds in grass	Specialized spp. associated with papyrus (e.g. some warblers), herons, rails, crakes, jaçanas	Same species remain	Same species remain; many, e.g. large hornbills, woodpeckers, barbets, now breed	Same species remain but some may retreat to forest edge; few breed

Fig 7b. Catenary formation in area of forest-savanna mosaic with swamps and rainfall of *c.* 1500 mm/year (Uganda).

		Run-off	Effective rainfall	Vegetation	Birds
Stage I	Undisturbed condition productive	10%	540 mm	Scattered tall acacias with long grass, e.g. *Themeda triandra*; canopy reduced by regular, hot, dry-season fires	Open country species, e.g. gamebirds, bustards, larks, grass-warblers; rather few bush species
II	Heavy grazing by livestock; productive, but cannot be maintained	50% +	300 mm	Scattered tall acacias persist, grass grazed down, no regular fires. Seedlings / suckers unpalatable to browsing species invade. Transition towards subdesert has begun	Open country species decrease (e.g. Ostrich, Secretary Bird, bustards); bush-loving species, e.g. small hornbills, bush shrikes, increase
III	Overgrazed; productivity reduced	66%	200 mm	Tall trees are lopped; further invasion by smaller, bushy acacias and some succulents. Ground is bare, gullies begin, soil loss is severe. Cattle die out, replaced by goats	Bush-loving species increase; most open country species now gone
IV	Overgrazing end-point; productivity reduced economically irreparable, badly damaged physically by gullying	70%	180 mm	Tall trees are dead, ground covered by uneatable succulents. Canopy largely composed of low shrubby acacias which do not prevent run-off. Gullying severe	Bush-loving species dominant, e.g. *Tockus* hornbills, bush shrikes, small weavers, sparrows; many species but different from those of Stage I

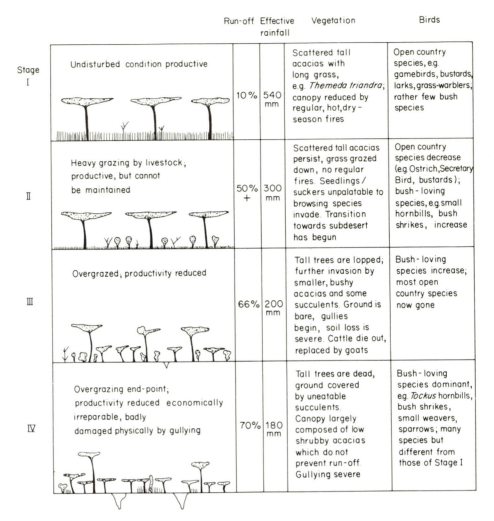

Fig. 8. Stages in degradation of habitat (perennial *Acacia*-grassland with rainfall of 600 mm/year). (N.B. This is semi-diagrammatic and perhaps exaggerated, but the run-off and effective rainfall figures are realistic and related to recent experimental work.)

years ago. Then, even a small population of human hunter/food gatherers could set fire to enormous areas, probably affecting hundreds of square kilometres per head of population. Such fires would be started deliberately, either to smoke out beehives, or simply to clear long grass so that people could move about unhindered.

Within the last 5000–6000 years pastoralists dependent on livestock, and cultivators dependent on crops have further affected and modified the vegetation over vast areas. For instance, virtually the whole of the once luxuriant cedar and olive forests that covered the northern third of Ethiopia has been destroyed by cultivators in the last 2000–3000 years. Camels, unknown to the ancient Egyptians, have enabled widespread human occupation of desert and subdesert environments within the last 2000 years.

Within the last 100 years, and especially within the last 30 years, as an unintended result of improved law and order and the success of veterinary medicine, misuse of the environment by humans, especially with livestock, has accelerated at a catastrophic pace. Forest clearance, swamp drainage and other such practices have affected

or will affect certain habitats ever more swiftly. If population trends continue, which currently show an annual increase of at least 2% with no indication of slowing down at present, about 3·6 million hectares of hitherto virgin forest or woodland will have to be destroyed annually by cultivators in order to survive (Brown 1980).

The normal result of such human usage is a 'derived' type of vegetation, recognizable because it bears no clear relationship to the drainage pattern or topography, but is scattered in patches over the landscape (Vesey-Fitzgerald 1974). Where the human population is not too dense such a situation may result in a mosaic of habitats capable of supporting an even greater variety of birds than would have occurred under strictly natural conditions. The general trend, however, is to destroy the natural climax vegetation and substitute for it a lower and usually less productive vegetative type, which sometimes severely erodes the land until it eventually becomes a virtual desert.

For instance, the loss of 60% or more of incident rainfall from bare ground reduces an actual rainfall of 600 mm/year to an effective rainfall of 240 mm/year, thus changing perennial grassland to what is effectively semi-desert (Fig. 8). If severe soil loss occurs, such trends may be irreversible, at least in historical time. Sometimes, however, the end result of such human misuse may actually be more favourable to birds than the original condition, for instance when excessive numbers of livestock eat down grass, so suppressing fierce annual fires, but encouraging the invasion of unpalatable trees and shrubs which may eventually come to dominate the original grassland as thicket.

The most vulnerable of all habitats are probably the small 'island forests' near the summits of inselbergs in otherwise semi-arid country, which are vital for the survival of several very local species. However, larger areas of tropical rain forest are also extremely vulnerable, and are being exploited at an ever increasing pace. Swamps and wetlands too are threatened by exploitation, drainage, river diversion, flood control, and development of hydro-electric power, most notably in the Zambezi–Kafue system at present, and perhaps most importantly in southern Africa generally, though the Nile system has also been much affected. Irrigation schemes following such developments may also increase risks to birds from toxic chemicals. On the other hand, however, the development of new dams, impoundments and irrigation schemes may create new areas of habitat attractive to water birds in what was once arid and unproductive terrain.

Although no African bird species is known to have become extinct in Africa within the last 50 years, certain species are now threatened with early extinction, and the prospects for some of these, for example the Waldrapp *Geronticus eremita*, seem precarious. More species will inevitably be threatened with extinction in the immediate future unless deliberate steps are taken to conserve them. This would involve the conservation of adequate undisturbed areas of suitable habitat, often threatened at present, such as the Arabuko–Sokoke Forest in coastal Kenya, or the forests of the Usambara Mountains in Tanzania. From the viewpoint of human survival, little useful purpose will be served by destroying the last remnants of such forests or other habitats, as the number of human beings who could thereby survive is insignificant in relation to the increase of the population as a whole.

1.4 Noteworthy Bird Habitats in Africa

The interacting climatic and topographical factors so far described have resulted in a number of widespread habitat types in Africa. These generally intergrade with one another with no definite dividing line, though in some cases, notably at the boundary between deciduous woodland and tropical forest, the change is often abrupt. Within the major habitats innumerable minor variations may be described, usually on the basis of particular associations of plants; for instance, Acocks (1953) describes over 70 veld types in South Africa alone. However, for our purposes simplification into a smaller number of basic main habitats, and subtypes within

these, is necessary. We use the classification of Keay (1959), which includes over 30 definable main habitats and subtypes in Africa south of the Tropic of Cancer (see Fig. 3).

Before describing these major habitats, however, some remarkable or unique areas of outstanding ornithological interest deserve special mention. Especially notable concentrations of mainly aquatic birds occur on the Banc D'Arguin off the coast of Mauritania, and in the delta of the Senegal River and associated swamplands. Both are important wintering areas for huge numbers of Palearctic migrant waders and ducks, while they also are breeding areas for both species of flamingoes and the Great White Pelican *Pelecanus onocrotalus*. Other very large wetland areas of outstanding interest include the Niger inundation zone in Mali; the swamps around Lake Chad; the Nile Sudd region in southern Sudan; the Wembere swamps of Central Tanzania (with enormous, seldom visited colonies of many species of herons, ibises and storks); the seasonally inundated plains of Lake Rukwa in South Tanzania; the Bangweulu swamps and the Kafue flood plain (now threatened by development for hydro-electric power) in Zambia; and the Okavango delta swamps in Botswana. The swamps from the Sudan to Bangweulu are the range of the spectacular African endemic Shoebill *Balaeniceps rex*, and all such wetlands support large populations of water birds vulnerable elsewhere, such as several large colonies of Great White Pelicans. Interference with some of these aquatic ecosystems or major wetlands for human usage may be inevitable, but will certainly have adverse effects on the remarkable bird communities they now support.

Africa includes within its boundaries the second largest freshwater lake in the world, Lake Victoria, and the world's second deepest lake, Lake Tanganyika (which is not remarkable for its bird life). Along both arms of the Rift Valley in western Uganda, Zaïre, Kenya and Tanzania lie chains of freshwater and alkaline lakes of unique biological interest. The best known, Lake Nakuru, supports one of the world's greatest ornithological spectacles, that is, an irregular population of 1·5 million Lesser Flamingoes *Phoeniconaias minor* (Vareschi 1978), together with large concentrations of other water birds. The flamingoes do not breed there but on the forbidding, scorching hot, crystalline soda mudflats of Lake Natron in North Tanzania, also one of this chain of Rift Valley lakes, but at a much lower altitude and with much higher temperatures. Four neighbouring lakes in the Ethiopian Rift, Zwai, Langano and Abiata (which are interconnected), and Shala are also of exceptional interest, and have been the sites of some important recent studies on large water birds.

The four major river systems of Africa, the Niger, Nile, Congo and Zambezi, with their associated flood plains form aquatic threads traversing all other habitats from the densest forest in Zaïre to the Sahara desert. These, and other very large rivers such as the Senegal, Volta, Benue, Shari, Rufiji, Kafue, Cunene, Limpopo and Orange support characteristic bird faunas including bee-eaters, plovers, pratincoles and skimmers; and in some cases they may act as migration routes. None of the major African waterways is as large as the Amazon, but collectively they are much more varied than the Amazon system.

The Ethiopian highlands form the largest montane massif in Africa, totalling some 70,000 km² above 1500 m, and are bisected by the Rift Valley. Of 25 endemic species, 21 are montane, and most of these are common and widespread over this huge highland massif. The mountain massifs of Hoggar and Tibesti in the Sahara are also very large, but, with no endemics, their ornithological interest is much less. The highlands of East Africa and eastern Zaïre are also very extensive, but are more divided into individual mountain massifs separated from each other by impassable lowland barriers. They include all the highest peaks in Africa, Mt Kilimanjaro (5894 m), Mt Kenya (5199 m) and the Ruwenzori Range (5119 m), all with glaciers and alpine zones almost devoid of vegetation. They and other lower but still lofty mountains, such as Mt Meru in Tanzania, Mt Elgon on the Kenya–Uganda border, and the Virunga volcanos in the Uganda–Zaïre–Rwanda border area, are remarkable for their extraordinary Afro-alpine vegetation, including many species of giant groundsels *Senecio* spp., giant *Lobelia* spp., everlasting *Helichrysum* spp., alpine heaths *Erica* and *Philippia* spp., and the heath-like composite *Stoebe kilimandsharica*. Single mountain ranges or peaks may support endemic species or subspecies. The mountain ranges of Cape Province are botanically even more remarkable, the Cape maccia or fynbos forming a unique plant group. They support a number of endemic bird species, and one endemic family, the Promeropidae (sugarbirds), here has its main centre of distribution.

Probably the most varied and ornithologically rich area on the continent is that stretching from the eastern border of Zaïre in the Ituri/Bwamba forest to Kenya and Tanzania. This area includes many high mountains, both arms of the Rift Valley and associated lakes, and stretches of all types of habitats from tropical lowland forests to lava deserts. Of some 1850 species found in Africa as a whole, 1315 (or 71%) occur in Kenya, Uganda and Tanzania. Kenya, with 1030 species (including seabirds), is the richest and most ecologically varied of the three East African countries.

Having stressed the special interest of some of these remarkable habitats and areas, it must be admitted that most of the rest of Africa has been well summed up in the ribald phrase 'miles and miles of bloody Africa'. In much of the rest of the continent one can travel for hundreds, even thousands of kilometres through flat or gently undulating terrain, the skyline perhaps broken only by an occasional inselberg and the landscape covered with a blanket of essentially similar vegetation, thornbush, acacia steppe with thickets, broad-leaved woodland, or forest. Visibility from the roadside can vary from 10 m or less inside tropical forest to 200–300 m in more open woodland, expanding to further horizons in acacia steppe, and closing in again to 50–100 m in thornbush. Nevertheless, such vast areas of often still relatively wild and untouched habitat (especially in South Central Africa) have their charm, and, for ornithologists, their characteristic inhabitants.

Excluding the relatively small montane areas, wetlands, rivers and swamps, the majority of the African land mass totalling 30·3 million km² may be divided between the main habitat types shown in Table I, as defined and mapped by Keay (1959), and shown in Fig. 3.

These extensive vegetation types are the truly charac-

Table I. Main habitat types of Africa in order of ascending rainfall and productivity.

	km² (in millions)
1. Desert.	8547
2. Subdesert steppes and scrub (Karoo and tropical types).	2530
3. Grass steppes with abundant *Acacia* and *Commiphora* spp. and thorny thickets.	4671
4. Broad-leaved deciduous woodlands or savannas, subdivided into:	
(a) undifferentiated relatively dry types, e.g. mopane *Colophospermum mopane* woodland;	3869
(b) *Isoberlinia* (northern) and *Brachystegia/Julbernardia* (southern) woodlands;	3979
(c) undifferentiated, relatively moist types, with abundant *Combretum*, *Terminalia* and *Vitex* spp., and tall *Hyparrhenia* grass as the ground layer.	1304
5. Forest–savanna mosaic, usually with 'gallery forest' in valleys and broad-leaved woodland on ridges.	1502
6. Moist or wet lowland tropical rain forest.	2515

teristic habitats of African bird species. In them the more widespread species may inhabit vast areas, without having to adapt to great ecological variety. Even among these major types, however, the same bird species often do not inhabit similar vegetation both north and south of the equator. Some are extremely widespread in both northern and southern vegetation types, for instance the Helmeted Guineafowl *Numida meleagris*, Namaqua Dove *Oena capensis*, Grey Hornbill *Tockus nasutus* and Green Wood-Hoopoe *Phoeniculus purpureus*. In some cases the northern and southern forms differ to some extent, and it is not easy to know whether they should be treated as conspecific or not. For instance, the southern Yellow-billed Hornbill *T. flavirostris leucomelas* differs in voice and display from the northern *T. f. flavirostris*, and perhaps they would not interbreed. They inhabit thornbush, and are accordingly effectively isolated from each other by intervening belts of woodland.

Some very local bird species are confined to restricted areas of habitat not apparently very different from others of similar general type. An area of acacia steppes near Neghelli and Mega in South Ethiopia, not obviously different in vegetation from many others (dominated as in the Serengeti Plains by *Acacia tortilis*, with *Themeda/Cynodon* in the grass layer), harbours three very local endemic species: Stresemann's Bush Crow *Zavattariornis stresemanni*, the White-breasted Swallow *Hirundo megaensis* (whose nest is unknown), and the newly discovered Sidamo Lark *Mirafra sidamoensis* (Erard 1975). Species such as these which are unaccountably absent from apparently suitable habitat are as intriguing and interesting as the unexpected occurrence of a species in apparently unsuitable or unusual habitat. Such questions will engage and puzzle students of distribution for decades to come.

1.5 The Kinds of Birds in Africa

Of *c.* 1850 species of birds found in Africa, none is resident in every part, and the most widespread are a handful of Palearctic migrants, like European Swallows *Hirundo rustica*, which nest in North Africa, can occur practically anywhere in the Sahara during migration and winter throughout sub-Saharan Africa. A great many species are restricted by habitat; many others are endemic to one or another region of Africa, the areas with the greatest endemicity being the Abyssinian massif, Mt Cameroon, the East African highlands, the Somali and the Namibian (South West African) arid zones, and the Gulf of Guinea islands, particularly Príncipe and São Tomé.

Especially well represented are bustards (16 species in Africa out of 22), coursers and relatives (10/16), sandgrouse (10/15), honeyguides (11/13), larks (47/69), shrikes (55/74), *Cisticola* grass warblers (36/37), ploceine weavers (101/112) and estrildines (66/100) (Moreau 1966). Other groups well represented are long-legged waders, ducks, diurnal birds of prey, francolins, plovers, pigeons, doves, cuckoos, swifts, kingfishers, bee-eaters, hornbills, barbets, swallows, bulbuls, thrushes, babblers, warblers and glossy starlings. Some, such as corvids and flycatchers, are not especially varied but include some species that are easily seen. Still other groups, such as parrots, trogons, woodpeckers, broadbills and pittas, are poorly represented.

Of *c.* 1850, *c.* 50 species are irregular or vagrant visitors and *c.* 95 are regular visitors to Africa without ever breeding there. Waders feature importantly among them; for instance, numerous members of the family Scolopacidae visit the continent but only one, the African Snipe *Gallinago gallinago nigripennis*, is indigenous. Locally, wintering waders and wildfowl can greatly outnumber native birds, while over much of the West African Sahel zone Palearctic land birds are almost as numerous in the winter or dry-season months as the resident birds. A further 90 or so Palearctic species, which have breeding populations in North Africa, winter in tropical Africa, some abundantly, some sparsely.

The bird fauna of North Africa is overwhelmingly Palearctic in affinity. Some 165 Palearctic species breed there (mainly in Northwest Africa) without extending into sub-Saharan Africa either as migrants or residents. They include endemics such as Dupont's Lark *Chersophilus duponti*, Moussier's Redstart *Phoenicurus moussieri*, Tristram's Warbler *Sylvia deserticola* and the recently discovered Kabyle Nuthatch *Sitta ledanti* (Vielliard 1976). Several birds clearly of Afrotropical (or Ethiopian) provenance also reside there, like the White-rumped Swift *Apus caffer* and the Black-headed Tchagra *Tchagra senegala*.

About 1450 species are resident south of the Sahara, i.e. in Afrotropical Africa as distinct from Palearctic Africa. A few of them, notably herons, are widespread in both the Afrotropical and the Palearctic regions. About 6 species nesting irregularly or sparsely in South Africa are otherwise strictly Palearctic, such as the Booted Eagle *Hieraaetus pennatus* (Brooke *et al.* 1980) and European Bee-eater *Merops apiaster* (Fry, in press). There is considerable affinity between tropical African and Oriental Region birds, most of the shared species being the larger non-passerines. Two orders are endemic to sub-Saharan Africa (6 species of mousebirds, Coliiformes, and the Ostrich *Struthio camelus*, Struthioniformes) and 13 families and subfamilies: the Hamerkop *Scopus umbretta*, Shoebill *Balaeniceps rex*, Secretary Bird *Sagittarius serpentarius*, guineafowls (7 species with 1 also occurring in North Africa), turacos (18), wood-hoopoes (6), bush-shrikes (39), helmet-shrikes (9), rockfowls (2), sugarbirds (2), buffalo-weavers (2), parasitic weavers (9) and oxpeckers (2).

Sub-Saharan Africa is also characterized by numerous endemic genera and species; notable among the genera are the Congo Peacock *Afropavo*, the pygmy rails or flufftails *Sarothrura*, the crowned cranes *Balearica*, the Standard-winged and Pennant-winged Nightjars *Macrodipteryx*, the fishing owls *Scotopelia*, the casqued and ground hornbills *Ceratogymna* and *Bucorvus*, the Ground Woodpecker *Geocolaptes* and, to name a single songbird, the long-claws *Macronyx*.

1.6 The Numbers of Birds in Africa

The population density of birds in Africa may be expected to reflect broadly the productivity and seasonality of vegetation in any area, while the fact that birds are extremely mobile to some extent overcomes the perennial poverty of desert environments. Certain habitats, notably shallow lakes and marshes, may either temporarily or permanently support population densities far exceeding those of the areas around them. Lake Nakuru, for instance, only *c.* 4000 ha in extent, supports 1·5–2 million birds or 375–500/ha. It is surrounded by *Acacia* woodland with a population of perhaps 40 birds/ha. The lake supports about a hundred times as many birds as the woodland, and the biomass of the lake's large water birds is at least 1000 times that of an equivalent area of the woodland, populated mainly by small passerines. Not all aquatic areas are so productive. Lakes Tanganyika and Malawi, both very deep lakes in the southern Rift Valley, lack the abundant phytoplankton typical of Lake Nakuru and similar lakes, and consequently support less animal life. These very large deep lakes are almost devoid of bird life on their open waters, while water birds are not even very common round their shores.

Adequate, accurate and sufficiently varied census data are not available to permit anything better than an informal 'guesstimate' of the total number of birds within Africa. Palearctic migrants entering Africa have been estimated by Moreau (1972) at *c.* 3750–5000 million. He considered that this figure would be a good 'order of magnitude' estimate, as it was based upon numerous census figures from Europe by competent ornithologists. He dismissed, however, as impracticable any attempt to compute the numbers of resident species, as the available census data were so fragmentary. More data are now available and we consider that it is possible to arrive at a very approximate preliminary estimate of the number of birds in Africa.

In the most arid habitats, deserts, the numbers of birds are very small, but are unlikely to be much lower than in the extremely arid habitats of the Arabian desert close to the empty quarter. Here the overall numbers were estimated (Brown 1969) to be *c.* 1 bird/4 ha, varying from 1/6·6 ha on open barren stony desert to 1/1·6 ha in relatively well vegetated wadis, averaging overall *c.* 25 birds/km². The low density of birds in deserts means that despite their vast extent, they form a comparatively small fraction of the total population.

Other scattered estimates suggest that, once trees and bushes appear in the vegetation, the number of birds per area unit rises rapidly, in relation to overall productivity, reaching a maximum of something approaching 100/ha in tropical rain forest. In their 10-year study of acacia-grass steppe in Senegal, Morel and Morel (1978) found a mean annual density (residents and Palearctic migrants) of 5·8 birds/ha or 580/km². Beals (1970) found 46 nesting pairs of 40 species in a 2 ha study area of semi-arid *Acacia* woodland in Ethiopia, and recorded 102 species altogether, so that the overall density was greater than 46 breeding birds/ha. For East Africa there are estimates of over 80 birds/ha in *Acacia–Combretum* thornbush and 30 birds/ha in coastal scrub (EANHS records; L. H. Brown, personal estimates). In two recent studies of tropical forests (Zimmerman 1972; Britton and Zimmerman 1979), 63–73 birds/ha have been recorded in the Kakamega and Arabuko Forests in Kenya. Neither is remarkably rich in birds compared to some taller forests, so these figures may be minimal for forests. They suggest that 60–100 birds/ha would be a reasonable estimate in such environments. In some artificial environments, for instance developed gardens in rural suburbs, bird numbers can be extremely high. In a garden at Karen (L. H. Brown, pers. obs.) they are regularly of the order of 150–200/ha, but many are visitors from surrounding areas attracted by fruit or flowers and are not permanently present. Conversely, large areas of crop monoculture, whether annuals such

Table II. Distribution of bird populations of Africa.

Habitat	Estimated total area (km²)	Density/km²	Total in millions
1. Desert	8,547,000	25	214
2. Subdesert steppe/scrub	2,530,000	125	316
3. Acacia–grass steppe	4,671,000	1500	7007
4. Broad-leaved woodlands			
(a) Relatively dry types	3,869,000	2500	9673
(b) *Isoberlinia/Brachystegia*	3,979,000	3500	13,927
(c) Relatively moist types	1,304,000	4500	5868
5. Forest–savanna mosaic	1,502,000	6000	9012
6. Lowland rain forest	2,515,000	8000	20,120
7. Other habitats, montane, etc.	1,082,000	2000	2164
8. Lakes, rivers, swamps	301,000	7000	2107
	30,300,000		71,311

as maize or wheat, or perennials such as tea or oil palms support very few birds per hectare.

Working from these figures, and using the main habitats described in Section 1.4, we do not consider it unreasonable to suggest that there may be a total population of the order of 70,000–75,000 million birds in Africa, calculated as shown in Table II.

If these figures are even approximately correct, it is clear that the role of Palearctic migrants as possible competitors for food with residents has often been overstressed. Continent-wide, and year-round (since the migrants spend only about half the year in Africa), only about one bird in 20 would be a migrant. Even if the respective figures were 5000 million Palearctic migrants and 50,000 million residents, only one bird in 10 would be a migrant.

The local effect of migrants is, however, greater than these figures suggest. Rather few of them enter tropical forest. Probably about two thirds of the total remain north of the equator, where the African savannas are much broader than those south of the Gulf of Guinea, spanning 55–60° of longitude as compared to 25–30° in the south. However, most of the population of certain species, for instance the European Bee-eater *Merops apiaster*, the Hobby *Falco subbuteo* and the Steppe Buzzard *Buteo b. vulpinus*, winters south of the equator; and more may do so than is at present supposed (Moreau 1972).

The effect of immigrants from the Palearctic region is in some areas, notably West Africa, compounded by large-scale north–south movements in dry and wet seasons by intra-African migrants. In the savannas of the Ivory Coast, intra-tropical migrant raptors such as the Black Kite *Milvus migrans* and Grasshopper Buzzard *Butastur rufipennis* outnumber and exceed in biomass even large resident raptors such as the Vulturine Fish Eagle *Gypohierax angolensis* and the African Harrier Hawk *Polyboroides typus* for a short season (December–March) when food is abundant. The effect is magnified during this period by grass fires, which make more food available (Thiollay 1975–77). The onset of rains, initiating swarms of alate termites and ants, may also affect the timing of migration and the abundance of migrants (Thiollay 1970).

Migrants, either Palearctic or intra-African, thus locally and seasonally, and in certain families (notably ducks, waders and some raptors), greatly outnumber local residents. The resident ducks in the Senegal estuary number less than half of the winter migrants and do not compete for food in the breeding season when the Palearctic migrants are absent. The Palearctic waders wintering in Langebaan Lagoon, South Africa, enormously outnumber any residents and are present in summer, when the residents could be expected to breed; actual competition for food is, however, apparently small. The fact that such very large numbers of migrants can be accommodated in several parts of Africa without seriously affecting the numbers and breeding of local residents suggests that in such situations food supplies are superabundant. Even in tropical West Africa migrants are unlikely to affect residents breeding in the rainy season, as at that time they are absent from the area.

1.7 Movements of Birds within Africa

Three main types of movements, more or less interlocking or overlapping, are seen among African birds:

(i) The arrival and departure of Palearctic migrants. Arrival begins about August and continues until November, peaking in September–October. Return migration begins about February, and is virtually complete by late April. A few migrants, probably mainly immatures, may oversummer in the tropics. Many of these Palearctic migrants actually spend more of their lives in tropical or warm parts of Africa than in their northern breeding quarters. This applies to both those that winter in tropical latitudes and those that pass on further to the southern tip of Africa to winter in the warm southern summer.

Moreau (1972) listed and mapped the ranges, as then known, of 187 Palearctic species migrating to Africa. Thirty-seven of these, chiefly larger non-passerines (e.g. Squacco and Purple Herons *Ardeola ralloides* and *Ardea purpurea*, Black Kite *Milvus migrans*, Great Spotted Cuckoo *Clamator glandarius* and Alpine Swift *Apus melba*), also have races or populations resident in Africa, some of them migrants within the continent itself. The Red-rumped Swallow *Hirundo daurica* is one of the few passerine species with breeding populations both in the Palearctic and Africa. At least four species, the White and Black Storks *Ciconia ciconia* and *C. nigra*, Booted Eagle *Hieraaetus pennatus* and European Bee-eater *Merops apiaster*, have populations breeding both in northern and southern Africa.

(ii) Intra-African migration. For convenience we here use Moreau's definition (1972) of a migration as a regular two-way movement over 250 miles (400 km) or more, between a breeding range and a non-breeding range, performed annually and normally related to regular seasonal factors. In fact, regular movements over shorter distances occur, for instance on the Transvaal between highveld and lowveld. This type of migration has often in the past been regarded as mere local movement in response to changes in food supply (e.g. Thomson 1942), but in recent years its true nature has been more widely recognized. The phenomenon is much easier to identify and has been much more fully studied in West Africa (Chapin 1932–54; Douaud 1957; Elgood, Fry and Dowsett 1973) than in East or South Africa, though in some cases at least it is also quite apparent in South Africa. In East Africa the extremely broken topography and the complications of the various rainfall regimes make intra-African migration much more difficult to observe and study.

Some intra-African migrants, for instance Abdim's Stork *Ciconia abdimii*, Wahlberg's Eagle *Aquila wahlbergi* and the Pennant-winged Nightjar *Macrodipteryx vexillarius*, travel regularly to and fro across the equator. Of these, Abdim's Stork breeds just before or in the rains in the northern part of its range and 'winters' in the southern part, passing through the equatorial Inter-Tropical Convergence Zone in October–November and March–April, seasons during which some rain may be expected; it thus spends most of its life in moist conditions. Wahlberg's Eagle breeds mainly (but not entirely) south of the equator, moving into its main breeding range in August and returning northwards in March–April to 'winter' in parts of Africa as yet not firmly identified, but probably in savannas of southern Sudan and Chad. Of species making such trans-equatorial migrations, a few, at least, such as Wahlberg's Eagle, breed both in the northern and southern parts of their total range.

In the West African tropics, where the northern tropical rainfall regime results in a very clear alternation of 4–8 months of dry season and 4–8 months of wet (the length depending on latitude), at least 70 species are now known to perform regular north-south migrations. Some movements are very obvious and clear-cut, for instance those of the White-throated Bee-eater *Merops albicollis*. Others are much less obvious and have been detected partly by mist-netting in recent years. Some of these migrants, e.g. the African Swallow-tailed Kite *Chelictinia riocourii* and the Carmine and White-throated Bee-eaters *Merops nubicus* and *M. albicollis*, breed in the northern parts of their range and migrate south into the moister parts in the dry season. Others, such as the Black Kite *Milvus migrans* and Red-necked Buzzard *Buteo auguralis*, migrate south in the dry season, breed in the southern part of their range, and return north after breeding. The fierce annual fires in the moister Guinea savannas between January and March may affect some of these migrants, notably the Grasshopper Buzzard *Butastur rufipennis* (Thiollay 1971, 1975–77). Fuller details are given in the species texts, but there is still much to learn about intra-African migrations of this type.

Many species that breed in South Africa in summer (September–April) migrate northwards during the austral winter. Though less severe than the Eurasian winter this nevertheless results in snow and low temperatures on the higher mountain massifs. Some of these southern African migrants may travel as far north as the equator, or even beyond, but most probably go no further than tropical South Central Africa.

A few species may perform all three of the types of movement mentioned. European members of the Black Kite *Milvus m. migrans* migrate into Africa, to the equator and sometimes beyond, in the Palearctic winter. Here they mingle with the northern tropical members of the Black Kite *M. m. parasitus*, which migrate southward in September–October, breed, and then move north again. These northern members of this race are indistinguishable from the southern members, which also migrate south in September–October, breed and move north again in March. It is not known where these southern breeding kites spend the austral winter, but some are suspected to reach the equator in June–July when the northern tropical members of their race are absent.

Altitudinal movements also occur in East and South Africa. In Kenya the Olive Pigeon *Columba arquatrix* and several sunbirds *Nectarinia* spp. descend in the rains (April–July) from the high mountains of the Aberdares (where it is very cold and wet at that time) to the warmer drier regions of the Rift Valley. Although such movements, apparently regular, do not come within Moreau's definition of migration because of the relatively short distance covered, they are in fact regular movements undertaken by most or all members of a population.

While much remains to be learned about intra-African migration, it is certainly a more regular and clearly defined phenomenon than mere local movement dictated by food supplies, as has often been stated in the past. It has recently been discussed in detail by Curry-Lindahl (1981).

(iii) Irregular, nomadic movements, especially of species of arid localities. Considering that at least 10 million km² of Africa are desert or semi-desert it is not surprising to find that many species move about very irregularly, taking advantage of temporarily favourable conditions to breed, sometimes in large numbers, then moving away again. The movements of these species are unpredictable, follow no regular pattern, and may not occur every year, so they are not true migrations (*sensu* Moreau) but are more properly described as nomadism.

Species performing this type of movement in the tropics include the Harlequin Quail *Coturnix delegorguei*, which breeds in enormous numbers when local conditions are favourable and may then not appear in similar numbers in the same locality for years. Its movements in southern Africa are more regular, and near Lake Victoria are sufficiently predictable to permit trapping in large numbers for food. The Wattled Starling *Creatophora cinerea* breeds in large numbers in some years but not annually in the same localities; so do several weaver birds such as the Chestnut Weaver *Ploceus rubiginosus* and the Fire-fronted Bishop *Euplectes diadematus*. The Red-billed Quelea *Quelea quelea* also performs irregular movements, breeding in enormous numbers in some years and not at all, or in lesser numbers, in others. Its economic importance as an agricultural pest has led to intensive study, which has shown that there are at least three more or less discrete populations, each with a more or less regular pattern of movement and breeding.

Some species with wide ecological tolerance may be permanent residents in one part of Africa, and nomadic, opportunistic breeders in another. The Wattled Starling is a regular breeder in some parts of Cape Province, and has become so in recent years as a result of perennially available food supplies (Uys 1977). The wide-ranging Black-shouldered Kite *Elanus caeruleus* is permanently resident on the highveld near Johannesburg, though its numbers fluctuate. In East Africa it is more or less nomadic, fluctuating widely in numbers from one year to another; and in Senegal it may be even more irregular, numerous in some years and absent in others (Morel and Poulet 1976). These irregular movements are probably associated with rat plagues, themselves irregular, but generally occurring in response to erratically fluctuating rainfall. Even the pedestrian Ostrich *Struthio camelus* breeds very regularly in the dry season in the moister parts of its range in East Africa, but is opportunistic, breeding usually in the rains, in the more arid parts of it, for instance the Namib Desert (Sauer and Sauer 1966; B. C. R. Bertram, pers. comm.).

2. Some Possibilities for Research

Prior to 1950 ornithological research in Africa depended to a large extent upon the enthusiasm of amateurs who happened to take an interest in particular groups or species, so that some, e.g. large raptors or the genus *Cisticola* among warblers, have become well-known, while others, apparently equally interesting, remain little known, e.g. rollers and bustards. The number of ornithologists long resident in Africa, amateur or professional, has probably decreased since the early sixties except in South Africa. However, it is equally true to say that probably a greater proportion of those now resident for short periods are interested in natural history in one form or another, especially ornithology, and can often carry out more effective short-term research work than could be done before. Many problems, especially perhaps concerning such subjects as migration, which depend to a great extent on long-term co-ordination of records from regularly manned stations, may remain obscure until more permanently resident African scientists become available and interested. The flood of literature recently published on African ornithology (e.g. no less than 1300 titles listed by Fry (1979) for the years 1975–78) certainly does not suggest any lack of interest.

Naturally, every naturalist has his or her particular interests; but given the present situation in Africa there seems little point in duplicating or elaborating on work which has already been quite thoroughly carried out for some very well known species when, close at hand, there may be other species about which very little is known, though they may be common and easily observed. The limited number of professional or amateur observers who are at present interested, and who have the time and opportunity to carry out part-time research, might often direct their efforts to better advantage if useful subjects for research were pinpointed. Innumerable examples will emerge from the texts on individual species of areas where a purposeful study would quickly be repaid in new information; here we mention a few broader subjects, where it seems to us that some co-ordinated concentration would rapidly advance our uneven knowledge.

The level of available knowledge varies greatly for different African countries. The avifauna of former British territories used to be the best known, largely because many British colonial officers were interested in birds. Professional ornithologists have never been numerous except in South Africa, and even there they have only become so within the last 20 years. A much larger number, too, of competent interested amateurs in South Africa has meant that the avifauna there is now much better known than in almost any other part of the continent. There is also extensive French literature, notably on North and Northwest Africa, and fine studies are also available from Mauritania, Senegal, the Ivory Coast and Gabon. Zaïre has been quite well covered, not only by Belgian scientists but also by the indefatigable J. P. Chapin of the American Museum of Natural History. Former Portuguese, Spanish and Italian territories were and still are much less well known. Ethiopia, only briefly colonized by the Italians, is better known than some other countries. This has largely come about because of the intrinsic interest offered by its mountain massif, the largest in Africa, which attracts many scientific expeditions; and latterly because of the efforts of several resident expatriate scientists.

African scientists interested in birds are as yet very scarce, and political conditions and recent social instability have greatly affected or reduced the opportunities for research in many countries. While it is to be hoped that this is only a temporary phase and that research will flourish better in the future, especially when more African scientists become involved, the present appears quite a good time to sum up what is now known about African bird species, and to suggest some lines of research that can profitably be explored by those in a position to do so.

2.1 Collecting, Systematics and Distribution

Up to the outbreak of World War II most of the published papers on African ornithology were mainly concerned with the details of systematics and distribution. They were often mere lists of specimens taken, giving very little information on such subjects as habitat preference, food, voice, behaviour, or nesting habits. Following the war, more attention was paid to field habits and behaviour, to such an extent that at the present time purely collecting activities have come to be frowned upon. This attitude is almost as unbalanced as the former concentration on collecting specimens and comparing minutiae of plumage differences or measurements without recording much about field habits. There is still room for collecting; but in the present conditions of generally increasing threats to bird populations it should be done with care, and with the aim of obtaining as much detailed information as possible from every specimen collected.

We have stressed the special interest of certain systematic problems; for instance, what are the true affinities of the Hamerkop *Scopus umbretta* or the Secretary Bird *Sagittarius serpentarius*, or the rockfowl *Picathartes*, or the Rockjumper *Chaetops frenatus*? Problems of this sort are not likely to be solved by collecting a few more skins, but require a more detailed and multipronged ecological, ethological, vocal and anatomical approach. However, it is also true to say that there are few major taxa which would not repay further study, probably involving some collection. Shrikes and starlings are two major groups obviously in need of further detailed study.

All that we would say here is that 'old style' collecting, involving killing a bird and just preparing its skin for a museum drawer, is usually now inadequate. Collecting should be extended to include any and every detail that may be of interest to other ornithologists. We know that we have the support of many modern taxonomists in this view. Good modern examples of the type of approach we have in mind have recently been provided by Ash (1979) who watched his new serin species *Serinus ankoberensis*, and found and described its nest before collecting it; and Wilson and Ball (1979), who extracted a great deal of interesting data, including such little recorded details as wing-loading, from 36 species of birds in Darfur, without collecting more than one or two individuals of any but common species.

There is certainly still room for what might be called 'old-style' collecting expeditions. At least 18 new species have been described from Africa in the past two decades, some by means of taxonomic splitting but all as the product of improved collections. They include two from Mt Nimba in Liberia, the distinctive Liberian Flycatcher *Melaenornis annamarulae* (Forbes-Watson 1970) and Eisentraut's Honeyguide *Melignomon eisentrauti* (Louette 1981), the Gola Malimbe *Malimbus ballmanni* from Sierra Leone (Wolters 1974, see also Field 1979), the Sidamo Lark *Mirafra sidamoensis* from Ethiopia (Erard 1975), the Kabyle Nuthatch *Sitta ledanti* from Algeria (Vielliard 1976) and the Ankober Serin *Serinus ankoberensis* from Ethiopia (Ash 1979). We might also mention a new genus and species of Bay Owl *Phodilus prigoginei* found long ago in Kivu, Zaïre (Schouteden 1952) but still known only by the single original specimen.

Another owl, the Sokoke Scops Owl *Otus ireneae*, first collected in Kenya in 1964 (Ripley 1966), is already threatened with extinction because of the smallness of the forest area it is known to inhabit, and none but males have ever been collected or seen. It may exist in the Boni Forest north of the Tana River, but this area is largely unknown. A well-equipped expedition to the little known forests of Southwest Ethiopia, already shrinking rapidly through human encroachment, would almost certainly discover new subspecies, if not full species, and extend our understanding of the range of others.

Available knowledge of the systematics of African species has recently been summed up in two monumental works, 'An Atlas of Speciation in African Passerine Birds' (Hall and Moreau 1970) and 'An Atlas of Speciation in African Non-passerine Birds' (Snow 1978). Although they do not cover subspecific variation in detail, these atlases pinpoint the known localities of all available specimens in museums and many sight records. Africa is now better served in this respect than any other continent. While there are still areas (e.g. Somalia, Angola, North Mozambique) where our knowledge is still relatively poor, there is a very solid body of information available as a starting point.

2.2 Nests and Eggs

The nests and eggs of many African species, some quite common, widespread or locally abundant, are still unknown. For instance, the eggs of the Bristle-crowned Chestnut-wing Starling *Onychognathus salvadorii* have never been seen, though its nesting sites are known, and there is a breeding record with young. Nothing is known of the breeding of the endemic and locally com-mon Rüppell's Chat *Myrmecocichla melaena*. Even more surprising, the eggs of several common barbets such as the Black-throated Barbet *Lybius melanocephalus*, widespread in East African thornbush near Nairobi, still remain to be described.

While we recognize that in some cases it will be desirable to deposit a clutch of eggs in a reputable museum for record purposes, we also feel that anyone locating the first nest of such a species will do more good by recording as much as possible of the breeding habits than by immediately collecting the eggs. A careful description of the nest and of the colour and size of the eggs can be made without taking them, and can nowadays easily be supplemented by colour photographs. If opportunity permits, more detailed observations can then be made. Notable examples of the value of such 'forbearance' when a nest is first discovered have recently been provided by Brosset and his co-workers in Gabon (Brosset 1971; Brosset and Erard 1976). Once a nest and its site have been discovered, others can later make fuller observations. Useful observations can also be made when there is no possibility of preserving the eggs. For instance, a 24-hour observation of the first known nest of the White-winged Dove *Streptopelia reichenowi* established that both sexes incubated and that certain displays were performed at nest-relief, while available descriptions of its voice were also found to be wrong (Brown 1977).

It is useless to collect eggs unless the identity of the parents is certain, which in skulking forest species may not be possible without collecting or trapping the birds. If the eggs are collected, it is also desirable (within limits) to collect the nest as well, as such specimens can be useful for comparative studies of nest-building methods and materials. Careful measurements at least should be taken and details recorded. (This may necessitate regularly carrying a small steel tape measure and calipers as well as a notebook.)

In species which are obviously common little harm can be done in taking a clutch or several clutches, but clearly this should be avoided in scarce, local or threatened species. Unfortunately, these are the very species found most attractive by private egg-collectors. Even collections in cabinets in museums have sometimes been rifled of their more valuable contents by unscrupulous individuals. A reputed clutch of Osprey's eggs (*Pandion haliaetus*), said to have been collected on the Berg River and the only 'probable' record of the Osprey breeding in South Africa, is now missing although it was seen quite recently.

2.3 Breeding Seasons

The breeding seasons of birds in Africa, and the factors affecting them, are still very imperfectly understood. Temperature and day-length, which together virtually dictate breeding in spring in temperate localities, are not or are less important in tropical Africa. Breeding seasons are much more likely to be affected by the alternation of wet and dry seasons, but these do not always affect the same species in the same way in different parts of Africa, and may not always be related to the availability of certain food supplies.

Nest record schemes are in operation in East and South Africa, and the East African data have now been completely analysed, including over 86,000 records for 783 species, excluding five highly gregarious species for which the accumulated records total millions (Brown and Britton 1980). The much larger set of records in the South African scheme has not been analysed, except for a few individual species.

In other parts of Africa breeding records have sometimes been collected in review papers, handbooks, or annotated check lists (e.g. Morel and Roux 1962; Benson *et al.* 1971; Archer and Godman 1937–1961). While we have made use of all such sources in preparing the texts, it is clear that, especially for colonial species, records are very incomplete, perhaps describing only one or two nests in a large colony without adequate details, such as clutch size and laying dates, in the colony as a whole. For instance, it has been difficult to locate good detailed records of Abdim's Stork *Ciconia abdimii*, though this is the commonest and most characteristic breeding stork in northern tropical Africa.

It has been repeatedly stated (and is generally believed) that the breeding seasons of birds are primarily or solely controlled by the availability of food supplies, this being the ultimate factor governing the laying date (e.g. Lack 1954, 1966; Immelmann 1971; Maclean 1976). We do not think that the situation is quite as simple as this. In much of tropical Africa, while breeding seasons can normally be related to weather conditions, they have seldom been related to adequately detailed quantitative studies of available food supply. A study in which the ornithologist has been able to obtain the collaboration of specialists in other disciplines is that of Thiollay (1975–1977) on raptors in the Ivory Coast, and this study supported the 'food supply' theory. In other cases, however, and there are several instances among large raptors, herons and storks, when a species breeds at the height of the dry season in one area, and at the height of the rains in another area, it is difficult to believe that food supplies will be optimum at those times in both areas. In some species, notably those breeding on sandbanks in large rivers, the availability of a site, or special conditions affecting a site, appear to over-ride possibly optimum food conditions. Some species also may breed in one year and not in others, though the food supplies may appear to be similar in non-breeding years. There is hardly a single species which would not repay more detailed study, especially if it occurs in a wide variety of habitats and in several different climatic regimes.

2.4 Voice and Song

Several workers are very active in this field, and a discography of African bird songs is available (Chappuis 1980). There is also a national collection of voice recordings in the Transvaal Museum, Pretoria, and another (not generally available for use) in Nairobi. Such studies have become possible in recent years through the increased sophistication and availability of modern tape-recording equipment. From the texts on individual species, where we have stated whether (to our knowledge) a species has been recorded and quoted the source, it will be clear that there is still plenty of scope for 'collecting' bird voices on tape.

Such recordings can be useful in determining the validity of certain species, though of course voice alone is not an infallible guide. For instance, the late M. E. W. North, a pioneer in this field in Africa, recorded the Boran Cisticola *Cisticola bodessa* and the Rattling Cisticola *C. chiniana*, and thought they were probably different species, though scarcely distinguishable in plumage. Very careful plumage comparisons have subsequently shown that they are in fact both good species, indistinguishable in the field except by voice (Ash 1974). Likewise, North suggested that, on the basis of its voice, the Slender-tailed Nightjar *Caprimulgus clarus* was a distinct species, and not, as generally stated in available handbooks, a race of either the Long-tailed Nightjar *C. climacurus* or the Mozambique Nightjar *C. fossii*, whose voices are completely different. He also thought, on the same grounds, that the bird generally known as the Lesser Brown-necked Raven *Corvus ruficollis edithae* was a distinct species, the Somali Crow *C. edithae* (North 1962).

Research on voice and song can usually be done without disturbing the bird, though it may be necessary to trap or handle it to determine what it is. Some species otherwise extremely hard to study can be induced to approach very close, even show themselves in the open by playing recordings of their voices made on the spot, e.g. the pygmy rails or flufftails, genus *Sarothrura* (Keith *et al.* 1970). A new extension of the range of the Red-chested Pygmy Crake *Sarothrura rufa* to Togo has recently been made by analysing a recording of the calls of frogs, in which the voice of the rail could be heard in the background, and comparing it with a sonagram from elsewhere (Erard and Vieillard 1977). The value of records of songs and calls is greatest when studying species of forest or dense undergrowth, normally hard to see. Birds otherwise almost undetectable may then be found to be quite common.

2.5 Daily Routine and Energy Budgets

Although the way a bird behaves by day may be generally known, it can very seldom be analysed quantitatively, on the basis of many detailed observations from dawn to dark. One has only to pick almost any common species to realize that a detailed analysis of the time spent resting, preening and feeding is seldom possible from the available data. In some species, notably large, very active birds of prey, swifts, and many skulking species of undergrowth or thickets, the difficulties appear almost insuperable. However, in other species, notably in some large water birds and even some birds of prey, they could often be easily recorded. Even a few days or hours of concentrated observation can be useful. Valuable studies of this sort have recently been carried out by Tarboton (1978) on the daily activities of the Black-shouldered Kite *Elanus caeruleus*, and by Whitfield and Blaber (1978–1979) on various fishing birds at Lake St Lucia.

Data on such subjects can be recorded in two ways: (a) by the 'focal animal' method in which an individual is observed for as long as possible and its activities recorded and analysed; and (b) by the 'instantaneous scan' method in which the activities of all individuals of a species observed are recorded, however briefly they may be seen. The first method is obviously more suited to large, relatively inactive birds, or species such as the Ostrich or Secretary Bird which can be kept in view for long periods. The second method is of value with, for instance, large mobile species such as eagles that may be seen only rarely and briefly. In the case of the African Fish Eagle *Haliaeetus vocifer* there is good agreement between the results of detailed observation of the daily routine of individuals and scattered records collected in the course of population surveys (L. H. Brown, unpub.). The instantaneous scan method should thus be useful for other large birds not easily watched for long periods.

In some larger birds small radio transmitters attached to the body can be used to determine nocturnal and diurnal activity patterns. Such methods are particularly valuable for nocturnal species, or birds inhabiting dense growth where they cannot long be kept in view. Although of most use for nocturnal species, they could also be used to study large forest hornbills or turacos, which cannot long be watched by an observer on the forest floor. Instruments can be devised which inform the recorder not only where the bird is but what it is doing, i.e. flying, perching, feeding, and so on.

2.6 Food and Feeding Methods

As with daily habits, although these can often be generally described, they cannot often be described quantitatively. Much of the available data on food comes from the lists of stomach contents sometimes recorded on museum skin labels, or in expedition reports. The amount of food needed related to bodyweight, the time and energy required to collect it, and the strategies adopted are often scarcely, if at all known. Clearly, such studies can form part of wider studies on diurnal behaviour, as suggested above.

In many species the food brought to the nest for the young is known, but that eaten by the adults when not breeding is unknown or little known. In some cases the method of analysis, e.g. of the pellets of owls or large diurnal raptors, or collections of bones, are subject to bias, since they tend to over-emphasize what is indigestible or too large to swallow. However, provided the possibility of such a bias is recognized and allowed for, almost any method can produce at least some useful results. Since, as has been mentioned, the availability of food supplies is often supposed to be the most critical factor controlling breeding seasons or movements, it is desirable that more precise data on food actually eaten should be available. At present the data on which general statements are based are often sketchy and anecdotal at best, if not actually inaccurate. Ostriches, for instance, are not omnivorous or insectivorous as is often stated, but basically vegetarian.

2.7 Ringing, Marking and Migration Studies

A great deal of information now exists on the movements of Palearctic birds in Africa, usually as a result of the recovery in Africa of birds ringed in the Palearctic, but also of birds ringed in Africa and recovered in, or on the way to, their Palearctic breeding haunts. Data for intra-African migrants are, however, much more scanty, though some records exist which support more general ideas formulated from field observation.

The recovery rate of birds ringed in Africa is usually much lower than in temperate Europe or North America, no doubt because of the vast spaces involved and the small numbers of people who can recognize a ring and take the trouble to return it to its source. Most ringing has been done in South Africa, where 900,000 birds of 603 species have been ringed since 1948. There are also active groups of ringers in Northwest Africa, Senegal, Nigeria, Kenya and Zambia, while J. S. Ash has ringed over 40,000 birds in Ethiopia, and other ornithologists have carried out ringing for specific purposes. The extraordinarily interesting data recently obtained from Ngulia in Tsavo National Park, Kenya (Pearson and Backhurst 1976) have underlined how little we know about how even common migrants behave. The fact that these results were, and continue to be, obtained as a purely fortuitous by-product of building a game-viewing lodge in a particular locality with certain weather conditions further underlines the mystery surrounding many species. The regular wintering grounds of common Palearctic migrants as diverse as the Honey Buzzard *Pernis apivorus* and the House Martin *Delichon urbica* are still obscure.

Colour markings, with conspicuous and easily readable plastic rings, leg tags or patagial tags, has in some large species provided much more information than could be hoped for from ringing recoveries alone. In the Cape Vulture *Gyps coprotheres* far more information about movements and survival has been obtained in recent years through colour marking than in many previous years when the young were ringed. Marking a number of young Great White Pelicans *Pelecanus onocrotalus* with coloured leg streamers at Lake Shala in Ethiopia (which must be done with great care and only at the end of the breeding season because of the extreme shyness of the birds) has shown that the young, which disappear almost at once from the neighbourhood of the breeding colony, disperse widely in any direction (Urban and Jefford 1977). Such colour marking techniques deserve wider experimentation and use.

Most of the available data on weights of birds, and much on moults have come from ringers, most of whom automatically weigh the birds they catch, partly to relate weight to stored fat and other indications of their migrating condition. Results from South Africa are at present being collated by SAFRING. Ringers could often, however, record much more information than they usually do, e.g. on wing area and wing-loading, proportion of immatures to adults, and sex ratios. They could (and some do) also collect parasites, take blood samples and body condition measurements. When mere speed is not the main consideration (as it may be when large numbers have been caught), there is scope for more detailed recording of information possibly not of direct interest to students of migration.

Mist netting in thick forest and elsewhere has shed much light on the relative abundance of species in certain habitats, some species otherwise very hard to see being then found to be quite common, such as the Sokoke Pipit *Anthus sokokensis* (Britton and Zimmerman 1979) or skulking forest species in Uganda (Okia 1976). There are, however, many areas where such work has not been carried out at all. It evidently should only be carried out by those trained in the necessary techniques, for in the wrong hands mist nets may result in obvious abuses, for instance the trapping of birds for sale to aviaries abroad, which usually results in heavy loss of life, if not when caught, then certainly in transit.

Ringing and mist netting are at present rather well controlled in Africa, and in South Africa the policy is to discourage odd individual efforts at 'ring and fling' and to concentrate ringing schemes near main centres where results are most likely to be obtained. For unknown reasons, more recoveries are obtained from Francophone Africa than former British colonies, and good co-operation is also obtained from the USSR.

2.8 Numbers and Census Data

We have already observed that it is at present impossible to make a good estimate of the number of birds in Africa because of the paucity of good census data, relating to different habitats and different times of year. This is one field where available data could rapidly be augmented by well directed efforts by competent observers, and even by visitors to Africa for short periods. Some estimate of the number of birds in any habitat (except in very crowded aquatic situations or dense forest) can be made in a few hours. A large number of such estimates, collated over a period of time and related to habitat and seasons, would enable a better estimate of overall populations than is currently possible.

Various techniques can be used, depending on the circumstances. Actual counts of species and numbers of individuals can be made in reasonably open habitat. In forest or woodland, especially at certain seasons, good estimates of the numbers of some species can be made by locating singing males, using the techniques applied in the Common Birds Census organized by the British Trust for Ornithology. At the equator dawn song occurs on every day of the year; but the numbers of individuals and species singing vary from dry to wet seasons. Roadside counts have often been used for raptors, and rollers, for instance (Brown and Brown 1973), but are subject to bias in that large, more conspicuous, perching or aerial species such as the Bateleur *Terathopius ecaudatus* are seen more often than their actual abundance warrants. Such counts are possibly most useful to determine general trends; for instance, counts made over 10 years along the Nairobi–Mombasa road have shown that both Bateleurs and Tawny Eagles *Aquila rapax* (the species most likely to nest in large trees) have been reduced by human occupation and destruction of the habitat in recent times (C. H. Brown, pers. obs.).

A few species, generally those considered to be threatened, have been more or less accurately counted, e.g. the Jackass Penguin *Spheniscus demersus* in South Africa, and the Waldrapp *Geronticus eremita* in Northwest Africa. The Sokoke Scops Owl *Otus ireneae*, discovered in 1964 and thought to be very rare, has now been estimated at 1300–1500 pairs in its known range (Britton and Zimmerman 1979). Lesser Flamingoes *Phoeniconaias minor* have been estimated at at least two million (Tuite 1981) and possibly as many as five million (Brown 1975) in Africa. The density per unit area of several large birds of prey such as Wahlberg's Eagle *A. wahlbergi* and the Tawny Eagle has now been estimated in several areas, so that by extrapolating the results a reasonable estimate of the total population may be made. For instance, there are about 12 million km² of habitat suited to the Tawny Eagle; and if the species were uniformly distributed at estimated densities of 24 km² per pair, the total African population might be about 500,000. There is evidently enormous scope for research on population density, numbers related to particular habitats, and kindred subjects.

2.9 Pesticides and Their Effects, and Other Contaminants

The effects of using organochlorine pesticides in Europe and North America are now well documented, and it has been shown that they have far-reaching adverse effects on populations of birds and other animals living in areas where they are used. These effects were probably brought most sharply into focus by the decline of the Peregrine Falcon *Falco peregrinus*, and a few other sensitive species which could thus indicate quite clearly the level of environmental contamination (Hickey 1969). Quite large quantities of organochlorine pesticides are still used in Africa for malaria control, control of crop pests in irrigation schemes, locust control and dryland agriculture. It is, however, difficult to arrive at any clear indication of their effects because of a lack of good information on the amounts used and where (which some of the users and suppliers are reluctant to divulge) and lack of good studies on the degree of contamination of birds in the African environment.

The few published studies of the level of organochlorine residues in birds include several on birds of prey, generally regarded by reason of their position at the top of the food chain as sensitive indicator species. Some of these results have been more reassuring than otherwise, surveys in Kenya, for instance, indicating that the residue levels in some Rift Valley lakes were among the lowest on record (Kallquist and Meadows 1977; Greichus *et al.* 1977). However, the levels of contamination are higher in some areas than in others, e.g. in South Africa and Zimbabwe (Whitwell *et al.* 1974; Peakall and Kemp 1976).

Very large areas may be sprayed, almost indiscriminately by, for example, some international aid donors, in a manner which would not nowadays be tolerated by environmentally conscious societies in developed countries. Such schemes are usually aimed at controlling disease vectors, e.g. Tsetse Fly or *Simulium* (involved in the transmission of river blindness or onchocerciasis). Some such wholesale spraying operations are known to have had disastrous effects on animal life other than the target organisms (Koeman *et al.* 1978), and it would be very surprising if they did not. They have even been used in ecologically sensitive areas such as the Okavango Delta, and studies are needed to ascertain whether such activities have long-term adverse effects and, perhaps more important, whether the management applied thereafter will maintain any improvement that may have resulted for the human population. Direct spraying of breeding colonies of queleas, usually with less persistent organophosphorus compounds, may have adverse effects on birds of prey or on other species that roost or feed in the same area. However, if such spraying is done with care, damage to other than the target species is unlikely to be severe.

Although the use of organochlorine pesticides in agriculture receives the most publicity, many other human activities are dangerous to bird life. They are most likely to be serious in industrialized areas such as South Africa, but here the technology that can reduce the adverse effects is also available. Such adverse effects include the electrocution of large birds on power lines, e.g. Cape Vulture *Gyps coprotheres* (preventable by modifications in the design of pylons); threats to certain Karoo species by open-cast coal mining; threats to wintering areas important to large populations of Palearctic waders by the development of a deep water port; and threats to the endangered Jackass Penguin *Spheniscus demersus* by guano mining and oil pollution.

In all such cases it is necessary for ornithologists and other naturalists to learn in advance what plans exist, for a threat often arises suddenly without allowing any previous consultation with those concerned. Secondly, the seriousness of the threat to populations of any species must be objectively assessed; evidently they may be more important in the case of a species with a small and local population, such as the Slaty Egret *Egretta vinaceigula*, than in common and widespread species. Finally it is necessary to make clear and, if possible, reasonable recommendations that are likely to be accepted rather than to attempt to fight hopeless losing battles when these are not necessarily vital. It often seems reasonably clear that 'progress' and development will be pushed through whether ornithologists like it or not; but in other cases adequate prior information and careful factual surveys should lead to sensible reasoned recommendations which may well meet with acceptance. It must also be remembered that some of the results of human development may benefit some species. Martial Eagles *Polemaetus bellicosus* and Lanner Falcons *Falco biarmicus* now breed on electric pylons in Transvaal (Dean 1975; A. Kemp, pers. comm.) in areas where they could not breed at all in former times for lack of nesting sites. Adverse results usually outweigh beneficial ones, but any beneficial results should at least be noted and appreciated.

2.10 Longer Term Studies

Many of the subjects so far mentioned concern the sort of research that may not involve long-continued study in the same place. For those in a position to undertake long-term research there are many obvious subjects and a lengthy discussion of possibilities would be inappropriate; only a few subjects are therefore mentioned here.

(a) In view of the possibly over-rated numbers of migrants in relation to residents, further study of the role of migrants would be welcomed, especially concerning competition for food, niche occupation, and habits in Africa compared to their breeding range.

(b) Community studies in specific areas could be undertaken to see what the total population composition is and how the species are related to one another, what inter-dependency may exist directly or indirectly, and whether co-evolution with other animals or plants is evident. If such inter-dependencies exist, the advantages or disadvantages might be more closely investigated.

(c) Intercontinental comparisons of families or communities in similar habitats are needed to define further what factors are uniquely African and what factors are common to other areas in shaping species. For instance, there appear to be none of the remarkable lek passerines (cotingas and manakins in South America and birds of paradise in Australasia) in African forests; but nomadism is likely to occur in Australian and African arid and semi-arid habitats.

(d) The relationships of diet, and its quantity and quality, to annual cycles of moult, breeding and body condition could be examined to determine any shortages of essential constituents, to relate food supplies to environmental conditions and to ascertain more critically what factors limit abundance, or control the timing and success of breeding attempts.

(e) The study of individually marked populations to determine population dynamics, including age at first breeding, variation of breeding success with age, adult and juvenile survival, site tenacity and social organization would be extremely useful. Some work along these lines has already been done, but much more is needed.

We would stress that while there is plenty of scope for advanced scientific study in Africa, there is also still plenty of scope for what in Europe or North America might be called elementary ornithology. There are few bird species in Europe or North America whose nest and eggs have never been described, but in Africa there are scores. If known at all, the nest may never have been observed for any length of time, and there may be no photographic or other records of breeding behaviour or plumages. There is still abundant scope in Africa for straightforward observation of what may seem unimportant and insignificant details; and perhaps the emphasis in research should still be on gathering such missing details, rather than on more advanced fields of research of principal interest only to specialists. Any observant person, particularly in the less well-known areas of Africa, should be able to add to some area of our knowledge of African birds. It has even been done by people detained as prisoners or spies (Toschi 1950; Tyler 1978).

3. Scope, Content and Layout of the Text

3.1 Existing Reference Works

No single modern work exists covering the birds of the whole of Africa, the last to do so being Anton Reichenow's 'Die Vögel Afrikas' (1901–03, 1905). Classification of the birds of Africa south of the Sahara has been dealt with by Sclater (1924, 1930), White (1960–63, 1965), Hall and Moreau (1970) and Snow (1978). There are many regional handbooks dealing, for instance, with tropical West Africa (Bannerman 1930–51); the former Belgian Congo (Chapin 1932–54); the former British Somaliland and the Gulf of Aden (Archer and Godman 1937–61); Kenya and Uganda (Jackson and Sclater 1938) and the former Rhodesia (Priest 1933–36). The most recent series is that of Mackworth-Praed and Grant (1957–73), which deals with the whole of Africa south of the Sahara, in three sets of volumes, dealing with (i) Northeast and East Africa, (ii) the southern third of Africa and (iii) West Africa and the Congo. This arrangement necessitates the repetition of similar information on many of the same species in each of the three sets of regional volumes. There are also a number of field guides (which enable bird-watchers to identify *some* of the birds they may see in an area); and two notable regional works, one dealing with North and Northwest Africa (Etchécopar and Hüe 1967) and one with South Africa south of the Limpopo and Cunene Rivers (McLachlan and Liversidge 1978). If many of these older regional works can be obtained at all, their price is now extremely high as they are collectors' items; and none of them is much less than 20 years out of date. A complete list of major regional works is given in the bibliography of this volume.

Several of these existing works, moreover, were based either wholly or partly on information acquired from museums in Europe or America, and the authors sometimes had very limited experience of the countries they were writing about. An exception was J. P. Chapin and his work on the former Belgian Congo (Chapin 1932–54). In his book, knowledge derived from museum specimens was augmented by field expeditions, by published field notes, and by correspondence with a scatter of amateur ornithologists living in Africa. None of the existing handbooks takes cognizance of the flood of new published material (not to mention the mass of unpublished detail known to exist) which has appeared in recent years.

This new handbook is prepared by field ornithologists mainly *for* field ornithologists, though taxonomy and systematics have not been forgotten. We have in fact tried to stress particular points where further detailed study could help to elucidate long-standing and difficult taxonomic problems, either with single species, such as the Hamerkop *Scopus umbretta* and Secretary Bird *Sagittarius serpentarius*, or with families or genera, such as the shrikes Laniidae. However, our emphasis is primarily on ecology and behaviour. We feel that such an emphasis is now necessary because, over the last 20 years or so, the study of African birds has moved deci-

sively away from the former, mainly geographical, distributional and taxonomic approach towards detailed field observations on, for instance, habitat preferences, food and feeding methods, daily routine, migration and breeding habits. We therefore feel that the time has come to try to draw together what is known of the living bird.

3.2 Scope of the Work

We cover all species occurring in the area shown in Fig. 9, i.e. the entire continent of Africa and its adjacent islands. These include Socotra, Zanzibar and Pemba, Bioko (Fernando Po), São Tomé, Principe and Pagalu (Annobon) in the Gulf of Guinea. The more distant oceanic islands, such as the Azores, Madeira, the Canaries and Cape Verdes, however, are excluded. Madagascar, with Aldabra, Comoros, Mascarene Islands and the Seychelles, form a separate zoogeographical subregion, and it is intended that this will be covered in a further volume.

We are aware that in adopting this arrangement we are including those parts of Africa adjacent to the Mediterranean normally regarded as part of the Palearctic zoogeographical region; and excluding parts of southern Arabia, such as North and South Yemen, normally regarded as part of the Afrotropical (or Ethiopian) zoogeographical region. Despite the likelihood of some criticism, we have adopted this approach for several reasons:

(i) Africa is a striking geographical entity, the only continent which spans the whole latitudinal and climatic range from the northern to the southern subtropics. To most people Africa means the continent of Africa, not those parts of Africa south of the Sahara. We agree with Moreau (1966) that to ignore the bird faunas of some 8.7 million km² of Africa in and north of the Sahara 'passes by much that is of interest, and is unrealistic when viewed against the background of immense climatic changes known to have transformed so much of this part of Africa in the last few thousand years'. It thus seems ridiculous not to regard the huge Sahara desert as part of Africa, while the mountains of the Atlas and Cape ranges are ecologically similar, and even share some of the same botanical elements.

(ii) So little has been recorded in recent years about birds in either North or South Yemen that anything known about species inhabiting southern Arabia, but typical of the Afrotropical region, will probably have been recorded in the African part of their range.

(iii) While it is true that some 165 species breeding in North and Northwest Africa do not extend either as residents or migrants to the Afrotropical region, they have not usually been studied in great detail in their North African range, while their ecology there may differ markedly from that in, say, Finland. There are also many species which breed in North Africa and which either reach Africa south of the

Sahara as migrants, or have tropical breeding races.

(iv) Africa is a main wintering ground for a large proportion of migrant Palearctic species; a few, e.g. the Wheatear *Oenanthe o. leucorhoa*, reaching North Africa from Greenland. The movements and habits of many of these Palearctic winter migrants have often been studied in far greater detail in their African winter range than has been possible in their eastern winter range, which includes India, Burma, Malaysia and Indonesia.

Our approach necessitates some repetition of information already contained in the publication 'The Birds of the Western Palearctic' (Cramp and Simmons 1977, 1980 and continuing) for some purely Palearctic species which do not enter Africa south of the Sahara. In view of the need to reduce unnecessary duplication to a minimum, such purely Palearctic species have been treated in less detail than species that are properly of the Afrotropical region; and we have concentrated on their habits in North and North-west Africa as far as they are known. For Palearctic migrants in Africa we have concentrated on their habits within their African range (where they often spend most of the year) and have omitted all detail about breeding habits. For some other species, the Ostrich *Struthio camelus* for instance, which now barely occurs in the Western Palearctic and is at present typically African, we have provided as much detail as space allows.

Place names, particularly those of larger political regions and of countries, are subject to change. We use what appear to us to be the most commonly used and best understood names (see Fig. 9) and trust that, where a term used is considered by some to be inappropriate, it will cause no offence.

3.3 Content and Layout of the Text

We have tried to lay out the text, within the rather strict limits of wordage and space available, so that the essential information concerning a species is presented in a logical manner. This necessitates a compressed, terse style, some use of generally accepted abbreviations or symbols (e.g. ♂ male and ♀ female), and, where possible, compression of available data into figures rather than words.

(i) Nomenclature and Systematics

We adopt the orders and families and the sequence used by Voous' 'List of Holarctic Bird Species' (1973–1977) and his proposed sequence to be used in the forthcoming new edition of 'A New Dictionary of Birds' (Campbell and Lack, in prep.). In certain instances, however, we have used our own arrangement, e.g. Order Falconiformes. At the generic and species level we follow Hall and Moreau (1970) and Snow (1978) for birds of Africa south of the Sahara. For areas not covered by these works we largely follow Peters *et al.* (1934–1979). At the subspecies level we again generally rely on Peters *et al.*, updated where necessary by more recent findings.

(ii) Layout of Texts

Under each order heading we give a brief description of the main characteristics, and indicate whether it is divided further into suborders or superfamilies and how many families there are. Under each family heading we give a somewhat fuller description of its main features, make clear whether it is endemic to Africa, and detail the number of genera and species included. In some cases we subdivide families into subfamilies.

Under most genera we give a description, with the salient characteristics and numbers of species.

The species texts are laid out as follows:

Species heading. At the head of each species account the scientific name and authority, and English and French names are given, followed by the original name and citation.

We have given what we think is the most generally accepted English name world-wide. If this name is not generally accepted, e.g. in South Africa, where another name is often in general use, we give both names. Thus *Aquila verreauxi* is generally known as Verreaux's Eagle, but in South Africa and Zimbabwe it has long been called the Black Eagle. Some such local names can be misleading in a wider context. For instance, in South Africa the Cape Rook *Corvus capensis* is officially called the Black Crow, to distinguish it from the Pied Crow *Corvus albus*, though this would not serve in Somalia where the Somali Crow *C. edithae* (or *C. ruficollis edithae*) is also black. Our spelling of English names has been guided largely by Parkes (1978).

Since much of tropical Africa is Francophone we have given the French name, based upon Devillers (1976–78) as the most complete list. We have avoided using purely local names or names in languages not widely understood, even though some may be nicely expressive or onomatopoeic, for instance 'Ndundu', the Kikuyu and Kamba name for the Southern Ground Hornbill *Bucorvus leadbeateri*, which resembles the bird's call.

Range and Status. Here we describe briefly the range of the species in Africa and its status. We first indicate whether it is resident, a Palearctic winter migrant, or an intra-African migrant (it may, of course, be all three, e.g. the Black Kite *Milvus migrans*). We then briefly describe the habitats preferred by the birds within the whole of their range because some birds, particularly aquatic species, may not be found everywhere within the broad area delineated. Regarding status we have tried to give an indication of relative abundance. Thus, 'very abundant' means that more than 100 of any species would be seen daily in its preferred habitat; 'abundant' that one should see 10–100 daily; 'common' that 1–10 would be seen daily; 'frequent' that a species is quite often seen or heard, but some effort is needed to locate it; 'uncommon' that 10 or fewer would be seen in a year; 'rare' that a species is so scarce one would be lucky to see a specimen in several years, or even a lifetime; and 'vagrant' that only a few records exist. The status and

Fig. 9. Political map of Africa.

numbers of any species can vary from one part of its range to another; thus the Pink-backed Pelican *Pelecanus rufescens* is common or rare in South Africa but locally abundant in Nigeria or Kenya.

Few African birds have been accurately counted, but where we know of any figures we give them. We also mention whether a species is considered to be acutely threatened with extinction, endangered, somewhat threatened, or not in danger at all, these facts being dependent on recent surveys, or the work of the International Council for Bird Preservation (ICBP). Several African countries now maintain their own 'Red Book' of endangered species, although a bird endangered and needing protection in one country may be abundant in another, and so not endangered as a species.

In almost every case, a distribution map is given in this section, the exceptions being a few species confined to one island, where a map is needless, or rare vagrants. These maps cover the whole continent, and very occasionally may show more than one species, with areas of overlap defined by the different types of shading used. The maps are based on the two atlases of speciation in African birds (Hall and Moreau 1970; Snow 1978), but the small scale prohibits the use of symbols to show exact localities. Scale also prohibits the location of a species in relation to the vegetation of Africa, and the mapping of subspecies, and breeding and non-breeding ranges, other than in a few unusual cases. The ranges of seabirds off the coasts of Africa are imperfectly known, therefore the ranges shown are approximate.

Description. For all species we have given a fairly full description of the plumage of the adult male; of the female if different; and of the immatures and downy young where these details are known. Since all species are also illustrated in colour these descriptions are terse and brief, but we think adequate. (See pp. 30 and 31 for the terms used for parts of African birds.)

In polytypic species we have described the best known and most studied race in Africa, which may not be the nominate race. For instance, in the Great Cormorant *Phalacrocorax carbo* we have not described in full the nominate race *P. c. carbo* of Europe, but the resident African race *P. c. lucidus*, the White-breasted or White-necked Cormorant.

We have tried to indicate accurately the colours of soft parts, bill, cere, eye, bare facial skin, feet and legs, as these are very often among the points first noticed about a bird by field observers. Such colours may also vary in the breeding season, and where this occurs we describe the changes seen.

Measurements are taken from standard works such as Cramp and Simmons (1977, 1980), McLachlan and Liversidge (1978) and Brown and Amadon (1968), supplemented by more recent data. Specific sources are quoted only if the information has been gathered from other works than these. Whenever possible, measurements include sample size, averages and extremes. We begin with the flattened wing from the carpal joint to the tip of the longest primary, then the tail from the base to the tip of the longest tail feathers (usually, but not always the central pair), and the tarsus. We also give,

when available, measurements of weight, wing-span, and other details that may be of interest. (N.B. Measurements of size are given in millimetres and of weight in grams unless otherwise stated.)

The description is followed by a list of recognized subspecies (if any). For each we give the diagnostic characters, and the wing measurements and weights if known.

Field Characters. This section is designed to aid field identification. If a bird is unmistakable, only a few characters are listed and the section is brief. If, on the other hand, it can easily be confused with other species, we give more comprehensive information on how to distinguish it. Some details of description, e.g. bill or eye colour, may here be repeated if diagnostic. We have given the fullest details for closely allied species or those whose ranges overlap. Line illustrations of some diagnostic details have occasionally been provided.

Voice. We first state whether to our knowledge the voice of a species has been recorded and, if so, quote a number referring back to the discography given in each volume (for this volume see p. 507).

Phonetic renderings of calls in most books are unsatisfactory, partly because there is no universally accepted method of expressing bird calls in human syllables, and partly because hardly any two listeners will agree on the exact character of a call. Nonetheless we have taken advantage of such recordings as are available and our own field experience in trying to express calls phonetically. Sonagrams have not been used in most cases as they require training in interpretation and occupy much space.

In addition to vocal calls, birds sometimes make mechanical noises, good examples being the aerial display of the Flappet Lark *Mirafra rufocinnamomea* or the whirring display of the Broadbill *Smithornis capensis*. Where necessary we have described these, defining, if known, the context in which they are used, e.g. the bill-clattering of storks in mutual displays.

General Habits. This section broadly concerns what the bird does when not breeding or when away from the nest. We have first attempted to define how well known these habits are: (a) scarcely known—the species may have been collected, but no detailed field observations have been made and its calls may still be undescribed; (b) little known—a few scattered observations have been published; (c) well known—much is known about its general habits but few quantitative data have been published; (d) very well known—the general habits have been very well recorded and some quantitative data may be available; (e) intimately known—the species has been thoroughly studied and its habits have been analysed quantitatively.

Habits are usually described in the following sequence: (a) type of habitat preferred, some species being very tolerant and others confined to single habitats; (b) roosting and foraging; (c) movements (if any) within Africa, with approximate dates of arrival and departure at selected localities; (d) any special aspect of behaviour which helps to distinguish the bird from others.

Food. The preferred food is listed, if possible quantitatively, by number and by weight. Usually it can only be generally indicated, and space does not permit full lists for species whose food is very well known. If any special method of feeding applicable to that particular species and no other is known we describe it fully here, for instance the mode of opening molluscs used by the Openbill Stork *Anastomus lamelligerus*, or the filter-feeding of flamingoes.

Breeding Habits. In purely migrant Palearctic visitors this section is omitted altogether. In those Palearctic species which breed solely in North and Northwest Africa with no tropical races, breeding biology is dealt with only briefly, as it will have been much more fully dealt with in other handbooks dealing specifically with the Palearctic region. In mainly marine species which breed somewhere within our geographical limits, but which have not been thoroughly studied in our area, we include salient points derived from other studies. In those species (by far the majority) which are resident somewhere within Africa and the adjacent islands we provide all the detail we can, commensurate with the space available to us.

We again begin by categorizing the current state of our knowledge on each species: (a) unknown—the nest has never been found; in a few such cases the site may be suspected and if so we detail these; (b) little known—a few nests and eggs may have been found, but little detail is recorded; (c) well known—many nests and eggs have been found, and there is good general detail on sites and seasons, but no long-sustained observations at the nest have been made; (d) very well known—as (c), but at least one nest has been watched throughout most of one breeding season and the shares of the sexes and rate of development of young have been recorded; (e) intimately known—several or many nests of many individuals have been watched for long periods in several places, giving good quantitative detail on all aspects of breeding behaviour.

Following this brief definition of the state of our knowledge (which may differ in different parts of Africa) we describe the course of the breeding season in the following sequence: (a) areas chosen; (b) song, courtship and display associated with breeding; (c) nest and nest-building, giving details of sites, size, materials used and share of the sexes in building; and, if remarkable (e.g. the nest of the Hamerkop *Scopus umbretta*), the method of construction; (d) eggs and incubation, giving as full details as are available of number, size, colour, weight, laying seasons, incubation period and behaviour of the parents during this; (e) development of the young during the fledging period, including details of their appearance and weight, if known, at different ages; (f) behaviour of the parents during the fledging period, including details of the share of the sexes in rearing young; (g) the post-fledging period with information on the behaviour of young and adults after leaving the nest; (h) statistics of survival, in terms of young reared per pair per year overall or per successful nest, and the implications of such statistics on longevity. Data on the adolescence of the young and their survival rate to maturity may in a few cases (e.g. the Marabou Stork *Leptoptilos crumeniferus*) be available, and are included here.

References. Where possible, a few key references are listed at the end of each account. The aim of this is to help anyone interested in a particular species to go straight to the most comprehensive papers concerning that bird in our full bibliography at the end of each volume. (Many other relevant works will usually be given in the references cited in any such paper as well as those listed by us.) No references are quoted in the text unless information of quite exceptional or unusual interest is mentioned, in which case the author and date of the source are quoted. In the bibliography itself the full details of all the references consulted, whether mentioned in the species accounts or not, have been listed, grouped under family headings (N.B. this has not always been possible in the case of L. H. Brown's text). A list of the main general and regional references and checklists used is also given here. Sometimes Ph.D. theses not subsequently published in any well known journal are the only good source of detail, and where this is so we have cited their whereabouts.

(iii) Illustrations

Almost all species are illustrated in colour and, with a few exceptions, principal sex, age and seasonal differences are shown. Several subspecies are illustrated if these are markedly different from one another, but the illustration of all known variations of plumage or every recognized subspecies has not been possible.

Where feasible, all members of a genus, or of several related genera, are shown on one plate; sometimes we have departed from the strict systematic sequence in order to make illustrations more useful in a particular area when comparing similar-sized or coloured species. Occasionally a bill or head is shown again separately on the main plate in order to help with identification, and these illustrations may be on a different scale from the rest of the plate. Eggs are not illustrated.

In addition, line drawings of important postures and displays are occasionally given in the text to clarify our descriptions of these.

References

Acocks, J. P. H. (1953). Veld types of South Africa. *Bot. Surv. S. Afr. Mem.* **28**.

Archer, G. and Godman, E. M. (1937–1961). 'The Birds of British Somaliland and the Gulf of Aden'. Vols 1–2. Gurney and Jackson, London. Vols 3–4. Oliver & Boyd, London.

Ash, J. S. (1974). The Boran Cisticola in Ethiopia. *Bull. Br. Orn. Club* **94**, 24–26.

Ash, J. S. (1979). A new species of serin from Ethiopia. *Ibis* **121**, 1–7.

Bannerman, D. A. (1930–1951). 'The Birds of Tropical West Africa'. Vols 1–8. Crown Agents, London.

Beals, E. W. (1970). Birds of a *Euphorbia-Acacia* woodland in Ethiopia: habitat and seasonal changes. *J. Anim. Ecol.* **39**, 277–297.

Benson, C. W., Brooke, R. K., Dowsett, R. J. and Irwin, M. P. S. (1971). 'The Birds of Zambia'. Collins, London.

Britton, P. L. and Zimmerman, D. A. (1979). The avifauna of Sokoke Forest, Kenya. *J. E. Afr. Nat. Hist. Soc.* **169**, 1–16.

Brooke, R. K., Martin, R., Martin, J. and Martin, E. (1980). The Booted Eagle, *Hieraaetus pennatus*, as a breeding species in South Africa. *Gerfaut* **70**, 297–304.

Brosset, A. (1971). Premières observations sur la reproduction de six oiseaux africains. *Alauda* **39**, 112–126.

Brosset, A. and Erard, C. (1976). Première description de la nidification de quatre espèces en forêt Gabonaise. *Alauda* **44**, 205–235.

Brown, L. H. (1969). A bird count on the Arabian 'Jol'. *J. Bombay Nat. Hist. Soc.* **66** (2), 327–337.

Brown, L. H. (1975). Population, ecology and the conservation of flamingos—East Africa. *In* 'Flamingos' (Kear, J. and Duplaix-Hall, N. Eds), pp. 38–48. T. & A. D. Poyser, Berkhamsted.

Brown, L. H. (1977). The White-winged Dove *Streptopelia reichenowi* in SE Ethiopia, comparisons with other species, and a field key for identification. *Scopus* **1**, 107–109.

Brown, L. H. (1980). The conservation of African birds: threats, problems and action needed. Proc. IV Pan-Afr. Orn. Cong., pp. 345–354. South African Ornithological Society, Johannesburg.

Brown, L. H. and Amadon, D. (1968). 'Eagles, Hawks and Falcons of the World'. Vols 1, 2. Hamlyn, Feltham.

Brown, L. H. and Britton, P. L. (1980). 'The Breeding Seasons of East African Birds'. East African Natural History Society, Nairobi.

Brown, L. H. and Brown, B. E. (1973). The relative numbers of migrant and resident rollers in eastern Kenya. *Bull. Br. Orn. Club* **93**, 126–130.

Brown, L. H. and Cochemé, J. (1969). 'A Study of the Agroclimatology of the Highlands of Eastern Africa'. FAO/UNESCO/WHO, Rome.

Campbell, B. and Lack, E. (Eds) (in prep.). 'A New Dictionary of Birds'. Revised ed.

Chapin, J. (1932–1954). The birds of the Belgian Congo. *Bull. Am. Mus. Nat. Hist.* **65**, 75, **75A**, **75B**.

Chappuis, C. (1980). List of sound-recorded Ethiopian birds. *Malimbus* **2**, 1–15, 82–98.

Cramp, S. and Simmons, K. E. L. (Eds) (1977, 1980). 'The Birds of the Western Palearctic'. Vols I, II. Oxford University Press, Oxford.

Curry-Lindahl, K. (1981). 'Bird Migration in Africa. Movements between Six Continents'. Academic Press, London and New York.

Dean, W. R. J. (1975). Martial Eagles nesting on high tension pylons. *Ostrich* **46**, 116–117.

Devillers, P. (1976–1978). Projet de nomenclature francaise des oiseaux du monde. *Gerfaut* **66**, 153–168, 391–421; **67**, 171–200, 337–365, 469–489; **68**, 129–136, 233–240, 703–720.

Diamond, A. W. and Hamilton, A. C. (1980). The distribution of forest passerine birds and Quaternary climatic change in tropical Africa. *J. Zool., Lond.* **191**, 379–402.

Douaud, J. (1957). Les migrations au Togo (Afrique occidentale). *Alauda* **24**, 146–147.

Elgood, J. H., Fry, C. H. and Dowsett, R. J. (1973). African migrants in Nigeria. *Ibis* **115**, 1–45, 375–411.

Erard, C. (1975). Une nouvelle alouette du sud de l'Ethiopie. *Alauda* **43**, 115–124.

Erard, C. and Vieilliard, V. (1977). *Sarothrura rufa* (Vieillot) au Togo. *L'Oiseau et RFO* **47(3)**, 309–310.

Etchécopar, R. D. and Hüe, F. (1967) 'The Birds of North Africa.' Oliver & Boyd, London.

Field, G. D. (1979). A new species of *Malimbus* sighted in Sierra Leone and a review of the genus. *Malimbus* **1**, 2–13.

Forbes-Watson, A. D. (1970). A new species of *Melaenornis* (Muscicapinae) from Liberia. *Bull. Brit. Orn. Cl.* **90**, 145–148.

Fry, C. H. (1979). Coded bibliography of African ornithology 1975–1978. *Malimbus* Suppl. No. 1, 100 pp.

Fry, C. H. (in press). 'The Bee-eaters: Evolutionary Biology of the Meropidae'. T. & A. D. Poyser, Calton.

Greichus, Y. A., Greichus, A., Ammann, B. D. and Hopcraft, J. (1977). Insecticides, polychlorinated biphenyls and metals in African lake ecosystem. III. Lake Nakuru. *Bull. Environ. Contam. Toxicol.* **19(4)**, 454–461.

Hall, B. P. and Moreau, R. E. (1970). 'An Atlas of Speciation in African Passerine Birds'. British Museum (Natural History), London.

Hickey, J. J. (Ed.) (1969). 'Peregrine Falcon Populations: their Biology and Decline'. University of Wisconsin Press, Madison.

Immelmann, K. (1971). Ecological aspects of periodic reproduction. *In* 'Avian Biology' (Farner, D. and King, J., Eds) Academic Press, London and New York.

Jackson, F. J. and Sclater, W. L. (1938). 'The Birds of Kenya Colony and the Uganda Protectorate'. Gurney and Jackson, London.

Kallquist, T. and Meadows, B. S. (1977). Pesticide levels in the Kenyan environment. *Afr. Environ.* **2(4)**, 163–170.

Keay, R. W. J. (Ed.) (1959). Vegetation Map of Africa. Oxford University Press, London.

Keith, S., Benson, C. W. and Irwin, M. P. S. (1970). The genus *Sarothura* (Aves, Rallidae). *Bull. Am. Mus. Nat. Hist.* **143(1)**, 1–84.

Koeman, J. H., Boer, W. M. J. D., Feith, A. F., de Iongh, H. H. and Spliethoff, P. C. (1978). Three years' observation on side effects of helicopter applications of insecticides used to exterminate *Glossina* species in Nigeria. *Environ. Pollut.* **15**, 31–59.

Lack, D. (1954). 'The Natural Regulation of Animal Numbers'. Clarendon Press, Oxford.

Lack, D. (1966). 'Population Studies of Birds'. Clarendon Press, Oxford.

Livingstone, D. A. (1975). Late Quaternary climatic changes in Africa. *A. Rev. Ecol. Syst.* **6**, 249–280.

Louette, M. (1981). A new species of honeyguide from West Africa (Aves, Indicatoridae). *Rev. Zool. Afr.* **95**, 131–135.

Mackworth-Praed, C. W. and Grant, C. H. B. (1957, 1960). 'Birds of Eastern and North Eastern Africa.' 2 vols. Longmans, London.

Mackworth-Praed, C. W. and Grant, C. H. B. (1962, 1963).

'Birds of the Southern Third of Africa'. 2 vols. Longmans, London.

Mackworth-Praed, C. W. and Grant, C. H. B. (1970, 1973). 'Birds of West Central and Western Africa'. 2 vols. Longmans, London.

McLachlan, G. R. and Liversidge, R. (1978). 'Roberts Birds of South Africa'. Trustees of the John Voelcker Bird Book Fund, Cape Town.

Maclean, G. L. (1976). Factors governing breeding of African birds in non-arid habitats. Proc. XVI Int. Orn. Cong. pp. 258–271. Australian Academy of Science, Canberra.

Moreau, R. E. (1966). 'The Bird Faunas of Africa and its Islands'. Academic Press, London and New York.

Moreau, R. E. (1972). 'The Palaearctic-African Bird Migration Systems'. Academic Press, London and New York.

Morel, G. J. and Morel, M.-Y. (1978). Recherche ecologique sur une savane sahelienne du Ferlo septentrional, Sénégal. Etude d'une communanté avienne. *Cah. ORSTOM* (sér. Biol) **13**, 3–34.

Morel, G. J. and Poulet, A. R. (1976). Un important dortoir d'*Elanus caeruleus*, Accipitridae, au Sénégal. *L'Oiseau et RFO* **46(4)**, 429–430.

Morel, G. and Roux, F. (1962). Données nouvelles sur l'avifauna au Sénégal. *Oiseau* **32**, 28–56.

North, M. E. W. (1962). Vocal affinities of *Corvus corax edithae*, 'dwarf raven' or 'Somali crow'? *Ibis* **104**, 431.

Okia, N. O. (1976). Birds of the understorey of lake-shore forests on the Entebbe Peninsula, Uganda. *Ibis* **118**, 1–13.

Parkes, K. C. (1978). A guide to forming and capitalizing compound names of birds in English. *Auk* **95**, 324–326.

Peakall, D. B. and Kemp, A. C. (1976). Organochlorine residue levels in herons and raptors in the Transvaal. *Ostrich* **47**, 139–141.

Pearson, D. J. and Backhurst, G. C. (1976). The southward migration of Palaearctic birds over Ngulia, Kenya. *Ibis* **118**, 78–105.

Peters, J. L. *et al.* (1934–1979). 'Check List of Birds of the World'. Vols 1–10, 12–15. Museum of Comparative Zoology, Cambridge, Massachusetts.

Priest, C. D. (1933–1936). 'The Birds of Southern Rhodesia'. 4 vols. William Clowes, Edinburgh.

Reichenow, A. (1901–03, 1905). 'Die Vögel Afrikas'. 4 vols. J. Neumann, Neudamm.

Ripley, S. D. (1966). A notable owlet from Kenya. *Ibis* **108**, 136–137.

Sauer, E. G. F. and Sauer, E. M. (1966). The behaviour and ecology of the South African ostrich. *Living Bird* **5**, 45–75.

Schouteden, H. (1952). Un Strigidae nouveau d'Afrique noire: *Phodilus prigoginei* nov. sp. *Rev. Zool. Bot. Afr.* **46**, 423–428.

Sclater, W. L. (1924, 1930). 'Systema Avium Ethiopicarum'. Parts 1 and 2. British Ornithologists' Union, London.

Snow, D. W. (Ed.) (1978). 'An Atlas of Speciation in African Non-passerine Birds'. British Museum (Natural History), London.

Snow, D. W. (1980). Regional differences between tropical floras and the evolution of frugivory. Proc. XVII Int. Orn. Congr. Berlin, 1978. pp. 1192–1198.

Tarboton, W. (1978). Hunting and the energy budget of the Black-shouldered Kite. *Condor* **80**, 88–91.

Thiollay, J.-M. (1970). L'exploitation par les oiseaux des essaimages de fourmis et termites dans une zone de contact savane-forêt en Côte-d'Ivoire. *Alauda* **38(4)**, 255–273.

Thiollay, J.-M. (1971). L'exploitation des feux de brousse par les oiseaux en Afrique occidentale. *Alauda* **39**, 54–72.

Thiollay, J.-M. (1975–1977). Les rapaces d'une zone de contact savane-fôret en Côte d'Ivoire. 1. Presentation du peuplement. 2. Densité, dynamique et structure du peuplement. 3. Modalités et succès de la reproduction. 4. Modes d'exploitation du milieu. *Alauda* **43**, 75–102, 387–416; **44**, 275–300; **45**, 197–218.

Thomson, A. L. (1942). 'Bird Migration: A Short Account'. H. F. and G. Witherby, London.

Toschi, A. (1950). Sulla biologia del *Lanius collaris humeralis* Stanley. *Ric. Zool. Appl. Caccia* **2(4)**, 65–136.

Tuite, C. (1981). Flamingoes in East Africa. *Swara* **4(4)**, 36–38.

Tyler, S. J. (1978). Some observations of birds in Fah, northwest Eritrea. *Bull. Br. Orn. Club* **98**, 80–87.

Urban, E. K. and Jefford, T. G. (1977). Movements of juvenile Great White Pelicans *Pelecanus onocrotalus* from Lake Shala, Ethiopia. *Ibis* **119**, 524–528.

Uys, C. J. (1977). Notes on Wattled Starlings in the Western Cape. *Bokmakierie* **29**, 87–89.

Vareschi, E. (1978). The ecology of Lake Nakuru (Kenya). 1. Abundance and feeding of the Lesser Flamingo. *Oecologia (Bul.)* **32**, 11–35.

Vesey-Fitzgerald, D. F. (1974). 'East African Grasslands'. East African Publishing House, Nairobi.

Vielliard, J. (1976). La Sitelle kabyle. *Alauda* **44**, 351–352.

Voous, K. H. (1973). List of recent Holarctic bird species. Non-passerines. *Ibis* **115**, 612–638.

Voous, K. H. (1977). List of recent Holarctic bird species. Passerines. *Ibis* **119**, 223–250, 376–406.

White, C. M. N. (1960). A checklist of the Ethiopian Muscicapidae (Sylviinae). Part I. *Occ. Pap. Nat. Mus. Sth Rhod.* **3** (24B), 399–430.

White, C. M. N. (1961). 'A Revised Checklist of African broadbills, pittas, larks, swallows, wagtails and pipits'. Government Printer, Lusaka.

White, C. M. N. (1962). A checklist of the Ethiopian Muscicapidae (Sylviinae). Part II. *Occ. Pap. Nat. Mus. Sth Rhod.* **3** (26B), 653–738.

White, C. M. N. (1962). 'A Revised Checklist of the African shrikes, orioles, drongos, starlings, crows, waxwings, cuckoo-shrikes, bulbuls, accentors, thrushes and babblers'. Government Printer, Lusaka.

White, C. M. N. (1963). 'A Revised Checklist of African flycatchers, tits, tree creepers, sunbirds, white-eyes, honey eaters, buntings, finches, weavers and waxbills'. Government Printer, Lusaka.

White, C. M. N. (1965). 'A Revised Checklist of African Non-passerine Birds'. Government Printer, Lusaka.

Whitfield, A. K. and Blaber, S. J. M. (1978). Feeding ecology of piscivorous birds at Lake St. Lucia. Part 1: Diving birds. *Ostrich* **49**, 185–198.

Whitfield, A. K. and Blaber, S. J. M. (1979). Feeding ecology of piscivorous birds at Lake St. Lucia. Part 2: Wading birds. *Ostrich* **50**, 1–9.

Whitfield, A. K. and Blaber, S. J. M. (1979). Feeding ecology of piscivorous birds at Lake St. Lucia. Part 3: Swimming birds. *Ostrich* **50**, 10–20.

Whitwell, A. C., Phelps, R. J. and Thomson, W. R. (1974). Further records of chlorinated hydrocarbon pes residues in Rhodesia. *Arnoldia* **6(37)**, 1–8, ..., wing

Wilson, R. T. and Ball, D. M. (1979). M... *Bull. Br. Orn.* loading and food of western Dar... *Club* **99**, 15–20. ...ng, III. *Bonn. Zool. Beitr.*

Wolters, H. E. (1974). A... des Museums A... The avifauna of the Kakamega **25**, 283–... Kenya, including a bird population

Zimmer... *Am. Mus. Nat. Hist.* **149(3)**, 257–339.

THE PARTS OF AFRICAN BIRDS

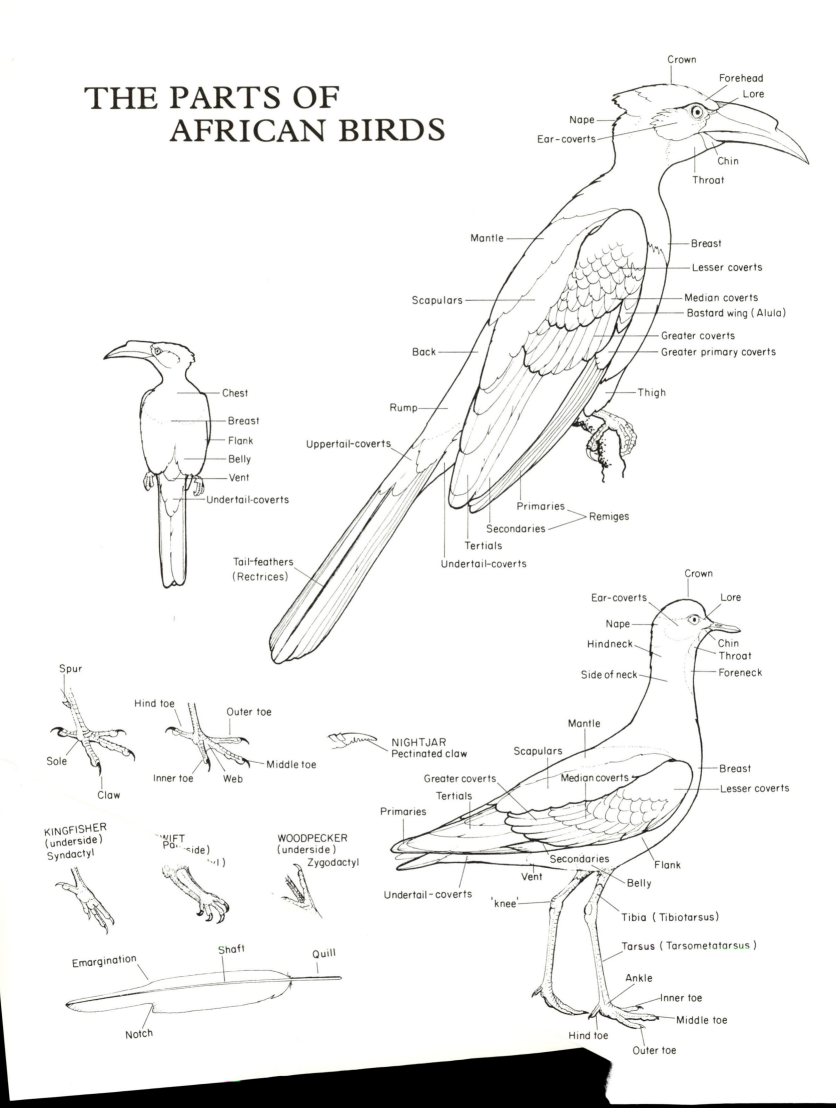

Crown
Forehead
Lore
Nape
Ear-coverts
Chin
Throat
Mantle
Breast
Lesser coverts
Scapulars
Median coverts
Bastard wing (Alula)
Back
Greater coverts
Greater primary coverts
Thigh
Rump
Uppertail-coverts
Primaries
Remiges
Secondaries
Tertials
Undertail-coverts
Tail-feathers
(Rectrices)

Chest
Breast
Flank
Belly
Vent
Undertail-coverts

Crown
Ear-coverts
Lore
Nape
Chin
Hindneck
Throat
Side of neck
Foreneck
Mantle
Scapulars
Breast
Greater coverts
Median coverts
Lesser coverts
Tertials
Primaries
Secondaries
Flank
Vent
Belly
Undertail-coverts
'knee'
Tibia (Tibiotarsus)
Tarsus (Tarsometatarsus)
Ankle
Inner toe
Middle toe
Hind toe
Outer toe

Spur
Hind toe
Outer toe
Sole
Inner toe
Web
Middle toe
Claw

NIGHTJAR
Pectinated claw

KINGFISHER
(underside)
Syndactyl

SWIFT
Pa...side)
...l)

WOODPECKER
(underside)
Zygodactyl

Emargination
Shaft
Quill
Notch

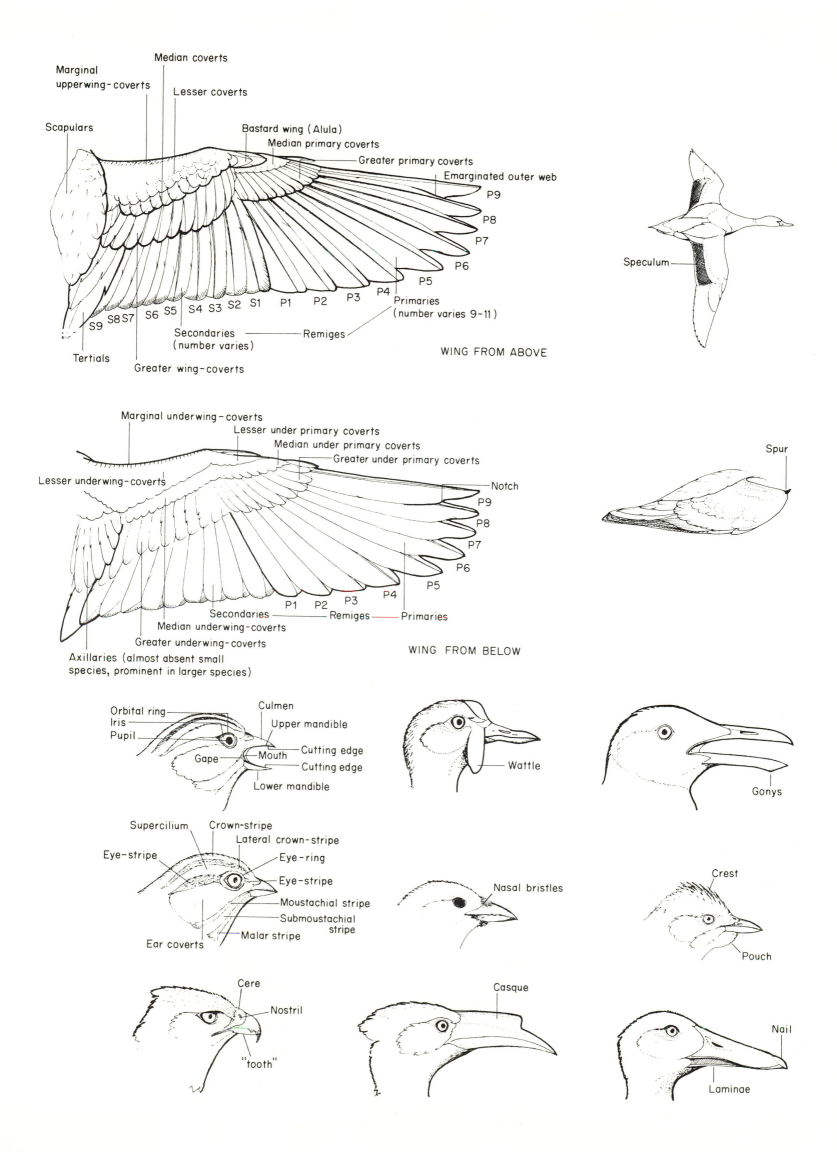

Marginal upperwing-coverts

Median coverts

Lesser coverts

Scapulars

Bastard wing (Alula)

Median primary coverts

Greater primary coverts

Emarginated outer web

P9

P8

P7

P6

P5

P4

Primaries (number varies 9-11)

S9 S8 S7 S6 S5 S4 S3 S2 S1 P1 P2 P3

Secondaries (number varies)

Remiges

Tertials

Greater wing-coverts

WING FROM ABOVE

Speculum

Marginal underwing-coverts

Lesser under primary coverts

Median under primary coverts

Greater under primary coverts

Notch

P9

P8

P7

P6

P5

Lesser underwing-coverts

P1 P2 P3 P4

Secondaries

Remiges

Primaries

Median underwing-coverts

Greater underwing-coverts

Axillaries (almost absent small species, prominent in larger species)

WING FROM BELOW

Spur

Orbital ring

Iris

Pupil

Gape

Culmen

Upper mandible

Cutting edge

Mouth

Cutting edge

Lower mandible

Wattle

Gonys

Supercilium

Crown-stripe

Eye-stripe

Lateral crown-stripe

Eye-ring

Eye-stripe

Moustachial stripe

Submoustachial stripe

Malar stripe

Ear coverts

Nasal bristles

Crest

Pouch

Cere

Nostril

"tooth"

Casque

Nail

Laminae

Order
STRUTHIONIFORMES

Huge or very large flightless birds, including the largest living. Comprises 2 suborders: Struthiones, containing the monotypic family, Struthionidae, Ostrich; and Rheae, South American rheas.

Suborder STRUTHIONES

Family STRUTHIONIDAE: Ostrich

Huge flightless birds, the largest living. Head and neck largely naked, covered with downy feathers. Beak rather short, rounded at tip, adapted for plucking vegetation. Eye exceptionally large, the largest of any terrestrial vertebrate (diameter 50 mm), protected by long eye-lashes (Walls 1942). Body, wings and tail with soft plume-like feathers, lacking barbules; ♂♂ conspicuously black and white, ♀♀ all dull grey–brown. Thighs almost naked; tarsus in ♂♂ with large, brightly coloured frontal scutes or shields; foot with 2 toes, inner with long stiff nail, much larger than outer, adapted for swift running; also used in attack, fighting and defence against predators. ♂ has a penis (grooved), unusual in birds.

The monotypic family has only 1 species, *Struthio camelus* Ostrich. Now endemic to Africa, extended to Arabia until 1968, and formerly more widespread. Despite its extraordinary interest, has been little studied in detail until recently.

Genus *Struthio* Linnaeus

Plate 1

(Opp. p. 34)

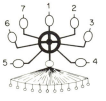

(1) Truth
(2) Benevolence
(3) Brotherly love
(4) Harmony
(5) Spirit (soul)
(6) Justice
(7) Peace

Struthio camelus Linnaeus. Ostrich. Autruche d'Afrique

Struthio Camelus Linnaeus, 1758. Syst. Nat. (10th ed.), p. 155; North Africa.

Range and Status. Africa generally south of the Sahara south to Cape Province; extends also to S Morocco, northern Sudan and southern Egypt (Wadi Gemal, 24° 40′N, 35° 06′E: Amer *et al.* 1980; S. M. Goodman, pers. comm.). Distribution broken in Central Africa by belt of *Brachystegia* woodland in S Tanzania, Zambia, Angola, Mozambique. In most of range frequent, locally common, even abundant where protected.

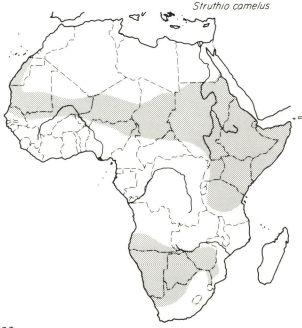

Struthio camelus

Northern and western nominate race *S. c. camelus* severely persecuted during 20th century, believed to be rapidly decreasing. E African *S. c. molybdophanes* and *S. c. massaicus* less persecuted. Southern *S. c. australis* extinct in most of former range as wild bird, confined to Namibia and national parks. Domesticated in Cape Province, but there hybridized with introduced *S. c. camelus*, becoming feral on farms.

Persecuted for meat, skins (for making fancy leather), feathers and eggs. Eggshells are used to make necklaces and waist-bands, and to carry water (Bushmen, Sudanese); also believed to have magic properties, protecting equally Muslim houses in W Africa (Salvan 1967) and Ethiopian Orthodox Churches against lightning (1 egg on each of the exposed points of a 7-pointed star, see margin illustration) (Negere 1980). On graves, eggs specify number of enemies killed by the deceased man in his lifetime (Burdji, S Ethiopia); also serve as engraved death gifts (Bushmen), and are valued as symbols of ritual and creative force, W Asia to Niger (Schüz 1970). Although greatly reduced recently and threatened by increasing direct persecution and destruction of habitat by overgrazing, no living race is threatened with imminent extinction. Domesticated population, Oudtshoorn district, South Africa, *c.* 90,000 (Shapiro, pers. comm.).

Description. *S. c. camelus* Linnaeus: W Africa from S Morocco and Mauritania east to Awash Valley in NE Ethiopia, Omo River in SW Ethiopia; south to S Sudan and N

Uganda. ADULT ♂: head, upper 75% of neck, sides of body and thighs nearly naked, pinkish. Crown bald, ringed with short stiff brown feathers extending down hindneck. Collar of white feathers between naked neck and lower neck. Lower neck, body, entire wing-coverts black. Wing- and tail-feathers pure white, loose, plume-like. Upper bill yellowish, lower mandible red; eye brown; legs reddish, with brighter red tarsal scutes. ADULT ♀: much duller; naked parts dirty grey-brown, downier than in ♂. Body feathers dark brown, edges paler; wing- and tail-feathers paler, greyish. In breeding season neck and bill of ♀ become brighter red, tarsal scutes also brighter. SIZE: bill, 130–140; wing, *c*. 900; tail, *c*. 490; tarsus, 450; inner toe without nail, 138. WEIGHT: ♂ 100–130 kg; ♀ 90–110 kg. (All feather measurements approximate, owing to loose structure.)

IMMATURE: attains adult height at *c*. 12 months but is lighter, *c*. 80% of adult weight (90 kg); rather darker than, but resembles ♀, ♂♂ become darker, acquiring whitish wing and tail in 2nd year. Attains full black and white plumage at *c*. 2 years, but not necessarily fully mature sexually.

DOWNY YOUNG: down spiky, resembling hedgehog, buff, tipped black; lines of black spots down sides of neck. Develops into immature plumage by emergence of feathers beginning at *c*. 3 months.

S. c. molybdophanes Reichenow. NE Ethiopia and Somalia west to near Awash Valley in Ethiopia and to Omo River in Ethiopia, south in Kenya to Tsavo East National Park. The most distinct race. Crown bald, like *S. c. camelus*. Bare skin of neck and thighs blue-grey, not pinkish. Tail white. A broad white neck ring; body plumage in ♂♂ strikingly black and white, lighter grey in ♀♀. Rather larger.

S. c. massaicus Neumann. E Kenya from south of Tsavo East to S Samburu District in west, south to Katavi grasslands in Tanzania. Crown not, or only partly bald. Neck and thighs pinkish grey, flushing bright red in breeding ♂♂; narrow white neck ring; wing- and tail-feathers white. Similar in size to other races.

S. c. australis Gurney. Southern Africa from Zimbabwe–Botswana to Cape Province; now found as pure wild bird only in Namibia and northern parts of original range. Crown not bald; neck grey, flushing red in breeding ♂♂; tarsal scutes then bright red. Tail dull brown to bright cinnamon-brown. No white ring. Possibly heaviest (♂♂ up to 150 kg), but not tallest race.

Other races have been described—*S. c. syriacus* of Arabia (extinct), and *S. c. spatzi* of NW Africa distinguished by somewhat smaller size but now merged with *S. c. camelus*. Ostriches have sometimes been split into 2, even 4 spp. on basis of bald or feathered crown, colour of neck and egg-pore characters. Blue-necked *S. c. molybdophanes* certainly most distinct race, perhaps unable to integrate in wild state with either *S. c. camelus* or *S. c. massaicus*. Distribution is analogous to reticulated giraffe (*Giraffa camelopardalis reticulata*) of same general area. However, domesticated *S. c. australis* in South Africa were crossed with *S. c. camelus*; hybrids fertile, remaining fertile when feral on farms. *S. c. molybdophanes*, introduced Nairobi National Park, bred with wild *S. c. massaicus* producing fertile hybrids. Specific rank for any race therefore doubtful.

Field Characters. Unmistakable, a huge terrestrial pedestrian bird; ♂♂ black and white, ♀♀ grey-brown, ♂♂ standing 2·0–2·2 m when fully erect, ♀♀ somewhat smaller. Young distinguished from any other ground bird by gregarious habits; spiky, buff, black-tipped down; normally accompanied by adults when small enough for confusion with e.g. large bustards.

Voice. Recorded (6). Varied, many calls not analysed. Normally silent, but breeding ♂♂ vocal. Commonest call

a deep, booming trisyllabic 'ohh-oooh-oooooo' descending in pitch at end; variable among individuals. Uttered mainly by day, especially early morning, occasionally at night, audible up to 3 km. Boom at other ♂♂ or to attract ♀♀, also when alone in territory. Of many calls, commonest a soft 'booh' or 'twoo', possibly contact call; also associated with anxiety and distraction display. In addition, hoarse guttural calls 'hrup', hisses (associated with distraction display), beak snapping and stomach rumbling, also used in threat or aggression (Sauer and Sauer 1966b). Chicks in anxiety utter entirely different, melodious, trilling 'quirrrr-quirrrr' calls.

General Habits. Very well known. Preferred habitat is open short-grass plains and semi-desert, commonly at densities of 1/5–20 km². Where protected and with little predation (Nairobi National Park), densities reach maximum, 0·6–0·8/km²; density affected by predation and persecution as much as food supply. Often quite common in open arid semi-desert or true desert with annual grasses (Namibia, NE Kenya, N tropical Africa). Avoids tall grass more than 1 m high, and any dense woodland, but in N and NE Africa *S. c. camelus* and *S. c. molybdophanes* readily traverse desert scrub up to 3 m high, and *S. c. molybdophanes* commonly enters thick thornbush taller than itself. *S. c. australis* occurs in open mopane woodland. Desert-adapted; in wild, largely or entirely independent of free water.

Mainly diurnal, but may be active by moonlight. Roosts squatting on ground at night, and frequently sits or squats by day also. Most active early morning and late afternoon, but heat-tolerant, able to raise body temperatures in hot conditions (Schmidt–Nielsen 1972), often walks about completely exposed in heat of day, seldom seeking shade (unlike many antelopes). Cannot run fast on wet slimy ground. Adapted to a variety of habitats from over 80 mm/year rainfall (*massaicus*) to under 200 mm/year (*australis*, *molybdophanes*, *camelus*). In arid habitats is independent of free water for months at least, possibly years, but in captivity and at artificial waterholes drinks freely and regularly (cf. behaviour of oryx and gemsbok in N Kenya and Kalahari).

By day walks about, normal pace *c*. 80 strides/min, each stride 75 cm, at 3·6–4·0 km/h. Trots when alarmed or in aggressive display at *c*. 30 km/h; when really alarmed, sprints, often jerking from side to side, at up to 60–70 km/h. Diurnal activity not fully analysed, but evidently variable according to habitat, must walk further to feed in arid areas. Breeding adults normally spend little time feeding, doing so in short spells throughout the day. Even in areas recently burned can soon find adequate food. When standing erect, eyes are *c*. 2·0–2·2 m above ground; tallest of keen-sighted animals in grassland except giraffe. Running ostrich immediately alerts most antelopes, which may then bolt without determining original cause of alarm (if any). May be able to run if necessary to escape predators at night.

When feeding, alternates bouts of plucking food at or near ground level with suddenly alert attitude, head raised to full stretch of neck, looking round intently.

Single birds look up more often than those in flocks or groups, which benefit from vigilance of one bird. Extremely keen-sighted, detects danger when feeding much more readily than many antelopes in same habitat. Probably spends not more than 20% of daylight actually feeding, and food requirements obtained relatively easily.

Outside breeding season somewhat sociable, in groups with open membership, individuals leaving and rejoining at random; groups usually 2–5. In breeding season adult ♂♂ and laying ♀♀ usually solitary, with groups of immatures or non-territorial adults. Immatures and subadults more gregarious than full adults. Large herds of 40, sometimes up to 100, usually composed of immatures after separation from adult escorts. Adults not often in pairs outside breeding season. In Namib desert apparently strongly social (up to 600 together) near waterholes, with dominance hierarchy among individuals (Sauer and Sauer 1966b).

In moister parts of range (e.g. near Nairobi) may be almost sedentary, individuals found in same areas over successive years. In more arid areas more or less nomadic, tending to concentrate near water in dry season, dispersing over wider areas in rains (Tarangire: Lamprey 1964). *S. c. camelus* in W Africa probably moves south in dry season, returning north in wet to more arid parts of range. Must have some vegetation, and in deserts most likely to occur in relatively well vegetated valleys or depressions, but traverses absolutely barren salt flats and sandy areas.

Displays mainly seen in breeding season, but non-breeding birds close to one another may stretch neck and bite at others, hissing or grunting. Erect tail, conspicuously white in ♂♂, usually denotes social dominance, lowered head with pendent tail indicates submissive attitude.

Food. Supposedly omnivorous, in fact almost exclusively vegetarian. Highly selective, prefers dicotyledonous plants but eats all parts of both herbs and grasses. Plucks or strips seed-heads of grasses, flowers of Compositae, seed-pods of e.g. *Aloe* spp. (unpalatable to other animals). Selects flowers and pods of acacias rather than leaves (Robinson and Seely 1975) and feeds on fallen figs (Archer and Godman 1937). Can become a pest in wheatfields, plucking whole heads of grain. May feed at up to 2 m above ground occasionally, but most food gathered from ground to *c.* 0·5 m above. May eat locusts and grasshoppers when available (Salvan 1967), but evidently not dependent on protein-rich animal food for breeding, as suggested (Sinclair 1978). In deserts,

in
0   12

0   30
cm

Plate 1

Struthio camelus Ostrich (p. 32)
Race *camelus*: 1. ADULT♂, 2. IMMATURE,
3. FULLY GROWN IMMATURE ♂, 4. ADULT ♀.
5. ♀ incubating, hiding in cover – note ring of abandoned eggs and shells.
Race *molybdophanes*: 6. ADULT ♂ (N.B. thighs usually more bluish than shown here).
7. *S. c. camelus* at 7 days, 8. 21 days,
9. 42–44 days, 10. 90–100 days, 11. 4–5 months,
12. SUBADULT (10 months).

Sagittarius serpentarius Secretary Bird
(p. 437)
13. ADULT, 14. from behind, 15. in flight,
16. IMMATURE.

feeds much on succulents. Captives mainly fed on lucerne (South Africa); and captive chicks relish meat (Hurxthal 1979). Food requirement *c.* 3·5 kg/day in captivity. Water requirement in wild nil. Captives pick up many curious objects, and wild birds usually ingest stones or grit.

Breeding Habits. Very well known. Ostrich breeding behaviour is unique with complex communal aspects. Although well studied in 3 areas, Nairobi National Park, Tsavo West Park and Namib Desert (Hurxthal 1979; Sauer and Sauer 1966b; B. Bertram, pers. comm.), many details still obscure. Strategies and timing vary according to habitat, regular breeding occurring in moister parts of range, and more irregular, adventitious or opportunistic breeding in arid areas (e.g. Namib, N Kenya).

Basic social pattern appears similar. Adult ♀♀ outnumber adult ♂♂ 1·2–1·8. Breeding population consists of : (i) territorial, fully adult ♂♂, nest-owners 1 per 3·4 ♀♀ (Nairobi); (ii) non-territorial, fully adult ♂♂, who may sometimes mate with ♀♀; (iii) 'major' ♀♀, mated to territorial ♂♂ in monogamous bonds, sometimes renewed for several successive years, the only ♀♀ to incubate eggs; however, territory of such major hens embraces parts of several ♂ territories; (iv) 'minor' hens which wander

Plate 2

Diomeda exulans Wandering Albatross (p. 39)
1. ADULT white form (above), 2. IMMATURE, plumage stage 2 (below), 3. (above), 4. IMMATURE, stage 5, white form (above) (adults of other forms look very similar to this), 5. ADULT white form (below), 6. IMMATURE, stage 5, white form (below).

Diomedea cauta Shy Albatross (p. 41)
7. ADULT (above), 8. ADULT (below),
9. IMMATURE (above).

Diomedea chrysostoma Grey-headed Albatross (p. 41)
10. ADULT (above), 11. IMMATURE (above), 12. ADULT (below), 13. IMMATURE (below).

Diomedea chlororhynchos Yellow-nosed Albatross (p. 42)
14. ADULT (above), 15. ADULT (below).

Phoebetria palpebrata Light-mantled Sooty Albatross (p. 43)
16. ADULT (above).

Phoebetria fusca Sooty Albatross (p. 43)
17. ADULT (above).

Diomedea melanophrys Black-browed Albatross (p. 40)
18. ADULT (below), 19. IMMATURE (below), 20. ADULT (above).

Macronectes giganteus Southern Giant Petrel (p. 44)
21. ADULT (white morph), 22. ADULT (dark morph).

Macronectes halli: Northern Giant Petrel (p. 45)
23. ADULT.

Heads: 24. *D. melanophrys*; 25. *D. chlororhynchos chlororhynchos*; 26. *D. bassi*; 27. *D. chrysostoma*; 28. *D. cauta cauta*; 29. *D. c. salvini* (IMM); 30. *D. exulans*; 31. *P. palpebrata;* 32. *P. fusca;* 33. *M. halli;* 34. *M. giganteus.*

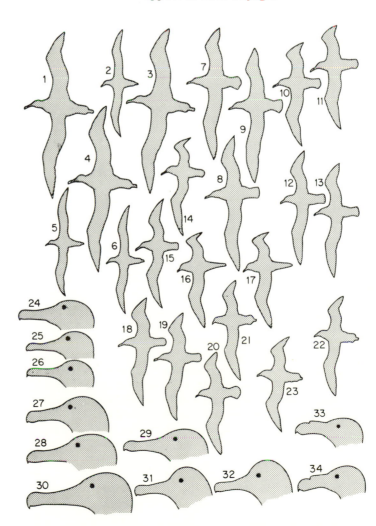

in
0   12
0   30
cm

Scale applies to birds in flight

through many ♂ territories, lay eggs in several nests, and do not regularly incubate eggs. May lay in nests of ♂♂ who have not mated with them. In Namib Desert ♂♂ are said to have 'harems' of ♀♀, but in E Africa regular bond is with 1 hen only; termed 'facultative monogamy' (Hurxthal 1979).

Early in breeding season, territorial ♂♂ occupy areas of 2–15 km². Highest density recorded (Nairobi National Park) 1/0·7–2·8 km², av. 2 km² (in c. 800 mm rainfall, Acacia–Themeda grassland); Tsavo Park av. 14 km², in av. 600 mm rainfall (territories here possibly larger because of heavier predation, rather than food supply). Territorial ♂ defends area from other ♂♂ for c. 5 months (Nairobi, May–Sept). In breeding ♂♂, colours of neck, bill, legs, tarsal shields more intense, normally becoming brighter red. In immediate ♂–♂ aggressive encounters necks swell and flush still brighter red; also when displaying to ♀. Territorial ♂♂ walk about, sometimes booming; are very alert to intruders or to approaching ♀♀, running towards them with breastbone held low, head and neck low, stretched forward, tail up. Tail feathers in massaicus and australis often stained bright red with earth, but in molybdophanes remain white in similar terrain; camelus not studied.

Active breeding ♂♂ have red cloacal opening and enlarged penis, often displayed. Territorial ♂ displays include: 'wing-flapping', when wings of standing ♂♂ are alternately flipped downwards then raised again, usually with erect tail and erected neck-ruff; 'formal approach', head and neck straight and upright, erected neck-ruff, wings lowered, tail expanded into ball-shape while ♂ moves towards another of either sex; 'kantle', when ♂ lies down, spreads wings and alternately raises and lowers them with head and neck weaving laterally, head rhythmically thumping on back; 'full threat', when ♂ closely approaches another ♂ or ♀, wings spread, raised high, tail erected, neck swollen and brighter red, bill clapping. Formal approach, kantle and full threat used both in ♂–♂ aggression and in courtship, full threat often precedes copulation; wing-flapping normally in mild ♂–♂ aggression. Immature or subadult ♂♂ also 'dance' in groups, running about swiftly, wing-flapping; or spin like ballerinas 'waltzing'. Such behaviour not related to territory.

♀♀ ready to copulate solicit approaching ♂ with wings partly spread and gently vibrating primaries lowered, head held low. ♂ responds by lowering wings. Tails held low, heads and necks raised and lowered. Soliciting ♀ first approaches ♂, then turns and often walks slowly away. At copulation, ♂ approaches ♀ (who drops to ground) snapping bill and tapping with feet; places right foot right of centre of her back, left on ground beside her. Then drops gently onto her back, everts grooved penis and, after penetration, rolls or sways rhythmically with side to side movements resembling kantle. Wings are vibrated, accompanied by deep rhythmic grunting or groaning; bill is snapped, upper neck partially inflated, body feathers erected. Full copulation takes c. 1 min, after which one or both stand up; ♀ may remain lying after ♂ has stood up. ♂ penis is engorged when withdrawn, visible as he stands, if copulation is successful.

Pair may then remain together or separate; sometimes ♂ then leads ♀ to nest.

NEST: ♂ begins nest well before mating and ♀♀ accept site selected by ♂; may be on bare ground, or in vegetation. ♂ scrapes irregularly with feet, sits down, pecks at, but does not feed on vegetation. When scraping, ♂ lies and scratches with feet behind him. ♂♂ seldom dig with beak; ♀♀ often do after accepting nest. ♂ solicits acceptance of ♀ by lowering and fluttering wings, movements resembling those of ♀ soliciting copulation. Most sites are in open situations with good view, often at edge of treeless drainage lines, usually roughly in centre of territory.

Major hen begins laying, and all hens lay on alternate days. Minor hens move through many territories (up to 7) and may lay in nests of ♂♂ with whom they have not mated. These lay in nest at same time as major hen, and later; visits to nest brief, usually in early evening (16.40–17.00 h); associated with laying, do not incubate or guard.

Where predators (especially Egyptian Vultures Neophron percnopterus, jackals, hyenas) are abundant, nest must be guarded by day during laying by major hen; minor hens play little part. Predators repelled by direct attack, but many nests lost before incubation begins. In Serengeti National Park nest predation by Egyptian Vultures may attract other mammalian predators by smell. Estimated 75–80% of nests affected Tsavo Park, fewer in Nairobi National Park.

EGGS: clutch of major hen 5–11, av. 8; minor hen 2–6, av. 3·7 in any nest (Nairobi). Up to 18 minor hens may lay in same nest, usually 2–5. Max. number of eggs which can be incubated 19–25, av. 21; therefore major hen's av. clutch comprises less than half total nest contents. If many hens lay in same nest any eggs in excess of 19–25 are surplus, and are ejected or laid beside nest, which becomes surrounded by ring of unincubated eggs. Maximum number recorded (Nairobi) 78, of which 21 incubated. Surplus eggs commoner in areas of high population density. This system results in wastage of eggs not incubated and different genetic characters in offspring of 1 nest. Rounded ovals, thick-shelled; yellowish when first laid, becoming white or cream later. Those of different races distinguishable by pore structure: small in camelus; larger and purplish in molybdophanes; deep and purplish in massaicus and australis. SIZE: individually small relative to ♀ bodyweight; probably varies according to age of ♀, young hens laying smaller lighter eggs: 48 eggs (camelus), 142–175 × 120–145 (158·5 × 131·0); 27 (molybdophanes), 144–173 × 111–126 (158 × 125); 28 (massaicus), 142–165 × 120–142 (154·5 × 127·5); 29 (australis), 136–160 × 119–135 (151·4 × 126·2) (Schönwetter 1960); (molybdophanes), 150–169 × 124–135 (159·5 × 128·8) (Leuthold 1977); 51 (australis), 135–158 × 110–130 (148·1 × 121·6) (McLachlan and Liversidge 1978). WEIGHT: normal range 1300–1900, but 780–1580 recorded (Sauer and Sauer 1966a), av. c. 1500, shell weight 300 (20% of egg weight). Single egg c. 1·5% of ♂ bodyweight; of clutch, 12–15%. Captives can be induced to lay up to 90 eggs by continual removal. Major hens can recognize own eggs, possibly by pore structure, size and shape, and these are never, or seldom ejected from nests with minor hens' surplus eggs (Bertram 1979).

Laying dates: breeding season highly variable. In moister areas (E African plains) (*massaicus*) concentrated June–Oct, laying peaking in Aug, in mid–late mid-year, long, cool, dry season. N Kenya: (*molybdophanes*) Jan, Feb, Mar (dry), July, Aug; (*camelus*) Feb, Mar, Aug–Dec, mainly dry. Sudan and W Africa, Chad: (*camelus*) Nov–Feb, most nests Dec–Jan (dry). South Africa: (*australis*) any month Feb–Nov, mainly dry. In Namib Desert, adventitiously, variable, laying end of dry season–early rains (Sauer and Sauer 1966a). Most breeding occurs in dry weather, incubation often beginning when grass is long with chicks hatching before main rains break.

Incubation begins *c.* 16 days after 1st egg laid by major hen. Usually carried out by major hen only, but in very hot conditions ♂ may relieve her by day (Siegfried and Frost 1974). Incubates from 1·0–1·5 h before sunset to 2–3 h after sunrise (*c.* 66% of day). Feeds for only *c.* 3–4 h of daylight, while ♂ can feed most of day; apparently does not suffer from this, however. Either parent may be killed on nest by e.g. lions. Incubation period: 45–46 days.

Eggs hatch in 9 h; lacking egg-tooth, chick breaks free by muscular spasms. In wild nests hatching period is 3–5 days, much shorter than egg-laying period. Synchronization of hatch as in related *Rhea* spp. (Brunning 1974) may possibly be assisted by inter-egg communication. Chicks hatch with a yolk reserve, *c.* 25% of bodyweight, absorbed over 4 days. Cannot walk well for 24 h but normally leave nest, accompanied by parents, within 3 days, when can run quickly 5–10 m. Back height of chicks enables reasonably accurate age estimates. Chicks 1 week old are *c.* 33% of parental tarsus height, head *c.* 50% of tarsus height. At 21 days, back *c.* 50% of parental tarsus, head level with tibio-tarsal joint. At 42 days, back height level with parental tibio-tarsal joint, head higher than parental belly; still entirely downy. At 90 days, back height about level with parental belly, head below parental back; tufts of feathers showing on tail and wings. At 4–5 months feathered, mottled grey and brown, tarsal scutes developed, *c.* 50% of adult size. Weight increases to 3 kg at 3 weeks, 5 kg at 6 weeks, 10 kg at 10 weeks, 45 kg at 6 months, reaching 85 kg at 1 year (based on captive birds: Smit 1963).

In Nairobi area and elsewhere broods from many nests join to form 1 large creche, accompanied and guarded by 1 or several adults. Broods from nests up to 12 km apart thus merge. Creching is assisted by nearly simultaneous hatching of many nests, and 'out of season' young may be attacked by adults (Sauer and Sauer 1966a). When merging, separate assorted broods gradually approach one another over a few minutes to *c.* 1 h. Merging is accompanied by vigorous display, in which adults suddenly lower head and run towards others, wings moved in rowing motion. Several run about agitatedly together, displays somewhat resembling threat and distraction displays. Displays of 1 or more escorts apparently repel others and assist merging; behaviour of captive adults suggests parents of older broods readily accept younger chicks, but older chicks repelled by escorts of younger ones. In Nairobi National Park all broods from all nests eventually join 1 creche; similar behaviour apparently general elsewhere. Very large groups of 100–300 (max. recorded 380) are usually escorted immatures.

Adults, not necessarily parents, accompany broods for up to 9 months, protecting them by distraction displays. On approach of predator or e.g. vehicle, escort runs swiftly away, then collapses, with flopping wings, swaying neck. When closely approached rises and runs on. More conspicuous ♂ more likely to perform distraction displays while ♀ escapes with chicks, but ♀♀ also perform. Alternatively, both sexes may threaten predator, running towards it with lowered head, opened wings. After escorts leave, chicks remain in large herds of assorted ages.

Despite large clutch, of which max. 25, more usually 21, eggs are incubated, heavy egg and chick losses result in low breeding success. Predation by birds and mammals, especially Egyptian Vulture (on eggs), jackals and hyenas, severe. In Nairobi National Park, of 1719 eggs in 27 incubated nests, 1102 (64%) were surplus, 617 incubated. 19 nests which hatched produced 204 chicks (33% of incubated eggs), 7·5 chicks/incubated nest. Survival rate of chicks estimated at *c.* 12%, i.e. *c.* 0·9 survivors/incubated nest. Since each incubated nest concerns an adult ♂, a major hen and 3–4 minor hens (*c.* 6 adults), survival equals *c.* 0·15 young/adult/year in this favourable situation. With some further mortality before sexual maturity, adults must live 8–10 years to replace themselves, 12–14 years altogether. Mortality, hence longevity, likely to be even higher elsewhere. If severe natural predation is aggravated by human persecution, numbers must decline. As largest numbers of surplus eggs not incubated (up to 52 in 1 nest) occur in dense populations, demand for eggs might best be satisfied by taking otherwise doomed peripheral eggs not incubated, or by commercial production. Value of domesticated bird, South Africa, *c.* R 150 (1979) of which 48% skin, 40% feathers, 12% carcass.

References
Bertram, B. (1979 and pers. comm.).
Hurxthal, L. (1979).
Sauer, E. G. F. and Sauer, E. M. (1966a, b).

Order
PROCELLARIIFORMES

A diverse order of enormous to very small, highly pelagic birds characterized by horny, plated, hooked beaks with external tubular nostrils, short legs, webbed feet, hind toe vestigial or absent, thick plumage, wings usually of high aspect ratio and a strong smell of musk. Wings have 11 primary feathers, 1 very small; 10 secondaries in southern storm-petrels, varying from 13 to 40 in others; usually 12 rectrices, 14 to 16 in fulmars. The order is comprised of 4 families: Diomedeidae (albatrosses): Procellariidae (fulmars, gadfly-petrels and shearwaters); Hydrobatidae (storm-petrels) and Pelecanoididae (diving-petrels). All spend most of their lives at sea, returning to land for only brief periods in order to breed.

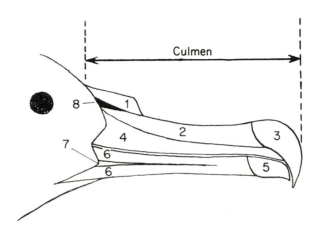

Typical petrel bill: 1. nostrils; 2. culminicorn; 3. maxillary unguis; 4. latericorn; 5. mandibular unguis; 6. ramicorn; 7. sulcus; 8. naricorn (after Serventy *et al.* 1971).

Family DIOMEDEIDAE: albatrosses

Enormous to very large seabirds spanning 2·0–3·5 m. Wandering Albatross *D. exulans* and Royal Albatross *D. epomophora* are not only the largest albatrosses, but also the largest marine birds. Wings very long, with 27–40 secondaries; legs short, placed far back on body. In flight feet are carried open on either side of tail. Bill large, with short tubular nostrils placed either side of culmen. Breed on islands and mainland peninsulas, mostly in southern seas. When not breeding, range the oceans and may annually circumnavigate globe. In the air much time spent in gliding flight, rising against wind, then turning to descend downwind at speed to wave level before ascending again. Fly deep into wave-troughs, wings tipping water, then bridge wave-crest, gaining height from wind deflection off wave, before descending into next trough. Also utilize vertical wind currents created by air displacement behind moving ships and may cover long distances in this way, occasionally settling on water to retrieve waste from ship's galley. Take-off from water in windy conditions fairly direct but in low wind involves lengthy scramble with feet running on surface and wings beating. Feed on cephalopods (squid, cuttlefish), mainly caught at night, fish and dead marine animals including whales. Silent at sea except when squabbling over food, then make a variety of guttural squawks. 2 genera, *Diomedea* (11 spp.) and *Phoebetria* (2 spp.) of which 5 *Diomedea* spp. and both *Phoebetria* spp. occur in African waters (Grey-headed Albatross *D. chrysostoma* and Light-mantled Sooty Albatross *P. palpebrata* rarely) as non-breeding visitors, mainly south of 28°S.

Genus *Diomedea* Linnaeus

Bodies white, with black and white or predominantly blackish wings, those in the latter group being known as mollymawks. Several have dark mark through top of the eye giving bird frowning appearance, most strongly in Black-browed Albatross *D. melanophrys*. Tails have 12 feathers. Specifically identified by bill colouring and underwing patterns, though immatures can easily be confused at sea. 11 spp., 5 in African waters as non-breeding visitors.

Diomedea exulans Linnaeus. Wandering Albatross. Albatros hurleur.

Diomedea exulans Linnaeus, 1758. Syst. Nat. (10th ed.), p. 132; Cape of Good Hope.

Plate 2

(Opp. p. 35)

Range and Status. All waters south of about 14°S, rarely to northern hemisphere. Fairly common off Namibian and South African coasts in southern winter.

Diomedea exulans

Description. *D. e. exulans,* ADULT ♂: (all-white stage) entirely white except for black primaries and secondaries; bill pink to horn yellow, tip yellow; eye dark brown; legs and feet flesh pink to mauvish. Adult ♂♂ of some populations never attain wholly white plumage; upperwing remains blackish with white wedge-shaped patches in centre of basal half; mantle and back have variable number of dark-tipped feathers; tail dark. Below body is white, speckled with dark-tipped feathers and a broad band of dark speckling across chest (the so-called 'leopard' stage). ♀♀ may attain predominantly white plumage or mature at 'leopard' stage, thus non-white plumage cannot be used as an age criterion and widespread belief that immature ♀♀ breed is unfounded. SIZE: (10 specimens) wing, ♂ 590–674 (644), ♀ 585–611 (601); tail, ♂ 186–202 (195), ♀ 177–200 (187); tarsus, ♂ 115–128 (121), ♀ 111–119 (115); culmen, ♂ 156–173 (168), ♀ 157–167 (161); middle toe and claw, 161; length, 135 cm; wing-span, 272–328 cm. WEIGHT: ♂ 6·25–11·30 (9) kg, ♀♀ smaller.

IMMATURE: progresses from predominantly chocolate brown with white facial mask in 1st year through 4–7 primary plumage stages depending on final plumage acquired (see above). Body below progressively whitens from central belly-patch, both body and underwing retaining variable speckled effect. Above, whitening starts on mantle and back, then cap and finally tail; upperwing develops wedge-shaped white patch (see above) which progressively extends to shoulder, then primaries. Time taken for entire process through to all-white stage probably 10 years.

Field Characters. Enormous, very long-winged seabird, much larger than any other except Royal Albatross *D. epomophora.* Either pure white with black primaries and secondaries, or white with dark upperwing having wedge-shaped white patch, and dark breast-band. Variations of darker plumage more common than all-white. All-white adult almost indistinguishable at sea from Royal Albatross, but on underwing, leading edge from carpal joint to tip is either all white or with narrow dark line only, whereas Royal Albatross has broad dark line. At all other stages distinguishable by fact that white of upperwing progresses as central wedge or strip, leading edge whitening only at last stage, if at all, whereas Royal Albatross upperwing whitens from leading edge backwards. 1st-year birds can be confused with giant petrels and sooty albatrosses, but white facial mask and larger size diagnostic.

Voice. Recorded (13, 23, 25). A harsh croaking when competing for food at sea.

General Habits. Well known. Most common in southern African waters Apr–Aug. Readily follows large ships, alighting on water to retrieve scraps, less commonly near fishing boats, where cannot compete with smaller, more nimble birds (Sinclair 1978). Most frequent western Cape and Namibia, fairly frequent Indian Ocean, exceptionally to Mozambique.

Food. Squid and fish, also ship's galley refuse.

References
Elliott, H. (1969).
Bourne, W. R. P. (1977).
Clancey, P. A. (1978a).
Harrison, P. (1979).

Diomedea epomophora Lesson. Royal Albatross. Albatros royal.

Diomedaea (sic) *epomophora* Lesson, 1825. Ann. Sci. Nat., Paris, 6, p. 95; no locality, probably Australian waters.

Not illustrated

Range and Status. Australian waters and subantarctic. Few probable sight records in region 37°S. Seen off South Africa July 1980 (J. Sinclair, pers. comm.), also Gough Island Nov 1980 (S. Keith, pers. comm.); may occur more often in Atlantic but go unrecorded due to difficulty in separating it from Wandering Albatross *D. exulans.*

Description. *D. e. sanfordi* Murphy, ADULT♂: entirely white except for black upper surface of wing, and broad dark line on leading edge of underwing from carpal joint to tips. Eye dark brown; bill flesh-pink, cutting edges blackish, nail light horn; feet bluish white, webs blue-grey. SIZE: (5 ♂♂, 12 ♀♀) wing, ♂ 590–630 (615), ♀ 593–639 (616); tail, ♂ 182–200 (190), ♀ 175–197 (189); tarsus, ♂ 112–120 (117), ♀ 111–120 (114); culmen, ♂ 156–168 (163), ♀ 151–170 (197); middle toe and

Diomedea epomophora

X Sighting

X

claw, ♂ 151–162 (157), ♀ 146–158 (151); length 107–122 cm; wing-span 305–351 cm.

IMMATURE: wholly white-bodied, sometimes a few dark-edged feathers on crown and back, and small black spots on tips of tail feathers; upperwing blackish brown.

Field Characters. Difficult to distinguish from Wandering Albatross, but broad, dark leading edge to underwing from carpal joint to tip diagnostic; at close range dark cutting edge to bill, all-white tail. Young birds separated from similar ages in Wandering Albatross by all-white body, and upperwing whitening from leading edge rearwards, not from central area outwards as in this species.

Voice. Not recorded. Nothing described for birds at sea.

General Habits. Well known in Australian waters, scarcely known elsewhere. Probably circumnavigates the globe in southern seas but records few.

Food. Cephalopods and fish.

Plate 2
(Opp. p. 35)

Diomedea melanophrys **Temminck. Black-browed Albatross. Albatros à sourcils noirs.**

Diomedea melanophris Temminck, 1823. Pl. Col. livr. 77, pl. 456; Cape of Good Hope.

Range and Status. All waters south of *c.* 20°S, occasionally crosses equator. Recorded Mombasa harbour (Bednall 1956). Commonest albatross off Cape in southern winter.

Description. *D. m. melanophrys,* ADULT ♂: entirely white except for sooty brown central back and upperwings; a dark streak above eye. Tail above and below dark grey; underwing white edged with sooty brown, broadly and irregularly on leading and trailing edges. Bill yellow, tipped orange-pink to reddish; eye brown; legs and feet grey-flesh but ranging from purplish to whitish. Sexes alike. SIZE: (♂♀) wing, (26 specimens) 462–543 (516); tail, (7) 189–215 (200); bill, (29) 110–124 (118); tarsus, (27) 80–90 (85); length, 84–94 cm; wing-span, 214–244 cm. WEIGHT: *c.* 3 kg.

IMMATURE: duller, drabber; top of head and neck grey initially, later becoming white leaving lower neck bluish grey; underwing initially with little white, slight paling in central area only, later with narrow central white area; bill blackish grey, tip darker, becoming horn-coloured first on sides, then at base and progressively more yellow until only black tip remains.

Field Characters. Most common albatross in southern African seas. Adult distinguished by orange-yellow bill, broad dark leading and trailing edges to underwing. Grey-headed immatures separated from other grey-headed species by bill colour, largely dark underwing.

Voice. Not recorded. Silent at sea except for occasional throaty cries of 'waak' during disputes over food. When excited this call repeated 3 or 4 times.

General Habits. Well known. Fearless of man, approaching closely to small fishing boats for fish and to large ships for galley waste, landing alongside and often diving to a depth of several metres to obtain fish on lines (Nicholls 1979, Oatley 1979). Approaches close to harbours and breakwaters in rough weather.

When loafing at sea mutual preening occurs and other display behaviour. 2 birds face each other, heads lowered, wings partially opened. Heads then rise together quickly followed by rapid bill-fencing. This is followed by elaborate wing-arching and head-bowing, ending with bills pointing vertically upwards. Most successful albatross at trawler nets, stealing fish from gannets and other smaller birds, and squabbling.

Food. Fish, cephalopods, crustaceans, offal.

References
Sinclair, J. C. (1978).

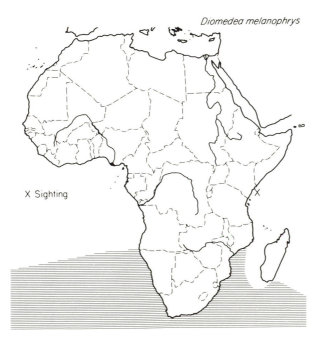

Diomedea melanophrys

X Sighting

X

Diomedea cauta Gould. Shy Albatross. Albatros à cape blanche.

Plate 2

(Opp. p. 35)

Diomedea cauta Gould, 1841. Proc. Zool. Soc. London (1840), p. 177; Bass Straight, Australia.

Range and Status. All waters south of *c.* 14°S. Fairly common on Namibian and South African seaboards in southern winter.

Description. *D. c. cauta,* ADULT ♂: crown white, sides of head to eye-level greyish, a dark mark over eye from front to rear. Nape and mantle to rear edge of wing dusky and encircling neck as darker collar; rest of back white. Tail dark grey; underbody white; undertail dark grey; underwing white narrowly edged dark brown, a dark patch encircling leading edge at shoulder. Bill pale greenish grey, tipped yellow, skin at base orange-pink; eye dark brown; legs and feet bluish grey. Sexes alike. SIZE: wing, ♂ 523–583 (556); tail, 188–220 (205); culmen, 117–135 (128); tarsus, 80–95 (88); middle toe and claw, 121–139 (131); length, 99 cm; wing-span, 198–244 cm. WEIGHT: *c.* 3 kg.

IMMATURE: similar but bill light grey, black-tipped; head and neck grey, throat white.

D. c. salvini (Rothschild). Differs in having grey head with white cap; primaries entirely black giving larger black area to underwing; bill grey-sided, ivory above and below, yellow tip to upper mandible, black tip to lower, becomes paler overall with age.

Diomedea cauta

Field Characters. Marginally larger than other mollymawks but best distinguished in flight by white underwing, and on water by bill colour. Most adults seen in African waters are pale-headed race *cauta* with yellow-tipped grey bill. Grey-headed immatures distinguishable from adult Grey-headed Albatross *D chrysostoma* and immature Black-browed Albatross *D. melanophrys* by light grey, black-tipped bill and white underwing.

Voice. Not recorded. At sea heard to emit fairly loud, drawn-out 'waaak' when feeding in vicinity of fishing boats with others (Sinclair 1978).

General Habits. Well known. Despite its name, is not shy. Follows fishing boats closely and will take bait or offal over which it will quarrel noisily. Sometimes dives several metres and swims underwater to obtain offal (Nicholls 1979). Pairs on water have been seen to give bill-rubbing displays and make 'croaking' sounds.

Food. Cuttlefish, fish, fish offal, barnacles and other crustaceans.

References
Swales, M. K. (1965).
White, C. M. N. (1973).
Cooper, J. (1974).

Diomedea chrysostoma Forster. Grey-headed Albatross. Albatros à tête grise.

Plate 2

(Opp. p. 35)

Diomedea chrysostoma Forster, 1785. Mém. Math. Phys. Acad. Sci. Paris, 10, p. 571; vicinity of the Antarctic Circle and in the Pacific Ocean.

Range and Status. All waters south of *c.* 28°S. An uncommon visitor to southern African waters, recorded once Namibia; small numbers regularly eastern Cape and Natal coasts (Samuels 1979).

Description. ADULT ♂: entire head to throat and nape blue-grey, grading into brown mantle and back to form continuous band with dark upperwing; rest of body white. Tail dark grey both surfaces; underwing white, edges broadly edged with dark brown, leading edge widest, and mottling into white area. Bill glossy black, a yellow line running the lengths of culmen ridges and bottom ridges of lower mandible; bare skin at base of bill orange-yellow; eye brown, a dark spot in front of and above eye, a white rim encircling lower eyelid; legs and feet pale flesh to blue-grey. SIZE: wing, ♂ 480–555 (510), ♀ 473–523 (504); tail, ♂ 175–205 (195), ♀ 175–199 (189); culmen, ♂ 106–122 (114), ♀ 108–119 (115); tarsus, ♂ 79–91 (86), ♀ 79–89 (85); middle toe and claw, ♂ 117–138 (126), ♀ 111–131 (122); length, 81–84 cm; wing-span, 214 cm. WEIGHT: 3·75 kg.

IMMATURE: similar but central area of underwing dusky, white ill-defined; bill mostly wholly dark olive-grey, the

Diomedea chrysostoma

ventral lower mandible tending to buff; feet grey with pinkish webs or pink washed dorsally on toes with fleshy grey. SIZE: wing, 539; culmen, 116; tarsus, 80.

Field Characters. In flight short neck and downward tilt to bill give distinctive shape. Adult separated from all forms of Shy Albatross *D. cauta* by broad dark margins to underwing; from young Black-browed *D. melanophrys* and Yellow-nosed *D. chlororhynchos* by solid grey of head (including throat) and bill colour. Immature, with pale head, grey nape and hindneck, and partial dark neck-band, very similar to immature Black-browed; best distinguished by solid blackish bill (in Black-browed, tip is always darker than rest of bill), with narrow line of pale horn on ridge of lower mandible.

As both species mature, identification becomes easier: base of Black-browed's bill becomes lighter brown, while black bill of Grey-headed acquires yellow ridge to culmen and tip of upper mandible.

Voice. Not recorded. No calls at sea known.

General Habits. Well known, but nothing specifically recorded for African waters. Tends not to follow ships but congregates at fishing vessels.

Food. Lampreys, squid and fish.

References
Bourne, W. R. P. (1977).

Plate 2
(Opp. p. 35)

Diomedea chlororhynchos Gmelin. Yellow-nosed Albatross. Albatros à bec jaune.

Diomedea chlororhynchos Gmelin, 1789. Syst. Nat. 1, p. 568; Cape of Good Hope.

Range and Status. All waters south of *c.* 15°S on west coast and 25°S on east coast. Commonest albatross in eastern Cape and Natal waters May–Sept.

Diomedea chlororhynchos

Description. *D. c. bassi* (Brooke *et al.* 1980): breeds Prince Edward, St Paul and Amsterdam Islands; occurs Indian Ocean and to unknown extent into western Cape waters. ADULT ♂: head and entire body white except for pale grey eyebrow and cheeks, and brown central back, the latter forming a continuous band with dark brown upperwings. Back of head and nape very pale pearl grey in fresh plumage, observable only at close range. Uppertail brown; underwing white with broad dark leading edge, very narrow dark trailing edge; undertail brown. Bill glossy black with broad yellow band length of culmen-ridge, tip pink; gape and bare skin at base of bill orange; eye brown, a small dark area in front of

and over eye; legs and feet bluish or pinkish blue. Sexes alike. SIZE: wing, (14 specimens) 465–499 (488); tail, (15) 185–210 (197); tarsus, (15) 78·7–86·6 (82·1); culmen, (15) 111·2–124·2 (118·7); middle toe and claw, (Serventy *et al.* 1971) (8) 107–113 (110); length, 71–81 cm; wing-span, 178–206 cm. WEIGHT: (15) 2490–2930 (2640).
IMMATURE: similar but bill wholly black.
D. c. chlororhynchos Gmelin. Breeds Tristan group and Gough Island; occurs Namibia and W coast of Cape at least to Cape Agulhas. Differs in head colouring: frons white, cheeks, ear-coverts, hind crown, nape and back of neck to mantle smoky grey. Immature has white head. SIZE: wing, (27) 483–520 (501); tail, (27) 178–214 (195); culmen, (27) 107·6–121·8 (114·6). WEIGHT: (26) 1780–2840 (2199).

Field Characters. Somewhat smaller and more slender than Black-browed Albatross *D. melanophrys* but this only apparent when seen together; best distinguished by black bill, narrow trailing edge to underwing. Nominate race, with grey wash on back of head and neck, distinguished from immature Black-browed and Grey-headed *D. chrysostoma* by bill colour, lack of neck-band, and underwing pattern; from adult Grey-headed by white throat, lack of yellow on lower mandible, and underwing pattern.

Voice. Recorded (23), but nothing described for birds at sea.

General Habits. Well known. Less bold than other mollymawks. Will approach fishing boats but flies in, seizes fish or squid, and quickly flies away, consuming meal away from other feeding birds. Mutual preening, bill-rubbing and bowing have been seen between swimming pairs.

Food. Mostly cephalopods; also shrimps and fish.

References
Cooper, J. (1974b).
Sinclair, J. C. (1978).
Brooke, R. K. *et al.* (1980).

Genus *Phoebetria* Reichenbach

The sooty albatrosses: 2 spp., both occurring in African waters as non-breeding visitors and characterized by being wholly sooty brown, smaller and more elegant than *Diomedea* spp.

Phoebetria fusca (Hilsenberg). Sooty Albatross. Albatros brun.

Plate 2

(Opp. p. 35)

Diomedea fusca Hilsenberg, 1822. Froriep, Not. 3, col., p. 74; Mozambique Channel, Eastern Africa.

Range and Status. All waters south of *c.* 30°S. Uncommon visitor to South Africa May–Sept.

Description. ADULT ♂: entirely uniform sooty brown, darker about head, quills of primaries and rectrices showing whitish at close range. Bill black with yellow line on sulcus, visible at close range; eye brown, incompletely circled by white ring, broadest posteriorly; feet pale grey. Sexes alike, ♀ smaller. SIZE: wing, ♂ (9 specimens) 481–516 (502), ♀ (4) 497–515 (503); tail, ♂ 241–265 (255), ♀ 237–253 (245); culmen, ♂ 111–116 (113), ♀ 110–114 (112); tarsus, ♂ 76–85 (81), ♀ 76–83 (80); middle toe and claw, ♂ 119–125 (120), ♀ 112–120 (117); length, 84–87 cm; wing-span, 204 cm. WEIGHT: *c.* 2·5 kg.

IMMATURE: has a barred, buff-coloured nape and dark primary shafts.

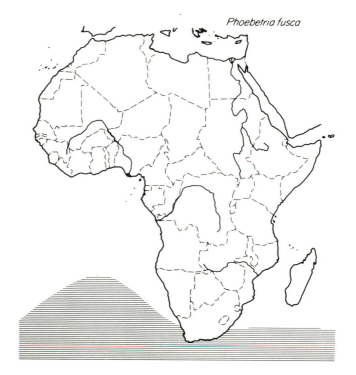

Phoebetria fusca

Field Characters. A small, elegant albatross, slender-winged with cigar-shaped body. Tail is usually held closed, flight light, buoyant, on flexible wings. Differs from Light-mantled Sooty Albatross *P. palpebrata* in having uniform body colouring and, at close quarters, by yellow not blue lines on bill; from young of giant petrels by generally slender appearance, slender bill, longer pointed look of tail and graceful flight, soaring and gliding interspersed with powerful wing-beats, especially in calm weather.

Voice. Recorded (13, 23), but nothing described for birds at sea.

Food. Squid, fish, crustaceans and carrion.

General Habits. Little known. Sometimes follows ships for long periods.

References
Swales, M. K. (1965).

Phoebetria palpebrata (Forster). Light-mantled Sooty Albatross. Albatros fuligineux.

Plate 2

(Opp. p. 35)

Diomedea palpebrata Forster, 1785. Mém. Math. Phys. Acad. Sci. Paris, 10, p. 571; Indian Ocean south of Prince Edward and Marion Islands.

Range and Status. All waters south of *c.* 33°S. Very rare visitor to Cape; 2 records, plus 1 partially decomposed corpse.

Description. ADULT ♂: entire head blackish; mantle and central back ash grey grading to brownish grey lower back. Tail grey-black with pale quills; upperwing brownish grey, primaries grey-black, underwing same. Bill black with pale blue line on sulcus; eye brown, incompletely encircled by white ring, broadest posteriorly; legs and feet bluish grey. Sexes alike, ♀ smaller. SIZE: wing, ♂ (12 specimens) 503–552 (524), ♀ (8) 490–526 (511); tail, ♂ (249–294 (271), ♀ 236–376 (267); culmen, ♂ 103–117 (111·4), ♀ 98–117 (109); tarsus, ♂ 80–87 (83·2), ♀ 78–84 (81); middle toe and claw, 120–238 (124·3), ♀ 116–125 (121); length, 79–89 cm; wing-span, 208–224 cm. WEIGHT: a little under 3 kg. IMMATURE: has all-black bill.

Field Characters. Dark, slender-winged, elegant albatross with cigar-shaped body. Slightly larger than Sooty Albatross *P. fusca*, bill shorter (Berruti 1976); also differs in having pale mantle and, at close range, blue line on bill, not yellow. Differs from immature giant petrels in having more slender proportions, slimmer bill, pointed appearance of tail and more graceful flight.

Voice. Recorded (13, 23, 25), but nothing described for birds at sea.

Phoebetria palpebrata

General Habits. Little known. Usually alights on water to feed but may also plunge from the air for food below the surface.

Food. Squid, euphausiids and other crustaceans, fish and carrion.

References
Swales, M. K. (1965).
Cooper, J. (1974a).

Family PROCELLARIIDAE: fulmars, shearwaters, petrels and prions

A diverse group of very large to medium-sized, long-winged pelagic birds. Includes many genera and species, some with world-wide distribution. Of 11 genera and 28 known species occurring in African waters, only 3 species breed on islands within our limits. Characterized by single nasal tube on top of bill and hind toe represented by sharp claw or nail. Plumage colours mostly drab but variable; flight identification difficult. Bill shape, size and leg colours important in hand. Sexes similar. All highly aerial birds adapted for very long periods at sea, mostly southern oceans, and little contact with land. Breed on islands and mainlands colonially or singly, in burrows or on surface. Flight at sea typically stiff-winged on lift provided by wind deflection off waves. Many species gather around fishing boats in large numbers to retrieve offal.

Genus *Macronectes* Richmond

The genus *Macronectes*, together with the genera *Daption*, *Fulmarus* and *Thalassoica*, are known collectively as the fulmarine-petrels. 6 spp. are found in African waters. Of robust appearance, they are buoyant and efficient gliders feeding on crustaceans, squid, small shoaling fish and carrion, which is either obtained by snatching it from the water's surface in flight or, more commonly, by settling nearby and swimming to the food source. In the water they float lightly and peck-feed.

Macronectes includes 2 spp., *M. giganteus* and *M. halli*, both non-breeding visitors to southern African waters, known collectively as the giant petrels. They are as large as the smaller albatrosses, and therefore the largest members of the family Procellariidae. Their bills are very robust, longer than the head, with large nasal tubes half as long as the culmens; they have short, fan-shaped tails with quills.

Plate 2
(Opp. p. 35)

Macronectes giganteus (Gmelin). **Southern Giant Petrel; Nellie; Stinker. Pétrel géant.**

Procellaria gigantea Gmelin, 1789. Syst. Nat. 1, pt. 2, p. 563; Staten Island, off Tierra del Fuego.

Range and Status. All waters south of *c.* 25°S regularly, occasionally further north, accidental to N Africa. Common visitor to South Africa, less common to Namibia, present all year but commonest Indian Ocean seaboard in southern winter.

Description. ADULT ♂: variable, 2 distinct morphs. (i) Dark morph has grey-brown colouring overall grading to paler head and whitish face, often mottled; plumage becomes paler with age. (ii) White morph is entirely white with dark spots, sometimes patches, randomly scattered; occasionally pure white. ADULT ♂: (both morphs) bill pale yellowish with pale green tip; eye usually pale grey, sometimes dark brown; legs and feet blackish to blue-grey. Sexes alike, ♀ smaller. SIZE: wing, ♂ (16 specimens) 500–565 (527), ♀ (19) 462–526 (498); tail, ♂ 166–189 (180), ♀ 162–184 (171); culmen, ♂ 90–105 (99), ♀ 78–101 (92); tarsus, ♂ 92–103 (96), ♀ 80–100 (88); middle toe and claw, ♂ 109–143 (130), ♀ 113–147 (125); length, 86–100 cm; wing-span, 185–206 cm. WEIGHT: 3–5·89 kg.

IMMATURE: entirely blackish brown or speckled with rusty brown; eye brown. Immature white morph as adult.

Field Characters. Huge marine birds approaching albatross in size but body stouter, wings shorter, bill shorter, thicker. Differs from Sooty Albatross *Phoebetria fusca* in having heavy pale bill, rounded tail, less elegant proportions; from Northern Giant Petrel *M. halli* by usually paler head and pale green tip to bill, but can be confused at distance.

Voice. Recorded (13, 15, 25). Generally silent at sea but may emit croaking sounds when quarrelling over food.

General Habits. Well known. Readily flocks to fishing vessels for discarded offal and occurs at seal colonies during culling operations, this and Northern Giant Petrel being the only petrels to feed both on land and at sea. Both morphs occur on South African coast, dark more common then white, both outnumbered by Northern Giant Petrel on west and Namibian coasts.

Food. A wide variety of animal matter: crustaceans, cephalopods, fish, offal, carrion, eggs and chicks of other marine birds; also ship's refuse.

Macronectes giganteus

References
Johnstone, G. W. (1974).
Bourne, W. R. P. and Warham, J. (1966).
Shaughnessy, P. D. and Sinclair, J. C. (1979).

Macronectes halli Mathews. **Northern Giant Petrel; Nellie; Stinker. Pétrel de Hall.**

Macronectes giganteus halli Mathews, 1912. Bds. Austr. 2, p. 187; Kerguelen.

Plate 2

(Opp. p. 35)

Range and Status. All waters south of *c.* 25°S regularly, occasionally further north. Commonest South African west coast and Namibian coast in southern winter, but present all year.

Description. ADULT ♂: variable but generally dark grey-brown overall except for whitish face freckled grey-brown; sometimes dark grey with paler feather edges giving freckled appearance. Head occasionally darker or white, but no white morph. Bill yellowish brown, sometimes reddish along culmen-ridge towards tip, which has dark smudge; eye pale grey; legs and feet blue-grey. Sexes alike, ♀ smaller. SIZE: ♂ (10 specimens) 498–550 (505), ♀ (5) 430–517 (489); tail, ♂ 170–190 (180), ♀ 167–185 (175); culmen, ♂ 93–106 (101), ♀ 87–108 (95); tarsus, ♂ 89–103 (96), ♀ 92–97 (94); middle toe and claw, ♂ 131–152 (141), ♀ 134–152 (140).

IMMATURE: dark brown, eye dark brown.

Field Characters. Huge marine bird approaching albatross in size but body stouter, wings shorter, bill thicker. Young birds distinguished from Sooty Albatross *Phoebetria fusca* by bulkier, less elegant form, shorter wings, thicker bill and rounded tail. Adults have less white about head than Southern Giant Petrel *M. giganteus* and dark tip to bill. No white morph.

Voice. Not recorded. Silent at sea except for croaking noises when squabbling over food.

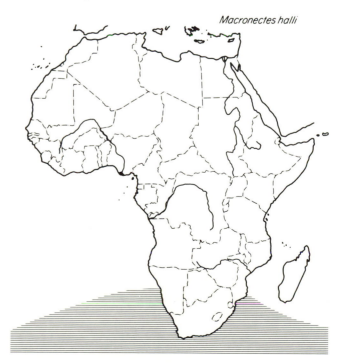

Macronectes halli

General Habits. Well known. Like Southern Giant Petrel, flocks to fishing boats and seal colonies at culling time. Feeds at sea or on land, being attracted to carrion. Apparently outnumbered by Southern Giant Petrel on east coast but outnumbers that species 30:1 at most gatherings on Atlantic coast. At trawler nets is extremely bold and aggressive, hurling itself into the mass of feeding birds and scattering all others, even pecking or shaking small species (Sinclair 1978).

Food. A wide variety of animal matter: crustaceans, cephalopods, fish, offal, carrion, eggs and chicks of other marine birds; also ship's refuse.

References
Bourne, W. R. P. and Warham, J. (1966).
Johnstone, G. W. (1974).
Shaughnessy, P. D. and Sinclair, J. C. (1979).

Genus *Fulmarus* Stephens

Medium-sized fulmarine-petrels having robust bills with long nasal tubes, thick necks and short, rounded tails with 14 feathers. White to pale grey, gull-like; sexes alike but ♂♂ larger, bills bigger. Accomplished gliders, flight action strong, wing-beats stiff, fairly rapid. 1, possibly 2 spp., are non-breeding visitors to African waters.

Plate 3
(Opp. p. 50)

Fulmarus glacialoides (Smith). Southern Fulmar; Silver-grey Petrel. Pétrel argenté.

Procellaria glacialoides A. Smith, 1840. Ill. Zool. S. Afr. Aves, pl. 51; Cape seas.

Range and Status. Uncommon visitor to South African waters. Widely distributed south of *c.* 30°S. Commonest Indian Ocean seaboard, July–Jan peaking Sept, most probably young birds, occurrences vary from year to year.

Description. ADULT ♂: head white; entire upper surface of body, tail and wings silver-grey. Trailing edge of secondaries and entire primaries sooty brown with distinct white 'flash'

at base of primaries. Rest of body, underwing and undertail white except for thin sooty brown margin to trailing edge of wings and tips of underwing-coverts adjacent to primaries. Bill flesh-pink to yellow, black at tip, nasal tubes blue; eye brown; legs and feet flesh or pinkish blue, stained brown. SIZE: wing, ♂ (5 specimens) 331–348 (339), ♀ (6) 315–332 (325); tail, 127–137 (132), ♀ 116–129 (124); culmen, ♂ 46–48 (47), ♀ 42–47 (44); tarsus, ♂ 52–57 (55), ♀ 50–54 (52); middle toe and claw, ♂ 66–74 (71), ♀ 65–70 (66); length, 46–51 cm; wingspan, 114 cm. WEIGHT: 52·5–90·0 (Serventy *et al.* 1971).
IMMATURE: similar but smaller (wing, 326: Mougin 1967).

Fulmarus glacialoides

Field Characters. Fairly large, long-winged, thick-necked, gull-like petrel with prominent white upper-wing-patches. Fast wing-beats alternate with sustained glides. This and Northern Fulmar *F. glacialis* are palest petrels in African seas, Antarctic Fulmar palest. Pinkish bill diagnostic.

Voice. Recorded (13, 15). Normally silent at sea.

General Habits. Usually solitary in African waters. Will attend ships for refuse but does not follow them. Occurrences in South African waters poorly understood, frequency of dead specimens, many young, suggests possibility of occasional 'wrecks' as in Australia.

Food. Crustaceans, cephalopods, fish and ships' refuse.

References
Serventy, D. L. *et al.* (1971).
Harper, C. and Kinsky, F. C. (1978).
Cooper, J. (1979).

Plate 3
(Opp. p. 50)

Fulmarus glacialis. Northern Fulmar. Pétrel fulmar.

Recorded off Portugal, Spain and Madeira; may occur N African coastline.

Genus *Thalassoica* Reichenbach

Medium-sized fulmarine-petrel of distinct white and chocolate brown colouring, compressed bill, tail with 12 quills; 1 sp.

Thalassoica antarctica (Gmelin). Antarctic Petrel. Pétrel antarctique.

Procellaria antarctica Gmelin, 1789. Syst. Nat. 1, p. 565; Antarctic Circle.

Plate 4

(Opp. p. 51)

Range and Status. A bird of antarctic pack ice, very rare in South African waters; occasional non-breeding visitor to southern African seaboard south of 30°S. 25 known records (Cooper 1979), mostly beached corpses, between July–Jan, peaking Sept, most apparently young birds.

Description. ADULT ♂: forehead to lower back chocolate brown, rump, uppertail-coverts and uppertail white, the tail broadly tipped brown. Upperwing chocolate brown over entire leading half and white over entire trailing half, except for brown tips and thin trailing edge. Chin, throat and sides of face brown, fading to white over rest of body and undertail-coverts; undertail brown; entire underwing white thickly edged brown. Bill brown, pale olive at sides; eye brown; legs and feet flesh. Sexes alike. SIZE: wing, ♂ (18 specimens) 300–330 (318), ♀ (26) 292–325 (310); tail, ♂ 105–130 (119), ♀ 108–122 (117); culmen, ♂ 36–40 (39), ♀ 33–37 (35); tarsus, ♂ 38–46 (43), ♀ 38–48 (43); middle toe and claw, ♂ 59–65 (62), ♀ 53–64 (58); length, 42–46 cm. WEIGHT: 509–768.
IMMATURE: like adult, bill darker.

Field Characters. A boldly patterned, piebald petrel. Can be confused only with Pintado Petrel *Daption capense* but differs from it in lacking mottled, patchy appearance above and is much whiter below.

Voice. Not recorded. Normally silent at sea.

General Habits. Little known; poorly recorded for African waters. Attends whale carcasses and (probably) fishing boats. Feeds by hovering over water, head to wind, and making flat plunges with wings outspread; also while swimming. In flight wing-beats short, strong and rapid.

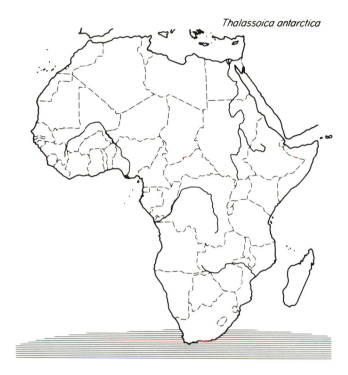

Thalassoica antarctica

Food. Crustaceans, pteropods, cephalopods, fish and medusae.

References
Cooper, J. (1979).

Genus *Daption* Stephens

Name is an anagram of the Spanish word 'pintado'—painted (Watson 1974). Medium-sized fulmarine-petrel of stocky appearance and pied plumage pattern. Bill broad, nasal tube relatively short, aperture appears single; skin beneath lower mandible bare (feathered in other fulmarine-petrels); outermost primary longest; tail with 14 quills; 1 sp.

Daption capense (Linnaeus). Pintado Petrel; Cape Pigeon. Pétrel damier.

Procellaria capense Linnaeus, 1758. Syst. Nat. (10th ed.), p. 132; Cape of Good Hope.

Plate 4

(Opp. p. 51)

Range and Status. Very common non-breeding visitor to African waters in southern winter to *c.* 25°S. Recorded Mombasa (Sinclair 1979). Commonest petrel in Cape seas.

Description. *D. c. capense*, ADULT ♂: entire head to sides of throat, nape and mantle black; back to tail-coverts white, spotted black. Tail white with broad black terminal band; upperwing black with 2 large white patches (inner primaries and primary wing-coverts, inner greater wing-coverts); scapulars white spotted black as back. Chin and throat white or speckled, rest of underparts white; undertail as uppertail; underwings white, broadly edged with black. Bill black; eye brown; legs and feet black, white patches on inner toes occasionally. Sexes alike. SIZE: wing, (38 specimens) 225–275 (258); tail, 90–107 (94); culmen, 28–33 (30); tarsus, 38–47 (45); middle toe and claw, 52–60 (57); length, 40 cm; wingspan, 81 cm. WEIGHT: 340–485.

IMMATURE: like adult.

Field Characters. A small, chunky petrel with unmistakable pied plumage pattern; 2 white patches on each wing. Flies with rapid wing-beats or sails with rigid wings. On sea floats buoyantly, tail high. Differs from larger Antarctic Petrel *Thalassoica antarctica* in having more dappled upper surfaces. Distinguishable from below by black bill, white chin and throat, broader black tail-band.

Voice. Recorded (3a, 13, 15, 23). A harsh, rattling 'cack-cack, cack-cack...'.

General Habits. Well known. Occurs in flocks, especially when feeding, when quarrelsome, pugnacious. Outnumbers most other petrels at fishing boats, taking small scraps, often those dropped by feeding albatrosses. Feeds mainly from surface, but can dive. In wake of ships, or when trailing fishing bait, uses hydroplaning action for prolonged periods, wings spread like glider, feet running on surface, breast resting lightly on water (Murphy 1936).

Food. Fish, crustaceans, cephalopods, also much offal obtained by scavenging.

References
Sinclair, J. C. (1978c).

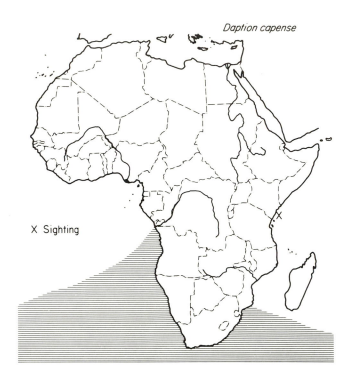

Daption capense

X Sighting

Genus *Pterodroma* Bonaparte

Small to medium-sized petrels known as 'gadfly-petrels' because of their swift, dashing flight. Bills short, thick, black, with short nasal tube, aperture directed upwards; tarsus only slightly compressed and rounded in front; tails broad when spread; necks thick and chunky. Colouring often darkish grey above, white below, forehead mottled, eye-patch often present and dark 'M' mark on upperwing in several species. At sea usually solitary, feeding from surface on squid and crustaceans. 5 spp. in African waters as non-breeding visitors: *P. macroptera* fairly common, *P. lessonii*, *P. brevirostris*, *P. incerta* and *P. mollis* uncommon.

Plate 5
(Opp. p. 82)

Pterodroma macroptera (Smith). Great-winged Petrel. Pétrel noir.

Procellaria macroptera A. Smith, 1840. Ill. Zool. S. Afr., Aves, pl. 52; Cape seas.

Range and Status. Fairly common visitor chiefly in southern summer to Atlantic seaboard south of *c.* 10°S and Indian Ocean to *c.* 19°S.

Description. *P. m. macroptera*: breeds Tristan, Gough, Marion, Crozets and Kerguelen Islands. ADULT ♂: wholly blackish brown above and below; some individuals have paler brown throat. Bill black, short and stout; eye brown; legs and feet black. Sexes alike, ♂ slightly larger. SIZE: wing, (7 specimens) 304–317 (309); tail, 121–129 (125); culmen, 34·0–37·2 (34·9); tarsus, 41–43 (42); middle toe and claw, 58–62 (60); length, 38–43 cm; wing-span, 102 cm. WEIGHT: 568.

IMMATURE: indistinguishable from adult.

Field Characters. Large, stubby-billed petrel with long narrow wings used in distinctive scythe-like backward rake. Larger and browner above than Kerguelen Petrel *P. brevirostris*. Flight often swift and powerful, wheeling in broad arcs to great heights above sea. When flying low over water can be confused with White-chinned Petrel *Procellaria aequinoctialis*, but distinguished by bounding flight, black bill.

Voice. Not recorded. Normally silent at sea.

General Habits. Little known. A shy, solitary species, paying no attention to ships.

Food. Mostly cephalopods; some fish.

References
Tuck, G. and Heinzel, H. (1979).

Pterodroma macroptera

Pterodroma lessonii (Garnot). White-headed Petrel. Pétrel de Lesson.

Plate 4

Procellaria Lessonii Garnot, 1826. Ann. Sci. Nat., Paris, 7, p. 54, pl. 4; Falkland Islands.

(Opp. p. 51)

Range and Status. 1 beached bird recorded Natal, Oct 1945. Recent sight records off Natal (1) and western Cape (8) (J. C. Sinclair and S. Keith, pers. comm.) suggest it may not be rare in South African waters, July–Nov.

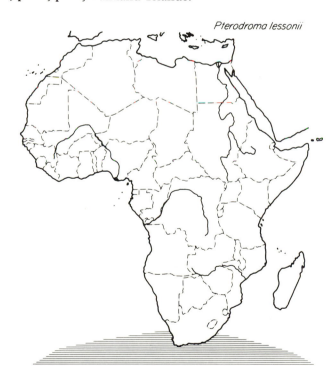

Pterodroma lessonii

Description. ADULT ♂: forehead and forecrown white, grading to pale grey on nape and darker grey on back. Upperwing brownish black; uppertail white, peppered grey and contrasting with back; a dark mark before and below eye, otherwise face and entire underparts white, including undertail; underwing grey, sometimes paler towards trailing edge, darker on leading edge and tips. Bill short, black; eye dark brown; feet flesh-pink, blackish on joints and outer halves of webs and toes. Sexes alike. SIZE: wing, (15 specimens) 292–317 (306); tail, 125–140 (134); culmen, 35–40 (38); tarsus, 38–48 (43); middle toe and claw, 60–69 (64); length, 41–46 cm; wing-span, 109 cm. WEIGHT: 536.
IMMATURE: indistinguishable from adult.

Field Characters. A fairly large petrel characterized by white head and underparts, dark wings. Differs from Grey Petrel *Procellaria cinerea* in having lighter head and white undertail-coverts. Wings appear sharply angled to form 'M' shape.

Voice. Not recorded. Silent at sea.

General Habits. Little known. Only occasionally follows ships. Normally solitary. Flight can be wild, erratic, towering high in sky, but normally fairly sedate, 6–16 m above water.

Food. Squid, fish and crustaceans.

Plate 4

(Opp. p. 51)

Pterodroma incerta (Schlegel). Schlegel's Petrel; Atlantic Petrel. Pétrel de Schlegel.

Procellaria incerta Schlegel, 1863. Mus. Hist. Nat. Pays-Bas, Rev. Méthod. Crit. Coll., livr. 4, Procellariae, p. 9—
'Mers australes, côtes de la Nouvelle Zélande, et Mers de l'Australia.'

Range and Status. Rare visitor to South African waters north to at least 26°S in Indian Ocean (Sinclair 1978c) *(for map see p. 52)*.

Description. ADULT ♂: entire upperparts brown, rump, wings and tail darker; sides of face, chin to lower neck, flanks, undertail-coverts, undertail and underwing brown; chest to belly white. Bill black; eye brown; legs and feet flesh-pink, brown on outer toes and webs. Sexes alike. SIZE: wing, 310–322 (316). Further data lacking. Regarded by some as conspecific with White-headed Petrel *P. lessonii*.
IMMATURE: no characteristics known.

Field Characters. A fairly large, stoutly built, dark brown petrel with white lower breast and belly; in worn plumage throat appears whitish. In pattern of underside resembles Soft-plumaged Petrel *P. mollis* from which can be distinguished by dark vent and undertail, uniform brown upperwing and more sedate flight.

Voice. Not recorded. Silent at sea.

General Habits. Little known. Normally solitary. Will circle ships, occasionally following.

Food. Probably predominantly squid.

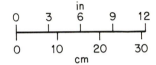

Scale applies to birds shown from above

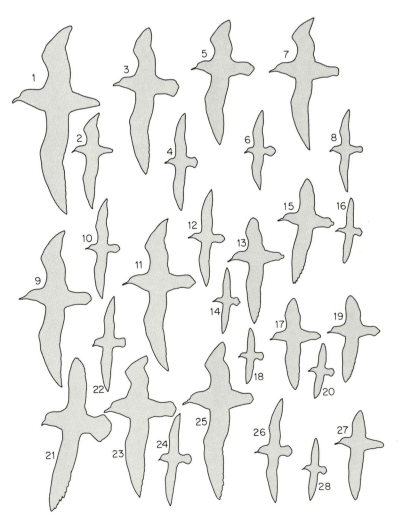

Plate 3

Procellaria aequinoctialis White-chinned Petrel (p. 57)
1. ADULT (above), 2. (below).

Puffinus carneipes Flesh-footed Shearwater (p. 61)
3. ADULT (above), 4. (below).

Puffinus pacificus Wedge-tailed Shearwater (p. 60)
5. ADULT (above), 6. (below).

Puffinus griseus Sooty Shearwater (p. 62)
7. ADULT (above), 8. (below).

Calonectris diomedea Cory's Shearwater (p. 59)
9. ADULT (above), 10. (below).

Puffinus gravis Great Shearwater (p. 61)
11. ADULT (above), 12. (below).

Puffinus puffinus Manx Shearwater (p. 63)
Race *yelkouan*: 13. ADULT (above), 14. (below).
Race *puffinus*: 15. ADULT (above), 16. (below).

Puffinus assimilis Little Shearwater (p. 65)
Race *baroli*: 17. ADULT (above), 18. (below).
Race *boydi*: 19. ADULT (above), 20. (below).

Fulmarus glacialis Northern Fulmar (p. 46)
21. ADULT (above), 22. (below).

Fulmarus glacialoides Southern Fulmar (p. 46)
23. ADULT (above), 24. (below).

Procellaria cinerea Grey Petrel (p. 58)
25. ADULT (above), 26. (below).

Puffinus lherminieri Audubon's Shearwater (p. 64)
Race *persica*: 27. ADULT (above), 28. (below).

Pterodroma brevirostris (Lesson). Kerguelen Petrel. Pétrel de Kerguelen.

Plate 4

(Opp. p. 51)

Procellaria brevirostris Lesson, 1831. Traité d'Orn., livr. 8, p. 611. No locality; type from Cape of Good Hope.

Range and Status. Rare visitor Cape and Natal coasts, southern winter (*for map see p. 52*).

Description. ADULT ♂: entirely dark grey, slightly darker on tail, around eyes and upperwing surface; underwing pale grey on primaries, paler towards bases, almost white on inner leading edge. Bill black; eye dark brown; legs and feet dusky black, tinged purple. Sexes alike. SIZE: (4 ♂♂, 12 ♀♀) wing, ♂ 242–260 (252), ♀ 250–265 (258); tail, ♂ 104–111 (108), ♀ 101–114 (107); culmen, ♂ 26·4–27·5 (26·9), ♀ 25·5–28·5 (26·6); tarsus, ♂ 37–39 (38), ♀ 34–40 (38); middle toe and claw, ♀ 46–52 (49); length, 33–33·5 cm; wing-span, 81 cm. WEIGHT: 312–340.

IMMATURE: said to have thicker bill than adult, becoming narrower, more compressed with age.

Field Characters. All-dark gadfly-petrel with short, stout bill and high forehead. Easily confused with dark form of Soft-plumaged Petrel *P. mollis* but has paler bases to primaries on underwing and almost white inner leading edge to wing. Flies with more twisting and turning than Soft-plumaged Petrel and soars to greater heights, hanging into wind; appears larger-headed, thicker-necked than that sp., primaries narrower. In low winds flies rapidly in weaving, bat-like fashion near surface. Resembles large swift.

Voice. Recorded (3a, 13, 23). Silent away from breeding sites.

General Habits. Little known. Normally occurs singly. Is attracted to ships but does not follow in their wake. Will rest on water and makes dives from surface.

Food. Mostly cephalopods, some crustaceans.

References
Sinclair, J. C. (1978a).

Plate 4

Pterodroma lessonii White-headed Petrel (p. 49)
1. ADULT (above), 2. (below).

Pterodroma incerta Schlegel's Petrel (p. 50)
3. ADULT (above), 4. (below).

Pterodroma mollis Soft-plumaged Petrel (p. 52)
Race *madeira*: 5. ADULT (above), 6. (below).

Pterodroma brevirostris Kerguelen Petrel (p. 51)
7. ADULT (above), 8. (below).

Daption capense Pintado Petrel (p. 47)
9. ADULT (above), 10. (below), 11. foot detail.

Thalassoica antarctica Antarctic Petrel (p. 47)
12. ADULT (above), 13. (below), 14. foot detail.

Halobaena caerulea Blue Petrel (p. 53)
15. ADULT (above), 16. (below).

Pachyptila vittata Broad-billed Prion (p. 54)
17. ADULT (above).

Pachyptila turtur Fairy Prion (p. 55)
18. ADULT (above).

Bills: 19. *Pachyptila crassirostris* Fulmar Prion (p. 56) (large geographical variation in bill size; 20. *P. belcheri* Thin-billed Prion (p. 55); 21. *P. turtur*; 22. *P. vittata macgillivrayi*; 23. *P. v. salvini*; 24. *P. desolata* Dove Prion (large geographical variation in bill size).

Note: owing to plumage variation within species and between adults and immatures, and the tendency of skins to shrink, rendering measurements somewhat unreliable, bill size and shape should be used as the principal guide for identifying prions in the hand.

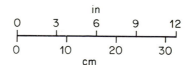

Scale applies to birds shown from above

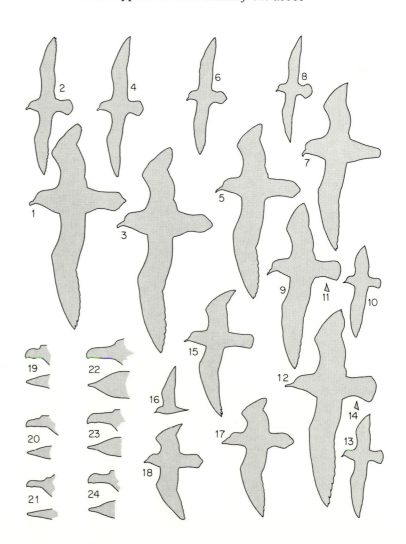

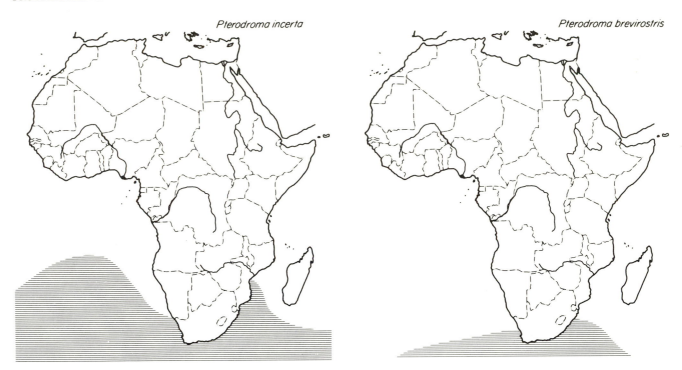

Pterodroma incerta

Pterodroma brevirostris

Plate 4

(Opp. p. 51)

Pterodroma mollis (Gould). Soft-plumaged Petrel. Pétrel soyeux.

Procellaria mollis Gould, 1844. Ann. Mag. Nat. Hist., 13, p. 363; South Atlantic lat. 20°S to 40°S.

Range and Status. Scarce non-breeding visitor to W African seaboard north of equator; regular and fairly common South African and Namibian waters in southern winter. Beached individuals collected Inhaca Island, Mozambique 25°1′S (Lawson 1963).

Description. *P. m. mollis*: breeds Tristan, Gough, Marion group and probably Antipodes Islands. ADULT ♂: crown dark grey-brown, feathers of forehead edged white giving pale, scaly effect, nape light grey. Rest of upperparts slate-grey but scapulars and wing-coverts blackish forming inconspicuous dark band across wing; tail grey, outer feathers paler. Dark cap extends to below eye, otherwise sides of face, chin and entire underbody including undertail white except for ill-

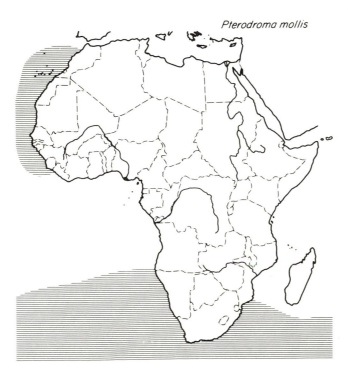

Pterodroma mollis

defined, sometimes incomplete, grey band across chest; underwing grey, coverts darker, inner leading edge of wing pale. Bill black; eye brown; legs flesh-pink, feet pink and blackish. Rare dark form has wholly blue-grey body but paler below, mottled on belly and flanks; chest-band, eye-mark and undertail darker. Sexes alike in both forms. SIZE: wing (15 specimens) 240–260 (252); tail, 102–120 (111); culmen, 27–30 (28); tarsus, 33–37 (35); middle toe and claw, 49–52 (50); length, 32–37 cm; wingspan, 83–95 cm. WEIGHT: 202–304 (254).

IMMATURE: indistinguishable from adult.

P. m. feae (Salvadori). Breeds Cape Verde Island and Bugio, Desertas Islands off Madeira and Porto Santo Islands off W Africa. Band across chest is broken, less well-defined. SIZE: wing (18), 263–273 (268·4); culmen (19), 26–30 (28·4).

P. m. madeira Mathews. Breeds highlands of Madeira, migrates to W Africa south to 9°N. Like *P.m. feae* but smaller. SIZE: wing, ♂ 247, 248, ♀ 251, 254. WEIGHT: 295–355.

Field Characters. A dark grey gadfly-petrel with white body and dusky chest-band or chest patches. Flight fast with erratic careening action. Smaller than Schlegel's Petrel *P. incerta*, chin and throat white, upperwing less uniform; best distinguished at distance by white vent and undertail, more twisting flight. Dark form differs from Kerguelen Petrel *P. brevirostris* in being paler on underbody with chest-band and undertail darker, inner leading edge of underwing not obviously paler, and in having different flight.

Voice. Recorded (29). Silent at sea.

General Habits. Little known. Occurs singly or in flocks. Inquisitive and will follow ships, sometimes settling on sea to retrieve refuse, e.g. offal.

Food. Squid and small fish.

References
Swales, M. K. (1965).
Sinclair, J. C. (1978a).

Genus *Halobaena* Bonaparte

Small, medium-grey petrel resembling a prion but bill and freckled forehead reminiscent of typical *Pterodroma* spp. Tail square-cut and wings more narrow and pointed than prions, outer 2 primaries equal in length; 1 sp.

Halobaena caerulea (Gmelin). Blue Petrel. Pétrel bleu.

Plate 4

(Opp. p. 51)

Procellaria caerulea Gmelin, 1789. Syst. Nat. 1, p. 560; southern ocean lat. 58°S.

Range and Status. Rare non-breeding visitor to South Africa. Several seen W Cape coast Sept 1969 (Voous 1970) and E Cape coast June 1979 (Samuels 1979).

Description. ADULT ♂: forehead mottled, crown to nape and around eyes blackish, mantle to tail-coverts medium grey. Tail medium grey, outer feathers and broad terminal band white; upper-wings medium grey, a broad, darker band running from outer primaries, along leading edge to 'wrist' and then backwards to end of scapulars forming an indistinct M-mark. Lores, cheeks, ear-coverts and underparts white, a dusky patch on sides of chest. Bill blue; culmen and nasal tubes black; eye brown; legs and feet lilac-blue, webs pale flesh. Sexes alike. SIZE: wing, (40 specimens) 200–224 (215); tail, 83–95 (89); culmen, 24–28 (26); tarsus, 28–36 (32); middle toe and claw 38–42 (41); length, 28–32 cm; wing-span, 58 cm. WEIGHT: 170–226.

IMMATURE: browner above, forehead greyish, feet pale lilac with dark stains on outer toes.

Field Characters. A small, medium-grey petrel with white underparts, incomplete collar, dark crown and unique white end to square tail. Easily confused with prions but greyer, less blue, lacking their black tail-tips, M-mark on upperwing less bold, crown and nape dark, flight less erratic, more steady.

General Habits. Well known. Gregarious at sea. Stays close to water with much gliding. On take-off patters over surface. Unlike prions, follows ships and accompanies whales.

Halobaena caerulea

Voice. Not recorded. Silent at sea.

Food. Mainly shrimps, small cephalopods and small fish.

Genus *Pachyptila* Illiger

Small petrels, blue-grey above, white below, with dark M-marks on upperwings (from behind) formed by blackish colouring on outer primaries, leading edge to 'wrist' and across wing-coverts to scapular ends. Tails wedge-shaped with dark terminal bands of varying widths on the central feathers (on all feathers in *P. turtur* and *P. crassirostris*). Bills are mostly blue-grey, culmen and nasal tubes darker; eyes brown; legs and feet blue, webs flesh-coloured. The skin under the lower mandible is distensible, forming a pouch. All spp. are so alike that specific identification at sea is almost impossible unless shade of plumage, width of tail band, and facial features can be seen. In the hand, identification is established by bill configuration (see Plate 4). Immatures of larger prions have narrower bills, resembling those of smaller species. Are peculiar in having a row of comb-like lamellae on each side of the palate within the upper mandible. In *P. vittata* these are so developed as to be visible on closed bill, but in others are rudimentary. Wings have 1st functional primary longer than, or equal to 2nd; 12 tail feathers. In general larger species are darker, heads larger.

At sea prions often move in flocks, sometimes large ones. Flight rapid, speeding flocks rising and falling, twisting and turning, the undersides alternately flashing white and disappearing. Feed using hydroplaning action in which bird's belly rests lightly on the surface, wings are raised up and feet drive it forward while bill is held underwater and used in a scooping action (Murphy 1936). Prions dive well, plunging and reappearing with great rapidity; do not follow ships. Food is zooplankton strained from the upper water through the lamellae of the bill. 6 spp., all reaching African waters as non-breeding visitors.

Plate 4

(Opp. p. 51)

Pachyptila vittata (Forster). **Broad-billed Prion. Prion de Forster.**

Procellaria vittata G. Forster, 1777. Voyage World, 1, pp. 91, 98; lat. 47°10′S.

Range and Status. Occurs Cape and Natal seas regularly in southern winter.

Description. *P. v. macgillivrayi* (Mathews): Indian Ocean. ADULT ♂: overall colour darker than other prions, size larger. Distensible chin pouch pinkish mauve. Bill widest of all prions, culmen less than twice as long as broad at base and perceptibly bowed at sides, grey in colour, palatal lamellae yellow, visible on closed bill. Sexes alike. SIZE: (4–23 specimens) wing, 197–214 (206); tail, 95–100 (98); culmen, 32–37 (34); width of bill, 18·2–22·6 (20·6); tarsus, 33–36 (35) middle toe and claw, 41–42 (41·5); length, 28–32 cm.
  IMMATURE: as adults but bill weaker, narrower.
  P. v. salvini (Mathews). Crozet, Prince Edward and Marion Islands to Cape seas. As nominate race but bill narrower, blue in colour. SIZE: wing, 182–199 (189); bill width, 14–17 (16). Also known as Medium-billed Prion, and sometimes treated as full species.

Field Characters. Separated from other prions only by very broad bill and darker colouring.

Voice. Recorded (23). Silent away from breeding grounds.

General Habits. Little known. Gregarious; less agile in flight and weaves less than other prions. Feeds mainly by hydroplaning.

Food. Mainly cephalopods and pteropods, probably also some crustaceans.

Pachyptila vittata

Plate 4

(Opp. p. 51)

Pachyptila desolata (Gmelin). **Dove Prion; Antarctic Prion. Prion de la Désolation.**

Procellaria desolata Gmelin, 1789. Syst. Nat. 1, pt. 2, p. 562; Desolation Island = Kerguelen Island.

Pachyptila desolata

Range and Status. Commonest prion in South African and Namibian seas, *P. d. desolata* outnumbering *P. d. banksi* 3 : 1; latter not known on western seaboard.

Description. *P. d. desolata* (Gmelin): breeds on Kerguelen Island and Crozet (east). ADULT ♂: prominent blackish stripe in front of and below eye to ear-coverts contrasts with white eyebrow. Lores freckled black, forehead black, corner of gape black, giving dark facial pattern; grey patch on either side of upper breast. Bill twice as long as width at base, sides straight, colour blue-grey. Sexes alike. SIZE: wing, (100+ specimens) 171–201 (186); tail, 72–104 (86); culmen, 24–30 (27); width of bill, 11–16 (13·5); tarsus, 28–35 (31·5); middle toe and claw, 29–39 (34); length, 25–30 cm.
  IMMATURE: like adult.
  P. d. banksi Smith. Breeds South Georgia, South Sandwich, South Orkney, South Shetland, Heard Island and Antarctica. Has broader bill than nominate race. SIZE: wing, 170–194 (182); width of bill, 13·6–15·4 (14·4).

Field Characters. Appears similar in flight to Thin-billed Prion *P. belcheri* but wing-beats slower, more purposeful, especially in calm weather. Head tucked into shoulders, wings held forward, give thick-set long-tailed appearance.

Voice. Not recorded. Silent at sea.

General Habits. Little known. Highly gregarious, may occur in thousands. Mass wrecks of many hundreds reported Natal coast July–Aug 1954 (Clancey 1955), July–Aug 1979 (J. Spearpoint, pers. comm.)

Food. Euphausiids and other crustaceans (especially the amphipods *Euthemisto antarctica*, *Euphausia*), pteropods, small cephalopods and polychaete worms; also individual larger prey taken from surface.

Pachyptila belcheri (Mathews). Thin-billed Prion; Slender-billed Prion. Prion de Belcher.

Plate 4

(Opp. p. 51)

Heteroprion belcheri Mathews, 1912. Bds. Austr. 2, p. 215 and text figs p. 224; Geelong, Victoria, Australia.

Range and Status. Recorded once in Cape, twice in Natal.

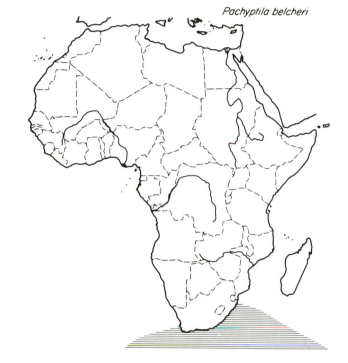

Description. ADULT ♂: head pattern distinct, white lores and eyebrows contrasting with narrow bluish grey stripe below and behind eye. Bill narrow, elongated (3 : 1), sides straight viewed from above, blue in colour. Sexes alike. SIZE: (10 specimens) wing, 180–191 (187); tail, 86–97 (92); culmen, 23·7–28·3 (25·9); width of bill, 9·8–11·4 (10·6); tarsus, 31–34 (33); middle toe and claw, 38–42 (40).

Field Characters. The palest prion with distinctive white lores and eyebrows.

Voice. Not recorded. Coos, and loud, harsh alarm notes uttered by birds captured at sea.

General Habits. Little known. Flight very agile and erratic, even in calm weather. Flies low over water, generally in small flocks. Feeds mainly at night, picking food from surface while gliding on stiffly outstretched wings.

Food. Amphipods, small squid and other crustaceans.

Pachyptila turtur (Kuhl). Fairy Prion. Prion colombe.

Plate 4

(Opp. p. 51)

Procellaria turtur Kuhl, 1820. Beitr. Zool. Vergl. Anat., Abth. 1, p. 143; no locality.

Range and Status. Scarce visitor to Namibian and South African seaboard in southern winter.

Description. ADULT ♂: face and eyebrow white, a dusky smudge extending from front of and below eye to encircle ear-coverts, corner of gape black; tail-band wide, covering half of tail and extending to all feathers. Bill narrow, fairly short, blue. Sexes alike. SIZE: (10–20 specimens) wing, 165–186 (174); tail, 80–93 (85); culmen, 21·0–23·6 (22·7); depth of culmen at nostril, 6·4–7·2; width of bill, 10·0–11·1 (10·6); tarsus, 28–32 (31); middle toe and claw, 38–41 (40); length, 25–28 cm. WEIGHT: 100–126.

IMMATURE: has weaker, narrower bill.

Field Characters. The smallest prion. Flies with head tucked in, wings held forward like Dove Prion *P. desolata*, but differs from it in having shorter bill, and from all other prions in having very wide tail-band. M-mark on wing very bold.

Voice. Not recorded. Silent at sea.

General Habits. Scarcely known. Feeds by picking food from surface during day-time.

Food. Small squid and crustaceans.

Plate 4
(Opp. p. 51)

Pachyptila crassirostris. **(Mathews). Fulmar Prion. Prion fulmar.**

Pseudoprion turtur crassirostris Mathews, 1912. Bds. Austr., 2, p. 221; Bounty Island.

Pachyptila crassirostris

X Sighting   X

Range and Status. 1 record (1841) Cape of Good Hope.

Description. ADULT ♂: M-mark on upperwings broad and pronounced; tail-band wide extending to full width of tail. Facial pattern indistinct. Bill short, stout, the nail large, deep and wide, little space between it and nasal tube. Sexes alike. SIZE: (7 specimens) wing, 180–187 (182); tail, 87–100 (91); culmen, 21–24 (23); depth of culmen at nostril 7·2–7·7; tarsus, 30–33 (31); middle toe and claw, 38–42 (41).

Field Characters. Black marks on wings and tail very conspicuous.

Voice. Not recorded. Silent at sea.

General Habits. Little known. Flight most erratic of all prions, with unique 'loop-the-loop' manoeuvre. Food picked from surface.

Food. Crustaceans, pteropods, squid; rarely fish.

Genus *Bulweria* Bonaparte

Closely related to *Pterodroma* but separated on osteological grounds, the lachrymal bone being free within the nasal cavity (fused to the nasal and frontal bones in *Pterodroma* spp.) and the limb bones being of different proportions (Olson 1975). Contains 3 spp., 2 occurring in African waters as non-breeding visitors. Both these have tails more wedge-shaped than most *Pterodroma* but otherwise, and for purposes of identification, they belong to the same group. Olson (1975) has proposed that *Bulweria* should be recognized at subgeneric level.

Plate 5
(Opp. p. 82)

Bulweria bulwerii **(Jardine & Selby). Bulwer's Petrel. Pétrel de Bulwer.**

Procellaria bulwerii Jardine & Selby, 1828. Ill. Orn. pt. 4, pl. 65 and text; Madeira.

Bulweria bulwerii

X

X Sighting   X

Range and Status. Offshore Atlantic seaboard south to Gulf of Guinea. Isolated sight records off Cape. Few onshore records. Commonest Apr–Oct, dispersing southwards Nov onwards.

Description. ADULT ♂: entirely sooty brown, paler on cheeks and throat and greater upperwing-coverts; tail markedly wedge-shaped. Bill black; eye dark brown; legs and feet pale flesh, dusky on outer webs. SIZE: wing, ♂ (29 specimens) 191–207 (200), ♀ 193–209 (199); tail, 103–114 (108), ♀ 102–116 (109); culmen, ♂ 19–23 (21·6), ♀ 20–22 (21·1); tarsus, ♂ 24–29 (27·8), ♀ 25–30 (27·1); toe, ♂ 25–32 (29·1) 26–32 (28·6); length, 26–28 cm; wing-span, 68–73 cm. WEIGHT: (breeding) 87–98 (93).
IMMATURE: indistinguishable from adult.

Field Characters. Small, all-dark; more like storm-petrel than gadfly-petrel, but lacks white rump. Heavy wedge-shaped tail and pale bars on upperwing diagnostic at sea. Bill fairly short, heavy.

General Habits. Little known. Seldom flocks; feeds mostly singly, well out to sea, and nocturnally. Flight fast with careening action.

Voice. Recorded (29). Silent at sea.

Food. Mainly planktonic animal life.

Bulweria fallax Jouanin. Jouanin's Petrel. Pétrel de Jouanin.

Bulweria fallax Jouanin, 1955. Oiseau, 25, p. 155; northwestern Indian Ocean lat. 12°30′N, long. 55°E.

Plate 5

(Opp. p. 82)

Range and Status. Occurs Gulf of Aden (penetration of Red Sea uncertain), south to at least 8°S, 58°E (Bailey 1964, 1966; Gill 1967). 1 record for Kenya. Further distributional data lacking.

Bulweria fallax

Description. Small (36 cm) all-dark gadfly-petrel with long, wedge-shaped tail. No good available measurements published. Considered by some to be conspecific with Bulwer's Petrel *B. bulwerii*.

Field Characters. Apparently differs from Bulwer's Petrel only in being larger in size. Probably indistinguishable from it at sea, but range overlap unlikely. Flight fast and mobile, with short, stout bill pointed downwards, differing in these respects from the longer-billed, slower-flying dark morph of the Wedge-tailed Shearwater *Puffinus pacificus*.

Voice. Not recorded. Unknown.

General Habits. Scarcely known.

Food. Nothing specifically recorded but probably plankton.

References
Tuck, T. and Heinzel, H. (1979).

Genus *Procellaria* Linnaeus

Large shearwaters with rounded tails; narrow, robust, well-hooked bills, always pale-coloured, nasal tubes prominent with apertures directed forward; dusky or black legs. Southern Hemisphere burrow breeders in temperate or subantarctic waters, showing marked post-breeding east–west dispersal. 4 spp., 2 recorded in African seas.

Procellaria aequinoctialis Linnaeus. White-chinned Petrel; Cape Hen; Shoemaker. Puffin brun.

Procellaria aequinoctialis Linnaeus, 1758. Syst. Nat. (10th ed.), p. 132; Cape of Good Hope.

Plate 3

(Opp. p. 50)

Range and Status. Common visitor to all waters south of *c.* 30°S, less commonly to *c.* 20°S on Atlantic seaboard. Numbers greatest in southern winter.

Description. *P. a. aequinoctialis*: breeds mainly islands in southern seas. ADULT ♂: entirely dark sooty brown with variable amount of white on chin and throat. Tail short, wedge-shaped. Bill greenish horn with dark patch on culmen; legs and feet black. Sexes alike. SIZE: wing (35 specimens) 339–409 (372): tail, 113–140 (124): culmen, 48–56 (52); tarsus,

56–72 (63); middle toe and claw, 79–90 (83); length, 51–59 cm; wing-span, 135–147 cm. WEIGHT: *c.* 1500. Partial albinism not uncommon—irregular patches of white on abdomen level with trailing edge of wing (Nicholls 1978).
    IMMATURE: indistinguishable from adult.

Field Characters. A large pale-billed petrel, dark with white chin. Flight smooth and powerful with much soaring, wing-beats measured, slow. Differs from young of giant petrels in smaller size, slender bill, wedge-shaped tail.

Procellaria aequinoctialis

Voice. Recorded (13). When feeding from trawler nets a high pitched trill and aggressive 'kek, kek kek' sounds have been recorded (Sinclair 1978c).

General Habits. Well known. Common Cape and Natal waters. Bold and aggressive, follows fishing boats and settles alongside for scraps. Visits and will often follow large ships.

Food. Cephalopods, fish, crustaceans and offal.

References
Gibson-Hill, C. A. (1949).
Rowan, A. N. *et al.* (1951).
Brooke, R. K. and Sinclair, J. C. (1978).

Plate 3
(Opp. p. 50)

Procellaria cinerea Gmelin. Grey Petrel; Pediunker. Puffin gris.

Procellaria cinerea Gmelin, 1789. Syst. Nat. 1, p. 563; New Zealand seas lat. 48°S.

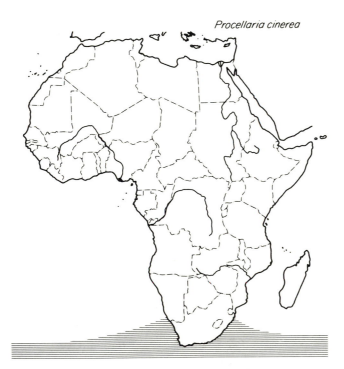

Procellaria cinerea

Range and Status. Visitor to Cape seas in southern summer, rarely north to Natal.

Description. ADULT ♂: top of head and nape dark greyish brown, mantle ash-brown, remainder of back and upperwing greyish brown, darker at tips. Tail dark brown; body below eye and wing-level white; underwing and undertail ash-brown. Bill pea-green laterally, horn-coloured at tips, blackish on central culmen and nostrils; eye brown; legs and feet grey-flesh, blackish on joints and outer sides, webs yellowish. Sexes alike. SIZE: wing, ♂ (6 specimens) 341–350 (346), ♀ (5) 340–355 (347); tail, ♂ 110–124 (116), ♀ 114–118 (116); culmen, ♂ 46–48 (47), ♀ 45–49 (47); tarsus, ♂ 58–61 (59), ♀ 58–61 (59); middle toe and claw, ♂ 72–75 (74), ♀ 72–76 (74); length, 50 cm; wing-span, 117 cm. WEIGHT: *c.* 1·3 kg.
IMMATURE: similar to adult.

Field Characters. A large petrel, grey-brown above and white below but with dark underwing, which distinguishes it from Cory's Shearwater *Calonectris diomedea*. Differs from White-headed Petrel *Pterodroma lessonii* in having dark top of head and dusky undertail-coverts, from Atlantic Petrel *P. incerta* in having pale bill and throat, greyer upperparts.

Voice. Recorded (13). Silent at sea.

General Habits. Well known. Generally solitary but groups gather at fishing vessels. Dives readily from 5–10 m. Can swim well underwater. Usually ignores larger ships.

Food. Cephalopods, fish, offal and ship's refuse.

Genus *Calonectris* Mathews and Iredale

Medium-sized shearwaters between *Procellaria* and *Puffinus* but more adapted to aerial, gliding life than *Puffinus*. Bill long (as long or longer than tarsus), strong, pale in colour, nasal tubes not bevelled, opening forward; tarsus rounded, not laterally flattened; tail rounded or wedge-shaped. 2 spp., 1 in African waters (Mediterranean) as breeding resident.

Calonectris diomedea (Scopoli). Cory's Shearwater. Puffin cendré.

Plate 3
(Opp. p. 50)

Procellaria diomedea Scopoli, 1769. Annus I Hist.-Nat., p. 74; Tremeti Islands, Italy, Adriatic Sea.

Range and Status. Mediterranean, breeding various islands including offshore Tunisia where abundant locally Feb–Nov; non-breeding visitor North and South Atlantic, commonly Morocco to Mauritania, Namibia to Cape, (scarce Gulf of Guinea) and to Indian Ocean northwards to Natal in southern summer, mostly occurring Cape Peninsula westward where sometimes in large numbers.

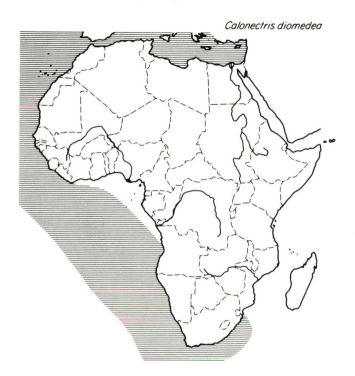

Calonectris diomedea

Description. *C. d. diomedea*: breeds Mediterranean Islands. ADULT ♂: head to just below eye, hindneck and mantle pale brownish grey; rest of upperparts sooty-brown, with a prominent white wedge on inner web of primaries. Uppertail-coverts usually paler, forming crescent shape and contrasting with dark tail; chin and throat faintly grey, rest of underparts white with faint grey barring on flanks and sides of undertail-coverts; undertail dusky-brown; underwing white, leading and trailing edges and primaries dusky-brown. Bill pale horn-yellow tipped dark; eye brown; legs and feet pale reddish flesh, outer sides of tarsus, outer toes and webs dusky, the tarsus cylindrical. Sexes alike, ♂ slightly larger. SIZE: wing, ♂ (9 specimens) 339–351 (346), ♀ (5) 330–347 (339); tail, ♂ 127–135; tarsus, ♂ 50–57; culmen, ♂ 45–55 (Kuroda 1954). WEIGHT: (breeding ♂ and ♀) (12) 560–730 (654).
    IMMATURE: indistinguishable from adult.
    DOWNY YOUNG: covered in brown down, chin and throat sparsely covered in white down.
    C. d. borealis (Cory). Breeds off Portugal, Madeira, Desertas, Porto Santo, Salvages, Canaries and Azores. Larger than *C. d. diomedea*, bill stouter, longer, pinkish; head and mantle slightly darker grey; at distance central back appears sandy, contrasting with wings (Bourne 1955). SIZE: wing, ♂ 361, 367. WEIGHT: ♂ (26) 940–1130 (1014).
    C. d. edwardsii (Oustalet). Breeds Cape Verde Islands. Smaller, with small dark bill. Appears darker, more uniform on mantle, more hooded appearance to head, centre of back and wings uniformly dark (Bourne 1955). SIZE: wing, ♂ (9) 298–321 (313).

Field Characters. Large, heavy-bodied shearwater, brown above, white below, with long pale bill. Flight strong but somewhat heavy, lumbering, wing-beats slower than in smaller species. Will soar in strong winds. Distinguished from Great Shearwater *Puffinus gravis* by more uniform upperparts, lack of pale collar, no 'dark-capped' effect (brown top of head grades gradually into pale throat), and all-white underwing (Great Shearwater has dark line across underwing from carpal joint to base of wings). Sometimes has pale band at base of tail like Great Shearwater. Similar-sized Grey Petrel *Procellaria cinerea* has brown underwing, dark vent.

Voice. Recorded (2a, 29). Normally silent at sea. At colonies noisy, calling mostly at dusk and dawn. Described as harsh, rasping, sobbing scream 'kaa-ough' or 'koo-ough' uttered 3 or 4 times with distinct sighing audible at close range. Copulation call of ♂ 'ka-ka-ka-ka' (Lockley 1952).

General Habits. Well known. After breeding moves south into Atlantic during Oct–Nov, spending southern summer in S Atlantic. Largest numbers off South Africa 30°–40°S, 10°–20°E, smaller numbers to Indian Ocean (Ross 1973). Nominate *C. d. diomedea* most common but *C. d. borealis* recorded twice E Cape. Although most return northwards *c.* Mar, some remain at least until May (Harrison 1978).

Food. Fish, fish spawn, cephalopods, crustaceans, latter especially popular with *C. d. diomedea*. Offal taken near fishing boats. Follows whales and schools of predatory fish to retrieve food scraps, and will follow fishing boats for same reason. Feeds mostly by surface-skimming in flight.

Breeding Habits. Little known N Africa; account chiefly based on data from elsewhere where well known. In Atlantic nests in tunnels on grassy slopes; at Dragonada Island (Crete) mostly under stones, cement slabs, apparently not excavating burrows (Mallet and Coghlan 1964).

Courting birds sit facing and preening each other, nibbling heads and bills. During copulation harsh calls are uttered; following copulation ♀ nibbles ♂'s tail and stern.

NEST: usually in huge, dense colonies, apparently with no competition for nest-sites. No territorial behaviour known. If tunnels are excavated this is done by both sexes.

EGGS: invariably 1. Ovate to elliptical; dull white (*C. d. diomedea*). SIZE: (85 eggs) 63–74 × 42–53 (69 × 45). WEIGHT: (calculated) 74.

Laying dates: May.

Incubation carried out by both sexes, ♂ first; spells av. 6·4 days, later 6 days. Period: (25 records) 52–55 (53·8) days. Earliest eggs hatch Crete 13 July, peaking 15–18 July.

Chick develops 2nd coat of slightly darker, longer down after *c.* 10 days. Egg tooth lost after *c.* 3·5 weeks, tail feathers emerge at *c.* 2·5 weeks, secondaries at 3·5 weeks, primaries at 4 weeks. Body feathers appear first on head and upperparts, predominate on back when primaries emerge. WEIGHT: day 1 (9 chicks) 53–82 (70); from days 2–3 until *c.* day 21 av. daily increase less than 15 g; thereafter more rapid, reaching peak weight of 660–1040 (843) at 44–89 days (usually 70–75). Chicks then emerge from nests, exploring immediate surroundings at night. No longer fed at this stage and lose *c.* 11% in weight (Round and Swann 1977). Leave nest 1–11 (av. 4·7, 19 records) days after last feed.

For first few days, 1 adult remains in nest with chick; thereafter chick left alone, adults visiting only at night; *c.* 50% of chicks visited any night fed by both parents. Feeds weigh 50–65 g day 15, increasing to 30–215 g by day 45, 90–160 g day 65; not fed after day 75.

Breeding success for *C. d. diomedea* unknown, but less than 1 reared per pair overall.

References
Bourne, W. R. P. (1955).
Kuroda, N. (1954).
Mallet, G. E. and Coghlan, L. T. (1964).
Round, P. D. and Swann, R. L. (1977).

Genus *Puffinus* Brisson

Small shearwaters, more aquatic, less aerially adapted and sturdier in build than *Procellaria* or *Calonectris*. Shorter wings and compressed tarsus aid underwater swimming but necessitate less gliding, more flapping flight. Bill long, slender, but shorter than *Calonectris*, nasal tubes open dorsally. Tarsus laterally compressed (almost cylindrical in *P. pacificus*), sharp-edged in front, pale flesh to blue or dusky. Tail long, rounded or wedge-shaped. Numerous species in both hemispheres, some making extensive transequatorial migrations. 7 spp. in African seas, 2 breeding, 5 non-breeding.

Plate 3
(Opp. p. 50)

Puffinus pacificus (Gmelin). Wedge-tailed Shearwater. Puffin fouquet.

Procellaria pacifica Gmelin, 1789. Syst. Nat. 1, p. 560; Pacific Ocean.

Range and Status. A tropical shearwater occurring as non-breeding visitor mostly Sept–Mar Indian Ocean seaboard, north to Gulf of Aden, south to Cape seas.

Description. ADULT ♂: entirely dark brown, darker on primaries and tail, slightly paler on chin and throat. Bill pale pink to lead-grey, dark on upper ridge and tip; eye brown; feet pale flesh. Rare pale morph is white below with dusky undertail-coverts, dark margins to white underwing. Sexes alike, both morphs. SIZE: wing, (20 specimens) 280–308 (290); tail, 119–138 (126); culmen, 36–41 (38); tarsus, 42–48 (46); middle toe and claw, 57–59 (58); length, 41–46 cm; wing-span, 97–104 cm. WEIGHT: 285–425.

IMMATURE: indistinguishable from adult.

Field Characters. All dark shearwater with pointed tail, which appears wedge-shaped only when spread, well-angled wings, dark bill. Smaller, slighter and proportionately longer-tailed than Flesh-footed Shearwater *P. carneipes*, wing-beats faster, interspersed with long twisting glides.

Voice. Recorded (7). Silent at sea.

Puffinus pacificus

General Habits. Well known. Usually travels singly but forms into small flocks when feeding. Occasionally follows ships. Usually flies low over water, below 10 m, making best use of wind differentials. Feeds mostly by flying close to water, sometimes touching water with outstretched feet, head and neck plunged down several centimetres, momentum then regained by vigorous flapping and foot-paddling. Fish eaten without interrupting flight. Often feeds on surface from sitting position, sometimes making shallow surface dives, rarely submerging. Frequently dips in flight in pursuit of flying fish, sometimes accompanied by vigorous foot-strokes. May rest on water after feeding.

Food. Cephalopods, crustacea and small fish.

References
King, W. B. (1974).
Sinclair, J. C. (1978b).

Puffinus carneipes Gould. Flesh-footed Shearwater. Puffin à pieds pâles.

Plate 3
(Opp. p. 50)

Puffinus carneipes Gould, 1844. Ann. Mag. Nat. Hist. 13, p. 365; Islands off Cape Leeuwin, western Australia.

Range and Status. Scarce non-breeding visitor. Most occur on Indian Ocean seaboard Cape north to Kenya, also recorded southwest Cape, most in southern summer.

Description. ADULT ♂: entirely dark brown; tail darker, rounded. Bill flesh-coloured, tip blackish; eye brown; legs and feet flesh-pink. Sexes alike. SIZE: wing, (12 specimens) 294–317 (309); tail, 102–112 (107); culmen, 39–44 (42); tarsus, 49–54 (51); middle toe and claw, 65–70 (67); length, 40–46 cm; wing-span, 99–107 cm. WEIGHT: 696–768.
IMMATURE: indistinguishable from adult.

Field Characters. Large, all-dark shearwater with pale bill and feet, rounded tail. Flies effortlessly, soaring and gliding close to sea's surface. In windy conditions soars and wheels in the typical shearwater cork-screw motion. Differs from Wedge-tailed Shearwater *P. pacificus* and Great-winged Petrel *Pterodroma macroptera* in having heavier build, pale bill and feet, less angled wings.

Voice. Recorded (23). Makes a high-pitched sound when squabbling over food.

General Habits. Little known, particularly in African waters. Usually occurs singly in Indian Ocean. Will approach fishing vessels for food. Dives to water at angle of 45 for food, striking surface with feet and breast, then feeds from surface; occasionally makes awkward shallow dives.

Puffinus carneipes

Food. Crustaceans, squid and small fish.

References
Sinclair, J. C. (1978c).

Puffinus gravis (O'Reilly). Great Shearwater. Puffin majeur.

Plate 3
(Opp. p. 50)

Procellaria Gravis O'Reilly, 1818. Greenland Adjacent Seas, Northwest Passage, p. 140, pl. 12, fig. 1; Cape Farewell and States Hook to Newfoundland.

Range and Status. Scarce non-breeding visitor to W African waters most Aug–Sept, between 36°N and equator, probably when moving south. Not recorded Gulf of Guinea; present Namibian and South African waters to about 25°E Oct–Jan, but uncommon.

Description. ADULT ♂: head-cap dark, otherwise upperparts brown except for pale collar and broad white uppertail-coverts forming crescent shape. Underparts white, central belly with large dusky patch, flanks and vent also dusky; underwing white with dark border, broadest on trailing edge; underwing-coverts tipped dark forming line from carpal joint to base of wing; undertail dark brown. Bill blackish, long, well-hooked; legs and feet pale flesh to bright pink, brown on outer edges. Sexes similar. SIZE: wing, ♂ (10 specimens) 318–348 (332), ♀ (6) 301–334 (318); tail, ♂ 113–126 (117), ♀ (8) 109–120 (113); culmen, ♂ 43–50 (46), ♀ 43–47 (44); tarsus, ♂ 58–63 (59·8), ♀ 57–60 (59); middle toe and claw, 68–77 (71·6), ♀ (5) 68–71 (69·4); length, 43–51 cm; wing-span, 100–118 cm. WEIGHT: (breeding) 715–950 (834).

Field Characters. Large, long-winged shearwater, dark above, white below. Best distinguished from

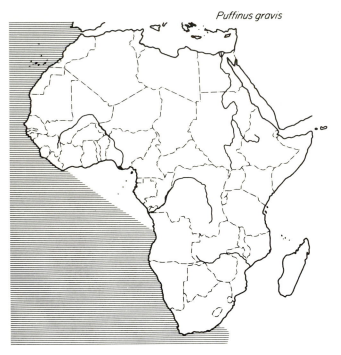

Puffinus gravis

Cory's Shearwater *Calonectris diomedea* by dark bill, blackish cap contrasting with white face, pale collar, and underwing pattern. White uppertail-coverts not diagnostic as some Cory's Shearwaters have these. Dusky belly-patch diagnostic if seen, but more easily identified by characters given above.

Voice. Not recorded. At sea utters harsh cries, screams and raucous squawks when squabbling over food.

General Habits. Little known. Less aerial than other shearwaters, often resting on surface in rafts, making shallow dives. Flight near surface powerful, deliberate, on stiff wings with much gliding and banking. Wing-beats more rapid than Cory's, less rapid than Manx Shearwater *P. puffinus*. Food obtained mostly during day-time by pursuit-diving, pursuit-plunging and surface-seizing. Prey swallowed on surface. Follows and feeds on surface-swimming fish shoals and follows whales and porpoises. Will approach fishing vessels, but is often indifferent to ships. Does not normally associate with other shearwaters in same range.

Food. Mainly fish and cephalopods; also fish offal discarded from fishing boats, sand-eels and crustaceans.

References
Rowan, M. K. (1951).
Voous, K. H. and Wattel, J. (1963).

Plate 3

(Opp. p. 50)

Puffinus griseus (Gmelin). Sooty Shearwater. Puffin fuligineux.

Procellaria grisea Gmelin, 1789. Syst. Nat. 1, pt. 2, p. 564; New Zealand.

Range and Status. Common non-breeding visitor to much of African coast. Occurs W Morocco late northern summer. Uncommon W Africa with records from Pagalu (Annobon), Bioko (Fernando Po) (Jan) and Liberia. All year Atlantic coast south of equator and common Namibian and South African seas in southern winter (many non-breeding individuals July–Aug: Phillips 1963.

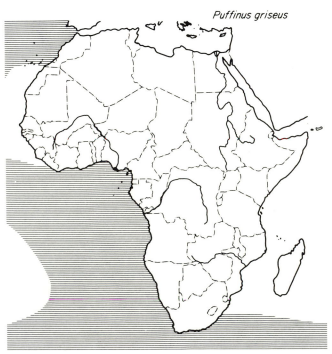

Puffinus griseus

Description. ADULT ♂: entirely sooty brown or dark grey except for pale area in centre of underwing. When visibility is good, scapulars and upperwing-coverts appear lighter, due to pale edges of feathers. Bill long, blackish; eye dark brown; legs and feet slate, webs tinged purple. Sexes alike. SIZE: (♂ ♀) wing (10 specimens) 283–304 (296); tail, 80–94 (88); culmen, 41–44 (42); tarsus, 53–57 (55); middle toe and claw, 62–70 (66); length, 46–53 cm; wing-span, 107 cm. WEIGHT: 635–954.
IMMATURE: indistinguishable from adults.

Field Characters. Large, dark shearwater with long narrow wings, long body and bill. Differs from Flesh-footed Shearwater *P. carneipes* and Wedge-tailed Shearwater *P. pacificus* and Great-winged Petrel *Pterodroma macroptera* in having pale centre to underwings, long narrow bill and wings which appear to be set well-back on body.

Voice. Not recorded. Flocks feeding at sea make a cackling sound resembling distant human voices.

General Habits. Well known. Often occurs in flocks at sea, frequently with other shearwaters. Seen in flocks of 200–300 flying east south of South Africa late Mar (van Oordt and Kruijt 1953). Feeds commonly behind trawlers but does not usually follow large ships. When fishing will plunge from surface while swimming, or in flight from height of 3–5 m, descending at angle of 45°, wings *c.* 30% extended, feet spread in front of breast, striking water with feet and breast then diving below from surface. Sometimes drops from height, stalls briefly *c.* 0·5 m above surface, then plunges head-first at angle of 60–70° above horizontal. Once submerged, swims deeply and well, descending at *c.* 45° to surface.

May ascend by bursting from surface directly into flight. Has fast, direct flight-action with powerful beats of rigid wings, rising and falling at no great height above waves.

Food. Mainly cephalopods, crustaceans and fish; also sand-eels, crab larvae and dead or mutilated squids.

References
Brooke, R. K. and Sinclair, J. C. (1978).
Brown, R. G. B. *et al.* (1978).

Puffinus puffinus (Brünnich). Manx Shearwater. Puffin des Anglais.

Procellaria puffinus Brünnich, 1764. Orn. Bor. p. 29; the Faeroes, north Atlantic Ocean.

Plate 3

(Opp. p. 50)

Range and Status. Entire Mediterranean, breeding on many islands; locations inadequately documented but certainly offshore Morocco, plus extralimital N Atlantic breeding islands. Common Atlantic coast of Morocco July–Aug as non-breeding visitor, less common or rare Atlantic seaboard south of about 30°N, but southern African western seaboard as scarce visitor in southern summer, stragglers eastern Cape to *c.* 34°S (Brooke and Sinclair 1978).

Description. *P. p. mauretanicus* Lowe: breeds western Mediterranean islands. ADULT ♂: entire upperparts, including sides of head to below eye, and tail dull grey-brown. Underparts, including underwing, variably dusky off-white to grey-brown; usually throat, sides of breast, flanks, undertail-coverts and axillaries dusky, no great contrast between brown and white on sides of head as in other races, underwing margins slightly darker; undertail grey-brown. Bill blackish, lower mandible paler, cutting-edge tinged green; eye blackish brown; legs and feet pale pink with black markings. Sexes alike. SIZE: wing, (19 specimens) 235–256 (246); tail, 70–79 (74·8); culmen, (25) 36–42 (38·4); tarsus, (24) 46–51 (48·1); toe, (9) 52–56 (54·6). WEIGHT: ♂ (6) 490–565 (537), ♀ (7) 472–550 (506). Larger than either *P. p. puffinus* or *P. p. yelkouan* but mensural data lacking.

IMMATURE: indistinguishable from adult.

DOWNY YOUNG: covered in light brown down, paler below.
P. p. puffinus (Brünnich). Breeds islands in eastern and western Atlantic, also Madeira and Azores. Upperparts darker, black wearing to brown-black; underparts white, dusky on flanks; underwing white, primaries and secondaries dark brown; undertail dark brown. SIZE: wing, ♂ 239, ♀ (breeding) 235.
P. p. yelkouan (Acerbi). Breeds on islands off southern France, Corsica, Sardinia, Tunisia (?), Italy, Sicily and in the Adriatic and Aegean Seas. Similar to *P. p. mauretanicus* but smaller, tail shorter. SIZE: wing, 235; tail, 69·9.

Field Characters. Long-billed, small-headed, medium-sized shearwater, dark above, pale below, but contrast less marked in *P. p. mauretanicus*. Wing-action rapid, stiff-winged, between bouts of gliding and wheeling, or, in high winds, on almost motionless wings, sometimes mounting up to 10 m above sea. Easily confused with similar dark and white shearwaters, especially smaller Little Shearwater *P. assimilis* and Audubon's Shearwater *P. lherminieri*, but outer wings appear longer, flight action generally less fluttering. Larger *P. p. mauretanicus* can be confused with Sooty Shearwater *P. griseus* but has less contrast between body and underwing, body paler. All races distinguishable from

Puffinus puffinus

much larger Cory's Shearwater *Calonectris diomedea* by dark, slender bill, darker cap and feet protruding beyond tail in flight. Swims buoyantly, head, wings and tail held high.

Voice. Recorded (1a, 2a). Silent at sea. Breeding birds highly vocal in and out of burrow. Mainly nocturnal, but calls sometimes heard from burrows by day. Considerable individual variation, especially in pitch. Returning birds give loud flight-call over colony and this is returned by mate in burrow, thus 2 individual voices are possibly recognizable. Inside nest-chamber pairs make quiet, conversational sounds. *P. p. puffinus* at breeding grounds in flight, on ground or in burrows, except moonlit nights, variety of raucous, piercing, rapidly repeated crows, coos, croons, howls, screams, often in duet and especially prior to egg-laying. Commonest call 'cack-cack-cack-carr-hoo' (Lockley 1959); also 'goch-och-aarka-a' (Cramp and Simmons 1977). Young utter piping calls, but when nearly full-grown calls resemble those of adults.

General Habits. Little known. Gregarious at all times, highly so at breeding grounds, large flocks gathering offshore at dusk. At sea usually in smaller flocks, larger aggregations at feeding areas. Roosts at sea. Feeds diurnally by pursuit-plunging, pursuit-diving and surface-seizing. *P. p. mauretanicus* of western Mediterranean, suspected of breeding Islas Chafarinas, Morocco and Zembra and Zembretta, Tunisia (Heim de Balsac and Mayaud 1962, Jarry 1969), and *P. p. yelkouan* of eastern Mediterranean occur year-round those waters, with some post-breeding dispersal through Straits of Gibraltar into Atlantic, probably by majority of *P. p. mauretanicus*, after which it moves northwards. Nominate *P. p. puffinus* migrates after breeding to western South Atlantic, juveniles and adults July–Sept returning to breeding areas Feb–Apr, possibly via southern Africa, but most remaining well off-shore.

Food. Small fish, especially young herrings, sprats, pilchards and anchovies. Also cephalopods, small crustaceans and offal.

Breeding Habits. Well known. Intensively studied N Europe, less so in Mediterranean. In *P. p. mauretanicus* monogamous pair-bond generally life-long, but no evidence of pair association at sea.

NEST: in burrows 1–2 m long (sometimes less) excavated by both sexes using bills and feet, sometimes occupying ready-made rabbit burrow. Nest chamber lined with vegetation. More than 1 pair may use burrow entrances, but nest chambers are separate. Pairs are faithful to colony which is situated on flat ground or slope, close to sea or up to 2 km away. Courtship behaviour little known due to nocturnal and subterranean habits but courtship feeding and mutual preening recorded. Copulation occurs on ground and in burrows.

EGGS: invariably 1; broad ovals, matt white. SIZE: (100 eggs) 56–68 × 39–45 (61 × 42); WEIGHT: (10) 52–63 (58).

Laying dates: Mar–June.

Incubation carried out by both sexes, ♂ taking 1st spell. Of 288 recorded spells av. length was 5·9 days with 6–12 spells per nest. Period: 41–45 (43) days.

Young remain in nest chamber, brooded by 1 parent first few days and fed at intervals on partially digested fish remains, particularly sprats and sandeels. Thereafter, visits by both parents occur at night only, at intervals averaging 1·7 days (2613 visits). Deserted by parents at *c.* 60 days, 8–9 days prior to leaving nest. Fledging period: 62–76 days.

Breeding success: of 56 eggs laid, 78% hatched; of 44 chicks hatched, 95·5% fledged. 1st year mortality unrecorded. Immatures usually return to colony of origin in 2nd, 3rd and 4th years of life, associating in burrows part of that season or even entire season without breeding (Cramp and Simmons 1977). Majority do not breed until at least 5th year. Adult survival 1964–65 at least 96% (Harris 1966b).

Plate 3

(Opp. p. 50)

Puffinus lherminieri (Lesson). Audubon's Shearwater; Dusky Shearwater; Baillon's Shearwater. Puffin d'Audubon.

Puffinus [sic] *lherminieri* Lesson, 1839. Rev. Zool., Paris, 2, p. 102; Antilles.

Puffinus lherminieri

Range and Status. Tropical waters all oceans, but little dispersion from breeding grounds. Breeds islands Persian Gulf, probably islets southern Red Sea, but firm confirmation lacking. Occurs regularly, fairly common in Gulf of Aden and Red Sea. Rare non-breeding visitor to seaboards of southern and E Africa to Natal.

Description. *P. l. persica* (Hume): Red Sea, Gulf of Aden and Indian Ocean to at least Kenya coast. ADULT ♂: entire upperparts sooty black, including head to a line below eye, level with gape. Underparts, including underside of wings, white; undertail-coverts black with a few central white feathers. Bill slate-grey, culmen and tip black; iris dark brown; legs pink, feet flesh to yellowish white with outside tarsus and outer toe mainly black and webs pale yellow. Sexes alike. SIZE: (26 specimens, *P. l. lherminieri*) wing, 200–216 (208); tail, 82–94 (87); tarsus, 39–43 (40); culmen, 26–32 (30).

IMMATURE: similar to adult.

DOWNY YOUNG: brownish grey to pearly grey above, white below; bill slate-grey; iris black; legs and feet pink with black outer toe and posterior part of tarsus.

P. l. bailloni (Bonaparte). Seaboards of southern and E Africa to at least E London. Overall darker but with lighter axillaries; bill thinner.

Field Characters. Small, dark brown or black and white shearwater. Separated from very similar Little Shearwater *P. assimilis* by brownish black, not blue-black, above; black, not white, ear-coverts; undertail-coverts more white; and flesh-coloured, not bluish, feet.

Voice. Not recorded in Africa. During breeding season, Bermudian birds utter loud characteristic 'capimlico capimlico capimlico capim-capim ca-ca-ca ca-ca-ca'; 'cat howls' and 'uncanny see-saw cries' also recorded. Young give plaintive, liquid-sounding note and a 'pipeep-pipeep-pipeep'.

General Habits. Little known in African waters, better known Americas. Normally seen flying near sea surface, rising with rapid wing-beats, then gliding and banking down to water. Dives freely. Feeds day and night. Settles on surface, especially when sea calm. After alighting, may take passing fish. Normally pelagic although occurs within 1–2 km of mainland (E Africa). 1 recorded inland, near Nairobi, 450 km from coast (J. Williams, pers. comm.). May be attracted to ship's lights at night but does not follow ships by day. Usually solitary although occurs in small groups around breeding areas and in plankton-rich areas with upwellings and strong currents.

Food. Not recorded in African waters; elsewhere fish, squid and cuttlefish.

Breeding Habits. Scarcely known in Africa; no recent records Red Sea. Breeding behaviour probably similar to that of *P. l. lherminieri* of western Atlantic, i.e. colonial, nesting on rocky offshore islets.

Nocturnal at breeding area. Courtship displays include: frequent visiting of future nest-site by pair, some remaining for long periods; circling each other in flight; rubbing bills together; uttering loud calls (see under Voice).

NEST: in narrow rock crevices, tunnels, burrows, or under dense vegetation; no special lining.

EGGS: 1; subelliptical, elongated; white, smooth with no gloss. SIZE: (39 eggs, *P. l. lherminieri*) 49–57 × 34–41 (53 × 36).

Laying dates in Africa unknown.

Incubation begins with 1st egg; by both parents equally with each taking turns of 8–10 days. Period: 51 days.

Young grow rapidly; by 30 days covered with soft pearl-grey down and almost same weight as parent. At 45 days feathers show; 55 days, losing down, head and body fully feathered; 63 days, nearly full-grown; 69 days fed for last time by parent; 70–71 days, much wing-beating; 72 days, 1st flight.

Both parents brood chick day and night for 1st 3–4 days; 1 parent remains with it during day for 1st week. Chick fed every night by 1 or both parents. Parent arrives 1 h after sunset; feeds chick 1st 30 min; then sits near nest most of night before departing 1–2 h before sunrise.

References
Harper, C. and Kinsky, F. C. (1978).
Palmer, R. (1962).
Penny, M. (1974).

Puffinus assimilis (Gould). Little Shearwater. Petit Puffin.

Puffinus assimilis Gould, 1838. Synop. Birds Australia, pt. 4, app., p. 7; New South Wales.

Plate 3

(Opp. p. 50)

Range and Status. Occurs regularly as non-breeding visitor to W African shores between 10° and 36°N, and to South African waters in small numbers all year where status still uncertain.

Description. *P. a. baroli* (Bonaparte): breeds Azores, Porto Santo (Cima and Baixo), Desertas (Bugio), Salvage and Canary Islands; occurs W Africa. ADULT ♂: entire upperparts slate-black. Underparts, including face and ear-coverts, white except for dark margins to wings, wider on trailing edge; white of face extending above eye and over ear-coverts. Bill blackish; eye dark brown; legs and feet chalk-blue, edges of webs dusky. Sexes alike. SIZE: wing, (7 specimens) 176–190 (184); tail, (14) 67–78 (71·8); culmen, (8) 24–28 (26·1); toe and claw, (12) 37–44 (40·9). Further measurements lacking.

P. a. tunneyi Mathews. Breeds on islands off coast of south-western Australia. Birds breeding on St Paul and (?) Amsterdam Island, south Indian Ocean, doubtfully assigned to this subspecies; recorded South African seas. Underparts entirely white; dividing line occurs at eye level; bill grey-black. SIZE: wing, (25) 169–184 (174).

P. a. elegans Giglioli and Salvadori. Breeds Tristan group (Tristan da Cunha, Nightingale and Inaccessible) and Gough, also other islands in Pacific; recorded South African seas. Upperparts slate-grey, pale edges to feathers of back; under-

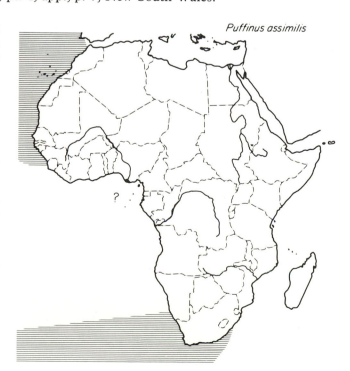

Puffinus assimilis

parts with dusky belly and vent; bill dull blue-grey; feet blue with black line down outer toe, webs pinkish with thin black margins. SIZE: wing, (94) 158–203 (190·5). WEIGHT: 170–275 (226).

Field Characters. Small, black and white shearwater with short bill. Flies fast, low, with rapid fluttering action. Differs from Audubon's Shearwater *P. lherminieri* in having white face and ear-coverts.

Voice. Not recorded. Silent at sea.

General Habits. Well known. Normally does not stray far from breeding islands and returns to nest-sites regularly throughout year where it spends much time on surface. 1 specimen *P. a. elegans* recorded roosting on exposed rocks among Jackass Penguins *Spheniscus demersus* on St Croix Island, Port Elizabeth during southern winter 1978 and 1979. Calls believed to be of this species heard at night on same island coincided with presence of this individual; same calls also heard Dec 1979 and Jan 1980, but breeding there not proven (Randall 1978; R. M. Randall, pers. comm.).

Food. Small fish, cephalopods and crustaceans.

References
Brooke, R. K. and Sinclair, J. C. (1978).
Swales, M. K. (1965).

Family HYDROBATIDAE: storm-petrels

Very small (thrush-size) pelagic petrels. Wings long and proportionately broader than in Procellariidae, with 10 functional primaries, the 2nd being the longest and 10–14 secondaries. Tail fairly long, rounded square or forked. Bill usually slender, nail prominent, well-hooked, nasal tubes with single aperture. Plumage mostly black; white rump, belly or facial markings diagnostic for species. Sexes alike. Flight in mild winds rapid, erratic, bouncing, fluttering or skimming over surface of water; in strong winds flight more direct, swallow-like. Feed mostly in flight with legs dangling, fluttering or pattering on surface. Sometimes feed while swimming, seldom dive. Some species follow ships. Can be solitary or gregarious at sea. 8 genera, 18–21 spp., of which 9 probably reach African waters as non-breeding visitors.

Genus *Oceanites* Keyserling and Blasius

Black, square-tailed storm-petrels with white on tail-coverts, sometimes on abdomen; long-legged, feet with yellow webs; bill short, nasal tubes half length of culmen. 1 sp. in African waters.

Plate 5

(Opp. p. 82)

Oceanites oceanicus (Kuhl). Wilson's Storm-petrel. Océanite de Wilson.

Procellaria oceanica Kuhl, 1820. Beitr. Zool. Vergl. Anat. Abth. 1, p. 136, pl. 10, fig. 1; no locality; South Georgia designated by Murphy, 1918, Bull. Amer. Mus. Nat. Hist., 38, p. 128.

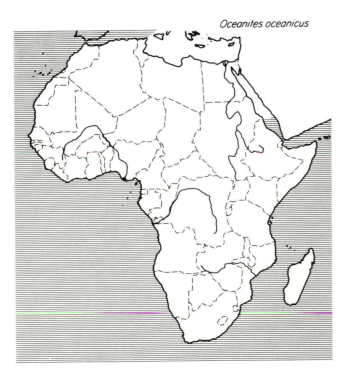

Oceanites oceanicus

Range and Status. Western Mediterranean, Atlantic, Indian Ocean and southern Red Sea seaboards. Most common storm-petrel in all African waters.

Description. *O. o. oceanicus*: breeds Tierra del Fuego, Falkland Islands, South Georgia, Bouvet (?), Crozet (?), Kerguelen and Heard Islands. ADULT ♂: entirely black except for white rump extending to lower flanks and lateral undertail-coverts, and a pale line extending diagonally across inner wing; tail square; bill black; eye brown; legs long, black, projecting beyond tail in flight, webs yellowish in centres. SIZE: (21 specimens) wing, 133–150 (142); tail, 52–67 (60·1); culmen, 10–13 (11·6); tarsus, 33–37 (34·7); middle toe and claw 25–29 (27·1); length, 15–19 cm; wing-span, 38–42 cm.

O. o. exasperatus Mathews. Breeds South Sandwich, South Orkney, South Shetland Islands and on Antarctica. SIZE: (30) wing, 147–163 (154).

Field Characters. Square tail, white rump and long legs diagnostic. Unlike Madeiran Storm-Petrel *Oceanodroma castro* and British Storm-Petrel *Hydrobates pelagicus* feet extend beyond tail in flight. Characteristically glides in swallow-like fashion, zig-zagging in wake of ships or hovering, wings held vertically, feet pattering on surface when feeding.

Voice. Recorded (13, 23). When feeding at sea utters an almost inaudible, rapid squeaking.

General Habits. Little known. Gregarious at sea. Is attracted to lights and fishing boats, following in their wake, but avoids concentrations of other birds at trawl nets.

Food. Small crustaceans, small squid and floating fish oil.

References
Bannerman, D. A. and Bannerman, W. M. (1963–68).

Genus *Garrodia* Forbes

Grey-backed, white-bellied storm-petrels with slightly rounded tails; legs do not protrude beyond tail in flight; bill short, nasal tubes half length of culmen. 1 sp. probable for Indian Ocean seaboard.

Garrodia nereis (Gould). Grey-backed Storm-Petrel. Océanite néréide.

Not illustrated

Thalassidroma Nereis Gould, 1841. Proc. Zool. Soc. London (1840), p. 178; Bass Strait, Australia.

Range and Status. Data on pelagic dispersal lacking but breeds on Gough, Crozet and Kerguelen Islands. Should be looked for in southern African waters of both oceans.

Description. ADULT ♂: entire head, nape and mantle dark slate; back, rump and uppertail pale grey; square-cut tail grey broadly tipped black. Chin, throat and upper breast dark slate, rest of underparts white; undertail as uppertail; upperwings dark slate, median coverts grey edged white; underwing-coverts white, rest dark slate. Eye dark brown; bill, feet and legs black. Sexes alike. SIZE: (8 specimens) wing, 121–130 (126); tail 53–62 (59); culmen, 12·2–13·2 (12·7); tarsus, 30–35 (31); middle toe and claw, 26–27 (27); length, 17–19 cm. IMMATURE: as adult.

Field Characters. A very small, grey storm-petrel. Black band at tail-tip conspicuous. Distinguished from all African storm-petrels except White-faced *Pelagodroma marina* by grey upperparts and lack of white rump; from White-faced Storm-Petrel by solid grey head without white on face or throat.

Voice. Not recorded. A crake-like call.

General Habits. Little known. Relatively non-migratory, normally remaining close to breeding islands. Seeks food with buoyant hovering action, occasionally with rapid 'darting to and fro' action.

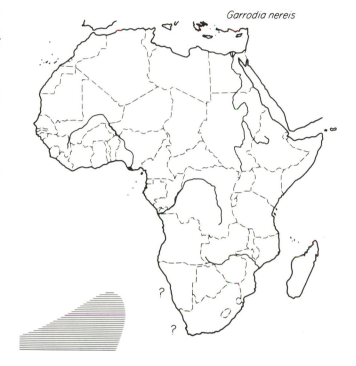

Garrodia nereis

Food. Little known but probably planktonic matter.

Genus *Pelagodroma* Reichenbach

Large, grey and white storm-petrels with slightly forked tails and legs projecting beyond in flight. Habits highly pelagic. 1 sp. African seas.

Pelagodroma marina (Latham). White-faced Storm-Petrel. Océanite frégate.

Plate 5

(Opp. p. 82)

Procellaria marina Latham, 1790. Ind. Orn. 2, p. 826; off the mouth of Rio de la Plata, Argentine.

Range and Status. Scarce visitor to W African Northern Hemisphere seaboard, probably Namibian and Cape seas but unrecorded, and Indian Ocean from approximately equator northwards to Gulf of Aden (*P. m. dulciae*). (Collected Cape Guardafui June–July.)

Description. *P. m. hypoleuca* (Moquin-Tandon): breeds Salvage Islands. ADULT ♂: forehead white, mottled grey; crown to hindneck dark grey; mantle, back and scapulars grey. Rump and uppertail-coverts lighter, ash-grey; slightly forked tail black, grey at base; upperwing dark greyish brown, primaries and primary coverts darker, secondary coverts paler especially in worn plumage. Dark grey patch extending from in front of and under eye rearwards over ear-coverts contrasts sharply with white face, eyebrow, chin and throat; rest of underparts white except for greyish on sides of chest, some flank feathers and undertail-coverts; underwing-coverts and axillaries white, rest grey-brown; undertail black. Bill black; eye brown; legs and feet black, webs yellow. Sexes alike. SIZE: (16 specimens) wing, 153–171 (161); tail, 68–84 (75); culmen, 16·6–18·2 (17·3); tarsus, 41·6–46·3 (44·2); middle toe and claw, 34·0–38·5 (36·4); length, 20–21 cm; wing-span, 41–43 cm. WEIGHT: (17) 42–60 (48·9).

IMMATURE: paler on head and rump, white-edged wing-coverts, white-tipped scapulars, secondaries and inner primaries.

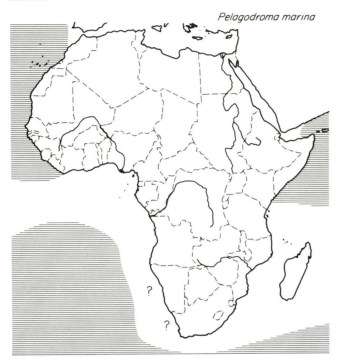

Pelagodroma marina

P. m. eadesi Bourne. Breeds Branco Island and Cima, Rombos Islands and Cape Verde Islands. Forehead whiter, greater contrast with crown, back paler; sides of neck whiter, forming incomplete collar; bill longer. SIZE: (11) wing, 154–169 (162). WEIGHT: (1 ♀) 52.

P. m. dulciae Mathews. Breeds on islands off eastern and southern Australia. Tail almost square-cut. SIZE: (14) wing, 158. WEIGHT: 55.

Field Characters. Differs from all other storm-petrels in having wholly white underparts and *white face* with dusky patch. Flight stronger than other storm-petrels, more prion-like with less fluttering, more banking to reveal underparts. Unique in its habit of swinging, pendulum-fashion, with long legs dangling over water, revealing yellow webs. Does not patter on surface, but touches water with feet in hopping action. Also glides on stiffened wings. Feet project beyond tail. Feeds with lowered legs and body splashing into water.

Voice. Recorded (29). Nothing described for birds at sea.

General Habits. Little known and surprisingly few pelagic reports. *P. m. hyoleuca* and *P. m. eadesi*, breeding Selvagens and Cape Verde Islands respectively, occur rarely offshore NW Africa, especially Morocco and Mauritania (not recorded south of equator) during non-breeding dispersal Aug–Nov. *P. m. dulciae* from Pacific and Australian waters occurs Indian Ocean to Red Sea May–Sept. Does not follow ships and seldom approaches coastlines; markedly pelagic, occurs singly or in small flocks.

Food. Chiefly planktonic crustaceans and some squid.

Genus *Fregetta* Bonaparte

Black and white storm-petrels, with distinctly pied underparts and white rumps. Tails very slightly forked, feet not projecting. 2 spp., 1 subantarctic, 1 subtropical, differing mainly in proportions of chin, back and rump markings.

Plate 5

(Opp. p. 82)

Fregetta tropica (Gould). Black-bellied Storm-Petrel. Océanite à ventre noir.

Thalassidroma tropica Gould, 1844. Ann. Mag. Nat. Hist. 13, p. 366; equatorial region Atlantic Ocean, lat. 6°33′N, long. 18°6′W.

Range and Status. Scarce visitor in southern winter to southern and western coasts of Africa.

Description. *F. t. tropica*, ADULT ♂: entire head and neck to chest, upper body, tail and upperwing sooty black except for white rump; chin sometimes mottled white. Rest of body white with black line running down centre of abdomen; underwing black, coverts white. Bill with prominent tubular nostrils black; eye brown; legs and feet black, claws narrow. SIZE: wing, ♂ (20 specimens) 154–167 (160), ♀ (6) 159–167 (163); tail, ♂ 72–77 (74), ♀ 72–76 (74); culmen, ♂ 14·0–15·8 (15·1), ♀ 14·5– 15·7 (15·1); tarsus, ♂ 40–42 (41), ♀ 42–44 (43); middle toe and claw, ♂ 28–29 (28), ♀ 28–30 (29) (Murphy 1936); length, 19–20·5 cm.

IMMATURE: indistinguishable from adult.

Field Characters. Flight erratic, the bird swinging from side to side and zig-zagging, exposing its white underside. Distinguished from Wilson's Storm-Petrel *Oceanites oceanicus* by white underparts, larger size and more stocky appearance; from White-bellied Storm-Petrel *F. grallaria* by black line down centre of belly, but this often hard to see and 2 spp. are easily confused.

Voice. Not recorded. Nothing described for birds at sea.

General Habits. Little known. Flies around or ahead of ships, occasionally in wake. Solitary or in small groups, sometimes with Wilson's Storm-petrel.

Food. Small cephalopods, crustaceans and fish picked from surface.

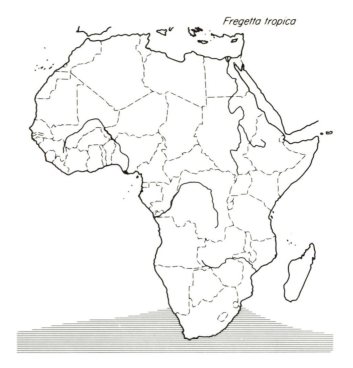

Fregetta tropica

Fregetta grallaria (Vieillot). **White-bellied Storm-Petrel. Océanite à ventre blanc.**

Procellaria grallaria Vieillot, 1817. Nouv. Dict. Hist Nat., nouv. éd., 25, p. 418; Australia.

Plate 5

(Opp. p. 82)

Range and Status. Visual Indian Ocean records for Durban, Mozambique Channel and north to 7°S.

Description. *F. g. leucogaster* (Gould), ADULT ♂: entire head and neck to chest sooty-black, mantle slightly lighter, back black, rump white. Tail black; rest of underparts white (the belly occasionally with irregular, black midventral line: Watson 1975) except for grey flecks on flanks and underwing-coverts. Bill black; eye brown; legs and feet black, toenails flattened, spade-like. SIZE: (63 specimens) wing, 146–163 (156); tail, 71–77 (74); culmen, 12·6–14·00 (13·2); tarsus, 33–37 (35); middle toe and claw, 20–23 (22) (Murphy 1936); length, 18·00–21·5 cm; wing-span, 43–48 cm. WEIGHT: 51. Sexes alike but ♀ from Signy Islands has longer wings than ♂ (178 *v.* 162·3) (Watson 1975). Birds from Lord Howe Islands have a dark morph entirely sooty black, only rump and bases of belly feathers white; intermediates (between both) occur (Serventy *et al.* 1971).

Field Characters. A black storm-petrel with white rump, belly and underwing, differing in this combination from all others. Dark morph resembles Wilson's Storm-Petrel *Oceanites oceanicus* but lacks pale wing-bar of that species. Flies with rapid wing-beats followed by glide on motionless wings held horizontally, bouncing with feet on water in side-to-side movement. Feet do not project beyond square-cut tail.

General Habits. Little known. Does not follow ships but is attracted by bright lights. Documentation for African waters lacking.

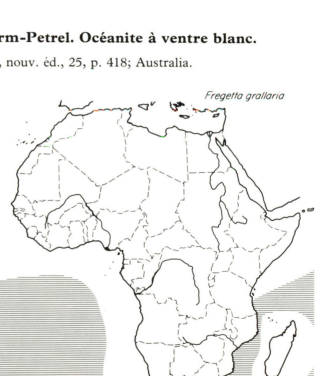

Fregetta grallaria

Voice. Not recorded. Nothing described for birds at sea.

Food. Small cephalopods, crustaceans and fish picked from surface.

Genus *Hydrobates* Boie

Black, short-legged, square-tailed storm-petrels with white on undertail-coverts and white bar on underwing; fluttering flight. 1 sp. in African seas.

Plate 5

(Opp. p. 82)

Hydrobates pelagicus (Linnaeus). British Storm-Petrel. Océanite tempête.

Procellaria pelagica Linnaeus, 1758. Syst. Nat. (10th ed.), p. 131; Coast of Sweden.

Range and Status. Formerly bred Tunisian islands but no recent evidence for N African coast. Otherwise occurs entire Atlantic and Indian Ocean coastline to Natal. Appears South African coastline chiefly Sept–Feb.

Description. ADULT ♂: black but with white rump patch extending to lower flanks and lateral undertail-coverts, narrow

Hydrobates pelagicus

whitish edges to tops of greater upperwing-coverts (less obvious in worn plumage) and fairly broad whitish edges to underwing-coverts; tail slightly rounded, appears square. Bill black; eye blackish brown; legs and feet black. SIZE: (19–20 ♂♂, 23–25 ♀♀) wing, ♂ 116–127 (120); tail, ♂ 47–56 (52·6), ♀ 46–61 (54·5); culmen, ♂ 9·5–11·5 (10·8); tarsus, ♂ 19·6–22·3 (21·5), ♀ 20·2–24·3 (22·1); toe, ♂ 17·8–21·0 (19·6); length, 14–18 cm; wing-span, 36–39 cm. WEIGHT: (breeding) 23·0–38·5.

IMMATURE: like adults but edges to wing-coverts broader, whiter.

Field Characters. Flight dainty, swallow-like when gliding, but fluttering and bat-like when hovering with wings raised, feet pattering on sea. Does not walk on surface like Wilson's Storm-Petrel *Oceanites oceanicus*. Differs from other dark storm-petrels in having white line on underwing. Feet do not project beyond tail. Freely alights on sea.

Voice. Recorded (2a). Nothing described for birds at sea.

General Habits. Well known. Prefers waters between littoral and deep ocean, less frequently inshore. Unaffected by severe weather conditions. Occurs in small flocks and sometimes follows in wake of ships.

Food. Surface crustaceans, small fish, medusae, cephalopods, oil and fatty materials.

References
Bannerman, D. A. and Bannerman, W. M. (1963–68).

Genus *Oceanodroma* Reichenbach

Large, fork-tailed storm-petrels; feet do not project beyond tail in flight; blackish brown in colour, with or without white rump patches. 4 spp. for African waters.

Plate 5

(Opp. p. 82)

Oceanodroma castro (Harcourt). Madeiran Storm-Petrel; Band-rumped Storm-Petrel. Océanite de Castro.

Thalassidroma castro Harcourt, 1851. Sketch Madeira, p. 128; Desertas Island, Madeira Isles.

Range and Status. Breeds Azores, Madeira, Cape Verde, Ascension, St Helena and other Atlantic islands, also Pacific islands. Non-breeding dispersal little known but highly pelagic, in deep tropical waters to *c*. 20°S. Frequent in Gulf of Guinea Feb–July, specimens collected São Tomé.

Description. ADULT ♂: entirely blackish brown with variable white rump extending to lower flanks and lateral undertail-coverts; upperwing-coverts slightly paler; tail slightly forked. Bill short, stubby, black; eye dark brown; legs and feet black. SIZE: wing, ♂ (18 specimens) 142–154 (148), ♀ (8) 149–161 (156); tail, ♂ 61–74 (67·2), ♀ 67–75 (70·1); culmen, 13·0–15·5

(14·4); tarsus, 21–23 (22·2); toe, 20·3–23·1 (21·9); length, 19–21 cm; wing-span, 44–46 cm. WEIGHT: 43·5.

IMMATURE: indistinguishable from adult.

Field Characters. Tail appears square, feet barely protrude beyond tip. Wings longer, more pointed than either British Storm-Petrel *Hydrobates pelagicus* or Leach's Storm-Petrel *O. leucorhoa*; larger, browner, but difficult to separate at sea. Flight direct, steady with even, high wing-beats between spells of gliding with wings held below horizontal. Less fluttery than British Storm-Petrel, less erratic than Leach's (Harris 1966). Patters with feet on sea but less regularly than other storm-petrels.

Voice. Recorded (29). Nothing described for birds at sea.

General Habits. Little known. Distinctly pelagic. Usually solitary, but may occur in flocks near breeding islands. Does not regularly follow ships. Feeds well away from land.

Food. Crustaceans, fish, oily scraps and refuse taken from surface.

References
Robins, C. R. (1966).

Oceanodroma castro

Oceanodroma monorhis (Swinhoe). Swinhoe's Storm-Petrel. Océanite de Swinhoe.

Thalassidroma monorhis Swinhoe, 1867. Ibis, p. 386; near Amoy, China.

Plate 5

(Opp. p. 82)

Range and Status. Breeds in Chinese and Korean seas, migrating to Indian Ocean west as far as Cape Guardafui and north to the Gulf of Aqaba in the Red Sea. Often treated as race of Leach's Storm-Petrel *O. leucorhoa*.

Description. ADULT ♂: entirely blackish brown, marginally paler on the under-surfaces, pale diagonal patch across the inner wings; tail well-forked. Bill black; eye brown; legs and feet black. Sexes similar. SIZE: specific data lacking; measurements usually lumped with those of Leach's Storm-Petrel.

IMMATURE: probably similar to adult.

Field Characters. An all-dark storm-petrel with deeply forked tail. Separated from very similar Leach's by lack of white rump; from Matsudaira's Storm-Petrel *O. matsudairae* only with great difficulty but latter shows white primary feather shafts towards end of wings, lacking in Swinhoe's. Best recognized by distinctive flight, bounding and swooping over water in tern-like fashion, never pattering.

Voice. Not recorded. Nothing described for birds at sea.

General Habits. Scarcely known. Probably much as for Leach's Storm-Petrel but specific data lacking.

Food. Nothing recorded but probably much the same as others in genus.

References
Tuck, G. and Heinzel, H. (1979).

Oceanodroma monorhis

Plate 5

(Opp. p. 82)

Oceanodroma leucorhoa (Vieillot). Leach's Storm-Petrel. Océanite culblanc.

Procellaria leucorhoa Vieillot, 1818. Nouv. Dict. Hist. Nat., nouv. éd., 25 (1817), p. 422; maritime parts of Picardy.

Oceanodroma leucorhoa

Range and Status. Entire African Atlantic coast. Arrives Africa late Nov; numerous Gulf of Guinea Jan; scarce Namibia and South Africa southern summer. Vagrant E Africa.

Description. ADULT ♂: entirely blackish brown (marginally paler on under surfaces) except for white rump patch divided in centre by indistinct grey line and pale diagonal patch across inner wings; tail well-forked. Bill black; eye brown; legs and feet black. Sexes similar. SIZE: (47–50 specimens) wing, ♂ 148–165 (158); tail, 74–91 (80·0); culmen, 14·2–16·6 (15·7); tarsus, 22·9–25·5 (24·0); toe, 22·5–25·6 (24·2); length, 19–22 cm; wing-span, 45–48 cm. WEIGHT: (non-breeding) 29·9.
IMMATURE: similar to adult but some have lighter edges to body feathers.

Field Characters. Comparatively large, fork-tailed storm-petrel with white rump, long wings. Differs from British Storm-Petrel *Hydrobates pelagicus* in having broad diagonal bar on wing and paler, browner plumage. Can be confused with Madeiran Storm-Petrel *O. castro* despite tail-fork. Most easily distinguished from all others by unique flight; darts and bounds over sea with constant changes of speed and direction, gliding, banking, hovering or hanging.

Voice. Not recorded. A rapid series of 8 or more staccato, chattering, musical notes with descending cadence sometimes heard at sea.

General Habits. Well known. Prefers shallow waters of continental shelf, occurring singly or in small flocks. Rarely follows ships, but is attracted to lights. Wing-beats deep; does not patter on surface.

Food. Crustaceans, molluscs, small fish, oily and fatty substances collected mostly while skimming surface.

Plate 5

(Opp. p. 82)

Oceanodroma matsudairae Kuroda. Matsudaira's Storm-Petrel. Océanite de Matsudaira.

Oceanodroma melania matsudariae [sic] Kuroda, 1922. Ibis, p. 311; Honshu, Japan.

Range and Status. Regular and frequent visitor to equatorial western Indian Ocean; collected July. Stragglers probably to E African coast.

Description. ADULT ♂: entirely sooty brown with pale primary shafts and long forked tail. Bill black; eye brown; legs black. Sexes alike. SIZE: (127 ♂♂ and ♀♀) wing, 178–194 (184); tail, 95–115 (103); culmen, 16–19 (17); tarsus, 25–29 (27); length, 25–5 cm; wing-span, 46–52 cm.

Field Characters. Large sooty brown storm-petrel with long wings having distinctive pale primary shafts, often visible as a pale patch; deeply forked tail; feet do not project. Can be confused with dark race of Leach's Storm-Petrel *O. leucorhoa* but larger, wings broader, with pale patch caused by white primary shafts; flight much slower. Forked tail not always visible at sea. In calm conditions flight slow, sluggish with short glides; in strong winds also slow but progresses downwind with long, swift glides. In all conditions suddenly changes to swift, erratic, low flight over water. Feeds by landing with wings raised or by settling.

Voice. Not recorded. Data lacking.

General Habits. Scarcely known. Breeds near Japan and subsequently disperses widely.

Food. No specific data but probably much as for other storm-petrels.

References
Bailey, R. S. *et al.* (1968).

Oceanodroma matsudairae

Order SPHENISCIFORMES

Flightless marine birds of the southern oceans. Characterized by stocky build, erect stature when walking, flipper-like wings, short legs, comparatively short tails and a dense covering of scale-like feathers. Bills stout, short to medium-long, moderately to very pointed, covered with a number of horny plates revealing relationship with petrels, less closely with Pelecaniformes. Colouring blackish above, white below. Sexes alike. Movement on land a shuffling walk in which both beak and stiff tail may be used as props, or series of hops and slides when on rugged terrain. On snow and ice lie prone and slide, using flippers and feet for propulsion. In water wings are used with oar-like action, feet aiding steering. In pursuit of marine organisms, swim underwater, sometimes to considerable depths, and may attain speed of 40 km/h, porpoising occasionally to breathe. On the surface float with head, sometimes tail, held high, most of body submerged. Breed in rookeries on islands, headlands and mainland sites, including Antarctica. Feed on fish, squid, euphausiid shrimps and other crustaceans. Order has single family, Spheniscidae.

Family SPHENISCIDAE: penguins

Of 6 genera, 3, *Aptenodytes*, *Eudyptes* and *Spheniscus*, recorded South Africa. *Spheniscus* resident, others straggle from southern seas.

Genus *Aptenodytes* Miller

Large to very large penguins, standing 1·0–1·3 m tall. Differ from others in being larger in size, and having long, slender, pointed, slightly decurved bills and yellow on upper breasts. 2 spp., 1 a rare straggler to Africa.

Plate 6

(Opp. p. 83)

Aptenodytes patagonicus Miller. King Penguin. Manchot Royal.

Aptenodytes patagonica J. F. Miller, 1778. Icon. Animal., pt. 4, p. 23; S. Georgia.

Range and Status. Ranges far in latitudes south of *c.* 34°S, rarely to Cape waters. 1 live specimen found on Cape coast Jan 1977 (33°47′S–18°27′E) and 1 probable sight record.

Description. ADULT ♂: head black with chrome-yellow, comma-shaped ear-patch; nape, back, tail and upper part of flippers silvery blue-grey grading to blackish edge between throat and flippers; underparts white, tinged orange on lower throat, suffused with yellow on upper breast; underside of flippers white, grey on leading edge and tips; bill black, basal two-thirds of lower mandible deep orange to pink; eye dark brown; feet grey-black. Sexes alike, ♂ larger. SIZE: flipper, ♂ 325–352 (332), ♀ 317–340 (329); tail, ♂ 55–95 (76), ♀ 40–75 (56); culmen, ♂ 100–105 (104), ♀ 97–107 (102) (Falla 1937); length, *c.* 100 cm. WEIGHT: 14–18 kg.

IMMATURE: crown feathers tipped grey; ear-patch pale yellow; pink of lower mandible ill-defined.

Field Characters. 2nd largest penguin. Stance erect, dignified. Walks, does not hop. When surface-swimming floats fairly high, much of back exposed, bill at angle of 30° above horizontal, flippers held sideways at right-angles to body. Long bill diagnostic in African waters.

Voice. Not recorded. At sea a monosyllabic 'aark'.

General Habits. Virtually unknown in African waters. The one certain specimen moulted shortly after capture (Cooper 1978a).

Aptenodytes patagonicus

Food. Cephalopods and fish.

References
Cooper, J. *et al.* (1978).

74

Genus *Eudyptes* Vieillot

Medium-sized penguins having yellow or yellow and red plumes on sides of heads, red bills and feet. 6 spp., 4 in New Zealand region, 2 more generally in subantarctic zone, breeding on a number of islands and visiting South Africa as rare vagrants.

Eudyptes chrysocome (Miller). Rockhopper Penguin. Gorfou sauteur.

Plate 6

(Opp. p. 83)

Aptenodytes chrysocome J. R. Forster, 1781. Comment. Phys. Soc. Reg. Sci. Götting., 3 (1781), pp. 133, 135–; Tasmania and Falkland Islands.

Range and Status. Subantarctic zone between 30°S and 50°S, occasionally more northerly. Uncommon visitor coast of South Africa (36 records), mostly moulting immatures Jan–Feb, adults all times. Of 25 specifically identified, 4 were southern race *E. c. chrysocome*, 21 northern race *E. c. moseleyi* (Cooper *et al.* 1978; Cooper 1980).

Description. *E. c. moseleyi* Mathews and Iredale: Tristan da Cunha, Gough and St Paul Islands east to New Zealand. ADULT ♂: entire head, including throat and neck, nape, back, tail and upperflipper black, a yellow stripe above eyes (not touching bill-base) extending over ears and terminating in long, drooping, straw-coloured plumes hanging over ears with long black crown feathers elongating laterally and projecting stiffly sideways; underparts white; underflippers white, a large triangular patch on tip, broad leading edge and elbow blackish. Bill short, stout, reddish brown, skin at base usually blackish; eye red; feet pale flesh, soles black. Sexes alike, but ♂ larger, bill deeper and heavier. SIZE: (15 specimens) flipper, 158–177 (165); tail, 65–90 (81); culmen, 40–53 (45); tarsus, 25–30 (28); middle toe and claw, 63–70 (66); length, 49–57 cm. WEIGHT: 2·0–2·75 kg to 4·5 kg in moult.
IMMATURE: at 1 year crest absent, superciliary present; bill dull brown; throat grey. At 2 years similar to adults but head-plumes shorter, stiffer.
E. c. chrysocome. Breeds Falklands east to Prince Edward, Marion, Crozets, Kerguelen, Heard and Macquarie Islands (south of *E. c. moseleyi* in African waters). Skin at base of bill usually pink; underflipper with black leading edge narrow, black tip small. SIZE: flipper, (20) 150–190 (171); tail, 72–104 (92).

Field Characters. Small penguin with somewhat stiff, long, black and yellow plumes protruding sideways from head. Bill, eyes and feet reddish. Distinguished from similar Macaroni Penguin by black forehead, fairly stiff lateral head-plumes, smaller size. Can walk normally but usually progresses in series of stiff-legged hops, especially on rocky terrain. Hops into water feet first. Indifferent to humans. At sea, with head-plumes wet, difficult to separate from other crested penguins. Yearlings lack conspicuous crest, but show eyebrow.

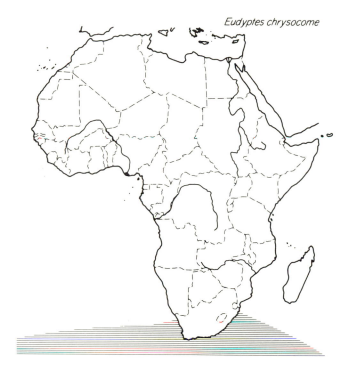

Eudyptes chrysocome

Voice. Not recorded. Harsh, staccato barks and brays, usually associated with threat displays.

General Habits. Scarcely known in African waters. All records onshore, frequently moulting birds; not yet observed at sea in southern African waters (Cooper 1980).

Food. Euphausiids, amphipods, cephalopods.

References
Cooper, J. *et al.* (1978).

Eudyptes chrysolophus (Brandt). Macaroni Penguin. Gorfou doré.

Plate 6

(Opp. p. 83)

Catarhactes chrysolophus Brandt, 1837. Bull. Sci. Acad. Imp. Sci. St Petersbourg, 2, col. 315; Falkland Islands.

Range and Status. Subantarctic and antarctic zones between c. 40° and 66°S, occasionally more northerly. Rare vagrant to South Africa. Immatures of nominate *E. c. chrysolophus* in mid-moult recorded onshore in Natal (30°–20°S, 30°–40°E) and Cape (34°–50°S, 20°–02°E), and an adult in moult at Bokoven, Cape, 33°57′S,

18°23′E. Early reports from Cape Seas (Ross *et al.* 1978) remain unconfirmed.

Description. *E. c. chrysolophus* Brandt, ADULT ♂: entire head including chin and neck, nape, back, tail and upperflipper black; forehead yellow-orange and, arising from this, a series of elongated lateral feathers drooping loosely along sides of head; a white patch at base of tail; underparts white; under-flipper white, two-thirds of leading edge, elbow and irregular

shape at tip black. Bill short, stout, reddish brown, a flesh-coloured triangle at corner of gape; eye dark brown; feet flesh-pink, whitish on upper surface, soles black. Sexes alike. SIZE: flipper, 170–210 (190); tail, 88–98 (93); culmen, 63–75 (69); tarsus, 38; length, 71–76 cm (Alexander 1963). WEIGHT: (moulting adult) 4250.

IMMATURE: 1st year birds smaller than adults; small yellow eyebrow; head-plumes absent; bill brown. In 2nd year head-plumes short, stiff.

Field Characters. Medium-sized penguin with heavy, reddish bill, lateral yellow-orange head-plumes arising from a patch on forehead and drooping loosely over eyes and ear-coverts. Walks on land slowly, head bent forward, flippers protruding sideways. Dives into water head first. Larger than Rockhopper *E. chrysocome*, head-plumes looser, less stiff, but at sea, with head-plumes wet, difficult to separate from this species.

Voice. Not recorded. At sea a harsh, nasal bark.

General Habits. Scarcely known in African waters. Onshore records only.

Food. Euphausiids, amphipods and cephalopods.

References
Alexander, W. B. (1963).
Cooper, J. (1979b).
Ross, G. J. B. *et al.* (1978).

Eudyptes chrysolophus

Genus *Spheniscus* Brisson

Medium-sized to small penguins with blackish bills and feet, bare pink skin around the lores and eyes, a white line extending from the eyebrow and encircling the ear-coverts, and pure white underparts surmounted by a black, encircling line from upper breast, down sides of body to feet. 4 spp. inhabiting mainly temperate to subtropical waters; *S. demersus* endemic to southern Africa.

Plate 6

(Opp. p. 83)

Spheniscus demersus (Linnaeus). Jackass Penguin; African Penguin. Manchot du Cap.

Diomedea demersa Linnaeus, 1758. Syst. Nat. (10th ed.), p. 132; Cape of Good Hope.

Range and Status. Africa's only endemic penguin. Breeds on 18 inshore islands on coast of Namibia and South Africa, ranging mostly around these western waters, occasionally north to Angola and east to Mozambique, exceptionally further north. Present population estimated 171,710 (Frost *et al.* 1976) but major decline this century. Dassen Island estimated to have once held 1,500,000 (Westphal and Rowan 1970), now holds 70,000 (Frost *et al.* 1976b). Original decline due to commercial egg exploitation and guano-scraping (interfering with nest-sites); since 1967, decline due to massive decrease in availability of major fish prey as result of over-exploitation by fishing industry and large-scale oil spills. Listed in South African Red Data Book and IUCN Red Data Book (1980) as vulnerable.

Description. ADULT ♂: forehead from base of bill, central crown, back of head, nape, mantle and rest of upperparts,

including flipper top and tail, black to side of body approximately level with shoulder; chin, foreneck, face, lores and ear-coverts black giving masked appearance; eyebrow, anterior portions of sides of neck and entire underparts below neck white; superimposed on this, an elliptical black band across breast and down each side of body, widening below flippers, plus a variable number of black spots on breast and belly, those between black band and black neck occasionally so dense as to form a second band; flipper below variously patched and spotted black and white. Bill black with irregular blue-grey vertical band across apical third; bare skin from near base of upper mandible, above and surrounding eye, pink (feathered white after moult); eye brown; legs and feet blackish with variable pink patches. Sexes alike, ♀ smaller. SIZE: culmen, ♂ (41 specimens) 57–65 (60·5), ♀ (25) 51·5–58·5 (55·5); bill depth at gonys, ♂ (41) 19·5–25·0 (23·0), ♀ (25) 19·0–23·5 (21) (Cooper 1972); flipper, ♂ ♀ 155–175; length, 63 cm. WEIGHT: ♂ (18) 3·6 kg, ♀ (18) 3·2 kg; variable over year, prior to moult generally 4·5–5·0 kg (R. Randall, pers. comm.).

IMMATURE: grey on dorsal surfaces fading to brownish

(sometimes almost white) before moult; face dark grey, blackish around eyes, streaked silver-white over eyebrow, ear-coverts and sides of neck; ventral surfaces white, washed dark grey over chin, across lower throat and lateral surfaces; bill dusky to grey-horn; legs and feet pale flesh. Birds *c.* 1 year old may undergo partial moult at sea when typical adult head, throat, neck and chest colour patterns are slowly acquired, although black and white side patterns not acquired at this stage (R. Randall, pers. comm.).

DOWNY YOUNG: up to 2 weeks old covered in grey down. In 2nd down usually grey-brown on dorsal surfaces; face, throat and belly white.

Field Characters. On land walks with upright, straight-backed gait, flippers away from body. On rocks hops over small gaps or slides down large inclines. Enters water generally from beaches, but jumps feet first from rocks when necessary. Swims on surface with head erect, bill at angle slightly above horizontal, back exposed, tail level with water surface or slightly above and flippers extended sideways just below surface. Distinct black and white head and black bill prevent confusion with any other penguin in African waters.

Voice. Recorded (6). A nasal, donkey-like bray plus various sighing sobs (throat) with breast heaving (Ecstatic display); growling when pecking and fighting; hissing by aggressive juveniles, all in colony. Braying heard at sea, especially during panic, in fog or on dark nights (Frost *et al.* 1976a).

General Habits. Well known. Normally gregarious, particularly when breeding. Ranges within 50 km of home islands, foraging to 15 km from mainland, exceptionally to 100 km (Liversidge and Thomas 1972). Most sea-going birds occur in cohesive groups (av. 8) and tend to act in unison, swimming, diving and swimming underwater together, indicating adaptive behaviour facilitating prey location and capture. Habitually forage by day, most returning to islands to roost; this may be a behavioural adaptation to avoid heat (Frost *et al.* 1976a) and predators (R. Randall, pers. comm.). Davies (1955) suggests normal on-surface swimming speed is 4–5 knots. When going to sea, birds tend to swim alternately on surface and underwater; when returning cover final few hundred metres to island with fast porpoising action, or mixture of surface-swimming and shallow dives. Porpoising also seen at sea in response to danger threat or other general panic. After night at sea sunbathing may occur during first 2·5 h following sunrise. Birds rotate bodies approximately 45° around long axis with one flipper held away from body, one foot raised with web spread, held above water and exposed to sun (Cooper 1977c).

Feeds mostly by day, groups swimming on surface and individuals performing head-dipping movements prior to diving as group. Dives obliquely; angled underwater-swimming in horizontal plane more usual than deep dives; submerges for short periods only (Siegfried *et al.* 1975). Frequently feeds in association with Cape Cormorant *Phalacrocorax capensis*, Cape Gannet *Sula capensis* and terns (R. Randall, pers. comm.).

Spheniscus demersus

All individuals return to home islands annually to moult, acquiring heavy fat deposits prior to 3-week period when landbound. Interval between moults 10·5–13·5 months, any time of year but bulk of population synchronized on any island, e.g. St Croix Oct–Dec (R. Randall, pers. comm.); 10·5 monthly intervals on Dassen Island (J. Cooper, in press).

Food. Under normal conditions of availability, as illustrated by Davies (1955, 1956) and Rand (1960) for 3-year period 1954–1956, average principal prey item percentage by weight was pilchards 46·3% (30–64%), anchovies 23·3% (19–31%) and horse mackerel 7·6% (3·16%). Other fish, crustaceans and cephalopods also taken. Pilchard population available to species has been decimated by commercial exploitation since late 1960s with result that local fishing industry has concentrated to a greater degree on anchovy and horse mackerel (Crawford and Shelton 1978). This situation will have had a marked effect both on the penguin's diet structure and its breeding success.

Breeding Habits. Intimately known. Breeds colonially, year-round, on offshore islands. Nests preferably placed in self-made, randomly spaced burrows in accumulated guano deposits or impacted, sandy substrate, beneath and between rocks, man-made structures (e.g. concrete breakwaters, foundations) or large items of jetsam. In face of population pressures and frequent absence of suitable burrowing surfaces many nests built above ground from available debris, closely packed next to one another in a hexagonal shape. This arrangement, giving optimum use of available space, may be a response to predation by Kelp Gulls *Larus dominicanus* (Siegfried 1977). On Dassen Island only 20% of eggs laid by surface nesters result in fledged young (Cooper, in press). Nest-site selection carried out by ♂, nest-building by both sexes.

Most behaviour in colony highly ritualized (see Eggleton and Siegfried (1977) for full account).

(1) ♂ 'Ecstatic display': territorial ♂♂ advertise ownership and availability for pairing by performing ecstatic display. Bird stands erect and slowly, deliberately, stretches head and bill skywards, bill opening as head is raised, flippers raised until nearly horizontal. Breast and base of throat heave silently, then develop into throbs, then full braying with head thrown back, bill wide open, flippers beating back and forth in time with deep rhythmic heaves of breast (see **A**). Ecstatic display also performed, but rarely, in sitting position, flippers held away from body and breast lifted clear of ground (**B**). Display may last few seconds or as long as 1 min, culminating in loud, raucous braying which is frequently taken-up by others in vicinity. Ecstatic display period may last 1 h or more with 12 or more displays in succession, typically occurring early morning, late afternoon and evening; most frequent early in breeding season. Display also made by mated ♂ alone or in company of mate, and after encounter with neighbour or rival on site. ♀ may give call only (R. Randall, pers. comm.) when aggressively motivated, i.e. when foreign penguin on nest-site. On approach of unmated ♀, attracted by ♂'s ecstatic display, ♂ terminates display abruptly.

A   **B**

(2) ♀♀ approaching ♂♂ may perform 'intermediate bow display'—body held forward, head bent forward and bill directed towards ground. Normally, prospecting, unmated ♀♀ will perform 'oblique stare bow' (OSB) in attempt to attract ♂—bill dropped onto or nearly onto breast, neck retracted or extended and arched over, bill pointing at ground; head is sometimes tilted to one side to direct bill obliquely at other bird, crest erect. If successful, ♂ approaches her in OSB, may go straight into 'arms act' and copulate (see below).

(3) ♂ Courtship displays: ♂ trying to attract ♀ will approach in OSB; she responds with OSB and he 'sidles' round her, both performing same actions. ♂ then returns to site, maintaining OSB, followed by ♀ doing same. At site ♂ crouches and performs 'vibrating head shake' (VHS) followed by symbolic 'nest-scrape'. VHS only performed by birds on nest-site, usually while sitting or crouching, less commonly, standing. Bird bows head, bringing bill close to body, directed downwards, the head vibrating from side to side. Primary function of VHS probably to appease aggression, and used as response to partner's bow greeting, or can constitute entire greeting ceremony, or is performed after aggressive encounter.

(4) Pre-copulatory displays: in nest-scrape activity penguin lies down, taking weight on breast-bone, and scrapes backwards with 1 foot. Used in scraping nest hollow, when bird is resettling on eggs, or as signal that ♂ is ready to form bond or copulate on nest. Prior to the arms act, ♂ approaches ♀ in 'intermediate bow' display: neck slightly extended, bill arched forwards varying from just below horizontal to almost dropped-bill position, eyes down, crest very erect, flippers held away from sides and vibrating slightly in attenuated patting movements (**C**). ♀ responds sometimes with intermediate bow, sometimes with OSB (**D**), then crouches and performs VHS if receptive. This is usually followed by arms act (**E**). If ♀ is standing, ♂ arches his head over

C

D   **E**

hers, resting chin and ventral surface of his neck on top of her head, pressing his breast against ♀'s back. Gently pats her sides with his flippers and attempts to push her into sitting position. If ♀ is already sitting ♂ mounts immediately. ♀ may also solicit ♂ while she is sitting in nest, by performing nest-scrape and VHS; ♂ then approaches her in intermediate bow (**F**) and mounts. ♀ not always receptive, especially in early pair-bonding. Unreceptive ♀ refuses to sit in response to arms act and will sometimes move away or, if already sitting, will stand and topple ♂ from her back. ♂♂ normally abandon copulatory attempts when refused. Rarely, refusal elicits aggressive response in ♂.

F

Copulation occurs on nest, sometimes elsewhere in colony or on landing beach. When ♀ assumes sitting position ♂ mounts, patting her sides with his flippers and treading her back with his feet. ♀ holds tail stiffly upright, cloaca everted, raises and holds head stiffly horizontal. ♂ bends head closely over ♀'s, usually vibrating his bill in manner similar to VHS, depresses his tail over ♀'s upraised tail and wags it from side to side until cloacal contact is made. ♂'s crest is erect during ejaculation. ♂ dismounts almost immediately.

Duration of successful copulation 69–228 s from mounting to dismounting. Copulation sometimes occurs while ♀ is incubating eggs. Promiscuous copulations occur and mated ♂♂ at pre-egg and guard stages copulate with prospecting ♀♀. Mated ♂♂ not observed to copulate with other than own mates, but unmated ♀♀ sometimes copulate with several ♂♂, some mated, before forming pair-bond with selected ♂. Copulation frequently elicits pecks and threats from neighbours and these can interrupt copulation. Frequently ♂, sometimes both, turn and threaten aggressive neighbour.

After dismounting ♂ stands beside ♀, motionless in characteristic, stiffly hunched posture with head bowed, sometimes crest erected, flippers away from body, occasionally one resting on ♀'s back. ♀ remains motionless for short time after copulation, sometimes does tail-shake and preens tail area. ♂ sometimes collects nest material while ♀ remains sitting in nest, intermittently performs nest-scrape and greets ♂ on his return with VHS.

Other displays made at nest-site include 'mutual ecstatic', 'extreme bow' and 'bill-slapping'. In mutual ecstatic display 2 birds stand facing or at angle to one another, flippers held against or slightly away from sides, necks extended, feathers of throats and crests sometimes erect, eyes down and bill wide open. Both call with raucous braying similar to calls in ecstatic display. Body posture variations include vertical stance, bill pointed upwards; horizontal stance with body bent well forward, neck arched downwards, bill close to ground, or intergradations between these extremes. Mutual ecstatic display may be performed when pairs reunite or may follow on from extreme bow and VHS.

In extreme bow display, primarily a non-aggressive greeting act between mated birds, the neck is extended and arched towards mate, chin and crest feathers very erect, eyes down and flippers away from body. Neck more arched than in intermediate bow display, and bill directed downwards, not towards mate.

Bill-slapping occurs between fighting birds at nest-site, between mated pairs (i.e. if ♀ refuses copulation), rarely between chicks and parents when former are losing their down (see below). In bill-slapping birds stand facing each other, sometimes stretching forward, bills side-by-side and crossed, heads are then shaken rapidly from side to side causing bills to make sharp contact with each other. Can occur independently or as part of aggressive encounter, i.e. pecking, interlocking bills, pulling and twisting in effort to push opponent sideways or down.

NEST: made of seaweed, twigs, feathers, stones, bones, or guano, collected before laying, and in incubation and fledging periods. Birds steal from other occupied or unattended nests, wandering far from own territories. ♂ collects most material, sometimes pair together, by lowering body from shoulder and pelvis, reaching forward with outstretched neck, holding head very close to ground, feathers sleeked, flippers held away from body. Returning through other territories, bird may walk or run with body stretched up, feathers sleeked, neck elongated, head above horizontal, flippers held out from body ('slender walk' posture); such birds may be pecked at but rarely retaliate. On reaching nest, drops material (sometimes with VHS), usually shakes head to remove particles. If mate present, typically bows head to mate, or towards place where material is to be deposited, performs VHS. Returning ♂♂ may bow and perform VHS to ♀♀, but not ♀♀ to ♂♂. If collecting material together, both may perform VHS simultaneously on return to nest.

EGGS: normally 2, sometimes 1, laid at 2–4 day intervals; chalky white. SIZE: (58 eggs) 62·8–76·4 × 48·3–55·9 (67·0 × 52·3) (Priest 1971). WEIGHT: (10) 99–118 (107) (R. Randall, pers. comm.).

Laying dates: all year with 1–2 peaks/year, e.g. Dassen Island (winter) June, (summer) Nov–Dec, with sub-annual cycle of 10·5 months after successful breeding (Cooper, in press); St Croix Island Jan–May (R. Randall, pers. comm.).

Incubation begins 1st egg; by both sexes, shares equal, in variable 1–3 day periods, occasionally up to 5 days, apparently varying related to food. Period: 38–41 days, av. 39 (Rand 1960).

Chicks hatch at intervals, eggshells not discarded; blind, helpless; weigh *c*. 60 g. First down retained to day 14, when weigh 325–710 g; second down develops days 14–30, and is lost days 40–60. Juvenile plumage develops on back as down shed, complete by days 70–80 when all down has disappeared. Chicks become aggressive to parents and other adults while losing down, lunging, pecking, or attempting bill-snapping. Aggressiveness may be triggered by mutual ecstatic display by parents, when returning with food, or when standing at nest-site. When food is scarce, chicks abandoned by parents for long periods form into creches at *c*. 30 days (probably for warmth and protection), returning to nests in late evening to await parents' return; especially applicable to chicks reared on surface (R. Randall and J. Cooper, pers. comm.).

When food is plentiful, 1 parent always stays with chick by day, both by night. Nest-relief normally every 24 h, usually in late afternoon, when returning mate feed chicks. Chicks fed by regurgitation; parent bends down, bill directed downward, gape wide open. Chick begs by touching or pecking sides of parent's bill, or gripping it in own, stretching forward towards parent with flippers held out sideways, calling soft 'peep-peep' when small, louder, more strident 'peeeep-peeeep' when larger (R. Randall, pers. comm.); finally inserts head into parental bill to receive food. Mutual ecstatic display of parents may also stimulate chicks to beg. Parent which has just fed chicks usually remains overnight, relieved adult going to sea next morning. When food scarce reliefs may only occur every 2–3 days, when younger, and sometimes older chick dies of starvation. If parent does not guard chicks up to 25 days, they are killed by Kelp Gulls *Larus dominicanus*.

Chicks leave home island at 70–118 days, normally *c*. 85. Parents continue feeding up to night before departure, returning to nest to feed even after chicks have left. Usually, chicks leave before 08.00 h, following stream of sea-going adults, attaching to various groups. May follow adults, or be driven away aggressively, then swims off alone, remaining away about one year, before returning to moult. Some may return after 7 months and feed near home island before moulting; others do not return until 18 months old. After moulting young leave again, but in next 3–4 years spend progressively longer periods at home island.

1st year mortality 80–96% (av. 89%) over 4 years, St Croix Island, near Port Elizabeth (R. Randall, pers. comm.). From St Croix, move mainly towards W Cape, rarely northwards towards Natal; recoveries of ringed birds from Dyer's Island, Marcus Island, and Lamberts Bay. First recorded breeding at exactly 4 years old (St Croix).

References
Eggleton, P. and Siegfried, W. R. (1979).
Frost, P. G. H. *et al.* (1976b).
Siegfried, W. R. (1977).
Siegfried, W. R. *et al.* (1975).

Illustrations reproduced with permission from Eggleton and Siegfried (1979).

Order
GAVIIFORMES

Family GAVIIDAE: divers

Medium to large diving birds found on fresh and salt water. Sole modern family in order, with single genus *Gavia*. Relationships to other avian orders remote; superficial relationship to Podicipediformes (grebes) due to convergence. Breeding plumage strikingly patterned; non-breeding plumage dull grey and white. Sexes alike although ♀♀ generally smaller. Bill long, straight and pointed; front toes fully webbed; body elongated, legs set far back, neck short. Awkward on land, but strong fliers. In flight extended neck sweeps downward, giving hunch-backed appearance, with feet projected beyond tail and held together, sole to sole. On water usually swim low, often raising themselves to flap wings. When preening or bathing, turn over on side or back. Swim well under water, diving from water surface. Seize (do not spear) fish with bill in underwater pursuit, using feet and occasionally wings for propulsion. Swallow small fish underwater. Circumpolar in Northern Hemisphere; 4 spp. with 3 occasionally reaching North Africa in Palearctic winter.

Genus *Gavia* Forster

Gavia stellata (Pontoppidan). Red-throated Diver; Red-throated Loon. Plongeon catmarin.   Not illustrated

Colymbus Stellatus Pontoppidan, 1763. Danske Atlas, 1, p. 621; Tame River, Warwickshire, England.

Range and Status. Palearctic winter visitor, uncommon to rare in Gibraltar Straits off Morocco; least rare of 3 *Gavia* spp. in Africa.

Description. ADULT ♂ (non-breeding): upperparts pale grey finely spotted with white. Head and neck white and grey with noticeable white face and eye-ring. Underparts white with little brown on flanks and undertail-coverts. Slender, slightly up-tilted bill dark slate grey. ADULT ♂ (breeding): head and sides of neck dark grey, back of crown and neck narrowly striped black and white, extending to bolder stripes on sides of breast. Foreneck dull vinaceous red. Rest of upperparts mainly uniform dark grey-brown. Flanks and undertail-coverts brown; rest of underparts white. Bill dull blue-grey; dark stripe along culmen; eye vinaceous red; legs grey-black. Sexes alike except ♀ smaller. SIZE: wing, ♂ (12 specimens) 265–310 (292), ♀ (10) 257–308 (281); tail, ♂ (10) 42–57 (53·4), ♀ (10) 47–54 (50·1); bill, ♂ (11) 48–61 (55·1), ♀ 46–55 (51·3); tarsus, ♂ (10) 66–82 (75·1), ♀ (10) 65–77 (70·8). WEIGHT: (winter) ♂ (6) 1170–1456 (1341), ♀ (9) 988–1302 (1144); (summer) ♂ (7) 1370–1900 (1729), ♀ 1410–1613 (1477).

IMMATURE: similar to non-breeding adult but duller brown, bill noticeably paler.

Field Characters. A small diver with a distinctive up-tilted bill. In non-breeding plumage, face whiter than other divers; at close range small spots on back. In breeding plumage, grey head, reddish patch on front of neck and plain brown back diagnostic.

Voice. Not recorded in Africa. Rather silent outside breeding season. A 'wailing' or 'barking' occasionally given in winter, and call notes uttered in migration. Croaking, cackling, wailing, cooing and moaning calls given during breeding season.

General Habits. Little known in Africa, well known in Europe and North America. In Africa occurs almost

Gavia stellata

exclusively in the sea, often along coast. More sociable than other divers, concentrating in groups of 50–200 or more, especially in migration. Migrates day or night. No courtship in winter flocks. General habits like those of other divers, but rises more easily from water.

Food. Fish, also crustaceans, molluscs and occasionally plant material.

References
Cramp, S. and Simmons, K. E. L. (1977).

Not illustrated   *Gavia arctica* **(Linnaeus). Black-throated Diver; Arctic Loon. Plongeon arctique.**

Columbus arcticus Linnaeus, 1758. Syst. Nat., (10th ed.), p. 135; Sweden.

Range and Status. Palearctic winter visitor, rare along Mediterranean and Atlantic coasts of NW Africa.

Description. *G. a. arctica* (Linnaeus), ADULT ♂ (non-breeding): upperparts dark brown, paler on crown and hindneck; scapulars sometimes with pale spots. Underparts and sides of head white; spots or streaks across sides of chest and along top of flanks. Bill grey, with darker culmen. ADULT ♂ (breeding): crown, hindneck and sides of head grey; lower face dark grey, shading into black chin and throat. Narrow transverse patch of short, vertical white streaks across throat; sides of neck and chest striped black and white. Rest of upperparts blue-black; mantle and scapulars with 4 areas of transverse white spots. Upperwing- and uppertail-coverts spotted white. Underwing and underparts mainly white with top flanks partly black. Straight bill black; eye red; legs grey-black. Sexes alike except ♀ smaller. SIZE: wing, ♂ (10 specimens) 294–343 (324), ♀ (10) 282–337 (309); tail, ♂ (10) 53–67 (58·7), ♀ (8) 51–61 (57·8); bill, ♂ (9) 52–68 (60·7), ♀ (10) 52–68 (60·2); tarsus, ♂ (10) 72–89 (82·2), ♀ (10) 71–87 (78·8). WEIGHT: (winter) ♂ (3) 1316–2607, ♀ (1) 1688; (summer) ♂ (2) 3310, 3400, ♀ (3) 2037–2471.

IMMATURE: like non-breeding adult but upperparts paler brown, without white-spotted upperwing-coverts; bill slate grey; eye light brown.

Field Characters. Slightly bulkier, longer-bodied, heavier-headed than Red-throated Diver *G. stellata*. In breeding plumage grey, chequered black and white upperparts, and black throat and foreneck diagnostic. In non-breeding plumage has darker upperparts than other divers. Also distinguished from Red-throated

---

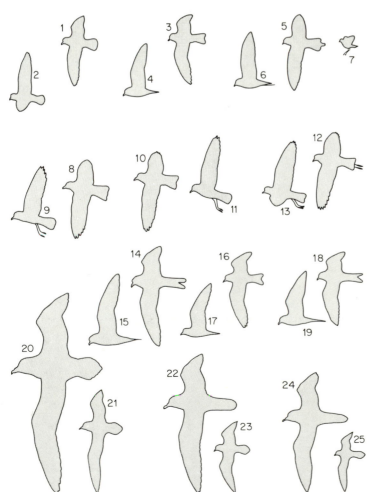

in
0	3	6	9	12

0	10	20	30
cm

Scale applies to birds shown from above

Plate 5

Hydrobates pelagicus British Storm-Petrel (p. 70)
1. ADULT (above), 2. (below).

Oceanodroma castro Madeiran Storm-Petrel (p. 70)
3. ADULT (above), 4. (below).

Oceanites oceanicus Wilson's Storm-Petrel (p. 66)
5. ADULT (above), 6. (below), 7. with feet dropped.

Fregetta grallaria White-bellied Storm-Petrel (p. 69)
8. ADULT (above), 9. (below).

Fregetta tropica Black-bellied Storm-Petrel (p. 68)
10. ADULT (above), 11. (below).

Pelagodroma marina White-faced Storm-Petrel (p. 67)
12. ADULT (above), 13. (below).

Oceanodroma matsudairae Matsudaira's Storm-Petrel (p. 72)
14. ADULT (above), 15. (below).

Oceanodroma monorhis Swinhoe's Storm-Petrel (p. 71)
16. ADULT (above), 17. (below).

Oceanodroma leucorhoa Leach's Storm-Petrel (p. 72)
18. ADULT (above), 19. (below).

Pterodroma macroptera Great-winged Petrel (p. 48)
20. ADULT (above), 21. (below).

Bulweria fallax Jouanin's Petrel (p. 57)
22. ADULT (above), 23. (below).

Bulweria bulwerii Bulwer's Petrel (p. 56)
24. ADULT (above), 25. (below).

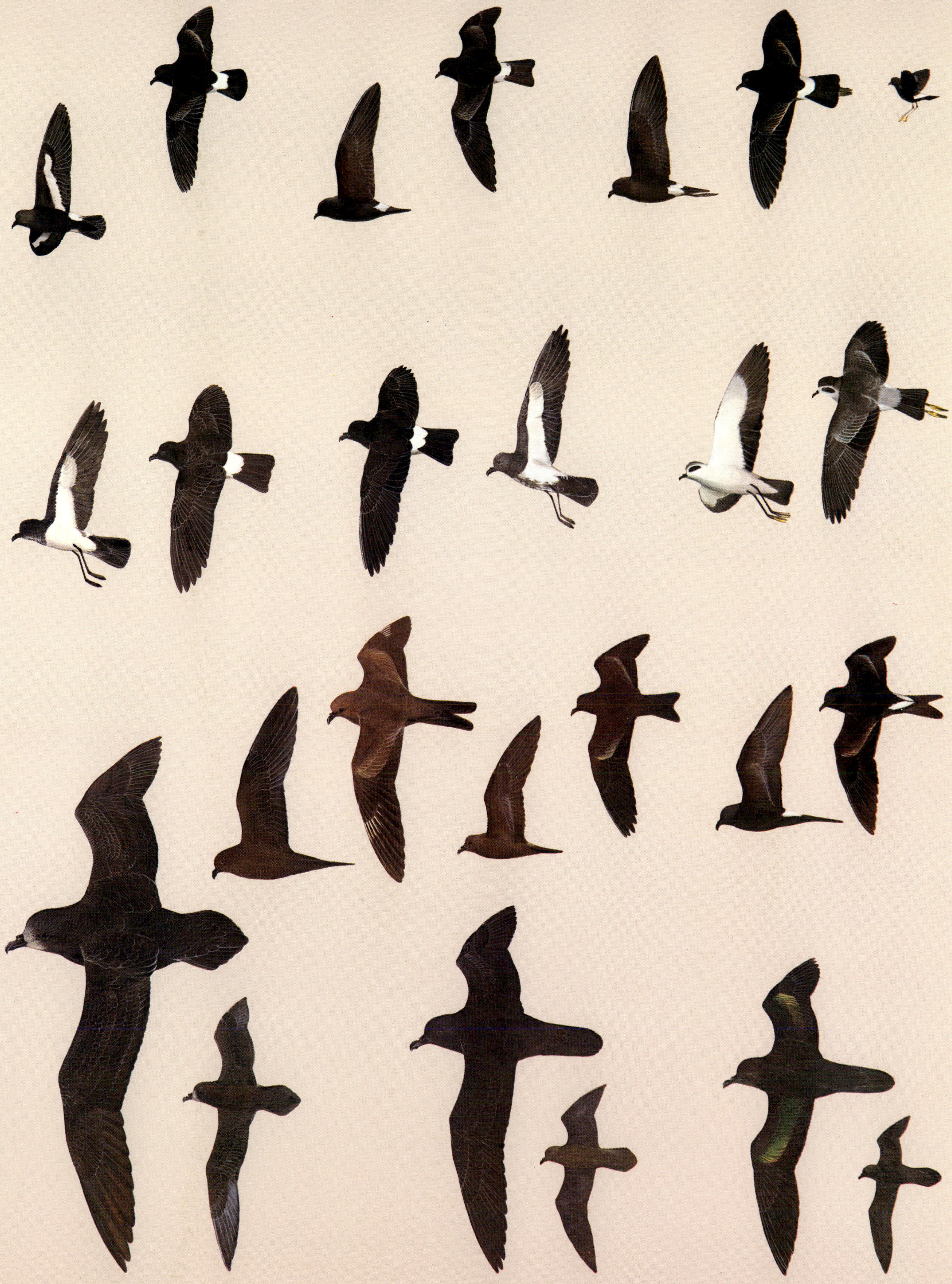

Diver in winter plumage by straight bill, and from Great Northern Diver *G. immer* by slender bill and thinner neck with no indented half-collar. Wings not raised as high in upstroke as Red-throated Diver.

Voice. Not recorded in Africa. Mostly silent in winter. In breeding season gives wailing, moaning, growling, croaking calls.

General Habits. Little known in Africa, well known in Europe and North America. In winter almost exclusively on coastal salt waters. Tends to migrate in pairs although sometimes in small flocks. General habits like those of other divers.

Food. Probably almost entirely fish during winter season.

Reference
Cramp, S. and Simmons, K. E. L. (1977).

Gavia arctica

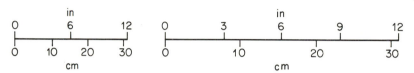

Left-hand scale applies to penguins (not head details), right-hand scale to grebes (not birds in flight)

Plate 6

Aptenodytes patagonicus King Penguin (p. 74)
1. ADULT.

Spheniscus demersus Jackass Penguin (p. 76)
2. and 3. ADULTS swimming,
4. JUVENILE, 5. ADULT.

Eudyptes chrysocome Rockhopper Penguin (p. 75)
6. ADULT head, side view, 7. ADULT head, from above, 8. ADULT.

Eudyptes chrysolophus Macaroni Penguin (p. 75)
9. ADULT head, side view, 10. ADULT head, from above, 11. ADULT.

Tachybaptus ruficollis Little Grebe (p. 85)
Race *capensis*: 12. ADULT (breeding), 13. ADULT (non-breeding), 14. DOWNY YOUNG, 15. ADULT (non-breeding) from rear, 16. ADULT (non-breeding) in flight.

Podiceps nigricollis Black-necked Grebe (p. 91)
17. ADULT (breeding), 18. ADULT (non-breeding), 19. JUVENILE, 20. DOWNY YOUNG,
21. ADULT (non-breeding) in flight.

Podiceps cristatus Great Crested Grebe (p. 88)
Race *infuscatus*: 22. ADULT (non-breeding),
23. ADULT (breeding), 24. DOWNY YOUNG,
25. JUVENILE.
Race *cristatus*: 26. ADULT (non-breeding),
27. in flight.

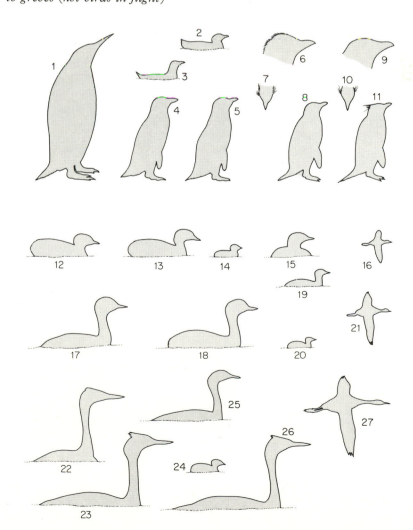

Not illustrated *Gavia immer* (Brünnich). **Great Northern Diver; Common Loon. Plongeon imbrin.**

Colymbus Immer Brünnich, 1764. Ornith. Borealis, p. 38; Faeroes.

Range and Status. Palearctic winter visitor, rare along coast from Algeria to western Morocco.

Gavia immer

Description. ADULT ♂ (non-breeding): upperparts dark brown-grey, mantle and scapulars with pale markings. Hind-neck darker than mantle. Underparts white. Lower neck with dark half-collar, ends of this sometimes almost meeting on foreneck. Bill grey with dark brown culmen. ADULT ♂ (breeding): head and neck black, with green metallic gloss; transverse row of 6–10 short vertical streaks on either side of neck. Rest of upperparts black with white spots, varying from small and round on mantle to large and square on scapulars. Breast and belly white; undertail-coverts dull black. Primaries and secondaries black, underwing-coverts white. Strong, straight bill black; eye vinaceous red; legs grey-black. Sexes alike except ♀ slightly smaller. SIZE: ♂ and ♀, wing (29 specimens) 331–400 (366), tail (21) 58–75 (66·8), bill (27) 72–89 (80·2), and tarsus (25) 83–100 (91·4). WEIGHT: ♂ (2) 3600, 3990; unsexed (3) 4250, 4350, 4480.

IMMATURE: like non-breeding adult but upperparts browner.

Field Characters. Largest of the 3 divers in Africa; about the size of a small goose. Bill strong and straight; neck thick. Dark head, vertical stripes on throat, light horizontal bands around neck, and back boldly covered with white spots diagnostic in summer plumage. Winter plumage resembles that of Black-throated Diver *G. arctica* but crown and hindneck usually darker than back. Distinguished from Red-throated Diver *G. stellata* by having no white spots on its back.

Voice. Not recorded in Africa. Mainly silent in winter quarters although short, abrupt, monosyllabic calls given when in flocks. A 'kwuk-kwuk-kwuk' given in flight. In breeding season gives 'wailing', 'laughing' and 'yodelling' calls.

General Habits. Little known in Africa, well known in Europe and North America. In Africa occurs along sea shores. Migrates largely by day. Found in single, small, loose groups, and, more rarely, larger flocks. Flight heavy, almost goose-like and noticeably slower and more powerful than other divers. Feeds any time of day, resting irregularly between feedings, usually on water but also on shore. When searching for food, regularly dips bill and forehead under water before diving. General habits like those of other divers.

Food. Primarily fish, size varying with locality and season; also crustaceans, and occasionally other invertebrates and plant material.

References
Cramp, S. and Simmons, K. E. L. (1977).

Order
PODICIPEDIFORMES

Family PODICIPEDIDAE: grebes

Small to medium-sized diving birds, feeding on fish and other aquatic organisms, apparently not closely related to any other birds, though superficially somewhat similar to Gaviiformes, divers. Bill normally sharp and pointed. Head often crested, or with conspicuous ear-tufts or neck-ruff in breeding plumage; necks normally long, slim. Body short and rounded, in larger species elongated. Plumage loose, fluffy, downy on back, smooth and silky on breast and belly. Wings small, narrow, flight feathers curved, tucked under body feathers when folded; 12 primaries, 17–22 secondaries. Flight feathers moulted simultaneously, causing temporary flightlessness; can fly fast and far, colonizing isolated habitats. In flight neck extends forward, feet project behind body, wing-beats very rapid. Tail short, downy, no normal tail-feathers. Legs set very far back on body, can scarcely stand or walk. Tarsi laterally flattened, serrated on rear edge. Toes broadly lobed, front 3 with small basal interconnecting webs; rear toe short, raised, flattened, lobe-like. Nails broad, flat; that of middle toe serrated.

The Order is almost cosmopolitan, most varied in the Americas. It comprises only 1 family, the Podicipedidae, grebes, with 6 genera and 17–21 species, according to the most modern revision (Storer 1979). 2 genera with 3 species occur in Africa, all African representatives of widespread Old World species, 1 also extending to America.

Grebes have been classified partly on the basis of their courtship displays and partly on anatomy (Storer 1963). They nest in water on aquatic vegetation, making flat pad-like nests of water weed. All species perform more or less complicated ritualized displays, more vocal in smaller, less ornamented species. Displays are mutual, performed by both sexes, including false copulation, ♀ mounting ♂. They fall broadly into 3 phases: (i) aggressive pair-formation displays performed on open water; (ii) 'water-courtship' performed by both sexes after their pair-formation; (iii) 'platform-courtship' performed on or near nest-platform by both sexes, including false and true copulation. Displays in African species are not well recorded, but several of those performed by same species in Europe have been seen (W. Dean, pers. comm.). Some common displays are (for full descriptions see Cramp and Simmons 1977, and references quoted therein): 'forward-threat'—bird, often with bill open, arches neck with head above water or extends it along water; 'hunched-back'—bird, with neck in, points bill slightly down, ruffs entire plumage and folds wings on back or tilts them forward somewhat; 'defence-upright'—bird erects neck, fully spreads tippets, holds crest vertically and points open bill downward; 'upright-advertising'—bird floats with neck erect and throat distended and makes croaking sounds; 'cat-display'—bird lowers head, erects crest and raises wings above back; 'ghostly-penguin'—bird holds body upright, with tail and rump submerged, and stretches head laterally forward; 'mutual penguin dance'—pair rises out of water facing each other, crests raised, breasts touching, then shake heads and may rush side by side over water in upright position; 'habit-preening'—bird preens when withdrawing from mate at end of high-intensity display; 'weed-ceremony'—birds withdraw, submerge slowly, collect weed underwater, swim towards one another, abruptly rise vertically face to face, shake heads, drop weed, and shake heads again; 'inviting'—♀, lying on nest, kinks neck, stretches it forward and utters inviting calls sometimes quivering wings; and 'copulation'—♂ moves head from side to side, mounts ♀ from behind and copulates, then dismounts over her head; in 1 sp. (Little Grebe *Tachybaptus ruficollis*), ♀ raises her head during copulation, rubbing ♂'s breast. (*All illustrations for this Order by Martin Woodcock after Cramp and Simmons (1977).*)

Genus *Tachybaptus* Reichenbach

Small grebe with short dumpy body, practically no tail, short neck and wings. Differs from *Podiceps* in lacking ornamental plumes on head and neck; in having a separate canal in the hypotarsus for the insertion of the tendon of the flexor perforatus digiti II muscle; and in certain differences in courtship displays, notably the absence of a 'discovery ceremony' (Storer 1963). Bill rather short, conical, blunted at tip. Outer toe nearly as long as middle toe. Downy young have no bald spot on crown. Found almost throughout Old World. 5 spp., 1 in Africa, *T. ruficollis*.

Tachybaptus ruficollis (Pallas). Little Grebe; Dabchick. Grèbe castagneux.

Colymbus ruficollis Pallas, 1764. Vroeg Cat. Raisonné Coll. Oiseaux, Adumbr. p. 6; Holland.

Plate 6

(Opp. p. 83)

Range and Status. Breeds NW Africa and occurs sporadically on seasonal ponds and oases in N Sahara (Kufra); also resident locally throughout Africa south of Sahara, from Senegal–Ethiopia thence south to Cape Province. Occurs any altitude from sea level to 3500 m (Ethiopia), commonest in highland areas of E Africa and in southern Africa; less widespread, more local W Africa. In most haunts common to abundant, occasionally very abundant, in thousands. In many E and southern African areas has increased greatly as a result of man-made dams and ponds; elsewhere stable.

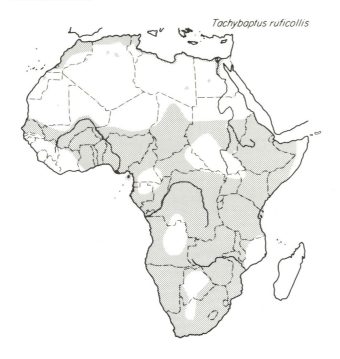

Tachybaptus ruficollis

Description. *T. r. capensis* Salvadori: Africa south of Sahara.
ADULT ♂ (breeding): crown and hindneck black extending
round eyes to chin; back blackish. Cheeks, sides and front of
neck dark rufous-chestnut. Upperparts and sides brown,
mottled white. Lower breast and belly white, flanks rufous
washed blackish. Bill short, black, with conspicuous pale
cream or yellow patch at gape; eye dark red; feet black. ADULT
♂ (non-breeding): paler, duller, greyer, chestnut areas becoming brownish white, black areas duller, brown areas, paler.
Sexes alike, ♀ slightly smaller. SIZE: wing, ♂ 100–107 (104),
♀ 95–102 (99); tarsus, ♂ 26–30, ♀ 24–26. WEIGHT: (14) 119–
188 (147) (Skead 1977b).
      IMMATURE: resembles non-breeding adult, with black
blotches and streaks on head and neck; eye brown.
      DOWNY YOUNG: top of head downy, not bald (as in *Podiceps*).
Above, brown, longitudinally streaked black; 3 conspicuous
white streaks behind eye. Chin and throat black, rest of underside white; eye dark brown.
      T. r. ruficollis (Pallas). Europe and NW Africa. Somewhat
smaller, paler. SIZE: wing, ♂ 95–106 (101), ♀ 90–102 (99).
WEIGHT: ♂ 131–266, ♀ 117–235, varying according to amount
of stored fat; lean birds av. ♂ 140, ♀ 130.

Field Characters. Smallest African grebe. Short stout
body with short neck; black crown; short, relatively
thick, somewhat blunted bill with conspicuous pale
patch at gape. Mainly rich dark chestnut and black
above, no conspicuous head-tufts in any plumage. Only
likely to be confused with Black-necked Grebe *Podiceps
nigricollis*, but is smaller than this species, darker,
shorter necked, and with distinctive bill-shape, straight,
rather blunt-ended, not sharp, flattened, slightly upturned. Immatures more difficult to distinguish, but in
all plumages show much darker underside than Black-
necked Grebe. Pale gape patch and bill-shape always
distinctive; dark brown eye diagnostic at close range.

Voice. Recorded (2a, 6, 14, 18, 19, 22a, 26, 27) Commonest call is courtship trill or whinny, uttered singly
or in duet; a long, high-pitched, slightly descending trill,
barely possible to syllabize, 'bi-i-i-i-i-i-i'. Other lower
calls audible at close range 'weet-weet-weet', or 'wee-

wee-wee' repeated; short clucks 'kyu-kyu', 'sweeet'.
Associated activities in Africa not described, but courtship trill uttered year-round near equator. Young emit
high-pitched, piping, squeaking, or wheedling calls.
(For fuller description with sonagrams of nominate *T. r.
ruficollis*, see Cramp and Simmons 1977.)

General Habits. Well known. In NW Africa *T. r. ruficollis* frequents ponds, lakes, usually shallow and with
vegetation, sometimes coastal estuaries, especially in
winter. In breeding season prefers shallow waters with
vegetated edges. Tropical African and South African
T. r. capensis frequents small ponds and dams, edges of
large freshwater or alkaline/saline lakes, coastal brackish
lagoons, river backwaters, rice fields, flood-plain ox-
bows and slow-moving rivers. Prefers shallow vegetated
waters but also found in thousands far from shore in
deep alkaline water e.g. Lake Shala, Ethiopia, or far
out in Lake Naivasha, Kenya. Avoids dense tall aquatic
vegetation, but common in small or large lagoons
enclosed by tall *Typha* or papyrus; seldom marine or
estuarine. Commonest in aquatic habitats in woodland
or open country, but also occurs within forests if habitat
otherwise suitable.
      Normally in pairs or family parties, rarely solitary,
sometimes gregarious in flocks of 10–30, e.g. on Lake
Shala (non-breeding birds). In South Africa flocks of
up to 700 recorded, possibly post-breeding dispersal
(W. Dean, pers. comm.). In tropics pairs remain within
territory much of year at densities of up to 2–3 pairs/ha,
but small isolated bodies of water of less than 1 ha
usually support only 1 pair, sometimes temporarily.
Roosts among, or on floating aquatic vegetation, under
bushes. Not normally active at night, but may be so
under artificial light; non-breeding birds roost gregariously on rafts on water. Normally not shy in Africa;
can be watched at close range. Flies readily when
pressed, skittering along surface of water, usually for
30–50 m, often submerging when alighting. Although
flight apparently weak, ability to colonize isolated
temporary ponds when available indicates sustained
flight for long distances over unfavourable terrain when
necessary.
      Feeds at any time of day, submerging quietly, some-
times with upward jump, remaining submerged 10–50 s,
av. *c.* 16 s. Usually travels 5–30 m each dive, but
may emerge repeatedly in almost same spot. Readily
swims among underwater vegetation, e.g. water-lily
stems *Nymphaea*, bladderwort *Utricularia*, or pondweed
Potamogeton. May feed in association with several
diving or dabbling ducks, including Spur-winged Goose
Plectropterus gambensis, Cape Teal *Anas capensis*, Red-
billed Teal *A. erythrorhyncha*, Northern Shoveler *A.
clypeata*, Maccoa Duck *Oxyura maccoa*, White-backed
Duck *Thalassornis leuconotus*. When feeding thus, dives
are shorter than normal (7·4–20·4 s, av. 11·61 s) separated by shorter intervals (5·6–15 s, av. 7·7 s); 1·9–3·9
dives/min, av. 2·7 (Siegfried 1971; Skead 1977a; Burger
and Berruti 1977). Apparently benefits from foraging
activity of ducks in disturbing small organisms, as
deliberately follows ducks about. Such activity probably
common, as often observed if looked for. Often sun-

bathes, orienting body with back to sun, perhaps absorbing heat through dark skin (Storer *et al.* 1975).

Resident N African population possibly augmented by migrants in winter, but no evidence of large-scale migration to N Africa. Within Africa south of Sahara, resident on larger waters year-round, but (at least in E Africa–Zaïre, Zimbabwe and also W Africa) widespread dispersal following heavy rains, then utilizing seasonal ponds for breeding. Immediately colonizes new dams, often in 1st year; thereafter on larger dams may become permanent resident. Frequently appears on very isolated waters in subdesert or open grassland, indicating ability to disperse widely over inhospitable terrain to locate new habitats. Temporary ponds deserted as they dry, smallest without breeding, but may breed successfully on ponds filled for only 3–4 months. Birds then displaced by drought may retreat to larger waters, possibly breeding again there (Ruwet 1963) and augmenting regular resident population. Apparently regular resident, not migrating far in colder parts of South Africa, but regularly concentrates in winter at Barberspan, peak numbers July–Aug.

Food. Not analysed in detail in Africa, but includes small fish, frogs, tadpoles, water insects and larvae, small crustaceans, molluscs. Food mainly caught by diving but e.g. copepods caught on surface of water. Feeds on flying termites (Steyn 1964), usually when they have fallen into water, but occasionally rushes at and catches one still in flight.

Breeding Habits. Well known, but not intensively studied anywhere in Africa. Displays not described in detail, but may be similar to nominate *ruficollis* in Europe (described in detail, Cramp and Simmons 1977). Less elaborate than in *Podiceps*. 2 main phases, water-courtship and platform-courtship. Pair-formation in water-courtship involves wing-waving in upright position, followed by pattering over surface. Pairs usually face each other and assume 'hunched display' posture with head retracted, wings slightly raised, trilling loudly; sometimes rise in water with rapidly paddling feet. Other water-courtship includes food presentation and bill-touching. Later, courtship initiates nest-building with pair swimming about together holding weed in bill, mutually presenting weed.

Platform-courtship follows construction of nest or platform. Both sexes build and 1 or more partially completed platforms may be built, used for courtship, then abandoned. Mating occurs on nest or platform, ♀ lying with kinked neck stretched forward, uttering inviting call (see **A**). Responding ♂ waves head slowly from side to side, mounts from behind and copulates in upright posture, uttering buzzing calls, ♀ raises head during act, rubbing ♂ breast; ♂ dismounts over her head. Copulation often precedes egg-laying by some days.

NEST: Built near edge of lake, dam, or pond, usually in shallow water and attached to submerged vegetation such as branch of an inundated bush. A pad of usually soft aquatic vegetation, water weeds and algae, sometimes including some stiffer stems, *c.* 25–35 cm across and up to 15 cm thick. Structure *c.* 66% submerged,

A

with shallow central hollows; is continually moist and becomes heated.

EGGS: 2–8, laid successive, sometimes alternate days (7–8 may be product of 2 ♀♀); Cape 2–6, mean (128) 3·34; Transvaal–Natal 2–7, mean (74) 3·70; Zimbabwe–Namibia 2–8, mean (160) 4·15; Kenya 2–6, mean (15) 3·33 (clutch size apparently increases from South Africa north to Zimbabwe, then possibly decreases nearer equator). White or cream when fresh, soon stained brown in incubation; rather long ovals. SIZE: 32·0–39·5 × 23·8–28·8 (mean, 200, southern Africa 37·8 × 25·6). WEIGHT: *c.* 14–15 g; clutch of 4, 60 g (25–30% of ♀ bodyweight).

Laying dates: Cape July–Mar, odd records June; peak 156/257 Sept–Dec (spring); Transvaal, Orange Free State, Natal, all months, least May–Aug (dry, cold), peak 68/104 Oct–Jan (winter rains); Zimbabwe, all months, more widespread peak, 190/244 Dec–Apr (main rains) with subsidiary peak June–Aug (37/244), suggesting double-brooded; Kenya, E Africa, all months, peak Apr–Aug (44/56) especially May (16/56) in and just after main rains; Zaïre Dec–Mar on outlying ponds (rains) June–July on large dams and stable lakes (dry); Ethiopia Apr–June, Oct (early rains); Nigeria Aug, Sept, Oct, late rains; Senegal Nov–Jan (dry); NW Africa end Mar–late May (spring). Pattern in tropics appears to be peak breeding in rains, and also in dry season on more stable waters; in southern and NW Africa breeding spring-summer (EANRC; SAOSNRC; Ruwet 1963; Morel and Morel 1962).

Laying ♀ raises herself, appears to strain with quivering wings (Wood 1949). Both sexes incubate, and nest almost invariably has sitting bird on it. Eggs almost invariably covered with soft weed from nest-edge when bird disturbed, but sometimes left briefly exposed when bird leaves of own accord to feed. ♀ not fed on nest by ♂ but leaves to feed for 5–30 min at intervals. Approaching nest, both dive some distance away, and surface silently just beside it. Trilling displays decrease once incubation commences; behaviour then generally secretive. Wet water weed continually added by both sexes during incubation, often associated with nest-relief. No elaborate nest-relief ceremonies once incubation well advanced. Period: *c.* 24 days for clutch (Wood 1949); 1 record Natal 28 days (SAOSNRC), Palearctic 20–21 days (Cramp and Simmons 1977); further study in tropics needed.

Young leave nest almost at once; accompany either parent. Climb onto parents' backs at intervals, but usually swim near. Are fed bill to bill with food caught by either parent; solicit with cheeping calls. At 25 days have developed short wings and may then return to nest and perform wing-flapping. 1st attempt to fish themselves occurs at *c.* 29 days; parents may drop live food in water in front of young, perhaps to stimulate early fishing attempts. Young can feed themselves by *c.* 32 days, and parents may then leave them on temporary pools, perhaps returning later; may still feed young up to 42 days. Young full grown by 50 days, and can flutter and skid over water; heads then rufous (Wood 1949).

Breeding success not recorded, but broods of 2–3 in E Africa usually reduced to 1 or less by end of fledging period. Probably less then 1 young per nest reared, with some re-laying and 2nd broods, especially on larger, more stable waters. Oldest ringed bird (nominate *ruficollis*) 13 years.

References

Siegfried, R. (1971).
Wood, M. G. (1949).

Genus *Podiceps* Latham

Rather small to large grebes. Beaks straight, pointed, sometimes slightly upturned. Head and neck in breeding season adorned with conspicuous, brightly coloured feathers, often ear-tufts, crests or neck-ruffs. Necks long, slender. Secondaries almost as long as primaries. Tarsus shorter than middle toe with claw; middle toe much shorter than outer. Young striped, with brightly coloured naked patches on crown. Almost cosmopolitan; 2 regular resident African spp. *P. cristatus* and *P. nigricollis*. 2 others rare vagrants NW Africa, *P. grisegena* and *P. auritus*. Both African species well known, but more intensively studied in Europe.

Plate 6
(Opp. p. 83)

Podiceps cristatus (Linnaeus). Great Crested Grebe. Grèbe huppé.

Colymbus cristatus Linnaeus, 1758. Syst. Nat. (10th ed.), p. 135; Europe (Sweden).

Range and Status. In Africa distribution discontinuous. Nominate *P. c. cristatus* breeds Tunisia (*c.* 60 pairs), but now only winter migrant in small numbers to Morocco. Straggles to Senegal Delta. African *P. c. ruficollis* breeds Ethiopia (to 3400 m); highlands of E Africa and Zaïre; and in South Africa from Transvaal–Cape, at sea level. Recorded Zimbabwe–Zambia. Absent from many apparently suitable habitats, not breeding below 1500 m in Kenya or Ethiopia. Locally common, sometimes abundant, but numbers variable. In E Africa has been almost exterminated since 1950 in some former haunts by nylon gill-nets set for fish.

Description. *P. c. infuscatus* Salvadori: tropical Africa to Cape. ADULT ♂: crown black, feathers erectile. Sides of face white. Ear-coverts forming a long curved tippet or neck-ruff, basally chestnut, terminally black. Back of neck, back and upper wing-coverts blackish, streaked brown. Foreneck and whole underparts, including wing-coverts, pure silky white. Primaries blackish, secondaries white, forming a marked white patch in open wing. Bill black, tinged reddish; eye crimson; feet and legs dusky. SIZE: wing, ♂ 173–182 (176); tarsus, 56·5–64 (60). ♂ normally distinguishable by slightly larger size, longer neck; ♀ has paler chestnut, less well developed ruff; 'brighter' looking of pair (W. Dean, pers. comm.). Av. size decreases clinally from north to south, Ethiopian and E African birds averaging largest (wing, ♂ 179–186, ♀ 172–185) and South African smallest (wing, ♂ 173–181, ♀ 162–180); not considered adequate to justify racial distinction (Benson and Irwin 1964). WEIGHT: 492–775 (595).

IMMATURE: dull grey above, lacking any erectile crown or ear-tippets; below white. Eye brown, bill black.

DOWNY YOUNG: forehead black; a bare red patch on crown, occiput black. Above, grey-brown with longitudinal black stripes. Eye blackish.

P. c. cristatus (Linnaeus). Europe and W Asia, breeding N Africa. Larger (wing, ♂ 175–209 (195), ♀ 168–199 (184)). WEIGHT: ♂ 758–1490, ♀ 609–1380, varying greatly according to fat; av. lean ♂ 738, ♀ 609, av. fat ♂ 920, ♀ 830, or even more. Generally paler in breeding plumage. In winter becomes grey above, white below, ornamental plumes moulted. Immatures resemble non-breeding adults.

Field Characters. A large grebe, impossible to confuse with any other except rare vagrant Red-necked Grebe *P. grisegena* in NW Africa. Distinguished from any duck by tail-less, apparently wing-less body (wings hidden by feathers), long slim neck usually held erect, large conspicuous ear-tippets often spread making head appear large and broad. Immature is grey, slim, with long sharp pointed bill. Resembles no duck, but vaguely reminiscent of small darter or cormorant.

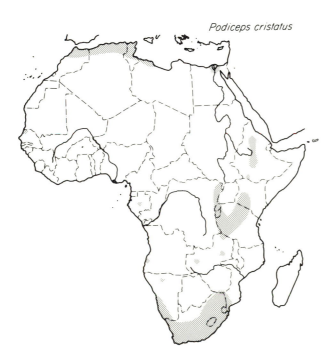

Podiceps cristatus

Voice. Not recorded in Africa. In Europe varied, most calls associated with particular activities. Loud 'barking', 'rah-rah-rah'; 'growling', drawn out 'gharrr' or 'ghorrr' repeated; 'snarling', loud prolonged 'gaaaaaa' usually with threat or fighting; 'twanging', a quiet metallic 'gung', repeated 2–3 times; 'clicking', hen-like 'cluck'; 'ticking', short 'ktik-ktik'; 'croaking' or 'crowing', loud, far-carrying, resonant 'grrr-owp' or 'ah-rrrrrr-oh' associated with advertising; 'mooing', cow-like 'eu-eue-u', pre-copulatory call; 'rattling', loud harsh series of 3 notes, accelerating, copulatory call. Young emit high-pitched wheedling 'queee-eeee-peep'; 'peeping', repeated 'peee-peee-peee', usually when being fed. Chick-like calls lost after 14 weeks (Europe), then emit duck-like croak 'er-er-er'; after 17 weeks calls like adult. General observations suggest African race utter similar calls, but appear much more silent than European; good details lacking.

General Habits. Well known. In Europe prefers cool to cold waters, and in Africa found only in highland localities with cool or cold water in tropics, descending to sea level only near Cape. Absent e.g. from Lake Victoria at 1225 m, despite apparently ideal habitat. Within discontinuous range frequents larger bodies of water, not less than 5 ha, but either alkaline or fresh acceptable; e.g. now abundant Lake Nakuru (strongly alkaline) as a result of introduced fish (*Tilapia grahami*) since 1960. Preferred habitat rather large open lakes edged with reeds, *Phragmites*, papyrus, or *Typha*, but may occur on alkaline waters with open short grass shores. Both in N Africa and in E and southern Africa able to colonize areas of rising water or large seasonal ponds, breeding in numbers for a few years, then reduced, or not at all.

Roosts on water and rests on water by day, apparently not climbing onto floating vegetation except to nest. Spends most of day swimming about, resting or preening on water, diving for food, often far out in shallow lakes. Also fishes in papyrus-enclosed lily lagoons but even then seldom swims among submerged vegetation. No detailed activity studies in Africa.

Migrant in winter to N Africa in small numbers. In tropical Africa resident year-round on most haunts, but in E Africa disperses from large lakes during rains, and may temporarily occupy and breed on large seasonal ponds of more than 5 ha. Apparently can fly long distances over inhospitable terrain to locate such sites. Population apparently fluctuates, rising in favourable years of high rainfall when breeding occurs on many waters, and in larger numbers than usual, falling again in drier years when little breeding takes place (Kenya, Transvaal).

Food. Almost entirely small fish, but also water insects, crustacea and young amphibia. Vegetable matter and feathers also found in stomachs. Formerly abundant on Lake Naivasha, Kenya (where all fish are introduced except indigenous but very small *Aplocheilichthys antinorii*—not apparently eaten), has now been all but exterminated by gill-nets; but at Lake Nakuru, with no fish prior to 1960 when *Tilapia grahami* were introduced, now very abundant, occurring in hundreds together. However, on some seasonal waters used for short periods, must feed mainly on organisms other than fish, probably young amphibia. Fish all caught underwater by diving, dives lasting 15–56 s, av. *c.* 20–25 s (Cramp and Simmons 1977). Length of dive probably affected by success. Food requirement *c.* 80 g/day.

Breeding Habits. Very well known, but in Africa intricate courtship rituals observed in European *P. c. cristatus* not described. Rituals possibly less intricate as breeding plumage retained year round, but said to perform many similar displays (W. Dean, pers. comm.). In Europe territorial, also in some regular African haunts, but also breeds gregariously in dispersed or rather closely spaced colonies, especially when rapidly rising water makes new habitat available (Dean 1977). Even then territorial, birds nesting close together must approach nest underwater.

Intricate courtship rituals observed in Europe include 3 main phases:

A

(1) Pairing phase, in which antagonism displayed to others. In most common threat display, head lowered, stretched out over water, ear-tippets raised, barking or growling calls uttered; this display often observed Transvaal (W. Dean, pers. comm.). At higher intensity, neck awash, may raise wings, ruffle back feathers and dive, swimming towards adversary underwater. May also adopt 'defence-upright' position—neck erect, ear-tippets spread and crest raised (see **A**). Submission indicated by head-wagging, preening and 'cat display', wings partly opened, tippets spread, crest erected (**B**).
(2) Water-courtship, comprising 4 highly ritualized mutual ceremonies initiated by either sex. (i) Advertis-

B

C

ing: floats or swims slowly, croaking or growling, neck erect, throat distended. (ii) Discovery ceremony: 1 bird dives and swims towards other, course detectable by ripples underwater; other watches, giving 'cat display'. (iii) 1st bird then emerges near other with back to it, in 'ghostly penguin' display—upright in water with tail and lower body submerged, head and neck bent forward (**C**), then turning to face partner; both then shake heads. Never rush together across water as climax of this ceremony, as in some other grebes. Then both raise heads high and, with tippets partly closed, perform rapid head-wagging. (iv) Weed ceremony: with intense head-shaking birds withdraw, preen, move apart with necks upright, crest depressed, tippets fully spread, giving twanging calls. When well apart submerge slowly, deliberately, both collect weed underwater swim towards one another and abruptly rise vertically, face to face; feet tread rapidly, heads wag from side to side, then drop weed and head shake again. This ceremony reported Transvaal, Lake Nakuru, but often with no weed (W. Dean, pers. comm.). Water-courtship is 'engagement period' in which ♂ may feed ♀; he is distinguishable as his head is held above ♀'s in several displays.

(3) Platform-courtship follows water-courtship; pair floats in one spot, and later construct there, or near it, one or more rudimentary platforms of weeds. Either sex may then solicit on platform, extending head and kinked neck forward with plumes depressed, immobile, giving twanging calls; this sometimes followed by rearing display when suddenly stands with neck arched down, bill near floor of platform, quivering wings (displaying white patches); partner brings nest material. Copulation performed by both sexes on platform. Bird on water erects crest, expands tippets, utters 'mooing call', leaps on partner's back, copulates quickly and dismounts over partner's head. Head-wagging and shaking follows.

Although all these complex rituals have not been described in Africa, most are probably performed, including head-shaking when pairs are facing one another, threat with head lowered, cat display and, commonly, weed ceremony. Observations suggest display less concentrated and obvious than in Europe, possibly because of protracted breeding season.

P. c. infuscatus apparently nests sometimes well apart from others and singly, but often in loose colonies, sometimes very close together, so that incubating bird can only approach own nest underwater to avoid attack.

NEST: constructed of *Phragmites* reeds, bulrushes, *Typha* and other material, usually mainly soft underwater vegetation supported by a few tough stems, anchored to underwater growth; may be right in the open or in thickets of e.g. *Typha*. Platforms *c.* 45 cm diameter basally, up to 30 cm deep, with most submerged, parts above water 28–45 cm across and 4–7 cm above water. No apparent difference between African and European nests. Built by both sexes in *c.* 8 days during courtship; egg-laying soon follows. Materials vary according to those available near site and in submerged grassland nest may be made of grass (Dean 1977). Nests in flooded sedges 10–60 m apart, av. *c.* 25 m, but in flooded grassland and bulrushes 1–5 m apart, av. 2·1 m (Dean 1977). This varies locally, but observations suggest that African race is more inclined to breed colonially than European *P. c. cristatus*.

EGGS: laid alternate days; 2–7 recorded South Africa, mean (63) 3·44; Transvaal (Barberspan) mean 3·6 (1974), 3·1 (1975); Kenya mean (20) 3·2 (apparently complete clutches of 1 recorded). 7 eggs suggest 2 ♀♀ laying in same nest as suspected in Europe; 5–9 recorded Morocco, clutch of 9 definitely 2 birds (Heim de Balsac 1952). Long ovals; at first white, soon stained brown. SIZE: (41 eggs, Transvaal) 49·5–58·4 × 29·0–39·0 (54·9–36·3) (Dean 1977); (125) 47·0–57·0 × 33·0–37·8 (52·9 × 35·5); NW Africa (*cristatus*) 48–60 × 36–38 (55 × 37). WEIGHT: (73) 35·0–43·0 (38·0).

Laying dates: Tunisia–Morocco May–June; Ethiopia May–Sept (rains); Kenya all months, but peaking Apr–June, in and just after long rains; Zambia rare records indicate breeding Sept–Feb, possibly 2 laying periods; Transvaal every month, but 280/308 records Mar–July (autumn–winter); Cape Jan–Feb, Apr–June, Aug–Dec, but 181/208 records Oct–Dec (spring). In Transvaal availability of cover in summer possibly most important factor regulating laying date (Dean 1977).

Both sexes incubate; details not recorded Africa, but in Europe either may sit for from 10–490 min. Incubation begins 1st egg. Period: Europe 28–29 days each egg, Transvaal (8 records) 27–30 days, av. 29. Both sexes add material throughout incubation, and nest becomes gradually sodden, sinking unless augmented. Adults almost invariably cover eggs if suddenly disturbed, but when leaving nest of own accord to feed may not, or will only partially cover; one parent usually present anyway. ♂ does not feed ♀ on or near nest.

Young leave nest almost immediately and swim with parents. Up to day 14 are carried on back of either parent, while other brings food; thereafter carried intermittently to day 21. Feeding rate (Europe) av. 12 times/h, up to 95 recorded. Broods of more than 1 young divided after 28–42 days; thereafter each parent tends 1 chick more than other ('in' chick and 'out' chick). Young can feed themselves at 56 days and fly at 70–79 days, but favoured chick may be fed up to 91 days and all are dependent for 70 days. These details not recorded fully in Africa.

Breeding success: Europe, av. 1·4 independent young/brood. In Africa broods reduces to av. 2·1 by 21 days, 1·9 by 28–56 days, 1·5 by 63 days, *c*. 1·5 young independent from av. clutches of 3·3, varying from year to year (Dean 1977). Allowing for failed nests, true breeding success to independence is *c*. 0·74–0·84/nesting attempt, *c*. 50% that in Europe. Kenya broods usually reduced from 3 to 1 or none near independence. In some areas young remain on same lake as adults (Lake Nakuru) but in others disperse after breeding completed, leaving some adults resident (Dean 1977). Young retain a stripy appearance until adult plumage assumed, crest appearing first, then neck-ruff (W. Dean, pers. comm.).

References
Cramp, S. and Simmons, K. E. L. (1977).
Dean, W. R. J. (1977).
Simmons, K. E. L. (1975).

Podiceps nigricollis Brehm. Black-necked Grebe; Eared Grebe. Grèbe à cou noir.

Podiceps nigricollis Brehm, 1831. Handb. Naturg. Vog. Deutschl. p. 963; Germany.

Plate 6

(Opp. p. 83)

Range and Status. Throughout Africa in suitable aquatic habitat. Distribution discontinuous, requiring highly productive waters, eutrophic, saline or alkaline, e.g. sewage lagoons. Not definitely recorded in many countries. Where it occurs, may not be permanent resident but seasonal or nomadic visitor. Usually scarcest of African grebes, but locally common, abundant, even very abundant. Probably no marked recent population changes, but may have increased slightly through man-made aquatic habitats.

Podiceps nigricollis

Description. *P. n. nigricollis* Brehm, ADULT ♂ (breeding): forehead, crown, neck, mantle and scapulars black, less intense on mantle; back dark brown, centre of rump and tuft on upper tail feathers black; tail below brownish. A patch of long, silky, bright golden feathers extends from below and behind eye through ear-coverts. Chin, throat jet black; upper breast mottled white and chestnut; sides of breast, flanks chestnut, mottled black and grey. Lower breast and belly pure silky white, feathers round vent pale brown, down-like. Primaries brown with black shafts, secondaries white, tipped more or less black, innermost black; upperwing-coverts dark brown, primary coverts grey, underwing-coverts white. Bill greyish black, sharp, slightly upturned; eye bright red with orange-brown ring; feet black externally, lighter, greenish or bluish below and on toes. ADULT ♂ (non-breeding): (plumage most often seen) generally paler, duller. Above greyish black, ear-coverts grey. Chin, throat white, a white half-collar almost encircling hindneck, lower throat and foreneck grey, rest of underparts white. Tail and wing as in breeding plumage. Bill paler; foot brown, grey-green to grey-blue inside. Sexes alike, ♀ slightly smaller. SIZE: wing, ♂ 127–139 (134), ♀ 124–136 (130), tarsus, ♂ 40–45 (43), ♀ 39–45 (42). WEIGHT: breeding ♂ 265–402, ♀ 231–298; non-breeding ♂ 366–450, ♀ 280; apparently fatter in non-breeding season (Cramp and Simmons 1977); 1 African specimen 298 (Skead 1977b).

IMMATURE: resembles non-breeding adult, but browner, generally paler, tinged olive above; sides of head mottled, upper neck tinged buff, flanks pale grey. By 1st year resembles non-breeding adult.

DOWNY YOUNG: above, brownish black invariably streaked paler; darker than other *Podiceps* spp. Crown black; sides of face striped black and white. A bare spot in centre of crown and lores bright pink to scarlet; bill pale flesh; eye brown; feet grey.

Field Characters. A small, round-bodied grebe with long thin neck; in Africa can only be confused with Little Grebe *Tachybaptus ruficollis*. Small square head, red eye, slim, pointed, straight bill, angled slightly upwards diagnostic. In breeding dress black head, neck and upperparts, with golden ear-tufts diagnostic. In non-breeding plumage much paler than Little Grebe, floats higher in water, displays much more white underside; slim neck, red eye, upturned straight bill diagnostic in any plumage. In NW Africa might be confused with very rare vagrant Slavonian Grebe *P. auritus*, but is smaller, has grey cheeks and shows less white underside. Downy young distinguished from those of Little Grebe by bare red patch on crown, and from Great Crested Grebe *P. cristatus* by generally dark back.

Voice. Not recorded; not well described in Africa. Normally silent except when breeding. Display trill then characteristic, audible at long range, clear mellow whistling 'bidder-widder-widder-widder-widder' or 'bi-devi-deidevide'. Copulation trill, intense, eerie, 'sih-sih-sih-si-si-urrrr'. Inviting call a low rapid 'goah'. Advertising call a whistled 'poo-eee' and 'click (chk)' audible only at close range; threat, a loud prolonged chittering; alarm 'whit' repeated 2–3 times; food call of young whimpering 'pie-eee' (Cramp and Simmons 1977); calls in Africa may be similar.

General Habits. Little known in Africa. Irregular, sometimes temporary, distribution, occurring on alkaline and freshwater lakes, sewage farm ponds; also on sea in NW Africa and at Walvis Bay. Often overlooked among more abundant Little Grebes. Has bred in

Kenya, South Africa, but largely unobserved in most of continent. Formerly bred in Tunisia, but no recent records; now mainly or entirely migrant to NW Africa.

Generally gregarious, usually observed in flocks outside breeding season; huge winter flocks recorded elsewhere seldom observed in Africa but seen at sea, Walvis Bay (W. R. Siegfried, pers. comm.). Behaviour little observed except when breeding, but e.g. at Lake Naivasha remains far out in centre of lake, seldom approaching shore; if typical this could explain why seldom seen near shores. Flocks spread over water in open pattern, often with Little Grebes in similar formation, species not segregated. Roosts on water at night, seldom entering thick cover, even by day, but may occur in lagoons sheltered by papyrus from open water. Flocks often identifiable by habit of resting and preening on side with white belly exposed and conspicuous (W. R. Siegfried, pers. comm.).

Feeds mainly as other grebes, diving to catch underwater organisms, duration of dives 9–50 s, av. *c.* 23–25 s. Feeds mainly by day. Also skims surface organisms off water with lateral movements of short, flattened bill. Ability to feed on surface organisms may enable it to live far out in open waters normally avoided by Little Grebe.

Movements within Africa not understood. NW Africa population now apparently entirely composed of small numbers of winter migrants. In South Africa some probably permanent residents, mainly summer breeding migrants, wintering localities unknown. Near equator (E Africa) occurrences irregular, no discernible pattern.

Food. Not detailed in Africa; includes small fish, aquatic insects and larvae, crustaceans, molluscs. Invertebrates probably more often taken than fish. Most stomachs contain feathers; in Europe only 7·6% contain fish (Cramp and Simmons 1977). Catches flying insects above surface.

Breeding Habits. Well known. Breeds in colonies, often in inaccessible sites in open water, but sometimes close to shore.

In Europe pair-formation occurs in flocks before breeding site is reached. Threat displays to rivals then include 'forward-threat' with neck arched, head above water, not stretched out or awash (see **A**); breast to breast fighting occurs. In water-courtship, performed by both sexes, pairs call in distinctive posture, heads up, crests raised. Nuptial displays include 'ghostly penguin' with body upright, tail and rump submerged, head stretched laterally forward; 'cat display' with

A

lowered head, crest erected, wings raised above back; 'mutual penguin dance' in which pair rise out of water facing each other, crests raised, breasts often touching (**B**). May then rush side by side over water in upright position (**C**); such mutual rushes more frequent in later stages. No food presentation ceremonies, or weed presentation or carrying observed (unlike most other grebes) (Cramp and Simmons 1977). Displays not fully described in Africa, but in early courtship pair face each other, shaking heads horizontally, then lower heads first to one side then the other. Then glide across water side by side, heads raised, white breasts showing; apparently resembles water-courtship, Europe (Clarke 1977).

B

C

Once site is selected, 1 or several platforms built, platform-courtship follows. This includes inviting, rearing with wings quivering, followed by copulation; either sex may invite or mount the other. Mounting preceded by copulation trill calls from active bird. True mating occurs some days before egg-laying.

NEST: built in open water but not free-floating, attached to some underwater growth; in 1 colony (Strandfontein Sewage Works: Broekhuysen and Frost 1968a), nests were attached to bushes, resulting in severe losses from fluctuating water level. Vary from slight structures of rushes, with algae and weeds on top, to quite substantial structures up to 0·5 m thick. This situation (Strandfontein) possibly abnormal as most nests were close to banks. More typical nests mere mounds of algae and other soft weed *c.* 15–20 cm across, based on underwater growth or e.g. submerged termite heap; nest cup barely above water level. Constructed by both sexes, taking normally less than 7 days, egg-laying following soon after construction. Material added throughout incubation.

EGGS: laid usually before midday, on consecutive days or at up to 72 h intervals; 1 record of 2 laid in same day. Complete clutches 1–7 recorded, mean (156) 3·62; excluding all clutches of 1–2 (125) 4·03 (SAOSNRC); 1–6, mean (27) 3·59 (Broekhuysen and Frost 1968b). SIZE: (84) 33·5–46·6 × 22·0–30·9 (37·8 × 25·5) (SAOSNRC); (246) 37·3–49·2 × 29·6–33·4 (43·49 × 29·45) (Broekhuysen and Frost 1968b). WEIGHT: *c*. 21 g; clutch of 4 *c*. 80 g, 25–30% of ♀ bodyweight.

Laying dates: Cape Oct–Jan, some in June, some Aug, peak Nov (12/31 SAOSNRC records); Transvaal Feb–June, peaking strongly Mar–Apr (138/158 records); E Kenya May–Aug, with peak June, at end of long rains.

Both sexes incubate; share uncertain. When leaving eggs less inclined to cover than other grebes, 24% completely, 37% partly, 39% uncovered; covering more thorough as incubation progresses. Incubation period: 20–22 days, av. 21 (as in European birds) (Broekhuysen and Frost 1968a).

All South African observations, Cape Province, indicate very poor breeding success, early losses probably stimulating re-laying in some pairs. At Strandfontein, eggs laid before 25 Sept in 16 nests; 29–30 Sept in 14 nests; after 11 Oct in 30 nests (Broekhuysen and Frost 1968a); Transvaal—no data. Such poor success (0–5%) probably abnormal, Kenya broods appear average on few records. In SW Cape broods 2–4 seen with parents (Brown and Morris 1960).

Young leave nest at once, are carried and fed by both parents. No details available for Africa; in Europe not fully recorded either, said to be independent of parental aid by 21 days (unlikely) (Cramp and Simmons 1977).

References
Broekhuysen, G. J. and Frost, P. G. H. (1968a, b).

2 other grebes exceptionally and rarely recorded winter vagrants NW Africa (not illustrated). They are:

Podiceps grisegena (Boddaert). Red-necked Grebe. Grèbe jougris.

Resembles Great Crested Grebe, *P. cristatus* but slightly smaller, stockier-looking, shorter-necked. In winter lacks white streak from bill to above eye, black of crown descending to eye level. Bill shorter, more conical, blackish at tip, basally yellow, not mainly yellow-orange. Eye brown, not red.

Podiceps auritus (Linnaeus). Slavonian Grebe; Horned Grebe. Grèbe esclavon.

Not illustrated

Slightly larger than Black-necked Grebe *Podiceps ruficollis*. In winter plumage very similar but adult and immature generally whiter, with white collar extending round hindneck, pure white cheeks below eye with no grey, small grey patch in front of eye; white lower cheek diagnostic.

Order
PELECANIFORMES

Large to very large, or enormous water birds, including some of the largest flying species (pelicans). Cosmopolitan, but most varied in the tropics, 2 families also temperate, even arctic. The Order is extremely varied, some of the different families appearing to be scarcely related to one another. However, all are large birds, feeding mainly on fish, with the common characteristic of all 4 toes being webbed (totipalmate). The very large webbed foot is also used to spread over the egg in incubation.

Considered by Sibley (1960) to be polyphyletic, the Order now contains 2 suborders: Phaethontes, including the Phaethontidae, tropicbirds; and Pelecani, including the Fregatidae, frigatebirds; Phalacrocoracidae, cormorants; Anhingidae, darters; Sulidae, gannets and boobies; and Pelecanidae, pelicans. The family Anhingidae has been regarded by Dorst and Mougin (1979) as a subfamily of the Phalacrocoracidae, but in view of its anatomical peculiarities we do not consider this sound, and have given our reasons under the family heading.

The Phaethontidae, Sulidae and Fregatidae are entirely marine or oceanic; Phalacrocoracidae are mainly marine, with some species common on fresh water; Pelecanidae mainly occur on fresh or brackish inland waters, with some marine spp.; and Anhingidae are basically inhabitants of fresh or brackish water, seldom marine. Large, conspicuous and often abundant, the Order includes some of the best known families and species in the world.

Suborder PHAETHONTES

Family PHAETHONTIDAE: tropicbirds

Large, mainly white, very beautiful seabirds; all tropical seas, mainly oceanic. Differ from all other Pelecaniform families in laying eggs without chalky covering; young downy at hatching, not naked; young seldom or never take food direct from parental gullet, but are fed by adult putting bill into chick's open beak. Possibly most closely related to Sulidae.

Bill stout, slightly decurved, pointed, edges in adults serrated; body rather stout; wings short, pointed, strong, beaten rapidly in flight; legs very short, can scarcely walk on land; tail moderately long, slightly wedge-shaped, the 2 central feathers prolonged into very long flexible white or red streamers (these may have a lateral stabilizing function in dives, but are also used in nuptial display). 1 genus, *Phaethon* Linnaeus, with 3 species. 1 (*P. rubricauda*) mainly Pacific; 1 (*P. lepturus*) pantropical; and 1 (*P. aethereus*) mainly Atlantic, but also found in Red Sea. Where 2 species breed together, *P. lepturus* is found with one or the other larger species, whose ranges are distinct.

Tropical birds seldom appear near mainland coasts and have not been studied within our limits. However, *P. aethereus* breeds on islands in the Red Sea, and *P. lepturus* on islands in the Gulf of Guinea and off the mouth of the Senegal River. The habits of all 3 are very similar. Breeding behaviour is briefly summarized in our accounts as a guide to stages of development for anyone visiting islands hitherto largely unexplored, e.g. in the Red Sea.

For general accounts of biology see Diamond (1975) and Stonehouse (1962).

Genus *Phaethon* Linnaeus

Plate 7

(Opp. p. 98)

Phaethon aethereus Linnaeus. Red-billed Tropicbird. Grand Phaéton.

Phaethon aethereus Linnaeus, 1758. Syst. Nat. (10th ed.), p. 134; tropical seas (Ascension).

Range and Status. Tropical Atlantic and E Pacific, NW Indian Ocean and Red Sea. Breeds on Ascension Island, Cape Verdes, Isles Madeleine off mouth of Senegal River and on islets in Red Sea. Has straggled north to Cape Spartel. Locally common to abundant at breeding grounds, rarely seen in open oceans.

Description. *P. a. indicus* (Hume): Red Sea and Gulf of Aden. ADULT ♂: mainly white; head white, feathers of crown basically black; a black streak from nape to eye curving downward to base of bill. Back, inner wing-coverts and rump white, with wavy black bars; outer wing-coverts white. Primaries black on outer webs, inner webs partly white; secondaries

black, tipped white; tertials black. Underside pure white. Tail white, central tail streamers white. Bill red; eye black; legs and toes yellow, webs black. Sexes alike. SIZE: wing, 267–293; tail, 189–242; central tail streamers, up to 550–555 (50% total length); wing-span, 852–880.

IMMATURE: lacks long adult tail streamers and has more black markings, otherwise similar, but bill pale green, not red (North 1946).

DOWNY YOUNG: white.

P. a. aethereus Linnaeus: Atlantic Ocean. Similar, somewhat larger. SIZE: wing, 305–315, central tail feathers, up to 600. WEIGHT: 650–700.

P. a. indicus has sometimes been considered a separate species *P. indicus*, but this is incorrect on present evidence.

94

Field Characters. Exquisitely beautiful seabirds of open seas, visiting island cliffs only to breed. At sea seen normally in small groups or singly, flying 10–30 m above water with quick, pigeon-like beats of wings. Behaviour something between tern and gannet, more like tern.

Distinguishable from White-tailed Tropicbird *P. lepturus* by its red bill, much larger size, more black on wing; from adult Red-tailed Tropicbird *P. rubricauda* by its white tail streamers and much more black in plumage. Immature distinguishable from that of Red-tailed by lack of tail streamers, pale green bill and larger size. The darkest, most heavily marked tropicbird.

Voice. Not recorded. Loud, harsh screams, described (*P. a. indicus*) as shrill piercing 'pirr-tati-tati-hay-hay-hay'; young 'ki-yi-ki-yi' (North 1946). Vocal near breeding grounds, mainly silent at sea. Downy young disturbed at nest emit extremely loud piercing rasping or reeling shriek, maintained for minutes on end.

General Habits. Well known. Like others, a bird of open blue water, seldom approaching shore except to breed. Feeds far out to sea, circling over water and diving to catch fish; may hover briefly before diving. Alternatively, swoops low over water, flattening out as if pursuing something seen below, then snatches from surface. Flying fish possibly caught in flight. Normally flies with quick wing-beats, seldom gliding or soaring. Tail streamers believed to function as lateral stabilizers in vertical plunge-dives (Stonehouse 1962). Except on breeding islands must roost on open water, but little recorded; when on water swims rather low.

Food. Fish, squid; in Atlantic flying fish especially, up to 25 cm long. Fish predominates, but diet varies locally; squid may be more important in Indian Ocean.

Breeding Habits. Scarcely known in our area; elsewhere intimately studied. Breeds mainly in holes and crannies in rocky cliffs, rarely (W Indies) amongst dense vegetation, never far inland. Sexual cycle (Ascension) 11 months if successful; moult completed at sea between cycles.

Near breeding colonies groups of 2–20 adults circle over sea calling loudly and excitedly. 2–3 break off from group and glide down to water, wings held stiffly below horizontal, tail streamers curving down. At Cape Verdes said to collect in flocks towards sunset and perform communal displays, wheeling high and calling excitedly. Nuptial display flights resemble other spp. with minor variations. Tail streamers may not be primarily nuptial plumes, but have a display function. After display, pairs go to nest cavity where ♂ mounts ♀; when copulation complete, both leave returning to sea.

EGGS: invariably 1, laid any time of day. Broad ovals, pale fawn to rich purplish brown, coated with water-soluble pigment rubbed off between poles. SIZE: (245 eggs, Ascension) 54·8–74·9 × 33·4–50·0 (45·2 × 64·5). Red Sea eggs (*P. a. indicus*) apparently differ, being clay-colour, rose or purple, darker at broad end, scrawled and dotted dark brown or black, sometimes forming a cap; SIZE: 53–64 × 34–48; no recent data. WEIGHT: 59–68, *c.* 9% of ♀ bodyweight.

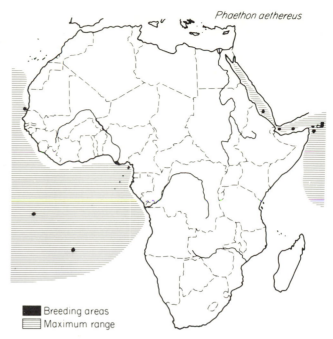

Phaethon aethereus

■ Breeding areas
▨ Maximum range

Laying dates: breeds year-round at Ascension, peaking Aug; in Red Sea little known, lays June on Dahlac Island, Mait Island. Few definite records but season in most breeding areas prolonged. Failure may result in re-laying (uncommon) 6–16 weeks after 1st egg.

Both sexes incubate in alternating periods of 6 days or more. Incubation period: 42–43 days.

Chick when hatched is covered with greyish down, tips of scapulars appear about day 13, secondaries day 22, primaries day 27, rectrices days 30–35, breast feathers days 23–24. Down shed 40–55 days, thereafter feathered. Increase in weight from 50 (days 1–5) to 190 (11–15 days) and maximum of 760–780 at 61–80 days, thereafter becoming lighter before 1st flight. Flies at 83–90 days and can at once fly strongly. Longest recorded fledging period, 110 days.

One or other parent stays in nest with chick all day and night when first hatched; attention time reduced from 82% in days 1–5 to 25% days 41–50, and then 21% up to day 60; thereafter parent on nest less than 10% of daylight. When disturbed, both reach forward and utter high-pitched raucous shriek. Young make 1st flight alone and leave islands at once; do not reappear until mature. Are fed by either parent at intervals of *c.* 1·5 days, mainly on fish; size of food brought increases with age of chicks; may be choked by fish too large to swallow. Parents do not fish near breeding islands.

At Ascension 169/345 eggs produced flying chicks in 18 months (51·5% of eggs laid); *c.* 30% of eggs were lost. Most chicks lost when small (less than 14 days old); few lost after day 40. Mortality not connected with food shortage, mainly due to fighting for nesting sites either with own species or *P. lepturus* (Ascension). Survival rate unknown thereafter. After chick flies, adults complete post-nuptial moult, begun before chick leaves; duration 19–29 weeks. Same individuals often repair and occupy same nest-site in successive cycles.

References
North, M. E. W. (1946).
Stonehouse, B. (1962).

Plate 7

(Opp. p. 98)

Phaethon rubricauda. Red-tailed Tropicbird. Phaéton à brins rouges.

Phaethon rubricauda Boddaert, 1785. Table Planches, Enlum., p. 57; Mauritius.

Range and Status. Indo-Pacific, not Atlantic; strictly oceanic, not breeding nearer Africa than Aldabra.

Description. ADULT ♂: pink-white, except for small black eye-streak, a few black markings near tops of primaries. Tail streamers red. Bill red; eye blackish; feet reddish with black webs. SIZE: wing, 310–358 (336); tail, 98–111 (102) (streamers to 370 beyond longest of other tail feathers); tarsus, 28–30 (29) (D. Snow, pers. comm.). WEIGHT: mean (18) 762.
IMMATURE: plumage has more black than adult.
DOWNY CHICK: white.

Phaethon rubricauda

■ Breeding areas
▭ Maximum range

Field Characters. The whitest, most spectacular of tropic birds, with red tail streamers and red bill. As large as Red-billed *P. aethereus* and much heavier than White-tailed *P. lepturus*. Almost pure white plumage and red tail streamers diagnostic.

Voice. Recorded (30). At sea silent; at breeding colonies a harsh disyllabic 'kell-eck'. Chicks utter piercing raucous scream when disturbed for minutes on end, and when begging continuous reeling call resembling Grasshopper Warbler *Locustella naevia*.

General Habits. Well known. Most oceanic of the genus; fishes far from land, probably further from shore than other species. Like others, seen in small groups or singly, diving or swooping to water to pick up surface organisms. Takes much larger fish and fewer squid than White-tailed Tropicbird (up to 330 mm long).

Food. Fish, especially flying fish, and squid.

References
Diamond, A. W. (1975).

Plate 7

(Opp. p. 98)

Phaethon lepturus Daudin. White-tailed Tropicbird. Petit Phaéton.

Phaeton lepturus Daudin, 1802. In Buffon's, Hist. Nat. (Didot) Quardr. 14. p. 319; Mauritius.

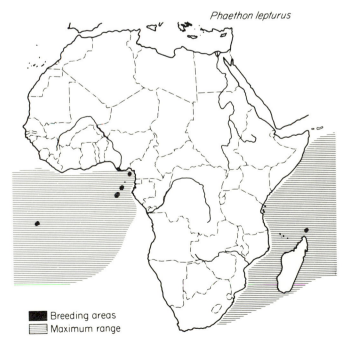

Phaethon lepturus

■ Breeding areas
▭ Maximum range

Range and Status. Oceanic, pantropical, including parts of Atlantic and Indian Oceans. Breeds Seychelles, Aldabra, not near E African coast. In Atlantic, Ascension, Cape Verdes and islets in Gulf of Guinea (at least formerly). Generally common to abundant near breeding islands, seldom seen at sea.

Description. *P. l. lepturus*: Indian Ocean. ADULT ♂: mainly white, sometimes tinged pink; a black streak through eye. Whole body above and below white, except long flank feathers streaked black. Wings white, outer primaries tipped black on outer webs. Median wing-coverts, inner secondaries and scapulars broadly tipped black, forming a broad black bar on inner wing. Rump, tail-coverts white, long white central tail streamers with black shafts. Bill yellow; eye black; feet mainly black, yellowish at base. Sexes alike. SIZE: wing, mean (chord) 337; tail, *c.* 180 (streamers to *c.* 850); tarsus, 20–22. WEIGHT: mean (59) 334.
DOWNY YOUNG: white, or greyish white.
P. l. ascensionis (Mathews): Atlantic Ocean. Slightly smaller. SIZE: wing, 253–265; WEIGHT: *c.* 320. Markedly sexually dimorphic, ♂♂ usually pink with intense yellow beaks, ♀♀

white with greyish beaks, but some pinkish. Fledged young has head densely mottled black, feathers of back white with 1–2 blackish bars (cf. 4–5 narrow black bars in Red-billed Tropicbird *P. aethereus*).

Field Characters. The smallest, most graceful tropic bird with most buoyant flight; tends to glide more than others. Much lighter, but not obviously smaller than others, except when seen together. Distinguished from adult Red-billed Tropicbird *P. aethereus* by yellow bill, much less black barring in plumage, but deep black inner wing bar. Distinguished from Red-tailed Tropicbird *P. rubricauda* by yellow bill, being much more black in plumage and having white, not red, tail streamers.

Voice. Not recorded. A harsh chatter, resembling calls of Red-tailed Tropicbird, but faster, more prolonged and higher-pitched 'kirrick-kirrick-kirrick'. Chicks when begging emit continuous reeling call, reminiscent of Grasshopper Warbler *Locustella naevia* or fishing reel; in alarm harsh raucous screams. Adults feeding young emit low 'chuck'. Silent except at breeding colonies, not very vocal even there (A. W. Diamond, pers. comm.).

General Habits. Well known. Fishes far from land but possibly nearer shore than larger species. Seen at sea singly or in small groups, circling over water, plunge-diving or swooping low to snatch something from surface; perhaps takes flying fish in flight. Little recorded far from breeding colonies.

Food. Fish and squid. At Ascension, mainly fish, especially flying fish 10–20 cm long; some squid. At Aldabra, fish 42% by number, but only 15% by weight; squid more important, 58·8% by number, 84·8% by weight. Diet varies locally, but prey taken is always smaller than in Red-billed or Red-tailed Tropicbird, thus reducing competition through overlap in prey.

Breeding Habits. Intimately known outside our limits. Successful cycles at Ascension vary from 251–335 days, mean (65 cycles) 268 days, but always less than 1 year. Adult post-nuptial moult is completed at sea between fledging of chick and return to breeding site.

Adults return to breeding islets 2–5 weeks before return to nest–site. New arrivals make brief visits, any time of day. Courtship includes flying in groups of 5–6 with others, calling. Rapid wing-beats alternate with long downward glides with wings rigid, tail streamers bent downward. 1 then flies into nest cavity, where joined by 2–3 others, 1 ♂ successful as mate. Adjacent cavities sometimes occupied simultaneously. Copulate in nest cavity; act brief, infrequent, ending with both birds flying away for hours; occurs up to 1 week before laying. ♀ may stay in nest several days before laying, sometimes with ♂.

NEST: in cavities, holes under rocks and, on Indian Ocean islands, on ground among tree buttresses, vegetation, even far from sea among masses of ferns or in holes in trees. Where 2 species breed together, intense competition favours larger (e.g. Red-billed Tropicbird, Ascension), but this species can use smaller cavities thus reducing competition with e.g. Red-tailed Tropicbird, Aldabra. In dense populations intense intra-specific fighting for available nest cavities occurs.

EGGS: invariably 1, laid any time of day. Broad ovals, pale fawn to rich purplish brown, coated with water-soluble pigment rubbed off in incubation between poles. SIZE: (811 eggs, Ascension) 46·4–62·2 × 33·9–41·3 (38·0 × 54·0); (Aldabra mean) 53·2 × 39·0. WEIGHT: (Ascension) *c.* 43; (Aldabra) 43·4 (10–13% of ♀ body-weight).

♂ begins incubating as soon as egg is laid, sometimes while still wet; thereafter either sex incubates in spells of 3–6 days, ♂ more often than ♀ (Ascension, 56% of total period). Incubation period: 41 days; either parent may be present at hatch, which takes *c.* 48 h.

Chick clad in silky greyish white down; eyes always closed. Weight at hatching 30, increasing to 125–180 by 16–20 days, reaching maximum 400 at 60 days, thereafter decreasing to 330 at 70–80 days. Aldabra chicks attain 121% of adult bodyweight before fledging. Scapulars appear day 11, secondaries day 17, primaries days 18–20, tail feathers days 26–28; down shed days 30–60, then largely feathered. 1st flight 71–80 days. Exercises wings freely before 1st flight and can fly strongly immediately; if not, may be caught and killed by e.g. frigatebirds (Stonehouse 1962).

Adults give 1st feed within 12–16 h. Parental attention is rapidly reduced from 72% in days 1–5 to 17% days 21–30, thereafter less than 10%. Chicks left alone suffer heavy mortality from competing adults of own or other species. Both parents feed chicks on fish and squid *c.* every 1·5 days. Smaller items in early feeds, 30–50 g at day 11–20. In this species chick may take food direct from parental crop (Ascension: Stonehouse 1962) thus resembling most Pelecaniformes.

Nest losses variable, often heavy. Of 821 eggs (Ascension), 426 lost as eggs (51·9%), 146 as chicks (17·8%) and 249 (30·3%) flew. Aldabra (overall success) 47·5% of eggs laid fledged chicks. Most chicks lost in first 14 days, usually through competition with adults of this species or Red-billed Tropicbird for nest space. Protracted breeding season with no marked peaks may favour higher fledging success when larger co-existing species not breeding. Re-laying in 10–12% of all cases may follow loss of egg or chick, at intervals of 24–79 days, depending on stage of loss of egg or chick. If 2nd egg or chick is lost, parents abandon breeding ground.

Adults begin post-nuptial moult when still feeding chicks and complete it at sea, returning in full plumage for new breeding cycle. Chicks not seen again until mature.

References
Diamond, A. W. (1975).
Stonehouse, B. (1962).

Suborder PELECANI

Family SULIDAE: gannets and boobies

Robust, thick-necked marine birds with cigar-shaped bodies; stout conical bills, not obviously hooked, cutting edge serrated, nostrils closed, facial and gular skin bare, especially in boobies; wedge-shaped tails with 12–16 pointed feathers; long, narrow, pointed wings with 10 functional primaries, 9th or 10th longest, *c.* 28 secondaries; short legs, fully webbed feet. Adult plumage predominantly black to dark brown and white, immature plumage markedly variable; sexes similar.

Boobies, smaller than gannets, are predominantly pantropical, breed mostly on islands, nest on ground, some species on cliffs or in trees. Most food obtained by plunge-diving, impact cushioned by special air-sac system beneath breast and abdomen skin, fish caught under water. Gannets occur predominantly in temperate waters; cliff or ground nesters on off-shore islands and headlands. 1st year gannets migrate to tropics, adults mostly sedentary in southern species, nomadic in northern.

Adult social displays well-developed; monogamous, form long-term pair-bonds maintained at nest-sites, which are strongly defended in colonies. Clutches have 1–2 eggs, rarely 3 or 4, incubated, as in other Pelecaniformes, beneath highly vascular feet. At sea often gregarious, flying long distances to fish shoals. Boobies return to roosting islands, gannets mostly roost at sea. 1 genus, 9 species, 5 occurring in African waters, of which 3 breed.

in
0 ──────── 12
0 ──────── 30
cm

Scale applies to all flying birds (except No. 2)

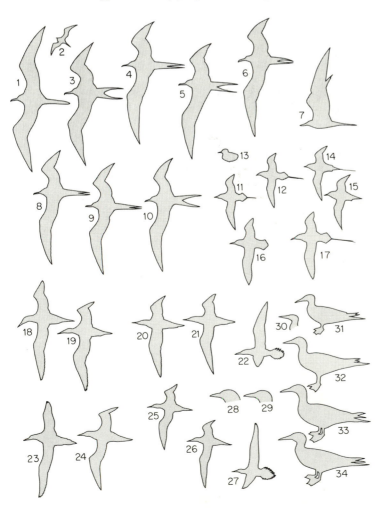

Plate 7

Fregata magnificens Magnificent Frigatebird (p. 129)
1. ADULT ♂, 2. in flight displaying red gular pouch, 3. ADULT ♀, 4. IMMATURE.

Fregata minor Greater Frigatebird (p. 130)
5. ADULT ♂, 6. ADULT ♀, 7. IMMATURE.

Fregata ariel Lesser Frigatebird (p. 131)
8. ADULT ♂, 9. ADULT ♀, 10. IMMATURE.

Phaethon aethereus Red-billed Tropicbird (p. 94)
Race *indicus*: 11. IMMATURE, 12. ADULT, 13. DOWNY YOUNG.

Phaethon lepturus White-tailed Tropicbird (p. 96)
14. ADULT, 15. IMMATURE.

Phaethon rubricauda Red-tailed Tropicbird (p. 96)
16. IMMATURE, 17. ADULT.

Sula bassana Northern Gannet (p. 99)
18. ADULT, 19. EARLY IMMATURE.

Sula dactylatra Masked Booby (p. 103)
20. ADULT, 21. IMMATURE (above), 22. IMMATURE (below).

Sula capensis Cape Gannet (p. 100)
23. ADULT, 24. EARLY IMMATURE.

Sula leucogaster Brown Booby (p. 106)
25. ADULT (above), 26. ADULT (below), 27. with tail spread.

Heads: 28. *S. leucogaster* (DOWNY YOUNG).
29. *S. dactylatra* (DOWNY YOUNG).
30. *S. leucogaster* (ADULT ♀).

Standing birds: 31. *S. leucogaster* (ADULT ♂).
32. *S. dactylatra* (ADULT). 33. *S. capensis* (ADULT).
34. *S. bassana* (ADULT).

Genus *Sula* Brisson

Although some authorities regard *Sula* as being applicable only to boobies (6 spp.) and use *Morus* for gannets (3 spp.), we have included both gannets and boobies in *Sula*. Of the 6 booby spp., 3 are known to occur in African waters, *S. sula*, *S. leucogaster* and *S. dactylatra*, the first as a non-breeding visitor, and the other 2 as breeding residents. Of the 3 gannet species, 2, *S. bassana* and *S. capensis*, occur in African waters, the last-named as an endemic breeding resident.

Sula bassana (Linnaeus). Northern Gannet; North Atlantic Gannet. Fou de Bassan.

Pelecanus Bassanus Linnaeus, 1785. Syst. Nat. (10th ed.), p. 133; Scotland.

Plate 7

(Opp. p. 98)

Range and Status. N Atlantic, breeding north of 48°N. Dispersal Nov–Mar generally southerly, occurring as non-breeding visitor W Africa where numerous on continental shelf to 10°N, largely 1st years, some remaining until 2nd year, small numbers to Mediterranean same period.

Description. ADULT ♂: body plumage thick, quilt-like. Entire head yellow-buff, paler on forehead and chin, deepest on crown, fading on upper neck and lower nape; rest of plumage white except for black primaries. Bill bluish white with black dividing lines on cutting edge, culmen and base running into black skin on lores, around eyes, malar and long gular streak; eye pale blue-grey; eye-ring cobalt blue; legs and fully webbed feet grey-black, toe-ridges greenish, tending to yellowish. Sexes alike except that toe-ridges in ♀ tending to bluish, ♂ larger. SIZE: wing, ♂ (23 specimens) 460–515 (491), ♀ (23) 460–520 (485); tail, ♂ 210–250 (223), ♀ 210–240 (220); culmen, ♂ 95–103 (99·3), ♀ 92–101 (97·4); tarsus, ♂ 58–64 (60·2), ♀ 58–64 (60·3); toe, ♂ 100–110 (106), ♀ 100–114 (104); length, 87–100 cm; wing-span, 170–180 cm. WEIGHT: ♂ (27, breeding) av. 2932, ♀ (27, breeding) av. 3067.

Plate 8

Phalacrocorax carbo Great Cormorant (p. 108)
Race *maroccanus*: 1. ADULT.
Race *lucidus*: 2. IMMATURE, 3. ADULT ♂ head (non-breeding), 4. ADULT ♀ head (breeding), 5. ADULT.

Phalacrocorax nigrogularis Socotra Cormorant (p. 111)
6. IMMATURE, 7. ADULT.

Phalacrocorax capensis Cape Cormorant (p. 112)
8. IMMATURE, 9. ADULT, 10. ADULT head (breeding), 11. IMMATURE head.

Phalacrocorax aristotelis Shag (p. 115)
12. ADULT, 13. ADULT head (breeding), 14. IMMATURE.

Phalacrocorax neglectus Bank Cormorant (p. 114)
15. ADULT, 16. ADULT head (breeding).

Phalacrocorax pygmaeus Pygmy Cormorant (p. 116)
17. IMMATURE, 18. ADULT, 19. ADULT head.

Phalacrocorax africanus Long-tailed Cormorant (p. 117)
20. IMMATURE, 21. ADULT head with breeding crest, 22. ADULT (breeding), 23. ADULT head (non-breeding).

Phalacrocorax coronatus Crowned Cormorant (p. 118)
24. ADULT head (non-breeding), 25. ADULT (breeding), 26. IMMATURE.

Scapular feather tips: 27. *P. coronatus*.
28. *P. africanus*.

Anhinga melanogaster Darter (p. 120)
29. DOWNY YOUNG, 30. IMMATURE, 31. ADULT ♀, 32. ADULT ♂.

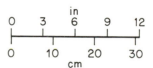

Scale does not apply to head or feather details

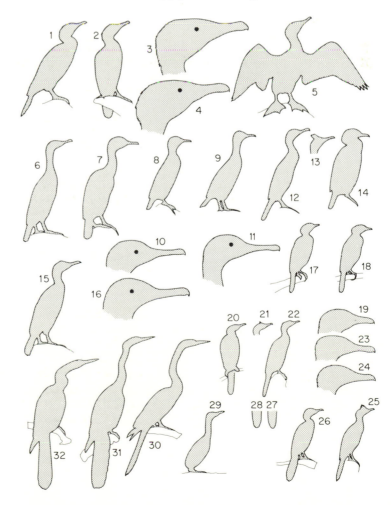

Sula bassana

IMMATURE: entirely blackish brown speckled white, darker on primaries, lesser wing-coverts and tail; bill dark horn-brown; bare facial skin brown; eye grey-brown; legs and feet brownish black. SIZE: wing, ♂ 474, ♀ 479. WEIGHT: at fledging 3650. Immature plumage during 4 years to full adulthood complicated and confusing, lower body increasingly invaded by white, then head, neck, breast and wing-coverts, lastly secondaries and tail, but great variation in age groups due to variable progress of moults. Head shows yellow by 3rd year, when underparts predominantly white; adult bill colour attained by late 2nd or 3rd year (Nelson 1964).

Field Characters. Sleek, predominantly white seabird with yellowish head, stout conical bill and pointed tail, wings narrow, stiff and centrally placed on body, primaries black. Wing-beats fast (3/s), shallow. Larger than boobies, yellow head diagnostic.

Adults distinguished from Cape Gannet *S. capensis* by shorter black streak down throat, white secondaries and tail; immatures not easily distinguishable from Cape Gannet, showing variable degrees of dark plumage, often with white belly. Probably impossible to distinguish two at sea.

Voice. Recorded (1a, 2a). Mostly silent at sea but a rapid, excited 'urrah' when competing for food.

General Habits. Very well known. Usually occurs off-shore in vicinity of fish shoals or fishing boats. Not highly gregarious at these times but numbers aggregate at food source, probably attracted by plunge-diving of others. Roosts at sea in African waters. Sometimes fly in long line or float in groups, especially immatures. Dives vertically and repeatedly from 10–40 m (Gurney 1913, Reinsch 1969), submerging for 5–20 s. Adults and young do not necessarily associate and young out-number adults in W African waters. Prey usually caught below surface after plunge-diving or from swimming start, swallowed on surfacing. Offal also taken while swimming, and other swimming birds robbed.

Food. Fish up to 30·5 cm long, but normally less than 25 cm.

References
Nelson, J. B. (1978)

Plate 7
(Opp. p. 98)

Sula capensis (Lichtenstein). Cape Gannet; South African Gannet; Malagash. Fou du Cap.

Dysporus capensis Lichtenstein, 1823. Verz. Doubl. Zool. Mus. Berlin, p. 86; Cape of Good Hope.

Sula capensis

Range and Status. Africa's only endemic sulid. Breeds South Africa and Namibia between 24°38′S and 33°50′S. Adults mostly sedentary ranging within 500 km of breeding colony; young of 2 years and less migrate to Gulf of Guinea, a few to Mozambique, exceptionally Kenya (Broekhuysen *et al.* 1961), those initially moving up east coast then returning south again before moving north up west coast (M. J. F. Jarvis, pers. comm.). Present population much reduced by human factors; estimated 353,000 (Rand 1959, 1963a, 1963b), though evidence of local population increases in 1978 (Randall and Ross 1978). Economic value as producer of guano well established. Afforded full protection at colonies but killed at sea by fishermen both off South and W Africa.

Description. ADULT ♂: entirely white but for yellow-buff extending from bill-base over entire head and nape, deepest on crown, palest on chin, fading on throat; black primaries, secondaries and tail. Eye silvery-white; eye-ring cobalt; bill pale blue-grey with black dividing lines on cutting-edge, culmen and base running into black skin on lores, around eyes, malar and long (13–19 mm) gular streaks; legs and fully webbed feet blackish, toe ridges pale blue to pale greenish. Sexes alike, ♂ larger, gular streak longer. SIZE: wing, ♂ (20 specimens) 450–510 (480), ♀ (16) 477–510 (477); tail, ♂ (16) 180–205 (189), ♀ (30) 191–206 (191); culmen, ♂ (43) 88–97 (92), ♀ (51) 91–97 (94) (Rand 1959a); wing-span, 171–185 cm; length, 84–94 cm. WEIGHT: (start of breeding) ♂ (23) 2722; (during incubation) ♂ (10) 2634, ♀ (10) 2679; (after chick-rearing) ♂ (22) 2579, ♀ (20) 2605.

IMMATURE: a variety of brown plumages. 1st-year birds blackish brown speckled white, most heavily on upper surfaces; wing-tips and tail black; bill and legs blackish without prominent lines. Succession of immature plumages complicated and irregular but relatively uniform plumage of 1st year increasingly invaded by white commencing on lower body, then head, neck, breast and wing-coverts.

DOWNY YOUNG: covered in pale grey down; bill, facial area and feet dull blackish.

Field Characters. Sleek, predominantly white sea-birds with yellowish heads. Flight stiff-winged with strong, fairly rapid wing-beats, thick neck with bulbous head and conical bill stretched forward. Yellow head separates it from smaller boobies, all black tail, black secondaries and longer gular streak from Northern Gannet *S. bassana*. Immatures at all stages probably inseparable from nothern counterparts, especially at sea.

Voice. Recorded (2a, 6). ♂♂ have higher pitched voices than ♀♀. Normally silent at sea but excited individuals at fishing aggregations utter 'warra warra' sounds (Sinclair 1978). At colonies where paired birds recognize calls of mates, basic call a rasping 'arrah-arrah'; this also uttered by incoming birds and delivered at various intensities, together with low moans and grunts, during pair-greeting, mutual preening activities and fighting. Sky-pointing activity accompanied by 'oo-ah' and variations of this, often high-pitched, sometimes uttered at take-off. Very small chicks give 'yapping' sound like puppy when uncomfortable; at all ages have loud begging calls.

General Habits. Well known. Preferred fishing haunts Benguela and Agulhas Currents, seldom beyond continental shelf. Occurs in flocks of a few individuals to 1000 or more (Siegfried 1976) according to food abundance, feeding by day, roosting at sea, though few always present at colonies. Normally forages from *c*. 20 m above water. On sighting fish, wings are partially folded and bird plummets at steep angle, wings being stretched out behind prior to hitting water. Underwater swims mainly with feet. Fish swallowed on surfacing. When fish abundant, birds either take flight immediately after surfacing, then plunge repeatedly from lower height, or dive again while swimming.

Aggregations of many hundreds may occur around fishing boats when nets are being hauled-in, usually birds settle on water to seize spilled and injured fish. Those entangled in nets often killed. During annual June northward migration of pilchards on Natal coast gannets accompany moving shoals in large numbers to Mozambique waters.

Food. 51% by weight of all fish pilchards (*Sardinops ocellata*), 20% maasbankers (*Trachurus trachurus*), 12%

anchovies (*Engraulus japonicus*), 5% mackerel (*Scomber japonicus*) and *c*. 2% cephalopods (Rand 1959). Davies (1955) gives similar data, but maasbankers and mackerel each 16% of total.

Breeding Habits. Intimately known (Javis 1971b) Lambert's Bay Island, Cape Province. Breeds on offshore islands of South Africa and Namibia Sept–Apr. Colonies of few hundred on smaller islands up to 40,000 estimated on Malagas Island, Saldanha Bay. Always on flat ground, nests placed closely, just beyond peck-range. Individuals show great fidelity to breeding colony and even to nest-site. Islands frequently shared with cormorants and penguins which use more rocky localities. Cycle can be separated into approximate stages as follows:

(i) ♂ arrival. Gannets return late Sept, ♂♂ establish nest-sites, frequently fighting others to gain or maintain possession. Fights involve bill-gripping and pushing or pulling opponent, and may be intense and prolonged occasionally resulting in damage to head, neck and eyes, more usually in exhaustion of both. After fight bird adopts pelican posture in which bill is pointed downwards close to body.

(ii) Soliciting mates. ♂♂ solicit ♀♀ by adopting stretched-neck stance, bill pointed at ♀ and head slowly shaking side-to-side, plus small bows. If ♀ approaches head-shaking becomes more rapid. Advertising ♀ moves in sky-pointing attitude (see **A**), lowering head occasionally. If ♀ accepts ♂ both stand facing, breasts touching, wings partially spread, necks stretched skywards and

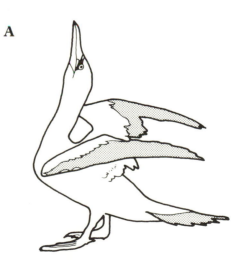

A

heads shaken a few times before dipping over each others backs while calling loudly in mutual greeting ceremony. Pair-bonds normally life-long.

(iii) Nest occupation. From this point nest-site is never left unattended though partner may be absent 2 days. Lone birds at nest may engage in solo bowing in which head is shaken to the accompaniment of loud calling and then placed under body, neck arched, or perform comfort movements in which bird flaps wings vigorously and shakes feathers with head and neck stretched at an angle of 45° to horizon and head rotated side-to-side.

(iv) Ritual displays. Returning birds fly low over colony to locate nest, calling and dipping head in direction of nest. This sometimes repeated one or more times before final approach in which bird heads into wind calling loudly and repetitively. In final vertical descent wings are flapped rapidly, tail splayed and depressed, and feet lowered with spread webs to decrease forward speed. Landing usually soft on windy days, hard and awkward on still days, the birds often overbalancing forward. ♂ initiates mutual greeting ceremony by biting ♀ on back of head or neck, the latter deflecting neck in anticipation (**B**). Alternatively bills are briefly locked together before ♀ deflects head. ♂ may initiate copulation by biting ♀ on back of head, receptive ♀ usually crouches on nest prior to this. ♂ then mounts ♀ and continues to bite until end of mating, which lasts *c.* 20 s. ♀ shakes head vigorously before and after mating. Copulation usually stimulates nest-building.

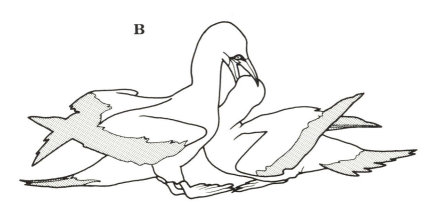

B

Sky-pointing, in which neck is stretched upwards, bill vertical, is used as appeasement posture by birds wishing to leave crowded colony. Direct take-off from nest-site only possible in strong winds, otherwise birds must move to take-off area at edge of colony, passing through other territories in process. Sky-pointing gannet steps forward slowly, wings held away from body, sometimes held at higher level above back. If sky-pointing maintained, little aggression shown by neighbours, but departing bird frequently becomes impatient towards edge of colony and dashes forward, wings flailing, to be viciously pecked by all in path. On reaching clear ground bird may swallow hard before proceeding to take-off area where more sky-pointing and wing-flapping precedes flight. Bird then faces into wind and hops forward, wings extended. As speed increases wings are flapped and both feet rowed backwards and forwards simultaneously in leaping action, distances up to 10 m being required to become airborne.

NEST: built of guano, sticks and seaweed (often dropped by passing cormorants) collected close to nest; no material carried in flight. Usually built by both sexes. ♀ stands in nest and reaches out to pull material towards her, depositing it with bill-quivering movement. ♂ stands beside nest and performs same action. After depositing material head is shaken vigorously, perhaps to dislodge particles from bill. Rarely ♂ walks short distance, collects material, drops it at ♀'s feet, or she

takes it from him. Such ♂♂ are frequently pecked at by neighbours or are threatened with open bills. Nesting pairs often preen each other on head and neck, interrupted by head-scratching with foot.

EGGS: usually 1, rarely 2. Elongated ovals, pale blue turning white, covered with thick chalky layer, soon stained brownish. SIZE: (100 eggs) 64·8–85·2 × 42·6–48·2 (76·13 × 48·22). WEIGHT: not recorded.

Laying dates: Oct–Dec after first copulation at peak period between 12.00 and 15.00 h. Some laid Sept, some Jan–Mar. If first clutch lost, relaying frequent. Of 41 pairs laying before Nov, 18 relaid, another 18 probably did; of the first 18, 6 lost egg when 1 day old and relaid again at 12 (2), 15 (2), 16 and 24 days; 2 lost when 2 days old were replaced 2 and 25 days later. The rest relaid at 20–55 days.

Incubation begins with 1st egg, carried out by both sexes. Webs are placed over egg, then covered by body feathers as bird sits. In hot weather bird may stand with webs covering egg; in rare clutches of 2, 1 web covers each egg. Periods by ♂ av. 45 h, by ♀ 38 h in first 22 days, 43 and 40 h respectively in 2nd half of incubation period. At nest-relief, returning bird sky-points frequently, moving towards or away from sitting mate; if mate unwilling to leave, sky-pointing may continue or mutual preening ensue. Sitting bird leaving also sky-points, and moves backward off nest; mate then drops head with bill lowered to breast (pelican posture) and moves to nest. Incubation period: 44 days.

Av. hatching success (1966–67) 85% (55 eggs). Chicks av. 30 h between pipping shell and full emergence. Helpless, cannot walk or move much; weight unknown. By 10 days can solicit food from parent by vigorous begging behaviour, pointing bill upwards towards parent's, swaying and retracting head, touching parent's bill. Chick reaches peak weight (*c.* 3190 g) at *c.* 80 days, decreasing slightly to *c.* 2894 g at fledging (1004 records, 2 seasons). Fledging period: 93–105 days, av. (15) 97·2. Young leave nest at *c.* 96 days, moving to edge of colony late morning/early afternoon, joining other young in take-off area. Some such young may return to nest for food, or may be fed where they are. In next few days play together or indulge in long bouts of wing-flapping, stimulated by windy weather, jumping into the air or running forward, often falling in ungainly fashion. When airborne fly directly to sea. Chick's plumage development not studied in detail but considered to be almost identical with that of Northern Gannet *S. bassana*. Immature birds attain adult plumage earlier than northern counterparts. At 2 years (31 specimens) plumage adult except for few individuals with some black feathers on wing-coverts and near preen-gland and some traces of grey on bill. 12 of same sample recaptured when 3 years old, all except 2 with full adult plumage (M. J. F. Jarvis, pers. comm.).

Both adults care for and feed chicks. For first 30–45 days are brooded continuously on top of, or between parents' webs. In first 20 days brooding periods av. (♂♂) 28 h, (♀♀) 31 h; 21–40 days ♂♂ 18, ♀♀ 19·5 h; 41–60 days, ♂♂ 18, ♀♀ 16 h; 61–80 days ♂♂ 13, ♀♀ 11; 81–100 days ♂♂ 10, ♀♀ 10. In whole cycle ♂♂ incubate somewhat more than ♀♀, ♀♀ tend chicks slightly more.

Chicks not attended continuously after 45 days, sometimes left unattended overnight. Parent feeding chick bends head downwards, opens bill wide, placing it over chick's head, enabling it to reach inside. Larger chicks thrust head into parental bill as soon as it is opened. Fed on regurgitated fish, initially in liquid form; within a few days fed on broken, undigested fish, later on entire fish. Adults preen chicks sporadically, mainly on head and back.

Overall breeding success estimated at *c.* 75%. In 129 nests where chicks hatched in first half of 1966–67 season 125 fledged; earlier breeding more successful, 96·9%. After first flight no evidence of post-fledging dependence or parental instruction; young presumably learn to plunge-dive by imitation. Young migrate north soon after independence, most returning to colony in second season after fledging. Post-fledging mortality highest in late-fledged chicks. Sexual maturity reached at 3–4 years, but mortality before then may be up to

93%; of 451 young ringed in colony, only 31 recovered in same site 2–3 years later. Adults and young do not necessarily associate, young outnumbering adults in W African waters.

Mortality caused by: (i) intentional killing by fishermen, both near home and on wintering grounds. Birds on water have difficulty in taking flight, and are easily chased, caught and killed; this is probably a major cause of mortality in W African waters. Fishermen also use nail-studded planks baited with fish, towed behind boat; diving gannet either breaks neck or is impaled. Bills are also tied up, so that gannets starve. (ii) Accidental killing —some gannets become entangled in nets, or are hooked on lines near fishing boats, or plunge onto deck of laden boats. (iii) Oil pollution, which is potentially the greatest hazard, especially in neighbourhood of breeding islands.

References
Jarvis, M. J. F. (1971a,b,c, 1974, 1977).
Nelson, J. B. (1978).

Sula dactylatra Lesson. Masked Booby; Blue-faced Booby. Fou masqué.   Plate 7

Sula dactylatra Lesson, 1831. Traité d'Orn. livr. 8, p. 601; Ascension Island.   (Opp. p. 98)

Range and Status. Pantropical, all oceans. Scarce visitor to Atlantic seaboard; 1 record for Gulf of Guinea (Santaren Island: Robins 1966). Locally common to uncommon east coast, breeding Red Sea (NE Haycock Island), Gulf of Aden (Mait and Kal Farun), Somali coast (Jazirat Sabuniya, near Socotra), Latham Island south of Zanzibar and others more easterly. Rare straggler south of *c.* 10°S. Breeding populations small to very small—*c.* 240 adults, Mait 1942, *c.* 100 pairs total, Kal Farun and Jazirat Sabuniya (Ripley and Bond 1966), larger Latham Island, 1000–2000 birds nesting Mar 1951, 500–550 nests all stages Nov 1971 (Gerhart and Turner 1978). Populations much reduced this century by human disturbance and rats.

Description. *S. d. melanops* Heuglin: breeds Red Sea, Gulf of Aden and Indian Ocean. ADULT ♂: entirely white except for black primaries, distal half of secondaries, humerals and tail. Bill orange-yellow to yellow-green, blackish at base, merging with black facial and gular skin, giving masked effect; eye yellow; legs and feet lead grey. Sexes alike. SIZE: wing, ♂ (6 specimens) 407–430 (421); tail, 169–180 (176); tarsus, 51–58 (56); culmen, 97–104 (100·7); wing-span, 160·170 cm. WEIGHT: 1480–1660 (1565).

IMMATURE: head, neck, back, tail and wing-coverts brown, speckled white; underparts and collar across hindneck white; bill whitish horn, blackish at base; facial and gular skin blue to blackish. Adult plumage attained in *c.* 32–33 months.

DOWNY YOUNG: sparsely covered in white down overlaying greyish or purplish skin; facial skin often blue-grey.

S. d. dactylatra Lesson. Breeds Atlantic and Caribbean Islands. Differs marginally in size and has straw-coloured to greenish yellow bill. SIZE: wing, ♂ (9) 406–433 (424), ♀ (7) 417–440 (429).

Field Characters. A large, robust heavy-looking booby, dazzling white with black tail and primaries, and black hind half of inner wing. Flight action powerful, wing-beats rapid, gannet-like. Adult distinguished

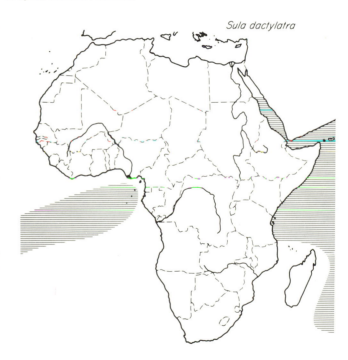

Sula dactylatra

from gannets by dark facial mask and lack of yellow head, from other white boobies by black tail. Immature can be confused with immature Brown Booby *S. leucogaster* but has more white at base of neck and on hind collar, brown plumage more speckled.

Voice. Not recorded. A bugle-like double honk, ringing and high-pitched, when commencing feeding dives. Noisy at colonies; sexes differ. Early and late in breeding season ♂ shouts or whistles from vantage point; a thin whistle, becoming harder and thinner with increased effort. When relaxed or advertising voice more flute-like, descending in pitch at end of call 'whee-ee-oo' when advertising, duration 2–3s. ♀ has loud shouting or honking voice variable in pitch and amplitude. Syllables usually short, descending in pitch. During intense interactions shouts become frenzied. On site may produce soft, conversational notes. Juveniles possess ♀-type voice, retained by ♂ for almost 3 years.

General Habits. Well known. A bird of deep waters, seldom on continental shelf. Flight strong, steady, usually *c.* 7 m or more above sea. Can achieve 70 km/h. Will circle ships few times but does not follow. Usually singly or in pairs, sometimes small groups when feeding. Tends to avoid association with other species. When foraging flies fairly high over sea, bill pointing directly downwards, searching below rather than in front. Prior to diving often hovers, tail fanned, feet held down and angled sideways, wings moving at tips. Dives steeply, even vertically, making half-twist in gravity dive or occasionally with rapid wing-beats in powered dive. Headlong plunges recorded from high as *c.* 100 m, but normally probably 15–35 m, plunging more heavily and diving more deeply than other boobies, enabling larger fish to be caught. Prey obtained by aerial pursuit or plunge-diving.

Food. Predominantly flying fish and squid, also other fish varying with location and abundance. Fish of 10–20 cm in size most common but larger fish taken, exceptionally 41·3 cm (Kermadec Islands).

Breeding Habits. Intimately known, but not studied in African waters. Breeding cycle basically annual, but varies geographically, sometimes aseasonal. Breeds usually in small colonies, preferring barren slopes or flat ground, frequently on coral sand. Although colonial, breeds in small scattered loose groups, well separated.

Pair-bonds not strong, irrespective of earlier successful mating. ♂♂ arrive first at colony, most obvious late afternoon. ♀♀ return later, pairs thereafter formed spending more time together at nest-site than at any later stage of cycle. Pair-bond rituals include: (1) flight-circuiting—bird makes brief flights with wings held almost in a steep 'V' (see **A**); (2) wing-flailing—territorial

rivals suddenly lift and spread wings, then bring them sharply downwards; (3) jabbing with bills (actual contact rarely occurs); (4) yes/no head-shake—retracted head is nodded up and down and slightly sideways (**B**); (5) pelican posture—bill-tip is briefly tucked against upper breast, often with head held slightly backwards; (6) bill-up-face-away—back of head is directed towards mate. Pairs assert rights to site or territory in 3 weeks, sometimes longer. Typically about 44 pairs/8780 m², or av. 1 pair/200 m². Do not make nest, but sitting bird usually plucks surrounding vegetation, if any.

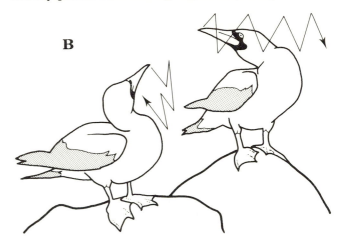

EGGS: 1–3, usually 2, laid at intervals of 2–12 days; av. (99 records) 5·3 days. Chalky white over hard blue surface, chalky covering rubs off, become nest-stained. SIZE: (12 eggs, Ascension Is.) 57·4–70·0 × 40·6–46·6 (60·4 × 44·4); (1, Mait Is.) 60·8 × 40·3. WEIGHT: av. 67·3.

Laying dates: (*S. d. melanops*) Mait Is. June–July (monsoon); Kal Farun Nov–Mar; Latham Is., recent data suggest Sept–Nov, peaking Oct, but other records give Feb–Mar, suggesting successive occupation by different groups (Brown and Britton 1980); Amirantes Apr–May. Lost clutches may be replaced in 30–45 days (Kure Atoll), same mates then remaining paired.

Incubation begins 1st egg; by both sexes, in spells of 12–24 h, regionally variable, probably according to food supply. Period: 44 days 1st egg, 43 2nd egg.

Eggs hatch *c.* 5 days apart; 2nd or younger chick dies in first few days, either trampled on or expelled by elder. At hatching 10 cm long, weighing 40–60 g, eyes open. 7–14 days, down covers back and flanks, but still thin and short; 14–21 days becomes more or less covered with thin down. 21–28 days, completely covered with thick 2nd down, *c.* 30% size of adult. 28–42 days large, fluffy, no feathers showing. Primaries erupt *c.* day 44, most showing by day 50; tail then sprouts. By 77 days, back feathered. All down shed by days 114–120, can then make sustained flights. Growth rates vary regionally, probably according to food abundance. At Kure Island 80-day-old young are *c.* 114% of mean adult weight; Galapagos birds at same age are same weight as adult; both fledge at adult weight. On Kure, chick measurements corresponded approximately with adults at following stages: tarsus and middle toe, days 45; culmen, days 70–80; primaries and tail feathers, *c.* days 120 (started flying at days 115–124); mean fledging

period 117·6 days. Very small chicks beg for food by nudging parent's lower mandible. Action becomes stronger, more vigorous as chick grows, becoming high-intensity begging in which head is laid back with bill pointing upward while being moved rapidly from side to side whilst nodding up and down and accompanied by 'aa-aa-aa' call, varying in pace and volume. Vigorous lunges often aimed at parent's bill about half way along its length while wings thrashed violently.

Chick guarded continuously, protected from predators and temperature extremes by either parent until *c.* 3–4 weeks of age. Brooding stints av. 18 h (Galapagos) in 1st week of chick's growth, decreasing gradually to av. 14 h week 9 onwards. Age at which young first left unattended variable; Galapagos 22–62 days according to season; Kure 29–84 (av. 60) days. In late stage of chick development adults stay only long enough to feed chick. Parents return with food late afternoon; chicks fed directly from parent's crop by partial regurgitation, av. 1·4 times/day on Galapagos. Parent may delay feeding for up to 1 h after return; other times may return, feed chick and depart within 20 min. On Galapagos parents fed chicks total of 120 days, 20–30 days of which young were free-flying. Adults do not interfere with elder chick's attacks and eventual displacement of younger.

Most chick loss occurs in weeks 3–4, when chick incompletely covered with down, and parents spend long periods away. Fledging success (Kure Is.) 79–83% of older chicks hatched. Free-flying juveniles fed by adults on or near colony for 50–60 days. Entire breeding cycle, if successful, 33–40 weeks.

Juveniles travel far from birth place and may breed on islands other than own. Fidelity to group strong but not absolute. 1st year mortality probably 50–60%. Annual adult mortality less than 10%. Life expectancy at least 17 years.

References
Nelson, J. B. (1978).

Sula sula (Linnaeus). Red-footed Booby. Fou à pieds rouges

Not illustrated

Pelecanus Sula Linnaeus, 1766. Syst. Nat. (12th ed.), 1, p. 218; Islands of Barbados, West Indies.

Range and Status. Pantropical, all oceans. Scarce, non-breeding straggler to W Africa (dead specimens only); and E Africa (1 record, Kilifi, Kenya, 1976: Britton 1977), regular to Port Sudan region May.

Description. *S. s. rubripes* Gould, ADULT ♂: white morph—entirely white except for variably yellow head and neck, blackish primaries, secondaries, primary coverts and major secondary coverts. Bill blue; eye brown; eye-ring purple-blue; facial skin green with pink flush, often reddish; legs and feet red to pink. Brown morph—buff to golden on head and neck, mantle and back brown, rump and tail pale grey, breast light buff-grey, rest of under-parts brown. Bill pale blue-green; eye brown; eye-ring azure blue; legs and feet red to pink. Sexes alike, both morphs, ♀♀ larger. SIZE: wing, ♂ (6 specimens) 375–383 (379), ♀ (2) 387, 419 (403); tail, ♂ (5) 212–243 (228), ♀ (2) 213, 245 (229); culmen, ♂ (7) 79–86 (83·3), ♀ (2) 83, 89·5 (82·6) (Nelson 1968); tarsus, 33–39 (36); toe, 78–79 (Serventy *et al.* 1971); length, ♂ (1) 682·5, ♀ (1) 686. WEIGHT: ♂ (4) 810–920 (874), ♀ (2) 930–970 (950).

IMMATURE: entirely dark brown; bill blackish; eye beige with some dark spots; facial skin blue; gular skin black to blue; legs and feet pink (Britton 1977).

Field Characters. A small, slender-bodied booby with long tail. Flight graceful, more flexible and faster than other boobies, tends to skim and shear the waves, often gliding for long distances. Normal white morph distinguished from Masked Booby *S. dactylatra* and gannets by white tail, red legs and absence of black humerals; dark morph adults and immatures difficult to separate from immature Brown Booby *S. leucogaster* except by smaller size and red feet.

Voice. Not recorded. No calls described for birds at sea but when squabbling over food probably make same grating 'karr-uk, karr-uk' in rapid series as when quarrelling in breeding colonies.

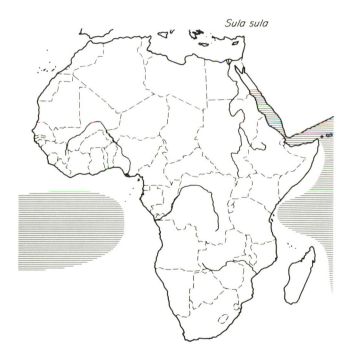

Sula sula

General Habits. Well known. Adults mostly sedentary in vicinity of home islands, young range widely in tropical seas. Fishing methods typical of family; regularly hover over bows of moving ships to seize displaced flying fish in swooping chase.

Food. Fish and squid.

References
Nelson, J. B. (1978).

Plate 7

(Opp. p. 98)

Sula leucogaster (Boddaert). Brown Booby. Fou brun.

Pelecanus Leucogaster Boddaert, 1783. Tabl. Pl. Enl. p. 57; Cayenne.

Range and Status. Pantropical, all oceans. In Atlantic occurs French Guinea to Gulf of Guinea, regularly breeding on, among other islands, Alcatraz, Principe, Sante Pedras, São Tomé, Tortuga and Pagalu. Occasional dispersal to approximately 15°N and 5°S on Atlantic seaboard. In Indian Ocean from Red Sea south to about 20°S, common to uncommon, breeding various islands in Red Sea and Gulf of Aden in colonies numbering from few dozen pairs to 6000–10,000 pairs (Zubair group); possibly also Latham Island, south of Zanzibar.

Sula leucogaster

Description. *S. l. plotus* (Forster): breeds Indian Ocean, Red Sea and Gulf of Aden; also Pacific Ocean. ADULT ♂: Entire head, throat, upper breast, mantle and all upperparts chocolate brown. Underbody from sharp demarcation on upper breast, undertail and underwing-coverts, white; undertail, distal part of underwing, narrow leading and broad trailing edges, brown; rest of underwing white. Bill yellow with pale flesh-colour at tip to greenish grey with a lighter tip; facial skin and gular region yellow to deep chrome yellow to whitish faintly tinged blue or greenish; eye dark; feet bright yellow to greenish. ADULT ♀: bill yellow shading to bluish horn at tip to greenish with paler tip; facial skin yellow, stronger in nuptial period, with conspicuous inky patch in front of eye; eyelids bright blue or yellow; feet pale yellow (♀♀ differ from ♂♂ and geographically in colouring of bare parts). SIZE: (Cocos Keeling Island) wing ♂ (4 specimens) 379–400 (390), ♀ (3) 385–418 (405); tail, ♂ 196–209 (203), ♀ 190–200 (194); tarsus, ♂, ♀ 40–47 (45); culmen, ♂ 97–99 (97·7), ♀ 100–110 (104·6); length, ♂ 780–784 (782), ♀ 755–830 (805). WEIGHT: (Indian Ocean, Christmas Island) ♂ (20) 962, ♀ (29) 1260.

IMMATURE: differs in having brown areas duller and paler than adults; underparts pale grey-brown; eye pale grey; bill dark grey becoming purple-flesh, greenish or yellow-green at base; facial skin grey; feet orange to dull yellow. Plumage becomes progressively darker on upper surfaces, paler on under surfaces, gular skin greenish.

DOWNY YOUNG: at first naked with slate-grey or pinkish mauve skin, sometimes with bluish blotches on body; bill pinkish on upper mandible, black on distal part, tip white, egg-tooth yellow.

S. l. leucogaster (Boddaert). Breeds Ascension Islands and western Atlantic. ADULT ♂: like *S. l. plotus* but head and mantle darker brown than rest of upperparts; bill pale flesh to pale blue-grey, yellowish at base; eye silver-white to grey; facial skin and gular pouch bright yellow to greenish (slate blue in Cape Verde birds); eye-ring dark or bright blue; legs and feet bright yellow to pale green or deep lime green. ADULT ♀: facial and gular skin, eye-ring, legs and feet pale yellow, a black spot before eye; (Cape Verde) face pale yellow with lead grey spot before eye. SIZE: wing, ♂ (13) 372–391 (381), ♀ (10) 384–415 (400). WEIGHT: ♂ (14) 850–1200, ♀ (26) 1100–1550.

Field Characters. A striking brown and white booby. Lighter, more agile on wing than gannets where both occur. Adults frequently confused with immature Masked Booby *S. dactylatra* but distinguished from it by greater extent of brown on throat and breast (on neck only in Masked Booby) and more even colouring of upper surfaces. Young are darker, more evenly coloured than young gannets; can be confused with young or brown morph of Red-footed Booby *S. sula* but lack of red feet and, usually evidence of breast dividing line in young Brown Booby diagnostic.

Voice. Recorded (1a). Sexes differ. In colonies or at sea when in dispute or aggression, ♂♂ utter high-pitched wheezy whistling resembling 'schweee', bill apparently closed. ♀♀ make loud, harsh, honking 'aar', strident and much repeated, bill wide open, that of young birds similar. These sounds used with little variation in variety of situations, becoming louder, more emphatic with increased aggressiveness or when returning to nest or roost. In latter case calling may commence in flight, increase in volume when landing and continue at decreased volume for some minutes. ♂♂ emit distinctive 'wheeze-whistle' when sky-pointing, preceded by 'swee-oo', head thrown back. Individual ♂♂ in colonies probably recognizable by distinct voices. During nest activities both sexes utter subdued conversational notes, ♂♂ a soft 'swoo', ♀♀ 'uh'. Nestlings utter various chuckling, clucking or gosling-like calls, particularly when with parents, more guttural version when importuning for food. Fledged, dependent young utter persistent ticking or clucking food-call when in sight of parents or when flying to colony.

General Habits. Well known. Fairly sedentary in vicinity of colonies, feeding mostly in shallow waters or regions of upwelling. Plunge-dives for food at shallow angle from low height with tail spread, wings held partly open until impact with water when wings extended backwards. May plunge into quite shallow waters or surf (Dorward 1962a, Simmons 1967b), into depths of only 1·5–1·8 m, from heights of 9–12 m, submerging for 25–40 s (Gibson-Hill 1947). Flying fish pursued in aerial chases from higher vantage points, often over bows of moving ship. Occurs singly or in small groups, larger local aggregations when food abundant. Maintains daily contact with roosting islands, often returning in small flocks flying in long lines or loose V-formations at low altitudes after day at sea. May closely approach mainland shores while fishing, e.g. in Massawa harbour (L. H. Brown, pers. obs.).

Food. Mainly fish, also squid and prawns. Flying fish, mullet, sea catfish, garfish, parrot-fish, sardines, anchovies and small-fry recorded. Av. size 5–7 cm, but up to 37 cm recorded (Stonehouse 1962, Dorward 1962a, Simmons 1967b). Sometimes piratical towards both own species and other boobies.

Breeding Habits. Little known African waters; intimately known elsewhere. Colonies frequently small, a few hundred pairs or less, sometimes large, up to many thousands of pairs. Same colony used year after year if undisturbed, same nest-site or site locality used repeatedly, probably for lifetime, even when not breeding in normally monogamous pairs.

Various pair-bond rituals performed by both sexes incorporating bill-pointing and bill-touching from

A

frontal position (greeting); bill-sparring and poking; symbolic feeding in which ♂ either inserts bill into that of ♀ or encloses hers in his (see **A**); mutual preening; bill-shaking followed by various appeasement postures, bill averted; bill-tucking in which bill is directed downwards and pressed against neck (**B**); bill-up-face-away with side or back of head directed towards mate (**C**); face-away action often incorporated in ceremonial 'parade-away' from mate with deliberate gait, tail cocked; at other times the same parade with bill pointed skywards or downwards, these actions often preceding flight.

Other rituals incorporate bowing by either partner, replied to by sky-pointing (**D**), usually by ♂ and accompanied by wheeze-whistle; stretch-up-and-stare initiated by ♂ and, if returned by ♀, followed by bowing and sky-pointing. Sky-pointing sometimes performed by flying birds (**E**) in response to salute by settled mate, and pair frequently perform flight circuit, ♂ behind ♀, during which ♂ sky-salutes and wheeze-whistles while gliding gracefully. Billing and bowing often precedes and initiates nest-building movements, objects are presented while giving persistent nest-calls and neck-crossing to reach other objects.

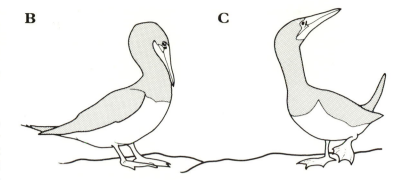

Nest activity often followed by mating ceremony: ♀ solicits by remaining still in nest, quiver-nibbling repeatedly at material in nest and ceasing to give nest-calls. ♂ mounts, rhythmically dipping bill towards back of ♀'s head while positioning, but never seizing it as gannets do. After copulation both sexes may bill-spar and ♀ may parade-away with bill averted then rejoin mate and arrange nest material (Murphy 1924; Dorward 1962a, b; Simmons 1967a, b, 1970).

NEST: consists of natural shallow depression in rock or one made by bird's feet in soft ground and lined to varying degrees according to location with grass, twigs and debris, mostly brought by ♂. Both sexes build; cup is shaped by rotation of bird's body, av. diameter 45 cm. Colonies typically more scattered, less closely packed than those of other boobies—on Christmas Island 36 nests and sites in 465 m² (1 nest/13·4 m²). Closer densities sometimes occur.

EGGS: 2, sometimes 1, occasionally 3; 2nd egg laid on av. 5·2 days after 1st. Clutch replaced if lost (av. delay 5 weeks), with up to 4 replacements. Oval, pale blue or greenish with chalky white covering, stained brown. SIZE: (48 eggs) 57–66 × 35·43 (Schönwetter 1960), (130) 50–67 × 36–40 (Stonehouse 1963). WEIGHT: 60–66 (av. 63) (Nelson 1978).

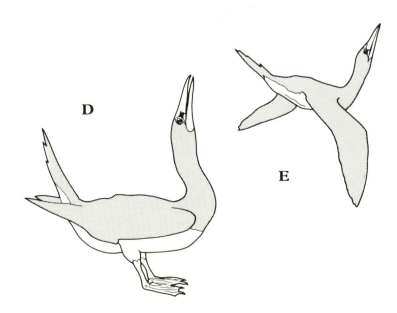

Egg-laying tends to occur at all times of the year according to locality with peaks at 8-month intervals, often associated with local food abundance.

Incubation begins 1st egg, carried out by both sexes in about equal shares. Period: 43–47 days, Ascension Island (Dorward 1962a); 42–43 days, Christmas Island (Nelson 1978).

Chicks hatch at 4–6 day intervals; eggshells discarded. Young helpless, naked, eyes closed, but may open on 1st day. By 7 days covered in sparse white down; between 14–28 days down thickens, chick becomes completely white, fluffy. By 30 days about half size of adult; face, gular skin, feet pale green, bill livid blue-grey. By 35 days covered in long white down, primaries 20 mm long, contour feathers sprouting. At 49 days still largely downy, almost adult size, primaries, scapulars and tail feathers conspicuous. By 63 days secondaries well-grown; at 70 days down thinning, still thick on head, neck, thighs, flank, and rump; bill blue, feet greenish. Down usually shed by 90–97 days, then in first juvenile plumage. Fledging period varies from 85–119 days (av. 95), probably according to food supply. Many can fly at 99 days, and most by 105 days.

Both adults brood, feed, and tend young. Up to 21 days, young are brooded on webs of feet; thereafter guarded up to about 36 days or more, depending on parental need to forage. If young stray from nest, not retrieved by adult, or fed away from it. Both parents feed small young by regurgitation; later apparently only ♀ until fledging.

Typically, only 1 chick survives from 2 eggs; fledged young returns to nest-site for unusually long period, av. 23 weeks, fed there by parents, depending on availability of food. 1st-year mortality probably 70%. Attain adult plumage in 4th year, probably first breed in 3rd or 4th year. Adult mortality thereafter probably less than 7%.

References
Nelson, J. B. (1978).

Illustrations for the Sulidae reproduced with permission from Nelson, J. B. (1978).

Family PHALACROCORACIDAE: cormorants and shags

Medium to large aquatic birds; more or less black with long neck and elongated body; fairly long, slender, laterally compressed, strongly hooked bill; short wings with 11 primaries, 8th and 9th longest, 17–23 secondaries; long and distinctly wedge-shaped tail with 12–14 pointed stiff feathers; short legs are set far back resulting in waddling gait. Pelvic girdle modified for powerful and rapid swimming; expert swimmers; swim low in water, often leaping forward half or totally out of water before diving. Plumage not fully waterproof. Often stand for long periods holding wings half-open for drying and thermoregulation. Feed mainly on fish caught by underwater pursuit; swim with feet, never with open wings. Large adductor muscles used to keep jaws shut when holding prey. Flight marked by uninterrupted flapping; rarely soar.

A world-wide family, mainly of tropical and temperate coastal and inland waters. 2 genera, 29 species; in Africa, the widely distributed genus *Phalacrocorax*. We maintain *Anhinga* in a separate family (see p. 119).

Genus *Phalacrocorax* Brisson

Characters as for the family. Of 8 African species, *P. carbo*, *P. aristotelis*, *P. capensis*, *P. neglectus*, *P. africanus* and *P. coronatus* are resident; *P. nigrogularis* may breed (Socotra) and *P. pygmaeus* is vagrant N Africa.

Plate 8

(Opp. p. 99)

Phalacrocorax carbo (Linnaeus). Great Cormorant; White-necked Cormorant; White-breasted Cormorant. Grand Cormoran.

Pelecanus Carbo Linnaeus, 1758. Syst. Nat. (10th ed.), p. 133; Europe, restricted to the 'rock-nesting form of the north Atlantic Ocean' by Hartert, 1920, Vögel Pae. Fauna, p. 1387.

Range and Status. Resident and Palearctic winter visitor, locally abundant to rare. 3 subspecies, the resident *lucidus* and *maroccanus* and the Palearctic visitor *sinensis*. The resident status of *sinensis* in Tunisia requires recent confirmation. The dimorphic form in E Africa is considered here to be *P. c. lucidus* (Urban and Jefford 1974), not *P. c. patricki* and *P. lucidus* (Williams 1966).

Description. *P. c. lucidus* (Lichtenstein): coastal from Mauritania (Banc d'Arguin) to Guinea-Bissau and Angola to Cape; inland Nigeria and Lake Chad to Sudan at 20°N, Ethiopia, thence south, mainly inland, through E and Central to South Africa where widespread both on coastal and inland waters. ADULT ♂ (non-breeding): overall black to brownish black with white throat, foreneck and upper breast. Forehead, crown and nape black, sometimes flecked grey, occasionally white. Hindneck, mantle, rump, tail and upperwing brown, distinctly edged with blackish green gloss. Cheek, throat, side and foreneck, and upper breast white to buff-white. Rest of underparts, including wings, flank and tail, black. Upper mandible black, lower mandible tan at base darkening to black at tip, both sometimes with vertical blackish bars; eye emerald; lores orange-yellow; gular pouch olive to buff-yellow; legs and feet black. Sexes alike. ADULT ♂ (breeding): plumage glossy black; erectile crest of stiff black feathers on crown. Either side of rump often with white spot. Lores orange; gular pouch olive to dark olive. ADULT ♀ (breeding): like ♂ but lores scarlet, scarlet-orange or orange. SIZE: wing, ♂ (7 specimens) 321–349 (344); wing, sex? (10) 304–350 (325); tail, 125–148 (140); tarsus, 48–61 (53); bill, 60–70 (66); bill, ♂ 64–70 (68). WEIGHT: ♀ 1590, 1820, 1930.

IMMATURE: above duller, often brownish; below, throat to undertail-coverts, whitish to greyish flecked with varying amounts of black and brown; eye brownish.

DOWNY YOUNG: naked at hatching, skin brown-black with pink on face; covered with dense black down at about day 6.

P. c. sinensis (Blumenbach). N Africa coasts and inland waters, Morocco to Egypt, Oct–Mar. SIZE: (large) wing, ♂ (38) 330–364 (347), ♀ 311–337 (325). Only chin, cheek and throat white.

P. c. maroccanus Hartert. Atlantic coast of Morocco and Mauritania. Intermediate between *lucidus* and *sinensis* with some white feathers on foreneck. SIZE: wing, 345, 355; bill, 70 (Vaurie 1965).

Populations of *P. c. lucidus* in E Africa, especially eastern Zaïre and western Uganda, dimorphic; some resemble *P. c. sinensis* with chin, cheek and throat white, neck and breast black; others represent all stages between white-breasted and all-black extremes. Individuals with dark neck mated to ones with white neck in Uganda (Urban and Jefford 1974).

Field Characters. The largest African cormorant, usually seen standing erect, often in large numbers along shore, on trees or on rocks. White lower neck and upper breast and, if present, white spot on either side of rump diagnostic.

Voice. Recorded (2a, 6, 18). Usually silent away from colony but sometimes utters guttural 'karrk' or 'korrk'. At colony, calls include: (1) while gaping—♂ a loud 'a/rrooo' or 'a/a/a/a/rrooo', ♀ a soft 'hrrr'; (2) early in breeding season just before departing from nest—1–2 'growls', later silent; (3) early in breeding season returning to nest—♂ a loud 'kro/kro/kro/kroo/kroa/kraa', ♀ a soft 'hhhhhhhhhh'; later both 'kro/kro/kro/kro'; (4) early in season while standing on nest—♂ a 'rooo' or snore-like 'hroooh'; (5) preparing to mate—♀ gargling sounds; and (6) threatening—a deep-toned 'hoik-hok-hok-hook'. Young begging for (1) food, a 'kra-wee; kra-wee' or 'kji-kji-kjik'; or (2) for water, an incessant and insistent 'kikikiki . . .'

General Habits. Intimately known. Usually gregarious. Inhabits any open water including alkaline and freshwater lakes, rivers, marshes, floodlands, and coastal bays, lagoons and estuaries. Roosts at nesting colonies or at major feeding area, collecting in large numbers at sunset, leaving again at sunrise. Flies in flocks of varying sizes with neck extended, feet under tail, and with fairly rapid wing-beats, often close to water. When over land, often flies several hundred metres above ground. During take-off from water, first splashes for several metres; from rocks or trees, swoops downward before airborne.

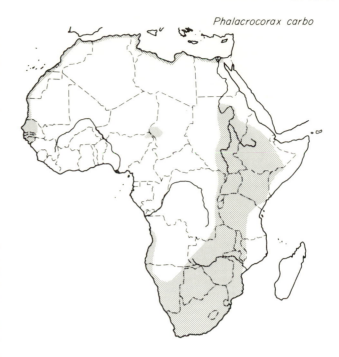

Phalacrocorax carbo

If alarmed when standing, straightens neck; if in water submerges body until only outstretched neck and head visible. Hops or makes short flights; rarely walks. Often stands, sometimes facing wind, with wings stretched outward for drying, thermoregulation and, possibly, balance. When standing, usually faces sun throughout daylight hours; as temperature increases, pants, flutters gular pouch, drools, wets legs and feet with guano, and shades young, occasionally regurgitating water over chick's body and into gaping mouth.

Usually solitary feeder, doing so throughout day with peak activity at Lake St Lucia 06.00–08.00 h; 2·3 h/day or 19% day spent fishing (Whitfield and Blaber 1979b). When feeding, dive is either preceded by a distinct jump bringing whole body out of water, or submerges immediately. Pursues and catches fish underwater. At Lake St Lucia submersion time 14 (4–30) s. Captures fish between mandibles with hook of upper mandible, often penetrating lateral surface of prey. Surfaces and swallows prey head first. At Lake St Lucia, fishes between 10–200 m but also up to 1 km from shore. At St Croix Island, Algoa Bay, South Africa, the population breeding on the island feeds both in the sea around the island and in estuaries on the mainland 15 km away (R. Randall, pers. comm.). In Ethiopian Rift Valley no details, but appears to fish anywhere along shore (if water deep enough to dive in) to several km from shore, often in large groups, sometimes mixed with other species.

Other than migration of *P. c. sinensis* from Palearctic to Africa, this species tends to be sedentary in Africa although some local movement reported (e.g. on Namibia's coast birds captured 140 km from where ringed (H. Berry, pers. comm.) and in South Africa birds captured 500 km south of where ringed at Barberspan).

Food. Mainly fish (tilapia, mullet, hottentot-fish, clinids) and occasionally frogs, crustaceans and molluscs; also *P. capensis* nestlings (Berry 1976a). Fish at Lake St Lucia ranged from 1–214 g (most 10–20 g) in weight (Whitfield and Blaber 1979).

Breeding Habits. Intimately known. Colonial, up to 1000 or more pairs breeding together, sometimes with darters, other cormorants, herons and spoonbills, in trees over or near water; sometimes on ground.

Nesting activity commences when ♂♂ establish and display on old or new nest-site territories. ♂ waves wings, opening and closing them about twice a second to reveal and cover white rump patches. During wing-waving draws head in, points bill slightly skyward and raises tail obliquely; does not call. If ♀ lands next to ♂, he shifts to gaping (see **A**). ♀ responds by gaping (**B**), placing head and bill halfway back to tail (not all the way back as in ♂) and produces a different call (see under Voice). When gaping, both place body horizontally and droop wings; ♂ spreads tail cocked up and slightly backward; ♀ droops it downward. Both preen each other, entwine necks, and, pointing closed bills upwards, slowly wave stretched heads and necks from side to side.

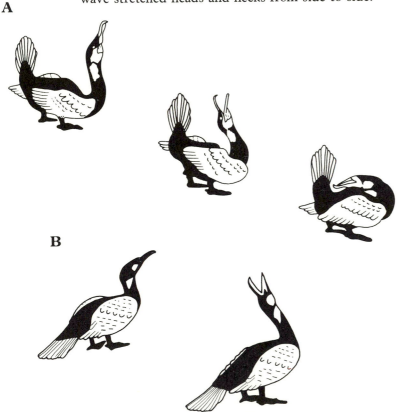

A

B

♂ collects most of nest material which he presents to ♀ who builds nest. Before departing from nest, either performs pre-flight display with head, throat and upper neck distended, crest raised and closed bill tilted up and forward. On returning, performs post-flight display with head and neck flattened laterally, crest raised, closed bill pointed forward and slightly downward. Both hop about vicinity of nest and perform kink-throat display with throat having angular appearance due to forward protrusion of hyoid bones.

No distinctive pre- or post-copulatory displays occur. At copulation, ♀ flattens body with bill pointed forward; ♂ closes wings and holds ♀'s head or neck with bill.

NEST: made of sticks and branches, usually with shallow central depression lined with grass, reeds, rushes, water-lily stems, seaweed, feathers, or human litter (fishing lines, plastic, broken glass) (H. Berry, pers. comm.). Structures sometimes touch; placed 0·5–5 m above water or ground. 25 nests (Ethiopia), outside rim 40 × 39 (33–47 × 35–50); inside rim 24 × 24 (21–28 × 21–30); deep central depression 4 cm (1–7); thickness from top to bottom 20 (13–27) cm, but occasionally some 1 m thick.

EGGS: 1–6, usually 2–3, laid at intervals of 23–24 h; Ethiopia mean (96 clutches) 2·24; E Africa (13) 3·23; Natal (60) 3·03; South Africa (472) 2·54 (Urban 1979, EANRC, SAOSNRC). Long ovals, greenish blue with chalky outer layer. SIZE: (193) 53–72 × 34–42 (64 × 40). WEIGHT: (4) 57–67 (60).

Lays mainly in rains, or all year round with peaks in rains, often in dry season. Laying dates: Morocco Apr–May (spring); Mauritania, Senegal, Guinea-Bissau Oct–Jan (dry); Nigeria Dec–Feb (dry); Kenya, Uganda 12/12 months, probably peaking Apr–June (main rains); Tanzania, Rwanda, Burundi Apr (rains); Zaïre Feb–Mar (rains); Zambia Feb–Sept; Malawi Mar–Aug; Zimbabwe Aug–May with peak Apr–May (end rains); Namibia Jan, May, July–Oct, Dec; South Africa year-round peaking Transvaal May (end rains to early dry season) and Cape Aug–Nov (spring).

Incubation usually begins with 1st egg, but sometimes not until clutch complete. Both parents incubate. In first few days parent (sex?) sitting on nest angles tail *c.* 45° above horizontal axis. Incubation period: 28–29 days (Ethiopia), 27–28 (Natal) (Urban 1979; Olver and Kuyper 1978).

Nestling from hatching to *c.* 2 weeks active only when being fed. At 3 weeks covered in chocolate-brown down; primaries up to 5 cm. From 3 weeks on, varies from all white to no white breast and abdomen. At 4 weeks active, jabs at neighbours and siblings, and often leaves nest; during heat of day hangs head and neck over the shady side of nest (**C**). At 5–6 weeks occasionally flies a few metres. At 7 weeks underparts from throat to undertail-coverts whitish; upperparts brown. At 8 weeks fledged and flies nearly as well as adult, but takes about twice as long to rise from water. Weighs (Natal) 38 g at hatching, 320 at 7 days, 1016 at 14 days, 1544 at 21 days, 2045 at 28 days, 2150 at 35 days and no further increase at 42 days.

Both parents usually at nest at hatching time; at least 1 at nest until nestling 1–2 weeks old; 1 parent at nest only at feeding time when nestling 2–8 weeks. Newly hatched to 2–3 week-old young are fed at irregular intervals throughout daylight. After 3 weeks usually fed once a day, often near sunset. Young seem to recognize parents; parents recognize young and feed them by regurgitation. Young beg for food with kink-throat display, closed bill and persistent calling (**D**); put head into parent's bill when feeding. Beg for water by waving mouth upwards, wide open (**E**); parent then fetches water.

C

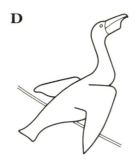
D

E

Major causes of mortality are predation by the Marabou *Leptoptilos crumeniferus*, African Fish Eagle *Haliaeetus vocifer*, Black Kite *Milvus migrans*, Kelp Gull *Larus dominicanus* and Fan-tailed Raven *Corvus rhipidurus*. Young are also pushed out of nest by larger siblings or jump out of nest to avoid predators.

Breeding success: (Natal) 60 nests, 186 eggs laid, 139 eggs hatched (74·7%), 96 young fledged (51·6% of eggs laid), 1·6 young/nest; (Ethiopia) 1·57 young/nest; E Africa, 1 or less young/nest by fledging.

References
Olver, M. D. and Kuyper, M. A. (1978).
Urban, E. (1979).
Urban, E. and Jefford, T. (1974).
Whitfield, A. K. and Blaber, S. J. (1979).

Illustrations reproduced with permission from: (A and B) van Tets (1966); (C, D and E) Jefford and Urban (in prep.).

Phalacrocorax nigrogularis Ogilvie-Grant and Forbes. Socotra Cormorant. Cormoran de Socotra.

Plate 8

Phalacrocorax nigrogularis Ogilvie-Grant and Forbes, 1899. Bull. Liverp. Mus., 2, p. 3; Socotra.

(Opp. p. 99)

Range and Status. Uncommon migrant to Gulf of Aden and Red Sea coasts of Somalia and Ethiopia; suspected breeder Socotra (Bailey 1966).

Description. ADULT ♂: entirely black. Head, neck, back, rump and underparts with slight purple gloss; mantle, scapulars and upperwing-coverts glossed dark bronze-green with black tips to feathers except glossy upperwing-coverts. Tail grey-black. Underwing brown-black. Bill grey-black with pale tip and greenish tinge at base of lower mandible; bare face skin black; eye dark emerald, eyelid black with yellow beads; gular pouch black, sometimes brown or grey-green; legs and feet black, toes pink. Sexes alike. At onset of breeding, many white filoplumes on head, neck, behind eyes and on rump; those behind eyes form white tufts, those of rump long. SIZE: wing, ♂ 288, 296, ♀ 284, immature ♀274, unsexed adult 304; tail, ♂ 85, immature ♀ 83–84; bill, ♂ 69, 73, immature ♀ 74, unsexed adult 77; tarsus, ♂ 73, 75, immature ♀ 73, 74, unsexed adult 86.

IMMATURE: brown to grey-brown above, mantle feathers with dark centres, scapulars edged paler; brownish white below. Bill grey-green; bare face dull yellow; eye steel grey; gular pouch pink; legs and feet dusky.

DOWNY YOUNG: naked at hatching, later covered with white down.

Field Characters. Medium-sized, long-billed, marine cormorant with dark plumage. In breeding season white tufts behind eyes and a scattering of white feathers on neck and upperparts.

Voice. Not recorded.

Phalacrocorax nigrogularis

General Habits. Scarcely known. Marine, largely in Persian Gulf where resident all year, and gregarious, at times in flocks of 10,000. Roost in large numbers on sand beaches. Fly in loose V-formation, often close to water. Movements in Persian Gulf complex; difficult to separate regular feeding from seasonal movements.

Occurs also in Arabian Sea and Gulf of Aden, sometimes in large numbers; and in southern Red Sea (1 collected Assab, Ethiopia).

Food. Fish (species?) (Ripley and Bond 1966) from 3–7 fathoms of water.

Breeding Habits. Unknown in Africa but suspected to nest Socotra with discovery of 1 poorly ossified skull of pre-fledging juvenile with date unknown (Bailey 1966) except not breeding Mar–June (Ripley and Bond 1966). Tens of thousands breed Mar, Persian Gulf islands.

NEST: a scrape on ground or slightly raised heap above ground. Structures almost touch, with 250 nests in 1000–1500 m².
EGGS: 2–3; oval, pale blue with chalky covering with dark brown spots at large end. SIZE: 56–59 × 38–41 (57 × 39); WEIGHT: 48 g.

References
Bailey, R. (1966).
Meinertzhagen, R. (1954).
Ripley, S. D. and Bond, R. (1966).

Plate 8

(Opp. p. 99)

Phalacrocorax capensis (Sparrman). Cape Cormorant. Cormoran du Cap.

Pelecanus capensis Sparrman, 1788. Mus. Carls. fasc. 3, no. 61, False Bay.

Range and Status. Resident, abundant to locally not uncommon, in coastal and offshore marine habitats from Congo River south and east to Durban. Most numerous along Namibian coast between 21°45'S and 23°20'S. Very abundant South African west coast with stable population of over one million due to prey availability in nutrient-rich Benguela current. In 1956 (Crawford and Shelton 1978; Rand 1960, 1963), there were 1,102, 482 with over 175,000 on Cape Islands, 9000 on Namibian islands, and more than 900,000 on Namibian guano platforms; 1974 (Berry 1976a), platforms with at least 1,053,000.

Description. ADULT ♂ (non-breeding): overall blue-black, sometimes brown with lighter brown throat. Head and neck with varying amount of white filoplumes. Upper mantle, wings and scapulars bottle-green edged with blue-black, giving scaly appearance. Black tail strongly graduated, giving short-tailed appearance. Bill black; gular area black, white or pale yellow; lores yellow; eye grey to blue; beads on eyelids blue; legs and feet black. Sexes alike. ADULT ♂ (breeding): overall blue-black with general sheen. Eye bright turquoise; beads on eye-lids bright blue; gular area deep yellow-orange. SIZE: (10 specimens) wing, 245–275 (254); tail, 86–100 (95); tarsus, 56–63 (59); culmen, 50–56 (54). WEIGHT: ♂ 1306, ♀ 1155; mean species weight, 1230.

IMMATURE: brown with lighter brown throat and underparts.

DOWNY YOUNG: black naked skin with pink on extremities and underside.

Field Characters. A sleek dark marine cormorant, usually seen in large numbers. Yellow-orange gular area, yellow lores, short-tailed appearance and habit of jumping clear of water before diving diagnostic.

Voice. Recorded (1c, 2a, 6). When not breeding, calls much reduced. During breeding season: (1) a soft croak repeated at intervals by both sexes when flying in formation and brooding; (2) a repeated low-pitched clucking by ♂ during courtship; ♀ answers with a 'gra-gra-gra'; after pair formed, call of ♂ like ♀; (3) both sexes, a hissy cluck which intensifies into a short, sharp explosive croaking, likened to a bark, when threatening. Nestlings utter (1) a 'pew-pew-pew' until eyes open; (2) a 3-syllabled, high-pitched musical warbling when soliciting; and (3) a series of high-pitched, squeaky 'tchew-tchew-tchew'.

General Habits. Very well known. Gregarious in large numbers all year. Inhabit coastal waters usually up to 10 km out, but recorded up to 70 km from mainland. Also in lagoons and channels leading from brackish pools.
Flocks of hundreds to thousands fly low across water in long undulating lines. When coming upon a shoal of fish, settle. Then feed with great activity with as many as 120,000 individuals diving and flying in 'leap-frog' fashion. Dive from swimming position; sometimes first jump clear of water. Remain submerged for c. 30 s. Av. duration of foraging bout 20–32 min; feed twice daily when fish available. Often found in feeding groups with penguins and terns. When seeking food for young, normally fly in one direction for c. 40 km with flight speed along Namibian beach in calm weather 75 km/h (Berry 1976a).

Phalacrocorax capensis

Roost in large numbers on islands or guano platforms, arriving in long undulating lines late afternoon to sunset; leave shortly after sunrise and fly to sea again in long undulating lines. Departure delayed if foggy. Typically, first fly short distance, settle on water and bathe for av. 68 s (Berry 1976a). Sometimes roost at sea.

In non-breeding season disperse widely along coast in large flocks, probably following large fish shoals. Travel long distances north and south along west coast of Africa and east and west along Cape coast from Congo River in west to Durban in east. Of 33 ringed recoveries in excess of 100 km (Berry 1976a), farthest north, Mariquita, Angola (14°40′S, 12°09′E), ringed Walvis Bay guano platforms (22°54′S, 14°31′E); farthest east, Sundays River (33°43′S, 25°50′E), ringed Saldanha Bay (33°00′S, 17°56′E); farthest travelled, 1430 km (ringed Cape Cross guano platform, 21°45′S, 13°56′E; recovered Hermanus, 34°25′S, 19°16′E) and longest time between ringing and recovery, 9·05 years.

Food. Feeds on highly active pelagic shoaling fish, mainly pilchard (*Sardinops*), anchovy (*Engraulis*), maasbanker (*Trachurus*) and inshore shoaling *Ammodytes*; occasionally crabs, lobsters, mussels and cephalopods; and, rarely, littoral fish. Major fish, pilchard (80% by number, 84% by weight), anchovy (12% by number, 15% by weight) (Berry 1976a); pilchard, maasbanker and *Ammodytes* (81% of diet) (Williams and Burger 1978). Daily intake 133–266 g or 11–22% bodyweight (Berry 1976a).

Breeding Habits. Very well known. Breeds in colonies of up to 120,000 individuals on cliff-edges and flat inner areas of off-shore islands, guano platforms, estuarine sand islands, and edges of man-made salt evaporation pans. Nests placed on ground or tops of bushes up to 3 m high; often in areas of reduced or drier air movement than those where the Bank Cormorant *P. neglectus* nests (Berry 1976a). Prefers to nest on cliff ledges, less on flat inner areas of island.

Courtship begins when ♂, sitting on potential nest-site, gapes by throwing head back so neck lies on back; at same time erects and fans tail, extends bright orange-yellow gular area and makes low-pitched clucking. Keeps this position for several minutes; does not wave wings. When ♀ arrives, ♂ moves head slowly forward until neck is fully extended; ♀ responds with 'gra-gra-gra'. Copulation takes 5–15 s, and is followed by preening and passing of a feather or debris. Both threaten intruders by rapid sideways shaking of head in a withdrawn position, interspersed by striking towards intruder with bill. Either bird walks with 'high-stepping' gait; hops with neck in S-shape, feathers on neck erected, open bill pointed downward and gular pouch extended; leaves nest with look, crouch and leap. 24 h activity of courting bird (Namibia) includes 42% night and 8% day resting, 10% display, 12% flying to feeding area, 6% feeding, 5% bathing, 5% gathering nest material and 12% defending territory (Berry 1976a).

♂ collects nest material mainly along high water mark or on storm beach, sometimes by diving, and brings it to ♀ who constructs nest. Takes up to 20 h to build nest (South Africa) (Williams 1978).

NEST: flimsy structure of seaweeds, sticks and stalks *c.* 30 cm across; cup 15 cm across. 3·1 nests/m² with distance between nests *c.* 30 cm (Berry 1976a). Often infested with ticks; over 1600 ticks in 1 nest (Williams 1978).

EGGS: 1–5, usually 2–3; mean (1626 clutches) 2·39 (SAOSNRC); laid at 2–3 day intervals. Long ovals, pale green with bluish tinge, covered with bluish white chalky layer. SIZE: (100 eggs) 47–61 × 33–38 (55 × 36) (Berry 1976a); (110) 49–58 × 32–37 (54 × 35) (SAOSNRC). WEIGHT: (14) 31–42 (37) (SAOSNRC).

Peaks in breeding timed with availability of abundant shoals of pelagic fish, particularly pilchards. Sudden interruption in mass breeding not uncommon, due to failure of food supply, particularly early in season, with birds either not breeding that year or moving elsewhere to breed. Laying dates: Namibia and South Africa Jan–Mar, Sept–Dec, but some throughout year, with peak Sept–Oct.

Both sexes incubate. Period: 22–23 days (Berry 1976a), 22–28 days (McLachlan and Liversidge 1978).

Weight of nestling increases from 24–31 (26) g at hatching to 51–64 (56) at 4 days and 190–250 (234) at 9 days; adult weight achieved at 40 days. Eyes open day 4. At 1 week covered in charcoal to dull black down; at 18 days quills emerging on wing and tail, and some white on lower neck, upper breast and leading edge of wing. At 5 weeks, leave nest-site and at 7 weeks form small bands of up to 10. At *c.* 9 weeks can fly but complete independence comes several weeks later.

Both sexes brood and feed young. Parent leaves nest at *c.* 06.00 h, returning 1–1·5 h (range 0·5–3 h) later with food which may be in its stomach 5 h before feeding young. Feeds naked and half-grown young 5–6 times daily by regurgitation; each feed lasts *c.* 3 min. As young grow, number of fishing excursions by parents increase. Little to no feeding activity at night.

Brooding adults and young raise and stretch wings, scratch head and neck, yawn, and fluff and shake feathers. Brooding adults control body temperature by fluttering gular area, drooling, drooping wings over edge of nest and on hot days holding them fully extended in a horizontal plane. Orient away from sun when hot (J. Cooper, pers. comm.).

Main predator, black-backed jackal *Canis mesomelas*. On guano platforms, adult Great Cormorants *P. carbo* and adult and nearly fledged Great White Pelicans *Pelecanus onocrotalus* eat *capensis* nestlings. Kelp Gull *Larus dominicanus* eats eggs and small young. Total effect of predators on cormorant population, however, negligible.

References
Berry, H. (1976a).
Rand, R. W. (1960).

Plate 8   *Phalacrocorax neglectus* (Wahlberg). **Bank Cormorant. Cormoran des bancs.**

(Opp. p. 99)   *Graculus neglectus* Wahlberg, 1855. Öfv. K. Vet.-Akad. Förh, 12, p. 214; islands off South West Africa.

Range and Status. Resident, locally common in marine habitats along coast from Swakopmund and Guano Islands (Namibia) to Cape Agulhas (South Africa) with total population *c.* 4000 (Crawford and Shelton 1978).

Phalacrocorax neglectus

Description. ADULT ♂ (non-breeding): overall black. Head, neck, lower mandible, rump, tail and underparts blue-black with green wash. Upper mantle, wings and scapulars bronze-brown with black edges. Varying amount of white on rump. Bill black, lighter towards tip; lores, base of bill and chin with black feathers; bare throat and area around eye black; eye brown above, green below; legs and feet black. Sexes alike. ADULT ♂ (breeding): with white filoplumes on neck. SIZE: (3 specimens) wing, 260–288; tail, 112–132; tarsus, 62–70; culmen, 54–57. WEIGHT: 1800 g.

IMMATURE: more bronzy with green wash. 1st year, brown to blue eyes; 2nd year, green eye; 3rd year, eye like adult.

DOWNY YOUNG: sooty black with varying amount of white down on head, neck, wings and rump.

Field Characters. A large, heavy, black cormorant with varying amount of white on rump.

Voice. Not recorded. Adult at nest utters a throaty alarm cry if approached.

General Habits. Scarcely known in published literature; habits studied in detail, however, but not yet published (J. Cooper, in prep.). Strictly marine, often in widely dispersed flocks or small groups foraging in littoral zones often among kelp beds close to and rarely more than 10 km from shore. Because of large size, has difficulty taking off from flat land surface and thus avoids beaches. Sensitive to disturbance, vulnerable to oiling and may be in competition with lobster industry (Siegfried *et al.* 1976).

Tends to forage solitarily close inshore, primarily in littoral zone, especially among kelp beds; occasionally fishes along sandy bottom inshore. Each feeding bout lasts *c.* 26–58 min (Siegfried *et al.* 1975).

Food. Wide range of food types, probably wider than other southern African marine cormorants; includes fish, crustaceans and cephalopods. Fish and invertebrates from the littoral zone form 82% of diet; takes benthic fish but hardly ever pelagic shoaling species (Williams and Burger 1978). Size of food *c.* 68 (5–214) g (Siegfried *et al.* 1975).

Breeding Habits. Scarcely known, or data unpublished (J. Cooper, in prep.). Colonial nester, building nest on top of isolated small pinnacles of rock or rounded granite islets, often well out to sea where exposed to cool wind and fine spray. Same nesting sites used year after year. Nests located almost always immediately adjacent to sea where high seas wash over them, necessitating rebuilding.

At courtship ♂, in one continuous movement, shoots head and neck first forward, then upwards and back so head rests in small of back and bill points skyward. Holding this position for a minute or so, ♂ then sweeps head and neck forward and down so bill points directly downward. This behaviour reveals and covers white rump, as in *P. carbo*. Other courtship behaviour not described but studied in detail (J. Cooper, in prep.). Collects nest material entirely by diving, not by walking along shore. Nest-relief of short duration.

NEST: made of seaweeds, primarily filamentous green algae with some *Ulva*, but also some feathers, sticks and bits of thread and similar human debris. 2 nests lacked parasites (Williams 1978); 1·3 nests/m² at Malagas Island, South Africa (Rand 1963).

EGGS: 1–3, mean (113 clutches) 1·84 (SAOSNRC). Long ovals, pale blue, with chalky white covering. SIZE: 51–67 × 33–40 (60 × 39). WEIGHT: 47 g.

Laying dates: Namibia and South Africa year-round, with main peak May–July.

Broods usually 1–2 chicks in successful nests. No published details available (J. Cooper, pers. comm.).

References
Rand, R. W. (1960).

Phalacrocorax aristotelis (Linnaeus). Shag. Cormoran huppé.

Plate 8

Pelecanus aristotelis Linnaeus, 1761. Fn. Svec., ed. 2, p. [23]; Sweden.

(Opp. p. 99)

Range and Status. Resident, coastal waters Morocco to Egypt; seldom inland. *P. a. desmarestii*, Mediterranean coasts: frequent Morocco to Tunisia rare Libya to Egypt. *P. a. riggenbachi*: frequent Moroccan Atlantic coast.

Description. *P. a. desmarestii* (Payraudeau): Mediterranean coasts of Africa. ADULT ♂: all dark, brown-black glossed with green. Head and neck glossed dark blue-green; short forward-curving crest on forehead; neck with numerous white tufted filoplumes. Mantle, scapulars and wing-coverts purplish with narrow black edges; tail sometimes tipped brownish white. Bill, yellow with black culmen and tip, not black and yellow as in nominate *aristotelis*, and longer, more slender than in nominate race; bare skin at base of mandible extensive pale yellow, not black with yellow spots as in nominate; eye bright emerald; skin around eyes, inside mouth and gape orange-yellow; legs black, feet brown with yellow webs, not black as in nominate. Sexes alike. SIZE: wing, ♂ (12 specimens) 243–271 (258), ♀ (11) 240–265 (249); bill, ♂ (6) 58–65 (61), ♀ (5) 61–65 (63); tail (nominate *aristotelis*), ♂ (6) 119–133 (129), ♀ (10) 114–125 (119); WEIGHT: (nominate *aristotelis*) ♂ 1930, 1760, 2145.

IMMATURE: above largely dark brown glossed green, below brownish white. Skin at base of mandible whitish; throat brown.

DOWNY YOUNG: naked at hatching, skin brown; after a few days, covered with dense brown down.

P. a. riggenbachi Hartert. Atlantic Morocco coast. Size similar to *desmarestii*, smaller than nominate *aristotelis*; soft parts like those of *desmarestii* but has shorter and more slender bill, like *aristotelis*.

Field Characters. Medium-sized, slender-billed marine cormorant with dark plumage and yellow gape. Distinguished from breeding Great Cormorant *P. carbo* by lack of white patch on sides of rump and lack of white on chin, throat or neck. Also has slimmer build, shorter neck, smaller head and faster wing-beats than Great Cormorant. At close range, short forward-curving crest diagnostic.

Voice. Recorded (2a). In Europe, usually silent away from breeding colony. At breeding colony, both sexes give clicking sounds from throat; ♂ also gives grunting 'ar(k)' in long continuous series, interspersed with clicks 'ar(k)-ik-ar(k)-ik'. Except for throat-clicking and hissing, ♀ voiceless. Young give squeaking 'weee-ik', begging 'weeeu' repeated several times and threatening 'we-AA'. ♀ starts losing voice when 35 days old.

General Habits. Little known in Africa; well known in Europe. Essentially marine, preferring rocky coastlines with fairly deep water. Usually does not range far from shore. Avoids shallow sandy or muddy inlets, estuaries, and brackish or fresh water. Often solitary,

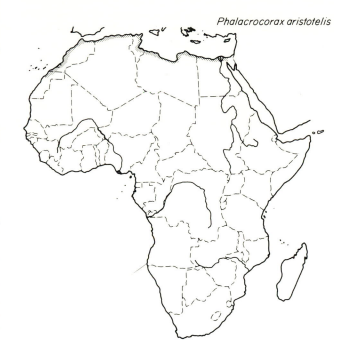

Phalacrocorax aristotelis

occasionally flocks at fish shoals. Spends much time resting and preening on rocks and cliff ledges; rarely rests on sand banks, trees, posts and piers. Roosts at nest-site, or on rocks and cliffs elsewhere in non-breeding season. Large numbers use same roost, but some roost singly. Flies low over water, rarely higher than 100 m. Some movement along African coast by individuals where no breeding occurs, but extent unknown. Also not known if individuals from Europe winter in N Africa.

Fish caught between mandibles underwater and swallowed upon return to surface, although small prey swallowed underwater. Normally a surface-diver, springing clear of water before diving; sometimes slides under surface without preliminary leap, or plunges from air. Remains underwater 5–100 s (mean 40 s); maximum 3–4 min. Dives to 18–21 m. Typically solitary feeder but flocks of 300–500 feed on dense fish shoals. Sometimes feeds 13–18 km from roosting or nesting areas (Cramp and Simmons 1977).

Food. Little known in Africa. In Europe, chiefly mid-water and bottom-living fish, especially sand-eels, herring and cod; also some crustaceans.

Breeding Habits. Scarcely known in Africa; well known in Europe. Breeds in colonies of variable size, usually small scattered groups; also solitary. Rarely shares nesting area with Great Cormorant, preferring sheltered overhanging ledges and flat rocks.

Courtship begins when all adult birds on rocks below colony alight or hop about, performing land-gape in which body is in upright posture, feathers flattened, head thrown back and beak opened wide and pointed upwards. ♂ either on rocks below colony or on nest-site performs dart-gape in which head is drawn over back, then rapidly and repeatedly darted upwards and forwards. When ♀ approaches, ♂ performs throw-back with neck laid backwards along back and beak pointed skywards. When ♀ beside ♂, he bows with head and bill pointed down and pressed to breast. Sometimes ♂ shows ♀ nest-site; other times several ♀♀ visit ♂ at nest-site. In greeting, bird at nest bows and gapes upward, moving head from side to side. Incoming bird, after giving nest material to partner, also gapes. Both also throat-click with head, neck, body and tail in semi-horizontal position over back or neck of partner. Copulation often preceeded by gaping and bowing. Mutual preening frequent during courtship and incubation.

NEST: a heap of seaweed lined with grass, built by both sexes. Av. size (*P. a. aristotelis*) 45–55 cm across by 15 cm high (Cramp and Simmons 1977).

EGGS: 2–3, laid at intervals of 24–36 h. Long ovals, pale blue with whitish chalky outer layer. SIZE: 52–77 × 35–41 (63 × 39). WEIGHT: 49.

Laying dates: Morocco Apr–June; Tunisia Feb; confirmation of recent breeding in Libya required (Bundy 1976).

Incubation begins with 2nd egg; carried out by both parents. Period: (Europe) 30–31 days. Both parents care for and feed young by regurgitation. When feeding, young put bill inside parent's bill. During last 10 days in nest and when out of nest, young very curious, investigating anything that moves. Fledging period: (Europe) 45–58 days (Cramp and Simmons 1977).

Breeding success: no data Africa; Europe 1·87 young/nest, the small, poorly built nests having poor breeding success because more eggs or young tend to fall out of them (Cramp and Simmons 1977).

References
Cramp, S. and Simmons K. E. L. (1977).
Etchécopar, R. D. and Hüe, F. (1967).

Plate 8

(Opp. p. 99)

Phalacrocorax pygmaeus (Pallas). Pygmy Cormorant. Cormoran pygmée.

Pelecanus pygmeus [sic] Pallas, 1773. Reise Versch. Prov. Russ. Reichs, 2, p. 712, pl. G; Caspian Sea.

Range and Status. In Algeria long extinct but once resident Lakes Fetzara and Halloula where it bred in 19th century; vagrant in Tunisia.

Description. ADULT ♂ (non-breeding): overall dark plumage; head, neck, mantle, back, rump and underparts black to dark brown. Small crest on forehead. Tail black. Flight feathers grey-black; scapulars and upperwing-coverts glossy grey with narrow black margins; underwing-coverts black. Chin often white; throat and foreneck pale brown. Bill, legs, feet and bare skin around eye and at corner of mouth black; eye dark. Sexes alike. ADULT ♂ (breeding): plumage black, speckled with many white filoplumes; head, neck and upper breast with definite velvety brown appearance. SIZE: wing, ♂ (11 specimens) 195–217 (206), ♀ (7) 193–208 (201); tail, ♂ (6) 137–145 (142), ♀ (5) 139–147 (141); bill, ♂ (6) 29–33 (31), ♀ (5) 27–31 (29); tarsus, ♂ (6) 37–40 (38), ♀ (5) 36–39 (38). WEIGHT: ♂ 650, 710, 870; ♀ 565, 640.

IMMATURE: like non-breeding adult but browner and with brownish white underparts and yellowish bill.

DOWNY YOUNG: naked at hatching, skin black, gradually covered with dark brown down.

Field Characters. Small, short-necked, round-headed, fairly long-tailed cormorant with dark plumage. Differs from Long-tailed Cormorant *P. africanus* in having black, not yellow, bill and absence of black subterminal spots on scapulars and upperwing-coverts. Immatures of these 2 spp. indistinguishable in field.

Voice. Not recorded. Silent except during breeding season.

General Habits. Scarcely known in Africa. In Palearctic mainly gregarious in small flocks but sometimes solitary. Usually in open standing or slow-moving freshwater. In Palearctic some migratory from Aug or Sept to Mar or Apr with 1 straggler to Tunisia (Sfax) (Etchécopar and Hüe 1967).

Food. Not recorded in Africa, but probably primarily small fish.

References
Cramp, S. and Simmons, K. E. L. (1977).

Phalacrocorax pygmaeus

X Vagrant

Phalacrocorax africanus (Gmelin). Long-tailed Cormorant; Reed Cormorant. Cormoran africain.

Plate 8

Pelecanus africanus Gmelin, 1789. Syst. Nat., 1, p. 577; based on "African Shag" of Latham, 1785, General Synop. Birds, 3, p. 606—Africa.

(Opp. p. 99)

Range and Status. Resident, widely distributed in freshwater lakes, rivers and swamps but also estuaries and mangrove creeks, mainly south of about 18°N from Mauritania and Senegal to Sudan and Ethiopia south to Cape. In 19th century in Egypt north to Faiyum. Replaced by Crowned Cormorant *P. coronatus* on rocky offshore islands washed by cold Benguela Current along west coast of southern Africa from Namibia to Cape.

Description. *P. a. africanus* (Gmelin), ADULT ♂: overall black. Forehead, crown, nape, side of head and neck velvety black. Forehead with tuft of stiff feathers black at tips, white at bases. Tuft of white filoplumes behind eyes and over ears. Mantle, back, rump and uppertail-coverts black scaled with off-white. Tail long, graduated, stiff and black with slight sheen. Primaries and secondaries black; upperwing-coverts and scapulars bronze-grey with broad velvety black tips. Underparts, including underwing, black. Bill yellow with black culmen and dark stripes on lower mandible; bare skin of face yellow, orange-yellow or red early in breeding season; eye ruby-red; legs and feet black. Sexes alike. SIZE: wing, ♂ (6 specimens) 206–219 (212), ♀ (8) 194–216 (207); tail, ♂ (5) 144–153 (149), ♀ (5) 139–164 (148); bill, ♂ (6) 29–33 (31), ♀ (8) 26–32 (30); tarsus, ♂ (2) 37, ♀ (4) 34–36 (36). WEIGHT: ♂ 440, 685, ♀ 550, immature ♂ 680.

IMMATURE: upperparts with brownish sheen; no crest. Wing-coverts and scapulars without black tips. Underparts whitish and streaked with varying amounts of buff and brown. Flanks and undertail often black. Eye light brown.

DOWNY YOUNG: at hatching has grey skin, pale yellow head, red throat, black line from nostrils across eye to ear opening, and black bill; later covered in fluffy jet-black down.

Field Characters. A small, long-tailed, short-necked dark cormorant with a short bill. Swims low in water with only head and neck showing, and sits on branches overlooking water, rarely on shoreline. Distinguished from *P. coronatus* by broad, not narrow, terminal tip on scapulars, juvenile being fully white below, and less well developed crest.

Voice. Recorded (2a). Usually silent away from colony or roost. At roost a bleating 'hahahahahaha', and at nest 'hissing' and 'cackling' sounds. Young produce an incessant throaty cackling when begging.

General Habits. Well known. Spends daylight hours alone or in small groups, mainly in freshwater habitats; sometimes coastal lagoons, estuaries and mangroves, less often inland alkaline lakes. Occurs more often on smaller rivers and ponds than Great Cormorant *P. corbo*. Swims low in water with only head and part of neck showing. If alarmed in water, almost immediately flies away, rarely dives for cover. Perches on branches overlooking water, often in wing-spread posture probably to dry feathers, balance, regulate body temperature, and possibly to inform others of location of a profitable fish area (Jones 1978).

Phalacrocorax africanus

Fishes in sheltered water 30–200 cm deep and within 100 m of shore, Lake St Lucia (Whitfield and Blaber 1979); mean depth 2·14 m, Lake Kariba (Birkhead 1978). Tends to feed alone although fishes with own species or in association with Pink-backed Pelican *Pelecanus rufescens* and Great White Pelican *P. ono-crotalus*. When diving in pursuit of fish, head is submerged followed by rest of body. Fish captured underwater between mandibles and swallowed head first after surfacing. Dives last 3–18 (mean 9) s. Fishes any time of day with peak activity 06.00–08.00 h and 15.00–17.00 h. Fishes 3·1 h/day or 26% of daylight, Lake St Lucia (Whitfield and Blaber 1979).

Roosts on *Typha*, *Phragmites*, or partly submerged trees or bushes, sometimes in large numbers of several thousands, often with Cattle Egret *Bubulcus ibis*, Darter *Anhinga melanogaster* and other cormorants. Flies to roost in compact groups rather than in lines or V-formation. Arrives 1 h before sunset, departs sometimes before sunrise but normally 0·5–1·5 h after sunrise, singly or in small groups of up to 20. Often first flies to communal day-time roost, then to feeding areas.

Well-marked movements in W Africa (e.g. Congo basin: Snow 1978; Nigeria: Elgood *et al.* 1973); present on large rivers when low, dispersing to pools during flooding. Individuals in northern tropics once considered to be migratory from central African breeding areas but this now thought unlikely with discovery of breeding in Mauritania, Senegal, Nigeria and Chad. Elsewhere in Africa movements irregular; little recorded.

Food. Mainly fish; also frogs (mainly frogs, South Africa), aquatic insects, crustaceans and small birds (young one in South Africa recorded with a *Coturnix* in its mouth: Duxbury 1963). May prefer long, cylindrical, slow-moving, lurking fish. Favourites include mormyrids, 41·0% (by weight) at Bangweulu swamp and Lake Mweru, Zambia (Bowmaker 1963); cichlids (*Haplochromis* and *Pseudocrenilabrus*) 66·1% (by number), over 70% (by weight) at Lake Kariba, Zimbabwe (Birkhead 1978); sole (*Solea*) and tilapia (*Sarotherodon*) at Lake St Lucia (Whitfield and Blaber 1979) and bottom-living squeakers (*Synodontis*), 75% of diet in Zambezi and Kafue rivers. Fish only (all *Tilapia* species of a very young age) fed to chicks (Tomlinson 1979).

Size of prey 1–15 g, mainly 3–4 g, Lake St Lucia (Whitfield and Blaber 1979); 8·0 (4–70·1) g in weight and 7·0 (2·3–19·0) cm long, Lake Kariba (Birkhead 1978); and 2–20 cm, Bangweulu and Meru. Av. daily food intake 80–85 g, *c.* 14% of bodyweight (Bowmaker 1963).

Breeding Habits. Well known. Nests on ground, in tufts of vegetation, partly submerged trees, reed beds or acacias far from water. In colonies, sometimes only 1 or 2 pairs, often with herons, storks, ibises, other cormorants and darters. Nests scattered throughout, not grouped within, mixed colony, but often nearer water than others.

Courtship little known. Displays include: (1) ♂, with neck arched, bill pointed forward and slightly up, waves wings *c.* 3 times/2 s; (2) mutual neck-rubbing; (3) head-shaking; (4) bill-touching; (5) mutual preening; (6) intertwining of necks; and (7) stick-offering.

NEST: a platform of twigs and other vegetation, *c.* 25 cm in diameter, 2–4 cm deep. Built 0·5–6 m above water or ground, touching or 1–2 m apart.

EGGS: 2–8; Ghana mean (59 clutches) 3·8; South Africa (107, Cape) 2·49, (53, highveld) 3·34; Zimbabwe (216) 3·25; Namibia (23) 2·3; Botswana (3) 4·23; total mean (435) 3·09. Pale blue to light green with chalky covering. SIZE: (304 eggs) 38–54 × 26–42 (44 × 29).

Breeding opportunistic, with eggs laid in many months; in rainy season often with first heavy rains, sometimes late in rains or early dry season in inundated areas. Laying dates: Mauritania Mar–Oct; Senegal Jan–Feb, Sept–Dec (mainly dry); Gambia July; Mali Oct; Ghana June–July (rains); Nigeria Jan–Feb (dry), Aug–Dec (end rains); Chad July; Niger Jan–Feb, Sept–Dec; São Tomé Nov–Dec; Cameroon Jan; Ethiopia Mar, May–Sept (rains); E Kenya Feb–Oct, Dec, peak May–June; W Kenya, Uganda Mar, May–Dec, peak Aug–Oct (end rains); Zaïre Mar–Apr, July; Tanzania May–June; Zambia Jan–Sept, Dec; Malawi Feb–Mar, May, Jul–Aug; Zimbabwe Jan–Dec, with major peak Feb–Mar; Botswana Mar–June; Mozambique Sept; Namibia Mar–June, Aug; South Africa Jan–Dec, peaking Transvaal, Oct–Dec (early rains), and Cape, Aug–Oct (spring).

Incubation begins with 1st egg; carried out by both sexes; period 23–25 days. Early in incubation, change-over takes 10–20 min, later 1–2 min. Young cared for and fed by both parents by regurgitation.

Survival data (Ghana): of 27 nests, 80% eggs hatched, 63% chicks survived to leave nest (Bowen *et al.* 1962).

References

Birkhead, M. E. (1978).
Bowen, W. *et al.* (1962).
Bowmaker, A. P. (1963).
Jones, P. J. (1978).
Whitfield, A. K. and Blaber, S. J. M. (1979).

Plate 8
(Opp. p. 99)

Phalacrocorax coronatus (Wahlberg). Crowned Cormorant. Cormoran couronné.

Graculus coronatus Wahlberg, 1855. Öfv. K. Sv. Vet.-Akad. Förh., 12. p. 214; Possession Island, South West Africa.

Range and Status. Resident, frequent to uncommon, on rocky coasts and islands of Namibia and South Africa from Swakopmund to Cape Agulhas. Often considered to be *P. africanus coronatus*. In keeping with the conclusions of Snow (1978) and others, we treat it as a separate species because it is ecologically distinct from the Long-tailed Cormorant *P. africanus* and, although it occurs close to this species, it does not integrate with it.

Probably less than 1500 birds on islands off South Africa and Namibia coasts. Thought to be declining, possibly because vulnerable to disturbance and oiling (Siegfried *et al.* 1976).

Description. ADULT ♂: overall plumage and soft parts very similar to those of Long-tailed, but slightly smaller in size (length 54 cm; Long-tailed 60 cm) with shorter tail, longer legs, scapulars and wing-coverts with broader black edges and narrower black tips. Crest always present. Lacks tuft of white filoplumes behind eyes. Gape yellow; eye red. Sexes alike. SIZE: (8 specimens) wing, 198–223 (210); tail, 115–168 (135); tarsus, 37–42 (39); culmen, 27–35 (31). WEIGHT: 800 g.

IMMATURE: much browner than immature Long-tailed.
DOWNY YOUNG: naked at hatching, dark pink to red skin turning dull black soon afterwards; later covered with black down except for light yellow crown. Bare skin of throat next to mandible on either side reddish, speckled yellow, and black underneath; legs and feet black.

Field Characters. A dark cormorant, distinguished from other coastal cormorants by small size, red eye, yellow gape and long tail. Difficult to distinguish from Long-tailed Cormorant; habitat preference probably best distinguishing character as Long-tailed not found, as Crowned Cormorant is, on rocky offshore islands and coasts washed by cold Benguela current. At close range diagnostic features include narrow, not broad, black terminal tip on scapulars, smaller size, longer crest, less scaly back, comparatively shorter tail, longer legs, and juvenile never fully white below.

Voice. Not recorded.

General Habits. Scarcely known. Confined to coastal islands and shorelines washed by cold water; does not occur inland. Habits probably very much like other coastal cormorants but details unrecorded.

Food. Clinid fish, pipefish, sole, shrimp and isopods. Captures slow-moving, benthic fish found close inshore; mean weight of meal 21 g (Rand 1960).

Breeding Habits. Little known. Breeds in small groups of *c.* 4 to *c.* 150 pairs on cliffs on mainland and islands, flat rocks, ledges, sometimes 2–2·5 m above ground in bushes and small trees, under guano platforms and on kelp wracks at high spring-tide mark on island beaches. Nests in sheltered, not exposed areas, but usually near other species. Some years no nests appear, while other years 4–150 nests recorded in same area (Williams 1978); elsewhere same nests used every year, becoming substantial platforms 50 cm or more thick. Courtship not described. Nest material gathered at high water mark rather than by diving.

NEST: a platform mainly of brown algae and sticks sometimes mixed with feathers, bones, rope, wire, netting and plastic bags. Inner diameter 12 cm with shallow depression 2–3 cm deep (Berry 1974); contains large number of ticks.

EGGS: 2–4; Walvis Bay mean, 2·5; Penguin, Shark and Long Islands (27) 1·93; South Africa (777) 2·42 (SAOSNRC). Long ovals, pale blue with chalky white outer layer. SIZE: (323 eggs) 41–58 × 28–35 (47 × 31).

Laying dates: Namibia Jan–Feb, Apr–June, Oct–Dec, mainly Oct–Feb and possibly year-round; South Africa year-round, peaking Aug–Dec (spring).

Phalacrocorax coronatus

At Walvis Bay, 71 chicks recorded in 28 nests, 2–4/nest, av. 2, ranging from newly hatched to fledglings. Once primaries present, young become very agile and move from nest.

References
Berry, H. (1974).
Rand, R. W. (1960).
Shaughnessy, P. D. and Shaughnessy, G. L. (1978).

Family ANHINGIDAE: darters

Large aquatic birds resembling, although slimmer than, most cormorants. Slender, serrated bill without hook; small head; long and slender neck with modified articular surface of 8th and 9th vertebrae forming S-shaped curve; tail long and strongly graduated. Wings broad and long; outer webs of central pair of rectrices and longest pair of scapulars with transverse grooves. Moves wings at intervals; soars. Flight feathers moulted nearly simultaneously, causing temporary flightlessness. Feed with slow, prowling progression underwater, piercing prey with a thrust of the mandibles; do not actively pursue prey. Tend to be less buoyant and can remain submerged in water longer than cormorants. Lack heavy musculature of hind limbs for rapid swimming underwater; hind limb muscles adapted for climbing and perching. A world-wide family in warm temperate and tropical latitudes. 1 genus, *Anhinga*, and, following Voous (1973), 2 species, *melanogaster* and *anhinga*.

Owre (1967a) has shown that major differences between darters and cormorants exist in feeding behaviour, ptilosis and post-cranial osteology and myology and has recommended they be retained in a separate family. We agree with Owre that differences between darters and cormorants are very major and so have followed his arrangement in retaining separate families for these groups, contra Dorst and Mougin (1979).

Genus *Anhinga* Brisson

Characters as for the family; in Africa *A. melanogaster*, with 1 subspecies, *rufa*.

Plate 8

(Opp. p. 99)

Anhinga melanogaster Pennant. Darter. Anhinga.

Anhinga melanogaster Pennant, 1769. Indian Zoöl., p. 13, pl. 12; Ceylon and Java.

Range and Status. Resident, widely distributed, common to locally abundant in freshwater lakes, rivers, swamps, marshes and reservoirs; frequent to uncommon in temporary inundations, brackish waters and coastal lagoons. South of about 18°N latitude from Mauritania east to Ethiopia and south to Cape.

Anhinga melanogaster

Description. *A. m. rufa* (Daudin), ADULT ♂ crown, nape and hindneck dark blackish brown. Side and fore-neck chestnut with lateral white stripe, edged blackish from cheek through top third of neck; inconspicuous plumes on stripe. Chin and throat buff. Mantle, back, rump, uppertail-coverts and underparts black to brown. Primaries and secondaries black; scapulars, tertials and wing-coverts black with white shaft streaks; underwing black. Bill greenish horn to yellowish brown; bare facial skin brown to yellow-brown; gular area creamy to greenish black; eye golden yellow, ringed yellow to brown; legs and feet brown to grey. ADULT ♀: crown, nape, hindneck and mantle brown; stripe less evident. ADULT ♂ (breeding): black colours become glossy; lateral white stripe evident; gular area greenish black. SIZE: wing, ♂ (8 specimens) 328–364 (349), ♀ (7) 331–360 (344); tail, ♂ (8) 229–253 (238), ♀ (4) 233–248 (239); bill, ♂ (12) 75–89 (81), ♀ (6) 71–78 (76); tarsus, ♂ (11) 41–46 (44), ♀ (7) 41–45 (42). WEIGHT: Adult ♂ (7) 948–1815 (1292), immature adult (5) 1055–1224 (1178), adult ♀ (2) 1358–1530 (1444).

IMMATURE: like ♀ but underparts buffish brown.

DOWNY YOUNG: naked at hatching then covered with white down; later buff to brown on head, neck and mantle; no neck stripe; underparts whitish to greyish; eye greyish; bill pale horn; feet dull whitish.

Field Characters. Large, dark, water birds, distinguished from cormorants by pointed bill and much smaller head, long thin neck, and long graduated tail often spread into fan-shape in flight. Neck conspicuously kinked during flight and when perched. Flies with a few rapid wing-flaps, then glides. Soars in thermals. Swims low in water, usually with only long neck and head showing.

Voice. Recorded (6, 18). Normally silent except at nest where it emits harsh croaking quack; may emit flock-integrating calls outside breeding season.

General Habits. Well known. Prefers shallow, still, freshwater lakes and rivers fringed with reeds and trees; also alkaline lakes; less often lagoons, estuaries, shallow inlets and forested streams. Often solitary, perching with tail hanging down and wings half-spread. Roosts in groups of 10–100 in trees, bushes and reed beds often with cormorants or herons. Leaves night-time roost 0·5–1·0 h after sunrise, flying to feeding area. May roost at foraging areas.

Solitary feeder; often stalks prey with neck retracted. When within range specially adapted neck muscles release a sudden forward thrust of neck, spearing prey with mandibles (see **A**). At surface shakes prey free, catches it in mid-air and swallows it head first. Appears to pierce smaller fish mostly by upper mandible, larger fish by both mandibles.

Becomes airborne from perch; rarely takes off from water and then with difficulty. After feeding, hops, waddles, scrambles and climbs from water onto bush, tree or bank. Enters water by climbing down into it, by diving into it from overhanging branches, or by a belly-landing on the surface. When swimming, often submerges whole body with only head and neck above the surface. Dives and swims slowly underwater for 30–60 s. Feet are used together when swimming underwater but alternately while swimming on surface. Belly and back plumage absorbs water quickly, reducing buoyancy, to permit slow submerged swimming among vegetation when searching for prey.

Flies fast, often close to the surface of water. Soars and circles to considerable heights singly or in groups. Passes through a flightless stage when all remiges (but not rectrices) moult at same time. Spreads wings to dry and thermoregulate.

Subject to local movements that require documentation.

Food. Mainly fish, but also frogs and aquatic arthropods. At Lake Kariba (Zimbabwe) takes a variety of prey species (only 31% fed on 1 sp. alone; cf. 86% of Long-tailed Cormorants *Phalacrocorax africanus*, same location), 8 (2–17) cm long, and mainly cichlids (*Pseudocrenilabrus*, *Sarotherodon*, and *Tilapia*; 90% by number, 70% by weight) (Birkhead 1978). At Lakes Victoria and Albert mainly *Haplochromis*, but also *Lates*, *Alestes*, *Bagrus*, *Haplochilichthys* and *Tilapia* (Cott 1961); in Zaïre (Katanga) *Barbus* (Ruwet 1963); and in S Africa (Barberspan) *Labeo* (Milstein 1975).

Breeding Habits. Well known. Nests usually in colonies of loose groups of 6 to several thousand pairs, often with cormorants, egrets and herons, in trees (*Acacia*, *Aeschynomene*, *Craeva*, *Sesbania*) and reed beds usually 1–6 m above surface of water.

At onset of breeding ♂ claims old nest or builds new nest-platform. From it, with bill pointed upwards at angle of 45°, stretches neck, head and tail raised 80° above horizontal, sometimes raising each wing alternately at least twice a second. ♀ circles several ♂♂, then lands next to a ♂ who points at her. If ♀ moves to nest, ♂ leaves, circles area, and returns, often with a twig, or clump of leaves or aquatic plants. Both point, intertwine necks, fluff feathers, preen each other, and snap-bow with head and neck in an inverted U-shape, spread tail held 80° above horizontal and wings slightly raised and vibrated rapidly. If ♀ leaves to circle area, ♂ waves wings and points. Copulation occurs when ♀ crouches on nest and lowers neck; ♂ with wings partly open mounts and grasps her bill or nearby stick. Mating occurs several times during first few days of pair-formation and may continue into incubation.

After pair formed, ♂ collects most of nest material; ♀ builds nest. At nest-relief, incoming bird emits several calls before landing; bird on nest, with head outstretched and pointed downward, produces similar calls. Bird on nest then extends head upward towards incoming bird. At nest-relief, both intertwine necks, snap-bow and point.

NEST: a platform of sticks, twigs and reeds, lined with finer twigs and bits of green reeds. 45 cm in diameter; av. height above ground (88 nests) 402 cm (SAOSNRC). Built in 1 day.

EGGS: 2–6, laid at irregular intervals; E Africa mean (52 clutches) 3·35; Ghana (45) 3·7; Zimbabwe (622) 3·25; Namibia and Botswana (20) 2·95; South Africa (111, SW Cape) 2·93, (39, Natal) 3·25, (17, Orange Free State) 3·0, (17, Transvaal) 3·82 (SAOSNRC). Very long ovals, pale greenish or bluish white with varying amount of chalky outer layer, sometimes with dark brown spots. SIZE: (164 eggs) 46–60 × 31–40 (53 × 35). WEIGHT: 37.

Laying dates: may be laid all year round, or seasonally; Gambia Aug; Guinea-Bissau July–Oct; Gabon Aug–Sept; Mali Mar; Ghana July, Sept; Nigeria June–Mar; Sudan Aug–Sept; Ethiopia Jan–May, July–Dec, peak Mar (early rains); Somalia Oct–Dec; E Kenya, N Tanzania year-round, peak May–Sept (end rains and mid-year dry season); W Kenya, Uganda, year-round, especially Aug–Jan, avoiding wettest months; S Tanzania Feb, Apr, June–July (dry); Zaïre July; Burundi, Rwanda Apr; Zambia, Malawi, Zimbabwe year-round or most months, peaking Feb–Mar (late rains); Botswana Jan, Mar (wet), July, Oct (dry), Dec (wet); Mozambique Oct; Namibia Jan–Apr; South Africa Jan–Dec. In most areas avoids heaviest rains and lays either at end of rains or in dry season.

Incubation details little known; begins 1st egg; by both sexes; period estimated 21–28 days (*c.* 22 days: SAOSNRC).

Young naked at hatching; at 2 days covered with white down, later turning buff-brown on head, neck and mantle. Primaries, secondaries and tail feathers appear at 3 weeks, when leave nest, well developed at 4 weeks. Rarely return to the nest at 5 weeks; fly short distances of up to 1·5 km at *c.* 7–8 weeks. Exact time of fledging not known.

Both parents brood and feed young about equally. Very young birds fed predigested food from parent's bill tip, later put bill into parent's bill when feeding. During 1st week young brooded continuously; 2nd week adult present but does not brood continuously. From 3rd week on, young left increasingly unattended except at feeding time.

Breeding success: (Ghana) of 26 nests, 89% eggs hatched, 72% chicks left nests; and in 2nd breeding wave, of 19 nests, 58% eggs hatched, and 40% chicks left nest (Bowen *et al.* 1962).

References
Birkhead, M. E. (1978).
Bowen, W. *et al.* (1962).
Owre, O. T. (1967).

Illustrations by Peter Hayman.

A

Family PELECANIDAE: pelicans

Very large to enormous water birds; among the largest flying birds. Plumage silky, usually white or grey, some black. Wings long, but of medium aspect ratio (6·7–7·4); outer primaries deeply emarginated both webs. Tail very short, heads tufted or crested (breeding). Bill long, upper mandible rigid, keeled above, ridged, grooved and serrated within, tip with strong hooked 'nail'; lower mandible loosely articulated, flexible, with muscular extensible dependent pouch attached. Legs short, set far back on body, adapted to swimming, giving ungainly appearance on land; feet very large. Bare skin of face, pouch, feet, brightly coloured, intensified in breeding season. ♂♂ always larger, sometimes much larger than ♀♀.

1 genus, *Pelecanus*; cosmopolitan, with 7, perhaps 8 species forming 3 superspecies separable by fishing habits (plunge-diving, solitary, or communal) and nesting (small, loose tree or large, packed ground colonies). The 3 African species represent 2 of these superspecies. 2, *P. rufescens* and *P. onocrotalus*, are mainly tropical residents, *P. onocrotalus* also migrant; 1, *P. crispus*, scarce Palearctic winter migrant. 2, *P. rufescens* and *P. onocrotalus*, thoroughly studied in most details.

Genus *Pelecanus* Linnaeus

Plate 9

(Opp. p. 146)

Pelecanus onocrotalus Linnaeus. Great White Pelican. Pélican blanc.

Pelecanus Onocrotalus Linnaeus, 1758. Syst. Nat. (10th ed.), p. 132; Caspian Sea.

Range and Status. Resident throughout on large alkaline or freshwater lakes, sometimes marine (Mauritania, South Africa); partial Palearctic winter migrant, N Africa. Locally very abundant; not threatened at present, but breeding colonies readily deserted, and very vulnerable to human interference.

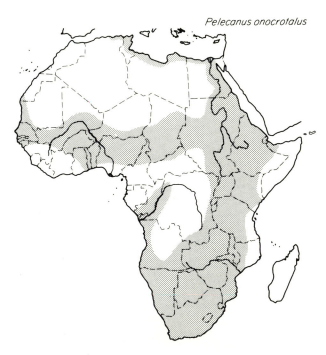

Pelecanus onocrotalus

Description. ADULT ♂: pure white, variously tinged pink, with secretion from uropygial gland. Wing feathers black, tail white. Bill bright yellow and bluish, tipped with red nail; pouch and feet bright yellow; bare facial skin pink; eye dark red-brown. ♀ similar, considerably smaller (10–15%), and much lighter. ADULT ♂ and ♀ (breeding): both develop swollen knobs at base of upper mandible and crests, that of ♀ normally being longer than that of ♂. Knob and bare skin of ♂ lemon-yellow, of ♀ rich orange, becoming pink in both once eggs have been laid. SIZE: wing, ♂ 650–735 (702), ♀ 605–618; tail, ♂ 150–210 (181), ♀ 135–190; tarsus, ♂ 130–150 (142), ♀ 115–135; span,

♂ 2720–3050 (2858), ♀ 2260–2655 (2644). WEIGHT: ♂ 9–15 (11·5) kg, ♀ 5·4–9 (7·6) kg, *c.* 66% of ♂ weight (Din and Eltringham 1977).

IMMATURE: pale brownish grey, mottled; head paler, primaries black, tail whitish. Bill grey; pouch blackish with ochre patches; feet grey-yellow.

DOWNY YOUNG: at first pink naked, then black naked, then covered with dense dark brown down. Pouch, bare skin, bill and feet black.

Plumage sometimes acquires brown colours through iron-staining, varying from yellowish breast-band at water level to dark orange-brown all over, whereupon scarcely recognizable as same species. Darkest birds normally seen at, or near, breeding colonies; reasons unexplained (Baxter and Urban 1970).

P. o. roseus (Gmelin) has been separated as a distinct race in Africa, being pinker and smaller. Recent measurements do not support this, however, and pink colour is merely secretion of uropygial gland. We therefore consider the species to be monotypic.

Field Characters. Adults immediately recognizable by almost pure white plumage contrasting strongly in flight with black primaries, bright yellow bill, pouch and feet, dark eye; crestless when not breeding. Pink-backed Pelican *P. rufescens* adult is much smaller, greyer. Dalmatian Pelican *P. crispus* adult much greyer, primaries white, bill black with red pouch, legs black, eye whitish. Immatures more difficult to distinguish; but Pink-backed generally much browner, much smaller and Dalmatian lacks dark wing feathers in flight.

Voice. Recorded (2a, 18). Not very vocal except at breeding colonies. Commonest call a loud deep 'moo', 'ha-oogh', associated with advertisement display; deep grunts, 'hunh-hunh-hunh', 'orrh-orrh-orrh', associated with aggression. Low grunts, 'huh-huh-huh', by parents to young. Small young utter yelping 'yewk-yewk-yewk' and larger young soliciting adults utter wailing 'yaaaa-ew' resembling wails of human children. A continuous roar or hum emanates from a large breeding colony, never ceasing entirely even at night.

General Habits. Very well known. Intensely gregarious, locally much more numerous than Pink-backed Pelican, but confined to larger bodies of water, often alkaline or saline, hence less widespread. Breeds on sea islands off Mauritania and South Africa, but mainly occurs inland, especially on lakes of E African Rift Valley. Roosts, rests and loafs in large flocks on the ground, not in trees as can scarcely perch on them except rarely if forced down by storms. On ground walks clumsily on short legs, swinging from side to side. In water swims swiftly, with strong paddling strokes, maximum speed *c.* 6 km/h.

When living temporarily in suitable habitat, is not dependent on daily thermals for activity, as is tree-roosting Pink-backed Pelican. From roosts on shore commences fishing soon after daylight, and may have caught requirements 1–2 h later. Then spends most of day loafing, preening and bathing in favoured spots, in large flocks of 500–3000, often associated with other pelican spp., cormorants and other water birds. Normally inactive by night, but may fish singly on moonlit nights and locally may make regular nocturnal flights (K. Curry-Lindahl, pers. comm.). All night and most of day (21–24 h) normally spent roosting or loafing. Bathes in freshwater streams, alkaline lakes, vigorously ducking head and body and flapping wings.

Habitually fishes in groups, but often also singly. Single fishers may be relatively more successful, but group fishing involves more birds. Between 2 and 40 (usually 8–12) gather and swim forward in horseshoe formation, open end towards front, parallel to shore in shallow water. At intervals of 15–20 s, sometimes longer, all flip open wings and almost simultaneously plunge bills into centre of horseshoe; fish caught in about 20% of strikes. Group then swims on, sometimes joined by others, until satisfied individuals break off. When all are satisfied, collect on shore, resting and loafing in preferred roost area. Most morning fishing completed by 08.00–09.00 h, but may repeat in evening; sometimes fish all day. Occasionally several hundred gather in milling swarm, flapping frantically over one another to trap shoals of fish; or a long semi-circular line may form, bills open, held below water, moving slowly shorewards, trapping fish against land like animated seine-net. Bill is undoubtedly sensitively tactile, able to detect fish in opaque water; touch is e.g. gentle on bare human legs. Occasionally may scavenge on rubbish dumps (South Africa), and often associates with African fishing canoes, receiving some of catch.

Dependent on thermals to move from lake to lake. Then normally takes wing 1–3 h after daybreak, depending on weather. Alternately flaps and glides low over ground till thermal found, then spirals upwards to 1000 m or more above ground, afterwards flapping and gliding on chosen course in long V-shaped or curved skeins; flapping by one bird initiates flapping by next, all down the line. May use further thermals to regain lost height, and on arrival at destination usually descends swiftly from height with wings furled, circling and side-slipping, using spread feet as air-brakes, landing finally with heavy flaps. Able to fly for 8–9/24 h; may then cover 400–500 km/day. Eurasian birds may migrate to N Africa, and tropical birds undertake long movements from lake to lake, not well understood or observed, but definitely irregular, not always occurring at same time of year (E Africa). Such movements may be associated with breeding or variation in food supplies.

Food. Fish up to 600 g, especially cichlids (*Tilapia, Haplochromis*). Takes larger fish than Pink-backed Pelican, with some overlap. Can survive on abundant populations of very small fish, e.g. *Tilapia grahami*, Lake Nakuru, but when available large fish make up 90% of diet by weight. Food requirement estimated at 1200 g/day (10% bodyweight); full stomach contents 590 g (Uganda). At Lake Nakuru, population, av. 10,000 (85% of biomass of fish-eating birds), estimated to harvest *c.* 12,000 kg/fish/day, or 4380 t/year (Vareschi 1979). Can survive for several days without food when travelling, often resting for night on alkaline lakes lacking any fish.

Breeding Habits. Intimately known. Nests in few, scattered, regular colonies of 1000–30,000 pairs, sometimes opportunistically in huge numbers in sites only occasionally available. Some colonies far from water or rocky mountains, others on islands in lakes or alkaline mudflats. Regular colonies known: Mauritania (1), Senegal (1), Nigeria (1, abandoned ?1980), Chad (1, abandoned ?1980), Ethiopia (1), Kenya (1, since 1968), Tanzania (1), Namibia (1), South Africa (2). Other, possibly less regular colonies have been observed in Zambia, Botswana, Mali, probably elsewhere. Total breeding population may av. 50,000–60,000 pairs, but numbers in colonies fluctuate widely (Ethiopia, 3000–14,000), av. *c.* 6000–8000, over 9 years (Urban, in press)). May suddenly abandon colony through failure of food supply, human disturbance, or even heavy storms, leaving eggs, small and large young. Very shy of humans at breeding colonies, but do not react to e.g. hippopotamuses. Colonies normally on more or less inaccessible islands or in wet swamps, probably to avoid mammalian predators. Colonies should never be approached by humans, except when exercising great care.

Large colonies consist of discrete groups laying synchronously; Ethiopia, a maximum of 4000–6000 pairs at one time in colonies totalling 10,000–14,000 pairs. May breed continuously for up to 2 years or longer, or be more regularly seasonal, depending on area; can evidently breed opportunistically at will given suitable but unusual conditions. When one group vacates an area, others immediately occupy it. Colonies may be triggered by breeding of flamingoes especially, ibis and herons, which are then wiped out by much larger pelicans.

At onset of breeding cycle, both sexes develop a swollen knob on forehead and a crest. Sexes immediately distinguishable as bare skin of ♀ is orange, of ♂ pale yellow. Groups of ♂♂ collect on shore and do 'head-up' (see **A**, p. 124), raising bill skywards, sometimes spreading yellow pouch ('spade-pouching': Feely 1962), 'mooing' and thrusting bills towards centre of group, occasionally interlocking bills; such groups noisy, conspicuous. Single, or several ♀♀ ready to mate join such groups and are immediately pursued by one or several ♂♂ on ground or on water. 1 ♂ normally soon becomes dominant and repels others by 'head-up' and mooing call. Pair-formation rapid, probably occurs afresh each year. Mated pair then lands, walks along shore in 'strutting walk' (**B**), heads held high, wings partly spread; yellow pouch of ♂ spread and fluttering, that of ♀ closed. May then stand about, or proceed almost at once to join a laying group. ♀ selects nest-site, where she remains; mating process and site selection may occupy only a few hours.

A

No pre-copulatory display recorded. Successful copulation only on land, but ♂♂ may attempt copulation in water, forcing ♀ right under. ♀ normally accepts ♂ squatting on future nest-site; ♂ seizes her neck in bill, mounts and copulates in 3–5 s, flapping wings for balance. Copulation frequent in nest-building and before egg-laying, thereafter ceases. Knob shrinks immediately after pair-formation and normally disappears when eggs have been laid; crest retained longer. Any 'knobbed' birds indicate breeding in vicinity.

NEST: ♂ only collects nest material, walking 50 m or more to low bushes, shrubs, or picking up grass, sticks, feathers, often robbing other nests. May scoop out nest-hollow by sideways sweep of flexible lower mandible (**C**), Material collected in pouch is brought to nest-site (**D**), deposited before ♀, who draws it towards herself making small, slight nest, 35–60 cm across (av. 46·4). Pair-formation precedes laying by only 3–4 days, and additional nest material is added after eggs laid. Nests practically contiguous, 48–107 cm apart, av. 77 cm; sitting birds often touch.

EGGS: 1–3, normally 2; Ethiopia mean (over 500 clutches) 1·88; Natal (9) 1·89; Seal Island (1931, SAOS NRC) mean (42 clutches) 1·91, but recent South African clutches av. smaller, 1·62 (Cooper 1980). Any nests with 4–5 eggs laid by 2 ♀♀. Probably laid on successive days. Pale bluish white with chalky covering, soon stained brown. SIZE: 86·8–98·5 × 53·5–64·0 (60·2 × 92·3).

Laying dates: (season varies) Mauritania mainly Oct–Jan (dry season), also Mar, Apr, Sept; Senegal Dec–Mar (dry); Mali Jan (dry); Nigeria Oct–Dec (dry); Cameroon Sept–Dec (mainly dry); Chad Dec–Jan (dry); Ethiopia Sept–July, peaking Dec–Jan (dry); Kenya (since 1968) mainly in main rains, peaking Apr–June, sometimes continuing year-round; S Tanzania June–Sept (after height of main rains but in inundation period); Zambia Aug–Sept (dry); Botswana July–Aug (dry); Namibia, Etosha Pan July–Sept (dry), near Walvis Bay Sept (dry); South Africa, Natal May–July (dry), Cape area Sept–Oct (spring). To summarize, prefers dry seasons, but may breed in rains, or opportunistically, sometimes year-round. Inaccessibility of nest-site probably more important than any other factor. No clear connection with food supply except in South Africa, where fish abundance coincides with breeding. One colony (Tanzania 1962) abandoned suddenly, apparently through loss of food supply.

Incubation begins with 1st egg, incubated under spread feet. Both sexes incubate, in spells of 24–72 h, associated with inability to fly far except on thermals. Some feeding grounds very distant (160 km) from colonies. At nest-relief, arriving bird lands outside main mass, walks into it, lunging with bill at others; arrives at nest, usually from in front, part-spreads wings; raises head well above horizontal, sometimes nearly vertical; then bows. Relieved bird stands, shuffles backwards, sometimes raises head; other then squats on nest, but both shuffle back and forth several times. Relieved bird then walks out of colony and takes off normally from open ground. Incubation period: estimated at 33–35 days in wild state, 30 days in captivity.

Newly hatched chick naked pink, days 1–3; naked black, days 4–14. Days 14–28 covered with dark chocolate-brown down, bill, pouch, feet black. Days 28–42 down becomes paler brown, feathers erupt, first wing and tail feathers, then body feathers. Can now walk; leaves adult breeding groups, forming into tightly

B

C

packed groups, known as pods, of 10–100 individuals. Pods move about by day and for some hours after dark. Days 56–70, young leave pods, walk about singly, are free swimming and practise wing-flapping. No weights for wild birds available, but a captive increased from less than 200 g to 13·9 kg, at 63 days, thereafter decreasing to 10·9 kg at 98 days (Portmann 1937). Wild young also appear to lose weight, becoming slimmer before first flight at 70–75 days. Large walking young can recognize its own parents from afar, runs to meet it, waving wings frantically, weaving head, biting own wings, sometimes falling, apparently in distraction behaviour. When parent alights, young pursues it, and when it stands still, seizes bill, forces parent to crouch, thrusts bill far down parental oesophagus and opens it to obtain food, stretching parental throat skin.

Either parent broods newly hatched young continuously in 24–72 h spells. Brooding reduced days 7–21, ceasing by day after about day 21, continuing at night. Parents shade chicks from sun during the day by turning backs to it and often spreading wings. First feeds delivered to naked pink young from inverted bill-tip, placed far back between legs; inverted red upper mandible nail acts like cup to receive regurgitated liquid matter, probably predigested fish. Undigested fish can be retained by parent (in stomach?) for up to 48 h. Black naked young reach up into parental pouch, held vertically, seeking red opening of parent's oesophagus.

Parent can locate its own young in a pod and recognize it; young sometimes cannot locate its parent. Locating young, adult reaches out, sometimes to middle of pod, siezes young by neck, violently shakes it and thus activates it to feed from pouch. Large walking young can recognize own parent, which on alighting seeks a convenient open place to feed. Parent will only feed own young, others repelled. Parent crouches or lies, young thrusts head far down parental throat, opening bill, and then violently struggles to obtain food, often dragging parent about helplessly (especially large ♂ young with smaller ♀ parent).

Eggs predated by Egyptian Vulture *Neophron percnopterus*, and young taken by eagles reduce total reared by, at most, 5–10%. Most predation occurs on periphery of tightly packed groups, synchronous laying thus helping to reduce it. Brood losses from sibling aggression apparently slight (unlike Pink-backed Pelican); only a little desultory pecking observed, unless adults are forced off nests, when predation and pecking at once increase. Although most (over 90%) eggs hatch, surviving broods av. 1·50 young by day 7, and by day 60 all successful adults are feeding single young. Estimated overall breeding success in successful colonies *c.* 0·8–1 young per pair breeding, but may be reduced by sudden mass desertions, and not all adults breed annually.

Young make first flights independent of adults. Do not then normally accompany adults to fishing grounds, but disperse widely at random for several hundred km. Before first flight they perform communal fishing behaviour of adults, so can presumably feed themselves at once. In some colonies maturing young consume all rotting carcasses floating in water, or scavenge them on land. Shortly after first flight young become much whiter, harder to distinguish with certainty from adults, as pouch and feet soon become yellow. Perhaps attain sexual maturity at 3 years. Possible life-span hard to estimate because of variable proportion of total adult population breeding annually (33–100% of maximum Lake Shala), while some may also be double-brooded in prolonged breeding over more than 1 year (Kenya). If 50% of adults breed, rear 0·8 young/pair and young suffer 50% mortality before sexual maturity, adult breeding life would be about 10 years. Captives live much longer.

References
Brown, L. H. and Urban, E. K. (1969).
Din, N. A. and Eltringham, S. K. (1974a; 1977).
Feely, J. M. (1962).
Urban, E. K. (in press).
Vesey-Fitzgerald, D. F. (1957).

Illustrations by Martin Woodcock after Brown, L. H. and Urban, E. K. (1969).

D

Plate 9
(Opp. p. 146)

Pelecanus rufescens **Gmelin. Pink-backed Pelican. Pélican roussâtre.**

Pelecanus rufescens Gmelin, 1789. Syst. Nat., 1, p. 571; West Africa.

Range and Status. Resident; widespread south of lat. 20°N; Gambia east to Gulf of Aden; south to Cape Province. On rivers, marshes, flood plains, lakes, not usually within dense forest. Tropical Africa common, locally abundant; South Africa considered threatened.

Pelecanus rufescens

Description. ADULT ♂: generally pale grey, mottled; head tufted. Face, throat and underparts whiter, back and rump pinkish, belly washed pink. Primaries blackish, secondaries grey-brown, edged grey. Tail (20 feathers) greyish white with black shafts. Bill grey or pink, nail orange or pink; pouch flesh-colour transversely striped yellow; bare facial skin, greyish flesh-colour; eye black or brown; feet yellowish. Sexes alike, ♀ smaller. ADULT ♂ and ♀ (breeding): develop a longish grey crest, a black patch round eye and pink skin above, yellow below; eyelids in ♂ yellow, ♀ orange. Pouch deep yellow, striped vertically blackish, inside deep red; feet red. Sexes almost identical. SIZE: wing, ♂ 595–615 (605), ♀ 545–580 (560); tail, ♂ 160–185 (172), ♀ 140–180 (166); tarsus, ♂ 90–100 (96), ♀ 75–100 (87); span, ♂ 2260–2415 (2339), ♀ 2160–2360 (2242). WEIGHT: ♂ 4·5–7·0 (6·0) kg; ♀ 3·9–6·2 (4·9) kg.

IMMATURE: browner than adult, head white, tufted; neck and wing-coverts brownish, back white; wing feathers brown, edged white; tail brown; bill grey; pouch yellow-green; facial skin grey; feet greyish pink.

DOWNY YOUNG: whitish, becoming greyer.

Field Characters. Much smaller, generally greyer than adult Great White Pelican *P. onocrotalus*; would not occur with Dalmatian Pelican *P. crispus*. Adult also distinguished from Great White Pelican by grey bill, pinkish, not bright yellow feet and pouch. In flight much less contrast between dark wing feathers and grey wing-coverts, pinkish back rarely visible. Immature is smaller in size, has browner plumage (including tail), grey beak, greenish yellow pouch, greyish pink feet distinctive.

Voice. Not recorded. Adults largely silent; 'blowing noises' (Serle 1943) and guttural calls at breeding colonies. Young emit loud begging calls resembling lowing of cattle.

General Habits. Very well known. Frequents almost any aquatic habitat; lakes, large rivers, dams, seasonal ponds. Prefers fresh water, but also occurs on alkaline or saline lakes and lagoons, sometimes in estuaries. Seldom actually on open sea-coast.

Roosts usually in trees, sometimes on ground, for 14–15/24 h; may fish on moonlit nights or by artificial light. Gregarious at roost, separating into smaller parties or singles to fish, becoming gregarious again when loafing, e.g. on sandbanks after feeding. Perches easily on trees. Fishes morning and evening, preferring quiet backwaters, weed-grown lagoons to open waters. Can survive sometimes on small areas of water, e.g. artificial dams or small ponds, because it is solitary.

Habitually fishes singly, first searching with head and neck raised, then retracting head and neck onto back, approaching prey cautiously, slowly, body low in water. Suddenly shoots out head and neck, capturing prey in about 40–50% of strikes. Occasionally fishes communally, in manner of Great White Pelican, in deep water or e.g. against banks where fish may be trapped. Spends only about 15–20% of daylight fishing. When not fishing, gathers in groups with other pelicans and cormorants, on regularly used 'loafing' grounds, e.g. sandbanks, rests, preens, often lies down. Bathes in fresh water vigorously, flapping wings, ducking head and body (Din and Eltringham 1974a).

Normally resident where it occurs, with local movements perhaps connected with varying water conditions, or resort to breeding areas. In W Africa some movement south in dry season, returning north in wet season. In flight, less dependent on strong thermals than heavier Great White Pelican, but breast muscles (7% of body-weight) do not permit sustained flapping flight. If travelling far alternately flaps and glides until it finds a thermal, then spirals up to 1000 m or more above ground, thereafter gliding without effort to other areas. Soars with emarginated primaries and tail spread.

Food. Fish of any size up to 400 g, especially cichlids (*Tilapia*, *Haplochromis* spp.). Larger fish more important by weight, but many small fish and fry taken. Some overlap in preferred prey size with Great White Pelican; where both are common, ecological separation is achieved and competition reduced by different feeding methods and preferred size of fish. Pink-backed Pelican normally takes fish of 80–290 g and large numbers of fry, cf. few fry and fish up to 500 g in Great White Pelican. Both take abundant *Haplochromis* spp. of similar size. Fish once caught in pouch seldom escape, swallowed with head raised, bill pointing skyward. Estimated food requirement: 776 g/day (14% of bodyweight). Av. full stomach contents *c.* 450 g. Normally catches daily, but can survive several days without food (Din and Eltringham 1974a).

Breeding Habits. Intimately known (Kenya–Uganda). Nests in colonies of 20–500 pairs in trees, rarely on ground (islands) reeds, low bushes. Large colonies composed of several groups each laying synchronously. Traditional sites resorted to annually, perhaps for centuries. May miss 1–2 years entirely, or occupy a fresh site briefly, but normally breeds yearly, with much less fluctuation in total numbers than Great White Pelican. Tall trees preferred, e.g. baobabs, *Bombax*, *Chlorophora*, large *Ficus* spp. May also use *Acacia*, *Euphorbia* (Zaïre, Uganda). Breeding colonies sometimes near but often unaccountably far from aquatic feeding grounds. Often shared with storks, ibises, herons, especially Marabou *Leptoptilos crumeniferus* and Yellow-billed Stork *Mycteria ibis*. Often breeds in populated areas close to man, in towns and villages (N Nigeria, Senegal); does not desert nest readily when disturbed.

At onset of breeding, flocks soar over site. ♂♂ collect in breeding trees and display, in groups or singly, often flying from tree to tree and fighting with bills interlocked. ♂ selects nest-site and there displays actively; these displays including especially (1) 'bill-clapping'—throws bill over back, thrashes wings and claps mandibles 25 times/min, accelerating to 30/min, if ♀ appears; (2) 'mouth open'—sits with pouch fully expanded, beak open, displaying yellow exterior and red interior; then points bill at passing pelicans, thrashing wings slightly. ♂♂ also bow, arching head down to breast with expanded pouch, or wag heads slowly from side to side, usually near other pelicans. Advertisement displays (1) and (2) attract ♀♀ to nest-site; new pairs probably formed annually. Displays are adapted to arboreal situations.

After ♀ accepts nest-site she remains there while ♂ collects all nesting material. Twigs, sticks torn off live bushes, collected from ground or other nests, carried in bill or pouch; softer material added later.

NEST: usually constructed anew each year. A small structure (the sitting bird overflowing it), *c.* 0·5–0·6 m across by 0·2–0·4 m deep, completed in 7–8 days. ♂ continues bringing some material after eggs laid. In crowded colonies nests may touch, but are well separated in most; defended territory is nest and immediate surroundings. May be at any height from 10–50 m above ground in trees. Becomes solidified with droppings of young, but usually collapses through rains later or is destroyed by other pelicans. Continual re-occupation of same site may kill nesting trees, forcing a move, but seldom far.

No pre-copulatory displays known. Mating occurs on nest or site, chiefly in morning or early afternoon, av. 1·5 times/h, lasting 5–10 s. ♀ remains 2–3 days in nest before laying, which occurs 10–12 days after building commenced.

EGGS: 1–3, usually 2; Kenya–Uganda mean (182 clutches) 1·99; laid at intervals of 1–4 days, mean 2·2 days. Pale bluish white with chalky covering. SIZE: 72–93 × 50–54 (82·1 × 54·6). WEIGHT: 90–144 (119·8).

Laying dates: (breeding season varies with locality) South Africa, Zimbabwe, Malawi, Zambia, few records, South Africa mainly Dec–Jan (summer rains). Gambia July–Jan; Zaïre June–July; Nigeria, W Africa, end of rains, Sept, Oct, Nov, young leave Feb–Mar (dry), colony may be re-occupied, laying again Aug (peak rains) (Serle 1943); W Kenya–Uganda Aug–Nov, peaking Aug–Oct, late rains, young fledge dry season Jan–Feb; E Kenya, Tanzania, end of long rains May–June, young fledge dry season, Sept. Most breeding starts late rains, young leaving nest in dry seasons. No clear connections with food supply established.

Incubation begins with 1st egg, resulting in different sizes of chicks with long laying intervals. Thereafter by both sexes, normally in 24 h spells, associated with difficulty in flight except on thermals towards mid-day. Incubation period: normally 30 days, 1 record 33–34 days. Hatching from chipping to emergence takes 24 h (Din and Eltringham 1974b).

Newly hatched chick pink, naked, helpless days 1–7; days 8–14 white down grows on back, days 14–21 covers body. Days 22–28 blackish wing and tail feathers and scapulars emerge; body feathers days 29–35. Down copious till day 42, thereafter reduced; day 56, covered by feathers. Weight increases slowly at first to 200 g at day 7, then rapidly to 5200 g at day 50, reaching maximum 5800 g at 70 days; may be reduced before first flight at av. 84 days. Wing-flapping frequent days 65 onwards. Culmen grows regularly throughout; humerus and manus nearly full length by days 45–50; foot full size day 42. Tail grows rapidly, increasing from 150 to 200 mm just before 1st flight, usually a short flap from branch to branch, made alone; becomes proficient flier in *c.* 7 days.

Adults brood chick closely days 1–7, thereafter brooding reduced, ceasing by days 10–12, parent then shading chick; may brood at night. After day 30, when young partly feathered, chicks left alone most of day. Both sexes brood and feed young; in days 1–7 are fed up to 30 times daily on small, partly digested fish dropped into nest. Feeds reduced to 10–25/day, days 7–21; 4–5/day days 22–42; thereafter once daily, or sometimes less. After day 14 chicks reach up into, and thrust whole head and neck into adult's throat to feed. In late stages feeds may take 10–20 min to deliver, sometimes in 2 spells with a rest between.

Young solicit parent by turning towards it, thrusting head back and forth, flapping wings and calling; if refused may peck at adult's bill, face, feet or breast. Young may bite own wings and branches in possible distraction behaviour when not fed. Adults feed only their own young though others solicit; young 40 days old can recognize own parents approaching in flight.

Nest mortality is heavy through sibling aggression and starvation. With 2–3 day laying interval elder young soon dominates younger, forces it to nest edge, bites and attacks it. Then dies of wounds, starvation, or from falling out of nest. From av. clutches of 1·98 (Uganda), 1·9 young hatch, but 0·95 young/pair/year fledge. Elsewhere, breeding success may be even lower, 0·55 young/pair in W Kenya; Sokoto, N Nigeria, 30 nests, 70 eggs,

12 chicks = 0·40 young/pair/year (Mundy and Cook 1974); overall, probably *c.* 0·8 young/pair/year fledge. Little nest-predation recorded, even from often associated Marabous. Young which fall to ground may be eaten by lions, leopards, hyenas, jackals, pythons, possibly monitor lizards; never fed by parents on ground. Young hatched from single-egg clutches, or in odd nests rather than large synchronous groups, may actually have a better chance of survival.

Young depend on parents for food for 2–3 weeks after first flight, then leave colony, usually joining parents on fishing grounds. Attain sexual maturity in, perhaps, 3 years. Assuming 80% of adult population breeds annually, 0·8 young/pair/year fledge, and 50% mortality before sexual maturity, adult breeding life must av. 6·25 years to maintain population. Captive individuals live much longer.

References
Burke, V. E. M. and Brown, L. H. (1970).
Din, N. A. and Eltringham, S. K. (1974a, b; 1977).

Plate 9
(Opp. p. 146)

Pelecanus crispus Bruch. Dalmatian Pelican. Pélican frisé.

Pelecanus crispus Bruch, 1832. Isis von Oken, col. 1109; Dalmatia.

In Vol. 1 of the Peters' List 1979, *P. crispus* has been classed by Dorst and Mougin as a race of the eastern Spot-billed Pelican *P. philippensis*. Since neither of these species has been thoroughly studied in the field, and since *P. philippensis* appears to form a more appropriate species pair with the African *P. rufescens* on what little is known of its habits, we do not consider it justifiable to discard the long accepted name *P. crispus* for the Dalmatian Pelican, unless detailed study of the habits of both this species and *P. philippensis* renders this desirable.

Range and Status. Uncommon winter migrant to Egypt; vagrant in Algeria and Rio de Oro. Breeds Palearctic, Balkans–Russia; formerly much more widespread, now rarest Palearctic breeding species, reduced to 500–600 pairs (no accurate estimates), perhaps increasing somewhat with recent protection.

Description. ADULT ♂ (winter): head, neck, body and folded wings, greyish white, tinged bluish below. Hind crown and neck with a curled crest, crop-patch straw-coloured. Outermost primaries blackish at tips, inner and secondaries greyish, edged whitish above, below largely white or pale grey. Tail pale grey. Bill mixed yellowish grey; pouch red-orange; facial skin white; eye white-pale yellow; legs dark grey-blackish. ♀ similar, slightly smaller (size difference less marked than in Great White Pelican *P. onocrotalus*). ADULT ♂ and ♀ (breeding): both assume brighter colours, pouch becomes dark red-orange, bill pale yellow with orange terminal nail, bare facial skin purple. SIZE: wing, ♂ 690–800 (745), ♀ 670–780 (725); tail, ♂ 230–250, ♀ 230; tarsus, ♂ 130–135, ♀ 130; bill, ♂ 390–450 (420), ♀ 350–430 (390); wing-span, ♂ up to 3·08 m. WEIGHT: ♂ 10·5–12 kg, ♀ 10 kg.

IMMATURE: above dull mottled grey-brown, below dirty white, wing feathers brownish; becomes whiter with age. Bill grey; pouch greyish yellow; eye whitish; legs blackish.

Field Characters. Very large, as large as Great White Pelican *P. onocrotalus*, 25% bigger than Pink-backed *P. rufescens* (with which it would not normally overlap). Readily distinguished in all plumages by curly crest, whitish eye, dark grey or blackish legs, red-orange pouch, and in flight by mainly white or pale grey underwing, darker only on outer primaries. Immatures more like Great White Pelican, but distinguishable by whitish eye, blackish legs, generally whitish underwing with darker outer primaries. Rarely, adult Great White Pelicans have white wing feathers, but are still separable by yellow legs and pouch, dark eye.

Pelecanus crispus

Voice. Not recorded in Africa. Usually silent outside breeding season although may produce grunts; noisy when fishing.

General Habits. Scarcely known in Africa, little known in Eurasia. Often in large flocks, mainly in fresh water but also coastal habitats, e.g. sheltered coast-line. Roosts on ground, never in trees; feeds in large groups. Habits similar to those of Great White Pelican.

Food. Entirely fish; in Europe mainly *Cyprinus*, *Perca*, *Aspinus*, *Rutilus* and *Esox*.

References
Cramp, S. and Simmons, K. E. L. (1977).

Family FREGATIDAE: frigatebirds or man'o'warbirds

A highly specialized family of very large, mainly oceanic seabirds occurring in all tropical seas. Unmistakable, an extreme flying form, with very long wings sharply bent at carpal joint; high aspect ratio; large pectoral muscles; very light bones, adapted for prolonged effortless soaring or swift attacks; wing-loading lower than in any other seabird. Tail very long, deeply forked; bill long, strong, sharply hooked; tarsi extremely short, feet with all webs deeply indented, little used for swimming. Sexually dimorphic, ♂♂ always smaller and darker than ♀♀, with brilliant red inflatable throat pouch used in display. Roost and breed on land (bushes, trees); can alight accurately on a branch but scarcely walk. All species have similar habits, obtaining food usually by snatching it from near surface, sometimes by taking it away from e.g. boobies; occasionally kill young or adults of smaller seabirds. All lay 1 egg; have long (44–55 days) incubation periods, very long (150–210 days) fledging periods; poor breeding success (20% of eggs laid, variable locally). Often re-lay after failure 1–3 times. Free-flying young depend on parents for food up to 1 year, so that if breeding succeeds, birds cannot breed annually.

1 genus *Fregata* with 5 species, 2 confined to single islands; *F. magnificens* largest, chiefly Western Atlantic; *F. ariel* and *F. minor* mainly Indo-Pacific. None breed on islands in our area, but *F. ariel* rumoured in Gulf of Aden. Following details therefore concern recognition only. See Nelson (1975) for comparative biology data.

Genus *Fregata* Lacépède

Fregata magnificens Mathews. Magnificent Frigatebird. Frégate superbe.

Fregata minor magnificens Mathews, 1914. Austral Avian Rec., 2, p. 120; Barrington Island, Galapagos Islands.

Plate 7

(Opp. p. 98)

Range and Status. Atlantic Ocean, chiefly in west, but breeds Cape Verde Islands; uncommon or rare off W African shores.

Description. ADULT ♂: entirely black, glossed purplish above, paler, more violet below. Gular pouch scarlet. Bill greyish; eye blackish; feet black. ADULT ♀: mainly dark brown, little glossed. Throat dark brown, extending to breast in deep V; breast and upper belly white. Wing and tail feathers black. Bill bluish, feet purplish pink. SIZE: (mean) wing, ♂ 633, ♀ 650; tail, ♂ 431, ♀ 431; bill, ♂ 112, ♀ 121. WEIGHT: ♂ c. 1500, ♀ c. 1550.

IMMATURE: head, neck, breast white, spotted all over brown; plumage paler than that of adults.

Field Characters. Unmistakable; a very large, almost all-dark seabird with very long pointed wings sharply angled at carpal joint, very long forked tail. Normally seen soaring high over water or islands, able to maintain position for long periods without wing-flaps. Can alternate this 'still' soaring with swift flight, wings deeply beaten, e.g. when chasing boobies; seldom alights on water.

Fregata magnificens

Not illustrated   *Fregata aquila* (Linnaeus). Ascension Frigatebird. Frégate aigle-de-mer.

Pelecanus Aquilus Linnaeus, 1758. Syst. Nat. (10th ed.), p. 133; Ascension Island.

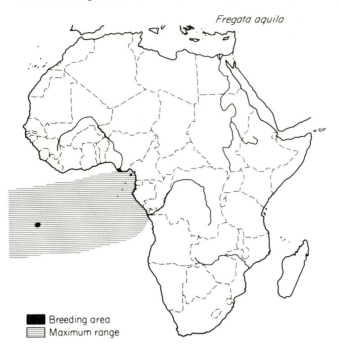

Fregata aquila

■ Breeding area
▨ Maximum range

Range and Status. Ascension Island and south tropical Atlantic Ocean; vagrant western African coast from Gulf of Guinea to mouth of Congo River.

Description. ADULT ♂: all black including underparts and undersides of wings, with much glossy metallic sheen; breast and belly duller. Tail forked, ventral part of quill-shafts ivory-white. Eye brown; bill bluish; chin and pouch red; feet and toes black. ADULT ♀: similar but less glossy green above; underparts browner, sometimes breast to belly almost white. Eyes and bill as ♂; no gular pouch, skin of chin and centre of throat red; feet black, toes red. SIZE: (5 ♂♂, 4 ♀♀) wing, ♂ 552–581 (562), ♀ 587–607 (598); tail, ♂ 357–402 (384), ♀ 393–411 (405); bill, ♂ 87–96 (92), ♀ 99–106 (103).
    IMMATURE: generally brown; head, neck and breast to belly white with rusty tinge.

Field Characters. Difficult to distinguish in the field. Somewhat smaller than Magnificent Frigatebird *F. magnificens* with ♂ having smaller bill. ♀ unique among frigatebirds, usually having brown and not white breast.

Plate 7   *Fregata minor* (Gmelin). Greater Frigatebird. Frégate du Pacifique.

(Opp. p. 98)   *Pelecanus minor* Gmelin, 1789. Syst. Nat., 1, p. 573; Christmas Island, eastern half of Indian Ocean.

Fregata minor

■ Breeding areas
▨ Maximum range

Range and Status. Indo-Pacific Ocean, off E Africa from Aldabra south to Mauritius. The species most likely to be seen off E African Coast, recorded Kenya–Natal and Cape Province, but rare near coast.

Description. *F. m. aldabrensis* Mathews, ADULT ♂: all black, glossed bronzy on crown and mantle; throat pouch scarlet. Bill slate blue; eye blackish; feet red. ADULT ♀: duller dark brown; throat grey, merging into white breast; upper belly white extending along base of wing; larger. SIZE: (mean) wing, ♂ 600, ♀ 610; tail, ♂ 427, ♀ 386; bill, ♂ 104, ♀ 117. WEIGHT: ♂ 1000–1450 (1201), ♀ 1215–1640 (1427). ♂ lighter (84% of ♀ weight), relatively much longer-tailed than ♀.
    IMMATURE: pure white throat, head and lower neck white spotted or streaked rufous, separated from pure white lower breast by broad rusty band; paler brown than adult, with a pale bar on upper wing.

Field Characters. Distinctly larger than, but hard to distinguish from Lesser Frigatebird *F. ariel* in most plumages if alone. ♂ entirely black, no white on underside, and has red, not black feet. ♀ whiter below with greyish throat merging into upper breast, but distinction difficult except at close range. Pure white throat and broader breast band should distinguish immature at close range.

Fregata ariel (G. R. Gray). Lesser Frigatebird. Frégate ariel.

Plate 7

Atagen ariel G. R. Gray (ex Gould MS), 1845. Gen. Birds. 3, p. (669), col. pl. (185); Raine Island, Queensland.

(Opp. p. 98)

Range and Status. Western Indian Ocean, in our limits recorded from Gulf of Aden and Red Sea (Massawa); less likely to be seen off E African Coast.

Description. *F. a. iredalei* Mathews: Aldabra. ADULT ♂: all black, with small white bar on flanks extending to axillaries; throat pouch scarlet. Bill grey or blackish; eye black; feet black to reddish brown. ADULT ♀: mainly dark brown, with buffy white collar extending to upper neck, chest, flanks; throat black clearly demarcated from upper breast. Upperwing-coverts brown. Bill pink or blue; feet reddish. Larger. SIZE: (av.) wing, ♂ 538, ♀ 553; tail, ♂ 325, ♀ 324; bill, ♂ 83, ♀ 87. WEIGHT: ♂ 625–875 (754), ♀ 760–955 (858). ♂♂ only slightly longer-tailed than ♀♀.

IMMATURE: neck and head mainly rusty brown, upper breast rufous separated from white belly and flanks by narrow darker band.

Field Characters. When seen on wing with Greater Frigatebird *F. minor* appears only slightly smaller, though much lighter. Alone, ♀♀ hard to distinguish with certainty. White underwing bar of ♂ and darker black feet diagnostic. At close range, blackish throat clearly demarcated from white upper breast distinguishes ♀; band across lower neck of ♀ chestnut or brownish, not black. Immature in 1st plumage is redder on head and neck than that of Greater Frigatebird, but later virtually indistinguishable except by size.

References
Diamond, A. W. (1975).

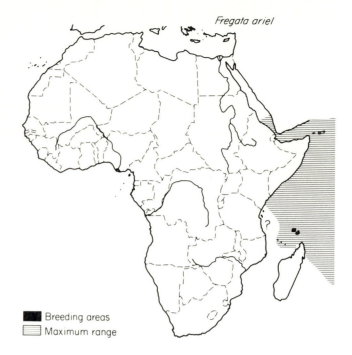

Fregata ariel

■ Breeding areas
▤ Maximum range

Order
CICONIIFORMES

A diverse order of mainly large to very large water birds, some storks and herons terrestrial. Characterized by long legs adapted for wading and walking; partially webbed or unwebbed toes, sometimes very long; long bills (in some highly specialized, adapted for feeding on particular aquatic organisms). Most varied in tropical latitudes, feeding mainly on fish, less often insects, molluscs, amphibia, or other aquatic organisms.

The order now comprises 3 suborders (Mayr and Cottrell 1979): Ardeae, herons, egrets and bitterns; Scopi, containing only the extraordinary Hamerkop (which perhaps deserves ordinal rank); and Ciconiae, storks, Shoebills, ibises and spoonbills. This new arrangement underlines the lack of obvious relationships between herons, Hamerkop and storks, and between this order and the Pelecaniformes (though such a relationship has been suggested for the Shoebill, Balaenicipitidae: Cottam 1957). However, this order is evidently closer to the flamingoes, Order Phoenicopteriformes, while they form a link between it and the ducks, swans and geese, Anseriformes.

One suborder, the Scopi, Hamerkop, is endemic to Africa, and one family, Balaenicipitidae, Shoebill, is an endemic monotypic family. Herons, storks, ibises and spoonbills are all well represented in Africa. Being large, common, often conspicuous water birds, many have been rather fully studied, though some of the smaller, more cryptic, nocturnal bitterns are still little known.

Suborder ARDEAE

Family ARDEIDAE: herons, egrets and bitterns

Medium-sized to very large wading birds with slim body; ♂ larger than ♀. Long neck with kink at 6th vertebra. Long legs with bare lower part of tibia. Tarsus with large scutes in front, rarely reticulate. Long toes with small web between middle and outer toes. Long, broad wings; 11 primaries, 15–20 secondaries. Short, square or rounded tail; undertail-coverts nearly as long as tail feathers. Long, straight, sharp bill; nostrils long slits. Lores bare. Oil gland small with short tufts. Many with ornamental plumes on head, back or chest. Moult poorly known with irregular moult of primaries.

Fly with strong regular wing-beats and neck retracted. Stand upright; walk with striding gait. Usually found at water's edge, especially with gentle slope; some found in deeper water while others mainly terrestrial. Basic feeding methods include: (1) stand and wait (see **A**); (2) wade or walk slowly while stalking prey (**B**), sometimes foot-stir (**C**) or wing-flick to startle prey; (3) disturb-and-chase by running about, flushing prey (**D**); (4) surface-dive; (5) hover above water, then dive; and (6) plunge-dive from perch. (*Illustrations reproduced with permission from Voisin (1978).*)

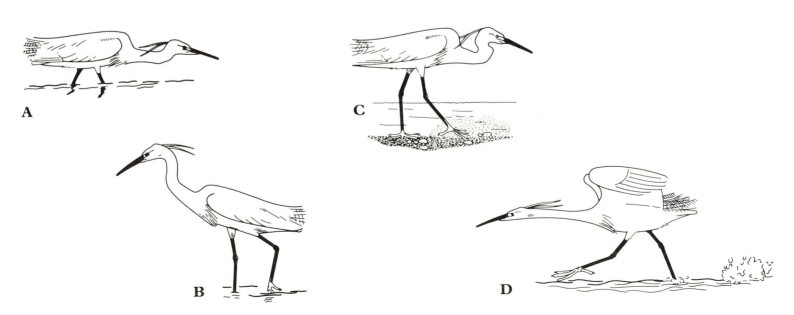

World-wide from fairly high temperate latitudes to tropics with most species tropical. Genera, species, common names and order in this book are those of Hancock and Elliott (1978) with 17 genera and 61 species from 2 subfamilies, Botaurinae and Ardeinae.

In Africa, 10 genera, 21 species, including 1 non-breeding visitor from Madagascar, and 20 residents with 8 having Palearctic populations wintering in Africa (see Hancock and Elliott 1978.)

Subfamily BOTAURINAE

Bitterns, with stout body and neck, relatively short legs, 8–10 tail feathers, inner toe longer than outer, 2 pairs of powder-down patches, ornamental plumes not well developed, and cryptic plumage. Tend to be secretive and to keep in cover. When alarmed, assume upright concealing 'bittern stance' with head and bill vertical and eyes peering forward. Visual displays poorly known and probably less well developed than Ardeinae and correlated with secretive behaviour.

Key nuptial plumage features include: (1) *Botaurus*, erect plumes of neck and breast and exposed scapular tufts; and (2) *Ixobrychus*, ruffling of crown, neck and back feathers, and colour changes of soft parts, such as legs turning bright orange, eyes red and base of bill and bare facial skin orange-red, even bluish, in some species.

Genus *Botaurus* Stephens

Large bitterns; plumage brown or buff with many dark streaks. Sexes alike; immature similar to adult. Strictly marsh birds, rarely perch in trees. ♂ makes loud booming call in breeding season. World-wide, 4 species. In Africa, 1 species with resident and wintering Palearctic populations.

Botaurus stellaris (Linnaeus). Eurasian Bittern. Butor étoilé.

Ardea stellaris Linnaeus, 1758. Syst. Nat. (10th ed.), p. 144; Europe—restricted type locality, Sweden.

Plate 11

(Opp. p. 162)

Range and Status. Resident and Palearctic winter visitor, uncommon to rare in freshwater marshes. Nominate subspecies resident Algeria, Tunisia and Morocco (present breeding status N Africa uncertain); and Palearctic winter visitor Libya, Egypt, Sudan, Ethiopia, Kenya and northern Zaïre west to Nigeria. *B. s. capensis* resident eastern half of southern Africa from southern Tanzania and Zambia to Cape; also Angola, Namibia and Botswana.

Description. *B. s. stellaris* (Linnaeus): Africa south to near equator. ADULT ♂: golden brown, mottled and barred black above with black crown and nape. Loose ruff on neck. Moustache streak dark brown to black; chin and throat creamy-buff. Mantle black with tawny margins; back, rump and tail with lighter margins. Below pale yellow-buff with dark to rufous-brown vertical stripes on breast; fewer on belly, nearly absent on vent and undertail-coverts. Breast feathers droop. Flight feathers black, barred rufous to rufous-buff; inner secondaries and upperwing-coverts buff; under-wing-coverts buff with grey mottling. Bill greenish yellow with culmen brown to black at top; eye yellow; legs and feet green. Sexes alike. SIZE: wing, ♂ (21 specimens) 335–357 (346), ♀ (16) 296–327 (311); tail, ♂ (11) 112–126 (117), ♀ (8) 96–110 (104); bill, ♂ (20) 61–74 (69), ♀ (16) 60–68 (64); tarsus, ♂ (11) 97–109 (102), ♀ (9) 87–95 (91). WEIGHT: ♂ 966–1940, ♀ 867–1150.

IMMATURE: like adult but browner and moustache and crown less extensive; mantle and shorter scapulars less boldly patterned.

DOWNY YOUNG: with long cinnamon-tawny, rufous-brown or

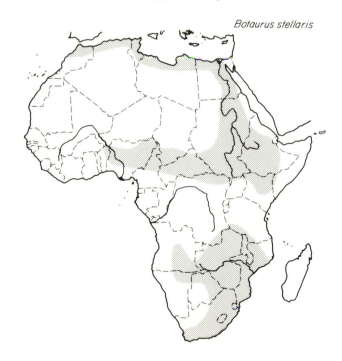

Botaurus stellaris

rufous-buff down. Bill pale green to pinkish yellow; eye dark brown; legs pale green to pale pink.

B. s. capensis (Schlegel). From near equator south to Cape. Slightly smaller (wing, 6 specimens, 280–310); darker above with flight feathers more narrowly and irregularly barred; even spotted.

Field Characters. Stocky, thick-necked heron. Plumage golden brown with distinct black margins. Crown, nape and malar stripe black; underparts broadly streaked dark brown. Distinguished from immature night heron by larger size and lack of white spots on wings. Very secretive, when booming more often heard than seen.

Voice. Recorded (2a). Migrants silent, residents heard rarely in breeding localities. ♂ gives deep distinctive booming call by inflating oesophagus with neck stretched forward and downward, then raised. Produces deep, slow, resonant 'uprumb' or 'up-up-(up)-rumb', not loud, but sometimes audible up to 3–5 km away; preceded by 2–3 short grunts and sometimes by bill-clattering. Repeated at 1–2 s intervals, usually 3–4 times. ♀ sometimes responds with soft, booming 'wumph'. Both also utter harsh 'kwow' or 'kwah', and in flight 'kau'.

General Habits. Little known in Africa; well known in Europe. Solitary and secretive, among reeds, rice fields, grass and papyrus, especially tracts or fringes overgrown with tall vegetation. Scarce along sea coasts. Local and uncommon, heard more than seen; active by day and dusk. Walks slowly and deliberately in somewhat crouching posture, can run quite well. May stand motionless for some time before taking next step. Roosts solitarily at night in dense cover, mostly on floating beds of reeds; rarely in trees. Flies with long bill and legs extended, low over reeds in owl-like manner with rounded, down-bent wings. Sometimes circles, soaring to great heights. When alarmed, assumes 'bittern stance'. If flushed, emerges from cover with neck extended, retracting it in flight. Flies short distance, then returns into reeds. Feeds largely within reed cover, taking prey when wading slowly or when standing.

Palearctic migrants winter in NW Africa and south of Sahara to about equator, with most southern localities being Niapu (Zaïre), Ilorin (Nigeria) and Lake Naivasha (Kenya). Most northern localities of *capensis* are Mweru Marsh (Zambia) and Lake Rukwa (Tanzania). Not known whether resident populations in NW Africa disperse south of Sahara after breeding season; migratory movements in southern Africa mainly in southwest.

Food. Fish, frogs and aquatic insects. In Europe diet varies with locality and season but primarily fish (especially eels) and amphibians; also small mammals, birds and crustaceans.

Breeding Habits. Little known in Africa; well known in Europe. Breeding season begins with booming advertising call of ♂. ♂ probably strongly territorial for several months, excluding other ♂♂ but including several nesting ♀♀ since this bittern is probably polygamous with 1 ♂ having several ♀♀. Density of ♂♂ varies from a maximum of 1♂/ha in favourable localities to 1♂/40–50 ha or more. Booming given from regular calling place, both day and night, but mostly in evening throughout breeding season. May erect plumes of neck and breast when booming. Birds more often heard than seen at this time. ♂♂ often answer one another; booming also attracts ♀♀. ♀ sometimes answers booming ♂ with similar but softer call. ♂♂ highly aggressive in defence of territory, some have been found dead of stab wounds. Some engage in aerial battles, circling in flight and trying to stab each other. As season advances several birds perform courtship flights over reeds, flying for 10 min to heights of *c.* 65 m (Hancock and Elliott 1978). Copulation takes place immediately at end of flight when ♂ drops into reeds and mounts ♀ crouched in reeds; copulation not confined to nest. Occasionally some expose tuft of pale shoulder plumes, usually hidden by the closed wing; significance of this posture uncertain but may be a threat display, or may be given when booming or prior to copulation as in the American Bittern *B. lentiginosus* (Palmer 1962).

NEST: built only by ♀; a mass of rushes, nearly side by side or scattered over marshes with water depth of at least 30 cm. Nest platform 30–40 cm in diameter and 10–15 cm high. Often situated near ♂'s calling place, with each nest 50–500 m apart.

EGGS: 3–4, sometimes 5; laid at 2–3 day intervals. Regular ovals, pale olive green to brown. SIZE: (100 eggs, *B. s. stellaris*) 48–58 × 34–41 (53 × 39); WEIGHT: 42.

Laying dates: mainly in rains, recorded South Africa Sept–Jan; no recent records Algeria (E. Johnson, pers. comm.).

Incubation begins with 1st egg, by ♀ only. Period: 25–26 days.

When 15–16 days old, young wander from nest. After a few weeks are very active but may take several more weeks to fly. Fledging period: 50–55 days.

♀ parent only feeds young, although ♂ may bring food near nest for ♀ to collect. ♀ regurgitates food onto nest, from which young pick it up. After 15–20 days young are fed away from nest.

References
Hancock, J. and Elliott, H. (1978).

Genus *Ixobrychus* Billberg

Small bitterns with variable colour patterns; ♀♀ of some species duller than ♂♂ and heavily streaked like immature. Bill very pointed, much serrated before tip. Nostrils slit-shaped. Long neck covered with long feathers. Perch and nest in bushes and trees more often than large bitterns. ♂ produces low call but does not boom. Worldwide, 8 species. In Africa, 2 residents, 1 having Palearctic population that winters in Africa.

Ixobrychus minutus (Linnaeus). Little Bittern. Blongios nain.

Plate 11

Ardea minuta Linnaeus, 1766. Syst. Nat. (12th ed.), p. 240: 'Helvetia, Aleppo', restricted type locality, Switzerland.

(Opp. p. 162)

Range and Status. Resident and Palearctic winter visitor frequent to uncommon in reed beds and papyrus swamps and marshes. *I. m. payesii*, resident from Senegal to Somalia south to Cape. Nominate *I. m. minutus*, resident Morocco, Algeria and Tunisia and Palearctic winter visitor across Sahara south to Cape, but mainly eastern half of continent. *I. m. podiceps*, vagrant from Madagascar to Zanzibar.

Description. *I. m. payesii* (Hartlaub): Africa south of Sahara. ADULT ♂: crown, slightly crested nape, mantle, back, rump, tail, primaries, secondaries and scapulars black with green gloss. Sides of head and neck chestnut to rufous; chin, throat, upperwing-coverts and underparts pale buff; underwing-coverts white. Outermost primary shorter than 2nd or 3rd primaries. Bill yellow to greenish yellow, culmen darker; lores normally yellow, dull red in courtship; eye yellow, orange or reddish brown; legs and feet green, back of tarsus and soles yellow. ADULT ♂ (breeding): colours intensify during courtship. ADULT ♀: duller than ♂. Crown, nape and tail black, less glossy green, hindneck red-brown; rest upperparts, including flight feathers, brown tinged rufous and narrowly streaked pale buff. Upperwing-coverts browner. Sides of neck sometimes rufous-brown; foreneck and chest buff streaked with pale brown. Rest underparts buff, streaked dark brown. SIZE: wing, ♂ (7 specimens) 135–142 (139), ♀ (5) 141–150 (145); tail, (28) 36–50 (45); bill, (28) 43–55 (48); tarsus, (28) 40–46 (43).

IMMATURE: similar to ♀ but duller and reddish with upperparts more mottled, underparts with darker brown streaks.

DOWNY YOUNG: upperparts with reddish buff down, underparts, white down. Bill pink; orbital area and hindneck bare; eye dark brown; legs pale yellow pink.

I. m. minutus (Linnaeus). Breeds NW Africa, migrant to rest of Africa. Larger (wing, ♂ (15 specimens) 149–157 (153), ♀ (12) 142–153 (148)); adult ♂ with pale buff sides of head and neck. Outermost primary about equal to size of 2nd and 3rd primaries. Eye yellow. Downy young pinkish buff above, white below. WEIGHT: adult ♂ (11 specimens) 145–150 (149), ♀ (7) 140–150 (146).

I. m. podiceps (Bonaparte): Zanzibar. Smaller than other 2 subspecies (wing, 122–128); adult ♂ darker with deep russet of neck extending over whole of underparts and wing-coverts, becoming chestnut on upperside neck. ♀ and immature also darker.

Field Characters. A small, thick-necked, secretive bittern. Most often seen taking off or in flight. On rising, both sexes show white wing-patches which contrast with otherwise dark upperparts, while Dwarf Bittern *I. sturmii* has solid dark upperparts and wings.

Voice. Recorded (2a, 14). Advertising call of ♂, a hoarse or croaking, short, muffled, often repeated 'crick' or 'kekekekee'; both sexes give other squawking and yipping notes.

General Habits. Little known in Africa; well known in Europe. In swamps, marshes and wet grasslands, along streams and rivers, and in mangroves. Solitary or

Ixobrychus minutus

in pairs, except in migration when *I. m. minutus* in groups of up to 30 roost together day or night. Active at dusk and by night; often seen flying over reed beds by day. Skulking and secretive. Sometimes moves quickly in crouched posture through thick vegetation, climbing reeds to perch motionless with bill pointing upright in bittern posture. Rises in flight with feet trailing. Flies short distances with fast wing-beats interspersed with long glides; enters cover with glide followed by sudden bank to one side.

Except for movements due to fluctuating water levels, *I. m. payesii* sedentary. *I. m. podiceps* rarely emigrates from Madagascar to Zanzibar in dry season. *I. m. minutus* from Europe and N Africa passes through N Africa mainly Mar–June and Aug–Oct, with numerous records in widely dispersed oases indicating they cross Sahara on broad front.

Food. Fish, amphibians, insects and other small arthropods but diet varies with locality, availability and time of year. Of 8 stomachs in Zaïre, fish in 4; also frogs, spiders, shrimp and various insects (Chapin 1932).

Breeding Habits. Little known in Africa; better known in Europe. Solitary nester although 2–3 pairs in same pond with nests 50 m apart. ♂ chooses nest-site and builds most of nest; drives off ♂ intruders by chasing and flight attacks. Attracts ♀ to nest by advertising call. Copulation occurs at nest; not preceded by any special display. Nest-relief ceremony includes much ruffling of feathers with raising and lowering of crest and opening and closing of tail. Other courtship displays unknown.

NEST: a small flat platform of roots and stems *c.* 10 cm from water or on ground.

EGGS: 2–5; Zimbabwe mean (5 clutches) 3·8; Namibia (1) 2; South Africa, SW Cape (1) 3, Natal (4) 2·25 (SAOSNRC); white. SIZE: (10 eggs) 32–37 × 25–26 (34 × 25) (SAOSNRC); WEIGHT: (*I. m. minutus*) 13.

Breeding occurs in late rains, and dry season just after rains. Laying dates: Morocco, Algeria, Tunisia and Egypt May–July (but no recent records); Gambia Sept; Guinea-Bissau Aug; Sierra Leone Aug–Oct; Mali Sept; Ghana July–Sept; Nigeria June–Sept; Gabon Aug–Oct; Zaïre Jan, May–Sept, Dec; Sudan June–Sept; Kenya May–June; Uganda Mar–July, Nov–Dec; Zambia Mar–Apr, June; Malawi Apr–May; Mozambique Sept; Zimbabwe Feb, Sept, Nov–Dec; Namibia Mar; South Africa, SW Cape Sept–Nov, Natal Oct, Dec.

Incubation begins with first egg; carried out by both sexes. Period: 17–19 days (*I. m. minutus*).

Both parents tend and feed young. During nesting period one parent always in attendance at nest with both parents caring for young. Uses 'bittern stance' on nest when observed. When threatened, turns side-on to intruder with wings spread and lifts wing nearest to it and lowers the other. Young leave nest at 17–18 days; fledged at 25–30 days (*I. m. minutus*).

References

Cramp, S. and Simmons, K. E. L. (1977).

Plate 11
(Opp. p. 162)

Ixobrychus sturmii (Wagler). Dwarf Bittern; Rail Heron. Blongios de Sturm.

Ardea Sturmii Wagler, 1827. Syst. Av., *Ardea*, no. 37; Senegambia.

Range and Status. Resident, uncommon to rare, preferring banks of rivers, streams and freshwater ponds, but also marshes, wet grasslands and mangroves south of about 16°N from Senegal to Ethiopia south to mainly eastern Cape. Intra-African migrant, present in southern and probably northern parts of range mainly in wet season.

Description. ADULT ♂: upperparts from crown to tail, sides of face and neck, and upper and underwings slate grey. Elongated plumes on head and neck. Throat to breast pale buff, heavily streaked black; belly darker buff streaked grey. Bill, black to dark green above, yellow below. Lores and orbital area bluish to yellowish green. Eye red-brown to wine red. Legs and feet greenish to yellowish brown in front, yellow behind and on toes; occasionally legs and feet bright orange in courtship. ADULT ♀: similar but paler than ♂ with more rufous on belly; eye yellow. SIZE: wing, 6 specimens, 154–169 (162); tail, 48–56 (53); culmen, 39–42 (40); tarsus, 44–51 (49). WEIGHT: 142.

IMMATURE: paler and duller than adult with feathers of upperparts tipped buff; more russet underparts. Bill dull yellowish grey; eye orange-red; legs and feet yellow.

DOWNY YOUNG: pale pink skin covered with ginger down, 1 cm long; slightly longer on crown. Bill dull pink; eye dark brown; legs and feet pinkish yellow.

Field Characters. A very small bittern with uniform slate upperparts and pale, but heavily streaked underparts, usually suddenly seen flapping up and out of bush or tree. Yellow feet diagnostic. Instantly distinguished on rising from Little Bittern *I. minutus* by solid slate grey upperparts and wings, and from Green Heron *Butorides striatus* by much smaller size and much darker upperparts.

Voice. Not recorded. May give loud croaking or grunting cry when flushed.

General Habits. Little known. Solitary or in pairs, largely nocturnal, in bushes or trees along edges of dams, lakes, ponds, rivers and streams in forested and savannah country; also in grassy and reedy marshes, margins of temporary pools and seasonally inundated grasslands and mangroves. Flight slow and heavy, with

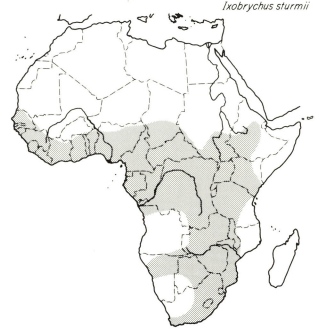

Ixobrychus sturmii

legs dangling. Sometimes assumes 'bittern stance'. Hunts both day and night, mainly at night.

Moves to southern Africa in Nov in wet season, leaves in Apr in dry season (Benson and Irwin 1966). In South Africa (Nyl flood plains) erratic seasonal migrant, occurring along flood plains only when fully inundated; arrives few weeks after flooding usually mid-Jan and remains 4–5 months (W. Tarboton, in prep.). Does not appear at all if flooding occurs late summer. In northern part of range probably moves into areas north of equator May–June in rains, leaving Sept in dry season. Populations near equator may be sedentary but probably augmented by off-season migrants from both northern and southern populations.

Food. Insects, crustaceans, crabs, small fish, frogs. 2 stomachs (Zaïre) held a tiny fish, a small frog, pieces of crabs, a spider, a grasshopper and a water bug (Chapin 1932). 3 nestlings (South Africa) regurgitated several small frogs when handled (W. Tarboton, in prep.).

Breeding Habits. Well known. Solitary nests although sometimes a few together are seen (South Africa, Nyl, 2–3 nests within 15 m: W. Tarboton, in prep.; Kruger National Park, 17 nests together: K. Newman), usually on margins of flood plains when flood water inundates acacia woodland. Nests on horizontal or down-sloping branch in trees or bushes, usually with thorns and surrounded by, or overhanging water (South Africa, Nyl, mean height above water (23 nests) 1·6 m, range 0·6–3·7 m; most commonly in *Zizyphus mucronata* and *Rhus pyroides*: W. Tarboton, in prep.). Built in 1–2 days.

Courtship not described.

NEST: a flimsy saucer-shaped platform of dry twigs and coarse dry grass stems, 23–38 cm across and 7 cm thick.

EGGS: 2–5; Zimbabwe and Namibia mean (48 clutches) 3·3; South Africa, Transvaal (16) 3·1 (SAOSNRC). Very pale blue to pale green. SIZE: (13 eggs, Nyl, South Africa) 33–37 × 26–29 (36 × 28); (25 eggs, SAOSNRC) 33–40 × 26–29 (36 × 28); WEIGHT: 19–20.

Breeds mainly in rains, also early in dry season probably in inundated areas. Laying dates: Senegal Sept; Sierra Leone July; Mali Aug–Oct; Ghana July; Zaïre Dec–Jan; Kenya May–June; Zambia Jan, Mar; Zimbabwe Jan–Mar, Sept–Nov; Namibia Feb–Mar, Aug; South Africa Jan–Apr, Sept–Dec.

Incubation begins before clutch is complete. Period: 14–15 days.

Parents feed young from about sunset onwards by regurgitation. At 7 days young adopt 'bittern stance' with bill pointing upward at angle of 45°. After 7 days leave nest when approached but return when left alone. At 11 days, flight feathers appear.

Hatching success: of 8 clutches (Nyl), 4 failed, and of 30 eggs, 14 hatched (W. Tarboton, in prep.).

References
Tarboton, W. R. (in prep.).

Subfamily ARDEINAE

Typical herons with 3 major groups (1) tiger herons (*Tigriornis*), (2) night herons (*Gorsachius* and *Nycticorax*) and (3) typical egrets and herons (*Ardeola, Bubulcus, Butorides, Egretta* and *Ardea*). Legs long, except in *Nycticorax*. Usually 12 tail feathers. Outer toe longer than inner. 3 pairs of powder-down patches on breast, rump and thigh with a 4th pair on back in a few species. Ornamental plumes usually well developed and include 3 types: (1) lanceolate, long in comparison to width, with barbs of vanes interlocked; (2) filamentous, long and 'hairy' with barbs almost entirely free; and (3) aigrette, loosest of all with barbs and barbules elongated and free.

Key nuptial plumage features include: (1) *Tigriornis*, colours of bare areas especially obvious, spreading of white crest feathers and possibly also primaries and tail feathers, but little known; (2) *Gorsachius*, crest of slightly elongated black lanceolate feathers, lanceolate scapular plumes forming a conspicuous white patch on back, and soft parts of varying colours but poorly documented; (3) *Nycticorax*, crest of short black feathers including 2–3 long white lanceolate plumes; plumage becomes bluish black; soft parts of varying colour (e.g. black bill, crimson eye and blue-black orbital skin); (4) *Ardeola*, crest and back with lanceolate plumes long except *rufiventris*, and soft parts of varying colours but not well documented; (5) *Bubulcus*, buff ornamental plumes on crown, nape, mantle, foreneck, and chest with plumes on mantle especially long, bill bright orange to red, lores purple-pink, eyes red and feet dusky red; (6) *Butorides*, short lanceolate crest feathers but long lanceolate scapular plumes, lores yellow to pink, legs reddish to orange, bill glossy black and eye deep orange; (7) *Egretta*, aigrettes often but not always on back, long lanceolate plumes on crest, back or breast and soft parts of varying colours; and (8) *Ardea*, lanceolate feathers on crest and/or back and soft parts of varying colours.

Visual displays common; may include: (1) 'upright display' in which standing bird erects body and neck, inclining them slightly (see **A**, p. 159); sometimes angles bill and head downward and may erect crown but not other plumes; (2) 'forward display' in which bird crouches, retracts neck, points bill forward, erects plumes, opens and closes wings, flips tail up and down, and sometimes strikes intruder (see **A**); (3) 'snap display' in which bird holds body at or below horizontal, extends neck forward with bill pointing downward, bends legs until head and neck are at same level, may erect plumes or seize stick, then snaps mandibles together (**B**); (4) 'stretch display' in which bird first stretches body and neck up with bill pointed skyward, then, holding neck and bill in this position, bends legs, lowers body and inclines head backward (see **B**, p. 159); normally does not erect crown plumes; (5) 'flap-flight' display (**C**) in which bird flies from displaying area with neck curved, legs and body held

A

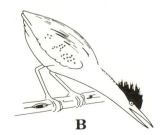

B

C

45° to horizontal, legs dangling, and beats wings slowly; (6) 'bowing display' in which bird, often with twig in bill, stretches up with bill drawn in near neck, lowers head in front of body without moving rest of body, then stretches up again (see **A**, p. 164); and (7) 'wing-touch display' in which bird, in a standing position, touches closed wing with bill (see **C**, p. 159). (*Illustrations on p. 137 reproduced with permission from Meyerriecks (1960).*)

Genus *Tigriornis* Sharpe

1 of 3 genera in the world forming a well-characterized group, collectively known as tiger herons or tiger bitterns. 3 pairs of grey (not white) powder-down patches; tarsus reticulate. In Africa, 1 species.

Plate 11
(Opp. p. 162)

Tigriornis leucolophus (Jardine). White-crested Tiger Heron. Onoré à huppe blanche.

Tigrisoma leucolopha Jardine, 1846. Ann. Mag. Nat. Hist., 17, p. 86; 'Western Africa' = Old Calabar or Bonny Rivers region (Nigeria).

Range and Status. Resident, usually uncommon in equatorial rain forest between 8°N and 5°S and 13°W and 28°E from Sierra Leone east to Cameroon, Central African Republic, Gabon and Zaïre.

Tigriornis leucolophus

Description. ADULT ♂: crown and nape black; feathers of nape partly concealing white crest plumes. Face, chin, neck, mantle, back, rump, tail and upperwing transversely barred black and buff; barring of tail and tip of primaries whiter. Underparts buff streaked and spotted black. Long and slender bill blackish brown above, yellowish green below; facial and orbital skin green; eye yellow; legs brown with back of legs and toes yellow. ADULT ♀: similar but buff bars narrower making bird appear darker. SIZE: wing, ♂ (9 specimens) 255–282 (268), ♀ (4) 251–270 (260); tail, 120–130 (125); culmen, ♂ (9) 90–115 (103), ♀ (4) 80–90 (85); tarsus, 80–86 (83).
IMMATURE: similar to adult but barring much broader.
DOWNY YOUNG: covered with yellowish down later turning whitish; 60 mm on crown.

Field Characters. Similar size and appearance to large bittern, but appears more slender than other large bitterns. Distinguished from all other herons by transversely barred black and buff plumage, and white crest feathers.

Voice. Not recorded. Utters a single or double, loud, hollow-sounding note repeated slowly and regularly for several min, like bittern boom, usually at dusk or night. Silent when departing due to disturbance (K. Curry-Lindahl, pers. comm.).

General Habits. Scarcely known. Solitary, at least partly nocturnal, retiring forest species. Prefers swampy places and smaller shaded streams flowing through thick forest; sometimes inhabits forested river banks and dense mangrove swamps. Freezes in bittern-like posture or flies when surprised.

Food. Small fish, crustaceans, spiders, various insects, frogs, lizards and snakes.

Breeding Habits. Well known. Solitary nester; courtship behaviour unknown. Fully fledged captive in Gabon spread white crest feathers and tail feathers and primaries 'peacock-wise', pointed beak with neck retracted and rhythmically moved from side to side (Bannerman 1930).
NEST: a loosely constructed twig platform *c.* 6 m above ground in a tree.
EGGS: clutch size unknown, but only nest found contained 1 egg. Beige-yellow with scattered reddish brown spots and obscure greyish violet secondary blotches. SIZE: 55 × 45.
Tends to breed in rains but varies between May–July in west and Nov–Jan in east of range, ensuring that feeding of young generally coincides with peak water levels. Laying dates: Sierre Leone Sept–Oct; Liberia Oct; Cameroon Mar, May; Gabon Jan.
Incubation period: at least 29 days, perhaps more (A. Brosset, pers. comm.).

References
Brosset, A. (1971).

Genus *Gorsachius* Bonaparte

Night herons with stocky body and short legs; solitary all seasons of year, inhabiting wooded streams. Strictly nocturnal. 4 species; 1 in Africa.

Gorsachius leuconotus (Wagler). White-backed Night Heron. Bihoreau à dos blanc.

Plate 11

Ardea Leuconotus Wagler, 1827. Syst. Av., *Ardea*, no. 33; Senegambia.

(Opp. p. 162)

Range and Status. Resident, widespread, usually uncommon to frequent in forests near water from Senegal to western Ethiopia to eastern Cape.

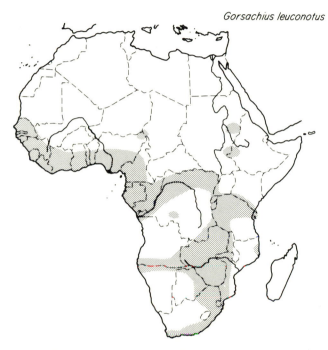

Gorsachius leuconotus

Description. ADULT ♂: crown and nape black with thick black plumes terminating in short crest; mantle, back, rump and tail blackish brown. Wings brown; primaries slate. White lanceolate scapulars forming white patch on back, conspicuous in flight. Face black; chin white; throat and neck rufous-chestnut becoming duskier on upper breast. Rest of underparts brown, belly whitish. Bill black, base of lower mandible with some yellow; lores pale blue to greenish yellow; huge eye yellow in non-breeding season, brown, red, chestnut or amber in breeding season; surrounded by large pale lemon yellow patch; legs and feet, green to orange-yellow. Sexes alike. SIZE: (6 specimens) wing, 262–274 (267); tail, 109–120 (112); culmen, 57–62 (60); tarsus, 68–79 (72).

IMMATURE: buff-brown speckled and streaked like other night herons but more spotted on back and wings, darker, unstreaked forehead and crown, less streaking on side of face, and with some white scapulars developing before moulting; white back plumes present.

DOWNY YOUNG: olive-brown, with buff tips to feathers and creamy buff down showing through. Bill greenish grey; eyes brown; legs greenish grey, yellowish on feet.

Field Characters. A night heron with dark head, large white patch around huge eye, rufous neck and brown body; smaller than Black-crowned Night Heron *Nycticorax nycticorax*. In flight white triangular patch on back conspicuous.

Voice. Not recorded. Usually silent, but at night utters a growling call with a clashing 'taash-taash-taash'; also a toad-like 'kroak' when alarmed.

General Habits. Little known. Solitary or in pairs; active at night in forests with dense vegetation along quiet, tree-fringed streams, rivers and mangroves; occasionally among reeds along rivers and marshes. Widespread but uncommon; seldom seen except when flushed, flying up and down streams at dusk, or standing motionless on floating rafts of tangled water weeds (Hancock and Elliott 1978). By day inactive in dense marshland vegetation or on branches of thickly foliaged trees some 15–18 m tall (Hancock and Elliott 1978).

Possibility of migratory movements correlated with onset of rains suggested by known breeding locations and by data (location and date) from collected specimens, but more information needed (Hancock and Elliott 1978).

Food. Feeds on fish, amphibians, molluscs and insects. Food generally similar to that of Black-crowned Night Heron with ecological separation of 2 unknown. 2 young birds, taken from nest when 4 days old, fed successfully on diet entirely of small cyprinid and cichlid fishes (Junor 1972).

Breeding Habits. Little known. Solitary breeder. Courtship and nest-building behaviour unknown. Nests on low tree branches including euphorbia that project 30–60 cm over water; rarely on branches just above water or shrubs on rocks (Hancock and Elliott 1978).

NEST: large (25–30 cm), saucer-like, of sticks and reeds.

EGGS: 2–3 (sometimes up to 5) laid at at least 48-h intervals; Zimbabwe mean (27 clutches) 2·6; South Africa, E Cape (6) 2·7 (SAOSNRC). Pale greenish white to bluish. SIZE: (17 eggs) 44–48 × 33–37 (46 × 36); WEIGHT: 28.

Breeding mainly in rains or early in dry season with peak in flooding. Laying dates: Nigeria Sept–Oct; Gabon June; Guinea-Bissau Aug; Zaïre Oct; Kenya May–June; Tanzania Mar, July; Zambia Jan, Mar, Oct; Zimbabwe Jan–Apr, June, Aug–Dec; Mozambique Sept; South Africa Jan, Mar–Apr, July–Dec.

Incubation period: 23–26 days. Both parents seen together at nest. Fledging period: 40–41 days in captivity; young leave nest at *c.* 6–8 weeks in wild.

References
Hancock, J. and Elliott, H. (1978).

Genus *Nycticorax* T. Forster

Night herons, medium-sized. Crest of short plumes with a few long ones arising at rear. Bill stout. Relatively short legs; only small part of tibia bare. Tarsus reticulate in front. Small oil gland with longer tufts than other herons. Adult black, grey and white; immature brown and streaked. Somewhat gregarious when roosting and nesting. 3 species; 1 in Africa, with 1 subspecies.

Plate 11

(Opp. p. 162)

Nycticorax nycticorax (Linnaeus). Black-crowned Night Heron. Bihoreau gris.

Ardea nycticorax Linnaeus, 1758. Syst. Nat. (10th ed.), p. 142; southern Europe.

Range and Status. Resident and Palearctic winter visitor, common to frequent along rivers, lakes, marshes and coastal area from Senegal to Ethiopia southward to Cape; also in N Africa. Rare to absent in drier central and western areas of southern Africa and equatorial forest belt of W Africa. Palearctic birds occur alongside resident populations probably south to about equator. Partially migratory in southern Africa. Only *N. n. nycticorax* in Africa.

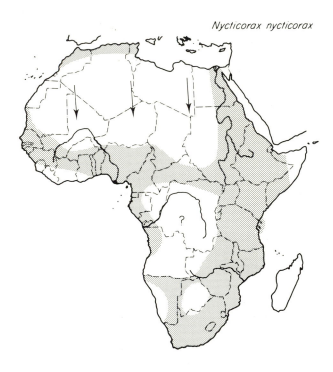

Nycticorax nycticorax

Description. *N. n. nycticorax* (Linnaeus), ADULT ♂: distinctive black, grey and white plumage. Crown, nape, mantle and scapulars black, glossy bottle green, turning bluish black in breeding season. 2–3 long white nuptial plumes extending from crown over hindneck and back. Hindneck, back, wings, rump and tail light grey. Forehead, area above eye, cheeks and underparts, including underparts of wings, white. Bill greenish black, turning black in breeding season; bare skin around eye greenish, turning blue-black at onset of breeding; large eye crimson; legs and feet pale yellow but red briefly during courtship. Sexes alike. SIZE: wing, (27 specimens) 278–308 (291); tail, (16) 103–119 (111); tarsus, (10) 68–84 (75); culmen, (27) 64–78 (71). WEIGHT: (125, Camargue) 339–780 (535).

IMMATURE: 1st-year birds, including fledged juveniles, dark brown above, spotted and streaked buff and white, underparts grey streaked dark brown; older 1st-year birds with fewer white spots and streaks above. Bill yellow; eyes orange-yellow; legs yellow-green. 2nd year immature more like adult but black areas of adult browner; underparts washed with brown and grey; eye brown-red; bill green-black.

DOWNY YOUNG: covered largely in brown down, crown darker with white-tipped, hair-like down giving appearance of a crest; white down on abdomen.

Field Characters. A medium-sized, stocky, black, grey and white heron with short legs and large head; often sits in a hunched position. Black head and crown with greatly elongated white plumes and large reddish eyes distinctive. Immature resembles Eurasian Bittern *Botaurus stellaris* but smaller with broadly streaked underparts and many white spots on upperparts, including wings. In flight, large round wings giving a stumpy appearance with toes projecting only slightly beyond tail.

Voice. Recorded (2a, 19). Generally silent away from colony especially during day. At dusk, or when flushed from day-time hiding place, gives single or series of hoarse, harsh 'quock' sounds. Calls at African colonies similar to those produced by European and American populations: include (1) advertising call with a clicking 'plup', then a twanging 'buzz', (2) high, variable, harsh, rasping, threatening 'kak-kak-kak', (3) an alarm 'squok', (4) a low 'wok-wok' when alerting and mobbing, (5) a sonorous 'kak-kak' when alighting, and (6) soft 'wok-wok' when greeting or before copulating. Also bill-snap and bill-rattle. Food-calls of young include a cackling 'kak-kak-kak' and a 'chip-chip-chip'.

General Habits. Well known in Africa, especially well known in Europe and North America. Often gregarious, skulking, largely nocturnal, usually seen flying at dusk, or sitting on a tree or bush near water, or on floating masses of vegetation. In breeding season, also active daylight hours, particularly early morning and dusk. Spends day in dense vegetation of marshes, swamps, lakes, rivers and coastal mangroves, roosting in flocks of 2–6 to 200, often in same place year after year. After emerging from daylight hiding place, almost always perches 5–25 min in exposed position along periphery of roost before taking off. In South Africa, leaves roost 11–21 min after sunset (Siegfried 1966c). Often fly in pairs, wing-beats faster than those of larger herons. Returns to roost at, or just before, sunrise.

Feeds largely at night. Possibly territorial on feeding ground. Waits for prey but also wades slowly through water searching for it. Prey located by sight and caught by rapid strike of bill. Some hover, dive or swim when feeding. At nesting colony eats chicks of other herons, sometimes by drowning them (K. Curry-Lindahl, pers. comm.); feeds own chicks mainly on small fish and large insects.

In Camargue, southern France (Watmough 1978) other herons, especially Little Egrets *Egretta garzetta*, attack night herons during day and steal their food; after dark, large number of night herons successively feed on same area, suggesting that they feed at night to avoid competing with other herons. When competitive species are absent, adults and newly fledged young may feed in day-time, but this is unusual.

In Palearctic winter most leave N Africa, moving widely across Sahara with European and Asian birds. Birds ringed France, Spain, recovered Senegal, Gambia, Sierra Leone, Mali; ringed Hungary, Czechoslovakia, recovered Guinea, Niger; and ringed Russia, recovered Cameroon, Chad, Sudan. Local movements recorded in southern Africa as Cape Province-ringed bird recovered in Mozambique (McLachlan and Liversidge 1978).

Food. Feeds on fish, frogs, snakes, lizards, crustaceans, molluscs, insects, spiders, small mammals and birds.

Breeding Habits. Well known in Africa; especially well known in Europe and North America. Colonial, 10–1000 pairs with other herons, ibises, darters and cormorants. Tend to nest together in trees or bushes, occupying centre or top of colony.

Both sexes arrive at colony at about same time, often in same flock. Courtship starts when ♂ leaves inactive flock and chooses one or more territories, building nest platform on at least one. On nest or nests, performs upright, forward and snap displays, and gives advertising calls. Several ♀♀ approach displaying unpaired ♂, cautiously at first, and also perform these displays. Next, ♂, with white plumes erect, does main pairing display, the song dance display, in which he stands erect with neck extended in line with body, but bill held horizontally, and lifts feet alternately; then bends legs to lower body and starts to call when bill almost level with feet; continues forward movements crouched with neck over side of nest, then stands up. Repeats entire performance 3–4 times in succession until joined by ♀ who fans head and neck feathers and moves white nape plumes at angles to one another. ♂ follows suit; he also performs bowing display. Both sexes do wing-touch display; no flap-flight display has been recorded.

Pair-formation may last 2–26 days but is completed within *c.* 30 min once ♀ permitted to stay at nest. ♂ then collects the majority of nest material, ♀ constructs nest. When either returns, both perform 'greeting ceremony' in which both assume horizontal position with necks stretched, white plumes erected, and touch bills; this display preceded by loud call when either sex returns to nest. Copulation at or close to nest-site, often following greeting ceremony. Billing and mutual preening occur before and after copulation.

NEST: flimsy platform of sticks and reeds, barely large enough to accommodate sitting bird; built in low trees, bushes, reedbeds over or near water; often collapse in incubation causing losses.

EGGS: 3–6, laid at 2-day intervals; E Africa mean (7 clutches) 3·3; Zimbabwe (17) 2·8; South Africa, SW Cape (73) 2·4, OFS (7) 2·4, Transvaal (25) 2·2 (SAOSNRC). Pale blue-green, rounded at both ends. SIZE: (26 eggs) 45–53 × 32–37 (49 × 35); WEIGHT: 34.

Laying dates: N Africa Apr-June; Mauritania May; Senegal July–Dec; Guinea-Bissau May–Dec; Mali Aug–Sept; Gambia July–Sept; Ethiopia Apr, Aug–Sept; Kenya–Uganda Feb–July, peaking Apr–June; Tanzania Feb–June; Zaïre Nov–May; Rwanda Apr–May; Zambia Jan–Apr, Aug; Malawi Nov; Zimbabwe Jan–Apr, Aug–Dec; Namibia June–July; South Africa Jan, Aug–Dec. Most records in rains or late in rains in inundated areas; N Africa spring.

Both parents incubate (mainly ♀ ?); by day 1 parent on nest for several hours with no nest-reliefs. Incubation period: Europe 21–22 days, Zimbabwe 24–26 days, South Africa *c.* 22 days (SAOSNRC).

Both parents feed and attend young, at first by direct regurgitation into chicks' beaks, later onto nest from which young collect it. Young develop first feathers at 12th day; leave nest readily at 20–25 days; can fly at 40–50 days.

Irregular, not annual, breeding and heavy nest losses due to pythons, monitor lizards, or hippopotamuses shaking eggs and young out of nests, result in low replacement rate in some areas, e.g. Kisumu, 30 pairs laid, but only 1 young seen flying from *c.* 100 eggs. In successful E African nests, mean (58 broods) was 2·08. Overall, probably 1 young/pair/year (L. H. Brown, pers. comm.; EANRC).

References
Voisin, C. (1970).
Watmough, B. R. (1978).

Genus *Ardeola* Boie

Small, stocky, short-legged herons with relatively short and slender bills; includes the pond herons. Typical plumage of most is cryptic on ground, with white flashing wings on take-off. Filamentous feathers common. Tarsi scutellate, claws relatively long.

Several opinions on generic position of Rufous-bellied Heron *Ardeola rufiventris*. In first half of 20th century *Erythrocnus* was used. In 1958 the South African Bird List Committee used *Butorides*. Bock (1956) and Curry-Lindahl (1968, 1971) concluded on different grounds that *rufiventris* has more in common with *Ardeola*, the pond herons, than with *Butorides*. Payne and Risley (1976) suggested *rufiventris* may be a link between *Butorides* and *Ardeola*. Hancock and Elliott (1978) and Payne (1979) placed *rufiventris* in *Ardeola*, and we have done so as well.

Plate 11

(Opp. p. 162)

Ardeola ralloides (Scopoli). Squacco Heron. Crabier chevelu.

Ardea ralloides Scopoli, 1769. Annus 1 Historico-Nat., p. 88; Carniola.

Range and Status. Resident and Palearctic winter visitor, frequent or common to locally abundant, along lakes, marshes, large rivers and smaller ponds; rare along coasts and in estuaries from Mauritania to Ethiopia south to Cape; also N Africa. More numerous south of equator; some evidence of movements between African mainland and Madagascar. Palearctic visitors from Eurasia and N Africa cross Sahara on broad front, augmenting resident populations at least to equator. We follow Cramp and Simmons (1977), Hancock and Elliott (1978) and Payne (1979) in not considering populations of central and southern Africa a separate subspecies, *A. r. paludivaga* Clancey.

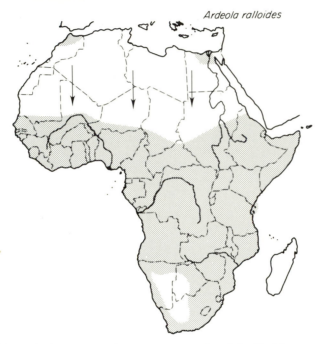

Ardeola ralloides

Description. ADULT ♂: crown, nape and neck buff with overlay of black, brown and grey filamentous crest feathers. Mantle and scapulars dull buff brown. Back, rump, tail and upperparts of wings white washed with some yellow. Chin and throat white. Buff foreneck and breast and white belly and underpart of wings streaked brown. Bill greenish yellow, black at tip; lores yellowish green; eye yellow; legs and feet yellow-green. ADULT ♂ (breeding): crest with long black-edged white feathers; mantle cinnamon-buff with longest feathers drooping over wings and tail. Breast and rest of underparts without brown streaks. Bill china blue with black tip; lores blue to green; eyes rich yellow; legs and feet bright red. Sexes alike. SIZE: wing, ♂ (9 specimens) 208–234 (225), ♀ (9) 209–228 (216); tail, ♂ (8) 73–84 (81), ♀ (9) 66–84 (73); bill, ♂ (8) 62–70 (65), ♀ (9) 58–65 (62); tarsus, ♂ (9) 51–62 (58), ♀ (9) 54–59 (56). WEIGHT: (23) 230–370 (300).

IMMATURE: like non-breeding adult but mantle earth brown; no long crest or mantle plumes; breast more strongly streaked; belly greyish; and wings tinged or mottled brown.

DOWNY YOUNG: a mixture of grey, buff and white down; eye olive with yellow; bill yellow with dark tip; lores green-yellow; legs olive in front, pale yellow behind.

Field Characters. Smallish, thickset, short-legged heron, mainly brownish buff. Bittern-like when standing. On take-off sudden appearance of white wings, rump and tail contrasting with dark upperparts distinguishes it. Resembles Cattle Egret *Bubulcus ibis* but has dark back contrasting with white wings in flight, dark bill and streaked head; also Cattle Egret always appears white at distance. In flight more rapid wing-beats and less frequent gliding than egrets.

Voice. Recorded (18, 19). Mainly silent but at dusk, especially in breeding season, utters 'kaar', 'kak', 'charr', 'rrra', 'kwang', 'kaak' and 'kok'. Begging call of young: 'kri-kri-kri-kri'.

General Habits. Well known. Often common but inconspicuous due to secretive habits and cryptic colouring. Prefers vegetation associated with still fresh water of ponds and edges of sluggish rivers and streams, perched on or among papyrus and reeds. Usually solitary, although parties of up to 20 recorded. Gregarious when roosting, often with mixed species. Roosts dusk to dawn but some roost in day. Feeds individually, occasionally in groups, in shallow water any time of day. Normally feeds by slow stalk and swift jab.

Resident populations north of equator greatly augmented by Palearctic winter visitors. In Nigeria during Palearctic winter numbers increase from small to very large (Moreau 1967); Uganda increase 10-fold in Sept and 30-fold in Oct–Nov (Mann 1976). Palearctic populations move across Sahara on broad front, being recorded in oases in Niger, Chad, Libya and Sudan. Birds ringed in Spain, recovered Mauritania; in France —Guinea and Sierra Leone; in Yugoslavia—Nigeria and Cameroon; in Bulgaria—Nigeria; and in Russia— Zaïre. Southern limit of Palearctic visitors unknown but south into Zaïre, Rwanda and Burundi at least where they mix commonly with common resident populations. Present in SE Zaïre only May–Nov in non-breeding plumage and appearance in Zambia in flocks up to 20 in early rains in July suggest seasonal migratory movements (Benson *et al.* 1971a; Prigogine 1975).

Food. Prefers relatively small insects, although diet includes a variety of invertebrates and vertebrates including grasshoppers, beetles, butterflies, spiders, crabs, molluscs, fish (up to 10 cm long) (Hancock and Elliott 1978), frogs and oddments such as a White-throat *Sylvia communis* (Backhurst and Pearson 1977).

Breeding Habits. Well known in Africa, better known in Palearctic. Usually colonial, small to large numbers (2000 nests, Tanzania: Stronach 1968) often in heronries with other species, sometimes alone.

Courtship not studied in Africa but probably like Palearctic populations and pond herons of Asia. Begins when ♂ claims site and builds small nest where he performs flap-flight display, upright display, forward display, stretch display, and snap display, snapping bill loudly. ♀♀ at first driven away but one eventually joins ♂. Both then perform stretch display, billing, mutual preening and stick-passing. Copulation occurs at or near nest; no precopulatory display except occasionally stretch display.

NEST: bulky but compact structure of sticks, grass and reeds, usually on branch over water or concealed in thickets or reedbeds. Usually sited within 1 m of water, rarely above 1·2 m, and, in mixed heronries, usually in thicker cover than other species. Built by ♂♂ in 1–3 days.

EGGS: 2–4, laid in usually 1, sometimes 2 days; E Africa mean (8 clutches) 2·9; Senegal (9) 2·4; Zambia, Zimbabwe and Botswana (16) 2·3; South Africa, Transvaal (37) 2·7 (SAOSNRC). Regular ovals, greenish blue. SIZE: (10 eggs) 36–41 × 27–31 (38 × 29) (SAOSNRC); WEIGHT: *c.* 16.

Laying dates: Morocco, Tunisia, Egypt Apr–May; Algeria May–June; Senegal July–Dec; Sierra Leone Aug–Oct; Mali Mar, June–Oct; Gambia July–Sept; Nigeria Mar–Aug, Oct; Ghana July; Chad Feb; Sudan July, Nov; Ethiopia Mar–June, Aug–Sept; W Kenya–Uganda Jan–July, Aug, peaking Apr; Tanzania Jan, May; Zaïre May–Aug; Burundi, Rwanda Apr; Zambia Jan–June, Aug–Oct, peaking Mar; Zimbabwe Jan, Sept–Dec; Namibia May; Botswana June; Mozambique Oct; South Africa Jan–May, July–Dec, peaking Feb–Mar (Nyl flood plain, Transvaal). Lays mainly in rains, or at end of rains in inundated areas, but many W African records in dry season, and in W and South Africa breeds spring and early summer.

Incubation begins when clutch complete; by both sexes, roles not detailed in Africa. Aggressive to other birds when incubating, and if any bird (including other, sometimes larger, herons) approaches, incubating bird raises neck- and back-plumes, squawks and strikes at intruder. Incubation period: Europe 22–24 days; not recorded Africa, but Madagascar 18 days.

Both parents attend and feed young. Feed by regurgitating food into mouths of young, later onto nest from which young pick it up. Brooding continues in early stages. Young move out of nest and freeze in undergrowth when 2 weeks old. Fledging period: Madagascar 35 days; in Europe young leave nest at 35 days but can fly only at 45 days. Survival, E Africa, usually 1–2 young/nest.

References
Cramp, S. and Simmons, K. E. L. (1977).

Ardeola idae (Hartlaub). Malagasy Pond Heron; Madagascar Squacco Heron. Crabier blanc.

Plate 11

Ardea Idae Hartlaub, 1860. Journ. f. Orn. 8, p. 167; east coast of Madagascar.

(Opp. p. 162)

Range and Status. Non-breeding migrant, uncommon to frequent in eastern and central Africa. Known north to about equator in Kenya, west to 24°E in Zaïre and south to 16°S in Zambia and 20°S in Zimbabwe. 25 specimens in the Tervuren Museum from Zaïre and Rwanda, suggest that, in Central Africa at least, this heron may be more common than thought.

Description. ADULT ♂: crown and nape broadly streaked with black; mantle, scapulars and inner secondaries brown with buff shaft streak enlarging at feather tip. Sides of head, throat and breast yellow narrowly streaked blackish brown. Back dusty brown; rump, tail, belly and flight feathers whitish. Tips of outer flight feathers and tail of immature sooty brown. Bill grey with some greenish tinge and black tip; legs and feet green to greenish yellow. Sexes alike. ADULT ♂ (breeding): entirely snow-white including long plumes on nape, back, foreneck and breast. Bill deep cerulean blue with black tip; lores green; eye yellow; legs rose pink, toes green. Pale buff-yellow wash on upperparts disappears when full breeding plumage attained. SIZE: wing, 210–262 (236) (McLachlan and Liversidge 1978); 7 adults 230–254 (245), 17 immatures in first winter plumage 211–244 (227) (Prigogine 1976); tail, 77–101 (89).

IMMATURE: like non-breeding adult but back dull brown; inner secondaries with well defined shaft streaks.

Ardeola idae

Field Characters. Adult ♂ in full breeding dress seen Mafia Island, 22 Feb 1915, and Pemba Island, 12 Oct 1942; otherwise immatures and adults only recorded in non-breeding plumage in Africa (Turner 1980). These resemble Squacco Heron *A. ralloides* Malagasy Pond Heron but stockier and heavier, particularly around neck, and without dull buff-brown colouring; also has heavier and broader bill, heavier, darker (almost dark chocolate brown) mantle; darker, broader streaking; and brighter yellow toes, sometimes with pink and red feet. Separation in field rather difficult. In hand, dull brown back and inner secondaries with well defined shaft streaks, also blunt, square-cut wing-tips (4 outer, longest primaries nearly equal in length), not pointed (2nd primary from outside longest) as in Squacco Heron.

Voice. Not recorded. A croak more raucous, less shrill than that of Squacco Heron; also a nasal rather musical rattled 'burr' when approached by a Cattle Egret *Bubulcus ibis*.

General Habits. Little known. Thought to be more closely related to pond herons of Far East than to Squacco Heron (Hancock and Elliott 1978), but habits apparently similar to this species, and tends to occur alongside it although adapted more to wooded rather than open habitats, flying up into trees when disturbed. Migrates to eastern half of tropical Africa in non-breeding season, May–Oct, with some 1st-year birds remaining in Africa during breeding season.

Food. Scarcely known in Africa. Solitary feeders, especially along banks of small streams, but also along lakes, ponds and reefs at low tide. In Aldabra feed mainly with egrets on inland pools and edges of lagoons (Benson and Penny 1971). Food recorded in Madagascar and Aldabra includes fish, frogs, skinks, geckos, grass-hoppers and beetles.

References
Hancock, J. and Elliott, H. (1978).
Prigogine, A. (1976).
Turner, D. (1980).

Plate 11
(Opp. p. 162)

Ardeola rufiventris (Sundevall). Rufous-bellied Heron. Héron à ventre roux.

Ardea rufiventris Sundevall, 1851. Öfv. K. Vet.-Akad. Förh., Stockholm, for 1850, p. 110; 'Caffraria superior' = Mooi River, Potchefstroom, Transvaal.

Range and Status. Resident in central and southern part of continent from Angola to Kenya south to eastern Cape. Known as far north as Entebbe and Lake Kioga, Uganda (K. Curry-Lindahl, pers. comm.). Common in flood plains of western and northern Zambia and Okavango delta of Botswana; elsewhere rare to uncommon.

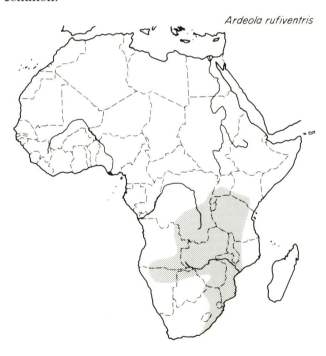

Ardeola rufiventris

Description. ADULT ♂: general colour dark slate-grey with chestnut-red on shoulders, uppertail-coverts, rump, tail and belly. Crown and sides of head medium bluish grey, merging to darker slate-grey on neck and mantle. Slack plumes on back up to 10 cm long; lower back dark brownish grey. Flight feathers black. Chin and throat dark slate-grey. Bill yellow with black tip; lores and bare orbital area yellow; eye yellow, sometimes with an orange outer ring; legs and feet bright orange-yellow, toes sometimes with reddish tinge. ADULT ♀: general colour sooty brown; plumes on back up to 7–8 cm long.

Chin, throat and lower neck buffish brown with buff to whitish stripe from chin to base of foreneck. Chestnut-red shoulders, rump, tail and belly as in ♂; belly lighter. Lores and orbital area pale yellow, almost white. Bill horn-brown with basal two-thirds of lower mandible greenish or orange-yellow. SIZE: 17 specimens, wing, 198–321 (216); tail, 70–83 (75); tarsus, 51–66 (57); culmen, 56–75 (62).

IMMATURE: similar to ♀ but streaked buff-brown on side of head, neck and breast but not belly.

DOWNY YOUNG: at hatching covered with grey down on back, dirty white underneath. Bill pale pink with reddish brown tip; tarsus pale pink.

Field Characters. A dark heron, smaller than Squacco Heron *A. ralloides* but larger, thicker-necked, longer-winged and heavier-billed than Green Heron *Butorides striatus*. Resembles the larger Black Heron *Egretta ardesiaca* but has chestnut-red tail, rump, belly and shoulder patch and bright yellow legs, rather than black legs with orange toes. Yellow bill with black tip, and yellow loral and orbital bare skin striking in field, even in flight, when yellow feet also clearly visible.

Voice. Not recorded. Described as a rasping 'kraak', a muffled, crow-like 'kar' or 'caw', a 'cherr-cherr' when chasing another individual; a 'twaa' when approaching nest with food; and a soft 'po-po-po' when calling young.

General Habits. Well known. Solitary, sometimes in small groups of 5 or so, associated with seasonally wet grasslands, marshes and flood plains; sometimes along river banks, edges of lakes, lagoons and reedbeds. Feeds by day, sometimes at night, typically in horizontal stance, along landward margins of vegetation bordering a wetland and in shallows, sometimes with other water birds. When flushed, flies short distance usually into a nearby leafy tree. When hiding, assumes a bittern-like posture but with bill pointing straight ahead, not up. When not foraging, several perch in trees, sometimes some distance from water.

May be partly migratory or some movements at least associated with seasonal flooding. Thus, in Bangweulu area (Zambia) regular but only Dec–Aug; regular Katanga (Zaïre) Dec–July, rare Sept–Nov; Amboseli (Kenya) Oct; and South Africa (Nyl flood plain) most months year but only when flood conditions prevail.

Food. Fish (including *Barbus* and *Tilapia* spp.), frogs, insects and worms.

Breeding Habits. Very well known, but courtship behaviour not described. Colonial nesters in reedbeds, *Phragmites*, *Cyperus*, stunted ambatch trees, and thickets of *Ficus* in or near water, with 60–800 nests in Bangweulu (Zambia) area (Mwenya 1973); sometimes with other herons, storks and darters.

NEST: a small platform of reed stems, twigs and leaves; 25–35 cm in diameter, 10–12 cm thick and 1·0–3·5 m above water.

EGGS: 1–4 laid at *c.* 2-day intervals; Zambia mean (41 clutches) 2·3; Botswana (24) 1·9; Zimbabwe (46) 2·6 (SAOSNRC); South Africa (7) 1·8; Transvaal (8) 3·5 (SAOSNRC). Pale blue without any markings. SIZE: (40 eggs) 29–41 × 25–29 (37 × 28).

Breeds in rains and in dry season when flooding occurs. Laying dates: Uganda Apr–May; Zambia Jan–June, Aug (most Mar); Zaïre Dec–Jan; Malawi Dec; Zimbabwe Jan–Apr, July–Dec; Botswana Aug; Namibia Sept; South Africa Feb–Mar, May, Dec.

Incubation begins immediately after 1st egg; share of sexes unknown; period unrecorded.

Not known if both parents feed young. Small young fed by regurgitation, presumably throughout day.

Young hatch within 2-day intervals. Open eyes, body length 8·5 cm and culmen 1·5 cm at 2 days. Bill dark red, tarsus greenish yellow and down on back dirty black at 4 days. Move around nest, body length 14·2 cm and culmen 1·7 cm at 5–6 days. Young soon become quite active, sometimes leaving nest to swim short distances. Body length 17·0 cm, primaries 0·4 cm, down on back darkens slightly and reddish tinge on crown at 11–12 days. Feathers begin to replace down by 14 days. Spend daytime out of nest but return to it at night at 17 days. Body length 27·8 cm and primaries 5·2 cm at 19 days. Tail 1·3 cm, eye brown and tarsus yellow at 20 days. 33% adult size and fly a few metres at 24 days. 75% adult size and fly strongly at 32 days. Only weight recorded, 170 g, that of dead 16-day-old chick.

Behaviour of young includes frequent begging with mouth open, lower mandible distended, and uttering of 'cheep' calls; frequently wipe bill, explore-peck and pick up food; crawl even when very young using wings as props; stand at 7 days; hop and run when disturbed; remain immobile in nest or jump from it and crouch in reeds when alarmed; defaecate outside nest.

Of nests with av. clutch size of *c.* 3 (Zambia), av. chick content (22 nests with no eggs remaining) 1·5. Death rate high due to hanging between reed stems when leaving nests, starvation, ejection from nest by older sibling and also by predators, including Nile Monitor *Varanus niloticus* and African Marsh Harrier *Circus aeruginosus*.

References
Uys, J. M. and Clutton-Brock, T. H. (1966).

Genus *Bubulcus* Bonaparte

Small, stocky, white herons with short stout bill, buff on breeding plumage and distinctive habit of following large hooved mammals in order to feed on the disturbed insects.

Bubulcus ibis (Linnaeus). Cattle Egret; Buff-backed Heron. Héron garde-boeufs.

Ardea Ibis Linnaeus, 1758. Syst. Nat. (10th ed.), p. 144; Egypt.

Plate 10

(Opp. p. 147)

Range and Status. Resident and intra-African migrant, common to abundant, in damp and dry open fields, flooded plains and short grassy margins of rivers and lakes. Breeding populations (1) in Morocco, Algeria, Tunisia and Egypt; (2) between 10–16°N from Senegal east to Red Sea coast; (3) between 16°S and the Cape from Namibia east and south to Botswana, Zimbabwe, Mozambique and South Africa; and (4) in Uganda, Kenya, Tanzania and Rwanda. Passage migrant across Zaïre forest belt moving north Apr–May and south Nov–Dec. Some movement along Red Sea from Egypt southward, across Mediterranean between Morocco and Spain, and along NW Morocco coastal area. Movements across Sahara unknown.

Description. *B. i. ibis* (Linnaeus), ADULT ♂ (late in breeding season and non-breeding season): largely white with little to no buff on crown and nape. Bill, lores and eye yellow; legs and feet dark green-brown. Sexes alike, except feathers on lower throat and mantle creamy white and slightly elongated in ♂, not elongated in ♀. ADULT ♂ and ♀ (breeding): buff or pale rufous crown, nape and elongated ornamental plumes of mantle, foreneck and chest; mantle plumes nearly reach tail. Rest of plumage including wings and tail white. Bill bright orange, coral red, or red; lores purple-pink; eyes red; legs and feet coral red to dusky red, feet sometimes dusky yellow. SIZE: wing, ♂ (20 specimens) 241–266 (253), ♀ (20) 240–258 (248); tail, ♂ (20) 79–93 (88), ♀ (20) 74–93 (86); bill, ♂ (12) 52–60 (56), ♀ 52–58 (54); tarsus, ♂ (20) 70–85 (77), ♀ (20) 70–81 (76). WEIGHT: (4) 325–387 (345).

IMMATURE: like non-breeding adult but no buff or elongated feathers; plumage can have grey cast. Bill, legs and feet black.

DOWNY YOUNG: at hatching, white down on head, back and wings but not on nape, throat and along spine. Body skin olive-green. Bill and orbital area green, horn or pale flesh; eye white to pale yellow; legs and feet pale yellow-green.

Bubulcus ibis

Field Characters. At distance, small stocky white heron with short neck, stout yellow bill and yellow legs and feet. At close range breeding birds with buff on crown, foreneck and mantle conspicuous. Stand with neck hunched into shoulder. When walking, neck extended forward or diagonally upward, not in slender curve. Region under jaw enlarged to give distinctive heavy jowl. Distinguishable from Little Egret *Egretta garzetta* and white phase of Reef Heron *E. gularis* by lack of long, slim black bill; from Yellow-billed Egret *E. intermedia* by smaller size and lack of blackish feet; and from Squacco Heron *Ardeola ralloides* by habits, habitat and having basically white, not brownish or buff plumage when at rest.

Voice. Recorded (2a, 6, 19). Simple, unmusical and throaty calls given at colony or roost; relatively silent elsewhere. Include: (1) 'rick-rack' call, by both sexes, a croaking sound with 1st syllable louder and higher-pitched; early in breeding season, quieter, hoarser, slow-

Left-hand scale applies to all standing pelicans and Nos. 1–3 in flight; centre scale to Nos. 17–23 in flight; right-hand scale to flamingoes (not head details)

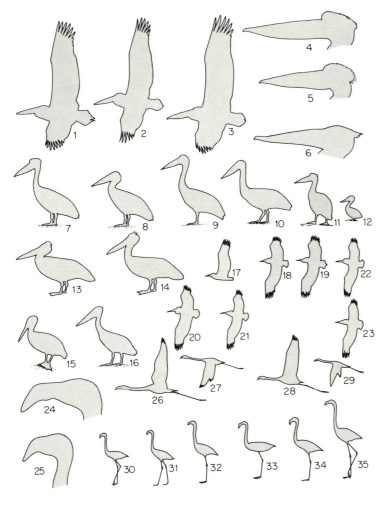

Plate 9

Pelicans

Adults in flight from below: 1. *Pelecanus onocrotalus* Great White Pelican (p. 122).
2. *P. rufescens* Pink-backed Pelican (p. 126).
3. *P. crispus* Dalmatian Pelican (p. 128).

Heads: 4. *P. onocrotalus* (breeding ♂). 5. *P. onocrotalus* (breeding ♀). 6. *P. rufescens* (breeding).

Standing birds: *P. onocrotalus* 7. ADULT ♂, 8. ADULT ♀, 9. IMMATURE, 10. 6–8 week old JUVENILE, 11. ADULT with iron-stained plumage, 12. DOWNY YOUNG. *P. crispus* 13. ADULT (breeding), 14. IMMATURE. *P. rufescens* 15. ADULT, 16. IMMATURE.

In flight: *P. onocrotalus* 17. IMMATURE from side, 18. IMMATURE from above, 19. ADULT from above. *P. crispus* 20. ADULT from above. *P. rufescens* 21. IMMATURE from above, 22. ADULT from above, 23. with worn plumage.

Flamingoes

Heads: 24. *Phoenicopterus ruber* Greater Flamingo (p. 212) ADULT. 25. *Phoeniconaias minor* Lesser Flamingo (p. 216) ADULT.

In flight: *P. ruber* 26. ADULT from below, 27. from above. *P. minor* 28. ADULT from below, 29. from above.

Standing birds: *P. minor* 30. IMMATURE, 31. ADULT (non-breeding), 32. ADULT (breeding). *P. ruber* 33. IMMATURE, 34. ADULT ♀ (non-breeding), 35. ADULT ♂ (breeding: note larger size).

pitched 'ruk-rok'. The 'rick-rack' call given during greeting ceremonies, when returning to nest and at roost, but rarely when feeding. (2) Brief but harsh 'raa' and 'kraah' calls used as threats by both sexes. (3) A soft and muffled 'thonk' given by ♂ early in breeding season especially to approaching ♀♀. (4) A low-pitched alarm 'kok' given singly or in a series. (5) Chatter calls including: (a) 'nasal chatter' by unmated ♂, a 1–2 s phase of 5–12 nasal notes descending in pitch and volume; (b) 'soft chatter' not descending and uttered by recently mated pair; and (c) loud harsh 'kakakakakak' in greeting ceremonies by mated birds. (6) A soft 'ow' followed by a 'rooo' by unmated ♂ during stretch displays. (7) 'rooo' by mated ♀ doing stretch display. (8) Young make 'ziz-ZIT' food call, raspy squeaky threat call, discomfort 'eeeh' call, and a recognition-appearance 'chirp' call. Adults make loud thudding sounds with wings during flap-flight display, but make no bill noise during snap display.

General Habits. Intimately known. Gregarious, usually in flocks of 10–20 in close association with livestock and game mammals. Sometimes follows plough; attracted to grass fires with several hundred individuals of mixed age and sex gathering around locally abundant food. Least aquatic of herons, spending daylight hours away from water in pastures, semi-arid steppes and arable fields; not usually found in coastal, marine, forested and high mountain environments. Daily cycle includes (1) morning flight to feeding grounds, mostly less than 19 km but can be up to 60 km from roost; (2) late afternoon and early evening flights, 1 h or so before sunset, to watering places and assembly areas, 1–10 km from roost; and (3) evening flights to roost in trees or on ground (Blaker 1969a; Cramp and Simmons 1977). Roost-bound flights follow water courses or cut directly across country, sometimes in close, fairly low-flying groups in V-formation. Wing-beats rather rapid and shallower than other herons.

Plate 10

Bubulcus ibis Cattle Egret (p. 145)
1. ADULT (non-breeding), 2. ADULT (breeding).

Egretta garzetta Little Egret (p. 154)
3. dark morph, 4. white morph.

Egretta intermedia Yellow-billed Egret (p. 156)
5. ADULT (non-breeding).

Egretta alba Great Egret (p. 157)
6. ADULT (non-breeding).

Egretta gularis Western Reef Heron (p. 153)
Race *dimorpha*: 7. dark morph, 8. white morph.
Race *asha*: 9. white morph, 10. dark morph.

Ardea melanocephala Black-headed Heron (p. 165)
11. ADULT, 12. IMMATURE, 13. in flight

Heads: 14. *B. ibis* (breeding), 15. *B. ibis* (non-breeding), 16. *E. alba* (breeding), 17. *E. intermedia* (breeding).

Egretta ardesiaca Black Heron (p. 151)
18. ADULT standing and in fishing posture.

Egretta vinaceigula Slaty Egret (p. 152)
19. ADULT.

Ardea cinerea Grey Heron (p. 161)
20. IMMATURE, 21. ADULT (non-breeding).

Ardea purpurea Purple Heron (p. 160)
22. IMMATURE, 23. ADULT.

Ardea goliath Goliath Heron (p. 167)
24. IMMATURE, 25. ADULT.

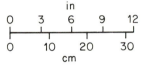

Scale applies to standing birds

Roosts normally hold a few hundred to 2000, sometimes 10,000 birds often with other herons, ibises and cormorants; found alone on occasion or in small groups (Siegfried 1971a). Roost as a single unit in reedbeds, on trees or on ground, normally near water but sometimes close to or in villages. Each bird tends to use same perch night after night; little aggression among roosting birds.

Feeds usually in loosely associated flocks on wet or dry land or shallow water, normally alongside or following cattle, African buffalo and hippopotamus; also follows African elephant, rhinoceros, zebra, giraffe, eland, topi and waterbuck. More efficient foraging with large mammals than when foraging alone. Often seen back-riding, probably for vantage perch but sometimes to feed on ticks. Feeds also in vegetable gardens.

Common method of foraging is steady walk interspersed with stabs and dashes. Before striking, sometimes wriggles neck, sways head or shakes body. Slack feeding activity in middle of day; feeds mainly mornings and afternoons.

In late 19th and early 20th century confined to subtropical and tropical Africa. With increase in intensive livestock farming has spread southward into Cape where breeding colonies established 1920s and 1930s. Pronounced migrant, following the rains to breed in rainy season. Birds ringed South Africa, recovered Central African Republic (farthest distance from colony, 4216 km: Morant 1980), Uganda, Zaïre, Zambia, Malawi, Mozambique and Tanzania. About 80% of South African birds move north Mar–Apr; 20% remain in South Africa (K. Newman, pers. comm.). Migrants of southern population remain east of Zaïre forest in E Africa; those from northern breeding populations remain in Zaïre forest belt and along western coastal areas. Movements of mainly resident E. African individuals not known. Birds ringed Spain, recovered Morocco, suggesting some movement across Mediterranean Sea. Seasonal visitor Mauritania, Oct–Jun.

Food. Mainly insects, especially grasshoppers and earthworms; not uncommonly spiders and frogs; also crustaceans, molluscs, fish, lizards, snakes, young birds, rodents and palm-nut pulp. Eats earthworms in rainy season; ground-dwelling, grass-chewing insects throughout year. One stomach contained 682 grasshoppers (Siegfried 1971b). Feeds on calliphorid flies but not bees attracted to fallen mangoes (Smalley 1979). Chicks fed centipedes, grasshoppers, distyoperans, isopterans, a few frogs (*Rana* spp.), lizards (*Mabuya striata*, *Nucros taentolata* and *Agama kirkii*) and blind worms (*Zygaspis quadrifrons*) (Tomlinson 1979).

Breeding Habits. Intimately known. Colonial, in trees often far from feeding grounds and sometimes in villages and reedbeds; in small to large numbers (up to 10,000 pairs: Stronach 1968) often with other herons, ibises, spoonbills, darters and cormorants. Sometimes nest only with Long-tailed Cormorant *Phalacrocorax africanus* (Kenya). Colonies may be used from year to year.

Nesting starts when small groups of ♂♂ take up one or more territories, seize twigs, spread wings, raise crests, stand hunched with back plumes erect, prance from foot to foot; also perform upright, forward, stretch and flap-flight displays. Usually do flap-flight display within 2–10 m of territory, beating wings to produce loud 'thud' sounds. ♂♂ also make 'rick-rack' and 'chatter' calls. Several ♀♀ gather within 8 m radius, perched 1–2 m above ♂. Eventually approach ♂, attempting to land on his back or to stand next to him to bite his back feathers. At first ♂ repulses ♀♀ but within 3–4 days permits a ♀ to remain, the pair then being formed within a few hours. At this time mutual back preening, twig-shaking (usually ♂) and stretch display (usually ♀) take place.

After pair has formed, ♂ followed by ♀ usually moves to another site where nest-building begins. Usually no pre-copulation display except crouching by ♀. ♂ collects nest material, up to 300 m away; ♀ builds nest. Greeting ceremony with fully erected back plumes and flattened crest occurs whenever one returns to nest.

NEST: a saucer-shaped platform of dry, brittle sticks 20–25 cm in diameter, 12–25 cm high; occasionally with a thin grass lining and 1·2–2·5 m over water. Nest-building and egg-laying take about 11 days.

EGGS: 1–7 laid at 1–2 day intervals; Ghana mean (89 clutches) 2·6, E Africa (55) 2·6, Zimbabwe (76) 2·2; Botswana (7) 2·1; South Africa, SW Cape (1976) 2·58, OFS (332) 2·5, Transvaal (290) 2·48, Natal (184) 2·2 (SAOSNRC). Pale green or blue, somewhat pointed towards one end. SIZE: (105 eggs) 41–51 × 30–35 (44 × 34) (SAOSNRC).

Breeding mainly in or just after rains. Laying dates: N Africa mainly spring, Morocco Apr–June; Algeria and Tunisia May–June; and Egypt Apr–Sept. W Africa mainly rains, Senegal May, Aug–Dec; Guinea-Bissau July–Sept; Gambia May–Sept; Ghana June–Sept; Mali May–Nov; Niger July; Nigeria May–Sept; São Tomé June–July, Oct–Nov; Cameroon Apr; Chad July–Sept; Congo, Zaïre Apr, Aug. E Africa rains but also dry season, Sudan May–June; Ethiopia June–Aug; Kenya Mar–June, Sept–Oct; Uganda Mar, June, Sept–Oct; Tanzania Feb, Apr–May. Southern Africa, Zimbabwe Jan–Apr, Aug–Sept, Nov; Mozambique Jan, Nov; Namibia June–July; Botswana Oct, Dec–Jan; South Africa, SW Cape Aug–Dec with peak Sept–Oct, OFS Oct–Dec with peak Oct, Transvaal Sept–Jan with peak Dec, Natal Aug–Jan with peak Nov–Dec.

Incubation by both parents who change over 1–4 times a day; starts with 1st or 2nd egg. Period: 22–26 (23·7) days.

Young hatch at 1–2 day intervals and thus differ in size. For first 5–8 days peck and grab weakly at any part of adult's bill. Thereafter begging becomes more intense with chicks waving wings, bobbing head, neck and body, quivering head with open bill and attempting to seize base of parent's bill. Later even chase parent. Leave nest at *c.* 20 days; begin to fly at 25 days; fledged at 30 days and independent at 45 days. Bill turns black at 5–10 days, then gradually becomes yellow during 2nd and 3rd month. Completely feathered at 7 weeks; tail full-grown at 8 weeks. Legs become dark green to black before fledging. Feathers remain largely white until 5 months when some buff colour on head.

Young cared for and fed by both parents; not left unattended until about 10 days old. When young less than 10 days, each parent collects food once per day but feed young several times per day. Older young fed on av. 1·5 times per day.

Breeding success, Cape Province, 34% eggs laid produced fledged young, or av. 0·43 young/pair successfully raised (Siegfried 1972b). Main losses due to eggs falling out of nest, starvation in first 2 weeks of hatching, and predation by *Varanus* lizards, pythons, night herons, and at least once by Vervet Monkey (*Cercopithicus aethiops*). Ghana, 37 nests, 62% eggs hatched, 46% chicks survived to leave nest (Bowen *et al.* 1962); E Africa 1–2 young normally fledged in successful nests (L. H. Brown, pers. comm.).

Normally breeds when 2 years old but sometimes when 1 year old. Mortality, 1st year birds, 37%; thereafter, annual av. 25% (Siegfried 1970).

References
Blaker, D. (1969a).
Siegfried, W. R. (1966a, b; 1970; 1971a, b, c, d, e, f; 1972a, b, c; 1978).
Skead, C. J. (1966).

Genus *Butorides* Blyth

Small, stocky, short-legged herons with rather short and heavy-looking neck, large bill, and claws more strongly curved than *Ardeola*.

Butorides striatus (Linnaeus). Green Heron; Green-backed Heron. Héron vert.

Ardea striatus Linnaeus, 1758. Syst. Nat. (10th ed.), p. 144; Surinam.

Plate 11
(Opp. p. 162)

Range and Status. Resident, frequent to common, in mangroves along seashores and estuaries, and thick underbrush along rivers, streams, and lakes from about 16°N from Senegal to Sudan south to eastern Cape; also along Red Sea coast north to Egypt.

Description. *B. s. atricapillus* (Afzelius): Africa south of Sahara from Senegal to Sudan south to eastern Cape excluding Red Sea coast. ADULT ♂: generally dark above, pale below. Crown and nape black glossed green, forming elongated crest. White patch behind eye edged below with black. Hindneck and side of neck grey. Scapulars long, glossed green and lanceolated. Back and tail dark grey. Chin white; centre of foreneck and upper breast rufous-brown; rest of underparts grey. Upperwing dark grey, outer webs glossed green and edged with cream to white; underwing grey. Upper mandible black, lower yellow-green, dark at tip. Lores dark blue or greenish; eye yellow; legs grey-brown in front, yellow behind. Sexes similar, ♀ duller. ADULT ♂ and ♀ (breeding): besides lengthening of crest and scapular plumes, bill is glossy black, lores yellow, eyes deep orange and legs bright yellow-orange to red-orange. SIZE: wing, (16 specimens) 167–190 (179); tail, (16) 57–70 (64); culmen, (15) 55–65 (61); tarsus, (10) 44–47 (46). WEIGHT: 193–235.

IMMATURE: brown above, crown slightly glossed green, wing fawn with white spots. Crest and scapular plumes small. Throat, foreneck and breast buff with brown spots and streaks; rest of underparts grey. Soft parts like non-breeding adult.

DOWNY YOUNG: skin black, covered with light grey down with white along centre of throat and underparts; bill yellow; lores and eye greenish yellow.

B. s. brevipes (Ehrenberg). Red Sea coasts Egypt, Sudan, Ethiopia and Somalia. Darker; crown, nape, back and scapulars more bronzy green, less bright green.

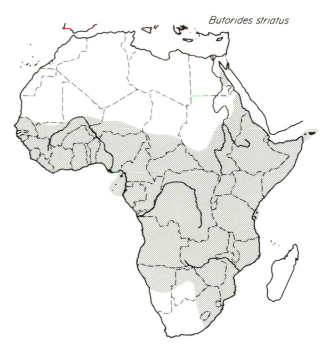

Butorides striatus

Field Characters. A small heron with dark green crown, back and wings, and grey on neck and underparts. Immatures with browner underparts spotted fawn and white, buff underparts streaked with dark brown. Crown noticeably erectile. Often stands in horizontal posture with tendency to extend head and neck even in flight. In flight, a small dark heron with protruding orange-yellow legs.

Voice. Recorded (2a, 6, 18). Largely silent but when flushed a single, rather explosive 'tyah' or 'kyah'. At nest harsh croaks when disturbed. Call of adults prior to nest-site selection a harsh, sneezing, 'tchaa-aah', sometimes with an explosive 'hoo'. 'Skows' and 'skeows' during courtship. On arrival at nest and on reaching nest prior to feeding young, a long drawn 'tchee-unk'; also harsh calls and a single chicken-like 'cluck'. Calls of young from egg near hatching soft croaking or thumping; older young a soft, croaking 'toc-toc-toc-toc' between parental feeding visits and a hiss when disturbed.

General Habits. Well known. Largely solitary and retiring, inhabiting dense mangroves or thick underbrush alongside rivers, lakes and streams. Runs about roots and branches with relative ease. Occasionally in open flood plains. Equally at home in salt or fresh water; ventures freely into open water. Usually seen in hunched position; walks with body held almost horizontally and legs bent. Bobs or flicks tail in the vertical plane at any or all times except when roosting. Often raises crest. Occasionally adopts 'bittern stance'.

Roosts solitarily in trees or rocks, often during day or during rising tide, flying to feeding grounds at sunset or at ebb tide. In mangrove creeks, active day or night. Feeds alone day or night. Hunts by stealthy stalking or waiting motionless until prey comes within reach, then lunges forward to capture it cross-wise in bill. If on a branch above water, stretches neck down and jabs forward, even diving and completely submerging when striking at fish. Sometimes stands in centre of stream in 'bittern stance' and snatches dragonflies which approach or land on its bill (K. Newman, pers. comm.). Uses bait to catch fish. Has been seen to fly to heaps of maize meal, collects a piece, drops this in water and watches it float past, then retrieves it and tries again. Method not usually very successful; only strikes if small fish are attracted, sometimes successfully; large fish ignored. Method used by day, and by few birds (Shrives and Carberry, pers. comm.; W. J. Eggeling, unpub.).

Very little information on movements. Basically sedentary but some dispersion from Red Sea breeding localities; in Kenya Backhurst and Pearson (1977), having seen them at dawn several times in Dec, suggested they have been attracted to lights of a game lodge (Ngulia) during nocturnal movement; also recorded in South Africa (Nyl) where erratic seasonal visitor in flood years (W. Tarboton, pers. comm.).

Food. Fish, especially mud-skippers in mangrove swamps; also crabs, shrimps, molluscs, water insects, grasshoppers, dragonflies, spiders, frogs and reptiles.

Breeding Habits. Well known in Africa; intimately known in North and Central America (see Palmer 1962). Normally nests solitarily usually *c.* 1 m above water in low bushes or branches of mangroves, acacias, figs or other small trees. Sometimes in loose colonies with 5–15 nests in same tree or neighbouring trees. Rarely with other herons.

Courtship in Africa poorly described but probably nearly identical to that of Green Heron of North America (Curry-Lindahl 1971) in which both sexes arrive at nesting area about same time. ♂♂ select territories and, from them, repeatedly utter 'skow' call, with ♀♀ then roaming from ♂ to ♂ and making high-pitched 'skeow', even answering ♂♂. If ♀ attempts to land, ♂ repulses her with forward-threat and upright displays. ♂ next shifts to snap and stretch displays; ♀♀ stop roaming and each settles near a ♂. Both then do flap-flight display in which displaying birds leave territory, fly in large circle and land near starting point. Often perform this aerial display with neck held in kinked position, crest and scapulars erected, and legs dangling. Pair established at about this time. Copulation occurs only in territory; preceded by mutual stretch display, feather-nibbling, twig-passing and billing.

NEST: display site used as nest-site. ♂ collects nest material; ♀ builds nest in 3 days. Generally well hidden; a loose, flimsy structure of twigs, sticks and reeds with shallow cup about 30 cm in diameter.

EGGS: 2–4, laid at 2-day intervals; E Africa mean (19 clutches) 2·37; Zimbabwe (114) 2·7; South Africa, Natal (4) 2·8, Transvaal (11) 2·6 (SAOSNRC). Pale blue-green. SIZE: (43 eggs) 33–41 × 27–30 (37 × 28) (SAOSNRC); WEIGHT: 17.

Breeds largely in rains but also dry season. Laying dates: Senegal Feb–Mar, June–Dec; Gambia May, July–Sept, Nov–Dec; Guinea-Bissau Apr–May, July–Sept; Liberia Oct; Sierra Leone May, July–Sept; Ivory Coast June; Mali Jan–Mar, Aug–Oct; Ghana June–Sept; Nigeria Apr–Oct; Gabon June–Sept; Sudan June–Sept; Ethiopia Apr; Kenya Apr, June, Sept–Oct, Dec; Tanzania Jan–Feb, Apr–May, July–Aug; Uganda Apr–June, Sept–Oct, Dec; Zaïre Oct–Dec; Zambia Jan–June, Aug–Oct; Malawi Jan–Feb, Dec; Zimbabwe Jan–June, Aug, Oct–Dec; Botswana July; Mozambique Aug–Sept; South Africa Jan–Dec.

Incubation by both sexes; period 21–25 days.

Eyes of young open at hatching. Maintain upright posture at 2 days. Tail-flipping and 'bittern stance' done by 5–6 days. 1st wing-flapping movements by 7–8 days. Climb by 1st week; jump from branch to branch by 15 days. Make short flights by 21 days. Fly when 34–35 days.

Both sexes care for young for 1 month or more after leaving nest. Young fed about 1 day after hatching when parents drop regurgitated food into young's open mouth, or occasionally onto nest if seized when young are older. By 1 week young vigorously beg and seize parent's bill. For 1st week young brooded almost constantly; by 3 weeks young no longer brooded.

Survival, E Africa, probably less than 2/nest.

References
Cowles, R. B. (1930).
Meyerriecks, A. J. (1960).

Genus *Egretta* T. Forster

Small to medium-sized herons, often white or having white phase. Tarsus scutellate. In Africa, 6 species, 2 with Palearctic populations that migrate to Africa in winter. Of the 6, 2, *ardesiaca* and *vinaeigula*, have long lanceolate plumes on crown, nape, back and breast but no aigrettes. The remaining 4 have long lanceolate plumes and also aigrettes with *intermedia* having them on back and breast, and *gularis*, *garzetta* and *alba* on back. *Gularis* and *garzetta* have 2–3 narrow elongated filamentous plumes on nape. *Intermedia* and *alba* do not have ornamental plumes on crown or nape.

Egretta gularis dimorpha considered *E. garzetta dimorpha* by Cramp and Simmons (1977) and *E. dimorpha* by Payne and Risley (1976) and Payne (1979). We follow Hancock and Elliott (1978) and Snow (1978) by treating *dimorpha* as a race of *E. gularis*. Caution is needed when referring to Little Egret/Reef Heron in E African literature. Dark morph Little Egret *E. garzetta* (e.g. Britton 1975) in all likelihood *dimorpha* and treated here as Western Reef Heron *E. gularis dimorpha*.

Egretta alba has characteristics in common with both *Egretta* and *Ardea* and, because of this, is sometimes placed in *Casmerodius*. Similarities with *Ardea* include relatively large size, lack of plumes on head and several skeletal characteristics, and with *Egretta* all-white plumage, loose long aigrette feathers on back and similar displays. Until more studies clarify the situation, we place *alba* in *Egretta* (as have Cramp and Simmons 1977; Hancock and Elliott 1978; Snow 1978) rather than *Ardea* (Curry-Lindahl 1971; Payne 1979; Payne and Risley 1976; Tomlinson 1976) or *Casmerodius* (Mock 1978).

Egretta ardesiaca (Wagler). Black Heron; Black Egret. Aigrette ardoisée.

Plate 10

(Opp. p. 147)

Ardea ardesiaca Wagler, 1827. Syst. Av., *Ardea* no. 20; Senegambia.

Range and Status. Resident; normally uncommon, occasionally locally abundant, in shallow water along edges of lakes, rivers, marshes, flooded plains, mangroves and tidal flats, south of 17°N from Senegal to Ethiopia southward, mainly down eastern half of continent. More common north of, than south of, Zambezi River. In W Africa at least, more common along coasts and lower river valleys, less so inland.

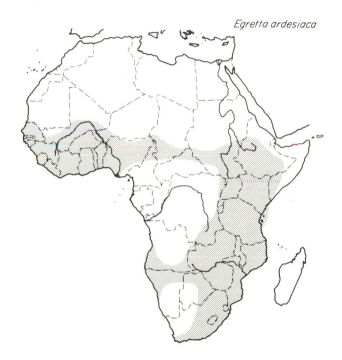

Egretta ardesiaca

Description. ADULT ♂: black with bluish or slate grey tinge. Long lanceolate plumes on crown, nape, neck and mantle. Primaries broad, sharply emarginated with outer webs broad. Secondaries, scapulars, axillaries and underwing-coverts broad and long; outer half of secondary shaft soft and 'degenerate'. Bill black; eye bright yellow; legs black; feet yellow to orange-yellow, sometimes red at onset of breeding. Sexes alike. SIZE: wing, ♂ (18 specimens) 244–273 (266), ♀ (9) 235–263 (249); tail, 90–101 (96); tarsus, ♂ (15) 78–89 (85), ♀ (7) 78–89 (85); culmen, ♂ (17) 58–69 (65), ♀ (8) 56–66 (62) (Benson *et al.* 1971b).

IMMATURE: duller, more brown-black, with no long plumes.

DOWNY YOUNG: covered in black-grey down; crest of white down; skin green with yellow throat and abdomen; eyes dark brown; legs greenish yellow; feet yellow.

Field Characters. An all-black heron with black bill and legs, contrasting yellow eyes and feet. Distinguished from dark morph Reef Heron *E. gularis* by dark, not white, throat and black, not pale-coloured, bill and legs; and from Rufous-bellied Heron *Ardeola rufiventris* and Slaty Egret *E. vinaceigula* by black legs, yellow feet, not yellow or dark grey-yellow legs and feet. Is decidedly smaller than Reef Heron or Little Egret *E. garzetta*; overall colour darker than dark morphs of these 2 spp. Habit of forming feeding canopy with spread wings, short legs, rapid wing-beats and swift flight also diagnostic.

Voice. Not recorded. Harsh cries when defending nest and a low cluck.

General Habits. Well known. Usually in groups of 5–50 but 100 or more reported (Mwenya 1973); sometimes solitary. Visits a variety of shallow fresh and salt water habitats, including swamps, edges of rivers, lakes, flooded grasslands, mangroves and tidal mudflats. When in brackish areas along coast or in alkaline lakes, tends mainly to be observed at freshwater inlets.

Diurnal; last to go to roost (Tree 1966); Mida Creek (Kenya) roosts with Little Egrets at high tide. Will erect all its plumage, shake itself vigorously, then allow feathers to return to normal. Some local movements, e.g. present Sierra Leone only Dec–June; also wetlands Zimbabwe plateau only Oct–Feb, thereafter returns to swamps of Zambesi and Limpopo.

Feeds by canopying. Forms canopy on sunny and overcast days and at dusk; also reported to do so at night (Mackworth-Praed and Grant 1952). Walks a few paces, stops, lowers head, then rapidly flings wings forward and slightly overlapped to form a black canopy that shades water in front of head. Wing-tips only a few cm from, or touching, water surface; holds this pose for 2–3 s, then returns wings to normal position, moves forward and canopies again. While canopying, wiggles toes presumably to attract or disturb prey. Sometimes moves slowly when canopying. At Mida Creek (Kenya) regularly feeds in small pools on exposed mudflats where walks up to pool, canopies and, under canopy, works bill rapidly 'like needle of sewing machine' (L. H. Brown, pers. comm.). Swallows small prey either while canopying or after returning to standing position. Canopies in rapid succession in many places if feeding intensively. Feeds in isolation from other birds; also feeds socially with 70 or more in a group, canopying, unfolding, then canopying again as they follow a school of fish. Occasionally feeds with Great Egrets *E. alba*, Little Egrets and Reef Herons. Also canopies in mudflats from which most water has drained at low tide, and a captive bird canopied over plate of food (Milon *et al.* 1973).

Reasons for canopy not clear but heron in canopied position is probably waiting for prey to take shelter in shadow of canopy. Canopy may eliminate reflection from water surface, greatly improving ability of bird to see into water, and may have effect of obscuring from the fish any sudden movement of striking bird.

Food. Mainly fish but also crustaceans and aquatic insects.

Breeding Habits. Well known. Colonial in groups of 5–50 up to 1500, often scattered among nests of other herons, cormorants, ibises and darters. Nests located 1–6 m above water in a variety of trees including mangroves and ambatch; also in reedbeds.

Courtship behaviour largely undetermined. One possible courtship display reported when two birds followed one another at fast run, stopped, canopied and, without fishing, ran and canopied again (Cooper 1970).

NEST: a solidly constructed platform of sticks and twigs.

EGGS: 2–4; South Africa mean, Transvaal (4 clutches) 2·3 (Tarboton 1979), Natal (7) 2·7 (SAOSNRC). Blue-green to dark blue. SIZE: (14 eggs) 42–48 × 32–34 (46 × 33); WEIGHT: 28.

Breeding correlated with rainfall, especially with increased water level, nest-building reaching peak several weeks after start of rains. Laying dates: Senegal Aug–Sept; Gambia June; Guinea-Bissau Sept; Ghana July–Aug; Mali Jan–Mar, Aug–Oct; Nigeria Feb–Apr; Kenya Feb–Mar, May–June; Tanzania Feb–Mar; Zambia Mar–June; Botswana Feb–Apr, June; Zimbabwe Jan; South Africa Dec–Jan.

Incubation, parental care and fledging period undescribed. Adults show marked aggressiveness towards own kind and other species when on nest. If approached, strike at intruder generally with head-plumes raised. When young birds start hunting, begin by spreading one wing; later canopy with both wings.

Many nests systematically watched have not been successful, possibly due to predation by Pied Crow *Corvus albus* (Grimes 1967) and special vulnerability to human predators.

References

Benson, C. W. *et al.* (1971b).
Cooper, J. (1970).
Grimes, L. G. (1967).
Milstein, P. le S. and Hunter, H. C. (1974).

Plate 10
(Opp. p. 162)

Egretta vinaceigula (Sharpe). Slaty Egret. Aigrette vineuse.

Melanophoyx vinaceigula Sharpe, 1895. Bull. Brit. Orn. Cl., 5, p. 13; Potchefstroom, Transvaal.

Range and Status. Resident and uncommon with restricted distribution in marshes and flood plains of Okavango delta and Chobe National Park (Botswana), Caprivi Strip (Namibia), Kafue Flats, Zambezi River north to Bangweulu swamps and Nchelenge District (Zambia) (Dowsett 1979) and, probably, southeastern Angola; no longer South Africa. Possible summer (Dec–Jan) visitor Malawi and northern Mozambique (Day 1978).

First known to science in 1895 on basis of 3 specimens collected at Potchefstroom (South Africa); a 4th specimen collected at Kabuta in Caprivi Strip in 1948, and recently a pair from Xugana (Botswana).

Description. ADULT ♂: overall pale slate grey. Head, hind and side of neck, mantle, back and tail slate grey. Plumes on hindneck narrow; those on mantle and back extending beyond tip of tail with conspicuous twist to tips. Chin, throat and foreneck wine red becoming deep buff with wear. Plumes of chest slate grey or slate grey and wine red. Abdomen and flanks uniform black or mixed with wine red. Primaries and secondaries slate grey with white bases to shafts. Underwing buffish and pale slate grey. Bill black with a pale keel to lower mandible; ring of black feathers around pale yellow eye; legs yellow to yellowish green with slightly pale short toes. Sexes alike. SIZE: wing, ♂ (4 specimens) 229–242 (237), ♀ (1) 226; culmen, ♂ (4) 53–60 (57), ♀ (1) 56; tarsus, ♂ (4) 82–86 (84), ♀ (1) 76. WEIGHT: 340 (Benson *et al.* 1971a; Irwin 1975). IMMATURE and DOWNY YOUNG plumages unrecorded.

Field Characters. A slate-grey heron, rather like a dark Little Egret *E. garzetta* with a slender neck and bill, yellowish legs and feet. Lacks short, dumpy appearance of Black Heron *E. ardesiaca*. Wine-red throat and neck visible only at close range.

Voice. Not recorded. A triple harsh 'kraak kraak kraak' uttered during aggressive behaviour towards its own or other species (H. Elliot, pers. comm.).

General Habits. Little known. Normally solitary in marshes and receding flood plains. Preferred habitat seems to be extensive shallow inundation zones especially where water level is falling. Forages often where grass tall enough to conceal birds. Does not enter open water as often as Little Egret. Known to perch in trees and feed with other aquatic species. Feeds alone, in pairs, or in groups up to 8, stalking and stabbing prey, not forming canopy like Black Heron. Occasionally breaks into sort of run or partly opens wings when striking. Foot-stirs with both feet up to 25% of foraging time (H. Elliott, pers. comm.).

Seasonal movements possible since it disappears from Chobe area in rains, and by midsummer influx in western Okavango.

Food. Fish 5–10 cm long and also probably dragonflies and perhaps snails (H. Elliott, pers. comm.).

Egretta vinaceigula

+ 1895 Potchefstroom record

Breeding Habits. Scarcely known. One nesting colony of 8 pairs known from a reedbed in Botswana in May; nests 1 m above water but contents unknown.

References
Benson, C. W. *et al.* (1971b).
Irwin, M. P. S. (1975).
Milewski, A. V. (1976).
Vernon, C. J. (1971).

Egretta gularis (Bosc). **Western Reef Heron. Aigrette gorge blanche.**

Ardea gularis Bosc, 1792. Actes Soc. Hist. Nat. Paris 1, p. 4, pl. 2; Senegal River.

Plate 10

(Opp. p. 147)

Range and Status. Resident, locally common, in a variety of coastal habitats; rare inland. *E. g. gularis* along W African coast from *c.* 25°N lat. from Mauritania south to Gulf of Guinea islands and Gabon. *E. g. asha* along coasts of Red Sea, Gulf of Aden and Indian Ocean from Egypt to Kenya; also Socotra; occasionally inland on lakes in Rift Valley (Uganda, Kenya, Ethiopia) and upper Nile. *E. g. dimorpha*, migrant along Tanzania and Mozambique coast, nests Aldabra and Madagascar. Area of overlap between *asha* and *dimorpha* on E African coast remains to be ascertained, but one *asha* reported as far south as Dar es Salaam; possibly intergrades on coast of Somalia (Hancock and Elliott 1978).

Description. *E. g. gularis* (Bose): W Africa. ADULT ♂: dark morph—black to slate grey upperparts, wings and underparts except white chin and throat, and occasionally white belly. Primary coverts with variable amount of white. Bill heavy, horn-brown with yellow at base of lower mandible; upper mandible down-curved at tip. Lores and orbital area greenish yellow to olive-green; eye yellow. Legs greenish black, feet yellow to orange-yellow. ADULT ♂ (breeding): 2–3 slate grey filamentous plumes on nape; lanceolate plumes on chest, back and scapulars; aigrettes on back. White morph—rare (e.g. of 900 birds Banc d'Arguin, 2 or 3 white: Etchécopar and Hüe 1967), all white; bare parts as above. Sexes alike. SIZE: wing, (23 specimens) 244–285 (265); tail, (11) 82–101 (91); bill, (21)

Egretta gularis

+ Vagrants

79–89 (84); tarsus, (19) 82–94 (90). WEIGHT: ♂ (1) 400. (Measurements combine sexes, adults and juveniles.)

IMMATURE: dark morph—light brownish grey with white chin and throat, variable white on wings; rest of underparts mottled off-white. White morph—like non-breeding adult.

DOWNY YOUNG: down of crest white, sides of face, neck and upperparts grey; wing, flanks and underparts paler; skin grey.

E. g. asha (Sykes): Red Sea south to Kenya. Slightly larger than nominate race, wing (10 specimens) 272–311 (288) (Vaurie 1965); weight, ♂ 638, ♀ 644 (Owre 1967). Dark morph more ashy grey. Bill yellow, sometimes tinged greenish grey, but apparently horn-brown on the north Somalia coast (Archer and Godman 1937). Legs and feet like nominate race but suffused with olive to apple green, especially immatures; feet reddish orange in courtship. The white morph, with bare parts very similar in colour, predominates at the north end, the dark morph at the south end of the Red Sea; and particoloured specimens seem more common than in other races.

E. g. dimorpha (Hartert) Tanzania and Mozambique. Slightly larger than *asha*; dark morph with less white, sometimes without white on chin; bill black, similar to that of Little Egret *E. garzetta*, but some yellow at base and longer, heavier and down-curved at tip, not straight and slender like *garzetta*; yellow feet with yellow extending halfway up tarsus. White morph has bare parts like those of dark morph.

Field Characters. Medium-sized herons, usually seen foraging on sea coasts. Dark morph distinguishable from similar but rare melanistic or dark morph Little Egret by heavier, distinctly downward curving bill, by conspicuous and well-defined white chin and throat and, in *gularis* and *asha*, by brown or yellow bill. White morph *dimorpha* separated with difficulty from normal Little Egret by conformation of bill, as noted above, and tendency towards paler and more extensive yellow on toes and tarsus and a pale yellowish patch near the gape. Separation of white morph *gularis* and *asha* from Little Egret by colour of bill and/or legs is comparatively easy. There are also differences in the colour of the lores and of the nuptial flush between the 2 species, but these are too slight to be readily detected.

Voice. Not recorded. Normally silent. At breeding colony calls include deep cries uttered in greeting; rasping contact calls; harsh squawks; and a warning 'co-oi' when nesting bird is disturbed. Also bill-snapping.

General Habits. Well known. Found in small groups, but frequently solitary. Prefers rocky and sandy coasts and reefs; also salt marshes, mudflats, estuaries, tidal creeks, mangroves and lagoons. Roosts mangroves, rocky cliffs and islets, sometimes in large numbers (500–1000 on 1 roost, Nigeria: Elgood *et al.* 1973), usually at night. Feeds by day, but, depending on tides, also at night. Normally solitary feeder, maintaining feeding territory along shore. Moves slowly with head and neck level with body, or in an upright pose; sometimes crouches flat in water or on coral. Often in water with seaweeds or silty substrate; stirs bottom with feet, then rushes at prey. Sometimes raises wings forming partial canopy like Black Heron *E. ardesiaca*. White morphs tend to feed in groups usually in open situations; dark morphs singly in mangrove-sheltered creeks (Hancock and Elliott 1978).

Some dispersal from breeding colonies along Red Sea, and probably inland, accounting for Rift Valley sightings. In Nigeria and Gambia most seen Sept–Feb, possibly due to movements to breeding colonies.

Food. Mainly fish, crustaceans and molluscans; also crickets, grubs and earthworms.

Breeding Habits. Well known. Nests in mangroves, on boulders, and sometimes inland beyond mangroves, in small colonies of *c.* 12 pairs, sometimes up to 100, occasionally solitarily; seldom with other species.

Courtship poorly described. ♂ establishes territory and builds display platform; several ♀♀ watch as ♂ performs upright, forward, snap and stretch displays. ♀♀ approach ♂ with one eventually being accepted by him. Light and dark morphs often pair. After pairing, mutual billing and preening, stick-passing, stretch display and stroking display in which both face each other and rub necks or heads together. Copulation on nest. Stretch display important when greeting.

NEST: a platform of twigs and seaweed *c.* 30 cm in diameter, 15–20 cm high. ♂ collects material; ♀ constructs nest.

EGGS: 2–4 (W Africa), 3 (Red Sea). Oval, smooth, pale blue-green. SIZE: (6 eggs, *E. g. asha*) 45–49 × 34 (47 × 34); (*E. g. gularis*) 44 × 32.

Lays in rains: Mauritania Apr–Oct; Senegal May–Oct; Gambia July–Oct; Sierra Leone July–Aug; Guinea-Bissau Mar–Sept; Ghana July–Aug; Nigeria Jan; São Tomé Aug; Ethiopia Apr–July; Somalia Apr–May.

Incubation begins with 1st egg; by both sexes. Period: 23–26 days.

Both parents feed and care for young. Food is regurgitated. Young move out of nest after *c.* 15 days; fly *c.* 45 days. Both light and dark chicks seen in same nests in Red Sea region but colour of parents not recorded (Hancock and Elliott 1978).

References
Hancock, J. and Elliott, H. (1978).
Owre, O. T. (1967).

Plate 10

(Opp. p. 147)

Egretta garzetta **(Linnaeus). Little Egret. Aigrette garzette.**

Ardea garzetta Linnaeus, 1766. Syst. Nat. (12th ed.), p. 237; 'in Oriente' = Malalbergo, NE Italy.

Range and Status. Resident and Palearctic winter visitor, locally common along margins of coastal and inland water habitats. Breeding areas scattered all over Africa except in equatorial forest regions of western Africa and Saharan, Somalian and Namibian deserts. Palearctic migrants widespread from N Africa south to equator. Only nominate race in Africa (*dimorpha* considered *E. gularis dimorpha* in this book—see above).

Description. *E. g. garzetta*, ADULT ♂: white morph—all white. Bill straight, slender and black; lores grey-green; eye yellow; legs black; feet greenish yellow. Dark morph—all slate grey including chin; soft parts like white morph; few reliable specimens collected or observed. Sexes alike. ADULT ♂ and ♀ (breeding): 2–3 filamentous plumes on nape; lanceolate plumes on foreneck, breast, mantle and scapulars; aigrettes on mantle and scapulars nearly reach tip of tail; lores orange to mauve-red; legs orange-yellow to bright red. SIZE: wing, ♂ (17 specimens) 245–303 (280), ♀ (17) 251–297 (272); tail, ♂ (16) 84–113 (98), ♀ (14) 81–101 (94); bill, ♂ (17) 67–93 (84), ♀ (17) 68–89 (80); tarsus, ♂ (17) 78–112 (101) ♀ (17) 88–110 (97): WEIGHT: Palearctic adults 280–614.

IMMATURE: like non-breeding adult without ornamental plumes.

DOWNY YOUNG: covered in white down; upper mandible black, lower light; eye grey; legs green.

Field Characters. Entirely white, medium-sized heron with a slender, straight black bill, black legs and conspicuous yellow feet. Black bill and yellow feet distinguish it from Great Egret *E. alba* which usually has yellow bill (except during the peak of the breeding season when its bill becomes mostly black), black feet and a black gape line behind eye. Distinguished from Yellow-billed Egret *E. intermedia* by black not yellow bill; from Cattle Egret *Bubulcus ibis* by black, not yellow, bill and legs and absence of buff in plumage; and from Reef Heron *E. gularis* by slender and straight, not down-curved and heavier, bill. Rare dark morph distinguished from dark morph Reef Heron by straight bill and absence of well-defined white chin. Differences between Reef Herons and Little Egrets more fully discussed under Reef Heron.

Voice. Recorded (2a, 18, 22a, 26). Usually silent away from roost and colony. At South Africa colony calls include grating 'aaah' at take-off; 'da-WAH' at greeting; gargling 'ggrow' when threatening; long, gargling sound and brief loud hollow 'dow' when ♂ advertising; descending 5–9 hollow 'po' calls when breeding birds (sex ?) are advertising (?); nasal chatter when ♂ twig-shaking and when both sexes greeting; and 'ow' during downward movement of stretch display. Also rattles bill during flap-flight display.

General Habits. Well known. Usually solitary except when roosting in trees or flying to roost. Occupies variety of habitats including flood plains and edges of marshy rivers, lakes, estuaries and mangrove creeks. Favours open areas with shallow fresh water. Leaves roost at dawn, returns at sunset; sleeps during night. Roosts at high tide with Grey Heron *Ardea cinerea*, Goliath Heron *A. goliath*, Black Heron *E. ardesiaca* and Great Egret *E. alba* (L. H. Brown, pers. comm.). At Luanda Harbour (Angola) occurs in large numbers (1000), gathering around incoming fishing boats (W. Tarboton, pers. comm.).

Feeds chiefly by walking through water, making quick movements here and there and snapping prey. Also stands and waits to catch passing prey or agitates water and mud with one foot to locate prey. In calm, clear water, walks and stabs prey when seen. In vegetated areas and on open tidal flats, runs from place to place, sometimes opening and closing wings, disturbing and capturing prey. In areas with much wave-action stands and waits for movement of prey in trough of each

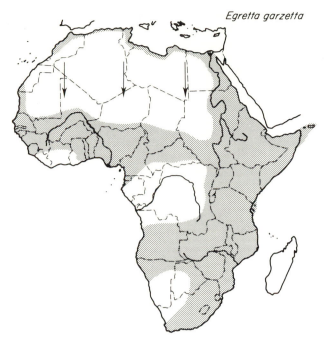

Egretta garzetta

wave. In coastal South Africa feeds 65% day (7·8/24 h); feeds in water 10 cm deep; disturbs and chases 54%, walks slowly 31%, and stands and waits 15% (Whitfield and Blaber 1979).

Birds ringed France, recovered Senegal, Gambia, Mali; Spain, recovered Guinea; Yugoslavia, recovered Nigeria; and Russia, recovered Nigeria, Cameroon. This suggests Palearctic migrants fly at least to equator with those from western Europe tending to winter in western W Africa and those from eastern Europe in eastern W Africa. Common passage migrant N Africa Mar–May and Aug–Sept with some wintering there, e.g. Libya, some Dec–Feb. Move across Sahara in broad front. Non-breeding birds remain south of Sahara during Palearctic summer, e.g. some Sierra Leone, rains (July) and dry season (Dec); Ethiopia, along Red Sea coast in Palearctic autumn. Definite seasonal movements southern Africa with reduced numbers in winter (Witwatersrand, numbers Mar–Apr 10% of those in summer months); also one caught 1840 km northeast of Rondevlei (South Africa) (McLachlan and Liversidge 1978).

Food. In coastal South Africa crown crab, snails, bivalves and fish (usually less than 1 g); food recorded elsewhere includes frogs, shrimp, insects, lizards, fish and, rarely, small birds. Occasionally follows cattle like Cattle Egrets. In Luanda Harbour (Angola) when gulls not present scavenges by hovering with dangling legs, stretching down and picking up floating fish with bill (Brooke 1971a).

Breeding Habits. Very well known. Colonial nester near water, in trees, bushes, reeds and sometimes on rocks or cliffs. Sometimes in own colonies ranging from a few to 100 nests, but more often with Black-crowned Night Heron *Nycticorax nycticorax*, Squacco Heron *Ardeola ralloides*, Cattle Egret *Bubulcus ibis* and Glossy Ibis *Plegadis falcinellus*; 1500 Little Egret nests among 50,000 nests recorded Tanzania (Stronach 1968).

Courtship begins when several ♂♂ and ♀♀ form mobile groups with ♀♀ following ♂♂ who defend and advertise from a succession of small territories. With all plumes erect, ♂ walks about each site, (1) uttering gargling and 'dow' advertising sounds and nasal chatter, (2) performing forward and upright displays, (3) shaking twigs, and (4) making short flap-flights and longer circle-flights of 30–300 m. Makes extended flights, as do other individuals (sex?), with neck stretched 20–30° above horizontal and scapular plumes raised first 5–10 m after take-off. ♀♀ attracted to displaying ♂; perch nearby, peering at him with necks extended. Several ♀♀ repeatedly fly towards him only to be threatened and supplanted; ♀♀ occasionally perform wing-touch display at this time. ♂ next performs stretch display, raising only scapular aigrettes and not 2–3 filamentous plumes of nape and lanceolate plumes of breast and back. Pair-formation occurs after few days (exact manner not described), and, if ♀ allowed to stay, bond established in a few hours. Both then perform flap-flight display and rattle bills. ♂ then collects nesting material, ♀ builds nest. When greeting at nest, sitting bird extends neck upward towards newly arrived mate and gives 'de-WAH' and chatter calls. Both then stand with all plumes erected and rattle bills. Little display before copulation; during copulation ♀ stands with legs only slightly bent.

NEST: a flimsy to solid platform of sticks and reeds 30–35 cm in diameter and 10–15 cm in height.

EGGS: 2–4, laid at 24–48 h intervals; E Africa mean (19 clutches) 2·6; Namibia (2) 2·5; South Africa, SW Cape (93) 2·5, OFS (4) 3·3, Natal (7) 2·9, Transvaal (10) 2·4 (SAOSNRC). Regular ovals, greenish blue. SIZE: (267 eggs) 41–54 × 31–38 (46 × 34); WEIGHT: 28.

Laying dates: Morocco, Algeria, Egypt Mar–July (spring); Mauritania Aug–Oct; Senegal Aug–Dec; Gambia Jan, July, Nov–Dec; Mali Jan, July–Sept; Nigeria Jan; Ethiopia Aug–Sept; E Kenya Jan–July; W Kenya, Uganda Jan–June, peaking Apr; Tanzania Jan–June, Sept; Zambia Feb–July; Zimbabwe Jan–Nov, Mozambique Jan–Nov; Botswana May–June; Namibia Jan–Mar, Oct–Dec; South Africa, SW Cape Aug–Jan (peaking Dec), E Cape Oct–Nov, OFS Oct–Dec, Natal Oct, Dec–Jan, Transvaal Sept, Nov–Jan, peaking Dec (SAOSNRC). Most laying in main rains or late in rains in tropics, spring and early summer N and NW Africa.

Incubation begins with 1st egg; performed by both sexes; period 21–25 days.

Both parents attend, feed and care for young during fledging period; also feed well after fledging. Feed small young by regurgitation into their bills, later onto nest from which nestlings pick it up.

Half-grown young have grey-black bill and greyish white eye. Leave nest after *c*. 30 days and can fly at 40–50 days. Heavy mortality due to starvation and falling from nest or branches. In Kenya, 8 pairs laid 24 eggs, 1 young fledged, but better success likely elsewhere. 1 ringed bird (South Africa) lived 9 years 11 months (McLachlan and Liversidge 1978).

References

Blaker, D. (1969b).
Voisin, C. (1976, 1977).

Plate 10

(Opp. p. 147)

Egretta intermedia (Wagler). Yellow-billed Egret; Intermediate Egret. Aigrette intermédiaire.

Ardea intermedia Wagler, 1829. Isis, vi, p. 659; Java.

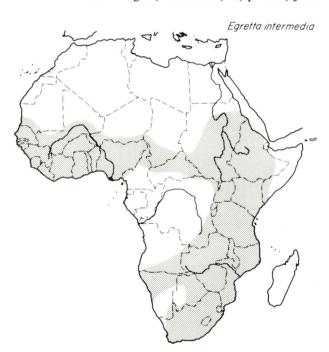

Egretta intermedia

Range and Status. Resident, widespread and locally common south of about 18°N in a variety of freshwater and coastal habitats; possibly migratory. In western Africa, mainly Sudano-Guinean and Sahelian zones between 12° and 17°; in eastern Africa, Sudan and Ethiopia south to Cape.

Description. *E. i. brachyrhyncha* (Brehm), ADULT ♂: overall white with creamy tinge. Relatively short bill orange-yellow to yellow; lores and eyes yellow; legs, bare part of tibia yellow, rest of leg from tarsal joint and feet black. Sexes alike. ADULT ♂ and ♀ (breeding): moderate crest on hind crown and nape but no long plumes. Aigrettes on lower foreneck and breast; those of scapulars extended well beyond tip of tail, sometimes to feet in ♂. Bill red, yellow-orange at tip; lores and orbital area bright green; eye ruby; bare part of tibia crimson, rest of leg black. SIZE: wing, (5 specimens) 305–318 (311); tail, (5) 118–132 (125); bill, (8) 66–78 (71); tarsus, (7) 104–110 (107).

IMMATURE: like non-breeding adult.

DOWNY YOUNG: white; bill yellow; eye pale yellowish brown; legs greenish grey.

Field Characters. A medium-sized white heron with yellow bill and mainly black legs. Looks like a small Great Egret *E. alba* and difficult to distinguish from it, but has shorter and deeper bill, shorter and thicker neck and shorter legs. At close range, black line of gape ending immediately below, not 1 cm beyond, eye, and legs greenish yellow above joint, not uniform black. In flight, scapular plumes ordinarily reaching a little, not far, beyond tip of tail as in Great Egret. Easily distinguished from white morph Little Egret *E. garzetta* and Reef Heron *E. gularis* as they have black bill and legs and yellow feet; much smaller Cattle Egret *Bubulcus ibis* has shorter all-yellow legs, heavy jowl, short neck and, if adult, buff crown, mantle and throat.

Voice. Recorded (19). Calls strikingly different from other herons, tending to be faint with hoarse buzzing quality. During greeting ceremony buzzing, 2-syllabled call and staccato stammering. When collecting and bringing sticks to ♀, ♂ emits a reedy 'whooee-whoee'. When flying from nest both usually silent but sometimes give a deep 2-syllabled croak. Also clatter bills.

General Habits. Well known. Sometimes gregarious, in loose groups of 12–50, but frequently solitary. Occupies flooded plains, rain ponds, margins of fresh and alkaline lakes, river and stream banks, swamps and mudflats of estuaries and coastal lagoons; also dry grasslands if water close by.

Active during day, sometimes in association with Cattle Egrets, Little Egrets and Great Egrets; roosts at night in trees, including mangroves. Shyer and more wary feeder than other egrets. Primarily an aquatic feeder; in 2 years Blaker (1969b) recorded 68% feeding in shallow water, 32% in pastures near water. When feeding, walks slowly, then lunges downward when prey sighted. Sometimes tilts head and neck to one side when hunting. Occasionally hovers just above water, capturing prey with bill.

Some local movement, possibly migratory. One ringed Rondevlei (South Africa, 34°05′S, 28°06′E) recovered Mongu (Zambia, 15°16′S, 23°08′E) (Benson *et al.* 1971a). Dry season visitor Sierra Leone, Nov–July, and southern Nigeria, Nov–May. Arrives Sudan with first rains May–June to breed. Numbers increase Uganda Sept–Oct and largest numbers southern Ghana at peak rains May–July. Has increased range and abundance in W Africa since 1950s (Macdonald 1978b).

Food. Mainly fish and amphibians but also small aquatic and sometimes terrestrial invertebrates. One breeding bird in Tanzania reported to have killed nestling of Squacco Heron *Ardeola ralloides* (Stronach 1968).

Breeding Habits. Very well known. Nest almost always in mixed, sometimes large colonies in trees over water or reedbeds. Numbers of *intermedia* nests within mixed colonies vary from 50 (Zambia) to 150 (Tanzania) to 1000 (Ethiopia).

Courtship similar to that of Little Egret, but calls have hoarse buzzing quality and no mobile groups of unmated ♂♂ and ♀♀ formed. ♂ defends small territory against all conspecifics, and from it performs upright, forward, flap-flight, twig-shaking, snap and stretch displays; also does longer circle flights. ♀♀ attracted to ♂, but at first are repeatedly driven off. After bond established, the pair spends long inactive periods at nest, interspersed with mutual preening, neck entwining, back-biting and bill-clattering. ♂ collects nest material, often stealing sticks from other nests nearby in mixed colonies; ♀ builds nest. During copulation ♀ stands with legs only slightly bent. When alighting at nest ornamental back plumes reared and fanned.

NEST: a structure of sticks, reeds and rushes, usually lined with grass; *c.* 0·6–0·8 m across and 0·2–0·4 m deep. Built in trees, bushes and reedbeds.

EGGS: 2–3, rarely 4–5; E Africa mean (7 clutches) 2·6; Zimbabwe (33) 1·8; South Africa, SW Cape (57) 2·0; Transvaal (62) 2·5 (SAOSNRC). Ovals, smooth or lightly pitted; pale greenish blue. SIZE: (23 eggs) 54–44 × 37–33 (48 × 35); WEIGHT: 31.

Breeding in rains, just after main rains, or in dry season. Laying dates: Senegal July–Oct, Dec; Guinea-Bissau Aug–Oct; Mali Sept–Jan; Nigeria Jan–Mar, Dec; Congo Aug; Sudan May–June; Ethiopia Aug; Kenya Mar–Aug, Nov, peak Apr; Uganda Aug–Sept; Tanzania Jan–Feb, June; Zambia Jan–Apr, Aug–Sept, Dec; Zimbabwe Jan, Mar, Sept, Nov; South Africa, SW Cape Jan, Sept–Oct, OFS Dec, Transvaal Sept–Feb with main breeding Sept–Nov (SAOSNRC).

Both parents incubate but changeovers infrequent; in 12·5 h on 3 days with 3 nests in view constantly only 1 nest-relief noted (L. H. Brown, pers. comm.). Period: 24–27 days.

Young leave nest when 3 weeks old. Fledging period about 35 days. Breeding success higher in Kisumu (Kenya) colony than in other species observed, despite predation by *Varanus* lizards and pythons (L. H. Brown, pers. comm.).

References
Blaker, D. (1969b).
Macdonald, M. A. (1978b).

Egretta alba (Linnaeus). Great Egret; Great White Egret. Grande Aigrette.   Plate 10

Ardea alba Linnaeus, 1758. Syst. Nat. (10th ed.), p. 144; Europe subsequently restricted to Sweden.   (Opp. p. 147)

Range and Status. Resident and Palearctic winter visitor on open water of various coastal and inland habitats. Resident form, *E. a. melanorhynchos*, locally common to frequent, south of Sahara from southern Mauritania, east to Ethiopia thence south to Cape. Palearctic winter, *E. a. alba*, rare to uncommon, Mediterranean coast from Morocco to Egypt; apparently rarely crosses Sahara.

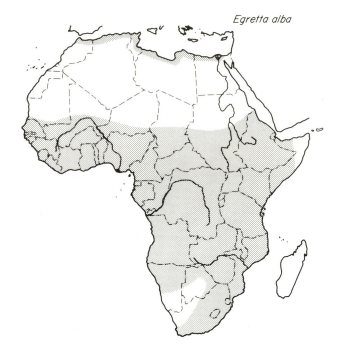

Egretta alba

Description. *E. a. melanorhynchos* (Wagler): Africa south of Sahara. ADULT ♂: entire plumage white. Feathers of nape slightly elongated. Bill yellow, black line of gape extends at least 1 cm behind eye; lores and orbital area olive-green; eye pale yellow; legs and feet black. Sexes alike. ADULT ♂ and ♀ (breeding): long aigrette plumes from scapulars extending far behind tip of tail. Lanceolate feathers on lower foreneck and upper breast, but no ornamental plumes on crown or nape. Bill black with varying amount of yellow at base; lores and orbital area bright emerald green; eye brilliant red. SIZE: (8 specimens) wing, 343–396 (383); tail, 131–163 (147); tarsus, 134–170 (149); culmen, 104–116 (108). WEIGHT: 1110.

IMMATURE: like non-breeding adult without ornamental plumes.

DOWNY YOUNG: down white, elongated on crown to form crest; bill and legs greenish grey.

E. a. alba (Linnaeus): N Africa. Slightly larger, wing, ♂ (10 specimens) 410–485 (438), ♀ 400–450 (429). Tarsus black sometimes with yellowish sides.

Field Characters. A large, slender, long-necked egret, all-white with black legs and feet and slim bill, yellow in non-breeding season, black in breeding season. May be confused with Little Egret *E. garzetta* and Reef Heron *E. gularis* (white morph) but much larger and even slimmer with more snake-like neck, narrower wings, and black legs. In early courtship also distinguished from Little Egret by yellow bill. Distinguished from Yellow-billed Egret *E. intermedia* by having slimmer, longer bill, larger size and longer, more kinked neck. At very close range, distinguished from all egrets by black line of gape extending well behind eye. In flight, long legs extend well beyond tail.

Voice. Recorded (2a, 6, 18, 19). Mostly silent away from colony or roost, although utters a deep raucous croak, much deeper than other egrets. At Zimbabwe colony calls include: (1) loud, very deep guttural 'aahrr' warning; (2) nasal stammering, by ♂ during stretch display; (3) 'croak-croak' by ♂ when circle flying; (4) 'craa craa craa' by both when greeting at nest; (5) nasal wheezy noises by ♀ during copulation; (6) 'ket ket ket' by young when begging; and (7) 'cheeraa, cheeraa' squeaking noise by young when asserting themselves. Non-vocal noises include mechanical bill clack during snap display and 'thud' of wings during flap-flight display.

General Habits. Well known in Africa; very well known in North America. Commonly occurs singly but also in small parties in a variety of habitats including salt pans, estuaries, lagoons, coral reefs (sometimes several miles offshore), rivers, freshwater lakes, and flooded grasslands. Most often seen by itself, standing or slowly wading through shallow water. In flight, legs extended well beyond tail. Flight lighter and more buoyant than that of Grey Heron *Ardea cinerea*; wingbeats slower than in Little Egret.

Active during day, but may feed during moonlit nights. Fly in small parties to roost at night, often with cormorants, darters, African Spoonbill *Platalea alba* and other herons and egrets in large trees in villages, or on the edges of lakes, lagoons and mangroves. Fly to roost 1 h before sunset; leave at sunrise. Other instances, roost in groups any time of day, doing so according to tides. Same roosts used for many years, possibly by same birds.

Feeds in swift water up to belly-deep, but more often in pools on coral reefs and sandbanks. Largely a solitary feeder, usually in deeper water than other egrets. Highly territorial away from nest or roost, chasing conspecifics from fishing areas. At Lake St Lucia (South Africa) fishes 7·6 h/day or 63% of daylight hours (Whitfield and Blaber 1979; at Mida Creek (Kenya) fishes c. 50% of time dependent upon low tides (L. H. Brown, pers. comm.). Stands and waits for prey in upright posture, with head and neck held about 45° above water level. When prey sighted, adopts stand-and-wait position with body held horizontally, and head and neck partially retracted. Strikes from standing position. Sometimes tilts head towards shaded side of body, striking into shadow. On wave-washed shoreline, walks slowly through waves with head and neck fully extended and, when striking, head and part of neck disappear below water surface. Sometimes moves vegetation in a slow deliberate manner with one foot. Captures fish, usually cross-wise, in bill, holds it for 2–3 s, then swallows it head first. At Lake St Lucia used 'walking slowly' 71% of feeding time, 'stand-and-wait' 19% and 'disturb-and-chase' 10% (Whitfield and Blaber 1979).

Although rarely crosses Sahara, one ringed Russia, recovered Central African Republic, and another at Chad suspected to be Palearctic migrant. Definite post-breeding dispersal of resident population; evidence includes (1) dry season (mid Dec–mid Jan) visitor, Sierra Leone, with few non-breeding individuals remaining during rains; (2) resident all year on coast, Ghana, but scarce Aug–Apr; (3) present Namibia only Oct–Dec (1970–1972); and (4) Kenya (Ngulia, Tsavo National Park), 12 seen at night 5 Dec 1973, circling in mist, lit-up by game lodge lights (Backhurst and Pearson 1977).

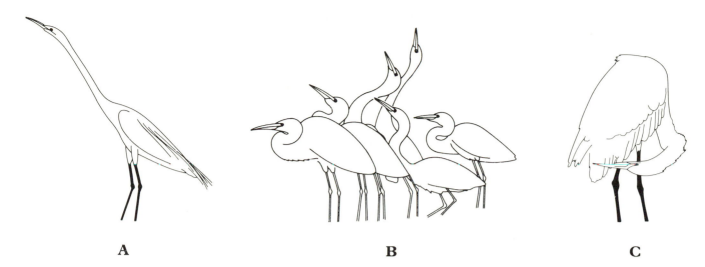

A   B   C

Food. Predominantly fish and amphibians, but also aquatic and terrestrial insects and small mammals. At Lake St Lucia 50% of food Mozambique tilapia, 1–45 (most 5–10) g (Whitfield and Blaber 1979). Only fish (*Clarias gariepinnus*, *Serranochromis robustus*, *Tilapia rendalli* and *Barbus* spp.) fed to chicks Lake Kyle, Zimbabwe (Tomlinson 1979).

Breeding Habits. Very well known. Largely colonial, in groups of 50–200 nests, some solitary or in small groups of 2–3. Nests usually 1 to 4–5 m high in trees overhanging water or sometimes in villages; occasionally in reeds close to water. Sometimes nests with cormorants, darters and other herons and egrets.

Courtship starts when ♂, after flying about colony for a period of time, claims small territory. Builds small platform on it from which he displays and which serves as the future nest-site. When displaying, assumes hunched neck position with aigrettes fanned over back and at intervals walks about stiff-legged, shaking twigs and producing advertising calls. Also performs upright (see **A**), forward, flap-flight, snap, stretch (**B**) and wing-touch (**C**) displays. Makes circle flights, returning with neck extended about 20° above horizontal and uttering guttural 'croak-croak'. ♀♀ attracted to displaying ♂ who at first chases all conspecifics away. By third day, ♂ makes elaborate circle flight and upon returning presents a stick to ♀ who moves onto platform. Both perform greeting ceremony, using stretch display; ♀ accepts stick and places it into nest. Pair-bond established at about this time. Thereafter, ♂ collects nest material (93% of time, Zimbabwe); ♀ builds nest (98%). Arrival of ♂ accompanied with greeting ceremony followed by mutual bill-grasping, back-biting with preening, and copulation with ♀ in crouched position.

NEST: a platform of sticks and twigs, lined with fine rushes and plant stems. 20 nests (Zimbabwe) outer diameter 34 (29–41), depth 12 (9–15); distance between nests (15) *c.* 2·5 m with 2–5 nests in 1 tree.

EGGS: 2·5, laid at 2-day intervals; Kenya mean (8 clutches) 3·4, Zimbabwe (31) 3·7, South Africa, Natal (31) 3·1 (SAOSNRC). Regular ovals, pale blue, rather coarse in texture. SIZE: 44–66 × 31–55 (40 × 56); WEIGHT: 61.

Breeding coincides with rains (Ethiopia, Kenya), end rains (Niger, Mali), inundation and flooding, or dry season (Nigeria). Laying dates: Mauritania Apr–Aug; Senegal July–Oct, Dec; Guinea-Bissau July–Sept; Gambia June, Aug–Dec; Mali July–Oct; Niger Sept–Oct; Ghana July–Sept; Nigeria Sept–Feb; Congo Apr, Aug; Ethiopia Mar, June–July; Kenya Feb–Aug, peak Apr–June; Uganda, W Kenya Mar, June; Tanzania Jan–Feb, June; Zambia Jan–June, Aug–Sept, Dec; Zimbabwe Jan–Mar, Sept, Nov; Botswana Jan, June; South Africa Dec–Mar, May–June.

Incubation usually begins with 1st egg; by both parents, with changeover 3 times a day in morning, mid-day and evening. Period: 24–27 days, av. 26·4 (Tomlinson 1976, 1979).

Young stand on feet at *c.* 15 days; fly short distance at 40 days; fly 200 m at 45–50 days; and leave colony with parents at 50–60 days.

Both parents care for and feed young with changeovers in morning and evening; one parent with or near young until 30 days old. Initially parents regurgitate food on centre of nest; chicks feed directly off nest. At about 10 days chicks actively feed from parents' bill. Parents shade young from mid-day sun by standing with wings drooped over them and with back directed towards sun; from rain by crouching over them; and from intruders by performing upright display in which brooding bird, from a sitting position, stretches neck vertically upward, raises bill about 45° above horizontal, erects feathers on head, neck and throat, and utters deep guttural 'aahr'. Takes about 90 days for pair to raise a brood from advertising stage to departure of young.

Breeding success: out of 31 clutches comprising 121 eggs, 94 hatched, or 77·6% success (Zimbabwe). At Kisumu (Kenya), heavy losses of young due to habit of young leaving nest after which they become impaled on acacia thorns; 9 nests comprising 27–30 eggs produced 13 young able to fly (L. H. Brown, pers. comm.).

References

Mock, D. W. (1978).
Tomlinson, D. N. S. (1979).

Illustrations reproduced with permission from Mock (1978).

Genus *Ardea* Linnaeus

Medium to largest of all herons, all with lanceolate crest and scapular plumes. In Africa, 4 species form 2 groups: *purpurea*, *cinerea* and *melanocephala* with primaries darker than rest of wing and crest and scapular plumes long; and *goliath* with primaries the same colour as rest of wing, and short crest and scapular plumes.

Plate 10

(Opp. p. 147)

Ardea purpurea Linnaeus. Purple Heron. Héron pourpré.

Ardea purpurea Linnaeus, 1766. Syst. Nat. (12th ed.), p. 236; 'in Oriente' = River Danube.

Range and Status. Resident and Palearctic winter visitor, widespread throughout continent, locally common to uncommon in reedbeds and other dense marshy vegetation. Palearctic individuals indistinguishable from resident birds, migrate south to equator, chiefly wintering W Africa. Breeding colonies mainly in eastern part of continent from about equator southward, except those in Senegal, Mali, Morocco and Algeria. 1 subspecies, *A. p. purpurea*, in Africa.

Ardea purpurea

Description. *A. p. purpurea* Linnaeus, ADULT ♂: overall dark. Forehead to hindneck black with 2 lanceolate plumes on nape. Sides of head and neck reddish buff. Black line from gape along side of head to nape and another from gape down side of neck. Throat and foreneck white; lower half of latter with elongated black spots grading into white and chestnut lanceolate feathers. Mantle dark purplish grey; lanceolate feathers of scapulars grading light grey to tawny. Back to tail dark grey. Shoulder patches, breast and belly deep chestnut, latter with black. Undertail-coverts black with white streaks. Primaries and secondaries black; rest of upperwing with some chestnut; leading edge of wing buff. Underwing dark, mainly grey to rufous-chestnut. Long slender bill buff with brown culmen; lores and orbital area yellow-green; eye yellow; legs and feet dark brown, back of tarsus and soles yellow. Sexes alike. ADULT ♂ and ♀ (breeding): lanceolate feathers of scapulars pale; bill bright buff-yellow. SIZE: wing, ♂ (13 specimens) 357–383 (371), ♀ (9) 337–372 (355); tail, ♂ (13) 118–136 (125), ♀ (8) 112–127 (119); bill ♂ (13) 120–131 (126), ♀ (8) 109–123 (116); tarsus, ♂ (13) 113–131 (122), ♀ (8) 112–125 (118). WEIGHT: ♂ 617–1218, ♀ 525–1135.

IMMATURE: more mottled with upperparts brown and pale rufous, underparts white streaked brown. Crown rufous; stripes on side of head and neck very small or absent.

DOWNY YOUNG: dark brown to grey down above, white below; conspicuous white crest. Skin greenish yellow; bill dirty yellow; eye yellow-grey.

Field Characters. A medium-sized, slim, thin-headed and thin-billed heron with rufous neck, dark grey upperparts and chestnut and black underparts. In flight, appears dark, the neck with a downward bulge and legs projecting considerably beyond tail. Black streaks on sides of head and neck noticeable at close range. Generally rufous colour with dark grey upperparts distinguish it from Grey Heron *A. cinerea* and Black-headed Heron *A. melanocephala*; resembles Goliath Heron *A. goliath*, but half the size, much slimmer and has black, not rufous crown.

Voice. Recorded (18). Other than harsh deep 'kwaak', 'aark' or 'krreek', usually silent away from colony, but may call in flight, e.g. to roost. At colony (Zimbabwe) (1) high-pitched squawk during forward display; (2) low, guttural 'craak-cr-ra-raak' by incoming bird; (3) musical 'whoop' and loud 'clack-clack-clack' (♂) and low 'craak' and soft 'crak-crak-crak' (♀) during greeting when performing stretch display. Bill-clattering during mutual preening. Food call of young up to 10 days, a continuous 'chik ...', later a raucous 'chak ...'.

General Habits. Very well known. Usually skulking and solitary in dense vegetation of swamps, marshes and margins of lakes; occasionally coastal mudflats and edges of mangroves. Well adapted to dense marshy vegetation with long toes and claws for walking on floating vegetation and grasping reeds and twigs; has camouflage plumage and adopts 'bittern stance'.

Feeds alone, standing on floating vegetation, river bank or in shallow water with body nearly horizontal and neck stretched 60° above horizontal. Peers into water for long periods. Also wades slowly with beak horizontal and close to water. Catches fish sideways in bill with rapid strike of head and neck; swallows fish head first.

Crepuscular; roosts and rests communally day and night in reedbeds and bullrushes with a few to 100 other Purple Herons. Travels to roost singly or in small parties. Flies with 114 wing-beats/min (Cooper 1971).

Common passage migrant Egypt–Libya and along Red Sea coast Sept–Oct. Data indicate cross Sahara on broad front (Moreau 1967). Most birds in tropical Africa north of equator probably Palearctic migrants, as few breeding colonies known here. Birds ringed France, recovered Mali, Senegal, Sierra Leone, Nigeria; Holland, recovered Mauritania, Senegal, Sierra Leone, Mali, Nigeria; Russia, recovered Nigeria, Sudan and Cameroon—all confirm this. Odd individuals may oversummer, e.g. an immature ringed France recovered Mali July. In Uganda common all year but noticeable fluctuations, especially Sept, probably Palearctic migrants.

Food. Largely fish but also frogs, lizards, snakes, rodents and birds. In Zimbabwe feeds on *Clarias, Labeo, Tilapia, Alestes* and *Haplochromis*. Once observed spearing and swallowing ♂ Black-headed Weaver *Ploceus cucullatus* (Wood 1970).

Breeding Habits. Very well known. Nests in small, loose colonies, in groups of 2–3 pairs, or singly, in well concealed sites in reedbeds 1–3 m from or on ground, in thickets of semi-aquatic figs 3–4 m above ground, in mangroves, or on floating vegetation. Sometimes nests with other herons.

Available data on western Palearctic populations suggest Purple Heron is very similar to Grey Heron in displays and other social behaviour but details lacking. Type and details of pair-formation largely undescribed although it is known that ♂ chooses nest-site where does upright and forward displays. Only heterosexual behaviour reported by Tomlinson (1974b) in form of greeting ceremony at nest-relief. When returning partner lands, bird on nest turns side-on or away from mate, slowly rises, then does stretch display with bill pointing skyward and gular region puffed-out, the latter feature being unique to the Purple Heron. Returning bird also does stretch display, then moves to nest. Sometimes bird on nest sways bill from side to side and bobs head and tail up and down before leaving nest. Both then pass twigs, back-bite and preen mutually. Flap-flight and snap displays not described although almost certainly occur.

NEST: both sexes build nest, a loosely constructed pile of bulrushes and reeds. In bulrushes constructed by bending number of bulrushes over towards each other to form base for nest; in reeds built in middle of number of closely growing reed stems. Diameter (37 nests) 15–76 cm (35·6), thickness (35 nests) 10–46 cm (17·8).

EGGS: 2–5, laid at 1–3 day intervals; East Africa mean (22 clutches) 2·6; Botswana (15) 2·9; (Fraser 1971);

Zimbabwe (113) 3·3 (Tomlinson 1975); South Africa, SW Cape (24) 2·5, Transvaal (40) 2·1 (SAOSNRC). Regular, pointed ovals, pale blue or blue-green. SIZE: (113 eggs) 50–60 × 37–44 (55 × 40); WEIGHT: (35 eggs) 39–59 (47·4).

Laying dates: Morocco Mar; Algeria May (spring); Senegal July–Oct, Dec; Mali Oct–May; Ghana May (rains); Kenya Feb–July, peaking in Apr–May (rains); Uganda Mar, June; Tanzania Jan–Feb; Zaïre Mar–May; Zambia, Malawi, Mozambique Jan–Mar, June–Aug; Zimbabwe Jan–Feb, Apr, July–Dec; Botswana Aug; South Africa Jan–Dec, peaking Sept–Oct. Most breeding in tropics in rains, some in dry seasons.

Incubation begins with 1st egg; carried out by both parents with infrequent nest-reliefs by day. Period: 25–27 (25·7) days.

Young, 0–5 days, covered with soft down, weigh 75 g (4 days). 6–9 days, spiky pin feathers visible, 160 g (8 days). 10–11 days, feathers break through pin sheath and appear on throat, abdomen, back and leading edge of wings. 12–20 days, feathers cover bare patches of skin with most down gone, 375 g (16 days). 20 days, dark feathers on neck, chest and back; primaries start to grow; very agile and leave nest, returning only at feeding; 500 g. 37 days, strong fliers. 45–50 days, attain juvenile plumage and fledge. 55–65 days, independent.

Both parents care for and feed young until well after fledging. Parents change over and feed very young chicks 3 times daily. When chicks 15 days old, parents change over twice each day in morning and evening. Very small young pick up food from floor of nest until 10 days old; thereafter take food directly from adult's bill.

Main predators: (Lake McIlwaine, Zimbabwe) Clawless Otter *Aonyx capensis* feeding on well developed young, African Marsh Harrier *Circus ranivorus* feeding on eggs and very young chicks; (Botswana) Black Crake *Limnocorax flavirostra* feeding on eggs; and (Kenya) monitor lizards feeding on young.

Breeding success: Lake McIlwaine (Zimbabwe) 1969/1970, 35 nests, 113 eggs laid, 57 chicks hatched, 31 survived to 20–24 days or 27% success; 7 heronries, 47 pairs raised 45 chicks. In 1970–1971 18 pairs raised 7 chicks, or less than 1/breeding adult. Lake Victoria, 1 or less by flying stage (L. H. Brown, pers. comm.).

References
Tomlinson, D. N. S. (1974a, b; 1975).

Ardea cinerea Linnaeus. Grey Heron. Héron cendré.

Ardea cinerea Linnaeus, 1758. Syst. Nat. (10th ed.), p. 143; Sweden.

Plate 10

(Opp. p. 147)

Range and Status. Resident and Palearctic winter visitor, widespread, normally frequent, locally common to uncommon in shallow fresh, brackish and, less often, salt water with vegetated banks or open areas. Palearctic visitors occurring south to equator indistinguishable from residents. Breeding colonies largely in southern Africa, north to about equator, and in NW Africa.

Description. *A. c. cinerea* Linnaeus, ADULT ♂: overall black, white and grey. Forehead to top of crown white; sides of crown and nape black, nape with 2–3 long narrow black plumes. Back to tail grey. Throat and sides of face below eye white. Neck grey to white, tinged buff at base; foreneck with 2 black streaks terminating on white breast. Shoulder patches and sides of breast black. Belly black; rest of underparts mainly white. Primaries and secondaries black, leading edge of wing at carpal

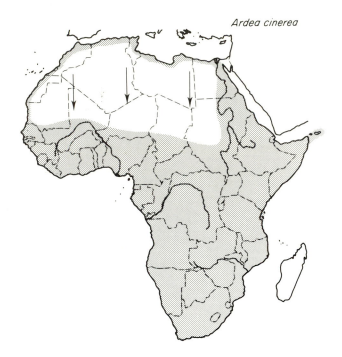

Ardea cinerea

joint white; rest of upperwing and underwing blue grey. Bill, lores and eye yellow, tinged green round eye; leg brown with some yellow on back of tarsus and tibia. ADULT ♂ (breeding): mantle and scapulars with long greyish white lanceolate plumes, lower foreneck and breast with long white lanceolate plumes. Bill and eye deep orange to vermilion; tibia and tarsus red. Sexes alike. SIZE: wing, ♂ (20) 440–485 (457), ♀ (12) 428–463 (443); tail, ♂ (20) 161–187 (174), ♀ (12) 157–174 (166); bill, ♂ (26) 110–131 (120), ♀ (19) 101–123 (112); tarsus, ♂ (23) 136–172 (151), ♀ (16) 132–153 (141). WEIGHT: ♂ (17) 1071–2073 (1505), ♀ (13) 1020–1785 (1361).

IMMATURE: overall greyer, paler than adult. No white crown, black shoulder patch, wedge on sides of breast and belly, or ornamental plumes. Forehead to crown dark grey; nape dull black with feathers moderately elongated. Sides of face grey, chin white. Neck dark grey; foreneck with brown-grey streaks; underparts mainly grey but with some brown-grey streaks. Bill and upper mandible brown, lower mandible yellow; legs greenish grey.

DOWNY YOUNG: above brownish grey down, below white; head with crest. Bill grey; eye yellow; legs green-grey.

A. c. monicae Jouanin & Roux. Based on 2 specimens from Banc d'Arguin, Mauritania (de Naurois 1975). Smaller, wing, 395–422; paler, light areas of head and neck pure white, not pale grey. Appears a somewhat doubtful race.

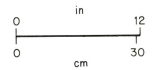

in
0   12
0   30
cm

Scale applies to standing birds

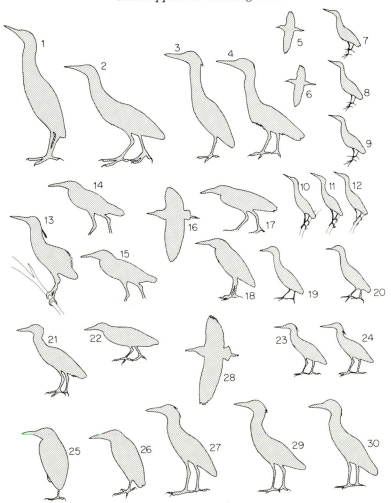

Plate 11

Botaurus stellaris Eurasian Bittern (p. 133)
Race *stellaris*: 1. ADULT.
Race *capensis*: 2. ADULT.

Tigriornis leucolophus White-crested Tiger Heron (p. 138)
3. IMMATURE, 4. ADULT ♀.

Ixobrychus minutus Little Bittern (p. 135)
Race *payesii*: 5. ♂ in flight, 6. ♀ in flight, 7. IMMATURE, 8. ADULT ♀, 9. ADULT ♂.
Race *minutus*: 10. IMMATURE, 11. ADULT ♀, 12. ADULT ♂.

Ardeola ralloides Squacco Heron (p. 142)
13. ADULT (breeding), 14. ADULT (non-breeding), 15. IMMATURE, 16. IMMATURE in flight.

Ardeola idae Malagasy Pond Heron (p. 143)
17. ADULT (non-breeding), 18. IMMATURE.

Ixobrychus sturmii Dwarf Bittern (p. 136)
19. IMMATURE, 20. ADULT.

Ardeola rufiventris Rufous-bellied Heron (p. 144)
21. ADULT, 22. IMMATURE.

Butorides striatus Green Heron (p. 149)
Race *atricapillus*: 23. IMMATURE, 24. ADULT.

Nycticorax nycticorax Black-crowned Night Heron (p. 140)
25. IMMATURE (back), 26. IMMATURE (front), 27. ADULT (breeding), 28. ADULT in flight.

Gorsachius leuconotus White-backed Night Heron (p. 139)
29. IMMATURE, 30. ADULT.

Field Characters. Large, slim, black, white and grey heron, larger than all but Goliath Heron *A. goliath*. Especially distinctive features are white top of head contrasting with black eye stripe, white neck, black streaks in front and black shoulders. Distinguished from Goliath Heron and Purple Heron *A. purpurea* by lack of rufous in plumage, and from Black-headed Heron *A. melanocephala* by white, not black, crown and neck, by uniformly grey, not contrasting white and black, underwings and by relatively much longer bill.

Voice. Recorded (2a, 18). Away from colony loud harsh 'frarnk'. At breeding colony more vocal; calls include (1) sharp 'rwo' by unpaired ♂ when advertising at nest-site; (2) short soft 'hoo' at height of stretch display, followed by longer, gargling 'oooo' when crouched, given by both sexes; (3) loud, harsh squawking 'quooo' during forward display, by both, and louder 'schaah' in flight when ♂ chases intruder; (4) low, soft nasal 'go-go-go' when mildly alarmed, given by both; (5) series of grunting squawks, diminishing in volume, often ending in a clucking, by incoming ♂ or ♀ before landing at nest; (6) growling or wailing sound, increasing in volume during copulation, mainly by ♀; and (7) young food call, chittering by very small young, later 'chak-chak-chak . . .' endlessly in short phrases and in concert when begging from parent, or left alone in nest and hungry. Non-vocal sounds include single sharp 'clop' at climax of snap display, mainly by ♂; 1 or more bill-snaps when foes meet or when mates greet; and bill-rattling during pair-formation or when pair at nest.

General Habits. Well known in Africa, especially well known in Europe. Usually solitary, sometimes in small flocks of 5 or so; commonly walks near or wades in shallow fresh or salt water; also frequents open grasslands. Occasionally swims, up to 10 min at a time.

Depending on feeding routine, active day or, less often, by night. Feeds at night by moonlight but usually early morning or late afternoon (Whitfield and Blaber 1979. On Kenyan coast feeding routine dependent on tides, roosting at high tide. Defends feeding territories but will feed with other species. When feeding, stands-and-waits for long periods; sometimes wades and walks. Partially retracts head and neck before lunging at prey. Normally captures fish cross-wise in beak; swallows it head first. When hunting Lake St Lucia, stand-and-wait procedure 53%, wade and walk slowly 47%; did not disturb-and-chase (Whitfield and Blaber 1979). Sometimes flies slowly over lake and hovers. Upon sighting prey, drops into water, head and feet first, to capture it (Taylor 1957).

Roosts communally or solitarily at midday near feeding areas, or at night in trees, cliffs, low rocks, islets or along shore; sometimes near or in nesting colony. When returning to roost or nest, drops down in long spiral flights. Flight slow and heavy; flies with 142 wing-beats/min (Cooper 1971).

Plate 12

Balaeniceps rex Shoebill (p. 191)
1. ADULT, 2. DOWNY YOUNG.

Ciconia abdimii Abdim's Stork (p. 180)
3. ADULT.

Scopus umbretta Hamerkop (p. 169)
4. ADULT.

Ciconia ciconia White Stork (p. 183)
5. ADULT, 6. head of IMMATURE.

Ciconia nigra Black Stork (p. 178)
7. ADULT, 8. IMMATURE.

Ciconia episcopus Woolly-necked Stork (p. 181)
9. ADULT.

Mycteria ibis Yellow-billed Stork (p. 173)
10. ADULT (breeding), 11. (non-breeding),
12. IMMATURE.

Ephippiorhynchus senegalensis Saddle-billed Stork (p. 185)
13. ADULT ♂, 14. head of ADULT ♀.

Anastomus lamelligerus African Open-bill Stork (p. 176)
15. ADULT.

Leptoptilos crumeniferus Marabou Stork (p. 187)
16. ADULT (breeding), 17. (non-breeding) showing 1 of its 2 inflatable airsacs, 18. IMMATURE.

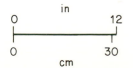

Scale applies to all birds except No. 17

Mainly nocturnal migrant in small parties, sometimes in flocks of 200–250. Common passage migrant N Africa late Aug–early Nov and late Feb–Apr. Some winter N Africa but most cross Sahara to remain generally north of equator although known south to 4°S in Zaïre. Some Palearctic birds oversummer. Most birds in tropical Africa north of equator probably Palearctic migrants as few breeding colonies known here. Records confirm this—birds ringed Sweden, recovered Mali, Upper Volta; Netherlands, recovered Senegal, Guinea, Sierra Leone, Mali, Upper Volta; France, recovered Senegal, Guinea, Sierra Leone; Switzerland, recovered Senegal, Guinea, Sierra Leone, Mali, Upper Volta, Togo, Nigeria; Germany, recovered Togo, Nigeria; Poland, recovered Mali, Upper Volta, Ethiopia; Czechoslovakia, recovered Mali, Upper Volta; Hungary, recovered Mali, Upper Volta, Togo, Nigeria; and Russia, recovered Senegal, Guinea, Sierra Leone, Mali, Upper Volta, Sudan, southern Egypt and Kenya.

Food. Fish, amphibians, reptiles, small mammals and insects; sometimes crabs, molluscs, worms, small birds and plant material. Diet (St Lucia Bay) mostly mullet and tilapia, 1–110 (most 10–20) g (Whitfield and Blaber 1979). Only fish (*Tilapia, Clarias, Serranochromis* and *Labeo* spp.) fed to chicks (Lake Kyle, Zimbabwe) (Tomlinson 1979).

Breeding Habits. Well known in Africa; intimately known in Europe. Usually nests in colonies, rarely solitarily, sometimes with other herons and cormorants, in trees (including mangroves), reedbeds and occasionally on ground. 2–15 nests in one tree; sometimes on tops of trees (Tomlinson 1979).

Both sexes return to colony area at about same time. Courtship begins when ♂ takes up small territory on tree which may be old nest and later serves as new nest. ♂ defends displaying site, threatening with forward and upright displays and making flap-flights. When returning from flight, does alighting display, uttering characteristic call and flying in with powerful wing-beats, neck arched and feathers raised, especially crest- and neck-plumes. Advertises on site by calling at frequent intervals during day, and by performing stretch, snap and twig-shake displays. A succession of ♀♀ visit ♂. When ♀♀ approach, ♂ becomes very excited,

A

performing stretch, upright and forward (see **A**) displays. If ♀ remains, ♂ gradually becomes less aggressive and does many snap displays, up to 40 in succession (Cramp and Simmons 1977). Pair-formation usually follows. After pair-formation, ♂ rarely does snap display. ♀ occasionally does stretch display. Both do bill-rattling, and mutual billing and preening with ♂ initiating latter.

When either bird returns to nest, incoming bird performs alighting display; bird on nest responds with upright or stretch display. Both birds wave wings at this time. Copulation takes place with ♀ standing; up to 3 times a day, lasts up to 16 s and continues until most or all eggs laid. Pair-bond lasts 1 season with paired ♂♂ showing tendency to be promiscuous at times (Cramp and Simmons 1977).

NEST: constructed of sticks, centre often lined with grass. May be large or relatively small structures barely accommodating sitting bird. At Banc d'Arguin nests on ground on tufts of grass, or in small depressions, with stones and dust removed by scratching, surrounded by bones and dried vegetation.

EGGS: 3–6, laid at 2–3 day intervals; E Africa mean (10 clutches) 3·5, Zimbabwe (337) 2·6; Namibia and Botswana (65) 2·9; South Africa, SW Cape (98) 2·8, OFS (15) 2·0, Transvaal (41) 2·7, Natal (3) 2·7 (SAOSNRC). Regular ovals, pointed at ends, greenish blue or blue. SIZE: (137 eggs) 53–72 × 34–46 (60 × 73) (SAOSNRC). WEIGHT: 61.

Lays mainly at height of rains, sometimes almost year-round (Mombasa). Laying dates: Egypt Feb–Apr (spring); Mauritania Apr–Nov; Mali Jan–May; Nigeria Jan, May–June; Ethiopia Aug–Sept; Kenya Apr–Oct, Dec, but mainly in main rains Apr–May, and not regular annually; Tanzania Jan–Feb, June, Aug; Zambia Feb–Aug, Nov–Dec; Malawi Sept, Nov (dry); Zimbabwe Jan–Dec with most Aug–Jan; Angola Mar, July–Aug; Namibia Feb, July–Dec; South Africa Jan–Dec with main breeding July–Sept. Good recent data Morocco, Algeria and Tunisia lacking.

Incubation begins 1st egg; carried out by both parents with infrequent nest-reliefs by day. Greeting ceremony at nest-relief includes crouching by sitting bird, followed by stretch display, with erected crest and, sometimes, loud calling. Incubation period: 23–28 days, av. *c.* 26.

Young hatch with eyes open; soon afterwards beg by calling. At *c.* 7 days, pins of growing feathers appear. Are fully feathered at *c.* 28 days, but some down remains on crown and nape. Spend most of time on nest standing or dozing, waiting to be fed. Grasp bills of siblings or trample on dozing ones. Clean bills with tongues, search for apparently non-existent food in nest, mock-hunt twigs, play with objects, flatten themselves in nest when danger threatens, preen, gular-flutter in heat, shade and perform upright, forward and snap displays. At 20–30 days may leave nest and climb about on adjacent branches. Can fly at 50 days but continue to return to nest area until they become completely independent at 60–70 days.

Both parents brood, care for and feed young. Brooding is continuous or regular up to 18 days when chicks are part-feathered; thereafter one or both parents at nest guarding them up to 29–30 days. Parents then visit nest only briefly to feed young; also shelter young from rain or hot sun. Feed chicks, even very small ones, by regurgitating food onto nest. Older young bite or snatch at parent's bill to stimulate regurgitation of food. Young are fed 3–4 times/24 h, most frequently just after dawn and in the evening.

Breeding success: Europe (Britain), 3·1 hatched from mean clutch of 4·1 and 2·5 fledged; most losses caused by infertile eggs or deaths of small chicks (Cramp and Simmons 1977). E Africa, much lower; does not breed annually in same sites but at Mombasa breeds all year round. 1·2 young reared/successful nest, probably averaging less than 1/pair/year overall (L. H. Brown, pers. comm.; EANRC).

Reference
Milstein, P. le S. *et al.* (1970).
Illustration reproduced with permission from this publication.

Ardea melanocephala Vigors and Children. Black-headed Heron. Héron mélanocéphale.

Plate 10

Ardea melanocephala Anon. = Vigors and Children, 1826. In Denham and Clapperton's Travels, vol. 2, App. xxi, p. 201; near Lake Chad.

(Opp. p. 147)

Range and Status. Resident, widespread, locally common but with a patchy distribution in open moist habitats including grasslands, marshes, and margins of rivers and lakes, sometimes dry areas far from permanent water, south of about 17°N from Senegal to Ethiopia, thence south to Cape. Normally commonest large heron in most of Africa, often associating with man, breeding in towns; has probably increased through human developments, creating new open habitats and water sources.

Ardea melanocephala

Description. ADULT ♂: overall black and grey with white throat. Top and sides of head down neck blue-black; nape with 1 to 3 long lanceolate plumes. Mantle dark slate grey; long lanceolate feathers of back and scapulars, terminally lighter grey. Rump and uppertail-coverts grey; tail dark slate grey. Chin and throat white, foreneck blue-black spotted white down centre. Rest of underside grey with long lanceolate feathers on foreneck and sides of upper breast. Occasionally chin and entire underparts black. Primaries and secondaries dark slate grey, rest of upperwing light grey with wing-edge white; underwing-coverts white. Upper mandible black, lower yellow to greenish yellow; base of bill and area around eye white; eye yellow; lores yellow and green; legs and feet black. Sexes alike. Eye ruby red in early courtship. SIZE: (9 specimens) wing, 387–410 (401); tail, 142–160 (157); tarsus, 118–180 (136); culmen, 85–106 (100). WEIGHT: ♂ 820, 935, 1420, ♀ 710, 1505, immature 850.

IMMATURE: top of head and neck dark grey to brownish grey; throat and breast with some rust-buff; rest underparts buff-white.

DOWNY YOUNG: covered pale grey down with bare patches throat and belly; crest on forehead. Eye yellow.

Field Characters. A black and white heron similar to, but smaller and relatively slimmer than, Grey Heron *A. cinerea*. Distinguished from it by black head and neck contrasting with white chin and throat; grey underparts; and in flight markedly 2-tone appearance with black flight feathers and white underwing-coverts. Conspicuous white patch at shoulder on standing bird. In contrast, Grey Heron has white crown and neck, white and black underparts, and uniform grey underwing pattern. Lack of rufous in plumage distinguishes it from Goliath Heron *A. goliath* and Purple Heron *A. purpurea*. At close range, bill shorter, upper mandible black, not yellow like that of Grey Heron; bill is deeper and shorter relative to size than in any other large African heron.

Voice. Recorded (2a, 3b, 6, 19). Away from roost or breeding colony a raucous croak, squawk, or loud nasal 'kuark'. At colony calls include (1) when landing, a loud 'kow-owk, kow-owk, kowk', followed by growl, a 'kwo-o-oh, kwo-o-oh' and a short 'kut-kut-kut'; the last also by relieved birds; (2) when performing forward display, a harsh 'keh' or 'kaah'; and (3) during stretch display, a soft 'how-oo' when at top of stretch, and a gentle gurgle 'roo-roo-roo-roo' when crouching. Hunger call of young bird, a 'kek-kek-kek-kek-kek' repeated again and again, high-pitched in young birds, deeper in older birds.

General Habits. Well known. When not at roost or breeding colony, usually solitary, but may fly in small parties. Basically a terrestrial species, preferring open grassy and cultivated ground in savannas, and, unlike other *Ardea*, often away from permanent water; but is also found on rivers, lakes, marshes, estuaries, coastal areas and forest clearings, but not closed forests.

Active during day but also partly nocturnal in habits. Feeds solitarily, walking slowly over open area, raising feet high. Every few steps, stretches neck with head and bill held horizontally. Upon sighting prey, moves head slightly forward, then strikes at and catches prey between mandibles. Sometimes moves neck in a series of sideway undulations 1–2/s as it prepares to strike.

Roosts colonially in groups of up to 100 in trees, reedbeds, papyrus, and floating papyrus-island (K. Curry-Lindahl, pers. comm.), usually returning to the same roost nightly. Sometimes flies daily up to 30 km from roost. Roosts may be separate from breeding colonies; may be near or in villages and large cities. Flies with 143 wing-beats/min (Cooper 1971).

In W Africa moves north in Sahel Zone in rains, June–Oct, returning south to Ghana, Nigeria, Chad, Cameroon and Zaïre in dry season, Oct–May. Similar movements associated with rains in central and SE Africa; for example, is present Zambia (Luangwa) rains, Nov–May, only. In South Africa, young disperse widely and rapidly; one ringed Witwatersrand, recovered 2·5 years later, Oct, Zimbabwe, 830 km NE (Hancock and Elliott 1978). May cross Sahara northwards as a vagrant but proof lacking.

Food. A variety of invertebrates and vertebrates, reflecting habit of feeding mainly on firm ground, but when associated with aquatic habitat often mainly fish and amphibians. 200 pellets contained 91% insect remains, 61% mammals, 59% lizards, snakes and frogs, 9·5% birds, 4·5% earthworms and 4% spiders (Taylor 1948). Of 52 pellets collected beneath breeding colony, 34 contained traces of rodents, 23 grasshoppers, 19 fish, 16 beetles, 10 birds, 5 vegetable material, 4 mammals other than rodents, 2 frogs and 1 crab (North 1963).

Occasionally scavenges, collecting fish offal left from lake-shore market; also bits of skull of duck and flamingo and goat hair recorded in pellets (North 1963). Recorded to have once stabbed at a nest of Red-naped Widowbird *Euplectes ardens* (L. H. Brown, pers. comm.). At Etosha (Namibia) photographed stalking, lunging at, sometimes spearing and swallowing Cape Turtle Dove *Streptopelia capicola*, Laughing Dove *S. senegalensis*, Namaqua Dove *Oena capensis*, buntings, finches, sparrows and wasps (D. Bartlett, pers. comm.). At Lake Kyle (Zimbabwe), adults seen carrying unidentified chicks to nests on 3 occasions; their chicks regurgitated lizards (*Mabuya quinquetaeniata*, *Agama kirkii* and young of *Varanus niloticus*), frogs (*Rana* spp.) and rodents (*Otomys* spp.) (Tomlinson 1979).

Breeding Habits. Very well known. Nests in large colonies up to 200 or more pairs, sometimes with other long-legged waders, 10–30 m up in eucalyptus, baobab, acacia, fig, palm, papyrus and floating papyrus-island (K. Curry-Lindahl, pers. comm.), with up to 35 nests in 1 tree. Also in reedbeds and on sandstone ledges, with those on ledges almost touching each other. Colonies often in villages or cities, e.g. Nairobi, Kampala.

Courtship not well documented but probably similar to that of Grey Heron. Individual unpaired ♂♂ claim a territory which is site of future nest. Threaten and advertise from it; reported to do upright, forward, stretch and twig-grasping displays but probably also snap and flap-flight displays. During stretch display when pointing bill skyward and when calling, white chin and throat especially obvious and crest and neck feathers raised. Other displays reported include bill-biting, neck-entwining and mutual preening but not bill-snapping and bill-rattling. Once pair has formed, ♂ collects nest

material, sometimes from distances of 1600 m; ♀ builds nest. Building takes up to 15 days. When returning to nest, incoming bird calls; bird on nest, or both birds, then do stretch display. Sometimes bird on nest does this display when mate away. Copulation occurs with ♀ crouched on nest.

NEST: bulky structure of sticks, lined with twigs, leaves, grass, castings of wool and hair; *c.* 0·5 m across and 0·2–0·3 m deep, varying according to site, often just large enough to accommodate sitting bird. Usually in high trees, including baobabs, bombax, eucalyptus, figs, tall acacias; sometimes in reedbeds, at any height from 1–20 m above ground or water, usually 8–15 m.

EGGS: 2–6, laid at 2-day intervals, perhaps more often; E Africa mean (13 clutches) 2·61; Nigeria (5) 3·2; Zimbabwe (20) 2·3; South Africa, SW Cape (57) 2·6, E Cape (25) 2·5, Natal (10) 1·5, Transvaal (218) 2·9, OFS (40) 3·1 (SAOSNRC). Regular ovals, pale blue. SIZE: (120 eggs) 52–73 × 39–44 (62 × 44) (SAOSNRC); WEIGHT: 60.

Lays mainly in rains, sometimes year-round, especially in towns, but even then peak falls in wet months; sometimes only in dry season. Laying dates: Senegal, Gambia Apr–June; Guinea-Bissau Apr–June; Mali Mar–Aug; Ghana May (rains); Niger July; Nigeria Jan–Feb (dry), Apr–Dec; Chad July–Aug (rains); Sudan June–July (rains); Ethiopia Apr, Aug–Sept (rains); Kenya–Uganda year-round, peaking Apr–May and Nov (rains); at Malindi Oct (dry); Tanzania Jan–June, Nov–Dec (rains); Zaïre year-round; Rwanda Apr–June; Burundi Apr–July; Zambia Jan–June, Nov–Dec (rains); Malawi Jan–Dec; Zimbabwe Jan–Apr, Aug–Dec; Mozambique Jan–June, Oct–Dec (wet and dry); Botswana Jan, Sept–Dec; Angola Jan, Aug; Namibia June, Aug (dry); South Africa, SW Cape, July–Jan, peaking Sept, E Cape, June–July, Aug–Jan, peaking Sept, Natal Jan–Feb, May–July, Sept–Dec, Transvaal Jan–Feb, April–Dec, peaking May and Oct, OFS Feb, June, Oct–Nov.

Incubation begins with 1st egg; by both parents; nest-reliefs infrequent and by day only. Period: 23–27 days (av. estimate 25).

Development of young poorly documented but probably like the large *Ardea* spp. When about half-grown, seen to perform stretch displays, play with twigs, and, with raised wings, stretch necks diagonally downwards. Fly at 40–55 days, thereafter returning to nest only to feed. Become independent at 60 days, crown is then dark grey, chin and throat rufous without black and white speckles on throat, and belly nearly white.

Both parents care for and feed young; feed young only at nest. Brooding is regular when young are small, later reduced, one parent standing on or beside nest, and shading chicks from sun. When parent with food lands at nest, raises neck as in stretch display, but keeps bill horizontal; young increase volume of hunger calls, bend legs, raise crest, open and flutter wings, then seize parent's bill near base, sometimes pulling its head towards floor of nest. Parent regurgitates directly into beaks of young, not onto nest floor, though food dropped may be retrieved by young. Young are guarded until 21 days old; thereafter adults remain at nest only long enough to feed young.

Predation sometimes severe from African Hawk Eagle *Hieraaetus spilogaster* and African Fish Eagle *Haliaeetus vocifer*, latter sometimes completely destroying colony. Herons rise shrieking in alarm when eagles appear; settle while eagle is feeding on young in nest, and again rise in alarm when it flies away. In one W Kenyan colony only 7 out of 545 eggs hatched, the rest predated on the ground; no young flew (Parsons 1977). Many young also fall from nests; available data suggest low breeding success common. E Africa, 1 or less at fledging (L. H. Brown, pers. comm.).

References
North, M. E. W. (1963).
Parsons, J. (1977).
Taylor, J. S. (1948).

Ardea goliath Cretzchmar. Goliath Heron. Héron goliath.   Plate 10

Ardea goliath Cretzchmar, 1827. Rüppell's Atlas Reise (Vögel), p. 39, pl. 26; 'Bahhar Abiad' = Bahr el Abiad or White Nile.   (Opp. p. 147)

Range and Status. Resident, normally frequent, sometimes common, in many areas uncommon. Prefers shallow shores of freshwater lakes but also marshes, rivers, estuaries and coastal areas, south of about 18°N from Senegal to Sudan and Ethiopia south to northeastern Cape. Occurs northward along Red Sea to about 24°N. Breeds mostly in E and southern Africa from Ethiopia to Natal, but also Gambia, Guinea-Bissau.

Description. ADULT ♂: overall slate grey and rufous chestnut. Head, face and hind and side of neck rich chestnut, darkest on top of head; a bushy crest on crown and nape. Chin, throat, foreneck and upper breast white, latter two streaked black, with lanceolate feathers on upper breast. Lower neck, back, tail and upperwings slate grey. Mantle and scapulars with lanceolate plumes. Underwing-coverts and underparts deep rufous-chestnut. Upper mandible black, lower horn; lores and orbital area yellow tinged green; eye yellow; legs and feet black. Sexes alike. Nuptial changes in colour not recorded although yellow eye with red rim may be courtship colour. SIZE: wing, ♂ (7 specimens) 570–630 (591), ♀ (8) 560–599 (575); tail, 200–235 (226); bill, ♂ (9) 183–208 (193), ♀ (10) 156–196 (177); tarsus, 225–238 (231). WEIGHT: ♂ 4310, 4345.

IMMATURE: similar to adult but paler, upperparts browner. Forehead dark grey to black; foreneck and breast with few black marks. Rest of underparts more mottled, rufous and paler with lower breast and belly buff-white streaked dark brown. Dark grey mottling under wings.

DOWNY YOUNG: covered in greyish white down; eye light green at hatching, later yellow; bill pale greenish brown; skin, legs and feet pale lime green.

Field Characters. A very large heron, about 1·5 m tall (one individual exactly 1·524 m tall: D. Mock, pers. comm.), with large and very deep bill, grey upperparts and mainly rufous-chestnut head, neck and underparts. Might be confused with Purple Heron *A. purpurea* but Goliath Heron nearly twice as large and has rufous, not black, crown and a thick, not thin, bill.

Voice. Recorded (1b, 2a, 6, 18, 19, 20b). Normal call is very deep, raucous 'kowoorrk-kowoorrk-woorrk-work-worrk' audible for 2 km; corresponds to 'frarnk' of Grey Heron *A. cinerea* but is a multiple call. What was thought to be a courting pair, away from nest at the edge of an oxbow lagoon and behaving in a manner similar to that described in the note on courtship in the Breeding Habits section below, was heard on two consecutive mornings between dawn and sunrise uttering a series of organ-like notes apparently in the form of a well

Ardea goliath

synchronized duet (H. Elliott, pers. comm.). In stretch display a 'krooo' when bill pointed vertically, and a series of deep grunts, a 'huh-huh-huh-huh', when in crouched stage (L. H. Brown, pers. comm.).

General Habits. Well known. Normally solitary, or in pairs, rarely gregarious, inhabiting shallow fresh and salt water of lakes, marshes, streams, rivers, estuaries and mangrove creeks. Usually does not wander far from water. Same bird seen daily in same locality. Roosts in trees, on floating vegetation (e.g. papyrus beds), and active soon after dawn if not at night (L. H. Brown, pers. comm.). Flight slow and ponderous with wings and legs sagging below horizontal. Capable of long flights, dispersing locally in response to seasonal changes in water, but no evidence of migration.

Usually feeds alone, spread thinly over large areas, *c.* 1/4 km² in Zambia (Dowsett and de Vos 1963/1964). Usually hunt among floating vegetation, although on Kenya coast (L. H. Brown, pers. comm.) fishes the rising tide, standing in deep swift running water up to belly. Moves from one fishing area to another by short walk or flight. At St Lucia Bay (Mock and Mock 1980) remains motionless about 76% time, takes 3–4 steps/min covering 1·2 m, moves av. 1·6 times/h. 56% of moves made by flying, with most moves less than 30 m. When landing on floating vegetation, slowly sinks without splashing or scaring fish. Spends 50–60% of daylight hours hunting; eats 2–3 meals/day. Hunts mainly by walking slowly, also uses stand-and-wait procedure but never disturb-and-chase. When sights prey, lowers body, head and neck about parallel with water. From this position, or with head and neck first partially retracted, strikes, normally totally submerging head. Usually skewers prey with mandible tips held 2 cm apart and often protruding 2–4 cm through other side of fish. At St Lucia Bay (Mock and Mock 1980) strikes infrequently, less than 1 strike/h with about 1 in 3 strikes being successful. May flap wings in air and against water surface when bringing large prey to surface. After capturing fish, may drop it on floating vegetation, stab it again, then swallow it or carry it ashore. At St Lucia Bay, of 107 captures, herons take av. 109 s (max. 308 s) after strike to swallow fish (Mock and Mock 1980). After swallowing, drinks for several min, vibrating bill in water, probably for cleaning purposes and not to attract fish. Then for *c.* 1 h stands, preens, suns itself and sleeps. Some prey is lost to fish eagles which dive at herons, forcing them to release prey.

Food. Chiefly large fish, e.g. mullet, tilapia, catfish, carp and eel; also frogs, lizards, snakes, rodents, crabs, prawns and floating carrion. Size of fish captured Lake St Lucia (Mock and Mock 1980) 15–50 cm (30), 500–600 g; sometimes smaller (Whitfield and Blaber 1979) 11–297 g (most 50–60).

Breeding Habits. Well known. Solitary or, rarely, colonial nester, nesting on trees overhanging water, on submerged or partly submerged trees, low bushes, mangroves, on ground, on cliffs and on flattened sedge or papyrus. As many as 3 nests on same tree; many nests often less than 20–30 m apart. Sometimes nests with other herons, cormorants and darters.

Courtship unknown but probably like that of Grey Heron. Two encounters reported. One, when landing on shore, immediately did stretch display which was similar, but more slowly performed than same display by Great Egret *Egretta alba* and Black-headed Heron *A. melanocephala* (L. H. Brown, pers. comm.). The other, when approaching another bird away from nest, extended neck; latter stretched neck with bill pointing down, called, lowered and extended neck until throat touched water, pointed bill at first bird, then called several times (Schuttee 1969).

NEST: a platform of sticks and reeds, *c.* 1–1·5 m in diameter, thickness varies according to site but may be up to 0·8 m thick; believed to be built by both sexes.

EGGS: 2–4; E Africa mean (12 clutches) 2·8; Zimbabwe and Zambia (78) 2·6; South Africa, OFS (16) 2·8, Natal (3) 3·0, Transvaal (5) 2·4 (SAOSNRC). Regular ovals, pale blue or blue-green. SIZE: (8 eggs) 69–77 × 50–59 (73 × 53); WEIGHT: 109.

Lays mainly in rains, but in several areas year-round with no obvious peaks. Laying dates: Gambia, Guinea-Bissau Aug–Sept (late rains); Ethiopia Feb–Apr, Nov; Somalia Sept–Dec; E Kenya Feb–Dec, perhaps peaking Apr–June (main rains); Uganda Apr, June, Sept; Tanzania Jan, July–Aug; Zaïre Jan–May, Dec; Zambia, Zimbabwe Jan–Dec; Malawi June, Sept–Oct (dry); Mozambique Jan–June, Oct–Dec; Namibia Aug–Sept; South Africa Jan, June, Aug–Dec (dry and into rains). Breeding in Egypt's Red Sea requires confirmation.

Incubation begins with 1st egg, by both parents; period estimated at 24–30 days.

Parental behaviour and development of young poorly documented. Both feed chicks (age?) twice a day by regurgitation. At hatching, young in same nest vary in size, e.g. 2 young, culmen, 2·0–2·5 cm; wing, 1·7–2·8; tarsus, 1·8–3·1. Soon after hatching can lift head and emit continual hissing noises. When 3–4 weeks, well feathered but unable to stand; flutter gular area and perform forward display; withdraw and crouch when intruder present. When 6–7 weeks, fully capable of moving from nest. Nestling period: reports vary, 81 days (Audin 1963); at least 58 days (Cooper and Marshall 1970); *c.* 40 days (de Naurois 1969); or *c.* 6 weeks (McLachlan and Liversidge 1978). Breeding success, E Africa, usually 1 and occasionally 2/pair (L. H. Brown, pers. comm.).

References
Audin, H. (1963).
Cooper, H. and Marshall, B. E. (1970).
Mock, D. W. and Mock, K. C. (1980).

Suborder SCOPI

Family SCOPIDAE: Hamerkop

A unique endemic African family. Medium-sized water birds, uniform brown. Wings rather long, broad, 10 primaries; tail short, 12 feathers. Head crested, lores feathered. Bill compressed, upper mandible curving over lower forming a hook; groove above nostril continued along culmen, bill appearing almost flat from side. 3 front toes partly webbed, middle toe in adults pectinated, hind toe free, somewhat above others. 1 genus and species, *Scopus umbretta.*

The family has been generally regarded as nearest to the Balaenicipitidae. However, although the bill superficially resembles both that of the Shoebill *Balaeniceps rex* and of South American Boat-billed Herons *Cochlearius*, behaviour indicates no close relations with either herons, Shoebill, or any other Ciconiiform family (Kahl 1967). Hamerkops resemble herons in having a pectinated middle toe, but lack powder-down patches or elongated nuptial plumes.

The free hind toe perhaps suggests affinities with flamingoes, but the Hamerkop resembles these in no other way. Resemblance of the bill to *Balaeniceps* and *Cochlearius* is likely to be due to convergent adaptation for feeding. Egg-white protein electrophoresis indicates that Hamerkops are closest to the Ciconiidae, but their ectoparasites suggest a link with the Charadriiformes. The nesting habits, with a huge domed nest, are unlike any other member of the Order Ciconiiformes. Though placed here, its true affinities are still obscure and further detailed studies are needed of all aspects of this unique bird.

Genus *Scopus* Brisson

Scopus umbretta Gmelin. Hamerkop. Ombrette du Sénégal.

Scopus umbretta Gmelin, 1789. Syst. Nat., 1, p. 618; Senegal.

Plate 12
(Opp. p. 163)

Range and Status. Resident in aquatic habitats throughout Africa from Senegal east to S Somalia thence south to Cape Province. Normally frequent to common, locally abundant. Numbers probably increasing due to man-made extension of aquatic habitats, e.g. dams, irrigation schemes. Never persecuted by Africans who regard it as having magic powers, or being of ill omen.

Description. *S. u. umbretta* Gmelin: tropical Africa from N Nigeria east to Somalia, south to Gabon, Zaïre and to the Cape. ADULT ♂: entire body dull brown, paler on chin and throat. Head strongly crested. Primaries darker brown. Tail brown, broadly barred subterminally with 5 other indistinct darker brown bars. Bill black; eye brown; legs black. Sexes alike, ♂ slightly larger. SIZE: wing, 297–316 (305); tail, 152–158 (156); tarsus, 69–73 (70); wing-span, 90–94 cm; wing-loading, 27–28 N/m² (Wilson and Wilson, in press). WEIGHT: 415–430.

IMMATURE: scarcely distinguishable from adult.

DOWNY YOUNG: covered with smoke-grey down. Bill blunt, brown; eye light grey; legs at first flesh-coloured, becoming brown. Head crested within 6 days. Middle toe not pectinated.

S. u. minor Bates. Coastal belt from Sierra Leone to southeastern Nigeria. Smaller, wing, 246–286; somewhat darker.

Scopus umbretta

Field Characters. Normally unmistakable, a plain brown, long-legged, strongly crested water bird. Flight buoyant, rather owl-like; agile among vegetation; in flapping flight, head is partially retracted, wing-beats 180–190/min. Glides with head extended. Soars well, when might be mistaken for medium-sized raptor, but short tail, rather broad wings, somewhat jerky flapping flight, conspicuous extended beak and call, when uttered, diagnostic

Voice. Recorded (2a, 6, 18, 19, 20a, 22a, 26, 28). Complicated; calls not well associated with behaviour patterns. Often silent when alone, but very vocal when with others, or in social and nuptial displays. In flight utters short, sharp, high-pitched, nasal 'yip' or 'nyip', alternatively 'kek' (Kahl 1967). In social and nuptial displays loud, nasal 'yip-purrrr', also 'yik-yik-yik-yirrrr-yirrrr'; or 'wek-wek-wek-warrrrk, wek-wek-warrrk', often repeated, uttered in duet or chorus. Better information needed on specific calls associated with behaviour.

General Habits. Well known. Entirely diurnal, but active dawn–dusk. Frequents any aquatic environment, lakes, large rivers, marshes, dams, temporary seasonal ponds, in all habitats from forest to semi-desert wherever water is available. Commonest in well-watered savanna or woodland, less common in forest; in semi-arid areas often only seasonally resident. A nest in semi-arid areas when dry indicates seasonal water and presence of Hamerkops.

Normally or often roosts in or near nest. Leaves just after dawn, dropping out of narrow nest entrance with closed wings, which are then immediately opened. Flies fairly high (50–100 m above ground) to feeding areas. In feeding areas frequents mainly shallow water, e.g. along sandbanks, reedy margins, floating vegetation. At midday frequently perches resting on trees, rocks or banks, feeding again in afternoon. Prefers to take flight from elevated situation, but from surface leaps upwards with rapidly beating wings. Returns *c.* 30–60 min before dark to roost and, if entering nest, flies low, then swoops up, closing wings neatly at last moment to enter in 'upward dive' (Kahl 1967). Contrary to some published suggestions, not active at night (Wilson and Wilson, in press).

Normally occurs in pairs, sometimes social groups of more than 50 reported, often 8–10 together. At least partly territorial, resident pairs occupying stretch of river or lake shore, but not actively aggressive to neighbours and territories certainly overlap (Wilson and Wilson, in press). No detailed population studies available, but population density perhaps regulated by availability of shallow water for feeding. On small rivers 1 pair/3 km (E Africa), but much commoner on e.g. some irrigation schemes (over 100 nests on 90 ha, 50% fit for use, 35 occupied by Barn Owls *Tyto alba*: Wilson and Wilson, in press). Relatively scarce on deep, large, fast-flowing rivers. Sedentary, pairs remaining in territory year-round, regularly roosting in nests, but some wet-season dispersal to seasonal ponds in semi-arid areas, perhaps breeding, then retreating to permanent waters. No evidence of regular migration anywhere.

Food. In southern Africa mainly amphibia, especially adults and young of clawed frog *Xenopus*; often taken in E Africa also. In Mali, and often in E Africa, mainly small fish (young *Clarias*, *Barbus*, *Tilapia* spp.). Availability of amphibia not critical for survival. Takes some aquatic invertebrates, and may scavenge fish scraps near villages.

Specialized bill is feeding adaptation. Normally feeds wading or standing in shallow water, watching intently, head sometimes cocked to side. May stir bottom with foot, or flash open wings, perhaps thus moving prey. Catches most prey among aquatic vegetation, or in clear water, by quick snatch, aided by hook on upper mandible; but does not grab mixed mass of prey and vegetation, sorting it out later, as Shoebill *Balaeniceps rex* does. Probes in mud with bill. Also often feeds in flight, flying slowly upwind just above water with deep wing strokes (slow flight assisted by very low wing-loading), dipping bill to take prey from surface, then also touching water with feet. Many thus take swarming tadpoles of *Xenopus*, but also small fish. May hover momentarily; success rate estimated 80% (Kahl 1967). Often washes captured prey before swallowing. Food requirement unknown, but stomach contents 22–24 g (Wilson and Wilson, in press), and in favourable habitat most individuals can easily obtain superabundant food. When catching small fish, is frequently robbed by Fish Eagle *Haliaeetus vocifer*, and must catch many before satisfying itself.

Breeding Habits. Very well known. Nests usually in trees overhanging water, less often on cliff ledges, banks, rock columns in midstream, on ground or sandbanks. Prefers permanent waters, but will use seasonal waters in arid areas. If available, dead tree actually standing in water often preferred. Nests at any height 1–20 m above water, usually 5–10 m.

NEST: extraordinary, huge for size of bird, domed with narrow round entrance hole. Entrance itself overhung by upper structure, inaccessible from rear. May be built annually or, more often, used several years in succession; sometimes several nests built in a year by 1 pair. Most pairs have 1–3 nests close together in territory, only 1 in regular use for roosting. May last many years, or collapse in less than a year or even within a few weeks.

Built by both sexes, methods observed in detail (Liversidge 1963; Wilson and Wilson, in press; L. H. Brown, pers. obs.). Most building done dawn to 10.00 h, sometimes also evening, 16.00–18.00 h. Wet weather preferred in some areas, building reduced in temporary dry spells, but in Mali building mainly in dry season. Both sexes collect material, usually within 100 m of site, returning time after time to any suitable source, e.g. pile of flood debris. Most material sticks, dead weed stems, reeds, grass, but large strong sticks up to 1·5 m long and 1·5 cm thick used in later stages. Share of sexes about equal, making trips at 50–120 s intervals, av. *c*. 25–30/h. Finished structure may contain 8000 items, weigh 25 kg, max. 50 kg (Wilson and Wilson, in press). Typical nest is *c*. 150 cm deep by 160 cm from rear to entrance, with internal chamber *c*. 80 × 30 cm, entrance passage 13–18 cm in diameter and 40–60 cm long, leading to nest depression 35 cm wide × 10 cm deep towards rear. Interior roughly, entrance tunnel smoothly plastered with mud, sometimes with broad ledge near entrance. Contrary to general belief, has only 1 chamber and entrance does not always face east. Building may be complete in 4–6 weeks, nest sporadically added to thereafter (Kahl 1967; Liversidge 1963; Wilson and Wilson, in press).

In 1st stage, an untidy mass of vegetation with central bowl is constructed in fork in 4–7 days, resembling stork or raptor nest; vegetation consists of sticks, reeds and weed-stems, mixed with mud, either adhering to material or specially collected in bill. Sides are then built up *c*. 15 cm above bowl with sticks. Birds then commence roofing with strong sticks, worked vertically into edge, slanting inwards, interwoven with others laid longitudinally; procedure broadly resembles raising hood of baby's pram or sports car. Birds work gradually forward, one often remaining within cavity, while other works on top; both may work together on one stick. When strong, stable roof of sticks thus completed, masses of other material added on top—reeds, weeds, grass, small sticks, rags, bones, plastic, paper, any rubbish. This mass of material may be added by both working continuously all one day, or may take longer. Finally, entrance chamber is fashioned with short sticks usually brought by one (probably ♂) while other remains within and works them into place. Entrance and nest chamber are then plastered with mud, leaving no sharp projections. Finished structure will bear weight of heavy man standing on top.

In early bowl stage nests sometimes usurped by Verreaux's Eagle Owl *Bubo lacteus* (attacked but not deterred by Hamerkops). Completed nests often usurped by Barn Owl, sometimes by Grey Kestrel *Falco ardosiaceus* (Wilson and Wilson, in press; Serle 1943), but these often use old or abandoned nests. Empty nests often used by Egyptian Goose *Alopochen aegyptiacus* and Knob-billed Duck *Sarkidiornis melanotos*, less often by African Pygmy Goose *Nettapus auritus* or Speckled Pigeon *Columba guinea*; goose-down at entrance often identifies occupant. Also used as day-time resting places by e.g. genets *Genatta* spp., monitor lizards *Veranus* spp. and large snakes, e.g. Spitting Cobra *Naja nigricollis*. Caution desirable when investigating with bare hands. When building adults are aggressive to e.g. cats, dogs, even large eagles. Other adults sometimes congregate nearby, or perch on edge (as if taking an interest), but do not build (Gentis 1976).

Completed nest in an African Mahogany tree *Khaya senegalensis.*
(*Drawn by Martin Woodcock from photographs kindly supplied by R. T. and M. Wilson, Mali.*)

Apparent social courtship displays common near nest. May involve up to 8–10 birds, composed apparently of several pairs, with outsiders. In pairs, larger (♂?) partner runs up to other, wings drooped and flicked part-open, crest rapidly rising and falling. Pair (?) then run in circles side by side, and repeated false mounting is performed, apparently largely indiscriminately, ♂–♀, ♂–♂, or ♀–♂. Soliciting bird crouches, other mounts, balancing with open wings; tail of lower bird raised and pressed against depressed tail of upper, no true copulation. May even face in opposite directions. Preferred site of such performances an open lawn, flat-topped water tank, boulder, dead tree, or sandbank. Usually occur at dawn and last 10–40 min, accompanied by loud calling in duet or chorus, but during nest-building may occur frequently and at any time of day (Wilson and Wilson, in press).

True pair courtship somewhat similar. One often flies with rapid bat-like flight at other (sometimes, but not always mate). In nest-building, mutual courtship and copulation frequent, 8–10 times/morning, accompanied by loud 'yip-purrrr' calling. Soliciting ♀ crouches, ♂

circles with flirting wings, crest rising and falling, then mounts. Copulation occurs on top of nest, or on branch nearby, or on ground up to 100 m away. False mounting of ♂ by ♀ also seen. Mating ceases when nest complete, but social displays with false-mating may occur at almost any time, not necessarily near nest.

EGGS: 3–7, laid at 24–48 h intervals, sometimes more often; 3–7 recorded South Africa; 3–5 normal E Africa; Mali, complete clutches 4–5, mean (10) 4·4; little variation with latitude. Nest may contain fertile incubated eggs and large young (Jackson and Sclater 1938). 1st egg may be laid before nest complete, or by *c.* 12 days afterwards. Eggs also often laid, then abandoned in completed nest before clutch complete. Chalky white, soon stained brown with mud. SIZE: (78 eggs, South Africa) 41·3–52 × 32·0–36 (46·0–34·8); (18, Mali) 42·9–47·7 × 33·4–35·6 (45·03 × 34·32); WEIGHT: (10) 25·2–29·7 (27·6) (Wilson and Wilson, in press); clutch of 4, *c.* 25% of ♀ bodyweight.

Laying dates: Senegal Nov, Mar (dry); Gambia Apr–June; Mali July–Jan, no obvious peaks (wet, extending into dry season); N Nigeria Jan–Apr (late dry); Ethiopia

Jan, Mar, Sept, Nov (dry and wet); Kenya, Uganda most months, no obvious peaks; Zambia, Zimbabwe, Malawi, 8/12 months, possibly peaking Feb–Mar (late rains) and July–Sept (dry); South Africa July–Jan, mainly dry. Dates difficult to establish accurately, as eggs or young must be seen in nest, but available data suggest (surprisingly in view of partly or largely amphibian diet) that more breeding occurs in dry than wet seasons, and that food supply may not be critical factor.

Incubation may begin when clutch incomplete, *c.* 4 days after laying 1st egg (Liversidge 1963), but this evidently not invariable. Both sexes incubate by day, each taking long spells off, leaving eggs uncovered; surface temperature of eggs low (Wilson and Wilson, in press). Roles at night unknown, but ♂ may roost in nest with ♀. Incubation period: *c.* 30 days (Liversidge 1963).

Newly hatched young covered with grey down, darker on back. Develops crest within 6 days, and at 5 days bill is as broad as deep, suggesting relationship with Shoebill (but beak of young Shoebill not similar). Head feathers develop first (Cowles 1930), head entirely feathered, crested like adult at 17 days when wing- and tail-feathers and dorsal contour feathers just appearing through down. Body largely feathered at 30 days. Weight increases steadily from *c.* 20 g at hatch to max. 600 g at 35 days, thereafter sometimes decreasing slowly to *c.* 500 g at 1st flight at 50 days (Liversidge 1963); but weight loss before flight not normal in broods of several young (Wilson and Wilson, in press).

Parental behaviour in fledging period poorly known, but both parents feed young. One or both parents roost in nest at night, but small young are soon left for long periods unattended by day, parents visiting to bring food. Internal temperature of very large nest varies little and is generally cooler than environment. Advantage of huge nest may be to permit both parents to forage and rear large broods (Siegfried 1975). However, this supposition not supported by available data on low average breeding success, or any recent observations (Wilson and Wilson, in press). Fledged young, after leaving nest, can return immediately, flying into narrow entrance with no difficulty. Return daily for 14 days after 1st flight and may roost together in nest for 1 month afterwards. Parents then depart too in some cases.

Good long-term data on breeding success, adolescence and survival lacking. However, non-breeding is frequent even when nests have been built (e.g. 4 nests built successive years, none used, Karen, Kenya); only 20 clutches laid in 64 nests, Mali (Wilson and Wilson, in press). Up to 3 nests may be built by 1 pair in 1 year and none used. Nests often collapse when soaked by heavy rains and are often taken over by Barn Owls, sometimes by Grey Kestrel; and monitor lizards eat many clutches. From 16 clutches, Mali, 9 lost all eggs, 20 eggs hatched in 6 others produced 15 fledged young, (1–4 recorded reared); equivalent to 0·94 young reared per clutch laid. Food supply in nestling period not considered critical (Wilson and Wilson, in press). In South Africa breeding may be more regular, successive broods reared annually (Cowles 1930). Available data suggest frequent non-breeding in nests constructed but not used (up to 78%); frequent egg losses (up to 50%); losses in nest of young up to 30–40%. If 25% of pairs breed, 50% lose all eggs and 60% of young hatched are reared, this equals 0·13 young reared per adult, necessitating mean adult life of perhaps 20 years. Better data required to assess true situation, but Hamerkop is probably long-lived.

References
Cowles, R. B. (1930).
Kahl, M. P. (1967).
Liversidge, R. (1963).
Wilson, R. T. and M. P. (in press).

Suborder CICONIAE

In the most recent arrangement (Kahl 1979) the 2 families Ciconiidae, storks, and Balaenicipitidae, Shoebill, are included in this new suborder.

Family CICONIIDAE: storks

An almost cosmopolitan family of large to very large long-legged water birds, most varied in tropical countries. The 17 species in 6 genera are arranged by Kahl (1971a, 1979) in 3 tribes, the Mycteriini containing the genera *Mycteria* and *Anastomus*; Ciconiini containing *Ciconia*; and Leptoptilini containing *Ephippiorhynchus*, *Leptoptilos* and the South American *Jabiru*. 8 species in 5 genera occur in Africa. Of these, 2 are mainly Palearctic, with populations resident in South Africa (White Stork *C. ciconia* with only a few pairs), and other populations resident in Europe, Asia and N Africa migrating to Africa in winter. The other 6 species are typically African, mainly tropical in distribution.

Being large and often abundant or at least common, all African storks are well known or very well known, 1, the Marabou *Leptoptilos crumeniferus*, studied in detail. All have long legs with unwebbed toes, bony beaks, in some species specialized for particular functions. All fly and soar well, usually with necks outstretched (unlike herons,

Ardeidae), but Marabous fly with heads retracted. Some are highly gregarious, others solitary. Most feed on fish or other aquatic organisms, but 3 *Ciconia* species are largely or mainly terrestrial, feeding on insects; and 1, the Marabou, feeds largely on carrion and is also an active predator.

The arrangement of storks by Kahl is largely based upon comparative study of displays, which are rather similar throughout the family, some displays being performed by all species. The most common forms of display are (for full descriptions see Kahl 1966a, 1971a, 1972a,b,c, 1973, and Cramp and Simmons 1977): (1) 'anxiety stretch' in which bird spreads wings, erects body and arches neck forward with bill 45–60° below horizontal (see **B**, p. 189); (2) 'forward threat' in which bird fully extends head and neck forward and clatters bill (**C**, p. 189); (3) 'up right' in which bird lifts wing-tips slightly, angles body and neck forward and upward at 60–70°, holds head high, and opens and shakes bill from side to side or up and down (**A**, p. 188); (4) 'aerial-clattering threat' in which bird flies at opponent with neck extended forward and clatters bill loudly (**D**, p. 189); (5) 'up–down' (see **A**, p. 184, and **F**, p. 189) in which bird first throws head upward (or all the way back until crown touches back and bill points toward tail), then brings neck and head forward and down, with bill pointing vertically down or slightly forward; clatters bill loudly and rapidly when bringing head forward; (6) 'balancing posture' in which ♀ holds wings fully open, body almost at horizontal axis, and head low with bill pointing down and sometimes agape (not *Ciconia*) (**B**, p. 175); (7) 'gaping' in which bird, often standing erect with neck extended vertically, opens bill for long periods (not *Ciconia*); (8) 'display preening' in which ♂ 'pretends' to strip down feathers of a partially open wing (*Mycteria* only) (**A**, p. 175); (9) 'swaying twig-grasping' in which bird bends over until bill reaches substrate, raises tips of wings slightly, then sways from left to right and back, shifts weight from one leg to another, and grasps lightly at twigs at end of each oscillation (*Mycteria*, *Leptoptilos*) (**E**, p. 189); (10) 'advertising-sway' in which ♂ bends forward until bill is pointed downward, almost between its feet, then shifts its weight back and forth from 1 leg to another, lifting each foot slightly at end of each oscillation (*Anastomus* only) (**A**, p. 177); (11) 'head-shaking crouch' in which ♂, when ♀ approaches, crouches on nest with tail high, then shakes his head back and forth; sometimes ♂ bends forward with tail high, head low and body axis *c.* 45° below horizontal before crouching on nest (*Ciconia* only) (**A** and **B**, p. 181); (12) 'copulation' and 'copulation clattering' in which ♂ steps on ♀'s back, hooks feet over her shoulders, lowers himself for cloacal contact, flaps wings for balance, places bill alongside ♀'s bill and clatters his bill; (13) 'flap-dash' in which 1 member of a foraging pair suddenly stands erect, then dashes wildly, flapping its wings vigorously (*Ephippiorhynchus* only); and (14) 'snap display' in which bird stands hunched, with neck drawn in, then raises bill quickly above horizontal without extending the neck and snaps it audibly once (*Leptoptilos* only). (*All illustrations for Ciconiidae by Martin Woodcock as follows: Yellow-billed, Open-bill and Abdim's Stork, after Kahl (1971a); White Stork, after Cramp and Simmons (1977); Marabou Stork, after Kahl (1966b).*)

Genus *Mycteria* Linnaeus

Medium-sized storks, with naked heads or faces; plumage mainly white with red or pink and black in wings. Generic characters include highly specialized bill with swollen base, rounder in cross-section than other storks, and pronounced downward curve at tip. Bill is sensitively tactile, specialized for feeding in opaque water with quickest known muscular reflex. Bill-clattering in display less than in typical storks (Kahl 1972c).

Mycteria ibis (Linnaeus). Yellow-billed Stork; Wood Ibis. Tantale ibis.

Tantalus Ibis Linnaeus, 1766. Syst. Nat. (12th ed.), 1, p. 241; Egypt.

Plate 12

(Opp. p. 163)

Range and Status. Resident; widespread in aquatic habitats, including alkaline lakes and marine mudflats throughout tropical Africa, less in forested areas; straggles to Palearctic Africa (Morocco; Egypt, early 20th century), and in South Africa occurs seasonally to Cape Province. Common to locally abundant, or very abundant near breeding colonies. Population probably stable, except possibly in South Africa.

Description. ADULT ♂: forehead and face naked; hindcrown and neck greyish white. Back, upperwing- and underwing-coverts, breast and belly white, more or less tinged pink with pinkish or reddish tips to some feathers. Wing-feathers and tail black. Bill long, slightly decurved, thick at base, bright yellow; bare skin of face orange-red; eye greyish brown; legs red. Sexes alike, ♀ slightly smaller. ADULT ♂ and ♀ (breeding):

colours intensify; bill becomes deeper yellow, bare facial skin bright red, white plumage is suffused pink and wing-coverts broadly tipped crimson, legs brighter red. SIZE: wing, 455–513; tail 168–183; tarsus, 197–229; bill, 205–242; span, 1500–1650.

IMMATURE: 1st-year birds generally greyish brown, with dull greyish yellow bill, dull orange face, brownish legs; wing- and tail-feathers dark brown. Subadults are paler versions of adults, with no pinkish flush, duller coloured soft parts, but black wing- and tail-feathers.

DOWNY YOUNG: dirty white, becoming snow-white at *c.* 10 days when 2nd down emerges.

Field Characters. A large, usually gregarious stork, with long deep yellow bill, bare orange-red facial skin and red legs. Can only be confused with White Stork *Ciconia ciconia*, but adults normally show some pink in

Mycteria ibis

plumage, and in flight black tail diagnostic. Outstretched neck in flight distinguishes it from any pelican and short, not wedge-shaped, black tail and long bill distinguish it from Egyptian Vulture *Neophron percnopterus*.

Voice. Recorded (19). Generally silent. At breeding colonies adults utter a 'fizzing' whining call, or hissing screams, said to resemble a squeaking hinge. Young beg with repeated, monotonous braying sound. Bill-clattering by adults, with very hollow sound, reduced cf. other storks, a few 'snaps' in 'up-down' display, short rattles in flight, true clattering only in copulation.

General Habits. Well known. Found usually in large swamps, along lake margins, larger rivers, irrigated rice fields, and other large areas of marsh or water. May occur at small pools or streams but not for long. To some extent gregarious, but never in very large flocks. Often associates with other storks, herons and pelicans at favoured resting places. Takes flight with strong quick wing-beats, but for travelling far rises on thermals to great height, then glides. Roosts on ground, sandbanks, lake margins, sometimes in trees, using favourite trees nightly, collecting from far around.

Where it occurs, always rather an inactive bird, spending much time resting by day, very often squatting on tarsi. Movements generally slow and deliberate except when threatening others. Feeds in shallow water, and evidently obtains food easily as only a small proportion of daylight spent feeding. Often feeds for a short time, then rests and feeds again when hungry. Habitually congregates at certain places to rest by day and on some E African tidal mudflats same place is used for many successive years, probably by same individuals as long as they live, disturbed only by exceptional tides.

Movements irregular, somewhat nomadic, poorly documented. In South Africa definitely migrant, arriving in Oct, departing in Apr, remaining through southern summer; all N African records spring and summer (Mar–Oct). Permanently present in Zimbabwe, Zambia and most of tropical E Africa, moving only locally. In W Africa, however, performs regular migrations, moving south in dry season and departing to north in wet season, arriving Oct–Nov, departing Mar; arrival may coincide with strong Harmattan winds. Elsewhere may move locally but not far. In some areas permanently resident, though probably congregating locally to breed.

Food. Frogs, small fish, some aquatic insects, worms, crustaceans, perhaps small mammals. Almost all food is caught in water by remarkable bill adaptation, involving quickest known muscular reflex. Generally feeds with bill immersed to near base, slightly open, while stirring bottom mud with one foot. May open one wing to shade water. When prey moves, bill instantly snaps. Alternatively, may walk along, plunging bill repeatedly into water and weeds, snapping any prey located. On tidal E African sandflats feeds in small pools, rarely picking up prey from dry sand; can apparently catch immediate requirements in a few min. Also, may associate with e.g. Great White Pelicans *Pelecanus onocrotalus* to fish, standing in line with part-open bill outstretched forward and sunk, awaiting movement of fish, which are then snapped up. Bill is undoubtedly intensely tactile, as most prey is invisible, caught in opaque or muddy water. Seized prey is manipulated, wriggling, between mandibles, then swallowed, usually alive.

Breeding Habits. Well known. Nests in small or large colonies, often or usually with other storks (especially Marabou *Leptoptilos crumeniferus*), herons and cormorants, singly or in small groups, 10–20 per tree at most, among these other species, seldom large discrete masses together. Nests normally in trees, usually tall acacias, baobabs, *Bombax* (often in villages, W Africa), high up or on top, not low down; but in flooded areas low trees acceptable.

♂ apparently chooses site, and when breeding ♀ approaches 'display preens' (see **A**) first one, then other wing, in front and behind, exposing bright and contrasting colours. ♀ perches in 'balancing posture' head held forward, bill gaping, wings part-spread (**B**); then closes wings, joins ♂, often still gaping. After pair-formation, and thereafter at nest-relief and when on nest, pair perform 'up-down', throwing head high, bill vertical, then lowering bill towards nest, swinging head from side to side, uttering 'fizzing' calls. At copulation ♀ holds wings open wide, ♂ mounts, clatters bill, and also clatters it laterally against that of ♀, with elements of 2 types of bill-clattering (of *Ciconia* and *Anastomus*). Bright colours of bare facial skin accentuated by retracting scalp, exposing greater area.

NEST: built quickly by both sexes in 7–10 days, usually afresh each year, though sometimes old structures persist. Rather small structure of sticks, lined with leaves, reeds and aquatic grasses, normally not more than 1 m across by 0·2–0·3 m thick. Nest material continues to be brought throughout cycle, accompanied by 'up-down' displays if pair on nest.

EGGS: 2–4, usually 2–3, laid alternate days; mean (45

A

B

clutches) 2·5. Dull white, glossless, without chalky covering, becoming nest-stained. SIZE: (36) 59·0–72·3 × 42·0–46·1 (66·0 × 44·0); WEIGHT: calculated 71, actual av. 77 (Mundy and Cook 1974).

Laying dates: Senegal, Gambia, Guinea–Bissau Nov–Dec (dry); N Nigeria late Aug–Sept (end rains); E Africa, Kenya–Uganda Mar–June, late long rains; Tanzania mainly Jan–Feb, some Mar–Apr, late in rains or in inundated areas; Zambia Feb–June, also Aug–Sept; Botswana Feb–Mar, Aug, Sept–Oct (suggesting more elastic breeding season in southern tropics); Natal–Lesotho June, Oct (dry). Most breeding apparently starts late in rains, or in deeply inundated areas, young leaving nest in dry seasons. Some laying also in dry season, young then leaving nest in rains.

Both sexes incubate, in long spells of several hours by day, bird not incubating feeding some distance away. Not known which sits at night, probably ♀. Incubation period: not recorded, probably *c.* 30 days.

Young hatched at intervals of 2 or more days; helpless, cannot stand, require continuous brooding at first. At 10 days 2nd down emerges, become pure white. At 21 days when part-feathered, suddenly become aggressive to intruders; thereafter can possibly defend nest against other storks (main danger) and release parents from attention. Towards maturity, walk out onto branches near nest, flap wings. Further good details lacking; fledging period *c.* 55 days.

Both adults brood, tend and feed chicks; brooding continuous at first, but soon reduced, adults then standing on nest with chicks until part-feathered, shading from sun as necessary. Young fed by regurgitating food direct onto nest floor where they will pick it up, but if extremely hungry reach up and take food as it pours from parental bill. Are given water by dribbling down bill. Food items seen regurgitated usually small, possibly young amphibia, small fish. Parental attention reduced after 21 days.

Comparatively few young fall to the ground and are lost; possibly slow deliberate movements help prevent losses. Breeding success in observed colonies relatively high; broods of 1–3 young recorded E Africa. From 33 nests, 1·33 surviving young/nest, *c.* 50% of eggs laid. W Africa, from 70 eggs in 30 nests, 30 chicks fledged, 0·4/egg and 1·0/nest; mean (63 nests) 1·17. However, since breeding population is certainly much smaller than total in E Africa, and breeding does not occur annually in traditional sites, real breeding success per pair overall is less than 1/year.

Young leave nest of own accord, require no parental help. Can at once perform specialized foot-stirring and feeding methods of adults. Then normally accompany adults on feeding grounds, not separating (as in some other storks). Composition of adult/young population can be broadly determined as recent immatures; sub-adults (? 2nd year); non-breeding, and breeding adults. Full adult plumage not attained until at least 3rd year and may not immediately breed.

References
Kahl, M. P. (1972c).
Mundy, P. J. and Cook, A. W. (1974).

Genus *Anastomus* Bonnaterre

Medium-sized storks, with highly specialized bills, curving lower mandibles in adults separated by a gap from upper, touching only at tip. Specialization is to utilize shelled molluscs as food. 2 species, 1 Asian, 1 African—*A. lamelligerus*.

Plate 12

(Opp. p. 163)

Anastomus lamelligerus Temminck. African Open-bill Stork. Bec-ouvert africain.

Anastomus lamelligerus Temminck, 1823. Pl. Col. livr., 40, pl. 236; Senegal.

Range and Status. Resident mainland tropical Africa, in all aquatic habitats in open country, seldom within forest. Intra-tropical, probably trans-equatorial migrant, breeding mainly south of equator from north of Namibia to Kenya–Uganda (but also Chad, Ethiopia). Dry season visitor to most of W Africa, from Sudan west to Mali; Senegal (whence described), not recently seen. When breeding, locally abundant to very abundant, otherwise frequent to common, locally abundant. Population probably stable.

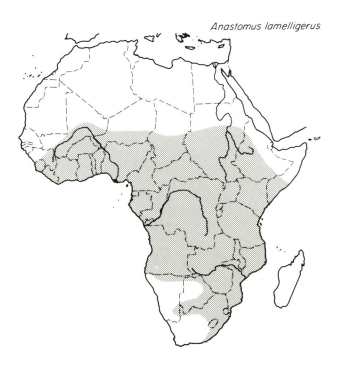

Anastomus lamelligerus

Description. *A. l. lamelligerus* Temminck, ADULT ♂: entirely black, glossed green and purple. Feathers of mantle and breast long, stiff, shining, glossed green, purple, or brownish. Underparts dull black, feathers prolonged into shiny filaments. Bill brownish, basally whitish; eye brown; bare skin blackish; legs and feet black. Sexes alike, no recorded size differences, but ♀♀ av. smaller. SIZE: wing, 370–433; tail, 165–206; tarsus, 133–165; bill, 153–194. WEIGHT: 1 ♂ 1250, 1 ♀ 1000, unsexed 970 (Blancou 1960). Highly specialized bill has curved lower mandible, upper nearly straight with a gap, 5·5–6 mm at widest in adults.
IMMATURE: duller than adult, hindneck speckled white, underparts brown; bill almost straight, shorter than adult, lacking curved lower mandible and marked gap.
DOWNY YOUNG: sooty black; bill black, eye brown, gular skin pink.

Field Characters. Unmistakable; a medium-sized, all-black stork, highly gregarious, and with extraordinary bill, mandibles meeting at tip but with a wide visible gap in centre (in adult); immatures have straighter bills but are also blackish.

Voice. Recorded (19). Loud, sonorous, rather raucous croaks or honks, 'horrrh-horrrh' audible at up to 100 m. Begging young emit high-pitched whining or braying

calls, resembling those of Yellow-billed Stork *Mycteria ibis*, but higher-pitched, more nasal 'resembling yelping of a litter of puppies' (Parsons 1974). Bill-clattering as in other storks physically impossible; but in copulation similar sounds are produced by rattling bills sideways against each other.

General Habits. Well known. A very gregarious stork of mainly large aquatic habitats, sometimes seen far from water when on movements. Frequents swamps, flood plains, rice fields, river shallows, lake edges and backwaters, normally needing large, wet or moist areas in which to feed. Stragglers may stay temporarily at small ponds. Normally travels in large flocks and roosts communally, but when feeding individuals disperse, well separated from others. May forage e.g. among floating vegetation, or by walking on backs of hippopotami. Roosts and rests in trees, often bare, collecting to roost from far around; same roost used nightly if birds in area for some time.

Movements not clearly understood, but breeds mainly south of equator, in rains and seasons of inundation, and north of equator is mainly a dry season visitor (Nov–May, occasionally later). Since these cannot be Southern Hemisphere breeding birds at that season, not all the population moves north of equator. Most that do leave when main rains break around May, stragglers remaining to July, some breeding in Chad Sept, Ethiopia Aug–Sept. More than one population unit may be involved. On migration travels in flocks, normally using thermals to gain height, then gliding on. However, can travel some distance by direct flapping flight, and will sometimes cross large bodies of water direct, alternately flapping and gliding.

Feeds in rice fields, swamps and on river sandbanks. Spends long periods by day resting on shores or in trees, often preferring leafless trees. Normally arrives suddenly in a locality in numbers, may remain for a time, breed (in Southern Hemisphere) and depart equally suddenly in flocks, perhaps leaving some stragglers behind.

Food. Snails (especially *Pila* spp.), freshwater mussels. Bill is highly specialized for the peculiar diet; upper mandible nearly straight, with 20–30 columnar pads 2–4 mm wide and 1–2 mm high along cutting edges near tip. Lower mandible curved in adult, forming a distinct visible gap, occasionally bent sideways so that tip does not meet that of upper mandible. Articulation of quadrate bones also specialized, with one long narrow condyle; all adaptations connected with specialized feeding techniques. No good recent evidence suggesting it can or does eat other than molluscan prey.

Early accounts of feeding which assumed molluscs were held in gap of mandibles where they were cracked or broken are erroneous. Snails are carried in bill-tip, not in mandibular gap. When eating snail, stork holds it underwater, so usually invisible, but thought to pin snail

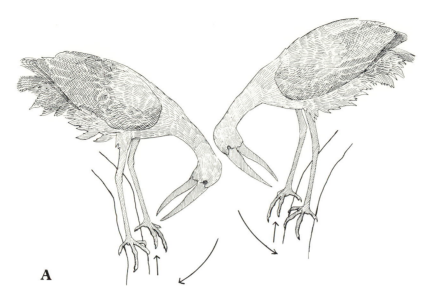

A

down with tip of upper mandible while blade-like lower mandible is inserted between operculum and shell, cutting columellar muscle and releasing mollusc from almost intact shell. When feeding on bivalves (freshwater mussels), inserts lower mandible between halves of shell near hinge, cuts main muscles, so relaxing animal and eats it almost without damaging shell. Also reported to leave bivalves in sun to open, then extracts flesh, but this evidently unnecessary (Kahl 1971b).

Breeding Habits. Well known. Breeds in small or large colonies in trees, often inundated in standing water on flood plains, sometimes with other storks, ibises or herons. Breeding highly adventitious, not occurring every year in same localities, but taking advantage of temporary unusual conditions some years.

Good details of early stages lacking, but male probably selects suitable site and there performs 'advertising sway', pointing bill down between feet, first one foot and then the other stiffly raised in swaying motion (see **A**). When pairs formed, both perform typical stork 'up-down' display, arching necks up and forward, bills widely gaping, then lowering bills to nest uttering loud raucous calls every 1–2 s. Both sexes build nest and add to it through incubation period and later; nest is continually wet or moist with regurgitated water. At copulation ♂, when mounting, clatters bill against side of ♀'s bill, producing sounds resembling normal stork bill-clattering.

NEST: small, 45–56 cm across, of sticks, reeds, or water weeds (*Polygonum senegalense*: Van der Heiden 1974). Normally built anew annually, but old breeding sites sometimes re-occupied.

EGGS: 2–5, normally 3–4, laid at 2-day intervals; Zimbabwe mean (27) 2·6 (SAOSNRC; Van der Heiden 1974). Dull white, soon becoming stained. SIZE: (14) 51–59·5 × 39·5–43·2 (54·7 × 40·5); WEIGHT: *c.* 50.

Laying dates: Chad Sept; Ethiopia (Lake Tana) Aug, Sept; Kenya–Uganda Jan–May, peaking Mar, also Aug–Oct; Tanzania mainly Jan–Feb, some Apr; Zambia mainly Feb, Mar, also Sept, Oct, Nov, Dec, Mar–July; Zimbabwe Jan, Sept–Oct, Dec; South Africa Feb–Mar.

Most nesting occurs late in rains, or at height of inundation on flood plains, but some (e.g. Zimbabwe Sept) at end of dry season or early rains. Birds may arrive at colony, build nests, then not lay. Breeding possibly correlated with emergence from aestivation of *Pila* snails, principal food (Kahl 1968). Freshwater mussels, most easily caught prey in dry season and low water, possibly inadequate food for regular breeding.

Both sexes incubate, one often standing on or beside nest while other sits; no good details. Incubation period: unknown, estimated 25–30 days.

Young when hatched lack exaggerated bill, but have wide gape enabling rapid ingestion of large meals. Young weighing 45 g can swallow snails weighing 5 g. A 15-day-old captive weighing 148 g ate 143 g of snails in 24 h (Kahl 1971b). Captive young select snails as preferred food and must be force-fed with anything else. 42-day-old captives cannot manipulate a snail. Flight feathers appear through down at about 25 days, body covered with feathers by 40 days. Good details lacking, but fledging period estimated 50–55 days.

Both parents feed young, regurgitating food onto nest where picked up by chicks. Also regurgitate water to chicks, wetting nest at same time. No good details of parental behaviour available, but both adults probably leave young to forage after about 20 days. Before then, 1 is usually on nest brooding, or perched beside it. Breeding success unknown, but total failure frequent, while in successful colonies broods of 2–4 may be reared; 1 Zimbabwe colony of 28 pairs reared av. 3/nest (Parsons 1974); in another (smaller), no chicks from *c.* 15 nests. Rather large clutch permits rapid increase if successful. In view of irregular adventitious breeding not involving entire adult population, overall breeding success almost certainly less than 1/pair/year.

Immatures leaving nest have nearly straight bills, but must soon feed unaided on snails or mussels; bill curvature develops over several years.

References

Kahl, M. P. (1971b; 1972b).

Genus *Ciconia* Brisson

This genus now includes the former genera *Dissoura* and *Sphenorhynchus* following Kahl (1971a). Medium-sized to large storks, some mainly terrestrial, feeding on insects. Plumage mainly black and white. Often highly gregarious, migrating and feeding in flocks, and breeding in colonies. Fly with neck fully extended. 2 species, White Stork *C. ciconia* and Black Stork *C. nigra*, have Palearctic populations, migrating to Africa in winter and southern African breeding populations. 1, Abdim's Stork *C. abdimii*, is an intra-African trans-equatorial migrant, and 1, Woolly-necked Stork *C. episcopus*, is a solitary, rather local resident within the tropics. All species are well known or very well known, the Palearctic breeding populations of *C. nigra* and *C. ciconia* better known there than in Africa. The commonest and most characteristic in tropical Africa, *C. abdimii*, is the least well known (see Kahl 1972a).

Plate 12

(Opp. p. 163)

Ciconia nigra (Linnaeus). Black Stork. Cigogne noire.

Ardea nigra Linnaeus, 1758. Syst. Nat. (10th ed.), p. 142; Sweden.

Range and Status. Breeding populations both in Palearctic and southern Africa, part of Palearctic population migrating to Africa in winter. South African birds may also leave breeding areas in non-breeding season. Palearctic population much larger than South African, but has decreased in western part of its range. Uncommon-frequent winter migrant E and NE Africa; in South Africa frequent, locally common. South African breeding population considered stable, perhaps increasing.

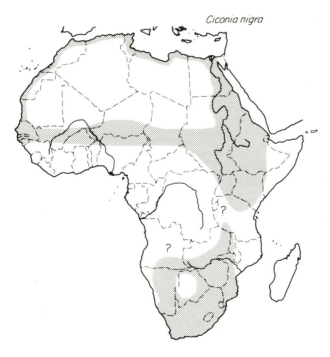

Ciconia nigra

Description. ADULT ♂: whole upperside, head, breast and wing-coverts black, glossed greenish on back, purplish on wing-coverts. Lower breast, belly and elongated undertail-coverts white, strongly contrasting. Wing- and tail-feathers black. Bill bright red, yellowish at base of upper mandible; bare facial skin red; eye dark brown; legs red. Red legs and face darker in non-breeding season. Sexes alike, ♀ somewhat smaller. SIZE: wing, 520–600 (539); tail, 190–240; tarsus, 180–280; bill, 160–190; wing-span, 1440–1550. WEIGHT: adult *c.* 3000, juveniles 2400–2500.

    IMMATURE: yellowish green bill and legs; orbital skin grey.
    DOWNY YOUNG: white with yellow bill, pale pinkish legs.

Field Characters. A large stork, 95–110 cm, rather smaller than White Stork *C. ciconia*, but much larger than Abdim's Stork *C. abdimii*. Distinguished from all but Abdim's by black and white plumage; from Abdim's by red bill, red legs, larger size, black (not white) uppertail-coverts. Immature resembles Abdim's more, but Abdim's has whitish legs with reddish feet and tibio-tarsal joint, and pale yellow bill with blue base; is also more gregarious. Much darker, generally, in adult and immature plumage than immature Yellow-billed Stork *Mycteria ibis*.

Voice. Recorded (2a). Not described for southern Africa where very silent even when breeding; Palearctic migrants in Africa silent. In Palearctic breeding areas more vocal than White Stork, most often calling 'chee-lee-chee-lee'; in threat a prolonged piping 'feeeeeeh' or 'fleeeeee'. Weak bisyllabic whistles in 'up-down' displays, and thin mewing 'hiiio-hiiioh'. Young utter repeated begging calls variously rendered 'ha-chi-chi', 'ge-ek, ge-ek, ge-ok'; 'gogogo'; soft 'pitjau'; later whining 'quieeeeee'; and, when fledged, hissing 'ooi-ooi-oooi'. In alarm, hoarse gasping 'ziap' and young ♂♂ utter deep growling 'ua-ua-ua'. Some bill-clattering by both sexes and young in excitement and display, but less constant and important than in White Stork (Cramp and Simmons 1977). In Africa little noted, but whistling 'kweee-ooo' or tremulous 'kwee-rrrooo' by adults and croaking calls by young (Fincham 1971).

General Habits. Well known. Throughout range much less common and gregarious than White Stork, but in South Africa breeding population exceeds that of White Stork. Normally rather solitary, seen singly, in pairs, or small groups (rarely as high as 30). Groups (possibly of immatures) may roost communally in South Africa, flying many km to roost, sometimes with Woolly-necked Storks *C. episcopus*. Prefers neighbourhood of water, streams, rivers, marshes, or small ponds, but may also be seen in open dry grassland (highland, Ethiopia). Habitually feeds alone, or, at most, in pairs or small groups, in long grass, reeds, stream verges. Catches little food far from water, but some large insects in grassland.

Palearctic population enters Africa mainly through Suez and Gibraltar, but also crosses Mediterranean on broader front. Most Palearctic birds occur in E and NE Africa, relatively common W Ethiopia on Sudan border; scarce south of equator and W Africa. Individuals from same brood have been recovered to southwest and southeast of Danish ringing site. Peak of southward migration at Bosphorus mid- to end-Sept, present E Africa Oct–Apr. Peak return migration Mar–Apr, *c*. 2 weeks later than White Stork.

Southern African population remains mainly in breeding areas, but moves locally outside breeding season, e.g. from high to lower altitudes, and to marshes, rivers and estuaries some distance from breeding localities. No general northward winter movement noted in southern Africa. Transvaal population breeding in highlands migrates to low veld in non-breeding season (summer) then frequenting larger rivers.

When feeding behaves much as White Stork, walking about slowly and stabbing at suitable prey, but feeds mainly in shallow water. Is reported (Portugal) to shade water with wings, standing with wings open, then darting forward to seize fish in manner of several other storks; this not reported in Africa.

In flight can soar well, but easily rises from ground by flapping, and is much less dependent on thermals than White Stork to gain height. Roosts on cliff or trees, either alone or with mate; and in breeding season in southern Africa on nesting cliff. Is active most of daylight, but rests beside water when not feeding, often for hours.

Food. Mainly fish, caught in shallow water; some amphibia, crabs, small reptiles, a few small mammals and nestling birds. Is much less dependent than White or Abdim's Stork on large insects, and does not normally associate with locust swarms or outbreaks of army worm (*Spodoptera*). Catches some grasshoppers and other large insects in grassland. Young fed mainly on fish. Fish are normally caught with a quick stabbing motion of bill.

Breeding Habits. Very well known; studied more fully in Palearctic than in southern Africa. Not known to breed NW Africa. In Palearctic, breeds mainly in trees, but in South Africa normally on cliffs and, rarely, in trees growing on cliffs; once recorded on nest of Hamerkop *Scopus umbretta* and often adopts cliff nests of large raptors. In southern Africa invariably a solitary nester, with nests spaced *c*. 8 km apart when available sites not limited. Recorded nesting from near sea level to at least 2000 m in Lesotho Highlands. Lack of cliff nest-sites often limits population in otherwise suitable habitat.

♂ may arrive first at nest, but often both arrive together. Since solitary nesting requires no repulsion of others, little threat display at nest. Mutual displays include ♂ performing 'head-shaking crouch' on nest in incubating posture at approach of ♀. When ♀ alights, execute mutual up-down display, heads first raised, then lowered towards nest, sometimes with bill-clattering. In mutual greeting, white undertail-coverts may be con-

spicuously spread. Pair may also stand horizontally, wings slightly depressed, quickly tossing head up and down, at same time depressing, widely spreading, and raising and lowering white undertail-coverts, keeping black tail feathers closed. These displays are unlike those of White Stork. Mutual displays begin about 2 weeks before egg-laying, continue as long as pair encounter each other on nest. At copulation ♂ walks round ♀, who adopts horizontal stance; ♂ then mounts slowly from behind. No calls heard at nest in southern Africa, but bill-clattering recorded (W. Tarboton, pers. comm.).

NEST: large stick structure, used year after year. Rather loose flattish mass, up to 2 m across by 0·5 m thick depending on site, with shallow central cup often lined with 'resurrection plant' *Xerophyta* (= *Vellozia*). Normally easily distinguished from raptors' nests by profuse white droppings on rock wall behind. Built by both sexes, who may pair for life.

EGGS: usually 2–4 (southern Africa, 2–5), laid at 2-day intervals; mean (90) 2·78 (SAOSNRC). Dull white, long ovals. SIZE: (47) 60–74 × 45–56 (69·0 × 48·7); WEIGHT: *c*. 86.

Laying dates: Cape Aug–Sept; Transvaal, Orange Free State, Natal, Lesotho June–Sept, peaking July; Zimbabwe Mar–Aug, peaking June–July (27/37 records) Malawi July; Zambia May–June. Lays mainly in winter or cool dry season; in Cape in spring.

Both sexes incubate; nest-relief by day accompanied by mutual displays. When one incubating, other is far away foraging. ♀ probably incubates at night. Incubation period: not recorded South Africa; in Europe 35–38 days, possibly more.

Young hatch asynchronously; helpless, require close attention days 1–10. At 25 days can shuffle on tarsi and defaecate over nest-edge, but cannot stand. Feathers have appeared through down by 30–35 days, and by 45 days mainly feathered, can stand and walk about. Fledging period: Europe 63–71 days, southern Africa similar. Young reported to be fed directly at first on food regurgitated by adult, but this probably erroneous, as in all storks adult regurgitates food into nest where it is picked up by young (M. P. Kahl, pers. comm.).

One or both parents remain on nest entire time days 1–15; thereafter one parent normally on guard, shading or standing with chicks, while other is away foraging. Brooding in first 7 days almost continuous, but thereafter largely reduced by day, ceasing about 30 days after hatch. Parents continue to roost or perch near nest even when young are large.

Young leave nest on their own, soon becoming independent of parents. Broods 1–3 may be reared; little detailed data on productivity, but in 24 pair/years, Transvaal, 4 years no breeding, 39 young reared in 20 breeding years; 1·95 young per pair which bred, similar to or better than Palearctic records (31–92% of eggs laid producing young: Cramp and Simmons 1977).

References
Cramp, S. and Simmons, K. E. L. (1977).

Plate 12

(Opp. p. 163)

Ciconia abdimii Lichtenstein. Abdim's Stork; White-bellied Stork. Cigogne d'Abdim.

Ciconia abdimii Lichtenstein, 1823. Verz. Doubl., p. 76. Dongola, Sudan.

Range and Status. Intra-tropical trans-equatorial migrant, breeding from Somalia, Ethiopia, Uganda and NW Kenya to Senegal, migrating in non-breeding season, mainly east and south commonly to the Zambezi and Transvaal, less often to Cape Province. Common, locally very abundant, in very large flocks. Population probably stable.

Ciconia abdimii

Description. ADULT ♂: head, neck, back and upperparts of wings black glossed purple and green. Lower back, uppertail-coverts, underside from breast to belly and inner underwing-coverts white. Wing- and tail-feathers black, primaries glossed greenish. Bill pale green, tip red; eye brown; bare skin on face grey-blue, red in front of eye and below bill; legs and feet dull green; a 'garter' round tibio-tarsal joint red. ♀ similar, somewhat smaller, recognizable when pair together. ADULT ♂ and ♀ (breeding): assume bright blue base of bill, blue bare skin on forehead; other soft parts become brighter coloured, bill yellowish. SIZE: wing, ♂ and ♀ 400–475; tail, 167–205; tarsus, 117–136; bill, 103–127 (that of ♂ deeper, thicker at base).

IMMATURE: duller, browner than adult, less glossy. Bill and legs darker, duller coloured.

DOWNY YOUNG: pale grey or whitish.

Field Characters. A small, intensely gregarious stork, rarely seen singly, usually in large to enormous flocks of up to 10,000. Distinguished from Black Stork *C. nigra* by white lower back and uppertail-coverts, green bill and legs, with red garter at tibio-tarsal joint; and by gregarious habits. Otherwise unmistakable.

Voice. Not recorded. Normally silent except at breeding localities. At nest utters a weak double whistle 'heep-heep' in 'up-down' mutual display, followed by bill-clattering with bill pointed skywards.

General Habits. Well known. Gregarious, rarely seen in groups of less than 10, usually far larger flocks; often associates with White Stork *C. ciconia*. Basically terrestrial, feeding in open grassland, pastures, cultivation, and normally unafraid of men, who rightly regard it as beneficial. When available, congregate in large numbers near locust swarms or outbreaks of army worm (*Spodoptera*) caterpillars; attends grass fires. Otherwise spreads out over wide expanses of country, each bird foraging singly for some hours, then rejoining others to rest, preen and roost. Near midday flocks often soar to great height, soaring effortlessly, almost invisible, often later returning to same feeding area; such flights possibly have thermoregulation functions.

Movements are strongly seasonal and ensure that this stork rarely spends much time in dry conditions. After breeding in the wet season in the northern tropics May–Aug, moves first east then south (West African populations), or south (East African populations), often in huge flocks through the equatorial 2-season rainfall belt in Sept–Oct, arriving in the southern tropics early in the rains, Nov. Remains in southern range till Mar, when rains decrease, then moves north again through E Africa about the beginning of the long rains, Mar–Apr. Reaches breeding quarters in northern tropics late in dry season or as heavy rains commence, usually Apr–May. In Senegal birds arrive in Apr before rains have begun and leave Oct–Nov, apparently spending little of the dry season there, apart from scattered records. Some may migrate right across the main forest belt without stopping, or may alight and feed on e.g. airfields. Further details of movements desirable, but W African birds first move east and then south, or travel southeast direct across the forest, which is seldom observed.

Although they can fly with sustained flapping flight for several km if necessary, they habitually use thermals, like White Storks, to rise to great heights and then glide on. Can cross wide bodies of water by flapping, with alternate glides. Often descend to feed in selected areas from great height, with wings half-closed, swerving from side to side and alighting with a short run. When not feeding gather beside pools, water-holes, wells or swamps. Roost in trees, or on rock cliffs. Leave roost soon after dawn when in feeding areas, but on migration may await thermals before taking off for more sustained flights. Descend to feed some time during the day when migrating, except possibly when crossing forests.

Food. Especially grasshoppers, locusts, crickets and other large insects. Locusts are now less available through control, but this has apparently had no serious effect on population. Feeds on swarms of Army Worm (*Spodoptera*) caterpillars when available. Feeding on swarms, gobbles insects as fast as possible until gorged. When in more open formation walks steadily along, snapping up items as seen, sometimes running a few paces. Takes a few mice, frogs, lizards, small fish, molluscs, crabs, but mainly dependent on insects in grasslands.

A

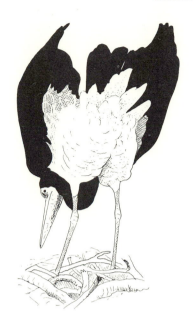

B

Breeding Habits. Well known in early part of cycle only. Breeds in small or large colonies, sometimes singly, sometimes associated with other large birds such as Marabous *Leptoptilos crumeniferus* or Pink-backed Pelican *Pelecanus rufescens* in same tree. Colonies do not normally exceed 20 pairs and are usually widely scattered. Frequently breeds in association with man in villages, and is welcomed by African tribesmen in breeding range as harbinger of rains.

♂♂ arrive first, re-occupying old nests if available, or selecting a new site. When ♀ arrives, ♂ does 'head-shaking crouch' in nest with wings part-opened, bill lowered towards structure, wagging head rapidly from side to side (see **A** and **B**). If ♀ alights, both perform mutual 'up-down' greeting displays, with wings widely spread, bill first pointing downwards, whistling, then raising bill vertically and clattering 8–15 times. Such mutual displays continue whenever one alights on the nest with the other, or at intervals when both are present. With ♀ present, ♂ brings most nesting material, while she remains on structure. Egg-laying follows within 10–14 days.

NEST: most often in trees, sometimes on cliffs (e.g. on island in Lake Shala, Ethiopia), occasionally actually on huts, the basket-like structures being made for them (Lake Chad: Salvan 1967). Used repeatedly if it does not collapse, not necessarily by same birds. 1–1·5 m in diameter and 20–30 cm thick, made of large sticks, lined with grass and some green leaves. Sticks are gathered from the ground, usually near colony, some-times some distance away, or stolen from nests of other birds, or other storks in the colony. Material may be added through most of the breeding cycle.

EGGS: usually 2–3, sometimes only 1, usually laid at 2-day, sometimes 3-day, intervals; mean (16 clutches) 2·2. Chalky white, soon becoming stained, green inside when held up to light. SIZE: 54·6–64·8 × 40·8–45·3 (60·4–43·1); also recorded (41) 56·2–64·1 × 40·1–45·8 (59·6 × 43·3) (Serle 1943), and (21) 55–63·5 × 39·7–47·1 (58·3 × 42·5) (Schönwetter 1960); WEIGHT: *c.* 58.

Laying dates: earliest laying occurs, W Kenya Jan–Mar; usually May in main parts of range at height of early rains. Both sexes incubate, share not established in detail. Nest-relief accompanied by mutual 'up-down' displays.

Incubation begins with 2nd egg. Period: (in captivity) 30–31 days (Bigalke 1948).

Young light grey or whitish; forehead black; completely downy up to 15 days. Fledging period probably *c.* 50–60 days, and entire cycle from nest-building to flight of young *c.* 90–100 days. Southward movement of young and adults could begin from Aug onwards. Nest losses occur through fighting at nests when too close together. Small young said to be fed by regurgitation, later pick up food dropped in nest. Better details of all stages of breeding cycle after egg-laying needed.

Reference
Kahl, M. P. (1972a).

Ciconia episcopus (Boddaert). **Woolly-necked Stork. Cigogne épiscopale.**   **Plate 12**

Ardea episcopus Boddaert, 1783. Table Planches Enlum., p. 54; Coromandel Coast.   (Opp. p. 163)

Range and Status. Resident tropical Africa south of Sahara to South Africa; aquatic and marine habitats. Generally uncommon to rare in most areas, but population probably stable.

Description. *C. e. microscelis* (Gray), ADULT ♂: forehead white, woolly; crown dark blue, streaked white on occiput. Neck covered with soft white woolly feathers. Back, wings, breast and sides black, glossed bluish on wings, purplish on mantle and below. Belly and specialized long undertail-coverts white.

Ciconia episcopus

Wing-feathers black. Tail forked, shorter than stiff undertail-coverts, black. Bill black, red along culmen; bare facial skin grey; eye dark red; legs black. Sexes alike, little size difference. SIZE: wing, 440–485; tail, 180–214; tarsus, 140–171; bill, 135–168. WEIGHT: unrecorded.

IMMATURE: lacks white forehead, duller, browner generally than adult.

DOWNY YOUNG: grey, bill black, red at tip, legs black. Eye dark brown.

Field Characters. A rather large, mainly black stork, distinguished from all others by white woolly neck, black bill and legs. Could only be confused with Black Stork *C. nigra*, but has white neck, black bill and legs. Not gregarious like Abdim's Stork *C. abdimii*; found mainly near water.

Voice. Not recorded. Largely silent; at nest said to make raucous calls and bisyllabic whistles, very like calls of Abdim's Stork in 'up-down' display. Young, begging, utter a sound 'like a file being used on a metal pipe'. Infrequent bill-clattering at e.g. nest-relief.

General Habits. Little known. In most of range an uncommon, usually solitary species preferring water-sides, either freshwater or marine; in E Africa commonest along sea coast, rare inland. Normally seen in pairs or solitary, rarely in small flocks. On migration in flocks of 6–65 birds to as many as several hundred in Zaïre (K. Curry-Lindahl, pers. comm.). Apparently sometimes in large flocks of up to 200 near southern extremity of range (Zimbabwe). Although uncommon, is widespread; may appear in almost any aquatic habitat. Also sometimes seen in grasslands. Avoids deeply forested country, even when water available, except during migration when visits clearings in the Congo lowland rainforest (K. Curry-Lindahl, pers. comm.); prefers wooded areas.

Apparently mainly resident, but some certainly migrate, though movements not well documented. In W Africa moves irregularly north and south between northern and southern savannas, avoiding rains in wetter areas. Passes through Darfur Apr–May moving north. Southern African records suggest southward movement Apr–June (early dry season) and northward migration Feb–Mar, perhaps of tropical African populations.

Feeds at low tide on E African coastal coral reefs and mudflats in creeks. Alternatively, may feed in grassland near coast (e.g. Mombasa Airport). Also in river flood plains, swamps, near small rivers, ponds and dams; perhaps more inclined to feed in grasslands in southern part of range. Attends grass fires to feed on burned insects, and recorded at carrion. When feeding, walks slowly and sedately, picking up small items. Spends long periods standing still, resting. Roosts in trees, pairs often using the same tree night after night when resident in certain localities.

Food. Mainly animal, especially large insects and larvae, molluscs, crabs, some fish, frogs, lizards. Oil palm fibres found in stomachs; not well documented. Young at one nest were fed toads, a crab, and many larvae of an aquatic hover-fly (Anthony 1977).

Breeding Habits. Well known. Solitary, but sometimes more than one pair fairly close together. Nests on trees; site repeatedly used if not disturbed. In contrast to many storks, shy and easily disturbed when nesting.

♂ probably arrives first, takes possession of old nest if any; mate arrives up to 1 month later, sometimes at same time. No obvious nuptial displays recorded, and recent observations do not substantiate spectacular display flights reported. Pair feed together near nest, visiting it at intervals. In possible precopulation display ♂ and ♀ walk round on nest, necks bent, heads and bills touching, preening each other and bobbing heads; actual copulation not observed. On analogy with Black Stork, specialized undertail-coverts should have some display function but none recorded.

NEST: often built on lateral limb of large shady tree, 30–50 m above ground. Large stick structure, *c.* 1 m across by 0·3 m deep, lined with finer twigs and dry grass. Both sexes build and continue to add nesting material well into fledging period; nests may be abandoned because of disturbance, or a new nest built and not used. Care needed in observation at this season.

EGGS: 2–4, usually 3–4, laid at intervals of 2–5 days. Dull white, sometimes nest-stained. SIZE: 60–67 × 41·2–43·2, mean (4) 63·5 × 42·4; WEIGHT: calculated 59, actual (2) 55 (Anthony 1977).

Laying dates: Zululand June–Aug (dry); Natal Nov; Zimbabwe Sept (dry); Zambia Aug–Sept (dry); Uganda Nov, Dec, Feb, Mar (dry); N Nigeria Jan (dry). Throughout range apparently lays in dry season, often late, producing flying young in following rains.

Incubation begins with 1st egg; by both sexes, with nest-relief about every 4 h by day. Often not accompanied by any ceremony, but sometimes sitting bird, observing mate approaching, clatters bill; when relief arrives, both stand, clatter bills and move heads up and down, sitting bird also opening wings. Such ceremonies uncommon, resemble those of Black Stork. Incubation period: 30–31 days.

Young hatch at intervals, but despite wide size difference, apparently no sibling aggression. Runts may be successfully reared 10 days after others flown. When first hatched body grey, neck buff; at 7–10 days bodies darker, neck white; at 15 days first feathers emerge on crown; at 20 days wing and back feathers; thereafter black and grey. At 33 days feathers well developed, can move about on nest; much mutual preening. Day 40 onwards, move out onto branches, exercise wings. Well developed chicks fly clumsily at 55 days, but weaker chicks may not until 65 days. Broods of up to 4 may be reared.

An adult normally remains on or near nest up to day 30; thereafter young left largely alone. Both adults attend young. Large young out of nest return to solicit adult arriving or flying past with 'filing' begging call, and head bobbing up and down. Feeds apparently rather rare, irregular; good details of feeding behaviour lacking.

Young and adults remain roosting near nest for *c.* 21 days after flight; young then disperse, not accompanied by parents. Scanty records suggest breeding success *c.* 1·5 young/pair/year, with broods 1–4 recorded; may have been reduced by human interference or predation, in cases known.

Reference
Scott, J. A. (1975).

Ciconia ciconia (Linnaeus). White Stork. Cigogne blanche.

Ardea ciconia Linnaeus, 1758. Syst. Nat. (10th ed.), p. 142; Sweden.

Plate 12

(Opp. p. 163)

Range and Status. Palearctic migrant and resident. Breeds Palearctic from Netherlands to E Russia and China, including NW Africa from Tunisia to Morocco; occasional sporadic breeder South Africa. Still locally common to abundant, or very abundant, but decreasing in most of Palearctic breeding range, especially temperate Europe from Holland to Switzerland. Locally very abundant winter migrant to Africa, some not passing equator; a few immatures or injured stragglers may summer in Africa. May have been adversely affected in winter range by toxic sprays used for locust control.

Description. *C. c. ciconia* (Linnaeus): Europe and Africa. ADULT ♂: head, body and secondary wing-coverts white; elongated chest feathers forming ruff. Scapulars, primary coverts and wing-feathers and alula black, glossed green or purple. Bill bright red; eye brown; legs bright red. Sexes alike, ♀ slightly smaller with thinner bill. SIZE: wing, ♂ 536–630, ♀ 530–590, av. 580 ♂ and ♀; tail, ♂ and ♀ 218–251 (227); tarsus, ♂ and ♀ 213–225 (220); bill, ♂ 150–190, ♀ 140–170; wing-span, 1550–1650 , ♂♂ larger. WEIGHT: 2610–4400 (3571), ♀ 2275–3900 (3325).
IMMATURE: shorter bill than adult; bill black with reddish base, eye grey, legs dull red.
DOWNY YOUNG: white, showing black bar on wings; bill black, iris grey, legs greyish yellow.

Field Characters. A large stork distinguished from all others in Africa by mainly white plumage contrasting strongly with black wing-feathers. Red bill distinguishes it from Yellow-billed Stork *Mycteria ibis*, which also has red legs. Immatures have darker, shorter bills, duller red legs, but normally occur with adults.

Voice. Recorded (2a). Adults practically mute, can utter only a weak hiss. Young utter begging call resembling mewing of cat, cheeping sounds and harsh hissing. Bill-clattering by adults, especially in mutual display; young also clatter bills from downy stage.

General Habits. Well known. In Africa principally a Palearctic migrant, entering Africa either via Gibraltar

Ciconia ciconia

or through Bosphorus and Suez; seldom crosses Mediterranean. Travels in large flocks, circling on thermals or up-currents to gain height, then gliding until another thermal permits lost height to be regained. Flocks settle in grasslands to feed, spreading out into looser formation or breaking into smaller groups. Roosts gregariously in trees at night and normally only flies when thermals permit, but may feed close to night-time roost without flying far.

W European, Iberian and NW African breeding populations winter W Africa from Mali to N Nigeria, apparently crossing Sahara non-stop on broad front. Population breeding east of Alsace in Europe and in Middle East travel via Bosphorus to Sudan–Somalia and south to Cape Province. Relative numbers *c.* 60,000 for western and 350,000 for eastern populations, based on counts.

Migrant flocks enter Africa late Aug–early Oct, movement Sept. Eastern population reaches southern Africa Nov, most remaining till Feb. Return migration peaks Gibraltar and Bosphorus late Feb–early Mar; most have left southern Africa by late Feb, some remaining till Mar; still common Kenya in Mar. A few remain all Palearctic summer Apr–Sept. Breeding populations in NW Africa arrive early Feb, laying at latest Algeria early Apr.

When feeding, spreads out through grassland and walks steadily along, striking prey at intervals. Feeds rapidly, taking up to 45 large items/h or 30 small items/min. At abundant food sources, especially locust hopper swarms, formerly concentrated in large numbers; this now seldom occurs, however, because of effective locust control. Habit of associating with locusts may have led to ingestion of toxic substances, perhaps accelerating rate of decrease, but modern locust control methods less likely to have adverse effect. When satisfied, flocks again gather, if available, often near water and rest until feeding again; avoids feeding in hottest hours of day.

Food. Entirely animal, including especially mice, small reptiles (snakes, lizards) amphibia, fish, large insects (especially Orthoptera). Occasionally, young of ground breeding birds, scorpions, molluscs (in some areas important). Diet varies according to availability, but in Africa large insects (especially grasshoppers and locusts) probably more important than large items. In wet conditions takes many frogs, tadpoles, but in most areas large insects predominate. Universally regarded as highly beneficial by Africans and Europeans alike and, with Abdim's Stork *C. abdimii*, known as 'locust-bird'.

Breeding Habits. Little known in Africa; intimately known in Europe. African behaviour probably similar to European summarized below.

In Europe and N Africa nests are placed on buildings, pylons, huts, or artificial structures specially erected, occasionally on trees. Same site used year after year, not necessarily by same pair. In Morocco, nests on low grass huts 4–5 m above ground to minarets, or tall pylons up to 30 m above ground; usually solitary, but sometimes in loose colonies, or several nests close together. South African nests all in trees.

♂ arrives first, takes possession of nest and may accept first ♀ to arrive, often but not always mate of previous year, suggesting faithfulness to site rather than partner. ♂ vigorously defends site from other ♂♂ and juveniles. Displays frequently, performing 'up-down' with bill-clattering, in which head thrown up and back, sometimes touching back (see **A**), and then returned forward more slowly, clattering continuously, usually ending by touching nest material. In threat to other ♂♂, wings partly opened, moved slowly up and down. When it sees ♀, especially if a stranger, ♂ performs 'head-shaking crouch' at nest. If ♀ alights, both perform up-down with bill-clattering. Copulation occurs almost at once, ♂ and ♀ walking round slowly until ♀ stops, allowing ♂ to mount. He maintains balance by waving wings, and she nibbles his neck feathers during act, accompanied by soft bill-clattering. Later, mutual display by both sexes occurs repeatedly on arrival of one or other at nest, with up-down and bill-clattering. This continues throughout cycle, more intense in earlier stages.

A

NEST: large pile of sticks, reeds, earth, 1–2 m high and 80–150 cm across, relatively small when new, increasing with age. New nest can be built in 8 days. Built by both sexes, ♂ beginning repair when he arrives. Building continues through entire cycle and even after young fledged. Material gathered from up to 500 m away.

EGGS: 1–7, usually 2–5, laid at intervals of 1–4 days; Holland mean (80) c. 3·9; SW Cape (22) 2·95 (SAOSNRC). Dull chalky white. SIZE: 65–82 × 47–56 (73 × 52); WEIGHT: 96–119 (111).

Laying dates: N Africa, spring, beginning Feb, latest laying early Apr; SW Cape Sept–Nov.

Young hatch asynchronously. Brooded almost continuously by either parent days 1–10, thereafter mainly shaded. At first largely helpless, cannot stand or move much, becoming more active after 10 days. Can stand at day 22, but flap wings from day 14. Defaecate into nest to day 15, thereafter ejecting clear. Feathers appear through down at about 30 days, feathered by 45 days, thereafter usually left alone in nest. Fledging period: 58–64 days, Europe.

Either parent feeds or broods or tends young by day, perhaps ♀ by night. Bird not brooding returns with food at intervals and often changes over with mutual bill-clattering. Food at first dropped into nest and picked up by young; after day 12 young may sometimes sieze parental bill and feed from it direct. Feeds given every hour days 1–10, every 2 h days 10–15, thereafter less frequent.

Young leave nest alone; dependent on parents another 7–20 days, then leave area. Parents remain another 15–30 days. Breeding success variable, 12–20% failing in good years, 50% in bad. Brood size: 1·3–2·6 av. 2·0, *c.* 50% of eggs laid. Few South African records suggest similar success rate. Some young (*c.* 13%) first breed at 2–3 years, most (87%) at 4–7 years. Most breed within 25 km of natal site. Birds breeding first at 4–7 years are more successful than younger birds, and breeding success is better in years when adults return early. Probably 30% of young die before 2 years old; thereafter av. 21% mortality. Oldest ringed bird, 26 years. Comparable data from NW Africa needed. 1 ringed young from South Africa recovered on Tanzania–Zambia border, 3300 km from natal site (McLachlan 1963).

Reference
Cramp, S. and Simmons, K. E. L. (1977).

Genus *Ephippiorhynchus* Bonaparte

Very large, tall, slender storks of aquatic habitats; plumage black and white. Bill long, slender, laterally compressed, brightly coloured in the African species *E. senegalensis* with a bright yellow frontal shield or saddle. Legs very long. 2 species, one African, the other Asian extending to Australia.

Ephippiorhynchus senegalensis (Shaw). Saddle-billed Stork; African Jabiru. Jabiru du Sénégal.

Plate 12

Mycteria Senegalensis Shaw, 1800. Trans. Linn. Soc., 5, p. 35, pl. 3; Senegal.

(Opp. p. 163)

Range and Status. Resident throughout tropical Africa and warmer parts of southern Africa. Favours aquatic habitats, normally in open or semi-arid country rather than forest, but may occur there. Widespread, but never more than frequent to common, often uncommon. Population probably stable, but could easily become threatened.

Description. ADULT ♂: head and neck black, glossed green, purplish on base of neck. Base of neck, back, uppertail-coverts, marginal wing-coverts, and whole underside white. Upper and underwing-coverts and scapulars black, glossed green, contrasting strongly with white primaries and secondaries; tail black, glossed green. Bill long, slightly upturned, blade-shaped; distal (20 cm) bright red, a black band across centre, basally bright red, surmounted by a bright yellow frontal shield, edged tiny black feathers. A pair of small pendent yellow or red wattles ('stirrups') at base of bill (in both sexes). Eye brown; legs black, with a red 'garter' at tibio-tarsal joint and red feet. ♀ differs in having a bright yellow eye and is obviously 10–15% smaller. SIZE: (measurements not separated in published works) wing, 600–670; tail, 250–288; tarsus, 311–365; bill, 273–334; yellow shield, 48–85; span, up to 2·7 m.

IMMATURE: 1st-year birds largely grey, lacking bright colours or any obvious frontal shield above grey bill. 2nd-year birds are duller, greyer versions of adult, without a bright yellow frontal shield, but bill dull red and black.

DOWNY YOUNG: white; bill short, grey or black.

Ephippiorhynchus senegalensis

Field Characters. The tallest African stork, spectacular in adult plumage, as large as a Marabou *Leptoptilos crumeniferus*, but slimmer, neater, more graceful. Adults unmistakable, strikingly black and white, especially on wing. 1st-year young resemble young of Yellow-billed Stork *Mycteria ibis* in having grey plumage and grey bills without shield, but are much larger; 2nd-year immatures, again, unmistakable. Normally solitary, at most in small groups.

Voice. Recorded (6). Adults apparently completely silent. Young emit 'weak vocalizations' (Kahl 1973); bill-clattering reported in related Black-necked Stork *E. asiaticus*, not heard in Saddle-billed Stork.

General Habits. Well known. Widespread, may occur in any aquatic habitat, on large or small rivers, lake shores, flood plains, swamps, either alkaline or fresh as long as they contain fish. Normally rather shy and wary, but can become very tame, allowing close approach when accustomed to e.g. vehicles in national parks.

Forages singly or in pairs. Fishes (i) by standing still in water and stabbing any fish that come within range in manner of a heron; (ii) by walking about in reeds and shallow water, repeatedly jabbing bill into water, fish contacted is then seized; (iii) repeated probing in mixed weeds and dirty water where prey invisible, sometimes stirring with one foot in manner of *Mycteria* spp.; bill then undoubtedly has tactile function, closing rapidly on unseen prey. Preferred methods are (i) and especially (ii), but is more versatile feeder than sometimes supposed.

Generally resident in favoured areas, not migratory, though to some extent nomadic, moving from place to place in e.g. flood plains or large expanses of swamp. May be basically territorial where resident, not tolerating other pairs within home range. Roosts on trees, sometimes near nest-tree; pair usually roosts together even if apart by day. 1st- and 2nd-year young often remain in parental home range, tolerated by adults until adult themselves. Takes flight easily from ground with quick, powerful wing-flaps and, once aloft, soars easily, rising on thermals in manner of other storks.

Food. Principally fish, caught either by stabbing in open water or by seizing amongst vegetation and shallow water. Can swallow up to at least 500 g. Catfish often taken when they surface for air. Snips off spines of large catfish before swallowing (Morris 1979). Also frogs, small reptiles, small mammals, reputedly young birds, some molluscs, probably insects. Fish normally washed, and large ones taken to the bank before swallowing head first. Drinks water after swallowing.

Breeding Habits. Well known. Nests singly, never in colonies. Same site resorted to annually, though does not necessarily breed each year in known localities. Nests invariably in trees near water, usually thorny acacias, sometimes other species, but normally right on top of tree in full sunlight, not within canopy. Tree may be quite low if surrounded by inaccessible swamp, but most nests are 20–30 m above ground. Many sites used for consecutive years.

Pair-bond is probably lifelong; courtship unspectacular, or non-existent. Pairs feed together near nest, and one may do 'flap-dash', dashing through water with wings spread, showing striking contrasts, returning to mate and standing with wings spread for some moments. Other courtship details lacking, but pairs probably infrequently perform 'up-down' on nest (as in related Indian species).

NEST: large, flattish structure on top of tree, c. 2 m wide by 0·5 m thick, cup large enough to hide sitting bird completely. Both sexes build. Constructed of sticks, lined with reeds, with much earth included, and finer material (sedges). When nest complete, copulation occurs; no spectacular ceremony, ♂ merely mounts, legs crooked, tibio-tarsal joints hanging down, so ♀ takes whole weight; duration 5–7 s.

EGGS: 1–5, usually 2–3; mean (54 clutches) 2·8 (SAOSNRC). Laying interval not recorded, probably at least 2 days (based on varying size of young). Dull white, slightly glossy, slightly pitted. SIZE: 75·6–81·3 × 56·0–58·0; av. (6) 80·0 × 57·0; WEIGHT: c. 146 (Schönwetter 1960).

Laying dates: Natal Mar, July; Transvaal Mar–July; Zimbabwe Jan–Apr, July, peaking Feb–Mar (20/22 records); Zambia Mar–May, Aug; Kenya–Uganda Jan, Apr, May, June, Oct; Ethiopia possibly Oct, Nov. Most southern African records (28/33) are late in rains, in E Africa both in rains and dry season; laying perhaps timed so that young leave nest late in a dry season.

Both sexes incubate, in spells of several hours, varying from 1 h 25 min to 5 h 50 min; sometimes both are on nest together. ♂ may incubate more than ♀ by day and sometimes sits into dusk, but ♀ may take over just at dusk or ♂ may sit at night. When incubating, either may stand, turn round, resettle after looking briefly at eggs. No greeting ceremonies when mate passes in flight near nest. Incubation period: not accurately recorded, estimated 30–35 days (J. Hayes, unpub.).

Good details of chick development lacking. At hatch greyish white, helpless, unable to stand, continuously brooded by parent. At 45 days still largely downy, with dark feathers showing on wings, black bill; from now on left much alone. Fledging period not accurately recorded, estimated at least 70 days, possibly nearer 100. Breeding cycle possibly longer than that of Marabou.

At hatch either ♂ or ♀ may eat eggshells. Chicks brooded closely days 1–10. Fed by either parent by regurgitating food onto nest, chicks sometimes catch fish from adult's beak. Chicks are also watered, with water dribbled down parental bill. Food sometimes regurgitated into nest, then re-swallowed by attendant parent.

Breeding success not recorded. Does not necessarily breed annually. 1–2 young normally fly from average clutch of 3. Larger broods recorded South Africa, 4 plus 3 in successive years, Zimbabwe (Vernon 1975). Since non-breeding is frequent and some nests fail, overall breeding success probably not more than 1·0 young/pair/year, possibly averaging more in southern Africa.

Genus *Leptoptilos* Lesson

Very large to huge storks, bulky, clumsy-looking when on the ground. Distinguished from all others by nearly naked head and neck, sometimes brightly coloured; distensible air sacs on throat and upper back; bill long, strong, conical, but surprisingly light; a ruff of feathers at base of neck surrounding dorsal air sac; undertail-coverts fluffy, specialized (Marabou down). Wings are very long and adapted for soaring; tail relatively short. Largely terrestrial, feeding on carrion and scavenging, but also frequent in aquatic habitats. 3 tropical species, of which 2 Asian, 1 African.

Leptoptilos crumeniferus (Lesson). Marabou Stork; Marabou. Marabout d'Afrique

Plate 12

Ciconia crumenifera Lesson, 1831. Traité d'Orn, livr. 8, p. 585; Senegal.

Range and Status. Resident tropical Africa from Senegal–Somalia, south to Botswana; rare in South Africa. Breeds Botswana north to Ethiopia and Somalia and west to Senegal. Frequent to common in most of range, locally abundant or very abundant near large colonies and in towns. Probably increasing through association with humans, and scavenging on rubbish dumps; total Uganda population estimated 4000–5000 in 1971.

Description. ADULT ♂ (non-breeding): head and neck naked, mainly red or pink, with sparse filamentous black feathers. Ruff at base of neck white. Mantle, back, upperwing- and underwing-coverts slate-grey, coverts glossed green. Body below, white. Wing and tail black, glossed green. Bill horn-coloured to pinkish, mottled blackish; eye brown; legs black. 2 inflatable air sacs, 1 on throat long, pendent, reddish, other on upper back, normally hidden in ruff, orange-red when inflated. Sexes alike, ♂ larger. ADULT ♂ and ♀ (breeding): wing-coverts and back acquire waxy blue-grey bloom; secondary wing-coverts clearly bordered white; undertail-coverts enlarge, become more fluffy. Colours of bare skin intensify, becoming brighter red on neck and throat pouch, on head black in front of eye, magenta on occiput, with scabs of dried blood appearing like warty black skin round base of bill, and 2 lines of blackish warts ('earrings') extending from hindneck round ear. Sides of head orange-red, lower neck in front pink, behind pale blue. Colours of bare skin also often intensified in displays. SIZE: wing, ♂ 70·5–79·4 (74·5), ♀ 63·1–70·9 (67·8); tail, ♂ 27·8–35·8 (32·3), ♀ 24·0–30·2 (28·2); tarsus, 26·6–31·9 (29·3), ♀ 24·5–28·3 (26·6); bill, ♂ 27·9–34·6, ♀ 24·1–31·4; wing-span, ♂ av. 263 cm, ♀ 247 cm; ♂ max, 287 cm. WEIGHT: ♂ 5·6–8·9 kg (7·1), ♀ 4·0–6·8 (5·7). Adult bill length increases slowly with age; reputed spans of 4 m or over can be discounted.

IMMATURE: 1st-year bird has more black hairy feathers on head, wing feathers dark brown with little gloss; feathers of coverts with paler margins, appearing in rows. 2nd-year birds, flight feathers and coverts mainly brown, sometimes pale. Subadults develop black wing feathers, more or less glossed, becoming completely black and glossy in the 3rd year. Colours of bare skin in younger birds yellower or pinker, black round base of bill, fewer black spots on head and face; 'ear-rings' less pronounced. Mature young are smaller than adults in all dimensions by about 5% (Pomeroy 1977).

Field Characters. Unmistakable; a very large, bulky, heavy-bodied stork with bare neck, often with pendent throat pouch visible; long conical bill. Plumage black above, white below, legs black, but often whitened with dried excrement. Flies and soars with head and neck retracted, or extended on short flights. Distinguished from any soaring vulture by long, projecting bill and legs, white underside and underwing. Unlikely to be confused with any other stork when soaring, but dark underwing-coverts distinguish it from White Stork *Ciconia ciconia* and Yellow-billed Stork *Mycteria ibis*. Very much larger than either.

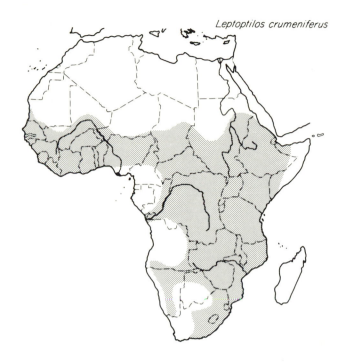

Leptoptilos crumeniferus

Voice. Recorded (2a, 19). Usually silent away from nest, apart from bill-clattering, usually associated with threat. At nest a variety of squealing, whistling, whining, or mooing calls and grunts, associated with various displays; a loud nasal 'Mwaaa' by adult threatening human intruder. Begging calls of small young, high-pitched chitter, developing at 2–3 weeks to hollow nasal squawks, later a hoarse stuttering nasal bray; in threat repelling adults, utter rapid, hiccuping distress calls, usually successful. Most sounds impossible to syllabize in any known language. Bill-clattering, loud, hollow-sounding, frequent both in threat and nuptial displays; young attempt it without making much sound.

General Habits. Intimately known. Usually more or less gregarious, sometimes single. Frequents both aquatic and terrestrial habitats, preferring open or semi-arid areas; rare within forested areas and true desert. Often associates with man near fishing villages and refuse tips, and sometimes breeds in villages. Roosts gregariously, at same site nightly, gathering from far around. Usually roosts for 14–16/24 h, from 1–2 h before dark to 1–2 h after sunrise in tropical localities; probably cannot fly far except on thermals and by gliding.

On rubbish dumps, lake shores and similar areas spends many hours standing almost still, occasionally pacing slowly a short distance. Often squats on breast, and when sun emerges on cool days turns back to it and spreads wings; at midday wings held horizontal. Spread wings also associated with threat displays. In commonest, attacker advances with jerky gait, bill pointed at opponent, back feathers erected, tail spread, throat pouch distended. Subordinate usually retreats, but if actually attacked with bill thrust forward and clattered, compresses feathers, raises head high, gapes and shakes head from side to side as if warding off opponent.

When taking wing from ground, lowers head and neck, takes a short run, then flaps to take off; from branches takes off with a single spring of bent legs. Flaps to gain access to thermals, or for short distances. With thermals, rises to great heights, becoming almost invisible, up to 1500 m or more above ground. Can cross large bodies of water (e.g. Lake Victoria) aided by thermals, or fronts of thunderstorms. In good thermal conditions, may be on wing for much of day, travelling long distances.

Frequents carrion in company with vultures in small numbers, ratio usually less than 1:10; but can rarely dominate these or carrion-eating eagles such as Tawny Eagles *Aquila rapax*, which may pirate food from it. At carcass normally stands on outskirts and runs in to snatch dropped morsels, but sometimes enters throng of vultures and tears at carcass with them. Steals scraps from all except Lappet-faced Vultures *Aegypius tracheliotus*. May remain with small vultures (Egyptian *Neophron percnopterus* and Hooded *Necrosyrtes monachus*) after larger vultures have left carcass, cleaning up scraps. On rubbish dumps not only cleans up scraps but kills rats that would otherwise infest them; therefore a valuable scavenger in many tropical towns.

Movements vary in different parts of Africa. Some appear almost permanently resident. Southern populations probably move north towards equator after breeding Apr–July, and northern populations move south after breeding Aug–Sept. In Uganda and Zaïre near equator southern and northern birds augment probably permanent populations, each at different seasons. In W Africa some, probably non-breeding birds move south into moister savannas in dry season Nov–Mar. Extent of west–east migration or movements, if any, unknown. Locally is nomadic, moving from one favourable feeding locality to another at any season (Pomeroy 1978b).

Food. Virtually any animal matter from termites to dead elephant. Probably originally fish, amphibia, crustacea and other aquatic organisms, and carrion. Carrion still important in places, nowadays greatly augmented by human scraps and refuse in towns, fishing villages and dumps of fish scraps. While normally a scavenger, can also be an active predator, catching rats and mice with swift snap. Kills adult Greater and Lesser Flamingoes (*Phoenicopterus ruber* and *Phoeniconais minor*) by walking along shore, causing flamingo flocks to pack in panic; Marabou then makes short flight and stabs flamingo in back. Once disabled, it is drowned, then torn to pieces and eaten by one or several Marabous in 3–4 min. Has serious adverse effect on colonies of Greater Flamingo by causing mass desertion (of up to 4500 pairs by 17 Marabous: Brown *et al.* 1973). Flamingoes tolerate and even repel 1–5 Marabous, but 6 or more cause mass desertion.

Often fishes somewhat like Yellow-billed Stork, walking in shallow water, bill submerged, partly open, probably locating prey by touch; or may repeatedly stab in water while walking. Also fishes by sight, seeing and stabbing prey. Birds, e.g. downy young flamingoes, always thoroughly soused underwater, then swallowed whole. Drinks after swallowing prey. Alate termites gobbled as they emerge, but beetles can be caught in flight; can make short agile runs in pursuit of prey. Bill is ill-adapted for tearing up large prey, but pieces are torn off by seizing body in bill-tip and shaking vigorously. Can swallow whole lumps of food of up to 1 kg.

Breeding Habits. Intimately known. Gregarious, breeding in colonies of normally 20–60, sometimes of several hundred, even several thousand pairs (Anderson 1949). Usually in trees, sometimes in towns or villages; some colonies on cliffs (Sudan, Tanzania). May associate especially with Pink-backed Pelican *Pelecanus rufescens*, less often with Yellow-billed Storks, occasionally with herons, cormorants. Same site is used annually, some colonies known for at least 50 years. May also change site in mid-season; several new or recent colonies associated with availability of human scraps from butcheries, or rubbish dumps.

Early in pair-formation, ♂ and ♀ threaten by angling body and neck forward and upward (see **A**), by spreading wings, erecting body and arching neck forward (**B**), by walking toward opponent with head and neck extended forward and clattering bill (**C**) and by flying at opponent with neck extended and clattering bill (**D**). When ♂ first takes up nest or suitable nest-site, performs 'swaying twig-grasping' display, in which he bends to touch nest or branch with bill, with dorsal air sac inflated, wings raised to produce depression in back; then sways to and fro 5–10 times in 3 s, lightly grasping twigs with bill (**E**). If ♀ attracted, she settles and gives 'balancing' display, wings fully opened, body horizontal, tail cocked, underwing-coverts fluffed, head low and bill vertical, uttering high-pitched squeals. ♂ may at first repel or attack her. She usually persists, however,

A

and both then perform many 'snap' displays, with bill slightly raised and snapped sharply once. This may be followed by mutual 'up-down', head thrown up to vertical, then brought slowly down to tibia or tarsi, wings arched, tail-coverts fluffed, dorsal sac inflated, accompanied at first by grunts, whistles, moos and, as head descends, by mutual bill-clattering (**F**). This remains commonest mutual display at nest thereafter. Copulation soon follows pair-formation. ♂ mounts from side, slowly, balancing with open wings; both lower bills to *c.* 45° below horizontal, ♂ clatters his vigorously, and ♀ utters series of low moans; copulation lasts av. 14·4 s (19 observations).

NEST: ♂ may collect first sticks during pair-formation, usually from ground, or from any available empty nest. Later, ♀ remains on nest while ♂ makes repeated trips, 6–8/h; bouts of stick-collecting interspersed with rests and mutual displays, ♀ occasionally brings sticks, but usually works those brought by ♂ into nest. New nest built in 7–10 days; a flat platform *c.* 1 m in diameter, 0·2–0·3 m thick, with shallow central cup, lined with smaller sticks and green leaves. May be 3–40 m above

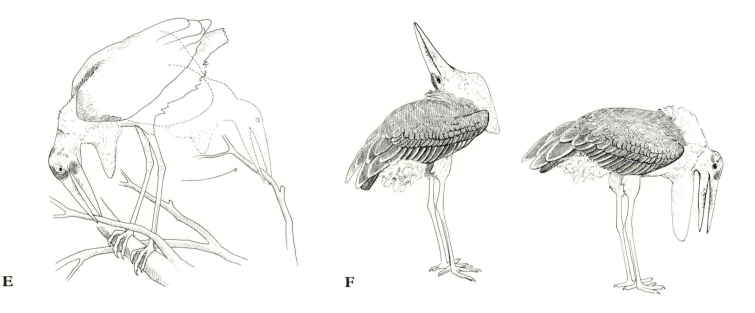

ground, usually 10–30. More sticks brought later throughout season, but most then brought by ♀. One or other adult normally remains at nest-site until after chicks have flown; even occupied nests would otherwise be robbed of sticks by others in colony.

EGGS: 1–4, usually 2–3, laid at intervals of 1–3 days; Okavango, Kenya, Uganda, Zimbabwe mean (108 clutches) 2·4. Dull chalky white, soon stained. SIZE: (22) 71–84·5 × 50–62 (79·1 × 55·6) (Schönwetter 1960; SAOSNRC); WEIGHT: calculated c. 138.

Laying dates: Zimbabwe June–Sept; Botswana July–Aug (dry); Zambia, S Tanzania June–July, height of dry season; W Kenya–Uganda Oct–Dec, peaking Nov, varying year to year occasionally later, up to Mar, in warmer of 2 dry seasons; Sudan Nov; Ethiopia–Somalia Oct–Nov (late rains—dry); W Africa Dec–Feb, dry season. In equatorial 2-season rainfall zone breeding cannot be completed in 1 short dry season; but in northern and southern tropics breeding usually begins in dry season and ends in rains. Young may fledge at end of dry season (E Kenya) or in height of rains (S Tanzania, Zambia) (Pomeroy 1978b).

Both sexes incubate for about 84% of daylight; ♂♂ 48%, ♀♀ 36%. ♂♂ incubate more often at night than ♀♀(c. 2·5:1). Incubation period: 29–31 days, av. 30·3 days (6 eggs in 4 different nests); hatch normally takes 24 h; 52–95% of eggs hatch, av. 72% (Kahl 1966a).

Small young weak, down sparse, brooded almost continuously day and night days 1–15, less on warm days. Newly hatched young weigh 94–96 g. Days 1–10 down sparse, pale grey; 2nd heavier snow-white down grows in c. 8 days, covering body by 20 days; entirely white down to 35 days. 36–50 days, black feathers growing in; days 51–65 become predominantly black, feathered, bare skin of face becomes rosy. 66–130 days, feathered, main growth is in flight feathers and muscle development. Can stand and flap wings at 17 days, hover over nest at 65 days, make short flights in tree day 95; 1st recorded flight from tree day 98, usually later. Small young in nest solicit parents for food by squatting on tarsi, with open wings and cocked tail, nodding head up and down, and chittering; this develops by degrees into movements resembling normal 'up-down', with loud hoarse nasal bray. Unattended chicks repel strange adults by squatting with tail cocked, giving rapid hiccuping distress call, 2/s; this usually succeeds, but if intruder persists young lunge with beaks, uttering loud rasping scream and could then be dangerous to humans examining nest.

Adults brood young almost continuously days 1–10. Thereafter brooding reduced, increasing in rain or cold weather, until little brooded after day 30; shaded in hot sun. Young may then be left alone in nest and can defend it, but usually a parent remains on or near nest to end of fledging period. Both sexes brood, tend and feed young, ♂♂ more than ♀♀ (55%, cf. 45% in 386 records). ♀ later spends more time guarding nest and may leave to forage herself when ♂ brings food. Food is regurgitated into nest and picked up by young; rarely, a scrap may be offered in bill-tip and taken by young. Most feeds occur between 10.00 h and 15.00 h, coinciding with daily thermal activity. Food requirement of young (estimated from captives) increases from under 100 g/day, days 1–10, to 500–600, days 60–65. Runts from clutch of 3 rarely reared (Kahl 1966a; Pomeroy 1978a).

Young make 1st flights at 95–115 days, but remain dependent on parents to 130 days or more. Feeding now reduced, but flying young at first return to nest to be fed 4–5 times daily; thereafter become independent. Fledged young among adult assemblies can barely compete, standing round edges, making occasional rushes to try to get a scrap; this behaviour is analogous to large vultures. Young fledged in early rains may also find amphibia easy to catch.

Breeding success: av. c. 0·9 young/nest in Uganda colonies; 36% of eggs laid in Kenya produced fledged young. However, only c. 50% (56%) of adults in population breed annually, so this equals effectively c. 1 young/4 adults/year. Age structures of population based on plumage (4566 birds): 601 juveniles, 1–2 years (13·16%); 703, 3–4 years (15·4%); adults 3263 (72%), of which 56% breed. Estimated mortality of young fledging to end year, 72%; in years 2–3, 28%/year; years 4 and after, av. 8%. First attain full adult plumage after 4 years, but not necessarily sexually mature; age at first breeding unknown. Maximum calculated age would exceed 25 years (Pomeroy 1978a).

References
Kahl, M. P. (1966a, b; 1971a).
Pomeroy, D. E. (1975; 1977; 1978a, b).

Family BALAENICIPITIDAE: Shoebill

Very large marsh birds, endemic to Africa, found locally in tropical swamps. Unique characters are a huge, swollen, bulbous bill tipped with strong hooked nail, the mandibles with sharp edges. Legs with very long toes, supporting the bird when walking on submerged vegetation. Plumage grey. Affinities rather obscure. Heron-like attributes include powder-down patches, flight with retracted neck and possibly some displays. Stork-like characters include breeding habits, many displays and defaecation on the tibiotarsal joint. Possible Pelecaniform attributes include the hooked bill-tip and some anatomical features. On balance, appears most closely related to storks, notably the Marabou *Leptoptilos crumeniferus*, which also flies with retracted neck, but is best retained in its own monotypic family. See Fischer (1970) for a general summary.

Genus *Balaeniceps* Gould

Balaeniceps rex Gould. Shoebill; Whale-headed Stork. Bec-en-sabot du Nil.

Balaeniceps rex Gould, 1850. Athenaeum, no. 1207, p. 1315; Upper White Nile.

Plate 12

(Opp. p. 163)

Balaeniceps rex

Range and Status. Sudd region of S Sudan west to Aweil area, east to Baro-Akobo Swamps of W Ethiopia, thence south through Uganda to Katanga in S Zaïre and Zambia (Bangweulu and Kafue flood plains); perhaps straggles to W Kenya, and recently sight-recorded Botswana (Mathews 1979). Locally frequent, even common, but generally threatened severely in Sudanese range by agricultural development, water diversion, competition for habitat from humans and livestock and, in particular, capture of young for zoos. Total numbers may not exceed 1500. Not directly persecuted by Sudanese or other African people, but nevertheless severely threatened.

Description. ADULT ♂: head grey to blue-grey, crown ashy. Above, generally ashy grey, slightly glossed greenish, feather margins paler; lesser wing-coverts paler grey, lanceolate feathers on lower neck with black shafts. Belly and undertail-coverts nearly white. Primaries dark slate-grey, becoming blackish near tips; secondaries slate, slightly glossed green. Bill enormously enlarged, bulbous, with central dorsal keel ending in large hook, mandibles sharp-edged, pinkish or yellowish, irregularly streaked darker; eye grey to bluish white, or pale yellow; legs blackish. Sexes alike, ♀ slightly smaller. SIZE: wing, *c.* 780; tail, 258; tarsus, 245; bill, 191.

IMMATURE: bill less swollen; plumage darker, rather more brown; otherwise similar.

DOWNY CHICK: silvery grey to white, lacking extremely enlarged bill, but with wide gape.

Field Characters. Unmistakable, a very large, grey, stork-like bird frequenting swamps, with huge bulbous swollen bill. In flight, head and neck retracted like a heron, not outstretched like storks; grey above and mainly grey below. Could only be confused with Goliath Heron *Ardea goliath*, but lacks any chestnut and has huge swollen bill.

Voice. Recorded (19). Normally silent. At nest utters a high-pitched whining or mewing call 'beeeeeeh'; young utter hiccuping begging calls. Bill-clattering by both sexes, individually distinguishable in tone, accompanied by shaking head from side to side.

General Habits. Well known. Frequents large freshwater swamps overgrown with vegetation, grasses, reeds and papyrus; rather rarely seen in open. Local within such habitat, not found throughout. Walks easily over submerged and floating vegetation, aided by long toes. Occasionally perches in trees, but normally roosts in swamps. Mainly or wholly diurnal, not fishing at night, except possibly in moonlight.

Basically solitary, though several may fish near one another in favoured places. No communal fishing (as reported), each bird fishing alone, though possibly close to others. Is active soon after dawn, but normally flies far only after thermals permit soaring flight, thus

resembling Marabou *Leptoptilos crumeniferus*. As far as is known is largely sedentary, each bird remaining in or near home range most of the year. Flood waters, however, make local movements to accessible fishing grounds necessary and may then be more gregarious, several congregating in small areas.

Spends most of its time among aquatic vegetation, rather rarely flying to other localities. In flight soars well with head and neck retracted like a heron, but otherwise resembles stork. Takes flight with a sharp spring from vegetation, and must flap heavily for some distance before locating thermals suited to soaring.

Preferred fishing sites are in floating or rooted vegetation on edges of open water channels, or channels with sparse emergent vegetation. Vegetation usually tall enough to hide Shoebill from below, but not above bird's back. Tall dense vegetation avoided, and floating vegetation must support Shoebill's weight. Forages also in shallow open water, sometimes away from water on moist ground covered with vegetation. Favoured feeding places are defended against other Shoebills; normally fishes alone but temporary gatherings near shallow drying pools occur without social behaviour (Guillet 1979).

Walks on aquatic vegetation very slowly and deliberately, often sinking in up to tibio-tarsal joint, sometimes deeper. At each pace foot is raised and folded, then advanced and outspread to support weight. Gait is slow, deliberate and stately. Fishing birds normally stand motionless for long periods, intently regarding water. When not fishing, may rest almost immobile for long periods, occasionally blinking or moving head, preening etc. Daily energy requirement is probably low.

When fishing, moves very slowly and quietly, deliberately placing feet, or stands motionless for 30 min or more. Normally holds head with beak pointing vertically downwards, facilitating binocular vision. When fish or other prey sighted, Shoebill thrusts head forward, tenses neck; when prey located, hurls whole body forward head first, wings outstretched. Open bill grabs prey located and vegetation together; vegetation is then separated from prey by working mandibles. Prey is often decapitated, sometimes swallowed head-first, with beak vertical. Cannot immediately recover and strike again if unsuccessful (Guillet 1979). After swallowing prey Shoebill invariably drinks water, scooping it and swallowing with mandibles tilted at 45°. Fishing method suggests that bill is an adaptation to catching fish or other prey among submerged vegetation rather than an indication of systematic relationships.

Food. Fish, frogs, water snakes, possibly some mammals and young waterbirds. Fish include especially lungfish, bichirs and catfish (which often surface to gulp air in stagnant water). Bill is not used (as reputed) to excavate aestivating lungfish from mud. Water snakes frequently taken, also young freshwater turtles, large amphibia. Small aquatic mammals rarely taken, and rumours of eating lechwe calves probably unfounded.

Breeding Habits. Very well known (Zambia). Nests singly, in swamps, not necessarily in tall vegetation. Sometimes several pairs in one suitable area, but well apart, not forming true colonies. Nests in floating vegetation, usually in deep water, but in Sudan sometimes solidly based on termite hills temporarily surrounded by flood water. Same area, sometimes same nest, used for many successive seasons.

Nuptial display in wild undescribed. Captives perform many stork-like displays, e.g. standing on nest and swaying side to side, stretching neck and beak, mandibulating nest material. Both sexes bring nest material, swaying from side to side. Mutual displays include: raising and lowering head (resembling 'up-down' of storks); bowing; mutual greeting with bill-clattering, as in storks. Soaring above nest-site may be advertisement display, but not well studied.

NEST: large flattish structure of any aquatic vegetation up to 2·5 m across, with upper part above water about 1 m across and shallow central cup. Continually added to throughout breeding season by both birds, it becomes sodden, sinking deeper unless on solid foundations. Nest material usually gathered within 10 m of nest, rarely brought from a distance. Surrounding vegetation normally tall enough to hide sitting bird, sometimes in tall papyrus, more often swamp grasses or sedges. Has been suggested that older, more experienced adults breed in the most remote sites, younger birds in more accessible places (Guillet 1978).

EGGS: 1–3, usually 2, laid at intervals of up to 5 days. In Sudan, 50% or more clutches, 1 egg only (A. Guillet, pers. comm.). Dull white when fresh, becoming stained in incubation. SIZE: (4) 80·1–90·0 × 56·9–63 (85·7 × 59·4); WEIGHT: c. 164.

Laying dates: Sudan, when flood waters in Nile Sudd subside; in Bahr el Ghazal region Oct–Nov; later, Feb in Al Buhayrat (main Nile system); Uganda, said to breed Lake Kyoga in main rains Apr–June; Zambia, lays late Apr–early May, when flood waters subside, perhaps sometimes later, up to July. No re-laying after loss known, and vulnerable to disturbance in Sudan at nest-sites.

Both sexes incubate, ♂ taking one or more long spells by day, ♀ incubating at night, perhaps 75% of 24 h. Both may spend night on nest together. Incubate head to wind and frequently stand up to move or turn eggs with bill or feet. When settling again often use bill-tip as balancing prop. In hot weather water eggs 3–4 times daily, collecting a beakful and pouring it over eggs; wet nesting material then often added. Incubation period: c. 30 days.

Newly hatched chick clad in uniform silky silvery grey down. Lacks exaggerated bill, but has wide gape, large head and marked hook at bill-tip. At first helpless, feeble. Days 1–35 mainly or entirely downy, cannot stand, brooded or shaded by an adult. Days 35–75 feathers emerging through down, can stand, shuffle or sit on tarsi; now requires little brooding by adult. Days 75–95, feathered, left alone for long periods; if parent present seldom or not shaded. At about 95 days chick or chicks walk off nest without parental encouragement, returning to roost in nest up to day 105. Although little obvious sibling aggression, normally only 1 young survives from clutch of 2–3.

Both adults feed, brood and tend the chicks, ♀ probably more than ♂. At first, parent broods all night and most of day, but day-time brooding ceases after day 40, possibly brooding by night up to day 75. Thereafter both parents largely absent, but ♀ especially may rest for some hours with chick on nest by day. Feathered chick is left alone in nest at night. Chicks less than 30 days old are watered (4–5 times daily on hot days) by parent pouring quantities of water over them from capacious bill (see **A**); chick drinks some direct, or from its down. Watering ceases in cool weather and after 30 days, when chick can reach nest-edge to drink.

A

Adult bill structure necessitates newly hatched chick feeding itself on offered food. Fish swallowed head-first are regurgitated tail-first, then champed between sharp mandibles till soft, when chicks can bite off small portions. Prey is sometimes dropped, picked up and remasticated before again presenting. After 30 days prey is dropped in nest, picked up and swallowed whole by chicks. Prey requirement increases from 1–3 items in early fledging period to 5–6 items towards end; both adults then largely occupied hunting.

Chick leaves nest at 95 days, but roosts there until about 105 days, thereafter moving away, accompanying parents. Can just fly at 105 days but still entirely dependent on parents to 112 days, probably longer. Attempts unsuccessfully to catch own fish at about 112 days; bill is then not fully developed.

Breeding success unknown, but since normally only 1 chick reared from 1–3 eggs and complete losses occur, probably less than 1 young/pair/year. Age to sexual maturity unknown, probably at least 3 years. Main threat to survival is human interference, especially taking young for zoos (up to 500 reported 1978: anon.) and increasing invasion of habitat by humans and livestock, latter involving burning.

References

Buxton, L. *et al.* (1978).
Fischer, W. (1970).
Guillet, A. (1978, 1979).

Illustration by C. H. Fry after Buxton et al. (*1978*).

Family THRESKIORNITHIDAE: ibises and spoonbills

Fairly large to medium-sized wading and terrestrial birds with elongated body, long neck, moderately long legs, and long and broad wings. 11 primaries with 8th and 9th longest, 11th minute; 20 secondaries. Tail short, square or slightly rounded. Lower half of tibia bare; toes of medium length, webbed at base with hind toe slightly elongated. Bill long; nostrils slit-like. Oil gland feathered; no powder-down patches. 2 moults per cycle with moult of primaries descendant or serially descendant. In flight, legs and neck extended. Gregarious or solitary. Sexes alike but ♂♂ larger. World-wide in warm temperate and tropical habitats usually with standing or slow-moving fresh water; also along open and forest areas.

13 genera, 28 species, in 2 groups: (i) ibises with long slender, down-curving bill; (ii) spoonbills with straight bill with flattened terminal 'spoon' when adult, although at hatching nestling's bill resembles that of ibis. In Africa, 5 genera, 10 resident species of which 3 have Palearctic populations that migrate to Africa in Palearctic winter.

Genus *Plegadis* Kaup

All-dark glossy ibis with decurved bill, long neck and long legs. Relatively small; resembles a large curlew. Head and throat feathered; lores naked. 3 species; in Africa, the widely distributed *P. falcinellus*.

Plegadis falcinellus (Linnaeus). Glossy Ibis. Ibis falcinelle.

Tantalus falcinellus Linnaeus, 1766. Syst. Nat. (12th ed.), p. 241; Austria.

Plate 13

(Opp. p. 210)

Range and Status. Resident and Palearctic winter visitor, uncommon to locally common, over many areas of continent in fresh and coastal shallow water habitats. Most Palearctic birds winter south of Sahara probably to equator. Wide discontinuous breeding distribution with nesting in Mali, Kenya, Tanzania, Zambia, Namibia and South Africa.

Description. ADULT ♂: overall dark. Head and neck sooty brown with white streaks. Mantle, scapulars and shoulders chestnut, glossed purple. Back to tail black, glossed metallic green and purple. Underparts from breast to vent brownish black with some chestnut and purple. Wings dark metallic green, glossed purple. Bill olive brown; naked face, orbital area and lores purplish black bordered with narrow white line along forehead and cheeks; eye dark hazel; legs and feet brown with greenish cast. Sexes alike. ADULT: ♂ and ♀ (breeding): overall more metallic sheen, head and neck rich chestnut brown; crown, forehead and chin tinged black with purplish gloss. Underparts rich chestnut. Naked face, orbital area and lores pale cobalt at onset of breeding. SIZE: wing, ♂ (7 specimens) 280–306 (297), ♀ (7) 267–281 (273); tail, ♂ (6) 96–111 (106), ♀ (7) 90–99 (94); bill, ♂ (11) 126–141 (132), ♀ (8) 106–114 (110); tarsus, ♂ (18) 101–113 (107), ♀ (13) 82–90 (86).

IMMATURE: similar to non-breeding adult but overall more sooty with green, but no chestnut or purple gloss on upperparts. Head and neck browner; sometimes large white spots on forehead and crown. Underparts brown.

DOWNY YOUNG: sooty black down with some white on crown and throat. Bill pink, with base, tip and middle band black; bare face pink; eye grey-brown; feet pink.

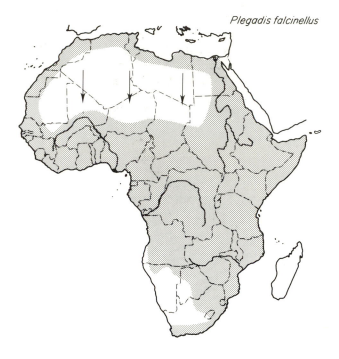

Plegadis falcinellus

Field Characters. A small dark ibis with long, down-curved bill and long, slender legs and feet. Speckled black and white head and neck of non-breeding birds; metallic reflections and chestnut head, neck, mantle and underparts of breeding birds; and legs and feet projecting slightly beyond tail diagnostic. Have characteristic flattened outline in flight with bill and legs outstretched, but slightly drooped and wing-beats rapid, interspaced with short glides. Sometimes mistaken at a distance for dark curlew but legs and neck longer; stands more upright and walks like a heron.

Voice. Recorded (2a). Generally silent but in flight utters harsh, low-pitched, crow-like 'graa-graa-graa' and subdued chattering and grunting. Grunts, guttural cooing, croaks and 'kwuk-kwuk-kwuk-kwuk' at nest.

General Habits. Well known. Gregarious in small flocks of up to 30, frequenting shallow rivers, lakes, marshes, flooded areas and coastal lagoons. Often roost communally at night in large numbers, sometimes thousands, often with herons and other ibises in trees or on ground, sometimes far from water; daily fly to and from feeding areas which may be some distance away. Feeds usually in small parties, by probing in mud; sometimes catches fish in shallow water. Swims short distances. Once reported to raise wings forming umbrella, then wade slowly through water like Black Heron *Egretta ardesiaca* (Lochhart 1975).

Flight purposeful, direct, with some flying high in broad circles, then making rapid descent with legs dangling. Fly most often in long lines but also compact groups or in a V-formation. Some spend Palearctic winter in N Africa; most cross Sahara in broad front Mar–May and Aug–Oct to about equator, within some areas (Nigeria, Ethiopia) containing flocks of over 100 in Oct–Mar. Palearctic birds ringed in Hungary, recovered Algeria and Egypt, and in Russia, recovered Sudan and Niger with latter recovered 75 days after

being ringed Sea of Azov. Post-breeding dispersal in southern Africa probably similar to that of Sacred Ibis *Threskiornis aethiopica*, with one Witwatersrand-ringed nestling (South Africa) recovered in southwestern Zambia (Tarboton 1977). Also, not present all year Kenya (L. H. Brown, pers. comm.).

Food. Mainly insects; also worms, leeches, molluscs, crustaceans, fish, frogs and small reptiles.

Breeding Habits. Well known. Colonial, almost always with other water birds, with nests scattered at random among nests of other species or in groups of 5–10 to sometimes 100; nests near water or over water in reedbeds, bushes and trees.

Courtship poorly described. Displays reported include mutual bowing, preening and billing at nest-site. Copulation occurs on nest immediately after construction and on branches and reeds. At nest-relief, both stand erect, rub bills and do much calling.

Both sexes build nest in 2 days with ♂ collecting material, ♀ building nest.

NEST: a compact pile of twigs or reeds, lined with finer green vegetation. Diameter 30 cm, cup depth 5–8 cm; some twigs up to 80 cm long.

EGGS: 2–3, occasionally 4–7, laid at 24 h intervals; South Africa mean, SW Cape (14 clutches) 3·7, Transvaal (83) 2·1. Bright blue to dark blue-green. SIZE: (133 eggs) 45–59 × 33–40 (52 × 37); WEIGHT: 38.

Laying dates: Algeria, Morocco, Egypt June (late spring or summer), but no recent records; Mali Mar, July–Sept; Kenya May–Aug, peaking in coastal, inundated areas May–June (end rains); Tanzania Apr (end rains); Zambia Feb; Namibia Aug (dry); Zimbabwe Jan; South Africa, SW Cape Sept–Nov, Transvaal Sept–Jan with peak Oct–Dec in summer rains. In most areas lays rains, or late in dry season, in flooded areas late in, or just after main rains.

Incubation begins before, sometimes after, completion of clutch. Both parents incubate with ♀ mainly at night but also sometimes part of day. Changeover usually once every 12 h. Incubating parent on nest 95% time. Incubate by sitting on nest with neck extended, with neck drawn close to body in a tight 'S', or with head resting on back. Period: 20–23 (21) days.

Both sexes care for and feed young at changeover about every 6 h when brooding small young. Very small young fed 8–12 times/day by regurgitation with young placing bill into parent's mouth. Sometimes food regurgitated onto nest when young older. Parents on nest 90% time until young 4–5 days old. One parent with young until 9–14 days. When 2 weeks old, young move to end of limbs of bush where nest located but return to it to feed; fed 5–8 times/day. At 21 days chicks often out of nest. At 6 weeks, can fly and obtain own food but still occasionally fed by parents; roost at old nest. At 7 weeks, fly to feeding areas with parents.

References
Miller, L. M. and Burger, J. (1978).

Genus *Bostrychia* Reichenbach

Medium-sized ibises with predominantly brown plumage with bronze and greenish iridescence, especially on wing-coverts. Head and neck feathered except bare area from beak to behind eye. Bill red or partly red, usually shorter, less decurved than in other ibises. Commonly produce harsh noises in flight. Confined to Africa, 4 species, 3 with nuchal crest.

Bostrychia hagedash (Latham). Hadada; Hadeda. Ibis hagedash.

Tantalus hagedash Latham, 1790. Ind. Orn. 2, p. 709; Cape of Good Hope.

Plate 13

(Opp. p. 210)

Range and Status. Resident, locally common to frequent along wooded streams in savanna country and open forests, Senegal to Ethiopia south to Cape; extending range westward in South Africa with construction of reservoirs.

Description. *B. h. hagedash* (Latham): southern Africa south of Zambezi Valley. ADULT ♂: generally dull brown with metallic reflections. Head and neck brownish grey; cheek with buff-white stripe. Mantle and back olive green to bronzy brown; rump and uppertail-coverts glossy bottle green; tail blue-black. Black primaries and glossy blue secondaries with some purple; major coverts bright iridescent greenish bronze, pinkish bronze to rosy purple in certain light. Underparts brownish grey. Bill black with basal half of culmen crimson, sometimes dark crimson (courtship?); eye brown with narrow outer ring of white; sometimes red; lores black; legs and feet greyish black to black with top of toes dull crimson. Sexes alike. SIZE: (17 specimens) wing, 334–370 (353); tail, 137–170 (154); bill, 117–153 (134); tarsus, 63–73 (68). WEIGHT: 1262.

IMMATURE: similar to adult but duller.

DOWNY YOUNG: pink skin with dark brown down; bill straight, black; legs and feet pale pink.

B. h. brevirostris (Reichenow). Senegal south through Zaïre and Kenya south to Zambezi Valley. Darker below, more brown, less grey; wing-coverts have greenish gloss, less bronzy. Bill longer, 126–163; wing 330–383.

B. h. nilotica Neumann. Sudan, Ethiopia, northwestern Zaïre, Uganda, and northwestern Tanzania. Similar to *B. h. brevirostris* but larger bill, 152–174; wing 335–392.

Field Characters. A plain brown ibis with greenish metallic gloss on back, especially upperwings. In flight, feet do not project beyond tail. Broad rounded wings flapped deeply, bill pointed downwards; wing-beats typically irregular, jerky, with one deep flap followed by several shallower flaps. At close range, white line on cheek diagnostic. Normally calls at take-off and in flight. Because of short legs, appears to stand low to ground.

Voice. Recorded (1a, 2a, 2b, 6, 8, 19, 20a, 20b, 22a, 26, 28). Chief call, given by both sexes when flying especially at dawn or near sunset, a 'haa-haa-de-dah' or 'haa-daa-daa'. When alarmed, a loud 'waaa', 'haaa' or 'kah-a-a-a'. Young give a 'hurrr-hurrr-hurrr'.

General Habits. Well known. A sedentary bird of open moist grasslands and savannas, especially along wooded river courses; less often marshes, flooded grasslands, edges of lakes, open forests, lawns in gardens, mangroves and coastal beaches. Usually in pairs, especially in breeding season but also flocks of 30 in non-breeding season with several flocks sometimes

Bostrychia hagedash

forming a large flock of 200 or so. Flocks wander several miles from roost but never fly in formation. Forages for food by probing in moist ground with long, curved bill; also takes food from soil surface, e.g. 60% diet by weight composed of animals obtained on soil surface (Raseroka 1975b).

Usually gregarious at roost, normally in small groups but sometimes up to 100 together; usually roosts only with other Hadadas although sometimes with other ibises or herons. Occasionally mated pairs roost apart from main flocks. Same roost used daily, even throughout year, with birds leaving at dawn, returning at sunset; often use same route going to or from roost. Usually very noisy leaving or returning to roost. At dawn, when leaving, vocal activity builds up with one bird calling, followed by one or many others. In large roosts, groups of birds call in unison, then are followed by another group elsewhere on roost (D. Manry, pers. comm.). When flushed, continue to utter Hadada call while flying from place to place. Sometimes a pair may call in unison, one bird calling first with second bird copying on third or fourth note (D. Manry, pers. comm.).

Food. Largely insects; also crustaceans, millipedes, spiders, snails and reptiles. Insects 96% by number and 58% by weight of animals ingested. Largest number, dipterans (62%), lepidopterans (15%); largest by weight, earthworms (18%), centipedes and millipedes (17%) (Raseroka 1975b); mainly coleopterous larvae and lepidopterous pupae (Ossowski 1952).

Breeding Habits. Very well known. Nests solitarily in a tree or bush standing in or near water, although sometimes far from water; also on telegraph poles. Same nest-site used year after year but not necessarily by same birds.

Courtship poorly recorded; begins when pairs remain together, calling, flying, billing, mutual preening, intertwining necks, collecting nest material, feeding and roosting. In billing, each grasps other's bill, then rattle bills while moving heads side-to-side and up-and-down; performed when birds are at nest, roost or at greeting time. Sometimes tap bill against partner's bill; often raise head and neck feathers. Both often touch bodies at nest. Occasionally, sitting bird shakes head rapidly from side-to-side and jibbers bill; partner then preens mate. Bird at nest jibbers bill when incoming bird approaches. ♂ probably collects nest material, ♀ builds nest, usually within 14 days but can be up to 1 month.

NEST: a basket-shaped structure, usually on a branch in fork of tree 1–8 m above water or ground (42% nests, 3·6–6·1 m; 28% 1·2–3·6 m; 3% above 12·2 m: Raseroka (1975a). Made of sticks and twigs and lined with lichens or grass, 20–45 cm in diameter, 13–15 cm thick, and 10 cm deep or less in centre. 1 nest, 112 sticks, weighed 1·2 kg.

EGGS: 2–3, sometimes 4, laid alternate days; South Africa mean (19 clutches) 3·2 (Skead 1951), (19) 2·9 (Raseroka 1975a), Cape (77) 2·8, Natal (78) 2·7, OFS (2) 2, Transvaal (18) 2·6; Zimbabwe (24) 2·2 (SAOSNRC); E Africa (39) 2·5 (EANRC); overall (276) 2·73. Rather broad ovals, buff or pale olive green, often heavily blotched and spotted red-brown, or blackish with purple undermarkings. SIZE: (172 eggs) 54–66 × 38–48 (60 × 42); WEIGHT: 55–62.

Laying dates: Guinea-Bissau May–Oct (rains); Gambia Jan–Mar (dry); Niger June; Nigeria June–July (rains); Ethiopia Sept; Kenya, Uganda year-round, with peak Mar–June (long rains); Tanzania Apr–July, Oct (mainly dry); Zambia Jan, Mar–Apr, July–Dec; Zaïre Jan–Dec; Zimbabwe Oct–Dec; Mozambique Dec; South Africa Jan–Dec (mainly in summer rains in southern Africa). In most areas has extended breeding season, sometimes year-round, but with tendency to peak in and after main rains.

Incubation begins 1st egg, sometimes when clutch complete. Both parents remain on nest for long spells, up to 3 h. Nest-reliefs unobtrusive, silent, one parent arriving and the other leaving without ceremony; sexes difficult to distinguish at nest with certainty. Period: 25–30 days.

Young require 24–48 h to hatch; adults throw egg shells out of nest. At days 3–4 eyes open; show first fear reaction. From early on, defaecate over rim of nest. At 7 days, most feathers emerging except on head and neck; unable to stand but can prop itself up on legs and belly. At 15–16 days, feathers with vanes appear on lower neck and head; legs light grey. At 20 days stand firmly on feet for first time. At 27 days have full covering of juvenile feathers with white cheek streaks. At 34 days walk on branches around nest. At 35 days fly short distances to trees surrounding nest. At 37 days on ground but remain near nest; fed by parents. At 49 days, leave nest area; no longer fed by parents; feed by probing.

Both parents brood and feed young by regurgitation, with chicks inserting heads into parent's mouth. Brooding continuous or regular up to day 7, thereafter reduced, but adults may stand on nest-edge by day and brood, or shelter young by night. Large feathered young left alone, but adults may roost near nest.

Mortality of young appears to be high in South Africa; from 17 nests with 67 eggs, 3 young fledged (Skead 1951; Raseroka 1975b). Losses are due to eggs falling from flimsy structure of nest and to eggs rolling, and young falling, out of nest. In E Africa better success recorded with av. 1·8 young/pair (Brown and Britton 1980).

References
Ossowski, L. L. J. (1952).
Raseroka, B. H. (1975a, b).
Skead, C. J. (1951).

Plate 13

(Opp. p. 210)

Bostrychia carunculata (Rüppell). Wattled Ibis. Ibis caronculé.

Ibis carunculata Rüppell, 1837. N. Wirbelth Fauna Abyssinien, Vögel, p. 49; Taranta Mts.

Range and Status. Resident, all over Ethiopian plateau from about 1500 m to highest moorlands at 4100 m.

Description. ADULT ♂: generally brownish black, glossed dull green above. Crown with dusky crest extending along nape and neck. Brown feathers on lores. Primaries black with bluish gloss, secondaries black with greenish gloss; upper wing-coverts white with black centres forming white wing-patch. Underparts brown. Bill, legs and feet dusky red; red pendent wattle from throat; eye pearly white with red ring. Sexes alike. SIZE: (7 specimens) wing, 358–380; tail, 150–180; bill, 110–127; tarsus, 63–66 (Moltoni and Ruscone 1942; Friedmann 1930).

IMMATURE: duller, paler than adult, with less white in wings; lacks wattles.

DOWNY YOUNG: covered in black-brown down; bare orbital area; straight bill grey, black at tip (Dorst and Roux 1972).

Field Characters. Unmistakable. A dark ibis on the Ethiopian highlands usually in flocks. In flight, makes loud raucous 'kowrr-kowrrr-kowrrr' calls, and shows extensive white upperwing-patch. Distinguishable from Hadada *B. hagedash* by large size, white or grey wing-patch, no white line on cheek, and, at close range, pendent wattles.

Voice. Not recorded. Normal call a loud, raucous, rolling 'kowrr-kowrrr-kowrrr' uttered on rising, often in chorus in flocks, audible at least 5 km away. Deeper and more growling than voice of Hadada. Calls alarm other animals, often needlessly. At dawn, roosting birds utter indescribable series of clicks, croaks, grunts and squeaks, finally leaving with loud, raucous, crowing calls as above.

General Habits. Well known. Roosts singly or in pairs in trees, more often in small or large groups on rock cliffs, often at site of breeding colonies. Leaves roost soon after dawn, small groups often amalgamating by day into large feeding flocks of 100 or more, foraging in open grasslands, marshes, open alpine moorland, or croplands and forest glades down to about 1500 m. Except when roosting on cliffs, normally found far from river courses. When feeding, walks about methodically, often in groups, probing ground regularly, perhaps locating some prey by ear. Sometimes accompanies herds of domestic animals, searching dung for beetles. When flock is flushed, all arise and call, continuing to do so as they fly away.

Food. Probably worms, insect larvae, larvae in dung; occasionally frogs, large insects, possibly mice (at least, their young).

Breeding Habits. Little known. Nests singly or in groups of 2 or 3 in trees and ledges of buildings; more often in small to large colonies on rocky cliffs, usually in river valleys. Few colonies known above 3000 m; those in trees found only at lower elevations (i.e. *c.* 1800–2000 m) in Rift Valley (Lake Awasa).

Courtship, nest-building, incubation and brooding behaviour not described. In one colony observed (L. H. Brown, pers. obs.), one bird was usually present on nest, suggesting territory occupation by ♂♂ as in *Geronticus*. This, plus colonial nesting on cliffs as well as solitary nesting in trees, indicates this species may be a link between *Bostrychia*, as typified by Hadada, and *Geronticus*. The tendency to nest in colonies in cliffs rather than alone in trees also indicates that this species

Bostrychia carunculata

may be much more like *Geronticus* than *Bostrychia*, despite its physical appearance.

NEST: a platform of branches and sticks, lined with soft vegetation, 50–60 cm in diameter. Sometimes nests nearly touch, other times are several metres apart. Nests are sometimes located to east for maximum exposure to sun in early hours of day which are very cold at high altitudes (Dorst and Roux 1972).

EGGS: 2–3; rough shelled and dirty white, variously marked brown. SIZE: 59–61 × 40–39 (60 × 39); WEIGHT: 50.

Laying dates: Mar–May, July, Dec, in little rains, main rains and dry season.

Fledged young feed away from nest and colony. All other aspects of biology of this ibis unrecorded.

References
Dorst, J. and Roux, F. (1972).
Urban, E. K. (1978).

Bostrychia olivacea (Du Bus de Gisignies). Olive Ibis; African Green Ibis. Ibis olive.   **Plate 13**

Ibis olivacea Du Bus de Gisignies, 1838. Bull. Acad. Roy. Sci. Lettres Beaux-Arts Belg. 4, p. 105; Liberia.   (Opp. p. 210)

Range and Status. Resident, widespread, uncommon, seldom seen, lowland forests Sierra Leone, Liberia, Ivory Coast, Principe Is., São Tomé, Cameroon, Gabon, Congo, and montane forests of eastern Zaïre, Kenya (Mt Kenya and Aberdares), and Tanzania (Kilimanjaro, Usambara Mts, Mt Meru).

Description. *B. o. olivacea* (Du Bus de Gisignies): Sierra Leone and Liberia. ADULT ♂: head and neck brown with pale shaft stripes. Crest brown with purple lustre extending to neck. Mantle, scapulars and rump dusky, with green-bronze lustre; uppertail-coverts and tail dark blue. Underparts brownish black washed green. Flight feathers black with blue

wash; innermost secondaries dusky with green-bronze lustre; wing-coverts glossed pinkish rose and green. Bill coral red; bare face, lores and orbital area blackish blue, pale brown from base of lower mandible to below ear-coverts; eye dark red to grey-brown; legs and feet yellowish green to pinkish brown or dull dark red. Sexes alike. SIZE: wing 330, 334; tail 147, 150; culmen 95, 96; tarsus 68, 73.

IMMATURE: similar to adult but duller and crest shorter.

DOWNY YOUNG: covered with brownish black down.

B. o. cupreipennis (Reichenow). Cameroon, Gabon, Congo and Zaïre. Neck and body more greenish, less dusky brown; wing, 309–355.

B. o. rothschildi (Bannerman). Principe Is. Crest a glossier purple and more graduated down to neck; rare if not extinct; wing, ♂ 328, ♀ 313.

Bostrychia olivacea

General Habits. Scarcely known. Shy, occurs singly, in pairs, or in groups or flocks of 5–12 in lowland forests along forest streams and rivers; sometimes also mangroves of W Africa and montane forests between 160 and 3700 m above sea level in E Africa (Britton 1980). Flies high above forest at dawn and dusk, calling. Often uses same routes daily travelling to and from roost and feeding areas. Prefers to roost in giant trees with dead tops; probably uses same one daily. Feeds quietly in glades and open forests.

The Spot-breasted Ibis *B. rara* and Olive Ibis are sympatric in W African forests but nothing is known about their ecological relationships; possibly their different sizes require different diets. Olive Ibis is also sympatric with Hadada *B. hagedash* in W Africa; however, Hadada is a bird of open woodlands, not dense forests. In E Africa Olive Ibis replaces Hadada altitudinally with the latter not being found above 1800 m, and the former from 1800 m to the upper timber line. Olive Ibis appears to be the only resident species in Africa found in lowland forests of W Africa and montane forests of E Africa.

B. o. bocagei (Chapin). São Tomé Is. Considerably smaller, wing 247–260; dull brown without gloss on wing-coverts.

B. o. akleyorum (Chapman). Mountains of Kenya and Tanzania. Larger, wing 343–372; brighter green.

Field Characters. A dark, forest-inhabiting ibis with long crest, short bill and fairly uniform, not scaly, underparts. Very difficult to see at all. Usually heard or seen flying high at dawn or dusk.

Voice. Recorded (2a, 14). Mainly strong, resonant, double squawk 'gar-wa gar-wa'; also 'aka-a', 'ka', 'kau', and a loud raucous clanging or honking, goose-like call heard long distance away. When alarmed, a single 'gar'.

Food. Beetles, grubs, worms, snails, snakes and some vegetable material from forest floor.

Breeding Habits. Scarcely known. Solitary breeder.

NEST: constructed of dead sticks on tree limb 7·5 m above ground; possibly also in holes in cliffs.

EGGS: 3; pale pea green stained with cinnamon rufous and marked with chestnut. SIZE: 56–58 × 40–41 (57 × 40); WEIGHT: 50.

Laying dates: Kenya June–Aug but no records since 1900; no records W Africa.

References
Meinertzhagen, R. (1937).

Plate 13

(Opp. p. 210)

Bostrychia rara (Rothschild, Hartert and Kleinschmidt). Spot-breasted Ibis. Ibis vermiculé.

Lampribis rara Rothschild, Hartert and Kleinschmidt, 1897. Nov. Zool., 4, p. 377; Denkera, Ghana.

Range and Status. Resident, widespread and little known in W African lowland forests from Liberia to Gabon and Zaïre; uncommon in most of its range, common in northeastern Gabon.

Description. ADULT ♂: overall brown. Crown with long, loose crest dark brown to black, glossed green crest extending to hindneck. All of neck, breast and belly red-brown edged black, resulting in spotted appearance. Mantle dark brown, edged buff, slightly glossed bronzy green. Back olive green. Rump to tail bluish green; tail slightly glossed with dark blue-green. Undertail-coverts bottle green. Primaries, secondaries and wing-coverts blue-black; scapulars and inner secondaries slightly glossed with bronzy green. Underwing black. Bill orange-red to dark red; forepart of face, lores and around eye, naked, black with a turquoise-green spot in front of, and

another behind, eye; a similarly coloured streak on face in line with lower mandible; eye dark brown; legs and feet pinkish brown. ♀ like ♂ but turquoise spots and streak smaller; bill shorter, not so red. SIZE: (10 specimens) wing, 270–290; tail, 112–120; bill, 115–130; tarsus, 56–65.

IMMATURE: similar to adult but duller, with shorter bill and crest; mantle and wings similar in colour.

DOWNY YOUNG: red or pale violet skin with blackish brown down; face black tinged blue; base of mandibles red.

Field Characters. A crested, forest-dwelling ibis, distinguished from all other ibises by conspicuously spotted neck and underparts. Differs also from larger Olive Ibis *B. olivacea* by greenish black, not purple, crest, and turquoise-green spots and streak on face.

Voice. Recorded (2a). Extremely noisy at dusk and sunset, even during the night, when utters loud raucous 'k-hah, k-hah' and a nasal 'haw'. Clatters mandibles during nest-relief and when threatening.

General Habits. Well known. In pairs, or singly, frequents small and large forested streams and wooded swamps, always above or near water. Feeds by day in forested swamps and muddy banks of forest streams and rivers by probing in mud with long bill.

Same roost-sites used year-round with 5–8 birds in same large leafy tree or 100–150 m apart. Returns to roost, which is always above or near water, shortly after sundown. For *c.* 1 h before settling on roost, flies around, calling and often changing perches. At roost, pair bow, lowering heads and bills with crests raised; touch bills and mutually preen. Leave roost shortly before dawn. Only noticeable when making raucous calls going to or leaving roost; silent and secretive rest of day. Occasionally active at night, especially in bright moonlight.

Food. Aquatic snails, worms, beetles, larvae and grubs.

Breeding Habits. Well known. Nests alone, in trees in back waters, swamps and marshes associated with rivers of lowland forests. Nests are situated 1–6 m above ground or overhanging water, not hidden but difficult to see from any distance because of foliage.

Whole nesting cycle is very secretive with small nests, little movement, quiet arrival and departure with no calling, and few nest-reliefs. Courtship behaviour observed includes bowing, touching bills, mutual preening and greeting at nest-relief. During nest-relief, bird at nest crouches, erects crest, fluffs breast and back feathers, lowers bill to breast and softly clatters bill. Incoming bird, upon landing, lowers bill and softly clatters it; touches mate's nape and bill. Crest feathers of incoming ♀ are erected, ♂'s are not. Except for barely audible clattering of bills, silent during nest-relief.

NEST: a circular platform on top of several lateral tree branches made of sticks, roots and lianes, edged with twigs and lined with dead leaves and fresh bits of epiphytes; 30 cm across, 5–15 cm thick, with cup 20 cm across. Smaller and less well made than nest of Hadada *B. hagedash*; resembles that of Olive Ibis.

EGGS: usually 2. Oval, richly coloured, smooth, slightly glossy, pale blue-green with many small brown spots, sometimes irregularly distributed all over, although usually concentrated at broad end. SIZE: av. 55 × 35 (Brosset and Erard 1976).

Nests built when water rises or when flood water high, not when water in rivers and marshes lowest. Breeds probably most of year with 2 peaks correspond-

Bostrychia rara

ing with rainfall peaks Mar–June and Sept–Dec; little breeding in dry season of Jan–Feb and none recorded in July–Aug. Laying dates: Gabon Jan–June, Sept–Dec.

Both parents incubate, ♀ at night, ♂ by day, starting *c.* 1–1·5 h after dawn and remaining for long spells, probably all day. Incubating bird moves very little; sits with head and neck retracted and bill buried in back feathers. Rises occasionally to turn eggs; sometimes remains standing in horizontal position with neck retracted and bill pointed upwards. Repels intruders by stretching out neck and making strong bill-clattering; usually crouches, however, and is silent and secretive. Incubation period: *c.* 20 days.

Both sexes brood and feed young. 1 parent at nest constantly days 1–7 with ♂ there until late evening when relieved by ♀. Probably *c.* 4 nest reliefs/day, 2 in morning, 2 in afternoon. During brooding, parents look after nest, often rearranging nest material and throwing debris into water. Stimulate small young to feed with bill. At 6 days blackish first down replaced by thicker white down, and wing- and tail-feathers appear. Young puts head in parent's mouth; fed by regurgitation. Feeding lasts 1–2 min and occurs as often as 6 times in 10 min. Adults and young, including newly hatched young, defaecate out of nest with parents holding young one in bill to prevent it from falling into water. Main predator probably man.

References

Brosset, A. and Erard, C. (1976).

Genus *Threskiornis* Gray

Medium-sized ibises with bare head and neck, the skin being black, white body plumage and patches of bare red (breeding) or grey-flesh (non-breeding) skin on sides of breast which extend as a stripe along the underside of the wing. 1 species in Africa.

Plate 13

(Opp. p. 210)

Threskiornis aethiopica (Latham). Sacred Ibis. Ibis sacré.

Tantalus aethiopicus Latham, 1790. Ind. Orn., 2, p. 706; Egypt.

Range and Status. Resident, common and widespread, margins of various freshwater habitats, grasslands, and cultivated fields and intertidal areas south of Sahara from Senegal to Ethiopia south to Cape. Bred in Egypt before 1850. 1 subspecies, *T. a. aethiopica*, in Africa.

Threskiornis aethiopica

Description. *T. a. aethiopica* (Latham), ADULT ♂: overall white with some black. Head and neck covered with bare wrinkled black skin; lower foreneck sometimes sac-like. Mantle grey in parts. Primaries and secondaries tipped with metallic greenish black. Wing edge, flanks and side of belly often tinged brownish yellow. Rest of plumage white. Long, decurved bill black at base, horn at tip. Eye brown; legs and feet black, legs tinged red. Sexes alike. ADULT: ♂ and ♀ (breeding): during courtship, scapulars and innermost secondaries have ornamental plumes, metallic blue-black, metallic greenish black, or glossed purple-violet. Has patch of bare blood red skin on upperwing along carpo-metacarpus, on underwing and on adjoining area of breast and flanks. Eye brown, ringed with deep red. SIZE: wing, ♂ (2 specimens) 380–385 (383), ♀ (3) 361–362 (362); tail, ♂ (3) 129–140 (134), ♀ (4) 127–135 (131); tarsus, ♂ (3) 100–116 (108), ♀ (5) 94–103 (98); bill, ♂ (7) 162–183 (170), ♀ (8) 135–157 (146). WEIGHT: ♂ 1530.

IMMATURE: similar to adult but head and neck have black, brownish black and white feathers; alula and greater primary coverts black. Eye brownish black; bill, legs and feet greyish black.

DOWNY YOUNG: head and neck covered with dense black down; crown has spot of white down. Rest of body covered with white down. Bare orbital area and lores white. Eye pale grey; bill, legs and feet pinkish white.

Field Characters. Unmistakable. A conspicuous, fairly large white bird with black head and neck, and long dark decurved bill. In flight, white wings with black trailing edges and legs and neck extended diagnostic. During courtship, dark ornamental plumes on back and blood-red bare skin on wings diagnostic.

Voice. Recorded (6, 18). Usually silent away from colony although sometimes utters harsh croak in flight. At colony (Ethiopia), produces squeals, squeaks, moans and inhaling/exhaling noises resembling 'whoot-whoot-whoot-whooeeoh' or 'pyuk-pyuk-peuk-peuk-pek-peuk'. During nest-building ♀ utters sharp 'whaank' 1–3 times which seems to attract ♂; copulation often follows. At copulation, ♀ produces 'hnhh-hnhh'. Adults utter a single 'turrooh' or 'keerrooh', falling in pitch, to call young. Nestling gives a repeated high-pitched screaming 'chrreeee-chree-eh-chrreeee' when begging for food; louder in older young.

General Habits. Very well known. Gregarious in groups of 2–20 to, occasionally, 100–300; sometimes solitary. Inhabits open moist areas close to inland bodies of water; also cultivated fields, dumps on outskirts of towns, plains, sometimes far from water, particularly after grass fires, along rivers in open forest, and coastal lagoons and intertidal areas. Walks slowly with body nearly horizontal and neck held more or less straight. Often flies in V-formation with neck extended, alternating wing-beats with glides, usually only a few metres above water or ground, 38·4 km/h (Ethiopia). Occasionally soars, sometimes returning to colonies or roosts from heights of several hundred metres.

Feeds during day, mainly in flocks on moist ground, including irrigated land, probing soft earth and mud. Flies up to 30 km away from colonies to feed (Clark and Clark 1979).

Roosts in hundreds on islets in rivers or floodlands, on trees near dams, at breeding sites, and sometimes in villages. Arrives at roost *c*. 1 h before sunset and leaves shortly after sunrise in groups of 2–9; silent when arriving or leaving roost.

Migrates several hundred kilometres north or south of equator to breed in rains, those north of equator moving north towards Sahara, and those south of equator moving south. At end of rains or early dry season, both groups return towards equator. 69 birds ringed in South African colonies were recovered Zambia (61, furthest distance 1336 km), Botswana (5) and Namibia (3) (Clark and Clark 1979; Dowsett 1969).

Food. Mainly grasshoppers, locusts, crickets and water beetles; also worms, molluscs, crustaceans, fish, amphibians, lizards, eggs of Great White Pelican *Pelecanus onocrotalus* and crocodiles, young of Cape Cormorant *Phalacrocorax capensis*, carrion and offal. At Pretoria (South Africa) mainly human, animal and vegetable refuse, and insects; in summer (Nov–Jan) animal food 50%, vegetable food 34%, and in winter (June–Aug) vegetable food 47%, animal food 34% of wet weight consumed (Clark 1979c). Regurgitated food from a 1-month-old chick (Ethiopia) included 22 dung beetle larvae, 2 lepidopteran larvae, 2 coleopteran adults, 1 bead, 1 small piece of bone, 1 seed, bits from a millipede, several small ants and 1 small piece of egg shell.

Breeding Habits. Intimately known. Nests in colonies of 50–2000 pairs in trees, bushes, or on the ground on islands. When with other ibises, storks, herons, or cormorants, nests in discrete tightly packed groups composed only of ibises; may sometimes mingle with spoonbills (Elmenteita, Kenya).

Courtship begins when parties of 10–50 birds, probably all ♂♂, visit potential nesting areas for 5–10 min to 1 h. In 1–2 days as many as 100 ♂♂ settle on 1 area where they establish pairing territories. When on territories, stand with tail-feathers spread, wings held slightly downward and ornamental plumes erected. Some feint at and strike each other's bills, and make wheezing, squeaking calls. Also perform: (1) forward threat, in which displaying bird adopts horizontal stance, extends head and neck towards opponent, then, with wings partly open revealing bright red skin, feints at opponent with open bill (see **A**); (2) modified forward threat, in which 2 or more ♂♂, standing side-by-side and usually facing same direction, open wings and point bills skyward; (3) stretch display, in which bird moves neck up and back in one smooth and rapid motion, then, with bill pointed skyward, flicks neck backward; this causes crown to touch mantle either to right or left, after which bird returns bill to normal position (**B**); (4) modified snap display, in which the bird, standing in a low horizontal position, suddenly extends neck forward and down but does not snap mandibles together; (5) pursuit flight, in which ♂ flies towards and chases opponent; and (6) supplanting attack, in which bird flies towards and forces opponent from perch.

A

1–2 days later much chasing and fighting occurs with the arrival of ♀♀ and additional ♂♂. If ♂ does not chase ♀ and she remains, pair is formed probably within a day. At this time both face each other, then bow with head and neck extended forward and downward; also intertwine necks and bills; preen (no mutual preening reported); occasionally nibble twigs; and perform stretch and, infrequently, snap displays.

New pairs probably formed annually; once established, ♂ and ♀ settle on nest territory, often 1–5 m away, both standing side by side with bodies pressed together. Copulation begins only after nest territory has been established. During copulation, ♀ crouches, ♂ places feet under her wings and she clamps wings together; then ♂ grasps and shakes ♀'s bill, moving partly opened mandibles up and down it. After copulation, both stand and preen.

B

After copulation period has started, ♂ usually collects nest material, ♀ usually remains on site and builds nest. When ♂ returns, both face each other with ♂ standing, ♀ crouching; they then angle bills skyward, bow and intertwine necks and bills. When nest is nearly finished, ♀ emits 1–3 sharp calls; ♂, standing nearby, moves to her and they may copulate.

NEST: a large pile of branches and sticks, up to 40 cm long, lined with leaves and grasses. Av. diameter, 10 Ethiopian nests, 34 (range, 28–43) cm; usually 20 cm thick. Nests are close together but rarely touch.

EGGS: 2–4, occasionally 5; Ethiopia and E Africa mean (535 clutches) 2·43; South Africa, SW Cape (291) 2·4, Transvaal (271) 2·0 (SAOSNRC). Dull white with faint bluish or greenish tinge, sometimes with dark reddish or brownish spots. SIZE: 56–70 × 38–48 (64 × 43) (Ethiopia, Uganda, South Africa); WEIGHT: 62.

Lays in rains or in dry season in flooded areas; often starts breeding after period of heavy rain. Laying dates: Senegal Nov–Dec; Gambia Jan, July, Nov–Dec (mainly dry); Guinea-Bissau Mar–Sept (rains); Nigeria Jan–Feb (dry), May–June (wet), Dec (dry); Mali July–Feb; Chad June; Sudan Mar, June–Aug (rains); Ethiopia Mar–June, Aug–Sept; Kenya Jan–June, peaking strongly W Kenya Apr, Rift Valley May–June, in and after long rains, also Aug, Nov; Uganda Feb, May, Nov; Burundi July; Tanzania Jan–Feb, May, Oct (mainly rains); Zambia, Malawi, Zimbabwe Jan–Sept, late in rains and into dry season; Namibia Apr, July, Aug (dry); South Africa Jan–Mar, May, Aug–Dec, with most breeding Aug–Jan.

Incubation begins when clutch complete (Ethiopia), or incomplete (Tanzania, Zambia). Both parents incubate, changing over at least once every 24 h. Incubate with back and tail directed towards sun, bill angled skyward 15–30° away from sun. Stand up *c.* every 20 min and in heat of day may remain standing for *c.* 20 min. Incubation period: 28–29 days.

Young remain in nest days 1–14, at first brooded, later shaded by standing adults. Leave nest at 14–21 days; congregate into loose flocks. Nest-site abandoned at this time. At 21 days *c.* 30–50% adult size with white feathers among black feathers of crown and neck; wing-feathers about half-grown; scapulars white and greater primary coverts black; bill greyish black, less than 50% adult length, and less decurved; eye brownish black; legs grey and enlarged at tarsal joint. At 35–40 days capable of some flight; at 44–48 days leave colony.

Both parents care for and feed young, with one always present first 7–10 days, remaining 24 h. Feed very small young at intervals throughout day by partial regurgitation with young putting head into parent's mouth. As temperature increases, parents shade very small young. When young 2 weeks and older, parents only with young once each day at feeding time. Recognize own young; young usually recognize parents.

Hatching success: Kisumu, Kenya (353 nests, 975 eggs: Parsons 1977) 43%; Schaapen Is., South Africa (54 nests: Manry 1978) 85%. Breeding success often very low, 0·05 young/nest (of 420 chicks hatched, 18 fledged, Kisumu, 1977), less than 1 young/nest (Kisumu, 1954: L. H. Brown, pers. comm.), 0·093 young/nest (Schaapen). Av. brood size (Ethiopia) at 21 days, 1·4 young/nest; at 39 days, 1·13 young/nest; at 44–48 days, 1·06 young/nest. Nesting success (Ethiopia) over 6 years, 35% (range 0–81%) pairs reared young.

Factors affecting breeding success include predation by fish eagles (each visited Kisumu colony 3·5 times/day; ate 7 eggs per visit: Parsons 1977) and Kelp Gulls *Larus dominicanus* (Schaapen: Manry 1978), abandonment of nests because of low rainfall (Kisumu), loss of eggs and young due to heavy rain storms (Ethiopia), and loss of young to falling out of nest, hanging themselves (Kisumu) or landing onto ground where they starve (Kisumu, Schaapen).

References
Clark, R. A. (1979a, b, c).
Clark, R. A. and Clark, A. (1979).
Parsons, J. (1977).
Urban, E. K. (1974a).

Illustrations by Robert Gillmor. Reproduced with permission from Cramp and Simmons (1977).

Genus *Geronticus* Wagler

Medium-sized all-dark ibises with bare head, face and throat, and enlarged crown. Iridescent plumage black with purple, bronze and green gloss; ruff on neck. Long, decurved bill and red legs. In mountainous regions, breeding takes place in colonies on cliff ledges. 2 species, 1 breeding in southeastern highlands of South Africa, 1 in Asia Minor and NW Africa.

Plate 13

(Opp. p. 210)

Geronticus eremita (Linnaeus). Waldrapp; Hermit Ibis; Bald Ibis. Ibis chauve.

Upupa Eremita Linnaeus, 1758. Syst. Nat. (10th ed.), p. 118; Switzerland.

Range and Status. Resident and Palearctic winter visitor. Once much more common; today rare in somewhat arid regions with rocky escarpments and open fields. Breeds Morocco, Algeria (since 1976: U. Hirsch, pers. comm.) and Turkey; once recorded in Egypt 1921 (U. Hirsch, pers. comm.). Distribution of winter population from Turkey not well known and erratic, but largely to Ethiopia; also Sudan and Somalia. Very local and declining: in Morocco, 1940, *c.* 500 breeding pairs and 38 known breeding sites; 1978, *c.* 90 breeding pairs at 13 known sites (Hirsch 1979a, pers. comm.). Turkey population, 1975, 250 pairs with only 6 wintering birds seen in Africa 1953–1979. Population (1979) seriously threatened, with known world population of fewer than 125 pairs (U. Hirsch, pers. comm.). Reasons for decline include use of pesticides on feeding grounds (181 ppm DDE in 20-day-old chicks, Turkey) and human disturbance (tourists, animal collectors and hunters, Morocco: U. Hirsch, pers. comm.).

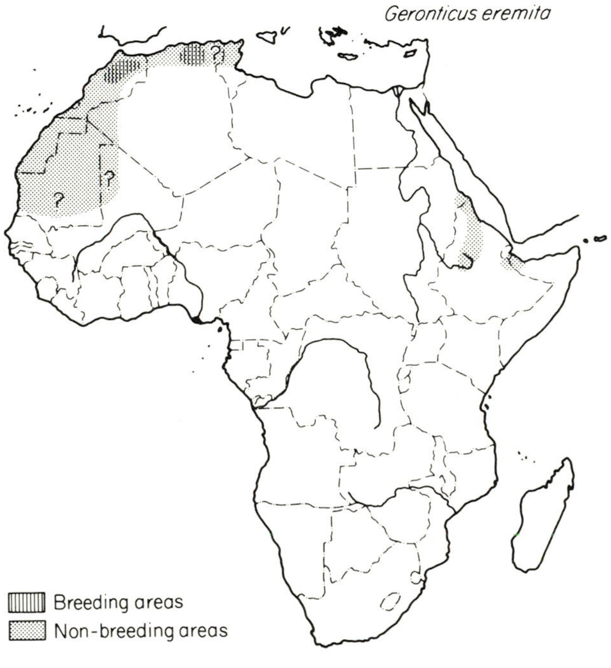

Geronticus eremita

Breeding areas
Non-breeding areas

Description. ADULT ♂: bare red head, face and throat except crown black with orange central streak. Plumage dark metallic green with purple gloss. Nape and neck with elongated ruff. Upperwing-coverts glossed copper and violet. Bill decurved, dull red; eye orange-red; legs and feet dirty red. Sexes alike. SIZE: wing, ♂ 403–420, ♀ 390–408; tail, ♂ and ♀ 196–220; tarsus, ♂ and ♀ 68–72; bill, ♂ 133–147, ♀ 115–131; bill, Morocco population, ♂ (16) 132–146 (141), ♀ (12) 128–145 (134); north-eastern population, ♂ (8) 126–132 (129), ♀ (5) 121–127 (124) (Siegfried 1972d).

IMMATURE: duller, less iridescent with no copper-tinted wing-patch. Head has greyish feathers. Eye yellow-grey to grey before 3rd year.

DOWNY YOUNG: grey-brown down above, paler below. Forehead, lores and orbital area bare. Bill pink with some black.

Field Characters. Virtually unmistakable. A dark ibis with bald red head, red bill and legs, and neck-ruff of long pointed feathers which wave in wind to give standing bird a shaggy appearance.

Voice. Recorded (2a). Normally silent when feeding but vocal at colony and roost. Calls include: (1) guttural 'jum' or 'jupe' when greeting partner and bowing; (2) low, stifled 'horr ... horr', followed by 'ouahh/yooohhh' by unmated ♂ at nest-site; (3) loud rumbling noises while displaying to approaching bird; (4) gobbling sounds at nest-relief; (5) high pitched 'gru', 'ga', 'gr' or 'gu' when alarmed; and (6) guttural repeated 'kyow' at winter roost. Young give 'lib, lib, lib' food-begging call. Non-vocal clappering made with bills during copulation.

General Habits. Well known. Gregarious throughout year in flocks of a few to over 100. Seen most often along dry creek beds, rocky slopes and ledges; also in cultivated fields, high meadows, pastures and valleys of mountain streams. Feeds on semi-arid ground with little vegetation in day-time, usually in loose, small groups, sometimes singly, or with Wattled Ibis *Bostrychia carunculata*, pecking at or into ground, under stones, into crevices and in tufts of vegetation. Sometimes sunbathes by orienting body up and down, or slightly backward and braced against ground by tail, and fully extending wings with remige edges on ground exposing belly and innerwings to sun (see **A**).

A

Flies to and from roost in flocks in V-formation with rather shallow wing-beats, often interspersed with glides on slightly bowed wings, and with legs not extended to end of tail. Roosts communally at night on trees, ledges and sometimes in fields where foraging. Sleeps on ledges above breeding areas or sideways on unoccupied parts of ledge. In Dec–Feb winter roost (Ethiopia), pre-roosting birds peck, croak and raise plumes at those landing.

Migration and movements of populations in NE and NW Africa poorly known. Birds from Turkey migrate, probably to NE Africa, mainly Ethiopia (Massawa–Asmara, 1951–1954; flock of 100 near Addis Ababa, 1952 (Smith 1970); 6 near Addis Ababa, 1977 (Ash and Howell 1977)); rare Somalia and Sudan. Of Moroccan

birds adults winter in Morocco (1979, flocks totalling 112 birds, only 4 young under 6 years old: U. Hirsch, pers. comm.) with young birds migrating in almost every direction to distant areas of Morocco, Algeria, Tunisia, Mauritania, and possibly across Sahara judging from recent sightings in Mali (2 near Lakes Takadji and Faguibine, 1971: B. Lamarche, pers. comm.).

Food. Mainly crickets, grasshoppers, locusts, earwigs, beetles, ants, woodlice, spiders, scorpions and molluscs; also frogs, tadpoles, snakes, lizards, fish, rodents, birds and mammals. Occasionally rhizomes of aquatic plants, berries and shoots.

Breeding Habits. Very well known. Breeds in colonies of 3–40 or more pairs, occasionally alone, on cliff ledges or in caves along inland water courses, or along sea among boulders on steep slopes, and on top of old buildings. Often nests with Chough *Pyrrhocorax pyrrhocorax*, Lesser Kestrel *Falco naumanni* and Black Kite *Milvus migrans*. Nests in shaded areas or on open ledges exposed to sun for less than 4·5 h/day; 15 cm–5 m apart. Certain spots on the breeding ledge are preferred and almost exclusively occupied by the oldest birds. Can breed when 3 years old but normally does not return to colonies to breed until 6 years old.

Courtship begins in mid-Feb or later when unmated ♂♂ appear at the colony, first circling over breeding area, then landing and standing at nest-sites for long periods. Defends site by pecking at rivals with open bill, often just touching tip of rival's bill; also, with mantle feathers raised especially, threatens by gaping with head retracted and bill lifted (**B**), then quickly lowers bill to ground with neck extended. ♀♀ then circle over colony; this causes ♂♂ to point up with neck extended and throat enlarged and to call. ♂ then lowers head with bill touching breast and utters first note of disyllabic call; then, raising bill sharply, utters second note. When another bird approaches, ♂ crouches, bites twigs, waves crest, makes rumbling sounds, sways from one foot to the other and passes bill under flanks several times. Other bird, if ♀, watches inactively but lowers head when ♂ approaches. ♂ again utters disyllabic call, then preens ♀'s back, neck and head. At first ♀ appears shy and may fly to another place in colony. Both eventually engage in mutual billing and entwining necks.

Pair-formation may take up to a week; once formed, ♂ collects nest material, ♀ builds nest within *c.* 1 week.

B

C

D

Both greet mate by bowing, which involves facing each other, simultaneously throwing head back to shoulder, then turning head to ground (**C** and **D**). Copulation, which ♀ solicits by lying prone with raised head, occurs daily, many times, until eggs hatch. During copulation ♂ rapidly shakes ♀'s bill in his bill while extending and flapping wings.

NEST: a loose platform of small branches lined with grass and stems.

EGGS: 1–7, usually 2–4, with nests on ledges usually having 2–3, those in holes mostly 4; laid at 1–3 day intervals. Ovals, rough and pitted, bluish white with small brown spots. SIZE: (46 eggs) 61–69 × 42–46 (63 × 44); WEIGHT: 68.

Laying dates: breeds in Palearctic spring, laying dependent on adequate rainfall, may not breed in dry years; lays Morocco, Algeria Mar–Apr.

Incubation begins with 1st egg; carried out by both parents. Period 24–28 days.

At 14 days first black feathers show through down and young begin to touch tip of parent's bill when begging. At 20 days beg at corner of adult's gape. Young often left unattended during day with 2 or more young from different nests then gathering together. When parents return, young run back to their nests to feed.

Fledged when 43–47 days; time of independence not known.

Both parents care for and feed young well after fledging. During incubation, adults regularly change over in middle of day or night. Parents assist in hatching, sometimes breaking off small pieces of egg shell and even pulling at chick. Feed young 10–20 min after hatching by lowering head and bill to side, clasping young's bill and guiding young's head to gullet where they are fed by regurgitation.

In Morocco, in good years, breeding success for clutches of 2–4 was as follows: 20% pairs reared on average no young, 60% 1 young, 15% 2 young, 5% 3 young. In poor (dry) years: 50% reared no young, nearly all rest 1 young. In 1968 and 1972 3 Morocco colonies with 13 nests holding 3–4 eggs each produced 39 fledged young, or at least 90% eggs laid resulted in fledged young (U. Hirsch, pers. comm.).

References
Hirsch, U. (1976, 1979a, b).

Illustration A reproduced with permission from Bauer and Glutz von Blotzheim (1966). Illustrations B, C and D by Robert Gillmor, reproduced with permission from Cramp and Simmons (1977).

Plate 13
(Opp. p. 210)

Geronticus calvus (Boddaert). Bald Ibis. Ibis du Cap.

Tantalus Calvus Boddaert, 1783. Tabl. Pl. Enlum., p. 52; Cape of Good Hope.

Range and Status. Resident, uncommon, breeding restricted to SE highlands of South Africa and Lesotho (900 m above sea level). Total population, 1971, *c.* 2000 birds (Siegfried 1971) with half of population in Orange Free State; formerly more abundant.

Description. ADULT♂: bald head, face, throat and nape beige; bright red crown domed posteriorly. Metallic bluish green feathers on neck form fluffy ruff. Upperwing-coverts metallic copper with violet iridescence. Rest of plumage dark metallic iridescent blue-green. Bill red; eye red to orange-red; legs and feet dull red. Sexes alike. SIZE: (7 specimens) wing, 369–403 (386); tail, 175–200 (191); tarsus, 66–73 (70); culmen, 140–152 (146). ♂♂ slightly larger with slightly longer bill and tarsus.

IMMATURE: plumage dark iridescent green. Feathered head, throat and nape light grey, finely streaked dark grey; no red on crown. No coppery wing-patches. Bill pinkish flesh, grey towards base. Lores dark grey. At 1 year old, similar to adult but wing-patches not so bright; some white on face at base

of bill; crown pinkish orange. 2 year olds, wrinkly red crown, less bulbous than adult; white face, throat, nape and especially orbital area with variable red spots; black ear openings; some indications of neck fluff.

DOWNY YOUNG: black skin with dark grey down darkest on crown; bill black with grey tip; eye dark blue; legs and feet blackish grey.

Field Characters. A dark iridescent green ibis with striking shiny red crown on bare white head. In flight, wings pointed and bill held directly ahead.

Voice. Recorded (6). Generally silent when foraging but vocal at colony. Common calls include: (1) a sharp, slightly resonant 'skē-ōhh', 'whē-ōhh', 'hū-ōhhh' or 'hē-ōhhh' in alarm and in flight. Birds at colony utter this as birds arrive or depart; departing or arriving birds also utter it. Sometimes 'whē-ōhh-yō' when evading attack by aerial predator. (2) 'skōlp', 'whōlp', 'whŭp', or 'yŭp' in flight, but not frequently heard; may serve to co-ordinate flock. (3) A piping 'ĕk-ĕk-ĕk . . .', 'ŭck-ŭck-ŭck . . .' or 'yĭp-yĭp-yĭp . . .' with bill usually pointed downwards or resting on back; the tail flicked with each note. Usually uttered by ♂, rarely ♀, on territory, by both during incubation, brooding and greeting; by ♀ during copulation. When greeting, bird utters series of piping notes that break into a loud 'ek-ek-ek-ek-ek, uhr-r-r!, ek-ek-ek-ek-ek, uhr-r-r! . .'. (4) A rasping 'skur-r-r-r' by ♂ before landing with nest material and, upon landing, a few emphatic, low moaning 'huhhhhh, huhhhhh' before releasing material. (5) High-pitched squeals by both during courtship and fighting. (6) Non-vocal bill-snapping by both when threatening, by ♂ prior to mounting ♀, and by both after copulation. (7) Young, a shrill 'shreeeee' when begging.

General Habits. Well known. Highly gregarious throughout year, scattered locally in small groups in upland or mountainous country with grasslands. Shy, but occasionally seen in villages. Forages mainly on burnt, mowed or heavily grazed fields, occasionally in tall grass, probing ground or turning over fallen leaves or cattle dung. During breeding season, adults range in a radius of possibly 20 miles from colony in search of food.

Bathes on fringes of reservoirs and in rivers, standing on submerged rocks. Sunbathes by orienting body up and down, or slightly backwards and braced against ground by tail, and fully extending wings with edges of feathers on ground, exposing belly and inner wings to sun.

Flies with much gliding in between flaps. If air currents are suitable, gains altitude rapidly with little or no wing-flapping. Having spiralled upwards for some time, descends again in long glide. About 30 min before sunset roost in groups of 40–150 at colony site, or elsewhere on cliffs or trees, with Cattle Egret *Bubulcus ibis*, Sacred Ibis *Threskiornis aethiopica* and cormorants; same roosts used for nearly 100 years (Pocock and Uys 1967).

Leaves nesting cliffs end breeding season in Dec–Jan with gradual dispersal of adults and juveniles from then until May. During this period, congregates in flocks of variable size, staying in one area for up to 1 week. Post-breeding dispersal unknown but probably limited to short distances (11 miles or more) according to food availability. Returns to colony from June until late Aug or Sept when colony size stable until following Dec–Jan.

Food. Insects, mainly grasshoppers, caterpillars, beetles; also snails, earthworms, frogs, small dead mammals and birds. Known to swallow buttons—155 buttons collected at and below nesting colony, diameter 10–23 (15) mm (Milstein 1974).

Breeding Habits. Intimately known. Nests in colonies of 2–60 or more on cliffs 30–100 m high, on hill-sides, by waterfalls, and in river gorges. Nesting sites usually on ledges, or in potholes or crevices with many accommodating 1–4 nests. Same site used annually by pairs for at least 2 years and probably for life. Number of breed-

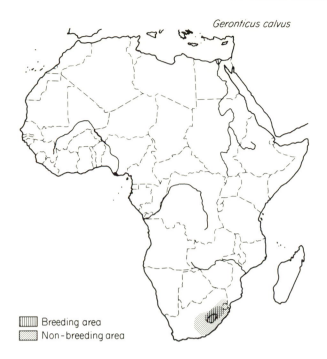

Geronticus calvus

||||Breeding area
||||Non-breeding area

ing birds fluctuates annually, with no breeding in years of subnormal rainfall.

In early winter (June) birds begin to spend more time at colony site; established pairs, especially ♂♂, spend much of day occupying or reoccupying nesting territory; potential new breeders immigrate to colony. Birds then forage only briefly, returning to colony sometimes by 11.00 h. ♂♂ defend against intruders and neighbouring pairs usually by bill-jabbing and bill-sparring.

Details on pair-formation difficult to determine because: (1) unpaired ♂♂ and ♀♀ copulate with different partners within minutes; (2) unpaired ♂ and ♀ associate for several days, behaving as a pair, then separate; (3) new pair moves from ledge to ledge performing court-ship behaviour; and (4) paired ♂♂ sometimes copulate with 'strange' ♀♀. Observed courtship behaviour includes: (1) mutual preening, mainly of neck plumage (not restricted to courtship); (2) either partner seizes mate's bill in own and wags head vigorously 2–4 times; (3) either partner, with twig in bill, vigorously wags head, while raising, lowering and turning head and bill sideways; sometimes both partners grasp same object and wag it together; (4) after a long separation, ♂ pecks with closed bill at ♀'s face, neck, body or wings; (5) in response to ♂'s pecking, ♀ crouches, extends neck vertically with nape towards him, presses bill against throat, and raises neck plumage concealing face and bill from him; sometimes ♀ extends neck with bill or side of neck resting on ground; (6) ♂ bites foot of standing ♀ to induce ♀ to adopt a prone position; frequently carried out by paired ♂ courting unpaired ♀; (7) ♀ stands or crouches, ♂ mounts her, grasps her bill in his and wags it repeatedly; copulation lasts 5–15 s. After dismounting, ♂ and sometimes ♀ stand erect with bill raised, snapping mandibles together; (8) upon return of mate, bird on nest flicks tail, makes piping notes, waves neck and brings nape in touch with back, pointing bill skyward; performed also during incubation and brooding; (9) either partner points and rapidly snaps bill at intruder; upon repelling intruder, both partners usually rub faces together, squeal and make squirming and reeling movements of neck.

♂ prepares nest-site, pressing breast into soil to make small depression; then scrapes backwards alternately with both feet. ♂ gathers most of nest material, ♀ builds nest.

NEST: a hollow mound of sticks and twigs *c*. 50 cm in diameter and 15 cm high; lined with soft vegetation.

EGGS: 1–3, laid at 2-day intervals; mean (21 clutches) 2·21 (Manry 1979), (307) 1·9 (Milstein and Wolff 1973), (78) 2·0 (Milstein and Siegfried 1970), (9) 1·8 (SAOSNRC), (53) 2·2 (SAOSNRC), overall (468) 1·96. Pale blue, spotted reddish brown. SIZE: 51–71 × 38–49 (63 × 43); WEIGHT: 68.

Laying dates: Aug–Oct (end dry season) apparently timed to permit chick development when maximum foraging ground (short grass with new growth over large areas) is available; 1 record Natal Mar (SAOSNRC).

Incubation begins 1st egg; by both parents, with reliefs usually twice daily in morning, midday and evening; bird sitting in evening usually sits all night although may changeover during night. Details of feather development not recorded. Young make 1st flight at *c*. 55 days; thereafter still dependent on parents for food for up to 2 months. Both parents alternate in guarding and feeding chicks. Nest-reliefs by either

usually twice daily, relieving bird feeding chicks. Young fed direct from parent's throat from hatching to independence. Adult brooding small young rests bill against nest-floor, opening bill to permit chick to insert its bill into parent's mouth for food. Older young, when begging, vigorously bob head, give shrill begging calls, tap ventral surface of parent's mandible, and insert head into parent's mouth.

Breeding success recorded, normally good, sometimes low. In 151 Transvaal nests, av. 1·8 young hatched, 1·6 large chicks; in 44 others, av. 1·7 medium-sized. In Natal, 1–2 large chicks in 55% of nests or *c*. 0·83 young/nest (Milstein and Wolff 1973, Manry 1979).

Success reduced by predation, principally humans taking chicks from nests. Losses also caused by parents accidentally kicking eggs out of nest when shaping nest-bowl. Once young hatch, starvation important cause of mortality; further mortality among young caused by falls.

References
Manry, D. (1979).
Milstein, P. le S. and Siegfried, W. R. (1970).
Milstein, P. le S. and Wolff, S. W. (1973).
Pocock, T. N. and Uys, C. J. (1967).
Vincent, J. and Symons, G. (1948).

Genus *Platalea* Linnaeus

Medium-sized long-legged waders, similar to ibises, but with flattened bill expanded towards tip forming flat spoon. Mandible edges smooth except for slight notching at tip; narrow groove from nostril along margin of upper mandible almost to tip; interior of spoon covered with sharp, lateral ridges, pointing inwards, obviously useful in grabbing prey. Chin, lores, area around eyes and part of forehead naked. Feeding method distinctive, sweeping bill from side to side in water. In flight, head and neck stretched forward, legs backward. 6 species in warm parts of world. In Africa, 2 species, 1 with Palearctic populations that migrate to Africa in winter.

Plate 13
(Opp. p. 210)

Platalea leucorodia Linnaeus. Eurasian Spoonbill; White Spoonbill. Spatule blanche.

Platalea leucorodia Linnaeus, 1758. Syst. Nat. (10th ed.), p. 139; Sweden.

Range and Status. Resident and Palearctic winter visitor mainly along coasts but also inland lakes and rivers. *P. l. balsaci* abundant coasts Mauritania; occasionally Senegal and Guinea-Bissau. *P. l. archeri* frequent to uncommon, coasts Sudan, Ethiopia, Somalia and probably Socotra; vagrant inland. *P. l. leucorodia* uncommon to rare Palearctic winter visitor N Africa south across Sahara to about 3°N.

Description. *P. l. leucorodia* Linnaeus: Africa south to about 3° N. ADULT ♂: all white. Forecrown between eyes feathered. Naked yellow to orange chin, throat, lores and round eyes. Base of upper mandible and narrow line on lores to eye black, bordered pale yellow or white. Bill black, tipped orange-yellow; eye carmine; legs and feet black. Sexes alike. ADULT ♂ and ♀ (breeding): yellowish buff collar; long, partially yellow-buff crest; and red band on naked skin bordering feathers of lower throat. SIZE: wing, ♂ (13 specimens) 386–412 (394), ♀ (10) 360–377 (370); tail, ♂ (25) 108–126 (117), ♀ (24) 108–118 (113); bill, ♂ (15) 195–231 (213), ♀ (24) 168–191 (182); tarsus,

♂ (24) 140–163 (149), ♀ (19) 123–141 (131). WEIGHT: 1323, 1463, 1960, 1130.

IMMATURE: similar to non-breeding adult but primaries tipped black; bill pink to dirty yellow; legs and feet dull yellowish horn; eye grey-brown.

DOWNY YOUNG: at hatching sparsely covered in white down; bill and feet orange; eye grey; bare area around eye, blue, and on chin and throat, pink.

P. l. balsaci de Naurois and Roux. Mauritania to Guinea-Bissau. Smaller, wing, ♂ (9) 364–390 (372), ♀ (8) 340–362 (352); bill all black; usually lacks yellow collar.

P. l. archeri Neumann. Sudan to northern Uganda and Kenya. Resembles *leucorodia* but smaller; wing 325–360.

Field Characters. Easily recognized as a spoonbill by spoon-shaped bill, all-white plumage, habit of moving bill from side-to-side in water when feeding, and extended neck in flight. Distinguished from African Spoonbill *P. alba* by black bill without red on upper mandible; feathered, not naked, area between eyes; yellow, not red, bare face; and black, not pink, legs and feet. Also diagnostic are alternating wing-flaps with short glides, slower than Glossy Ibis *Plegadis falcinellus*, but not as slow as *Ardea* herons.

Voice. Recorded (2a). Usually silent except at breeding colony when utters deep grunting 'huh-huh-huh' and, at nest-relief, groaning calls. Also clattering and snapping with bill.

General Habits. Well known but little observed in Africa. Gregarious throughout year when migrating, feeding, or going to and from roost and colony. Usually in small parties, but flocks of up to 100 when migrating. Does not usually associate with other long-legged waders. Occupies shallow water in coastal, brackish and freshwater habitats with fairly even depth, bottoms of mud, clay or sand, and gentle tidal or current changes. Roosts communally with mixed flocks of adults and fledged young together for long periods during day, preferring shallow water or short grassy areas but also shrubs and trees; sometimes communal roosts used for several years. Leaves roost at dusk, returning in morning. Feeding grounds up to 15 km away. Feeds at night but also by day in small flocks or singly, wading in water and sweeping bill from side-to-side. Sometimes makes loping runs after prey; swims short distances in deep water.

Migrating parties usually fly during day-time in single file or loose V-formation; sometimes soars in thermals. Overwinters Egypt to Morocco and, south of Sahara, in Mauritania, Senegal, Mali, Niger, Nigeria, Chad, Zaïre (extreme northeast) and Sudan. Passage of migrant, Sept and Mar, Morocco Atlantic coast with unknown destination, suspected to be Banc d'Arguin (Mauritania) where large numbers, up to 4000, of non-breeding spoonbills congregate, and where some marked Dutch birds sighted and recovered among wintering Banc d'Arguin population. Examples of other marked Palearctic birds: ringed Turkey, recovered Sudan, Egypt; Hungary, recovered Sudan, Niger, Tunisia, Libya and Egypt; Austria, recovered Tunisia, Libya, Egypt, Algeria; and Yugoslavia, recovered Tunisia, Libya and Egypt. Extent Palearctic migrants mix with African birds unknown but probably relatively small since European population not large. Some dispersion of subspecies *balsaci* along W African coast to Senegal and Guinea-Bissau; and of *archeri* along Red Sea coast of unknown extent.

Food. Mainly molluscs, crustaceans, aquatic insects and other invertebrates; also small fish and frogs.

Breeding Habits. Well known. Breeding occurs about 20° N along Mauritania coast (Banc d'Arguin) (colonies up to 1000 pairs) and Ethiopia and Somalia coasts (colonies of 20–40 pairs); in mangroves 3–5 m above water level (Ethiopia) or on clumps of *Salicornia*, 3–60 cm above ground or on tufts of grass on ground (Mauritania). Sometimes nests with Western Reef Heron *Egretta gularis*.

Courtship not well described. When defending territory, fights with bill, slashing and pecking at opponent;

Platalea leucorodia

sometimes turns from side to side alternately, avoiding opponent's slashes and showing yellow and red skin of throat. Makes clattering and snapping sounds by opening and closing mandibles. Threatens with crest feathers raised and bill open. Chases intruder on foot or in air, sometimes several birds together. Courtship behaviour includes: (1) raising crest feathers and pointing bill up, exposing bare skin on throat; (2) mutual preening, sometimes simultaneously by both partners; (3) greeting at nest with both birds erecting crest, making groaning moans with bill and sometimes bowing; (4) copulation, occurs frequently early in pair-formation with 11 attempts in 1 h (Mauritania) and with paired ♂♂ attempting to copulate with neighbouring birds; and (5) building nest, with ♂ collecting most material, ♀ building nest.

NEST: large pile of loose sticks, reeds, twigs and grass stems, 50–70 cm in diameter; often built close together.

EGGS: 3–7, generally 4 in Mauritania (once 7: von Westernhagen 1970), 3 in Red Sea, laid at 2–3 day intervals. Dull white, blotched and spotted red-brown and dark brown, with greyish undermarkings. SIZE: 250 eggs, 56–75 × 40–50 (67 × 46); WEIGHT: 76.

Laying dates: Algeria (not since late 19th century) May; Mauritania mainly end Apr–July, with isolated breeders Aug–Oct, before rains (replacement clutches may be laid if 1st is lost); Ethiopia Apr–Aug (rains, if any, in areas involved); Somalia Apr–June, Aug (mainly rains).

Details of incubation behaviour scanty. Begins with 1st egg; by both sexes with infrequent changeovers by day, not accompanied by elaborate ceremony. Period: 24–25 days (Mauritania).

Both parents care for and feed young by regurgitation, with young placing head into parent's mouth. Feed young largely early morning or evening. Development of young also poorly recorded but probably similar to that of African Spoonbill. Young beg by bobbing head up and down, and calling. Mobile young react to nearly every adult landing but usually stop if not parent. Young are highly sociable, engaging in much mutual billing; rarely fight. At about 3–4 weeks leave nest to wander about colony, but up to *c.* 5 weeks, return to nest at feeding time. Fly freely at 7 weeks; fed by parents until 10 weeks old.

No breeding success data for Africa; in Rumania, mortality of chicks varied annually from 17·2–100%,

losses being caused by rises in water levels, food supply and weather (Cramp and Simmons 1977).

References

Boswall, J. (1971).
de Naurois, R. (1969).
de Naurois, R. and Roux, F. (1974).
Dragesco, J. (1961).

Plate 13

(Opp. p. 210)

Platalea alba Scopoli. African Spoonbill. Spatule d'Afrique.

Platalea alba Scopoli, 1786. Del. Flor. Faun. Insubr. 2, p. 92; Cape of Good Hope.

Range and Status. Resident, widespread with patchy distribution, uncommon to common, south about 17°N from Senegal to Ethiopia south to Cape.

Platalea alba

Voice. Recorded (6, 19). Usually silent but utters guttural grunt, alarm 'wark-wark', double 'aark-ark', nasal 'kor', quacking note when flying, threatening hoarse 'kwaark', sometimes softly clatters mandibles, and at copulation 'moot-moot-moot'.

General Habits. Well known. Gregarious, usually in small parties of 3–30; occasionally alone. Rarely in contact with Eurasian Spoonbill. Shy; takes off quickly when disturbed. Always near water, especially large sheets of inland water; also estuaries and coastal lagoons. Feeds alone or in small groups of often up to 6, sometimes up to 10, and with other waders. Wades slowly through shallow water, sweeping bill from side to side in water, snapping prey in spoon, swallowing with backward jerk of head. Sometimes dashes about rapidly like Little Egret *Egretta garzetta*, chasing fish. Occasionally probes in mud. Rests along shore, sometimes in large numbers of up to 1000 with herons, ibises and flamingoes, standing on one leg with head tucked into scapulars. Usually flies in formation, with strong wing-beats, av. 225/min (M. P. Kahl, pers. comm.). In southern Africa more common winter than summer. Migratory movements little known but, at least in southern Africa, wanders large distances, e.g. one bird ringed Transvaal, recaptured several hundred km north in Zambia (McLachlan and Liversidge 1978).

Description. ADULT ♂: all white. Loose cream-coloured crest on nape and neck. Forehead, front of crown, area between and around eyes, lores, cheeks and throat bare; red on forehead and crown, grading to yellow around chin and throat. Upper mandible grey edged red, lower mandible slate black with yellow edges and spots; eye white to pale blue; legs and feet pink to bright red. Sexes alike, ♂ slightly larger. SIZE: (15 specimens, sex?) wing, 365–414 (384); tail, 105–152 (124); tarsus, 131–157 (144); culmen, 172–230 (193). WEIGHT: ♀ 1790.

IMMATURE: like adult but feathers extend further forward on forehead. Head streaked blackish brown; crest smaller; tips of primaries and underwing-coverts black. Bill dusky yellow to horn colour; feet black.

DOWNY YOUNG: at hatching, skin pink with white down; pink to orange bill without spoon; legs pink. Wing 13–21 (16), tarsus 20, culmen 18–24 (18).

Field Characters. Easily recognized by spoon-shaped grey and red bill and white plumage. Slightly larger than Eurasian Spoonbill *P. leucorodia*, distinguished by bare face and forehead being red, not yellow or orange; no feathers between eyes; and red, not black, legs and feet.

Breeding Habits. Well known. Nests colonially, sometimes 250 or more pairs together, often with cormorants, darters, herons, or Sacred Ibis *Threskiornis aethiopica*, on partly submerged trees, bushes, reeds and rocky islets.

Courtship scarcely known. Birds known to chase others in flight; threaten with bill outstretched and slightly opened; and bob heads. A pair, standing side-by-side but facing opposite directions, once seen to turn heads almost simultaneously and thrust them alternately above and below neck of mate several times. During copulation ♂ grasps and vigorously shakes ♀'s bill just behind 'spoon' (M. P. Kahl, pers. comm.) with both sometimes waggling bills from side to side and making clapping noises with them. After copulation, ♀ emits loud nasal hooting; both sexes preen themselves and their mate, intertwine bills and work on nest. During nest-building, mated pair appears to spend much time in close company, ♂ collecting nest material, ♀ building nest.

NEST: flat and oval with av. size (5 nests) 48 × 37

cm and cup 6–11 cm; made of sticks, creepers and reeds, often placed on existing platforms 25 cm to 6 m above water.

EGGS: 2–4, usually 2–3, laying interval unknown; mean E Africa (47 clutches) 2·8 (EANRC); Botswana and Namibia (5) 2·8 (SAOSNRC); South Africa (27) 2·6 (Whitelaw 1968), SW Cape (146) 2·5, OFS (6) 2·7, Transvaal (95) 2·7, Natal (19) 2·7 (SAOSNRC); overall (350) 2·9. Dull white to pale buff, more or less heavily blotched and spotted red-brown and dark brown, with greyish undermarkings. SIZE: (205 eggs) 57–82 × 40–48 (68 × 45); WEIGHT: 69.

Laying dates: Senegal Jan–Mar, Oct–Dec (dry); Guinea-Bissau Jan–Feb (dry), May (rains), Nov–Dec (dry); Sierra Leone Sept; Niger Oct; Mali Jan–Apr, Aug–Oct; Chad Jan–Apr; Nigeria Jan–Feb; Sudan Feb–Mar, Sept; Ethiopia July–Aug (rains), Oct; Kenya Feb–July, Sept–Oct, with major peak in rains (May), or in early mid-year dry season (June–July); Uganda Feb–June; Tanzania Feb–Mar, May (rains); Zambia Feb–July; Malawi Sept; Zimbabwe Jan–Apr, Sept; Botswana Mar–June; Namibia Feb–July, Oct (dry); South Africa, SW Cape Aug–Nov, Transvaal Jan, Mar–Nov, peaking May and Sept, Natal July–Aug, Oct (SAOSNRC). Most W African records east to Sudan are in dry season; E African and Central African in rains, sometimes in dry season.

Incubation begins when clutch is complete, or with 2nd egg. Both parents incubate, with ♀ sitting most of day, ♂ at night; rarely, changeover occurs by day. Birds often incubate with heads and bills tucked into back feathers, asleep; face wind if in exposed sites on islands. Incubation period: 25–29 days (av. 26).

Young at 3 days have grey skin; bill is thick and yellow with 2 latero-dorsal ridges; legs dark grey; wing 25–33, tarsus 26–34, culmen 26–31. At 4 days primaries sheathed with black tips visible. At 7 days primaries 11 mm long; indications of rectrices; wing 53–64, tarsus 56–68, culmen 39–44. At 9 days primaries 22 mm long; bill thick and ridged, slightly decurved; wing 70–85, tarsus 68–80, culmen 45–51. At 11 days, primaries 27 mm long, plumage entirely white; bill slightly flattened and spatulate at tip, decurved; wing 80–101, tarsus 83–92, culmen 54–61. At 14 days plumage white, except black-tipped primaries and black underwing-coverts; sufficiently well developed to leave nest when approached by intruder; wing 98–120, tarsus 85–101, culmen 65–85. At 21 days bill yellow with distinct spoon; partly abandon nest and wander in its vicinity; take short flights with much wing-beating. At 4 weeks, some aggression among chicks, make flights of 18–30 m. At *c.* 5 weeks, leave colony but some feeding by parents until young 46 days old.

Both parents feed young, mainly in evening and late afternoon but some throughout day. Feed by regurgitation with young placing head into parent's mouth. At least 1 parent with young until 16 days; thereafter parents only with young during day at feeding time, but roost at colony at night.

Breeding success: South Africa (Germiston), 59·5% eggs hatched (33 nests, 79 eggs, 47 hatched), 89·0% hatched survived 5–8 days (55 hatched, 49 5–8 days old), 49·1% reached flying stage (55 hatched, 27 able to fly), i.e. breeding success of *c.* 0·8 young/pair; E Africa (Kisumu, Elmenteita), less than 1 young/pair.

References
Whitelaw, D. A. (1968).

in
0   3   6   9   12

0   10   20   30
cm

Plate 13

Platalea alba African Spoonbill (p. 208)
1 ADULT (breeding), 2. IMMATURE.

Platalea leucorodia Eurasian Spoonbill (p. 206)
3. ADULT (breeding), 4. IMMATURE.

Geronticus calvus Bald Ibis (p. 204)
5. ADULT (breeding), 6. IMMATURE.

Geronticus eremita Waldrapp (p. 202)
7. ADULT, 8. IMMATURE.

Threskiornis aethiopica Sacred Ibis (p. 200)
9. ADULT (breeding), 10. showing enlarged foreneck,
11. IMMATURE.

Bostrychia carunculata Wattled Ibis (p. 196)
12. ADULT.

Bostrychia rara Spot-breasted Ibis (p. 198)
13. ADULT.

Bostrychia hagedash Hadada (p. 195)
Race *brevirostris*: 14. ADULT.
Race *hagedash*: 15. ADULT.

Bostrychia olivacea Olive Ibis (p. 197)
Race *olivacea*: 16. ADULT.
Race *cupreipennis*: 17. ADULT.

Plegadis falcinellus Glossy Ibis (p. 193)
18. ADULT, 19. IMMATURE.

Plate 14

Cygnus bewickii Bewick's Swan (p. 231)
1. ADULT and head detail, 2. IMMATURE and head detail.

Cygnus cygnus Whooper Swan (p. 230)
3. ADULT and head detail, 4. IMMATURE and head detail.

Cygnus olor Mute Swan (p. 229)
5. ADULT head, 6. IMMATURE head, 7. ADULT with DOWNY YOUNG, 8. IMMATURE.

Anser anser Greylag Goose (p. 234)
9. ADULT in flight from above and below,
10. ADULT standing and head detail.

Anser fabalis Bean Goose (p. 232)
11. ADULT standing and head detail, 12. ADULT in flight from above and below.

Anser albifrons Greater White-fronted Goose (p. 232)
13. ADULT in flight from above and below,
14. ADULT standing and head detail.

Anser erythropus Lesser White-fronted Goose (p. 233)

15. ADULT standing and head detail, 16. ADULT in flight from above and below.

Branta leucopsis Barnacle Goose (p. 234)
17. ADULT in flight from above and below,
18. ADULT standing.

Branta bernicla Brent Goose (p. 235)
19. ADULT in flight from above and below,
20. ADULT standing.

Branta ruficollis Red-breasted Goose (p. 236)
21. ADULT in flight from above and below,
22. ADULT standing.

Scale does not apply to head details or flying birds shown from below

Order
PHOENICOPTERIFORMES

A highly specialized order of large, generally rather slim, long-legged water birds. Plumage white, pink, red and black. Bills specialized for filter-feeding, either from the water surface or bottom mud (Jenkins 1957). Feet webbed; all swim freely. All make mud-mound nests, lay one egg and produce downy young with swollen, blood-rich legs, which leave the nest within a few days. All perform striking communal displays, unlike those of any other group.

The order perhaps forms a link between the long-legged herons, storks and ibises of the Order Ciconiiformes, and the short-legged, free-swimming, web-footed ducks and geese, Order Anseriformes. Possible relationships have been reviewed by Sibley *et al.* (1969), who concluded that there were more anatomical similarities between flamingoes and herons than between flamingoes and ducks. However, this review contains several major errors, notably the supposition that flamingoes do not voluntarily swim (all do). Similarities with the ducks and especially geese include webbed feet and readiness to swim; waterproof plumage; honking voices; downy young remarkably like goslings, which soon leave the nest; and feather lice. In the Ciconiiformes the feather lice are of the genus *Ardeicola*, but in flamingoes (inhabiting the same waters with both these other orders) are of the genera *Anaticola* and *Anatoecus*, typical of ducks and geese.

Although the similarities to ducks and geese appear greater on balance than to the herons, storks and ibises, we consider the flamingoes a highly specialized order, placed between the Ciconiiformes and Anseriformes, but clearly different from either. The order has only 1 family, Phoenicopteridae, with either 1 genus *Phoenicopterus* of 5, possibly 6 species; or 3 genera *Phoenicopterus* (2 species), *Phoeniconaias* (1) and *Phoenicoparrus* (2). The last is exclusively South American but both *Phoenicopterus* and *Phoeniconaias* occur in Africa, the Lesser Flamingo *Phoeniconaias minor* probably outnumbering all the rest of the world's flamingoes combined. For further study see Jenkins (1957), Kear and Duplaix-Hall (1975) and Sibley *et al.* (1969).

Family PHOENICOPTERIDAE: flamingoes

Genus *Phoenicopterus* Linnaeus

The largest flamingoes, ♂♂ standing up to 1·6 m. Adult plumage white, pink, bright red and black. Bill shallow-keeled (Jenkins 1957) the upper mandible covering, but not fitting closely into, the lower. Feed chiefly on invertebrates in bottom mud. 2 species, 1 *P. ruber* with races in America, Eurasia and Africa.

Plate 9
(Opp. p. 146)

Phoenicopterus ruber Linnaeus. Greater Flamingo. Grand Flamant.

Phoenicopterus ruber Linnaeus, 1758. Syst. Nat. (10th ed.), 1, p. 139; West Indies.

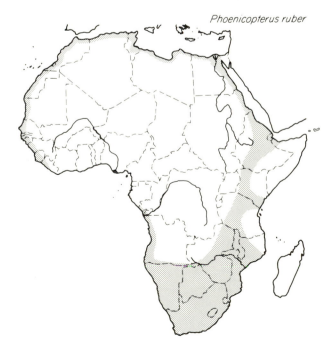
Phoenicopterus ruber

Range and Status. Occurs throughout Africa in suitable habitat, alkaline or saline lakes, estuarine lagoons. Highly gregarious, locally very abundant. Breeds in large colonies, sometimes, associated with Lesser Flamingoes *Phoeniconaias minor*. Regular breeding localities in Tunisia, Mauritania, Senegal, Kenya, Tanzania, Namibia, and less regular in South Africa. Largest recorded African colony (over 15,000 pairs) recently discovered, Botswana (Robertson and Johnson, in prep.). May be increasing in southern Africa due to increased man-made habitats, but perhaps decreasing in E African Rift Valley due to interference from Great White Pelicans *Pelecanus onocrotalus*. Elsewhere, stable or increasing; often benefits from man-made habitats such as salt works, sewage lagoons or large dams.

Description. *P. r. roseus* Pallas, ADULT ♂: general colour pale pink. Upperwing- and underwing-coverts bright scarlet. Primaries and secondaries black, strongly contrasting. Tail pale pink. Bill pink, terminal third black; eye yellow; legs bright coral pink. ♀ similar, decidedly smaller, especially shorter-legged. ADULT ♂ and ♀ (breeding): red colours intensify.

SIZE: wing, ♂ 406–464 (428), ♀ 360–396 (380); tail, ♂ 144–167 (154), ♀ 130–138 (135); tarsus, ♂ 291–373 (323), ♀ 232–280 (259); bill, ♂ 117–125 (121), ♀ 112–121 (116). WEIGHT: ♂ 3000–4100 (3579), ♀ 2100–3300 (2525) (Gallet 1950).

IMMATURE: generally brownish grey where adult is pink; upperwing-coverts brown, streaked darker, underwing-coverts whitish tinged pink. Wing-feathers dark brown, paler below, tail pinkish. Bill grey, tipped black; eye brown; legs grey. Assumes adult plumage at least 2 years, first becoming white tinged pink, with greyish head and neck, red and pink colours thereafter intensifying.

DOWNY YOUNG: pale silky grey, when first hatched, with swollen, blood-rich, bright pink legs and feet; these become blackish brown and shrink at *c.* 4–5 days; 2nd down dull grey-brown; eye blackish, bill grey.

Field Characters. Unmistakable as flamingoes; tall, long-legged, fragile-looking pink, red and black water birds, wading in shallows or swimming. Adults distinguished from Lesser Flamingoes by bright scarlet upper and lower wing-coverts, generally paler pink plumage, large pink bill tipped black. Much larger, especially much taller. Recent immatures much larger, taller, browner than Lesser Flamingo; subadults mainly white with black primaries, grey legs and bills.

Voice. Recorded (2a, 6, 18, 22a). Commonest call a loud, brassy, goose-like double honk 'ka-ha', often repeated in chorus in display, or at colonies. In alarm or pre-flight a long-drawn nasal 'kngaaaa' or 'pmaaaa'. Conversational babble when feeding 'kuk-kuk, ke-kuk . . .'. in chorus. In aggressive display to others in colony deep grunting 'hurrrh-hurrrh-hurrh' accompanied by swaying head and neck from side to side; and at hatch adults continuously call a high-pitched 'kurruck-kurruck-kurruck' to emerging chicks. Young emit repeated high pitched cries 'kewick-kewick' when begging for food.

General Habits. Very well known. Frequent mainly on saline or alkaline lakes, estuaries and lagoons. Seldom alights on fresh water and cannot survive there long. Normally very gregarious, occurring in thousands together, almost always in flocks of 100 or more; if seen singly probably sick or moribund.

Feeds mainly by day, but migrates largely at night. When feeding usually walks on bottom in shallow water, head submerged, raising head to breathe at intervals of 5–25 s. Sometimes stands in one place, working feet to stir bottom mud, but usually walks steadily along. In deeper water swims, upending like a dabbling duck to reach bottom, paddling behind with webbed feet to maintain position. Occasionally feeds on surface like Lesser Flamingo, sieving material from top few cm, with bills held steady or gently swung from side to side. Roost together in large flocks on sandbanks, islands, or standing in shallow water. Night vision poor, but better than human.

Greater Flamingoes spend much of the day wading about feeding, but often also rest on shore for hours, especially near midday or in high winds. Bathe in fresh water, and drink at mouths of streams and springs entering alkaline/saline lakes. In flight neck and legs are stretched out in front and behind. Flight is straight and direct, wing-beats powerful, speed *c.* 50–60 km/h. Move from place to place in large skeins, travelling perhaps 500–600 km/night between habitats. Rarely fly overland by day.

Population breeding in Europe (Camargue, Spain) migrates to N Africa in winter, mainly from Mauritania east to Tunisia, occasionally Egypt; not proven to migrate south of Sahara. In E Africa resident population may be augmented in winter by migrants from Afghanistan, Turkey, Iran, Iraq; no proven recoveries but 2 juveniles marked Iran and recovered Ethiopia suggest some movement to Rift Valley Lakes (Scott 1975). Within tropical Africa movements erratic, unpredictable, possibly, but not always, connected with locally abundant food supplies. South African birds tend to move northwards during colder periods. Perhaps 4 more or less discrete population units exist, centred on (i) Europe and Middle East migrating in winter to N and E Africa; (ii) in Mauritania and Senegal; (iii) in E African Rift; and (iv) in southern Africa.

Food. Mainly small aquatic invertebrates, in Africa especially chironomid larvae, copepeds (Ridley *et al.* 1955). In N Africa and Europe brine shrimp *Artemia salina* important. Can also subsist upon organic content of bottom mud and sometimes on dense bloom of blue-green algae (Lake Nakuru).

Mode of feeding distinct from that of Lesser Flamingo. Shallow-keeled beak (see **A**) is held upside down, and in shallow water is rapidly opened and closed, about 5–6 times/s, in 'gabbling' motion like that of some ducks. This sucks in and expels water and mud containing food organisms, which are caught on hairs fringing the beak on expulsion and are then conveyed to gut by long processes on tongue, which works continuously in a groove of the lower mandible like piston of pump (Jenkins 1957). Edges of mandibles also have fine striae of laminae, probably used for filter feeding on finer particles (**B**). Nature of food normally prevents competition with Lesser Flamingo where both occur.

A

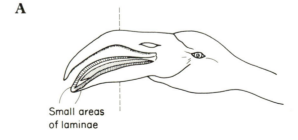

Small areas of laminae

B

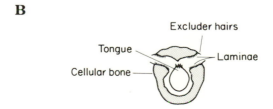

Excluder hairs
Tongue
Laminae
Cellular bone

C   D   E

Breeding Habits. Intimately known; studied both in Europe and Africa by several observers, and in captivity. Highly erratic, opportunistic breeders, not nesting annually in frequently used sites, but may breed twice within one year (Brown 1958). E African breeding population av. *c.* 3000 pairs over a decade, but in peak years may total 15,000–20,000 pairs. Largest known single colony of over 15,000 pairs recently discovered Botswana. Recent colonies in Kenya have been disrupted, or caused to desert, by attacks by Marabou Storks *Leptoptilos crumeniferus* and interference by Great White Pelicans, themselves apparently triggered to breed by presence of flamingoes. Tunisian and Mauritanian colonies poorly recorded, probably (Tunisia) less regular than E African. More frequent breeding reported in southern Africa in last decade perhaps indicates real increase in numbers.

F

G

Breeds in large colonies of 100–15,000 pairs in Africa (in India up to 500,000 pairs), usually 1000–5000 pairs. Normally observed on mudflats, but in E Africa also on bare rocky islands. Pre-breeding displays formalized and ritualistic, not necessarily followed by breeding. Start with ♂♂ collecting in groups, standing erect with body raised above horizontal, necks stretched upward, bills at 45° to horizontal (see **C**), flagging heads from side to side, calling continuously and in chorus. ♀♀ join group and behave in similar manner. Individuals then perform an irregular series of ritual actions, approximately in following order: (i) 'wing-salute'—bird stands bolt upright, beak vertical, flicks wings rigidly out to side, snaps them closed again (**D**); (ii) 'twist-preen' when bird lays head along back, partly opens wing, and appears to preen above and below wing (**E**); (iii) 'bow' or 'inverted wing-salute'—bird bends forward, lowering head towards water, flicks wings partly open and twists them forward to display bright red upperwing-coverts (**F**), closes them smartly, and resumes upright position; (iv) 'twist-preen' again. Occasionally, groups suddenly come together with loud chorus of honking calls, heads held over backs of others with necks and beaks hooked downwards ('hooking') (**G**). This apparently is pre-copulation display. Pairs about to copulate leave displaying group, ♀ walking in front, ♂ following, often 'hooking' over ♀'s back. She stops, he mounts, placing webbed feet firmly on her innermost wing-joint, maintains balance by flapping wings, dismounts forward over ♀'s head; she may continue feeding or walk forward, taking no obvious active part. Later, birds move to colony site, where territorial display consists of erecting long scapulars and back feathers, while lowering bill to nest-site; feathers also raised thus when incubating or brooding young. Threat display to others in colony includes hooking bill downwards, swaying neck from side to side, grunting repeatedly and erecting feathers in territorial display.

NEST: on mudflats truncated cones, usually 15–45 cm high, basal diameter 40–55 cm, with central depression *c.* 30–40 cm across (Uys *et al.* 1963); weight of excavated material 34·5–79 kg, av. 52 kg (Lake Magadi, 1962: Brown *et al.* 1973). On rocky islands slight collections of feathers, straw, grass, gravel, gathered with bill; if any mud available will make low mud cone. Both sexes build, excavating mud from around nest, creating a ditch often filled with water. Maximum density *c.* 1·5 nests/m², controlled by pecking distance between adjacent sitting birds. Thousands of pairs may construct nests and lay within a few days, but in E. Africa total laying period may last 6 weeks, with discrete groups laying together within 3–7 days. If space is limited, successive groups may re-occupy same island when young from first hatching leave it.

EGGS: normally 1, rarely 2 (15/2700 clutches) not always both laid by same bird. Pale blue, covered with thick chalky covering, soon becoming stained brown. SIZE: (28 eggs, E Africa) 80·5–96·5 × 55·0–58·0 (89·7 × 56·4); (135, South Africa) 79–103 × 48·3–54·1 (88·8 × 53·96); similar to Europe; WEIGHT: *c.* 140.

Laying dates: Tunisia Feb–Apr; Mauritania Apr–May; E Africa, most months, but peaking Kenya Mar–Apr, again June–July (early in and after long rains); Lake Natron, Tanzania, associated usually with Lesser Flamingoes, 1 record Feb, but mainly Aug–Oct (dry season); Namibia Apr–May; Botswana May–June; Natal Oct–Nov; Cape Province Sept–Dec, peaking Nov. No clear connection with food supply or regular climatic factors, except in Natal where first recorded breeding coincided with increased salinity and availability of food (Porter and Forrest 1974).

Both sexes incubate, taking almost equal shares, by night or day. Whichever is on nest in evening incubates at night, when few reliefs occur. At nest-relief by day, relieving bird alights in water, walks into colony striking left and right at threatening birds. On reaching nest partner rises and leaves without elaborate ceremony, walking to edge of group then flying away. Incubation period: (many records) 28 days. Hatch of chick may take only 1–2 h, and may be actively assisted by parent pulling eggshell away from chick.

Downy young at hatch cannot walk, barely stands; in a few hours stands and, despite swollen blood-rich legs, staggers. If on mud-cone nest, however, does not leave, unless forced to, for first 3–4 days. Continuously brooded first 2–3 days, but as soft swollen legs harden and become brown, walks freely, then joins creche of other young, shaded by adults. In rocky island colonies with no mud-mound nests, chicks may leave nests within 24 h, apparently with no ill effects.

Either parent may be present at hatch; continually rise and sit again, lowering head to egg, uttering trumpeting, high-pitched calls. Individual voices seem distinct and this calling may imprint parental voice on hatching chick. Chick is brooded mainly underwing for first 3–4 days of life, but parent repeatedly rises and settles again, continually calling. Chick thereafter recognizes parental voice, even at distance; and parent feeds only own chick, repelling others. After 4–5 days chicks collect in herds or creches, guarded and shaded by some adults, releasing others. Brooding thereafter ceases, except perhaps at night.

Chicks walk freely at 5–6 days, coinciding with hardening and darkening of legs. At 10–12 days develop coarser, thicker, woollier coat of down; downward curve of beak now clear. Swim freely from 12 days on, earlier if forced. Such walking young collect into large creches and are guarded, led and herded by adults. Feathers emerge at *c.* 30 days, and young are largely feathered by 50 days. At 40 days bills have pronounced downward bend and lamellae are visible inside. May then attempt filter feeding as in adults, but essentially still entirely dependent until bill fully developed at *c.* 70–75 days, coinciding with first flight. Flap wings at 60–70 days, often breaking them in crowded herds; are stimulated by wind and make first real flights at 75–80 days.

Feeds by adults to small chicks frequent, short, soon increasing with age. At first food is liquid regurgitated matter, partly, at least, a crop secretion containing red blood corpuscles (Studer-Thiersh 1966). Later, thick creamy pink or reddish fluid delivered in quantity; with large young, feeds take up to 18 min. Each adult feeds only own chick, repelling others, and chick recognizes adult's call and runs to it, sometimes up to 100 m. Parental attention decreases rapidly once chick's legs have hardened; *c.* 1 adult to 10 chicks up to days 20–30, reduced to 1/100 or more by day 30–40. Creches guarded by few adults (possibly birds which have lost own eggs or young), permitting both parents to forage, often far away. After day 50 chicks left entirely alone, in large packed herds. Feeds then normally given only by day, not more than once a day, rarely at night. Feeding chick invariably faces same way as adult, receiving food from adult's inverted bill-tip.

85–90% of eggs hatch, and breeding success in successful colonies varies from 25–75% of eggs laid, av. *c.* 40% of chicks fledged/eggs laid. Losses are caused by: diseases (unidentified); overrunning of small young by herds of bigger ones; some predation by e.g. Tawny Eagle *Aquila rapax*, fish eagles, and especially Marabou Storks. More than 6–8 Marabous can cause wholesale desertion of colonies of 4000–6000 pairs. Recently, Great White Pelicans associated with Kenyan breeding colonies having reduced breeding success virtually to nil, not through aggression or predation but apparently because they are attracted to breed on same islands and are larger and heavier. Similar association has been recorded at Etosha Pan and NW India (Berry *et al.* 1973), apparently with less completely fatal results.

In 12 years, 1956–1968, observed Kenyan colonies totalling 29,800 pairs in 6 breeding years produced 9300 young, av. 0·156/pair/year overall. Mortality from fledging to sexual maturity unknown, but possibly high. Greater Flamingoes therefore must be long-lived in wild, perhaps living 30–50 years as adults.

References

Brown, L. H. (1958, 1971).
Brown, L. H. *et al.* (1973).
Berry, H. H. (1972).
Berry, H. H. *et al.* (1973).
Uys, C. J. *et al.* (1963).

Illustrations by Martin Woodcock after Brown (1973) and Cramp and Simmons (1977).

Genus *Phoeniconaias*

Small flamingoes, standing less than 1 m high. Adult plumage deep pink, crimson and black. Bills deep-keeled, the upper mandible triangular in section, fitting closely into lower, the inner surface of both covered with a fine mat of laminae, adapted to feeding on microscopic algae and diatoms.

Some authors have recently merged *Phoeniconaias* (long accepted as a separate genus in the past) with *Phoenicopterus*. However, the general consensus of opinion among flamingo experts in 1973 was that the entirely different and much more specialized feeding methods, together with differences in display patterns, were sufficient to merit generic distinction (Kear and Duplaix-Hall 1975).

Plate 9

(Opp. p. 146)

Phoeniconaias minor (Geoffroy). Lesser Flamingo. Petit Flamant.

Phoenicopterus minor Geoffroy, 1798. Bull. Sci. Soc. Philom. 1, (2), p. 98 and pl., figs 1–3; Senegal.

Range and Status. Saline and alkaline lakes and lagoons of Africa south of Sahara, Persian Gulf and NW India. Nomadic within this range. The world's most numerous flamingo, total population estimated at 5–6,000,000, with at least 2,000,000 and possibly 4,500,000 in Africa. Numbers probably stable at present. There may be 3 discrete population units: one centred on Mauritania (small); the main bulk in the E African Rift from Ethiopia to S Tanzania; and the third centred on Etosha Pan and moving between Walvis Bay and Botswana. Recent evidence, however, indicates that the eastern and southern populations may not be separate units (Tuite 1981). No confirmation available from ringing results.

Phoeniconaias minor

Description. ADULT ♂: general colour deep rose-pink. Upper-wing- and underwing-coverts more or less blotched deep crimson, not solid red. Wing-feathers black, tail deep pink, undertail-coverts forming a red erectile tuft on either side. Bill dark red, tip black; eye yellow; legs and feet bright red. ♀ similar, distinctly smaller and lighter. ADULT ♂ and ♀ (breeding): all red colours intensify. SIZE: wing, ♂ 321–354 (334), ♀ 310–325 (319); tail, ♂ 120–142, ♀ 99–105; tarsus, ♂ 190–242 (205), ♀ av. 195. WEIGHT: ♂ c. 1930, av. ♀ c. 1590.

IMMATURE: 1st-year bird brownish grey, streaked on wing-coverts, breast and back. Wing-feathers dark brown to black-ish; bill and legs grey; eye blackish. Between 6 months and 1

year becomes almost white, bill and legs remaining grey. Pale pink birds are probably subadults of undetermined age.

DOWNY YOUNG: pale to dark grey, more variable than in Greater Flamingo *Phoenicopterus ruber*; albinos known. Bill blackish, eye black, feet and legs at first swollen, puffy, red, becoming shrunken, blackish within 5 days.

Adults moult at intervals to complete flightlessness, but may do so before, during, or after breeding. Flightlessness lasts c. 3 weeks in individuals, and 6–8 weeks among entire population of a lake. Usually occurs at breeding lakes (Lake Natron, N Tanzania), not elsewhere.

Field Characters. Adults always distinguishable from Greater Flamingo by darker pink plumage, upper and lower wing-coverts not bright scarlet but mottled and blotched deep dark red and bill dark red, not pink. Much smaller; in mixed groups in shallow water bodies of Greater Flamingoes stand above backs of Lesser Flamingoes. Immatures much smaller than those of Greater Flamingo, usually greyer. Small downy young recognizable by presence of incipient deep keel inside beak; otherwise almost indistinguishable.

Voice. Recorded (2a, 18, 19, 29). Quite distinct from that of Greater Flamingo. A high-pitched 'chissick', or 'kwirrick', resembling some calls of Greater White-fronted Goose *Anser albifrons*. Also, a low bleating murmur 'murrrh-errh, murrr-errh' especially when walking or resting. A rather shrill 'quie-ow' perhaps before flight. Calling to young at nest a high-pitched 'quaronk'; young utter squeaking begging calls. Massed flocks utter a low murmuring sound; and displaying flocks a loud deep roaring chorus.

General Habits. Very well known. Typically inhabits large alkaline or saline lakes and pans, sometimes estuarine areas; cannot survive long in fresh water. Intensely gregarious, normally occurring in huge flocks of hundreds of thousands, regularly exceeding one million on several E African lakes. Where both occur, mingles freely with Greater Flamingoes. Is normally sedentary on one or more lakes for some months, then may suddenly move out in enormous numbers, at night, to other haunts. Movements may be caused by failure of food supply, but sometimes are unconnected with such failure, and an abundant available food supply does not necessarily attract Lesser Flamingoes (Vareschi 1978).

At any temporary haunt feeds both by day and night, more at night, preferring calm water. May feed while walking in shallows, but more often when swimming; cannot exploit available food supply in most lakes without swimming. In high winds and choppy water collects in huge flocks along shores, resting and preening; whole masses often observed with head under wing, apparently asleep. In such tightly packed flocks, up to 5–6 birds/m². Feeds for *c.* 12·5/24 h and rests mainly by day. On strongly alkaline lakes drink relatively fresh water if available daily, deliberately flying to known permanent or temporary sources (e.g. runoff water from sudden rainstorms), taking a few sips, then moving away. Any relatively fresh water suffices, even if very hot (e.g. from geysers), at up to 65–70°C. Bathes vigorously in freshwater stream outlets, submerging whole body, head and neck, flapping wings vigorously in manner of ducks.

Not regularly migratory within range, but nomadic, moving from one haunt to another at night. Rarely flies by day away from lakeside haunts, but regularly flies in late evening and early night, sometimes moving out, sometimes returning to present haunt. Flight straight and direct, legs and long neck outstretched, at *c.* 50–60 km/h. At such speed, cannot travel more then 600 km/night, which supports likelihood that W African, E African Rift Valley and southern African populations are discrete, or mainly discrete. E African population known to move between Ethiopia and S Tanzania, probably also Zambia (Lake Mweru), but separated by more than 1000 km from pans in Botswana, with very few records in Zimbabwe between. W African population small, no records indicating regular movement to E Africa, but may be maintained by periodic incursions (Cramp and Simmons 1977). Rare records from airmen (H. Loeffler, pers. comm.) suggest some day-time movement at heights far above normal diurnal range of eagles, which otherwise prey on flying flamingoes and possibly prevent diurnal movement at low altitudes. When moving from lake to lake, fly in large skeins, usually invisible but audible from ground at night, in straggling V-formation. Stragglers then rarely descend to freshwater lakes, single or few birds found in such situations probably weak or moribund.

Food. Food mainly microscopic blue-green algae, especially *Spirulina (Arthrospira) platensis*; also diatoms (Ridley *et al.* 1955). Occasional, larger food items such as copepods, rotifers, chironomid larvae possibly swallowed by mistake. Bill is specialized to extract food in size range 40–200 μm, platelets inside mandibles av. 120 μm apart (Jenkins 1957). Cannot extract smaller, unicellular green algae often abundant in same water (Vareschi 1978).

Mode of feeding more intensely specialized than in Greater Flamingo. Normally requires calm water in which to feed, hence prefers to feed at night; in choppy water swollen, bulbous, extremely light lower mandible, uppermost when feeding, acts as float, rising and falling and permitting regular immersion of bill to certain depth. Large flocks in choppy water create local areas of calm where feeding is possible. Feeds normally either by walking in shallows or swimming, in either case with head and neck rhythmically swinging from side to side in scything curves, extracting food from top 3 cm of

water. Occasionally feeds on bottom in deeper water, possibly then taking diatoms from bottom mud. In very shallow water, places bill on side when very rapid pulse of water can be seen dribbling down it (15–17 pulses/s). Different mode of feeding and preferred food eliminates competition with Greater Flamingo where both occur.

Deep-keeled upper mandible fits tightly into lower, with a scarcely perceptible gap when feeding (see **A**). Tongue works in narrow groove in lower mandible, pumping water in and out. When sucked in, laminae on platelets lie flat, are erected when water is pumped out, catching microscopic algae (**B**). When sufficient caught, mandibles are worked against each other, apparently rolling collected masses of algae down onto tongue, where backward pointing processes automatically pull food into oesophagus as tongue pulses to and fro (Jenkins 1957). Mode of feeding is extremely efficient in suitable habitat, av. population of Lake Nakuru (*c.* 900,000 in years observed) extracting *c.* 60 tonnes (dry wt) of algae daily from 40 km² of water. Food requirement of individuals *c.* 60 g (dry wt) of algae/day (Vareschi 1978). In recent years, introduction of *Tilapia grahami* into Lake Nakuru may have upset nutrient balance of lake and prevented occurrence of previously known huge populations of Lesser Flamingoes. *T. grahami* can survive on unicellular green algae too small for Lesser Flamingoes.

A
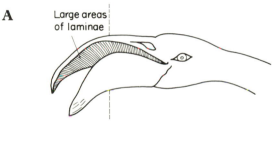
Large areas of laminae

B
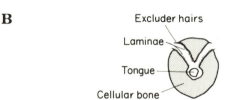
Excluder hairs
Laminae
Tongue
Cellular bone

Breeding Habits. Very well known, but inaccessible breeding sites have prevented very detailed study. An erratic, irregular breeder, in E Africa nesting in huge colonies of 50,000 to over 1 million pairs (largest known, Lake Magadi 1962, *c.* 1,200,000 pairs). Colonies so far reported: Mauritania small, *c.* 800 pairs only (de Naurois 1965); and in southern Africa smaller than in E African Rift (1200–50,000 pairs).

All known colonies on mudflats usually far out in large alkaline lakes or pans inaccessible to humans on foot (at Lake Natron temperatures of surface mud 55–65°C). Choice of site ensures little interference from mammalian predators, which at Lake Magadi, unusually accessible, caused local large-scale desertion.

Displays share several features with Greater Flamingo, but are basically different, much more intensely communal. In main feature, a group forms, at first apparently of ♂♂ with a receptive ♀, perhaps 10–12 suddenly gathering. Others of either sex join and original 10–12 increases to hundreds, later thousands together. These pack together tightly, with raised breast of one almost resting on back of bird in front. Within packed throng, individuals (a) raise heads vertically, flagging them from side to side (analogous to head-flagging in Greater Flamingo); (b) adjacent birds rapidly fence with beaks flicking from side to side, almost touching; (c) some adopt 'broken-neck posture' in which head and bill are lowered to breast with sharp bend in neck, as if broken about 2–3 vertebrae behind head. Necks are then raised straight into air, with feathers erected, possibly swollen, and with a flush of blood to skin. Whole displaying mass forms a darker red patch within large resting flocks. Massed birds are carried along swiftly on forest of twinkling red legs, and general impression is of an insensate mass of demented creatures moving along almost involuntarily.

On outskirts of such masses, individuals perform similar movements to those of Greater and other flamingoes; wing-salute, twist-preen and bow, or inverted wing-salute. Such movements are impossible in main packed displaying throng. Mating occurs near displaying masses, ♂ stalking behind ♀ with neck in 'hooking' posture over her back; mounts from behind, supporting himself by placing feet on her innermost wing joint, flapping wings for balance; dismounts over her head. She often apparently pays no attention, even continuing to feed with bill submerged. Intense communal mass display does not occur everywhere (2 main sites on Lake Nakuru); may continue for weeks, even months daily, and is not then necessarily followed by breeding, though displaying birds may be fat, in bright dark red plumage and with gonads enlarged (J. G. William, pers. comm.). Lake Nakuru is an important display ground, but no recorded breeding there in last 50 years. Apparently not vital for survival, as breeding has occurred at Lake Natron since Lake Nakuru was largely deserted by flamingoes in 1974.

Colonies on mudflats are of 2 types: (i) clumped colonies with masses of nests together; (ii) at Lake Natron, reticulate colonies with thin lines of nests along junctions of soda plates; apparently cannot excavate other than soft mud. Density varies according to site from 5–180 nests/100 m, av. c. 80, with 4–5/m² in tightly packed groups.

NEST: typical truncated cone of mud and soda crystals. In E Africa 20–40 cm high with basal diameter 45 cm, and slight hollow in top 15–20 cm across; weight 14–31 kg, av. c. 20. At Etosha pan 15–40 cm high, av. c 20; basal diameter 35–56 cm, av. 43; cup externally 22–30 cm, av. 25; internally 14–19 cm, av. 16–17; weight of excavated material 8–85 kg, av. c. 30. A colony of 500,000 pairs thus excavates c. 15,000 tonnes of mud. Temperature of surrounding mud at Lake Natron is 55–65°C, probably lethal to newly hatched young, but temperature of nest cup is c. 30–35°C, blood heat or less. Temperatures of environment less extreme at Etosha Pan, but still severe.

EGGS: 1, very rarely 2 (c. 1/300–500 cases), at least some being genuine 2-egg clutches. Pale bluish, covered with chalky layer, almost immediately stained brown by parental feet; any white eggs seen from air are fresh.
SIZE: (E Africa) 72·0–85·5 × 48·0–51·0 (78·5 × 49·3); (Etosha Pan) 75–85 × 47–53; WEIGHT: c. 115–120 (Schönwetter 1960).

Laying dates: Mauritania June–July (rains); E Africa (Lake Natron) mainly Aug–Oct, in some years continuing to Dec (late dry season and in short rains); Botswana June (dry season); Etosha Pan June–July, (dry season). In E Africa no clear connection established between food supply, climatic conditions and breeding, which is erratic and irregular, but mainly occurs late in cool dry season and short rains. At Etosha and in Botswana apparently in dry season following years of exceptional or high rainfall with extensive flooding of pans (Berry 1972; Robertson and Johnson, in prep.).

Both sexes incubate, in long spells, sometimes up to 24 h, perhaps even more. Whichever sex is on nest in evening incubates at night. No elaborate ceremony at nest-relief, relieving bird walking up to nest and partner leaving. In only colony observed closely (Lake Magadi, Kenya) most nest-reliefs occurred at night, but this is probably abnormal, necessitated here by distant feeding grounds and reluctance to fly overland by day. Eggs are predated by Egyptian Vultures *Neophron percnopterus* in colony, adults making ineffectual attempts to fight them off, but more vigorous than Greater Flamingo in same situation. Incubation period: estimated 28 days.

Chicks hatch 2–24 h after chipping; may be assisted by adults removing eggshells. Weigh 73–98 g at hatching, 70–75% of egg weight. At first remain on top of nest mound, not leaving voluntarily for 2–3 days. If they fall off, attempt to return to nest top and may be assisted by parent. Temperature of surrounding mud may be lethal. At first have swollen blood-rich legs, but these shrink and become blackish by 4–5 days old; can leave nest-mound and form into herds from 8 days old, guarded by relatively few adults, on surface of mud. Much more gregarious than Greater Flamingo chicks, forming herds of many thousands by days 10–12, steadily increasing. Thicker, woollier, brownish grey down develops at c. 14 days, and chicks then form into huge herds of up to 300,000 together, guarded and herded by 1–5 adults, which lead them away from possible danger. Startled young run together into circular mass, heads buried under each other. At Lake Natron and Etosha, downy chicks march up to 30–50 km across mudflats to lagoons of permanent water, forming enormous groups hundreds of thousands strong. March in long strings (up to 30 km long) with knots and groups scattered along them. Movement occurs suddenly, chicks of various ages together, mortality on march apparently slight. Same gathering grounds are used at Lake Natron at each breeding attempt. First feathers appear at 28–30 days, chicks are feathered by 50 days, practise wing-flapping and normally make first flights at 70–75 days. Can just fly if pressed at 65 days, and in abnormal situation of Lake Magadi (see above), fledging period prolonged to 90 days.

Each adult feeds only its own chick, despite huge creches; chick recognizes parental voice, perhaps imprinted during hatch as in Greater Flamingo. Either parent feeds chick on liquid regurgitated matter. Small chicks on nest are brooded, often underwing, and fed when they solicit by poking head out and calling, but more often when standing up on nest. May be brooded on mud after they leave the nest at 5–8 days, but very hot conditions in nesting grounds make shading more important than brooding. Adults assist young to return to nest top with bill if necessary. Once chicks have left nest and are in herds, feeds are relatively infrequent, longer and may be delivered at night only. Temporarily flightless adults must walk (at Lake Natron) to feeding areas, and at Lake Magadi breeding adults did not become flightless. By 21 days, large herds of 2000–3000 young attended by only 1–2 adults, so that both parents are free to forage. Chicks at gathering grounds are left entirely alone.

Predation by Egyptian and other vultures, and eagles slight (not more than 5% of eggs and young). Marabous *Leptoptilos crumeniferus* have no observed adverse effect on Lesser Flamingoes. Mammalian predation negligible in normal situations. Chicks can distinguish relatively harmless Black Kite *Milvus migrans* from actively predatory Egyptian Vulture while still downy. Breeding success in observed colonies, E Africa, varies from 5–70% of eggs laid, av. *c.* 41–43%. However, breeding irregular and does not involve whole adult population in breeding years. In 10 years, in an average population estimated at 1,500,000 pairs in E Africa, *c.* 319,000 pairs bred annually (1 in 4·7 pairs) rearing 139,000–149,000 young, *c.* 9% of adult pairs. Assuming 50% mortality before sexual maturity at *c.* 4 years, this would involve an average life as adults of over 20 years.

References

Berry, H. H. (1972).
Brown, L. H. and Root, A. (1971).

Illustrations reproduced with permission from Brown (1973).

Order
ANSERIFORMES

Medium to large aquatic, marine and terrestrial birds comprising 2 suborders, the Anseres with the large, cosmopolitan family Anatidae, and the Anhimae with the small South American family Anhimidae (screamers). Both have unspotted eggs and nidifugous, down-clad young. In the Anatidae the toes are joined by full webs, the hind toes small and placed high. In the Anhimidae the toes are only slightly webbed, the hind toe long and on the same level as the other toes.

Suborder ANSERES

Family ANATIDAE: swans, geese and ducks

Water birds with relatively long necks, blunt, rather spatulate or slender, straight, hooked bills, and short legs. Plumage colours highly variable, entirely white in some swans and geese, ornamental in many dabbling ducks, ♂♂ and ♀♀ with considerable diversity of plumage types. Bodies rather broad, rounded or elongated. Plumage thick, waterproofed by underlying coat of down; wings relatively small, broad and fairly pointed; tertials often long, brightly coloured. Tail short, square or slightly rounded, or with pointed central feathers, longest in diving species. Many duck species have distinct non-breeding (eclipse) plumage; flight feathers usually moulted simultaneously rendering birds flightless for 3–4 weeks. Adult birds feed on a wide range of vegetable and animal matter obtained by swimming or diving in water, grazing on land or in water, this varying widely with species. Some totally vegetarian or insectivorous. Many highly migratory from continent to continent; others travel shorter distances or are sedentary, movements of many being still unclear.

Many comfort movements, common to most Anatidae, are used in a social context as follows: (1) Body-shake which begins with lateral Tail-wag, moves forward to the wings which are vibrated rapidly while remaining folded, then to head which is lifted upwards to angle of c. 45° and rotated around its long axis. (2) Wing-shake differs from (1) in that Tail-wag and Head-shake absent; wings shaken vigorously while folded, mainly secondaries being involved. (3) Swimming-shake performed on water; bird wags tail vigorously, paddles feet hard, raising breast out of water, and shake moves forward over body until head and neck are stretched up and rotated as in Body-shake. (4) Head-shake in which the head is shaken laterally several times; often associated with Nibble-preening and Bill-dipping. (5) Head-flick, a very rapid action in which the head is jerked up, shaken laterally once or twice, and at same time rotated around the long axis before being returned to resting position. (6) Tail-wag, rapid and vigorous lateral wagging of tail, often while fanned. (7) Wing-flap, performed both on water and land; body raised almost vertical, then wings flapped a few times while fully opened. (8) Wing-shuffle and Tail-fan in which wings are repeatedly lifted a little from the sides, separately or simultaneously, while tail is fanned. (9) Bill-dip, bill is dipped into water and immediately withdrawn while swimming or standing at water's edge. Action common and closely linked with Nibble-preening, usual sequence: Bill-dip—Head-shake—Nibble feathers—Bill-dip. (10) Bathing occurs in all Anatidae, Head-dipping, Wing-thrashing and Somersaulting are main actions; often follows copulation.

Generally solitary breeders, nests concealed in vegetation near water or over water, sometimes in trees, tree holes, ground holes or on cliffs; some species colonial. Nests often lined with down plucked from ♀'s breast. Some species highly territorial, others with largely undefended home ranges. Monogamous pair-bonds formed in most species, but variation exists in duration of bond and degree of ♂ promiscuity. Social systems and displays associated with pair-formation complex, largely dissimilar in the 2 main subfamilies. Copulation occurs on water in majority of species, typically with ♂ grasping ♀'s nape with bill. Clutches especially large in species with reduced parental care; eggs large, covered with down when ♀ absent. Some species show tendency to lay eggs in nests of other anatids, this especially developed in stiff-tails and some pochards, while 2 ♀♀ frequently lay in one nest, large 'dumps' usually deserted. Single clutches, most replaced if first eggs lost. Incubation begins when clutch complete, incubation and fledging periods variable. Downy young precocial soon after hatching; led to water after leaving nest, mostly self-feeding.

Composed of 7 subfamilies with 42 genera and 145 species (Mayr and Cottrell 1979); the subfamilies Dendrocygninae, Anserinae, Tadorninae, Anatinae, Merginae and Oxyurinae in Africa.

All illustrations for this family by Martin Woodcock after Johnsgard (1962), except Anas sparsa *(after McKinney et al. 1978) and* Oxyura maccoa *(after Siegfried and Van der Merwe 1975).*

Subfamily DENDROCYGNINAE: whistling-ducks and White-backed Duck

Very goose-like ducks, but differ from geese mainly in having more specialized tracheal structure and whistling voices. Sexes almost identical, pair-bonds relatively permanent; downy young plumages distinctive. Sometimes referred to as 'tree ducks' but do not regularly perch in trees, rarely nest in tree-holes. Vegetarian, dive when foraging, keeping wings closed and commencing with coot-like jump. 2 genera, *Dendrocygna* and *Thalassornis*.

Genus *Dendrocygna* Swainson

Small ducks with fairly long necks held straight as in geese, broad rounded wings, primaries and secondaries of equal length, primaries emarginated; flank feathers frequently elongated and ornamental; long legs of which tibia half-naked, tarsus reticulated in front; large feet, webs indented, thumb long and low-placed, claws sharp; bill high and narrow, the nail large, hooked; no wing specula; 1 annual moult, wing-moult entire. Pair-forming displays simple, similar in both sexes. ♂'s courtship posture consists of swimming ahead of courted ♀ in aloof or haughty attitude as in swans and geese; this not well studied. Pre-copulatory displays range from mutual Drinking or Bill-dipping to mutual Head-dipping. Species which copulate on water have post-copulatory Step-dance accompanied by vertical Wing-raising and calling in which both rise vertically on water, feet treading hard, outer wings raised. Eggs small, rounded; incubation shared by both sexes. 8 species in New and Old Worlds, 2 in Africa.

Dendrocygna bicolor (Vieillot). Fulvous Whistling-Duck; Fulvous Tree-Duck. Dendrocygne fauve.

Plate 15

Anas bicolor Vieillot, 1816. Nouv. Dict. Hist. Nat. 5, p. 136; Paraguay.

(Opp. p. 226)

Range and Status. Resident south of Sahara, Senegal eastwards through Mali and Chad in narrow belt; from Ethiopia south to Cape Province over eastern half of continent. Distribution discontinuous throughout range. Breeding populations also in Kenya, Uganda, Tanzania, SE Zaïre, Zambia, Malawi, Zimbabwe and South Africa. Populations Senegal and Niger deltas variable, e.g. from few hundred Jan 1972 and 1974 to 23,000 Senegal delta Jan 1979 (Roux 1973; Browne 1979); 5000 July, SE Zaïre (Curry-Lindahl 1975); 15,000–50,000 July–Sept, Kafue Flats, Zambia (Clarke 1972; Douthwaite 1977). Present all seasons in flocks of up to 3000 S Malawi (Benson 1977); 1000–2000 Feb Transvaal (Clark 1974a); scarce in Cape Peninsula, breeding occasionally (Broekhuysen 1955; Langley 1979). Absent or accidental coastal and forested regions of W and Central Africa, Angola and southwestern arid regions.

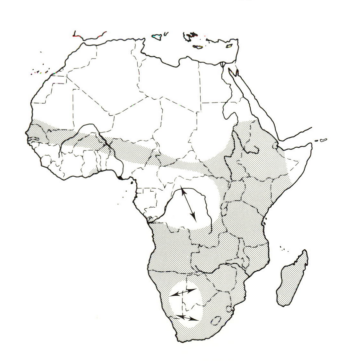

Dendrocygna bicolor

Description. ADULT ♂: from base of bill, forehead and crown to small crest rich rufous-brown; from crest down back of head and neck a blackish brown stripe; rest of head and upperneck tawny brown, more rufous around eyes and face; throat and neck white, the feathers markedly striated and exposing dark basal regions, giving streaked effect; back and scapulars dark brown, feather-ends fringed rusty; rump black; uppertail-coverts white, washed buff; tail black. Underparts from white neck pale fulvous becoming rich, deep fulvous over flanks, long flank feathers white on outer webs giving distinctive striped appearance; undertail-coverts white. Upperwing with lesser coverts dull reddish brown, rest of coverts and remiges blackish; axillaries and underwing-coverts blackish. Eye brown; bill, legs and feet slate grey. Sexes alike. SIZE: (12 ♂♂, 15 ♀♀) wing, ♂ 202–242 (216), ♀

203–235 (217); tail, ♂ 44·2–57·1 (49·2), ♀ 41·1–53·3 (43·4); culmen, ♂ 43·1–48·1 (46·2), ♀ 41·5–50·0 (46·1); tarsus, ♀ 52·1–57·2 (54·2), ♀ 50·1–58·9 (54·0). WEIGHT: (6♂♀) 540–916 (G. Morel, pers. comm.).

JUVENILE: similar to adult but paler below.

DOWNY YOUNG: white below, pale grey above; facial stripe ill-defined; cap darker grey. Bill dark grey; feet olive-green.

Field Characters. An erect-standing duck with dark brown upperparts and stripe down back of neck, also bold white stripes on flanks. In flight dark wings, feet protruding beyond tail, white uppertail-coverts showing distinct V-marking diagnostic. Distinguishable from White-faced Whistling-Duck *D. viduata*, with which it regularly associates, by lack of white face.

Voice. Recorded (2a, 6, 19). Normal call consists of 2 resonant notes often repeated, 'tsoo-ee' or tsu-ee', used in variety of situations. 2nd note shrill in ♀, shorter, lower-pitched and more resonant in ♂. During hostile behaviour a single harsh 'kee' repeated rapidly 4 or more times. Either call may be taken up by assembled flock, producing chorus. In breeding season, when disturbed in vicinity of nest or with ducklings, 1 of pair will fly around repeating single resonant 'szee' (Clark 1978a). Less vocal than White-faced Whistling-Duck.

General Habits. Well known. Fairly gregarious when not breeding, although less social than White-faced Whistling-Duck. Large flocks, compact, noisy and restless, newcomers attracted by incessant whistling and flapping of wings (Douthwaite 1977). Smaller groups mostly silent and unobtrusive, spending day afloat or loafing and preening on land. Feeds post-dawn, pre-nightfall, only casually during day. Wary, difficult to approach. When flying from water lift-off normally clear; wings produce muffled sound, noticeable in flocks. Cross-country flights have no marked formation, altitude *c.* 40 m, flight strong, less fast than some ducks.

Utilizes a variety of quiet waters, preferably with surface vegetation. Seldom present 1 locality all year, movements incompletely understood. Locally migratory in E Africa, some lakes May-Sept but others Aug-May; in Ruzizi marshes, Zaïre, Burundi, May-June and Nov-Mar (K. Curry-Lindahl, pers. comm.); probably regular movement from north southwards into South Africa for summer months, with most birds returning north again after breeding and before winter (A. Clark, pers. comm.). Moult recorded during Apr-July, Zambia (Douthwaite 1977); Apr-May, Transvaal; 5-10 months after breeding, Senegal (Roux *et al.* 1976-1977).

Food obtained by dabbling in marshy ground, partly flooded grasslands or on open water, head immersed (av. 5 s), or by up-ending similar period. Occasionally dives for food (submerged periods 5-20 s); sometimes for periods of 90 min continually. Among aquatic herbs flocks swim back and forth over same area; in grass swamp remain stationary. Birds aggregate in tightly packed groups in which they dive in quick succession, in water 30-170 cm deep (usually 45-90 cm).

Food. On Kafue Flats, Zambia, extremely large flocks feed on seeds and fruits of *Nymphoides indica*, *Ambrosia maritima*, *Echinochloa stagnina* and *Nymphaea capensis*. In 33 crops, 97% dry weight consisted of seeds and fruit, animal matter only 1% in crops of 4 birds.

Breeding Habits. Well known. Nests well concealed in lush grass near water, in marshy ground at edge of water, or in reeds or sedges. Sometimes several nests in same locality as little as 50 m apart (Clark 1976).

During breeding season Threat-flights occur; leading bird, usually ♀ of mated pair, is pursued by rival ♂, ♂ of pair lagging behind. Leading bird may alter course suddenly and frequently. After 4-6 min, in which height of 60 m sometimes reached, threatening bird breaks away, pair returns to water in long, graceful glides alighting next to each other. Should rival settle nearby, mated ♂ makes threatening move towards it, causing it to retreat. Chin-back threat display is used where 2-6 birds swim together with heads laid back and bills resting on necks, usually with crest raised.

During pre-copulatory behaviour, always in water, pairs face each other, ♀ with head fully raised, ♂ repeatedly dipping bill or head in water, bill tilted downwards as it is dipped. This behaviour sometimes prolonged (164 dips recorded). Head-dipping resembles feeding movement, frequently preceded by mutual feeding. When participants equally stimulated, ♂ quickly mounts, almost totally submerging ♀, and remains there briefly, wings spread. After dismounting both perform Step-dance (see **A**), lasting 1-2 s, bills held

A

pressed against throat. Then both bathe briefly and swim to bank where usually preen and Wing-flap. Mutual preening much less common than in White-faced Whistling-Duck.

NEST: constructed of surrounding vegetation, bowl formed of grass stalks or *Typha* leaves, with or without down lining, 0·2-0·5 m above water, dimensions not recorded. Both sexes build (observed in captivity: J. Kear, pers. comm.).

EGGS: 6-13, laid at daily intervals; South Africa mean (22 clutches) 10. Small regular ovals; white or very pale brown. SIZE: (74 eggs) 48·0-55·0 × 37·0-41·6 (51·5 × 39·8) (Clark 1974); WEIGHT: (100 eggs, captive birds) 41·5-59·0 (50·0) (J. Kear, pers. comm.).

Laying dates: months of low rainfall favoured north of Zambezi River, but wet season in southern Africa (Siegfried 1973). Senegal Apr, June, Sept, Nov; Ghana, Nigeria July-Sept; Kenya (coastal) Aug, (inland) June; Uganda May-June; Tanzania Apr; southern Zaïre Aug-Sept; Zambia Feb-Aug; Malawi June-Aug; Zimbabwe Feb-Sept; South Africa Dec-Mar.

Incubation carried out mostly by ♂. Period: 24–26 days.

Chicks leave nest within 36 h of first chipping. Can make dives of 5–8 s for food, or feed from surface. Brood size: (39 broods under 2 months old, South Africa) 1–12, av. 6 (Clark 1976). Wing- and tail-feathers appear and legs change from olive green to blue-grey day 35; juvenile plumage begins to appear on upper-back, flanks, front of neck day 40; remnant of downy cheek stripe still present, juvenile plumage nearly complete except for rectrices and remiges day 60; cheek-

stripe gone and 1st flight day 63 (Meanley and Meanley 1959). 100 day-old captive young weighed 22–38 g (29) (J. Kear, pers. comm.). Thereafter weight increases to *c.* 220 g day 33, *c.* 520 day 60, *c.* 650 day 365. Fledging period: *c.* 2 months.

Both parents attend chicks and keep them in thick cover while small.

References

Clark, A. (1974a, 1976, 1978a).
Douthwaite, R. J. (1977).
Meanley, B. and Meanley, A. G. (1958, 1959).

Dendrocygna viduata (Linnaeus). White-faced Whistling-Duck; White-faced Tree-Duck. Dendrocygne veuf.

Plate 15

Anas viduata Linnaeus, 1766. Syst. Nat. (12th ed.), 1, p. 205; Cartagena, Columbia.

(Opp. p. 226)

Range and Status. Resident south of Sahara, common in lowland tropical regions, less so in highlands. Generally absent from forested Zaïre and western regions south to western Cape with exception of sporadic visits by individuals and small groups (Siegfried 1965). In Senegal delta, Jan 1972 43,000, Jan 1974 6400 (Roux 1976), Jan 1981 22,000 (Dupuy and Fournier 1981). Central Niger delta, Jan 1972 21,000, Jan 1974 7700 (Roux 1976), Jan 1978 71,500 (Sanigho 1978). Most abundant resident duck Nigeria (Elgood *et al.* 1973; L. H. Brown, pers. comm.). Regular passage migrant eastern Zaïre and Burundi, Feb 4000–5000, Ruzizi marshes (K. Curry-Lindahl, pers. comm.); Kafue Flats, Zambia, numbers estimated 16,000 June (Douthwaite 1977); Zululand 5000 (Cooper 1960); Witwatersrand, Transvaal, 1000 (Clark 1974a).

Dendrocygna viduata

Description. ADULT ♂: entire frontal half of head from well behind eyes, chin and throat white; rest of head to mid-neck black, a variable black strip separating white throat and chin; lower neck and breast rich chestnut; upperback olive-brown, transversely barred rusty; scapulars greyish olive-brown, edged rusty; lower back, rump and uppertail-coverts and tail black with blue sheen. Underparts from lower breast over entire medial plane to tail black with blue sheen; lateral surfaces of breast and flanks white, washed with ochre and boldly transversely barred black. Upperwing lesser coverts deep chestnut, remainder of coverts dark bluish grey with olive overlay; remiges black, tertials as scapulars; axillaries and underwing-coverts black. Eye brown; bill black, a transverse bluish grey bar near tip; legs and feet bluish grey. Sexes alike. SIZE: (6 ♂♂, 6 ♀♀) wing, ♂ 216–222 (219), ♀ 221–225 (223·3); tail ♂ 54–58 (55·4), ♀ 53–59·1 (56·3); culmen, ♂ 47–49·1 (47·7), ♀ 45·3–48·9 (47·4); tarsus, ♂ 48·1–55·0 (52·6), ♀ 52–55·2 (52·9). WEIGHT: ♂ (12) 637, ♀ (15) 614 (G. Morel, pers. comm.).

JUVENILE: Similar to adult, but duller, lacks white face, black head and belly during 1st month approximately; face entirely white 3·5–4 months later, at which time difficult to distinguish from adult.

DOWNY YOUNG: dark brown above, yellow below, irregular patches on sides; characteristic *Dendrocygna* head markings of dark cap, white superciliary stripe, pale line from under eye to back of head.

Field Characters. A distinctive, long-necked, erect-standing duck with black and white head, rich chestnut breast, olive back and barred flanks; white face diagnostic. Floats high on water, undertail-coverts well

clear. All dark wings similar to those of Fulvous Whistling-Duck *D. bicolor*, but white face, lack of white on tail and, usually, continual whistling of flock characteristic.

Voice. Recorded (2a, 6, 14, 22a, 26). A highly vocal species. Usual call a sibilant 3-note whistle 'swee-swee-sweeoo', repeated after brief pauses. Used by individuals as contact call and flocks in variety of situations, e.g. when feeding, as prelude to fight, in flight and when settling. 3 clear notes normally descend the scale but occasionally merge, sometimes with variation in pitch or frequency. No sexual difference discernible. If disturbed at nest or with ducklings, will fly around repeating single note 'wheee'.

General Habits. Well known. Highly gregarious when not breeding. Preferred habitats large rivers, lakes, storage dams, deltas, flood plains, settlement pans, often with emergent and surface vegetation.

Main foraging periods (Transvaal grasslands) 2 h after dawn and before dusk; casual feeding at other times of day, but during winter months daylight feeding increases. Food obtained by dabbling in marshy or partly flooded grassland, sometimes on open water, head immersed av. 5 s, or by up-ending for similar period. Also dives for food, remaining underwater 5–10 s, no lateral underwater movement. Smaller feet less well adapted for diving than those of Fulvous Whistling-Duck (Siegfried 1973a).

Food usually obtained (Kafue Flats, Zambia) in shallow water by filtering or grubbing, in various feeding zones according to season, i.e. Dec–Mar fringing zone; Mar–May peripheral flood plain; May–June, Sept lagoon; June–Dec meander belt of river. Regardless of habitat, walking or standing preferred to swimming. Flocks of up to 400 seen feeding offshore, groups of 2–11 at shoreline. In W Africa feeds in rice fields; may become severe pest to young crops (L. H. Brown, pers. comm.).

Raises head with lateral head-shakes before taking flight; whistling commences and continues for short period after take-off. At rest, groups frequently mix with Fulvous Whistling-Duck, but in flight usually separate after take-off on reaching c. 60 m.

During non-breeding season, individuals in resting group on land may threaten others, jumping at opponent, bill open and wings flapping. Alternatively approaches with spread wings, whistling; this often precipitated by birds changing position in group. Threatened bird will take evasive action causing others nearby to react in similar manner, several leap-frogging over each other, legs dangling, whistling in chorus; also head and neck outstretched from withdrawn position towards opponent, bill opened, but crest not raised.

Flocks, sometimes of several hundred, subject to local movements according to food availability; irregular long distance movements in wet seasons also occur, up to 540 km recorded Zambia–Zimbabwe (Douthwaite 1977). Local movements also occur E Zaïre, Kenya, Ghana and Senegal (K. Curry-Lindahl, pers. comm.). Moult, with mature birds flightless, follows breeding: May–Aug Zambia (Douthwaite 1977); Apr–May southern Zaïre; May–July South Africa.

Food. Summer, Transvaal, grass, *Polygonum* seeds, *Spirogyra* and *Potamogeton* filaments. 34 crops (Kafue Flats) contained av. 92% dry matter composed of *Ambrosia maritima*, *Nymphoides indica* and *Nymphaea* seeds, *Echinochloa stagnina* fruits, and 8% rhizomes. Animal matter absent from most crops and never accounts for more than 3% dry weight.

Breeding Habits. Well known. Nests singly on ground, over water, or, exceptionally, in trees above water (Clark 1976); min. distance between nests 75 m.

Courtship behaviour simple. 1 of pair may elevate head and lift breast slightly in water as it swims towards rival; may also raise wings slightly from back. After departure of rival, paired bird continues to swim in this posture leading partner away. Threat-flights occur in which rival ♂ pursues ♀ of pair, ♂ partner following behind, birds giving normal whistle. Sometimes other individuals may join flight and numbers build-up to 5 or more. Mutual preening between pairs and within flocks more obvious than in other *Dendrocygna* spp.

Copulation occurs before flocks disperse for breeding. Pair swims 10–20 m away from main group, face each other, ♀ with head partially elevated, ♂ repeatedly dipping bill or head into water, bill tilted downwards when dipped. ♂ mounts, almost totally submerging ♀, remains there briefly, wings spread. This followed by Step-dance, bills pointing downwards but not close to throat, then both return to bank to preen, occasionally Wing-flapping.

NEST: Transvaal, placed in long grass 15–45 m from water; in *Typha* or sedge 0·2–1·0 m above water 1·0–1·5 m deep; or (1 record) in fork of tree 2·5 m above water (Clark 1976). Nigeria, in ground hollow scratched between tufts of grass, usually on untilled land well away from water (Bannerman 1938). In Transvaal, Natal and Zimbabwe constructed from vegetation in immediate vicinity, e.g. *Typha* leaves, grass stalks. On ground, well concealed; if over water, surrounding vegetation pulled down, partially obscuring nest. May contain traces of down, South Africa; no down recorded, Nigeria. Share of sexes in building not recorded, but presumably both participate as in other *Dendrocygna* spp.

EGGS: 4–13, laid at 24-h intervals; Zambia mean (65 clutches) 7·4, southern Africa (61) 7·1. Small, smooth, regular ovals; creamy white, tinged pink when fresh. SIZE: (75 eggs, South Africa) 45·5–52·7 × 35·0–41·5 (48·7 × 36·9) (Clark 1974a); WEIGHT: (100 eggs, captive birds) 27·5–52·5 (35) (J. Kear, pers. comm.).

Laying dates: (wet season preferred throughout range) Senegal Sept–Oct, Jan; Ghana May–Aug; Nigeria July–Oct; Chad June–Sept; Uganda June, Dec; Kenya Jan, Mar (coastal region July–Aug, Oct–Dec); Tanzania May; Malawi Feb–May; Zambia Dec–June; Zimbabwe Sept–Apr, peaking Jan–Feb; South Africa Oct–Apr, peaking Jan–Feb.

Incubation mostly by ♂. If disturbed, incubating bird flies off quietly, may alight nearby and perform distraction display. Period: 26–28 days (Johnsgard 1978), captive birds 28–30 days (Delacour 1954).

100 captive day-old chicks weighed 16·5–27·0 (22) (J. Kear, pers. comm.). Chicks normally leave nest within 48 h of hatching (Clark 1974a), apparently led to water at night in Nigeria (Bannerman 1938).

Carrying of downy young in parent's bill reported Zimbabwe but not confirmed (Jones 1978). Chicks attended by both parents, usually kept in dense cover until free-flying. If disturbed, ducklings dive, surfacing some distance away; parents flap across water in 'broken-wing' display, or, if cover inadequate to conceal brood, parents fly around calling. Half-grown ducklings seen to dive freely while parents remain on surface.

Brood size: (39 broods from hatching to 2 months) 2–13, av. 6. Av. percentage of juveniles in flocks on Transvaal highveld in summer of good rains assessed at 55%, in summer of poor rains 9·8%; av. brood sizes 7·9 and 5·3 respectively. Juveniles tend to remain in family groups with parents during non-breeding season.

References
Clark, A. (1974a, 1976, 1978a).
Douthwaite, R. J. (1977).
Johnsgard, P. A. (1978).

Genus *Thalassornis* Eyton

Small, long-necked duck with conspicuous nail to sharply tapered bill, white back, reticulated surface to tarsi and plumage similarities to stiff-tailed ducks (Oxyurinae). Eggs glossy brown (unique among the Anatidae), and unusually large.

A monotypic genus placed by Eyton (1838) with the stiff-tailed ducks. Delacour and Mayr (1945) reduced the stiff-tails to tribal rank (Oxyurini). Johnsgard (1967) suggested affinities with whistling-ducks, supporting this with behavioural evidence from breeding birds, e.g. unusual tracheal structure, whistling voices, nest defence and large share of incubation by ♂♂, and post-copulatory behaviour. Anatomical evidence (Raikow 1971), analysis of duckling vocalizations (Kear 1967) and feather protein analysis (Brush 1976) further support the view that the White-backed Duck is a stiff-tail-like whistling duck. Tail not used under water as in true stiff-tails, but species nevertheless better adapted for diving and swimming underwater than *Dendrocygna* spp., being closer in this and other adaptive features to the Oxyurinae. Nominate *T. l. leuconotus* in Africa.

Thalassornis leuconotus Eyton. White-backed Duck. Erismature à dos blanc.

Thalassornis leuconotus Eyton, 1838. Monogr. Anatidae, p. 168; Cape of Good Hope.

Plate 16

(Opp. p. 227)

Range and Status. Resident Ethiopia to Cape, mainly in eastern non-forested half of continent, but extending south of Sahara to W Africa. Localized and sedentary on quiet waters from sea level to high inland plateaux. Seldom very abundant. Senegal and Chad small irregular numbers, but does breed; up to 500 Lake Naivasha, Kenya (Meadows, in press) and on Kafue Flats, Zambia (Douthwaite 1977); in South Africa frequent but unpredictable.

Description. *T. l. leuconotus* Eyton, ADULT ♂: crown, nape, hindneck black, feathers finely edged and barred buff; mantle, wing-coverts, scapulars blackish brown, boldly spotted and barred white, buff and tawny brown; upper back black, feathers broadly edged white, lower back white; rump and uppertail-coverts black, feathers broadly fringed white; short tapered tail blackish brown, feathers edged and laterally notched buffy white. Face buff, densely and coarsely speckled black (darkest around eyes), a white patch from lores extending downwards past gape to tip of chin; rest of chin dusky, scaled with buff; sides of head and neck with fore-throat dull deep buff extending to entire breast, breast feathers all heavily barred sub-apically with dark brown, boldest over lateral surfaces, on central breast long feather-tips have obscure barring giving unmarked appearance; thighs dark brown, feathers narrowly fringed white or buffy white. Undertail-coverts blackish brown, broadly tipped white; primary coverts brown; primaries light grey-brown, whitening over inner vane: secondaries pale brown, tipped buffy white; tertials blackish brown barred rusty; underwing-coverts pale brownish, broadly edged white; axillaries pale buff. Eye brown; bill blackish slate, speckled green and yellow, cutting edge of upper mandible and much of under mandible dull yellow; legs and feet grey. ADULT ♀: very similar, but smaller. Head smaller than ♂'s, nape feathers less dense, bill less profusely covered with flecks (Wintle 1981). SIZE: (8 ♂♂ and ♀♀) wing, 163–171 (169·7); tail, 47·5–53·0 (49); culmen, 36–39 (37·1); tarsus, 36·5–39 (38·3); length 38–43 cm. WEIGHT: ♂ (3) 650–790, ♀ (4) 625–765 (Britton 1970).

JUVENILE: generally darker, less distinctively marked, face and neck more heavily spotted; loral patch smaller, duller.

DOWNY YOUNG: around eye on cheek, crown, nape and hindneck blackish; rest of upperparts, flanks and wings deep olivaceous-buff, rest of facial surface, ear-coverts, plus entire sides of neck deep tawny olive; apex of chin blackish; rest of throat and breast pale pinkish grey-buff; underparts and thighs blackish grey, transected laterally by pale stripe. Small claw on alula 1st 4 weeks.

Thalassornis leuconotus

Field Characters. A brownish duck with low squat body, longish neck, rather bulbous head, sharply tapering, well-hooked bill. Whitish spot at base of bill visible at some distance. When swimming, back appears slightly humped at shoulder level, lower back and tail sloping downwards into water, head usually well clear of shoulders. Short wings, no speculum, white back and feet protruding beyond tail diagnostic in flight.

Voice. Recorded (2a). Main call 'tit-weet', a double note, 2nd longer syllable lower than 1st, uttered in variety of situations. Whistling calls on water uttered by both sexes; loudest, apparently an alarm note, is loud double whistle; also a conversational or contact call of 3–5 notes uttered as rising series of soft whistles. ♂ wishing to be relieved from incubation utters soft, trilling, flute-like whistle; ♀ approaching in response utters same sound. Also whistles in flight, resembling *Dendrocygna* spp. ♂♂ hiss loudly in aggressive situations. Downy young utter soft, low twitter while feeding and preening, and a single sharp distress note uttered slowly, repeated regularly. Sonograms resemble those of *Dendrocygna*, but have no similarity with those of *Oxyura* spp.

General Habits. Well known. Highly aquatic, inhabiting fresh water pans, quiet pools and backwaters of lakes, marshes, swamps and inland deltas fringed with screens of emergent vegetation and rafts of water lilies to which it can repair if disturbed. Quiet, unobtrusive, resting or sleeping on the water some distance from shore, anchoring itself amidst floating or emergent vegetation or drifting on open water. When not breeding, congregate in groups of usually 20–100, distance between individuals 30–200 cm. During daylight most rest 3–4 h late morning, casual shorter spells other times. A foot-shake, similar to that of Maccoa Duck *Oxyura maccoa*, occurs while resting on water. Foot is brought out and waved, either returned to its resting place or left out, protruding from the side, webs expanded. Sometimes when disturbed will raise head and Wing-flap, and the sequence Nibble-preen, Shake and Wing-flap not unusual at this time; Wing-and-leg-stretch and Head-scratch are also seen.

Seldom flies during day except for short distances across water; longer flights 1–10 m above water by 2 or more occur in afternoon after rousing, prior to feeding. Pre-flight signalled by birds gathering, hesitating with heads raised and facing into wind, may Shake, Wing-flap or Head-shake. Good stretch of open water essential for take-off, birds frequently swimming downwind to suitable position. Take-off prolonged, bird paddling with feet on surface 3–7 m before becoming airborne.

Food obtained almost solely by diving, surface-feeding unusual. In water *c.* 30 cm deep diving times 12–14 s, 4–6 s on surface between dives; *c.* 60–90 cm deep diving times 15–20 s, 5–10 s on surface; *c.* 2 m deep diving times 25–30 s, 7–12 s on surface.

Movements little understood but apparently related to rainfall patterns throughout range. Local and seasonally regular movements E Zaïre and E Africa (K. Curry-Lindahl, pers. comm.). In southern Africa preference for often temporary pans causes birds to move to more permanent waters in drought periods. In Transvaal moves only following fairly consistent rains (A. Clark, pers. comm.), in Zimbabwe influx occurs during rains (Smithers *et al.* 1957), in Zambia in dry season Feb–

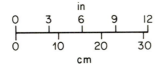

Scale does not apply to flying birds

Plate 15

Cyanochen cyanopterus Blue-winged Goose (p. 237)
1. ADULT and DOWNY YOUNG.

Alopochen aegyptiacus Egyptian Goose (p. 238)
2. ADULT ♂ and DOWNY YOUNG, 3. ADULT ♀.

Plectropterus gambensis Spur-winged Goose (p. 246)
4. ADULT ♂ and DOWNY YOUNG.

Sarkidiornis melanotos Knob-billed Duck (p. 249)
5. ADULT ♀ in flight, 6. ADULT ♂ (note size compared with ♀), 7. ADULT ♀ and DOWNY YOUNG.

Tadorna ferruginea Ruddy Shelduck (p. 240)
8. DOWNY YOUNG, 9. ADULT ♀ (non-breeding), 10. ADULT ♂ (non-breeding).

Tadorna cana South African Shelduck (p. 241)
11. ADULT ♂ in flight, 12. ADULT ♀, 13. ADULT ♂ and DOWNY YOUNG.

Tadorna tadorna Common Shelduck (p. 244)
14. ADULT ♂, 15. DOWNY YOUNG, 16. ADULT ♀ (head detail), 17. ADULT ♂ in flight.

Dendrocygna bicolor Fulvous Whistling-Duck (p. 221)
18. DOWNY YOUNG, 19. ADULT swimming and standing, 20. ADULT in flight.

Dendrocygna viduata White-faced Whistling-Duck (p. 223)
21. ADULT in flight, 22. ADULT swimming and standing.

Sept, peaking May–June. Bird ringed Lochinvar, Zambia, recovered 180 km northeast at Lukanga Swamp. Flightless birds in moult recorded 18 June–20 July (Douthwaite 1977).

Food. Aquatic vegetable matter, mainly water-lily seeds. In 2 separate samples at Lochinvar, Zambia, from 4 birds feeding on flood plains Mar–Apr, the other from 4 feeding in lagoon May–Sept (3-year period), 97% dry weight of 7 guts comprised aquatic herbs, seeds and vegetative parts of water-lilies (Douthwaite 1977). Stomach contents of wild chicks suggest preference for *Chironomid* (gnat) larvae, normally obtained from mud in shallow waters (J. G. Williams, pers. comm.) and *Polygonum* seeds.

Breeding Habits. Little known. Nests mainly over water in emergent vegetation or on ground in waterside vegetation, or floating. Pair-bonds probably permanent. No ♂ courtship display or conspicuous pair-bonding behaviour observed, except possibly when 1 bird, probably ♂, swims to another calling, then both swim parallel while calling. Also, 2 birds swim side by side, heads partly up and held stiffly, smaller bird (presumed ♀) dives and swims underwater and larger bird swims to join it when surfaced; smaller bird then dips bill, larger bird does same, both then swim off, heads erect. 2 birds may swim around in 1·5 m circle, bill-dipping frequently.

Copulation observed between 16.20 and 17.10 h following feeding. Pair swims away from main group

Plate 16

Pteronetta hartlaubii Hartlaub's Duck (p. 248)
1. DOWNY YOUNG, 2. ADULT standing, swimming and in flight.

Nettapus auritus African Pygmy Goose (p. 251)
3. DOWNY YOUNG, 4. ADULT ♂, 5. ADULT ♀, 6. ADULT ♂ in flight.

Marmaronetta angustirostris Marbled Teal (p. 273)
7. ADULT in flight, 8. DOWNY YOUNG, 9. ADULT swimming and standing.

Anas sparsa African Black Duck (p. 262)
10. ADULT standing and in flight, 11. ADULT swimming with DOWNY YOUNG.

Anas capensis Cape Teal (p. 256)
12. ADULT swimming, 13. ADULT in flight, 14. ADULT standing with DOWNY YOUNG.

Anas undulata Yellow-billed Duck (p. 260)
15. ADULT standing and in flight, 16. ADULT swimming with DOWNY YOUNG.

Anas erythrorhyncha Red-billed Teal (p. 265)
17. ADULT standing, swimming and in flight.

Anas hottentota Hottentot Teal (p. 267)
18. ADULT ♂ standing and in flight, 19. ADULT ♀.

Anas smithii Cape Shoveler (p. 270)
20. ADULT swimming, standing and in flight.

Netta erythrophthalma Southern Pochard (p. 276)
21. ADULT ♂, 22. ADULT ♀, 23. ADULT ♂ in flight.

Netta rufina Red-crested Pochard (p. 275)
24. ADULT ♂, 25. in flight, 26. ADULT ♀ with DOWNY YOUNG.

Oxyura leucocephala White-headed Duck (p. 287)
27. ADULT ♂, 28. ADULT ♀, 29. ADULT ♂ with DOWNY YOUNG.

Oxyura maccoa Maccoa Duck (p. 289)
30. ADULT ♀, 31. ADULT ♂ in flight and swimming.

Thalassornis leuconotus White-backed Duck (p. 225)
32. ADULT standing and in flight, 33. ADULT swimming with DOWNY YOUNG.

Scale does not apply to flying birds

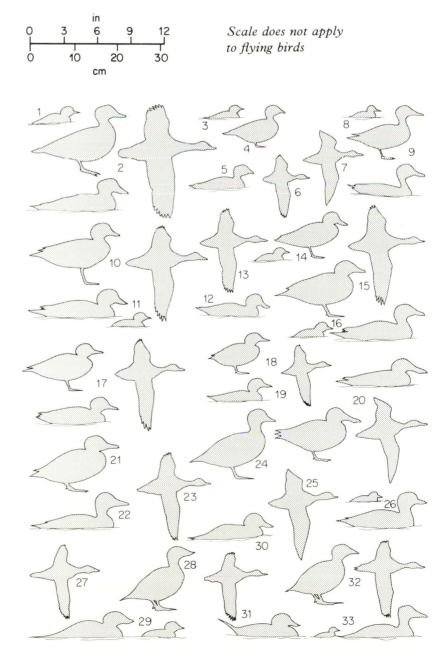

side by side, heads up and breasts slightly raised for short distance. Bill-dipping then commences, heads sometimes almost completely immersed. Also swim round in circle with heads and necks on water, body low. Immediately following Bill-dipping ♀ swims low in water with head forward; may swim completely round ♂. Copulation follows; ♂ beats wings causing some splashing. Following copulation whistles loudly once and both birds perform *Dendrocygna*-like Step-dance side by side, treading water with feet, body held vertically above water, wing furthest away from other bird raised. ♂ seen to bow forward 3 times, almost touching water with bill during water treading. Following this both birds seen to remain motionless few seconds, ♀ then Wing-flaps and Preens before both swim off side by side, heads erect.

NEST: on grass tuft on small floating island of vegetation or in reed or papyrus beds. Positioned close to water with ramp often leading to nest, or with approach channel between nest and open water, and up to 45 cm above water, usually less. Nest usually concealed by overhanging vegetation, sometimes old nest of coot or grebe used as base. Constructed from available plant life, frequently shredded reed leaves, sedge or water weeds, sometimes with surrounding vegetation bent over to form bower, usually lined with fine grass or other finer vegetable matter, very occasionally some down or few feathers. Continually built up during incubation by addition of fresh vegetation; entrance always covered by vegetation if possible. 2nd 'spare' nest sometimes built few metres away. Structure *c.* 30 cm wide by 23 cm high with interior cup 15–20 cm across by 5–10 cm deep; sometimes cup only built into base of reeds or sedges. Floating nests occasionally constructed in water 60–300 cm deep. Nest-building carried out by both sexes in captivity (J. Kear, pers. comm.).

EGGS: 4–10, laid at 24 h intervals; southern Africa mean (74 clutches) 6·75. Large, glossy, smooth ovals; rich coffee brown to chocolate brown with darker markings. SIZE: 57·0–69·2 × 46·5–53·0 (63·5 × 49·3); WEIGHT: (31 eggs, captive birds) 77–94 (81) (J. Kear, pers. comm.); *c.* 11·8% av. ♀ body weight.

Laying dates: Transvaal highveld all months, peaking Aug, Nov–June (wet and dry); Transvaal lowveld and Natal all months, peaking Dec–Mar (wet); Zim-babwe Feb–Aug, peaking June; Botswana Nov–Sept, peaking Apr; Zambia Dec–Aug, peaking Jan–Feb (wet), Apr, June (dry); Malawi Apr, June–Aug; Kenya all months, peaking June (late long rains) and Aug (dry); Uganda Apr. Breeding most regions apparently peaks when waters high and stable.

Incubation normally begins with completion of clutch, sometimes before; carried out by both sexes, ♂ performing greater part. Period: 29–33 days (in captivity), 36 days (1 wild record). 2 birds sometimes observed on nest. When not incubating ♂ remains close to nest and defends it, acting aggressively towards other waterbirds and humans. Incubating ♀ will quietly slip away from nest at approach of humans, whereas incubating ♂ will remain on nest a while. When ♂ finally leaves nest, he threatens intruder, hissing fiercely, and may even make attacks (usually abortive) or beat water with wings. In Threat posture bird lies low on water, neck partially submerged, head thrust forward towards object of aggression, bill opened, scapulars ruffled, wings raised and spread, feet paddling rapidly to agitate water. ♀ may also adopt this posture (observations of captive birds: J. Kear) with very rounded back. Attack or Threat usually followed by general body shake.

Ducklings feed themselves, swimming and diving freely within 20 h of first pipping of egg. Weight at hatching 54 g; at day 27 young *c.* half size of parents; day 34 fully feathered except for flight feathers; day 55 indistinguishable from adults. Fully grown day 114.

Parents drop flight feathers when young 7 weeks old. Young accompanied and guarded by parents at least until fully grown, ♂ with brood 90% fully grown seen to adopt same threatening behaviour as used when guarding nest. Small chicks brooded on nest by either parent; ♂ may break down side of nest to allow chicks to re-enter or chicks may climb up adjacent vegetation and drop into nest. Small young often kept in cover of emergent vegetation. Brood size Witwatersrand, Transvaal, 1–7.

References
Clark, A. (1969a, 1979).
Elwell, N. H. and McIlleron, W. G. (1978).
Johnsgard, P. A. (1967).
Kear, J. (1967).
Wintle, C. C. (1981).

Subfamily ANSERINAE: swans and geese

Moderately large to very large waterfowl (long-necked swans, moderately long-necked geese) with no iridescent coloration; tarsal surfaces reticulated; voices loud, honking. In swans, *Cygnus*, adult plumages white or black, partially pied in 2 species, patterns of downy young simple. True geese, *Anser* and *Branta*, variously coloured, white and black patterns often predominating. Sexes alike.

Many highly migratory; all vegetarian, food being obtained mostly from below water in swans, by terrestrial grazing in geese. Pre-flight in true geese and some swans signalled by call rather than head movements. Pre-copulatory display mutual Head-dipping. Both sexes call as copulation is terminated, both then rise up in water while extending head and neck vertically, with or without lifting or extending wings. In true geese, possibly also swans, ♂'s courtship consists of swimming ahead of ♀ with neck extended. Pair-forming involves the frequent use of the Triumph-ceremony, mutual Chin-lifting and loud calling.

6 genera, of which 3, *Cygnus*, *Anser* and *Branta*, represented in Africa.

Genus *Cygnus* Bechstein

Large, long-necked waterfowl. Plumage mostly white; young grey; neck longer than body (thus differing from ducks and geese); bill strong, deep at base; lores bare; legs short, feet large. Voices vary from muted to loud, trumpeting and honking.

Walk heavily; dive to escape danger. Flight powerful with neck fully extended, wing-beats slow and regular, often producing audible sounds; flocks usually form staggered lines or V-formations. Pre-flight signalled by erect necks, take-off often laboured and prolonged. Courtship behaviour simple; includes (1) Threat-busking display in which (*C. olor*) half-opened wings are raised so that secondaries and tertials form arch over back with head thrown well back between wings, or (*C. cygnus* and *C. bewickii*) wings are spread away from body with head and curved neck held low; and (2) Triumph-ceremony in which both sexes stretch their necks upwards and forwards and call loudly.

5 species, of which 3 Palearctic winter rarely N Africa where their exact status is uncertain due to mis-identification.

Cygnus olor (Gmelin). Mute Swan. Cygne tuberculé.

Plate 14

(Opp. p. 211)

Anas Olor Gmelin, 1789. Syst. Nat., 1, p. 502; Russia.

Range and Status. Palearctic winter migrant from south USSR to Egypt where uncommon; also Algeria. Introduced feral populations exist Egypt, possibly elsewhere N Africa, also eastern Cape Province, South Africa, where now established as wild breeding species. Not normally hunted or otherwise molested and South African population of a few hundred birds stable.

Cygnus olor

Description. ADULT ♂: entirely white. Bill orange-red, tip, cutting edge, base, nostrils and knob on forehead black; eye hazel; legs and feet black. Sexes alike. ♂ larger. SIZE: wing, ♂ (12 specimens) 580–623 (606), ♀ (10) 533–589 (562); tail, ♂ (6) 205–246 (224), ♀ (10) 190–232 (211); bill from knob, ♂ (12) 74–88 (80·6), ♀ (13) 69–79 (74·2); tarsus, ♂ (12) 107–118 (114), ♀ (10) 99–114 (104); toe, ♂ (11) 147–166 (158), ♀ (10) 134–150 (142); length, 145–160 cm; wing-span, 208–238 cm. WEIGHT: (England) ♂ (59) 9·2–14·3 (11·8) kg, ♀ (35) 7·6–10·6 (9·7) kg.

JUVENILE: dingy brown above, whitish below with some white on cheeks, scapulars and centre of mantle to rump; bill lacks knob, grey becoming suffused with pink, then dull orange; feet grey becoming black. Plumage progressively whitens but traces of brown may remain until 2nd winter.

DOWNY YOUNG: upperparts pale grey, underparts white; bill black, nail pale horn; feet dark grey; skin in front of eye feathered.

Field Characters. Huge white swan differing from other swans in having gracefully curved neck, wings usually arched over back when swimming, reddish bill. Takes off from water with heavy flapping, feet pattering on surface; from ground take-off even more laborious and in boggy conditions may be grounded. Once airborne flies strongly and purposefully, neck outstretched and wings producing distinct whining sound.

Voice. Recorded (6). Generally silent but hisses in anger. Otherwise occasional hoarse, explosive snorting or grunting 'whrrk' or 'hrrrk'.

General Habits. Little known in Africa; intimately known in Europe. Introduced populations mostly sedentary within 50 km of breeding territory. May congregate in groups of 60 or so when in moult. Seen mostly on or near water, including flooded lands and estuary flats. During day mated adults normally swim in pairs or family parties, sometimes several pairs in loose association, feeding and preening. Feeds by immersing head and neck, or by up-ending in water 1 m deep; also grazes or dabbles at water's edge and grazes occasionally in flood lands. Roosts on ground, usually on island or bank, protected, if possible, from predators by water.

Food. Mainly aquatic vegetation; also frogs, toads, tadpoles, molluscs, worms, insects and larvae regularly taken. Daily intake of moulting adults 3·6–4 kg of wet vegetable food.

Breeding Habits. Little known in Africa; well known in Europe. Nests solitary, on ground, usually within 100 m of water, frequently at water's edge. Territorial during breeding season; less so at other times. Non-breeding, unmated and young birds gregarious all year. Pair-bond usually life-long. Breeding pairs establish and defend territories with aggressive display. When repulsing a rival, both sexes perform Triumph-ceremony and Threat-busking display; also lift chins up and down and make snorting calls. Sometimes when performing Threat-busking display, each bird swims towards opponent, paddling with both feet simultaneously, causing jerking motion. Attacks may occur on fringe of territory, occasionally developing into fights in which snorting opponents use wings and bills. Loser either flies off or adopts submissive posture in which entire plumage is sleeked, wings pressed firmly against body and neck stretched forward with bill pointed downwards and touching water.

When greeting, pair face each other on water, touch breasts, fluff upper head feathers, sometimes raise secondaries and turn heads back and forth. Before copulating, both alternately dip heads below water, preen or rub backs or flanks, sometimes up-end, hold necks upright and close together, and keep wings low, even in water. When copulating, ♂ pushes neck and body over ♀'s and mounts, grasping her neck feathers in bill. After copulation both often utter hoarse, muted cries while rising half out of water, sometimes breast to breast, necks extended, bills pointed up, then down, then side to side (see **A**). May also bathe, preen and tail-wag afterwards.

NEST: on island, edge of reedbed, or bank; built of reeds, rushes and other water-side plants to form large mound with shallow depression lined with soft vegetable matter and a little down. 1–2 m across (up to 4 m if in water) by 60–80 cm high; depression 5–15 cm deep. Both sexes build with ♂ frequently selecting site and preparing foundation. Vegetation obtained in vicinity of nest, ♂ plucking and passing material over shoulder to ♀ who arranges it and forms bowl with breast, bill and feet. Av. completion time 10 days. ♀ continues to add small amounts of material during incubation. Most nests normally well spread out, though may be as close as 2 m. Nests may be used year after year.

A

EGGS: 5–8 (range 1–11), laid at 48 h intervals, mostly early morning. Rounded; pale green with chalky covering when fresh, becoming scratched and stained brown or yellow during incubation. SIZE: (88) 100–122 × 70–80 (113 × 74); WEIGHT: (80) 294–385 (354).

Laying dates: South Africa Sept–Oct.

Incubation by ♀ though ♂ sits during laying and while ♀ is feeding; otherwise eggs covered with nest material when ♀ off. Period: 35–41 days (av. 36). Replacement clutches laid 2–4 weeks after loss of eggs. Hatching synchronous 24–36 h; shells left in nest.

Chicks active and mobile, cared for by both parents. While small, often carried on especially ♀'s back on water and brooded at night by ♀ on land or nest. Self-feeding but parents may free vegetation from both bank and underwater.

Young sometimes driven from territory at c. 6 months or may stay with parents until winter flocking, remaining with flock when adults next breed. Fledging period 120–150 days (Europe). Starvation most important cause of mortality first 2 weeks after hatching (Europe).

References
McLachlan, G. R. and Liversidge, R. (1978).

Cygnus cygnus (Linnaeus). Whooper Swan. Cygne chanteur.

Anas Cygnus Linnaeus, 1758. Syst. Nat. (10th ed.), p. 122; Sweden.

Plate 14
(Opp. p. 211)

Range and Status. Rare Palearctic winter visitor to Algeria, Tunisia and Egypt, often well into spring.

Description. ADULT ♂: entirely white, head, neck and underparts sometimes stained rusty. Lores and bill over entire basal half of culmen extending forward laterally in wedge below nostril yellow, anterior half from nostril forward and entire base black; eye brown; legs and feet black. Sexes alike, ♀ slightly smaller. SIZE: wing, ♂ (17 specimens) 587–635 (610), (14) 562–615 (583); tail, ♂ (16) 151–182 (169), ♀ (15) 151–181 (167); culmen, ♂ (19) 98–116 (106), ♀ (15) 92–111 (102); tarsus, ♂ (21) 116–130 (123), ♀ (22) 104–119 (113); middle toe and claw, ♂ (21) 142–172 (156), ♀ (22) 129–155 (141); length, 145–160 cm; wing-span, 218–243 cm. WEIGHT: (<10) ♂ 10·8 kg, ♀ 8·1 kg (winter mean: Owen 1977).

JUVENILE: grey-brown, whitish around eye and on underparts; bill pinkish at base, blackish at tip but variable; legs and feet pale flesh-grey. In 1st winter and spring becomes whiter but still mostly grey above; base of bill becomes bluish white then yellow; feet black.

Field Characters. Swims with straight, stiff neck and walks well, no waddling action, differing in this from Mute Swan *C. olor*. Similar to Bewick's Swan *C. bewickii* but much larger, heavier in build and has larger bill with more yellow at base; flattened head profile diagnostic. In flight wings make swishing sound (not loud soughing of Mute Swan) and loud call uttered frequently, deeper and louder than that of Bewick's Swan.

Voice. Recorded (6). Loud, musical, trumpeting 'hou-hou', 2nd syllable higher pitched; uttered by individuals in swimming and flying flocks and repeated several times with short pauses. Individual contact calls on land or water high-pitched, monosyllabic 'ang' or 'huck'; high-pitched 'wak' in anxiety.

General Habits. Little known in Africa, well known in Europe. Gregarious in winter. Frequents coastal waters, lakes and lagoons, indulging in much underwater grazing well away from shorelines. Will also graze on land. On local journeys groups fly low in diagonal lines, V-formation or loose straggle, flocks usually containing young. Feed by immersing head or up-ending in both fresh and saline waters, or grazing on land.

Food. Aquatic vegetation; also grasses, roots, shoots and green crops.

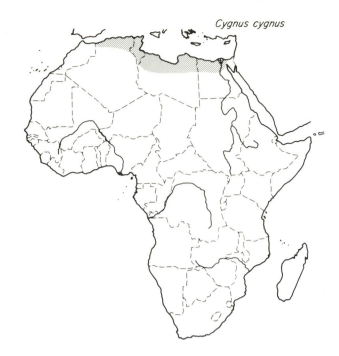

Cygnus cygnus

Cygnus bewickii Yarrell. Bewick's Swan. Cygne de Bewick.

Cygnus Bewickii Yarrell, 1830. Trans. Linn. Soc. London, 16, p. 453, pl. 24, England.

Plate 14

(Opp. p. 211)

Range and Status. Rare Palearctic winter visitor to N Africa; exact range uncertain but collected Algeria and Libya.

Description. ADULT ♂: entirely white; bill variably yellow on basal half, black on anterior half (pattern acquired for life, enabling individuals to be recognized annually); eye brown; legs and feet black. Sexes alike, ♀ smaller. SIZE: (captive specimens, Europe) wing, ♂ (93) 485–573 (531), ♀ (92) 478–543 (510); tail, ♂ (9) 141–164 (151), ♀ (15) 139–164 (152); culmen, ♂ (94) 81–108 (94·7), ♀ (94) 75–100 (90·9); middle toe and claw, ♂ (16) 118–141 (128), ♀ (21) 110–130 (121); length, 115 cm; wing-span, 180–211 cm. WEIGHT: (winter, England) ♂ (96) 4·9–7·8 (6·4) kg, ♀ (95) 3·4–7·2 (5·7) kg (Scott *et al.* 1972).
JUVENILE: grey-brown, whiter on underparts; bill variable, tip dark, base pinkish; feet dark grey to blackish.

Field Characters. Adult and juvenile very similar to, but smaller than, Whooper Swan *C. cygnus*. Yellow bill patch less extensive, head more rounded, neck appears shorter and body more stocky at all ages. Swims with straight neck, walks easily.

Voice. Recorded (6). Noisy on water or land, a crooning or goose-like honking. Less vocal in flight, a monosyllabic 'hong' or 'hung'.

General Habits. Little known in Africa, well known in Europe. When present, probably in small groups frequenting estuaries, lakes, lagoons. Present in severe

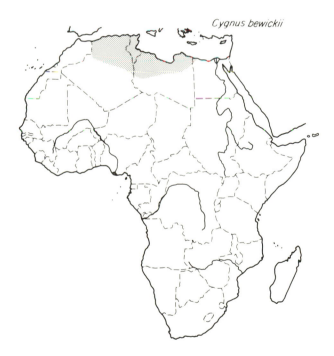

Cygnus bewickii

European winters only. Feeds by head-dipping or up-ending in water, or grazing and digging with feet on land.

Food. Aquatic vegetation; also various herbage, rhizomes, roots and tubers.

Genus *Anser* Brisson

Moderately large, large-headed, thick-necked geese with longish legs placed forward. Bills high, narrow, with serrated edges and strong nails; tails longish, rounded. Predominantly brown in colour, feathers pale-edged forming regular transverse lines on upperparts; vents white; heads and necks dark brown, neck feathers lanceolate, projecting in vertical ridges and furrows; bills and feet orange or pink. Sexes alike, ♂♂ larger. All highly gregarious; flocks fly in staggered lines or V-formations, graze diurnally on grasslands, croplands; family units close-knit within flock.

Migratory Holarctic genus of 10 species, 4 in N Africa as winter migrants.

Plate 14

(Opp. p. 211)

Anser fabalis (Latham). Bean Goose. Oie des moissons.

Anas Fabalis Latham, 1787. Gen. Syn. Birds, Suppl., p. 297; Great Britain.

Range and Status. Fairly common Morocco and Algeria in Palearctic winter, occasional sightings Egypt; vagrant Niger Delta (Lamarche 1980).

Anser fabalis

X Vagrant

Description. *A. f. fabalis*, ADULT ♂: head and neck very dark brown, grading to dull medium brown over entire upperparts, including scapulars and sides of body, feathers with buff tips; back and rump black-brown; uppertail-coverts white; tail black-brown, narrowly margined and broadly tipped white. Belly and thighs grey-brown, feathers broadly tipped white; vent, sides of rump and undertail-coverts white; upperwings lacking distinct pattern, coverts dull medium brown as upperparts, contrasting slightly with blackish remiges, greater and

median coverts broadly tipped white; underwing dark grey. Bill long, heavy, orange-yellow with black tip and variable amount of black extending from base; eyes dark brown, no eye-ring; legs and feet orange–yellow. SIZE: wing, ♂ (87 specimens) 452–520 (481), ♀ (73) 434–488 (460); tail, ♂ (5) 126–139 (132), ♀ (2) 127–137 (132); bill, ♂ (93) 57–70 (63·6), ♀ (75) 55–66 (60); tarsus, ♂ (21) 76–90 (82·2), ♀ (11) 73–80 (76·7); toe, ♂ (12) 82–94 (88·6), ♀ (11) 78–84 (82·7); length, 66–84 cm; wing-span, 142–175 cm. WEIGHT (winter) ♂ (68) 2690–4060 (3198), ♀ (58) 2220–3470 (2843).

JUVENILE: darker, feather tips dull coloured only, wing-coverts appear marbled rather than streaked, legs and bill less bright.

A. f. rossicus Buturlin. Neck shorter; bill deeper-based, finer-pointed, orange-yellow confined to small patch behind nail. Smaller; wing, ♂ 430–478 (454); tail, 113–136 (125).

Field Characters. Large, tall, long-billed, long-necked brown goose. Differs from Greylag *A. anser* in having very dark head and neck, orange feet; from Greater White-fronted *A. albifrons* and Lesser White-fronted *A. erythropus* in larger size, lack of white on head or black on belly, orange bill at all ages.

Voice. Recorded (22b). Least vocal of group. Flight call of flock reedy, bassoon-like 'ung-ank' or 'bow-wow'.

General Habits. Little known in Africa. Wintering populations gregarious, forming flocks sometimes of hundreds exploiting grasslands, farmlands. May also occur in family groups, then prone to mix with other geese. Roosts on feeding grounds or on small nearby waters. Generally frequents less open waters than other *Anser* spp.

Food. Grasses, cereals, various agricultural crops obtained by diurnal grazing. Also root crops.

Plate 14

(Opp. p. 211)

Anser albifrons (Scopoli). Greater White-fronted Goose. Oie rieuse

Branta albifrons Scopoli 1769. Annus 1, Hist. Nat., p. 69; northern Italy.

Range and Status. Regular visitor to Nile Delta during Palearctic winter; then most common goose in Egypt; accidental elsewhere N Africa.

Description. *A. a. albifrons*, ADULT ♂: around base of bill and forehead white; rest of head and neck dark brown; mantle, scapulars, sides of body and flanks dark brown,

feathers with grey-tinged centres, buff-edged, paler at tips; back and rump dark grey, longest feathers tipped white; uppertail-coverts white; tail grey-black edged white. Breast, belly grey-brown, feathers broadly tipped buffy white, entire region with heavy, black transverse blotches and bars; vent, sides of body and undertail-coverts white, contiguous with uppertail-coverts; upperwing no obvious pattern, coverts dusky grey, lesser, inner median and greater coverts tinged brown, greater and median coverts broadly tipped white; remiges black, primaries grey basally; underwing and axillaries dark grey. Bill pink, middle of culmen and basal half under mandible tinged yellow, nail white; eye dark brown, eye-ring black to yellow; legs and feet orange. SIZE: wing, ♂ (20 specimens) 399–444 (428), ♀ (14) 393–415 (404); tail, ♂ (15) 106–217 (119), ♀ (12) 102–127 (113); bill, ♂ (32) 43–50 (46·4), ♀ (31) 39–47 (43·3); tarsus, ♂ (26) 69–80 (73·5), ♀ (26) 63–74 (68·6); toe, ♂ (26) 69–82 (74·2), ♀ (26) 63–74 (68·6); length, 65–78 cm; wing-span 130–165 cm. WEIGHT: ♂ (238, winter, Netherlands) 1757–2650 (2130), ♀ (287) 1430–2240 (1905).

JUVENILE: as adult but lacking white on head and black on underparts, generally browner, more uniform.

Field Characters. Deep-chested, square-headed, grey-brown goose with white base to pink bill; orange legs. Larger, longer-billed than Lesser White-fronted Goose *A. erythropus* with less white around bill base, this marking being entirely absent in larger Greylag Goose *A. anser*. Young only separable from young of Lesser White-fronted Goose by larger size.

Voice. Recorded (22b). Flight calls high-pitched, more hurried than other *Anser* spp., 'kow-lyow' or lyo-lyck'. Feeding flocks utter low buzzing.

General Habits. Little known in Africa, well known elsewhere. Frequents delta wetlands with preference for fresh water, often lingering until May. Flies freely when disturbed, circling widely at medium height. Known in

Egypt for thousands of years and depicted on many ancient monuments.

Food. Mostly diurnal grazer, feeding on variety of vegetable matter, including crops.

Anser albifrons

Anser erythropus (Linnaeus). Lesser White-fronted Goose. Oie naine.

Anas erythropus Linnaeus, 1758. Syst. Nat. (10th ed.), p. 123; northern Sweden.

Plate 14

(Opp. p. 211)

Range and Status. Winter vagrant to NE Africa, mostly Egypt.

Description. ADULT ♂: almost identical to Greater White-fronted Goose *A. albifrons*, but smaller, more petite, white at bill base more extensive over forehead; eye-ring yellow; black blotching of belly less extensive. SIZE: wing, ♂ (8 specimens) 370–388 (378), ♀ (7) 361–387 (373); tail, ♂ (4) 98–108 (104), ♀ (7) 97–110 (102); bill, ♂ (13) 31–37 (33·6), ♀ (17) 29–34 (31·3); tarsus, ♂ (13) 59–68 (63·7), ♀ (15) 57–63 (61); toe, ♂ (13) 59–67 (62·5), ♀ (19) 56–63 (59·7); length, 53–66 cm; wing-span 120–135 mm. WEIGHT: (Europe) ♂ (6) 1800–2300, ♀ (4) 1400–2150.

JUVENILE: lacks white forehead, black blotches on belly and pale feather edging on upperparts.

Field Characters. Small dusky brown goose with white patch on forehead, pink bill and orange feet. Differs from larger Greater White-fronted Goose in having more extensive white forehead, yellow eyelids and paler, less black-marked belly. Short bill gives head rounded appearance. Young almost inseparable from young of Greater White-fronted Goose, but smaller, shorter-billed.

Voice. Recorded (22b). Contact call 'kah'. Other calls not loud, but high-pitched, squeaky 'kyu-yu-yu' or 'ouiou-ou-ou'.

General Habits. Scarcely known in Africa but similar to those of Greater White-fronted Goose.

Food. Mainly shoots, leaves and stems of grasses and sedges; grazes like other *Anser* spp.

Anser erythropus

Plate 14

(Opp. p. 211)

Anser anser (Linnaeus). Greylag Goose. Oie cendrée.

Anas Anser Linnaeus, 1758. Syst. Nat. (10th ed.), p. 123; Sweden.

Range and Status. Regular visitor Morocco–Tunisia Oct–Mar; occasional east of Tunisia, status unclear; also Mali (K. Curry-Lindahl, pers. comm.). Single case of breeding on Lake Fetzara, Algeria considered accidental by wounded bird (Etchécopar and Hüe 1967).

Anser anser

Description. *A. a. anser*, ADULT ♂: entire head, neck, mantle, sides of body and flanks grey-brown, paler at shoulder, except for head and neck all feathers edged buff-white; back and rump grey; uppertail-coverts to sides of rump white; tail grey edged white. Breast and underparts pale buff-grey grading into brown flanks, all feathers edged buff-white, small black blotches irregularly scattered on belly; vent and undertail-coverts white, contiguous with rump; upperwing with scapulars, tertials and inner secondaries grey-brown, all feathers edged buff-white; wing-coverts pale blue-grey, whitish to-

wards leading edge; speculum brown, edged white, remiges blackish; underwing-coverts dark brown. Bill orange, nail pink; eye brown with orange eye-ring; legs and feet flesh. SIZE: wing, ♂ (7 specimens) 448–480 (465), ♀ (16) 412–465 (442); tail, ♂ (14) 130–149 (139), ♀ (10) 120–139 (129); culmen, ♂ (32) 59–74 (66·6), ♀ (24) 58–65 (61·5); tarsus, ♂ (32) 78–93 (84·7), ♀ (24) 71–87 (78·8); toe, ♂ (32) 84–102 (91·6), ♀ (24) 80–97 (85·7); length, 75–90 cm; wing-span, 147–180 cm. WEIGHT: (winter, Scotland) ♂ (94) 2600–4560 (3509), ♀ (75) 2160–3800 (3108).

JUVENILE: plumage more mottled, less clearly defined feather edges.

A. a. rubirostris Swinhoe. Head, neck, upperparts and flanks whitish rather than buff; forewing paler; bill longer, pink except for white nail. Slightly larger: wing, ♂ 436–513 (468); bill, 59–78 (68·8).

Field Characters. Difficult to separate from other grey geese but noticeably paler in colour than Bean *A. fabalis*, Greater White-fronted *A. albifrons* and Lesser White-fronted *A. erythropus* Geese with noticeably pale forewing in flight, on ground greater bulk and combination of orange bill and pink feet diagnostic.

Voice. Recorded (6). Contact call soft, low, nasal cackling, 2–7 syllables uttered in flock by grazing birds. In flight loud, high-pitched, sonorous honking 'aahng-ung-ung'.

General Habits. Little known in Africa, well known in Europe. Gregarious, flocks arriving early autumn, frequenting cultivated fields, marshes, river mouths. Members of flock maintain continual conversational calls. Both *A. a. anser* and *A. a. rubirostris* recorded in Tunisia (Rooth 1971).

Food. In winter quarters grazes diurnally largely on grasslands and local agricultural crops according to availability.

Genus *Branta* Scopoli

Medium-size geese, smaller than most *Anser* spp., quicker in their movements, more vocal, necks longer and thinner, bills smaller and always black, as are legs and feet; tails slightly rounded. Plumages predominantly black, white and brown, elaborately patterned, neck-furrows absent. Sexes alike, ♂♂ slightly larger. Gregarious in winter quarters, wholly or partially maritime in habits, moving between feeding areas in loose, compact flocks.

Migratory geese closely related to genus *Anser*; 5 species, 3 in N Africa as visitors during Palearctic winter.

Plate 14

(Opp. p. 211)

Branta leucopsis (Bechstein). Barnacle Goose. Bernache nonnette.

Anas leucopsis Bechstein, 1803. Orn. Taschenb. Deutschland, 2, p. 424; Germany.

Range and Status. Accidental Morocco and Egypt.

Description. ADULT ♂: forehead, sides of head, chin and throat creamy white; crown, neck, mantle, chest, upper breast, back and rump black; rest of upperparts ash-blue, feathers tipped broadly black with white edges; sides of body and flanks

pale grey, broadly edged white; thighs and sides of back black, blotched white; sides of rump, tail-coverts, belly and vent white; tail black; upperwing-coverts ash blue, all coverts tipped broadly black with white edges giving parallel barred effect; underwing grey. Bill, legs and feet black; eye brown. SIZE: wing, ♂ (23 specimens) 388–429 (410), ♀ (19) 376–410 (392); tail, ♂ (22) 116–134 (126), ♀ (18) 113–130 (119); bill,

♂ (32) 28–33 (29·6), ♀ (28) 27–32 (28·6); tarsus, ♂ (31) 67–80 (72·4), ♀ (28) 64–72 (67·8); toe, ♂ (24) 57–68 (62·6), ♀ (22) 54–63 (58·2); length, 58–70 cm; wing-span, 132–145 cm. WEIGHT: (winter, Netherlands) ♂ (33) 1370–2010 (1672), ♀ (35) 1290–1785 (1499).

JUVENILE: black line through eye joining crown, face more dusky, rest of plumage duller, less clearly marked.

Field Characters. A white-faced, black-necked goose with black and white transverse lines over upperparts. Differs from Brent Goose *B. bernicla* in having white face, much paler wings and body.

Voice. Recorded (22b). Resembles dog barking. Shrill, monosyllabic 'gnuk' varying in pitch. When feeding flocks utter low-pitched, muffled 'hoog'.

General Habits. Scarcely known in Africa, well known in Europe. Fly in compact, formless flocks between feeding sites, frequenting marshes and grasslands close to sea. May rest on sea but habits far less marine than those of Brent Goose. Flocks noisy and quarrelsome. Food obtained by grazing day or night.

Food. Leaves, grasses, mosses, seeds.

Branta leucopsis

Branta bernicla (Linnaeus). Brent Goose; Brant. Bernache cravant.

Anas Bernicla Linnaeus, 1758. Syst. Nat. (10th ed.), p. 124; Sweden.

Plate 14

(Opp. p. 211)

Range and Status. Rare vagrant to Atlantic coast of Morocco; small numbers regular Algeria, Tunisia, Libya; rare Egypt.

Description. *B. b. bernicla* (Linnaeus), ADULT ♂: head, neck, upper mantle, chest and upper breast black; triangular patches on sides of neck white; mantle grey-black, the feathers narrowly edged pale grey-brown; scapulars, back, rump and wing-coverts grey-black; sides of back and rump and uppertail-coverts white; lower breast, belly dark grey, feathers edged paler; on sides of body and flank feathers darker grey with brown tinge and contrasting white edges; vent, undertail-coverts white; remiges and rectrices black; wings dark grey. Bill, legs and feet black; eye dark brown. SIZE: wing, ♂ (18 specimens) 330–353 (340), ♀ (13) 317–335 (324); tail, ♂ (17) 90–101 (94·6), ♀ (14) 86–95 (90·8); bill, ♂ (17) 32–38 (34·9), ♀ (14) 29–33 (31·7); tarsus, ♂ (17) 60–67 (63·7), ♀ (13) 56–61 (58·1); toe, ♂ (16) 55–62 (58·4), ♀ (13) 51–57 (54·3); length, 56–61 cm; wing-span, 110–120 cm. WEIGHT: (27, winter, Britain) 1420.

JUVENILE: as adult but lacks white neck patch; more prominent barring on mantle, scapulars and wings.

Field Characters. When swimming appears all black except for white neck mark, otherwise shows pale belly and white ventral region. Distinct from any other goose in Africa.

Voice. Recorded (22b). Mostly silent, but flocks can be noisy on water and in flight, a hard, brief trumpeting 'rott, rott, rott', or soft monosyllabic 'ronk'.

General Habits. Little known in Africa, well known in Europe. Gregarious and maritime in winter quarters, feeding on tidal flats, resting on sea at high water and at night. Feeding rhythm related to tidal cycle; will feed by moonlight. Generally more aquatic than other *Branta* spp. Flies swiftly, like other geese, but seldom in V-formation.

Food. Marine vegetation; also small shellfish and other invertebrates obtained by grazing in shallow water, pulling up and tearing underwater plants; will up-end or feed with head submerged while swimming.

Branta bernicla

Plate 14

(Opp. p. 211)

Branta ruficollis (Pallas). Red-breasted Goose. Bernache à cou roux.

Anser ruficollis Pallas, 1769. Spic. Zool., fasc. 6, p. 21; Lower Ob, Siberia.

Range and Status. Vagrant to Algeria and Egypt in Palearctic winter. Probably common formerly as depicted in ancient Egyptian frescos.

Description. ADULT ♂: from gape to above lores a large, white, oval patch touching eye; throat, chin, rest of face to above eyes, forehead, crown, nape and rear neck black; on both sides

Branta ruficollis

of head a large triangular chestnut patch encircled by white line which descends down side of neck; entire foreneck, chest and breast rich chestnut; a white line encircling entire body level with mantle; rest of upperparts and underparts to legs black except for irregular white line bordering sides and flanks, 2 white lines across wing-coverts; uppertail-coverts, thighs, vent and undertail-coverts white; tail black. Eye brown; bill, legs and feet black. SIZE: wing ♂ (8 specimens) 355–379 (367), ♀ (7) 332–352 (343); tail, ♂ (8) 98–121 (109), ♀ (8) 96–107 (102); bill ♂ (9) 23–27 (24·9), ♀ (8) 22–26 (24·2); tarsus, ♂ (8) 58–65 (61·3), ♀ (8) 54–61 (57·1); toe, ♂ (9) 50–59 (54·2), ♀ (8) 49–53 (51·4); length, 53–56 cm; wing-span 116–135 cm. WEIGHT: ♂ (3) 1200–1456, ♀ (2) 1060, 1130.

JUVENILE: similar, chestnut cheek-patch smaller or absent.

Field Characters. Small, thick-necked, small-billed goose having elaborate black, white and chestnut plumage pattern. Unmistakable.

Voice. Recorded (21a). Main call in flight or from feeding flocks shrill, loud, staccato double shriek 'kee-kwa' or 'kik-wit'. Hisses frequently while feeding.

General Habits. Scarcely known in Africa, well known in Europe. In winter quarters frequents coastal regions but less aquatic, more terrestrial than other *Branta* spp. Swims readily on fresh and salt water; roosts at night on water. Feeds by grazing, cropping with rapid head movements. Highly gregarious.

Food. Coastal grasses, sedges, wheat and maize crops.

Subfamily Tadorninae: sheldgeese and shelducks

6 genera representing a transition between true geese and ducks with *Cyanochen* and *Alopochen*, the sheldgeese, and *Tadorna*, the shelducks, in Africa. Most species have scutellated frontal patterns to tarsi; some (possibly all) undergo 2 body moults annually. Sexual dimorphism in many adult plumages, being especially marked in some shelducks. Plumages mostly black, white and chestnut with distinct barring or colour patches, and metallic specula; shelducks have pure white wing-coverts. Pre-flight signalled by lateral Head-shakes and repeated Chin-lifting. Most species highly aggressive, many maintaining and defending territories while breeding, some pairs occupying territories all year. Courtship often terrestrial, less elaborate than in Anatinae and lacking communal courtship. Pair-bonds fairly strong in sheldgeese, less strong in shelducks. Unlike true geese, pair-forming behaviour conspicuous, akin to basic pair-forming behaviour in Anatinae, with ♀♀ Inciting ♂♂ to attack other ♂♂ or ♀♀ and selecting their mates on basis of ♂'s reaction to this. ♂♂ typically respond by overtly threatening or attacking indicated victim, then return to ♀♀ and display to them. This involves calling in an erect attitude as in Anserinae Triumph-ceremony, accompanied by spreading or lifting folded wings to display specula. Pre-copulatory mutual Head-dipping seen in most, if not all shelducks, while in many sheldgeese and shelduck species post-copulatory behaviour involves calling by both sexes while ♂ (to a lesser extent also ♀) lifts wing on opposite side to partner, as in whistling-ducks. Other heterosexual displays include Puffing, Bowing, High-and-erect often with wing-raising and strutting gait, Bill-dip, Ceremonial-drinking, Mock-preening (in form of Preen-behind-wing) and Pursuit-flights.

Genus *Cyanochen* Bonaparte

A monotypic genus resembling the South American *Chloephaga* in appearance, behaviour and temperament; closest to Andean Goose *C. melanoptera*. Neck thick, moderately long; tail graduated; bill short, not deep at base; legs short; general colouring ash grey, green specula formed by secondaries, not greater wing-coverts. Inciting consists primarily of calls; if visual signals exist, lack directional basis.

Cyanochen cyanopterus (Rüppell). Blue-winged Goose. Ouette à ailes bleues.

Plate 15

Bernicla cyanoptera Rüppell, 1845. Syst. Übersicht Vögel Nord-Ost-Afrika's, p. 129; Shoa, Ethiopia.

(Opp. p. 226)

Range and Status. Endemic to highlands of Ethiopia above *c.* 1800 m where fairly common. Not threatened by hunting as not eaten for religious reasons; future pressures resulting from human expansion possible.

Description. ADULT ♂: entire head and neck brownish ash, paler on forehead, face and throat; mantle and underparts mottled dusky brown and pale grey, most feathers of underparts with pale centres; back slate grey grading to pale brown on uppertail-coverts; vent and undertail-coverts white; tail rounded, black; upperwing-coverts pale slate blue, a small white patch at bend of wing; primaries black; secondaries glossy green; tertials brown; underwing-coverts white extending from knob of shoulder to body, the fore-edge grey. Eye dark brown; bill and legs black. SIZE: wing, ♂ (samples unknown) 368–374, ♀ 314–334; tail, ♂ 160–164, ♀ 135–142; culmen, ♂ 32–33, ♀ 30–31; tarsus, ♂ 70–73, ♀ 51–65 (Delacour 1954). WEIGHT: (captives) ♂ (2) 2000, 2360, ♀ (3) 1305–1500 (1420) (J. Kear, pers. comm.); ♀ (1) 1520 (Lack 1968).

JUVENILE: like adult, generally duller.

DOWNY YOUNG: upperside black-brown with 4 irregular silvery white markings on each side; underside silvery white throat to tail, including undertail; large black patch from bill to behind eye; sides of head, eyebrow to cheek, with golden yellow wash; bill, legs and feet black.

Cyanochen cyanopterus

Field Characters. Medium-size, thick-necked, short-legged grey goose with pale blue wing-patch. In flight white underwing-coverts form white spot extending from carpal joint to body (Blaauw 1927); tail rounded. Feathers on hindneck slightly lengthened as are feathers of upperwing-coverts, which are often carried loosely. When relaxed, standing or walking, has habit of resting back of neck on mantle, mantle feathers loose, tail depressed. Cannot be confused with any other duck in its restricted range.

Voice. Recorded (1a, 17). Both sexes have similar, high-pitched, almost whistling voices. Normal mild alarm call of ♂ a soft, scarcely audible 'whew-whu-whu-whu'. When alarmed into reluctant flight, a nasal bark 'penk-penk-penk-penk' is uttered at take-off, not in flight. When ♂ display-struts to ♀ utters rapidly repeated whistle 'wheee-whu-whu-whu-whu-whu-whu'; both sexes utter rapid 'wi-wi-wi-wi-wi-wi' after ♂ has threatened other waterfowl.

General Habits. Little known. Sedentary, pairs constantly together, usually inhabiting same area, probably territorial. In Bale and Arussi mountains lives in marshes, bog pools, swamps and streams with abundant grassland surroundings, usually avoiding open or deep waters; may occur in open Afro-alpine moorland up to 4000 m or more. In most suitable ranges occurs sparsely in pairs, less often in small groups, but in Web Valley marshes more common, 30 pairs seen in 40 km in 1966 and possibly 200–300 pairs estimated in entire valley (L. H. Brown, pers. comm.). During July–Sept rains flock in groups 50–100 or more, moving to lower altitudes, probably undergoing moult at this time. Consorts with Egyptian Goose *Alopochen aegyptiacus*, but gener-

ally discrete groups within mixed flocks. Confiding by nature, permitting close approach, *c.* 10 m. If disturbed, fly-off low down, not fast, one behind another, settling again within short distance (Von Heuglin, quoted by Delacour 1954), flying back to favourite haunt when intruder has passed.

♂♂ frequently threaten other waterfowl, swimming or standing erect with neck outstretched and held high but with wings closed and inconspicuous. After such threat ♂ returns to mate rapidly whistling 'wi-wi-wi-wi-wi-wi-wi . . .'; ♀ responds in same manner and both stand together with necks outstretched diagonally, heads close together, bills almost touching. Little aggressive behaviour recorded in ♀♀. Pre-flight movements involve lateral Head-shaking and Chin-lifting. In captivity nocturnally active.

Food. Riverside grasses and other herbage obtained by grazing. Also worms, insects, larvae, snails.

Breeding Habits. Little known; following data taken partially from captive studies. Nest built on sedge clump, under bush, probably at night. ♂ seen acting aggressively towards other ♂♂ and continually displaying to mate early Mar at headwaters of Webbi Shebelle River. ♂ struts round ♀ with head and neck bent over its back, bill pointing skywards or even behind, exposing blue-grey wing-patch and green secondaries and uttering rapidly repeated whistle (see Voice).

NEST: constructed by ♀ (captive bird: M. Lubbock, pers. comm.).

EGGS: 4–9; elongated, cream-coloured (captive birds: Johnsgard 1978). SIZE: 70 × 50 (Johnsgard 1978); WEIGHT: (90 eggs, captive birds) 73–92 (81) (J. Kear, pers. comm).

Laying dates: Mar–June, Sept.

Incubation (in captivity) carried out by ♀ only. Period: 30 to 34 days (Johnsgard 1978).

Chick weight increases from *c*. 52 g day 1 to *c*. 88 g day 5 (J. Kear, pers. comm.). Day 21 feathers start emerging; day 28 underside and shoulders feathered, legs become blue-black; day 38 blue wing-patch visible, tail well developed; day 42 completely feathered but wing feathers and coverts still short; day 85 almost adult size, fully fledged; day 176 start of 1st moult.

In captivity both parents defend young (M. Lubbock, pers. comm.).

Sexual maturity probably attained at 2 years (Johnsgard 1978).

References
Blaauw, F. E. (1927).
Brown, L. H. (1966).
Loeffler, H. von (1977).
Urban, E. K. (1978).

Genus *Alopochen* Stejneger

Fairly large sheldgoose common to most of Africa. Plumage generally chestnut and white; superficially resembles *Tadorna* but much larger, heavier-legged, longer-necked. Feathers of nape and hindneck rather long, loose; upperwing-coverts white, conspicuous; secondaries metallic green; tail longish. 1 sp., the Egyptian Goose *A. aegyptiacus*.

Plate 15

(Opp. p. 225)

Alopochen aegyptiacus (Linnaeus). Egyptian Goose. Oie d'Egypte.

Anas aegyptiaca Linnaeus, 1766. Syst. Nat. (12th ed.), 1, p. 197; Egypt.

Range and Status. Resident, common to locally abundant, mainly south of Sahara. Most common southern and E Africa; substantial population increase South Africa during this century as result of dams, irrigation schemes. Absent in western forested regions except major waterways. Wet season migrant to southern Algeria, Tunisia, parts of Sahara; no recent confirmed breeding records. In Egypt, where once common entire Nile Valley and regarded as sacred in ancient times, now largely confined to Upper Egypt where still fairly common. Formerly found over most of Africa, Middle East and southern Europe.

Description. ADULT ♂: frons, forecrown, cheeks, chin, throat and entire foreneck pale stone-grey; a large chestnut-coloured oval patch encircling eye, sometimes continuous as narrow

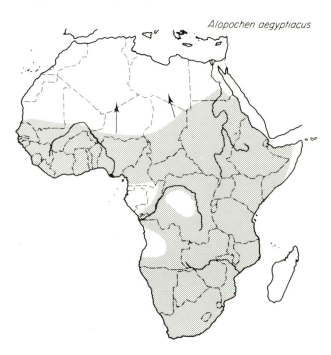

Alopochen aegyptiacus

chestnut band surrounding entire bill base; central crown, nape, rear neck and ear-coverts variably pale to medium chestnut; lower neck encircled by chestnut collar, broadest posteriorly; lower neck, flanks and entire underparts to vent pale stone-grey with fine transverse grey barring, mantle and sides of neck suffused with rust, a small irregular chestnut patch on centre of breast; mantle and scapulars reddish brown to dark brown vermiculated with buff or grey; rump and uppertail-coverts blackish; upperwing-coverts white, secondary coverts with a black subapical bar; primary coverts and primaries black; secondaries metallic green, inner webs duller; axillaries and underwing-coverts white; vent and undertail-coverts white washed pale yellow. Bill pink, dark brown at base and sides of upper mandible, around nostrils and on nail, deep maroon along cutting edge; eye orange; legs and feet bright pink. Sexes very similar, ♀ marginally smaller. SIZE: wing, ♂ (6 specimens) 378–406 (392), ♀ (7) 352–390 (375); tail, ♂ (6) 116–130 (123), ♀ (6) 111–131 (121); bill, ♂ (7) 46–54 (49·6), ♀ (10) 43–52 (47·9); tarsus, ♂ (7) 80–95 (85·5), ♀ (10) 73–85 (80·2); length, 63–73 cm; wing-span, 134–154 cm. WEIGHT: ♂ av. *c*. 2500, ♀ av. *c*. 2040.

JUVENILE: duller, more dusky about head and neck, eye-patch vestigial or absent; breast patch absent.

DOWNY YOUNG: crown, hindneck, streak behind eye to nape, upperparts, thighs, and sometimes indistinct spot on cheek dark cinnamon-brown; forehead, wide streak over eyes, sides of head, large spots on wing and sides of back and underparts white or pale grey; eye yellow-brown; bill and feet yellow-grey.

Field Characters. A large goose-like duck with chestnut and pale grey plumage, prominent eye-patch, pink bill and legs. On ground distinctive, unmistakable. Swims with rear end held higher than shoulders. In air white wing-coverts striking; similar to Ruddy Shelduck *Tadorna ferruginea* and South African Shelduck *T. cana*, differing in having pale not reddish body.

Voice. Recorded (6). Generally silent except in social situations. Sexes have totally different voices. ♂ emits husky, wheezing sound, produced with force, head and neck extended forward during all display situations, intensity and rapidity of sound depending on degree of excitement. ♀ makes harsh, nasal, high-pitched 'hur-hur-hur-hur . . .' often speeded-up in staccato manner, produced with neck extended forward.

Young utter high, rapid calls in groups of 6–7 notes. In distress, these are higher-pitched and faster than in true geese (J. Kear, pers. comm.).

General Habits. Well known. One of the commonest, most widespread duck species in Africa, at home in wide variety of wetland habitats except forests. On small waters occurs in small family parties; on large waters, especially during non-breeding season, flocks of up to 100 or more recorded South Africa when undergoing wing moult; Ethiopia often seen in flocks all year (L. H. Brown, pers. comm.); Niger delta 1600 Jan 1972 (Roux 1973). Found in most freshwater habitats up to 4000 m (Ethiopia; Kivu volcanoes, Zaïre), generally absent coastal regions. Subject to considerable seasonal movements, 1100 km in South Africa (McLachlan and Liversidge 1978), probably further in Nigeria, Chad, where trans-Saharan movements take place to Algeria, Tunisia in wet season; patterns not fully understood. Small part of population remains dispersed in pairs on small permanent waters throughout year.

Normal flying speed 60 km/h (Reardon 1977). Feeds by grazing on land. Non-breeding flocks well integrated and synchronized, individual distance maintained, mated pairs and juvenile groups tending to remain together within flock. Adults and fledged young undergo moult at same time. Post-nuptial moult occurs throughout year, 2 marked peaks in Jan–Mar and July–Aug (Geldenhuys 1975). Moults apparently related to breeding and local wet seasons; wing moult usually takes place on large waters, where birds dive capably if pursued. When not in wing moult flocks fly at sunset to communal grazing grounds, returning to roost after a few hours.

Food. Grasses, other plant leaves, seeds, maize stubble and young growing crops. Small amounts of various animal matter probably taken accidentally. Major crop pest in Cape Province and Orange Free State some years.

Breeding Habits. Well known, especially South Africa. Nests singly, sites highly variable, on ground or any convenient platform, hole or structure.

Courtship behaviour begins within flocks up to 4 months prior to dispersal to breeding territories. At this time aggressive interactions occur between ♂♂ and between ♀♀. Paired and pairing ♀♀ attack unpaired ♀♀ soliciting their mates. If ♂ approaches ♀, greets her by Ceremonial-drinking; may swim high in water, turning sideways to reveal yellow undertail-coverts. If not rejected, initiates Triumph-ceremony, stretching neck upwards and forwards. ♀ signifies acceptance by adopting similar posture and uttering Incitement calls. Pair may then perform full Triumph-ceremony, calls and movements escalating and sometimes leading to crossing of necks. In presence of rival, ♂ will suddenly spread wings; mutual Wing-spread display is normal climax

to Triumph-ceremony. Pre-copulatory display consists mainly of mutual Head-dipping, increasing in tempo, with neck-crossing, before ♀ assumes Prone-posture and ♂ mounts. ♀ may initiate copulation by adopting Prone-posture without preliminary display. Copulation normally takes place while birds swimming, sometimes while standing in shallow water or on land. Both sexes frequently call while copulating (Eltringham 1974). On dismounting ♂ may retain hold on ♀'s nape as both call, before releasing her and adopting High-and-erect posture, often raising far wing; alternatively or subsequently both may Preen-behind-wing (Eltringham 1974) and perform mutual Bathing.

Breeding pairs maintain discrete territory of up to 1 ha on large waters. During establishment and maintenance of territory fighting occurs, mainly between territorial ♂ and intruder. Displays occur in following broad sequence: (1) Threat display, Wing-showing by ♂; (2) Bent-neck posture, head lowered against breast, bill pointing down and neck with feathers erected, drawn-in; (3) Forward-posture, wings slightly opened, head and neck stretched horizontally forward, bill opened and directed at rival, ♂ utters wheezing Threat-call before pursuit. ♀ may display in same way, more usually attacks without preliminaries. Territorial pairs assume Wing-spread display directed at overflying conspecifics, whole body erect, fully spread wings lifted, calls loudly. In full attack Wing-spread display used just prior to contact if rival stands ground. When fighting, combatants stand or swim breast to breast, attempting to grasp or bite base of hindneck while beating with wings or striking with feet. Appeasement signalled by erect posture, neck held slightly backwards from vertical, bill horizontal, feathers of neck sleeked, wings hidden in flank pockets thus concealing white secondaries. Victorious birds perform Triumph-ceremony, usually initiated by returning ♂ who places himself in front of ♀. This display also used in greeting after pairs temporarily separated.

NEST: on ground in dense vegetation, under bushes or in tunnel in vegetation; also holes in embankments, caves, cliff ledges, tree cavities, church steeples and other buildings up to 60 m above ground, in or on nests of other species, e.g. darters, herons, crows, eagles and Hamerkop *Scopus umbretta*. Ground nests constructed of grass or reeds, other sites usually simple depression without material. All nests lined with down, 23–45 cm wide by 7–10 cm deep, built by ♀ only. Site close to, or far as 1 km away from water.

EGGS: 5–11, in captivity lays at 24 h intervals; southern Africa mean (654 clutches) 6·74. Smooth, glossy, regular ovals; cream-coloured. SIZE: (277 eggs) 57·9–75·8 × 46·0–57·7 (68·4 × 51·33). WEIGHT: (100 eggs, captive birds) 78·5–110 (98) (J. Kear, pers. comm.). Single-brooded, clutch replaced if lost.

Laying dates: N Africa Mar–Apr; Sudan June, Sept; Ethiopia July–Aug, probably also Feb–Apr; Senegal July–Oct; Nigeria Jan, Sept; Uganda Jan–Oct; Kenya Lake Turkana Apr, May, Sept; rest of Kenya all months, no pronounced peaks; Tanzania all months, no peaks; southern Zaïre June–Aug; Zambia Jan–Nov; Malawi Jan, Aug (2 records); Mozambique July–Oct; Zimbabwe all months, peaking June–Sept; South Africa all months, peaking Aug–Sept. In southern Africa marked tendency for breeding in late dry season (Geldenhuys, in press).

Incubation begins at clutch completion, by ♀ only. Period: 28–30 days. Hatching synchronous, eggshells left in nest.

Young leave nest within 24 h of hatching. In elevated sites called from nest by ♀ below, all jump in quick succession over water or land (Milstein 1975b). Weight at 1 day old (22 captive chicks) 45·0–59·5 (54) (J. Kear, pers. comm.). 1st contour feathers emerge as blood sheaths at days 17–21 in flank, tail, scapular and breast regions; feathers on forehead, cheek, crown, throat, nape and abdomen emerge almost simultaneously days 21–26; primary and secondary remiges, and feathers of back and rump appear by week 4. Flight possible at c. 11 weeks. Plumage undergoes continual change until 1st wing moult when adult plumage acquired. Characteristic brown eye-patch just evident at 3 months, complete

5 months; breast spot usually present at 5 months, but variable.

Cared for and defended by both parents, brooded by ♀ while small. Stay with parents several weeks, or even months after fledging, variable.

Hatching success from 5 clutches, 43 eggs (98%) (electric incubator, SW Cape). Breeding success in Uganda: of 62 broods producing total of 402 young, 243 successfully raised; av. survival rate 60·4% at day 60 after 1st sighting over 5-year period. Annual survival rate fluctuated 4·6%–80·4%. Broods with no survival, 26%; with 100% survival, 23%. Main predators *Milvus* kites, monitor lizards; also barbel (*Protopterus* spp.), hinged tortoises, snakes, various mammals (Eltringham 1974). 1st breeding takes place at probably 2 years.

References
Eltringham, S. K. (1974).
Geldenhuys, J. N. (1981b).
Siegfried, W. R. (1962a).

Genus *Tadorna* Fleming

Goose-like, with long bodies held horizontally; short, thick necks (except *T. tadorna*). All show limited sexual dimorphism, ♀♀ with more white on heads than ♂♂.

3 species in Africa, 1 endemic to South Africa, 2 in northern Africa as both winter migrants and breeding species.

Plate 15
(Opp. p. 226)

Tadorna ferruginea (Pallas). Ruddy Shelduck. Tadorne casarca.

Anas ferruginea Pallas, 1764. In Vroeg, Cat. Raisonné Coll. Oiseaux, Adumbr., p. 5; no locality = Tartary.

Range and Status. Breeding resident and non-breeding Palearctic migrant to N Africa, and western Sahara to Sudan and Ethiopia; vagrant Kenya. Formerly common, widespread, now extinct as breeding species many regions. Atlas Mountains possibly 1000 pairs; southern Sahara several hundred pairs; Iriki, Morocco, c. 50 pairs wet seasons only, otherwise absent. Algeria, Tunisia scarce, non-breeding visitor (Jacobs and

Ochando 1979); absent Libya. Once (1930) fairly common Nov–Apr Lower and Upper Egypt and Suez zone, common Nile Valley of northern Sudan (1955), recent information lacking. Recently discovered breeding Saneti Plateau of Bale Mountains, Ethiopia; 1st breeding recorded south of Sahara (Ash 1977a).

Tadorna ferruginea

Description. ADULT ♂ (breeding): head and neck cinnamon-buff, pale to creamy on face and lores, darkest on neck; a thin black collar at base of neck; mantle, scapulars and back rich cinnamon, latter 2 with fine grey vermiculations; rump, uppertail-coverts and tail black with green sheen. Chest and entire underbody orange–brown to chestnut, richer on breast, paler on undertail-coverts; upperwing-coverts white, often strongly washed pink-buff or creamy yellow; primary coverts, remiges black glossed green; outer tertials chestnut on outer webs, inner webs grey, inner tertials rufous-cinnamon, inner webs buff, grey, or vermiculated with both; underwing and axillaries white; greater primary coverts grey. Eye dark brown; bill, legs and feet dark grey to black. ADULT ♂ (eclipse): very similar, but collar narrower or absent. ADULT ♀: as ♂ but from near base of bill, around and behind eye, white; no collar. SIZE: wing, ♂ (9 specimens) 354–383 (366), ♀ (6) 321–369 (399); tail, ♂ (8) 116–135 (125), ♀ (6) 112–122 (118); bill, ♂ (11) 41–49 (44·4), ♀ (9) 35–43 (39·5); tarsus, ♂ (11) 59–64 (61·5), ♀ (10) 52–57 (54·6); toe, ♂ (11) 60–69 (64·5), ♀ (10) 55–59 (57·2); length, 61–67 cm; wing-span, 121–145 cm. WEIGHT: ♂ 1200–1600, ♀ 925–1500.

JUVENILE: resembles adult ♀ but duller, back browner.

DOWNY YOUNG: crown, nape and all upperparts, including lateral breast and thigh patches, dark olive grey; forehead, sides of heads, all underparts and patches on sides of mantle and back white, a blackish streak from eye to hind crown. Eye brown; bill grey-black; feet grey-black.

Field Characters. Small-billed, chestnut-coloured, long-bodied, goose-like duck. Unlikely to be confused with any other species in Africa except larger Egyptian Geese *Alopochen aegyptiacus* in flight; wing patterns closely similar but Ruddy Shelduck thicker-necked, more rufous.

Voice. Recorded (2a). Whining, nasal trumpeting or whooping. Loud, penetrating 'ang' used all occasions including flight, or more prolonged, high-pitched 'ah-onk' and repeated, ascending 'ka-ha-ha'. Tone of ♀ voice harsher than that of ♂. Inciting call a repeated 'gaaa'; alarm call 'hä-hä'. ♂ Threat call loud, prolonged 'chorr' and a 2-syllabled 'cho-hoo' in response to ♀'s Inciting, or given prior to and following copulation.

General Habits. Little known in Africa; well known in Europe. Occurs all altitudes on inland freshwater lakes, marshes, rivers, streams and tarns; exceptionally to 4000 m (Ethiopia). Semi-arid terrain with little water often preferred, avoiding tall grass or dense herbage. Less aerial and aquatic than many ducks, spending much time on land grazing. Normally pairs or family parties, sometimes large flocks but these largely prevented by basic aggressiveness; very noisy. Wary or tame, according to degree of persecution. Roosts at night on water in groups or family parties, feeds by day, grazing on land, dabbling, scything and up-ending in water.

In NW Africa may moult and overwinter near nesting grounds where water available, but during cold weather general exodus from mountains to coastal plains occurs. Concentrations in Moulouya delta, Morocco, July–Sept presumably moulting birds. Northward movement to Guadaquivir delta in Spain Aug–Oct, returning Feb–Mar much reduced recent years, otherwise only known instance of African breeding species migrating to Europe. Birds visiting northern Nile Oct–Apr probably wintering individuals from Black Sea area. Breeding populations in Ethiopian highlands probably resident (Ash 1977a), numbers augmented by non-breeding visitors some years; seen in pairs Jan–Mar, thought to be preparing to breed (L. H. Brown, pers. comm.).

Food. Plant and animal material, probably varying seasonally. On land various grasses, thistles, sprouting greens, grain and millet crops; also picks up locusts and other terrestrial insects. At edge of water brine shrimps, other crustaceans and molluscs, also worms, fish, frogs and spawn, frequently in brackish water.

Breeding Habits. Little known in Africa, well known in Europe. Nests in holes, cavities, in various situations on ground or elevated, dispersed or tending towards gregariousness when available sites closely spaced; nest only defended.

In usual *Tadorna* manner ♀ takes initiative in pair-formation by Inciting; ♂ responds with Threat-call, assumes High-and-erect posture. Pre-copulatory display involves mutual Head-dipping, ♂ frequently giving 2-syllabled call. Copulation takes place in water of swimming depth; ♀ starts calling before ♂. After ♂ begins calling remains mounted few seconds, still holding ♀'s nape, then slightly raises folded wing on side opposite ♀ and slides off to 1 side in High-and-erect posture. Both then bathe. Feeding territory, which is strongly defended, not necessarily adjacent to nest-site.

NEST: frequently located far from water. Ready-made holes in banks, among rocks, hollow trees, old buildings or cliffs. Shallow depression formed by ♀ and lined with down, occasionally some grass.

EGGS: 6–12 (records of 16 probably 2 ♀♀), laid consecutive days; Europe mean, 8. Oval; creamy white, semi-glossy. SIZE: (110 eggs) 62–72 × 45–50 (68 × 47); WEIGHT: (100 from captive birds) 65–99 (81) (J. Kear, pers. comm.).

Laying dates: N Africa mid-Mar to mid-Apr; Ethiopia Apr–May.

Incubation by ♀ only, begins with completion of clutch. Period: 28–29 days.

At 1 day old, 36 captive young weighed 42·5–55·0 g, av. 48 g (J. Kear, pers. comm.). Can feed themselves in shallows on aquatic insects. Fledging period *c*. 55 days, young independent soon after.

Both parents care for young, may carry them from nest to water on back, also while swimming, but rare (Johnsgard and Kear 1968). In Ethiopia young broods deserted by accompanying parent on being approached by observer, parent (always 1) flying off without displaying undue distress (Ash 1977a).

1st breeding takes place at probably 2 years.

References
Ash, J. S. (1977a).
Cramp, S. and Simmons, K. E. L. (1977).

Tadorna cana (Gmelin). South African Shelduck. Tadorne à tête grise.

Plate 15

Anas cana Gmelin, 1789. Syst. Nat., 1, p. 510; Cape of Good Hope.

(Opp. p. 226)

Range and Status. Very common; endemic southern Africa south of 19°S, especially arid Orange Free State (OFS) and southern Cape Province; at least partially migratory, distances up to 1000 km reported (K. Curry-Lindahl, pers. comm.). Numbers stable, but small population of *c*. 42,000 vulnerable through reliance on mammal burrow nest sites (Geldenhuys 1981b).

Description. ADULT ♂ (breeding): head and neck ash grey, terminating sharply at base of neck; mantle, back and scapulars deep chestnut, feathers pale-edged, long scapulars with dark brown inner webs; rump and uppertail-coverts black, rump with fine grey vermiculations; tail black; from lower neck to lower breast pale cream-yellow grading to chestnut on flanks and belly; sides of rump black, vermiculated buff; undertail-coverts pale chestnut; upperwing with greater coverts white, washed grey, feathers sometimes with black vane edges; middle and lesser coverts white; alula, primary coverts and primaries blackish; secondaries with outer webs metallic green, inner webs blackish, tertials chestnut with inner webs

Tadorna cana

brown; underwing with axillaries and coverts white, broadly tipped black at base of primaries; primaries and secondaries tipped white. Eye dark brown; bill black; legs and feet black or dark grey. ADULT ♂ (eclipse): body plumage dull chestnut, finely vermiculated, lower neck and breast dull khaki-yellow, all colours less brightly contrasting. ADULT ♀ (breeding): head and neck grey, darker than in ♂, a variable, irregular white area on face, forehead and chin, this normally extending to 2 cm behind eye in wedge-shape at eye-level, sometimes extending over ear-coverts and laterally down nape, also over throat, exceptionally entire head white; on wing greater secondary coverts mostly as in ♂; middle and lesser secondary coverts pure white, or with light grey or brown feather edging; feet usually blotched pink; otherwise as breeding ♂.

SIZE: wing, ♂ (5 specimens) 345–365 (355·8), ♀ (5) 315–335 (326·2); tail, ♂ 120–136 (125·9), ♀ 120–129 (124·5); culmen, ♂ 42–48 (45·2), ♀ 39–54·5 (42·4); tarsus, ♂ 56–60 (58), ♀ 52–58 (56); length, *c.* 61 cm (Clancey 1967). WEIGHT: (Barberspan) ♂ (171 specimens) 1032–2032 (1527), ♀ (215) 872–1835 (1229) (Dean and Skead 1979).

JUVENILE: like adult ♂, but colouring duller. Immature ♀ initially has white rings around eyes and base of bill, this progressively increasing.

DOWNY YOUNG: crown and all upperparts to tail dusky brown; wing with white bar; on sides of back immediately behind wing an elongated white blotch, 2 large white patches on rump near base of tail; cheeks, sides of neck, chin and entire underparts white. Eye brown; bill grey, tinged olive on lower mandible, nail paler; legs and feet buffy brown, toes grey.

Field Characters. Medium-sized, long-bodied, chestnut-coloured duck with grey head or white face; on water long body distinctive. Superficially similar to Egyptian Goose *Alopochen aegyptiacus* but smaller, shorter-necked, shorter-legged and with grey head or white face. ♀ has similar white face to White-faced Whistling-Duck *Dendrocygna viduata* but larger size, quite different proportions and stance, and grey, not black, head prevents confusion. In flight bold white wing pattern striking, this similar to that of Egyptian Goose but smaller size, grey head and richer colouring diagnostic.

Voice. Recorded (6). When calling together ♂♂ utter deep 'hoogh', 'how' or 'honk' at intervals; ♀♀ alternate with harsher 'hark'. ♂'s response to ♀'s Inciting involves 1 of 2 calls; single syllable 'korrr' (Threat) or 2-syllable 'ka-thoo' (sexual call) while assuming High-and-erect posture. Utterances loud during display. Both sexes also heard to hiss when accompanying broods or threatened by humans.

Young ♂♂ aged *c.* 2 months still 'peep' whereas ♀ voice has 'broken' by this time. Downy young give high-pitched, disyllabic distress calls (7 in 2·5 s) and contact twitter, very slow, 2nd syllable higher in frequency than 1st (J. Kear, pers. comm.).

General Habits. Very well known. On any water, though seasonal brackish pans of western OFS favoured if filled by summer rains. Both sexes undergo 2 body moults and 1 wing moult a year. For wing moult ducks move northeast Nov–Dec to large, fresh, deep-water lakes and dams: 17 in OFS, 3 in Transvaal, 3 in Cape Province. At these times form flocks of few hundred to *c.* 5000 of moulting and 1st-year birds. Maximum counted at known wing-moult waters *c.* 30,000 (25,000 in OFS), or about 70% of total South African Shelduck population. Soon after completion of wing moult on large waters, majority of birds move southwest to seasonal, shallow, brackish pans.

In most flocks ♀♀ outnumber ♂♂. Non-breeding flocks comprise paired and single birds. These highly nomadic during dry season, numbers varying from 10–800. In resting non-breeding flocks unpaired birds occupy centre, paired birds being spaced on edges. Pairs seldom fight but maintain few square metres spacing. Solitary nomadic pairs move restlessly from pond to pond, apparently searching for suitable territories. Territorial pairs frequently tolerate other pairs forming part of loose flock, whereas presence of solitary pair elicits much calling and agitation.

Plant food obtained by dabbling, scything and head-dipping in shallows or grazing on land. Animal food obtained by scything and digging on exposed mudflats, by head-dipping and by dabbling on surface. Often feeds on agricultural land, but moulting and breeding birds confined to permanent waters. When feeding in stubble fields flights undertaken regularly 30 min before, and 1 h after, both sunrise and sunset. In contrast, much greater time and effort needed to obtain adequate amounts of filamentous algae as this only present in small quantities. Flock sizes according to food taken: invertebrates 30–173 birds; submerged hydrophytes 33–620 birds; cereal seed 58–700 birds.

Food. Vegetable and animal matter according to season. Winter and spring (dry and late dry season) entirely vegetable: maize seed 62·3% and sorghum seed 11·6% gleaned from stubble fields after mechanical harvesting; algae 26% obtained by dabbling in water. Mid-summer (wet season): oesophagi of 14 flightless ducks from moult flock in deep water all empty; gizzards contained very small amounts of food (0·5 ml per gizzard) but included filamentous algae and insect remains. Further

8 shelducks found dead or dying on lake shore having both oesophagi and gizzards empty. Prior to and immediately following flightless period birds recorded to make feeding flights to nearby stubble fields: 16 oesophagi examined were stuffed with seed, av. 42 ml (594 seeds) per bird. Late summer-autumn: animal and plant material formed 55% and 45% respectively. Tendipedid larvae and pupae and *Conchostraca* and *Notostraca* crustaceans most important animal food items.

Breeding Habits. Very well known. Monogamous, pair-bonds long-lasting or permanent. Nests below ground in mammal burrows.

Most birds move to small, permanent fresh waters to breed in dry season (June–July). Pairs aggressively defend territories with loud calls, chasing and occasionally fighting. ♀♀ actively compete for mates. Single bird pursuits usually involve 2 ♀♀ with ♂ of pair following. Displays are normal *Tadorna* combination of ♀ Inciting and aggression between ♂♂. In Inciting display, ♀ stretches out neck, holds head low, calls and makes repeated lateral Bill-pointing movements over shoulder towards ♂. ♂ then gives 1- or 2-syllable Threat calls as he jerks head up and back into characteristic High-and-erect posture. In Threat display ♂ partly spreads wings, showing white patches, fans tail, holds head forward, stretches neck out and calls. Pairs establish territories on *c.* 5 ha of water area. This area used by pair for all daily routines and rearing of brood; vigorously defended against conspecifics. Pre-copulatory behaviour consists of Head-dipping, resembling bathing, by ♂, often accompanied by 2-note call. Copulation takes place in water. ♀ starts calling several seconds before ♂ calls and dismounts. ♂ then lifts wing vertically on side opposite ♀, displaying white patch for several seconds while in High-and-erect posture. Both then bathe. ♀ seeks nest-site on land, usually far from open water, ♂ follows 10–20 m behind her; ♂'s function mainly defence of area against other pairs.

NEST: in chamber at end of disused mammal burrow, distance from entrance as much as 9 m (Edelstein 1932). In sample of 14 nests, 11 in aardvark holes, 3 in spring hare *Pedetes capensis* or porcupine *Hystrix africaeaustralis* burrows. Distance from water territory (9 nests) 85–1700 m. Nest-site does not form part of normal territory.

EGGS: estimated 1–15 (Delacour 1954), assumed av. 10, probably laid at 24 h intervals. Cream-coloured. SIZE: 65–71 × 46–59. WEIGHT: (50, captive birds) 74·5–99·5 (89) (J. Kear, pers. comm.).

Laying dates: mid May to late Sept (dry season), peak last week July to mid-Aug. 90% of ♀♀ laid eggs 2nd week July – end Aug. During egg-laying ♂♂ occasionally seen on territories in early morning.

Incubation by ♀ only, main period July–Sept, peak Aug. ♀ then quiet, in contrast to noisy behaviour prior to egg-laying. Nest-site guarded by ♂ while ♀ incubating; if approached by humans on foot becomes excited, at first running away making hissing sounds, then taking-off, circling overhead. Period: *c.* 30 days.

Chick weight at 1 day old (9 captives) 52–61·5 (56·5) (J. Kear, pers. comm.). Chick development (captive birds) week 6 head and neck covered in grey feathers; lower neck and breast area tawny orange, separated from neck by clear demarcation. Week 7 ♀♀ distinguished by white rims around eyes and base of bill, these gradually expanding weeks 7–11 (at 3 months have merged); at weeks 11–12 ♂♂ may also show white rim at bill base, this absent from 3 months. Feather growth: day 18 1st contour feathers visible as small pin-feathers in regions of flanks, tail. Week 4 immature feathers present in breast, flank, abdominal and scapular regions, primary and secondary remiges just emerging as blood quills; duckling still predominantly downy. Week 5 blood sheaths have appeared as lesser, middle and greater wing-coverts; tail, breast, flank and abdominal regions show well developed but still immature feathers; 1st feathers emerge on back, neck, crown and forehead, rest of head still downy. Week 6 mature feathers present on breast, flanks and abdomen plus certain regions of head, neck. Week 8 young bird almost completely covered with mature contour feathers, including wings; down still adhering to tops of nape feathers, feathers of back and rump regions not quite fully developed. Flight possible at week 10. Av. weight increases from *c.* 60 g day 5 to 978 g day 54. At 8 months av. ♂ weight (6 specimens) 1174 g, ♀ (8) 933 g (Siegfried 1966).

On leaving nest burrow parents with brood quickly and quietly cross ground to water, ♂ leading, ♀ attending to chicks, sometimes making hissing sounds. Family bond very strong first 5 weeks, parents solicitous of young, remaining with them even if humans approach within 20 m. During 1st half of parental care period, family stays roughly within territory, still vigorously defended against conspecifics. Territorial area may expand as young grow and wander further afield, depending on proximity of other shelduck family groups. Brood sizes of young arriving at territories: 1–11, av. (0–1 week) 6·4 (1976, Karoo), 8·0 (OFS highveld 1974); overall brood size both areas 7·4 (0–1 week), 5·8 at week 10 when independent. Family groups start to break up weeks 9–10. Dependent young present on breeding waters 3rd week June – end Dec; maximum broods present 1st 2 weeks Oct. Breeding densities: mean (Karoo) 4·0, (OFS highveld) 8·6 broods per 100 km². Breeding success: 1·7–1·8 ducklings per full-grown duck reach independent stage. Survival: av. rate for ducklings 75%; 7 out of 139 broods (5%) reaching territories subsequently disappeared; 6 at week 1–2, 1 at weeks 2–3. Total mortality rate 26% (Karoo, OFS highveld) 15% in 1st 4 weeks. Survival rate of ducklings over 4-year period, both study areas, 68%–83% (76%) High reproductive success of breeding population countered by high mortality of full-grown birds, including juveniles and subadults (Geldenhuys 1981b).

References
Geldenhuys, J. N. (1976c, 1977, 1979, 1980, 1981a, b).
Johnsgard, P. A. (1965, 1978).
Siegfried, W. R. (1966, 1967).

Plate 15
(Opp. p. 226)

Tadorna tadorna (Linnaeus). Common Shelduck. Tadorne de Belon.

Anas Tadorna Linnaeus, 1758. Syst. Nat. (10th ed.), p. 122; Sweden.

Range and Status. Palearctic breeding and non-breeding visitor to N Africa. Morocco fairly frequent south to Sous depression; Algeria and Tunisia common, isolated breeding wet years; scarce visitor east to Nile Valley; also Senegal. Birds observed in Cape Province considered feral (Clancey 1976).

Tadorna tadorna

X Vagrant

Description. ADULT ♂ (breeding): entire head, upperneck glossy blackish green; below this, from sharp demarcation, entire body and upperparts white except for broad chestnut band encircling mantle and breast, broadest below, and black band along length of underparts from breast to vent; tail white, broadly tipped black; undertail-coverts cinnamon; outer scapulars, primaries and secondaries glossy blackish green; coverts white. Eye brown; bill with prominent fleshy knob on forehead bright red; legs and feet deep flesh. ADULT ♂ (eclipse): duller, patterns less clear-cut; face, throat and forehead speckled white; chestnut breast-band duller, edges ragged; belly-stripe and uppertail-coverts speckled white; bill flesh, knob much reduced. ADULT ♀: similar to ♂, smaller. Colours less bright; lores whitish; breast-band narrower, ragged-edged; bill flesh. SIZE: wing, ♂ (33 specimens) 312–350 (334), ♀ (28) 284–316 (303); tail, ♂ (27) 96–115 (108), ♀ (27) 89–106 (96·9); culmen, ♂ (37) 50–58 (53), ♀ (36) 44–50 (47·3); tarsus, ♂ (34) 52–60 (55·8), ♀ 46–54 (50); toe, ♂ (34) 57–64 (60·1), ♀ 51–59 (54·2); length 58–67 cm; wing-span 110–153 cm. WEIGHT: ♂ 830–1500, ♀ 562–1085.

JUVENILE: top of head, hindneck and all upperparts dark grey-brown; forehead, around eye, face, throat, foreneck and all underparts white, a grey wash on flanks and belly; white of wing-coverts tinged grey; bill grey-pink; legs and feet grey.

DOWNY YOUNG: crown, nape, all upperparts and wings dark grey-brown; forehead, small spot above eye, face, ear-coverts and entire underparts and flanks to sides of back white, a dark grey-brown vertical patch from thighs upwards; spot on mantle white. Eye brown; bill and feet grey.

Field Characters. A white duck with green-black head and neck, broad chestnut band around breast, blackish side-stripes from folded secondaries, reddish bill, feet; ♂♂ with knob on forehead. Larger, longer-necked than other shelducks, more boldly patterned. In wing moult body appears entirely white. Striking pied flight pattern with chestnut breast band diagnostic. Confusion in flight with Red-breasted Merganser *Mergus serrator* possible but whiter body and wings, dark scapular stripes diagnostic. Flight goose-like, wing-beats slower, more deliberate than most ducks. On land walks easily, fast.

Voice. Recorded (2a, 22b). ♂ has variety of clear, melodious whistling notes rising in pitch and falling gradually, often used in conjunction with threat and courtship postures, 'sos-thiu' (in flight), 'piu-pu', 'whee-o' or 'whee-ee'. During antagonistic encounters rapid, rhythmic 'wheesp-wheesp-wheesp . . .'; long whirring version given with Whistle-shake display. ♀ calls harsher, fast, nasal 'ak-ai-ai-ai', loud, insistent, up to *c.* 12 notes/s given in variety of situations, in flight and when settled. Alarm call harsh 'quack-wack-wack-wack'; also various softer calls. Both sexes rather quiet when not breeding; in breeding season characteristic chattering of ♀♀ audible over large distances.

Young cheep continuously while still in nest, beginning as soon as eggs chip. Contact call, a soft trill; high-pitched piping (rhythm similar to 'ak ak' call of ♀) uttered when out of nest and separated from parents (J. Kear, pers. comm.).

General Habits. Little known in Africa, well known in Europe. N African birds occur in small, sedentary, isolated populations; also post-moult wintering flocks from SE Europe, arriving Oct–Dec, returning Mar. Numbers in Algeria *c.* 4000–7000 varying from year to year; flocks some regions maximum *c.* 5000, normally 1500–3000 (Jacobs and Ochando 1979). Favour warm, semi-arid, mild maritime climate with decidedly salt or brackish water, e.g. estuaries, shallow coasts, inland seas and lakes, sand or mud flats with daily tidal cycle, muddy channels; less often, open sea. Rise easily from water or land, fly in V-formations or staggered lines. Pre-flight signals lateral Head-shaking, probably Chin-lifting (Johnsgard 1965). Food obtained in shallow water by scything, dabbling, head-dipping, up-ending or by surface-digging in exposed mud, dabbling if surface wet, foot-trampling to dislodge live prey.

Food. Mostly molluscs, insects, crustaceans. Small amounts water plants and algae also taken. Main items vary with season, locality and food abundance, but sea-shrimps, prawns, crabs, sand-hoppers and snails especially sought.

Breeding Habits. Little known in Africa, well known in Europe. Nests in holes in variety of situations, often close together, even in same hole.

Pair-formation frequently takes place in flock, ♀ Inciting ♂ in typical *Tadorna* manner, ♂ responds by Bowing before attacking rival; may remain stationary in Head-down posture, or walk, run or fly at rival, biting if contact made. On ♂'s return from victorious encounter both perform exaggerated Preen-behind-wing (see **A**), sequence usually Bill-dip, Head shake, Preen.

A

Copulation on water preceded by vigorous Head-dipping or shallow dives by both sexes while swimming rapidly. ♀ may adopt Prone-posture, motionless on water, ♂ usually Preening-behind-wing before mounting. As ♂ dismounts ♀ calls, ♂ pulls her head back, both rotating slightly in water, ♂ assumes High-and-erect stance, opposite wing to ♀ slightly raised. Both then bathe, preen. Pairs form territories, usually on muddy shore which is used for feeding, especially during ♀'s spells off nest when incubating. Some territory used repeated seasons, ♀ particularly attached. Pairs then prospect for nest-site, ♀ leading, ♂ following, mainly early mornings.

NEST: in variety of ready-made cavities in ground, rabbit burrows in dunes, trees up to 5 m above ground, old buildings, banks, walls, close to or up to 1 km away from water. Nest-cup lined with down by ♀, also grass or other vegetation in open sites.

EGGS: 8–10, laid at daily intervals; Kent, England mean (95 clutches) 9. Rounded ovals; smooth, creamy-white, little gloss. SIZE: (175 eggs) 61–71 × 43–40 (66 × 47); WEIGHT: (100, England) 65·5–92·5 (78) (J. Kear, pers. comm.).

Laying dates: Europe May–July; N Africa mainly June.

Incubation by ♀ only, starts with completion of clutch. Eggs covered with down when left. ♂ remains in feeding territory where joined by ♀ 3–4 times daily. Period: 29–31 days.

After 24 h, weight of 36 captive young ranged from 44·5 to 58·0 g, av. 49 g (J. Kear, pers. comm.). Remain in brood 15–20 days then usually join creche, though sometimes remain with parents until fledged; fully independent at fledging.

When young emerge from burrow are led to water nursery area, which is distinct from feeding territory now abandoned. Both parents defend young but frequently desert them before fledging.

Mature at 2 years, ♀♀ breeding at this age, ♂♂ at 4–5 years.

References

Jacobs, P. and Ochando, B. (1979).
Johnsgard, P. A. (1978).

Subfamily ANATINAE: perching, dabbling and diving ducks

A large subfamily of 17 genera and 70 species of waterfowl distributed throughout temperate and tropical regions and represented in Africa by 8 genera, 24 species. Of these, 13 species are in *Anas*, 4 in *Aythya*, 2 in *Netta* and 1 each in *Plectropterus*, *Pteronetta*, *Sarkidiornis*, *Nettapus* and *Marmaronetta*. *Plectropterus* (Spur-winged Goose) and *Sarkidiornis* (knob-billed or comb ducks) differ markedly from most others in the subfamily by being larger and having goose-like proportions, a lack of marked sexual dimorphism or eclipse plumage, and courting displays which are either inconspicuous or absent. Except for the large size, these characteristics are shared also by *Pteronetta* (Hartlaub's Duck) and *Nettapus* (pygmy geese). By contrast *Anas* species, also known as surface-feeding or dabbling ducks, stand apart from the others as being slender-bodied ducks with a horizontal stance dictated by their short, centrally placed legs, which result in an easy, though waddling gait, and in having a highly developed courtship display ritual. *Marmaronetta* has many aberrant features and can be regarded as an *Anas*-like duck with pochard-like characteristics. Pochards are medium-sized waterfowl in 2 genera, *Netta* with 3 species, *Aythya* with 12 species. Chief characteristics separating pochards from *Anas* are their large heads, large flat bills, bulky bodies, large feet, and legs well spaced and set far back on the body resulting in an upright stance and, in *Aythya* especially, clumsy gait on land. All pochards dive with considerable ability, feeding mostly underwater. Pair-forming displays are slightly less varied than in *Anas*. Major displays of ♂ pochards are: Sneak, in which ♂ extends head along water, or inclines head forward, bill towards ♀, while giving a nasal call; Head-throw, in which the head is thrown backwards; Downward-sneeze, in which head is drawn into shoulders, bill directed forwards or sideways at ♀ and sneeze-like calls given; and Kinked-neck display which incorporates a vocal utterance while neck is held with a distinct bend in it, head low. ♀ Inciting display similar to that of *Anas*; pre-copulatory Head-pumping used in *Netta*, in others Bill-dipping and Preen-dorsally. Prone-posture of ♀♀ differs from *Anas* in that head is held forward diagonally, not flat on water. Post-copulatory displays include characteristic Bill-down posture, in which head is held forward with bill close to water, by ♂ only or by both sexes together.

Genus *Plectropterus* Stephens

A large, powerful, goose-like, African perching duck differing from true geese in having larger, coarser feet and longer legs, bill and neck. Predominantly black and white, feathers large, loose, those on upperparts with strong metallic sheen, a long, sharp carpal spur present in both sexes, ♂♂ with conspicuous knob on forehead. White wing-coverts function as threat signals as in shelducks and sheldgeese. Otherwise ritualized displays rudimentary or lacking, voices weak. Frequent large rivers, swamps and lakes, congregating in large numbers in dry season. Non-migratory but seasonal movements dictated by rains.

Plate 15
(Opp. p. 226)

Plectropterus gambensis (Linnaeus). Spur-winged Goose. Plectroptère de Gambie.

Anas gambensis Linnaeus, 1766. Syst. Nat. (12th ed.), 1, p. 195; Gambia.

Range and Status. Resident south of Sahara extending north along Nile to Abou Simbel in Egypt where recorded Mar. Migratory over most of range. In Senegal delta influx occurs Jan (6900 in 1976); Lake Chad Feb–May; Zambia (Luangwa Valley) chiefly Oct–Mar (K. Curry-Lindahl, pers. comm.). Seasonally common to very common most large inland waters.

Plectropterus gambensis

Description. *P. g. gambensis* (Linnaeus): tropics north of *c.* 15°S. ADULT ♂: entire plumage basically blackish, wings with marked iridescence. Facial region to forehead, forecrown, including knob, cheeks and orbital ring devoid of feathers, skin bright carmine pink to purplish; ear-coverts, chin, throat, front of neck and rest of underparts, including flanks and undertail-coverts, white; tail black with green iridescence; wing with prominent carpal spur; upperwing lesser coverts and shoulder edged white, remainder of wing black; remiges strongly shot with green and pinkish violet; underwing-coverts and axillaries brown and white; rest of remiges black. Eye dark brown; bill deep pinkish red, nail whitish; legs and feet deep pinkish red. ADULT ♀: smaller; knob of forehead smaller or absent, bare facial skin less extensive (these both increasing with age); general colouring less iridescent, white area on wings less extensive. SIZE: wing, ♂ (specimens unknown) 530–550, ♀ 422–440; culmen (from nostril), ♂ 59–63, ♀ 57–59; length, 75–100 cm. WEIGHT: ♂ 5·4–6·8 kg (rarely to 10·0 kg), ♀ 4·0–5·4 kg (Johnsgard 1978).

JUVENILE: both sexes lack bare facial skin and enlarged bill; browner on face and neck, body feathers fringed brown; white areas on wings and underparts restricted.

DOWNY YOUNG: yellow-brown above; buffy below, face lighter with indistinct brown eye-stripe; light band on sides of body, light patches on wings and scapulars. Eye dark brown; bill and legs blue-grey.

P. g. niger Phillips. Africa south of *c.* 15°S. ADULT ♂: white areas on face and underparts much reduced; on face variable amount of white freckling behind eye, on cheeks, chin; white underparts much reduced, commencing only on central breast as variable narrow patch widening on belly. ADULT ♀: usually with white on belly and undertail-coverts only. Many individual variations. SIZE: wing, ♂ 530–533, ♀ 500–503; culmen, 70–76; wing-spur, ♂ 20, ♀ 18·2 (McLachlan and Liversidge 1978). JUVENILE: lacks any white plumage.

Field Characters. Large black and white or predominantly black goose-like perching duck with pink bill and legs. Legs and neck markedly longer than in true geese; mature ♂♂ have variable size knob on forehead, less pronounced in *P. g. niger*. Larger, coarser than any Palearctic geese, even in event of range overlap confusion unlikely. In flight broad wings with white shoulder patches, white belly, otherwise dark plumage, diagnostic. Swims with rear end held higher than shoulder level.

Voice. Recorded (2a, 6). ♂ has weak, whistling voice; may utter soft, high-pitched bubbling 'cherwit' in flight or when aroused. Also squeaky, 4-syllable 'chi-chi-chi-chi' when approaching ♀ in courtship. Huffing 'chu-chu' uttered if threatened, plus 'tchic-tchic-tchic...'. ♀ silent much of time; utters high-pitched 'chi-chi-chi-chi...', with quick bill-lifting movements when disturbed.

General Habits. Little known. Subject to marked seasonal movements, sometimes hundreds of kilometres. In dry season large flocks gather at permanent water, these often undergoing wing moult, e.g. Niger Delta 1500; Senegal Delta 1170 Jan 1972 (Roux 1973); *c.* 2000 moulting birds at Barberspan, W Transvaal, June–Aug; wing moult 6–7 weeks. Dives readily and swims underwater if pursued when flightless. In wet season disperse in small groups or pairs to breed on smaller waters, e.g. floodlands, pans. Regularly perches in trees to roost or loaf, more often seen resting on sandbanks of large rivers, feeding in flooded grasslands, swamps, pastures, often with Egyptian Goose *Alopochen aegyptiacus*. Rests by day, flies to feed early morning, evening or night; flocks usually fly in staggered lines, occasionally V-formations. Wary, difficult to approach. Pre-flight signalled by lateral Head-shakes and Chin-lifting.

Food. Shoots and seeds of grasses, grain, tuberous crops, lucern, fallen fruit, soft parts of aquatic plants and other vegetable matter obtained by grazing on land. Small fish also recorded (Clancey 1967). Frequently major crop pest.

Breeding Habits. Little known. Nests singly in wide variety of ground and elevated situations. Dominant ♂♂ frequently seen with 2 or more ♀♀, suggesting species is polygynous (Douthwaite 1978; Clark 1980a). Courtship behaviour little known. ♂ approaches ♀ with fluffed scapular feathers, Wing-shaking while uttering squeaky 4-syllable call; this appears to be courtship display or form of Triumph-ceremony. No ritualized Threat displays known but, when disturbed, often stretches both wings above back, as in stretching comfort movement; action displays spurs and white wing-patches, may function as simple Threat display. When attacking ♂ runs rapidly over ground, often gaping as he spreads or flaps wings, attempts to strike opponent with formidable wing-spurs. Following attack returns to ♀ behaving as described above. Copulatory behaviour unknown, seen to occur once on water (Prozesky 1959). Pair-bonding activities probably virtually lacking (Johnsgard 1978).

NEST: in Senegal in trees, tree-holes or on ground. Tree sites 20–100 cm high in trees 3–4 m tall; 18 in *Belanites aegyptiaca, Acacia senegal, A. seyal* or *Cadaba farinosa*, generally on west or southwest of tree. Often well camouflaged, occasionally with tunnel entrance through *Belanites* thorns, frequently 2–5 km from water. Ground nests in long grass, simple depression in sand; 40–45 cm across, 8–9 cm deep in centre of bowl. Before laying ♀ collects grass stems and sticks which are added to bowl, more added gradually as eggs laid and more plucked from immediate surroundings and added, with down, while ♀ incubating. Bowl lining *c.* 2 cm thick (Treca 1979, 1980). In southern and E Africa, where trees often unavailable, nests mostly on ground amidst long grass or reeds near water, less often in trees, tree boles (one 5 km from water), cliffs, termite mounds, Aardvark *Orycteropus afer* burrows and old nests of other birds, e.g. African Fish Eagle *Haliaeetus vocifer* (9 m from ground), Hamerkop *Scopus umbretta*

and Social Weaver *Philetairus socius*. ♀ only builds. Few nests Senegal re-used subsequent year.

EGGS: 6–14 (37 recorded Senegal, 27 southern Africa; probably laid by at least 2 ♀♀); laid at daily intervals or slightly less; South Africa mean (55) 6·5; Senegal mean (1978) 17·5, (1979) 12·4. Regular ovals; glossy ivory or pale brown. SIZE: (50 eggs, *P. g. gambensis*) 68·0–86·2 × 51·0–58·8 (74·5 × 55·3); (*P. g. niger*) 67·0–77·0 × 51·0–58·3 (71·34 × 54·45). WEIGHT: (27, *P. g. gambensis*) av. 125 g; (*P. g. niger*) 122 g.

Laying dates: most regions during or following major rains. Senegal, Mali Sept–Dec; Nigeria Aug–Nov; Uganda all months, peaking Jan–Mar; Kenya Jan–June; Zambia all months, peaking Jan–Mar; Malawi Jan–May, peaking Mar; Zimbabwe, South Africa Aug–May, peaking Dec–Feb (Cape Province Aug–Oct).

Incubation by ♀ only. Easily abandons nest if disturbed at beginning of incubation well advanced may sleep deeply during spells. ♂ may or may not remain near nest; may perch in tree and warn of danger (Treca 1979). Period: 30–33 days.

In both sexes wing spur apparent at week 4, *c.* 3 mm long; week 10 exceeds 10 mm; upper mandible remains slate blue first 6 weeks; week 7 rosy tint apparent; week 9 bill brownish red. Weights of 2 captive young increased from 90 g (♂) and 87 g (♀) day 5 to 3000 g (♂) and 2451 g (♀) day 70. Young remain with parent at least until dry season flocking. Young of 2·5 months in Senegal still unable to fly, diving under water or hiding in reeds in response to danger.

Brood size southern Africa 1–10: hatching success apparently low (Clark 1980a). Role of ♂ parent in brood care apparently variable. Frequently pair-bond does not persist beyond egg stage (Johnsgard 1978). Of 23 broods (South Africa) 17 attended by ♀ only, 6 by 2 adults (presumably both parents). In Senegal reaction to danger by ♂ accompanying brood recorded, both parents flying overhead, ♂ calling 'tchic-tchic-tchic'. In E Africa both parents seen to accompany young; thought to be response to possibility of predation by, for example, crocodiles (Pitman 1965).

References
Browne, P. W. D. (1979).
Clark, A. (1980a).
Siegfried, W. R. (1964).
Treca, B. (1979, 1980).

Genus *Pteronetta* Salvadori

A fairly large, broad-winged, short-legged perching duck, wings with bony knobs at metacarpal joint, ♂♂ with swollen base to bill when breeding. ♀♀ smaller than ♂♂, sexual dimorphism slight. A forest species, prone to perching in trees.

Considered by Delacour (1959) to be congeneric with the 2 other perching ducks of rain forest, the South American Muscovy Duck *Cairina moschata* and the Asian White-winged Wood Duck *C. scutulata*, on grounds of plumage similarity, body proportions, wings having bony knobs, breeding ♂♂ having swollen bill caruncles, ♂♂ being larger than ♀♀ and their having similar habits and temperaments. We agree, however, with other authorities that the numerous plumage and behavioural differences (Johnsgard 1965) and skeletal peculiarities (Woolfenden 1961) of this species warrant the retention of monotypic genus.

Plate 16

(Opp. p. 227)

Pteronetta hartlaubii (Cassin). Hartlaub's Duck. Ptéronette de Hartlaub.

Querquedula Hartlaubii Cassin, 1859. Proc. Acad. Nat. Sci. Philad. p. 175; Camma River, Gabon.

Range and Status. Resident, common in forested regions from Sierra Leone south to Zaïre and east to SW Sudan.

Pteronetta hartlaubii

Description. ADULT ♂: head and upperneck black, a square white patch on forehead (this feature variable, individuals with more extensive white over face or entire top of head not uncommon in NE Zaïre); rest of body rich chestnut grading to dark olive brown on longer scapulars, rump and tail; upperwing-coverts china blue, rest olive brown, secondaries bordered blue-grey, tertials bordered black; underwing dark. Bill black with greyish or yellowish band near tip and spot below nostrils, base becomes swollen in breeding season; eye reddish brown; legs and feet dark brown with yellow tinge, webs blackish. ADULT ♀: similar but smaller, duller, little or no white on forehead, bill pinkish grey with band and spots. SIZE: wing, ♂ 270–281, ♀ 248–266; tail, ♂ 100–115; culmen, ♂ 46–48, ♀ 44–47; tarsus, ♂ 44–46. WEIGHT: (captive birds) ♂ (4) 925–1140 (976), ♀ (2) 770–805 (788) (J. Kear, pers. comm.).

JUVENILE: duller, feathers pale-edged.

DOWNY YOUNG: blackish above; yellow below, chin, neck and face with orange tinge; yellow patches on wings, sides of back and rump; strong black streak through eyes, black spot in ear-coverts; black cap nearly reaches eyes in a point.

Field Characters. A long-bodied, chestnut coloured duck with black head, short legs set well forward. In flight bright blue upperwing diagnostic. Confusion with other ducks unlikely as forest habitat and range shared by few species.

Voice. Recorded (17). A quickly repeated quacking 'ko-ko-ko-ko', a conversational 'whit-whit-whit' and variations of grating calls 'ka-ka-kerr' or 'karr-karr', but normally very silent. Pairs heard to make raucous noises, ♂ gives a succession of harsh, low, wheezy whistles similar to those of Mallard *Anas platyrhynchos*, ♀ a series of clucking cackles; also a quiet, high-pitched wheezing noise by ♂ and a loud quacking call by ♀ uttered frequently.

Downy young in distress utter series of evenly spaced calls (10 in 2 s) on downward scale. Contact calls, in groups of 3 notes, are faster than distress calls (9 in 1 s) (J. Kear, pers. comm.).

General Habits. Little known. Of sedentary disposition, frequenting streams and small rivers in rain and gallery forests and well-wooded savannas. Occurs singly, in pairs or small goups; larger groups (*c.* 15) recorded on pools of larger rivers in certain seasons, possibly moulting at this time (Johnsgard 1978). Perches readily on branches of large trees. Apparently feeds mostly in evening in forested streams bordered by thick vegetation.

Food. Little known. Much aquatic animal matter, e.g. insect larvae (mainly dragonflies), freshwater snails, small bivalve molluscs, shrimps, spiders; also small seeds.

Breeding Habits. Scarcely known. No nests recorded in wild. Pairs seen to face each other while perched on bough of trees, bow, rub bills and heads and make raucous noises (Delacour 1959). Similar behaviour described for captive birds, including circular movements of head while calling, but sounds, though similar to those made by both sexes in wild, are said to be quiet, not raucous, in these cases. Captive birds established a strong pair-bond and were highly territorial (Jones 1972).

NEST: site presumed to be hollow in forest tree as chicks are known to have sharp claws and are able to climb well (chicks bred in captivity able to climb out of wooden keg, clinging to sides with claws; this ability lost after 2 days). In captivity nest lined with pale grey down (Johnstone 1960).

EGGS: (all data from captive records) 7–11 (8 clutches); pear-shaped, creamy. SIZE: (2) av. 53 × 40 (Johnstone 1960). WEIGHT: (2) av. 51 (Johnstone 1960).

Incubation (in captivity) by ♀ only. Period: 30–32 days (Jones 1972; Johnstone 1960).

Young recorded Aug–Nov in wild. Captive-bred young became fully feathered at 8 weeks, at which point adult ♂ began to threaten them; usually both parents defend young in captivity (Jones 1972; M. Lubbock, pers. comm.). Av. weight at 1 day old (10 captives) 28 g (J. Kear, pers. comm.).

Both sexes mature at 1 year (captive pair: Johnstone 1960).

Genus *Sarkidiornis* Eyton

A monotypic genus of perching ducks with 1 subspecies each in the Old World and South America, *S.m. melanotos* occurring throughout tropical Africa, Madagascar, India and SE Asia. ♂♂ very large, with fleshy caruncle or knob on upper mandible, ♀♀ considerably smaller and lacking knob. Colours basically glossy blue-black above, white elsewhere. Prefers pools within open woodland, and grassy ponds or floodlands in savanna country; primarily vegetarian and sometimes a pest in croplands. Single brooded, dominant ♂♂ forming pair-bonds with 2 or more ♀♀. When not breeding may form large flocks, often of a single sex.

Sarkidiornis melanotos (Pennant). Knob-billed Duck; Comb Duck. Canard casqué.

Plate 15

(Opp. p. 226)

Anser melanotos Pennant, 1769. Ind. Zool., p. 12, pl. 11; Ceylon.

Range and Status. Resident Africa south of Sahara; highly mobile, wide-ranging. Senegal delta concentrations occur Oct–Mar/Apr; Jan 1972 *c.* 690, Jan 1974 *c.* 540 (Roux 1976), Jan 1981 850 (Dupuy and Fournier 1981); Mali (central Niger delta) Jan 1973 *c.* 2500 (Roux 1976), Jan 1978 15,000 (Sanigho 1978); Sudan May–Nov; NE Zaïre Nov–Feb (non-breeding); Kenya flies south Dec–Jan; Luangwa Valley, Zambia Nov–June; locally migratory in South Africa. Regular E Zaïre forests along rivers and lakes (K. Curry-Lindahl, pers. comm.), absent other dense forest and arid areas; locally common to abundant well-watered savanna.

Description. *S. m. melanotos*, ADULT ♂ (breeding): entire head and neck, including upper base of comb, white, many feathers tipped black giving spotted effect, densely so over crown and hindneck, variable; an orange-yellow wash over sides of hindneck, sometimes extending to ear-coverts, cheeks; nape to upper breast white; rest of upperparts except rump, but including tail, black strongly shot with blue, green and purple, this extending in narrow oblique line downwards and forwards between lateral breast and flanks; rump pale grey; flanks and underparts white with pearl-grey wash; wings, both surfaces, blackish shot with blue, green and purple. Eye dark brown; bill, with prominent nail, black, comb slate-grey; strongly clawed feet pale grey-brown. ADULT ♂ (non-breeding): comb much reduced; lacks yellow wash on head. ADULT ♀: much smaller than ♂. Lacks comb; bill grey; upperparts less iridescent, more drab; rump white; otherwise as ♂. SIZE: wing, ♂ 349–370 (359), ♀ 263–293 (286); tail, ♂ 130–150 (137·3), ♀ 100–120 (110); tarsus, ♂ 56–67 (59·8), ♀ 42–50 (47); culmen, ♂ (with knob) 45–60 (51), ♀ 42·5–48 (44); length, ♂ 79 cm, ♀ 64 cm (McLachlan and Liversidge 1978). WEIGHT: ♂ 1300–2610, ♀ 1230–2325 (Johnsgard 1978); 1 captive 1300 (D'Eath 1967).

JUVENILE: like ♀ but head and neck more heavily speckled, often almost black; underparts washed ochreous.

DOWNY YOUNG: crown, nape, hindneck, entire upperparts and wings blackish; sides of head yellow-ochre, a thin, often incomplete, blackish stripe from lores through eye; entire underparts yellow–ochre, a dark patch above legs; eye dark brown; bill slate-grey, tip yellow; legs and feet grey, webs yellowish.

Field Characters. Large, goose-like, pied duck, ♂♂ with fleshy black protuberance on upper mandible. Walks with distinct swaggering waddle. Swims with humped back, tail well clear of water. Flies in groups, V-formations or staggered lines, with steady, powerful wing-beats.

Sarkidiornis melanotos

Voice. Recorded (2a). Varied, usually associated with displays. ♂ in Head-high display utters 'hissing' sound; in high intensity Head-high pursuing ♂ utters weak, wheezy whistling in flight; wheezing also made by ♂ in Supplant-bow. During Threat ♂ utters harsh 'guk-guk'; in high intensity fighting rival ♂♂ make sound similar to creaking of unoiled wagon wheel (Siegfried 1979). ♀ utters a soft, clucking 'guk-guk' when Inciting and soft, melodious 'caroo-oo' in Coquette-call. When prospecting for nest-site and when inciting ♂ to follow, utters 'huark' Going-away-call, walking or flying. ♀ also makes soft whining when feeding with mate, and loud, sharp squealing when alarmed.

Chicks call from nest with continual harsh 'whirr, whirr'; in distress utter a series of rapid, evenly spaced notes (14 in 2 s), accent on descending note (J. Kear, pers. comm.).

General Habits. Well known. Frequents marshes, temporary pans in woodland, woodland-fringed lagoons in inundated flood plains and river deltas. Flocks, sometimes large, form in dry (non-breeding) season. Sexes frequently segregated when not breeding. At the onset of rains flocks break up and disperse to breeding grounds. Seasonal movements considerable, e.g. Zimbabwe to Mozambique, Zambia, Zaïre, Tanzania, Chad (3879 km), 2 to Sudan (3600 km); bird ringed NW Senegal to Mali (900 km) (K. Curry-Lindahl, pers. comm.). Habitually perches in trees, especially dead ones. Food obtained by grazing on land, or dabbling and wading in shallow water with emergent vegetation. Mated ♀♀ may devote more time to dabbling than their harem-masters (mated ♂♂) who concentrate on stripping grass seeds. 2 harem-masters, each with 3 ♀♀, spent 9·8 and 10·0 h feeding in a 14 h day (Siegfried 1979).

Food. Grass seeds, water-lily seeds, crops (sometimes agricultural pests, rice fields, W Africa), locusts, aquatic insect larvae.

Breeding Habits. Well known. Breeds singly or in groups (harems), usually in tree cavities; same cavity may be used from year to year. Breeding occurs when climate hot in areas of relatively high rainfall, though this may be unevenly distributed annually, seasonally and locally. Non-breeding frequent in years of poor rainfall.

Monogamous in marginal habitats (e.g. South Africa) or polygynous in optimum breeding habitats (Zimbabwe northwards). ♂ harem-masters form pair-bonds with 2 or more ♀♀ at same time (harem polygyny) or with 2 or more ♀♀ in succession (successive polygyny), or may be involved in both forms of polygyny during breeding season. Pair-bonds apparently formed on breeding grounds. Dominant ♂ protects ♀♀ in his harem, but does not defend a 'territory' or nest site. Pair-bonds last at least as long as ♀ laying cycle.

Unmated ♀♀ join harems temporarily, where they are tolerated by mated ♀♀ but relegated to low place in ♀ dominance order. Harem-master reacts with acceptance, courtship or overt aggression.

Unmated ♂♂ cluster around areas occupied by harems and keep watch from elevated perches, descending and raping mated ♀♀ or courting unmated ♀♀ whenever possible. These attempts countered by continual vigil of harem-master and mated ♀♀. When aggressively challenged by harem-master, intruding ♂ normally concedes but remains close by.

Aggressive displays by harem-masters during interactions with other birds are: (1) Wing-flap, directed at other ♂♂ or ♀♀ within c. 100 m, 1–6 evenly spaced slow, stiffly executed wing flaps, body and head erect. (2) Head-high, aggressive ♂ struts on tips of 'toes' or swims sideways towards antagonist, posture erect, wings slightly raised displaying conspicuous metallic sheen. (3) Supplant-bow, ♂ performs, from Head-high posture, exaggerated, stiffly executed, slow bow, crest and scapulars raised, tail fanned, wings slightly spread. Head then raised rapidly while bird shakes wings and returns to Head-high stance. Performer advances sideways towards rival. (4) Wing-shake also used to threaten other ♂♂. If intruder stands ground, fighting ensues. If rivals are evenly matched may last 1 min or longer. Birds face one another, heads held below breasts in Supplant-bow posture while circling each other with slow, stiff-legged sideways gait for c. 5 s. Rivals may utter sound like creaking wheel. Stalemate broken when 1 ♂ lifts head in Head-high posture; facing each other both rear up and strike with wings, thrusting and bumping with breasts. Do not grip or peck. Contest ends when 1 bird topples over or retreats; victor pecks at it as it escapes.

Courtship displays by ♂♂ towards ♀♀ include Body-shake and Breast-preen. When approaching ♀, courting ♂ may perform exaggerated Drinking and Turning-back-of-head. Head-down-end-up serves as both pre-copulatory and post-copulatory display. ♂ draws in head and holds bill, pointing downwards, against breast, wings slightly spread and raised posteriorly. Holds position several seconds while aligning body laterally to ♀'s. May occur while swimming or standing. If ♀ receptive to ♂'s display she assumes Prone-posture, neck and head stretched forward on water. ♂ mounts from side, gripping ♀'s neck. Treading lasts few seconds only. ♂ dismounts forward over side of ♀, swims or walks off, rather rapidly, for more than 1 m, tail held up, general posture similar to Head-down-end-up. ♀ performs vigorous wing-flapping, then either bathes or feeds with mate.

♀ displays include: Inciting, quick chin-lifting movements while calling with a soft clucking 'guk-guk', open bill directed towards desired ♂; and Going-away posture used to encourage ♂ to follow, ♀ walks or flies towards ♂, then deliberately turns and goes away, calling 'hu-ark'. ♀♀ threaten ♂♂ by adopting erect posture, bill up, wings slightly raised, nape feathers erect, and harsh 'guk-guk' call may be given. Also used by ♀ with brood towards intruders and by paired ♀ towards strange, unmated ♀♀.

NEST: in tree cavities usually close to water, sometimes up to 1 km away. Suitable cavities occur in dead trees, subsequently hollowed by wood-boring insects. ♀♀ prospect for cavities all hours of day, greatest activity occurs for 3 h in early morning; clamber along branches, peering into all crevices, sometimes compete for suitable sites. In Mali and Sudan large *Acacia albida* trees favoured, alternatively Hamerkop *Scopus umbretta* nests, trees usually standing in flood plains or rice fields; nest cavity 7–12 m high. If nest placed on ground, depression is strewn with long grasses, white down and other fine materials (Wilson and Wilson 1980). ♂♂ take no part in selection or preparation of nest-site.

EGGS: 6–20 (up to 54 recorded, probably laid by several ♀♀, although 1 nest with 20 eggs was incubated by single ♀ in Mali); tropical Africa 6–11; Zambia and southern Africa 8; probably laid at daily intervals. Oval; glossy, brilliant white (Mali), yellowish (South Africa). SIZE: (6 eggs, Zambia, Zimbabwe) 53–56 × 43–44·5 (54·6 × 44·0); av. (Sudan) 55·6 × 38·5; av. (Mali) 58·3 × 40·6. WEIGHT: av. (Sudan) 46·2; av. (Mali) 55·5 after 8–10 days' incubation (Wilson and Wilson 1980; SAOSNRC).

Laying dates: Mali July–Sept; Nigeria Sept; Sudan end June–early Sept; Uganda Aug; Kenya Feb; Tanzania Feb–Mar; Zambia Nov–June; Zimbabwe Dec–Apr, peaking Feb.

Incubation probably begins with completion of clutch, by ♀ only. Incubating ♀ feeds after dawn and late evenings (Mali), periods av. 90 min. Incubation period: 28–30 days.

Chicks may leave nest on parent's back (Pitman 1965); in Mali seen to jump from nest to ground on being called by ♀ within 36 h of hatching. Weight 10 nestlings (Mali) av. 38·2 g; body length 26 mm; bill 15·5 mm. Fledging period: *c.* 10 weeks. Remain with parent until moult exodus. Broods may consolidate in loose creches on larger pans. Predation high (N. Zaloumis, pers. comm.).

♀ calls chicks from nest in early morning (delaying if predators nearby), then leads brood to water. Brood attended by ♀ only but harem-master maintains vigilance over territory area.

References

Siegfried, W. R. (1979).
Wilson, R. T. and Wilson, M. P. (1980).

Genus *Nettapus* Brandt

Diminutive cavity-nesting, perching ducks represented in Africa, Asia and Australia by 1 species in each region, *N. auritus* being widely distributed in tropical Africa and Madagascar. All are characterized by very small size; short, deep-based, sharply tapering bills; predominantly white and glossy green plumage; whistling voices; and a marked preference for secluded pools with water-lilies, on which they feed.

Nettapus auritus (Boddaert). African Pygmy Goose. Sarcelle à Oreillons.

Anas aurita Boddaert, 1783. Tabl. Pl. Enl. p. 48, pl. 770; Madagascar.

Plate 16

(Opp. p. 227)

Range and Status. Resident Senegal and Ethiopia southward. Distribution over entire range sporadic, dictated by rainfall and habitat availability. Uncommon but widespread Senegal delta (Browne 1979); abundant Lake Tana, Ethiopia; rare Kenya highlands (L. H. Brown, pers. comm.). In southern Africa through northern Namibia and Botswana (very common Okavango delta: Brown and Seely 1973; estimated 10,600 ± 4400 July–Oct 1978: Douthwaite 1980), Zimbabwe, Mozambique and eastern subtropical regions of South Africa; dry season flocks *c.* 1000 N Zululand (W. Tarboton, pers. comm.). Straggler to interior of South Africa and arid regions Botswana, Namibia.

Nettapus auritus

Description. ADULT ♂: forehead, face, chin, throat and foreneck white; crown, nape and hindneck metallic greenish black, shot with violet and blue; sides of neck from behind ear-coverts pale sea-green, bordered black; lower hindneck deep tawny, vermiculated with metallic green; rest of upperparts dark metallic green; tail black; breast and flanks deep tawny; centre of breast and belly whitish; undertail-coverts blackish; on upperwing lesser and median coverts broadly tipped white forming, with white secondaries, a broad white patch on wing; primary coverts, primaries, tertials, black; axillaries, underwing-coverts blackish grey. Bill bright yellow, nail black; eye brown; legs and feet grey. ADULT ♀: generally duller; lacks pale green neck-patch; neck white, speckled dusky; bill lacks black nail. Slightly smaller than ♂. SIZE: wing, ♂ 150–165, ♀ 142–158; tail, ♂ 62–70; culmen, ♂ 25–27, ♀ 23–25; tarsus, ♂ 25–28 (Delacour 1959); length, 30·5–35·5 cm. WEIGHT: ♂ (1) 280 (Britton 1970), 290 (McLachlan and Liversidge 1978); ♀ 260 (Lack 1968).

JUVENILE: as adult ♀, less distinctly marked.

DOWNY YOUNG: black above, white below; black streak through eyes, black spots below eyes and on cheeks; white bar and white spot on wings; bill and feet black; tail long, stiff.

Field Characters. A very small duck with dark green upperparts, tawny flanks, white face and short, deep, yellow bill. Frequently remains motionless among lilies and emergent vegetation, difficult then to detect. Flies swiftly and low, wing-patches diagnostic. Unlikely to be confused with other species.

Voice. Not recorded. In ♂ a soft twittering whistle, 'choo-choo' and 'pee-wee'. Also a repeated, 2-syllable, subdued 'tsu-tswi ... tsu-tswi ...' (W. Tarboton, pers. comm.). ♀ utters weak quack, and during courtship in captivity a twittering whistle, sharper than that of ♂, has been noted (Alder 1963).

General Habits. Little known. Frequents flood pans, natural pans and pools with clear water, emergent vegetation and water-lilies. Semi-gregarious, normally seen in groups of 10–200. Food mainly gathered from water surface, or dived for; observed to feed during daylight hours (Clancey 1967). Seldom walks on land but will perch on logs and trees. When alarmed flies short distance only; if wounded will hide underwater, bill only above surface. Nomadic during dry season in regions of seasonal rainfall. In N Botswana migratory, highest counts being made Dec (during breeding season) and lowest Mar–Apr. Possibly a moult migration from which birds returned July (Douthwaite 1980).

Food. Principal diet water-lily seeds (*Nymphaea*) but only eaten when ripe (red or black); also other aquatic vegetation and insects. Birds caught in the wild regurgitated fish (M. Lubbock, pers. comm.).

Breeding Habits. Little known. Nests singly, in holes, in trees (including artificial nest logs: K. Newman, pers. obs.), ant hills or cliffs, nests of Hamerkop *Scopus umbretta*, grass clumps or other location with suitable cavity (even thatch of occupied hut: Pitman 1965). Probable courtship display described in which ♂ swims past ♀, turning head slightly to show pale green patches on sides (Delacour 1959). On land displaying ♂ holds bill well down and utters musical 'chip, chip, chirrup, chiroo'. Head-bobbing accompanied by whistle (from ♀ while ♂ displays and as greeting to ♂: Alder 1963) and Pursuit-flights also observed (N. Zaloumis, pers. comm.). ♂ and ♀ search for suitable nest-site together.

NEST: cavity may be lined with vegetable material including leaves and moss (McLachlan and Liversidge 1978), sometimes white down (Pitman 1965; N. Zaloumis, pers. comm.). Cavity size varies according to site but nest log (*Euphorbia ingens* stem) recorded South Africa measuring 60 × 21 cm with horizontal oval entrance hole 7 × 8 cm and internal cavity 12 cm in diameter fixed to tree 4·2 m above ground at water's edge (W. R. Tarboton, pers. comm.; K. Newman, pers. obs.). Tree-hole nests often up to 10 m above ground and 1 observed at 20 m (Pitman 1965).

EGGS: usually 9 (Pitman 1965), occasionally up to 12 (Delacour 1954); ivory-white. SIZE: (14) av. 43·3 × 32·9 (McLachlan and Liversidge 1978). WEIGHT: (2, laid in captivity) av. 27 g (Zaloumis 1976).

Laying dates: Nigeria July–Aug; Uganda June–Oct, Jan; Kenya coast July; Tanzania June; southern Zaïre probably July–Oct; Zambia, Zimbabwe Sept–Mar, peaking Jan, Feb (Boulton and Woodall 1974); Botswana, South Africa Oct, Feb.

In wild state ♀ only seen to incubate (W. R. Tarboton, pers. comm.). Under artificial conditions 1 egg in electric incubator hatched in 23 days 13 h; weight when fresh 27·1 g, at 23 days 21·3 g; hatching weight of chick 17·5 g. 2nd egg under Bantam hen hatched in 24 days 1 h; weight when fresh 26·5 g, at 23 days 20·3 g; hatching weight of chick 15·3 g (Zaloumis 1976). 2 wild broods of 6 observed Zimbabwe; newly hatched brood of 8 recorded Uganda (Pitman 1965).

References
Clancey, P. A. (1964).
Delacour, J. (1959).

Genus *Anas* Linnaeus

Fairly slender-bodied; legs short and placed centrally, giving horizontal stance. Bright, often metallic, wing specula in both sexes; long pointed wings; flattened bills with distinct laminae; fairly short, pointed tails, the central rectrices sometimes elongated. ♂♂ of temperate breeding species usually exhibit bright plumages, this alternating with less bright eclipse non-breeding plumage during flightless post-breeding moult and contrasting with dull, cryptic colouring in ♀♀. In tropical and subtropical breeding species ♂ and ♀ plumages tend to be identically sombre with no obvious eclipse phase.

Usually gregarious when not breeding; found in shallow water rich in submerged, emergent or floating vegetation and invertebrate animal life. Food, both vegetable and animal, obtained by pumping surface water through the bill where food is sieved out through laminae (Dabbling), tipping forward with head and neck immersed (Head-dipping), tipping foward with head immersed and rear-end raised vertically (Up-ending); occasionally by diving with aid of wings and by grazing on land. Pre-flight signals include lateral Head-shaking and repeated vertical Head-thrusting. Take-off from land or water accomplished with ease, flight moderately fast to very fast. Northern species tend to migrate annually over considerable distances, normally at night, while African endemics are subject to less extensive seasonal movements associated with annual rainfall patterns; nomadism in some.

Normally monogamous of seasonal duration in Palearctic migratory species, but often long-term in tropical resident or nomadic species. In early nesting stages pairs typically occupy home-ranges which overlap with those of other pairs. Within home-range 1 or more small areas frequented for feeding and loafing by ♂ while ♀ laying or incubating and by ♀ when off nest; in some species defended by ♂. Pair-formation starts in flocks following assumption of nuptial plumage, and terminates during incubation when ♂♂ flock again. Courtship behaviour involves many highly ritualized displays, mainly by ♂♂, to lesser extent by ♀♀, initially in flocks, then in pair-formation and maintenance. In addition to forming pair-bonds with eventual mate ♂♂ display to or rape other ♀♀, often after flight in which several ♂♂ chase single ♀. In communal courtship several ♂♂ typically display to 1 or more ♀♀ on water; displays often elaborate, consisting of secondary and major forms. ♂♂ first assume Courtship-intent posture with each ♂ aligning its body parallel to ♀. Secondary displays, forms of basic comfort movements, include Upward-shake and Wing-flap, which involve brief lifting of body vertically clear of water as feet tread and shaking head laterally with bill inclined downwards; and Head-flick.

Major displays usually more elaborate, often with vocal accompaniment; include at least 3 actions (based on those of Mallard *A. platyrhynchos*): (1) Water-flick or Grunt-whistle in which bill immersed with forward-back shaking action causing small droplets of water to be flicked backwards and upwards in high arch. Forebody then lifted from water with neck well arched and bill remaining close to surface while loud, sharp whistle followed by deep grunt emitted, then normal swimming posture resumed. During this action bird usually moves backwards. (2) Head-up-tail-up in which ♂ gives loud whistle, thrusts head with indrawn chin backwards and upwards while simultaneously curving tail upwards, rump feathers ruffled, causing the bird to appear short and high. Simultaneously, folded wings are lifted to expose speculum and curled rump feathers. Action lasts *c.* 1 s, head alone remaining high for a moment, head feathers erected, bill directed at courted ♀. Next, ♂ shoots away over water, stretched flat in Nod-swimming position, head and neck extended on surface, moving in circle around ♀. In final phase ♂ returns to normal swimming position but with head raised and turned away from ♀ to display dark nape patch caused by erection of nape feathers. In this Turn-back-of-head posture ♂ swims in front of ♀, inducing her to follow (ceremonial Leading-display). (3) Down-up movement in which ♂ thrusts bill into water in lightning action and immediately jerks head upwards while keeping breast low in water. This action raises water droplets; when head is highest, breast deepest, whistle is emitted. Following action, quick 'raebraeb' call is uttered with raised chin. Down-up not usually directed at ♀ but may be performed simultaneously by 2 or more ♂♂ in courting party, ensuing 'raebraeb' palaver temporarily terminating social displays. Nod-swimming also performed by ♀ of certain species during communal courtship; may initiate ♂ courtship activity and culminate in several ♂♂ chasing preferred ♀ in Courtship-flight.

As bonds form in communal courtship the following major displays of pair-courtship become apparent: (1) Turn-back-of-head and ♀ Inciting; (2) Bill-dipping; (3) Ceremonial-drinking; (4) various Mock-preen displays including highly ritualized Preen-behind-wing in which colourful speculum briefly exposed, also Preen-dorsally, Preen-back-behind-wing and Preen-belly; (5) Bridling-display, performed on land or water, in which ♂ throws head backwards onto mantle, with bill directed skywards, while rounded breast raised high; on water rear-end may be submerged during this action; (6) 'Raebraeb' palavers in which both sexes utter similar calls while Chin-raising towards each other, necks outstretched. ♀ displays, though less numerous than those of ♂, include Inciting, in which ♀ directs bill towards ♂, often over shoulder, while uttering characteristic Inciting-call. Marked differences in calls with ♀♀ typically louder and coarser. Decrescendo-call (a series of 2, 3 or 4 notes with downward inflection) also characteristic of genus. Pre-copulatory displays consist typically of mutual Head-pumping; copulation normally occurs in water. Rape, lacking any preliminary displays, may occur on land. Post-copulatory behaviour of ♂ includes Burp-display, in which ♂ extends neck vertically, moves head up and somewhat back, and calls; also Bridling and Nod-swimming, often followed by mutual Bathing.

Mated ♂ will pursue single ♀ or pair intruding into a 'waiting area' (3-bird Flight) and attempt to bite or buffet intruding ♀ from below and behind. ♂ of intruding pair usually lags behind. Flights usually of short duration, or prolonged by participation of other 'territorial' ♂♂. Mated ♀♀ will defend themselves from strange ♂♂, especially during incubation period and when escorting young. Gesture-of-repulsion used, and utters broken series of single, sharp 'gaeck' sounds. This call also given by ♀ when pursued by ♂♂ in flight.

Nests on ground, usually in dense vegetation, well concealed shallow depressions, normally lined with down plucked from ♀'s breast, who alone builds. Eggs unmarked, creamy, bluish, greenish or greyish; clutches 6–12, eggs laid daily, replaced after loss, incubation by ♀ only. Young cared for by ♀ only in most species, ♂ sometimes in attendance when brood young, but in several African endemics with long-term pair-bonds ♂ also accompanies young; only ♀ broods them, however. In these species young aggressively defended by both parents, otherwise main anti-predator reaction is injury-feigning distraction display by ♀. Young mature at 1 year.

37 species world-wide. Of 15 in Africa 6 are endemic, 7 occur as non-breeding or occasional breeding visitors from Palearctic region and 2 as vagrants from North America.

Anas penelope Linnaeus. Eurasian Wigeon. Canard siffleur.

Anas Penelope Linnaeus, 1758. Syst. Nat. (10th ed.), 1, p. 126; Sweden.

Plate 17

(Opp. p. 290)

Range and Status. Palearctic migrant to N Africa and south through Nile Valley to E Africa during northern winter; rare Libya. Common to abundant Ethiopia, northern Sudan; less common Kenya and Tanzania; rare W Africa generally, small numbers only to northern Nigeria and Chad, maximum count 300 Lake Chad 1969–1970 (Roux 1970).

Description. ADULT ♂ (breeding): forehead creamy yellow; head and neck chestnut with glossy green patch behind eye, blackish throat; upperparts vermiculated grey; uppertail-coverts white, vermiculated grey; tail blackish, edged white; chest, sides of breast vinaceous pink; breast and belly white; flanks vermiculated grey; vent, undertail-coverts black; forewing white; primaries grey-brown; elongated scapulars vermiculated grey; speculum dark green, broadly edged black; underwing and axillaries dusky grey to greyish white. Eye brown; bill small, grey-blue, tip black; legs and feet blue-grey to yellow-brown, webs dusky. ADULT ♂ (eclipse): like ♀, but upperparts darker, flanks richer rufous; white forewing present and noticeable on sides at rest. ADULT ♀ (breeding): head, neck, breast, and upperparts rufous-brown, barred or

spotted blackish with paler pink-buff edges to feathers, flanks similar, paler; uppertail-coverts grey to sepia; underparts white; undertail-coverts with dark marks; wing-coverts grey-brown; speculum blackish, glossed green; underwing grey-brown with paler markings; axillaries greyish; bill, legs duller than ♂. ADULT ♀ (non-breeding): head heavily spotted; mantle, chest, flanks, back, rump with only few dark bars; scapulars broadly edged cinnamon; tail dark grey, edged off-white. SIZE: wing, ♂ (45 specimens) 252–281 (267), ♀ (19) 242–262 (250); tail, ♂ (19) 102–119 (106), ♀ (13) 86–95 (90·7); bill, ♂ (84) 32–38 (34·7), ♀ (51) 31–37 (33·8); tarsus, ♂ (49) 37–44 (39·5), ♀ (40) 35–41 (38·6); length, 45–51 cm; wing-span, 75–86 cm. WEIGHT: (juveniles included) (Russia, Nov–Mar) ♂ 400–820, ♀ 400–780; (Russia, Oct) ♂ 670–1090, ♀ 600–910.

JUVENILE: similar to adult ♀, more heavily streaked and barred on head. ♂ assumes white forewing in 2nd winter.

Field Characters. Small-billed, short-necked, medium-sized dabbling duck with peaked forehead, pointed tail and short legs. Breeding ♂ with cream-yellow forehead, chestnut head, pinkish breast, grey flanks with white bar, grey upperparts. In flight white

Anas penelope

forewings, rufous head, grey upperparts distinctive, differing from ♂ Smew *Mergus albellus* in having pointed, not rounded, tail and white V-shaped upper-tail-coverts. ♀ and eclipse ♂ separated from other brown ducks in flight by monotone wing-colouring above and below, white V-shaped uppertail-coverts and white belly, pointed wings.

Voice. Recorded (2a). ♂ call a loud, musical 'whee-OO' uttered singly or in long series. Multi-syllablic 'wip . . . wee . . . wip . . . weu' given as Threat-call, in flight and in Raebraeb-palaver. ♀ utters distinctive repeated purring or grating growl of varying loudness, 'krrr-krrr' in variety of situations. Decrescendo-call, 1–3 syllabled 'KRRR-kw' of decreasing volume.

General Habits. Well known in Africa, intimately known in Europe. Birds in N and E Africa, especially Tunisia, originate in west-central Siberia; origins of W African birds unknown. Some individuals remain in winter quarters through breeding season.

Favours shallow, sheltered waters, often maritime salt marshes, estuaries, tidal flats and other coastal habitats, or lagoons, lakes, floodlands and reservoirs, space and good visibility essential. In Ethiopia occurs on shallow coastal waters and plateau lakes, in Kenya mostly restricted to highland waters. Highly gregarious, densely packed flocks form where present in numbers (single flock of 4200 counted on Lake Adele, Ethiopia, Jan 1969; E. K. Urban, pers. comm.); wary, well-coordinated, prone to much calling. Swims low in water, rising straight up on take-off; flies with rapid wing-beats, flocks in tight formations or straggling lines. Movements between feeding or loafing grounds occur day or night, flocks usually travelling at no great height. Gregarious feeder, day or night, depending on degree of disturbance or tides. Feeds by grazing on land, from water's surface and, less often, underwater by immersing head and neck.

Food. Almost entirely vegetable matter; leaves, stems, stolons, bulbils, rhizomes and seeds. Small amounts of animal matter consumed, depending on availability, e.g. algae, amphipods, fish spawn.

Plate 17
(Opp. p. 290)

Anas strepera Linnaeus. Gadwall. Canard chipeau.

Anas strepera Linnaeus, 1758. Syst. Nat. (10th ed.), p. 125; Sweden.

Range and Status. Non-breeding Palearctic migrant to NE Africa, Nile Valley to Sudan; Ethiopia sporadic occurrences to over 2500 m in highlands and southern movement in autumn (Eritrea); rarely Kenya and Tanzania (Backhurst *et al.* 1973); W Africa rarely to Senegal delta (Morel 1980), vagrant Upper Volta, Nigeria, Cameroon, Zaïre; not recorded Lake Chad region since 1929. Breeds occasionally Morocco, Algeria.

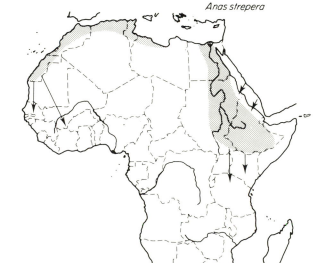

Anas strepera

Description. *A. s. strepera*, ADULT ♂ (breeding): entire head grey-buff, crown, nape darker; mantle, back and flanks grey with fine, paler vermiculations; scapulars buff, centres dark grey; back, upper rump black tinged olive, vermiculated whitish; lower rump, tail-coverts black; tail dark grey; upper breast white heavily barred with black crescents; lower breast, belly, vent white; upperwing mouse grey, inner secondaries white, others black or mouse grey, tipped white; greater wing-coverts black; median coverts chestnut; underwing-coverts and axillaries white. Eye dark brown; bill lead-grey; legs and feet dull orange-yellow, webs dusky. ADULT ♂ (eclipse): like ♀, greyer, upperparts darker, less heavily marked; wing-coverts remain chestnut. ADULT ♀: head similar to that of ♂; breast, upperparts and flanks streaked buff or marked heavily with darker brown feather centres, bars and edges; underparts white. Eye dark brown; bill olive-grey on culmen, yellow-ochre on sides; legs and feet yellow-brown to orange-yellow, webs dusky. SIZE: wing, ♂ (24 specimens) 261–282 (269), ♀ (14) 243–261 (252); tail, ♂ (13) 81–92 (86.0), ♀ (9) 77–84 (80.2); bill, ♂ (60) 39–46 (42.4), ♀ (48) 37–43 (39.8); tarsus, ♂ (42) 38–42 (40.3), ♀ (34) 36–42 (38.8); length, 46–56 cm; wing-span, 84–95 cm; WEIGHT: (Russia) ♂ (22, Mar) 605–950, ♀ (9, Mar–Apr) 650–820; (Oct) ♂ 800–1300, ♀ 800–1000.

JUVENILE: resembles adult ♀ but underparts boldly streaked and spotted.

DOWNY YOUNG: upperparts including crown and nape, sepia, light patches on wing, sides of back and rump; sides of head and underparts cream-buff, sometimes tinged cinnamon on breast; eye brown; bill grey, edges of upper mandible flesh; legs and feet dark grey, yellow-buff on sides of tarsus and toes.

Field Characters. Small, inconspicuous, grey-brown duck. Breeding ♂, when swimming, appears mealy grey, black (not white) around tail, with black bill; ♀ and eclipse ♂ similar, bill with orange sides more extensive than that of ♀ Mallard *A. platyrhynchos*, profile less heavy. In flight shows small black and white patch on secondaries, also chestnut bar and black back in ♂, otherwise plain upperparts. These features, plus white underwing and belly in both sexes, separate it from other similar brown ducks.

Voice. Recorded (2a). ♂ emits 1–4 low whistles uttered separately; short low whistle followed by loud, short grunt; long loud whistle followed by long grunt; multisyllabic series of grunts and whistles 'raeb-zee-zee-raeb-raeb'; chattering series of repeated grunts and whistles. ♀ calls are Persistent-quacking and Decrescendo-call; similar to those of Mallard, but more nasal in quality.

General Habits. Little known in Africa, intimately known in Europe. Shy, retiring, gregarious when not breeding but seldom occurs in large flocks. Most of day spent loafing, preening, on shore, otherwise on open water. Pairs maintain discreet distance in flocks. Dispute display mainly Open-bill threat, neck extended; lateral Head-jerking also performed by ♂♂ Chin-lifting in both sexes frequent, especially in pair disputes, often involves Pair-palaver. Food obtained mostly by swimming with head submerged, less often by up-ending. Also grazes.

Food. Mainly vegetable; roots, leaves, tubers, buds and seeds of pondweeds, sedges, rushes, grasses; also algae. Small amount of animal matter, including insects, molluscs, annelids, amphibians and spawn, plus small fish. Takes cereal grains on land. Ducklings eat surface invertebrates for first few days and thereafter aquatic invertebrates until essentially herbivorous at 3 weeks.

Breeding Habits. Little known in Africa, well known in Europe. Nests often as close as 5 m; placed on ground close to water in dense vegetation.

Pair behaviour involves highly ritualized Pair-palaver; Courtship-flights originating from groups on water; much fighting between ♂♂ as pairs attempt to drive other ♂♂ away; 3-bird flights; and Decrescendo-

calling by ♀♀; ♀♀ also engage in Persistent-quacking in spring. Mock-preening displays are used, especially Preen-behind-wing by ♂, to lesser extent by ♀; also Turn-back-of head (see **A**) and ♀ Inciting (**B**). Bill-dip and full Ceremonial-drinking occur mainly when mates meet again after separation, and especially after antagonistic encounters. At times, pair also touch each other briefly with bills. From initial stage of pairing, birds sometimes engage in pre-copulatory displays, this often leading to full copulatory sequence. Pre-copulatory and copulatory behaviour much as in other *Anas* spp. Following copulation ♂ usually Bridles, swings round to face ♀ as she starts post-copulatory Bathing, performs Burp or Head-high display, then Bathes.

NEST: in tussocks, thick bushes, rushes, tall grass. Slight hollow on ground lined with grass, leaves, then down; 20–30 cm across, cup 18–20 cm across by up to 7 cm deep; built by ♀ who gathers material near nest.

EGGS: 6–15 (mean, Europe, 9·96). Blunt ovals; pale pink. SIZE: (200 eggs) 51–59 × 35–44 (55 × 39). WEIGHT: (100, captive birds) 35–55 (44) (J. Kear, pers. comm.).

Laying dates: Morocco, Algeria mid-Apr–June.

Incubation begins with completion of clutch, by ♀. While ♀ is laying ♂ remains alone in activity centre, spends over 50% of time Burp-calling. Incubation period: 24–26 days.

Fledging period: 45–50 days; ducklings are independent at or just prior to fledging; breed at 1 year. Cared for by ♀, brooded while young.

Anas crecca Linnaeus. Green-winged Teal; Common Teal. Sarcelle d'hiver.

Plate 17

(Opp. p. 290)

Anas Crecca Linnaeus, 1758. Syst. Nat. (10th ed.), p. 126; Sweden.

Range and Status. Palearctic winter migrant to N Africa and northern tropics. N Africa fairly common to abundant, most occur in severe European winters, ranging from Morocco-Egypt (Jan counts, Algeria: 1975, 15,682; 1977, 7074; 1978, 9359); Nile Valley all regions; Sudan common to c. 6°N; Ethiopia common, maximum most waters c. 100; small numbers to E Africa; small to moderate numbers Senegal (Jan 1972, 500), Lake Chad (1970–1971, 1200), Nigeria; vagrant Mali, Burundi, Zaïre.

Description. *A. c. crecca*: Europe, Asia and Africa north of equator. ADULT ♂ (breeding): entire head chestnut with metallic green eye-patch, outlined creamy white from in front of eye to nape, the outline extending forward to bill-base; upperparts and flanks grey, vermiculated dark grey, a prominent white horizontal scapular stripe bordered black; breast cream, spotted blackish; central lower breast and belly white; undertail yellow-buff, bordered black; tail black; upperwing medium grey-brown, speculum metallic green bordered broadly with buff in front, narrowly with white at rear; underwing grey and white. Eye dark hazel; bill slate; legs and feet

Anas crecca

X Vagrant

combination of small size, rather pointed wings with uniform colouring, pale-bordered green speculum diagnostic.

Voice. Recorded (22b). Calls of ♂ in evidence especially winter and spring, main note penetrating, melodious, far-carrying whistle 'prip-prip', 'krick-et' or 'kedick', just discernibly 2-syllabled. ♀ gives various forms of quacking, high-pitched or squeaky, not far-carrying. Also high-pitched Decrescendo-call of 4 notes. In both sexes wings cause whistling note in flight.

General Habits. Well known. Main flocks arrive N Africa Oct–Nov, further cold weather movements from Europe any time during winter, exact origin of N and W African birds unknown; those in Nile Valley, Ethiopia to E Africa, from USSR. Favours wide variety freshwater habitats, occasionally sea; in N Africa lakes, lagoons, slow-flowing streams, even small pools; in northern tropics small pools on edges larger waters, river deltas, mountain tarns, pools in floodlands, can be highland or coastal waters. Flocks generally 30–40, sometimes hundreds on larger waters; often rest out of water, even perching in trees; disperse to individually preferred feeding grounds at night. Flocks react to flying predators with loud whistles by ♂♂. If on land, fly to water, regrouping and swimming off in tight pack; may fly over water in close formation until predator leaves. Food obtained by walking slowly filtering mud with bill, swimming with head and neck submerged, upending, picking items off surface of water, sometimes by skimming surface with bill; rarely dives.

♂♂ frequently outnumber ♀♀. During pair-formation hostile encounters occur between ♂♂, which are far more quarrelsome than in other *Anas* spp. Threaten with Chin-lift, accompanied by whistles, rapid Head-shakes and Open-bill threats, these frequently leading to chasing and fighting. ♀♀ threaten ♂♂ during pairing, often with Inciting display in which sideways neck-jerking of head is repeatedly made towards rejected ♂. Communal courtship usually involves 5–7 ♂♂, 1 ♀; other ♂♂ strongly attracted by displaying group. Pre-flight signals involve Head-shakes and Head-thrusts.

Food. In winter mainly seeds 1–2·6 mm long, chiefly sedges, bulrushes, pondweeds and grasses but varies with locality. Some aquatic insects and larvae also taken, plus crustaceans.

olive-grey, webs darker. ADULT ♂ (eclipse): resembles ♀ but upperparts darker, more uniform. ADULT ♀: entirely brownish; head with dark crown and eye-streak, rest of head and neck buffy brown with darker streaking, chin and throat white; upperparts, flanks and undertail-coverts buffy brown, heavily blotched dark brown, darker when not breeding; lower breast and belly white; tail brown; wing as ♂ but speculum bordered white both front and back. Eye dark brown to light hazel; bill dark slate or olive-grey on culmen and tip. SIZE: wing, ♂ (34 specimens) 181–196 (187), ♀ (22) 175–184 (180); tail, ♂ (14) 64–71 (66·9), ♀ (10) 62–69 (64·7); culmen, ♂ (85) 34–40 (36·4), ♀ (50) 32–38 (34·9); tarsus, ♂ (38) 29–32 (30·4), ♀ (32) 28–31 (29·8); length, 34–38; wing-span, 58–64. WEIGHT: (USSR and France, Jan–Mar) ♂ (300) 200–371, ♀ (285) 185–400.

JUVENILE: similar to adult, somewhat darker, more uniform above; lower breast and belly spotted; bill pink-horn.

A. c. carolinensis Gmelin. N America; recorded once Lake of Imfout near Oued Oum-er-Rbia, Morocco. ADULT ♂ differs from nominate race in having large white crescent on side of breast at shoulder height.

Field Characters. ♂ is small, compact grey duck with chestnut head and green eye-patch; ♂ and ♀ eclipse small brown-speckled duck with dark bill, white underparts. Breeding ♂ distinctive; non-breeding ♂ and ♀ best separated from other small brown ducks, e.g. Garganey *A. querquedula*, Gadwall *A. strepera*, by well developed dark eye-stripes, dark crowns, white chins. In flight

Plate 16

(Opp. p. 227)

Anas capensis Gmelin. Cape Teal; Cape Wigeon. Sarcelle du Cap.

Anas capensis Gmelin, 1789. Syst. Nat., 1, pt. 2, p. 527; Cape of Good Hope.

Range and Status. Resident south of *c.* 17°N, occasionally more northerly in Libya. Distribution pattern patchy, scarce over much of range. Rare west of 5°E; small, but regular occurrences Ghana, Nigeria, Lake Chad flocks up to 300 (Viellard 1972); Sudan scarce wet season migrant; Ethiopia common to abundant; E Africa present all year, common only on Rift Valley soda lakes; rare extreme southeast of Zaïre; occasional records S Mozambique and Angola coast; fairly common to very common southern Africa except central Botswana; scarce Natal.

Description. ADULT ♂: entire head and neck pale ash grey closely speckled grey-brown, densely before eyes and on nape, lightly at base of bill, on chin and foreneck; all upperparts dark chocolate brown, feathers broadly edged creamy buff; rest of body pale ash grey, all feathers with central areas dark brown giving spotted effect; upperwing dark brown, speculum iridescent green with black surround and bold white border. Bill rose pink grading to blue-white tip, including nail, base of bill black broadening laterally and around nostrils; eye orange to light brown, occasionally yellowish; legs and feet dirty yellow, joint, webs, blackish. Sexes alike, ♀ slightly smaller. SIZE: (52 specimens, ♂ and ♀) wing, 168–206 (193·8);

tail, 53–74 (64·3); tarsus, 32–40 (37·0); culmen, 36–44 (39·6); length, 45·7 cm; wing-span 78–82 cm. WEIGHT: ♂ (31) 352–502 (419), ♀ (25) 316–451 (380).

JUVENILE: closely resembles adult, but less speckled below.

DOWNY YOUNG: forehead, crown, nape and entire upper-parts ash grey; a grey patch under eye, lores to ear-coverts, sides of head otherwise white; over upper breast a grey suffusion grading to white over rest of underparts and extending to large circular shape over sides of body to level with wing-base and encircling bold grey patch. Bill dusky, pinkish towards tip; eye dark brown; legs and feet dull, dusky pink.

Field Characters. A small, pale grey duck with pink upturned bill. In good light appears almost white. Sits high on water. Flight agile, much twisting and turning; displays bold white speculum with green centre. Unlikely to be confused with any other duck within its range.

Voice. Recorded (2a, 6). ♂ call normally a husky whisper, sounding like a nasal squeak; ♀ gives a low quacking; both usually silent. During pair-formation ♀, while Inciting, calls 'ke-ke-ke-ke-ke'. Mated ♀♀ utter 5-syllabled Decrescendo-call 'che-che-*che*-che-che', accent on 3rd syllable. Displaying ♂♂, and sometimes ♀♀, utter Burp-whistle, a 2-syllabled nasal 'P-ZHH', 1st note short, contrasting with longer, descending 2nd note.

General Habits. Well known. Normally seen in pairs or small groups but flocks of several hundreds occur when moulting. Prefers shallow vleis, lagoons, salt pans, sewage settlement pans and tidal mudflats with preference for brackish waters, soda lakes. Nomadic, making complex long distance movements. Regular occurrence Ghana and Nigeria suggests dry season movements north (Hall 1976; Macdonald and Taylor 1976).

Swimming birds bob heads and lower tails slowly when nervous or alert; if further disturbed swim to deeper water or take off in long gradual ascent, circle round and resettle near by.

Feeding occurs throughout daylight hours with most activity 13.00–17.00 h. Food mainly obtained by up-ending or swimming with head and neck submerged. May also stir up mud in shallows, feeding on creatures thus disturbed on surface. 1 of few *Anas* spp. adapted for diving as dives with wings closed in manner of diving ducks. Diving for food far less common, however, than other feeding methods (accounted for less than 19% total feeding activity at Barberspan, W Transvaal).

Adults undergo complete post-nuptial moult for period of 23–24 days, when flightless birds usually retire to deep waters; sometimes retire to *Typha* beds, loafing on matted stems and leaves (D. M. Skead, pers. comm.). If disturbed make for deeper water, neck and head stretched out, body half-submerged; when pressed will dive and swim up to 6 m underwater with wings closed.

Food. Animal and vegetable matter. Analysis by bulk of 39 stomachs, SW Cape, summer and autumn (Sept–Apr): 17% leaves, stems and seeds of *Potomogeton*

Anas capensis

pectinatum; 83% animal matter (insects 63%, crustacea and *Xenopus* tadpoles 10%. Oesophagi of 13 adults, Barberspan and district, showed aggregate percentage 99% animal matter, 1% vegetable matter. Most important food items Coriscidae adults 33%, Ostracoda 33% and Chironomidae larvae 26% (D. M. Skead, pers. comm.).

Breeding Habits. Very well known in SW Cape. Nests singly, on ground, with marked preference for island sites; well concealed where adequate vegetation present. Irregular, opportunistic breeder, breeding varying with erratic and sporadic rainfall.

Pair-bonds long-lasting and probably related (though not exclusively so) to this species' need to take advantage of unpredictable breeding opportunities. Non-breeding birds, paired and unpaired, gather on permanent waters taking part in social courtship whole year round. Peak activity May, to lesser extent Nov at Barberspan (D. M. Skead, pers. comm.); in SW Cape pair-formation occurs towards end July. Pairs travel together and initiate early nesting in response to erratic presence of short-lived habitat. Pale grey plumages of adults and downy young blend well with preferred brine-encrusted saline pans, devoid of emergent vegetation. Social courtship behaviour includes characteristic Nod-swimming followed by Preen-behind-wing, also Burp, Head-up-tail-up and Preliminary-shake. ♀ follows ♂ closely, Inciting if other ♂♂ show interest in her; ♀ places herself between mate and unmated ♂ and, facing latter, thrusts bill into water and, with bill still submerged, make series of semi-circles opposite unwanted ♂, actions accompanied by 'ke-ke-ke-ke' call. On land Inciting performed with back arched, tail depressed, neck stretched in direction of unwanted ♂, head held horizontally, semi-circles traced while in this position. In pre-copulatory displays both sexes face each other and nod heads vigorously. ♀ then settles low in water while ♂ grasps her neck and begins to tread. Mating always occurs on water. This followed by Bridling where ♂ pulls his head back to middle of back, whistles, and settles low in water for few seconds, after which vigorous bathing, preening, wing-flapping, and more whistling take place.

NEST: site selection and construction by ♀ only, ♂ usually following behind. Construction begins 2–10 days prior to laying of 1st egg and continues during egg-laying period. Initially a hollow depression, nest is gradually built up from base with dry vegetable matter, obtained in immediate vicinity, main structure being finished prior to completion of clutch. ♀ then lines it completely with down plucked from breast while still laying, continuing to do so during incubation, especially on outer rim of nest. Main structure 22·9 cm wide by 7·5 cm deep; inner bowl 10·2–15·2 cm wide by 5·7–6·4 cm deep; down lining 3·8 cm thick. In deep undergrowth narrow tunnel is formed by passage of ♀ to and from nest. Sample of 165 nests showed tendency for concealment under bushes or trees, 40% having cover from above and on all 4 sides. Degree of concealment directly correlated with nest success; only 20% destroyed by, for example, predators and flooding.

EGGS: 6–11, laid at 24 h intervals; SW Cape mean (138 clutches) 8·4; Transvaal mean (39 clutches) 7·0. Ovoid, rather pointed at small end with smooth, matt surface; pale to deep cream colour. SIZE: (531 eggs) 46·2–54·8 × 33·0–39·4 (49·7 × 35·9). WEIGHT: (46 eggs, captive birds) 25·5–39·0 (30·5) (J. Kear, pers. comm.).

Laying dates: extended breeding season over much of range; Sudan June–Sept; Ethiopia Jan, Mar–May; Kenya Apr–May; Tanzania Aug. In southern Africa laying recorded all months, peak in late wet season Aug–Nov SW Cape; Transvaal, Botswana, Namibia Apr–Aug (dry season). Wet season laying may show 2 peaks (Sept and Nov) and may vary slightly from year to year.

Incubation by ♀ only, beginning with completion of clutch. ♀ covers eggs with down when leaving to feed, does not defecate on eggs when flushed. ♂ remains in vicinity of nest throughout incubation. Period: 26–30 days. Period between pipping and hatching c. 30 h.

Weeks 1·5–3 down on young already faded, lighter patches appearing; weeks 3–4·5 still predominantly downy but patches of feathers visible, tail feathers completely visible; weeks 4·5–6 predominantly feathered, downy still nape and rump; weeks 6–8 completely feathered, some down still present on nape; week 8 fully feathered, resembles adult, able to fly. Secondaries and primaries also lost at approximately 6 months and duck then flightless for replacement period (34 days for primaries, 28 days for secondaries). Weights of captive reared young: on hatching 23·4; 1 week 28·4; 4 weeks 188·0; 8 weeks 377·0; 12 weeks 453·0.

Both parents care for young, ♂ remaining with ♀ and brood until young reach flying age, frequently drive off other ♂♂. While with newly hatched young, parents usually remain in defended area for long period. If approached slowly may swim off with brood; if startled ducklings dive and scatter, while ♀ resorts to injury-feigning. Amalgamation of several broods into creches known.

Hatching success in SW Cape: 94% of 850 eggs and 97·3% of 72 eggs. Survival of av. brood of 8 after 1 week, 7·1.

References
Brand, D. J. (1961, 1964).
Siegfried, W. R. (1974).
Skead, D. M. (1977b).
Winterbottom, J. M. (1974).

Plate 17
(Opp. p. 290)

Anas platyrhynchos Linnaeus. Mallard. Canard colvert.

Anas platyrhynchos Linnaeus, 1758. Syst. Nat. (10th ed.), p. 125; Europe.

Range and Status. Palearctic winter migrant to N Africa and breeding resident small numbers Morocco, Algeria, Tunisia; visitor to Nile Valley south to Sudan and Ethiopia. Fairly common N Africa (Algeria 1975–1978, annual counts c. 1600–3200); northern tropics, including W and E Africa, vagrant only.

Description. *A. p. platyrhynchos*, ADULT ♂ (breeding): entire head bottle green; mantle and scapulars, finely vermiculated grey and white, lower mantle suffused cinnamon-buff, scapulars variably black and buff on edges; back black, finely vermiculated pale grey; rump and tail-coverts black glossed blue-green; tail black centrally, outer feathers mainly white, 2 black feathers curling upwards; lower neck with narrow white collar; chest, upper breast rich mahogany; flanks, underparts white, vermiculated grey; wings above mainly grey-brown, speculum blue or purple, thinly edged black, boldly bordered white back and front; underwing-coverts and axillaries white. Eye dark brown; bill olive-green to bright yellow, nail black; legs and feet orange-red. ADULT ♂ (eclipse): like ♀ but bill yellower; build heavier, crown darker, breast less streaked, face and neck paler. ADULT ♀: basically brown, streaked, spotted or mottled darker brown or blackish overall; crown, nape, and eye-stripe darker than eyebrow, sides of head and neck; upperparts darker than underparts, individually variable; wing as ♂. Bill dull orange to olive, nail black; eye and feet as ♂. SIZE: wing, ♂ (13 specimens) 272–285 (279), ♀ (13) 257–273 (265); tail, ♂ (14) 80–91 (85·8), ♀ (12) 81–90 (84·5); culmen, ♂ (58) 51–61 (55·4), ♀ (48) 47–56 (51·8); tarsus, ♂ (45) 42–48 (45·3), ♀ (37) 41–46 (43·4); length, 50–65 cm; wing-span, 81–98 cm. WEIGHT: ♂ (269) 850–1572, ♀ (114) 750–1320.

JUVENILE: similar to ♀ but duller, underparts more narrowly streaked; crown, nape and upperparts darker in ♂; bill red-brown; feet orange.

DOWNY YOUNG: crown, nape, streak through eye and upperparts, including flanks to thighs, dark sepia; eyebrow, cheeks, sides of neck and rest of underparts yellow-buff, paler on throat; streak on rear wing, spots on back and rump pale yellow; eye brown; bill flesh, spotted black, nail pink-white; feet dark olive-grey.

Field Characters. Large, heavily built duck, ♂ with green head, green-yellow bill, mahogany breast, grey body, reddish legs; ♀ brown, well mottled darker, with olive bill, reddish feet. In flight both show blue or purple white-edged speculum, ♂ with green head and black back and rump contrasting with otherwise grey upperparts. ♀ and eclipse ♂ at rest closely similar to several other *Anas* ♀♀, but large size, long bill and head, orange-red legs distinguish them. In flight blue speculum and white underwing-coverts conspicuous.

Voice. Recorded (2a). ♂ utters 'raehb' call in variety of situations: quiet, spaced, drawn-out sounds as alarm or contact call, in response to ♀'s Decrescendo-call; Raebraeb-call a faster series of 'raehb' notes in 2-syllabled phrases, accent on 2nd syllable, characterizes antagonistic encounters between ♂♂, and Pair-palavers. Also single, loud, high-pitched whistle uttered on water, and wheezy, 3-note 'chachacha' during communal courtship. ♀ calls more varied, basically loud quacks. Also various soft, quiet Maternal-calls uttered before eggs hatch and when ♀ with brood. Contact call of downy young, soft, fast, high-pitched 'pipi' notes, irregularly spaced. Distress call, loud, high-pitched 'peeca' notes, harsher and more evenly spaced.

General Habits. Well known in Africa. Gregarious when not breeding, occurring on all types of water habitat, fresh or salt, large or small, where water less than 1 m deep. Prefers well-vegetated pools, with either submerged, floating or emergent vegetation, but is also tolerant of open waters with mudflats, spits, e.g. irrigation networks, sewage-farms. Tolerant of man and disturbance and adapts to ornamental ponds in cities. Birds in N Africa thought to originate Baltic, upper Volga and central Europe; those in NE Africa from SW Russia. Movements to winter quarters start Aug, peak numbers reaching Africa Nov–Dec.

Flocks few dozen to several hundred, composed of pairs, trios, unpaired birds, generally more ♂♂ than ♀♀, this further influenced by tendency of ♀♀ to move further south. Roosts both nocturnally and diurnally, communally when not breeding. Rests and preens on land, loafing on any available shoreline or mudflat. Often flies considerable distances to feeding places early morning, late evening. Food obtained in water while swimming by pecking, sieving with bill on surface, up-ending, diving (especially young birds); on land by grazing and grubbing. Within flock Diving-play occurs; mass bathing accompanied by dashing-and-diving rushes across water, short flights, sudden dives characteristic. Pre-flight signalled by Head-shakes, Head-thrusts, usually facing into wind, neck erect, accompanied by calls from ♀♀. In presence of danger members of flock utter warning calls, with neck sleeked, head held high.

Food. Omnivorous, varying with locality, season: seeds, cereals, various aquatic and waterside vegetation, roots; also insects, molluscs, crustaceans, annelids, amphibians, fish.

Breeding Habits. Well known in Africa, intimately known in Europe. Non-colonial breeder but nests only 1 m apart tolerated; usually placed near water on ground in dense cover, but highly variable. Monogamous pair-bonds of seasonal duration.

Social courtship occurs over many months, peaking Oct–Nov, Feb–Mar. Courtship on water occurs in bouts of up to 15 min, ♂♂ in groups, ♀♀ on periphery. Routine involves persistent swimming manoeuvres. Water-flick (see **A**), Head-up-tail-up (**B**) and Down-up (**C**), plus elements of antagonistic behaviour between ♂♂. Displays stimulated by ♀ Nod-swimming, Head-nodding or Inciting while swimming among groups of

Anas platyrhynchos

♂♂. Pursuit-flights take form of typical 3-bird flights, group-flights (5–15 ♂♂ chasing single ♀) and Rape-intent flights. Pair-formation behaviour sometimes seen during communal courtship when ♂ leads while ♀ follows, often Inciting. When mates rejoin after temporary separation perform Pair-palaver, ♂ Raebraeb-calling in Chin-lift posture while ♀ Incites; Mutual Ceremonial-drinking; various mock-preen displays including Preen-behind-wing, Preen-dorsally, Preen-belly and Preen-breast. Copulation preceded by mutual Head-pumping. ♀ then adopts Prone-posture, stretching out head and neck along water, slightly droops wings and raises tail. Following copulation ♂ dismounts and quickly Bridles, then Nod-swims around ♀, sometimes with brief spells of Leading, finally bathes and Wing-flaps; ♀ also bathes and Wing-flaps.

NEST: placed in ground cover as available, often against post or tree, under bushes, brambles, or in tree cavities up to 10 m high, or artificial nest boxes. Shallow depression with low rim of grasses, leaves, small twigs, well lined with down; internal diameter 17–22 cm, depth 6–14 cm; built by ♀ from materials near nest, these often added during laying or incubation.

EGGS: (Europe) 4–18, usually laid at 24 h intervals, but sometimes 2–3 days; mean (95 clutches) 12·6. Blunt ovals; grey-green or buff. SIZE: (500 eggs) 50–65 × 37–46 (57 × 41). WEIGHT: (200 eggs, England) 42–59 (51) (J. Kear, pers. comm.).

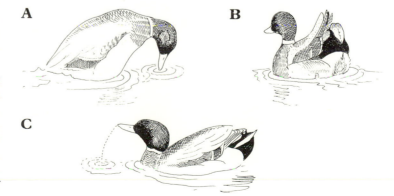

A

B

C

Laying dates: Morocco, Algeria Mar–June.

Incubation begins with completion of clutch, by ♀ only, ♂ sometimes nearby in early stages. Eggs covered with down when ♀ off; will defend nest against predators and humans.

Young leave ground nest at 14–21 h, hole nests 20–25 h. Fledging period: 50–60 days; becomes independent at or just before fledging.

Young cared for by ♀, brooded while small, defended. Leads brood to water and food; while leading moves slowly, uttering occasionally quiet Maternal-calls, louder on appearance of danger or if ducklings give distress call, e.g. if cold, wet, hungry or lost. If brood becomes dispersed ♀ runs back and forth until reunited. Unidentifiable, wet ducklings sometimes killed by mother. 1st breeding takes place at 1 year.

Plate 16
(Opp. p. 227)

Anas undulata Dubois. Yellow-billed Duck. Canard à bec jaune.

Anas undulata Dubois, 1839. Ornith. Gallerie, 1, p. 119, pl. 77; Cape of Good Hope.

Range and Status. Resident mostly on eastern half of continent, Ethiopia south to Cape. Most abundant duck many parts of range, especially temperate regions. Numbers in southern Africa estimated at tens of thousands; e.g. dry season maximum for well-counted waters *c.* 13,000 multiplied by birds on move and populations on uncounted waters, possibly 52,000–65,000. Frequents open waters up to 3890 m Ethiopia (Ash 1977). Subject to both limited local and long distance movements.

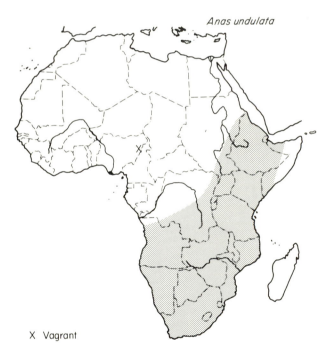

Anas undulata

X Vagrant

Description. *A. u. undulata* Dubois: S Uganda and Kenya south to Cape. ADULT♂: entire head, neck blackish grey, pale-edged feathers giving streaked effect, crown and face darkest; rest of plumage, including tail, upper wing, dark olive-brown, feathers broadly edged white to creamy, broadest on breast, flanks and underparts giving almost white effect at distance; speculum iridescent green, bordered broadly front and back with black, narrowly edged white; underwing whitish. Eye chestnut; bill bright yellow with black central patch on culmen, black nail and base of gape, undersurface black; legs and feet deep red-brown, blackish or yellowish. ADULT ♀: smaller, bill paler yellow; forehead more steeply sloped; speculum less bright, less wide. Undersurface of lower mandible black, mottled yellow. SIZE: (100 live ♂♂, 100 live ♀♀, Barberspan, Transvaal: Day 1977) wing, ♂ 532–635 (583), ♀ 497–579 (535); tail, ♂ 90–109 (100), ♀ 86–108 (97); culmen, ♂ 46–56 (52), ♀ 44–54 (49); tarsus, ♂ 39–51 (45), ♀ 39–48 (43);

length, ♂ 532–635 (583), ♀ 497–579 (535). WEIGHT: ♂ (7839) 533–1310 (965), ♀ (6080) 600–1123 (823) (Dean and Skead 1979).

JUVENILE: similar to adult, but head streaking coarser, darker, feather edges more buffy, underparts more heavily spotted.

DOWNY YOUNG: crown and upperparts greyish olive-brown, 2 panels of primrose yellow either side of central line, either side of back, 1 on sides of rump; face primrose yellow, a dusky line through eye from lores across sides of head to nape, a dusky smudge on ear-coverts; underparts pale primrose yellow, darkening over breast, thighs; wings olive-brown, edged primrose.

A. u. rueppelli Blyth. Upper Blue Nile and Ethiopian lake region, N Uganda, N Kenya (1 specimen from Cameroon). Darker, browner, feather margins less broad; bill deeper yellow.

Field Characters. Medium-sized grey-brown duck with bright yellow bill, pale edges to brown feathers of upperparts, rest of body with ashy, speckled appearance. In flight green speculum clearly visible. Yellow bill diagnostic, confusion with others unlikely.

Voice. Recorded (2a, 6, 14, 17, 18, 21c). ♂ emits various low whistles while swimming, audible at close range during Grunt-whistle and Down-up displays; also a seldom heard, weak, nasal 'whaarp-whaarp'. ♀ has 5 calls uttered while swimming or on ground: (1) Inciting call, loud, trembling 'queggeggeggegge'; (2) loud Decrescendo-call, 'quaegaegaegaegaeg', accent on 2nd syllable, decreasing in following syllables; (3) Going-away call, loud, evenly spaced 'quacks' when pair takes wing; (4) Persistent-quacking, loud, monotonous 'qua-qua-qua-qua ...' (16–20 calls per 10 s period) uttered on ground or on wing prior to laying; (5) loud, broken series of single 'gaeck' calls uttered by ♀ when incubating or escorting brood.

General Habits. Very well known. Frequents open waters of estuaries, slow-running rivers with pools, lakes, flooded lands, coastal lagoons, artificial reservoirs and dams, pans and sewage disposal impoundments where does not utilize highly acidic habitat or waters with high concentrations of sodium chloride, but tolerant of other salts even when pH is 10 or more. In southern Africa large numbers congregate towards middle and end of dry season (Jan–May SW Cape, May–Nov Transvaal, Orange Free State); flocks disperse to breed at onset of first major rains. Local movements to alternative waters within same region during rains, considerable and random to *c.* 50 km or less. Movements over greater distances, recorded Barberspan, W Transvaal, birds travelling up to 1100 km (Dean 1977).

Flock sizes highly variable, from few birds to many hundreds. Non-breeding birds spend day loafing on water, in shallows or at shoreline, feeding mainly early morning, late afternoon, although may graze in inundated grasslands much of day. Food obtained by swimming and filtering with bill, with head and bill immersed, by up-ending, and occasionally by diving or grazing. Movements take place mostly evenings, nights, pairs or small groups moving to new waters.

Peak post-nuptial wing moult occurs Nov–Feb in SW Cape, Apr–July in Transvaal, *c.* 3–4 months after breeding peaks. Av. interval between successive moults SW Cape 334 days (sample 10). Flightless birds swim away to deeper water if pursued, dive if pressed.

Food. Mainly plant matter, principal items varying with locality, availability. On Kafue Flats, Zambia (7 adults) main items *Sacciolepsis*, *Vossia* and *Echinochloa* fruits, *Spirogyra* filaments, *Nymphoides* and *Nymphaea* seeds, and *Najas* stems and leaves; also often *Echinochloa* leaves (Douthwaite 1977). At Barberspan, W Transvaal, in non-breeding adult and flying juvenile ♂♂, plant matter 83%, animal matter 17%, mainly *Potamogeton* plants and chironomid larvae; in non-breeding adult ♀♀, plant matter 71%, animal matter 29% (*Potamogeton* plants, chironomid larvae and also mayflies). In winter months, after harvesting, spilled maize and sunflower seeds. In non-flying juveniles, plant matter 29%, animal matter 71%, mainly Dytiscid larvae, *Bulinus*, grasshoppers and *Lagarosiphon* and *Eleocharis* plants (Skead 1980).

Breeding Habits. Well known in South Africa. Nests singly in dense vegetation on ground near water. May be closely spaced, distance of 12·1 m recorded, but normally greater than this.

Communal courtship takes place mostly early morning, early evening, occurs in flocks with increasing frequency towards end of dry season; basically typical *Anas* displays, e.g. Head-flick, Preen-back-behind-wing, Grunt-whistle and Down-up. Pair-courtship displays also basically *Anas* actions and especially similar to Mallard *A. platyrhynchos* with few specific variations, such as independent Nod-swimming by both sexes. Adult ♀♀ perform Nod-swimming when associating with group of displaying ♂♂, finally lowering head and neck forward onto water and swimming rapidly round and through group. Inciting, Preen-behind-wing, Drinking and Head-pumping also performed by ♀♀ as courtship or pair-bond maintenance actions. Courtship actions by adult ♂♂ include: (1) Preliminary-shake; (2) Drinking; (3) Bill-dip; (4) Bathing; (5) Wing-flap (independent action not to be confused with Wing-flap after bathing); (6) Attack; (7) Flight; (8) Preen-behind-wing; (9) Preen-dorsally; (10) Jump-flight; (11) Fluttering-

flight; (12) Head-up-tail-up; (13) Neck-jerking, in which 1 or more ♂♂ swim quickly past ♀, heads and necks high and rapidly jerking back and forth, each attempting to get in front of ♀ before Leading her; (14) Leading or Turn-back-of-head; (15) Independent Nod-swimming.

Copulation preceded by Head-pumping. After copulation ♂ bridles, then Nod-swims around or away from ♀; ♀ bathes.

NEST: sited among rushes, reeds, dense grass, lucerne, arum lilies, sedge, thistles, or in the matted rootlets of willow trees; marked tendency to build within tuft of vegetation. Frequently screened from above by overhanging vegetation, some with tunnel access through surrounding grass; occasionally recorded in unusually exposed or vulnerable position. Southern Africa placed within 20 m of water, often much closer, few in waterlogged conditions or actually floating; Kenya nests usually some distance from water. External dimensions vary, largest in waterlogged conditions, usually 25–104 cm wide by 7–15 cm deep, internal cup 18–21 cm across by 9–11 cm deep. Down lining added at start of incubation, greatest quantities at clutch completion. Of 65 nests, 9 with full clutches contained only small amounts of down or none. All have layer of fine grass or water weeds. Built by ♀ only.

EGGS: 4–12, laid at 24 h intervals: South Africa mean (35) 7·8. Blunt-ended; immaculate ivory, pale creamy yellow or buff with light sheen. SIZE: (104 eggs) 49–63 × 34–45 (54·9 × 41·3). WEIGHT: (64, captive birds) 44–62 (54·9) (J. Kear, pers. comm.).

Laying dates: South Africa occurs throughout the year, peaking at onset of rains and coinciding with maximum invertebrate food availability for young in newly flooded lands. W Cape July–Sept, E Cape Aug–Oct, Transvaal Dec–Jan; Zambia all year, peaking May–June; Kenya Jan, Apr–July; Uganda (Ruwenzori) June–Aug, N Uganda July; Ethiopia Aug–Sept, possibly July–Dec.

Incubation carried out by ♀ only who sits closely in face of disturbance, flushing only at last moment. Down pulled over eggs when nest left voluntarily. Period: 26–29 days.

Chick development: (5 hand-reared newly-hatched ducklings) first evidence of feathering *c.* day 30; day 37 feathers replacing down on scapulars, tail, sides of breast and entire undersurface, primary feathers just visible; day 42 primary feathers *c.* 25 mm long, uppertail-coverts have emerged; day 50 primary feathers 39 mm long, secondaries more developed, speculum visible as distinct black bar bordered front and back by clear white bands; day 56 *c.* 25 mm of primary webbing visible; day 57 speculum broadening and green coloration evident, 50 mm of primary webbing visible; day 68 1st flight of 3 ducklings (Day 1977). At 1 day old, 37 captive young weighed 28–40 (32) (J. Kear, pers. comm.).

Young chicks normally attended by ♀ only 1st 3 weeks, bond between ♂ and ♀ seldom persisting after egg-laying, although broods with 2 adults in attendance recorded, sexes and relationship not determined. Adults with multiple broods also known. Young remain with parent at least 6 weeks after fledging. ♀♀ escorting broods or off nest during incubation, if harassed by ♂♂ intent on rape, respond with Gesture-of-repulsion.

Av. brood size (ducklings wholly or partly in down) 5·2, representing post-incubation loss of 3/brood or 37·5% of eggs in clutch; e.g. through infertility, early chick death. Mortality in older broods not known. Adult mortality rate in ringed Transvaal (Barberspan) birds 1955–1969 calculated at 46·3% (Siegfried 1970a). Adult

♂♂ outnumber adult ♀♀ by 3:1, as opposed to juvenile ratio of 4:1 (Dean and Skead 1977b).

References:
Day, D. H. (1977).
Dean, W. R. J. (1978).
Rowan, M. K. (1963).
Siegfried, W. R. (1970a).
Skead, D. M. (1976, 1980).

Plate 16

(Opp. p. 227)

Anas sparsa Eyton. African Black Duck. Canard noir.

Anas sparsa Eyton, 1838. Mon. Anat. p. 142; South Africa.

Range and Status. Resident south of the Sahara, nowhere numerous. Inhabits rivers, streams and mountain sponges Cape to Ethiopia in east, Cameroon, Gabon, rarely Nigeria in west; scarce Angola and Namibia, elsewhere localized.

Anas sparsa

Description. *A. s. sparsa* Eyton: Cape Peninsula to Zambia and Mozambique. ADULT ♂: dark sooty-brown, face, front and sides of neck plus breast paler, underparts tending to buff with feathers edged light brown, giving mottled effect; long scapulars and uppertail-coverts barred white giving boldly spotted effect; tail crossed by 2 rows of white spots; neck with a central white bar in some; breast with dark transverse lines; wings, with prominent carpal spurs, dark brown above; secondary coverts with apical third white, broadly tipped black forming wing-bar, secondaries with outer webs metallic blue-green, tipped black and white, inner webs brown; tertials dark brown, barred white; underwing with coverts brown, broadly tipped white, axillaries white. Bill slate grey, nail and culmen ridge black, base of lower mandible pink and, frequently, a narrow pink rim at base of mandible; eye brown; legs, feet dull orange. Sexes similar, ♀ smaller. SIZE: wing, ♂ (22) 245–272, ♀ (20) 232–248; culmen, ♂ (22) 45–51 (47), ♀ (20) 43–46 (44); tail, ♂ (22) 100–115 (110), ♀ (20) 90–100 (93); tarsus, ♂ (22) 41–45 (43), ♀ (20) 29–42 (40); length, ♂ (22) 510–570 (545), ♀ (20) 480–530 (510). WEIGHT: ♂ unrecorded; ♀ (4, breeding) 760–1077 (Britton 1970; Siegfried 1968a).

JUVENILE: more brown than adults; spots on tail buff; belly barred white; 1st year birds with broad white edges to primary coverts, sometimes retained as narrow edges into 2nd year.

DOWNY YOUNG: black above with 3 pairs of yellow spots laterally on back and rump; buffy white below, with black collar on upper breast; chin, throat and foreneck white; face with complicated pattern of black and pale yellow lines; whitish eyebrows, a black line through eyes and another from bill to black patch on ear coverts, a third line underneath; bill black; legs pale dusky, yellowish in front.

A. s. leucostigma Rüppell. Angola, Zaïre, E Africa, Sudan Ethiopia and Cameroon. Bill, except black nail and culmen, pink; bars and spots on upperparts buff, narrower.

A. s. maclatchyi Berlioz. Gabon lowland forests. Smaller, darker than other races, spots of upperparts much smaller, buff-coloured; bill black with small pink zones near tip and base. SIZE: wing, 220. WEIGHT: ♂ (2) 1081 (Todd 1979).

Field Characters. A dark brown duck with white or buff-spotted upperparts, dark bill (with or without pink patches), orange legs. Longish tail and shortish neck give impression of elongated, low-swimming duck. In flight displays blue-green speculum. Spotted upperparts diagnostic.

Voice. Recorded (2a, 6, 17, 26). Contact calls given by lone birds in flight and on land or water. ♂ utters Repeated-calls 'weep . . . weep . . . weep', less noisy than Persistent-quacking of ♀. Persistent-quacking also given by ♀ when pair in flight together. Decrescendo-calls directed by ♀ towards ♂ consist of relatively few notes (5–8) and decrescendo is often poorly defined. In Mutual-greeting ♀ utters loud double calls (usually 4) 'ga-ga, ga-ga, ga-ga, ga-ga' and ♂ responds with irregularly spaced peeping calls. Pairs also give flight-intention calls, increasingly loud, rapidly repeated notes, 'ka ka ka ka . . .', by ♀ and rapid peeping calls, 'pee-peep, pee-peep, pee-peep . . .' or 'pepepepepe . . .', by ♂ (McKinney *et al.* 1978). In contrast to ♀, ♂ voice weak, almost inaudible.

General Habits. Well known. Sedentary and territorial with permanent home range. Inhabits mostly streams and rivers with stony bottoms in well-wooded valleys; also exposed streams and sponges on mountain plateaux up to *c.* 4000 m; and, to a lesser extent, sandy-bottomed estuaries, dams and shallow pools in open country.

Diurnal; always roosts at night whilst daylight hours are spent mostly feeding, sleeping and preening. Feeds by dabbling, head-dipping and up-ending, especially on stony river-beds in order to remove weeds attached to boulders. Territorial pairs forage only in territory (usually less than 1 ha), whereas non-territorial birds use a much larger area (often more than 890 ha) (Ball *et al.* 1978).

Before nightfall throughout year in SW Cape (and presumably elsewhere) moves from rivers to large open waters, especially dams, to roost, returning to rivers early morning. Ducks involved are mostly single birds and juveniles, a few pairs without territories, and, occasionally, territorial pairs, greatest numbers recorded summer and autumn, Oct–Mar. During 30 min before nightfall fights take place between ♂♂ and between ♀♀ involving groups of 2–4 birds any age, with aerial pursuits occurring. Interactions decline with onset of darkness.

Body, tail and wing moults occur regularly in alternating cycles. Exact duration of flightless period unknown, but observations on wild birds indicate limited flight capability *c.* 25–26 days from start of moult. ♂♂ begin wing moult *c.* 1 month before ♀♀, who start only after brood reared, sometimes delayed by late broods until mid-summer.

Food. Mainly vegetable matter and chironomid larvae and pupae. Small fish, e.g. *Barbus trimaculatus* up to 10 cm long and *Salmo gairdneri* up to 20 cm long recorded in wild and at fish hatchery respectively (Milstein 1977a), but normally daily fish intake probably small.

Breeding Habits. Well known. Solitary nester on or just above ground on riverbank or stream-edge. Pair-bonds long-term or permanent.

Characteristic *Anas* courtship behaviour rare, some displays completely lacking. Grunt-whistle, Head-up-tail-up displays used rarely by ♂♂ courting ♀♀. Head-flick, Drink, Swimming-shake, Wing-flap and Head-dip also recorded, mostly at dusk. ♀♀ may give prolonged bouts of quacking, approach and associate with calling ♂♂ (differing in this respect from other *Anas* spp. in which ♂♂ are primary mate-seekers). Mild preliminary actions performed by birds competing for mates include Feather-erection, Wing-raising, and prolonged Swim- and Walk-offs. Once pair-bond established, ♀ greets ♂ by producing loud 'ga-ga' call with bill open, head and neck stretched toward him. ♂ shows little overt interest in ♀; may respond by lowering head and giving peeping calls or may give open Bill-threat.

Mated birds territorial throughout year with territories 200–700 m along stretch of river, held for several years; only territory-holders attempt to breed. Pairs are highly intolerant of intrusion by other adult Black Ducks but will tolerate young white-bellied birds (Frost *et al.* 1979). When rebuffing intruder, pair may first perform Swim-off or Walk-off, or closely approach while performing noisy Mutual-greetings. ♀ may advance towards intruder in hunched posture, swimming alongside and forcing it to veer away (see **A**). Other deterrent actions include bill-rubbing movements on chest, false sleeping postures and ritualized head-dipping/feeding movements.

A

Aggressive expulsion flights also used to warn off outsiders, these involving maximum of 4 birds and mostly observed prior to breeding season, reaching peak June. When fighting, pair and rival stand erect in water attempting to grasp each other by back of neck while delivering repeated blows with both wings (**B**). Encounters last several minutes, causing birds to bleed at carpal joints, and end when one flees by diving, hiding in vegetation or flying off.

B

Copulation initiated by either sex. Pre-copulatory behaviour may include (1) ♂ rushing at ♀ and roughly pecking at base of her neck; (2) ♀ assuming Prone-posture in front of ♂; (3) both performing vertical pre-copulatory Head-pumping; (4) Crash-diving, in which 1 or both suddenly submerge with open wings and much splashing for several seconds, then surface some metres away. ♀ may surface in Prone-posture, whereupon ♂ mounts. On dismounting, ♂ may perform Bridling after fashion of Mallard *A. platyrhynchos*. ♀ remains in Prone-posture or bathes. Mutual-greetings occurs after ♂ has displayed. Rape and Rape-intent flights not recorded (McKinney *et al.* 1978).

NEST: frequently placed in flood debris on river bank or in matted grass on ground, thickly lined with down (3 nests examined contained 1115, 579 and 517 down feathers, and 11, 5 and 2 contour feathers respectively: Siegfried 1964a). Presumably built by ♀ only.

EGGS: 4–8, laid at 24-h intervals; South Africa mean (42 clutches) 5·9. Smooth, slightly glossed, elongated; light cream to buff-yellow. SIZE: (27 eggs) 57·3–65·5 × 40·2–48·8 (63·5 × 45·0). WEIGHT: (5, captive birds) 66·5–71 (68) (J. Kear, pers. comm.).

Laying dates: SW Cape July–Dec, peak Sept; Zimbabwe, Zambia May–Aug; Malawi Apr–Aug, peak July; Zaïre Feb, Apr–June; Tanzania Nov; Kenya Dec–Feb, June–July, Oct; Uganda (Ruwenzori region)

Nov–Jan, (northern region) Dec–Jan, May–Aug; Ethiopia Jan–July.

Incubation by ♀ only; eggs covered with down when absent. Period: 28 days.

Advanced young develop as follows: tail feathers emerging day 21; primaries and secondaries day 30; also juvenile down; scapulars erupted by day 39 (appearance at this stage untidy); down shed days 40–70, then largely feathered; day 86 plumage fully developed.

Young usually only accompanied by ♀, who may bring them back to nest at night or in bad weather. ♂ remains in home range, joining ♀ and young on night roost; rarely accompanies them during day.

References
Johnsgard, P. A. (1978)
Siegfried, W. R. (1968a, 1974).
Siegfried, W. R. et al. (1977a, b).

Plate 17

(Opp. p. 290)

Anas acuta Linnaeus. Northern Pintail. Canard pilet.

Anas acuta Linnaeus, 1758. Syst. Nat. (10th ed.), p. 126; Sweden.

Range and Status. Palearctic winter migrant south to Nigeria, Chad, Sudan, Kenya; resident, occasionally breeding, Morocco, Tunisia. Visitors common to abundant seasonally throughout most of range: Algeria av. 8000 recent years (Jacobs and Ochando 1979); W Africa in Senegal Delta 80,000 Jan 1971, 55,000 Jan 1972, 90,000 Jan 1974 (Roux 1973, 1976), 52,500 Jan 1981 (Dupuy and Fournier 1981); Mali, internal Niger Delta, 27,000 Jan 1972, 75,500 Jan 1974 (Roux 1976), 495,000 Jan 1978 (Sanigho 1978); very abundant also Nigeria, Niger, Chad (5600 Dec 1971: Roux 1976), S Sudan; Ethiopia common to abundant plateau lakes, mountain tarns to 3600 m (Moreau 1972; Urban and Brown 1971); Kenya few hundred to c. 1000 major waters recent years (Meadows, in press); also Uganda, Tanzania, rarely Rwanda, Burundi (K. Curry-Lindahl, pers. comm.); stragglers to Zambia, Zimbabwe, Transvaal.

Description. *A. a. acuta* Linnaeus, ADULT ♂: entire head, throat, upper neck, nape and hindneck black-brown except for vertical white stripe behind ear, this descending and widening into white foreneck, breast and belly; upperparts, nape to uppertail-coverts, and flanks, vermiculated grey; upper scapulars black, elongated lower scapulars with black centres, cream edges; long, pointed tail black, edged white; undertail-coverts black with broad, cream-buff band in front;

Anas acuta

upperwing grey-brown, speculum metallic green, glossed bronze and shading to black at rear, rich buff border in front, white at trailing edge; underwing-coverts off-white. Eye yellow-brown to yellow; bill pale blue-grey, nail, base and strip over culmen black; legs and feet grey, webs black. ADULT ♂ (eclipse): as adult ♀ but upperparts greyer, more uniform. ADULT ♀: generally as other *Anas* ♀♀, somewhat paler and greyer; flanks with bold crescentic marks; belly whitish; speculum browner than that of ♂, buff bar reduced; legs and feet green-grey. SIZE: wing, ♂ (20 specimens) 267–282 (275), ♀ (12) 254–267 (260); tail, ♂ (8) 172–189 (179), ♀ (7) 95–113 (104); culmen, ♂ (55) 47–56 (50·9), ♀ (31) 44–51 (46·7); tarsus, ♂ (40) 40–45 (42·6), ♀ (30) 39–43 (41·0); length, 51–66 cm (excluding 10 cm long tail feathers of ♂; wing-span 80–95 cm. WEIGHT: ♂ 550–1300, ♀ 400–1050.

JUVENILE: as adult ♀ but darker above without pale feather edges; more heavily streaked, spotted below; cheeks, sides of neck paler; bill dark grey.

DOWNY YOUNG: crown, nape, eye-stripe, irregular cheek-stripe, upperparts, tail and thighs sepia-brown; eyebrow, stripe below eye, cheeks, rear of wing, patches on sides of back and rump, all underparts, white, some buffy tinge to head areas; eye brown; bill dark grey-horn, nail and base of lower mandible flesh-coloured; feet olive-grey.

Field Characters. Long-necked, long-tailed duck. ♂ with distinctively patterned plumage, long pointed tail; unmistakable. ♀ has shorter tail than ♂; separated from other *Anas* ♀♀ by more slender proportions, and from ♀ Mallard *A. platyrhynchos* and Gadwall *A. strepera* by bill colour and less warm, greyer plumage. In flight, white underbody, white trailing edge to secondaries and pale wing-linings, pointed wings and tail diagnostic.

Voice. Recorded (2a). Similar to Mallard. ♂ utters 'geeeeee' call, long, drawn-out, rising and falling as neck is raised and lowered during Burp-display, usually with soft flute-like whistle at peak of movement. Other whistles given during Water-flick, Head-up-tail-up and Bridling-displays. ♀ gives Decrescendo-call, series of deep, loud quacks with decreasing amplitude and pitch; Inciting-call, rattling or chuckling sounds described variably as 'arrrrrrrrr', 'RARRerrerr' and 'kuk-kuk-kuk-kuk-kuk' ('kuk' notes also uttered during flock disputes); Repulsion-call, harsh, deep, cackling 'kak-kak-kak-kak'; Distraction-call, 'gaak', 'keek-keek', or softer 'kee-kee' when with brood.

General Habits. Well known. In N Africa frequents sheltered coastal estuaries and nearby inland waters, also some sub-Saharan lakes, e.g. Iriki, Morocco, where perhaps several hundred pairs breed some years. Marked annual fluctuations all regions, main flocks arriving N and W Africa Oct–Nov, month later in east, departing Feb–Mar. Birds ringed Russia, recovered Tunisia, Mali, Chad, Nigeria; Finland, Algeria; Senegal, France, Italy, USSR. Pre-flight signals chiefly Head-shakes or Head-thrusts with soft calls; fly regularly, sometimes to great heights. Birds generally shy, wary, inactive by day, feeding nocturnally. Flocks roost on water, or on land if undisturbed. Food obtained mainly in depths of 10–31 cm (inland waters), 20–30 cm (coast), by up-ending or by swimming with head submerged, this facilitated by long neck. Will occasionally dive for food or feed on land, digging with bill.

Food. Wide variety of plant and animal materials: seeds, tubers and rhizomes of pondweeds, sedges, docks, various grasses, various algae, cereals, rice, potatoes; aquatic insects, molluscs, crustaceans and amphibians.

Breeding Habits. Little known in Africa, well known in Europe. Nests on ground, usually away from water, nests well spaced or as close as 2–3 m. Monogamous pair-bonds of seasonal duration.

In Communal-courtship (several ♂♂ around single ♀) major displays include Chin-lift, Burp, Water-flick and Head-up-tail-down, these introduced by Upward-shake. Burp often alternates with Chin-lift, this being a Threat-display in which bill is rapidly raised and lowered with stretched neck, accompanied by loud calling. Water-flick accompanied by whistle, no grunt. Aerial-pursuit flights, often initiated by ♀, similar to those of other *Anas* spp., but may last over 1 h, cover many kilometres, and often take place high in sky. Flight frequently ends with ♀ descending rapidly, often far from water; rape or attempted rape by 1 or more ♂♂ follows. ♂♂ also harass ♀♀ on ground, ♀ may take short evasive flight or take refuge in cover. Paired birds carry out most comfort movements together, Preen-behind-wing being most ritualized action. Exploratory-flights by pair over nesting cover occur morning, evening. Prior to copulation ♀ first assumes Prone-posture on water, ♂ responds by Head-pumping. Post-copulatory display of ♂ usually Bridling. Each pair characteristically occupies large home-range overlapping with other pairs; joint use of restricted feeding areas frequent, thus no territorial defence takes place.

NEST: on ground in low cover, sometimes on bare ground; distance from water usually *c*. 200 m or as much as 1–2 km; also recorded near water. Slight hollow, sometimes lined with vegetation, always with down; built by ♀ only from immediately available materials.

EGGS: 6–12, laid at 24 h intervals; Finland mean (39 clutches) 8·3. Ovals; yellowish white to yellowish green. SIZE: (75 eggs) 48–60 × 36–42 (55 × 39). WEIGHT: (81, captive birds) 34–50 (42) (J. Kear, pers. comm.).

Laying dates: Morocco, Tunisia Apr–June.

Incubation begins on completion of clutch, by ♀ only, but ♂ often close by.

Fledging period 40–45 days, independent about this time. First breed at 1 year, some in 2nd year.

Young cared for by ♀, ♂ sometimes in attendance in early period. Brooded by ♀ while small and defended using distraction displays.

Anas erythrorhyncha Gmelin. Red-billed Teal; Red-billed Duck. Canard à bec rouge.

Plate 16
(Opp. p. 227)

Anas erythrorhyncha Gmelin, 1789. Syst. Nat., 1, p. 517; Cape of Good Hope.

Range and Status. Resident Ethiopia and S Sudan to E Africa, S Zaïre and southwards to Cape; Angola records mostly coastal. Considered most abundant duck in southern Africa (Siegfried 1970a); e.g. Witwatersrand, S Transvaal, 1200; Barberspan, W Transvaal, 4712 (Sept 1975); Kafue Flats, Zambia, 29,000 Aug 1971 (Douthwaite 1977); Lake Ngami, Botswana, 500,000 (Smithers 1964); common to abundant elsewhere within its range in suitable habitat.

Description. ADULT ♂: top of head from bill and below eye dark brown, this extending downwards behind ear-coverts, over nape and rear neck; rest of head from sharp division below eye buff-white, an increasing amount of brown speckling invading ear-coverts posteriorly and upper neck; upperparts, including scapulars, dark olive-brown, narrowly, but clearly, edged cream-buff; neck speckled brown, sometimes almost solid brown; breast and underparts to vent buff-white, all feathers with dark brown crescentic centre-patches giving heavily speckled appearance, boldest on flanks; upperwing dark olive-brown; speculum, covering entire secondaries and tips of secondary coverts pinkish buff, a narrow black line inset from leading edge. Eye umber brown; bill bright carmine-pink with brown culmen-ridge and nail; legs and feet slate-grey. Sexes alike. SIZE: wing, (6 ♂, 6♀) ♂ 218·5–228 (223·8), ♀ 207–216·5 (211·5); tail, ♂ 81·5–90 (85·1), ♀ 74–80 (76·3); culmen, ♂ 42–46·5 (44·3), ♀ 41·5–47 (43·5); tarsus, ♂ 35–37 (36·0) ♀ 30–37 (33·4); length, 43–48 cm. WEIGHT: ♂ (1366) 345–954 (591), ♀ (1177) 338–955 (544).

Anas erythrorhyncha

JUVENILE: similar to adult but duller, underparts less white, more buffy, bill dull brownish pink.

DOWNY YOUNG: top of head, nape and upperparts dark olive-brown; over either side of back and lower rump 2 small primrose yellow panels; face pale yellow-buff, a brown streak running from lores, through eyes, to back of head, dark smudge on ear-coverts; below pale buffy yellow with olive-brown extended down over flanks; wings dark olive-brown, trailing edge fringed primrose.

Field Characters. A smallish, petite duck with bright red bill, dark brown cap contrasting with whitish face, dark brown upperparts and pale underparts; in flight creamy speculum obvious. Distinguishable from Hottentot Teal *A. hottentota* by red bill, larger size.

Voice. Recorded (2a, 6). Not very vocal. ♂ utters soft, swizzling 'whizzzt'; ♀ a loud 'quaaaak'. Utterances during display include Burp by ♂; a soft 'geeeee', and a trembling 'gueggeggeggegge' by Inciting ♀. Other ♀ calls are Persistent-quacking as in Yellow-billed Duck *A. undulata* but quieter, and Gesture of repulsion, a quiet whistle. All ♀ calls similar to those of Yellow-billed Duck but softer, audible only at close range.

General Habits. Well known. Occurs especially on open, shallow, fresh waters containing large amounts of submerged, floating and peripheral vegetation; lakes, marshes, flood plains, large dams and other similar impoundments. Throughout range, peak gatherings occur towards end of dry season or at start of rains. In Orange Free State and Barberspan, W Transvaal, numbers lowest during rains, peaks usually Sept–Oct (late dry), but may remain at high level if summer dry. In Zimbabwe numbers peak following years of above average rainfall. Highly social, flock sizes from few hundred to many thousands. Sedentary, with local, short distance movements; also partly nomadic population, dry season movements of which incompletely understood. Birds ringed Barberspan recovered south as far as Cape Town (*c.* 1126 km), northwards to Kafue Flats, a similar distance, and NW to Santa da Bandeira in Angola (*c.* 1800 km), many other recoveries over shorter distances in all directions (Dean 1977). Birds ringed in Zambia recovered South Africa, Zimbabwe, Botswana and Namibia. In Kenya numbers peak in northern winter, birds arriving from unknown sources to supplement large resident population; thought to come from north or northeast (Meadows, in press). Usually feeds in pairs or small flocks, largely nocturnally during rains. At low flood levels birds take aquatic invertebrates by day, leaving the area to graze on aquatic herbs by night.

Food. Mostly aquatic plants, seeds, fruits, stems, rhizomes and invertebrate animal life, this differing by season. On Kafue Flats, Zambia, during temporary summer flooding mid-Nov–mid-Feb, sample of 8 crops contained 45% (dry weight) animal matter, 32% vegetable (mainly leaves), 23% seeds. From mid-Feb until floods recede (sample 28) seeds comprised 85%, other vegetable matter, mainly rhizomes 10%, animal matter 5%. Principal animal matter molluscs, crustaceans and beetles. Percentage occurrence of food in oesophagi of 23 non-breeding adults (Barberspan, W Transvaal)

76% animal matter, 24% plant material. At Barberspan birds tend to leave at sunset *en masse* to feed on maize spilled during harvesting (Skead 1977b).

Breeding Habits. Well known. Nests singly on ground in thick vegetation near water.

Courtship displays typically *Anas* in character, many being close to those of Yellow-billed Duck, although less conspicuous. Communal courtship occurs mostly early mornings, with some activity at sunset. Groups of 3–15 ♂♂ and 1 ♀ slowly mill about on the water; a single bird will swim away from flock, others all follow, it then turns and swims back through flock with no apparent display. ♂ Leading, Burp and Chin-lifting displays occur infrequently, the latter a hostile display, which may culminate in Attacks or Fights, while aerial displays in the form of the usual Group-flights occur mostly at the start of and during breeding. Inciting is only ♀ display recorded during Communal courtship, this is a stiff-necked display when ♀ is being closely followed by ♂♂ which often attempt to Lead the Inciting bird. Copulatory behaviour involves mutual Head-pumping, sometimes by 1 sex only; this rapid, members of pair usually fairly far apart. When ♀ adopts Prone-posture, ♂ quickly swims to her and mounts. Copulation time 6–18 s, after which ♂ Bridles (see **A**), then swims away short distance from ♀ (**B**) while she Bathes.

A

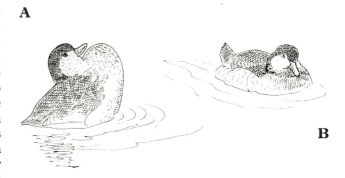

B

NEST: lush grass, rushes, reeds or other waterside herbage; always close to water. Built by ♀. Starts as bowl-shaped depression in vegetation where ♀ lays 1st egg; immediately available vegetable matter then collected by her while on nest, sides added to gradually as clutch is laid, longer grass or other herbage pulled down as canopy over nest. Day before clutch completion few down feathers added to nest, greater quantity of down plucked from ♀'s breast, and some contour feathers added immediately following clutch completion. Structure 15·3–17·7 cm wide by 6·4–10·2 cm deep; down lining 1·3–3·8 cm thick.

EGGS: 5–12, laid at 24 h intervals; SW Cape mean (12 clutches) 10. Smooth ovals; buff or cream coloured. SIZE: (69 eggs) 46·0–54·1 × 35·1–41·0 (50·5 × 37·8). WEIGHT: (20 eggs, SW Cape) 36–40 (38).

Laying dates: SW Cape June–Nov, peaking Oct–Nov (winter rainfall); Transvaal Nov–May, peaking Apr (summer rainfall); Botswana Dec, Mar (2 records); Namibia Jan; Zimbabwe all months except Oct, Dec, peak Jan–Apr (summer rains); Zambia Dec–May, peak Jan–Feb (summer rains); Malawi Feb–Apr; Tanzania

Mar–May (following main rains); Kenya Jan–Aug (following main rains, extending into dry season); Ethiopia Oct, possibly Mar–July.

Incubation begins with completion of clutch, by ♀ only. ♂ remains nearby, joined by ♀ when she leaves nest to feed or preen. ♀ leaves nest normally twice daily between 07.00 h and 10.00 h and between 16.00–18.00 for periods of 30 min to 2 h, av. time (39 observations) 1·5 h morning and afternoon. Eggs first covered with down and grass. Eggs turned on av. every 40 min by means of bill and feet; ♀'s sitting position changed at least every 30 min. When flushed from nest ♀ readily performs 'broken wing' display. If surprised will defecate on eggs when flushing (Siegfried 1962b).

Chicks 1st contour feathers emerge as blood sheaths days 11–17 after hatching. 1st feathers begin to grow in regions of flanks, tail, scapulars and breast. Feathers emerge on forehead, cheek, crown, throat and nape almost simultaneously at *c.* week 3; remiges appear weeks 3–4. Flight possible at *c.* 8 weeks. Juvenile plumage undergoes continual change until 1st wing moult when bird acquires full adult appearance.

Some paired birds maintain a long bond, others a short one. ♀ with brood accompanied by ♂ occurs most frequently on waters where conspecifics absent; generally ♂ does not accompany brood. South Africa mean brood size, 7·2 at 0–1 week (26 broods) and 5·9 at 1–3 weeks (30 broods).

References
Dean, R. J. and Skead, D. M. (1979).
Siegfried, W. R. (1962b, 1974).
Skead, D. M. (1976).

Anas hottentota Eyton. Hottentot Teal. Sarcelle hottentote.

Plate 16

Anas hottentota Eyton, 1838. Mon. Anat. p. 129; Western coast of South Africa near Orange River, Cape Province.

(Opp. p. 227)

Range and Status. Resident from Ethiopia southwards to eastern Cape; extend westwards only via northern Botswana to Namibia, 1 record E Angola; isolated breeding population northern Nigeria and Chad. Very abundant Kenya during northern winter and especially during local dry years; Tanzania present in thousands Lake Kitangiri June, Aug–Oct 1955 (C. D. W. Savage, pers. comm.); Ruzizi marshes, Zaïre and Burundi, common May, Oct–Feb; Kafue Flats, Zambia, small numbers all year, increasing slightly Oct–May with max. 500 Dec–Mar; South Africa uncommon to locally common.

Description. ADULT ♂: top of head from bill blackish brown forming distinct cap from below eye, extending down nape to upper rear neck as narrow line; rest of head, including chin, throat, upper neck, buff-white, patch of dusky mottling behind ear-coverts and over upper neck to hindneck. Mantle and anterior scapulars dark brown, broadly fringed with grey-buff giving scaled effect; long scapulars blackish shot with metallic blue, inner web with dull buff shaft-streak; lower back and rump glossy black, feathers narrowly fringed buff; lower rump and uppertail-coverts pale buffy brown, finely vermiculated black; tail with outermost feathers light buffy brown, finely peppered blackish brown, remainder of feathers dark brown, edged paler. Entire underparts buff-white, washed vinaceous, feathers with dark brown centres giving spotted effect on breast and sides, becoming barred on belly; long flank plumes plain buff; undertail-coverts pale buff, heavily vermiculated black; upperwing-coverts blackish brown shot with dull metallic green and blue; primaries and coverts blackish, secondaries with basal two-thirds bright metallic green forming speculum, this merging into black, trailing-edge white; underwing with axillaries white; underwing-coverts along edge of wing blackish, rest white. Eye dark brown; bill grey-blue, under mandible darker, culmen ridge and nail blackish; legs and feet blue-grey. ADULT ♀: underparts less buff, belly not barred; speculum less extensively green, more brown; bill duller. SIZE: (27 specimens, ♂ and ♀) wing, 149·5–157 (152·2); tail, 55–63 (59·3); culmen, 32–37·5 (35·5); tarsus, 26–29 (27·1); length, 33–35·5 cm. WEIGHT: ♀ (3) 216–282 (243) (Skead 1977b).
JUVENILE: as adult ♀ but duller.

Anas hottentota

DOWNY YOUNG: sepia brown on upperparts except for buff-yellow, broken, horizontal stripe above eye; chin, throat, cheeks and neck to nape buff-yellow except for oblong patch of sepia brown on lower cheek; on sides of body 3 buff-yellow oblique stripes; undersurface from neck to tail light buff; bill grey; nail flesh pink; feet grey.

Field Characters. Smallest African duck; dark-capped, dark-backed with spotted breast, buffy underparts and grey-blue bill. When swimming flank feathers frequently overlap wing forming distinct zig-zag line at junction. Green speculum edged white noticeable; underwing white. Differs from Red-billed Teal *Anas erythrorhyncha* mainly in having bluish, not red bill.

Voice. Recorded (1d, 21b). During courtship ♂ emits 3–5 soft metallic notes in quick succession, like clock ticking; used in Head-up posture, also in first movement of Burp. This call also given by both sexes when disturbed. When disturbed ♂ or ♀ may also emit harsh 'ke-ke' or 'ke-ke-ke', or resonant 'tze-tze' or 'tze-tze-tze'. This primarily a ♀ call, heard in flight, at take-off, prior to settling, or in social groups when 'ke' or 'tze' sound repeated 5–7 times, reducing in intensity with successive notes.

General Habits. Very well known. Favours shallow freshwater marshes and ponds fringed with reeds or papyrus with floating leaf-plants; also sewage pans. Occasionally large open waters devoid of emergent vegetation.

Most active early mornings and evenings, resting middle of day. Frequently rests out of water, sleeping with head tucked into scapulars or bill resting on breast, often standing on 1 leg, in discrete groups or mixed duck assemblies. Food obtained mainly by swimming with bill immersed, but also by swimming with head immersed, up-ending and walking with bill immersed.

Sedentary or makes movements of apparently only local nature. In Kenya annual influx thought to originate from north and northeast (Meadows, in press). In Tanzania thousands Lake Kitangri June and Aug–Oct 1955 (C. D. W. Savage, pers. comm.). On Kafue Flats, Zambia, small numbers present all year, these increasing slightly Oct–May with peak Dec–Mar when maximum of 500 seen; 6 ringed birds recovered within 260 km, 2 others recovered northern Botswana 500 km and 700 km southwest.

Wing moult recorded Aug–Sept (Zambia).

Food. Invertebrates, seeds and various other vegetable matter, seasonal differences marked. On Kafue Flats, Zambia, vegetable matter predominates when waters are high and stabilized late Nov–May, e.g. 55% seeds and fruits, 36% animal matter and 9% vegetable detritus. When water levels fall (June–Nov), animal matter increases to 92%, with seeds and fruit only 4% and vegetable detritus 4%. Principal animal matter crustaceans, gastropods, coleopteran adults, dipteran larvae and pupae.

Breeding Habits. Well known. Nest in clump of vegetation over water, singly, but sometimes closely spaced.

Communal courtship occurs any time of year; in groups of 1 ♀ and 2 or more ♂♂. Displays include Burp, Wing-flap, Drinking, Threat and occasionally Swimming-shake. When ♂ makes aggressive approach to ♀, she takes to air with rest of group following. Flight lasts up to 5 min; group may resettle in same place when more Burp displays and Wing-flaps follow, sometimes precipitating Flight again. Paired birds exhibit 3 types of behaviour: (1) ♂ threatens ♀, swimming quickly towards ♀ with bill open; ♀ makes no counter-move but swims off side by side with ♂; (2) both perform Head-pumping while swimming; (3) ♀ Incites—head moved up, forward and back, sometimes directed over shoulder, the forward movement mostly directed at unwanted ♂. Pre-copulatory behaviour involves mutual Head-pumping (emphasis on downwards movement with bill tilted slightly down). After copulation ♂ may leave ♀ without displaying or may give Swimming-shake, a delayed Wing-flap coinciding with same action in ♀, or a Burp prompted by presence of other ♂♂. ♀ usually Bathes; may perform Swimming-shake and/or Wing-flap.

NEST: in clump of *Typha* or *Phragmites* reeds, in *Cyperus cyperoides* sedge or other emergent vegetation with leaves from surrounding plants pulled down to form dome, leaving entrance hole or tunnel with ready access to water. Lined with large amounts of dark brown down, capable of covering eggs with layer 25 mm thick; when bird incubating, down pushed aside to form girdle around inside of nest bowl. Structure *c.* 150–180 mm across top of bowl; placed 150–760 mm above water, av. *c.* 500 mm over water 380–500 mm deep. Share of sexes in nest-building unknown.

EGGS: 6–9, laid at 24-h intervals; Zimbabwe 6–9 (5 nests); Transvaal 6–8, mean (7 clutches) 7·1. Cream or yellow-buff. SIZE: (Witwatersrand) 43·2–45·6 × 33·0–33·5 (44·2 × 33·3); (26, Zimbabwe) 41–48 × 31–34 (44·0 × 32·5) (Thomas and Condy 1965). WEIGHT: (7, captive birds) 26–30 (28) (J. Kear, pers. comm.).

Laying dates: South Africa all months, peaking (Witwatersrand) Jan–Apr (wet season); Zimbabwe Apr–May, peaking May, also Aug (dry season) (Boulton and Woodall 1971); Malawi June–Aug (dry); Zambia Dec–Sept (late rains and dry season); Kenya Feb, June–Oct (dry season) (Brown and Britton 1980).

Incubation begins with completion of clutch; by ♀ only. Period: 25–27 days (Witwatersrand). Covers eggs with down before leaving nest; if disturbed may defaecate on eggs on leaving. Leaves in mornings for approximately 1 h; ♂, who remains close by during incubation, joins ♀ when she calls on leaving nest and both go off to feed. When pair meet ♂ greets ♀ with Burp or by Drinking.

Broods, Witwatersrand, 1 to 7, usually 3. ♀ conceals ducklings in reedbeds. ♂ sometimes accompanies ♀ with brood (twice in 17 observed broods; Siegfried 1974). Weight of young, 1 day old (11 captive chicks), 14–17 (16) (J. Kear, pers. comm.).

References
Clark, A. (1969b, 1971).
Douthwaite, R. J. (1977).
Thomas, D. D. and Condy, J. B. (1965).

Anas querquedula Linnaeus. Garganey. Sarcelle d'été.

Plate 17

Anas Querquedula Linnaeus, 1758. Syst. Nat. (10th ed.), p. 126; Sweden.

(Opp. p. 290)

Anas querquedula

Range and Status. Palearctic migrant mainly to northern tropics. In N Africa present Nov and especially Feb as trans-Saharan passage migrant. In Ethiopia locally rare to common (Eritrea commonest passage migrant Aug–Oct and Apr). Kenya common Nov–Mar/Apr, total annual wintering population estimated at 20,000 (Meadows, in press). W Africa from S Mauritania–Senegal to Chad abundant Sept–Mar (Jan 1971 and 1972 numbers estimated at 200,000 and 135,000 Mali delta, 93,000 and 94,000 Senegal delta). Small numbers south to Zambia, Malawi; vagrant to Zimbabwe, South Africa.

Description. ADULT ♂ (breeding): forehead and crown to below eye black-brown; mantle to uppertail-coverts black-brown, feathers edged and barred pale; tail black with grey bloom, feathers edged white; from in front of eye to nape a broad, tapering, curved white stripe; cheeks and foreneck golden brown, flecked white; chin and throat with black patch; breast and sides of upper mantle pink-brown, barred black (crescent-shaped marks) sharply divided from vermiculated grey flanks and white belly; undertail white with dark brown bars and spots; scapulars elongated, drooping, striped grey, dark green, black and white; forewing pale blue-grey; speculum green, edged white, broadest in front; underwing with dark leading edge. Eye dark brown; bill grey-black; legs and feet dull grey. ADULT ♂ (eclipse): as adult ♀ but brighter, belly and throat whiter. ADULT ♀: entirely buffy brown with darker streaking and blotching; dark brown crown and eye-stripe contrasting with pale patch at base of bill and pale eyebrow; underparts white; forewing greyish; speculum green-brown; bill green-grey. SIZE: wing, ♂ (34 specimens) 190–211 (198), ♀ (16) 184–196 (189); tail, ♂ (28) 60–73 (66·1), ♀ (17) 58–69 (62·6); culmen, ♂ (70) 38–43 (39·6), ♀ (34) 36–40 (38·0); tarsus, ♂ (38) 29–33 (31·3), ♀ (20) 28–32 (30·1); length, 37–41 cm; wing-span, 60–63 cm. WEIGHT: (USSR, June–July) ♂ (13) 320–430, ♀ (6) 290–350.

JUVENILE: like adult ♀ but underparts mottled and streaked with brown.

Field Characters. Small, slender-necked, flat-crowned duck; ♂ with conspicuous white eye-stripe on dark brown head, white flanks contrasting with brown breast distinctive. ♀ and eclipse ♂ speckled brown, similar especially to Green-winged Teal *A. crecca* and Gadwall *A. strepera* but crown of Gadwall darker, facial markings more prominent, a shorter-necked more compact duck. In flight combination of small size, blue-grey forewing and white-bordered green speculum diagnostic, as is dark leading-edge from below.

Voice. Recorded (22b). Main call of ♂ mechanical-sounding, strident 'klerrep' or 'rrar . . . rrar . . . rrar' like stick being drawn across railings, this produced in broken bursts on water, land or in flight, especially during courtship rituals. ♀ has number of calls: pre-flight a harsh 'gack', tempo increasing just before take-off; alarm call 'krrrt'; Inciting-call disjointed series of single 'gaeg' notes; Decrescendo-call a rapid series of quacks.

General Habits. Well known. Occurs mainly shallow fresh waters to *c.* 2600 m in Ethiopia; normally avoids coastal regions except when migrating, favouring sheltered waters with low emergent vegetation, e.g. water-lilies, water-grass, also flooded grasslands, deltas. Feeds day or night, usually whilst swimming with head submerged, sometimes up-ending. Flocks often dense, well co-ordinated, in flight manoeuvring with speed and agility, often close to water. Surprisingly, therefore, no pre-flight signal has been identified (Johnsgard 1965). Rises easily from water, flying with rapid wing-action.

W African populations originate Europe and Russia, travelling via Spain, Italy, or straight over Mediterranean, apparently do not linger N Africa. In east, birds seen moving south-southwest near Alexandria across Red Sea and off tip of Sinai; regular autumn passage recorded Ethiopia.

Communal courtship common in winter quarters where majority form pairs. ♂♂ swim in Courtship-intent posture, windpipe bulging in throat, while performing Ceremonial-drinking, Upward-shakes, Wing-flaps and Mock-preening (especially Preen-behind-wing in which conspicuous blue wing-patch briefly displayed on side nearest ♀). Major displays become more frequent as display bout progresses, Burp-drink performed in varying degrees of intensity. In simple form ♂ raises head slightly, calls, drinks, while in most elaborate version head is flung back so that crown touches lower back, bill pointing up, then rapidly returned to starting position after call is given. This Laying-head-back display unique in *Anas*, superficially similar to Head-throw in pochards. ♂ responds to ♀ Inciting with Turn-back-of-head while Leading. ♀♀ also Preen-behind-wing and, if particularly responsive to ♂ display, may also perform ♂-like Laying-head-back.

Food. Insects and larvae, especially waterbugs, caddis-flies, waterbeetles, Chironomidae midges; also molluscs, crustaceans, worms, leeches, frog spawn, tadpoles and fishes. Also a variety of aquatic plant material, buds, leaves, roots, tubers and seeds. In Senegal *Nymphea* seeds 26%, wild *Graminea* 39%, Cyperaceae 15%, rice 10% and Characae oogoniums 7% (Treca 1981).

Plate 16
(Opp. p. 227)

Anas smithii (Hartert). Cape Shoveler. Canard du Cap.

Spatula smithii Hartert, 1891. Kat. Vogelsammlung Mus. Senckenberg. Naturforschendengesell. Frankfurt, p. 231; Cape Province.

Range and Status. Resident southern Africa. Most common or abundant SW Cape Province, Orange Free State, Transvaal; uncommon E Cape, Natal and arid NW; Botswana common NW region only; Namibia uncommon; Angola rare; Zimbabwe uncommon, south only; vagrant Zambia (D. R. Aspinwall, pers. comm.), Zaïre, Tanzania (K. Curry-Lindahl, pers. comm.). Old reports for N Africa, Ethiopia, Kenya suspect; pair recorded Morocco Apr 1978 (Duff 1979) probably escapees.

Anas smithii

X Vagrant

Description. ADULT ♂: head, neck and underbody dull off-white, all feathers with dark brown central patches (except pure white throat) giving all-over mottling, fine on head and neck, darker, streakier on crown; underparts dark brown, feathers edged and faintly barred cinnamon; tail dark brown, outer feathers edged cinnamon; primaries brown; speculum blue-green, broadly edged white; upperwing-coverts conspicuous pale grey-blue; underwing pale brown, secondaries tipped white. Eye light yellow, more intense when breeding; bill black, longer than head, flat, broad and spatulate with long bristle-like lamellae conspicuous as mandible fringes; legs and feet yellow, orange-yellow when breeding. ADULT ♀: slightly smaller, paler, less contrasty; head darker, ventral and dorsal body surfaces mottled brown; speculum (without white surround) and blue shoulder-patch duller. Eye dark sepia; bill dark grey; legs and feet yellow-grey. SIZE: (32 ♂♂, 26 ♀♀, live specimens) wing, ♂ 222–253 (238·1), ♀ 208–238 (226·4); tail, ♂ 63–98 (76·4), ♀ 61–81 (69·9); culmen, ♂ 56–65 (60·6), ♀ 52–60

(56·5); maximum bill width, ♂ 28–32 (30·4), ♀ 26–31 (28·3); tarsus, ♂ 37–43 (41·1), ♀ 34–41 (38·0). WEIGHT: ♂ 584–830 (688·3), ♀ 467–691 (597·8) (SW Cape: Siegfried 1965); ♂ (27 specimens) 522–680 (603), ♀ (24) 492–665 (572) (Barberspan, W Transvaal: Skead 1977b).

JUVENILE: similar to adult, but duller.

DOWNY YOUNG: upperparts dull olive-brown, darker over crown and nape, broad pale yellow lines on back near wings and tail; sides of head pale buff, a dark streak from bill through eye extending to nape, darkish patches on cheek extending to ear-coverts; underparts pale yellow-white. Eye dark brown; bill black with reddish tip; legs and feet dusky.

Field Characters. Medium-sized, dull grey-brown duck with long spatulate bill; swims with forepart of body deeply sunk, bill pointed downwards. Rises almost vertically from water; flies fast (70 km/h) displaying pale blue wing-patches, head and neck held in downward slope, wings appearing to be set far back on body. Could be mistaken for ♀ or eclipse ♂ Northern Shoveler *A. clypeata* in rare circumstances of range overlap; probably inseparable in flight.

Voice. Recorded (2a, 6). In non-breeding season ♂ utters single, loud, 'rrar'; ♀ gives Decrescendo-call, or 1 long note followed by up to 14 short ones. Calls associated with early courtship are: (1) in ♂♂, Repeat Call, series of quiet hoarse cries with rising inflection, 'cawick' or 'po-huk'; these sometimes interspersed with Fast-calls, a machine-gun-like rattling, 'rararararara'; (2) in ♀♀, a many-syllabled rippling chatter, rising in pitch when Inciting, similar call used when with brood and threatening other ducks; and (3) by either sex, a hoarse 'chachachacha' during Hostile-pumping. During copulation ♂ makes rhythmical, wheezy 'th' or 'cuay' sounds. Following copulation ♂ may utter single, loud nasal call followed by several quieter calls. Paired ♀♀ give Persistent-quacking, after being flushed during the pre-laying period or during laying; may continue for several minutes. In sample of 8 counts, rate was 62 notes in 37·5 s or 1·7 quacks/s (McKinney 1970). Downy young utter typical *Anas* distress calls but faster (1-day-old chicks gave c. 8 calls/s; J. Kear, pers. comm.).

General Habits. Well known. Gregarious, usually occurs in small groups when not breeding. Seldom associates with other species; if in mixed flocks maintains discrete group. Does not disperse when disturbed and seldom flies in heterogeneous company with other species. Essentially bird of fresh water but tolerates tidal estuaries, saline lagoons, pans. Prefers temporary sheets of open, shallow water and marsh remaining after flooding. Common on highly alkaline waters (pH 10), sewage disposal ponds where water fertility high; seldom on deep lakes, swift-running waters, farm dams and reservoirs except as temporary refuge.

Food obtained day or night mostly by surface-dabbling, head and neck stretched forward, bill submerged while duck paddles along rapidly. Other methods include submerging head completely and swivelling neck back and forth, occasionally immersing forebody as far as shoulders, but not lifting tail; sweeping bill from side to side; snapping at insects; up-ending occasionally; diving rare. Co-operative swimming circle, peculiar to shovelers, frequently used; 2–7 birds swim in circle close behind one another, each feeding from water stirred up by bird ahead. Occasionally dabbles in bottom mud or sand at water's edge and in shallows; young birds observed up-ending near shoreline over beds of semi-submerged vegetation.

Most numerous in SW Cape winter rainfall region in winter–spring (May–Sept), reverse applying Orange Free State and Transvaal summer rainfall regions. Nomadic and subject to restlessness (Siegfried 1965), but no clear pattern of movements. Some south–north movement indicated, this subject to variation dependent upon irregular climate of central parts of South Africa (D. M. Skead, pers. comm.). South African birds recovered Namibia, up to 1680 km away (K. Curry-Lindahl, pers. comm.).

During post-nuptial moult birds retire to large, open waters rich in natural foods. Bird flightless *c.* 30 days; SW Cape July–Dec (peak Oct–Nov); W Transvaal mainly Oct–Dec, Apr–July, also Jan. When in moult swims particularly low in water. If disturbed makes for open water; if chased dives and swims submerged, sometimes revealing only head and bill between dives.

Food. At SW Cape (summer/autumn) mainly animal matter, including snails, insects, crustaceans and *Xenopus* tadpoles; also leaves, stems and seeds of water plants including *Potamogeton pectinatus* (Brand 1961). At Barberspan, W Transvaal, only aquatic insects and crustacea (D. M. Skead, pers. comm.). Juveniles feed mainly on aquatic insects for 1st 3 weeks after hatching.

Breeding Habits. Well known. Monogamous, pair-bonds apparently seasonal, although evidence suggests some mated birds stay together longer (Skead 1977b). Nests on ground singly; nest-crowding not uncommon where suitable sites scarce, i.e. in semi-arid northern parts of breeding range and on islands of SW Cape waters (Siegfried 1965); 31 nests recorded on 1 island *c.* 190 m².

Pair-formation entails various displays in air, on water, or on land (Siegfried 1965; McKinney 1970). Displays mostly simple and typical of genus, mainly in form of Head-pumping. Frequent courtship actions are: (1) Lateral-dabbling, in which ♂ dips bill into water in series of dabbling actions with back and flank feathers raised, speculum sometimes exposed,

while laterally positioned to ♀; (2) Jump-flights, in which 1 ♂ emerges from courting group (several ♂♂ and 1 ♀), swimming few metres in front of ♀, turning broadside to show himself and continually trying to lead her away. All other ♂♂ attempt same action while keeping pace with ♀; leading ♂ suddenly flutters into air with slow wing-beats making muffled fluttering sound, wing colours in evidence, inducing ♀ to follow; (3) Group-flights, typically composed of 1 ♀ and small group of ♂♂, often follow Jump-flights; ♂♂ constantly jostle for best position to display wing colours to ♀.

Courtship in paired birds or pair-bonding actions typical of *Anas* species with few variations. These include: (1) Turn-back-of-head; (2) Display-feeding, in which Head-pumping ♂ approaches ♀, uttering low guttural calls before both swim in circle, head to tail, bills straining water; (3) Swimming-shake; (4) Washing-and-diving, in which ♀ follows ♂ after Mutual Head-bobbing in underwater swim (duration *c.* 5 s); may be followed by leap-frogging on surface, dashes, vigorous Bathing and Wing-stretching, and nodding or swimming in unison; (5) Expulsion-flight, in which territorial ♂ chases single or mated birds into air; (6) Hostile Head-pumping, by pairs or territorial ♂, usually directed at intruding conspecifics (may lead to fighting). Preen-dorsally, Preen-behind-wing and Bathe-and-wing-flap occur rarely. Rape seldom successful; territorial ♂ usually repulses intruding ♂, ♀♀ also fight and repulse attacker. Pre-copulatory behaviour as in other *Anas* spp.

♂ and ♀ prospect for nest-site together, but ♀ chooses this. Site determined more by abundance of suitable food than by available cover. Prefers areas near very fertile, shallow water rich in *Daphnia*. Of 191 nests, 82·2% placed in vegetation not exceeding 30·5 cm high. 93% of nests recorded (SAOSNRC) built less than 10 m from water, none more than 100 m. At De Hoop Vlei, 72 nests placed on islands, 26 in open veld (grassland), 11 in pastures, 3 on embankments. At Cape Flats, where few islands available, 50 nests were in pastures, 12 on embankments, 11 on islands, 6 in open veld (Brand 1961).

NEST: constructed by ♀ from shallow scrape clawed in earth 2–10 days prior to egg-laying. Following 1st egg nest is built-up from grasses surrounding immediate site, increasing in size as more eggs laid. During nest-building and egg-laying ♂ remains nearby and accompanies ♀ whenever off nest. Down from ♀'s breast added to sides, but not base of nest during egg-laying, greatest amount added following final egg. While sitting ♀ bends any surrounding vegetation inwards to form canopy over nest; this present in 21·7% of 112 nests studied at De Hoop Vlei Cape. Nests in SW Cape not well concealed, nest destruction by mammalian and, to lesser extent avain, predators consequently high (32·9% of 91 nests). In contrast nests at Barberspan, W Transvaal, generally well concealed, even in low grass (D. M. Skead, pers. comm.).

EGGS: 5–12, laid 24-h intervals, usually between 08.00 and 10.00; mean 9·36. Cream, tinged green. SIZE: (350 eggs) 48·4–59·5 × 36·6–41·1 (53·4 × 38·7). WEIGHT: (85, captive birds) 34–43·5 (38) (J. Kear, pers. comm.).

Laying dates: Barberspan, W Transvaal, all months of year, peaking Jan, Apr, Aug–Sept; De Hoop Vlei, SW Cape, Aug–Nov, peaking Sept; Cape Flats July–Dec, peaking Oct.

Incubation by ♀ only, begins when clutch complete. Period: 27–28 days. ♀ leaves nest twice daily for periods of over 60 min, but frequency and duration of absences lessens as incubation proceeds. In early stages, when leaving nest voluntarily, first covers eggs with down, then leaves inconspicuously. If surprised, springs off suddenly, leaving eggs uncovered, and expels foul-smelling liquid excrement over them. May alight on water nearby and feign injury. Liable to desert nest if disturbed by man in early stages of egg-laying. More tolerant of disturbance later in incubation but will desert as result of flooding.

Young hatch at short intervals; brood remains in nest until dry (1–2 days) unless disturbed, whereupon immediately led to water. Av. chick weight at hatching (71 captive young) 30·0; week 6 (60) 458·9; week 12 (60) 528·0. Plumage development in 1st 8 weeks (captive birds): week 1·5–2 down already faded, lighter patches appearing; week 4·5–6·5 predominantly feathered, patches of down still present; week 8 completely feathered, able to fly. From c. week 10 1st immature plumage moulted. Complete moult cycle takes c. 20 weeks.

Chicks cared for by ♀. When in danger may lead young to dense cover and then perform injury-feigning. Known to brood very small young under wing in cold weather. Some ♂♂ continue to associate with mates for limited period while ducklings are small; isolated records of brood-accompanying ♂♂ driving off conspecific ♂♂. Hatching success: De Hoop Vlei, SW Cape, 89·6% (448 eggs); Cape Flats, 96·1% (355 eggs).

References
Brand, D. J. (1961, 1964).
McKinney, F. (1970).
Siegfried, W. R. (1965, 1974).
Skead, D. M. and Dean, W. R. J. (1977a, b).

Plate 17
(Opp. p. 290)

Anas clypeata Linnaeus. Northern Shoveler. Canard souchet.

Anas clypeata Linnaeus, 1758. Syst. Nat. (10th ed.), p. 124; Sweden.

Range and Status. Palearctic migrant to Africa north of equator, particularly N, NE and E Africa. Mid-season counts recent years Algeria 1975, 1977–1978 av. 8000 (Jacobs and Ochando 1979); Ethiopia up to 6000 along 4 km of Lake Abiata shoreline, most abundant duck there; Kenya dry period minimum estimate 22,000, mainly Lake Naivasha, appreciably less wet years (Meadows, in press). W Africa fairly common (Morel 1972); Senegal Delta 6600 1973 (Morel and Roux 1973); 13,200 Jan 1981 (Dupuy and Fournier 1981); Mali (Central Niger Delta) 2230 Jan 1978 (Sanigho 1978); Lake Chad 10,500 1970 (Roux 1970). Stragglers south to Zambia, Malawi, Botswana, Zimbabwe, Namibia mostly singles, South African records largely suspect (Clark 1977).

Description. ADULT ♂ (breeding): entire head dark green; centre of mantle dark sepia, feathers edged white on upper mantle, olive-grey on lower; outer scapulars white, longer ones with blue outer webs, blackish inner webs; inner scapulars blackish with green gloss, longer ones with broad white shaft-streaks; back and rump with blackish centres; tail dark olive-sepia, feathers edged white; neck, breast, sides of mantle white; flanks, underparts and vent chestnut, separated from black undertail-coverts by white band; upper forewing bright pale blue, separated from green speculum by white bar, primaries and coverts brown; underwing-coverts white. Eye yellow to orange; large spatulate bill lead black; legs and feet orange. ADULT ♂ (eclipse): as ♀ but upperparts darker, flanks more rufous, forewing and speculum brighter, eye yellow. ADULT ♀: very similar to other *Anas* ♀♀ but distinctive wing pattern as in ♂; large bill olive-grey or dark brown, sides yellow-brown; eye brown to straw-colour; legs as ♂. SIZE: wing, ♂ (27 specimens) 239–249 (244), ♀ (18) 222–237 (230); tail, ♂ (26) 76–86 (81·7), ♀ (15) 72–80 (75·8); culmen, ♂ (61) 62–72 (66·1), ♀ (47) 56–64 (60·7); tarsus, ♂ (48) 35–40 (37·2), ♀ (39) 35–38 (36·0); length, 44–52 cm; wing-span, 70–84 cm. WEIGHT: (USSR and Netherlands, Oct–Nov) ♂ (2) 560–950, ♀ (3) 600–800.

JUVENILE: as adult ♀, upperparts more uniform, underparts streakier; wing brighter in ♂; eye sepia to grey-brown; bill olive-brown, sides orange-brown; legs and feet yellow to orange.

Field Characters. Spatulate bill distinguishes both sexes, all age groups. Breeding ♂ further distinguished by green head, white breast, chestnut flanks. Heavy-bodied, short-necked ducks which swim with forebody low in water. In flight blue forewings, green speculum edged white in front, plus large bill and wings set

Anas clypeata

well-back, diagnostic, Possible confusion only with Cape Shoveler *A. smithii* in rare cases of range overlap. ♀ or eclipse Northern Shoveler paler, more rufous, bill larger; may be inseparable in flight unless bill sizes apparent.

Voice. Recorded (22b). Weak, not easily heard. Most common note uttered by ♂ quiet 'took', plus louder, nasal 'paay' and wheezy 'whe' or 'thic'. These used singly or in series in variety of situations, faster and louder in Threat and during pair-formation. ♀ gives Decrescendo-call, 1–4 long notes each with downward inflection in descending pitch followed immediately by 3–9 shorter single quacks 'gack-gack-gack-ga-ga-ga...', last 2 notes muffled; great variation in duration and pattern; various 'quack' calls, given singly or in series in other situations; Inciting-call, rapid, rippling chatter, rising in pitch as head raised.

General Habits. Well known. Favours mainly fresh, mud-bottomed shallow waters rich in invertebrate life, typically in open grassland, from sea level to 2900 m in Ethiopia. Gregarious in Africa, flocks usually of 20–30, or several hundred in favoured areas; roosts communally, nocturnally. Food collected mostly by surface dabbling, neck stretched forward, sweeping surface with side to side movements of bill to filter small organisms. Also feeds while swimming with head and neck immersed, up-ending and diving. Single birds or small groups also swim together surface-feeding in small circles, head to tail.

Main pre-flight signals lateral Head-shaking and vertical Head-thrusting in erect posture, facing into wind. From *c.* Jan ♂♂ start to assemble in courting parties, *c.* 12 ♂♂ to 1 ♀. Displays simple, easily overlooked, ♂♂ attracting ♀'s attention with lateral body displays—Lateral-dabbling (dabbling as when feeding), Head-dip (submerging head and neck briefly) and Up-end (immersing entire front of body)—all with back and flank feathers erected, blue speculum partially exposed. May also adopt lateral Head-high posture with series of Repeated-calls. Non-lateral displays by ♂ include Leading and Jump-flights, latter producing rattling wing noise and speculum display. Inciting, close to preferred ♂, main ♀ pairing display.

1st arrivals Africa Oct, greatest numbers late Nov to early Dec, greatest concentrations many regions Jan. Ringing recoveries indicate birds N Africa originate Europe, E Russia; W Africa mainly from Europe; Egypt, and NE and E Africa probably mostly from USSR. Main return movements Feb–early Mar; small numbers remain throughout northern summer, in Ethiopia at least (Urban 1970).

Food. Various invertebrates, also vegetable matter. Main items: crustaceans, molluscs, insects and larvae (caddisflies, waterbeetles, dragonflies, flies), seeds of aquatic plants, duckweed. To lesser extent: annelids, amphibian spawn, tadpoles, spiders, fish and vegetative parts of plants.

References.
Clark, A. (1977).
Moreau, R. E. (1972).
Morel, G. J. (1972).

---

2 other *Anas* spp. winter vagrants to Africa (not illustrated). These are:

Anas americana Gmelin. Eurasian Wigeon. Canard siffleur d'Amerique.

Senegal (Roux *et al.* 1976–77). Adult ♂ resembles European Wigeon *A. penelope* but forehead and crown white, green patch round and behind eye and hindneck; vermiculations on mantle, scapulars and flanks pink and dark grey. Adult ♀ almost indistinguishable from ♀ Wigeon except head and neck greyer; axillaries white.

Anas discors Linnaeus. Blue-winged Teal. Sarcelle soucrourou.

Recorded Morocco (Cramp and Simmons 1977) and Senegal (Roux *et al.* 1976–77). Adult ♂ with conspicuous white crescent-shaped mark in front of eye; forewing blue. Adult ♀ like Garganey *A. querquedula* but has bluer forewing, larger dark bill and yellow legs.

Not illustrated

Genus *Marmaronetta* Reichenbach

Although markedly like a dabbling duck in appearance, this monotypic genus exhibits aberrant features and behaviour more akin to *Aythya* than *Anas*. Bill long and narrow, high at base; crest feathers elongated; pochard-like displays; and lacks metallic speculum.

Marmaronetta angustirostris (Ménétriés). Marbled Teal; Marbled Duck. Sarcelle marbrée.

Plate 16

Anas angustirostris Ménétriés, 1832. Cat. Rais. Obj. Zool. Recueillis Voyage Caucase, p. 58; Lenkoran, Caspian Sea.

(Opp. p. 227)

Range and Status. Resident and non-breeding visitor to N Africa, non-breeding visitor to Sahara, NW and W Africa. Numbers highly irregular, unpredictable: 1500 maritime Morocco 1964; 125 Morocco 1972; 361 Algeria Jan–Feb 1975 (only 31 same months 1978). Apparently present Tunisia Palearctic summer,

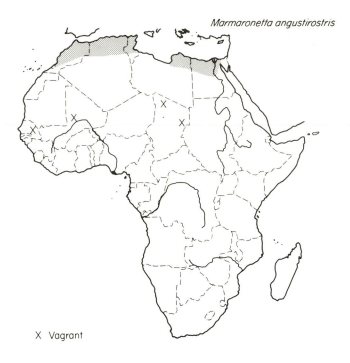

Marmaronetta angustirostris

X Vagrant

deserting in winter, no breeding recorded since 1968; Egypt small numbers only in winter. Occurs in south and west of Sahara in variable numbers (1500 on temporary flood south of Tafilalet May 1970); very small, but regular numbers Senegal, Nigeria, Mali, Chad. Rarest Palearctic dabbling duck, numbers greatly decreased since 19th century throughout its range.

Description. ADULT ♂: generally grey-brown, all feathers having cream-coloured centres, dark grey-brown edges, giving overall spotted effect; paler below; dark smudge extends from front of eye to nape; nape feathers elongated to form pendant shaggy crest; secondaries pale brown fading into grey-brown tips; primaries pale silver-grey; no speculum. Bill blackish, base dull grey-green, a pale transverse line near tip; eye brown; legs and feet green-brown, webs blackish. ADULT ♀: as ♂, but slightly smaller, crest smaller or absent, a dull olive-green triangular patch basally at sides of upper mandible. SIZE: wing, ♂ (9 specimens) 195–215 (207), ♀ (10) 186–206 (198); tail, ♂ (4) 67–73 (69·8), ♀ (3) 67–68 (67·7); bill, ♂ (9) 42–47 (44·2), ♀ (11) 35–40 (37·4); length, 39–42 cm; wing-span, 63–67 cm. WEIGHT: (India) ♂ 535–590, ♀ 450–535.
  JUVENILE: like ♀, but duller, markings ill-defined.
  DOWNY YOUNG: crown, narrow streak through eye, hindneck, upperparts and thighs dark fawn-brown; streak over eye, hindneck, rest of head, underparts and ill-defined patches on wing and sides of back and rump pale buff-yellow; eye brown; bill and feet green-grey.

Field Characters. A small, pale grey-brown duck marbled with cream spots, and with dark eye-patch, blackish bill. Differs in these diagnostic features from Cape Teal *A. capensis*, with which in extreme south of range overlaps. Lack of speculum diagnostic in flight.

Voice. Recorded (2a). Few calls weak and seldom used. Main call of ♂ heard in courtship display and following copulation, a nasal squeak 'eeeeep'. ♀ call similar to that of ♂; also weak, high-pitched whistling 'pleep-pleep'; no Decrescendo-call in ♀.

General Habits. Little known in Africa. Gregarious, ♂♂ gathering together to moult on breeding grounds even when ♀♀ incubating; larger flocks are of both sexes other times, except possibly pre-breeding. Migratory and dispersive, movements little understood. Birds ringed Coto Doñana, Spain, recovered NW Morocco, others at least partially sedentary N Africa. Seasonal and periodic displacements enforced by fluctuating water levels otherwise less migratory than *Anas* spp. Occurrences in many regions apparently dictated by availability of suitable habitat (small or medium-sized, shallow, well vegetated freshwater pools). Frequents floodlands, brackish, saline or alkaline lagoons, reservoirs, irrigation networks and slow-flowing rivers, foraging on banks and even in fields, but location influenced by preference for instant access to shelter in fringe vegetation. Obtains food by dabbling in shallow water on surface and in vegetation; also up-ends and dives, or grubs in shore mud.

Food. Seeds, tubers, shoots of aquatic plants, worms, molluscs, aquatic insects and larvae.

Breeding Habits. Little known. Nests singly, on ground under bushes and in thick vegetation, never far from water. Observations of captive birds suggest pair-bonds are re-formed each autumn and winter, so birds probably already paired on arrival at breeding grounds.

Communal courtship behaviour in captive birds occurs over long period between autumn and spring; in wild birds has been seen Jan and Mar. ♂ displays differ considerably from those of most *Anas* spp., being more akin to those of pochards. These include general Body-shake, Bill-shake, and sequence of Neck-stretch, pause, and quick withdrawal of head downward and backward into scapulars while uttering a weak 'eeeep'. ♀♀ may also perform Neck-stretch sequence. ♂♂ often extend heads and necks forward over water towards another bird, and turn backs of heads towards Inciting ♀♀ as they swim ahead of them. Inciting behaviour in ♀♀ consists of threatening 'rushes' directly towards another bird, followed by a rapid swim back towards mate or potential mate. Decrescendo-call is apparently lacking. Both sexes perform Display-drinking, generally as prelude to copulation rather than as part of basic pair-forming patterns. Prior to copulation both birds of pair perform series of Bill-dipping, Bill-shaking and Dorsal-preening displays, often in synchrony or near-synchrony. After treading, ♂ calls once with head fully extended diagonally, then draws head back, points bill downwards and swims in partial circle around ♀ (Johnsgard 1965).

NEST: slight depression in ground under bushes, in thick, dry grass. Constructed of dry grasses and lined with small amount of down; built by ♀ only.

EGGS: 7–14, laid daily. Oval; pale straw-coloured. SIZE: (100) 42–51 × 32–36 (46 × 34) (Schönwetter 1960). WEIGHT: (100 eggs, captives) 25·5–34·5 (29).

Laying dates: Tunisia mostly May–June (Jarry 1969); Senegal (1 record) Apr (Dupuy and Sylla, in press).

Incubation carried out by ♀. Period: 25–27 days from completion of clutch.

Young are active, self-feeding. Cared for by ♀, brooded when small. Age at 1st breeding, 1 year.

Genus *Netta* Kaup

Medium-sized pochards with bodies, bills and legs longer and narrower than in *Aythya* species. Take off from water with some difficulty, but gait on land less clumsy, stance more upright than that of *Aythya*. Less well adapted to diving than other pochards. Plumage colours variable in ♂♂, but glossy purple-black or blue-black breasts and red eyes common to all. ♀♀ similar, dull brown with few distinctive markings. 3 species, 2 in Africa.

Netta rufina (Pallas). Red-crested Pochard. Nette rousse.

Plate 16

(Opp. p. 227)

Anas rufina Pallas, 1773. Reise Verschiedene Provinzen Russischen Reichs, 2, p. 713; Caspian Sea and lakes of the Tartarian Desert.

Range and Status. Palearctic winter migrant Morocco to Egypt, least common towards east. Small numbers may breed infrequently Morocco, Algeria, Tunisia, Libya, but status uncertain; rare on Nile, occasionally south to 25°N.

Description. ADULT ♂ (breeding): head with short bushy crest rich golden chestnut, paler and more golden on crown; upperparts and wings dull brown to grey-brown, a white crescent, sometimes concealed, on shoulders; back black; tail dull brown; neck, breast, central belly-stripe and vent black; flanks white, upper flanks barred brown; upperwing with broad white stripe along leading edge to beyond carpal joint; secondaries and primaries white, often tinged pink; central area of wing and tips of flight feathers dull brown. Eye red; bill deep pink to bright vermilion, nail pink; legs and feet orange-red to vermilion, joints and webs dull black. ADULT ♂ (eclipse): resembles ♀ but differs in having red bill, red eye, larger looking head with bushier crest, greyer body and whiter wing-stripe. ADULT ♀: top of head from below eye, nape, rear neck dark brown with sharp division from grey-white lores, cheeks, ear-coverts and upper throat; upperparts otherwise dull light brown; underparts light brown, upper breast darker; belly, vent grey-white; flanks barred whitish; upper wing-pattern similar to that of ♂, leading-edge stripe narrower, duller; underwing, axillaries whitish. Eye red-brown, darker in winter; bill grey, edges and patch near tip pink; legs and feet pink, webs dusky. SIZE: wing, ♂ (16 specimens) 255–273 (264), ♀ (14) 251–275 (260); tail, ♂ (15) 67–76 (70·6), ♀ (15) 62–74 (68·4); culmen, ♂ (25) 45–52 (48·2), ♀ 42–50 (46·6); tarsus, ♂ (25) 42–47 (44·1), ♀ (26) 40–45 (42·2) length, 53–57 cm; wingspan, 84–88. WEIGHT: (USSR, Feb ♂ 900–1170 (av. 1135), ♀ 830–1320 (av. 967).

JUVENILE: very similar to adult ♀, but darker, underparts more mottled, though this soon lost. Rudimentary crest gives ♂♂ larger-headed appearance, bills become pink in 1st winter.

DOWNY YOUNG: crown, hindneck and upperparts including sides of body olive-brown; spots on wing, flanks and rump pale yellow; rest of head from above eye, and entire underparts pale yellow; flanks tinged grey, belly and vent white; eye dark brown; bill dark brown, tip pink; legs and feet dark grey.

Field Characters. Large, rounded chestnut head of ♂ with pink bill, black breast and underparts, brown upperparts and white flanks unmistakable; in flight bold white span-wise stripe on leading-edge of wing, white flight feathers and underwing diagnostic. ♀ at rest or swimming resembles ♀ or juvenile Black Scoter *Melanitta nigra*, but has longer, less squat bill, generally paler appearance, whiter face. In flight pale facial patch and upperwing stripe diagnostic.

Voice. Recorded (22b). Rather silent except in courtship. ♂ utters hoarse, repeated 'bät' on water or in flight; also 'chru' or harsh, resonant 'chik' repeated 4–5 times. During courtship and as a warning, ♂♂ utter

Netta rufina

quiet 'geng', usually in phrases, several notes one after the other. Sneeze call is loud, rasping wheeze resembling stifled sneeze. ♀♀, 2 main calls, both variable. 'Gock' or soft 'guk-guk'; and a grating 'kurr' or 'kur-r-r'.

General Habits. Little known in Africa, well known in Europe. Seeks quiet waters and large lagoons with protective vegetation, usually avoiding sea. Roosts day or night, usually on water, but sometimes on shore, never far from water's edge. When alarmed, stretches neck vertically and calls continuously.

Food obtained by diving, dabbling on surface, upending and foraging with head immersed. Feeds mostly early mornings and evenings, mostly in 2–4 m of water; dives last 6–10 s, maximum recorded 13·7 s.

Food. Mainly stems, leaves, roots, seeds and buds of aquatic plants, occasionally aquatic insects and larvae, small fish, tadpoles and spawn, also crustaceans and molluscs.

Breeding Habits. Little known in Africa, well known in Europe. Nests usually well dispersed, though sometimes as close as 30 m; situated on ground in dense vegetation close to water.

Communal courtship occurs throughout winter, usually on water, involving several ♂♂ crowding around single ♀ and following her. 4 major ♂ displays: (1) in

Sideways-sneeze ♂ withdraws neck, lowers head, turns it in direction of ♀ with quick lateral movements of head, jerks crown towards ♀ while uttering Sneeze-call with bill open. (2) In incomplete Sneak-display ♂ lowers crest, points bill towards ♀ while stretching neck out over water and gives nasal call. (3) In Neck-stretch ♂ elevates head and raises crest while calling. (4) ♂ ceremonially leads ♀ while performing Turn-back-of-head. Antagonistic behaviour between ♂♂ involves (1) Forward-display with head and neck stretched horizontally above water, bill open; (2) Attack-intent with head held low and thrust forward as Threat-call is given; and (3) Threat, in which bird rushes across water at opponent. ♀ Incites by alternately threatening rejected ♂♂ with exaggerated forward tossing of head in their direction and repeatedly turning in Neck-stretch posture towards favoured ♂, this accompanied by calling. Secondary displays include Courtship-drinking,

Bill-dipping, Upward-shake, Head-flick and Wing-flaps. Intensive swimming chases, during which ♂♂ perform Sideways-sneeze, frequently followed by Pursuit-flight, several ♂♂ chasing single ♀ in air.

Courtship-feeding, unique to species, occurs in well-established pairs with ♂ diving and bringing up food. Presents this to ♀, waits for her to swim to him, or places it on water in front of her; also performs Preen-behind-wing and Ceremonial-drinking during courtship. Pre-copulatory behaviour by ♂ involves Bill-dips, Head-flick, Preen-dorsally (see **A**), followed by Head-pumping; ♀ usually Head-pumps (**B**), then gradually assumes Prone-posture, body and tail low in water, neck stretched forward diagonally. After copulation ♂ performs single Sideways-sneeze directed at ♀, then swims round in Bill-down posture. ♀ typically bathes.

NEST: under bush or in dense vegetation, sometimes on matted reed island in water. Simple depression on ground lined with grass, leaves, rushes and down, 28–45 cm across by 10–20 cm deep. Built by ♀ only, using materials within reach.

EGGS: 6–14 (av. 8–10; up to 39 recorded in dump nests); laying interval unknown. Broad, rounded; cream-yellow or pale green. SIZE: (150) 53–62 × 39–45 (58 × 42). WEIGHT: (101, captive birds) 47–60 (56) (J. Kear, pers. comm.).

Laying dates: Algeria May–June.

Incubation begins when clutch complete, by ♀ only. Eggs covered with down when ♀ off nest. Period: 26–28 days.

Young self-feeding, cared for by ♀, brooded while small. Fledging period: 45–50 days; are independent c. same time. 1st breeding can take place at 1 year old, but usually 2.

Plate 16
(Opp. p. 227)

Netta erythrophthalma (Eyton). Southern Pochard; Red-eyed Pochard. Nette brune.

Anas erythrophthalma Wied, 1832. Beitr. Nat. Bras. 4, p. 929; eastern Brazil.

Netta erythrophthalma

Range and Status. Resident southern and eastern half of Africa north to Ethiopia; common to abundant altitudes up to 2400 m. Flocks 800–5000 W Cape, 7500 Kafue Flats, Zambia, 1300 Lake Naivasha, Kenya. South African populations known to undertake local and long distance migrations.

Description. *N. e. brunnea* (Eyton), ADULT ♂: plumage glossy. Forehead, crown, nape and hindneck blackish; scapulars, back, dark umber-brown finely mottled with golden specks; lateral lower back, uppertail-coverts, tail as back; face, side of head, upper neck and throat warm vinaceous brown; rest of neck, breast, lateral breast and underparts to tail blackish; flanks rich chestnut; base of primaries and secondaries white forming speculum bounded posteriorly by brown tips. Bill pale grey-blue, nail prominent, black; eye bright vermilion; legs and feet grey. ADULT ♀: head, crown, nape and hindneck medium brown, tending to bronze; forehead and chin broadly white, extending to lower cheeks, throat and upper neck and from there upwards in broad whitish crescent shape to behind eye; scapulars, back, nape and wing similar to ♂, paler; lower neck, breast and flanks fulvous brown; underparts fulvous mottled or barred white or dull grey-brown. Bill olive-grey, nail darker; eye red-brown; legs and feet grey. No ♂ or

♀ eclipse. SIZE: wing, ♂ (24 specimens) 202–228 (217·5), ♀ (23) 201–221 (208·9); tail, ♂ (28) 52–66 (59·0), ♀ (31) 52–68 (56·5); culmen, ♂ (32) 40–48 (44·0), ♀ (32) 38–49 (43·3); tarsus, ♂ (32) 35–44 (39·6), ♀ (32) 36–44 (39·6); length, 51 cm (Middlemiss (1958b). WEIGHT: ♂ (577) 592–1010 (799), ♀ (463) 484–1018 (763) (Dean and Skead 1979).

JUVENILE: as adult ♀, but colours paler, facial markings less pronounced, ill-defined; ♂ rather darker on lower neck, chest and abdomen.

DOWNY YOUNG: upperparts, crown, sides of chest, sides of thigh, flank-patch above thigh sepia brown with strong olive tinge; a faint brown streak across ear-coverts; forehead, sides of head, rest of underparts pale sulphur yellow. Eye pale grey; bill pale pinkish grey; legs and feet dark olive-grey.

Field Characters. ♂♂ dark, bronze-brown ducks with paler flanks, blue-grey bills and red eyes; ♀♀, paler brown with a characteristic white crescentic mark on sides of head, from eye to upper neck level, and white throat and bill-base, thus differing from ♀ Maccoa Duck *Oxyura maccoa* which has horizontal white facial marks. In flight wings appear to be set well back on body, white speculum extending almost full wing-span.

Voice. Recorded (6). Not highly vocal. ♂ in flight utters 'prerr . . . prerr . . . prerr'; soft, almost hissing, vibrant 'quack'; and croaking, deep and low, 'phreeeooo' associated with Head-throw display. Courtship call 'eerooow' like rapid winding of watch spring. ♀ in flight utters nasal 'krrrrrow' with downward inflection, frequently repeated, and 'quarrrk'; on water same 'quarrrk' made when threatening and harsh 'rrrr-rrrr' when Inciting.

General Habits. Very well known. Adult ♂♂ outnumber ♀♀ 1·4:1 most flocks, juvenile ♂♂ outnumber juvenile ♀♀ 1·6:1 (Dean and Skead 1977). Most active early mornings, evenings, rest of day spent resting on shoreline. Feeds mainly during day, sometimes at night. Food obtained by diving, up-ending, occasionally by foraging at water's edge. May also feed on water's surface with bill or entire head submerged.

Occurs on clear, permanent or temporary waters with or without emergent vegetation, rarely temporarily flooded pans or shallow ponds; seldom seen on land. In South Africa numbers lowest Mar–Aug (dry season), at peak Oct–Nov (early wet season), suggesting existence of 2 populations, 1 migratory. Ringing recoveries suggest dry season movement northwards to Zimbabwe, Zambia, Malawi, Botswana, southern Mozambique and Kenya. In Zambia annual influxes at Lochinvar, Kafue Flats, mid-May; numbers build up Lake Bangweulu after Sept, reaching peak of many thousands Dec. In Kenya peak population occurs northern winter with large influx most years Oct, departing Feb (Meadows, in press).

Wing moult occurs SW Cape after influx of birds from north in Aug–Sept. Birds flightless 1–2 days prior to dropping feathers, and further 1–2 days after development of new sets. Total flightless period *c.* 31 days. During moult flocks keep to open waters or close to beds of emergent vegetation, solitary birds use cover of reeds and sedges. Evasion during moult is by diving, underwater distances of *c.* 100 m recorded, sub-

merged times up to 30 s. If pursued merely surfaces head before diving again.

Food. Primarily seeds of water lilies, bladderwort, duckweeds, bulrushes and similar aquatic or shoreline plants. Also some beetles, snails, ants, crustaceans.

Breeding Habits. Very well known. Nests singly, usually near water, occasionally in grass on land.

Courtship displays include (1) ♂ Courtship-call, in which head, with crown feathers raised to form a peak, is lifted slowly, but not to full extent, and returned to original position while soft 'eerooow' call is uttered. Occurs while ♂ is swimming in courting group; ♀♀ do not react. (2) Head-throw (see **A**) in which head is rolled from withdrawn position back in line with body until back of head touches mantle; then returned. Call similar to Courtship-call is made. (3) Courtship-flights conspicuous; may be precipitated by ♂ rushing aggressively at ♀; ♀ takes off and is followed by 1 or more ♂♂. Lasts 3–5 min, birds may or may not return to point of departure. Principal ♀ display is Inciting, in which head is thrown up and forward to fullest extension of neck and then withdrawn, accompanied by harsh 'rrrr', repeated as ♀ swims. ♂♂ seen to respond by swimming ahead and Turning-back-of-head or display preening behind wing.

A

Copulation is preceded by mutual Head-pumping, ♂ performing occasional dorsal preens. After copulating ♂ swims away in Bill-down posture, feathers on head peaked (A. Clark, pers. comm.).

NEST: in rank waterside vegetation, emergent vegetation over water, or long grass away from water; well hidden, usually with access tunnel through vegetation. Occasionally recorded in exposed positions in sedge, on dam wall, in old antbear hole and in old nests of other waterbirds. Constructed of grasses, sedges or waterweeds, or reeds which are frequently folded down to form bower. Basin-shaped, lined with small, finely textured grey-fawn down and some small feathers; down lining variable, sometimes small amounts only. Size variable, *c.* 17·5–28 cm across by 10–23 cm deep, inner bowl *c.* 18 cm across by 8 cm deep. Nests over water are *c.* 28 cm above surface. Built by ♀ only.

EGGS: 5–15, laying interval unknown; South Africa and Zambia mean (103 clutches) 6·7. Equally rounded both ends; creamy white to light brown with pink tinge, very smooth, slightly glossed, small pitting visible. SIZE: (42) 50·8–59·6 × 40·1–46·5 (56·3 × 43·7). WEIGHT: (19) 59 (Schönwetter 1960).

Laying dates: mainly towards end of wet season. SW Cape Jan, Mar–May; E Cape May–Jan, peaking Sept; Transvaal mainly Dec–Apr, peaking Feb; Orange Free State Feb–June, peaking Feb; Namibia, Botswana Feb–Mar; Zimbabwe Feb–Oct; Zambia Dec–June; Tanzania Apr; Kenya May–July; Uganda Nov.

Incubation begins with completion of clutch, by ♀ only. ♂ not seen near nest during incubation. ♀ usually leaves nest well in advance of intruder's approach, moving unseen through grass tunnels without sound or display. When leaving nest before clutch complete eggs covered with mixture of down and plucked grass, most grass on top, entire layer level with surrounding grass,

providing good camouflage. Incubation period: 20–21 days.

After hatching, young active, led to water as soon as dry, dive well. In danger are able to remain below water against plant stem with head only protruding. Fledging period unknown. Brood normally attended by ♀, but ♂ has been seen with ♀ attending chicks on water.

References
Clark, A. (1966).
Middlemiss, E. (1958b).
Williams, J. G. (1965).

Genus *Aythya* Boie

Typical pochards with short, heavy bodies; large heads; long bills, flattened, wider at tip in some; legs set well back on body; large feet, causing clumsy gait on land; wings broad, less pointed than in typical Anatinae; wing-beats fast; take off from water difficult; good divers. Typical habitats all year standing fresh water 1–15 m deep (Greater Scaup *A. marila* exception, marine in winter); waters with dense marginal vegetation tolerated, even in forests.

12 species in 3 groups: (1) typical pochards, including Common Pochard *A. ferina*, (2) white-eyed pochards, including Ferruginous Duck *A. nyroca*, (3) scaups, including *A. marila* and Tufted Duck *A. fuligula*; 4 species visit Africa in Palearctic winter, 2 species formerly bred N Africa.

Plate 17

(Opp. p. 290)

Aythya ferina (Linnaeus). Common Pochard. Fuligule milouin.

Anas ferina Linnaeus, 1758. Syst. Nat. (10th ed.), p. 126; Sweden.

Range and Status. Palearctic winter migrant N Africa and northern tropics. Formerly bred N Africa. Migrant numbers highly variable, 166,000 Tunisia and Algeria Nov 1971 (Johnson and Hafner 1972); 246 Algeria 1975, 8426 1977 (Jacobs and Ochando 1979). Greatly reduced recent decades W Africa (Moreau 1972), 420 Senegal Jan 1973, 1500 Jan 1981; 400 Mali Jan 1973; 250 Chad

(Roux 1973; Dupuy and Fournier 1981) stragglers to Gambia. Small numbers winter Nile Valley, Sudan, Ethiopia; very small numbers to Cameroon, Zaïre, Uganda and Kenya annually, stragglers to Tanzania.

Description. ADULT ♂ (breeding): head, upper neck uniform chestnut-brown; upper mantle, back and tail black; rest of upperparts vermiculated pale grey; lower neck and entire breast black; flanks and underparts vermiculated pale grey like upperparts, except black vent; upperwing grey with paler stripe running along entire length. Eye bright red; bill dark grey with pale grey band across middle; legs, feet dull grey, webs blackish. ADULT ♂ (eclipse): duller, upperparts all pale, flanks and underparts browner; breast, back, tail region dull brown, not black; eye more orange-red. ADULT ♀: head, neck mainly yellow-brown, variable, darkest on crown; sides of face and ear-coverts paler with dark mottling sometimes on cheeks, throat, a pale streak behind eye; back, scapulars and sides coarsely vermiculated grey-brown; uppertail-coverts dark brown, flecked white; neck and breast yellow–brown, variable, broad white feather-tips, centre of lower breast whiter; under-tail-coverts greyish, well flecked with white; upperwing as ♂; eye red–brown; bill and feet as ♂. SIZE: wing, ♂ (19 specimens) 212–223 (217), ♀ (22) 200–216 (206); tail, ♂ (23) 51–58 (54·2), ♀ (23) 51–57 (53·0); culmen, ♂ (62) 43–52 (47·1), ♀ (47) 42–48 (44·9); tarsus, ♂ (52) 37–42 (39·5), ♀ (47) 36–41 (38·8); length 42–49 cm; wing-span, 72–82 cm. WEIGHT: (France, Dec–Feb) ♂ (119) 585–1240, ♀ (202) 467–1090.

JUVENILE similar to ♀, but generally duller, less grey vermiculation on upperparts, underparts barred or mottled grey, white or buff.

Field Characters. Chestnut head, with black and grey body of breeding ♂ diagnostic, unmistakable. Differs from Red-crested Pochard *Netta rufina* in that head noticeably peaked on crown, grey bill, sloping forehead. In flight grey upperwing with paler secondaries and primaries distinctive; feet protrude beyond tail. Eclipse ♂ can be distinguished by chestnut head with sloping forehead, greyish body. ♀ has same shaped head and grey-banded bill; in flight, upperwing same as ♂. Possibility of confusion with ♀ Southern Pochard *Netta erythrophthalma* where ranges overlap, but Common Pochard ♀ lacks clear white lores and crescentic facial mark of the southern species.

Voice. Recorded (2a). Largely confined to courtship, calls are weak, low-pitched, inaudible at distance.

2 principal ♂ courtship calls: (1) a soft whispered nasal sound 'wiwierr', 'hip-sierr' or 'meeyo-oo-oo' and (2) a louder, triple 'kil-kil-kil' (sometimes 1–2 syllables) descending slightly in pitch. Also a soft, low whistle, frequent soft piping 'quee-week', or soft, whistling half-piping, half-cheeping 'djudjn' or 'djudjidji'. ♀ utters 2 sounds during courtship: (1) 'pack' or 'back', or explosive 'pwook'; and (2) 'brerr' or 'err' call. Also continual 'gagagagag-grA-grA ...' on water in presence of ♂♂, a 'wuk-uk-uk' and 'gurr' given as warning to young.

General Habits. Little known in Africa, well known in Europe. Gregarious, often common to very abundant winter quarters, arriving N Africa Oct–Nov, ♂♂ often preceding ♀♀, sometimes large flocks taking up resi-

dence on fresh and brackish waters, dams, marshes, weirs and lakes, numbers fluctuating annually. Though common in coastal regions, seldom uses marine habitat, preferring fresh to brackish waters. Also occupies suitable habitat at higher altitudes, even Saharien plateaus of Atlas Mountains. Normally prefers open waters several hectares in extent, uncluttered by surface vegetation but rich in submerged plant and animal life. Spends much of day resting on open waters, often in compact groups, seldom ventures far inland from shore-line. When alerted on water, birds stretch necks vertically, tending to swim or dive from danger rather than fly. Pre-flight signals consist of Chin-lifting, Head-flicking. Commonly seen using strong, fast flight at sunrise and sunset.

Feeding mainly nocturnal. Adults dive with or without preliminary jump, sometimes foot-paddling before diving (see also Southern Pochard). Usual diving depth for feeding 1–2·5 m, ♂♂ preferring deeper waters to ♀♀. Av. diving times 15·4 s in 0·9 m; 24 and 28·6 s in 3·0–3·4 m and 3·7–4·0 m respectively. Also feeds by upending, or with head and neck immersed, or dabbles.

Food. Vegetable and animal matter including seeds, rhizomes, buds, shoots, leaves and tubers obtained chiefly by diving; also crustaceans, molluscs, annelids, insects and larvae, frogs, tadpoles and small fish. Young feed on insects, especially flies, and seeds floating on surface.

Aythya nyroca (Güldenstädt). Ferruginous Duck; White-eyed Pochard. Fuligule nyroca.

Plate 17

Anas nyroca Güldenstädt, 1770. Novi Commentarii Acad. Sci. Imp. Petropolitanae, 14 (1769), p. 403; southern Russia.

(Opp. p. 290)

Range and Status. Palearctic winter migrant to N Africa and northern tropics. W Africa variable, irregular, some years totally absent; in east small numbers winter Ethiopia, Sudan, rarely to Kenya. Recent counts: Algeria 6 (1975), 9 (1977), 8 (1978) (Jacobs and Ochando 1979); Senegal 230 (Jan 1972; Roux 1973); Mali 42 (Jan 1972: Roux 1973), 925 (Jan 1978: Sanigho 1978). Marked numerical decline in Africa recent decades. Formerly bred N Africa.

Description. ADULT ♂ (breeding): head, neck and breast reddish brown, almost mahogany; upperparts black-brown, wings glossed dull green; tail brown; small white spot on chin; dark band surrounding lower neck; flanks paler, yellow-brown streaked darker; underparts and undertail-coverts white; upperwing brown with broad white stripe running full span over primaries and secondaries, this bordered by brown trailing edge; underwing mainly white. Eye white; bill slate grey, paler towards tip, nail black; legs and feet olive-grey. ADULT ♂ (eclipse): upperparts duller, olive-brown; breast less rufous; flanks paler; undertail remains white; eye white, thus differing from ♀. ADULT ♀: similar to eclipse ♂ but duller, browner; sides of head, neck, more golden brown; breast duller, darker than ♂; flanks paler; wing as ♂; eye brown; bill leaden-black; legs and feet as ♂, duller. SIZE: wing, adult ♂ (31 specimens) 180–196 (188), ♀ (8) 178–185 (182); tail, ♂ 50–60 (54), ♀ 50–55 (52·7); culmen, ♂ (58) 38–43 (40·3), ♀ (28) 36–40 (38·2); tarsus, ♂ 31–35 (32·7), ♀ (29) 30–34 (32·2); length, 38–42 cm; wing-span, 63–67 cm. WEIGHT: (USSR,

Sept), ♂ (5) 440–540, ♀ (3) 470–540.

JUVENILE similar to adult ♀, but breast duller, less rufous; underparts, and vent, mottled white. Becomes like adult after 1st winter moult, eyes turn grey by Mar in immature ♂.

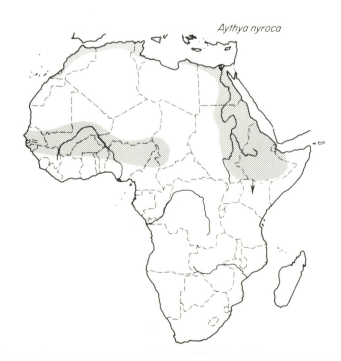

Aythya nyroca

Field Characters. Small, brown ducks with distinctive peaked heads, white vents. ♂ could be confused with ♂ Southern Pochard *Netta erythrophthalma* where ranges overlap, especially as mixing likely, but white eye and vent distinctive. ♀ similar to ♀ or juvenile Tufted Duck *A. fuligula* which, however, has rounded, crested head, white facial patch, no white vent. Flight pattern, with distinctive white wing-stripe, white underwing, belly and vent, similar to those of both Greater Scaup *A. marila* and Tufted Duck but former shows black foreparts, grey back in ♂, white facial patch in ♀ and both lack white vent. Latter species also has dark foreparts in ♂, white facial patch in ♀, and both sexes have dingier wing-stripe and lack white vent.

Voice. Recorded (2a). Mainly associated with courtship. ♂ calls: (1) quiet, soft 'wock'; (2) louder, hoarse 'wück' or 'wückwück'; (3) louder and much rarer 'witt'; (4) Coughing-call, a high-pitched 'WEE-whew'. ♀ calls harsher, louder than ♂'s: 'gek' ('dü' when uttered quietly). Flight calls loud, harsh growling or croaking 'aark', repeated *c.* 2 notes/s.

General Habits. Little known in Africa, well known in Europe. Frequents waters with good natural cover, tolerating heavier vegetation than most Anatinae; secretive and tends to skulk in this habitat much of the time, although larger flocks may frequent more open waters. Not given to flying unless essential. Repeated Chin-lifting only pre-flight behaviour recorded. Not generally gregarious or inclined to mix with other species. Roosts communally, sleeping both on water and on shore, resting during day; most active during evening.

Feeds mainly early morning and evening. Food obtained from water's surface by swimming with head submerged, or by upending or diving. Usually feeds in shallow water with rich littoral vegetation, mostly 20–70 cm deep, but can be up to 1·6 m; dives last 40–50 s, often less.

Arrives Oct–Nov, remaining in N Africa or continuing southwards. Status and movements of resident populations, formerly common (Etchécopar and Hüe 1967), now unclear.

Food. Chiefly various pondweeds and sedges; also small fish and spawn, tadpoles and frogs up to 3 cm long, annelids, molluscs, crustacea and insects, including especially dragonflies, waterbugs, caddisflies, waterbeetles and flies.

Plate 17
(Opp. p. 290)

Aythya fuligula (Linnaeus). Tufted Duck. Fuligule morillon.

Anas Fuligula Linnaeus, 1758. Syst. Nat. (10th ed.), p. 128; Sweden.

Range and Status. Palearctic winter migrant to N, NE and W Africa south mainly to equator; rare straggler to Malawi. Annual counts Algeria *c.* 9000 in 1977 (Jacobs and Ochando 1979); Senegal, Mali, N Nigeria, Chad usually small numbers, e.g. Lake Chad 60, Feb 1963 (Moreau 1972); Ethiopia common to locally abundant, 1000 on 4 km Lake Abiata shoreline Mar 1965 (Urban 1970): Sudan fairly common; Kenya maximum *c.* 1000 (Meadows, in press).

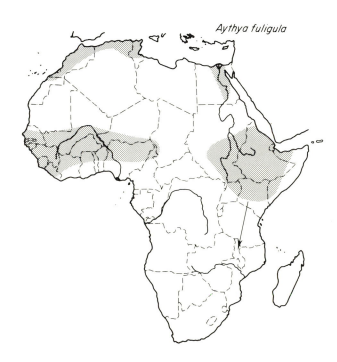

Aythya fuligula

Description. ADULT ♂ (breeding): head including long, drooping crest at back, neck, breast, lateral breast and nape black glossed purple; upperparts black glossed green; tail, vent, undertail-coverts dull black; flanks and belly white; upperwing black with broad white stripe along entire length, dingier towards tips; underwing mostly white. Eye golden yellow; bill pale slate-blue, tip and nail black with pale band anteriorly; legs and feet lead-blue, joints, webs blackish. ADULT ♂ (eclipse) resembles ♀ but dark parts blacker, underparts whiter, lacks white at base of bill. ADULT ♀: variable; head and upperparts dark blackish brown, redder on cheeks and neck, small white patch on lores; breast, flanks, underparts dark brown, yellower on flanks, redder on belly; undertail-coverts dark brown mottled white; wing as ♂; soft parts as ♂, bill sometimes darker. May show white flecking on breast; whiter flanks, belly; larger, whiter patch at bill-base. SIZE: wing, ♂ (46 specimens) 198–215 (206), ♀ (40) 193–205 (199); tail, ♂ (44) 49–58 (53·7), ♀ (39) 48–57 (52·7); culmen, ♂ (66) 37–44 (39·9), ♀ (73) 36–41 (38·6); tarsus, ♂ (40) 34–37 (35·5), ♀ (40) 32–37 (34·7); length, 40–47 cm; wing-span, 67–73 cm. WEIGHT: (France, Dec–Mar) ♂ (343) 400–950, ♀ (700) 450–920; (Netherlands and Denmark, Dec–Mar) ♂ (11) 835–1028, ♀ (8) 738–948.

JUVENILE: similar to adult ♀, less white on lores and undertail; ♂ with blacker head, white flecks on upperparts.

Field Characters. Small, short-necked, compact diving duck with rounded head, loose crest. ♂ black with white side panels, duller in eclipse, yellow eye at all times. ♀ dark brown, flanks paler, patch on lores and undertail-coverts whitish, crest less obvious. ♂ unmistakable, differing from ♂ Greater Scaup *A. marila* in having black back and crest all seasons. ♀ and juvenile similar to ♀ and juvenile Greater Scaup, but darker, especially on back, white patch on lores usually smaller, less clearly defined, and crest present. Flight pattern, especially that of ♀, similar to Greater Scaup and Ferruginous Duck *A. nyroca*, but Tufted Duck markedly smaller than Greater Scaup, smaller-headed, upperwing darker, facial patch smaller, underbody dark, not white as in Ferruginous Duck.

Voice. Recorded (22b). Rather quiet in winter quarters. Courtship calls of ♂ include mellow 'WHEE-oo', and rapid 3-note whistle 'WHA-wa-whew' also as flight call. ♀ with 3 courtship calls 'quack', 'gack', and 'karr', also soft 'kärr' or 'quaark quaark' diminishing in intensity, or 'körr'. Flight-call guttural 'bre-bre-bre'.

General Habits. Little known in Africa, well known in Europe. Prefers sheltered, shallow fresh waters free of floating vegetation. Readily accepts man-made waters and tolerates human presence. Highly gregarious, but flocks frequently of 1 sex. On water very active, continually jump-diving and bobbing to surface. Stands or sits on shore regularly. Flight fast, wing-beats rapid, causing whistling sound. Flies frequently and vigorously over wide radius of feeding area, and to considerable heights. Feeds chiefly by diving, with some surface-feeding, up-ending and wading-feeding. Prefers feeding in depths of up to 3 m, food usually swallowed underwater, ♂♂ remaining submerged longer than ♀♀. Diving times up to 40 s, usually 14–17 s.

Arrive early Oct, some individuals earlier. NW African birds from northern USSR and Iceland, more easterly populations from central and southern USSR, these also travel to NE and E Africa; origin of W African birds unknown. Many arrivals Dec–Jan in all regions. Departures Mar–Apr, individuals late as June.

Food. Omnivorous, variable according to locality and season. Mostly stationary or slow-moving items collected from bottom, e.g. molluscs, crustaceans, emergent plant materials (including seeds), aquatic plants, aquatic insects, small fish and their eggs.

Aythya marila (Linnaeus). Greater Scaup. Fuligule milouinan.

Anas Marila Linnaeus, 1761. Fauna Svecica (2nd ed.), p. 39; Lapland.

Plate 17

(Opp. p. 290)

Range and Status. Palearctic visitor to entire coast of N Africa in severe northern winters; rare.

Description. ADULT ♂ (breeding): entire head, breast, lateral breast and nape black, head with green gloss; upperparts vermiculated white and brown-black; rump, uppertail- and undertail-coverts black; flanks and belly white; upperwing brown with broad white bar along entire length, dingier towards tips; underwing mostly white. Eye golden yellow; large broad bill blue-grey, nail black; legs and feet olive-grey to lead-blue. ADULT ♂ (eclipse): head, foreparts and tail region dark brown, whitish patch at base of bill; upperparts and flanks browner; belly pale brown; bill darker. ADULT ♀: head brown, a large white facial patch surrounding bill-base forehead to chin; upperparts dark brown vermiculated whitish; flanks light yellowish brown; lower breast and belly white; wing as ♂; eye as ♂; bill darker than ♂; legs duller. SIZE: wing, ♂ (45 specimens) 219–237 (227), ♀ (35) 211–225 (217); tail, ♂ (45) 52–61 (56), ♀ (34) 51–60 (56); culmen, ♂ (46) 41–47 (44), ♀ (36) 40–45 (43); tarsus, ♂ (56) 38–42 (40), ♀ (45) 37–41 (39); toe, ♂ (58) 61–72 (66), ♀ (40) 61–68 (64). WEIGHT: ♂ (40) 744–1372, ♀ (35) 690–1312.

JUVENILE: like adult ♀, but less white about face.

Field Characters. Medium-sized, broad-bodied diving duck with large, wide bill and large head. ♂ distinctive, differs from otherwise similar ♂ Tufted Duck *A. fuligula* in having pale upperparts, no crest on head. ♀ distinguishable from ♀ Tufted Duck by larger white area on face, vermiculations on upperparts, paler underparts and flanks. In flight similar to Tufted Duck and Ferruginous Duck *A. nyroca* but larger, rounder-headed, with paler forewings, ♂ with pale back.

Voice. Recorded (20c). ♂ call, low, dove-like cooing, inaudible beyond few metres. ♀ call, loud, coarse 'kack', 'gock' or 'querr'; 'querr' or 'arrr' also given in flight, plus 'tuc-tuc-turra-tuc' and 'chup-chup-cherr-err'; all associated with courtship.

Aythya marila

General Habits. Little known in Africa; well known in Europe. In N Africa almost exclusively maritime, frequenting coastal bays and estuaries where indifferent to rough weather. May also occur on large coastal fresh waters. Flocks often of several hundreds, even thousands, closely packed, ♀♀ outnumbering ♂♂. Apparently, ♀♀ tend to winter further south than ♂♂. If undisturbed feed by day, otherwise at night, concentrating near mussel beds, sewage outfalls, seaweed beds. Food obtained chiefly by diving, using feet for propulsion, also dabbling and up-ending in shallows. Majority of dives take place in 0·5–3·5 m of water. Seldom seen on land, where walk is ungainly, but does rest on sand-banks, spits; swims low in water, tail trailing; rises with difficulty, flies with rapid wing-beats.

Food. Bivalve and univalve molluscs *Mytilus*, *Mulinia* and *Littorina* predominate in marine localities; also crustaceans, insects, annelids, small fish. Scavenges dead fish, waste grain and scraps. Inland also feeds on seeds and vegetation.

Subfamily MERGINAE: scoters, sawbills and other sea ducks

Predominantly marine diving ducks; medium to large, heavy-bodied, of rugged proportions with well-tapered, deep-based bills, narrow and having serrated edges in *Mergus*. ♂ plumages predominantly black or strikingly pied, heads usually glossy; ♀♀ and young markedly duller. Gait on land variable, laboured in some species. Actions on water powerful; all dive expertly, wing-action used when submerging. Flight rapid, usually low, whistling sound often produced by wings. Most species markedly gregarious at all times, chief food being animal matter often obtained by co-operative action.

Main pre-flight signals are lateral Head-shakes. Pair-formations occur annually within flocks during later winter with well-developed communal courtships occurring on water. Neck-stretch postures are common to most species; most common major ♂ displays are: Head-throw accompanied by call, in which head is thrown backwards, often resting momentarily on mantle, bill pointing skywards, before being returned to normal swimming position; Kick-displays, also performed with calls, in which bird tilts forward to raise rear-end while kicking water backwards with feet; Rushing or Steaming towards ♀; Turn-back-of-head and Head-turning. Secondary ♂ displays include Upward-shake, Wing-flap, various Mock-preens and lateral Head-shakes, while ♀♀ employ various Inciting displays.

5 Holarctic genera with 14 species; 6 non-breeding species from 3 genera in N Africa.

Genus *Melanitta* Boie

Sea ducks with well-rounded bodies, large heads and base of upper mandible markedly swollen. 3 species, of which 2 visit NW African coasts.

Plate 17
(Opp. p. 290)

Melanitta nigra (Linnaeus). Black Scoter; Common Scoter. Macreuse noire.

Anas nigra Linnaeus, 1758. Syst. Nat. (10th ed.), p. 123; Lapland, England.

Range and Status. Palearctic winter migrant to coastal waters of Atlantic, Morocco (Tangiers) to Mauritania (Nouadhibou), stragglers in Mediterranean east to Algeria.

Melanitta nigra

Description. *M. n. nigra*, ADULT ♂ (breeding): entirely glossy black except for grey underwing with black coverts; eye dark brown; narrow eye-ring dark brown or orange-yellow; bill, with swollen base to upper mandible, black with yellow or orange patch on upper mandible from around nostrils to base; legs and feet olive-brown to black. ADULT ♂ (non-breeding): similar, but duller, belly browner. ADULT ♀: dark brown, lower breast and belly paler, tending to whitish, flanks and undertail somewhat barred; a well-defined brownish white patch on cheeks, sides of upper neck and throat; bill green-black, sometimes with narrow strip of orange-yellow from between nostrils to nail. SIZE: wing, ♂ (91 specimens) 224–247 (234), ♀ (31) 216–239 (226); tail, ♂ (39) 82–103 (92·3), ♀ (24) 68–84 (74·7); culmen, ♂ (47) 43–51 (47·5), ♀ (32) 41–46 (43·4); tarsus, ♂ (69) 43–48 (45·4), ♀ (55) 41–46 (43·5); length, 44–54 cm; wing-span, 79–90 cm. WEIGHT: ♂ 642–1450, ♀ 600–1268; (Netherlands and Denmark, Oct–Apr) ♂ (14) 964–1339, ♀ (10) 973–1233.

JUVENILE: similar to adult ♀, generally paler, breast and belly whiter; small patch of orange-yellow around nostrils; wing, ♂ (30) 217–241 (226), ♀ (30) 206–226 (218).

Field Characters. Compact sea ducks of squat appearance, thick-necked and deep-billed, with pointed tails. ♂ entirely black with yellow bill-patch; ♀ dark brown with pale facial-patch. Swimming ♀ similar to Greater Scaup *Aythya marila* but lacks white lores, has thicker bill. All-dark flight pattern, ♀ with pale face, unique within African range.

Voice. Recorded (22b). Most characteristic sound in flock a monosyllabic whistling, piping or hooting, several calling simultaneously. Pitch variable, speed increasing with degree of excitement. Though ♂'s voice higher-pitched than that of ♀, latter harsher, coarser, distinguishable at sea.

General Habits. Little known in Africa, well known in Europe. Almost exclusively marine, flocks often densely packed, forming dense rafts of several hundred individuals; feeding groups smaller. Swims buoyantly, tail raised, head tucked into shoulders unless alarmed whereupon stretches neck, head pointed upwards, body lightly submerged. If swimming at speed bill pointed slightly above horizon. Take-off from water easier than in other scoters; flies with rapid wing-beats and whistling sound. Groups usually fly over water in long, wavering lines. Usually frequents open, rock-free, inshore waters, broad estuaries, seldom more than *c*. 2 km from land where depths 10–20 m and food readily access-ible. This obtained by diving, tail fanned, wings partially opened in rough conditions, otherwise closed. Chiefly day-time feeder, groups diving in synchrony, most dives 18–30 s, maximum 49 s (Dewar 1924). Pre-flight signals, Neck-stretch posture plus lateral Head-shakes. In early communal courtship ♂♂ may make infrequent aggressive skating approaches over water towards other ♂♂, head and neck stretched forward.

N European birds move southwest to African coast late Sept–Nov, daily movements *c*. 3900 towards Morocco recorded. Return movements late Feb–Apr.

Food. At sea mainly molluscs, especially blue mussel *Mytilus edulis* up to 40 mm long; fewer cockles, clams and other bivalves, also gastropods, occasionally crustaceans, including amphipods, small crabs.

References
Cramp, S. and Simmons, K. E. L. (1977).

Melanitta fusca (Linnaeus). Velvet Scoter; White-winged Scoter. Macreuse brune.

Anas fusca Linnaeus, 1758. Syst. Nat. (10th ed.), p. 123; coast of Sweden.

Plate 17
(Opp. p. 290)

Range and Status. Palearctic straggler to N African coast near Algiers and Mogador, Morocco, well south of normal wintering range; very rare.

Description. *M. f. fusca*, ADULT ♂: entirely black except for small white patch below and behind eye, and white secondaries. Eye grey-white; bill fairly deep at base, black with orange sides and tip; legs and feet red, webs black. ADULT ♀: entirely dark brown except for round, dull white patch between bill and eye and on ear-coverts, and white secondaries. Eye brown; bill olive-brown; legs dull red. SIZE: wing, ♂ (31 specimens) 269–286 (280), ♀ (7) 255–271 (263); tail, ♂ (26) 75–89 (81·2), ♀ 67–78 (73·4); culmen, ♂ (47) 41–51 (44·9), ♀ (27) 37–44 (40·8); tarsus, ♂ (43) 46–53 (48·8), ♀ 43–49 (45·8); length, 51–58 cm; wing-span, 90–99 cm. WEIGHT: (Dec–Jan) ♂ (9) 1517–1980, ♀ (11) 1360–1895.

JUVENILE: as ♀ but paler, more mottled; white head-patches whiter.

Field Characters. Fairly large black or dark brown sea-duck with thick-necked, squat appearance. White secondaries show as bar on folded wing when swimming, distinctive in flight and differing in this from smaller Black Scoter *M. nigra*.

Voice. Recorded (22b). Little heard at sea, no flock calling as in Black Scoter. Individuals make brief, harsh croaking or growling sounds, at times rising to higher-pitched piping or whistling.

General Habits. Little known in Africa, well known in Europe. Highly aquatic, more inclined to visit inland waters than other scoters but this not recorded in N Africa. Gregarious but flocks normally of 20 or less; often swims in single file, may occur in more broken water than Black Scoter, feeding among rocks, islands, otherwise keeps off-shore where reluctant to take wing. Swims less buoyantly than Black Scoter with which may associate, takes off with greater difficulty. Feeds by surface-diving with partly opened wings; groups diving in unison.

Food. Chiefly molluscs, otherwise similar to diet of Black Scoter.

References
Cramp, S. and Simmons, K. E. L. (1977).

Melanitta fusca

Genus *Bucephala* Baird

Bulbous-headed sea ducks with stout bodies, rounded as in other Merginae; bills tend to be shorter, flight patterns pied, and heads appear balloon-like against more slender necks. 3 species, 1 an occasional visitor to NW African coasts.

Plate 17
(Opp. p. 290)

Bucephala clangula (Linnaeus). Common Goldeneye. Garrot à oeil d'or.

Anas Clangula Linnaeus, 1758. Syst. Nat. (10th ed.), p. 125; Sweden.

Range and Status. Rare Palearctic migrant to Morocco, Algeria, Libya, only during severe northern winters.

Bucephala clangula

Description. *B. c. clangula*, ADULT ♂ (breeding): bulbous head blackish with green gloss, except for large white circular loral patch; neck white; back, rump, black; outer scapulars white, edged black; underparts white; upperwing black with bold white square patch on inner half over secondaries and coverts almost to leading edge; underwing grey. Eye yellow; bill black; legs and feet pale orange, webs blackish. ADULT ♂ (eclipse): like ♀ but head darker, more white on scapulars, wing-coverts. ADULT ♀: head entirely chocolate brown; inconspicuous white collar; breast and upperparts mottled blue-grey; rump black; tail grey-brown; underparts white with grey flanks and under-tail; upperwing as ♂ but white patch intersected by 2 black lines. Eye pale yellow-white; bill black with yellow band near tip; legs and feet as ♂. ADULT ♀ (eclipse): browner, head paler, collar absent. SIZE: wing, ♂ (31 specimens) 209–231 (220), ♀ (24) 197–207 (203); tail, ♂ (20) 78–91 (84·6), ♀ (25) 71–82 (77·5); bill, ♂ (57) 30–36 (33·3), ♀ (42) 28–31 (29·4); tarsus, ♂ (40) 37–41 (38·8), ♀ (46) 33–37 (35·1); length, 42–50 cm; wing-span, 65–80 cm. WEIGHT: (Denmark and Netherlands, winter) ♂ (9) 996–1245 (1136), ♀ (9) 707–860 (787).

JUVENILE: as ♀ eclipse, ♂♂ larger than ♀♀, white patch on folded wing larger.

Field Characters. Stocky, yellow-eyed, bulbous-headed duck with short stout bill. ♂ with distinct peak to crown of blackish head, white body with black back; ♀ with chocolate-coloured head, grey body, white collar. When flying, large head, short neck and pied underwing pattern diagnostic.

Voice. Recorded (22b). Usually silent except in courtship when ♂ utters loud whistling notes and ♀ occasionally utters weak screeching cry. ♂ gives short deep 'arr' on take-off and ♀ call is loud hoarse 'ah-ah-ah'. Wings produce vibrant rhythmic whistling in flight, audible over at least 1 km and similar to ringing sound of flat stone ricocheting over thin ice (Cramp and Simmons 1977).

General Habits. Little known in Africa, well known Europe. In winter range prefers sea or open sheets of fresh water. Indifferent to rough weather, spurning shelter. Swims buoyantly, neck tucked into shoulders or, if hurrying, with neck extended. Dives frequently, is active and restless, springing into flight directly from water. Shy, seldom mixes with other species. Swims underwater with great facility in still or fast-flowing water, disturbing stones at bottom at depths of *c.* 58 m. Dives last 15–20 s, ♂♂ having superior diving ability to ♀♀. Usually feeds by day, mainly by surface-diving. Food generally swallowed underwater.

Pair-bonds renewed annually during prolonged period of courtship in winter and spring; 80% of ♀♀ paired by Mar. Communal courtship well developed; ♂ displays include Head-up, Head-throw (see **A**) and Back-kick.

A

References
Johnsgard, P. A. (1978).

Genus *Mergus* Linnaeus

Fish-eating ducks having long, slender bills with straight or backward-facing teeth on both mandibles, the nail long, well-hooked. Heads markedly bulbous, usually well-crested; bodies long, slender; legs short, feet large. Sexual dimorphism marked, ♂♂ usually having strikingly pied breeding plumages with a non-breeding eclipse. Unique within the Anatidae in pursuing fast-moving prey under water. 3 species visit N African coastal waters.

Mergus albellus Linnaeus. Smew. Harle piette.

Mergus Albellus Linnaeus, 1758. Syst. Nat. (10th ed.), p. 129; Europe (Smyrna).

Plate 17

(Opp. p. 290)

Range and Status. Rare visitor Algeria to Egypt in very cold northern winters.

Description. ADULT ♂ (breeding): almost entirely white; mask surrounding eye to base of bill, loose feathers on sides of nape, mantle and central back black; 2 thin black lines running from mantle down side of chest in inverted V; flanks vermiculated grey; rump and tail grey-black; primaries and secondaries black, latter broadly edged white on trailing edge; inner tertials black, outer white; greater wing-coverts black, boldly tipped white; median wing-coverts white, lesser ones black. Eye red; bill short, grey; legs and feet grey. ADULT ♂ (eclipse): resembles ♀ but back blacker, though white patch on median wing-coverts retained. ADULT ♀: crown, nape and upper hindneck rich rufous brown; mask black; rest of head, throat, neck white; upperparts, tail, dull grey; breast and flanks mottled grey; rest of underparts white. Eye brown; bill and legs grey. SIZE: wing, ♂ (25 specimens) 197–208 (202), ♀ (10) 181–189 (184); tail, ♂ (24) 72–78 (74·8), ♀ (10) 65–73 (69·7); bill, ♂ (46) 27–32 (29·6), ♀ (33) 25–29 (26·8); tarsus, ♂ (46) 31–36 (34·0), ♀ (33) 29–32 (30·6); length, 38–44 cm; wing-span 55–69 cm. WEIGHT: ♂ (May) av. 622, (Jan) 950; ♀ 510–670; (USSR, Nov) ♂ 720–935 (814), ♀ 550–650 (572).
JUVENILE: like ♂, but lacks black mask.

Field Characters. Small, teal-sized, compact duck with striking plumage patterns. Breeding ♂ appears almost white in field, flight pattern markedly pied, head mostly white; ♀ and eclipse ♂ have diagnostic chestnut cap contrasting with white face and black mask.

Voice. Recorded (2a, 22b). ♂ utters soft, mechanical sounding rattle, high-pitched initially, then becoming lower and lower, 'kur-rik' or 'krrr-eck'. Also growling-humming 'troh'. ♀ utters rattling 'krrrr krrr', and low, hollow, rapid 'wok' or 'quok'.

General Habits. Little known in Africa, well known in Europe. Normally gregarious, preferring rivers and lagoons in N Africa, occasionally salt water in sheltered, shallow bays, estuaries and inlets up to 4 m deep. Man-made water catchments often used in winter.

Dives almost vertically or at long slant, submergence times usually less than 30 s (mean 18·2 s). Prey usually brought to surface before swallowing. Flocks often dive synchronously; co-operative fishing known to occur. Highly mobile, restless, frequently moving to new feeding and resting areas, and exploring other habitats. Groups fly in oblique lines or V-formations, in bunches over short distances. Swims buoyantly, dives easily and quickly; walks well with upright carriage.

Food. Fish, aquatic insects when available, some aquatic vegetation.

Mergus serrator Linnaeus. Red-breasted Merganser. Harle huppé.

Mergus Serrator Linnaeus, 1758, Syst. Nat. (10th ed.), p. 129; Sweden.

Plate 17

(Opp. p. 290)

Range and Status. Fairly common winter visitor to Algeria, Tunisia, occasionally to Egypt, Morocco, where more common than Common Merganser *M. merganser*.

Description. ADULT (breeding): entire head with large crest, upper and hindneck greenish black; mantle, inner scapulars black; outer scapulars mostly white; back, rump, tail-coverts vermiculated black and white; tail dark grey-brown; lower

Mergus serrator

neck, except hindneck, white; upper breast red-brown, heavily speckled black and forming broad band merging with mantle and black, white-spotted shoulder patch; flanks vermiculated black and white; rest of underparts white; upperwing black with large white patch incorporating secondaries and most of coverts, these intersected by 2 black bars; on underwing primaries and secondaries grey; rest of underparts white. Eye carmine; bill deep carmine, culmen and nail black; legs and feet deep vermilion. ADULT ♂ (eclipse): resembles ♀, back darker, wing pattern unchanged. ADULT ♀: entire head with large crest and neck ash-brown, redder on cheeks, pale almost white on chin and foreneck, black area before eye and a white streak below eye; mantle and upperparts generally dirty grey; underparts, grading from neck, and flanks mottled grey; upperwing brown with white on inner secondaries only. Eye pale brown to dull red; bill brown-red to orange-red; culmen dark brown; legs and feet dull orange-red, webs pale brown. SIZE: wing, ♂ (32 specimens) 235–255 (247), ♀ (14) 216–239 (228); tail, ♂ (34) 76–87 (81·2), ♀ (14) 73–81 (76·4); bill, ♂ (46) 56–64 (59·2), ♀ (28) 40–45 (42·7); tarsus, ♂ (45)

44–50 (47·0), ♀ (28) 40–45 (42·7); length, 52–58 cm; wingspan, 70–86 cm. WEIGHT: (Netherlands and Denmark, Nov–Feb) ♂ (11) 947–1350, ♀ (5) 900–1100.

JUVENILE: resembles adult ♀, crest shorter, plumage darker, especially on chest.

Field Characters. Medium-sized, tooth-billed duck with long, ragged, divided crest. Breeding ♂ with distinct pied plumage, brownish breast; ♀ duller, less distinctive, but darker than Common Merganser. In flight upperparts less white than Common Merganser, hindneck dark in ♂. Generally smaller in build, with more ragged head and thinner bill than Common Merganser. Head moves with foot action when swimming.

Voice. Recorded (22b). ♂ call a loud, rough, purring 'da-ah'; also single soft cat-like 'yeow'; and 'chit-up . . . pititee'. Alarm call a gruff 'gta' or 'gragrag'. ♀ call a harsh or croaking 'krrr-krrr', 'garr', 'gorr.'

General Habits. Little known in Africa, well known in Europe. Wintering birds in N Africa prefer marine habitats including salt coastal and estuarine waters, shallow, clear, sheltered bays and inlets, with sandy beds and spits, rocks or banks for resting. Tends to form flocks on brackish waters, otherwise occurs in small parties. Most feeding activity takes place early mornings and evenings, usually in water less than 3·5 m deep. Hunts in pairs or flocks, often co-operatively, driving fish into shallows where diving activity increases. Fish located by foraging on surface with head immersed, then pursued underwater using wings and legs for propulsion. Remains submerged up to 2 min, but normally less than 30 s. Prey mostly brought to surface unless in deep water; small prey also sometimes swallowed underwater. Spends much of time flying at low altitude as poorly adapted for walking.

Food. Mainly fish 8–10 cm long; also crustaceans and insects.

Plate 17
(Opp. p. 290)

Mergus merganser Linnaeus. Common Merganser; Goosander. Harle bièvre.

Mergus Merganser Linnaeus, 1758. Syst. Nat. (10th ed.), p. 129; Sweden.

Range and Status. Rare visitor to Morocco, Algeria, Tunisia, Libya and Egypt in northern winter.

Description. *M. m. merganser*, ADULT ♂ (breeding): entire head and upper neck green-black; centre of mantle black; back and rump grey; tail grey-black; outer scapulars, lower neck and underparts white, tinged cream, flanks sometimes greyish; upperwing black on outer half, white on inner, with black leading edge grading into tapering, inward-curving grey-black line running entire width of inner wing to tertials; underwing white. Eye dark brown; long, thin bill red, nail black; legs and feet red. ADULT ♂ (eclipse): as ♀, but wing pattern unchanged. ADULT ♀: crested head and upper neck chestnut, chin white; upperparts pale blue-grey, tail darker; underparts from lower neck white; flanks mottled grey and white; bill and legs red. SIZE: wing, ♂ (30 specimens) 275–295 (285), ♀ (23) 255–270 (262); tail, ♂ (27) 100–111 (105), ♀ (23) 95–106 (100); bill, ♂ (58) 52–60 (55·8), ♀ (43) 44–52 (48·7); tarsus, ♂ (58) 49–55 (51·7), ♀ (43) 44–51 (47·4); length,

58–66 cm; wing-span, 82–97 cm. WEIGHT: (Canada, Mar–Apr) ♂ (16) av. 1604, ♀ (2) av. 1106; (Canada, Jan–early Feb) ♂ (62) av. 1890, ♀ (21) av. 1390.

JUVENILE: resembles adult ♀, head colour less intense, crest shorter, white throat less distinct, general colouring duller grey; wing, ♂ 275, ♀ 252.

Field Characters. Largest of tooth-billed ducks. Long, low-lying duck with bulbous head, slender hooked bill. ♂ with blackish head and upperparts, white underparts, red bill; ♀ with rufous crested head, grey upperparts, white underparts. ♂ with pied upperwing, white neck, black head, ♀ with grey upperwing, white secondary patches, brown head. In flight distinguishable from Red-breasted Merganser *M. serrator* by white upper neck of ♂, grey, rather than brown, appearance of ♀. ♀ distinguishable from ♀ Smew *M. albellus* by broader wings, grey, not white, wing-coverts, larger size.

Voice. Recorded (22b). Used only in courtship or if alarmed. ♂ display call is guitar-like 'uig-a', or faint, high-pitched, bell-like note; warning or alarm call is hoarse 'grrr', 'wak' or 'karrr'. ♀ calls mostly harsh, loud 'karr karr' or quick cackling 'kokokokokok'. Flight call 'karr-r-r' also serves as alarm call.

General Habits. Little known in Africa, well known in Europe. Prefers deep, open, cool waters including marine outlets, but not sea. Seldom comes to land but flies freely, following river courses. Flight action rapid. Feeds by surface-diving, using legs for propulsion. Forages with head submerged, then dives and chases prey with head and neck held in straight line in front of body. Small fish may be swallowed while submerged, larger fish brought to surface; prey held across middle, then turned and swallowed head-first. Favours waters up to 4 m deep; duration of dives up to 2 m, normally 30 s. Hunts in pairs, small groups or flocks, forming lines to drive fish into shallows. Most active early morning, evening.

Food. Fish up to 36–46 cm long, av. 10 cm. Ducklings consume large quantities of insects before becoming adept at fishing.

Mergus merganser

Subfamily OXYURINAE: stiff-tailed ducks

Small to medium-sized diving ducks with no close affinities to others of the family Anatidae. Bodies broad and short; necks short and thick with loose, extendible skin which, in some ♂♂, can be inflated during sexual display; tails long, stiff and used for steering under water; wings broad, short legs placed well back on body, feet large; bills broad, wide, usually swollen at base. Dive with great facility, walk on land with difficulty, fly with rapid, jerky action. Plumage grebe-like, dense and shiny, sexual dimorphism marked in majority; speculum absent in all but 1 species. Highly aquatic, frequenting mostly warm, shallow, fresh or brackish waters, well fringed with emergent vegetation. 3 genera, 8 species; in Africa 2 species from 1 genus.

Genus *Oxyura* Bonaparte

Stiff-tailed ducks characterized by habit in ♂♂ of holding tails in vertical position, of inflating necks in some, swimming with heads and necks low in water and splashing water (Sousing) during courtship. ♂ uses Scatter-rushes or Ski when approaching ♀, aggressively at other ♂♂, and in courtship. Food predominantly vegetable, obtained mostly by diving, submerged periods prolonged. Sexual dimorphism usually marked, ♂♂ with bright blue bills when breeding, in eclipse resemble ♀♀. Few vocal utterances except subdued sounds in courtship. Eggs unusually large; nest duties and brood care by ♀ only; young independent before fledging. 6 species world-wide, *O. leucocephala* in N Africa, *O. maccoa* in E and southern Africa.

Oxyura leucocephala (Scopoli). White-headed Duck. Erismature à tête blanche.   **Plate 16**

Anas leucocephala Scopoli, 1769. Annus I Hist.–Nat., p. 65; no locality; probably northern Italy.   (Opp. p. 227)

Range and Status. Resident and Palearctic migrant N Africa; exact status resident N African populations uncertain, distribution discontinuous over entire range. Morocco no recent breeding recorded; Algeria small numbers, probably breeds Lake Tonga, El Kala region (15 counted 1977, 36 in 1978); Tunisia both resident and wintering populations, seasonally fairly common, 670 Lake Tunis Jan 1973, smaller numbers elsewhere; Egypt small numbers wintering, influx possibly from NW Africa.

Oxyura leucocephala

Description. ADULT ♂ (breeding): head white with black crown-patch; upperparts rusty grey with fine, transverse lines or bars of blackish brown; uppertail-coverts rich chestnut; tail dark brown; neck black, fading into chestnut breast; lower breast, belly, silver-white, mottled grey; flanks as upperparts; undertail-coverts grey-brown; wing grey-brown. Eye orange-yellow; bill sky blue; legs and feet lead-grey, webs and joints dusky. ADULT ♂ (eclipse): black crown more extensive, extending down nape; rest of plumage paler, barring more prominent; breast orange-yellow; bill grey. ADULT ♀: crown to below eye-level, nape, and broad line from gape to ear-coverts dark brown; rest of head, including broad line below eye from bill to nape, chin, cheeks and neck, buff-white; rest of plumage as breeding ♂, barring stronger, breast paler. Eye pale yellow; bill, feet and legs lead-grey. SIZE: wing, ♂ (10 specimens) 157–172 (162), ♀ (6) 148–167 (159); tail, ♂ (9) 85–100 (92·4), ♀ 75–93 (85·5); culmen, ♂ (17) 43–48 (45·5), ♀ (16) 43–46 (44·5); tarsus, ♂ (16) 35–38 (35·9), ♀ 33–37 (34·9); length, 43–48 cm; wing-span 62–70 cm. WEIGHT: ♂ 558–865 (737), ♀ 539–631 (593) (Johnsgard 1978).

JUVENILE: duller and paler than ♀ but variable, lacks chestnut tinge; eye pale grey to pale brown; bill pale lead colour; feet pale cinnamon-brown.

DOWNY YOUNG: head and neck dark brown, a distinct buff-white streak from bill-base, under eye, to ear; chin, throat, sides of neck, pale grey; upperparts, chest, flanks, dark brown; belly, vent, white; tail with long, stiff shafts; eye brown.

Field Characters. Medium-sized, dumpy, cinnamon-brown stiff-tailed duck with much white about head. Bill deep and swollen at base, compressed towards tip, tail fairly long. ♂ with clear white head, black crown patch, blue bill, tail often held up stiffly. ♀ with dark brown crown and facial streak. Attitude on water frequently squat, hunched, short-necked, or ♂ with neck and tail erect if displaying. Seldom flies but in air appears short-winged, heavy-bodied, coot-like. Unlikely to be confused with any other duck within its African range.

Voice. Recorded (2a). Silent except in courtship. ♂♂, when displaying to ♀♀, utter tickering-purr (sound likened to bouncing of ping-pong ball on table), and series of double, reedy notes resembling 'pipe-pipe'. ♂ utters harsh grunts during Flotilla-swimming. ♀ utters soft 'gek' during same activity; wheezy sound during post-breeding courtship and warning 'huu-rugru-u'; calls missing ducklings with low, rattling purr. Ducklings make buzzing 'whit whit' up to week 4, and low, twittering contact call.

General Habits. Little known in Africa, well known in Europe. Prefers shallow, fresh or saline waters, e.g. lagoons, lakes, well-fringed with aquatic vegetation, these usually with maritime influence. May occur also in rocky sea bays. Dives well and for long periods, swimming submerged 30 m or more. Food obtained mostly by diving or submerging in waters 1–2 m deep; submerged periods last up to 40 s, as many as 50 successive dives recorded. Also feeds by dabbling at water's edge. Degree of movements and origins of wintering birds uncertain. Usually gregarious when not breeding, ♂♂ gathering to moult while ♀♀ still incubating. Flocks roost on water. Pre-flight signal presumed to be lateral Head-flicks.

Food. Omnivorous; vegetable matter may predominate but animal matter not inconsiderable. Leaves and seeds of pondweeds, eel-grass, seeds of bulrush and crustaceans recorded.

Breeding Habits. Little known in Africa, well known Europe. Non-colonial, nests placed in thick vegetation close to water.

Flocks containing both sexes perform Flotilla-swimming when all move steadily forward, led by single ♂ or ♀ in Head-high posture, tail raised 45° or flat on water. Flock generally silent but ♀♀ may give soft calls, ♂♂ harsh grunts. Following lateral Head-shakes, individuals may Scatter-rush across water, then perform ritualized comfort movements such as Dip-diving, brief immersion with down-up movement; Head-rolling, head rubbed on shoulder; and Wing-shuffling and Dab-preening, bill repeatedly jabbed into breast feathers. Swim about giving tickering-purr calls. During pair-formation, competing ♂♂ give Open-bill-threat, often in Hunched-posture, scapulars raised, head thrust low over water towards rival; threat may develop into Hunched-rush at opponent, but physical contact rare, victim usually escapes by diving. After Hunched-rush ♂ returns to ♀ in same manner, swinging broadside to her in Sideways-hunch, first 1 side then other, until ♀ responds. These actions possibly succeeded by Head-high-tail-cock, head and tail slowly lifted in synchrony until tail at angle of just over 90°; may also Kick-flap, thrusting bill into water and lifting folded wings while legs kick vigorously backwards, Sideways-hunching then resumed at high intensity, bill open, making series of double 'Pipe-calls'; fully spread tail twisting sideways while vibrating it, folded wings slightly raised and lowered, between each Pipe-call. ♀'s reaction minimal; may give Open-bill-threat. Copulatory behaviour unknown.

NEST: platform of dead reed stems and leaves woven into base of standing reeds; may use old nest of Coot *Fulica atra* or Tufted Duck *Aythya fuligula*, adding more material. Vegetation may be bent over to form bower. Little or no down-lining. Built by ♀ only.

EGGS: 5–10, laid at day intervals (up to 15 recorded, laid by 2 ♀♀). Broad ovals; dull white. SIZE: (100 eggs) 63–73 × 48–54 (67 × 51). WEIGHT: (100, captive birds) 82–109 (94) (J. Kear, pers. comm.)

Laying dates: Algeria late May and June.

Incubation by ♀; ♂ usually deserts about this time. Incubated continuously with normal feeding bouts. Period: 25–26 days.

Young leave nest within 12 h of hatching, dive within 7 min of reaching water; duration of submerged periods increases until same as adults at 7 weeks. Weight at 1 day old (9 ducklings) 57–64·5 (60) (J. Kear, pers. comm.). When frightened, ducklings erect heads and tails while swimming away. Independent before fledging.

Young cared for by ♀ only, may return to nest for brooding. In first few hours on water ♀ swims from 1 duckling to another with head low, bill slightly open, scapulars smooth, strengthening family bond by touching each lightly on back of head with bill. If ♂ still present on water usually ignores young; once seen to make Sideways-hunch towards ducklings as they first appeared (Cramp and Simmons 1977).

References
Jacobs, P. and Ochando, B. (1979).

Oxyura maccoa (Eyton). Maccoa Duck. Erismature maccoa.

Erismatura maccoa Eyton, 1838. Monogr. Anatidae, p. 169; Indian Isles = S Africa.

Plate 16

(Opp. p. 227)

Range and Status. Resident south of *c.* 12°N (more northerly in Ethiopia). Fairly common Ethiopia, Kenya, Uganda, northern Tanzania, eastern Zaïre, Rwanda and Burundi, but rare coastal regions. Southern Africa uncommon Zimbabwe, common to locally abundant all other regions to SW Cape except arid and semi-arid zones and coastal Natal. Locally migratory Transvaal.

Description. ADULT ♂ (breeding): head, upper neck black; lower neck, mantle, scapulars, lower rump, uppertail-coverts bright chestnut; rump dark brown speckled lighter; breast, abdomen, vent, grey-brown, silver-white feather-tips giving almost white appearance; flanks pale chestnut, freckled lighter brown; wings grey-brown, primaries and outer secondaries uniform, rest strongly freckled ochreous-brown; no speculum; rectrices stiff, narrowly webbed, blackish brown. Eye dark brown; bill short, high and broad, bright cobalt blue; legs, feet, lead-grey. ADULT ♂ (eclipse): as ♀, but crown slightly darker. ADULT ♀: top of head to just below eye grey-brown, feathers tipped ochreous; below this a whitish line extending from lores towards nape (but not meeting it); below this a darker zone as crown extending back to upper neck; chin, throat, whitish grading into ash brown, lower neck with faint white bar; entire upper surface hindneck to uppertail-coverts grey-brown, finely vermiculated and freckled light brown and buff-white; breast, abdomen, vent, grey-brown, buff-white feather-tips giving silky white appearance; flanks ash-brown barred buff-white, slightly freckled; wings and tail as ♂. Eye dark brown; bill slate grey; legs, feet, grey-brown. SIZE: (2 ♂♂, 1 ♀) wing, ♂ 165, 173, ♀ 155; tail, ♂ 72, 73, ♀ 66; tarsus, ♂ 34, 34, ♀ 31; culmen, ♂ 40, 42, ♀ 36 (McLachlan and Liversidge 1978). WEIGHT: ♂ (1, Lake Nakuru) 820 (Britton 1970), ♀ (3) 516–580 (554) (Siegfried 1969).

JUVENILE: resembles adult ♀. From *c.* 7 months ♂♂ distinguished from ♀♀ by fading eye-stripe, brown feathers replacing ash-brown mantle. Later head begins to turn black, back becomes deeper brown; light collar retained until head and mantle feathers are as adult, but bill remains grey-black.

DOWNY YOUNG: muddy brown, an ill-defined pale patch above wing; entire side of head from level with eye white, intersected by narrow brown horizontal stripe from gape to nape; upper breast brown; rest of underparts white; eye brown, bill olive-grey; feet olive-grey, webs black. 2nd downy plumage light brown with head markings of adult ♀.

Oxyura maccoa

Field Characters. Small, squat, stiff-tailed duck with fairly short, thick-based bill. Breeding ♂ with bright chestnut plumage, black head, bright blue bill; ♀ and eclipse ♂ dull, speckled grey-brown pepper and salt pattern, a pale stripe below eye, whitish upper neck and throat. Swimming posture characteristic, body low in water, tail either trailing below surface or stiffly angled upwards at 45°. Wings short, set well back on body; highly aquatic, seldom seen walking or flying. ♀ and eclipse ♂ differ from ♀ Southern Pochard *Netta erythrophthalma* in having squatter appearance and horizontal, not vertical, crescent-shaped white facial markings.

(*Continued on p. 291.*)

Plate 17

All birds shown are ADULTS.

Anas penelope Eurasian Wigeon (p. 253)
1. ♀ in flight and swimming, 2. ♂ in flight and standing.

Anas strepera Gadwall (p. 254)
3. ♀ in flight and swimming, 4. ♂ in flight and standing.

Anas acuta Northern Pintail (p. 264)
5. ♀ in flight and swimming, 6. ♂ in flight and standing.

Scale does not apply to head details

Anas clypeata Northern Shoveler (p. 272)
7. ♀ in flight and swimming, 8. ♂ in flight and standing.

Anas crecca Green-winged Teal (p. 255)
9. ♂ in flight and standing, 10. ♀ swimming and in flight.

Anas querquedula Garganey (p. 269)
11. ♂ in flight and standing, 12. ♀ swimming and in flight.

Anas platyrhynchos Mallard (p. 258)
13. ♀ in flight and swimming, 14. ♂ standing and in flight.

Aythya ferina Common Pochard (p. 278)
15. ♂ standing and in flight, 16. ♀ swimming and in flight.

Aythya fuligula Tufted Duck (p. 280)
17. ♂ standing and in flight, 18. ♀ in flight and swimming.

Melanitta nigra Black Scoter (p. 282)
19. ♂ in flight, 20. ♀ in flight, 21. ♂ swimming, 22. ♀ swimming.

Melanitta fusca Velvet Scoter (p. 283)
23. ♀ in flight, 24. ♂ in flight, 25. ♂ swimming, 26. ♀ swimming.

Heads: 27. *M. nigra* ♀, 28. *M. fusca* ♀.

Aythya nyroca Ferruginous Duck (p. 279)
29. ♀ in flight and swimming, 30. ♂ in flight and standing.

Aythya marila Greater Scaup (p. 281)
31. ♀ in flight and swimming, 32. ♂ in flight and standing.

Bucephala clangula Common Goldeneye (p. 284)
33. ♀ swimming and in flight, 34. ♂ swimming and in flight.

Mergus merganser Common Merganser (p. 286)
35. ♀ swimming and in flight, 36. ♂ standing and in flight.

Mergus serrator Red-breasted Merganser (p. 285)
37. ♀ swimming and in flight, 38. ♂ standing and in flight.

Mergus albellus Smew (p. 285)
39. ♀ in flight and swimming, 40. ♂ in flight and swimming.

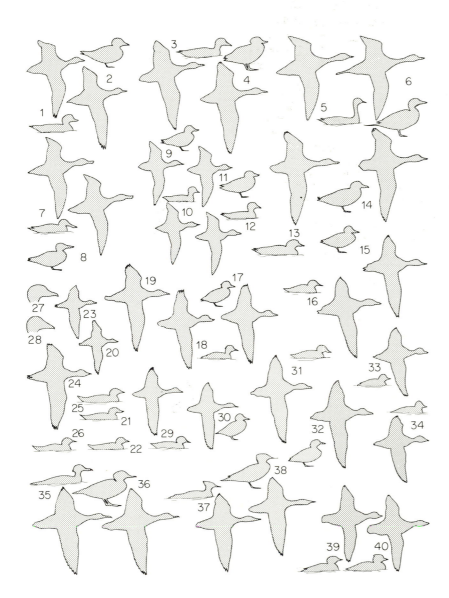

Voice. Not recorded. Generally silent. ♂'s basic sound a vibrating 'prrr....' of 2–3 s duration, used especially in Vibrating Trumpet Call and Independent Vibrating Trumpet Call displays. Also soft whistle during Neck-jerk display. In Threat display either sex may utter soft, grunting call.

General Habits. Intimately known. Prefers shallow, nutrient-rich waters with extensive emergent vegetation. In Ethiopia recorded at 3000 m in Bale Mountains (Loeffler 1977); in South Africa sea level to 2150 m (Clark 1974d), breeding at all these altitudes. In Witwatersrand, Transvaal, present all year, greatest numbers in summer (breeding period) coinciding with rains, lowest in winter (dry period) when non-breeding birds move to larger waters in Orange Free State (Clark 1974d).

During day, swims, dives, preens, bathes and occasionally displays. Rests more than 50% of any part of day (Siegfried *et al.* 1976), but more frequently for longer periods late morning and late afternoon. Mainly seen on open water, repeatedly using same area and often 'anchoring' itself to floating vegetation before sleeping. Probably sleeps all night except if ♂ defending territory. Feeds by straining soft, muddy ooze from bottom of ponds; obtained solely by diving.

Sedentary Maccoas moult remiges twice yearly; in SW Cape Jan and June. ♂♂ moult before and after breeding, ♀♀ before breeding, timing of 2nd moult not determined.

Food. *Polygonum* sp. and other seeds; Tendipedidae larvae and pupae, *Daphnia* and other invertebrates. Food ingested at rate of 96–97 mg (dry weight) per dive.

Breeding Habits. Intimately known. Nests singly, mainly over water in emergent vegetation.

♂♂ come into breeding condition well ahead of ♀♀, remaining sexually active at least 4 months. Promiscuous, no social courtship or pair-bond. Territorial ♂ may have 1 or more ♀♀ nesting in territory. ♀♀ generally aggressive towards ♂♂. Territories incorporate open water and emergent vegetation with frontage of *c*. 80 cm; ♂ displays aggressively at other ♂♂ many metres away and courts all ♀♀. Waters with breeding birds usually contain more ♂♂ than ♀♀ and more ♂♂ than territories.

Displays used to establish and maintain territories include: (1) Independent Vibrating Trumpet Call used by ♂ when patrolling territory, when out of sight of conspecifics, or in response to this call by another ♂, made up of 3 separate sequences as follows: (i) Neck-

Plate 18

Machaerhamphus alcinus Bat Hawk (p. 301)
1. IMMATURE, *2*. ADULT.

Haliaeetus vocifer African Fish Eagle (p. 312)
3. ADULT, *4*. 1ST YEAR IMMATURE, *5*. 2ND YEAR IMMATURE, *6*. SUBADULT.

Pandion haliaetus Osprey (p. 295)
7. IMMATURE, *8*. ADULT.

Pernis apivorus Honey Buzzard (p. 299)
9. ADULT ♀ (dark phase), *10*. IMMATURE , *11*. ADULT ♂.

Milvus milvus Red Kite (p. 310)
12. ADULT, *13*. IMMATURE.

Milvus migrans Black Kite (p. 307)
Race *migrans*: *14*. IMMATURE, *15*. ADULT.
Race *parasitus*: *16*. IMMATURE, *17*. ADULT.

Gypohierax angolensis Vulturine Fish Eagle (p. 316)
18. IMMATURE, *19*. ADULT.

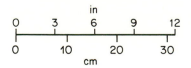

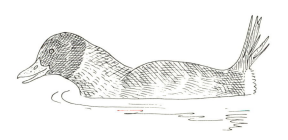 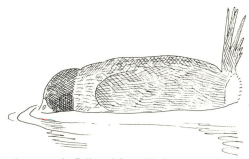

jerk—bird raises head, jerks it backwards and upwards with slightly opened bill pointing downwards; rest of body motionless *c.* 1 s while making soft whistling sound (this sequence sometimes omitted). (ii) Nucleus (may follow or be independent of (i))—bird thrusts head forward stretching out neck and uttering a vibrating 'prrr' of 2–3 s duration. During call, anteriorly stretched neck forms angle between 25° and 50° with surface of water, open bill held about horizontal, 'horns' on head erected. If preceded by (i), tail is fanned and erected while calling. (iii) Recovery—bird returns to posture in which head and bill held relatively low, body partially submerged. (2) Running-flight by ♂, in which bird 'runs' rapidly across water with wings flapping, feet pattering audibly on surface over 20–30 m within territory. (3) Threat, in which bird adopts Stretch-swim posture, head (and 'horns' on head) erect, bill directed forward; bird swims towards opponent; may utter soft grunt 'um-on'. (4) Fighting, common between rival ♂♂, occurring as much underwater as on surface; involves chases in which rivals may surface locked in combat, holding bills, striking with wings.

Main courtship displays are: (1) Ski, performed by ♂ when approaching ♀; tail held flat on water, back hunched, head drawn in against body, bill pointing downwards. Bird swims rapidly forward causing considerable 'bow wave'. (2) Leading-swim, a modified version of Stretch-swim, in which ♂ swims 1 m or more ahead of ♀, continuing to do so for up to 60 m if ♀ follows; ends when ♂ leads ♀ into cover. (3) Water-flicking, commonly performed by both sexes either stationary or backwards—swimming bird adopts Stretch–swim posture followed by rapid upward and backward jerk of head causing bill to splash water upwards and past bird's side. Usually several Water-flicks are alternated with other displays. When doing this display, ♂ orients body sideways to ♀ 49% of time, faces her 42% and away from her 9% (129 observations). (4) Sousing, in which ♂ sucks in air, causing neck to swell, then throws head and neck forward and down onto water several times until air disperses and neck normal size again. At first tail cocked upright, but later lowered onto water when body nearly submerged and neck flat on water. (5) Vibrating Trumpet Call, performed by ♂ only, often following Ski. ♂ Skis to ♀, performs neck-jerk, shuffles wings, then stretches neck vertically, sucking air into trachea and oesophagus. Head then thrust forwards and downwards, tail lifted and fanned. Differs from Independent Vibrating Trumpet Call in that head is lower, swollen neck stretched out on water and bill

half-submerged. Like this call, is uttered as ♂ moves backwards and displays underside of fanned tail. (6) Copulation, takes place following (5) provided ♀ responds with Water-flicking and/or lowering body into Prone-posture; ♂ mounts over side of ♀ after first seizing back of her head or neck. Copulation lasts *c.* 35 s, only head of ♀ protruding above water. ♀ usually moves forward 1–5 m, paddling with feet, sometimes thrashing vigorously with wings. Following copulation both Bathe, ♂ usually more intensively with more frequent Head-dipping and for longer periods. (7) Communal Diving, performed either by ♂ and ♀ or by 2 ♀♀, lasting up to 30 min. Cheek-rolling, Swimming-shake, Head-dipping, False-preening, Wing-flapping, Wing-shuffle and Tail-shake, evolved from comfort movements, all occur as components of the foregoing display sequences.

NEST: usually 5–40 m apart; in reeds, also waterside sedges, or hollow in sand under bush. Old nests of coots, *Fulica*, sometimes used. Made of flat dry reed leaves pulled down, criss-crossed and bent to form basin *c.* 20 cm wide, bowl 8 cm deep, small amounts of down often present. Eggs usually 8–23 cm above water. Constructed by ♀ only.

EGGS: (Transvaal) 4–8, normally 5, laid at 1–2 day intervals; (SW Cape) 4–10, mean 5·9; nests containing larger clutches attributed to 2 ♀♀, these frequently deserted; egg-dumping common. Rough, matt-surfaced; bluish white. SIZE: (54 eggs) 63·0–72·5 × 46·7–52·5 (66·9 × 50·5). WEIGHT: (5 eggs) 73–98 (88) (Siegfried 1969).

Laying dates: extended season most regions. Witwatersrand, Transvaal, all months, peaking Sept–Dec; SW Cape July–Apr, peaking Sept–Nov; E Africa dry and wet periods, 1 record each Mar, Apr, July, Aug, Sept, Oct.

Incubation by ♀ only, begins with completion of clutch. Incubating ♀ feeds frequently in short spells off nest alternating with longer bouts of incubation throughout the day. At night attentiveness higher, but feeding does occur. Bird sits facing nest entrance *c.* 50% of incubating spells. Longest spells occur when nest-air temperatures approach temperature of eggs in nest; ♀ becomes restless when nest-air temperature rises above incubation temperature of eggs. Egg desertion by ♀ before and during incubation not unusual. Intraspecific and interspecific nest parasitism in Maccoa Duck well authenticated; in Transvaal main host Hottentot Teal *Anas hottentota* (Dean 1970). Incubation period: 25–27 days.

Chicks remain with mother *c.* 5 weeks, may remain together as group at least 3 weeks after mother's departure. 2nd down appears at week 2; juvenile feathers begin to appear on flanks and wings weeks 5–6; down on mantle and hind quarters last to disappear; flight feathers last to develop (Clark 1964).

Mother of brood usually chases ♂♂ and other species away from proximity of ducklings although ♂ parent may occasionally perform Vibrating Trumpet Call to mate without being chased (Clark 1964). Family remains on open water throughout daylight hours, ♀ feeding assiduously, seldom resting. Small chicks brooded at night, returning to nest first few days after hatching.

References

Clark, A. (1964).
Siegfried, W. R. (1976).
Siegfried, W. R. and Van der Merwe F. J. (1975).
Siegfried, W. R. *et al.* (1976a, b, c).

Order FALCONIFORMES

A very large cosmopolitan order of *c.* 290 species, 93 found in Africa. Its correct arrangement is subject to disagreement, and 2 alternative arrangements have recently been proposed. The first, adopted here, is that of Stresemann and Amadon (in the 1979 revision of the Peters Check List of Birds of the World, Vol. I) in which the order is divided into 4 suborders: Cathartes, comprising only the New World vultures; Accipitres, the Osprey, kites, fish eagles, Old World vultures, hawks and eagles; Sagittarii, containing only the endemic African Secretary bird; and Falcones, the New World caracaras and cosmopolitan falcons. In the Peters List, this very large and varied assembly is placed between the Order Ciconiiformes and the small specialized Order Phoenicopteriformes. Since the latter are closely allied on the one hand to the Ciconiiformes and on the other to the Anseriformes, we here depart from the Peters List and place the Falconiformes immediately after the Anseriformes in the position it has traditionally occupied.

The alternative arrangement, based upon Voous (1973) is to accept that the Falconiformes are not 1 order but 3: Cathartiformes (New World vultures); Accipitriformes (Osprey, hawks, eagles, Old World vultures, and the Secretary Bird); and Falconiformes (caracaras and falcons). It is thus evident that the arrangement of this very large, complex and diverse order is still controversial. There is even some doubt that the Secretary Bird is correctly placed in it at all, as some authorities have suggested that it is more closely related to the Gruiformes. Pending further research, however, it is best included in the Falconiformes as usual.

All Falconiformes have hooked beaks for tearing flesh, and most have powerful talons for holding and killing prey, though in carrion-feeding vultures these are reduced. All but 1 Australian species are basically diurnal, though some are crepuscular, hunting at dusk (*Machaerhamphus*, *Elanus* and some *Falco* spp.). Very large eyes, almost immovable in their sockets, provide good binocular vision through 35–50° of arc. African species, varying in size and weight from 55–7500 g, feed on animals alive or dead, from termites to dead elephants; the largest eagles can kill prey up to 20 kg in weight. Many of the genera and species are specialized so as to exploit 1, or a few, food resources or a particular habitat. Most are entirely flesh-eaters though 1 sp. (*Gypohierax*) is basically vegetarian, and several others feed much on vegetable matter, notably oil palm pericarp. The various specializations and characteristics are discussed separately under genus headings below. (*All illustrations for this Order by Martin Woodcock.*)

Suborder ACCIPITRES

Includes all Old World diurnal birds of prey except those in the suborders Sagittarii and Falcones. In the arrangement of Stresemann and Amadon (1979), the suborder contains only 1 family, Accipitridae. All Accipitres build their own nests; lay eggs which show green inside when held up to the light; and when defaecating emit a stream of liquid matter, known to falconers as a 'slice', frequently shooting it under pressure for 1 m or more. Otherwise extremely varied, e.g. in wing-shape, number of wing feathers, shape and function of bill and feet, and other features.

Family ACCIPITRIDAE: Osprey, cuckoo falcons, honey buzzards, kites, fish eagles, Old World vultures, snake eagles, harriers, goshawks, sparrowhawks, buzzards, eagles

Now divided into 2 subfamilies, Pandioninae, containing only the Osprey, and Accipitrinae, containing the rest. In Africa 72 species in 32 genera, of which 12 are endemic, with 2 others (*Melierax* and *Polyboroides*) also typically African but extending outside Africa to Yemen and Madagascar. Until the recent revision of the Falconiformes by Stresemann and Amadon (1979), the Osprey *Pandion haliaetus* was usually given full family rank as the family Pandionidae and is still so treated by Voous (1973). The very large and diverse family Accipitridae was formerly divided into a number of other subfamilies, these being Perninae, Milvinae, Haliaeetinae, Aegypiinae, Circaetinae, Circinae, Polyboroidinae, Accipitrinae, Buteoninae and Aquilinae, a convenient arrangement now considered inappropriate as at least some of these former subfamilies do not appear to be closely related to those listed nearest to them.

Subfamily PANDIONINAE: Osprey

Large diurnal bird of prey inhabiting aquatic environments, feeding almost exclusively on live fish. The Osprey is regarded either as a subfamily akin to relatively primitive kites (Stresemann and Amadon 1979), or as a full family Pandionidae (Voous 1973), specialized, and placed after the Accipitridae. Since the Osprey appears to have certain kite-like characters we prefer the arrangements of Stresemann and Amadon (1979). Ospreys differ from other Accipitridae in having specializations for catching and holding fish, and in some other ways. Beak strong, arched, sharply hooked; nostrils long, slit-like, can be closed at will. Eyes large, prominent, directed forward; skull lacking a supraorbital ridge (as in some kites). Wings long, distinctly angled at carpal joint in flight; legs powerful, thick, feet with reversible outer toe and soles covered with sharp spicules; plumage mainly white and brown. 1 species, almost cosmopolitan, but, strangely, does not breed in Africa south of the Red Sea and Cape Gardafui; Palearctic individuals migrate to Africa in winter.

Genus *Pandion* Savigny

Pandion haliaetus (Linnaeus). Osprey. Balbuzard pêcheur.

Falco haliaetus Linnaeus, 1758. Syst. Nat. (10th ed.), p. 91; Sweden.

**Plates
18 and 30**
(Opp. pp. 291
and 451)

Range and Status. All of Africa in suitable aquatic habitats, sea coasts, estuaries, large lakes, large rivers, sometimes smaller waters. Breeds Mediterranean, Red Sea to near Cape Gardafui, coast of Somalia and Sudan, and islands off Atlantic Coast south to Cape Verde Is., not on Atlantic coast itself. Suspected to breed Senegal (Isles Madeleine: Dupuy 1972). Winter migrant to the rest of Africa; all formerly accepted breeding records south of Somalia–Cape Verde now rejected. Mediterranean breeding population now nearly extinct; Red Sea, Somalia–Sudan still common. As migrant, frequent to locally common.

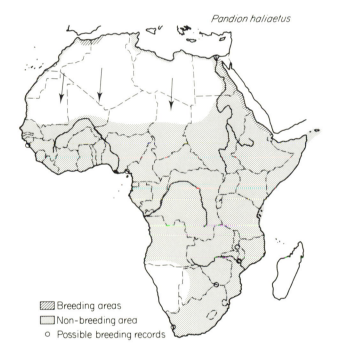

Pandion haliaetus

▨ Breeding areas
▢ Non-breeding area
○ Possible breeding records

Description. *P. h. haliaetus*, ADULT ♂: forehead dark brown, streaked white; crown white; hind crown and nape buff, streaked dark brown. A broad black band through eye above white throat. Rest of upperparts, including upperwing-coverts, dark brown, glossed purplish, feathers narrowly tipped whitish. Chin and throat white, lower throat and breast pale brown, forming a band across chest. Rest of body below white, underwing-coverts mottled brown and white. Outer primaries blackish, inner webs mottled brown;

inner and secondaries dark brown glossed purple, barred white on inner webs. Tail-feathers dark brown, tipped buff, inner webs of all but central pair white, broadly barred brown terminally. Eye pale yellow; cere grey-blue; legs blue-grey to greenish white. Sexes alike, ♀ larger. SIZE: wing, ♂ 450–510, usually 450–495 (469), ♀ 470–510 (495); tail, ♂ 187–210, (201), ♀ 194–232 (216); tarsus, ♂ 52–58 (56), ♀ 54–57 (56); wing-span, ♂ 1470–1663 (1590), ♀ 1540–1683 (1631). WEIGHT: ♂ 1120–1740 (1428), ♀ 1208–2050 (1627).

IMMATURE: resembles adult, but generally paler, more streaky above, with feathers more broadly tipped buff; eye yellow, cere and feet greyish. Adult plumage acquired at *c.* 18 months; age at 1st breeding *c.* 3 years.

DOWNY YOUNG: 1st down short, dense, brown above, creamy below, with pale buff streak from nape-tail. 2nd down brown above with central pale streak, below brown, speckled whitish. In open nests down pattern cryptic.

Field Characters. Almost unmistakable, more likely to be confused with large immature gulls than any hawk. Whitish head with broad black eye streak, dark brown above and generally white below with contrasting darker wing-feathers and tail in flight. Wings have pronounced bend at carpal joint in flight, resembling kites and some large gulls. Basically aquatic habits also distinctive.

Voice. Recorded (2a, 30). In Africa normally silent, but elsewhere (and presumably in N and NE African breeding areas) a short, rather melodius whistle 'chewk-chewk-chewk' or 'chip-chip'; voice of ♀ lower-pitched than that of ♂. In alarm at nest ♂ utters 'kip-kip-kip-kiweeek-kiweeek' and ♀, in mild alarm, a lower-pitched 'piu-piu-piu'. When soliciting copulation ♀ utters soft 'quee-quee-quee-quee' or long-drawn, shrill 'pseeeek-pseeeek'; similar, louder calls used when soliciting food. In mutual display, and in distraction, ♂, often carrying fish, utters frenzied 'chip-chip-chip-chereeeek-chereeeek'. Various other short, sharp whistling calls uttered, and a grunting call by ♀ defending nest. Small young utter shrill peeping, and larger young 'tyuck-tyuck-tyuck-yeeep-yeep-yeep', calls becoming more like adults' with age. Voice feeble for a bird of its size, used mainly in display and near nest.

General Habits. Well known in Africa, intimately known in Europe. May occur in any aquatic habitat, principally coastal marshes and estuaries, also larger inland lakes and rivers, sometimes on small ponds or dams. Usually solitary or in pairs, not gregarious in winter quarters, though several may breed on same island, and several may hunt in same estuary without conflict. Uncommon south of equator.

Resident, possibly partially migrant in Red Sea area and off N African coast. Most individuals seen in Africa are Palearctic migrants. Scandinavian, Finnish and British birds migrate south down west coast of Europe and tropical Africa to Senegal, Nigeria, Gabon, Zaïre, according to ringing recoveries. Birds occurring in E and southern Africa probably come mainly from Russia

and E Asia, but Swedish and Finnish birds recovered in Ethiopia and Zimbabwe. Earliest arrivals occur near equator Aug, remaining till May; odd individuals may oversummer. South Africa, mainly Oct–Mar. Southward movement from Red Sea may follow Rift Valley to Lake Turkana where birds seen moving south early Aug. Adults readily cross large bodies of water on broad front with flapping flight, and all reaching inland lakes must cross large tracts of dry land. Can soar easily and probably thus crosses such dry land areas unobserved, climbing to height, then flapping–gliding as needed. Entirely diurnal; but active soon after dawn to near dark if needed. Roosts preferably on trees, or on rocky cliffs, sandbars, islands.

Spends most of day perched, even when breeding. When fishing, usually very successful; soars over water at 50–150 m, circling and sometimes flapping. On sighting fish halts and hovers briefly, perhaps drops a little; then plunges, apparently head first, but at last moment before striking prey throws feet forward in front of head and usually crashes right in with heavy splash. Less often, picks smaller fish from surface with little splash. If attempt fails turns up abruptly from near water and hovers again, often pursuing same fish for some distance. If successful, may plunge in until entirely submerged, wing-tips only above water, and can take fish almost 1 m below surface. Rising, flaps vigorously to gain height, then shakes or shivers to dry itself, and flies off with fish, often some way, eventually settling to feed. Carries fish fore-and-aft, in line with body. Is often robbed by fish eagles but can withstand attacks from, for example, kites. In E African coastal waters often fishes only when tides are suitable, usually when rising over shallow sandbanks. Daily requirements apparently easily obtained, often in not more than 10–20 min, with 1–3 strikes/kill. Success rate varies from 25–90% of all dives elsewhere. Absence as a breeding bird inexplicable, since breeding sites and food supply widely available in tropical and southern Africa, many southern African habitats closely resembling Eurasian or American breeding areas.

Food. In Africa entirely fish; nothing else recorded. All caught alive, in fresh or salt water, but usually calm or shallow, not rough and deep. Can catch fish to maximum weight of *c.* 3 kg, but most much smaller, 200–500 g. Seldom, however, takes very small fish, usually securing good-sized catch with little effort. Food requirement (Scotland) *c.* 330–350 g/day/adult, *c.* 130 kg for pair and young in breeding cycle, perhaps 250–300 kg/pair/year; requirement possibly less in tropics, but no data available.

Breeding Habits. Little known in Africa, intimately known Europe and America. These results (briefly summarized here) probably similar, with minor variations, to Africa. In Mediterranean breeds on cliffs, isolated rock stacks; population now almost extinct. In Red Sea and Somalia breeds semi-colonially on sandbanks, small islands (e.g. 11 pairs recorded on Aibat Is.: Archer and Godman 1937); less often on cliffs, harbour installations; may be some distance (200–2000 m) from sea.

Most nests are on ground. E African nests at Lake Naivasha and South African ones at Berg River were reported to be in trees.

In nuptial display ♂ soars high, performing steep undulating dives, and swoops over nest-site, sometimes carrying fish, and sometimes flapping wings vigorously with fish dangling, remaining almost stationary, calling (frenzied 'chereek-chereek'). Feeds ♀ during courtship; incipient courtship feeding is seen in migrants along E African coast, so pair-bond may be maintained or formed in winter quarters. Copulation in Europe frequent before egg-laying, up to 7 times daily, then reduced; usually on or near nest.

NEST: enormous structures for size of bird, built of sticks, seaweed, driftwood; repaired annually, used for many years, in NE Africa as in Europe. May be up to 1·5 m high, 1 m thick at base, tower-like, tapering towards top, shallow central cup lined with dry grass and seaweed. Both sexes build in Europe; no African observations. ♂ arrives first, initiates building, brings more material than ♀ before incubation begins; later ♀ brings more. New material is added throughout nesting cycle.

EGGS: 1–4, usually 2–3 (Somalia normally 3); probably laid at 2–3 day intervals, av. clutch apparently no smaller than European. Broad ovals; colour varies greatly, buff, heavily marked brown, red-brown, dark red, with purplish or greyish undermarkings. SIZE: (12 eggs, Somalia) 56·0–64·5 × 42–45 (60·5 × 43·6), av. slightly smaller than in Europe; WEIGHT: *c.* 65 g (Archer and Godman 1937).

Laying dates: Somalia Dec; Red Sea possibly later, to Feb; Mediterranean (Morocco–Algeria) Jan–Feb, perhaps later.

Incubation mostly carried out by ♀—all night and 65–70% of daylight hours (Europe); fed near nest by ♂ throughout incubation, nest-relief usually associated with feeding. Incubation period: 35–38 days (Europe).

Hatch is signified by posture of ♀ sitting higher in nest, and by increased feeding rate by ♂. ♂ feeds himself, ♀ and brood up to at least 40 days after hatch. Food requirements rise from 2–3 fish/day in incubation to 4 just after hatch, then increasing to a maximum of 6, reduced to 4–4·5/day just before young fly. ♂ can catch all or most of this in relatively short fishing periods, still spending many hours a day perched. After day 42, when chicks part-feathered, ♀ assists in fishing.

Chicks hatch at intervals, at first brooded constantly by ♀, brooding reduced as they grow. When disturbed, lie flat in nest, cryptic back-striping helping to hide them from above. First feathers emerge *c.* 28 days; fully feathered by 40 days; first flight *c.* 50–59 days, but varies.

♀ alone broods young, almost continuously up to day 10, thereafter not by day; fed by ♂ while brooding up to day 40; ♀ then remains on or near nest, still dependent on ♂ for food. ♀ continues to feed young with food brought by ♂ up to 42 days old, when they can feed themselves; thereafter she kills prey too but in mid-fledging period ♂ must provide for up to 5 times his own requirements.

Young leave nest of own accord; at first remain nearby, roosting there for *c.* 7 days, then on trees in the vicinity. Are dependent on parents for food for *c.* 30 days after leaving nest, but when strong on wing accompany parents to fishing grounds. Little is known about post-fledging period, even in Europe.

Subfamily ACCIPITRINAE: cuckoo falcons, honey buzzards, kites, fish eagles, Old World vultures, snake eagles, harriers, goshawks, sparrowhawks, buzzards and eagles.

A very large diverse family, varying in size from 55–7500 g and specialized to exploit many different feeding niches. Species occur in all habitats from desert to tropical forest, at all altitudes from sea level to over 4500 m. Some prefer aquatic or marshy habitats. Of 72 African spp. in 32 genera (15 monotypic, 12 endemic), 10 are exclusively Palearctic migrants. Of 62 spp. breeding in Africa, 14–15 also breed in Palearctic, migrating to Africa in winter. Extremely varied, sometimes so specialized for one particular function that no broad generalization is really applicable. Of the 62 African spp. breeding in Africa, the nests of 3 (all inhabitants of tropical forest) and the eggs of a 4th are unknown. However, the remainder are more or less well known, many intensively studied both at and away from the nest. Among the best-known of African birds.

Genus *Aviceda* Swainson

A mainly eastern genus with 1 African representative *Aviceda cuculoides*. Small to medium-sized specialized 'kites'. Upper mandible with 2 'teeth'; head crested; nostril slit-shaped. Legs short, rather stout; tarsus shorter than middle-toe, partly feathered. Wings rather long, pointed. Adult and immature plumage different, adults strongly barred below, immatures streaked. Somewhat resemble goshawks and sparrowhawks.

**Plates
23 and 31**
(Opp. pp. 370
and 466)

Aviceda cuculoides Swainson. African Cuckoo Falcon. Baza coucou.

Aviceda cuculoides Swainson, 1837. Bds. W. Afri. 1, p. 104, pl. 1; Senegal.

Range and Status. Forested and well-wooded parts of Africa from Senegal to W and, rarely, SE Ethiopia (Sim 1979), south, especially down the east coast, to Knysna and George, Cape Province. Generally uncommon, but locally frequent to common, especially on migration in E Africa. Mainly resident, but at least partially migratory southern and E Africa.

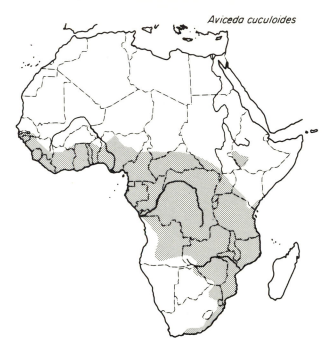

Aviceda cuculoides

Description. *A. c. cuculoides* Swainson: Senegal to E Zaïre and W Ethiopia, south to Nigeria and N Zaïre north of forest belt. ADULT ♂: blackish brown above, slaty on crown and mantle, feather bases white. Base of neck chestnut, uppertail-coverts black, tipped and barred white. Tail black, tipped white, with 3 broad grey bars. Throat, cheeks, upperbreast grey; rest of body below white, broadly barred chestnut, sometimes also on flanks. Underwing-coverts chestnut; rest of underwing white, barred black. Cere greenish; eye bright yellow; legs yellow. ♀ larger, usually much browner than ♂, chestnut bars on underside broader and paler than in ♂. SIZE: wing, 289–293; tail, 186; tarsus, 35–38.
　IMMATURE: above dark brown, many feathers edged buff, tail barred brownish grey. Below, whitish with large irregular dark brown blotches.
　DOWNY YOUNG: white.
　A. c. batesi (Swann). Forests of W and Central Africa from Sierra Leone to W Zaïre basin; darker, more heavily barred than *A. c. cuculoides*. SIZE: wing, ♂ (6) 273–301 (288), ♀ (7) 285–310 (293).
　A. c. verreauxi Lafresnaye. Tropical Africa from Angola and Central Congo to Kenya and south to Cape Province, possibly W Ethiopia. Much larger than *A. c. cuculoides* and has white bars on the chestnut underwing-coverts. SIZE: wing, 293–328 (305).

Field Characters. A secretive, retiring, but not necessarily shy species of woodlands and forests, resembling in appearance a forest *Accipiter* with longer wings, but with quite different mode of flight. At rest vaguely resembles a huge cuckoo, but unlike any falcon, except in having tomial 'teeth' on upper mandible (invisible in field). Differs from any *Accipiter* in having long, rather pointed wings which, when folded, almost reach tail-tip. Flight light, easy, graceful, often kite-like, not swift and direct as in *Accipiter*. Often found in undergrowth, but may also be seen in the open.

Voice. Not recorded. Normally silent. Most common call a single or double mew, explosive in tone 'tohew'; in breeding season a quick, whistling 'choo-titti-too' (syllabled 'mickey-to-you') uttered from perch; at nest soft 'pititiu-pititiu'. Soaring, a more plaintive, *Buteo*-like, but more explosive, 'peeeee-ooo' by both sexes and immatures. Young soliciting food a sharp 'pi-pi-pi-pi', and rapid staccato 'kwik-kwik'. Young also said to utter harsh querulous screams, but this seems unlikely. Voice basically resembles that of Honey Buzzard *Pernis apivorus*.

General Habits. Little known; most descriptions rather misleading. Bears no field resemblance to any falcon. Usually frequents dense cover, soaring or flying above it mainly in display. Perches within cover, sometimes in forest undergrowth, and characteristically remains still several minutes, searching intently above, below and around by turning and twisting head. Frequently perches on low branches making swoops to ground, almost in manner of some flycatchers, to catch an insect. When moving from tree to tree flies lightly, usually swoops low over ground, then flips up onto next perch. Soars and circles easily, flight leisurely, kite-like rather than *Accipiter*-like, again entirely unlike falcons, and unlike cuckoos either. Reluctant to fly across large open areas, but can cross wide areas of water.
　In many areas sedentary, permanently resident, but in coastal E Africa mainly a visitor, probably from further south July–Dec, when relatively common, and even slightly gregarious (several seen close together). Is definitely subject to movement in Transvaal, dispersing, possibly north, from breeding areas (W. Tarboton, pers. comm.). Most E African records June–Mar inclusive; but also breeds. Secretive, retiring habits, often in dense foliage, make good observations difficult.

Food. Insects, especially mantids, grasshoppers, large caterpillars and alate termites; mainly caught on ground, by a short downward swoop from low perch, also sometimes by swooping up into leafy canopy. Lizards, especially chameleons, killed by neatly biting skull (A. Diamond, pers. comm.). Occasionally preys on small birds and has been seen trying to catch a bat. Lizards probably most important prey by weight, especially when breeding (Weaving 1977).

Breeding Habits. Little known. In display, soars and circles, and performs steeply undulating, tumbling aerobatics, with sideways banking and twisting dives exposing chestnut underwing-coverts (W Africa: J. Elgood, pers. comm.). Several may soar together, calling, above forest.

NEST: all known nests are in trees, usually leafy ones, including eucalyptus (Weaving 1977). Usually high up, well hidden in foliage, small slight structures of eucalyptus leaves, leafy twigs, vines, sometimes looking like fallen debris. Both sexes build but one (probably ♀) often remains in nest while other collects twigs. ♂ may perch in tree, looking up, down and around, as if searching for prey; may then fly up to selected twig, grasp it in feet, nip it off with bill, and fall away, taking twig to nest (Brown and Bursell 1968). Final structure may be almost transparent, a small leafy cup lined with green leaves, 30 cm across by 2–25 cm deep; not large enough to hide sitting bird, resembles small nest of Honey Buzzard (Jeffery 1977).

EGGS: 2–3, usually 2; South Africa mean (4 clutches) 2. Pale greenish blue, spotted and streaked brown and chestnut, with lilac undermarkings. SIZE: (8 eggs, South Africa, *A. c. cuculoides*) 41·6–43·7 × 34·0–37·0 (42·8 × 35·1); (1, *A. c. verreauxi*) 42·3 × 34·8 (Schönwetter 1960); WEIGHT: *c*. 28 g.

Laying dates: South Africa Oct–Nov (rains); Zimbabwe, Zambia, Malawi Oct–Nov (rains); Kenya Nov; Nigeria June; all tropical records in rains.

Both sexes incubate; very unobtrusive near nest, again resembling Honey Buzzard. Some calling at nest-relief, or when bringing fresh twigs; no prey brought during incubation. Incubation period: estimated 32–33 days (Weaving 1977).

Young develops unusually rapidly for its size. At 16 days wings part-feathered, head and neck still downy 20 days, but mainly shed on rest of body. At 28 days perching outside nest, has flown by 30 days; disappears from nest area at once (Weaving 1977).

Parents brood and feed chick for first 10 days, thereafter it can feed itself on prey brought. Little detail on share of sexes. Observations suggest young thereafter remain dependent on parents for some time, though able to fly, being fed far away from nest, mainly on chameleons (A. Diamond, pers. comm.). In few recorded cases only 1 young reared. Failures common. In Transvaal, young and parents may remain together after post-nesting dispersal, in small groups.

References
Brown, L. H. and Bursell, G. (1968).
Jeffery, R. D. (1977).
Weaving, A. (1977).

Genus *Pernis* Cuvier

Medium-sized, rather lightly built, broad-winged, long-tailed hawks, superficially resembling *Buteo* spp. Bill weak, slightly hooked; nostrils slit-shaped, oblique; lores covered with scale-like feathers, some forms (not African) crested. Tarsus as long as middle toe, covered with hexagonal scales; claws slender, long, gently curved, sharp at first, but often blunted by digging. 1 sp. Europe, Asia, Africa; others in Far East.

Pernis apivorus (**Linnaeus**). **Honey Buzzard. Bondrée apivore.**

Falco apivorus Linnaeus, 1758. Syst. Nat. (10th ed.), p. 91; Sweden.

**Plates
18 and 30**
(Opp. pp. 291
and 451)

Range and Status. Palearctic winter migrant, does not breed NW Africa. Winter quarters still rather obscure, but probably mainly in W African and equatorial forest and *Brachystegia* woodland south of the equator, rarely south to Natal. Scarce E Africa. Abundant to very abundant autumn at Gibraltar and Bosphorus where most enter Africa; in winter range usually uncommon to frequent. A secretive bird difficult to record.

Description. *P. a. apivorus* (Linnaeus): Europe and Africa. ADULT ♂: extremely variable, several colour phases. Commonest has head and nape dark brown, bases of feathers white; sides of head grey, covered with scale-like feathers. Back, scapulars, upperwing- and uppertail-coverts dark brown, basally white; greater and primary coverts broadly tipped brown, edged whitish, basally barred white and brown. Body below mainly white, with brown streaks on throat, broad brown subterminal bars on remaining feathers. Underwing-coverts barred brown and white. Wing-feathers brown, narrowly tipped white, basally white on inner webs, with subterminal and other dark bars, broadest on primaries. Tail brown, tipped white, with broad subterminal and 2–3 narrower blackish bands, areas between bands vermiculated dark

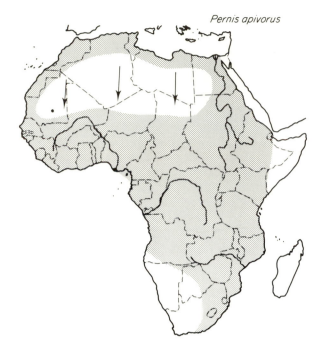

Pernis apivorus

brown. Wing-feathers below greyish brown, basally white, tipped and banded dark brown; tail below grey, with broad terminal and 2–3 other blackish bars, and thin wavy bars in intervening spaces. Eye yellow; cere yellow; legs and feet yellow. Sexes nearly alike in size. SIZE: wing, ♂ 370–425 (402), ♀ 372–447 (409); tail, ♀♂ 210–275; tarsus, 53–60. WEIGHT: ♂ (10 specimens) 510–800 (684), ♀ (8) 625–1040 (832); African birds (unsexed) 675–815 (Biggs *et al.* 1979).

Pale-phase adults are generally paler brown above, below mainly white with blackish shaft streaks and brown subterminal spots. Dark-phase birds still darker than normal, above darker, below more or less obscured by brown bars, sometimes almost uniform chocolate brown; tail- and wing-feathers as in normal phase.

IMMATURE: crown and nape creamy, streaked dark brown. Upperparts brown like adult, paler, feathers more broadly tipped whitish, especially on wing-coverts. Wing-feathers more broadly tipped white than adult. Below variable, palest birds almost white, with a few blackish shaft streaks, darkest uniform brown with darker shaft streaks, indistinctly barred brown on flanks, vent and undertail-coverts. Eye brown, cere and feet yellow.

Field Characters. Broadly resembles Common Buzzard *Buteo buteo* in size, often hard to distinguish from it, but has longer, somewhat narrower, wings and tail, and smaller head. Slender head stretched further forward in flight. At close range bright yellow eye and characteristic barred pattern of tail and wings is best guide; a broad, blackish, subterminal, and 2 other, dark bars seen in tail. In flight soars easily but differs from any *Buteo* or eagle in its frequent, kite-like, lateral twisting of tail at angle to body. Melanistic individuals and immatures resemble some smaller eagles but are distinguishable from them by bare yellow legs; does not closely resemble any breeding African *Buteo* spp.

Voice. Recorded (2a). In Africa, generally silent. In Europe normal call is rather explosive 'piha' or 'piuhu', more whistling than in *Buteo* spp. Long-drawn 'ku-weeee-ee-ee-eiu' by ♂. Other calls uttered at nest unlikely to be heard in Africa.

General Habits. Little known in Africa. Appears most common in forested or densely wooded country; but generally secretive, difficult to see, though not necessarily shy. Often spends some time on ground, alternatively perches well within cover of trees. On ground may walk about, eating insects, possibly termites.

Autumn migration into Africa from Europe and Asia begins late Aug, concentrated at Gibraltar and Bosphorus late Aug to mid-Sept. Far more enter Africa via Gibraltar than at Bosphorus (*c.* 120,000 : 25,000) and some also enter via Italy, Sicily, and Cape Bon, Tunisia. At concentration points thousands may pass in a day, peaks of 11,000–13,000 (Gibraltar) and 7300 in 7 days (Bosphorus) having been recorded (Cramp and Simmons 1980). Thereafter largely disappears or disperses, and is never gregarious in Africa proper. A scarce passage migrant in most of W Africa (Thiollay 1975c). Ringed birds from NW and Central Europe recovered Guinea–Zaïre, and 1 from E Germany in Ethiopia. Return migration more dispersed than southward, begins Apr, most in early May, complete by mid-May. On northward migration crosses Sahara in flocks non-stop, fasting, resting on ground when benighted (Heim de Balsac and Heim de Balsac 1949–1950). More cross the Mediterranean via Cape Bon, Malta and Sicily in spring than autumn (8100, 2–14 May: Thiollay 1977b) and suffer severe losses from shooting; said to be very good to eat. Migration routes and numbers vary from year to year.

Food. In Europe, underground nests of wasps and bees, dug out with feet. In Africa little known, but includes hornets' nests snatched from beneath eaves of huts, trees; termites, collected on ground or caught in flight; bee larvae. Also grasshoppers, locusts, wasps, possibly small reptiles and small birds. Better data needed. Lack of suitable food probably prevents breeding in hot dry Mediterranean summer in NW Africa.

Genus *Machaerhamphus* Westerman

Medium-sized, slender, lightly built aberrant 'kites'. Bill short, weak, keeled and with hook at tip; mandibles thin, gape very wide, adapted for swallowing prey whole. Eye very large, yellow; nostrils almost horizontal. Lores covered with thick velvety feathers, somewhat resembling *Pernis*; crest short. Wings long, narrow, pointed, falcon-like; some feathers have modified edges, as in owls, for silent flight. Tail rather long. Toes long, slender, especially middle toe, with long sharp talons.

Machaerhamphus alcinus Westerman. Bat Hawk. Milan des chauves-souris.

Machaerhamphus alcinus Westerman, 1851. K. Zool. Genootschap Natura Artis Magistra Amsterdam, Bijdragen Dierkunde, pt. 2, pt. 29, pl. 12; Malacca.

Range and Status. Found throughout tropical Africa in woodland or forest, rarely in more arid localities. Invariably local, at best frequent to uncommon, as often seen in towns as anywhere.

Description. *M. a. anderssoni* (Gurney), ADULT ♂: head dark brown with white streak above and below eye. Rest of upperparts dark brown. Wing-feathers brown, spotted white on inner webs. Tail brown, indistinctly barred paler. Throat white, with indistinct central streak. Rest of underside white, feathers of breast tipped brown, and of underwing-coverts spotted brown and white. Eye bright yellow; cere and gape bluish; legs bluish white. Sexes similar, ♀ averages larger. SIZE: wing, ♂ 324–338 (333), ♀ 336–360 (347); tail, 166–184; tarsus, 58–62. WEIGHT: (1 specimen) 650 g.

Dark-phase adults are wholly blackish, with white streak above and below eye, and a black median streak on brown throat; primaries unbarred, tail bars very indistinct. Feathers of nape and throat show white bases.

IMMATURE: browner than adult, showing more white below; eye dark brown, otherwise similar.

DOWNY YOUNG: white.

Field Characters. Although related to Honey Buzzard *Pernis apivorus* bears no field resemblance to it or any *Buteo* sp. In flight, most resembles very large dark falcon, with long, narrow, pointed wings and long tail, but more leisurely kite-like wing-beat. Usually seen only near dusk, when almost unmistakable. Perched by day, mainly blackish body, whitish throat with median dark streak, slim head and bill, and very large, bright yellow eyes are good field marks. Folded wings reach to near tail-tip. Rarely seen in flight by day, but then looks like huge dark falcon.

Voice. Not recorded. Normally silent, but at dusk and in nuptial display by day utters high-pitched broken whistles 'kik-kik-kik-kik-keeee' or 'kwieck-kwieck', kite-like in tone.

General Habits. Well known. Spends most of the day resting in leafy, shady trees, emerging only at dusk to hunt. Seldom flies by day, but may perform mutual nuptial displays in broad daylight, e.g. over Mombasa harbour. Towards dusk leaves roost, flies to chosen hunting area and there catches bats or other prey; may

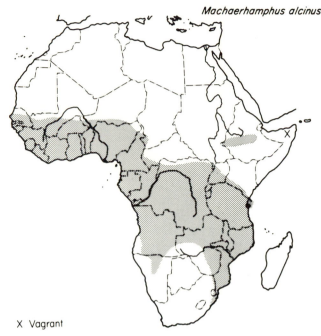

Machaerhamphus alcinus

X Vagrant

continue hunting until almost dark, sometimes, for example, hunting bats attracted to insects attracted to lights, well after normal dusk hours. Occasionally also hunts just after dawn.

For hunting, an open space is preferred, e.g. playing field, town square, beach, freshwater river or lake, tidal creek, against which bats can be sighted, pursued at speed and caught. It appears near such places towards dusk, at first flying round in leisurely kite-like fashion with rather slow wing-beats, but on sighting prey accelerates and attacks at speed, resembling swift falcon. Also catches bats near cave mouths where it either perches on trees, or flies to and fro, making repeated passes across mouth of cave to catch bats emerging at dusk. Roosts at night in trees.

Apparently resident wherever it occurs. With experience, the same individual can be located on chosen roost almost daily, and hunting over same areas in evening.

Food. Principally bats, selecting small species that can be caught in the feet and swallowed whole in flight, ignores larger bats, and never attempts to catch abundant large fruit bats such as *Eidolon*, *Epomophorus*, or even, apparently, extremely common cave guano bats *Otomops martienseni*. Takes some swifts and small hirundines, probably opportunistically as available in same habitat; a few other small birds, e.g. Emerald Cuckoo *Chrysococcyx cupreus* (W. Tarboton, pers. comm.), and some insects. Up to 70% of pellets contain bird remains (Fenton *et al.* 1978).

Hunting technique absolutely characteristic. Must have open space to permit swift pursuit. When bats emerge at dusk, hawk appears, flying or perched; when chance occurs, streaks across open and catches bat in feet, at once transferring it to mouth and swallowing it whole, in *c*. 6 s. Selects prey of preferred size, ignoring large or very small species, and consuming mainly bats in weight range 20–75 g (including *Eptesicus*, *Tadarida*, *Rhinolophus*, *Nycteris* spp.) Species such as *Miniopterus schreibersi* (of right size, but uses caves as night roost only) not often taken. Entire food requirements caught in 20–30 min at dusk, seldom hunting at dawn. 1 observed in Zambia foraged for 13–27 min (av. 18·3/night), made 57–113 passes across cave-mouth (av. 71/evening), and caught 4–11 bats (av. 7/evening), with about 50% of bats actually attacked caught. Food requirement estimated at 50–60 g/day, *c*. 10% of body-weight, amount caught daily varying from 30–80 g (Black *et al.* 1979). Long middle toe assists capture of swift-flying prey, and wide gape is adaptation which permits rapid swallowing of whole prey.

Breeding Habits. Well known; studied more fully in Far East than in Africa. At onset of breeding season pairs perform mutual nuptial displays in broad daylight, with swift aerial chases, rapid turning and diving, and sometimes mutual displays in which ♂ swoops at ♀ who turns on back and presents claws to his. Nuptial display performed at great speed, spectacular to watch, strong daylight no obstacle.

NEST: in trees, usually leafy, quite often in towns (where bats readily available). Same site used for several or many years and nest may be rebuilt in same tree if it collapses. Nest-tree is normally the same as, or close to, day-time roost-tree. When flying into nest-tree after display come in low, very fast and swoop up onto perch. Structure built of sticks, at any height up to 60 m (Africa usually 15–25 m); either in central fork or near trunk on large lateral limb, latter perhaps preferred. Built by both sexes, mainly ♀. Twigs broken off in flight, not collected from ground. May be large, up to 1 m across by 0·5 m deep, usually smaller; often not lined with green leaves, unlike other such raptors.

EGGS: 1–2 eggs laid asynchronously; interval not known. White, with a few faint markings. SIZE: (6 eggs, Zimbabwe) 57·6–64·0 × 43–48 (60·4 × 45·6).

Laying dates: Transvaal Nov–Dec (rains); Zimbabwe Sept–Nov (late dry–early rains); E Africa Apr–June (late rains–early dry); Uganda (1 record) Oct (early dry).

♀ alone incubates, sitting very close by day, leaving nest at evening to fly around, perhaps catching own prey in short period. Bold and likely to be aggressive near nest when disturbed. Period: estimated 30 days.

Newly hatched young brooded closely by ♀ by day; later in fledging period ♀ perches near, does not brood, full details lacking. Fed by ♂ at first, later by both parents. Both parents roost in tree later in fledging period. Young fly at 35–40 days, thereafter remaining near nest for a short time, then disappearing. In known instances, 1 young reared/year regularly, never more. Some non-breeding; overall success *c*. 0·8/year. Newly fledged immatures have much more white than adults, and perhaps white below signifies sub-adult stages, as most full adults appear to be dark-phase birds.

References
Black, H. L. *et al.* (1979).
Fenton, M. B. *et al.* (1978).

Genus *Elanus* Savigny

A very characteristic genus of small kites. Plumage grey and white patched with black, inhabiting open grasslands; almost cosmopolitan, but especially Australia. Head large, with supraorbital ridge; eyes large, red. Wings long, pointed. Tail short, square, or slightly indented. Bill short, gape wide. Tarsi short, 75% feathered, rest with round scales; talons rounded below. Pair of powder-down patches either side of rump. 4 spp., 1 African and Asian, 1 American, 2 Australian.

Plate 21

(Opp. p. 354)

Elanus caeruleus (Desfontaines). Black-shouldered Kite. Elanion blanc.

Falco caeruleus Desfontaines, 1789. Hist. Acad. Roy. Sci. Paris (1787), p. 503, pl. 15; near Algiers.

Range and Status. Breeds S Europe, NW Africa, and throughout tropical and southern Africa to Cape Province, in open grasslands, semi-desert, light woodland; rare in heavy woodland, but occurs in clearings or open spaces within former forest. In optimum habitat, common to abundant, usually frequent to common. Locally migratory and nomadic. Probably increasing through human activity, especially clearing of woodland and forest, and tree planting in open grasslands, providing new breeding and roosting sites.

Description. *E. c. caeruleus* (Desfontaines), ADULT ♂: forehead and streak above eye white, grey on head. Most of rest of upperparts pale grey, feathers at bend of wing white. Lesser and median wing-coverts, and a patch on outer edge of wing black. Primaries and secondaries blue-grey tipped blackish, shafts black. Central tail feathers grey, rest white. Whole underside, including cheeks, throat and underwing-coverts white, breast washed grey. Eye bright red; cere, gape, feet yellow. Sexes appear alike, but ♀ slightly larger and heavier. SIZE: wing, ♂ 260–278, ♀ 263–287; tail, 110–135; tarsus, 35–38. WEIGHT: ♂ (28) 200–270 (237), ♀ (27) 219–293 (258·5) (Biggs *et al.* 1979).

1ST IMMATURES: have breast and neck washed chestnut; nape streaked white, scapulars, wing-feathers and coverts dark brownish grey edged rufous, black shoulder-patch spotted white and is smaller than adult's. Eye yellow to pale brown. Complete body moult takes place within 3–6 months; wing- and tail-feathers within 1 year, becoming steadily greyer, less brownish; eye has become red by 6 months.

DOWNY YOUNG: pale brownish grey, eye dark, cere and feet yellowish white.

Field Characters. Not easily confused with other species; a small grey hawk, white below, rather stumpy-bodied when perched, but long-winged in flight; black shoulder in flight or when perched conspicuous. Most likely to be confused with ♂ Pallid Harrier *Circus macrourus* or ♂ Montagu's Harrier *C. pygargus*, but smaller, much shorter-tailed, lacks black wing-tips, and perches and hovers rather than flying low over grassland. Habit of hovering frequently characteristic.

Voice. Recorded (1e, 2a, 6, 19). Of little help in field recognition as calls weak, only audible at close range, when bird normally visible. Calls sexually distinct. Generally rather silent, except when breeding, when vocal. Utters whistles, screams, or short 'chipping' notes. Commonest ♂ display call (in butterfly display flight) shrill, 'weeet-weeet-weeet', or 'weep-weep'; this also contact call, with chipping 'tsip-tsip-tsip'. In alarm, or when attacking other kites or intruders, harsher screams 'shreeee-shreeee-shree' or chattering 'chit-it-it-it-it' recorded. ♀ soliciting copulation utters distinctive double whistle 'weeeee-egh', like begging calls of young; aspirated sounds 'weeee-eh', and 'whaaarh' also described (Van Someren 1956; W. Tarboton, unpub.).

General Habits. Intimately known; one of few raptors whose daily activities have been quantitatively analysed. Most abundant in open plains with long grass, such as South African highveld or E African grasslands; but occurs also in farmland, open patches or clearings in heavy woodland or forest (if large enough) and to edges of semi-desert. In wet years invades true desert with less than 200 mm annual rainfall. Found from sea level to *c.* 3000 m, but not normally in Afro-alpine moorland, despite abundance of rodent prey.

Roosts communally in small to large groups; normally 10–20, sometimes up to 100, rarely up to 500 (Morel and Poulet 1976); 2 such roosts in 76 km² in Transvaal (W. Tarboton, unpubl.). Some roosts regularly used, but individuals using them vary constantly. Leaves roost soon after dawn, flies to hunting territory, and may preen and perch for up to 2 h. Is then active for rest of day, normally hunting for *c.* 4 h daily, sometimes up to 9 h; same marked individual varied from spending 5·6–73·2% of daylight hunting on different days; av. in one study 54% daylight (Tarboton 1978a) may be generally too high (J. Mendelsohn, pers. comm.). Sometimes continues hunting late into dusk, aided by large eyes. Hunts chiefly by perching on trees, stubs, especially telegraph wires and poles, and by hovering over open spaces. When perching sits for long periods (71% of hunting time) but peers round actively. When prey sighted, drops in short glide, raising wings above back to make final attack. Hovers (29% of hunting time) with head to wind, body not strongly angled, short tail spread, long wings beating rather irregularly, not swiftly fanning as in kestrels. To catch prey, first descends slowly (parachute-like), then raises wings and plunges suddenly. Hovering may increase success rate of strikes from 10–15% to 20–35% and may permit capture of

Elanus caeruleus

larger prey, so extra energy expended (7 times as much as perching) is worthwhile (Tarboton 1978a); this may not be general (J. Mendelsohn, pers. comm.). Perching, requiring much less energy, is more efficient in terms of food secured/energy used.

Apparently permanently resident in some areas (notably South African highveld); individuals constantly change in any population. In most areas more or less nomadic, appearing in numbers in some years or months, perhaps breeding, then moving on. In same areas numbers may fluctuate by factor of 10 or more in successive years. Temporary abundance is probably associated with rodent plagues, kites congregating in areas where rodents temporarily abundant, and often associated with above average rainfall (E Africa). Since daily feed intake of non-breeding birds, estimated at 99·7 kcal, about equals theoretical maintenance requirements, breeding may not be possible unless rodents are abundant. No regular migrations documented, and nomadism hard to analyse, but probably associated with variable rainfall and seasonal changes in semi-arid grasslands. ♀♀ apparently more nomadic than ♂♂ (J. Mendelsohn, pers. comm.). In Transvaal marked individuals have moved as far as 645 km (in 69 days) and 915 km, but most stay within 50–100 km. Largest recorded roost concentrations (110 Kenya; 500 Senegal) were associated with rodent plagues.

Food. Almost entirely (90–95%) rodents in size range 40–90 g, especially *Rhabdomys*, *Otomys*, *Arvicanthis*. Less often, nocturnal *Praomys* taken at dusk. Some orthoptera recorded, especially in regularly burned W African woodlands (Thiollay 1978a); but probably unimportant by weight. Also, a few lizards and small ground birds. Daily food requirement estimated at 61 g, *c.* 25% of bodyweight; this provided by 1 *Otomys* or 2 *Rhabdomys-Praomys*. When rodents abundant can catch requirements easily, in 4/12 daylight h or less.

Breeding Habits. Intimately known; but many results not yet published (J. Mendelsohn, in prep.). Numbers breeding any locality vary greatly from year to year, apparently related to irregular rodent abundance, though connection not quantitatively established. Strongly territorial when breeding, vocal and aggressive, repelling other raptors much larger than itself, and other Black-shouldered Kites from defended area. Breeds in trees, 2–20 m above ground, most often in low thorny *Acacia* spp.; but broad-leaved trees and exotic pines also used.

Pre-laying period may occupy 21–75 days. Nuptial display not spectacular. Mutual soaring over nest-site, some chasing, and, by ♂, a fluttering descending flight (butterfly flight) towards nest or mate. Either sex may perch on trees, raising and lowering tail jerkily, calling; this is apparently threat display to mate, to intruders, other large birds, even aeroplanes; may also be seen when excited away from nesting area. ♂ feeds ♀ during courtship, near nest. Copulation occurs on or near nest-tree, sometimes on nest; takes *c.* 15 s. ♂ flies direct to soliciting ♀, who crouches, sometimes quivers wings, and calls; copulation becomes more frequent close to egg-laying.

NEST: new nest normally built annually; an old one occasionally rebuilt or may be taken over by another pair, then re-used by original builders. A thin, flat structure of sticks, usually not more than 30 cm across by 10 cm deep; not lined with green leaves, but shallow cup is lined with grass, or fine twigs. Both sexes build, ♀ more than ♂ in some observed cases, or she may remain in nest while ♂ brings twigs. New nests often built quickly, within 10 days, perhaps necessary to take advantage of temporary food abundance.

EGGS: 2–5 eggs, usually 3–4, laid at 2–3 day intervals; South African mean (70 clutches) 3·6, E Africa (24 clutches) 3·6, N Africa 4–5 recorded, may average larger. Cream to pale buff, blotched and spotted dark brown, purple, with grey undermarkings, often forming a cap at broad end. SIZE: (100 eggs, South Africa) 36·8–44·3 × 28·6–32·8 (40·1 × 31·7); (120) 35·0–43·0 × 28·5–33·0 (39·4 × 30·9) (Schönwetter 1960); WEIGHT: *c.* 21 g.

Laying ♀♀ weigh 320–333 g, weight reduced to normal later (W. Tarboton, unpub.); av. (clutch of 3) *c.* 25% of normal ♀ bodyweight.

Laying dates: South Africa all months, in some years little synchronized, in others synchronized: Cape peak July–Sept (early spring), Transvaal, 2 peaks, Sept–Oct (early dry season) and Feb–Mar (rains); Zambia–Zimbabwe Feb–Nov, perhaps peaking Apr–May (end rains); Kenya–Uganda most months, both dry and wet, with ill-defined peak late rains–early dry (E Kenya May–July); Ethiopia Feb–Apr (late dry); Nigeria Nov, Apr (late dry, early rains); N Africa Feb–Mar (early spring), Aug. Most laying apparently occurs late in rains–early dry season, but periods irregular. In good conditions can be double or multiple brooded, 1 marked ♀ made 6 attempts and laid 3 clutches (all unsuccessful) in 17 months (W. Tarboton, unpub.). Re-laying after natural failure may occur in 18–25 days.

Incubation begins with 1st egg, mainly by ♀, ♂ taking short spells by day, usually associated with feeding ♀. ♀ usually incubates 85–90% of daylight and at night; rarely, ♂ incubates up to 21% of daylight. ♂ feeds ♀ on nest, bringing up to 6 prey/day, usually first partly eaten by him. Prolonged failure to feed ♀ may result in her leaving to hunt herself, ending in failure; available data suggest abundant food essential for successful breeding. Breeding kites may tolerate others passing over territory, but not attempting to hunt within it. Incubation period: 30–33 (mean 31) days (J. Mendelsohn, pers. comm.).

Despite long laying period, hatching period much shorter; chicks vary less than expected in size. Little sibling aggression, but nest losses often severe. Chicks show feathers at 12–14 days, are largely feathered by 21 days, after 30 days perch on branches near nests. 1st flights at 33–37 (mean 35) days (J. Mendelsohn, pers. comm.).

During fledging period ♀ remains near nest, receives food from ♂, feeds chicks; ♂♂ not known to feed young. ♀ remains within 200 m of nest and may hunt and kill prey, but seldom feeds young on what she catches; main demand is on ♂ who hunts up to 1500 m from nest. Observations suggest food demand (2 items in 4 h at 14 days; 3 in 3 h at 22 days) increases through fledging period. ♀ later assists in feeding feathered young, starting earlier if food scarce (J. Mendelsohn, pers. comm.). Lack of food and predation (especially by Tawny Eagle *Aquila rapax*) most common cause of failure.

Young remain near nest for *c.* 6 days after first flight, usually in nest-tree, returning to nest-platform to feed. Thereafter perch near, making increasingly long flights, for up to 22 days. Then disperse in area, not necessarily very far; remain dependent 42–70 days. Complete a body moult in 3–6 months, retaining juvenile wing- and tail-feathers; can probably breed within 1 year of first flight, conceivably even earlier.

Breeding success not fully documented anywhere, but nest losses normally severe. Broods of 1–4 may be reared; but many attempts to breed do not result in eggs, incubation losses are heavy, and brood losses also heavy, but apparently less than in incubation. In 1 study area (Transvaal) 8/17 nests used, 9 abandoned; 42% of eggs hatched, and 75% of young hatched flew (W. Tarboton, unpub.). In other cases 30–50% failure before egg-laying, in incubation and in fledging period estimated (J. Mendelsohn, pers. comm.). If 50% of breeding attempts do not result in eggs, 60% of eggs are lost and 30% of young are lost in fledging period, this, with av. clutch of 3, equals 0·42 young/pair/breeding attempt, or 0·21/adult. Irregular breeding (little or none in some years, some areas) and mortality before sexual maturity would further reduce productivity. Implications are that adult Black-shouldered Kites may be moderately long-lived, perhaps up to 10 years.

References
Tarboton, W. (1978a).
Van Someren, V. G. L. (1956).

Genus *Chelictinia* Lesson

Small kites; grey marked black. Bill small, weak; wings long, pointed. Tail very long, deeply forked, outermost feathers greatly prolonged. Legs short, rather strong, talons sharply curved. This genus has sometimes been combined with *Elanus*, but has long forked tail, insectivorous diet and more gregarious habits.

Chelictinia riocourii (Vieillot). African Swallow-tailed Kite. Milan de Riocour.

Plate 21

Elanoides riocourii Vieillot, 1822. Gal. Ois. 1, p. 43, pl. 16; Senegal.

(Opp. p. 354)

Range and Status. The more arid parts of northern tropical Africa between *c*. lat. 8°N and 15°N, varying with season, from Senegal–Sudan, east to Ethiopia, Somalia and N Kenya as far south as Marsabit and Lake Turkana, rarely to near Nairobi. Migratory and nomadic, locally common to abundant, especially near breeding colonies. Numbers probably stable, but varying with natural factors.

Chelictinia riocourii

Description. ADULT ♂: forehead, eyebrow, white; a small black patch behind eye. Upperparts, including tail and most of wings, pale grey, washed sooty on upperback, outer scapulars with blackish margins. Primaries pale grey, secondaries white on inner webs. Tail grey, white on inner webs on all but central feathers. Whole underside including tail- and wing-feathers white, with a long black patch on underwing-coverts. Eye bright red; cere grey; legs yellow. Sexes similar, little size difference. SIZE: wing, ♂ 230–246, ♀ 230–254; tail, outermost feathers 170–216, central 92–100; tarsus, 28–33. WEIGHT: unrecorded.

IMMATURE: browner, with many feathers on back and secondaries edged rufous; tail much less deeply forked.

DOWNY YOUNG: dull pale grey, eye blackish (Davey and Davey 1980).

Field Characters. Unmistakable; a small, very beautiful kite, in flight resembling a tern more than a bird of prey. Almost all white below with black bar on underwing-coverts, and long, exceptionally deeply forked tail. Hovers and soars over open country, and tends to be gregarious. At rest very small and slim, tail feathers projecting far beyond folded wing-tips.

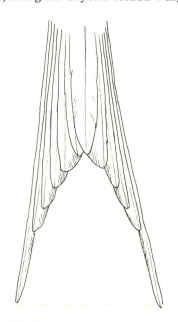

Voice. Recorded (19). Silent except at breeding quarters, where noisy, uttering rapid rasping calls 'tcheee-tchi-chi-chi-chi' or rapidly repeated 'to-ti-ti-ti-tri'; some softer whistles, and a feeble mew.

General Habits. Little known. Inhabits semi-desert areas of Africa from Senegal–Ethiopia south to Kenya, seldom occurring in rainfall exceeding 400 mm/year except when not breeding in dry season. A bird of open, sparsely grassed plains and deserts, only moving south into long grass savannas irregularly, not in all years.

Roosts on trees in small flocks, and is on wing most of the day. Soars and circles at 20–100 m above ground, continually turning into wind, poising motionless against wind, or hovering briefly with fanning wings; widely spread tail when poising probably assists slow searching flight. Supremely graceful in flight. Usually somewhat gregarious even by day, several hunting over same area, with other similar areas lacking any nearby. Not as gregarious as e.g. Lesser Kestrel *Falco naumanni* or Red-footed Falcon *F. vespertinus*, but much more than Black-shouldered Kite *Elanus caeruleus*.

Performs more or less regular north to south movements in W Africa, moving south as far as 8°N in lower Guinea savanna, arriving Nov, departing again north about Feb; arrival may coincide with strong Harmattan winds from the northeast, and birds do not come so far south all years. Then frequent mainly tree-less areas caused by human cultivation rather than dense woodland. Comes to grass fires to catch insects. Normally hunts over grassland or desert, plunging into grass to secure insects at intervals. In eastern part of range (Ethiopia–NE Kenya) less obviously migratory, present in both dry and wet seasons in some haunts, but not well documented; here perhaps moves south to breed in rains near Lake Turkana. In W Africa moves north to breed in rains in Sahel zone.

Food. Mainly insects in dry season, when not breeding. May also take a few small mammals and reptiles, lizards more important at breeding colonies. All are caught by dropping gracefully from hover, raising wings above back to drop more swiftly at last moment; at fires, disturbed insects caught on wing.

Breeding Habits. Little known; no colony ever studied fully. Nests colonially in trees (*Acacia*, *Balanites* recorded) in groups of 10–20 pairs, sometimes fewer. Same tree may be used repeatedly, but not in all years, and nests may be associated with those of other large

raptors (Brown Snake Eagle *Circaetus cinereus*, N Kenya) though this may be chance. However, often perches near such nests.

NEST: small, slight, *c*. 30–40 cm across, made of sticks; deep cup is lined with grass. Built anew each year, in trees, usually 5–8 m above ground, occasionally only 2 m. Extremely dense, thorny *Balanites* bushes may be selected when tall acacias available nearby (Davey and Davey 1980).

EGGS: normally 4. Pale sandy, speckled all over with red-brown. SIZE: 34·3–38·0 × 26·7–31·0 (35·4 × 28·6).

Apparently lays May–June (height of rains) almost throughout range. In N Kenya eggs recorded Mar, and breeding complete (young ready to leave) by 20 June.

Full details not available, but it appears ♀ takes larger share of incubation and feeds young. She is fed at nest by ♂, who also brings most prey to young. Food presentation may be accompanied by raising and lowering tail (in manner of Black-shouldered Kite) and excited chattering calls (Davey and Davey 1980).

References
Davey, P. and Davey, G. (1980).

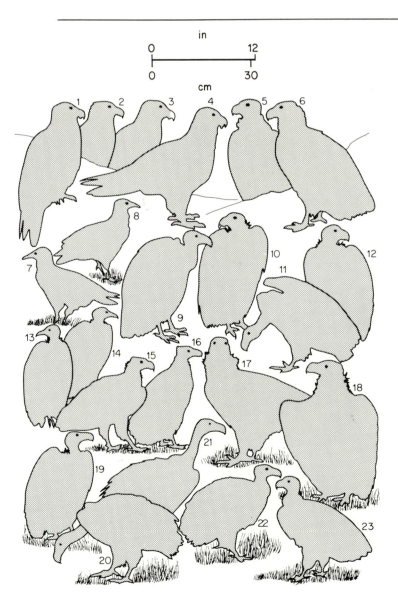

in
0 — 12
0 — 30
cm

Plate 19

Gypaetus barbatus Lammergeier (p. 318)
1. 1ST YEAR IMMATURE, 2. 2ND YEAR IMMATURE,
3. SUBADULT, 4. ADULT.

Aegypius monachus Cinereous Vulture (p. 335)
5. IMMATURE, 6. ADULT.

Neophron percnopterus Egyptian Vulture (p. 322)
7. ADULT, 8. IMMATURE.

Gyps fulvus European Griffon (p. 331)
9. ADULT, 10. IMMATURE.

Gyps coprotheres Cape Vulture (p. 333)
11. ADULT, 12. IMMATURE.

Necrosyrtes monachus Hooded Vulture (p. 324)
13. ADULT, 14. IMMATURE.

Aegypius occipitalis White-headed Vulture (p. 338)
15. ADULT, 16. IMMATURE.

Aegypius tracheliotus Lappet-faced Vulture
(p. 336)
17. IMMATURE, 18. ADULT.

Gyps rueppellii Rüppell's Griffon (p. 329)
Race *rueppellii*: 19. IMMATURE, 20. ADULT.
Race *erlangeri*: 21. ADULT.

Gyps africanus African White-backed Vulture
(p. 326)
22. ADULT, 23. IMMATURE.

Genus *Milvus* Lacépède

Typical large, fork-tailed, scavenging kites. Plumage brown and rufous, variable. Bill rather small, weak. Wings rather long, rounded at tips, in flight always sharply angled at carpal joint. Tail long, deeply or slightly forked, more so in adults than immatures. Legs short, tarsus with transverse scutes in front, reticulate scales behind; feet rather weak for size, but talons long, sharp, not strongly curved. 2 spp., 1 all Old World including Africa, 1 European–Asian, breeding NW Africa only.

Milvus migrans (Boddaert). Black Kite. Milan noir.

**Plates
18 and 30**
(Opp. pp. 291
and 451)

Falco migrans Boddaert, 1783. Tabl. Pl. Enl. p. 28, no. 472; France.

Range and Status. Throughout Africa, from NW Africa to Egypt and south to Cape Province. In almost any habitat, from subdeserts to dense forests, probably commonest in savannas and grasslands, but usually (90–95%) commensal with man. Regularly migratory, and locally nomadic. Abundant to very abundant, especially in north tropical African towns, less abundant south of equator. Away from towns only frequent to common. Probably increasing through association with man and his refuse.

Description. *M. m. parasitus* (Daudin): all tropical Africa to South Africa, except NE Africa, extra-limital Comoros and Madagascar. ADULT ♂: crown and nape brown, streaked black. Back and upperwing-coverts brown, washed rufous,

with dark shaft-streaks. Primaries black, secondaries brown, innermost with indistinct darker bars. Tail brown, paler towards tip, faintly barred lighter and darker. Underside, including underwing-coverts, uniform rufous-brown to dark cinammon. Bill bright yellow; cere yellow; eye brown; legs yellow. ♀♀ larger. SIZE: wing, ♂ 415–425, ♀ 425–450; tail, ♂♀ 240–270; tarsus, ♂♀ 50–60; span, 1330–1400. WEIGHT: ♂ 567–650, ♀ 584–765.

IMMATURE: duller brown above, but with paler head, more streaked. Below, browner than adult, with narrow, whitish shaft-streaks. Bill black, becoming yellowish at base, later fully yellow. Eye brown, cere and legs yellow.

DOWNY YOUNG: buff above, whitish below; first down long, silky, becoming thicker later, grey-brown above, buff below; eye brown, cere and legs from first pale yellow.

Racial variation is confused by sometimes separating this species into 2, *M. aegyptius*, the 2 African yellow-billed forms,

---

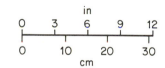

Plate 20

Circaetus gallicus European Snake Eagle (p. 340)
Race *gallicus*: 1. IMMATURE, 2. ADULT.
Race *beaudouini* (Beaudouin's Snake Eagle):
3. IMMATURE, 4. ADULT.
Race *pectoralis* (Black-breasted Snake Eagle):
5. IMMATURE, 6. ADULT.

Polyboroides typus African Harrier Hawk (p. 351)
7. ADULT, 8. IMMATURE.

Circaetus cinereus Brown Snake Eagle (p. 343)
9. IMMATURE, 10. ADULT.

Circaetus cinerascens Smaller Banded Snake Eagle (p. 346)
11. IMMATURE, 12. ADULT ♂, 13. ADULT ♀.

Circaetus fasciolatus
Southern Banded Snake Eagle (p. 344)
14. IMMATURE, 15. ADULT.

Dryotriorchis spectabilis Congo Serpent Eagle (p. 350)
16. ADULT, 17. IMMATURE.

Terathopius ecaudatus Bateleur (p. 347)
18. IMMATURE, 19. ADULT ♀ (light-backed phase),
20. ADULT ♂ (normal phase).

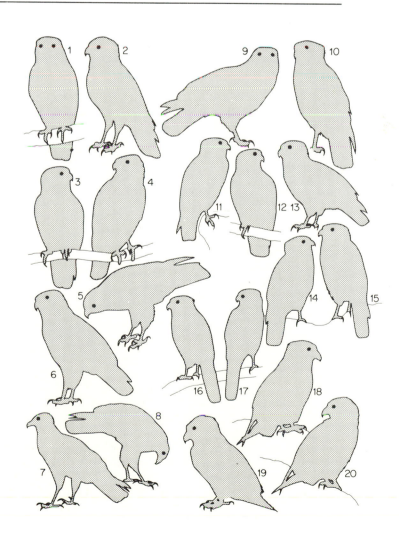

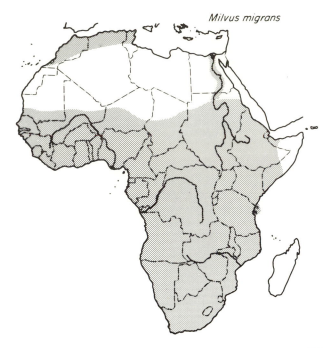

Milvus migrans

and *M. migrans*, all other Old World black-billed forms. This view is not generally accepted, and we consider that all Black Kites are of 1 widespread species *M. migrans* with 7 races, 3 occurring in Africa.

M. m. migrans (Boddaert). Breeds Palearctic, including NW Africa, migrating south in winter. Larger than *M. m. parasitus*. SIZE: wing, ♂ 426–463, ♀ 448–482; wing-span, *c.* 1500–1800. WEIGHT: ♂ 630–928 (807), ♀ 750–941 (850). Head markedly whiter, streaked black, body darker brown above and below, a marked greyish patch near carpal joint of wing in flight. Immatures more broadly streaked yellowish below.

M. m. aegyptius (Gmelin). Breeding Egypt–Red Sea, migrating to coastal E Africa in winter. Resembles *M. m. migrans*, but browner on head and neck, more rufous below, tail more rufous with 7–8 distinct darker bars. Bill yellow in adult, blackish in immature (like *M. m. parasitus*). SIZE: wing, ♂ 413–437 (423), ♀ 435–460 (452).

Field Characters. Can really only be confused with Red Kite *M. milvus*, which is decidedly smaller, much darker, less brightly rufous (especially on underwing), with shorter, less deeply forked tail. A medium-sized, generally darkish brown bird of prey with, in adult, tail always markedly forked even when spread; in immature fork barely discernible when tail spread. Wings always markedly angled at carpal joint; flight light, buoyant, alternate flapping and gliding when on straight course. Extremely agile, twisting long tail to steer expertly between trees, vehicles, huts and wires. Similar in size to small buzzard or smallest eagles; but can be distinguished from them by forked tail, yellow bill in adult (*parasitus* and *aegyptius*) and yellow naked tarsus. At rest somewhat like Grasshopper Buzzard *Butastur rufipennis*, but easily distinguishable from this by brown, not white, eye, forked tail and, in flight, by lack of rufous patch in wing. Booted Eagle *Hieraaetus pennatus* seen from above also has paler brown upper-wing-coverts, but is shorter-winged, holds wings straight when soaring and lacks forked tail.

Voice. Recorded (2a, 6, 8, 9, 17, 19, 26). A variety of moderately loud, quavering, repeated whistles, exact

functions of which (if any) not fully established by analysis. Most vocal in breeding season and at communal roosts. Commonest call a slow quavering 'killlll-errrrr' or 'quil-errrrr', (2nd trill lower-pitched) uttered when perched or in flight. In display, excitement, aggression, calls become higher-pitched and more staccato 'keeeee-yik-yik-yik' or 'queeeu-ki-ki-ki-ki'. Softer 'sio-kee-kee-kee' when bringing food. When perched, sometimes utters long-drawn mewing whistle 'wheeeeeuw'. Small begging young utter high-pitched 'pier' or 'wih-wih-wih', becoming more trilling and adult-like after 3 weeks, e.g. 'whirrrrrr'. Also low 'piu-piu' accepting food. Voices of races do not differ appreciably, and variations in renderings given elsewhere are often due to language differences (Cramp and Simmons 1980; Glutz von Blotzheim *et al.* 1971).

General Habits. Very well known. Despite ubiquitous distribution, and numbers which probably exceed any other African raptor, large or small, still not fully studied. Would qualify as the world's most successful and numerous diurnal raptor, very abundant in towns, and normally associated with small or large human communities, even very small ones. Seldom stays long in uninhabited areas, but must cross these on movements. May originally have been a woodland species, now chiefly adapted (90–95% of total population) to life with man. As long as humans and refuse available, adapts to any habitat from dense tropical forest to desert, even aquatic, e.g. in harbours.

Usually gregarious, except when breeding, sometimes even then. Roosts in large groups in towns; same site used nightly, often in eucalyptus. At dawn leaves roost to forage, travelling up to 30 km away from home roost; but in large towns principally forages in streets and markets. Near towns may follow lines of road to collect animals killed by cars. By mid-morning may have fed and may then gather in certain favoured places, usually open grass fields, where rests, preens. Returns towards roost in afternoon, gathering in circling, wheeling flocks 1–2 h before dark, often perching for some time before finally settling on night roost. In towns, is valuable scavenger, collecting any scrap of animal matter; often extremely bold, snatching food from plates, or scraps from among traffic. Kites themselves are so alert and agile they are seldom killed by vehicles.

Within Africa, 4 different interlocking movement patterns discernible: (i) *M. m. migrans* migrates south in winter, mainly to near equator, but occurs south to Transvaal. Breeds spring and early summer Palearctic, in Africa, only breeding in NW Palearctic; (ii) *M. m. aegyptius* breeds early spring Egypt; Dec–Apr N Somalia, migrating in non-breeding season south to Kenya–Tanzanian coastal regions. Extent inland of migration unclear, but probably includes W Ethiopia–Sudan border; (iii) northern populations of *M. m. parasitus* migrate south Oct, at end rains. Breed mainly in southern range and migrate north again Mar–May, summering north of *c.* 12°N, but in Mali and upper Volta also recorded breeding Mar–Apr, end dry season (Laferriers, nest records). A few remain year-round near equator; (iv) southern African population breeds in southern part of range in summer (Sept–Mar) and after breeding migrates north again, possibly reaching equator about June. These birds are, however, racially indistinguishable from northern, much more numerous *parasitus*. Kites breeding mid-year (June–Aug) near equator perhaps may be of the southern *parasitus* population. On migration, gregarious, travelling in flocks, or small groups at least, very seldom solitary.

Kites, often despised because of scavenging habits, are in fact supremely successful, adaptable birds, able to make use of almost any habitat and food supply, and valuable scavengers in tropical towns and villages, taking much refuse not specifically dumped for disposal elsewhere, e.g. on rubbish heaps.

Food. Any animal matter from insects to large dead mammals. Often arrive early at carcass, attracting larger species. Principally scraps of meat, skin, bones, and some vegetable matter collected in towns (e.g. cooked maize-meal). Catches termites and beetles in feet in flight, thereafter biting off abdomen, discarding hard thorax. Molluscs, crustacea, amphibia and small fish caught in shallow water, or sometimes fish from surface in harbours. In W Africa feeds much on oil palm peri-carp. Largest size of wild prey killed, small rats, young birds, poultry chicks, lizards. Pirates prey from other kites and raptors if it can, but often fails with larger more powerful species. Extremely agile and clever in catching live prey, aided by buoyant flight and high manoeuvrability imparted by forked tail, spread, closed, or twisted at will. Takes free-ranging untended young poultry, but on balance must be highly beneficial to man.

Breeding Habits. Very well known, but more intensively studied in Europe than Africa. Duration of pair-bond uncertain, perhaps life-long, as kites often appear still paired when on migration. Resident tropical races arrive at breeding grounds apparently paired.

Nuptial display begins within winter flocks. Main feature is twisting, weaving pursuit-flight, ♂ following ♀, calling, with rather measured deliberate wing-beats. May then soar in circles, ♂ above ♀; he may then dive at her, when she turns on back and presents claws. Rarely, pairs grapple claws and whirl downwards 'cart-wheeling' over and over. Such display is easily confused with pursuit flights connected with piracy. Intensifies when pair arrive at breeding locality, but seldom as active or vocal as in some other large raptors; much perching and calling near nest-site.

Usually nests in trees (invariable, tropical Africa), less often on buildings (Egypt, N Africa), rarely cliffs (where no trees available). Sometimes at least loosely colonial, 30–40 pairs in small area such as an oasis or plantation (*M. m. aegyptius*, Somalia) but usually well dispersed. Breeding population of large African towns (Ibadan, Nairobi, Addis Ababa) only a small fraction of total migrant flocks. Builds own nest, sometimes on foundation of another.

NEST: made of sticks; any height from 5–30 m above ground (usually 8–20 m), *c.* 0·5–0·8 m across, 0·3–0·5 m deep, roughly basin-shaped. Distinguished from

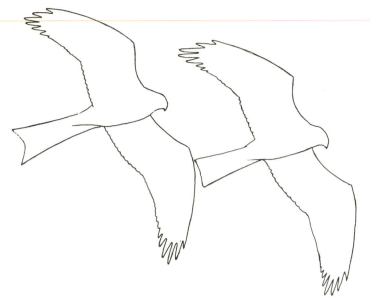

Flight silhouettes of (left) adult, (right) immature.

nests of all other large raptors (except Red Kite) by lining of scraps, dung, paper, bits of cloth, hair, skin, almost any rubbish, seldom green leaves. Built by both sexes; twigs snapped off in flight or collected from ground. Same nest is used for several years, and same general site usually re-occupied if same nest not actually used. Adults very aggressive at nest, often striking effectively and drawing blood with claws; attacks humans and, for example, cats.

EGGS: 1–4, normally 2–3, laid at 1 or 2 day intervals (Meyburg 1971); NW Africa mean (8 clutches) 2·26, South Africa (25) 1·8, E Africa (45) 1·98 (excluding 8 clutches, 2·19). Round ovals; dull white, sometimes unmarked, usually spotted and blotched brown, with greyish-purplish undermarkings. SIZE (100 eggs, *M. m. parasitus*) 49·5–58·7 × 38·6–46·6 (53·4 × 42·1); European *M. m. migrans* av. larger (53·6 × 42·8) and *M. m. aegyptius* (Somalia) 55·5–48·0 × 40·5–42·0 (51·6 × 41·6), rather smaller. WEIGHT: (*M. m. parasitus*) *c.* 53·5 g. Full details breeding in Africa unrecorded.

Laying dates: NW Africa (*M. m. migrans*) Mar–June, most Africa normally May; Egypt Feb–Apr; Somalia Dec–Jan (height of dry season), with perhaps a second peak Mar–Nov; W Africa Oct–Jan, mainly Dec, (early dry season); also Mali, upper Volta, Mar–Apr (end dry season) (Laferriers, nest records). E Africa chiefly Nov–Mar, but odd records May, June, Aug, Sept, Oct, suggesting birds of different origin; main peak Nov–Mar shows 2 sub-peaks Nov and Jan–Mar. Zambia–Zimbabwe Aug–Nov, peak Aug–Sept; South Africa (Natal–Transvaal) Aug–Nov, Feb, peak Oct, (Cape) Sept–Dec, peak Oct–Nov. In tropical Africa breeding occurs mainly in dry seasons, but sometimes (E Africa) in rains; affected more by migration pattern than other factors. At Cape and in N Africa nests in spring.

Incubation begins 1st egg; by ♀ mainly, ♂ takes only small share, but perches for long periods near nest. ♂ feeds ♀, and she also leaves nest to forage for herself. When ♂ incubates briefly, often associated with feeding ♀. Incubation period: (*M. m. parasitus*) estimated (once)

37 days, but better data needed; (*M. m. migrans*, Europe) 26–38 days recorded, usually 32–37, apparently varying with size of egg, clutch size (Cramp and Simmons 1980).

Newly hatched young weigh 42–45 g, 90 g by day 5. 1st feathers break through down *c.* 20 days, feathered by 30 days and can then walk about. Can feed themselves at 30–35 days but solicit food until late in fledging period. Move out on branches *c.* 40 days, fly at 42–45 days. Little apparent difference between temperate and tropical regions.

♀ broods chicks closely up to 5–6 days but after day 7 leaves them for long periods unbrooded, though perching near in same tree. ♂ at first brings all food, ♀

assisting after *c.* day 30. ♂ does not feed young, though they solicit him. 5–6 small kills required in later fledging period, usually dropped on nest by either parent, eaten by young unaided.

Breeding success unrecorded Africa; usually 1 per successful nest, rarely 2 (probably less than 1/pair/year); one acceptable record of 4 exists. Young remain near nest till *c.* 60 days old, then accompany parents to join other flocks. Better African data needed throughout breeding cycle.

References
Van Someren, V. G. L. (1956).

Plates 18 and 30
(Opp. pp. 291 and 451)

Milvus milvus (Linnaeus). Red Kite. Milan royal.

Falco Milvus Linnaeus, 1758. Syst. Nat. (10th ed.), 1, p. 89; southern Sweden.

Range and Status. Wooded parts of Europe, NW Asia and NW Africa; in Africa breeds only NW Africa. Mainly sedentary in subtropical Mediterranean, but some migrate from more northern localities. Frequent to common but always much less common, less of a town scavenger than Black Kite *M. migrans*. Numbers probably stable in NW Africa breeding range; may be threatened by deforestation and pesticides. Has recently been reported as rare migrant South Africa, reputedly also E Africa.

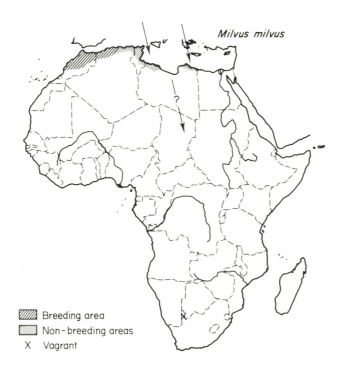

Milvus milvus

▨ Breeding area
▦ Non-breeding areas
X Vagrant

Description. *M. m. milvus*, ADULT ♂: crown and nape white, some rufous, streaked blackish. Neck and upperback brownish black, feathers broadly edged chestnut, appearing reddish. Back darker, reddish edges less distinct, scapulars browner with concealed dark bars. Uppertail-coverts chestnut with black shaft-streaks. Upperwing-coverts blackish brown, edged

chestnut. Primaries and secondaries brownish black, inner webs of primaries largely white, forming a conspicuous carpal patch; inner secondaries more rufous, barred blackish. Tail chestnut, tipped paler, buff on inner webs, outer feathers barred black, central only spotted. Sides of head, chin, throat, white streaked blackish. Underside of body rufous-chestnut, streaked black, nearly plain undertail-coverts. Underwing-coverts centrally dark, broadly edged greyish or rufous; tail below pale chestnut barred black. Base of bill and cere, eye and legs yellow. ♀ similar, but larger. SIZE: wing, ♂ 448–532 (490), ♀ 478–535 (503); tail, ♂, outer feathers 300–351 (327), innermost 220–250, fork 60–110 deep, ♀ outer 314–376 (343), central 220–260; tarsus, ♂ 52–55 (53·2), ♀ 51–54 (52·8); wingspan, *c.* 1750–1950. WEIGHT: ♂ (27 specimens) 757–1221 (957), ♀ (28) 960–1600 (1158), averaging heavier in autumn than spring.

IMMATURE: generally paler than adult, head more rufous, less streaked blackish. Above rufous brown, feathers broadly tipped buff. Underparts buff, with fewer black streaks. Eye brown, later becoming yellow; legs and feet duller yellow. Tail fork not so deep.

DOWNY YOUNG: on crown and nape down long, hairy, cream in colour; body above buff, creamy white below; 2nd down dense, more woolly. Eye light grey becoming yellow, cere pale grey, feet pinkish yellow or yellowish flesh. Eye colour of nestling a diagnostic feature distinguishing it from that of Black Kite.

Field Characters. Can only be confused with *Buteo* spp. and Black Kite. Much redder and paler generally than Black Kite, longer-winged and longer-tailed, with conspicuous whitish patch at carpal joint. Eye yellow, not brown. Long wings, angled at carpal joint, and long forked tail (in both immature and adult) distinguish it from any buzzard or eagle.

Voice. Recorded in Europe (see Cramp and Simmons 1980). Distinct from that of Black Kite. Main call a shrill, mewing 'weeeeooo-weeeeooo' somewhat resembling *Buteo* spp.; more musical whistling than Black Kite. When alarmed, sharper broken 'wee-ee-ee', first syllable emphasized; and in threat to others 'peee-pee-pee-pee' or 'peeeu-pee-pee-pee'. At copulation a more quavering 'glii-i-i-i-i' trilled. Nestlings utter thin, high-pitched piping calls, and just after fledging young utter whinnying 'weew-weeah-weeah-weee' (Cramp and Simmons 1980; Meyer 1958). Generally less vocal than Black Kite.

General Habits. Little known in NW Africa. Basically a woodland bird, which scavenges to some extent on human refuse and needs open spaces in which to hunt. Prefers deciduous woodlands but also frequents conifers. Not as gregarious as Black Kite, but tolerates others of own species, at least in small groups; several pairs may breed in same wood.

Flight exceptionally graceful, light, buoyant, soaring easily in circles, flying over woodlands alternately lightly flapping and gliding, and sometimes gliding close to ground against wind almost like a harrier (*Circus* spp). Continual sideways twisting of tail to turn and manoeuvre is conspicuous. Perches much on trees, but hunts mainly on the wing, and is surprisingly agile for its size and span. Sometimes frequents marshes and watersides, but less than Black Kite. Habits in NW Africa assumed to be similar to Europe, but little detail recorded.

Some birds from N European breeding localities cross into N Africa mainly via Gibraltar peaking there Oct–Nov; 1 ringed E Germany recovered Morocco. Some also cross via Bosphorus and Sicily–Cape Bon routes; most do not pass Sahara, but individuals have recently been seen South Africa and reported E Africa; their origin is obscure.

Food. Not recorded in detail in NW Africa. Elsewhere small mammals, birds, reptiles, amphibia, some fish, insects, carrion and scraps, the latter much less important than for Black Kite. A more active and vigorous predator, taking some large active birds, also often young of corvids and gulls. Cannot effectively compete with the smaller, but more numerous, more aggressive and adaptable Black Kite when both occur together. Analysis of several thousand prey items from W Europe gives 44·5% mammals, 34·5% birds, 8·2% other vertebrates and 12·4% invertebrates by number; mammals most important by weight, largest prey being young rabbits, hares.

Breeding Habits. Little known NW Africa, elsewhere intimately known. Same breeding area used annually for many years by different birds; pairs may breed only 200–300 m apart, but usually well dispersed. Display usually unspectacular, consisting of mutual soaring, weaving, flights above nesting area, sometimes calling. Few spectacular manoeuvres recorded, but occasionally ♂ dives at ♀ who may turn over; tumbling, whirling display with locked claws recorded in Spain (Cramp and Simmons 1980).

NEST: in trees, large structures of sticks, 6–30 m above ground, usually lower NW Africa. Usually or often built on foundation of another bird's nest; *c.* 0·6–1 m across by 0·3–0·6 m deep, similar to that of Black Kite, lined with rags, paper, plastic, hair, dung, bark, any refuse. Both sexes build, but mainly ♂; sticks collected from ground or trees, sometimes in flight, mainly in early morning and evening; ♀ usually remains in nest and works material. Fresh material continually added through breeding season. May sometimes usurp nests from other birds, or themselves be usurped by Black Kites. Nest repair occupies 2–3 weeks.

EGGS: (NW Africa) 2–3, av. 2·56 (18 clutches); European av. over 3; laid at 3-day intervals. Dull white, glossless, usually sparingly, sometimes richly spotted and blotched reddish or purplish. SIZE: (NW Africa) 52–62 × 42·5–46·0 (no different from Europe).

Laying dates: NW Africa early Apr–mid May.

Incubation begins with 1st egg, chiefly by ♀; ♂ may incubate for short spells if ♀ is away. ♂ feeds incubating ♀, but she also forages for herself. Incubation period: 31–32 days each egg (Britain), 38 days full clutch.

Young hatch asynchronously; not apparently aggressive to each other, despite marked size difference. 2nd denser down develops at 8–11 days. Show feathers at *c.* day 18–20, and are completely feathered by day 28 on body, downy on head. Weight increases from *c.* 50 g at hatch to 900–1120 at *c.* 49 days (about to fly). Fledging period usually 48–50 days (45–65 in recorded European cases). Dead young in nest may be eaten by siblings.

♀ alone broods young, closely for days 1–7, thereafter remains near to day 14, after which she assists ♂ in hunting, or collects prey from ♂ and brings it to nest. ♂ will not normally feed young. ♀ usually remains near nest for much of fledging period, may kill some prey, but most killed by ♂. Feathered young fed about every hour. After 1st flight young return to nest to feed for up to 15 days; thereafter remain near it for up to 21–30 days, then accompany parents in home range.

Breeding success in NW Africa unknown. In France and Germany, from larger clutches averaging over 3, 0·92/pair/year, 1·1/breeding pair and 1·5/successful nest. Success probably lower in NW Africa, where av. clutch smaller, but perhaps better than Britain (where av. clutch is 2·04, and success rate 0·52/pair/year, 0·67/breeding pair, 1·32/successful nest). Oldest known Red Kite 25 years 8 months (Switzerland) is oldest recorded ringed bird of prey.

Genus *Haliaeetus* Savigny

Large to very large birds of prey (eagles). Wings long, broad; tail short, 12 feathers (except Stellar's Sea Eagle *H. pelagicus* with 14). Bill large, strong, often deeply arched, laterally compressed. Tarsus short, feathered at base, with large transverse scutes in front, reticulate scales behind. Feet and toes powerful, with long very sharp talons, soles with sharp spicules. Cosmopolitan, except in South America; 8 spp., 1 African.

Plates 18 and 29
(Opp. pp. 291 and 450)

Haliaeetus vocifer (Daudin). African Fish Eagle. Pygargue vocifer.

Falco vocifer Daudin, 1800. Traité d'Orn., 2 p. 65; Keurboom River, Cape Province, South Africa.

Range and Status. Aquatic habitats throughout Africa south of the Sahara, coastal and marine, larger freshwater rivers and lakes. Occurs within forest and up to 3500 m, but most abundant in lowland freshwater areas. In most of range, common to abundant; in parts only frequent. Total population perhaps 100,000–200,000 adult pairs plus immatures; not normally molested or threatened.

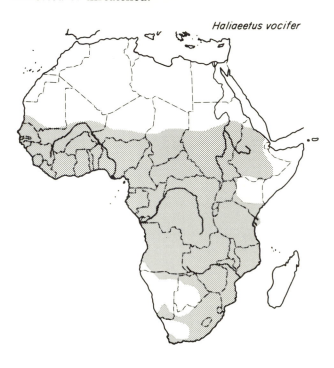

Haliaeetus vocifer

Description. ADULT ♂: head, back, chest and upper belly, white. Lower belly, undertail-coverts and lesser upperwing-coverts chestnut. Wing-feathers, greater upperwing-coverts and scapulars black, wing-feathers slaty below. Tail-feathers pure white. Bare facial skin and cere bright yellow; eye brown; feet and legs yellow. ♀♀ similar, rather larger, with deeper white chest. SIZE: wing, ♂ 510–540 (530), ♀ 565–605 (587); tail, ♂♀ 230–275; tarsus, ♂♀ 80–90; wing-span, ♂♂ 1906, ♀ 2370; wing-loading, 0·4–0·44 N/m². WEIGHT: ♂ 1986–2497, ♀ 3170–3630.

1ST IMMATURE: crown brown, tipped blackish, eyebrow and nape greyish. Rest of upperparts brown or blackish, feathers tipped black. Below, neck and chest white, heavily streaked brown and black; belly dark brown, streaked black; rest of underparts buff. Wing-feathers blackish; tail dirty white, broadly tipped brown. Variable; possibly sex-linked, ♂ generally darker than ♀. Eye brown; cere grey; legs pale yellow. 2ND YEAR: underside becomes pure white, some black streaks; a marked blackish eyebrow; underwing-coverts largely white, strongly contrasting with blackish wing-feathers; tail white with narrower brown tip. Eye brown; cere grey; feet greyish yellow. SUBADULT: (years 3–4) head, neck and breast white streaked black, becoming pure white; belly, under and upperwing-coverts black; darkest stage of plumage. Cere becomes pinkish; eye brown; legs yellow. Tail mainly white with indistinct brown tip becoming pure white. In pre-adult plumage, chestnut feathers grow in on belly and upper and underwing-coverts, eventually replacing black. Cere and legs become yellow; distinctive yelping voice acquired.

DOWNY YOUNG: white; cere greyish; legs grey-white.

Field Characters. Adult unmistakable; white head, neck and breast strongly contrasting with chestnut belly and coverts, black wings, tail white. Black wing-feathers at once distinguish it in flight from Vulturine Fish Eagle *Gypohierax angolensis*. 1st immature could be mistaken for some other large brown eagles, but is ragged-looking, and streaky brown and white rather than plain brown. All subadult stages recognizable by mainly white head and breast contrasting with black belly and mainly white tail, tipped brown. In flight, wings noticeably broad, deep, tail short and, when spread, scarcely extending beyond hind-edge of spread wing. Normally frequents aquatic habitats but (especially immatures) may appear far from water.

Voice. Recorded (1e, 2a, 6, 18, 19, 22a, 26, 28). Normally a loud, clear, far-carrying series of yelps 'weee-ah, hyo-hyo-hyo' uttered with head flung backwards towards tail and jerking back and forth, often in duet; in flight accompanied by deep wing-beats. Voice of ♂ is shriller than that of ♀ (treble : contralto); ♀ calls more often and initiates most duets. Adult call is not acquired by immature till late subadult (*c.* 3–4 years), but younger birds emit a cracked hoarse version. A low bark 'kwok-kwok' in anxiety near nest. In copulation ♀ (probably) emits distinctive low clucking calls. Noisy at all times, calls at first light, repeatedly thereafter, often when soaring. Voice is important in establishing territorial rights.

General Habits. Intimately known; one of few raptor species whose diurnal behaviour is quantitatively analysed. Normally frequents larger lakes, rivers, swamps and flood plains but also seashore and mangrove swamps. May temporarily inhabit quite small ponds/dams of 1 ha or less, but does not often breed on small waters. Frequents both alkaline and freshwater lakes, even some lacking fish, but breeds almost exclusively near freshwater or sea, rarely alkaline lakes. Is most abundant on lowland tropical lakes and large rivers, but may occur up to 4000 m (Ethiopian Highlands); and

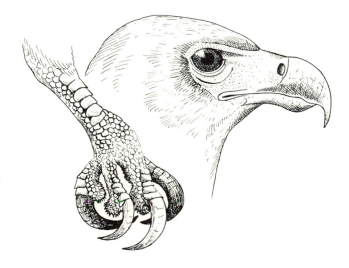

must cross large areas of arid country to reach isolated lakes (e.g. Mount Marsabit, N Kenya). Immatures and subadults more likely to appear in odd localities far from normal breeding haunts.

Diurnal activity (analysed from many dawn–dark watches in Kenya) shows this species roosts in trees and calls at first light. Before sunrise moves from roost to fishing perches in territory. Thereafter normally remains within territory, sometimes making distant forays to fishing areas. Spends 85–95% of daylight perched, 5–15% flying; ♂♂ fly, soar and make more fishing sorties than ♀♀. Of flying time, *c.* 36% spent soaring (partly in display), 9·5% in territorial flights, 23·5% flying perch–perch and 31% actively fishing. Fishing time in flight varies from 1 min (♀) to 65 min (♂ feeding young) per day and averages *c.* 8 min for both sexes. When perched, spends some of time actively fishing, intently watching water, but much of it idle, resting in shade or preening. Diurnal activity on same lake varies with locality from pair to pair, seasonally, according to habitat, and according to weather. Strong winds and rough weather stimulate soaring and sometimes assist fishing (Brown 1980). In some localities, e.g. South Africa, more time may be spent soaring or fishing (Whitfield and Blaber 1978).

Most common method of fishing is to perch, watching for prey, and make short strikes from perch of 10–30 m. Eagle glides down, levelling out near water and, on nearing prey, throws feet forward in front of head (see **A**), strikes down and backward, lifting fish cleanly from surface with powerful wing-flap. More rarely, plunges in, soaking breast and belly, even whole plumage. With heavy prey may lie with spread wings on surface, then take off dragging fish. Less often (♂ especially) makes short flights ('fishing sorties') out over water, circling for a few minutes, then returning to perch if unsuccessful. ♀ kills most often by short strikes. Occasionally, fish are caught from high soaring flight; but soaring birds are not usually hunting. When taking young water birds, eagle alights on nests and swallows or carries them off, sometimes snatching young from nests in passing flight. May entirely wipe out colonies of e.g. herons, egrets, spoonbills, cormorants (Parsons 1977; L. H. Brown, pers. obs.).

Is also strongly piratical; urge to piracy apparently compulsive. Attacks any other fishing birds seen with prey, from size of Goliath Heron *Ardea goliath* and Saddle-billed Stork *Ephippiorhynchus senegalensis* to Pied Kingfisher *Ceryle rudis*, including other fish eagles (even own mate or young) and Osprey *Pandion haliaetus*. Piracy is usually successful if attacked bird has prey; but large powerful birds such as Saddle-billed Stork may successfully resist. Huge pelicans completely helpless. ♀♀ of pairs pirate prey from ♂♂ more successfully than *vice versa*.

Normally sedentary, frequenting same territory year-round (80% regular occupation recorded). In some areas (e.g. parts of Lake Victoria) breeding pairs may move out of territory when not nesting, returning following year. Inundation of river flood plains may also necessitate or stimulate local movements. Also makes some long distance movements from lake to lake,

A

and can then cross high mountain ranges or broad deserts. Populations probably more mobile than is apparent from local observations. Easily mounts to great height on thermals, then gliding to destination.

Food. Mainly fish, of very large variety of surface species, mainly caught within 15 cm of surface, occasionally as deep as 0·5 m below. Most fish caught live, but will scavenge floating dead fish if hungry. Most fish taken weigh 200–500 g, but up to 3 kg recorded (Tomkinson 1975). Fish of up to 1·5 kg lifted clean from water at strike; can lift fish up to 2·5 kg, but large fish of 2·5–3 kg, normally planed along surface or dragged through water to shore, beached and eaten there. Daily food intake (estimated from dawn–dark watches) av. 135 g/day/adult, *c.* 5% of bodyweight (Kenya), must kill *c.* 150 g/day allowing for waste (10%).

Prefers and normally takes surface-feeding fish. In marine habitat particularly mullet, garfish; but also e.g. moray eels, wrasse, snappers, parrot fish stranded at low tide in coral pools and Porcupine Globe Fish *Diodon hystrix*. In fresh water, catfish, lungfish (which surface to breathe) most often taken, but also *Tilapia* spp. Catching efficiency varies from 1–14 strikes/kill, av. *c.* 7·5/kill (Kenya). Besides fish, takes many young water birds, occasionally adults. Can kill adult Greater and Lesser Flamingoes (*Phoenicopterus ruber* and *Phoeniconaias minor*), and cormorants and darters (perhaps taken underwater); adult small grebes also taken. Coots often attacked, but usually escape by packing and scurrying over water. Immatures especially feed on carrion, including, for example, kills of lions, wild dogs, but soon driven off by original predator. At carrion may itself suffer from piracy by e.g. Tawny Eagle *Aquila rapax* or Bateleur *Terathopius ecaudatus*.

African Fish Eagles can survive, but seldom breed, on waters lacking fish. Ability to catch enough food apparently is not a severe limiting factor on breeding population.

Breeding Habits. Very well known. Intensely territorial, pairs normally occupying territory year-round (80% occupancy recorded); sometimes more seasonal, arriving at onset of season, leaving after young independent till following year. Territory is defended vigorously from other Fish Eagles by calling, often in duet, when ♀ is most likely to call first. Others flying past below and in front of residents fiercely attacked; but if passing over high up may only elicit calls, and if behind shoreline territory normally ignored. Size of territory varies; in W Africa 1 pair/1–4 km of river; Uganda 1 pair/400–600 m of shore (Thiollay and Meyer 1978); Botswana (Okavango swamps) pairs c. 400–500 m apart, (Chobe River) 1/1·2 km; Transvaal (Nyl flood plain) pairs c. 9–10 km apart, each with c. 5 ha of fishing area (W. Tarboton, pers. comm.). Densest known populations, Kenya—1 pair/300 m of shore, occasionally still closer; 2 active pairs recorded only 60 m apart. Territorial behaviour most obvious in dense populations, where any available territory is occupied and defended, usually year-round. Fishing area included in territory varies from 3–15 ha (Kenya–Uganda); possibly larger in less densely populated areas.

Display is mainly vocal, some aerial. Dawn calling, and repeated calling by day is vocal territorial display. In flight, ♂♂ soar more than ♀♀ (2·9% of daylight compared with 2% for ♀♀); mount more easily, climbing higher in smaller circles. Pairs soar together above territory, usually between 09.00–12.00 h, sometimes later; aerial calling duets frequent, with head flung over back and deep graceful wing-flaps. ♂, if above ♀, may dive at her repeatedly; and occasionally pairs grapple talons and whirl downwards in spectacular series of cartwheels, more rarely spinning laterally like falling leaves. Near equator, display occurs daily year-round, elsewhere most obvious early in defined breeding season. Copulation may occur almost daily, whether breeding or not that year; up to 6 times in a morning when building nest. ♀ is usually more vocal than ♂, but when building ♂ may temporarily become more vocal and aggressive.

Normally nests in trees, selecting tall thorny acacias, euphorbias, or large figs with smooth scaling bark; more rarely on rock stacks, or bushes growing from cliffs or cliff edges (South Africa). Pairs have 1–4 nests, av. 1·4 (Kenya) usually near centre of territory; if more than 2, 1 normally disused and collapsing. Several nests may be close together in same or 2 adjacent trees.

NEST: large structure of sticks, papyrus fronds, often lined with papyrus heads and, sometimes, weaverbirds nests, seldom green leaves. New nest is a thin circle of sticks, c. 1·5 m wide and only c. 20–30 cm thick, but is added to annually, reaching maximum of c. 2 m × 1·5 m. Most nests not occupied for more than 10 years (1 case of 27 years; W. Tarboton, pers. comm.), very often less; collapse quickly when abandoned. Both sexes build, collecting sticks or fronds from ground, or breaking them off in flight. ♂ perhaps builds more than ♀, and often visits nest with sticks when ♀ absent. Nest repair or visits occur almost daily in continuously occupied territories; but a territory may be occupied by pair without any nest despite suitable trees, or occupied and defended in lagoons without any available nest-site.

Abandoned or unused nests often occupied by Egyptian Goose *Alopochen aegyptiacus* or Verreaux's Eagle Owl *Bubo lacteus*.

EGGS: 1–3 eggs, usually 2 (1 clutch of 4 reliably recorded); laid at intervals of 2–3 days; E and South Africa (86 clutches) 1·93; no appreciable latitude difference. White, slightly glossed, sometimes faintly spotted brown or grey. SIZE: 63·5–80·0 × 48·2–57·7 (72·2 × 54·5); WEIGHT: c. 120 g.

Laying dates: South Africa May–Oct, in Cape usually June–Aug (winter, wet); Transvaal, Natal, Botswana, Apr–Aug, especially May–July (winter, dry); Zimbabwe, Zambia, Malawi Feb–Oct, peaking Apr–June (end rains–early dry season); Tanzania May–July (dry); Kenya, Uganda all months, peaking in different localities at different times, e.g. W Uganda July–Oct (mid-year, dry season), Naivasha Mar–May (wettest months); Ethiopia Aug–Oct (late rains); N Uganda, Sudan, W Africa tends to peak Oct–Dec (dry season); Zaïre all months; Senegal, Mali, Nigeria Oct–Nov, perhaps Dec (early dry season). In areas with a single long dry season this is preferred; but in equatorial 2-season regimes, whole cycle cannot be completed in 1 short dry season. No good evidence that food supply affects season; climatic factors a more likely reason.

Incubation begins 1st egg; by both sexes, ♂ sometimes taking large share by day, perhaps incubating at night also. ♀ sits most; is not regularly fed by ♂, but hunts when off nest, and may leave eggs to pirate prey from own mate or another passing Fish Eagle. Incubation period: not accurately recorded, 42–44 days estimated.

Newly hatched young feeble, helpless, brooded continuously; but can take food almost at once. Sibling aggression less violent than in some other eagles, but elder usually eliminates younger by c. day 10; not connected with food shortage. Weight at 3 days, 70 g. 1st feathers break through down at 24 days when weight c. 1400 g. Feathering complete by 50 days, but eaglet cannot feed itself until 45–50 days old. Later development mainly in feather growth and muscular strength. Practise wing-flapping and short flights from 60–65 days, especially in windy weather; 1st real flight 65–75 days. Single eaglets may fledge before broods of 2 or more; 3 occasionally reared (2 cases in 140 Kenya records).

♀ broods young closely at first; ♂ also sometimes broods, but his main function is to bring prey. 1–3 fish brought/day. ♂ continues bringing most prey till young c. 50 days old, after which ♀ may also kill. ♂ may feed small chicks but does not feed large young. Daylight brooding reduced from c. 90% (and all night) days 1–4 to 25–30% by day 15, less than 5% by day 30. Thereafter ♀ usually remains near nest while ♂ hunts. By day 42 chick is left alone in nest at night, ♀ normally roosting near, sometimes ♂ also. In late stages either sex brings prey to nest and eaglet feeds unaided.

After 1st flight young return to roost in nest for up to 14 days; parents roost nearby. Young may then remain in parental territory up to 2 months, occasionally more, sharing adults' kills. Probably first kill for themselves c. 60 days after 1st flight, and are not attacked by parents while still dependent. Probably leave territory of own accord, not actually expelled; but at once harrassed if trespassing on neighbours. Since in contiguous breeding territories they are attacked by all adult Fish Eagles, where any such areas are available they seek areas of shore, lagoons and marshes lacking breeding pairs. May then be semi-gregarious, 5 or 6 together, roosting in groups of up to 30 (Morgan 1979); later become solitary. Recent immatures usually lose fish when attacked by adults or older immatures; but 2- and 3-year-old birds apparently can resist adult adversaries.

Breeding success variable, but generally low. In 265 cases 151 (57%) bred and 104 (39%) were successful. Overall av. 0·47 young/pair, 0·82/breeding pair and 1·19/successful nest. Individual success varies enormously, from 4 young in 3 attempts in 18 months, and 5 in 2 successive attempts, to nil, in adjacent pairs, some not even attempting (Kenya); 1 South African pair reared 9 young in 10 years (Steyn 1972a). Impossible to correlate these variations with food supply, which

apparently has little effect, pairs which fish successfully sometimes not breeding for several years.

Age classes of young as recorded by plumage stage (4217 records): overall *c.* 16% immatures and 84% full adults. Varies locally from 15–30% immatures. 16% immatures include 266 (63%) 1-year-old birds; 143 (3·4%) 2-year-old birds; 280 (6·64%) early and late subadults, necessitating adult life of 16–24 years. This seems improbable, but data from marked or identified individuals not available.

References
Brown, L. H. (1980).
Brown, L. H. and Cade, T. J. (1972).
Brown, L. H. and Hopcraft, J. B. D. (1973).
Steyn, P. (1960, 1972a).
Thiollay, J. M. and Meyer, J. A. (1978).
Whitfield, A. K. and Blaber, S. J. M. (1978).

Haliaeetus albicilla (Linnaeus). White-tailed Eagle; European Sea Eagle. Pygargue à queue blanche.

Not illustrated

Falco Albicilla Linnaeus, 1758. Syst. Nat. (10th ed.), 1, p. 89; Sweden.

Range and Status. Widely distributed Palearctic from Greenland–N Japan, south to Mediterranean. Decreasing or threatened in most of known range, small Mediterranean population almost extinct. Now only rare vagrant to N Africa, e.g. 5 definite records, Tunisia 1904–1970, 2 1963 and 1970; mainly immatures seen recent years.

Description. *H. a. albicilla* Linnaeus of Europe: details omitted as now only vagrant.

Field Characters. Not likely to be mistaken if seen. An enormous eagle with very broad, square-ended wings, very short, slightly wedge-shaped tail, longer, less wedge-shaped in juvenile. Bill heavy, powerful, in adult yellow, conspicuous at distance. Adult dark brown, head creamy, tail pure white; bare legs and bill conspicuously yellow. Immature (more likely to be seen) entirely dark brown, with paler mottlings on breast, pale patch on axillaries, and diffuse pale bar on inner wing-coverts. Frequents aquatic habitats, unlikely to be found in same habitat as Golden Eagle *Aquila chrysaetos*, from which immatures distinguished by shorter wedge-shaped tail, much larger size, broader wings, heavier bill.

Haliaeetus albicilla

X Vagrant

Genus *Gypohierax* Rüppell

Medium-sized eagles often of aquatic habitat; also in forests and woodland, but not arid areas. Bill large, powerful, nostrils oval; bare skin round eye and below bill. Wings rather short, very broad and rounded; tail short, rounded, *c.* 50% of wing-length. Tarsus bare, with reticulate scales. Talons short, but curved and sharp.

This monotypic genus is rather uneasily placed as a possible link between fish eagles (*Haliaeetus* and extra-limital *Ichthyophaga*) and the Egyptian Vulture *Neophron*. Partly aquatic, feeding on fish, but main diet oil-palm pericarp, in this way unique. Resembles fish eagles in having preference for aquatic habitats and taking some fish; vultures in its skeleton (resembling *Neophron* and *Gypaetus*), laying 1 egg, and having relatively long incubation and fledging periods. May not be closely related to either; further detailed study needed to establish possible relationships.

Gypohierax angolensis (Gmelin). Vulturine Fish Eagle; Palm-nut Vulture. Palmiste d'Angola.

Falco angolensis Gmelin, 1788. Syst. Nat. 1, pt. 1. p. 252; Angola.

Range and Status. Tropical Africa from Senegal east to Sudan, south to Angola, straggling to Orange Free State and Cape Province. In coastal mangroves, tropical forest and well-wooded savannas. Range largely, but not exclusively, coincident with that of oil palm *Elaeis guineensis*; rare where oil palms absent. Normally frequent, in W Africa locally common; uncommon to rare south of N Zambia and S Tanzania. Very local E Africa, in Kenya chiefly coastal. Numbers probably stable, or decreasing. Increased oil palm plantations, avoided but for feeding, probably do not balance effects of habitat destruction in W African forests.

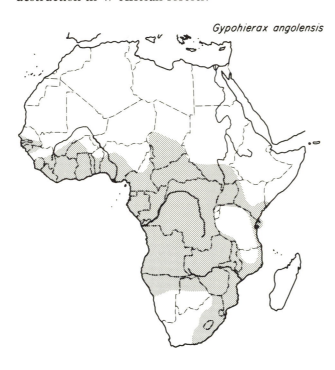

Gypohierax angolensis

Description. ADULT ♂: head, neck, back upperwing-coverts and underside white. Primaries white, tipped black; scapulars secondaries and greater wing-coverts black. Tail black tipped white. Bill yellow; cere grey; bare skin round eye and below bill red to orange; eye yellow; legs pinkish flesh to yellow. ♀ similar, scarcely larger. SIZE: wing, 397–445; tail, 188–210; tarsus, 75–85; span, *c.* 1300–1400. WEIGHT: ♂ (3 specimens) 1361–1710 (1505), ♀ 1712, unsexed 1698.

1ST IMMATURE: brown, darkest on back and scapulars, paler on wing-coverts, rump pale yellowish brown. Primaries black, tail dark brown with some pale tips. Bare facial skin yellow-orange; eye brown; legs whitish. This develops into adult plumage over 3–4 years; intermediate stages mottled brown, black and white; age classes not established.

DOWNY YOUNG: brown; eye brown; legs whitish; bare facial skin pale yellowish white.

Field Characters. Adult can only be confused with adult African Fish Eagle *Haliaeetus vocifer* or Egyptian Vulture *Neophron percnopterus*; unlikely to occur with the latter. Smaller than adult Fish Eagle, with white, not chestnut, upperwing-coverts, whole underside white, tail black with white tip, and, in flight, primaries tipped

black. Distinguished from Egyptian Vulture by white primaries and mainly black, square or rounded tail. When taking off, flaps wings much more rapidly than either, alternating with short glides. First immature most easily confused with Brown Snake Eagle *Circaetus cinereus*, less so with immature African Harrier Hawk *Polyboroides typus*, and some other brown eagles. At close range yellow or orange bare skin on face at once distinguishes it. Short, rather rounded wings and square tail distinguish it from Harrier Hawk, other brown eagles and immature Egyptian Vulture. Patchy, as opposed to streaky, black and white plumage and mainly white underside, smaller size and more rounded wings distinguish subadults from subadult African Fish Eagles.

Voice. Recorded (2a). Largely silent (cf. very vocal Fish Eagle). Rarely utters a growling, low-pitched 'pruk-kurrr'; on roost, duck-like quacking, resembling also copulation call 'kwuk-kwuk-kwuk'. In threat display a grating 'karrrrr'. Calls not well associated with specific activities.

General Habits. Well known. Unique among birds of prey in being mainly vegetarian, feeding largely on fleshy pericarp of oil palm fruit, discarding hard inside nut. Is consequently most abundant in range of oil palm, especially in W African mixed forest and cultivation, less common in Lower Guinea woodlands. Also often common in mangroves, harbours, here subsisting largely or partly on fish, crabs, molluscs, scraps. Benefits from scattered cultivation in mixed secondary forest increasing numbers of easily accessible oil palms; but does not favour oil palm plantations and is reduced by very dense human settlement (J. Thiollay, pers. comm.).

Usually seen perched on a tree, or soaring. Often tame and confiding, allowing closer approach than most raptors. Can fly at any time, independent of thermals. Roosts habitually on favourite trees in breeding territory, same trees used year-round. Leaves roost early morning, and spends much of day in forests, or along riversides, travelling up to 4 km away from nest/roost-sites, usually returning 3–4 h before dark to roost. Normally largely arboreal; in mangrove creeks or on

river flood plains spends more time on ground, walking slowly about, probably catching crabs and molluscs. Also perches near and flies over water, snatching small live fish from surface. In forests and savanna spends little time on ground, except after grass fires, when may walk about seeking burned animals.

Feeds most in early morning, from 07.00–10.00 h, little in evening. Rests in heat of day, usually in shade. When feeding on oil palm fruit, repeatedly visits same trees with ripe bunches, often at same time of day, and can probably obtain such food almost at will, going directly to fruiting palms. In Ivory Coast, spends 54% of day in forests, 41% along rivers, 5% on forest edges or in cultivation. 57% of foraging time spent in forest trees, 38% fishing, 5% on ground (Thiollay 1977a).

Almost completely sedentary throughout known range, remaining year-round in same area. Performs no long or regular seasonal movements, but local conditions, e.g. inundation of flood plains, may necessitate short irregular movements of a few km.

Food. Mainly pericarp of oil palms; also feeds on *Raphia* palm fruit, wild date (*Phoenix*), occasionally other fruits; of 705 fruits, 570 oil palm, 93 *Raphia*, 30 wild date. Oil palm fruit over 50% of diet by weight (Thiollay 1977a). When taking oil palm fruit, flies directly to fruiting tree, alights on frond, walks up it 'hand over hand' and pecks at bunch; then holds individual fruit in foot and eats pericarp. Feeding on *Raphia*, removes outer scales of large hard fruits and pecks at protein-rich pulp at base. Captives reject meat in favour of oil-palm pericarp; but suggestion that pulp (rich in vitamin A) is needed for survival is unfounded (Thomson and Moreau 1957). In main range 60% or more of diet is fruit; but in E Africa fish and crabs probably more important.

Apart from fruit, feeds on small fish, crabs, amphibia, molluscs and other invertebrates approximately in that order of importance. Live small fish easily caught by snatching from surface in feet in flight; also scavenges dead, floating and cast-up fish. Takes some birds, including large active species possibly when dead or dying (e.g. Black Kite *Milvus migrans*, Great Blue Turaco *Corythaeloa cristata*, hornbills, kingfishers, Barn Owl *Tyto alba*); also a few mammals, including, for example, a mongoose and a bat; some mammals taken as carrion (e.g. drowned Giant Rat *Cricetomys*). Odd items include young crocodiles, small snakes, lizards, scorpions, spiders. Most important food (apart from oil palm fruit) crabs, fish and amphibia, possibly more important in E Africa. River crabs may be main diet in localities where neither fish nor oil palms are common (Lake Manyara).

Breeding Habits. Well known; but no complete study of a nesting cycle recorded. Is territorial, pairs remaining near nest-site year-round, but defend only area 200–300 m from nest, maximum 500 m, foraging over up to 4000 ha outside defended area. Breeding density, Ivory Coast, in savanna forest mosaic, 4·8 pairs/1000 ha (208 ha/pair); but normal density much lower. Young and subadults can live in same areas as adults, unmolested (Thiollay 1975b).

Nuptial display not elaborate; adults repelling others from territory fly directly at them. Pairs sometimes perform quite vigorous aerial display, soaring together over site, or near neighbouring hilltop (if any available) with other eagles. ♂ then dives at ♀, who may roll over and present claws. Captives perform a possible threat display, bowing, partly opening wings, and uttering grating calls; similar displays not seen in wild birds. Such displays may suggest affinities with snake eagles or Bateleur *Terathopius ecaudatus*. Copulation occurs at or near nest-site, usually on branch of nest-tree; frequent just before egg-laying, with one bird (probably ♀) uttering low quacking or clucking calls, thus resembling fish eagles (Serle 1954).

NEST: always in trees, often tall ones, e.g. *Ceiba* (W Africa) and *Borassus* palms (Ivory Coast); in Angola large euphorbias (Dean 1974). Most nests are 10–20 m from ground, but may be 40 m in *Ceiba* (W Africa). In Ivory Coast 72 at 16–18 m, 28 at 19–21 m, mean 18·1 m (Thiollay 1976a). Nests are large, but not enormous, structures of sticks, usually *c*. 1 m across by 0·5 m deep. In *Borassus* palms built on leaf base below green fronds, in other trees usually in a high, shaded fork below or in canopy, not normally on lateral limbs. Are used for several successive years, becoming larger with age; but most exist for less than 5 years, and in *Borassus* palms often fall out earlier when tree sheds leaves (Thiollay 1976a). A new nest may take 4–6 weeks to construct. Both sexes build, and nests are lined with green leaves and, characteristically, oil palm racemes (Serle 1954).

EGGS: invariably 1; no clutches of 2 recorded. White, heavily marked with dark brown and chocolate, with lilac or grey undermarkings, unlike normal eggs of fish eagles or snake eagles, but somewhat like those of Egyptian Vulture. SIZE: (12 eggs) 62·0–78·3 × 48·5–57·0 (54·0 × 70·7); WEIGHT: *c*. 107 g (7·8% of ♀ bodyweight, relatively large for a raptor).

Laying dates: W Africa Nov–Dec (dry season) peaking (50/88 records) 16–30 Nov in Ivory Coast (Thiollay 1976a); E Africa, coastal, June–Aug, especially July–Aug (mid-year, cool dry season); Zambia-Malawi Aug (dry); Angola Sept (dry); 1 South African record of fledged young suggests laying Oct. In Ivory Coast, laying in early dry season coincides with abundant oil palm fruit in breeding season; but dry seasons also preferred E Africa, where oil palms largely absent. Dry season, with low clear water in rivers, may also facilitate fishing.

Good details of incubation and fledging periods lacking. Apparently only ♀ incubates (only ♀♀ shot on nests). Incubation period: at least 44 days. Fledging period also long for size of bird, estimated 90 days (Serle 1954). In Ivory Coast eggs laid 16–30 Nov, hatch 1–15 Jan, suggesting incubation period of *c*. 45 days; most young fly 1–15 Apr suggesting fledging period of 85–90 days, long for size of bird. No detailed data on roles of sexes in fledging period, or development of young. Recorded to re-lay within 12 months after failure; and rear young successfully (Serle 1954).

Breeding success, in optimum habitat and capacity population (Ivory Coast), 9/12 pairs laid 0·75 eggs/pair; reduced by losses to 0·58 chicks hatched/pair, of which

0·50 fledged/pair overall, 0·75/breeding pair and 1·0/ successful nest. Nest losses mainly due to predation or interference, 2 nests being taken over by African Hobby *Falco cuvieri*. In population as a whole, *c*. 40% are immatures and subadults, and available figures suggest relatively high survival rate of fledged young. Immatures occasionally pair with full adults. Perhaps first breeds in 4th year, so that mean adult life may not be more than 7–8 years. A captive has lived for 38 years (Thiollay 1975b, 1976a) but av. of 12 captives was 40 months (maximum 5 years).

References
Serle, W. M. (1954).
Thiollay, J. M. (1975b, 1976a, 1977, 1978).
Thomson, A. L. and Moreau, R. E. (1957).

Genera *Gypaetus*, *Neophron*, *Necrosyrtes*, *Gyps*, *Aegypius*: Old World vultures

This group of genera, all feeding mainly on carrion, seldom if ever killing live prey, and often, as a result, having reduced or blunt talons, were formerly placed in a subfamily Aegypiinae. All are apparently more closely related to each other than to either *Gypohierax* on the one hand or *Circaetus* on the other. *Gypaetus*, the Lammergeier, is a unique, specialized, monotypic genus hard to place, but probably most closely allied to *Neophron*, the Egyptian Vulture. *Neophron* and *Necrosyrtes*, the Hooded Vulture, have by some authorities (e.g. White 1965) been combined in *Neophron*, mainly because of similarities in bill structure and feeding habits. Their habits are otherwise so different that they are best regarded as separate monotypic genera. The genus *Gyps*, including the highly gregarious cliff-breeding griffons (3 spp.) now also includes the former genus *Pseudogyps*, white-backed vultures, with 12, not 14, tail feathers, differing also in having arboreal, less gregarious nesting habits. The genus *Aegypius*, formerly monotypic, now includes the former monotypic genera *Torgos* and *Trigonoceps* of Africa and the Asian *Sarcogyps*; they differ somewhat anatomically, but all have rather similar solitary habits and breed in trees, perhaps killing some of their own prey.

Most of these large, often abundant vultures have been thoroughly or very thoroughly studied, both in relation to their feeding habits and ecological separation into species groups, and their breeding habits. Several benefit from association with relatively primitive pastoral or agricultural cultures, becoming very abundant and commensal with man; but similar species suffer from association with civilization and development. The South African Cape Vulture *Gyps coprotheres*, and to a lesser extent the European Griffon *Gyps fulvus*, are threatened by modern sanitation, disposal of natural carrion, and other such developments. This has led to more intensive study of the group, but many results known to exist have not yet been published (P. Mundy, in prep.).

Genus *Gypaetus* Storr

Very large, long-winged, long-tailed, slim vultures; wings of relatively high aspect ratio and low wing-loading cf. other large species. Bill long, rather slender, but strongly hooked, gape extending to below eye, adapted for swallowing large bone fragments. Mandible with deep depression either side. Little bare facial skin, head feathered. A black tuft of downward pointing bristly feathers at base of upper and lower mandibles ('beard'); nostrils long, oval, obscured by bristles. Wings very long, pointed; tail very long, of 12 feathers, strongly graduated, wedge or diamond-shaped. Tarsus feathered nearly to toes; feet small, but claws sharp, more powerful grasping organs than in any other vulture. Overall biology of the genus world-wide has recently been thoroughly summarized by Hiraldo *et al.* (1979).

Plates 19 and 29
(Opp. pp. 306 and 450)

Gypaetus barbatus (Linnaeus). Lammergeier; Bearded Vulture. Gypaète barbu.

Vultur barbatus Linnaeus, 1758. Syst. Nat. (10th ed.), 1, p. 87; Africa, near Oran, Algeria.

Range and Status. 2 races; in all mountainous areas of N and NE Africa; absent wooded Central Africa, occurring again Natal, Lesotho, Orange Free State and extreme north of Cape Province. Normally uncommon to frequent, in Ethiopia common to locally abundant, sometimes more than 20 seen together; total estimated population of African race *G. b. meridionalis* 12,000. In NW Africa and South Africa uncommon to frequent, perhaps common at feeding stations. Population in most of African range probably stable even where uncommon; no recent severe decrease reported NW Africa (C. Vernon, pers. comm.).

Description. *G. b. meridionalis* Keyserling and Blasius: Yemen, Ethiopia, E and South Africa. ADULT ♂: forehead and forecrown white, separated from white cheeks by a black hairy band through eye, extending to black bristles at base of beak. Back, wings and tail blackish grey, feathers with white shaft-streaks. Underparts, including underwing-coverts, white, normally somewhat stained rufous by cosmetic activity. Wing-feathers blackish, tail-feathers dark brown. Eye pale yellow surrounded by red sclerotic ring; feet blackish grey; cere grey (hidden by bristles). Sexes alike, ♀ scarcely larger. SIZE: wing, ♂ (8 specimens) 743–787 (765), ♀ (20) 715–810 (770); tail, ♂ (26) 427–460 (443), ♀ (26) 437–469 (453); tarsus, ♂ 88–93, ♀ 89–93; aspect ratio, *c*. 8.

Adult plumage acquired in *c.* 7 years (Hiraldo *et al.* 1979) with 3 intermediate phases recognizable in the field:

1ST IMMATURE: head and neck blackish brown, contrasting with paler dull brown breast and belly; upperside dark brown with broad pale streaks sometimes coalescing into white patch on back. Eye brown; feet grey.

2ND IMMATURE: head and neck remain blackish brown, pale streaks on back disappear, becoming paler, more uniform brown; breast and belly more rufous-brown, contrasting strongly with blackish head and neck. Eye yellow, now with red ring; legs blackish. 1st moult of wing-feathers occurs in this stage, ends of primaries becoming rounded at 21–36 months.

SUBADULT (or PRE-ADULT): from 5–7 years. Odd white feathers develop on head and neck; head becomes clearly separated from paler, more rufous chest and belly by dark chestnut neck-ring. Eye whitish, sclerotic ring red as in adults.

DOWNY YOUNG: uniform greyish brown, eye brown, legs grey; 2nd down, thick, brown, darker on head.

G. b. barbatus (Linnaeus). NW Africa east to Egypt, Europe and Asia, is larger, paler rufous below, with blackish streaks on throat. SIZE: wing, (8 specimens, N Africa) 742–829 (799); WEIGHT: (14 specimens, Europe) 5000–9000 (5755) (Glutz von Blotzheim *et al.* 1971).

Rufous colour of all races is due to a powdering of iron oxide, acquired by cosmetic activities, which can be rubbed off. Feathers of underside are actually pure white, and full adults with white undersides may often be seen, perhaps especially in wet weather; captives lose rufous underside.

Field Characters. Almost unmistakable; a huge, very long-winged, gracefully soaring bird with long, diamond-shaped tail. Wings slim, almost falcon-like, pointed; in flight held just below horizontal, very seldom flapped. Head of adult shows white at long distance; at close range white with black streak through eye. At rest, very long folded wings produce marked 'hunched shoulders' silhouette; tips protrude almost to long tail tip. 'Beard' clearly visible at up to 300 m with naked eye. Young has similar silhouette, but is dark brown, with blackish head, and paler brown belly and breast. Long wedge-shaped tail distinguishes it from all but immature Egyptian Vulture *Neophron percnopterus*. Distinguished from this by being much larger (twice as large) and having beard. Much narrower-winged, slimmer, more graceful in flight than any large *Gyps* or *Aegypius* spp.

Voice. Recorded (2a). Generally silent, except near nest, even in potentially aggressive situations, e.g. when many together on rubbish dump (Ethiopia). Near nest not very vocal, but regularly utters shrill, kestrel-like 'cheek-acheek-acheek-acheek' (J. Guy, in prep.), e.g. at nest-relief. In aerial display said to utter shrill, whistling 'feeeeee' or 'peeeee'. Small young soliciting utter feeble 'wee-wee-wee' and large flying young soliciting utter piercing, high-pitched 'peee-yip-ee-yip-ee-yip' repeated, sometimes for long periods if not fed. Also (Europe) high prolonged trill when adults are long absent in stormy weather.

General Habits. Very well known. Throughout range, a bird of mountains, cliffs and gorges, occurring at any altitude from near sea level to summits of highest peaks in N Africa; in Ethiopia and NE Africa normally a bird of high mountains, seldom found below 1500 m, but in

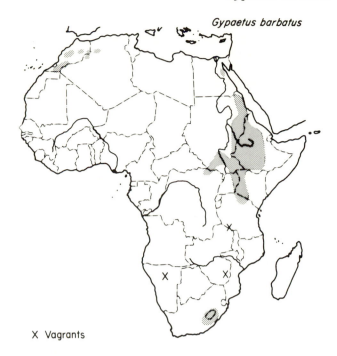

Gypaetus barbatus

X Vagrants

Danakil desert descending lower (to 300 m). In E Africa occurs almost entirely on or near isolated high mountains, some forested; scattered distribution, seldom below 2000 m. South Africa, now only in mountain massif of Lesotho–Natal (Drakensberg), normally 1500 m or over, up to highest peaks.

Roosts nightly in caves or ledges or rock cliffs, using same place night after night; often near nest-site, even when not breeding. Takes wing soon after dawn and (with lower wing-loading than other vultures) can mount to height on very gentle up-currents, often almost imperceptible. In Ethiopia often descends to frost-free levels to roost, ascending next morning to greater heights. In early morning flies slowly along contours of large cliffs, a few metres from rock face, rarely flapping wings, but gradually mounting until desired height reached. If wings flapped, a few slow, deep flaps alternate with long glides; but always prefers to glide long distance, gaining height by slow degrees.

Searches for food continually on wing, soaring at rather slow speed over and round mountain slopes, often close to ground. In Ethiopia, where most abundant, largely commensal with man, frequenting not only pastures on mountains but towns, rubbish dumps, and butchery or hotel refuse tips; 20–25 may be seen together. Arrives normally in towns *c.* 1 h after dawn, the same individuals frequenting the same towns daily, gliding and soaring most of the day above streets, and able to glide through small spaces between houses to pick up scraps. Low wing-loading aids slow flight and this huge bird can be astonishingly agile. It comes to carcasses, but cannot compete with larger, heavier vultures (*Gyps* and *Aegypius* spp.), and on refuse tips is easily repelled by dogs. One may waddle clumsily towards another with head lowered, wings slightly opened; but vigorous aggression at food sources not observed.

Has unique habit of staining white breast and belly rufous with iron oxide. Method not understood but possibly is acquired by dusting on ledges, or by bathing in springs or rivulets of iron-rich water, sometimes on huge cliff faces (Ethiopia). Will enter deep caverns and narrow gorges, perhaps to obtain such needs. Rufous colours persist most of time, but in wet weather may be washed off. 1 of an adult pair may temporarily appear pure white below, the other rufous.

Sedentary throughout range, non-migratory, able to survive in high mountain ranges in depths of winter, perhaps descending to forage in lowlands. In tropical and southern African haunts pairs completely sedentary; but individuals may travel up to 20 km daily to reach favoured feeding localities. Immatures in Ethiopia commoner in towns than in open mountainous country which contains many adult breeding pairs; survival probably assisted by availability of town refuse.

Food. Carrion—almost any scrap of meat or skin, and bones inedible to any other bird. If available, flesh or skin preferred to bones (Ethiopia). Long limbs of, for example, sheep disjointed, long bones swallowed; broad bones (scapulars) may be rejected. Most food carried in feet, sometimes in crop. Will enter thick bush to reach a carcass; and may repeatedly fill crop, regurgitating contents on nest, then returning for more. Often stores uneaten carrion in or near nest cavity until required (J. Guy, in prep.). Not proven, but suspected to kill some live prey, e.g. hyrax, monitor lizard, young dog. Recorded carrying and dropping live tortoises in Europe. Obtains fresh portions of dead domestic animals, but these are not necessarily killed by it (J. Guy, in prep.). Drinks frequently, at least once daily, possibly because of relatively dry diet. Food, composed largely of bones and hard skin, results in typically concreted hard white faeces, resembling those of hyaena *Crocuta crocuta*, immediately identifying regular roost ledges.

Most remarkable feeding habit is dropping bones on rocks to split them, then swallowing fragments (up to 25 cm long). Same dropping sites (ossuaries) probably used for centuries, become covered with bleached bone fragments. Flat rocks along cliff edges often selected, sometimes facing prevailing winds. Approaching ossuary, glides fast downwind, often increasing speed by dip or dive in flight, releasing bone 50–150 m above rock. Can regularly hit rocks less than 10 m square from up to 150 m above them. Then immediately turns into wind, descends and alights beside bone with quick, shallow, fanning wing-flaps. Often must alight quickly to avoid being robbed by more agile ravens or kites. If unsuccessful, retrieves bone, glides away, often regaining height on updraughts, then returns at height, sometimes after several minutes, to repeat. May repeat up to 11 times before abandoning bone, but usually 3–4 times. Sometimes snatches bones from other Lammergeiers; and has been seen to dive vertically 300 m after dropped bone, first passing, then turning up to catch falling bone in air. Habit of dropping objects appears almost compulsive; may repeatedly drop light objects, e.g. hare's foot, even lumps of moss, which could not possibly break on gentle impact. Bone dropping is probably not main source of food, most obtained direct from carcasses, or sources of scraps.

Breeding Habits. Very well known; studied in greater detail in Lesotho than elsewhere (J. Guy, in prep.). Nests invariably on high rock cliffs, usually in a cave (sometimes out of sight) or overhung ledge, seldom on open ledge exposed to sun. Ethiopian–Kenyan sites are at 2000–3700 m, some perhaps lower; Lesotho 1800–3000 m. Same nest-site is used for many years, sometimes same nest; but pairs may also have up to 7 alternate nests in adjacent caves.

Pairs frequent home range year-round, often or usually roosting on nest-cliff when not nesting. Size of home range not determined, but in Ethiopia 2 pairs bred within 3·5 km, suggesting av. home range of $c.$ 12·5 km². In Lesotho known sites are 20–30 km apart, suggesting $c.$ 625 km²/pair (J. Guy, pers. comm.). However, pair spends much of day in relatively small part of total range, within 500 m of nest-site, foraging far outside it; in Ethiopia many, often from distant sites, may congregate in towns. Ethiopian population (estimating an av. 100 km²/pair) is $c.$ 11,000–12,000 including immatures (Brown 1977); Lesotho, 50–100 pairs (J. Guy, pers. comm.).

At onset of breeding season pairs reported to perform spectacular displays, diving several hundred metres, shooting past nest-ledge, swinging up again. Also, mutual displays in which one dives at other, which turns on back and presents claws; such displays much more vigorous than in most large vultures, except Egyptian Vulture, which it resembles in this and nesting habits. Vigorous aerial displays evidently rather rare, not so far seen Lesotho, Kenya, Ethiopia. Before, and sometimes after, copulation, pairs face one another, bowing deeply and rapidly, ♂ then mounts and maintains balance by flapping wings. Afterwards pair may then strut about on ground or ledge, and mutual preening then frequent, each nibbling other's head and face. Often sunbathe close together on suitable ledges, mutual activities giving impression of close bond. Sexes difficult to distinguish with certainty except when copulating, owing to similar size.

NEST: normally very large, broad and flat, up to 3 m across by 1 m deep, usually shallower, with wide shallow depression 1·5–2·0 m across in centre. Made of sticks, lined with grass, moss, hair, skin, bones, rags, old clothing, dry dung. Not normally plastered and cemented with droppings (as in Egyptian Vulture), but usually stinks. Both sexes build, often spending much time in nest cavity together, and repeatedly visiting favoured sources of material. If several nests available, material from one may be used to build another. Nest-repair period, 3–4 weeks; copulation frequent, and much mutual preening at this time.

EGGS: 1–2, 2 perhaps more common; mean (8 clutches, E Africa, Ethiopia, Lesotho) 1·5; NW Africa (race *barbatus*) 1 clutch of 1, 2 clutches of 2 (Heim de Balsac and Mayaud 1962). Laying interval in wild not known, but in captivity 3–5 days (Glutz von Blotzheim *et al.* 1971). Broad ovals; buff or brownish ground, usually partly, sometimes entirely, obscured with dark red-brown, resembling eggs of some *Falco* spp. SIZE: (*meridionalis*) 83·5–88·1 × 66·5–68·2 (85·5 × 67·6), (*barbatus*, slightly larger) 82·0–89·0 × 54·2–70·1

(86.8×67.2); WEIGHT: *c*. 224 g (Schönwetter 1960), 1, Sofia Zoo, 235 g (Glutz von Blotzheim *et al.* 1971).

Laying dates: NW Africa end Dec–early Feb (late winter, as in Europe); Ethiopia Oct, Nov (end main rains–early dry, but also rains in SE Ethiopia, Bale Mts); Kenya Jan, Apr, July, apparently most often in height of long rains Apr–May; Uganda Jan (dry season); Lesotho and South Africa May, June, July, perhaps re-laying after early failure (late winter–early spring, dry and cold). In N and southern Africa lays late winter; in Ethiopia early dry season; in E Africa probably most in long rains, so that young are in nest during cool mid-year dry season.

Incubation begins 1st egg; would otherwise be frozen in N and southern Africa. By both sexes, each taking a large share, with 2–5 nest-reliefs per day. Exact shares not established as sexes not distinguished, but at 1 site 1 bird (♀?) incubated twice as much as other and probably at night. Nest-relief normally quick, not accompanied by any ceremony, sitting bird leaving as soon as relief arrives; nest never unoccupied more than a few minutes. Material rarely brought at nest-relief, or in incubation period. Incubating bird at intervals stands, turns through 180°, sometimes rolls or moves egg with bill, then sits again facing other way. Incubation period: not known exactly, between 45 and 55 days; probably nearer 55 as in European captives (race *aureus*) period is 55–58 days (J. Guy, in prep.; Glutz von Blotzheim *et al.* 1971).

Chicks hatch at intervals, in one case (perhaps abnormal) of 11 days (J. Guy, in prep.). No sibling aggression seen, but younger soon disappears; probably fails to obtain food and 2 never reared in known cases. Days 1–29, almost entirely downy, cannot stand, must be brooded by parent; but can pull at carrion when only a few days old and attempts to feed itself at 8 days. After *c*. 20 days, 2nd thick woolly down develops; wing-feathers sprout *c*. day 30. Days 30–60, young growing feathers, becoming more active; can feed itself on prey in nest by day 66; thereafter becomes more active, standing and walking about. From day 60 left alone in nest for longer periods, feathered, can feed itself. Wing-flapping and bounding about frequent towards end of period. Fledging period in one observed case 122 days, young making long 1st flight precipitately, as if accidentally. In other cases, 1st flight may be short, to a nearby ledge.

Days 1–30, either parent broods and feeds chick, 1, sometimes both, in nest cavity most of day. Feeds are frequent, relatively short, 7–9 times daily. Most food is flesh, usually fresh; bones may be offered, but often refused if too large. Adults feed themselves at same time. Days 30–60, parental attention somewhat reduced, but both still feed chick 3–7 times daily, longer, larger meals;

chick is not alone in nest for long before day 60. If not in nest cavity or on nest, usually one or both adults is perched nearby. In nest cavity, little brooding by day after day 30, parent standing beside young. Days 60–120, both parents forage outside nest area for longer periods, leaving chick alone in nest; but may still spend 1–2 h in nest cavity, and if not in nest cavity 1, probably most often ♀, spends hours perched near. Large quantities of carrion may accumulate in nest if a good source is readily available, adults making repeated collecting trips. Adults also secrete fluid to chick from beak, thus resembling other large vultures, e.g. Cinereous Vulture *Aegypius monachus* (Suetens and van Groenendaal 1967). Adults generally spend more time near nest than most large raptors.

After 1st flight young remains near nest, often returning to roost there, and dependent on parents for at least 30 days, possibly longer in Kenya. Normally perches on or near nest-ledge most of day, soliciting parents, or other large raptors passing, even calling at aeroplanes. After leaving nest area, may remain in neighbourhood up to 3 months, perhaps fed by adults some distance from nest, or locating own food sources. In Ethiopia recent immatures tend to concentrate near towns, refuse heaps, and other easy food sources, leaving mountainous breeding areas.

E African–Ethiopian records do not indicate regular annual breeding, perhaps averaging *c*. 1 attempt/2 years. Lesotho and N African pairs perhaps more regular; 1 Lesotho pair made 8 attempts (including 1 probable re-laying) in 7 years, but 3 young were injured by humans, of which 2 died and 1 was treated successfully and released Natal, surviving there; 4 flying young resulted from 8 attempts. Ethiopia–Kenya, av. 0.55 young/pair/year in 3 sites; never more than 1 per successful nest.

Flying young can be broadly grouped into 3 age-classes; recent immatures of 1 year or less; immatures in brown plumage, 2–5 years; subadults with partially white head, 5–7 years. Of 478 Ethiopian birds, 370 (77.4%) were adult, 108 (22.5%) immature. In Lesotho, despite apparently more regular breeding, percentage of surviving immatures is apparently lower, *c*. 10% (Rudebeck 1961; L. H. Brown, pers. obs.). Immediate pre-adult phase in Ethiopia may be *c*. 10% of all immatures, suggesting 90% mortality before sexual maturity. If sexually mature in 7th year (cf. Hiraldo *et al.* 1979) av. age of wild adults must be 18–19 as adults, 25–26 altogether; but if mortality is 90% before sexual maturity adults must live over 35 years.

References

Brown, L. H. (1977).
Hiraldo, F. *et al.* (1979).

Genus *Neophron* Savigny

Rather small vultures, adults black and white, 1st immature dark brown. Body slender, wings long, pointed, tail long, wedge-shaped, of 14 feathers. Beak slim, slightly hooked, nostrils long, horizontal. Bare facial skin extends to throat and mid-crown, nape and lower neck with lanceolate erectile feathers. Tarsus moderately long, claws long, outer and middle toe joined by partial web. Possibly rather remotely allied to *Gypohierax*, but on behavioural characters most closely allied to *Gypaetus*.

**Plates
19 and 29**
(Opp. pp. 306
and 450)

Neophron percnopterus (Linnaeus). Egyptian Vulture. Percnoptère d'Egypte.

Vultur Perenopterus [sic] Linnaeus, 1758. Syst. Nat. (10th ed.) p. 87; Egypt.

Range and Status. All the more arid parts of Africa from Morocco–Egypt, south to Senegal–Sudan, Kenya, N Tanzania. Absent from Central African *Brachystegia* woodland. Formerly also in drier areas of South Africa (e.g. Karoo), now rare there (15 sightings since 1945: Mundy 1978). Elsewhere, normally frequent to common, sometimes locally abundant in towns. Probably decreasing slowly through improved sanitation, but not at present threatened.

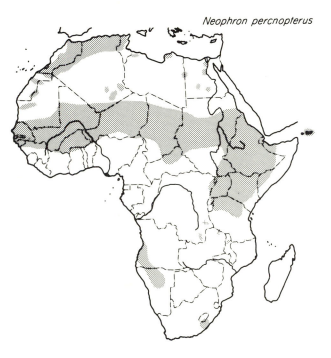

Neophron percnopterus

Description. *N. p. percnopterus*, ADULT ♂: entirely creamy white–pale buff, excepting black primaries and secondaries; primary and innermost greater coverts, which are black, greyish below; innermost secondaries which are grey on both webs. Bill dark brown; bare skin of face yellow-orange; eye red; legs yellow. Sexes similar, little size difference, ♀ slightly larger. SIZE: wing, ♂ (15 specimens) 470–536 (501·3), ♀ (16) 460–545 (508·6); tail, ♂ 232–251 (239·4), ♀ 240–267 (252·4); tarsus, ♂ 78·5–84·5 (81·6), ♀ 78–87 (83·1) (Europe: Glutz von Blotzheim *et al.* 1971); wing-span (2) 1642–1644. WEIGHT: 1584–2180 (1889); also (Europe) 1 ♂ 1975, 2 ♀♀ 1829–2200; European breeding birds possibly larger than African.

1ST IMMATURE: entirely dark brown, many feathers tipped buff, especially on lower mantle and scapulars. Tail greyish brown, broadly tipped buff. Eye brown, feet and bare facial skin blackish, becoming orange in 2nd year. In this year body and wing-coverts become paler, grey-brown. 3rd year, still paler, white areas of adult buff with brownish tinge basally. May breed while still not in full plumage, earliest at 4 years, latest at 6 years (Glutz von Blotzheim *et al.* 1971).

DOWNY YOUNG: 1st and 2nd down white, sometimes tinged pinkish; eye brown; bare skin and legs grey.

Field Characters. Adults unmistakable, creamy white or buff, with black wing-feathers, bare yellow face and, in flight, strongly contrasting black and white wings, long white wedge-shaped tail. Immatures could possibly be confused with immature Hooded Vulture *Necrosyrtes*

monachus, but are slimmer, have longer, narrower wings and long wedge-shaped tail, immediately diagnostic in flight. See also head details below (**A**, Hooded; **B**, Egyptian).

Voice. Recorded (2a). Normally silent, scarcely ever heard. Very rarely utters mewing sounds, whistles, low grunts and hisses in anger or excitement, e.g. in courtship. A high-pitched kite-like tremulous call 'gi-gi-gi-gi-gi' noted in Europe. Long grating calls in copulation. Begging young give feeble, piping calls.

General Habits. Well known. Occurs throughout deserts, subdeserts and more arid African savannas and open plains, not normally in rainfall exceeding 600 mm/year. Avoids densely wooded areas, but occurs in light *Acacia* woodland in Kenya–Tanzania. Often prefers mountainous country to flat lowlands, but this not invariable; requires cliffs for breeding. Occurs from sea level to 4500 m (Ethiopia). In parts of N Africa (e.g. Egypt, Ethiopia) common town scavenger, frequenting rubbish dumps and streets. In most areas solitary, in pairs, at most, small groups; sometimes in larger numbers in towns however, but even then individuals normally keep apart when feeding.

Roosts preferably on cliffs, returning nightly to same spot; sometimes on trees. Can fly soon after dawn, much less dependent on strong thermals than larger heavier vultures, and can thus reach carrion earlier. Frequents human dwellings, e.g. cattle enclosures, often sitting on ground or on trees for many hours daily, waiting for scraps. Cannot compete with larger vultures (*Gyps*, *Aegypius*) at carcasses, but forms species pair with Hooded Vulture with slim bill, eating scraps and picking meat from openings too small for heavier-billed species.

On wing, graceful, slim, with characteristic silhouette. Soars easily, often to great height, and can utilize smaller thermals than larger species, turning in tighter circles. Usually flies from roost to feeding area, remains there, often perched, much of day, and returns to roost at night. Prefers to roost in caves in cliffs if available, where numerous, often gregarious, more so than by day.

A

B

Most remarkable recorded habit is tool-using to break Ostrich eggs. First recorded South Africa, 19th century, more recently studied E Africa (Van Lawick-Goodall, J. and H. 1966; Boswall 1977). Vulture approaches Ostrich nest, selects stone, and rather irregularly and inaccurately hurls it at egg until cracked; can then insert slim bill into crack, exposing contents. Smell of cracked eggs may later attract other powerful mammalian predators (e.g. jackal, hyena), so that effect of vultures can indirectly be serious (B. Bertram, pers. comm.). Also smashes pelican or flamingo eggs by seizing them in bill, raising head and jerking downwards, hurling egg against hard ground or stones, repeating until broken. In flamingo colonies walks up to any selected nest and takes egg; adult flamingos ineffectually resist (Brown and Root 1971). Kills small downy flamingo chicks, and large downy chicks later recognize Egyptian Vulture as potential enemy and flee from it.

Near equator apparently sedentary, but European and most African birds wholly or partially migratory. European individuals migrate into N Africa, augmenting resident population through Gibraltar and Suez, movement beginning late Aug, peaking early–mid-Sept, continuing, but reduced, into Oct. Return migration less concentrated, beginning Feb, peaking Mar, continuing to May, even June; possibly breeding European adults return earliest. Movements within Africa not well documented but, for example, regular migrant Chad (near Abeche) in dry season Oct–May, leaving June, in rains (Salvan 1968). Within tropical Africa more or less nomadic, no clear pattern discernible.

Food. Carrion, meat scraps of any kind, birds' eggs and, in town, refuse and human excrement; a valuable scavenger despite somewhat revolting habits. At carcass with other large vultures cannot compete, and waits on outskirts to snatch dropped scraps when given opportunity (Kruuk 1967). Often remains at site of carcass after larger vultures have left, picking small remnants off bones, collecting scraps. May also eat flying termites when available, some insects, small molluscs.

Breeding Habits. Well known, but not studied in detail in Africa; European data summarized here. Nests in cliffs, steep banks, sometimes on buildings in towns, in Africa never in trees. Normal nest-site is an overhung ledge or small cave, sometimes deep inside in cliff face. Display is often more active than in larger vultures, including series of steep dives and upward swoops by single bird or pair but not generally spectacular. In pairs one may dive at other, which may roll and present claws. Mating occurs on cliffs, trees, or buildings close to nest, or in nest cave.

NEST: (Africa and elsewhere) small flattish structures of sticks, lined with skin, hair, dung, other oddments, usually becoming plastered and cemented with droppings, *c.* 0·7–1·5 m wide by 0·7–2·0 m deep, with shallow central cup 30–40 cm across. Same site used year after year, by generations of different adults. Both sexes build; in Europe nest repair period short, *c.* 10 days; possibly longer in tropical Africa; good details not available.

EGGS: 1–3, normally 2, laid at 2–4 day intervals, sometimes longer; NW Africa mean (46 clutches) 1·80 (Heim de Balsac and Mayaud 1962). Broad ovals; dull chalky white, rarely unmarked, usually heavily clouded, blotched and spotted brown and reddish brown, with grey or purplish undermarkings. SIZE: (100 eggs, Europe) 58·0–76·4 × 43·0–56·1 (66·0 × 50·4); WEIGHT: 81·5–97·0. African eggs within this range.

Laying dates: NW Africa–Algeria–Tunisia 21 Mar–21 Apr, Morocco–W Sahara later, 12 Apr–30 May (Heim de Balsac 1952); Ethiopia Jan–May, mainly Feb–Apr (late dry season); Sudan Feb–Apr (late dry); Nigeria Nov (dry); Kenya–Tanzania, Feb, Mar, May–July, peaking May–June (mid-year cool dry season); South Africa Dec, but no recent records. Breeds in spring in N Africa, in tropical Africa mainly in dry seasons, cooler of 2 preferred.

Incubation begins 1st egg: by both sexes, shares in Africa not established, but probably ♀ only at night; sexes difficult to distinguish. Period: estimated 42 days (Europe). Clutch may be replaced, if lost early in incubation, in another nest (Brosset 1961).

Long laying interval results in large size difference in young. No inter-sibling strife recorded, but only 1 young ever seen reared (E Africa). Full details of development not available. Fledging period: 77 days recorded (Europe: Rodriguez-Jiménez and Balcélls 1968). Both sexes brood small young and feed by regurgitating food onto nest, then feeding nestling if unable to feed itself. Brood young closely at first, and both often in nest together, especially in evening, when ♂ may roost with ♀ in or near nest-cave. After *c.* 40 days young left alone in nest by day, visited only to feed by day, parents returning to roost near or in nest cavity at night. Only 1 young reared from successful nests, but good details lacking. Breeding success certainly less than 1 young/pair/year as not all pairs breed and some fail after laying. Captive adults have lived for 23 years, and probably long-lived with sexual maturity at 5 years.

References
Glutz von Blotzheim, U. N. *et al.* (1971).
Lévêque, R. (1964).
Rodriguez-Jiménez, F. L. and Balcélls, R. (1968).
Van Lawick-Goodall, J. and Van Lawick-Goodall, H. (1966).

Genus *Necrosyrtes* Gloger

Medium-sized, brown vultures. Beak slender, somewhat resembling that of *Neophron*; nostrils long, nearly horizontal. Head and neck largely bare, covered with sparse down, brightly coloured. Lower throat, nape and hindneck with short woolly down, bordered with longer, fluffy feathers. Wings long, broad; tail short, slightly graduated. Tarsus rather long, feet weak lacking sharp claws, adapted for walking rather than grasping. Monotypic; endemic to Africa.

The genus has by some been combined with *Neophron*, but the only common character is the elongated bill, which is a feeding adaptation, due to convergent evolution. In many aspects of behaviour, notably nesting in trees, and in body shape and wing contours it is entirely different to *Neophron*. Apparently not very closely allied to any other African vultures.

Plates 19 and 29
(Opp. pp. 306 and 450)

Necrosyrtes monachus (Temminck). Hooded Vulture. Vautour charognard.

Cathartes monachus Temminck, 1823. Pl. Col. livr. 38, pl. 22; Senegal.

Range and Status. Throughout Africa south of the Sahara, in any habitat from desert to forest and coastal cities, in forest, however, local and only commensal with man. More widespread in savannas and grasslands, where not so dependent on man. Common to locally abundant, mainly in towns; perhaps locally increasing through dependence on human refuse, but has apparently disappeared in recent years from, for example, much of Sudan (Wilson, in press). South of equator much less common, not commensal with man.

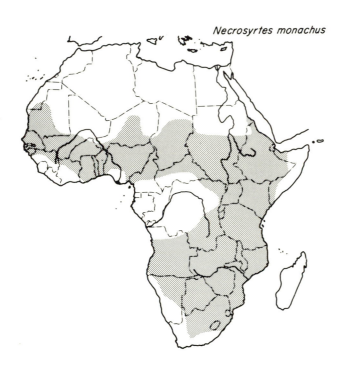

Necrosyrtes monachus

Description. *N. m. monachus* (Temminck): W Africa east to Sudan. ADULT ♂: head and neck pinkish, covered with thin grey down. Whole body, including wing-coverts, dark chocolate brown; wing- and tail-feathers blackish. Down of crop-patch and on thighs white, white feather bases also show through on underside. Iris brown; bare facial skin pink, flushing bright red when excited; legs pale blue-grey. ♀ similar, little size difference. SIZE: wing, ♂ 468–485 (474), ♀ 473–493 (484); tail, ♂ 214–224 (218), ♀ 212–230 (219); tarsus, ♂ 79–82 (81·2), ♀ 78–86 (82·5).

IMMATURE: resembles adult, but down of head dark brown, not whitish, bare skin paler pink; shows more white on crop, thighs and among feathers.

DOWNY YOUNG: head and neck pale brown, body greyish brown; eye brown; legs whitish.

N. m. pileatus (Burchell). NE Africa to South Africa; similar, not easy to separate, generally larger. SIZE: wing, ♂ 503–550 (513), ♀ 508–540 (521) (but some E African specimens smaller, 460–510); wing-span, 1696–1760; wing-loading, 45 N/m²; aspect ratio, 6·7 (Pennycuick 1972). WEIGHT: 1524–2102.

Field Characters. A medium-sized, generally dark brown vulture, with pink head covered with sparse whitish down (dark brown down in immature). In flight, long broad wings and short, almost square, tail immediately distinguish it from immature Egyptian Vulture *Neophron percnopterus*; most resembles a small version of Lappet-faced Vulture *Aegypius tracheliotus*. Head and beak noticeably slim in front of spread wings in flight, beak much more slender than any vulture except Egyptian Vulture.

Voice. Recorded (2a). Practically silent, but on nest or when excited utters thin querulous squealing cries. Begging call of young a soft 'chiu-chiu-chiu'.

General Habits. Well known. Occurs throughout tropical Africa south of Sahara from Senegal to N Somalia, south to Natal, in any habitat from hottest deserts to within tall rain forest; from sea level to 4000 m (Ethiopia). The common town scavenger all over W and NE Africa, in hundreds in any sizeable town south as far as Kampala (Uganda). In Kenya–Tanzania not a town scavenger, but associates with pastoralists at cattle kraals, obtaining scraps, and also feeds on natural carrion in uninhabited areas (e.g. Serengeti Plains). In southern Africa not commensal with man, but solitary, apparently wholly dependent on natural food supplies. Where abundant, gregarious, otherwise solitary.

Normally roosts in trees, using same tree nightly, often many on one tree. Leaves roost *c.* 1 h earlier than large *Gyps* spp., arriving on wing in Ethiopian towns between Black Kite *Milvus migrans* and Lammergeier *Gypaetus barbatus*. Then spends most of day foraging. Gregarious on rubbish dumps, and spends long periods waiting on trees near butcheries for discarded scraps and offal. Then many may quickly collect on ground, fighting for available food. Perches, or waits on ground near E African pastoralists' cattle kraals, sometimes with Egyptian Vulture; may obtain no food all day in such situations, occasionally gorges on dead stock.

At carcasses, unable to compete with larger vultures, *Gyps* and *Aegypius*. Forms a species pair with Egyptian Vulture (Kruuk 1967), feeding on scraps, or stripping meat with narrow bill from small openings. Is less aggressive than Egyptian Vulture but, like it, often remains at carcass remnant after larger vultures have left. Long slim bill also enables it to extract, for example, larvae from dung-beetle balls, and to feed on grubs in rice fields being cultivated. Adaptable in N Africa, able to exploit situations denied to other vultures; but in southern Africa not similarly successful.

Apparently sedentary in most of range, in W African semi-arid Sahelian zone leaving during rains June–Sept, perhaps for more arid areas (Salvan 1968). In much of W Africa no marked dry–wet season movements reported. Only vulture able to survive regularly in wet climates with rainfall over 2000 mm/year; but then entirely commensal with man.

Food. Carrion; any kind of meat, or scrap of skin, small bones, usually obtained in towns, where most abundant. Also, alate termites when available, large insect larvae, locusts. Has no specialized food habits, but adaptable. Valuable as a town scavenger.

Breeding Habits. Well known. Observations suggest pair-bond lifelong for any individual. Pairs normally sedentary in same area, seen daily, often roosting on or near nest nightly, even when not breeding. Not truly gregarious, but not aggressively territorial, many pairs clustering to breed on any available trees (Mundy and Cook 1972). Little obvious nuptial display, but before breeding, pairs soar sedately together, circling wing-tip to wing-tip. Rarely, one dives at other, which rolls clumsily and presents feet. Mating occurs many times daily, on trees, on the nest itself, sometimes on buildings, even on the ground. Both sexes flush bright red or purplish during the act. Pairs may occupy nest-site for weeks, even months, before laying, if they lay.

NEST: rather small structure of sticks, often not hiding sitting bird, *c.* 0·6 m wide by 0·3–0·4 m deep (maximum 1·0 × 0·75). Normally built in trees, selecting tall trees if available, sometimes in forests. In W African towns uses any available trees with some preference for thorny spp. (*Acacia*, *Balanites*) or *Borassus* palms. Rarely, on buildings or cliffs. Sometimes built on foundation of another species' nest. Shallow central depression, *c.* 0·4 m across, is lined with green leaves, grass, hair, bits of skin, rags; leaves brought at intervals through most of breeding season. Same nest used repeatedly for several years, and pairs may have more than 1 nest. Both sexes bring material, roles not established.

EGGS: almost invariably 1; only 1 clutch of 2 ever reported (Boughton-Leigh 1932). Rounded ovals, white, variously blotched brown, red-brown and grey, mainly at broad end, sometimes plain. SIZE: 64·0–82·1 × 48·0–59·1 (73·2 × 53·9); WEIGHT: 94–130 (W Africa, av. 108, cf. calculated weight of 120) (Mundy and Cook 1972; Schönwetter 1960).

Laying dates: W Africa, season extended, beginning late Sept, continuing till Apr, especially mid-Dec–mid-Mar (hot dry season); Sudan, N Uganda, Jan–Feb (hot dry season); Ethiopia–Somalia Oct–Dec (dry season); Kenya–Central Uganda Jan, Apr–July, Sept–Dec, with marked peaks late in both rainy seasons E Kenya; Zambia, Zimbabwe, Transvaal June–Aug, especially June–July (main dry season). Throughout range prefers to lay in dry season, but young from late layings are in nest in height of rains; where dry season is short, near equator, lays late in either rainy season. In W Africa many eggs become addled some years, perhaps because of cold nights (Serle 1943), but this evidently not invariable (Mundy and Cook 1972).

Both sexes incubate, constantly in attendance (Mundy and Cook 1972). In E Africa reportedly carried out mainly by ♀, ♂ taking short spells by day, ♀ always at night. ♂ in such cases feeds ♀ at nest, regurgitating food (Van Someren 1956). Adults may continue incubating addled eggs weeks after hatching is due (Serle 1943), but also may re-lay after early failure *c.* 6 weeks after losing 1st egg (Mundy and Cook 1972). Incubation period: E Africa, 46 days (1 nest); W Africa, av. 51 days (9 records).

Downy young are feeble, helpless and require close brooding. Wing-feathers just appearing at 14 days, back feathers 21 days, largely feathered by 40 days. Thereafter remains unusually long in nest, first climbing out onto branches at 95–100 days, making 1st flight at 120 days (Van Someren 1956). In W Africa fledging period estimated 89–130 days, usually 95–120 days (Mundy and Cook 1972). All records suggest unusually protracted period in nest after feathering complete. Young makes 1st flight unaided, then return to nest to roost for up to 30 days, thereafter probably independent. In towns can readily obtain food, but if forced to compete with adults at carcass may not succeed. Most young first fly in rains, when carrion is likely to be scarce.

Days 1–7 ♀, or both parents, brood young closely; ♂ brings food (Van Someren 1956). ♀, or either adult, sits very tight, will scarcely leave. Once young is part-feathered (after 21 days), ♀ also brings food, and probably both sexes normally do so. Food carried in crop, regurgitated onto nest-edge, then picked up and fed to chick; feathered young feeds itself on regurgitated food. Parents often perch near young in nest-tree and roost close to nest, throughout cycle. Experimental increase of clutches to 2 shows that pair can normally rear only 1 young even if 2 hatch (Mundy and Cook 1972).

Large numbers of non-breeding adults in some towns (e.g. in Ethiopia) suggest that many pairs do not breed annually. In W Africa perhaps more regular. Of 50 nests, 6 not used, 10 abandoned after courtship (32% non-breeding); 34 eggs laid resulted in 11–15 chicks reared, 0·22–0·30/pair overall, 0·32–0·44/breeding pair, 1·0/successful nest. Very low breeding success in apparently favourable situations (Sokoto: Mundy and Cook 1972) with dense adult population suggests long life-span.

References
Mundy, P. J. and Cook, A. W. (1972).
Serle, W. M. (1943).
Van Someren, V. G. L. (1956).

Genus *Gyps* Savigny

Very large, gregarious vultures, adapted for feeding on soft flesh and intestines (Kruuk 1967). Bill powerful, rather long, strongly hooked at tip, with sharp cutting edges; tongue stiff, channelled, with sharp serrations, assisting rapid feeding. Nostrils slit-shaped, nearly vertical. Head and neck bare, covered with thin down; neck long, adapted for thrusting deep into carcass. A ruff of feathers round base of neck, lanceolate in immatures, fluffy in adults; crop covered with short stiff feathers. Wings long, very broad, with 20 or more secondaries forming a nearly rectangular silhouette in flight. Tail short, slightly wedge-shaped. Tarsi strong, rather long, but shorter than long middle toe. Talons reduced, hind toe relatively small, feet adapted for walking rather than grasping (but have powerful grip).

Of the 7 spp. (4 African, 3 Asian–Indian), 2, formerly placed in the genus *Pseudogyps*, have 14 not 12 tail feathers, rather shorter sharper-edged bills, and breed in loose colonies or singly in trees. All others, except the Asian Long-billed Vulture *G. indicus*, breed in close colonies on cliffs; but since *G. indicus* breeds in trees it forms a link, and the genus *Pseudogyps* is not regarded as valid. There are, however, 2 distinct superspp., 1 containing the white-backed vultures *G. bengalensis* and *G. africanus*; the other the colonial rock-breeding griffons, with 5 spp., 3 found in Africa.

All African members are either well known or very well known with regard to their feeding habits and breeding behaviour. Since they suffer either directly or indirectly from development and civilization, they have been much studied in recent years. 2 African spp., *G. fulvus* and *G. coprotheres*, sometimes (but not by us) considered conspecific, are severely threatened throughout their range.

Plates 19 and 29 (Opp. pp. 306 and 450)

Gyps africanus Salvadori. African White-backed Vulture. Vautour africain.

Gyps africanus Salvadori, 1865. Not. Stor. R. Accad. Torino, p. 133; Sennar, Sudan.

Range and Status. Throughout tropical Africa in savannas, grasslands, thornbush and subdesert, sometimes in denser woodlands; most abundant woodlands with 500–800 mm annual rainfall. Not normally commensal with urban man, but associates with and sometimes dependent on pastoralists and dead domestic stock. Usually common, locally abundant to very abundant, hundreds together. The most numerous vulture in most grass plains and light woodland. In South Africa now much reduced, confined to National Parks and thinly populated ranches; elsewhere more stable, but probably decreasing; recently has apparently disappeared parts of N Sudan (Wilson, in press).

Description. ADULT ♂: bare head and neck black, with sparse yellowish or whitish down. Neck-ruff white, rather sparse. Mantle and scapulars brown, back and rump white. Lesser and median upperwing-coverts grey, edged sandy when worn.

Crop-patch chocolate brown, underparts of body dull rufous brown; underwing-coverts white, strongly contrasting with wing-feathers. Primaries, secondaries and tail-feathers black to blackish brown, paler on wing-feathers. Cere grey; eye dark brown; legs black. Sexes similar in size, ♂♂ perhaps averaging fractionally larger. SIZE: wing, 550–631 (610); tail 240–275; tarsus, 90–118; wing-span, 2120–2280 (2200); wing-loading, 77 N/m²; aspect ratio, 6·9. WEIGHT: (without crop contents) 4·25–6·25 (5·38) kg (D. Houston, pers. comm.; Pennycuick 1972).

IMMATURE: generally darker, browner than adult, head and neck with more conspicuous, whiter down; ruff thinner than adult, of tassel-like feathers, brown. Lower back brown, streaked white. Underside brown, feathers with light centres, producing streaked appearance; underwing-coverts mottled brown and white. Adult plumage is acquired by continuous moult, beginning at 10 months, continuing for at least 6 years. Recent immatures have flight and covert feathers with pointed tips. Older (3 years or over) have rounded, not pointed feathers, and shorter, stiffer ruff.

DOWNY YOUNG: when first hatched, down short, white, abdomen bare; 2nd down (14–21 days) thicker, sooty-grey. Eye brown, cere and legs grey.

Field Characters. The common large vulture in most savannas and grass plains. Normally can only be confused with Rüppell's Griffon *G. rueppellii* or Cape Vulture *G. coprotheres*. Differs from these in having rather shorter neck and shorter blackish bill, and adult has brown eye. Body plumage also is darker, more uniform brown than either, easily distinguished from adult or subadult Rüppell's Griffon by plain brown, not strongly scaled appearance. On taking off, white lower back of adult visible. In flight, adult easily distinguished from Rüppell's Griffon by strongly contrasting white underwing-coverts, less easily from Cape Vulture, which has buff coverts. Immature is mottled brown and white, but still generally paler than immature of adult Rüppell's Griffon.

Voice. Recorded (2a, 18). Normally silent, except at carcasses and at roosts, when utters hisses, and sometimes shrill, pig-like squeals. Throaty croaks at nest. Young utter whistling begging calls.

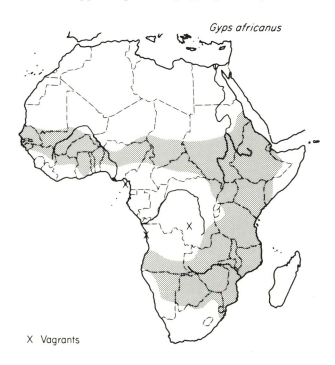

Gyps africanus

X Vagrants

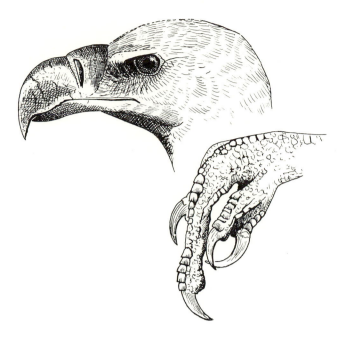

General Habits. Very well known. Favoured habitat open grassy plains and light *Acacia* woodland in rainfall of 500–800 mm/year; requires some tall trees for breeding. Becomes uncommon with increasing density of tall woodland, largely absent Lower Guinea savannas and central African *Brachystegia* woodland; but still common in dense thornbush. Normally in plains and lowlands rather than mountains, but occurs up to 3500 m (Ethiopia). Does not normally frequent towns, but may perch on outskirts, and is common near cattle kraals where dead domestic stock available.

Normally gregarious, at roosts and at carrion; more solitary when breeding. Roosts in groups on tall trees, often near breeding sites; but also on any available tall tree near temporary source of food. Unable to fly far without thermal aids, must normally remain on roost until 2–3 h after dawn and return 2–3 h before dark; but when roosting close to carrion may flap laboriously several hundred metres early morning, even in wet weather. Same birds use same roost perch night after night in well-used localities. Is normally on wing only 6–8 h in 24, probably perching for some of that time, or feeding with others at carcass. Often rests on ground, wings spread, towards midday, and regularly drinks water at favourite places.

At carcass, functions as species pair with Rüppell's Griffon or Cape Vulture in most of range, very rarely (W Africa) with European Griffon *G. fulvus*. Rather slender skull, and long neck and beak adapted to eating soft flesh and intestines, not able to penetrate skin of large carcass (Kruuk 1967). At carcass, squabbling, squealing mass of mixed vultures is composed of dominants temporarily in possession, satiated birds sitting nearby, and hungry new arrivals. New arrival usually alights some distance from carcass, then bounds towards others, head low, wings spread, sometimes feet outstretched; little calling is made, but chittering squealing calls uttered in immediate threat. Dominants at carcass spread wings, raise head and neck and hiss to repel others. Thrust head and neck into any orifice, and may go right inside large body, though generally perch-ing on top. Strip soft flesh and intestines of large animals rapidly, leaving bones and skin. When with other, somewhat larger *Gyps* spp. normally unable to repel them; but is often most numerous vulture present. Cannot withstand piratical attacks by Lappet-faced Vultures *Aegypius tracheliotus*, but can repel White-headed Vulture *A. occipitalis* and smaller Hooded and Egyptian Vultures (*Necrosyrtes monachus* and *Neophron percnopterus*). May gorge until almost unable to fly and full crop may contain 1000 g; but in natural situations must remain able to avoid attack by, for example, lions, hyenas. Having fed, usually withdraws some distance, then often remains for hours near carcass, standing or lying on ground, sometimes with wings spread and back to sun. May return later for further food and, in evening, if undisturbed, seeks nearest convenient roost-tree, perhaps feeding again next day.

Gliding flight studied in Serengeti (Pennycuick 1971a) indicates that normal forward speed is 13·2–23·0 m/s, av. *c*. 16–18 m/s (58–65 km/h); glides interspersed with periods of circling on thermals, reducing overall av. speed. In fast downward glide can attain *c*. 120 km/h. Surprisingly, is less efficient than man-made glider, with minimum sinking speed of 0·76 m/s at forward speed of 10 m/s, and maximum glide ratio of 15·3 : 1 at 13 m/s. Can turn in circles on thermals much smaller than are usable by glider, varying from 9–18 s per circle. Relatively low wing-loading compared with man-made glider thus permits more efficient use of small thermals, but less efficient cross-country gliding on larger thermals. Use of small thermals enables earlier foraging than would be possible for 'albatross-shaped' vulture; turn radius 14 m (cf. 21 m for latter). Relatively short wings with low wing-loading and low aspect ratio may thus have advantage in permitting earlier use of thermals, and in manoeuvring close to ground.

Normally sedentary within any large area of plains, not migratory; locally nomadic, congregating in areas with abundant food supply. In W Africa some southward movement occurs into more densely wooded areas in dry season Oct–Mar, returning north with Apr rains. Individuals may travel up to 50 km/day to reach food, not normally as far as Rüppell's Griffon. On wing soars occasionally to great height but normally seeks food, in areas of abundance, at 200–500 m above ground, more rarely 800–1000 m; very high birds possibly travelling, not foraging (D. Houston, pers. comm.). Regularly observes and follows other carrion birds, vultures, hyenas, even lions to locate food sources. Has recently associated in large numbers with game-culling operations, Kruger Park, South Africa (W. Tarboton, pers. comm.).

Food. Soft flesh and intestines of large dead wild animals or domestic stock; does not normally eat hides, but requires some bone in diet; bone flakes found in 47% of nests (Plug 1978). Does not take alate termites even when abundantly available. Disappears from areas where large carcasses no longer readily available, and has not generally adapted to human scraps and refuse. Food requirement estimated 315 g, *c*. 6–7% of adult bodyweight (Houston 1976).

Breeding Habits. Very well known, studied in E and South Africa (Houston 1976; Kemp and Kemp 1975a). Normally breeds in loose groups, but also often singly, most often in arid areas. Groups are commonest along rivers and streams with tall trees, e.g. 250 nests in 100 km, S Somalia, varying 1–6 per tree (North 1944). Colonies may be discrete and perhaps associated with favoured feeding ranges of lion prides (Timbavati Game Reserve: W. Tarboton, pers. comm.). Single nests found on old tall trees dotted through thornbush and light woodland.

Not strongly territorial, defending only a few square metres round nest itself. Nuptial display not spectacular, some slow circling in pairs near nest, less often than in other vultures. Pairs usually roost near nest for weeks, sometimes months, before laying. Copulation occurs on nest-tree, neighbouring trees, or nest itself, several times daily before egg-laying. ♂ mounts clumsily and maintains balance by wing-flapping; duration 25–35 s.

NEST: invariably in trees; may be at any height from 8–50 m from ground, mainly 15–25 m. Tall trees preferred, and thorny selected if available, e.g. *Acacia elatior*, *A. xanthophloea*, *A. tortilis*, *A. delagoensis*, *A. nigrescens* and *Terminalia prunoides*; sometimes large figs, or broad-leaved trees in forests adjacent to savanna areas. In thornbush, *Acacia* and *Terminalia* favoured, always taller than most in area. Nests reported on cliffs wrongly identified (Jackson and Sclater 1938). Usually built by vultures themselves, but sometimes use old nests of eagles, storks, Secretary Bird *Sagittarius serpentarius* and buffalo weavers (*Bubalornis*) (Kemp and Kemp 1975a). Structure rather small for size of bird, part of which often visible when sitting. Made of sticks, 45 cm–1 m in diameter, 15–90 cm thick, with shallow central cup 18–20 cm in diameter, lined mainly with grass, some green leaves and creepers. Sticks collected from ground or other nests, carried in bill; green branches detached with difficulty from nearby trees. Both sexes build, probably one most, shares not determined. Nests repeatedly used become cemented with droppings; most nests used for several or many years (1 record of 9 successive years), c. 2/3 re-occupied annually.

EGGS: almost invariably 1; 1 record of 2, Kruger Park, acceptable. Rounded ovals; white, rarely marked reddish. SIZE: (23 eggs) 83·6–96 × 63·2–74·5 (89·2 × 66·2); (33, Kruger Park) 82·4 × 67·6 (Kemp and Kemp 1975a). WEIGHT: c. 214 (4% of ♀ bodyweight).

Laying dates: W Africa–Sudan Oct–Nov, occasionally later (dry season); Ethiopia Oct–Mar (dry); Somalia Sept–Mar, especially Oct, Nov (dry or, in south, short rains); E Kenya Apr–June, again Dec–Jan (in or just after both rainy seasons); Tanzania (Serengeti), peak Apr–May (end rains); Zambia–Zimbabwe Apr–Oct, Jan, peaking Zambia May–June (early dry); Transvaal (Kruger Park) 14 May–30 June, variable, peaking later some years than others (Kemp and Kemp 1975a). Where 1 long dry and wet season alternate, most eggs laid early dry season, but in equatorial 2-season rainfall, eggs often laid rains, and entire cycle of 180 days must include wet periods.

Incubation by both sexes; share not well recorded. Both often present much of day, one perching near, other sitting. Nest-reliefs silent, brief, with no ceremony; other bird takes off when relief arrives. Incubation period: 56–58 days ± 1 day (Kemp and Kemp 1975a).

Chick can be heard in egg for 2 days before chipping, and egg may take 3 days to hatch. Hatching weight c. 150, increasing to 1000 at 20–25 days, 2000 by day 35, 3500 by day 45, 4000 day 65; thereafter growth slower, reaching maximum of 4500–4700 at 75–80 days. Entirely downy days 1–30; feathers begin to erupt day 35; wings and some upper contour feathers developed by day 48; largely feathered day 63. Thereafter main development in wing- and tail-feathers. Tarsus full grown at 55 days when can stand and feed itself; body growth complete by 90 days, but growth of wing- and tail-feathers still incomplete 112 days. 1st flight made unaided at av. c. 130 days nearest estimate 126 ± 2 days (Kemp and Kemp 1975a).

Adults brood helpless chick continuously days 1–7; thereafter chick often only shaded by day. Chick moves into shade cast by adult on open nest. Both parents brood and feed young, ♂ perhaps feeding more than ♀; shares not well recorded. ♂ may regurgitate food into nest where fed to young by ♀. Young can feed itself on regurgitated prey by day 45, when partly feathered. In later fledging period, one or other adult normally remains on nest while other forages; feeds then irregular, infrequent, sometimes by both parents almost simultaneously towards end. May be fed by more than 1 ♂ as more than 2 adults have been shot or seen at single nests (Houston 1976). Large, nearly fledged young sometimes left completely alone, adults not even roosting near, but usually 1 present to end of fledging.

Breeding success high in optimum habitat (e.g. Serengeti), c. 0·8–0·9 young/nest/year; but number of occupied nests per total of adult pairs not known. 1 nest reared 9 young in 10 years (Van Someren 1956). In Kruger Park, 68 occupied nests produced 43 young, i.e. 63% success (probably more realistic). Not all adults may breed, so real overall success may be still lower (Houston 1976; Kemp and Kemp 1975a).

Young after leaving nest dependent on parents for c. 1 month; after that join parents at carcasses, but have difficulty in competing, are more often attacked by adults than adults attack each other; may starve if food not abundant. Peak laying in Serengeti produces independent young c. Dec (rains) when food supplies not maximum; in Kruger laying peak May–June also produces young Dec–Jan (rains). Unlike Rüppell's Griffon in same area (Serengeti), may not be timed to produce flying young when food most abundant.

Population composition: of 1944 birds (Serengeti), full adults 933 (48%), immatures, 4–7 years, 447 (26%), 2–3 year olds 330 (17%), 1st-year birds 234 (9%) (Houston 1974). Depending on rate of mortality before sexual maturity, species must certainly be long lived. 50% mortality before maturity would produce only 4·5% adult replacements, necessitating mean adult breeding life at least 22 years.

References
Houston, D. C. (1974, 1976).
Kemp, A. C. and Kemp, M. I. (1975a).
Pennycuick, C. J. (1971a).

Gyps rueppellii (Brehm). Rüppell's Griffon. Vautour de Rüppell.

**Plates
19 and 29**
(Opp. pp. 306
and 450)

Vultur Rueppellii A. E. Brehm, 1852. Naumannia, 2, Heft 3, p. 44; Khartoum, Sudan.

Range and Status. More arid and mountainous areas of Africa south of the Sahara from Senegal east to Somalia and south to N Tanzania. Normally common to locally abundant or very abundant, hundreds together at carcasses or roosts. Probably stable, not threatened in most of range, but recently reported decreasing N Sudan; cause unknown.

Description. *G. r. rueppellii* (Brehm): Senegal east to Sudan, Kenya and Tanzania. ADULT ♂: head and neck dirty grey, covered with thin whitish down; ruff white. Feathers of back, upperwing-coverts, scapulars with dark centres edged whitish, producing a scaled appearance. Crop-patch deep chocolate brown. Underside, including underwing-coverts brown, feathers tipped creamy-buff. Wing- and tail-feathers blackish brown, washed chocolate. Bill dull reddish horn, tipped paler; cere and bare facial skin grey; eye yellow or amber; bare patch either side of crop blue-grey; feet slate colour. Sexes similar, little size difference. SIZE: wing, 670–710 (690); tail, 260–290 (274); tarsus, 102–110 (106); wing-span, (19) 2300–2500 (2410); wing-loading, 90 N/m²; aspect ratio 7·0. WEIGHT: (19) 6800–9000 (7570) (Pennycuick 1971b).

1ST IMMATURE: differs in having brown down on head and neck; body plumage darker, more uniform, lacking the scaly appearance. Feathers of underside centrally pale, appearing streaky; bill black, eye brown. This develops into adult plumage through an intermediate stage in which the beak becomes dull horn colour, the plumage of upperparts acquires scaly look, with cream feather edges, and streaks on underside disappear. Adult plumage acquired in not less than 7 years (Houston 1975).

DOWNY YOUNG: grey, becoming darker with age; soft parts undescribed.

G. r. erlangeri Salvadori. Ethiopia and Somalia; is paler, with more pronounced whitish feather edges. Larger: wing 625–665; wing-span 2395; weight (1) 6384.

Field Characters. The common large vulture of more arid tropical Africa, especially in mountains, in Ethiopia up to 4500 m or over. Absent from areas lacking any rock cliffs, and numbers depend on availability of gorges and cliffs. Adult easily distinguished in adult plumage from any other large vulture in its range by pale edges to many body feathers, yellow eye, dark reddish horn bill. Immatures more uniform, but darker, smaller than European Griffon *G. fulvus* in areas of possible overlap, N and NW Africa (Mali); also have dark brown crop area. Larger, paler, longer-necked, longer-billed than White-backed Vulture *G. africanus*. Long, thin, rather snaky neck distinguishes it from any *Aegypius* sp.

Voice. Not recorded. Not distinctive; normally silent, but at carcasses, hisses, grunts and querulous shrieks; said to utter loud harsh calls at breeding colonies and coarse grating calls at copulation. Begging call of young feeble, whistling.

General Habits. Very well known. A vulture mainly of mountainous country, or lowlands studded with large inselbergs, but occurs in open savanna reached by flight from mountainous areas. Dominant vulture in arid N Kenya, highlands of Ethiopia, and more arid savannas south of Sahara, but absent if no cliffs available. Often

Gyps rueppellii

very abundant at suitable roost sites, perhaps even thousands together (Mount Ololokwi, N Kenya), usually scores to hundreds.

Roosts nightly on cliff faces, usually very inaccessible. Starts to collect near roost 3–4 h before sundown; all have settled by 1 h before dark. Descends slowly from great height, circles, alights, often with difficulty, after a dive and upward swoop. Many may roost on same broad ledges, but also singly on small ledges or niches; same birds use same ledge night after night. Unable to fly far without thermal aid, but launches off high cliff faces 1–2 h after sunrise, occasionally earlier, and seeks updraughts over mountain ranges, or locates thermals rising from heated arid plains. Then mounts to height in spirals, gliding to foraging areas.

In areas of high ungulate concentration usually forages close to ground, below 300 m; but where ungulates scarce, forages from 300–1200 m above ground, commanding wider area in view. Occasionally flies higher, up to 2000 m; but such birds probably travelling, not searching for food. This species has the highest credible altitude record for any bird, 1 having been killed by a jet aircraft at 37,000 feet (11,300 m) above Abidjan (Laybourne 1974); this record not accepted by some authorities (D. Houston, pers. comm.). Forages over greater distances than White-backed Vulture in same area, travelling up to 150 km or more from roost or nesting areas; in many areas this is not necessary. Travels using a series of thermals, circling to gain height, then gliding. Gliding performance, as measured from glider, gave glide-ratio (over 34 km) of over 60:1. Av. speed (over 75 km) 47 km/h; would take *c.* 3 h to reach furthest foraging areas. With av. 8/12 h flying time, 5 h travelling and 3 h foraging daily permits a regular foraging range of *c.* 110 km from roost or nest-site (Pennycuick 1972).

Like other large vultures locates food by direct sight, cannot smell. Watches other carrion birds and vultures, and hyenas or lions. When feeding, normally forms species pair with White-backed Vulture, competing directly for same food, intestines and soft flesh, long neck enabling deeper penetration (Houston 1975). Larger, heavier, more powerful than White-backed Vulture; can dominate where both occur, but itself can be dominated by Lappet-faced Vulture *Aegypius tracheliotus*. Hungry bird alighting lands some metres from carcass, then bounds towards struggling mass, wings spread, scapular feathers erected into 'horns', head lowered and neck outstretched. In less active threat, one may walk towards another, head raised to full extent of neck, wings spread, stretching feet out forwards. Attacked bird nearly always gives way, but sometimes resists by itself opening wings, stretching neck. Rüppell's Griffon fights most often with its own species, next with White-backed Vulture (Kruuk 1967). When feeding, gulps food rapidly, aided by sharp edges to bill and long, scoop-like tongue edged with sharp serrations. Can gorge in a few minutes. Gorged birds, and those unable to obtain feeding place stand or sit about on outskirts of feeding group. When gorged, frequently lies or stands in sun, sometimes opening wings with back to sun. Occasionally roosts on trees near food, but usually leaves to return to favoured cliffs.

Normally sedentary within rather wide area, *c.* 100 km radius from roost-cliff; locally nomadic. Some regular north–south movement in dry season in W Africa, moving south to edges of woodland, retreating north again with early rains. Scarce in any kind of tall woodland, but abundant in dense thornbush in arid areas, e.g. N Kenya, Ethiopia, NW Somalia. In Ethiopia, may be at least partially commensal with urban man, and in Kenya often frequents cattle kraals where sickly domestic stock may die.

Food. Entirely carrion; adapted to eat soft flesh and intestines. Food requirement of captive birds *c.* 360 g/day (4·75% bodyweight); maximum crop contents 1500 g, crop still unnoticeable after ingesting 400 g. Adults can probably starve many days after gorging, immatures possibly more sensitive. Maximum daily food requirement of captive young *c.* 750 g days 40–60.

Breeding Habits. Very well known. Breeds in large colonies of up to 1000 pairs, usually less, on cliffs. Small colonies and occasional solitary pairs known. Any records of tree-nesting (e.g. Chad: Salvan 1968) doubtful.

Nuptial display not spectacular; pairs soar, circling close together near nest-cliff; but many birds so acting may not be mated. Paired adults perch together on or near nest-ledge for long periods. Copulation frequent (up to 6 times in 2 h) before and just after egg-laying, usually on cliff ledges near nest or on nest itself, sometimes on communal roost-ledges. Lasts 8–30 s, accompanied by distinctive coarse rasping call.

NEST: built on open rock ledges, or in niches, sometimes overhung. Small, slight structures of sticks, often smaller than sitting bird, *c.* 0·6 m across by 0·2 m deep, lined with grass and some green leaves. If sites abundant, are not necessarily used annually, but in some areas same site repeatedly used many years (Kenya, 1 for at least 20 years). With repeated use may be enlarged to 1·5 m across and up to 1 m deep; but even old nests often very small. Both sexes build, 1 (perhaps ♂) collecting most material, taking it to nest where arranged by mate. Most sticks are stolen from other nests, but some from bushes or trees; carried in bill.

EGGS: invariably 1; 1 record of 2 (Jackson and Sclater 1938) was possibly 2 birds laying in same nest. Broad ovals; white tinged green, occasionally slightly spotted brown. SIZE: (*G. r. rueppellii*) 86·5–102 × 63·4–70·5 (91·2 × 66·4), (*G. r. erlangeri*) av. larger, 96·0 × 66·5; WEIGHT: (*G. r. rueppellii*) 220 (2·7% of ♀ bodyweight), shell 20.

Laying dates: W Africa Oct, Nov, perhaps Sept (Mali) (dry season); Ethiopia Oct (early main dry season); N Kenya, N Tanzania, records in 10/12 months, peaking May–June (end long rains); Serengeti, Tanzania Dec–Feb, peaking Jan (height of rains). Laying dates in rains or early in long dry season produce young, *c.* 180 days later, end dry season or early following rains.

Both sexes incubate, shares not well established as not easily recognizable; reliefs occur about twice daily, suggesting either sex might sit at night, if present in evening. Incubation period: not exactly known, 55 days estimated by comparing with other *Gyps* spp. (Houston 1976).

When young hatch covered with thin grey down; 2nd down, developed by 21 days, thicker, woollier, darker grey. Feathers of back and upperwing-coverts appear at *c.* 25 days, cover upperbody by 35 days; feathers of underside develop later, by *c.* day 50. Wing- and tail-feathers visible by *c.* 35 days. After day 70 fully feathered, main development then in wing- and tail-feathers; can stand and walk about, but often cannot move far on precipitous nest-ledge. Make 1st flight at *c.* 110 days, and must immediately fly some distance, as in other cliff-nesting vultures. Weight increases from *c.* 180 g near hatching to over 7000 g at fledging; maximum food demand between 40–70 days, 600–800 g daily, reduced to 250–300 near fledging; details of feather development not well described, but maximum demand corresponds with most rapid feather growth.

Both sexes tend and brood young, reliefs occurring about once daily. Brooding continuous early stages, up to *c.* day 10, thereafter reduced, but an adult remains on or near nest till near end of fledging period. Either sex feeds young, and parents may deprive themselves to provide for young. Total requirement for parents and young in whole fledging period estimated at 900 g/day for 2 adults, plus up to 700 g/day for young, maximum *c.* 1600 g/day, 250–300 kg/fledging period. To provide chick's maximum demand adult must regurgitate full crop load, perhaps surviving itself by using stored fat. Adults lose weight through breeding season; fat reserves reduced from 21·0–3·7% (Houston 1976).

Breeding success in occupied nests apparently high; in 85 nests 75 (88%) hatched, producing 70 young (82%), or 0·82 young/breeding pair, 1·00/successful nest. Many non-breeding adults present some colonies, not possible to estimate proportion of adults in whole population breeding; true breeding success probably lower per pair overall.

Recent immatures cannot effectively compete with adults at carcasses, are attacked more often than theoretically expected. In Serengeti (optimum habitat), are believed to leave main breeding areas, moving to places where competition with adults reduced. Begin to moult within 10 months and are recognizable by pointed covert feathers, lanceolate or spiky ruff-feathers, darker bill, darker eye. Life-span at present impossible to estimate, but certainly long.

References
Houston, D. C. (1976).

Gyps fulvus (Hablizl). European Griffon. Vautour fauve.

Plates 19 and 29
(Opp. pp. 306 and 450)

Vultur fulvus Brisson = Hablizl, 1783. Neue Nord. Beytr., 4, p. 58; Samamisian Alps, Gilan, Iran.

Range and Status. Breeds Morocco, Algeria, Tunisia, especially southern parts; Egypt, including Sinai; and in southern Europe, some migrating from there to Africa in winter. Within tropical Africa only migrants occur, Senegal, Mali, N Sudan and N Ethiopia. Frequent to locally common near breeding localities; as migrant to tropical Africa uncommon to rare. Threatened and decreasing in much of European range, status in N Africa not very clear, but perhaps more stable.

Description. *G. f. fulvus*, ADULT ♂: head and neck bluish, covered with short thick whitish down. Ruff of loose creamy white feathers, crop patch of brown hair-like feathers encircled by white down. Back and lesser upperwing-coverts sandy to rufous-brown, sometimes dark greyish brown. Greater and primary wing-coverts blackish brown, edged paler. Below, including underwing-coverts, pinkish to pale rufous-brown, with pale shaft-streaks. Wing- and tail-feathers black to dark brown, browner on secondaries. Eye yellow to pale yellow-brown; cere grey; bill yellow-horn; feet and legs dark grey-brown. ♀♀ slightly larger than ♂♂. SIZE: wing, ♂ 685–750 (725); ♀ 725–775 (752); tail, ♂ 280–320 (300), ♀ 280–320 (304); tarsus, ♂ 107–119 (111), ♀ 107–119 (113); wing-span, (1) 2341. WEIGHT: ♂ 6·2–10·5 kg, ♀ 6·5–11·2 kg (max. recorded 15·0 kg, min. 4·25 kg).

IMMATURE: darker, more rufous above than adult, wing-coverts with noticeable paler shaft-streaks. Below, more rufous, with broad pale shaft-streaks. Ruff longer, feathers distinctly lanceolate, edged pinkish, with pale shaft-streaks. Eye brown; cere and legs grey. 2nd year birds may be still darker. Adult plumage acquired in *c*. 7 years.

DOWNY YOUNG: 1st down white, 2nd down above pale grey, below white, longer, thicker; eye yellowish grey; cere and legs grey.

Field Characters. A very large, gregarious vulture, generally pale rufous-brown, streaky below in immature. Adults immediately distinguishable from Rüppell's Griffon *G. rueppellii* by almost plain, not scaly-looking, rufous upperback and wing-coverts; also much paler and more rufous than uniform brown White-backed Vulture *G. africanus*. In flight, plain rufous underwing-coverts, not obviously mottled pale and dark, distinguish from Rüppell's Griffon. Adult White-backed Vulture has white underwing-coverts. Unlikely to be confused with anything but other griffons and would not occur in range of Cape Vulture *G. coprotheres*, which is very similar but for dark bill.

Voice. Recorded (2a). Practically impossible to render intelligibly in words. Generally silent, except at car-

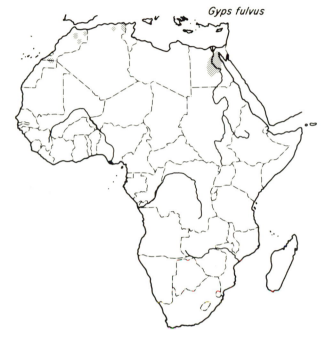

Gyps fulvus

casses and at breeding colonies. At carcasses loud hissing threat by dominants; subdominants utter sobbing sounds. Chattering calls rendered 'tetetet' or 'gegegeg'. Fighting, harsher, sharper 'kak-kak-kak'. At nest, grunting 'grak-grak' or 'kreh-kreh' in greeting. In copulation, loud harsh snarling 'achaaachachaaachaaach'. Adults utter whistling calls in anxiety at nest and begging young a feeble whistling 'pi-yi, pi-yi', older young a snarling screech like copulating adults (Fernandez 1975; Glutz von Blotzheim *et al.* 1971; Terrase and Boudoint 1960).

General Habits. Very well known in European range, little detail recorded in Africa. The common large vulture of N African mountain ranges, invariably a bird of mountainous country, descending to lowlands to forage. Gregarious at all times, roosting and nesting on rock cliffs, using the same site nightly, rarely roosting on trees. Roosts sometimes, but not always, on same cliffs as breeding colonies.

Like other griffons, normally remains on roost until mountain winds or warm rising thermals assist soaring flight. Then swiftly mounts to greater height and searches for food. Often tends to plane slowly along mountain ridges on updraughts, sometimes in small groups. When food located, either by direct sight or by watching other vultures and carrion birds, glides direct to source at speed. Can attain 140 km/h in fast glides, but normal flight *c*. 50–60 km/h. Returns to roost any time from mid-afternoon to evening, and is in flight for not more than 8/24 h, often less; but may travel 300–450 km in that time.

At carcass, normally must only compete with its own species or Cinereous Vulture *Aegypius monachus*. In tropical Africa rarely with White-backed Vulture, which is larger, so would probably dominate. With others at carcass, arriving individuals usually join a waiting group on outskirts, but if very hungry may directly challenge dominant birds in possession. Threat display then involves stretching forward head and neck; raising scapular feathers to form upstanding 'horns'; stretching feet towards opponent; and sometimes bounding towards it with open wings. Degree of aggressiveness is probably dependent on hunger, i.e. hungriest birds most aggressive. Dominance at carcass is only temporary as feeding places possessor at a disadvantage (and also, of course, reduces hunger). Congregations at a carcass normally include dominants and near-dominants in possession, hungry birds awaiting turn, and satiated birds resting after feeding. Often only a few birds are actually feeding, with many others near and little aggression; but sometimes a jostling, scrambling, bickering mass swarms over and inside carcass, feeding greedily. Feed until satiated when possible, then often rest nearby, sometimes spreading wings. Such feeding behaviour is typical of all *Gyps* spp. (Valverde 1959; Kruuk 1967).

Breeding adults often winter within breeding range, perhaps moving locally to lower levels. Some adults and many immatures migrate from Europe to Africa, entering Africa via Gibraltar or Suez. Gibraltar and N Morocco birds extend south to S Sahara, and occasionally Senegal (1 ringed Spain, recovered Dakar: P. W. P. Browne, unpub.); those entering via Suez to N Sudan and N Ethiopia. Autumn passage begins Aug–Sept with adults, immatures later, Oct–Nov. Return migration occurs Feb–May (Gibraltar) and appears less concentrated, migrants possibly mainly immatures and subadults. Does not normally migrate in large flocks, but small groups and individuals; but up to 18,000 pass Suez (Goodwin 1949) with up to 200/day at peak; these numbers probably since reduced (Goodwin 1949; Lathbury 1970; Safriel 1968).

Food. Soft flesh and intestines of large dead animals, nowadays usually domestic stock. Often cannot puncture skin of large fresh carcasses, but sometimes succeeds with hard sideways blows of head. Skull is relatively light-boned (Kruuk 1967), unsuited for penetration. Rapid gulping of soft flesh assisted by sharp edges of beak and channelled tongue with backward-pointing serrations.

Breeding Habits. Very well known in European range; not studied in N Africa in detail, presumably similar. Breeds in colonies on cliffs, usually of 5–50 pairs, sometimes more, maximum 100–150; reputed to breed occasionally in trees. Breeding cycle commences midwinter (Jan, or even earlier). Display not spectacular, slow circling in pairs near breeding site. Mating occurs on rock ledges near future nest-site, preceded by slow sinuous movements of head and neck; all movements slow and deliberate. ♂ mounts slowly, maintains balance by waving wings. Non-breeding birds may mate near site, but do not then nest (Terrasse and Boudoint 1960).

NEST: usually overhung ledges, protected from snow, 2–4 m apart. Only 10–20 m² defended from neighbours. Flattish structure of sticks, lined with some green leaves and oddments, 0·6–1·0 m across by 0–0·4 m deep, depth varying according to size of cavity, deeper in deep niches. Same site used repeatedly, probably by same birds; colonies continue to be occupied for centuries. Both sexes build, all material brought in bill; some material added throughout breeding season. Nest often becomes partially cemented with droppings (Terrasse and Boudoint 1960).

EGGS: almost invariably 1, rare clutch of 2 recorded probably laid by 2 ♀♀. Broad oval, smooth, fine-grained, white, occasionally flecked brown. SIZE: (100 eggs) 81·5–106 × 65·0–75·0 (92·17 × 69·89); WEIGHT: *c*. 252 g; 1 about to hatch 244 g.

Laying dates: Morocco Feb, Mar (Heim de Balsac and Mayaud 1962).

♀ remains on nest for several days before laying. Both sexes incubate: days 1–10 ♀ most, *c*. 88%; days 11–25 ♀ 77%, ♂ 23%; days 25–50 ♀ 57%, ♂ 43%; ♀ again most just before hatch. Incubating birds reluctant to leave because of cold; but ♂♂ leave more readily than ♀♀. At nest-relief, no elaborate ceremony, perhaps greeting calls and brief soaring together; reliefs occur about twice a day. Incubation period: 56 ± 2 days; in captivity 58–65 days. Non-breeding birds at colonies may outnumber breeders 2 : 1 (Fernandez 1975; Terrasse and Boudoint 1960).

Newly hatched young weighs *c*. 200 g, increasing to 600 g at 7 days. Can then emit weak cries. Days 6–25, becoming more active; days 26–50, rapid development, becoming more active and independent of parental attention, wing- and tail-feathers sprouting; eats eggshells. Day 51 to fledging, largely left alone, aggressive to intruders; partially feathered by 70 days, exercising wings. After 90 days may wander off nest-ledge if space available, visiting other nests, lying there with other young. Solicits adult with erected feathers, agitating whole body, uttering continuous raucous call like copulating adults, pecking at adult's beak; can feed itself on regurgitated food, but still solicits adults. 1st flight made independent of adults at 100–115 (usually 110–115) days.

♀ is normally on nest at hatch. Days 1–5, ♀ broods continuously; ♂ present *c*. 37% of time, but does not brood; only ♀ feeds small young on regurgitated liquid material. Days 6–25, brooding reduced, ♂ now also broods *c*. 16% of time, ♀ 76%, *c*. 8% uncovered. Adults regurgitate partly digested food into nest, young can feed on it by day 25. Days 26–50, an adult remains on nest, little brooding, ♂ and ♀ taking almost equal shares; now leave chick alone *c*. 30% of time. After 51 days, one or other adult on or near nest most of time, but not brooding or feeding chick, which feeds itself on regurgitated food; young often left alone in nest. Parents roost near nest at night.

After 1st flight young probably dependent on adults for short period, must then accompany adults to feeding grounds and compete for space at carcass. Breeding success not well established in Europe, but certainly less than 1 young reared per occupied nest, and less than 0·5/pair if non-breeding pairs included.

References
Fernandez, J. A. (1975).
Terrasse, J. F. and Boudoint, Y. (1960).
Valverde, J. A. (1959).

Gyps coprotheres (J. R. Forster). Cape Vulture. Vautour chassefiente.

Vultur Coprotheres J. R. Forster, 1798. In Levaillant's Naturg. Af. Vogel, p. 35, pl. 10; South Africa.

Plates 19 and 29
(Opp. pp. 306 and 450)

Gyps coprotheres

Range and Status. S and SW Africa from S Zimbabwe, E Botswana and Etosha Pan, south to Cape Province; main range now Transvaal, Lesotho. Straggles further north to Zambia and S Zaïre. Northernmost localities S Zimbabwe; westernmost Waterberg Mts, Namibia; southernmost near Bredasdorp. Said to avoid arid central Kalahari desert (McLachlan and Liversidge 1978), occurring in mountains and grasslands, or bushveld. Frequent, locally common to abundant near breeding colonies, or at carrion; but greatly reduced in last 20 years by direct persecution, shortage of carrion in ranching areas, frequent deaths from electrocution (Ledger and Annegan 1980), and possibly poor breeding success through inadequate bone in diet. In Transvaal *c.* 1270 pairs, perhaps 1500 pairs plus immatures and non-breeding adults altogether. Still apparently decreasing, threatened with extinction unless intensive conservation efforts succeed.

Description. ADULT: (sexes indistinguishable) head and neck naked, with sparse whitish down; neck-ruff pale buff. Back, rump and upperwing-coverts pale buff, some feathers with darker centres. Below, crop-patch dull brown, surrounded by white down. Body below pale buff to cream, almost white on undertail-coverts. Primaries blackish, secondaries blackish grey; secondaries below grey with white on inner webs, axillaries white. Tail above and below blackish brown. Cere grey; bare facial skin bluish; eye yellow to whitish; feet grey. SIZE: wing, 650–702 (683); tail, 300–345; tarsus, 90–105.

IMMATURE: generally darker, more streaky than adult. Down on head and neck buff; ruff brown, feathers more lanceolate, with pale centres. Back, uppertail- and upperwing-coverts brown, edged buff, appearing mottled or scaled. Below crop-patch brown, circled with white down; underside of body and underwing-coverts streaked brown and buff, feathers with pale centres edged darker, darkest on belly, palest less streaked on underwing-coverts. Primaries blackish above and below; secondaries dark brown above, tipped buff, below greyish brown. Tail above and below blackish brown. Cere and bare facial skin grey; eye brown; legs grey. In 2nd year and later becomes more uniform buff or cream, like adult; eye yellow by 3rd year.

DOWNY YOUNG: dull white, 2nd down greyer; eye brown; bill and feet pink when first hatched, becoming grey later.

This species has by some been regarded as a race of the European Griffon *G. fulvus*. However, as it is separated by thousands of kilometres from any European Griffons, with the very distinct Rüppell's Griffon *G. rueppellii* occurring between, with no intermediates, we prefer to treat it as a full species.

Field Characters. Unmistakable in any plumage, a very large, pale sandy or light rufous vulture with strongly contrasting blackish wings and tail. Would only occur at carcasses with White-backed Vulture *G. africanus* or *Aegypius* spp. Much larger, generally much paler, longer-necked than White-backed Vulture, no white patch on back. Immatures somewhat more difficult, but still generally much larger, paler; 1–2 year olds have ruff of lanceolate feathers, pointed coverts and brown, not yellow, eyes.

Voice. Not recorded. Almost indescribable in words. Usually silent, except at breeding colonies and carcasses. Then utters grunts, squeals, hisses, and querulous chattering calls, usually in threat or solicitation.

General Habits. Very well known, but little detail published. Preferred habitat is mountainous country, but descends to lowlands to feed. Occurs where only a few rocky mountains break otherwise flat lowlands (Botswana). Said to avoid most arid deserts, possibly because of food shortage, but this is questioned (J. Ledger, pers. comm.).

Like other rock-loving griffons, roosts gregariously on cliffs. Numbers at roosts in winter may exceed breeding pairs at same localities by 25% (Tarboton 1978b), and some roosts are not also breeding colonies. Arrives at roost 1–3 h before sunset, remaining on roost probably 14–16/24 h, depending on day-length. In mountainous terrain with strong updraughts (Lesotho), can fly earlier and may be moving 1 h after dawn, but in flatter country dependent on heat-produced thermals, usually unable to leave until 2–3 h after dawn. Then may leave almost simultaneously, all within 2 h (e.g. 07.30–09.30 h), mounting to height and gliding to foraging areas. These may be defined, within a certain range of breeding colonies or roost; extreme limit perhaps 150 km away, normally less.

In high mountains (Lesotho), often forages by gliding along ridges and faces of slopes, sometimes quite close to ground (50 m or less). Otherwise may mount to height and observe other vultures, following own species or White-backed Vulture to food source. In recent times, artificially fed at 'vulture restaurants' and visits these regularly, arriving 09.00–10.00 h (3–4 h after dawn), feeding for 30 min or less, then leaving. May follow regular routes to such feeding stations, but elsewhere must forage more at random.

Behaviour at carcass similar to European and Rüppell's Griffons. Hungry bird lands 5–10 m away, then bounds towards other feeding vultures with wings spread, neck outstretched, scapulars erected as 'horns'; also walks towards others, deliberately stretching feet forward, head lowered. Hungry birds usually become dominants for a short time, then are displaced by others. Recent immatures, as in other *Gyps* spp., unable to compete effectively. Probably cannot break unaided into large dead animals, but can tear into smaller carcasses, e.g. piglets. At 'restaurants', easily displaced by jackals, and associate with Pied Crow *Corvus albus*. These cannot feed until vultures have broken into carcasses, providing scraps; but are indifferent to jackals, continuing to feed when vultures cannot.

No regular movements reported, but in non-breeding season irregular dispersal. Only large vulture ringed in numbers at breeding colonies (3000 up to 1975), recoveries so far suggest that young disperse widely in any direction, but especially S–SSW, more movement southwards than northwards from breeding colonies. Maximum distance, *c.* 1200 km. Immatures may seek areas where adults are absent, perhaps reducing competition for available food.

Food. Carrion of any kind. Lack of dead large animals in most of former range has caused widespread decrease, and recently have been accused of sheep-killing, perhaps with some foundation owing to shortage of alternative food. Quality of food also important, studies suggesting that young require bone fragments (as would be naturally obtained from, for example, lion or hyena kills) to make healthy bone-growth (Mundy and Ledger 1976). A proportion in breeding colonies suffer from osteodystrophy (popularly called rickets), which has not been recorded in other *Gyps* spp. Food analysis shows that 'artefacts' (pieces of glass, china, etc.) may be mistaken

for bone and swallowed; only 13·3% of nests in wild areas contained bone flakes (Plug 1978). At 'restaurants' bone fragments now provided; no evidence as yet that this has any real effect.

Breeding Habits. Very well known; intensively studied in recent years following decline (P. Mundy, in prep.). Breeds in colonies on cliffs, of 5 to maximum of 350 pairs in known sites. Virtually every colony now known and several regularly counted (Mundy and Ledger 1975, 1976, 1977, 1978; Mundy *et al.* 1980). Ringed or otherwise marked birds of known age not so far seen breeding at colonies.

Adults assemble daily at breeding colonies, usually also communal roosts, some time before laying. Number of birds seen flying does not not determine number of breeding pairs as includes many immatures and subadults. Display not spectacular, largely mutual soaring near nest-sites, possibly followed by shallow dive with one following other. Sexes indistinguishable in field as similar in size. Mating occurs on or near nest-ledge several times daily before egg-laying.

Same nest-sites used annually, probably by same adults as long as one or other alive. This supported by record of 2 clutches of 2 eggs in same nest successive years (Mundy and Ledger 1975); individual recognition scarcely possible.

NEST: on ledges, not necessarily inaccessible, but often overhung; most require mountaineering equipment to reach. Built of sticks, weed or heath stems, bracken, grass; lined with grass and leaves. Most material gathered near colony, and any unused nest stripped by other adults. Small in size, av. *c.* 0·5 m across by 0·2–0·3 m deep, with shallow central cup; size varies according to site, some nests substantial, others (perhaps new) a mere scrape surrounded by a few sticks.

EGGS: almost invariably 1; several authentic clutches of 2 recorded, once at least in same nest successive years, presumed laid by same bird (Mundy and Ledger 1975). Broad white ovals. SIZE: (50 eggs) 83·2–98·0 × 63·2–72·5 (90·8 × 68·8); WEIGHT: *c.* 240 g.

Laying dates: Transvaal, Zimbabwe, Botswana Apr–June, with strong peak Apr, May (end rains); some records Cape Aug, Sept (early spring).

Both sexes incubate, shares not accurately recorded; period 53 days.

Details of development of young or parental behaviour not described. Presumably resembles European and Rüppell's Griffon, young entirely downy till *c.* day 30, feathered and able to walk by *c.* day 75, thereafter most growth in flight feathers. Some may weigh over 7 kg by early Sept (J. Ledger, pers. comm.) when ringing undertaken, well before 1st flight. Rarely, 2 chicks hatch, but not known to reach flying stage (Mundy and Ledger 1975). Fledging period said to be 150 days (McLachlan and Liversidge 1978), but probably shorter, 110–120 days. Little detail available on behaviour of parents at nest (P. Mundy, in prep.), but small young are brooded closely in the early stages, and thereafter one or both parents usually, or often, near nest. Both sexes feed young; presumably behaviour would resemble that of European Griffon in Mediterranean localities.

Decline in numbers has been attributed partly to poor breeding success and incidence of osteodystrophy among young. However, in 5 successive years, of 2412 nests examined, 2022 (82·1%) were occupied and 1900 contained well-grown chicks (94% of those occupied, 78·2% of all nests) (Mundy and Ledger 1975, 1978; Mundy *et al.* 1980). Proportion of dead chicks and those affected by osteodystrophy small (68 dead in 2022 occupied nests—3·3%). These figures suggest success little inferior to Rüppell's Griffon in optimum habitat, better than in some other large vultures. Overall breeding success is probably lower, as many non-breeding adults occur at colonies; may be *c.* 0·5 young per adult pair overall (Mundy and Ledger 1977), still not inferior to several other species. Decline may thus be due to poor

subsequent survival rather than poor breeding success.

Mortality, calculated from ringing recoveries, has been estimated at over 50% in 1st year and thereafter (Houston 1974). If this were correct, the species could not have survived for the last 20 years. Age structure of the immature population unknown at present, but mortality in years 1–2 an estimated 50%. Ringing recoveries and other data (more than for any other large vulture) suggest that few survive more than 2 years, but this figure may have been affected by ring loss. Oldest ringed bird recovered 12 years, but if reported mortality is general species must shortly become extinct.

References
Houston, D. C. (1974).
Mundy, P. J. and Ledger, J. A. (1975, 1976, 1977, 1978 and in prep.).
Mundy, P. J. *et al.* (1980).

Genus *Aegypius* Savigny

Medium-sized to very large vultures. Bill deep, strongly arched, adapted for feeding on tough material. Heads broad; either naked with lappets of bare skin in folds, or covered with woolly down. Neck relatively short; lower neck feathered, a ruff of fluffy feathers in some, or long lanceolate feathers covering crop. Body plumage mainly dark brown or black, with large areas of white in 1 sp. Wings long, broad, secondaries numerous; tail wedge-shaped, erectile in display. Lower body sometimes mainly downy, feathers sparse. Tarsi naked or partly feathered; toes long, feet more powerful than in *Gyps* spp.

The former monotypic genus *Aegypius* now contains 3 former monotypic genera *Torgos*, *Trigonoceps* and *Sarcogyps*, with 4 spp., 3 found in Africa. All are solitary nesters on tops of trees, and share certain display patterns. Variation in size and habits is considerable, but none are truly gregarious like *Gyps*, and the reasons for separating the 4 similar spp. as 4 monotypic genera are no longer considered valid.

Aegypius monachus (Linnaeus). Cinereous Vulture; Eurasian Black Vulture. Vautour moine.

Vultur Monachus Linnaeus, 1766. Syst. Nat. (12th ed.), 1, p. 122; Arabia (ex Edwards).

Plates 19 and 29
(Opp. pp. 306 and 450)

Range and Status. S Europe east to S China, mainly in mountainous country. Formerly may have bred Morocco, no recent records. Uncommon to rare winter migrant to N Africa. Threatened in European range, decreasing.

Aegypius monachus

Description. ADULT ♂: head and neck blue-grey, sparsely covered with blackish down, paler (whitish) above eye and on occiput. Neck-ruff of lanceolate dark brown feathers; crop-patch black. Body plumage above and below dark brown, becoming brownish grey on undertail-coverts. Primaries black, tail black above; tail- and wing-feathers below greyish black. Eye brown; cere purplish; legs pale blue-grey or whitish yellow. ♀♀ slightly larger, averaging heavier. SIZE: wing, ♂ 740–820 (776), ♀ 765–828 (795), extremes, (27 specimens) 740–834 (782); tail, 290–412 (365); tarsus, 107–140 (125); wing-span, 2535–2700. WEIGHT: ♂ (20) 7000–11,500, ♀ (21) 7500–12,500.

IMMATURE: differs from adult in more copious black down on head and neck, crop-patch dark brown, body plumage browner, much paler below than adult. Eye brown; cere pale mauve; legs grey.

Field Characters. A huge, blackish or dark brown vulture, with broad head covered in blackish or brown down, relatively short neck. Could only be confused with Lappet-faced Vulture *Aegypius tracheliotus*, but is darker and lacks bare pink skin and lappets. Distinguished from European Griffon *Gyps fulvus* by dark plumage, short neck, broad head; and in flight by dark colour, relatively long wedge-shaped tail.

Voice. Recorded (2a). Normally silent; at carcass croaks and hisses.

General Habits. Well known outside Africa; little recorded in N Africa. Occupies same feeding niche in mixed vulture groups as Lappet-faced Vulture, able to break into large carcasses unaided, dominating and robbing griffons of food, and able to eat sinews and dry skin not eaten by griffons.

Plates 19 and 29
(Opp. pp. 306 and 450)

Aegypius tracheliotus (J. R. Forster). Lappet-faced Vulture. Vautour oricou.

Vultur tracheliotus J. R. Forster, 1791. Levaillant, Reise Afr., 3, p. 363, pl. 12; Great Namaqualand.

Range and Status. Throughout more arid parts of Africa from NW Sahara east to NE Sudan, south to Cape Province and Namib Desert; straggles to Arabia; breeds Israel. Normally in plains, preferring subdeserts, but also, in E African–Ethiopian Highlands, sometimes to 4000 m. Frequent to common in most of range, commonest large vulture in subdesert SW Africa. Decreasing in Namibia, probably also NW Africa to N Sudan, but probably stable E and Central Africa. Not at present threatened, except in Namibia.

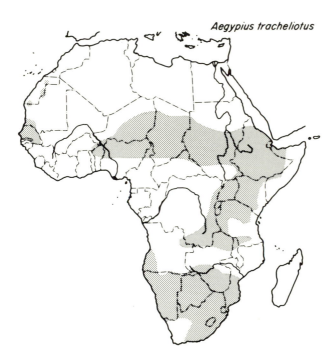

Aegypius tracheliotus

Description. ADULT ♂: head and neck naked, pink, with large fleshy ear-like lappets on sides of face. Ruff of short brown feathers; crop-patch dark brown. Body, above dark brown; below, upperbreast with short brown feathers surrounded with white down, feathers of lower breast and abdomen long, lanceolate, brown, edged whitish, more or less obscuring white body down; thighs unfeathered, covered with white down. Tail- and wing-feathers uniform dark brown to black. Eye brown; cere whitish; legs bluish grey; bill greenish brown, tipped yellowish. ♂ slightly smaller than ♀. SIZE: wing, ♂ 740–795 (770), ♀ 755–825 (782); tail, ♂ 330–375 (352), ♀ 335–360 (350); tarsus, ♂ 140–150 (146), ♀ 134–143 (140); wing-span, 2580–2660 (2640); wing-loading, 63 N/m²; aspect ratio, 6·8 (Pennycuick 1972). WEIGHT: ♀ (1) 6·8 kg, mean ♀♂ 6·6 (Pennycuick 1972).

IMMATURE: resembles adult, but neck skin paler, brownish, with some white down on head; thighs brownish.

DOWNY YOUNG: at first down sparse, white to buffy-white; 2nd down, emerging after 10 days, grey, thick, woolly; bare facial skin grey, eye brown, legs grey.

Some authorities recognize 2 races *A. t. tracheliotus* J. R. Forster of South Africa and *A. t. nubicus* (Smith) of tropical Africa north of Kenya. Differences are slight, mainly in the extent of wattles. The 2 populations would normally be separated by the broad belt of *Brachystegia* woodland; but we regard the species as monotypic.

Field Characters. Distinguished from any griffon at carcasses by bare pink head and neck, with large fleshy lappets, heavier head and massive bill; pink bare skin distinguishes it from Cinereous Vulture *A. monachus*, with which confusion rarely possible, except in NW Africa. In flight, very long broad wings, blackish appearance, wedge-shaped tail and white downy thighs distinctive. Most easily confused with Hooded Vulture *Necrosyrtes monachus* at long distance, distinguished from this by more white below, and heavier head and bill.

Voice. Recorded (2a). Normally entirely silent, even in threat display at carcass. Can emit a yelping call, growling sounds and grunts resembling 'guck-guck-guck'.

General Habits. Very well known. Inhabits semi-arid, semi-desert scrub, deserts and thornbush, where often the commonest large vulture. Also wooded grasslands in E Africa, and, in Ethiopia, plains on mountain plateaus, occurring up to 4000 m and breeding up to 2800 m. Rare in dense woodland. Normally solitary or, at most, in small groups; in some subdesert areas (Namibia, Somalia, N Chad) may be the commonest large vulture and is then more gregarious, up to 40–50 occurring together.

At carcasses forms a species pair with White-headed Vulture *A. occipitalis*, but much more powerful and aggressive (Kruuk 1967). Usually arrives later than other vultures, but is sometimes the first to break into a carcass with heavy sideways blows of powerful bill. When feeding with other vultures, normally remains on outskirts and attacks others, snatching flesh from them. Can dominate all other species, but itself is readily robbed by, for example, jackals. Threatening others, runs forward with head lowered, neck outstretched, feathers of back erected, wings partly spread and tail often cocked vertically. Attacked bird normally retreats or abandons prey; but struggle may ensue when one Lappet-faced Vulture attacks another. Seldom joins struggling throng of feeding griffons, but if hungry will force way into jostling mass and feed, scattering others. Feeding alone, powerful head and bill enables it to eat tough sinews, dry skin, small bones not utilized by griffons. Holds body down with feet and tears off large pieces of muscle and skin with great force (C. Penny-cuick, pers. comm.).

Roosts habitually on trees on open plains, a pair often close together on same or adjacent trees sometimes many successive nights. Unable to fly far without aid of thermal currents in flat country, but in mountains (e.g. Ethiopia) can easily ride updraughts to attain great heights. Normally is on wing for at most 8/24 h, usually less, but has lower wing-loading than griffons. If roosting near carcass can fly laboriously a few hundred metres by flapping. If carcass with feeding griffons located by day, often spends hours perched on ground nearby. After feeding, often spreads wings with back to sun. Also found in small groups alone in open country, when may have killed for itself or located a small dead animal.

Food. Chiefly carrion, mainly flesh; but can also eat sinews, bones and skin not eaten by griffons. Remains in nests suggest a preference for smaller dead animals (gazelles, reedbuck, duikers, hares) than griffons. In Namibia entirely carrion, small animals not necessarily preferred (R. Jensen, unpub.). Is suspected to kill small weak animals, e.g. gazelle calves, hares, probably by impact at strike, though not yet proven; grip is also powerful. In flamingo colonies (often raided) kills both adults and young, and eats eggs (Brown and Root 1971). Feeds also on locusts and flying termites swarming from holes, gobbling them on ground.

Breeding Habits. Very well known. Nests solitary, normally dispersed in individual territories; in Serengeti 1–10 (4·16) km apart (Pennycuick 1976); in Gone re Zhou, Zimbabwe, 0·7–5·9 (3·2) km apart (Anthony 1976) suggesting home range per pair 8–15 km² in optimum habitat; Serengeti, total range 43 km²/pair. Probably forages mainly within home range not travel-ling long distances like griffons. Where abundant (e.g. Chad: Salvan 1968), nests may be even closer together, even several nests in 1 tree reported, with active nests of African White-backed Vulture *Gyps africanus* in same tree (incorrectly identified as Rüppell's Griffon *G. rueppellii*: Salvan 1968).

No obvious forms of display known. Pairs often soar together, wing-tips a few metres apart, not very high above ground, suggesting mutual display and possible territorial function. Nests normally right on top of trees at any height from 3–15 m above ground, completely open to sun; occasionally on lateral branch of large trees growing on steep slopes. Thorny species preferred, various *Acacia* spp., *Balanites*, *Terminalia prunoides*; but also sometimes in broad-leaved figs, and cedar *Juniperus procera* (Ethiopia).

NEST: huge flattish structures up to 3 m across by 1 m thick (usually 2 m by 0·5–1·0 m), with broad shallow central depression *c.* 1 m across, lined with dry grass, later carpeted with hair from carcasses, skin. Pairs

normally have 1–3 nests, often only one; if several, may use them alternately. Used year after year if stable, often for many years; but new nests also built frequently (11/25 in 1 year, Serengeti: Pennycuick 1976). Un-stable foundation may cause collapse and desertion, or branches growing up around may make nest inaccessible (R. Jensen, unpub.). Both sexes build, carrying all material in bill. Nest repair at old nests consists of plac-ing a few sticks round rim, and re-lining with fresh grass in courtship period. One, or both birds usually roost in or beside nest, on nest-tree, sometimes year-round, more regularly as laying date approaches.

EGGS: almost invariably 1, clutches of 2 recorded Namibia (C. Clinning, pers. comm.). Broad oval; dull white, spotted and blotched brown. SIZE: 83–101·5 × 65·5–74·0 (91·1 × 68·6); WEIGHT: calculated 244 (Schön-wetter 1960); actual (3 eggs) 225–250.

Laying dates: S Tunisia, N Sahara Mar; Senegal Jan–Feb (early dry season) (Heim de Balsac and Mayaud 1962; Heim de Balsac 1954); Mali Dec; Chad Nov–Feb (dry); Ethiopia–Somalia Oct–late Feb, especially Nov–Jan (main dry); N Uganda, W Kenya May, June, Sept–Nov (wet and dry); E Kenya, N Tanzania May, July, Aug–Oct (mainly mid-year cool dry season); Serengeti, Tanzania, S Kenya Jan–Aug inclusive, peaking Apr–June (late rains); Gona re Zhou, Zimbabwe, May–June (end rains) (Anthony 1976); Namibia May–Aug, mainly May–July peaking at different times annually (R. Jensen and C. Clinning, unpub.). Where one long dry season prevails, normally lays at end rains, young leaving nest in late dry or early rains; in bimodal rainfall regime must sometimes lay or have young in rains.

♀♀ may sit in incubation posture for some time without an egg (R. Jensen, unpub.). Both sexes incubate, but share not determined, as hard to recognize. Nest-reliefs infrequent. Adults sit very tight, often not leaving unless tree is climbed (perhaps helping to protect egg from hot sun or predators, e.g. crows). Incubation period: estimated 53 days ± 1 day (R. Jensen, unpub.). Addled eggs may be incubated for 100 days or more, and replacement egg laid in another nest if 1st is lost early in incubation (Anthony 1976; R. Jensen, unpub.).

Newly hatched young weighs *c.* 200 g; very weak; has doubled in size by 8–9 days. 2nd thicker, darker grey down develops days 10–20, entirely downy till day 28–30 when wing-quills sprout. First contour feathers appear at 35 days, mainly feathered above by 50 days, largely feathered by 60 days; after 70 days feathered, growth thereafter in body, and wing- and tail-feathers. Weight increases to 1·7 kg day 20; 2·4 kg day 30; 3·4 kg day 40; 3·7 kg day 50; 4·0 kg day 60; 5 kg day 70; 7 kg day 90; increase then variable owing to large irregular meals. Can fly weakly at 115 days, normally flies 125–135 days; entire cycle from laying to 1st flight c. 185 days.

An adult remains at nest, brooding or sheltering chick for 97% of time up to day 20; 83% days 30–40; actual brooding reduced by day after day 10, when 2nd down emerges. From 35 days chick largely left alone in nest (Namib: R. Jensen, unpub.), not usually till later elsewhere, 50–60 days, when partially feathered. A parent still at nest for 40% of day days 60–80, Serengeti; thereafter 20% or less by day; but parents still often roost on nest or nest-tree; spend more time there than many large raptors, but apparently less than colonial cliff-nesting griffons. At first, probably only 1 sex (? ♂) brings food; later, after chick left alone in nest, either may do so. Most food in nests is small antelopes, gazelles, duiker, steinbuck, reedbuck, hares, perhaps some killed by adults (Pennycuick 1976; Anthony 1976).

After 1st flight young usually remain near nest for 1–2 months, still dependent on parents, which usually roost there; dependence may occasionally last 6 months (C. Clinning, pers. comm.). Newly fledged young cannot effectively compete with adults at carcasses, but can successfully compete with griffons, white-backed, or smaller vultures.

Breeding success in all estimates lower than in griffons. Serengeti 0·43 young reared per egg; Gona re Zhou 0·55 young per breeding pair; Namib 0·46 per occupied nest; overall average, 131 records, including some in optimum habitats, 0·46 young per breeding pair. Since not all pairs breed annually, real breeding success is probably lower, perhaps c. 0·35/pair overall. Nest losses occur through collapse of nest, theft of eggs by predators (sometimes aggravated by human disturbance) and predation of young in nests in low trees (by, for example, African wild cat: R. Jensen, unpub.).

Young disperse from breeding localities at random; ringed and window-marked young have been re-sighted up to 300 km from nesting site; but most re-sightings closer to nesting areas. No data on mortality rate of young after leaving nest, but low breeding success related to other vultures indicates that life must be long.

References

Anthony, A. J. (1976).
Pennycuick, C. J. (1976).

Plates 19 and 29
(Opp. pp. 306 and 450)

Aegypius occipitalis (Burchell). White-headed Vulture. Vautour à tête blanche.

Vultur occipitalis Burchell, 1824. Travels, 2, p. 329; note—Makwari = Matlowing River, Botswana.

Range and Status. Tropical Africa south of Sahara south to the Orange River, in semi-desert scrub, grasslands, sometimes woodlands. Normally frequent to uncommon, rarest of larger vultures in most areas. Probably stable except in parts of South Africa, where reduced, like other large vultures.

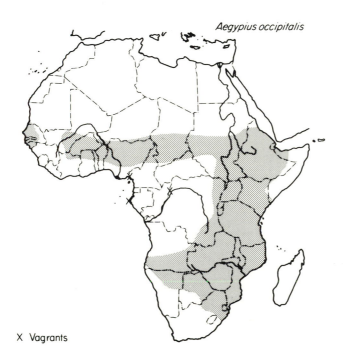

Aegypius occipitalis

X Vagrants

Description. ADULT ♂: top of head covered with thick white down, forming a peak behind head; bare skin whitish to pink. Lower neck, upperback to tail-coverts blackish brown. Below, crop-patch, lower body and thighs white, strongly contrasting with blackish band across chest. Upperwing- and underwing-coverts blackish brown. Primaries black, separated from coverts by narrow white line; secondaries white, forming a conspicuous patch. Tail-feathers black. Eye brown; cere bluish green; bill bright pink, tipped black; feet flesh-coloured. Sexes nearly alike. SIZE: wing, 610–643, tail, 265–295, tarsus, 95–110; wing-span, 2020–2195; wing-loading 54 N/m²; aspect ratio, 7·5 (Pennycuick 1972). WEIGHT: 4·76–4·82 kg recorded; mean (Serengeti) 4·7.

IMMATURE: generally darker than adult, down of head brownish, little white, but peaked on occiput; crop-patch white. Secondaries dark brown, innermost tipped grey, but a visible white line separates wing-feathers from coverts.

DOWNY YOUNG: white, with brown crop-patch and brown ring round crown.

Field Characters. Adults unmistakable—at rest white head and pink bill conspicuous and in flight white secondaries diagnostic. Smaller than any griffon, but with broader, distinctively triangular-looking head.

Immature resembles small immature Lappet-faced Vulture *A. tracheliotus*, but white crop-patch, reddish brown bill and, in flight, white line between secondaries and coverts distinctive.

Voice. Not recorded. Normally completely silent; but at carcasses utters shrill chattering calls.

General Habits. Well known. A scarce species of open semi-desert and lightly wooded grasslands all over Africa. Solitary or in pairs, usually seen singly, sometimes an immature with an adult. Is more inclined to enter dense woodland than Lappet-faced Vulture, at least in W Africa, but never as numerous—of *c.* 1 White-headed Vulture to 5 Lappet-faced and 50–200 griffons in most of range. Seems relatively more numerous in W than in E and southern Africa.

Roosts on trees, alone or in pairs, often near or at nest-site. Can probably fly earlier than other larger species because of relatively low wing-loading and can thus locate carrion earlier. Probably each pair forages within restricted area (C. Pennycuick, pers. comm.). In Serengeti arrives first at carcasses in 50% of cases, performing function of chief searcher, soon followed by larger, more aggressive species. Then cannot compete effectively with others (Lappet-faced, griffons) and feeds mainly by picking up dropped scraps. Attacks mainly its own species, seldom larger species. Also feeds on skin, sinews and similar tough material, thus forming a species pair with Lappet-faced, though much smaller and weaker (Kruuk 1967). Is often found feeding by itself on small carcasses, e.g. hares or gazelle calves, which it may have killed; sometimes in company with Lappet-faced Vulture in such situations.

Food. Carrion, utilizing dropped scraps and tougher materials, skin, sinews. Is strongly suspected of killing own prey, e.g. hares, gazelle calves, presumably by impact as feet are weak. Raids flamingo colonies killing young, sometimes adults; eats eggs. Also may kill lizards, guineafowl. Feeds on swarming termites emerging from holes and locusts, picking them from ground.

Breeding Habits. Well known. Breeds singly, widely spaced (av. over 400 km²/pair in Serengeti; 150 km²/pair, Timbavati, South Africa: W. Tarboton, pers. comm.); is possibly territorial. Nests normally on top of thorny trees, especially *Acacia* spp., but in W Africa baobabs also much used. No obvious forms of display known, but pairs roost together near or on nest-tree for some time before laying, and may soar together with wing-tips close, suggesting mutual display, resembling that of Lappet-faced Vulture.

NEST: large flat structures of sticks, lined with grass and hair, *c.* 1·5–1·7 m across by 0·5 m deep, resembling those of Lappet-faced Vulture and Secretary Bird *Sagittarius serpentarius*, but smaller than those of former. Normally built on top of an acacia at 5–10 m above ground, rarely up to 15 m, sometimes in baobabs, *Bombax* at greater heights (W Africa). No details on nest-building or share of sexes.

EGGS: invariably 1; broad ovals, white, unmarked or sparingly marked brown and greyish. SIZE: (22 eggs) 78·0–100·0 × 59·5–67·0 (85 × 64); WEIGHT: calculated 196 (Schönwetter 1960).

Laying dates: W Africa, Sudan Nov, Dec; Ethiopia–Somalia Oct–Mar, especially Nov–Jan (dry seasons); E Africa, Serengeti Mar–July, especially Apr–May, elsewhere Jan, Feb, May, July, Oct, Dec (preferring dry seasons); Zambia–southern Africa May–Aug, especially July–Aug (dry). Generally lays early in a dry season.

No good data on incubation period, but ♀ believed to incubate alone. Period: at least 43 days (Pennycuick 1976), probably longer.

Downy young is brooded closely by adult in early stages. Other data lacking, but fledging period probably *c.* 100 days; young remain near, often on nests, for months after they can fly. Scanty Serengeti data suggest *c.* 75% of eggs hatch and *c.* 50% of chicks hatched fledge; or 0·38 young/successful nest/year; even less per pair overall, as not all pairs breed annually. Must be long-lived to survive.

References
Kruuk, H. (1967).
Pennycuick, C. J. (1976).

Genus *Circaetus* Vieillot

Medium-sized to rather large 'eagles' unlike any other similar-sized raptors. Apparently not closely related either to other eagles or Old World vultures. Typified by noticeably large heads, with a hood or cowl of rather long feathers, partially or completely erectile. Eyes very large, usually strikingly yellow or whitish, even in immatures. Wings long, or rather short and rounded; tails moderately long to short. Tarsus long, naked, covered with round or hexagonal scales. Toes short, but strong, heavily padded below, with short, sharp talons, adapted to gripping slim snakes. Feed almost entirely on reptiles. 4 spp., 1 Eurasian and African, 3 African; 2 very well known, 2 little known. Formerly often called 'harrier eagles' from fancied resemblance to flight of harriers *Circus* (flaps alternating with short glides), but this name inappropriate as none even vaguely resembles harrier in habits. The name 'snake eagles' is preferred as all eat snakes.

Plates 20 and 30

(Opp. pp. 307 and 451)

Circaetus gallicus (Gmelin). European Snake Eagle; Short-toed Eagle (includes also Beaudouin's and Black-breasted Snake Eagles). Circaète Jean-le-Blanc.

Falco gallicus Gmelin, 1788. Syst. Nat., 1, p. 259; France.

Range and Status. European race *C. g. gallicus* breeds S Europe east to China, and in N Africa, migrating to northern tropical Africa, occasionally to equator (Kenya and Uganda) in winter. Other races (Beaudouin's Snake Eagle *C. g. beaudouini* and Black-breasted Snake Eagle *C. g. pectoralis*), tropical Africa from Senegal east to Ethiopia/Somalia south to Cape Province; also partially migratory or nomadic. Normally frequent to uncommon, usually in lowland plains but in Ethiopia–Kenya up to 2500 m.

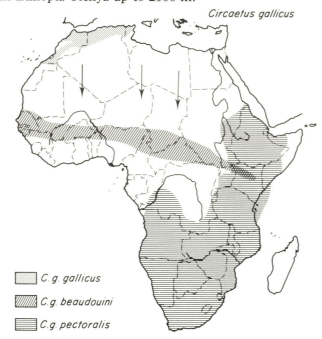

Circaetus gallicus

- ▨ *C. g. gallicus*
- ▧ *C. g. beaudouini*
- ▤ *C. g. pectoralis*

Description. *C. g. gallicus* (Gmelin): Europe and S Asia to N Africa. ADULT ♂: forehead, lores, area round eye white. Rest of upperparts including upperwing-coverts grey-brown. Cheeks, throat, breast brown, feathers basally white; breast and belly white, variously barred brown, sometimes almost unbarred, undertail-coverts white. Primaries black, whitish on inner webs; secondaries browner, white on inner webs; primaries with 2, secondaries with 2 or 3 narrow blackish bars; underwing-coverts largely white. Tail above grey-brown, all but central feathers white on inner webs, with 3 broad darker bars; below largely white, broadly barred darker. ♀ larger, usually more heavily barred below. Eye brilliant orange-yellow; cere dull greyish white; tarsus pale grey. SIZE: wing, ♂ 506–551 (523), ♀ 512–557 (535); tail, ♂ 256–280 (268), ♀ 266–315 (289), tarsus, ♂ 86–93 (90), ♀ 87–95 (91); wing-span, c. 1900. WEIGHT: ♂ 1815–1892, ♀ 1815–2324, 1 ♀ winter specimen 1304. Also records of ♂ 1180–2000 (1664), ♀ 1304–2324 (1735).

IMMATURE: resembles adult, but generally paler, more white on nape, throat and breast pale rufous. Underside white, feathers edged brown, subterminally barred brown on belly and thighs. Eye yellow, cere and feet pale grey. This plumage develops gradually to adult by darkening and becoming more distinctly barred.

DOWNY YOUNG: pure white; eye whitish, becoming yellow; cere, legs pale grey-blue.

C. g. beaudouini Verreaux and Des Murs. Tropical W Africa from Senegal east to W Ethiopia, south to N Uganda and W Kenya. Resembles *C. g. gallicus* above, but darker, bars on tail and wings more distinct. Below whole upperbreast grey-brown, lower breast and belly white with narrow transverse brown bars. Immature whitish on head and neck, largely white washed brown above, wings and tail light brown, barred darker. Subadults possibly first become bright rufous brown above and below, and later acquire grey-brown adult plumage. SIZE: smaller, wing, 475–502; ♀ not much larger than ♂.

C. g. pectoralis Smith. S Ethiopia and Somalia south to east and South Africa, as far west as Lake Victoria (where interbreeds with *C. g. beaudouini*). Above dark brown, almost blackish; throat whitish, breast plain, dark grey brown; rest of underside pure white. Immature dark brown above, rufous or cinnamon below. Subadult plumage obscure, but some probably almost indistinguishable from nominate *gallicus* (J. Ash, pers. comm.) and some South African subadults have a dark breast-band, brown bars on lower breast and belly. Downy young pure white. Larger than *C. g. beaudouini*, ♀ averages larger than ♂. SIZE: wing, 490–530; WEIGHT: ♂ (1) 2187; unsexed (46) 1178–2260 (1502) (Biggs *et al.* 1979).

These 3 races are sometimes regarded as 3 spp., *C. gallicus*, *C. beaudouini* and *C. pectoralis*. However, all 3 form mixed pairs (*gallicus* × *beaudouini*; *gallicus* × *pectoralis*; and *beaudouini* × *pectoralis*) near edges of their respective ranges; a mixed pair *beaudouini* × *pectoralis* is recorded nesting in W Kenya (♂ typical *pectoralis*, ♀ typical *beaudouini*). It is therefore preferable to regard all 3 as races of 1 widespread sp., varying especially in immature plumage (Brown 1974a).

Field Characters. Generally birds of open plains, or light woodland. At rest large cowled head, bright yellow eyes, rather long bare grey tarsus and erect stance distinctive. Distinguishable from Martial Eagle *Polemaetus bellicosus* by smaller size; confusion most likely to arise between this species and *C. g. pectoralis*, but latter has unspotted lower breast and belly. Dark, broadly barred tail of *C. g. beaudouini* distinguishes it from Red-necked Buzzard *Buteo auguralis*. In flight all races show white underwing, the feathers crossed by 2–3 narrow blackish bars, distinctive even in immature plumages. Martial Eagle in flight has dark mottled underwing-coverts, whereas snake eagles' are white; underwing of snake eagle always paler, less heavily barred. Immatures and subadults hard to distinguish except by experience; somewhat resemble those of Southern Banded Snake Eagle *C. fasciolatus* and Smaller Banded Snake Eagle *C. cinerascens*, but much larger, longer-tailed, longer-winged, with grey cere and legs.

Voice. Recorded (2a) in Europe; normally very silent. In display, and at nest utters melodious whistling or fluting calls, unlike hoarse crowing of other *Circaetus* spp. In display near nest fluting, buzzard-like 'hu-opp, hu-o-hu-opp'; 'piee-ou-piee-ou' or a high-pitched ringing 'quo-quo-quo' somewhat resembling calls of African Fish Eagle *Haliaeetus vocifer*. Soaring in display *C. g. pectoralis* utters rather harsh, high-pitched 'shreeee-ee-ee'; and at nest a melodious repeated 'wood-lay-ooo, weeu, weeeu'; in alarm or threat a sharper, deeper 'puoppp, puopp' and 'u-ok-ok, ue-ok-ok-ok'. Young in nest emit harsh squalling resembling other young *Circaetus* spp; and softer whistling 'cui-cui-cui' or 'wi-wi-wi' when begging; when larger, adult-like 'eee-op'. Calls can sometimes help distinguish sub-adults. (For various other renderings see Cramp and Simmons 1980.)

General Habits. Very well known. European and N African race inhabits open stony or lightly wooded hill-sides, subdesert steppes and fringes of true deserts (NW Africa). *C. g. beaudouini* normally inhabits woodland, sometimes rather dense, or open plains, seldom found in arid areas. *C. g. pectoralis* prefers open grass plains and lightly wooded *Acacia* or *Combretum* savannas; but also occurs in subdesert open thornbush, and in true deserts (Namib; Karoo).

All races more aerial than other snake eagles, soaring *c.* 20–100 m above ground, frequently hovering with gently fanning wings; the largest raptors that regularly hover. Alternatively, hunt from high perches, dead trees, pylons, telegraph poles, scanning ground intently, perching to hunt less often than other *Circaetus* spp. *C. g. beaudouini* perches more often than the other races, perhaps because of preference for more wooded habitat.

C. g. gallicus is completely migrant from breeding range in subtropical Mediterranean basin, migrating south in winter mainly to W tropical African range of *C. g. beaudouini*. Southward passage begins late summer (late Aug–early Sept) peaking mid-Sept to mid-Oct, stragglers until Nov. Moves in small groups or singly, not large flocks. Northward passage mid-Mar to early Apr (when reptiles first emerge from hibernation). European and W Asian birds enter Africa through Straits of Gibraltar and Suez, reaching *c.* 8–9 N in W Africa, occasionally approaching equator in E Africa (Lake Turkana). In winter quarters behave like close relatives (*beaudouini* and *pectoralis*). Although mixed pairs recorded with both other races, *C. g. gallicus* not proven to breed south of Sahara.

Other races may be mainly sedentary, migrate locally, or perform nomadic movements. Southern populations of *C. g. pectoralis* probably move north in southern winter to Zimbabwe (Apr–Sept) when local residents are breeding, but movements not well recorded; near equator sedentary. In W Africa *C. g. beaudouini* performs ill-defined N–S movements, flying south in dry season, north in rains; associated with grass fires and reduced cover. On migration may be somewhat gregarious, roosting together especially (Lorber 1971). Otherwise solitary, widely dispersed, though pairs often may be close together by day.

Mode of catching snakes not clear, but small snakes are lifted, wriggling, direct from ground, passed through feet in flight to head, then mangled with bill. Large snakes struck on ground, probably breaking back; thereafter disabled and gradually subdued. Eagles are not immune to venom, but snake strikes either at spread wing feathers, or long, rather downy underside plumage. Small snakes swallowed whole, almost at once, sometimes in flight, fed into beak head-first by feet; large ones dismembered, part-eaten on the spot and rest carried away.

Food. Mainly snakes, including, in Africa, venomous species. In some parts of Europe non-venomous species apparently selected, venomous vipers avoided (Boudouint 1953). In Africa large venomous cobras, mambas, vipers (puff-adders) taken. Also takes lizards, some amphibia, occasionally mammals and birds (hares, guineafowl). In S Europe and southern Africa prey *c.* 95% snakes, in E Africa more mammals and birds recorded (Brown 1952).

Snakes swallowed whole pass straight down into the gut and in captives can be felt as lump between legs (Steyn 1974). When torn up and eaten in pieces are retained in crop, as are mammals and birds. Digestion of snakes complete except for scales; castings small, ovoid, composed of scales and skin.

Breeding Habits. Of races *gallicus* and *pectoralis* very well to intimately known; of *beaudouini* little known, but probably similar. In tropical Africa pairs are very widely dispersed, each requiring several hundred km², but in Europe may nest within 1 km (Boudouint 1953). Same nesting area is used year after year but not same nest; new one normally constructed, sometimes several km from previous year's nest, but after some years same tree may again be used. In *gallicus* nest is normally on open hill-side; in *pectoralis* hill slopes also preferred, but not invariable, may nest on open flat plains.

In N Africa breeding begins Mar, when pairs arrive and become strongly territorial, repelling others; threat flight is described (France) in which the territorial bird flies towards intruder with head and neck held forward and outstretched wings held well up. Nuptial display is unspectacular, mainly mutual soaring and calling at height, occasionally undulating display flight without much wing-flapping. Display and nest-building period short in temperate N Africa, but prolonged for many months in tropical Africa. Mating occurs on trees near nest-site; may occur several times daily, accompanied by much calling. In 1 mixed *beaudouini* × *pectoralis* pair (W Kenya) both sexes, on sighting other overhead, raised wings above back and gently agitated them, repeatedly calling 'wood-lay-ooo-weeeu-weeu-weeu', possibly a pre-copulation display.

NEST: invariably small, of thin sticks, with rather deep cup lined with pine sprigs or green leaves, max. *c.* 1 m across by 20–25 cm deep. In N Africa usually in pine or evergreen oak, 3–10, usually 5–7 m above ground. In tropical Africa normally on *Euphorbia* crown or thorny flat-topped *Acacia* 5–15 m above ground, sometimes hidden among creepers barely large enough to accommodate adult. Both sexes build, ♀ remaining in nest while ♂ brings sticks, usually carried in beak not claws. In temperate climates nest is quickly finished but at equator sporadic building occurs for up to 18 months before laying.

EGGS: invariably 1, relatively large for size of bird. Round ovals; unmarked white. SIZE: *C. g. gallicus* (100 eggs, Europe) 66·0–83·4 × 53·0–63·1 (73·5 × 57·9); *C. g. pectoralis* (32 authentic eggs) av. 70·3 × 57·0 (P. Steyn, pers. comm.); WEIGHT: *c.* 136 (6·5–7·0% of ♀ body-weight).

Laying dates: N Africa (*gallicus*) Mar, Apr; N Nigeria (*beaudouini*) estimated Nov (Serle 1943); Ethiopia Nov, Dec; Kenya Feb, Mar, May, Dec; Zimbabwe Mar–Oct, peak July–Aug (dry); Zambia–Malawi May, June, Dec, possibly Jan, July; South Africa Sept. Season short and definite temperate N Africa, elsewhere widespread, but laying mainly in dry months.

Normally ♀ alone incubates, fed on or near nest by ♂; ♂ sits rarely for short periods, but often rests on trees nearby, or on nest with ♀. Despite small nest sitting adult hard to see or disturb; sits very tight, flat in nest, usually will not leave unless tree is climbed. This behaviour probably has survival value, especially in crowns of euphorbias. Incubation period: 47 days *C. g. gallicus*; longer, over 50 days in *C. g. pectoralis*. ♂ feeds ♀ with snake by holding out bill with snake's tail protruding; ♀ pulls it out, sometimes standing and straining back and swallows it head-first.

Newly hatched young weighs *c.* 90 g; has noticeably very large head, short beak, large fleshy cere, distinguishing it from other white downy eaglets but not from other snake eagles. 1st feathers appear at 15 days (*pectoralis*), apparently later (25 days) in *gallicus*. Develop rapidly on surface, covered in *pectoralis* by 28 days; upper surface of body is covered by 28–45 days, remaining downy below till much later. Young can swallow snakes up to 0·8 m long or small lizards when still entirely downy. In *pectoralis* underside feathered by 41 days; in *gallicus* apparently later. Thereafter main growth in feathers and in body; tarsus and bill almost

fully developed in *pectoralis* by day 48. Young *gallicus* practises wing-flapping at 45 days, *pectoralis* perhaps later. Young *pectoralis* increases in weight from 114 g at 2 days, to 157 at 5; 313 at 13; 654 at 21; 768 at 27; thereafter more slowly to 992 at 41; 1050 at 55; 1136 at 69 days. Conspicuous when standing, from 45 days reacts as adult to human approach, squatting flat in nest, barely visible. 1st flight made independent of adults at 70–75 days in *gallicus* and 90 days in *pectoralis* (Boudouint 1953; Steyn 1966).

Parental behaviour affected by rate of development of chick, notably dorsal feathering. Both parents brood in *gallicus*, ♀ most (Boudouint 1953); believed to be ♀ only in *pectoralis*. Brooding almost continuous days 1–7, thereafter reduced, and by day 15 chick mainly shaded, not brooded in *pectoralis*; brooding and shading continue till later in *gallicus* (possibly because of cooler climate). In *pectoralis* development of feathers on back and upperside permit parent to cease brooding or shading for long periods after day 28, and after day 45 in *gallicus*. Parental visits thereafter brief, to bring food; young left alone most of day and at night. Both parents bring food and either may feed small chick. Large snakes and lizards torn to pieces and fed thus, small ones deposited and swallowed whole. Arriving parent presents snake's tail, sometimes still wriggling; eaglet seizes it, both strain back, and part is withdrawn; process repeated until whole snake withdrawn, when either fed in pieces or swallowed whole, always head-first. Toads or frogs may be pulled out of beak by parent's claw, swallowed whole by eaglet. Large snake may take 5–7 min to swallow, and part of tail may protrude for some time.

Young makes 1st flight independent of parents, and leaves nest area soon afterwards; may perhaps return to roost (Steyn 1966). Possible advantage of long fledging period for size of bird is to produce young soon able to be independent. Breeding success in Europe and N Africa unrecorded; in Kenya breeding irregular, often unsuccessful, estimated 0·2–0·3 young/pair/year overall; apparently more regular Zimbabwe. Certainty difficult in view of small inconspicuous nest and frequent changes of site.

Post-fledging development of *pectoralis* (observed in captive young) shows gradual plumage change (Steyn 1974). A few blackish feathers appear on breast at 6 months; rufous colour of underside and head becomes drab grey at 8 months; first white feathers on sides of abdomen at 10 months. In 2nd year blackish feathers increase on breast, tail re-grown, and has 3 dark bars as in adult, underwing-coverts white by 21 months. Then resembles more ragged, browner version of adult. Full adult plumage possibly attained in 3rd year, brown spots on abdomen and brown thighs the last immature feathers to disappear.

References
Boudouint, Y. (1953).
Brown, L. H. (1952).
Steyn, P. (1966, 1974).

Circaetus cinereus Vieillot. Brown Snake Eagle. Circaète brun.

Circaetus cinereus Vieillot, 1818. Nouv. Dict. Hist. Nat., nouv. ed., 23, p. 445; Senegal.

Range and Status. Resident throughout woodlands and more arid thornbush of Africa south of Sahara, from Senegal east to Somalia, south to Cape Province and Namibia. Not found in dense forest or very arid areas. Normally frequent to uncommon.

Description. ADULT ♂: above and below uniform dark grey-brown; some have narrow black line above and below eye. Wing-feathers dark brown above, becoming white mottled brown at base of inner web; below uniform silvery (gunmetal) grey, unbarred. Tail dark brown, with 3 narrow grey bars, tipped white. Eye bright yellow; cere and legs grey to greyish white, ♀ similar, slightly larger. SIZE: wing, ♂ 490–508, ♀ 490–567; tail, ♀♂ 245–295; tarsus, 92–108; wing-span, *c.* 2000. WEIGHT: (26) unsexed 1540–2465 (2048).

IMMATURE: resembles adult, sometimes rather paler, showing more white feather-bases on nape and belly, feathers of back edged paler, appearing scaled. Some South African immatures have underside mottled brown and white, but tropical individuals usually appear brown.

DOWNY YOUNG: pure white; eye at first grey, becoming yellow, cere and legs almost white, bill pale grey, becoming blackish before flight.

Circaetus cinereus

Field Characters. The largest snake eagle, would normally only be confused with large brown Tawny Eagle *Aquila rapax* or spotted eagles, perhaps also smaller Wahlberg's Eagle *A. wahlbergi*. At rest conspicuously large cowled head, bright yellow eye, bare tarsus and upright stance distinctive. In flight, uniform silvery grey underside of wing-feathers, contrasting strongly with dark brown underwing-coverts diagnostic; 3 narrow pale bars in tail not obvious in many individuals, most clearly visible when flying away.

Voice. Not recorded. Hoarse, deep, crowing calls. In display, loud kok-kok-kok-kaaaw' uttered in flight, rarely when perched. At rest, throaty 'hok-hok' or 'kromp-kromp'. Begging young emit loud squalling 'eee-yaaa-aw' or 'kyaaaaa-aa-aa', somewhat gull-like; can utter deep 'hok-hok' at 60 days. Voice generally deeper, hoarser, than that of Smaller Banded and Southern Banded Snake Eagles *C. cinerascens* and *C. fasciolatus*, otherwise similar.

General Habits. Well known. A bird of woodlands, dense thornbush, occasionally near forest edges, normally avoiding very open country and arid areas. May occur in same habitat as 2 races of European Snake Eagle *C. gallicus beaudouini* and *C. g. pectoralis*, but usually ecologically separated from these, and from Smaller Banded Snake Eagle by hunting habits. Apparently sedentary wherever it occurs; but may perform irregular local movements, not well documented, e.g. breeding in Senegal in dry season, apparently moving north in wet.

Normally hunts from perches, on top of trees, e.g. euphorbias, remaining perched for long periods, intently scanning ground. Very often perches on dead trees in cultivation, and on baobabs in E African thornbush. Flies at intervals from perch to perch, usually

not very far, again remaining on new perch for some time; snakes apparently entirely caught on ground, large venomous species attacked as readily as harmless species. More powerful, less agile than European Snake Eagle races, more likely to kill and swallow snake on ground or perch than in air. Can soar well and in display often soars over mountain tops. Does not regularly hover, but can do so occasionally. Appears generally a sluggish species, usually seen perched. Little known about details of diurnal behaviour; but normally seen singly, pairs not remaining close to one another by day, or roosting near one another at night.

Food. Mainly snakes, including large venomous cobras, mambas (up to 3 m long), puff-adders; some large lizards (*Varanus* spp.). Also sometimes (Kenya) game-birds, guineafowl or francolins; occasionally poultry. Of 43 items recorded Zimbabwe 41 were snakes, 2 lizards. When killing large snakes, eagle drops on them, gripping body with short stout toes, possibly breaking back-bone. Snake continues to writhe and strikes repeatedly at eagles, usually hitting half-opened wings. Eagle finally paralyses snake by twisting pecks at spine; then mangles head and swallows prey head-first, even if venomous.

Digestion similar to that of European Snake Eagle, complete except for scales and skin, castings small; droppings hard distinctive white pellets rather than white liquid splash of most eagles.

Breeding Habits. Very well known, best studied of African snake eagles. Pairs widely dispersed, requiring probably up to 200 km² per pair, hence never very common. Same general area used annually, but nest may be up to 1–2 km from previous year's, so hard to locate definitely.

Display mainly soaring and vocal. One bird, probably ♂, may fly straight across sky, more often soars or circles over hill-top or escarpment, calling 'kok-kok-kaaauw'; voice audible at up to 3 km, instantly attracting attention to soaring bird. Much more vocal in display than any race of European Snake Eagle.

NEST: normally built on hill-side, escarpment, or hill-top, less often on flat plains. Small, slight structure, barely large enough to hide sitting bird, c. 1 m across by 15 cm deep, of thin, often pliant sticks; rather deep cup is copiously lined with green leaves. Fresh leaves added till mid-fledging period (c. 35 days after hatch). Usually placed on euphorbia crowns or flat-topped acacias, 4–12 m above ground; hard to see, especially in euphorbia crowns, or when placed in creepers. Nest normally used for 1 year only, in successive years building some distance away (up to 5 km) but same tree may be used again after several years. Occasionally uses nests of other raptors (Lendrum 1976).

EGGS: invariably 1, rounded, unmarked white, large for size of bird. Many accepted records doubtfully identified. SIZE: (12 authentic eggs: P. Steyn, pers. comm.) 69·5–78·6 × 58·2–66·0 (75·5 × 60·9); WEIGHT: (calculated) c. 140 g (Schönwetter 1960), c. 6·5% ♀ bodyweight; 1 definite record 170 g (Lendrum 1976).

Laying dates: W Africa–Sudan Nov–Feb (dry season); Kenya Feb–May inclusive (including dry and wet months); Zimbabwe, Botswana, Transvaal Dec–Mar inclusive, July, Aug, with peak Jan (12/19 records) (mainly in rains); season distinct from European Snake Eagle C. g. pectoralis in same area (P. Steyn, pers. comm.). Rains possibly unimportant except in W Africa.

Incubation by ♀ only, fed on nest by ♂, about once every 2 days. He only visits to feed, seldom perching near for long, or roosting anywhere near. ♀ sits extremely tight and, on approach of intruder, squats low, becoming almost invisible, will not leave until tree climbed. Incubation period: at least 50 days (Steyn 1972b), 52–53 days (Lendrum 1976); chick may take 3 days to hatch from first chipping.

Newly hatched young weighs c. 100 g (60% of egg weight); helpless, eyes partly closed; large head conspicuous. Weight increases to 390 g at 23 days, then rapidly to 908 at 35 days; thereafter more slowly, 1080 at 42 days, reaching over 2000 at 80 days (full adult weight). 1st feathers appear on back and scapulars 21 days, upperpart of body feathered by 35 days, under-side, rump and flanks still downy; eye changes from grey to pale yellow at 21–29 days. Can extract snake from parental crop at 19 days; stand at 35 days; and tear up snake when still partly downy at 37 days. Remains largely quiescent in nest, moving little; and after 40 days squats low at approach of human intruder. Often lies on side for long periods, watching other birds or parents in sky, and squalls in solicitation if hungry. Performs little wing-flapping until about to leave nest; then, stimulated by wind, makes cautious attempts to fly, rising a few metres, then suddenly collapsing, as if alarmed, in nest. 1st real flight made at 100–110 days, parents not present; then appears relatively much more mature than many true eagles at 1st flight.

Parental behaviour correlated with feather development of young. ♀ broods downy young closely up to day 10, ♂ only bringing prey. Thereafter brooding reduced rapidly by day, ♀ mainly shading chick. After 37–40 days, when eaglet part-feathered, left alone entirely by day and night, fed irregularly by either parent, 0–3 items per day. Parents neither roost nor perch near nest; and behaviour of young makes nest very hard to find. Snakes at first torn to pieces and fed thus to small eaglet. After 20 days, small snakes swallowed whole. Later, adult bends, presenting protruding tail; young seizes it, both strain back, part is withdrawn. Process repeated 2–4 times until whole snake withdrawn; then swallowed whole by young, always head-first. A large snake takes 7–10 min to swallow, part of tail often protruding after most engulfed.

Flying young remain only a few days near nest, then apparently accompany parents to feeding range. Not seen to be fed away from nest, but presumably require such assistance at first. Breeding in E Africa irregular, not every year, and success poor; 10 records av. c. 0·3 young/pair/year. In Zimbabwe apparently more regular, 4 young in 7 years, 0·57 young/pair overall. Combined av. c. 0·4 young/pair/year; but certainty always difficult because of inconspicuous nest and frequent moves. Probably is long-lived; age at sexual maturity unknown.

References
Brown, L. H. (1952–3).
Steyn, P. (1964, 1972b, 1975).

**Plates
20 and 30**
(Opp. pp. 307
and 451)

Circaetus fasciolatus Gurney. Southern Banded Snake Eagle. Circaète barré.

Circaëtus fasciolatus Gurney, 1861. Ibis, p. 130; Natal.

Range and Status. Resident coastal woodlands and forests of E Africa from S Somalia and N Kenyan border south to Natal and Zululand; seldom more than 20 km inland, but in Usambara Mts to near Amani (Tanzania) and recorded E Zimbabwe. Normally uncommon, at best frequent, but probably commoner than supposed, as hard to locate and see.

Description. ADULT ♂: crown, nape, dark greyish brown, becoming blackish, faintly tipped rufous on back and upperwing-coverts; uppertail-coverts blackish brown, some tipped white. Below, chin, throat, breast greyish brown; belly, thighs, undertail-coverts white, clearly barred brown; undertail-coverts almost white; underwing-coverts white, with a few brown bars. Primaries and secondaries dark brown, becoming whitish or greyish basally on inner webs, broadly tipped blackish, with 5–7 narrow dark bars; below grey, becoming whitish basally on inner webs, broadly tipped brown and with 5–6 narrow dark grey-brown bars. Tail, above black, tipped white with 3 visible grey-brown bands; below grey, tipped white, with broad subterminal and 3 other dark brown bars. Cere and a narrow band at base of bill yellow; eye cream to pale yellow; feet pale yellow, ♀ similar, more heavily barred, somewhat larger. SIZE: wing, ♂ 363–380, ♀ 371–390; tail, ♀♂ 245–270; tarsus, ♀♂ 76–87. WEIGHT: (2) ♂ 908–960 (943), (1) ♀ 1100.

1ST IMMATURE: crown dark brown, streaked white, nape paler edged white, feather bases white. Back and upperwing-coverts dark brown, faintly glossed purplish, greater coverts broadly tipped white. Below, chin and throat white streaked blackish, breast buffy white, narrowly streaked buff; flanks and thighs white, barred buff, undertail-coverts white. Primaries dull grey-brown above, white basally on inner webs, tipped blackish with 5 darker bars. Secondaries dark brown, basally white on inner webs, tipped white, with broad sub-terminal and 6 blackish bars; inner secondaries greyer. Tail above and below grey, pale basally, tipped white with sub-terminal and 4 other dark brown bars. Bill wholly black; cere and gape ochre-yellow; eye pale yellow; feet ochre-yellow.

Immature plumage in subadults apparently becomes notice-ably paler, almost whitish on head and neck in some in-dividuals; sequence of moults to adults unknown.

DOWNY YOUNG: undescribed; probably white, on basis of immature body down.

Field Characters. A small, rather stocky snake eagle, most resembling a giant African Cuckoo Falcon *Aviceda cuculoides*; not likely to be confused with any other except similar-sized Smaller Banded Snake Eagle *C. cinerascens*, from which distinguishable by 3 clear whitish tail bars, generally more heavily barred under-wing in flight, and pale belly and breast barred brown. From immature European Snake Eagle *C. gallicus pectoralis* can be distinguished by yellow cere and legs and more numerous heavier bars in underwing in all plumages, but subadults may be hard to recognize except by experience. Forest habitat helps; but it may occur with other snake eagles.

Voice. Not recorded. Adult utters a rather high-pitched, rapid 'ko-ko-ko-ko-kaw' not very loud; also sonorous single calls, at intervals 'kowaaaa' or 'kowaaaow'. Young in nest a loud, squalling 'kyaa-kyaa-kyaa-kyaa-kyaa', repeated for long periods at 1–2 min intervals; also, when handled, a hoarse 'tyuck-tyuck'. Voice very like that of Smaller Banded Snake Eagle, but less deep, hoarse and crowing than that of Brown Snake Eagle *C. cinereus*. Calls normally from perches, some-times in soaring flight.

General Habits. Little known; a secretive, retiring bird of heavy woodland and forests, not often seen in open, but sometimes, especially early morning, can be seen perched on dead trees in cultivation. Often betrays unseen presence only by repeated calling. Shy and difficult to approach in cover. In open cultivation behaves like Brown Snake Eagle, perching on dead trees, scanning ground carefully. Forest habitat and tendency to remain in dense cover normally distin-

Circaetus fasciolatus

guishes it from other snake eagles in same locality.

Probably is migratory from southern to northern parts of range in austral winter July–Oct, as is relatively numerous in N coastal Kenya at that time (as with several other species, including African Cuckoo Fal-con). May then be seen more often in open woodland or grassland. Rarely soars high in air, when again usually detected by calling.

Food. So far as known, entirely snakes and lizards, caught from perches. Rumours of taking birds and poultry require confirmation.

Breeding Habits. Little known, only a few nests ever found.

NEST: small structure of twigs, lined with green leaves, but some more solid than those of larger snake eagles. 1 example was *c.* 0·6 m across by 0·3 m deep. Built either in fork of a forest tree, well below the canopy, or sometimes on top of a tree among creepers. Not used repeatedly, and hard to locate, though pairs fre-quent same general area annually.

EGGS: 1, white to greenish white. SIZE: published measurements 60·1–66·5 × 47·8–55·5 are probably er-roneous, applying to other spp.; no good modern authentic measurements exist (P. Steyn, pers. comm.).

Laying dates: Kenya July, Oct; Mozambique Sept; Zimbabwe–Natal Oct; but all records require careful checking.

Both sexes may incubate, 1 ♂ having been shot off an egg near Beira in Sept 1907.

References
Brown, L. H. (1969).
Zimmermann, D. A. (1970).

**Plates
20 and 30**
(Opp. pp. 307
and 451)

Circaetus cinerascens Müller. Smaller Banded Snake Eagle. Circaète cendré.

Circaëtos [sic] *cinerascens* Müller, J. W. von, 1851. Naumannia, (1) Heft 4, p. 27; Sennar, Sudan.

Range and Status. Resident well wooded moist savannas, forest edges, and riverine forests of Africa south of Sahara from Sierra Leone east to W Ethiopia, E Kenya, south to Zambezi Valley and N Botswana (Okavango Delta). Normally uncommon; but in W Kenya frequent, perhaps commoner than Brown Snake Eagle *C. cinereus*. Locally threatened by habitat destruction along riversides.

Circaetus cinerascens

Description. ADULT ♂: above, mainly slaty grey, tinged brown; crown, upperback and upper wings paler grey-brown. Rump and uppertail-coverts brown, tipped white, forming a white bar at base of tail. Lores and cheeks whitish; chin white. Rest of underparts brown, indistinctly barred whitish on abdomen, thighs and undertail-coverts. Underwing-coverts white, with 3 narrower dark brown bars. Secondaries brown washed grey, basally whitish on inner webs, broadly tipped brown with 4 broad dark bars. Tail dark brown, tipped white, with one broad white bar. Cere and base of bill yellow; eye whitish yellow; legs yellow. ♀ similar, usually darker than ♂, less whitish barring on lower body, but bars more distinct; sometimes all dark brown with no noticeable barring below. Size similar, ♀♀ averaging slightly larger. SIZE: wing, 367–408; tail, 220–231; tarsus, 80–84.

IMMATURE: much paler than adults. Crown white streaked darker; upperparts pale brown broadly edged white. Below, mainly dirty white, some brown on belly and thighs. Tail whitish with broad black subterminal bar and concealed blackish base. Primaries whitish, tipped dark grey-brown, with 2 indistinct bars. Secondaries brown, grey-brown on inner webs, tipped dark brown, crossed 4 indistinct dark brown bars. Eye whitish; cere yellow; bill all dark brown; feet whitish.

1ST IMMATURE: apparently largely whitish, streaked and mottled brown. Probably assumes adult plumage first by becoming all dark brown, then assuming barring on belly and

thighs. All dark brown birds usually females, may be mated with obviously barred full adults. Can probably breed in this brown plumage.

DOWNY YOUNG: said to be greyish white. No good description.

Field Characters. A stumpy, small, short-tailed snake eagle, only likely to be confused with the Southern Banded Snake Eagle *C. fasciolatus*, but smaller, stouter, shorter-tailed; does not normally occur in same range. In all plumages except early immature, single broad white tail bar diagnostic. In adults, rather broad orange-yellow base to bill with bright orange cere is distinctive; all but bill-tip appears yellow. In flight at height, whitish inner webs of primaries and secondaries form a pale patch at carpal joint, at once distinctive from any plumage of Brown Snake Eagle (with which it occurs in same habitat). Fewer bars on underwing and single tail bar distinguish it in flight from Southern Banded Snake Eagle if seen together.

Voice. Not recorded. Very like that of Southern Banded Snake Eagle, but louder, more staccato; in aerial display loud, clear 'kok-kok-kok-kok-ko-ho' falling in pitch towards end. When perched, sometimes a series of loud, mournful calls, 'ko-waaaa', or 'ko-aagh', resembling some calls of Southern Banded Snake Eagle and Bateleur *Terathopius ecaudatus*. Voice of young unknown. Less vocal than either Brown or Southern Banded Snake Eagle, most often calls in flight, seldom from perches.

General Habits. Little known. In most of range prefers riverine woodland or forest strips passing through savanna, lighter woodland, or thornbush. Rare in arid localities, but may occur if riverine vegetation available (E Kenya). Range largely overlaps with that of Brown Snake Eagle, but habits separate it ecologically; may also occur with Southern Banded Snake Eagle, on eastern fringes of range. Normally seen perched for hours immobile on trees in riverine forest, but also perches on dead trees in cultivation, and kills snakes in open land near riverine strips. Normally a silent, rather secretive, but not very shy bird, often easy to approach closely when seen, and probably commoner than supposed.

In E and southern Africa largely sedentary; immatures certainly wander. In E Africa appears commonest Aug–Feb, suggesting some influx from elsewhere. In Ivory Coast, some evidence of southward movement into southern Guinea savannas June–Sept in main rains (Thiollay 1975c), returning north in dry season. No regular movements documented.

Food. Mainly snakes, usually small, thin, often tree snakes; but one seen with large venomous cobra longer than itself. Some lizards; frogs taken more often than by larger snake eagles. Catches snakes on ground or in trees, carries them, still writhing about eagle's head and neck, to tree, then perches, holding snake near head, until limp, hanging vertical. Snake may not be swallowed for 30 min or more after capture. Treatment of snakes similar to other snake eagles, mangling head, then swallowing whole, head-first. Will also collect dead snakes thrown out for it (P. Guhrs, pers. comm.). Droppings hard, white, lumpy, like other snake eagles.

Breeding Habits. Little known; some earlier published accounts doubtful. In display, soars high, usually over river valley rather than steep slopes, travelling in straight line or circling, calling repeatedly; as vocal as Brown Snake Eagle. Occasionally, spectacular vertical dives from great height, wings folded, preceded by 'ko-aaagh' call; this call perhaps specifically associated with display and courtship (P. Guhrs, pers. comm.).

♂ feeds ♀ near nest or nest-site almost daily; brings snake or frog, calls ♀ who flies to him; he drapes snake over favoured feeding limb, or places frog there; ♀ then swallows or tears up prey. Such courtship feeding may continue for up to 8 months without laying. Copulation

reported on ground, on river sandbanks, following tumbling descent from nest-tree with claws interlocked (P. Guhrs, pers. comm.).

NEST: in trees; said to build large stick nest, but such instances suggest use of another raptor's nest (cf. Brown Snake Eagle and Bateleur). All recently described nests in large trees near river banks or along backwaters, high up (15–18 m), but below canopy in shade, often built on or among creepers; thorny trees preferred, but not invariable. Small flattish structures 45–50 cm across by 20–25 cm deep, made of thin often pliable sticks, with shallow central cup 25 cm across, copiously lined with green leaves. ♀ being regularly fed near nest by ♂ may spend hours in incubation posture without an egg; ♂ normally roosts near nest-site in neighbouring tree.

EGG: reported 1 only; white, rough textured. SIZE: 66 × 55; all old records require checking.

Possible breeding dates, Zaïre Feb, Sudan Jan, Zimbabwe–Malawi Feb, Apr, Sept, in both wet and dry months. No further details available.

Genus *Terathopius* Lesson

A unique, monotypic genus considered to be a specialized offshoot of snake eagle stock. Typified by very long wings (about 25 secondaries) and, in adults, extremely short tail, feet projecting beyond tip in flight; tail:wing ratio (20%) is lowest of any raptor. Large, cowled heads with fully erectile feathers, rather short legs with stout toes and similar scutellation indicate relationships with *Circaetus*, further supported by deep crowing voice, and development of immature plumage. Sexually dimorphic; plumage of adults black, white and chestnut; of immatures brown, resembling some *Circaetus* spp.

Terathopius ecaudatus (Daudin). Bateleur; Bateleur Eagle. Bateleur à queue courte.

Falco ecaudatus Daudin, 1800. Traité d'Orn., 2, p. 54; Auteniquoi country, Knysna District, Cape Province (ex Levaillant).

Plates 20 and 29 (Opp. pp. 307 and 450)

Range and Status. Resident savannas, woodlands, grass plains and semi-desert thornbush throughout Africa south of Sahara, from Senegal east to Ethiopia–Somalia, thence south to Transvaal; straggles to S Arabia. Normally frequent to common, but much reduced or extinct in most of former southern African range, confined to National Parks and some ranches. Probably also reduced in much of tropical African range through destruction of habitat, notably large nesting trees, but good data lacking.

Description. ADULT ♂: (normal, or chestnut-backed phase) head, neck, breast, greater upperwing-coverts and belly black. Median and lesser upperwing-coverts brown, edged whitish. Back chestnut. Undertail-coverts chestnut; underwing-coverts white. Primaries black above, pure white below, tipped black, secondaries black, basally white. Tail-feathers chestnut. Bare skin of face and cere bright red; eye brown; legs red. ADULT ♀ differs in having all upperwing-coverts brown; secondaries above mainly grey, white on inner webs and below; flight-feathers with narrower black tips than ♂; and is slightly larger. SIZE: wing, ♂ 482–553 (515), ♀ 530–559 (539); tail, ♂ 98–124 (109); tarsus, ♂ 67–75 (73), ♀ 72–75 (74); wing-span, 1727–1772; aspect ratio, c. 8; wing-loading, 56–60 N/m² (♂♂ relatively longer-winged than ♀♀). WEIGHT: (10) 1820–2950 (2242); 1 ♂ 2250, ♀♀ may average heavier.

Light-backed, or cream phase adults have the back and tail pale brown or cream, not chestnut. ♀♀ of this phase have

secondaries washed grey, not all grey. This phase seems commonest in more arid areas, but may also be associated with old age.

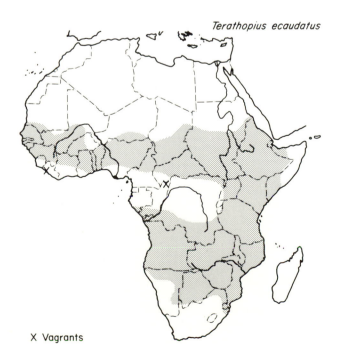

Terathopius ecaudatus

X Vagrants

1ST IMMATURE: all brown; pale brown, streaked darker on breast, and grey-brown on back. Wing- and tail-feathers blackish brown, no sexual differences visible. Cere and bare facial skin greenish blue; eye brown; legs grey. Wings broader than in adult and tail much longer (142–172); tail projects 50 mm beyond extended feet.

This juvenile plumage develops to adult over perhaps 6–7 years by repeated moults. At less than 2 years tail has moulted, is shorter (115–132 mm), now about equal to extended feet in flight. Otherwise uniform brown, darker on underwing-coverts. Subadults, 3–4 years old, are uniform dark sooty brown, with some gloss on back; bare face yellowish, feet pinkish; tail now shorter than extended feet. ♀♀ now show paler secondaries, but ♂♂ appear generally blackish brown. In pre-adult plumage, 5–7 years old, underwing-coverts become mottled dark brown and white, becoming gradually pure white as in adult; generally appear dark brown or blackish, with white mottling on underwing. Sexual differences on primaries and secondaries now evident. Bare facial skin and legs red as in adult. (Details based on captives: Brown and Cade 1972.)

DOWNY YOUNG: head, neck and underside buff; back and wings dark brown; cere yellowish white, wrinkled, eye brown, legs whitish.

Field Characters. Unmistakable in any plumage in flight because of exceptionally long, pointed wings, short tail, with feet actually protruding beyond it in adults. Lacking long tail, cants from side to side in flight to steer (hence name 'Bateleur' from term given to tightrope-walker using horizontal balancing pole). Perched black body, red face and legs, and very short tail diagnostic in adults; immatures resemble large short-tailed snake eagles, with cowled head, most like Brown Snake Eagle *C. cinereus*, but less uniform paler brown. Adults can be sexed by grey secondaries of ♀ at rest or from above; and in flight from below by narrow black trailing edge of white underwing in ♀, broader irregular trailing edge in ♂. Immatures can be classified in 3 age groups, as detailed by tail-length only; 1st year immatures have tail longer than extended feet.

Voice. Not recorded. Normally very silent; in aerial display and in piratical attacks a harsh, loud 'schaaaaa-aw', raucous tone resembling snake eagles. In distraction display or anxiety at nest, series of short sharp barks 'kau-kau-kau-kau' or 'ka-ka-ka-ka' accompanied by jerking body with half-spread wings. A harsh scream 'schaaaaa' possibly associated with threat. When perched, softer calls, 'kau-kau-kau-ko-aaagh' or 'kook-koaagh-koaagh', resemble some of those of banded snake eagles. Young emit harsh squealing squalls, 'kyup-kyup-kyup-keaaw-keeaw', when begging for food. Small eaglets give a melodious 'twip' unlike any adult call. In threat and nuptial display also makes mechanical sound with rapidly flapping wings like that of flapping sail 'whup-whup-whup-whup'; and when performing 360° lateral rolls a loud 'whurrup-whurrup-whurrup' is audible up to 1·5 km away.

General Habits. Very well known. Preferred habitat is broad-leaved woodland with long grass, dense *Acacia–Commiphora* thornbush, or *Acacia* savannas. Less common in open grass plains, semi-desert scrub and high mountains, but breeds at up to 2500 m at least and rarely may occur up to 4500 m (Ethiopia). Commonly seen because of largely aerial habits, is actually much less common than some other species more inclined to perch in cover.

Roosts on trees, pairs often roosting side by side on same branch, sometimes for several successive nights. In fine weather can fly soon after dawn, and thereafter spends much of day flying, regularly traversing same area back and forth, at air speed of 50–80 km/h, usually 50–150 m above ground, soaring higher at midday. May fly continuously for most of day, covering perhaps 400 km. Cannot easily fly after rain and avoids areas where heavy rain falls. Rarely utilizes thermal currents by day to mount to height, but may do so in nuptial display. Often follows lines of roads, crossing and re-crossing, apparently searching for road kills. Seldom perches on trees to rest, but may alight on ground and remain there some time, even hours, especially at water-holes, where it drinks and preens. Normally seen in flight, typically in straight line or wide curves (not circling), gliding steadily, sometimes with wing-tips swept back towards tail. Aerial performance is that of a high-speed glider, regularly searching large areas by day; one of the most extraordinary, spectacular and specialized of all land birds.

Apparently sedentary, especially near breeding sites in many areas, is also to some extent nomadic, perhaps even regularly migrant within tropics (Smeenk 1974). Sometimes disappears totally from otherwise suitable habitat, especially during rainy seasons. Juvenile and immatures often congregate, forming most of total population on, for example, large open flood plains, or extensive recently burned areas. Movements not well documented, but in W Africa some evidence of north to south movements in response to wet and dry seasons. Seasonally related transequatorial migration may be possible, but has not been proved.

Hunts by direct attack on suitable prey, sometimes with violent downward stoop for several hundred metres. Picks up carrion, especially road kills; attacks large snakes, including large puff-adders, and has been known sometimes to die of, or be affected by, snakebite (Moreau 1945; P. Davey, pers. comm.). Also compulsively piratical and violent, attacking vultures and other birds likely to have scraps of food, sometimes actually striking them, or forcing them to alight on ground. Contrary to published accounts a versatile and powerful predator, in habits resembling Tawny Eagle *Aquila rapax* more than any snake eagle.

Food. A wide variety of birds and mammals; not dependent on carrion or reptiles for preference. Takes mammals up to size of dik-dik (4 kg); many birds up to size of guineafowl; large reptiles to size of monitor lizard; some carrion, especially road kills; insects, e.g. dead grasshoppers, on burned ground, and alate termites, when swarming, taken on ground. In natural habitat, perhaps mainly a bird-eater. Middle toe, relatively longer than in *Circaetus* spp., supports bird-eating (cf. *Accipiter* spp.: Wattel 1973). Recorded details reflect available prey. In Tsavo Park (Smeenk 1974), 139 items included 62 mammals from size of shrew to dik-dik (27) and carrion of lion and large ungulates; 37 birds, from Common Bulbul *Pycnonotus barbatus* (30 g) to guinea-fowl and bustards (1200 g or over); some probably taken in flight, e.g. *Tockus* hornbills, rollers; 34 reptiles of which 26 were snakes, 2 monitor lizards. In Zimbabwe (Steyn 1980a) 236 items comprised 100 mammals (42% by number), including 54 hares *Lepus* spp., rats, small antelopes, porcupine, wildcat, jackal and mongooses (some taken as carrion); 113 birds (47·5% by numbers), including 24 doves, 12 francolins, 13 guineafowl, 16 glossy starlings; others varied from small shrikes to Spotted Eagle Owls *Bubo africanus*, and hornbills, rollers and kingfishers were present in both samples. Birds perhaps most important by number; mammals (including carrion and road kills) most important by weight; reptiles less important than either. Oddments include fish (catfish and tilapia) and invertebrates, including termites. Possibly takes more small helpless prey than above records indicate, as bias exists towards larger items in prey remains.

Breeding Habits. Intimately known; studied in several areas. Pairs frequent same breeding areas for many years (up to 30 in E Kenya) thus resembling typical eagles rather than snake eagles. Same nest-tree and nest used for many successive years, and if new nest built, usually near old one. Pairs require 140–200 km² Kenya, possibly less, 55–60 km², Kruger Park (Tarboton 1978b).

Nuptial display aerial, spectacular, ♂ diving at ♀ from height, calling loudly, flapping wings audible; she turns on her back and presents claws, then rolls to right herself as he shoots past. Attention is attracted by loud calling. Display not regular, and may occur far from nest-site. Similar performances apparently not always nuptial in function as may occur between 2 ♂♂, 2 ♀♀, or adults of either sex with immature. A rare possible advertisement display involves spectacular, rapid, 360° lateral rolls, repeated in less than 1 s, while proceeding in level flight, accompanied by loud 'whurrup' of wings. Apart from crowing voice, displays unlike those of snake eagles, much more vigorous.

Somewhat sociable, a third adult, usually ♂, may be present at nest with rightful pair (Brown 1955). This adult roosts with ♂ and appears when parents disturbed by intruders; but does not help in nest repair, incubation, or feeding young. Recent immatures have been recorded incubating eggs and often appear near nests; such 'triangles' perhaps are composed of 2 full adults with a recently mature subadult.

NEST: in trees, often in strip of riverine forest or woodland. When in open country, usually in an isolated tree larger than most in area; large thorny *Acacia* spp. often then selected, also baobabs, large *Terminalia* spp. May be 8–25 m from ground, usually 10–15 m. Usually built well inside leafy canopy, sometimes on lateral branch, not open to sky. Much more solid structures than those of typical *Circaetus* snake eagles, resembling nests of Wahlberg's Eagle *Aquila wahlbergi*, *c.* 0·6–0·7 m across by 0·3–0·4 m deep, of sticks, with deep central cup lined copiously with green leaves. Sometimes fouled with droppings, prey remains and smell like vultures' nests (W. Tarboton, pers. comm.). Both sexes build. Nest

repair normally takes 1–2 months before laying; but sporadic building may continue for up to 8 months without laying. A new nest takes 1–3 months to complete. Sometimes uses old nests of other birds of prey, those of Wahlberg's Eagles especially, also Crowned Eagles *Stephanoaetus coronatus*, but only if unoccupied.

EGGS: invariably 1; rounded oval, large for size of bird (as in snake eagles), usually unspotted chalky white. SIZE: (50) 74·2–87·0 × 57·0–68·1 (79·1 × 62·7) (Steyn 1980a); WEIGHT: *c.* 168 (6–7% of ♀ bodyweight).

Laying dates: W Africa Sept–Dec (dry season); Ethiopia June–Dec inclusive, avoiding driest months; Kenya–Uganda–Tanzania records 10/12 months, peaking in E Kenya (16/33 records) Feb, Mar, towards end of hottest dry season; Zambia Jan–Apr, Nov, with most in Jan–Feb (height of rains); Zimbabwe 9/12 months, with most Dec–Mar (49/69 records) late in main rains, dry season avoided (3/69 records June–Oct) (Steyn 1980a). Preference for breeding in rains some areas not explicable on grounds of food supply or availability.

Incubation mainly by ♀, sometimes ♂; individual ♂♂ vary in share. ♀ may be fed near nest by ♂, by aerial food pass occasionally, most often on tree near nest; or may leave herself to forage for long periods, with or without ♂ incubating. Egg can survive exposure for up to 6 h and remain fertile in warm tropical areas. 1 ♂ seen to attack baboon in nest tree, while ♀ remained in nest. Although sometimes appears to prefer nest-site close to road or path from which it can observe humans, violently resents human examination of nest, repeatedly swooping at intruder with loudly flapping wings. If unable to repel intruder, perches near and gives distraction or threat display, body jerking up and down, wings flapping, uttering short loud barks 'kah-kah-kah' or 'kau-kau-kau', *c.* 2/s (Moreau 1945). When photographic equipment erected near nest, will readily desert eggs or young (unique among large raptors in this respect). Photography should therefore not be attempted at nest. Incubation period: at least 52 days (Steyn 1980a), 55 (± 1) days, Kruger Park.

Newly hatched young (2 days) weighs 110 g (estimated 65% of egg weight); resembles young of snake eagles, apart from down colour. Cere becomes pale green at 8 days. Weight increases to 525 g at 14 days; 820 at 28; 1260 at 42; thereafter more slowly, reaching maximum 2035 at 70 days; slightly less, 1980, at 91 days. Feathers first appear on wing-coverts, scapulars, back of head; by 40 days forepart of body feathered, tail region and underside still downy; development closely resembles young *Circaetus* spp. Most of body feathered at 50 days, but underwing-coverts downy to 70 days, finally emerging at 85 days. Feather growth thereafter mainly in wing-feathers; primaries 4·5 cm at 42 days, 12·5 cm at 70, 23 cm at 90 days. 1st flight made normally at 110–115 days, shortest period 97 days; record of 125 days too long, probably not 1st real flight. Most often made without parental presence and may fly 1 km at first attempt (Steyn 1980a).

♀ normally broods small young alone; ♂♂ sometimes brood. Brooding 80% of daylight up to day 10, then steadily reduced to 5% of daylight by day 30. Thereafter, as in snake eagles, young left alone in nest day and night, coinciding with advancing feather development on upper surface. Nest is normally within or below canopy, so this feature apparently has little adaptive function. Both sexes then bring prey, ♂ taking larger share than in most raptors in 2nd half of fledging period (but individuals vary). Young fed daily in early stages, irregularly in latter half of period, at 1–3 day intervals. At end of period parents sometimes perch with food in sight of begging, squalling young, possibly in attempt to coax it from nest. Parents not usually visible near nest, but if human intruder climbs to it, they usually appear, performing violent diving threat displays.

Young sometimes leaves nest area after a few days, sometimes is attached to it for up to 90 days, perhaps longer. Young often seen near nest after 1st flight, may then be violently attacked by ♂, perhaps own parent. Recently fledged young may have been recorded incubating an egg probably laid by an adult, and are said to breed in immature plumage.

Breeding success in Kenya low, *c.* 0·5 young/pair/year; apparently more successful elsewhere, 56 Kruger Park records producing 0·66 young/egg laid, and in 4 Zimbabwe sites 0·77 young/pair overall; if human interference allowed for 0·86 young/pair/year. Overall average, including non-breeding pairs, perhaps 0·6–0·7 young/pair/nest. Young recently fledged range widely near nest-site, 1 marked bird ranging over 1347 km² (Snelling 1971).

Immatures form *c.* 30% of wild population. Of 2758 recorded all over Africa, 1971 (71·5%) were adults and 787 (28·5%) immatures. Of 1746 aged more precisely, 1101 were full adults (63%); 519 (29%) 1–2 year olds; 87 (5%) subadults of 3–5 years; and 39 (2·23%) were in pre-adult plumage. This suggests 97–98% mortality before sexual maturity at 7 years. Calculated adult age thus not less than 16 years, perhaps up to 23 years. 1 well known adult ♂ (Zimbabwe) believed to live for 20 years, recognized by its increased tolerance of observer and similar behaviour from year to year. Stable population could be maintained with productivity of 0·28 young/pair/year if these estimates reliable.

Captive Bateleurs become very tame, enjoy being stroked, bowing head to accept such grooming, emitting low whining squeals; no similar behaviour seen in wild birds to one another. Can be trained to fly to falconer's lure, but useless as falconer's birds as too likely to be lost.

References
Brown, L. H. (1955).
Brown, L. H. and Cade, T. J. (1972).
Moreau, R. E. (1945).
Smeenk, C. (1974).
Steyn, P. (1965, 1980a).

Genus *Dryotriorchis* Shelley

Specialized, forest-adapted snake eagle. Large head, short, very rounded wings, very long rounded tail (*c.* 70% of wing-length). Eyes very large, adapted for vision in dim light. Tarsi with rough reticulate scales, toes short, claws short and sharp. Probably more closely allied to *Circaetus* than to *Terathopius*, perhaps a link with eastern *Spilornis* snake eagles. 1 sp., very little known.

Plates 20 and 30
(Opp. pp. 307 and 451)

Dryotriorchis spectabilis (Schlegel). Congo Serpent Eagle. Serpentaire du Congo.

Astur spectabilis Schlegel, 1863. Ned. Tidjschr. Dierk, 1, p. 131, pl. 6; St George, Elmina, Ghana.

Range and Status. Resident W African and Congo Basin primary forests from Liberia east to Semliki Valley and Bwamba, W Uganda, south to Gabon and SE Zaïre. Uncommon, seldom seen, but possibly commoner than supposed. Reduced in Upper Guinea and elsewhere by destruction of primary forest.

Description. *D. s. spectabilis* (Schlegel): Upper Guinea forests from Liberia to S Nigeria and N Cameroon. ADULT ♂: crown, upperneck, blackish brown, feathers basally white; sides of neck and broad collar dark rufous-brown. Rest of upperparts dark chocolate brown. Cheeks light brown, throat buffy white with black moustachial streaks, and a black median streak. Underparts white, washed rufous (variable), with large round blackish spots; thighs barred sepia-brown and white, undertail-coverts pure white. Underwing-coverts mainly white, some brown, and black spots and bars. Primaries dark brown on outer, light brown on inner webs, tipped black and broadly barred blackish; below paler brown, tipped and barred dark brown. Tail light brown, with broad blackish bars. Eye dark brown or grey; cere, legs, feet yellow. Sexes similar. SIZE: wing, 295–315; tail, 245–268; tarsus, 66–70.

IMMATURE: crown and mantle basally white, feathers terminally rusty brown, tipped black. Below, whitish, spotted with round brown or blackish spots, disappearing with age. Upperwing-coverts brown, edged whitish; wing- and tail-feathers greyish brown, paler than adults, barred darker; eye brown, cere, legs and feet yellow.

DOWNY YOUNG: unknown.

D. s. batesi Sharpe. S Cameroon, Zaïre, W Uganda and Gabon (lower Guinea forests). Similar in size, wing, ♂ 282–307, ♀ 300–307; browner above and paler, centre of underside plain white, spots or bars only on flanks.

Field Characters. A slender, medium-sized, short-winged, long-tailed eagle with bare yellow tarsus, very large eyes. Distinguished from Cassin's Hawk Eagle *Spizaetus africanus* by bare yellow legs, relatively much longer tail, slimmer body with relatively large head, smaller overall size; from Black Sparrowhawk *Accipiter melanoleucus* by brownish collar, black moustachial and throat streaks, and 6 bars on long tail.

Voice. Not recorded. Quite vocal; with its prolonged series of sounds one of the most commonly heard raptorial voices in rain forests; at a distance sometimes resembles voice of turacos (K. Curry-Lindahl, pers. comm.). Said to utter a cat-like miaowing, and a low, nasal 'cow-cow-cow', repeated for long periods at intervals, often attracting attention.

General Habits. Scarcely known. Inhabits dense primary forest, apparently usually in understory, or on low boughs of taller trees where large eyes enable it to hunt in very poor light. Said to be rather harrier-like; but this barely possible in forest habitat. May be commoner than supposed as usually located only by voice.

Food. Little recorded. Snakes, lizards (especially chameleons), amphibians; possibly some small mammals, caught on ground by dropping from perches.

Breeding Habits. Unknown; calls may be advertisement display calls (cf. Southern Banded Snake Eagle *Circaetus fasciolatus* in cover); believed not to breed Zaïre Dec–May (dry-early rains).

References
Chapin, J. P. (1932).
Thiollay, J.-M. (1975a).

Dryotriorchis spectabilis

Genus *Polyboroides* Smith

Large, very light-bodied hawks with long, broad wings, and long tails. 2 spp., 1 Malagasy, 1 mainland Africa. Head small, beak weak, face bare. Legs long, with rough polygonal scales, outer toe short, claws thin, little curved, but sharp. Tibio-tarsal joint can bend 'backwards' through 70° enabling insertion into cavities (Burton 1978). Plumage grey and black in adult, brown in immatures; a short full bushy crest on head.

A highly specialized monotypic genus, in appearance resembling some Asian *Spilornis* snake eagles, especially the young. However, grey and black adult plumage, voice, several aspects of breeding behaviour, and nestling down suggest no close relationship to any snake eagle genus, but are more like *Accipiter* or *Buteo*. Resemblances to snake eagles may therefore be purely superficial.

Polyboroides typus Smith. African Harrier Hawk; Gymnogene. Serpentaire gymnogène.

Polyboroides typus A. Smith, 1829. S. Afr. Commercial Advertiser, 4 (13 May); no locality, South Africa.

Plates 20 and 30
(Opp. pp. 307 and 451)

Range and Status. Forests, woodlands, savannas, and sometimes thornbush of Africa south of the Sahara, avoiding interior of primary forests and rarely frequenting edges of semi-desert (Karoo). In eastern Zaïre, Rwanda and Burundi also cultivated habitats with eucalyptus. Generally frequent, locally common, especially in W. Africa and moister woodlands.

Description. *P. t. typus* Smith: South and E Africa from Sudan to Ethiopia and E Zaïre, south to Cape Province. ADULT ♂: crown, nape, back, grey, scapulars and upperwing-coverts with some black spots; uppertail-coverts barred black and white. Throat and upper breast plain grey, lower breast, abdomen, thighs, underwing- and undertail-coverts closely barred black and white, underwing-coverts separated from secondaries by white band. Primaries and outer secondaries black, inner secondaries basally grey, tipped black, freckled grey on inner webs. Tail black, tipped white with 1 broad

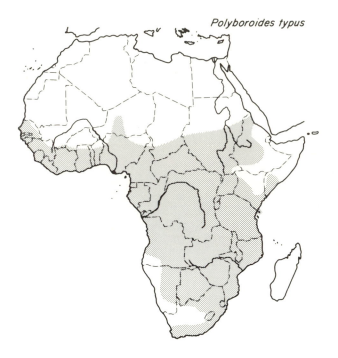

Polyboroides typus

white central band and a second, obscured, at base. Cere and bare skin round eye yellowish green, but flushes pink or red in excitement; eye dark brown, small; legs yellow. ♀ larger, usually more heavily spotted and barred than ♂. SIZE: wing, ♂ 443–464, ♀ 457–483; tail ♂♀ 280–320, ♀♀ average longer; tarsus, ♂♀ 83–100; wing-loading, 31–36 N/m². WEIGHT: unsexed 750–950, ♂ 642–720 (712), 1 ♀ 652.

1ST IMMATURE: above, dark brown, little barred or otherwise marked, feather margins and crest tipped buff. Primaries blackish brown, secondaries paler, basally mottled whitish, barred darker brown. Tail brown, with 5 darker brown bars. Abdomen, thighs, and undertail-coverts barred rufous and brown, underwing-coverts rufous mottled darker brown. Cere and gape yellow, bare facial skin grey, eye brown, legs yellow. Immatures moult directly into adult plumage by degrees over 2 years, becoming mottled or patched with grey, and acquiring yellow face. Probably are sexually mature at 3 years old.

DOWNY YOUNG: 1st down orange-buff, but darker, more chestnut on head, with long hair-like filaments, especially on head. Eye dark brown, cere and bare skin pale greenish yellow, legs dull brown. Down becomes longer, 2nd whiter down appears at *c.* 10 days, but remains hairy or silky rather than woolly-looking.

P. t. pectoralis Sharpe. W Africa from Gabon west to Gambia, north to S Sahara and W Sudan; smaller, darker, more heavily barred below. SIZE: wing, ♂ 373–396 (382), ♀ 379–405 (392). WEIGHT: ♂ 500–710 (564), ♀ 580–820 (711) (Thiollay 1977b).

A third race *P. t. prigoginei*, still darker, smaller, described from W Zaïre forests, is not admitted by Stresemann and Amadon (1979).

Field Characters. A large, broad-winged, long-tailed hawk, with noticeably slim small head and long tail with, in adult, single broad white central band. Grey barred plumage generally appears dark from below. Flight distinctive, very slow and buoyant, appearing at the mercy of gusts and air currents. Perched adults could possibly be confused with chanting goshawks *Melierax* spp.; but slim head, bare facial skin, white tail bar at once distinctive. Immatures, mottled brown and dark brown, are unlike any other hawk, most resembling

juvenile small snake eagles, but at once distinguishable by small head, bare facial skin.

Voice. Not recorded. Usually silent. In aerial display, and sometimes when perched, a long, tremulous mew 'su-eeeeee-oh', or 'su-eee, su-eeee'. Young in nest frequently call a sibilant, high-pitched 'sweeeee, sweeeee' alternating with high-pitched rapidly repeated 'pi-pi-pi-pi-pi' or 'ki-ki-ki-ki-ki'. Aggressive chick attacking sibling emits sharp harsh 'chet-et-et-et'. Statements that it emits a curlew-like 'kewee-keweee' in courtship flight erroneous.

General Habits. Very well known. A unique and peculiar bird, inhabiting for preference well-watered woodland, forest edges and moderately dense mixed cultivation; less common in tall dense forest, uncommon in semi-arid thornbush or subdesert, then found mainly along drainage lines with tall trees, and in gorges; but in South Africa breeds in cliffs on edges of treeless Karoo desert. Generally much commoner in W than I Africa; in optimum conditions pairs occupying 80 ha, with overlapping territories, foraging over 140–150 ha. In Transvaal 3–4 pairs in 76 km², with minimum hunting territories 5·3–5·5 km². In E Africa irregularly distributed. Adapts to townships and may breed in eucalyptus trees in towns. Abundance in W Africa connected with abundant oil palms, as in Vulturine Fish Eagle *Gypohierax angolensis* (Thiollay 1975a, 1978a; Thurow and Black 1980).

Forages in unique manner, by slow systematic searching. Leg can bend behind the vertical by 70° and through 30° from side to side (Burton 1978), permitting insertion into awkward hollows (see **A**). Small head permits insertion into narrow cavities behind, for

A

example, flaking bark of dead tree, where no other raptor can reach. In Ivory Coast forages mainly in wooded savanna, dense woodland and gallery forest, taking prey mainly from tree trunks, *Borassus* palm fronds and oil palms. Is active soon after dawn and spends 30–40% of daylight foraging, mainly morning and evening. Hunts systematically through range, frequenting certain places, e.g. groups of *Borassus* palms, regularly. May spend 30 min or more in 1 tree, but on average visits 31 trees/h obtaining prey in 6/31. Low wing-loading for its size assists slow searching flight. Clings to tree trunks or dry masses of *Borassus* palm fronds below growing canopy, flapping wings to maintain position and probing every possible cavity (**B**). Where oil palms abundant, visits these to feed on fruit, also locating animal prey among debris of fronds. Estimated to capture 24% of prey on tree trunks, 32% among *Borassus* palm fronds and 54% (including fruit) in oil palms (Thiollay 1972).

In Transvaal or E Africa, where oil palms scarce or lacking, forages much more widely, by low soaring, high soaring, perch hunting and hunting in canopy or on ground. Low soaring stimulates other birds, e.g. starlings to mob the hawk, so revealing locations of their nest, then robbed by hawk. In high soaring, at 30–100 m from ground, hawk locates prey then descends to near ground, flying low at speed to position of prey, suddenly slowing flight with spread tail to capture, for example, lizards. In perch hunting, hawk sits within canopy and scans area intently, thus often locating insect prey. In canopy and ground foraging, walks about on ground, or flies from tree to tree. Also clambers about on cliffs, walking along ledges, looking into holes and crevices (W. Tarboton, pers. comm.). Can thus locate bats and small hole-dwelling rodents, or nests of birds. Also regularly visits colonies of social weaver birds, hanging on nest or branch and tearing them open with bill; occasionally hovers to probe nest interior (Thurow and Black 1980). Is vigorously mobbed by many birds, especially drongos *Dicrurus* spp.; but by repeated passes over same area and repeated mobbing, the hawk locates nest and robs it, and is not repelled. Time spent foraging in suboptimum habitat may be only *c.* 4–5 h/day. In Transvaal hunts mainly from 06.30–10.30 h and again 17.00–18.00 h with long inactive period 11.00–16.00 h daily (Thurow and Black 1980).

Apparently completely sedentary throughout range, pairs present in territory year-round Ivory Coast (Thiollay 1975a), Guinea, Liberia, Zaïre, Rwanda and Burundi (K. Curry-Lindahl, pers. comm.). In E and South Africa may be more nomadic, but not known to perform any regular migrations.

Food. In W Africa, mainly oil palm fruit, supplemented by insects, arachnids, reptiles, small mammals, young and adult birds. Out of 5030 items, 4502 oil palm fruits; 22 beetle larvae; 22 reptiles (mainly skinks, *Mabuia* spp.); 38 mammals, mainly small rodents, largest a mongoose; 6 adult birds, including barbets, rollers, kingfishers, all probably taken in tree nest-holes; most young birds, except e.g. a chick of African Cuckoo

B

Falcon *Aviceda cuculoides*, also taken in holes. Oil palm fruit 86% by number, invertebrates 8·6%, mammals and birds 4·1% by number, but relatively more important by weight. In E and South Africa, where oil palms absent or scarce, depends entirely on animal food, mainly small mammals, young birds, reptiles and invertebrates. Also takes birds' eggs (from sparrow to Darter *Anhinga melanogaster*), stranded fish. In Transvaal, of 85 identified items with total biomass of 2005 g, there were 8 insects, 1 frog, 34 reptiles, 38 birds and eggs, 13 mammals; but mammals relatively most important by weight (44%, whereas birds 31%, reptiles 24%). Largest items bush squirrels *Paraxerus cepapi c.* 190 g; nestling birds 120 g; small monitor lizards 120 g. Feeds mainly on small, often helpless organisms, seldom catching adult active animals except when trapped in holes, or probably breeding or roosting (Thiollay 1976a; Thurow and Black 1980; W. Tarboton, pers. comm.).

Breeding Habits. Very well known; several nests studied throughout most of cycle (Thurow and Black 1980; Brown 1972). Pairs reside in territories year-round, and in dense populations are strongly territorial; on seeing others of same species take wing and perform aerial undulating displays (Thiollay 1976b). Aerial display before nesting consists of slow circling by 1 or pair, with gentle undulations in flight, and repeated calling. ♂, above, may gently touch back of ♀, when she rolls and presents claws. Display flights relatively unspectacular, average 20 min and occur up to 2 km from nest (Thurow and Black 1980). Copulation occurs on nest or on branch of nearby tree; ♀ solicits ♂ by calling as if begging, bends forward; ♂ sometimes places neck over her back, then mounts; duration 10–15 s, faces flushed bright red in both sexes before and during act. May occur also during incubation and fledging periods, reinforcing pair-bond.

NEST: mainly in trees in W Africa, usually high up. In Ivory Coast 100 nests ranged from 11–21 m above ground, av. 17·2 m; 97% in *Borassus* palms (evidently preferred when available). If *Borassus* not available, any other tall tree, usually below or inside canopy, in a main fork or on lateral branch, at up to 30 m above ground; tall trees preferred. In E Africa, usually in trees, including eucalyptus in towns, or trees growing from cliff faces, 5–20 m up; in South Africa mainly in trees often in eucalyptus, behind bushes growing from cliff faces, or on cliffs themselves; 1 in Natal on top of a spur of rock on summit of cliff, could be walked into. Nests not normally large, max. *c.* 1 m across by 0·3 m deep, often much smaller, a slight circle of thin sticks 0·5 m across by 0·2 m deep; invariably copiously lined with green leaves. When built at base of *Borassus* palm fronds, often hard to see and falls out frequently as fronds are shed. Nest built in trees used repeatedly for up to 5 years; area may then be entirely abandoned by birds (E Africa), but in South Africa some sites used for longer. Both sexes build, shares not well established. Green leaves brought throughout nesting cycle to late fledging period, often associated with nest relief; by either sex.

EGGS: 1–3, laid at 3-day intervals, morning or afternoon (Thurow and Black 1980); Ivory Coast mean (23 clutches) 1·17, E Africa mean (6) 1·5, South Africa–Zimbabwe mean (86) 1·71; 2 eggs commoner in south. Longish ovals; buff or cream, variously, usually richly, blotched and spotted brown, red-brown and choco-late, with grey or purplish undermarkings. SIZE: (44, *P. t. typus*) 50·6–61·4 × 40·0–46·4 (55·5 × 43·6) (SAOSNRC); (11, *P. t. pectoralis*) 50·2–62·5 × 40·0–46·0 (57·8 × 43·2) (Schönwetter 1960); WEIGHT: *c.* 57–60, clutch of 2 *c.* 15% of ♀ bodyweight.

Laying dates: W Africa (dry season), Ivory Coast 1 Dec–15 Feb, peaking 15 Dec–15 Feb; Nigeria Dec–Feb; Ethiopia Apr (rains); E Africa Jan–Apr, June, Oct, peaking E Kenya Oct (more records in rains than dry months; Zambia Sept–Dec (late dry–early rains); South Africa–Zimbabwe Aug–Dec, odd records Apr, May, peaking Sept–Oct (before and in early rains). In W Africa egg-laying coincides with abundant oil palm fruit, young in nest when lizards, grasshoppers abundant; South Africa young in nest when young passerines abundant (but mammals most important food by weight); E Africa observed peak does not coincide with food abundance, either for adults or young.

Incubation begins 1st egg, by both sexes by day, ♀ 80–90% by day, ♀ only at night. ♂ usually relieves ♀ mid-morning, often bringing green branch; may sit for 4–203 min, av. 59 min (1 nest), but at others may only take brief spells, usually when feeding ♀. ♀ also leaves nest to forage herself. Both may be on nest together and one push the other aside to incubate. Incubating bird moves frequently and rearranges egg. Incubation period: 36 days, hatching taking *c.* 24 h from pipping.

If 2 chicks hatch, violent sibling aggression occurs, elder normally eliminating younger early in fledging period. Elder strikes at head and back of younger,

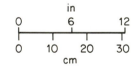

Plate 21

Elanus caeruleus Black-shouldered Kite (p. 302)
1. ADULT perched and in flight, 2. IMMATURE.

Chelictinia riocourii African Swallow-tailed Kite (p. 305)
3. ADULT perched and in flight, 4. IMMATURE.

Circus ranivorus African Marsh Harrier (p. 362)
5. ADULT ♂, 6. ADULT in flight, 7. IMMATURE.

Circus aeruginosus Marsh Harrier (p. 364)
Race *aeruginosus*: 8. ADULT ♀, 9. ADULT ♂, 10. IMMATURE.
Race *harterti*: 11. ADULT ♂.

Circus cyaneus Northern Harrier (p. 357)
12. ADULT ♀, 13. ADULT ♂, 14. IMMATURE.

Circus maurus Black Harrier (p. 356)
15. IMMATURE, 16. ADULT.

Circus macrourus Pallid Harrier (p. 358)
17. ADULT ♂, 18. IMMATURE, 19. ADULT ♀ in flight and head detail.

Circus pygargus Montagu's Harrier (p. 360)
20. ADULT ♂, 21. ADULT ♀ in flight and head detail, 22. IMMATURE.

forcing it to edge of nest and inflicting wounds; parent pays no attention, if on nest. Whiter 2nd down emerges at *c.* day 10; flight feathers appear at 14 days; largely feathered by 28 days, still downy on head and neck. Can feed itself on small items 25 days. Once feathered, remains alone in nest, usually advertising position by repeated calling. 1st flight of up to 1 km made independent of parents at 50–55 days, 1 accurate record of 52 days (Brown 1972a; Thurow and Black 1980). 2 young occasionally reared South Africa (W. Tarboton, pers. comm.).

♀ alone broods or shades chick 90% of day days 1–4, reducing to 50–55% by day 7 and 35% (21% brooding) by day 14. When not brooding remains perched on nest or in tree near it until *c.* day 28, when chick part-feathered; thereafter absent for over half daylight. In late fledging period neither parent roosts near nest. ♂♂ bring all prey up to day 28, ♀♀ remaining near nest; but thereafter ♀ also brings prey; she often leaves nest to receive prey at a distance from ♂. After day 35, visits by either parent brief, bringing food only. All small items carried in crop, largest items only in feet. Both adults very unobtrusive throughout breeding cycle, moving silently near nest and exchanging only soft low calls. When bringing prey or green branches, one or both flush bright red; flushing associated with any heightened emotion.

Young after leaving nest usually leaves vicinity, within 7 days if in forest, and thereafter not easily located.

South African observations indicate fledged young ranging over areas within 2 km from nest, occasionally returning to it in afternoon, fed by parent wherever it is. Makes early clumsy attempts at hunting on ground and in branches of trees, inspecting cavities; and becomes independent of parents *c.* 50–60 days after 1st flight. Parents then range further from nest-site and do not regularly appear near until following nesting cycle.

Breeding success, Kenya (8 pairs) 0·63 young/pair/year. Ivory Coast (32 pairs) 23 laid (0·84 eggs/pair overall); 81·5% of eggs hatched; 0·65 young per occupied nest fledged, or 0·47/pair overall including nonbreeders (Thiollay 1976b). Transvaal (12 successful nests) av. 1·17/nest. Average success apparently higher than in tropics (W. Tarboton, pers. comm.; Thurow and Black 1980). Average for whole of Africa may be *c.* 0·5–0·6 young/pair overall. Assuming 75% mortality before sexual maturity at 3 years, adults would require a breeding life of 6–8 years.

Although this species considered a probable link between Asian *Spilornis* snake eagles and harriers *Circus* spp. (Brown and Amadon 1969), the breeding cycle, with relatively short incubation and fledging periods, and young developing like a large *Accipiter* or a *Buteo* sp., suggest no close affinities with snake eagles.

References
Brown, L. H. (1972a).
Thiollay, J.-M. (1975b, 1978a).
Thurow, T. L. and Black, H. L. (1980).

Plate 22

in
0 — 3 — 6 — 9 — 12
0 — 10 — 20 — 30
cm

Accipiter rufiventris
Rufous-chested Sparrowhawk (p. 386)
1. ADULT ♂, 2. IMMATURE ♀.

Accipiter badius Shikra (p. 376)
3. ADULT ♂, 4. IMMATURE ♀.

Accipiter brevipes Levant Sparrowhawk (p. 379)
5. IMMATURE ♀, 6. ADULT ♂.

Accipiter ovampensis Ovampo Sparrowhawk (p. 382)
7. IMMATURE ♀, 8. ADULT ♂, 9. ADULT ♀
(melanistic phase).

Accipter nisus European Sparrowhawk (p. 384)
Race *punicus*: 10. IMMATURE ♀, 11. ADULT ♂.

Accipiter gentilis Northern Goshawk (p. 390)
Race *arrigonii*: 12. ADULT ♀, 13. IMMATURE ♂.

Micronisus gabar Gabar Goshawk (p. 366)
14. ADULT ♂ (melanistic phase), 15. ADULT ♀,
16. IMMATURE ♀.

Melierax metabates Dark Chanting Goshawk (p. 368)
17. ADULT ♂, 18. IMMATURE ♀.

Melierax canorus Pale Chanting Goshawk (p. 369)
Race *canorus*: 19. ADULT ♂, 20. IMMATURE ♀.
Race *poliopterus*: 21. ADULT ♀.

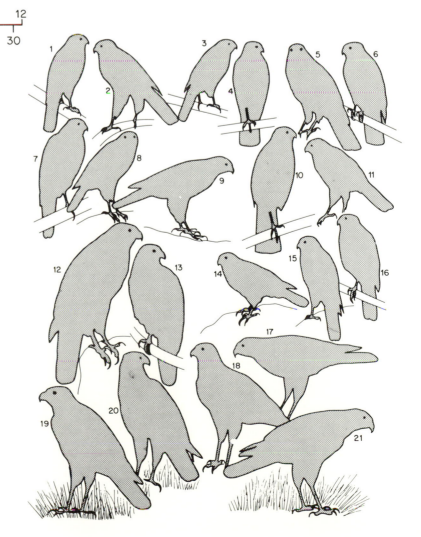

Genus *Circus* Lacépède

An extremely characteristic, cosmopolitan genus of moderate-sized, long-winged, long-tailed, long-legged hawks, inhabiting open country (moorlands, marshes, grasslands). Sexually dimorphic, ♀♀ always considerably larger than ♂♂. ♂♂ usually grey, or black and white, ♀♀ and immatures mainly brown. Bill short, gape wide. Head large, somewhat cowled, with distinct facial ruff and large ear-openings, sometimes with decided conch. Plumage generally rather soft, loose. Wings long; flight characteristic, buoyant, slow, bouts of flapping alternating with short glides. Wing-loading, low for bodyweight (25–30 N/m²), assists slow flight; can therefore traverse large stretches of open water more easily than soaring species. Tail long, usually somewhat graduated. Tarsi long, with frontal transverse scutes, reticulate scales behind. Toes short, talons rather long, sharp, foot adapted for grasping small active prey in thick cover. All but 1 (Australian) species nest on ground, laying unusually large clutches of unmarked pale blue or greenish eggs.

13 spp., 6 in Africa; include 2 endemic residents, *C. maurus* and *C. ranivorus*; 2 widespread Palearctic breeding spp. (*C. pygargus* and *C. aeruginosus*) breeding only N Africa; and 2 purely Palearctic winter migrants (*C. macrourus* and *C. cyaneus*). Curiously, none breed in apparently suitable habitat in grasslands or marshes in most of tropical Africa.

Plate 21

(Opp. p. 354)

Circus maurus (Temminck). Black Harrier. Busard maure.

Falco maurus Temminck, 1828. Pl. Col., livr. 78, p. 461; Cape of Good Hope.

Range and Status. Endemic South Africa; Cape Province north to Karoo desert, Natal, Orange Free State, Lesotho; more rarely Transvaal, Botswana (Lake Ngami), Kalahari desert and Namibia. Normally uncommon, locally frequent. Status obscure, but numbers probably stable.

Description. ADULT ♂: above, crown black; neck, back, most of upperwing and rump brownish black, browner near tail. Uppertail-coverts white, forming conspicuous white bar. Below, all brownish black with a few white spots on breast and belly, narrow white edges to belly and thigh feathers, and a few white bars on underwing-coverts. Primaries and primary coverts dark silvery grey, tipped black, white on inner webs; secondaries silvery grey, tipped black, white on inner webs, barred blackish on innermost pairs. Tail, above basally white, rest silvery grey, with 5 broad dark bars; below, white, strongly barred black. Cere orange-yellow; bare facial skin and eye yellow; legs orange-yellow. Not sexually dimorphic. ♀ similar, but larger. SIZE: wing, ♂ 331–347, ♀ 363–370; tail, ♂♀ 230–265; tarsus, 63–71. WEIGHT: not recorded.

IMMATURE: above chocolate brown, many feathers edged buff; nape white, sides of face and eyebrow buff. Below buff, mottled white on chin, streaked or spotted dark brown on chest, lower breast and belly unmarked buff. Wing-feathers brown, barred blackish; tail grey, white below, conspicuously barred black. Cere, eye, legs pale yellow.

DOWNY YOUNG: white; eye dark brown, cere flesh-coloured, a greyish ring round eye.

Field Characters. Unmistakable, the only mainly black harrier, with ♀ almost exactly the same as ♂. In flight, white uppertail-coverts contrast strongly with black body and barred black and white tail; underside of wing black and white. In field appears shorter-winged, heavier-bodied than African Marsh Harrier *C. ranivorus*. Immature Black Harrier always distinguishable from African Marsh Harrier by mainly white lower breast and belly, and strongly barred tail.

Voice. Not recorded. Resembles that of other harriers. Normally silent, except in nesting area. A shrill whistle 'seeeeeu' probably by ♂. Contact call near nest, mellow 'pi-pi-pi-pi'. Alarmed or excited near nest, a low chattering 'chek-ek-ek-ek-ek'.

General Habits. Little known. Essentially a harrier of dry country, frequenting more arid types of Cape maccia or fynbos, Karoo subdesert scrub, open plains with low shrubs, croplands; rarely, marshes with tall grass or reeds (*Restio* spp.). 60% of sightings in natural vegetation. Definitely prefers open ground; some bare ground apparently essential. Then behaves like other harriers, flying slowly upwind, 1–5 m above ground, veering from side to side, occasionally hovering briefly if prey located. May sometimes hunt among quite tall shrubs (e.g. *Protea* spp.), when relatively short wings may be advantageous, making it more agile. However, prefers open ground with low vegetation to any tall cover (F. Van der Merwe, pers. comm.).

Circus maurus

Breeding area

Non-breeding area

Movements rather little recorded, but analysis of 614 recent sightings indicates nomadism, and probably regular northward migration in non-breeding season. Some remain year-round in breeding range, and may then hunt over snow-covered ground (P. Steyn, pers. comm.). Seen less often in southern breeding range in non-breeding season Jan–July; but 83% of sightings north of breeding range in non-breeding season. Evidence of irregular, locally nomadic movements north and west to drier, warmer Botswana and Namibia in southern winter.

Food. No quantitative analyses available; but includes small birds to size of thrush; downy gamebird young; small mammals to size of rat; frogs; small reptiles; insects; birds' eggs and, occasionally, carrion (F. Van der Merwe, pers. comm.). All taken on ground in slow searching flight, dropping into cover to kill. May hover with widely spread tail, fanning wings. Prey caught in cover may be carried to open place to eat (Hustler 1976). Near nest, one parent passes food to other in typical harrier food-pass foot to foot, or is dropped and caught by other, upside down.

Breeding Habits. Well known. Pairs arrive at breeding haunts at least 1 month before nesting. ♂ soars high above breeding ground, performing undulating display, with calling at top of each upward swoop. Copulation on ground. Mating observed between 3 birds at 1 nest-site suggests bigamy or polygamy (as in other harriers) but similarity of ♂ and ♀ plumage makes proof of this difficult.

NEST: annually in same general area, not in same site; especially in drier parts of range (Namaqualand) same suitable places used annually. In successive years nests may be 30–50 m from previous site. Nests built on ground, dry sites preferred (11/17 records), sometimes in thick long grass or reeds, or low scrub. Rather small, flat structures, sometimes with base of thin sticks, more often made only with reeds and grass, finer in lining; *c.* 40 cm across by 5 cm deep, sufficient to protect eggs on moist ground. Normally flat, but lower edge may be built up on slopes.

EGGS: 2–5, usually 3–4, av. clutch 3·47 (F. Van der Merwe, pers. comm.). Laying interval unknown, but probably several days. Rounded ovals; plain dull bluish-white. SIZE: (7 eggs) 38·0–48·2 × 34·0–38·8 (44·7 × 36·6) (Schönwetter 1960); WEIGHT: *c.* 33 g.

Laying dates: Cape Province July–Nov, mainly Aug–Sept.

Probably ♀ alone incubates, called off nest to receive prey by ♂. Sits very tight, leaving only when intruder within a few paces; then reluctant to return if intruder in view. Incubation period: *c.* 35 days.

Chicks hatch asynchronously, but probably over shorter period than egg-laying as little size difference observed in downy young. Young at first brooded closely, probably by ♀, who is called off nest by ♂ to receive food in typical harrier food-pass. Partly feathered young 20 days old crawl down tunnels in surrounding vegetation when disturbed; in nest are aggressive, attacking, for example, foot of observer. When large, escape detection by hiding in tunnels. Once partly feathered, left alone in nest and both parents bring prey. Near end of fledging period, climb onto tops of reeds or bushes, practice wing-flapping. Fledging period: estimated 35–40 days.

Despite relatively small clutch for genus, breeding success apparently not much lower than other harriers. 25 eggs in 6 recorded nests produced 14–15 young, 2·2/occupied nest. However, frequent non-breeding occurs in established sites, possibly affected by rainfall, and overall breeding success would be lower (N. Macgregor and F. Van der Merwe, pers. comm.).

Circus cyaneus (Linnaeus). Northern Harrier; Hen Harrier. Busard Saint-Martin.

Falco cyaneus Linnaeus, 1766. Syst. Nat. (12th ed.), 1, p. 126; Europe, Africa = London (ex Edwards, pl. 225).

Plate 21

(Opp. p. 354)

Range and Status. Uncommon but regular Palearctic winter migrant N and NW Africa.

Description. ADULT ♂: above, entirely ash grey, but uppertail-coverts pure white. Sides of face, neck, throat and upper breast grey, paler on lower breast becoming white on belly, undertail- and underwing-coverts. Of 5 outermost primaries *c.* 65% black tinged grey on outer web, basally white. Inner primaries and secondaries grey on outer webs, largely white on inner, subterminally tipped brownish forming dark trailing edge. Tail above grey, plain on central pair, barred darker on outer pairs; below white, barred dark grey. Cere yellow; eye orange-yellow; legs yellow. ADULT ♀: crown, nape, back, upperwing-coverts dark brown, edged paler, appearing streaky. Uppertail-coverts white, a few rufous spots and bars. Sides of face pale brown, a ruff extending as blackish line across throat. Below, pale brown streaked darker; underwing-coverts buff streaked brown. Wing-feathers above brown, tipped blackish, heavily barred darker, whitish basally on inner webs; below pale brown to rufous, basally whitish, barred dark brown. Tail, central pairs grey-brown, outer rufous buff, all barred and broadly tipped blackish; below pale brown, barred blackish. Larger than ♂. SIZE: wing, ♂ 323–351 (338), ♀ 358–392 (376); tail, ♂ 202–224 (213), ♀ 222–255 (243); tarsus, ♂ 65–72 (69·3), ♀ 70–79 (74·5); wing-loading, 24–26 N/m². WEIGHT: ♂ 300–400 (346), ♀ 410–708 (527); young birds may be lighter.

IMMATURE: resembles ♀, but paler, broader buff edges to feathers, generally more rufous below. Eye brown in ♀♀, yellow in ♂♂; cere greenish, feet yellow. This plumage develops to adult by darkening in ♀, becoming partially grey in ♂; sexually mature at 2–3 years.

Field Characters. Could be confused in N Africa with Montagu's and (much rarer) Pallid Harrier (*C. pygargus* and *C. macrourus*). Adult ♂ at once distinguishable from either by broad, pure white uppertail-coverts, generally darker grey body, more black on primaries, no black bar on secondaries, no chestnut underwing markings, dark trailing edge on grey wing; also larger, with heavier build than either Montagu's or Pallid Harrier. Adult ♀ more difficult to recognize; but usually has broader and purer white uppertail-coverts, underparts more broadly

Circus cyaneus

Immatures distinguished from Montagu's Harrier by streaked, not plain underparts; and from Pallid Harrier by much heavier build, appearing relatively short-winged. Subadult ♀ always difficult to distinguish with certainty. Amount of white on uppertail-coverts not reliable guide.

Voice. Not recorded in Africa. In winter normally silent; may utter chattering cries 'chek-ek-ek-ek' or 'chuke-rukeruk', little different from other harriers.

General Habits. Little known in Africa, well known in Europe. Not normally confined to or preferring marshes, but often hunts over them. Flies low over open heaths, grasslands and crops, dropping on prey when located. Roosts communally on ground, like other harriers.

Food. Not well recorded N Africa; but includes small mammals, birds, probably insects. In breeding haunts takes more birds than other harriers and is a more active, swifter predator (Schipper 1973); but main food normally small mammals.

streaked than in Montagu's Harrier, with paler bases to wing-feathers. At close range lacks blackish ear-coverts of ♀ Montagu's Harrier, facial ruff less distinct.

References
Cramp, S. and Simmons, K. E. L. (1980).
Etchécopar, R. D. and Hüe, F. (1967).

Plate 21

(Opp. p. 354)

Circus macrourus (Gmelin). Pallid Harrier. Busard pâle.

Falco macrourus S. G. Gmelin, 1770. Reise Russland, 1, p. 48; Voronezh, Russia.

Range and Status. Palearctic winter migrant, mainly south of Sahara, some as far south as Cape Province. Up to 1950 often common, locally abundant, especially in W Africa. In recent years greatly reduced, probably due to pesticides and agricultural development in breeding range, perhaps aggravated by pesticides acquired while in winter range (especially on cotton irrigation schemes).

Circus macrourus

Description. ADULT ♂: forehead and eyebrow white; crown, back and upperwing-coverts pale grey, darker on mantle; uppertail-coverts white barred grey. Sides of face, throat, whole underside including underwing- and undertail-coverts white. 5 outer primaries narrowly tipped black, forming small black wedge, white basally, outer webs greyish, terminally browner; secondaries pale grey, white basally. Wings below white, except black primary tips. Tail, above central feathers pale grey, others white, barred grey; below white, indistinctly barred grey. Cere, eye, feet pale yellow. ADULT ♀: forehead and eyebrow whitish; crown and upperback dark brown edged rufous, basally white. Uppertail-coverts white, barred brown. Back and upperwing-coverts dark brown. Below buff, streaked chestnut, a blackish facial ruff extending round chin. Wing-feathers brown, paler below, becoming buff basally, barred dark brown. Tail with inner feathers brown, rufous buff on outer dark brown bars. Eye, cere, legs yellow. Larger than ♂.
SIZE: wing, 327–355 (340), ♀ 350–393 (371); tail, ♂ 199–222 (208), ♀ 222–251 (236); tarsus, ♂ 61–73 (66·5), ♀ 63–76 (71·8); wing-loading, (1) 27 N/m². WEIGHT: ♂ (3) 295–325, ♀ (3) 425–454; ♂ (14 adults and subadults) 235–416 (313), ♀ (4) 255–433 (379).
    IMMATURE: above brown, edged rufous, especially on lesser wing-coverts; a distinct rufous or buff collar; face white above and below eye, cheeks blackish. Upperwing-coverts pure

white. Below rich rufous, uniform, or streaked dark chestnut. Eye brown, cere greenish, legs yellow. Develops to adult plumage in 2–3 years. 2nd year ♂, darker grey above than adult, with some brown on head, nape, upperwing-coverts, and brown streaks below; tail with rufous bars. Eye becomes yellow earlier in ♂ than in ♀.

Field Characters. In most of winter range only likely to be confused with Montagu's Harrier *C. pygargus*. ♂ much paler, appearing almost gull-like; black tips of primaries much smaller; lacks any black bar on secondaries, or chestnut underwing markings. Much smaller, slimmer, paler, than ♂ Northern Harrier *C. cyaneus* and lacks obvious white uppertail-coverts. ♀♀ and immatures more difficult to distinguish, but at close range well-marked blackish ruff extending below chin is useful. Immature more streaky below than Montagu's Harrier, and immature ♂♂ lack any chestnut underwing bars. However, certainty of identification at any distance very difficult, except in adult ♂♂.

Voice. Not recorded. In winter quarters normally completely silent, but may utter chattering calls near roost.

General Habits. Well known. Mainly eastern European and Asian breeding range means that most enter Africa via Suez or across E Mediterranean, moving on broad front with little concentration, mainly to NE Africa, only a few reaching NW Africa. Southward movement begins late Aug-early Nov; most do not travel far south of equator. Presumably reaches W Africa by diagonal flights across Sahara, but a main migration route in E and NE Africa is down Nile and through Rift Valley, also down NE Ethiopian escarpment. Return passage takes more westerly course generally than southward, reaching Libya, and Tunisia at Cape Bon; birds ringed Cape Bon in spring recovered Italy to eastern Europe and USSR (Cramp and Simmons 1980). First autumn arrivals usually ♀♀ and immatures, followed by adult ♂♂. Latest spring stragglers are immatures and subadults. On migration flies singly, higher than when hunting, and readily crosses large stretches of open water. When migrating, may fly low (1–15 m above ground), sometimes in pairs or in groups of 3–15 birds, flying 5–15 m apart (K. Curry-Lindahl, pers. comm.).

Preferred winter habitat is open, short grass plains, but in W Africa also found in woodlands. Less likely to be found in rice fields, marshes, than Montagu's Harrier. In suitable habitat occurs from sea level to 4500 m (rarely). Hunts like other harriers flying low against wind, 1–5 m above ground (see **A**). Perches at intervals on ground, stones, posts or stumps, but is on wing much of day. Roosts communally, often with other species (especially Montagu's Harrier) in regularly used localities. In W Africa areas of stiff-leaved grass *Imperata cylindrica* often used, in E Africa *Pennisetum* spp. Sometimes occurs in marshes, but not regularly. Same individuals perhaps use same roost nightly for some time, ranging out to feeding areas daily. Before roosting, often perches near roost on ground.

Within winter quarters nomadic, attracted to abundant sources of food, e.g. locust swarms; attends grass fires, catching disturbed insects in flight. Behaviour in winter quarters very similar to Montagu's Harrier, but in E Africa is normally outnumbered by Montagu's Harrier by *c.* 2:1 (based on counts of adult ♂♂). Formerly was commonest wintering harrier in W Africa, east of Senegal, where Montagu's Harrier more numerous; now much reduced.

Food. Not well documented in winter quarters, but includes small mammals, small birds, and especially insects, notably grasshoppers; may take some frogs in irrigation schemes.

A

Plate 21

(Opp. p. 354)

Circus pygargus (Linnaeus). Montagu's Harrier. Busard cendré.

Falco Pygargus Linnaeus, 1758. Syst. Nat. (10th ed.), 1, p. 89; Europe = England (ex Albin).

Range and Status. Resident and Palearctic migrant; in Africa breeds Morocco, Algeria; not proven elsewhere. Uncommon breeder NW Africa; in winter quarters in E Africa commoner than any other harrier, outnumbering Pallid Harriers *C. macrourus* by *c.* 2:1. In W Africa formerly (up to 1950) little recorded, but recently found commoner than Pallid Harrier in Senegal. May have changed habits in last few decades. Formerly common, locally abundant; now at best frequent, locally common. Although greatly reduced, considered threatened, in W European breeding range, still relatively common in winter, E and NE Africa. Recorded as abundant, rice fields, Senegal, less common, occurring mainly north of 9° NE to Chad, Central African Republic, becoming commoner again Ethiopia–Kenya, suggesting main migrant streams do not fully mix in W Central Africa. Reduction probably due to pesticides in European and N African range, perhaps also acquired in winter range, especially on cotton irrigation schemes, where organochlorine pesticides still used.

Circus pygargus

Description. ADULT ♂: above, including upperwing-coverts, dull blue-grey, browner in worn plumage, paler on primary coverts. Uppertail-coverts grey, tipped and basally white, forming a broken white bar at base of tail. Sides of head whitish, with a slight ruff. Neck, chin, throat and upper breast grey like back; belly, undertail-coverts and underwing-coverts white, strongly barred chestnut on underwing-coverts, black on primary underwing-coverts. Outer primaries largely black, tipped grey, becoming grey-white on inner webs; inner primaries boldly barred black. Outer secondaries grey, inner webs white, barred black on both webs forming black wing-bar; inner secondaries grey. Below grey, broadly tipped black on primaries, barred black. Tail, above grey on central pair and outer webs of others; inner webs of outer feathers brownish, barred darker brown, or rufous on outermost pairs; below whitish, barred brown or rufous. Eye yellow, cere and feet yellow.

ADULT ♀: crown and upperside, including upperwing-coverts, dark brown, edged rufous; whitish on nape, primary coverts washed grey, uppertail-coverts white, subterminally barred or spotted. Face whitish, contrasting with dark brown ear-coverts. Below buff or pale rufous streaked rufous to dark brown; underwing-coverts buffy white, barred and streaked chestnut. Wing-feathers above brown, tipped and barred black; below greyish brown, tipped and barred blackish, axillaries white, barred chestnut. Tail, above grey-brown centrally, becoming more rufous on outer pairs, broadly barred blackish. Eye brown, cere and feet yellow. Larger than ♂. SIZE: wing, ♂ 346–393 (365), ♀ 355–391 (372); tail, ♂ 204–237 (218), ♀ 209–236 (225); tarsus, ♂ 52–62 (58·1), ♀ 56–65 (60·5); wing-loading, (2) 21 N/m². WEIGHT: ♂ (13) 227–305 (261), ♀ (6) 319–435 (348); ♂ 265, ♀ 345.

Rare melanistic adults are all brownish black, with some grey on upperparts, primary coverts, tail-coverts and tail, and on throat below.

IMMATURE: above like adult ♀, brown but generally darker, broader rufous edges to feathers. Uppertail-coverts white, often tipped rufous. Below, chin creamy; rest of underparts, including underwing-coverts and axillaries, deep almost uniform rufous brown, with darker shaft streaks, and dark centres to primary coverts. Wing above brown, paler basally, tipped and barred blackish, generally darker than adult ♀. Tail brown, broadly tipped and barred blackish, outer feathers more rufous. Eye brown, cere and feet yellow.

♂♂ moult to full adult plumage by 3rd year; intermediate stages partly grey, but already show chestnut bars and marks on paler underwing. ♀♀ grow paler, with narrower rufous edges on feathers above, streaky below. ♂ acquires yellow eye earlier than ♀, possibly as nestling.

DOWNY YOUNG: at first white, dark brown round eye, buff on wings and back; 2nd down deeper buff; down of melanistic phase dark brown. Eye brown, cere blue-grey, feet pale yellow.

Field Characters. Occurs with Pallid and (rarely) Northern Harriers *C. cyaneus* in African winter range. ♂♂ most easily recognized, both in adult and subadult plumage, by chestnut markings on underwings and sides; all 8 outer primaries wholly black, much more extensive than in Pallid Harrier but black bar on secondaries not always easily seen. White rump less extensive and obvious than in ♂ Northern Harrier. ♀♀ more difficult to distinguish, but are much smaller and slighter, appearing relatively longer-winged than Northern Harrier, and usually have less extensive white base of tail. ♀♀ and subadults generally difficult to distinguish with certainty from Pallid Harrier. Facial ruff is much less marked in this species, and Montagu's Harrier has large pale patch behind eye, but these distinctions only useful at close range; rather darker brown generally. Immature is plain dark rufous brown below, darker richer rufous than juvenile Pallid Harrier; this normally diagnostic if well seen, but hard to note in flight.

Voice. Recorded (Europe) (2a). In winter quarters normally silent. In breeding quarters ♂ utters mainly sharp staccato calls, ♀ high-pitched, sibilant calls. In courtship, ♂ utters sharp, clear, rapidly repeated 'kniakk-kniakk-kniakk', 'kett-kett-kett', or 'chek-chek-chek'. Food call of ♂ a longer drawn 'k-n-iakk' accented at end. Soliciting ♀ utters high-pitched whistling 'psiiiii' or 'piih-i' in courtship, when ♂ in display, and when soliciting food or in food-pass. In alarm near nest, low 'chuck-chuck' or 'chet-et' by ♂, similar lower-pitched 'chuck' by ♀. Small young utter high-pitched cheeping calls, and in nest later, high-pitched 'psiiii', like ♀; scream when handled in nest; on wing after fledging an alarm call like adults 'chet-et' or 'chuck-chuck', not so loud (Cramp and Simmons 1980, and authorities quoted therein).

General Habits. Well known. In winter quarters behaves like Pallid Harrier, both often found together, from sea level to 4000 m. Prefers open short grassland, and in W Africa winter distribution apparently more northerly, in drier Sahelian zone rather than moister Upper Guinean savannas and woodlands. Perhaps more inclined to hunt and roost in marshy areas than Pallid Harrier, but habits very similar.

Roosts communally on ground, often with Pallid, sometimes also with Marsh Harriers *C. aeruginosus*. Before roosting often collects in area 30 min before dark, and perches for some time, perhaps several close together, in open bare ground or on stones, termite-heaps. Individuals may use same roost nightly for some time, ranging out to foraging areas by day, but on migration succession of different individuals roost in same sight. Leaves roost early morning and begins hunting almost at once. Thereafter is on wing most of day, sometimes perching on stones, bare ground, or posts, usually not for long. Hunts like other harriers, flying low against wind, veering from side to side, in strong headwinds with ground speed little above walking pace. Checks or hovers briefly in flight in order to drop on possible prey in thick cover. Success rate not better than 1 kill out of 4 attacks.

Entirely migratory from breeding range. Apparently crosses Mediterranean and Sahara on broad front, where little observed, flying readily across large areas of open water. Southwest movement in Europe in autumn concentrates at Gibraltar, chiefly mid Aug–mid Sept, fewer recorded further east at Cape Bon and Suez, but large numbers migrate down NE Ethiopian escarpment, so many must enter Africa via Suez or across Red Sea. Data suggest 2 main migrant streams, with some concentration also via Sicily–Cape Bon and broad front movements between. Earliest arrivals W Africa mid-Sept (Elgood *et al.* 1973), NE Ethiopia early Oct, equator (Kenya) *c.* 15–20 Oct, South Africa late Oct–early Nov. Ringing recoveries Holland–Chad and Sweden–Nigeria. Despite apparent threat to breeding populations in Europe, still relatively abundant NE Africa in autumn; 2000 perhaps pass in Oct through only 10,000 km² of Tigrai plateau, Ethiopia. Recorded as abundant Senegal delta area in rice fields; apparently less common from N Nigeria east to Sudan, but little information. First arrivals mainly ♀♀ and immatures, adult ♂♂ 7–10 days later. Most remain north of equator, few reaching South Africa. Northward return migration begins late Mar, peaking in NE Ethiopia early Apr. Spring migrants readily cross Mediterranean, then appearing commonly in Greece and Malta suggesting westward swing by migrants entering NE Africa in

autumn. Numbers depart Cape Spartel across Straits of Gibraltar, usually in headwinds, peak passage early Apr (Evans and Lathbury 1973); some immatures summer Senegal, none recorded E or NE Africa. Most W European and NW African birds probably remain in W Africa in winter, not reaching E Africa, but many entering NE Africa in autumn may first move west, then north; spring passage at Cape Bon, Tunisia, considerable, all ringed birds moving northeast to Italy, Hungary, Bulgaria, Russia (Glutz von Blotzheim *et al.* 1971; Cramp and Simmons 1980).

Food. Little recorded in Africa; but hunting methods and preferences similar to Pallid Harrier. Includes small mammals, small ground birds (e.g. larks), lizards, probably amphibia (especially in and near irrigation schemes) and large insects, especially grasshoppers, mantids, locusts. In breeding quarters small birds, small mammals, lizards probably most important. Attends grass fires but generally abandons large burned areas, preferring to hunt in long cover. Almost all food taken on ground, but pursues insects and some small birds on wing, e.g. *Quelea* drinking at waterholes.

Breeding Habits. In NW Africa little known, presumably similar to other areas (summarized here). In Europe very well known, but not as intensively studied as some other harriers. ♂♂ leave wintering areas first, arriving at breeding grounds *c.* 7–10 days before ♀♀, in Morocco late Mar–early April. ♂♂ especially soar above breeding area, performing vigorous undulating displays. When ♀♀ arrive, both soar together. ♂ may then dive at ♀, who may roll and present claws. ♂ also performs spectacular vertical dives, first rising to 100–1000 m, then levelling out, followed by vertical plunge, calling repeatedly, twisting from side to side, tail fully spread, producing loud humming or whizzing sounds, resembling drumming snipe, but louder, flashing grey and black wings. May drop thus 30 m, level out and repeat, or continue to fall further; such vigorous displays performed most in fine weather. Several ♂♂ may display to 1 ♀; and bigamy or polygamy is recorded or suspected.

In NW Africa a rare breeder normally nesting in marshes, but not in tall reed-beds; sometimes in thick vegetation in dry areas. NEST: on ground, a flattish mass of reeds, sedges, small sticks, lined with finer reeds or grass, 20–25 cm across by 4–5 cm thick, often with an open trampled area round it. ♀ builds most or all of nest; but ♂ also brings some material. Nests normally singly, but sometimes in a diffuse colony. Details in NW Africa not well known.

EGGS: (NW Africa) 3–6, usually 3–5, laid at 36–72 h intervals; clutches av. *c.* 4, similar to Europe 3–10 (4·2), clutch of 10 laid by 2 ♀♀: Cramp and Simmons 1980). Rounded ovals; plain bluish white, rarely with sparse red-brown blotches or streaks (perhaps dried blood). SIZE: 38–46·5 × 32–42 (*c.* 42 × 37); WEIGHT: *c.* 24 g, clutch of 4 *c.* 27–28% of ♀ bodyweight.

Laying dates: Morocco, Algeria late Apr–early May (Heim de Balsac and Mayaud 1962); recent records lacking.

Incubated by ♀ alone, beginning with 1st egg; called

off nest to feed by ♂ up to 5–6 times daily. Incubation period: estimated 28–29 days each egg, 27–40 days clutch.

Young hatch over several days, eldest much larger than youngest. Newly hatched young cannot stand; but from 48 h begin to shuffle about and can stand at 12 days. 2nd darker buff down emerges at *c.* 5 days, first feathers at about 12 days. Feathers cover down by 21 days, fully feathered by 28 days. Fly first at 32–42 days, usually 35–40 days. Hide in surrounding cover once they can walk and practice wing-flapping when feathered, after 21 days.

♀ remains with young up to *c.* 20 days, brooding young at first, then standing with them. ♂ arriving with food calls ♀, who flies to him and receives it by food-pass foot to foot, or turns upside down to catch it in air. From *c.* 21 days (when young are feathered) ♀ also hunts; but may return to nest to shelter young from rain or hot sun. Prey requirement of av. brood rises from 5–6 items daily at first to 10–12 items per day.

For most of cycle, ♂ feeds himself, mate and several young. Brood losses among small young likely to be high, usually not more than 2 young reared/successful nest; no good details NW Africa, but in Europe *c.* 80% of eggs hatch, and 57% of young hatched fly, equivalent to *c.* 1·9 young reared/breeding pair.

After 1st flight young may return to nest to roost, and family may remain together for some time, even after parents have ceased to feed young. Communal roosting by several families begins soon after breeding, but ♂♂ may then separate and roost alone. ♀♀ and young leave breeding areas *c.* 14 days before ♂♂, arriving earlier in winter quarters. Breeding success and replacement rate in N Africa unknown; but ♂♂ can breed in following summer in partially mature plumage, normally at 2–3 years (Cramp and Simmons 1980).

References
Cramp, S. and Simmons, K. E. L. (1980).
Glutz von Blotzheim, U.N. *et al.* (1971).
Laszlo, S. (1939).

Plate 21
(Opp. p. 354)

Circus ranivorus **(Daudin). African Marsh Harrier. Busard grenouillard.**

Falco ranivorus Daudin, 1800. Traité d'Orn., 2, p. 170; South Africa (ex Levaillant).

Range and Status. Resident marshy areas of moister parts of Africa from Cape Province north to Kenya, west to Uganda, E Zaïre and Angola. Normally frequent, locally common. Reduced both in northern and southern parts of range by drainage of marshlands, but not yet threatened.

Description. ADULT ♂: very variable. Above, head, nape, back, upperwing-coverts dark brown, edged or streaked rufous, upperwing-coverts often banded white; uppertail-coverts brown, spotted and barred rufous, sometimes plain. Chin, throat, breast and belly white, becoming more rufous on thighs, streaked dark brown, sometimes plain dark brown; underwing-coverts white, streaked rufous-brown. Wing-feathers above grey, browner, more rufous on inner webs and secondaries, broadly tipped and barred blackish brown; below whitish, tinged rufous, secondaries greyer, tipped and barred

dark grey. Tail above centrally brown, more rufous basally and on outer pairs, with 7 broad blackish bars; below grey, tinged rufous, barred dark grey. Iris yellow; cere blue-grey; legs yellow. ♀ usually browner, darker than ♂, more rufous below sometimes more streaky. SIZE: wing, ♂ 340–368 (353), ♀ 365–395 (375); tail, 210–248; tarsus, 72–82. WEIGHT: 1 ♂ 423, 5 unsexed 405–590; av. (6) 567; 1 immature 606 (Biggs *et al.* 1979).

IMMATURE: above all dark brown, streaked rufous or white on nape and back; uppertail-coverts more rufous. Below dark rufous brown, streaked blackish on underwing-coverts, with a broad white band across chest. Wing-feathers plain dark brown. Tail above dark brown, faintly banded paler, more rufous on outer feathers; below grey, basally rufous, faintly barred darker. Cere greenish grey, eye pale brown, feet yellow.

DOWNY YOUNG: 1st down buff on head, darker on back, variable; 2nd down white on head and wings, body buff. Cere greyish, eye dark brown, feet pale yellow.

This species often regarded as a race of the European Marsh Harrier *C. aeruginosus ranivorus*. We follow Vaurie (1965) and Nieboer (1973) in regarding it as a good species (because of the body proportions, barred not plain tail in ♂♂, lack of marked sexual dimorphism and some apparent differences in display and breeding behaviour. Populations in tropical E and Central Africa north of Zambezi slightly smaller and considered by some to be *C. r. aequatorialis* Stresemann (Stresemann and Amadon 1979), but we feel measurements do not support this.

Field Characters. Only likely to be confused in same habitat with European Marsh Harrier. Smaller, much slimmer, paler brown generally. Adults lack pale crown and nape, and have barred tails; immatures have some white on nape, but broad white breast band then diagnostic. Distinguishable from any ♀ or immature of Montagu's or Pallid Harrier (*C. pygargus* and *C. macrourus*) at once by lack of white rump.

Voice. Recorded (6). Generally very silent, except near nest. Both sexes utter repeated 'tjurruck, tjurruck' bringing food to nest; whistling 'keee-u-keee-u' when

Circus ranivorus

soliciting. In nuptial display, high-pitched whistling 'feeeee-uw'. In alarm, loud ringing 'kek-kek-kek', resembling calls of Wattled Plover *Vanellus senegallus* (Malherbe 1970; W. Tarboton and A. C. Kemp, pers. comm.).

General Habits. Well known. Although mainly found near or in marshes and reedbeds, also hunts over open grasslands and cultivation. Roosts in marshes; usually solitary, gregarious roosting not recorded. Leaves roost early morning, thereafter flying slowly over marshes, along margins of lakes and dams, over dry areas (especially mountainous regions in Zaïre, Rwanda and Burundi), but often crossing these from one marsh to another, hunting on the way. Generally hunts singly, planing with wings held well above back, from 1–10 m above ground or marshes, often hunting at greater height than dry-land harriers (Montagu's or Pallid) in same area. Repeatedly traverses same ground in or near marshlands. When prey sighted, checks in flight, may hover briefly, then plunges with raised wings and extended feet into dense cover to catch prey; often abandons attempt before entering tall cover, halting and planing on. Also hunts by flying close to trees and bushes, repeatedly dashing down to branches to pick up prey. Sometimes soars high, not obviously displaying.

Apparently sedentary in all areas, migrating little anywhere. In E Africa pairs entirely sedentary in range, returning to roost in home marsh when not breeding. Occurs in E Africa at up to 3000 m, seldom below 1500 m, but, curiously, does not occur in similar clearly suitable highland marshes in Ethiopia. Temporary seasonal marshes may be occupied for hunting, sometimes also for breeding, abandoned when dry.

Food. Not quantitatively recorded, but varied, including small mammals and adult birds, some fledglings, lizards, frogs, insects. Takes birds as large as Red-billed Teal *Anas erythrorhyncha* (Cooper 1970), Speckled Pigeon *Columba guinea* and many doves (11 at 1 nest), notably Laughing Dove *Streptopelia senegalensis*; doves caught when drinking by rapid downwind flights low along river valleys (A. C. Kemp, pers. comm.). Feeds also on remnants of larger kills (flamingoes) of, for example, fish eagles. Most prey taken on ground or within cover, some taken on wing without stopping, insects and birds often caught on wing.

Breeding Habits. Well known. Breeds singly in marshes, the same marsh used annually, sometimes for many successive years. A small marsh of 1–2 ha surrounded by grasslands is adequate. Apparently not strongly territorial; but no loose colonies, or polygyny so far reported.

At onset of breeding season pair soars over marsh, rising to 100–300 m above it, repeatedly calling. ♂ then dives at ♀, who may sideslip, or turn on her back and present claws. ♂ also soars alone, descending from height in short undulating dives, regaining some height after each dive and repeating. Such diving flights are shallower, less steep and vigorous, more circling, than in European Marsh Harrier. No violent 'whirling' evolutions (as seen in Montagu's Harrier) reported.

NEST: solid flattish structures, often built in aquatic vegetation and up to 50 cm above water level. Very often surrounded by water, and base of nest may be partly submerged and sodden. Made of reeds, grass, some sticks, *c.* 1 m across at base, with shallow cup 25–30 cm across, lined with finer material. When same breeding marsh is used, 1 or several nests constructed annually, 1 of several finally used. ♀ collects most material; and material is added throughout incubation and early fledging period.

EGGS: 3–6 eggs, usually 3–4, laid at intervals of 2 or more days; mean (113 clutches of 3–6, probably complete) 3·63 (SAOSNRC). Plain bluish white. SIZE: (108 eggs) 39–54·7 × 31·0–40·6 (46·3 × 37·1); WEIGHT: 36·5–39 g (A. C. Kemp, pers. comm.).

Laying dates: SW Cape July–Dec, peak Sept–Oct; E Cape, Natal, Transvaal May–Nov, peak Sept–Oct (end dry season); Zimbabwe–Zambia Jan–May, peak Feb–Mar (late in rains); Kenya June–July (mid-year cool dry season). Apart from Zambia–Zimbabwe, most eggs laid in dry season, young often fledging in rains (SAOSNRC; EANRC).

Incubation begins 1st or 2nd egg. Unusually for a harrier, ♂ known to incubate (J. Pearson, pers. comm.); evidently unusual, as not observed in South Africa where ♀ normally incubates alone. Called off nest to receive food by ♂ in typical food-pass. Lack of marked sexual dimorphism may account for occasional records of ♂ incubating. Incubation period: at least 34 days.

Eggs hatch at intervals, eldest chick much larger than youngest. 1st buff down partly replaced by thicker white down on head and wings, day 9; still mainly downy, with dark ear coverts, blackish feathers on wing-coverts and back, day 15. Mainly feathered, active, can stand and feed itself, day 21; completely feathered except on head, day 25 on. Once active, hide in tunnels around nest in dry sites, but remain in nest and are aggressive to intruders over open water. Can fly 100 m by day 36; make 1st flights independent of parents days 36–41. Weight at hatch 21 g, increases to 126 day 9; 245 day 15; 350 day 25, thereafter more slowly, to 405 day 31. Tarsus and bill growth rapid to day 21 when tarsus 73 mm, bill 28 mm, thereafter slow, reaching 75 and 30·4 mm at day 31; days 21–36 most growth in flight feathers. These changes associated with ability to feed itself after day 21, releasing ♀ parent.

Early in fledging period ♀ remains on or near nest; aggressive to intruders, but in E Africa may leave chicks unattended for hours, even early in fledging period (J. Pearson, pers. comm.) ♂ brings prey, received in food-pass by ♀ as in other harriers; but 1 record (E Africa) of ♂ feeding young (J. Pearson, pers. comm.). An adult also seen to retrieve young that had fallen from nest in deep water (J. Pearson, pers. comm.). After day 21 ♂ also hunts; full details not available.

Losses of young apparently severe E Africa, usually only 1–2 young reared from 3–4 eggs; adequate data not available. Young follow parents for some time after 1st flight, then separate. Probably cannot breed until at least 2 years old.

References
Malherbe, E. (1970).

Plate 21

(Opp. p. 354)

Circus aeruginosus (Linnaeus). **Marsh Harrier. Busard des roseaux.**

Falco aeruginosus Linnaeus, 1758. Syst. Nat. (10th ed.), p. 91; Sweden.

Range and Status. Resident and Palearctic migrant; breeds NW Africa (*C. a. harterti*) (Morocco, Algeria, Tunisia). Nominate (*C. a. aeruginosus* migrates to tropical Africa and as far south as Zambia and S Zaïre, but only seldom to Zimbabwe or Botswana. Normally frequent, locally common, especially near communal roosts. Reduced in western breeding range recently but possibly less than some other harriers. NW African *C. a. harterti* apparently reduced by swamp drainage and cultivation (C. Vernon, pers. comm.), but has adapted to breed in dry vegetation (Pineau and Girard-Audine 1974).

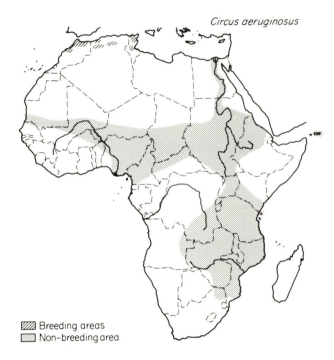

Circus aeruginosus

▨ Breeding areas
▨ Non-breeding area

Description. *C. a. aeruginosus* (Linnaeus): Europe and W Asia (most commonly seen race in most of Africa). ADULT ♂: crown, nape, cream to rufous-buff, streaked blackish; mantle, scapulars, back, dark brownish black, some feathers edged rufous; rump and uppertail-coverts paler, basally whitish tipped rufous, forming pale patch. Lesser and inner median wing-coverts buff, streaked blackish, forming a pale buff line at forward edge of wing. Median wing-coverts dark brown, edged rufous, variable; primary and outer greater coverts silvery blue. Below, chin, throat, breast buff, streaked brown, variable; rest of underside of body chestnut, edged buff to varying extent; underwing-coverts and axillaries paler rufous buff. Wing-feathers above chiefly silver-grey, forming (with coverts) marked pale patch in open wing, innermost secondaries brown. Tail above dull silvery grey, tipped white, inner edges of all but central feathers rufous; below, unbarred silvery grey. Eye yellow; cere and feet yellow.
ADULT ♀: crown and nape creamy, some dark streaks; mantle, back and rump dark brown edged rufous. Lesser and inner median wing-coverts buff, forming a pale line down fore-edge of dark wing. Below chin and throat creamy buff; lower throat and breast dark chestnut brown, broadly edged buff or cream, often forming a pale band across chest. Rest of underside dark chestnut brown. Primary coverts and wing-feathers blackish chocolate brown, primaries paler brown basally, tipped blackish, forming paler patch with dark trail-

ing edge, becoming darker with wear; wings below brown, axillaries and underwing-coverts more rufous than in ♂. Tail above dark brown, with some grey on central feathers and outer webs; below brown. Eye, cere and feet yellow. Much larger and heavier than ♂. SIZE: wing, ♂ 372–418 (393), ♀ 404–426 (413); tail, ♂ 213–237 (224), ♀ 225–252 (239); tarsus, ♂ 79–92 (84·7), ♀ 86–93 (88·4); wing-loading, (1) 30 N/m². WEIGHT: ♂ 405–667 (500), 540–800 (669); other of unknown age, ♂ 525–580 (552), ♀ 600–1105 (775); young ♀♀ may weight up to 1269.

IMMATURE: generally darker brown than adult ♀, lacking creamy head and breast-patch; some have creamy head, nape and leading edge of wing like adult ♀. Some pale brown streaks on hind crown. Wing-coverts dark brown, tipped buff, not forming a distinct pale line on fore-edge of wing. Whole underparts dark brown, some creamy edge to breast feathers and on chin. Wing and tail feathers dark brown, tipped buff, wing-feathers basally whitish, some rufous on inner webs of tail. Eye brown; cere and feet yellow.

♂♂ moult into full adult plumage over 2 years or more, by acquiring more silvery grey on wings and tail. ♀♀ remain brown but acquire creamy crown and forward wing-edge; both may breed before appearing to be fully adult.

DOWNY YOUNG: at first white on crown, throat, breast and belly, pinkish buff above; 2nd down buffy grey. Eye brown, cere and feet at first pinkish, becoming yellow later.

C. a. harterti Zedlitz. Morocco, Algeria, Tunisia. Darker above with, in adult ♂♂, conspicuous silvery grey wings and tail; head and nape whitish, streaked blackish. Below, much paler, clearly streaked brownish black. Slightly larger, wing, ♂ 375–487 (392), ♀ 401–424 (414).

Field Characters. Much larger, more heavily built than any other harrier, ♀♀ as big as Black Kite *Milvus migrans*, but longer-tailed. ♂♂ easily recognized by dark brown plumage, offset by silvery grey wings and tail; adult ♀♀ dark brown with creamy white head and leading edge of wing. ♂♂ cannot be confused with any other ♂♂, or immatures of any harrier in same range. ♀ with creamy breast-band might be confused with immature African Marsh Harrier *C. ranivorus* but generally darker and appear much larger, especially on wing. *C. a. harterti* ♂ distinguishable from *C. a. aeruginosus* ♂ by much more prominent grey patches on wing, and streaky underside; immatures difficult to distinguish.

Voice. Recorded (2a, 19). In winter quarters, almost silent. In breeding quarters, especially in display, vocal. Calls are of 3 types, chattering, wailing or whistling, and chuckling (as in other harriers). Chattering calls, mainly in threat, by ♂ 'ke-ke-ke-ke', by ♀ lower-pitched 'chek-ek-ek-ek'. In display in NW Africa *C. a. harterti* ♂♂ utter whistling, plaintive 'keeee-oo', ♀♀ responding with higher-pitched 'eeeeh-eh' from ground, or 'wheee-ah, wheee-ah'. Chuckling calls of ♂♂ when bringing food are hoarse, low, 'chuck-uck' or 'quek-quek-quek'. ♂♂ in tumbling display make loud rushing sounds with wings, accentuating visual effect. Food call of young, piercing 'peee-yah' and, when handled, angry-sounding chatter; with food, shrill 'ick-erick-erick'. Various variations on these main themes described by Cramp and Simmons (1980).

General Habits. Well known. *C. a. aeruginosus* is migratory from northern colder parts of range to tropical Africa, where it hunts in marshes and swamps, but may unexpectedly be found also *en route* to these in completely dry areas, at up to 3000 m, but less often than other migrant harriers. Roosts communally in marshes, often with other migrant harriers (Montagu's *C. pygargus* and Pallid *C. macrourus*) on, for example, islands in Nile (Meinertzhagen 1956). Leaves roost early morning, and thereafter flies over chosen hunting ground much of day, usually flying higher than plains-loving harriers, 10–30 m above ground, dropping into tall growth to catch prey. Rests on floating masses of vegetation, among reeds or papyrus, occasionally on stumps and posts. Moves back to roost area in late evening, often (like other harriers) perching on ground near before moving in to final roost.

Migration from N Europe begins late Aug with young birds of the year, followed by ♀♀, then ♂♂. Northern populations of nominate *aeruginosus* migratory, but southern and N African *harterti* remain near breeding areas, dispersing locally. Most migrants probably come from N European breeding range, leapfrogging over S European residents, which migrate little, if at all. Migrates on broad front, but some concentration Gibraltar, little at Bosphorus or Suez. Peak passage Gibraltar late Sept (Bernis 1975), first arrivals tropical Africa late Sept–early Oct, reaching equator mid-Oct, more often early Nov. Often follows coastlines and major river valleys in winter quarters. W European ringed birds recovered Algeria, Tunisia; Swedish, British and Finnish birds recovered Mauritania, Senegal, Chad. Return migration begins Feb–Mar and more then cross Mediterranean, common at Cape Bon, Tunisia; all migrants recovered from there moved northeast to Czechoslovakia and USSR. Peak spring passage late Mar, continuing to May. Migrants to E Africa presumed to come from E Europe and W Asia. Migrants are more gregarious than birds in winter quarters, especially at communal roosts, but usually move singly or, at most, in small parties.

Food. Not well known in Africa; elsewhere takes frogs, young marsh birds, mammals to size of young hare, and a few reptiles and insects. Wounded or sick adult water birds are taken; feeds also on abandoned kills of larger birds such as African Fish Eagles *Haliaeetus vocifer* or Marabous *Leptoptilos crumeniferus*. Fish are recorded, probably not taken alive. All prey is taken on ground, or in shallow water or dense aquatic vegetation, rarely caught in flight. Largest prey is taken by ♀♀, ♂♂ more active, hunting further from nest-sites. (For full details see Schipper 1977; Schipper *et al.* 1975.)

Breeding Habits. Of *C. a. harterti* little known; *C. a. aeruginosus* very well known, *C. a. harterti* probably similar. Breeds in Morocco both in coastal marshes and in riverine reedbeds some distance inland. Has also recently been found breeding in maccia away from marshlands, possibly because of drainage or preferred marshland habitat (Pineau and Girard-Audine 1974). In riverine *Phragmites* reedbeds, 2 or 3 pairs may breed within 200 m, forming a loose colony.

♂ in display mounts to great heights, higher than other harriers. Then performs a series of spectacular dives and upward loops, plunging down 40 m or more, regaining height, repeating many times, gradually descending. Several may display close together, and display is long-continued, accompanied by much calling. Spectacular aerobatics such as lateral spinning on axis or looping the loop are recorded elsewhere. Mutual displays with ♀ include soaring together over nest-site, ♂ often diving at her, when she rolls and presents claws. Mating occurs on ground, either on nest or on a feeding platform nearby.

NEST: normally in swamps, often among floating or submerged vegetation, but in NW Africa in recent years often among dense shrubs on dry ground, as formerly used swamps have now been drained (Girard-Audine and Pineau 1974). Large in wet sites, up to 70 cm across top by up to 20–25 cm deep, base often sodden. Recent NW African nests on dry ground (with 1 nest 90 cm from ground in broom brush), 90 cm across by 15 cm thick, made of branches 30 cm long, 1 cm thick, lined with finer grasses. Normal swamp nests made of sticks, reeds, dry grass. ♀ builds most, tearing up material in bill and carrying it in feet; but ♂ brings some material, and may construct false platforms used for feeding or mating. New nest normally built annually in the same general area; old nests occasionally re-used.

EGGS: (N Africa) 3–6, usually 4–5, laid at intervals of at least 2–3 days (clutch takes 7–14 days to deposit). Clutches may average smaller than in N Europe; *C. a. harterti* av. (7) 3·4, cf. 4–6, 70 European clutches (Cramp and Simmons 1980). Rounded ovals; plain bluish white. SIZE: (34 eggs, *C. a. harterti*) 47–51·4 × 37–40·2 (48·9 × 38·2) (Schönwetter 1960); WEIGHT: *c.* 39 g.

Laying dates: NW Africa mid Apr—early May (Heim de Balsac and Mayaud 1962).

Incubation begins 1st or 2nd egg; by ♀ alone, called off nest by ♂ to receive food in typical food-pass. Incubation period: no details *C. a. harterti*, but in European *C. a. aeruginosus* 33–38 days, av. 36 for each egg.

Young hatch over period, eldest always much larger than youngest, which usually dies. Downy days 1–7, when wing-feathers sprout; at 21 days largely, and at 28 days completely, feathered. 1st flight, preceded by wing-flapping from tops of reeds or bushes, at 40 days. Disturbed young crawl into surrounding dense vegetation if possible; otherwise very aggressive to intruders, lying on back, striking with feet and extending claws, hissing. Late in fledging period scatter widely from nest, especially in dry sites.

♀ remains on or near nest up to day 10, brooding or sheltering young. Then may leave for long periods by day, brooding at night. May continue to incubate large clutches, even with active growing young which hatched earlier. ♂ brings all food, calling ♀ off nest to receive it. Requirement increase from 3–4 items/young/day at 12 days to 4–5/young/day at 20–30 days. After 10 days ♀♀ also hunt, and ♂ may visit nest, especially if ♀ absent, or drop food in it for young more often than most harriers.

After 1st flight young remain in nest for 10–15 days; cannot fly strongly till 55–60 days old. Are then fed by parents near nest, flying to receive it. European young then become independent of parents, migrants moving south almost at once, others leaving nesting area. Family parties may rejoin to roost together. Breeding success of *C. a. harterti* not recorded, but recent nests on dry ground frequently failed (Pineau and Girard-Audine 1974); unlikely to exceed British av. of 1·5/nest; 1·9–2·2 young/pair recorded N Europe, but in Camargue, S France (perhaps more comparable), less than 1 young/pair/year (J. M. Thiollay, pers. comm.). Poly-

gamy known in *C. a. aeruginosus*, not recorded but probable in *C. a. harterti*. Life span unknown; oldest ringed *C. a. aeruginosus* 16·5 years. ♂♂ can breed in 2nd year, ♀♀ probably not until 3rd year.

References

Cramp, S. and Simmons, K. E. L. (1980).
Etchécopar, R. D. and Hüe, F. (1967).
Pineau, J. and Girard-Audine, M. (1974).

Genus *Micronisus* G. R. Gray

Small, short-winged, long-legged, long-tailed hawks of semi-arid country. Adult plumage grey above and on breast, finely barred dark grey and white below. Immatures brown, streaked and barred. Resemble a miniature version of *Melierax*, the chanting goshawks, and often merged with this genus (e.g. Brown and Amadon 1968; Stresemann and Amadon 1979); but differ in having a melanistic phase; being much smaller; feeding mainly on birds often caught in flight; and having white woolly down in nestlings. Resemble both chanting goshawks *Melierax* and the typical sparrowhawks and goshawks *Accipiter* in some features, perhaps closer to *Accipiter* in general habits, proportions of wing and body, mode of hunting (Black and Ross 1970) and plumage of downy young. We agree with Smeenk and Smeenk-Enserink (1975) that the Gabar Goshawk is best included in its own monotypic genus, endemic to Africa and S Arabia, pending further detailed study.

Plates 22 and 31
(Opp. pp. 355 and 466)

Micronisus gabar (Daudin). Gabar Goshawk. Autour gabar.

Falco gabar Daudin, 1800. Traité d'Orn. 2. p. 87; Zwart River, Cape Province, South Africa.

Range and Status. Resident throughout Africa south of the Sahara in thornbush, and woodland. Commonest in thornbush and light woodland, less so in heavy woodland, not in forest, but extending to subdesert scrub. Often the commonest small hawk in such areas, but seldom seen, frequent at best but probably more numerous than supposed. Numbers probably reduced by destruction of habitat, but not at present threatened.

Description. ADULT ♂: upperside including upperwing-coverts, and upperbreast plain slate grey; uppertail-coverts white. Belly, thighs and underwing-coverts white, closely

barred grey-brown; undertail-coverts pure white. Primaries and secondaries above dark brown, becoming whitish basally; primaries banded on inner webs, secondaries on both webs, below banded greyish and dark brown. Tail grey brown above, below white, tipped white, with 4 broad dark brown to black bars. Eye red-brown to dark red; cere orange; legs bright red. Sexes similar, ♀ often more heavily barred and larger. SIZE: wing, ♂ 183–204, ♀ 186–215; tail, ♂ 150–165, ♀ 175–185; tarsus, ♂ 42–50, ♀ 51–54. WEIGHT: ♂ 90–123, possibly to 150; ♀ 167–240 (Biggs *et al.* 1979).

A melanistic phase occurs in up to 25% (6·5% Transvaal: Kemp and Snelling 1973); all black, with no white uppertail-coverts; wing-feathers white below, banded black, tail-feathers barred grey and black above, black and white below. Rare intermediates also occur.

IMMATURE: crown brown, streaked white; nape, back, and upperwing-coverts brown; lower breast, belly, thighs, underwing- and undertail-coverts white, barred brown. Primaries barred darker brown, secondaries broadly tipped whitish; below brown barred darker brown. Tail above and below broadly barred dark and light brown. Eye yellowish, cere and feet pale orange.

DOWNY YOUNG: white, down woolly like *Accipiter*, not long and hairy as in *Melierax*. Eye dark brown, cere and legs pale yellow.

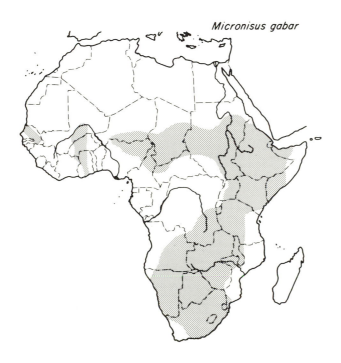

Micronisus gabar

Field Characters. Easily confused with several small *Accipiter* spp., especially Ovampo Sparrowhawk *A. ovampensis*, less so with Shikra *A. badius* and African Little Sparrowhawk *A. minullus*. Red, not yellow, legs diagnostic in adult plumage. Plain grey, not barred, breast, and white uppertail-coverts diagnostic if seen clearly. White rump, heavily barred tail distinguish it from Shikra when flying away; but Ovampo Sparrowhawk and African Little Sparrowhawk both have white or white-barred rumps. Distinguishable from Little Sparrowhawk by lack of any white bars on tail, more slender form, larger size and longer tail. Ovampo Sparrowhawk has white spots on tail shafts, but these hard to see in field. In melanistic phase easily confused with melanistic Ovampo Sparrowhawk, but red, not yellow or orange legs, strongly barred tail and wings, and lack of white spots on tail shafts distinctive. Immatures much browner than any young *Accipiter* spp., breast streaked, lower breast to undertail-coverts barred, not streaked. Care always needed in thick cover for conclusive identification.

Voice. Recorded (2a, 6, 18). Normally silent except in display. Then utters, from perch, reedy piping, 'kew-he, kew-he, kew-heee', and high-pitched, rapidly repeated chant 'sweee-pee-pee-pee-pee' or 'twee-twit-twee-twee-twit', these calls most resembling Didric Cuckoo *Chrysococcyx caprius*. Near nest, rapidly repeated 'twi-twi-twi-twi-twi', by either sex. Begging young utter feeble peeping calls. Voice, distinct from any *Accipiter* sp. of similar size, helps identification if heard.

General Habits. Well known. Inhabits any kind of woodland, but commonest in rather open thornbush (*Acacia–Commiphora*) or light *Acacia–Combretum* woodland. In N Kenya–Somalia extends into subdesert *Acacia* scrub, mainly along water courses. In South Africa mainly in *Acacia* thornbush, in Central Africa in any fairly open woodland, including *Brachystegia*. May occur in any wooded country with 100–400 mm annual rainful. Outnumbered locally by Shikra; but often commoner in habitat than any other small hawk.

Roosts in trees, active soon after dawn. Hunts both in flight and from perches within canopy, actively pursuing flying birds, or snatching them or lizards from ground. Bold, and will enter and breed in towns and villages. Tears open weaver bird nests to obtain young, and robs other nests of nestlings. Very short wings relative to very long tail probably an adaptation for swift hunting in thick cover.

In W Africa between 14°–17°N present all year although regular influx in rainy season (June–Oct) doubles populations; migration movements north–south; non-breeding population present dry season (Nov–Apr) on Ivory Coast (K. Curry-Lindahl, pers. comm.). Elsewhere in Africa, said to be locally migratory, but no good evidence; normally sedentary and resident in any area year-round.

Food. Mainly small birds to size of thrush (80 g), some lizards and insects. Young weaverbirds taken from nests, other young birds. Not well documented; is mainly a swift bird hunter unlike chanting goshawks, resembling *Accipiter* spp., but also often robs nests (Kemp and Snelling 1973).

Breeding Habits. Well known. Breeds in trees, usually thorny, at any height from 3–25 m above ground, usually 5–15 m. Same general area is resorted to annually, but new nest built each year. Early in breeding season ♂ (?) perches on branch of tree and calls at regular intervals, in this respect resembling chanting goshawk; then often found to be more common that supposed. No vigorous aerial displays described, but pairs chase one another among trees.

NEST: built mainly by ♀ (Van Someren 1956); usually a shallow cup of sticks, not more than 35 cm across by 10–15 cm deep, sometimes deeper; may occasionally use old nest of chanting goshawk (Smeenk and Smeenk-Enserink 1975). Lined with earth, pieces of rag, felted cobwebs, but not green leaves (unlike *Accipiter* spp.); normally covered with webs of colonial spiders, possibly deliberately placed there by the birds. Spiders' webs and lack of green leaves in lining normally distinguish it from nests of *Accipiter* spp.

EGGS: 1–4, most often 2, laid at 3–4 day intervals; mean (10 clutches) 2·33. Plain bluish white. SIZE: 33·5–45·0 × 29·0–34·2 (40·7 × 31·5); may average slightly larger in S than N Africa.

Laying dates: Transvaal, Zimbabwe, Botswana Aug–Jan, peaking Sept–Nov, especially Oct (71/116 records) (late dry season); Zambia Aug–Sept (late dry season); Kenya Mar, July–Nov, mainly Sept, Oct (late in cool mid-year dry season); Somalia Mar–June, peak 2nd half of Apr (late dry season); Nigeria Apr, May. Throughout range lays mainly late in dry season, with young in nest or leaving early rains; in E Africa cool mid-year dry season preferred.

Only ♀ known to incubate, probably fed near nest by ♂. Both sexes aggressive to other raptors near nest-site. Incubation period: 33 days.

Young hatch at intervals of 2–4 days; despite large size difference sibling aggression not observed. Brooded at first by female, who feeds them on prey brought by male to nest area. Tail- and wing-feathers sprout at 8 days, body feathers at 10 days. At 14 days, chicks have characteristic 'bib' of brown feathers, longitudinally streaked blackish on upperbreast and throat. By 19 days well-feathered, ♂♂ then distinguishable by smaller size and much greater activity. By 26 days fully feathered; ♂♂ may then fly about, ♀♀ later. Fledging period: *c.* 30 days (Kemp and Kemp 1976). In latter third of fledging period both sexes bring prey, main share by ♂.

2 young may be reared despite size differences, thus resembling *Accipiter* spp. Breeding success probably more than 1/pair/year.

References

Smeenk, C. and Smeenk-Enserink, N. (1975).
Van Someren, V. G. L. (1956).

Genus *Melierax* G. R. Gray

A distinctive genus of 2, perhaps 3 spp. of medium-sized, *Accipiter*-like hawks inhabiting arid countries. Endemic to Africa and S Arabia (Yemen). Adult plumage grey and black, with some white; immatures brown, barred below. Wings rather long and broad, rounded at tips; tail long, graduated. Legs long, slender; toes short, stout, with strong talons. Bills short, nostril round, with tubercle; bare skin of face, eye, cere and legs red in adults.

We agree with Smeenk and Smeenk-Enserink (1975) that Gabar Goshawk *Micronisus gabar* is not correctly placed in this genus, which apparently forms a link between harriers and typical goshawks and sparrowhawks *Accipiter*. The genus also resembles harrier hawks *Polyboroides* and the resemblances, especially in downy plumage, are perhaps not superficial. The 2 spp. are very much alike, but usually ecologically or geographically separated, with little overlap in range.

Plates 22 and 31
(Opp. pp. 355 and 466)

Melierax metabates Heuglin. Dark Chanting Goshawk. Autour-chanteur sombre.

Melierax metabates Heuglin, 1861. Ibis, p. 72; White Nile between 6° and 7°N.

Range and Status. Arid bushlands and drier woodlands of Africa from SW Morocco (*M. m. theresae*) east to Red Sea Province of Sudan, south to Angola, NE Natal and eastern Transvaal. Extralimital in S Arabia (*M. m. ignoscens*). Usually common, sometimes only frequent; numbers probably stable or decreasing slightly with local destruction of arboreal habitat.

Melierax metabates

X Vagrants

Description. *M. m. metabates* Heuglin: from Senegal east to S Sudan, Ethiopia, south to N Zaïre, N Uganda, western Kenya and parts of N Tanzania. ADULT ♂: crown, nape, back and upperwing-coverts slate grey, freckled white on wing-coverts, somewhat browner on back. Uppertail-coverts white, narrowly barred grey. Throat grey, freckled white; upperbreast grey. Lower breast, belly, thighs, undertail-coverts and underwing-coverts white, finely barred grey, bars browner on underwing-coverts. Primaries above terminally black, basally grey on inner webs, vermiculated and freckled white; secondaries grey, freckled and vermiculated white, innermost and scapulars plain grey; primaries below dark grey, and white. Tail graduated, central feathers black, tipped white, outer pairs broadly tipped and banded black and white; below central feathers grey, outer pairs becoming white barred grey. Base of bill and cere red; eye red-brown; legs red. SIZE: wing, ♂ 295–321, ♀ 305–325; tail, ♂ 200–220, ♀ 202–230; tarsus, 81–89; wing-span, ♂ (1) 1039. WEIGHT: ♂♂ 646–695, ♀ 841–852.

IMMATURE: above dull brown where adult is grey, wing-coverts edged paler. Chin and throat whitish streaked dark brown. Upperbreast pale brown, streaked darker brown. Lower breast, belly, thighs, undertail- and underwing-coverts barred brown and white, bars broader than in adult. Primaries dark brown above, grey-brown below and at tips, becoming whitish, narrowly barred darker on inner webs; secondaries above pale brown, faintly barred darker, below grey faintly barred darker below. Tail brown, barred darker brown, tipped whitish above, below grey, barred darker grey. Cere grey, eye yellow or yellowish white, legs dull yellow.

DOWNY YOUNG: greyish white, with long hair-like down on crown and back. Cere dark grey, eye grey, legs pale ochre yellow.

Subspecies differ only slightly from one another.

M. m. theresae Meinertzhagen. SW Morocco (Sous Valley). Darker generally, somewhat smaller, wing, ♂ 288–297, ♀ 315–323.

M. m. neumanni Hartert. N Sudan from Lake Chad to Blue Nile and Red Sea Provinces; wings more vermiculated than in *M. m. metabates*, otherwise very similar; a doubtful race.

M. m. mechowi Cabanis. S Tanzania to Mozambique, Angola and E Transvaal. Similar to *metabates*, but secondaries and greater coverts plain grey, unspeckled; legs, cere brighter, darker red. SIZE: wing, 295–323; WEIGHT: (69) unsexed 478–815; ♂ probably 478–700, ♀ 650–815 (Biggs *et al.* 1979).

Field Characters. Can only be confused with Pale Chanting Goshawk *M. canorus*, from which usually ecologically or geographically distinct. Where they overlap, normally distinguishable by generally darker grey colour, brighter red legs and cere, and, when flying away, barred, not pure white uppertail-coverts (often not easily seen). South Africa *M. m. mechowi* easily distinguished from nominate *M. c. canorus* by grey, not whitish secondaries. Immature is darker brown above, and below has streaked upperbreast, not plain grey-brown; both have uppertail-coverts white, barred brown. Much larger and longer-legged that the Lizard Buzzard *Kaupifalco monogrammicus* and lacks central white tail-band; twice the size of grey phase Gabar Goshawk *Micronisus gabar*, which also has pure white

uppertail-coverts. Great care needed in any area of possible overlap with Pale Chanting Goshawk; otherwise distinctive.

Voice. Recorded (2a, 19, 26). Generally silent outside breeding season; then utters 2 main calls; clear melodious whistling 'wheeeo-whew-whew-whew', or 'wheee-pee-pee-pee' uttered from a tree-top or other conspicuous perch, or in flight. Also a long-drawn, high-pitched 'kleee-u'; rapid 'klew-klew-klew' in excitement and young soliciting food utter shrill, repeated 'klee-klee-klee-klee' for long periods. Resembles voice of Pale Chanting Goshawk, possibly somewhat higher-pitched.

General Habits. Well known. Although generally more widespread than Pale Chanting Goshawk, has been less studied. Inhabits open woodland or thornbush, sometimes (in W Africa) taller Upper Guinea woodlands. Not completely ecologically distinct from Pale Chanting Goshawk; e.g. in W Kenya occurs in deserts west of Lake Turkana while Pale Chanting Goshawk occurs east of same lake. In some areas, e.g. Ethiopia, habitat is no guide to species occurring; but Dark Chanting Goshawk is more likely to be found in broad-leaved *Combretum* or similar woodland than Pale Chanting Goshawk.

Roosts in trees and hunts from elevated perches, tree-tops, summits of tall termite mounds and telegraph poles. In South Africa less inclined to perch on poles, more on trees, than Pale Chanting Goshawk. Spends long periods on same perch, watching intently, then may move to another perch not far away. Seldom soars except in breeding season in display. When moving flies with rapid wing-beats, then glides, usually sweeping up onto new perch from near ground. Generally more arboreal than Pale Chanting Goshawk but will also descend to ground, and walk about like miniature Secretary Bird *Sagittarius serpentarius*; can run very fast on ground. Catches most prey by a quick short stoop from an elevated perch; but can also swoop among trees in dense cover like *Accipiter*; less sluggish than usually stated.

In most tropical areas sedentary; but in W Africa some irregular movement south in dry season, north again in wet season. In northeastern Zaïre non-breeding birds Nov–Apr; in Nigeria, partially migratory with striking increase at Zaria Dec–Feb (K. Curry-Lindahl, pers. comm.). In southern part of this migratory range occurs in dense tall woodland. In South Africa,

perhaps somewhat migratory in E Transvaal, moving north, in winter to warmer localities. Movements not well documented, irregular, nomadic.

Food. Not quantitatively recorded. Mainly lizards, small snakes, small ground mammals, insects. Also gamebirds and doves, perhaps caught when drinking. Large items include full-grown guineafowl, mongoose, francolins, adult Yellow-billed Hornbill *Tockus flavirostris*. In Kruger Park associates both with honey badgers and troops of ground hornbills, watching for disturbed prey. Food caught mainly on ground, but probably can catch birds in flight.

Breeding Habits. Well known. Early in season ♂ sits on top of tree and 'chants' repeatedly; or soars, either alone or with ♀, over breeding area. Normally no spectacular displays, but once a violent, tumbling, twisting, harrier-like vertical descent observed. Better data needed.

NEST: in trees, usually thorny, mainly *Acacia*. Rather small, flat, but strong structures up to 50 cm across, built of sticks up to 50 cm long, with shallow depression in top 25–30 cm across. Sometimes cemented with mud and lined with pieces of dung, dried mud, rags, skin, stones, grass, not normally green leaves. Both sexes build, and roost in or near nest tree during building, which may be prolonged.

EGGS: 1–2 eggs, more often 1, laid (if 2) at intervals of 2 or more days. Plain bluish white. SIZE: (*M. m. metabates*) 48·8–54·5 × 38·7–43·6 (52·6 × 41·3), (*M. m. mechowi*) 48·8–59·3 × 38–45·5; WEIGHT: c. 48–52 g.

Laying dates: W Africa–Sudan Mar, Apr, May; Ethiopia Jan, May; Kenya-Uganda June, July; Zambia–Zimbabwe–Transvaal Aug–Oct, especially Sept–Oct. Most often lays late in, or in height of dry season. Only ♀♀ known to incubate; incubation period unrecorded.

If 2 eggs hatch, 1 young markedly larger than other, and usually only 1 survives. Emergent feathers are blackish on wings, brown on shoulders and tail-coverts. No good details available on parental behaviour, development of young, or duration of fledging period, but ♀ seems to spend most of time at nest, provisioned by ♂.

Reference
McLachlan, G. and Liversidge, R. (1978).

Melierax canorus Thunberg. Pale Chanting Goshawk. Autour-chanteur pâle. **Plate 22**

Falco canorus Rislachi, 1799. Diss. Falcone Canoro, p. 1; South Africa (ex Levaillant). (Opp. p. 355)

Range and Status. Resident; discontinuous, 2 races (*canorus* and *argentior*) in S and SW Africa, and *poliopterus* in Somalia, E Ethiopia, NE Kenya, south to Irangi, Tanzania. Overlaps with *M. metabates* in S Tanzania, Zimbabwe, Limpopo Valley and Angola; but NE population (*poliopterus*) perhaps specifically

distinct from southern (*canorus* and *argentior*). In most of range common, at least frequent, even abundant (10 or more seen daily), e.g. Namibia, Somalia (J. Ash, pers. comm.). Numbers probably stable but sometimes locally reduced by tree destruction by elephants (Tsavo area, Kenya).

Melierax canorus

Description. *M. c. poliopterus* Cabanis: NE Africa. ADULT ♂: crown, nape, upperback- and upperwing-coverts pale grey, palest on nape and upper back. Uppertail-coverts pure white, forming a conspicuous bar at tail-base. Below, chin, throat and upperbreast pale grey. Lower breast, belly, thighs, under-

tail-coverts and underwing-coverts white, narrowly barred dark grey, some undertail-coverts pure white. Primaries black, grey on inner webs, secondaries pale grey, narrowly tipped white and freckled on inner webs; below primaries black, basally grey, secondaries grey with much white basally. Tail above, central feathers black, outer pairs barred grey and white; basally white below. Cere orange-yellow or pink; eye red; legs red. SIZE: wing, ♂ 305–326, ♀ 325–340; tail, ♂ 210–250 (227), ♀ 235–252 (242); tarsus, ♂ 88–97 (93), ♀ 89–100 (94); wing-span, ♂ 976–1041, ♀ 1125. WEIGHT: ♂ (7) 514–581 (548), ♀ (3) 673–802 (724).

IMMATURE: crown, nape, upperback- and upperwing-coverts dull brown, palest on coverts, darkest on back. Uppertail-coverts white, barred brown. Below, upperbreast plain grey-brown; rest of underside including underwing-coverts barred brown and white. Primaries above dark brown, paler on inner webs, barred darker; secondaries brown faintly barred darker; primaries below greyish white, tipped dark brown narrowly barred dark brown; secondaries grey brown, tipped and barred dark brown. Tail above brown, barred dark brown, pale bars whitish or buff on outer pairs, below greyish conspicuously barred dark brown. Cere grey, eye whitish, legs pale yellow, becoming red before full adult plumage is assumed.

DOWNY YOUNG: grey, with long hair-like down on crown and back. Cere greenish, eye at first brown, becoming paler before leaving nest, legs pale yellow.

M. c. canorus (Thunberg). Cape Province north to E Orange Free State. Larger, with paler secondaries freckled with grey; wing ♂ 328–262 (346), ♀ 360–392 (372).

M. c. argentior Clancey. N Cape Province, Kalahari to Botswana and S Angola, east to western Transvaal and Orange

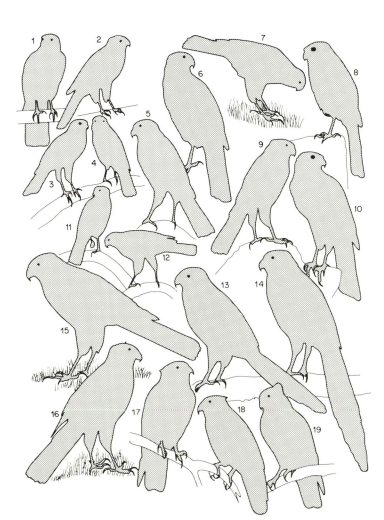

Plate 23

Accipiter castanilius Chestnut-flanked Sparrowhawk (p. 376)
1. IMMATURE, 2. ADULT ♂.

Accipiter minullus African Little Sparrowhawk (p. 380)
3. IMMATURE ♀, 4. ADULT ♂.

Accipiter tachiro African Goshawk (p. 373)
Race *macroscelides* : 5. ADULT ♂, 6. IMMATURE ♀.
Race *canescens*: 7. ADULT ♂, 8. IMMATURE ♀.
Race *tachiro*: 9. ADULT ♂, 10. IMMATURE ♀.

Accipiter erythropus Red-thighed Sparrowhawk (p. 379)
11. ADULT ♂, 12. IMMATURE ♀.

Urotriorchis macrourus Long-tailed Hawk (p. 391)
13. IMMATURE ♂, 14. ADULT ♀.

Accipiter melanoleucus Black Sparrowhawk (p. 387)
15. IMMATURE ♀, 16. ADULT ♂.

Aviceda cuculoides African Cuckoo Falcon (p. 298)
Race *verreauxi*: 17. ADULT ♀.
Race *cuculoides*: 18. IMMATURE ♂, 19. ADULT ♂.

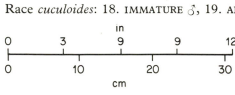

Free State. Still paler, more silvery grey, similar-sized: wing, same as *M. c. canorus*; WEIGHT: (245) (some *M. c. canorus* possibly included) 493–1000 (745·8); ♂ probably 493–750, ♀ 700–1000 (Biggs *et al.* 1979).

Smeenk and Smeenk-Enserink (1975) consider that these 2 southern races should be regarded as a separate species to *M. c. poliopterus*; but pending further field studies of South African forms we agree with Streseman and Amadon (1979) that specific rank is doubtful.

Field Characters. Very like the Dark Chanting Goshawk *M. metabates*, but generally (not always) found in more arid, less wooded country. Appears paler, generally rather larger and slightly longer-legged, cere and legs definitely paler red, tail bars less clear. Pure white rump when flying away is normally distinctive, but uncertain at distance. South African races easily distinguished by white or pale grey secondaries. Immature is best distinguished by plain brown, not streaked upperbreast; otherwise almost indistinguishable from Dark Chanting Goshawk as both have barred rumps.

Voice. Recorded (6, 18, 22a, 28). Rather silent, except in early breeding season; then gives melodious whistling 'chant', 'klueee-kli-kli-kli-kli-kli-klip-kleeep' from tree-top, alternatively rendered 'kleeeuw-kleeeuw-kleeeuw-klu-klu-klu-klu' or 'keeeuw-keeeuw, ki-ki, ki-ki' uttered perched or on wing by both sexes; possibly tones are sexually distinct. 'Sings' with soft melodious squeaking 'seee-seee-seee' uttered with fanned tail. A 'piercing squeak' and a 'fine trilling whistle' also noted (K. Curry-Lindahl, pers. comm.).♀ begging for food, a rapid 'ke-ke-ke-ke-ke' and, in alarm, either sex a long-drawn, quavering 'ee-e-e-e-e-e-e-e' resembling call of rock hyrax *Heterohyrax brucei*. Chicks begging utter rapid 'ke-ke-ke-ke-ke' and, in alarm, soft, whistling 'peeee-uuuuu'; first utter adult 'chant' at 7 weeks age (Smeenk and Smeenk-Enserink 1975). Calls generally rather more mellow and fluting than in Dark Chanting Goshawk, but if heard alone would not be diagnostic.

General Habits. Well known. Strikingly like those of Dark Chanting Goshawk, but rather more inclined to frequent open subdesert and arid thornbush, occurring in South Africa in true deserts (Namib), not often entering broad-leaved woodland, though quite common in *Acacia* wooded grasslands. Both may be found in ecologically similar habitat in different parts of range; but in areas of overlap habitat differences not well described. Pale species is more inclined to perch on, for example, telegraph poles in open than Dark species. In Kenya appear completely separated geographically, but not ecologically, both occurring in subdesert near Lake Turkana, Pale and Dark respectively to east and west of lake; and in Rift Valley in *Acacia-Themeda*

in

| 0 | 3 | 6 | 9 | 12 |

| 0 | 10 | 20 | 30 |

cm

Plate 24

Kaupifalco monogrammicus Lizard Buzzard (p. 394)
1. ADULT, 2. IMMATURE.

Butastur rufipennis Grasshopper Buzzard (p. 392)
3. ADULT, 4. IMMATURE.

Buteo oreophilus Mountain Buzzard (p. 397)
5. ADULT ♀, 6. IMMATURE ♂.

Buteo lagopus Rough-legged Buzzard (p. 400)
7. ADULT.

Buteo buteo Common Buzzard (p. 396)
Race *vulpinus* (Steppe Buzzard): 8. ADULT (pale phase), 9. IMMATURE, 10. ADULT (dark phase).

Buteo rufofuscus Jackal Buzzard (p. 401)
Race *archeri*: 11. ADULT, 12. IMMATURE.
Race *augur* (Augur Buzzard): 13. ADULT,
14. IMMATURE, 15. ADULT (melanistic form).
Race *rufofuscus*: 16. ADULT, 17. IMMATURE.

Buteo rufinus Long-legged Buzzard (p. 398)
Race *cirtensis*: 18. ADULT, 19. IMMATURE.
Race *rufinus*: 20. ADULT ♀, 21. ADULT
♀ (dark phase), 22. ADULT ♂, 23. IMMATURE.

Buteo auguralis Red-necked Buzzard (p. 400)
24. ADULT, 25. IMMATURE.

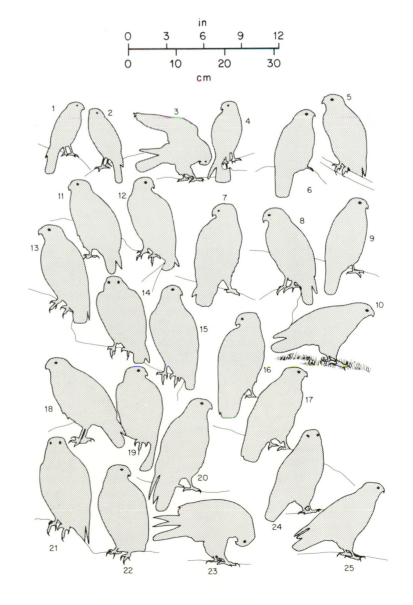

grasslands north (Dark) and south (Pale) of Mount Longonot. On field habits could practically be regarded as conspecific.

Normally sedentary throughout range, living in pairs in defined territories, of *c.* 1·2–2·1 km² in Tsavo National Park, Kenya; in Karoo much larger home ranges, but still mainly sedentary year-round in same localities, although reported to be at least partially migratory in southern Africa, travelling up to 770 km (K. Curry-Lindahl, pers. comm.). Roosts in trees, and soon after dawn is active, perching on series of hunting perches, tops of trees, telegraph poles, stumps, or tall termite mounds. Moves from perch to perch, usually not far, flying low and swooping up to new perch. Sometimes active through hot parts of day, but may rest in shade for hottest midday hours. Seldom soars, normally seen perched, or in short flight from perch to perch, or on ground.

Catches almost all prey on ground, by short swoop from elevated perch. However, can also catch some birds in flight, e.g. quail disturbed by humans, and attacks bustards, francolins (South Africa: W. Tarboton, pers. comm.). If swoop to ground fails, may then walk about, sometimes stamping on ground, e.g. at mouth of rodent burrow, resembling small Secretary Bird *Sagittarius serpentarius*; long legs maintain long tail above ground. Carries prey up to perch before feeding, usually in shade.

Food. Recorded items mainly lizards; but includes some birds, insects, small mammals. 91 recorded items in Tsavo included 51 lizards, 8 snakes, 6 birds (Crested Francolin *Francolinus sephaena*, quail, doves, small passerines), 2 mammals (small rodents) and 15 insects including dung-beetles. Food in South Africa not well recorded, but includes lizards, small mammals, some birds including e.g. bustards, francolins (W. Tarboton, pers. comm.). In Tsavo all recorded prey taken on ground, but has been seen to fly down Harlequin Quail *Coturnix delegorguei* in flight (Smeenk and Smeenk-Enserink 1975; L. H. Brown, pers. obs.). Follows honey badger, jackals, hoping to catch disturbed prey (Penz-horn 1976).

Breeding Habits. Well known. Pairs are dispersed through suitable habitat at regular intervals; only good details from Tsavo, Kenya, suggest territories of *c.* 1·2–2·1 km², but sometimes marked birds hunted outside territories. In other drier areas (e.g. Karoo) territories probably much larger, but not measured. Density at Tsavo probably near optimum, suggesting at least 50–60 pairs/100 km², in much of favoured habitat, similar most of semi-arid NE Africa.

At the beginning of breeding season pair becomes more vocal, calling frequently from close to nest-site. Display not generally spectacular, but includes mutual soaring to height, with wings held at strong dihedral, ♂ above diving at ♀ who turns over and presents claws. Resembles displays of some harriers and also *Accipiter* spp., but main display is *Accipiter*-like, calling from perch, or in flight near nest-site. Copulation takes place on trees near nest-site, or on nest, from early display throughout incubation and even into fledging period.

NEST: built annually in trees, often but not always thorny *Acacia* preferred, sometimes *Euphorbia* (E Africa). Vary from small to fairly large, 40–60 cm across by 15–25 cm thick, of sticks, lined with dung, grass, oddments (such as old nests of the Red-billed Quelea *Quelea quelea*), not green leaves. Built by both sexes, 1 new nest taking 4 weeks. Usually 3–8 m above ground, occasionally higher, depending on available trees; must have some trees to breed at all. Material added throughout nesting cycle, mainly by ♂ after eggs laid.

EGGS: 1–2, laid alternate days if more than 1; Kenya mean (9 clutches) 1·44, 1 more common than 2; 1 pair laid 3 clutches of 1 in successive seasons; South Africa 1–3 recorded. Broad rounded ovals; plain greenish white; SIZE: (*M. c. canorus*) 50·4–60 × 40·5–45·7 (55·8 × 42·9); (*M. c. poliopterus*) 49–57 × 39–42 (55·3 × 41·2); WEIGHT: 52–57 g.

Laying dates: Somalia Feb–June (dry); Ethiopia Feb; Kenya Aug–Oct, and again Feb–Mar (late dry seasons); Zimbabwe Sept–Nov (end dry); Transvaal June–Dec, most Sept–Oct (dry); Cape Aug. In many areas laying occurs late in dry seasons, with young in nest in the succeeding rains.

Incubation begins with 1st egg; mainly by ♀, ♂ rarely, if at all. Much incubation time spent standing, shading eggs, rather than sitting. Period: 36–38 days. Breed more than once a year, and sit on addled egg for more than 50 days; may re-lay if clutch lost.

Although no obvious sibling aggression between 2 young, only 1 ever known to survive; younger usually disappears soon after it hatches. Newly hatched chick is feeble, brooded or shaded by ♀ day and night. Wing- and tail-feathers appear between 14 and 21 days, patches of feathers on shoulders, back, rump, tail-coverts 21–28 days; at 28 days has very characteristic pattern of feathers below, a band of dark brown forming a V-shaped patch either side of breast, and 2 converging lines of banded feathers. Body feathers develop from these areas; hair-like crown and back feathers persist till 42 days, when young almost fully feathered. Fledging period: estimated 49–56 days (*c.* 53).

In first 3 weeks of fledging period ♂ provides all prey for himself, ♀ and young. ♀ broods chick for first few days but thereafter perches on branches nearby; does not really hunt but may collect small prey on ground. When ♂ brings food, sometimes passed from beak to beak but usually deposited by him and collected by her; ♂ seldom visits nest and will not normally feed small young, but may do so even when ♀ present. ♀ usually feeds first, then feeds young. Prey usually decapitated and part plucked if bird. Towards end of fledging period ♂ may bring food in absence of ♀, then may readily visit nest, and even feed chick. Food may be held by ♀ for up to 1·5 h, then may eat it herself without feeding chick.

After 1st flight young remain near nest for *c.* 14 days, returning to it for short periods; at this stage sometimes 'chant' like adults. Still fed by parents near nest, but learn to catch insects themselves before becoming independent *c.* 7 weeks after 1st flight. Adults then still in attendance, but young can catch own prey, and finally leave home range.

Breeding success poor in cases observed; pairs may breed twice in same year, or re-lay after clutch lost, but if successful normally 1 brood/year. Timing of season and success related to lizard abundance not clear. 3 young reared in 9 definite attempts (0·33/breeding attempt) but must actually be higher per pair per year because of repeat attempts, *c.* 0·5 young/pair/year. Drought, affecting prey abundance, may reduce breeding success.

References
Smeenk, C. and Smeenk-Enserink, N. (1975).

Genus *Accipiter* Brisson

The largest genus (45–47 spp.) of diurnal raptors. Cosmopolitan, most varied in Far East. 11 African spp., of which 7 endemic to Africa; includes 2 (*A. rufiventris* and *A. erythropus*) sometimes not accepted as good species. Most varied in forest, but also inhabit any type of dense woodland, not normally in semi-arid areas, where replaced in function by Gabar Goshawk *Micronisus gabar*. Bills short, small, but sharp. Bodies rather slender, wings short, rounded; tail long, sometimes graduated, normally 55–65% of wing length. Legs often long, rather thin, toes and talons long, sharp. Feed mainly on birds; but 1 spp. (*A. badius*) also largely on lizards.

The genus has been very thoroughly studied by Wattel (1973) who divides it into 7 main species-groups, on the basis of the relative proportions of wing, tail and legs, hunting habits, and geographical or plumage variations; at least 4 such groups represented in Africa. He accepts only 45 spp., considering *A. rufiventris* and *A. erythropus* to be subspecies of *A. nisus* and *A. minullus* respectively. We here follow Stresemann and Amadon (1979) in regarding these as good species, at least until detailed study can prove they are not; neither is well known. Of the African species, the nest of 1 (*A. castanilius*) is unknown; 2 (*A. nisus* and *A. gentilis*) are intimately known Palearctic forms, breeding in N Africa; 1 (*A. badius*) breeds in Asia and Africa, and is well known; and 1 (*A. brevipes*) is a Palearctic winter migrant. Of the remainder, 1 (*A. melanoleucus*) has been throughly studied, and 2 others (*A. tachiro* and *A. minullus*) studied in some detail and the 4th (*A. ovampensis*) is less well known. Generally secretive habits and habitat in dense cover make study more difficult. Forest species are suffering reduction through destruction of habitat, but none are at present threatened.

Accipiter tachiro (Daudin). African Goshawk. Autour tachiro.

Falco tachiro Daudin, 1800. Traité d'Orn, 2, p. 90; Knysna, Cape Province, South Africa.

**Plates
23 and 31**
(Opp. pp. 370
and 466)

Range and Status. Resident throughout forested and heavily wooded parts of Africa south of Sahara, from Sierra Leone east to N Ethiopia, thence south to Cape Province; also Bioko (Fernando Po). Normally the commonest, most easily seen *Accipiter* sp. in such habitats, more numerous than it appears, seen frequently to commonly. Habitat being steadily reduced by increased cultivation; but no known race at present threatened. Adapts to some extent to plantations, but prefers natural forest.

Description. *A. t. tachiro* (Daudin): South Africa north to S Angola, Zimbabwe and Mozambique. ADULT ♂: above, dark slate grey, paler on cheeks, sooty on back. Upperwing-coverts blackish brown. Chin and throat white, mottled grey. Rest of underside, including underwing- and undertail-coverts white, barred rufous to varying degree, less marked on undertail-coverts. Sides and thighs rufous-chestnut, indistinctly barred white. Primaries and secondaries above dark brown, whitish basally on inner webs, banded black, below grey, tipped darker, with 3–5 broad blackish bars. Tail above blackish brown, with 3 large white patches on central pairs, forming broken white bars; below grey with 3 broad blackish bars. Eye orange-yellow; cere yellow; feet yellow. ADULT ♀: much larger, usually browner, more heavily barred with dark brown rather than rufous bars below; tail bars less distinct, greyer. SIZE: wing, ♂ 200–225 (212), ♀ 240–257 (247); tail, ♂♀ 168–227; tarsus, ♂♀ 57–69. WEIGHT: ♂♀ (19) 230–510 (341·7); 1 ♂ 230, 3 ♀♀ 337–403; large ♂♂ possibly overlap small ♀♀.

IMMATURE: above dark brown, with some white on nape, feathers edged pale rufous. Below white to buff, with drop-shaped blackish spots on breast, flanks and underwing-coverts

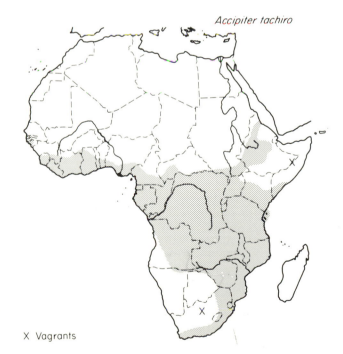

Accipiter tachiro

X Vagrants

barred dark brown, thighs closely barred and spotted sepia-brown, some chestnut intermixed. Wing-feathers brown above, greyish below, broadly barred dark brown. Tail above brown, tipped buff; below grey, with 4 black bars, lacking white bars of adult. Eye brown, cere and legs greenish. Probably assumes adult plumage in 2nd year by becoming more slaty or grey, and developing yellow eye, cere and legs.

DOWNY YOUNG: pure white; cere and feet pale yellowish, eye brown.

Subspecific variation is great, having in the past led to sub-division into 2, sometimes 3 spp. (*A. tousselenii* and *A. macroscelides*). All these intergrade, however, in a long series, and we recognize the following, grouped under possible species, and geographically:

(1) *tachiro* group

A. t. sparsimfasciatus (Reichenow). N Angola, S Zaïre, east to S Mozambique, thence north to S Somalia and west to Uganda, outside rainforests of Zaïre basin. Larger: wing ♂ 211, ♀ 252. Weight: ♂ (2) 227–235, ♀ (7) 300–509. Rather darker, more distinctly barred below, the whitish tail cross-bars indistinct. A melanistic variant occurs, difficult to distin-guish from melanistic *A. melanoleucus*, but usually browner, with distinct grey bars on tail. Probably the best-known race.

A. t. pembaensis Benson and Elliot. Pemba Island. Resembles *A. t. tachiro* more than *A. t. sparsimfasciatus*; in ♂ barring of underside pinkish brown, not greyish brown, white tail bars absent; ♀ greyer above, more rufous below; smaller: wing ♂ (4) 190–200, ♀ (1) 224.

A. t. unduliventer (Rüppell). Forests of E and N Ethiopia. Smaller than *A. t. sparsimfasciatus*; wing ♂ 184, ♀ 216; darker above, more heavily barred below, more washed rufous, tail spots larger, more distinct, forming 3 clear white bars.

A. t. croizati Desfayes. Forests of SW Ethiopia. Darker, browner, both above and below, than *A. t. unduliventer*. Similar-sized: wing ♂ 172, ♀ 217. Described from 2 speci-mens, marginally distinct.

(2) *tousselenii* group

A. t. canescens (Chapin). Forests of upper Zaïre basin, to W Uganda. The most extreme variation, above plain grey, tail with 3 clear white cross-bars; below grey on throat, pinkish rufous on breast and belly, underwing-coverts white, all almost unbarred. Immature almost pure white below, few spots. Smaller, wing ♂ 186, ♀ 216.

A. t. tousselenii (J. and E. Verreaux). Southern Cameroon to Gabon, and lower Zaïre basin. Head and neck clear grey, becoming darker on back; throat grey, clearly demarcated from breast and belly, which are washed with chestnut and barred chestnut on thighs. Tail almost black with 3 clear white bars and a white tip. Somewhat larger: wing ♂ 184–200, ♀ 203–302. WEIGHT: ♂ 150–235, ♀ 270–365 (Brosset 1973).

(3) *macroscelides* group

A. t. macroscelides (Hartlaub). Forests of W Cameroon west to Sierra Leone. More chestnut than *tousselenii* below, more heavily barred; tail with 3 clear white bars and white tip. Somewhat larger: wing ♂ 184–200, ♀ 213–302.

A. t. lopezi (Alexander). Bioko (Fernando Po). Small: wing ♂ 182–189, ♀ 214–216. Rich chestnut below, but distinctly barred; dark above, with three clear white tail bars. Inter-mediate between *tousselenii* group and *macroscelides* group.

Field Characters. The commonest, most often seen *Accipiter* sp. of any forest in Africa, but also emerging outside forest to hunt. Occurs widely alongside Black Sparrowhawk *A. melanoleucus*, and Chestnut-flanked Sparrowhawk *A. castanilius* in W African forests, and along edges with similar-sized Shikra *A. badius*. In highland E Africa–Ethiopia may occur with Rufous-chested Sparrowhawk *A. rufiventris*. Much smaller than Black Sparrowhawk, paler above, barred below; might be confused in melanistic plumage, but browner, with grey barred tail. Much larger than Chestnut-flanked Sparrowhawk, and has 3 clear, white tail bars, less broken than in Chestnut-flanked Sparrowhawk; difficult to distinguish in heavy forest, especially in Zaïre. Immediately distinguishable from Shikra by barred, not plain tail, and generally much more rufous more heavily barred below where they occur together. Rufous-chested Sparrowhawk is much more obviously rufous below than any race of this species in the same range.

Voice. Recorded (2a, 6, 8, 14, 18, 22a, 28). Distinctive, and in habitat diagnostic. Regularly vocal, morning and evening. A sharp rasping, rather high-pitched 'krit' or 'kwit', uttered at 2–3 s intervals, either perching or in soaring display, especially early morning and evening; often mimicked by robin chats *Cossypha* spp. and resembling some calls of Drongo *Dicrurus adsimilis*. At nest, a softer 'wheet', and a musical scream 'keeee-u'. Soliciting ♀♀ and young, a soft, long-drawn mew 'weee-ee-ee-uw'; and at dusk sometimes (probably ♀♀) long drawn 'weeeee-oh', higher-pitched, more musical than similar calls of Black Sparrowhawk.

General Habits. Well known; but only studied in any detail in E Africa. Generally the commonest *Accipiter* sp. in forests, living in deep forest, secondary growth, along riverine strips, in dense *Brachystegia* woodland, in mountain forests, and even in mangrove swamps. Normally, like most of the genus, skulking and difficult to see, remaining within canopy most of time, but may fly across open, especially early morning and evening; and may then fly high above forest. Frequently performs soaring displays above forest canopy (unlike other forest species) uttering distinctive call, when very conspicuous.

Roosts regularly in same area of forest, and is active at dawn, before sunrise, when it establishes its position by calling; falls silent after calling for a few minutes. Thereafter little seen, unless displaying, and remains within cover. Probably hunts most early morning and late evening, often obviously active hunting in semidusk conditions, inside dense forest. Near dusk, frequently displays aerially and calls, then flies into roosting area, often direct from some distance (300–500 m).

Hunts mainly inside forests, perching below canopy, making short flights from tree to tree flying low, sweeping up to another perch if disturbed. Regularly perches near waterholes in forest, waiting for possible prey coming to drink. Uses lines of riverine forest, plantations, or tall hedges as cover behind which to hide, flying along, then suddenly through or over them, surprising prey. Also may fly down prey such as doves in open flight above forest canopy; and may crash into dense vegetation in pursuit of prey. Not really shy, often permitting close cautious approach; but always secretive, even where never persecuted.

Apparently sedentary wherever it occurs, pairs regularly observed remaining in same area year-round.

Food. Not well documented. In E Africa, where studied, *c.* 66% birds and 30% mammals by number, mammals relatively more important by weight. Probably birds normally form most of diet. Kills mammals up to size of full-grown mole rat *Tachyoryctes* (*c.* 200 g) and birds at least to size of Green Pigeon *Treron australis* (240 g), doves and forest passerines possibly commonest prey. In W Africa takes forest mice, squirrels, small birds, insects. Takes some poultry in forest villages, up to 6 weeks old. Relatively stout legs perhaps adapted for taking forest mammals (Brosset 1973), but no positive evidence available, probably prefers birds. Captives trained for hawking can regularly take birds in weight range 90–600 g; and 1 ♀ could kill cock pheasants, perhaps 4–5 times its own weight (1600:350 g) by strangulation (Brosset 1969, 1973). Old birds perhaps learn to handle large prey by experience.

Breeding Habits. Well known to very well known; but studied only in E Africa in any detail (Van Someren 1956). Pair resident in territory year-round and regularly seen. Display at almost any time of year; normally consists of calling, 'krit', from prominent perch, or soaring in circles above forest, sometimes singly, sometimes pair together, calling at intervals; voice of ♀ lower-pitched than of ♂. When circling, glides interspersed with rapid flapping flight, which enables bird to gain height; display is in series of shallow undulations, and sometimes culminates in swift dive into tree-tops, especially in evening. May also fly with measured deep wing-beats, harrier-like, as in some other *Accipiter* spp. Is much more vocal and obvious in display than any other forest sparrowhawk, e.g. Black Sparrowhawk.

NEST: same nesting haunt is used year after year, but new nest normally constructed annually, 20–50 m from that of previous year. Built at any height from 6–20 m above ground, perhaps higher in tall forest, usually in a large fork below canopy, sometimes well hidden among creepers, often thorny. Adults very secretive when building; new nests difficult to locate unless general area known. Normally small structures, not more than 0·5 m across by 15–20 cm deep, of sticks,

with deep central cup, lined with green leaves, 23 cm across by 8–10 cm deep which almost conceals sitting bird; occasionally larger, up to 0·7 m across, 30 cm deep. Normally used only once, but occasionally old nests re-used (Van Someren 1956). Both sexes build, but respective roles little observed.

EGGS: 1–3, usually 2–3, laid at 3-day intervals; Natal mean (22 clutches) 2·4 (Dean 1971); Kenya, usually 2, of which 1 sometimes infertile. Round ovals, plain bluish or greenish white, sometimes sparsely marked brown and lilac. SIZE: (*A. t. tachiro*, South Africa) 41·8–48·4 × 34·6–38·7 (45·7 × 36·4); (*A. t. sparsimfasciatus*, E Africa) av. (6 eggs) 44·5 × 37·0 (Schönwetter 1960); WEIGHT: *c.* 34.

Laying dates: South Africa Aug–Dec, peaking Oct, Nov (late dry season or early rains); Zambia Oct, Dec (early rains); E Kenya Mar, Apr, July–Nov, peaking Mar–Apr and Oct–Nov (both rainy seasons); SE Zaïre Nov (dry season or rains); W Africa unrecorded. Prefers to lay late in dry season or rains, young in nest in rains.

Incubation begins 1st egg; by ♀ only in observed cases, fed by ♂ near nest. ♀ sits very tight, can hardly be induced to leave; but takes spells standing up, and leaves nest for brief intervals, especially when fed by ♂. Incubation period: recorded 28–30 days, short for genus.

Young hatch at 2–4 day intervals, varying considerably in size. No sibling aggression noted. Feathers break through down at *c.* 14 days. By 20 days are fully feathered and can feed themselves; may attempt to tear at prey by 6 days but may continue to be fed by ♀ until 28 days. First fly at *c.* 32 days. Before they fly are very noisy, continually mewing; nest not found earlier can then be located.

♀ broods young closely in early fledging period; ♂ brings prey, and ♀ feeds on same kills. ♂ does not feed young. After feathers appear ♀ perches near nest, but is not so obviously in close attendance as Black Sparrowhawk. In early stages leaves nest to receive food from ♂, but in later stages, after young feathered, takes part in killing and bringing prey. Roosts on nest with young in early fledging period; ♂ sometimes not far away (Van Someren 1956).

Young remain near nest after 1st flight, roosting in it, or in nest tree for up to 2 weeks; thereafter regularly found in nest area for up to 2 months, may become independent 60–70 days after 1st flight. Same pair been known to nest again 3 months after rearing one brood, twice within 1 year. Broods of 1–3 recorded. Breeding success in observed cases high, 12 eggs in 6 observed attempts, rearing 9 young; but other observations suggest frequent non-breeding, so these figures may be above average. Mean overall breeding success in these cases *c.* 2 young/pair/year, but av. probably lower; difficult to establish with certainty because of secretive behaviour, and regular change of nests.

Reference
Brosset, A. (1973).
Van Someren, V. G. L. (1956).

**Plates
23 and 31**
(Opp. pp. 370
and 466)

Accipiter castanilius Bonaparte. Chestnut-flanked Sparrowhawk. Autour à flancs roux.

Accipiter castanilius Bonaparte, 1853. Rev. Mag. Zool., Paris, ser. 2, 5, p. 578; 'South America' = Gabon.

Range and Status. Resident forests of W Africa from Nigeria–Zaïre basin and Gabon. Inhabits only dense forest. Habitat being reduced by human encroachment, but not at present threatened. No good data on numbers, but considered commoner in this habitat than Black Sparrowhawk *A. melanoleucus* (Brosset 1973).

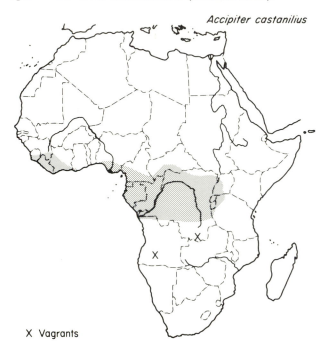

Accipiter castanilius

X Vagrants

Description. *A. c. castanilius* Bonaparte: S Nigeria to lower Zaïre basin, Gabon. ADULT ♂: above, including upperwing-coverts, black. Chin, throat white, barred grey. Breast, belly, flanks, thighs white, barred chestnut, almost wholly chestnut on sides; undertail-coverts white, underwing-coverts white barred grey. Wing-feathers above blackish, below grey, broadly tipped and barred darker, with large white spots on inner webs; scapulars and inner secondaries spotted and barred white, almost entirely white in inner secondaries below. Tail above black with irregular white bars, below grey, tipped black, with 3 broad blackish bands and 3 oval white spots on inner webs forming irregular white crossbars. Eye yellow to reddish brown; cere and legs yellow. ♀ browner above, more heavily barred, and with darker rufous flanks. SIZE: wing, ♂ 152–157, ♀ 174–183; tail, ♂ 130–136, ♀ 152–165. WEIGHT: ♂ (5) 135–150, ♀ (7) 152–200 (Brosset 1973).

IMMATURE: above brownish black, feathers of nape basally white, some buff edges. Below white to buff, with large drop-shaped brown spots on breast; flanks and thighs barred brown; undertail-coverts white, underwing-coverts white, sparsely spotted black. Wing-feathers above blackish, below grey terminally, becoming pinkish buff to white basally, with broad dark bars. Tail above dark brown tipped and broadly barred blackish, extreme tip whitish; below grey with broad sub-terminal and three broad dark cross-bars, some white on inner webs. Eye light grey-brown; cere and feet yellow.

A. c. beniensis Lönnberg. Forests of upper Zaïre basin. Similar, but larger: wing ♂ 162–167, ♀ 188–190.

Field Characters. Difficult to distinguish in overlapping range from African Goshawk *A. tachiro macroscelides*, but easily distinguished from *A. t. toussenelii*, much more chestnut barring below and on flanks. About 20% smaller, relatively longer-tailed, blacker above, more chestnut below than *A. t. macroscelides*. Also has 3 white tail bars, but is more spotted than barred white on tail, scapulars, secondaries. In hand, long slender middle toe, and dusky upperside of toes diagnostic. 3, not 2 white tail bars distinguish it from smaller Red-thighed Sparrowhawk *A. erythropus*.

Voice. Not recorded, undescribed.

General Habits. Scarcely known; a skulking species of very dense cover, rarely emerging into open; but readily takes young poultry near forest villages. Behaviour in natural habitat scarcely known, but probably much commoner than supposed. Within forest, flies low below canopy, causing instant alarm. Recorded (Brosset 1973) attending parties of forest birds, themselves attending columns of driver ants, presumably trying to catch small fleeing mammals or the attendant small birds. Trained captives in France killed birds from 40–300 g; natural food probably mainly birds, perhaps especially weavers of *c.* 40 g (Brosset 1973). Long middle toe indicates bird-killing (Wattel 1973).

Breeding Habits. Unknown, no nest ever found.

Reference
Brosset, A. (1973).

**Plates
22 and 31**
(Opp. pp. 355
and 466)

Accipiter badius (Gmelin). Shikra; Little Banded Goshawk. Epervier shikra.

Falco badius Gmelin, 1788. Syst. Nat., 1, p. 280; Ceylon.

Range and Status. Savannas and wooded grasslands of tropical Asia, and Africa south of Sahara. 2 races resident in Africa, *A. b. sphenurus* and *A. b. polyzonoides*, considered conspecific with Asian races, despite wide gap in range. Usually frequent to common, even in inhabited country; in equatorial savannas inexplicably uncommon. Sea level to 1500 m (in Transvaal), some-times higher (3500 m, Ethiopia) but usually prefers lowlands.

Description. *A. b. polyzonoides* Smith: South Africa north of Orange River north to Tanzania, S Zaïre. ADULT ♂: above, including upperwing-coverts, plain grey, some white spots on wing-coverts; cheeks grey. Below, throat white, finely barred grey; breast, belly, thighs, underwing- and undertail-coverts pale grey-pinkish, narrowly barred reddish brown, almost unbarred on undertail- and underwing-coverts. Wing-feathers above dark grey, whitish on inner webs, below grey becoming pinkish basally, with obscure, darker bars. Tail above, plain grey on central feathers, outer grey, broadly tipped and with 4 dark grey bars; below grey, with 5 darker bars and dark tip. Eye orange red; cere and legs yellow. ♀ larger, darker grey above, more heavily barred below. SIZE: wing, ♂ 165–184 (172), ♀ 184–200 (191); tail, ♂♀ 120–155; tarsus, ♂♀ 40–48. WEIGHT: ♂♀ (56) 75–158 (123) (Biggs *et al.* 1979).

IMMATURE: above, brownish grey, feathers edged paler. Below, white to buff, with drop-shaped streaks of dark reddish brown. Wing above brownish grey, obscurely barred darker; below pinkish rufous, barred darker. Tail above grey, below paler grey with broad subterminal and 3–4 darker brown bars. Eye brown, turning yellow then orange; cere and feet yellow to greenish yellow.

DOWNY YOUNG: buff to off-white, becoming greyish on upper body by 10 days; eyes dark brown, cere and feet yellow.

A. b. sphenurus (Rüppell). Tropical Africa from N Tanzania north to N Ethiopia, thence west to Gambia, in woodlands. Larger: wing, ♂ 171–192 (181), ♀ 183–200 (188). WEIGHT: ♂ 100–150 (122), ♀ 130–150 (141) (Thiollay 1977b). Darker, duller grey above, generally more rufous below.

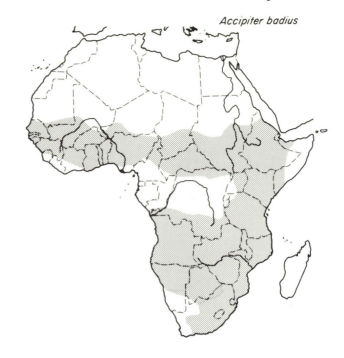

Accipiter badius

Field Characters. The common small hawk of most African lowland savannas and woodlands. Rather thick-set, short-legged for this genus. Adults readily recognized by plain, unbarred tail above, unless spread, when bars visible on outer feathers; no white tailbars or rump. Underside may appear almost wholly pinkish rufous, but when closely examined fine bars visible. Closely resembles the migrant Levant Sparrowhawk *A. brevipes*, but is darker and Levant Sparrowhawk has almost white underwing. Shikra *A. badius* has 5–6, not 6–8 bars in tail, seen from below. Immatures are brown, with less distinct spots or bars below than other small accipiters, have no white bars on tail or rump. In south most likely to be confused with Ovampo Sparrowhawk *A. ovampensis*, which is larger, has white spots on tail shafts, some white on rump and heavier barring below.

Voice. Recorded (1e, 2a, 6, 20a, 26). Very vocal, especially when breeding; distinctive in habitat. ♂ utters clear, bisyllabic 'kee-wit' or 'kee-wik', 2nd syllable higher-pitched; sometimes followed by short, sharp 'kwit, kwit'. ♀ 'kee-eh' or 'keew-keew-keew' falling in pitch, used when receiving food from ♂, and in other situations; also described as mellow 'kew-kew-kew'. In aggression or excitement, rapid 'kee-kee-kee-kee'; ♀ in alarm 'tu-wi'; and ♂ when copulating, rapid 'wi-wi-wi-wi'. ♀ in copulation calls repeatedly, loud, tremulous 'keveeeeeee'. Much more vocal near nest than most accipiters, calls frequently at most times (Smeenk and Smeenk-Enserink 1977; Steyn and Barbour 1973; Tarboton 1978c).

General Habits. Well known generally, but not described in detail away from nest. Frequents wooded grasslands, most abundant in tall grass broad-leaved woodland, e.g. *Combretum-Hyparrhenia*; but in South Africa also in lower, denser *Acacia*-dominated woodland. Population density may be high, W Africa 120 ha/pair (Smeenk and Smeenk-Enserink 1977) or 4·4

pairs/1000 ha (Thiollay 1975b). In Transvaal pairs spaced 1·5–7·3 km apart, av. 4·7 km (Tarboton 1978c), but affected by availability of eucalyptus groves. Much commoner and more obvious than any other small hawk in W African savannas, becoming quite common again south of Tanzania; but unaccountably rare in apparently suitable habitat in E Africa astride equator. May occur from sea level to 1500 m, occasionally higher (3500 m, Ethiopia), but prefers hot lowlands in moderate rainfall, 600–1200 mm/year, with long grass and scattered, deciduous, broad-leaved trees. Rarely enters thickets, but hunts along riverine forest edges.

When resident any area, roosts in same general area nightly, often calling soon after dawn, advertising position. Then moves from tree to tree in range, hunting exclusively from perches, taking all prey by a quick short dash from within cover. When moving from tree to tree, typically flies with undulating motion, a few quick flaps followed by short glide, finally swooping up silently to alight on a branch. Prefers to perch inside leafy canopy, where it searches for prey by looking up, down and to either side; however, takes practically all prey on ground (Smeenk and Smeenk-Enserink 1977; Thiollay 1977b). Not shy, will often allow close approach, and adapts well to intensively cultivated areas of high human population. In pursuit of prey may be very bold, dashing into buildings, or snatching lizards from walls. Has been trained for falconry in India, and will then take quails, not its natural prey in Africa.

In W Africa *A. b. sphenurus* is migratory within range, moving south in dry season, Oct–Mar, breeding, and moving north again in rains, Apr–Sept. Present all but 3 wettest months at 5°N; peak numbers Oct–Mar; at 10°N present year-round, but numbers reduced in rains, May–Aug. Breeding dates vary according to latitude, earlier further south. In South Africa is apparently resident year-round, and in E Africa no evidence of any movement; is unaccountably scarce in equatoral 2-season rainfall regime, but resident where it occurs.

Food. Mainly lizards, but some birds, a few small mammals and some frogs and insects, including termites. Of 464 identified items, 201 were lizards (with a few small snakes), 64 birds, 11 mammals, 6 amphibia, 182 insects and many unidentified. Lizards most important item by weight. Commonest species recorded are skinks *Mabuia* spp. in W Africa, small *Agama* spp., and, in South Africa, *Ichnotropis capensis*. Birds mainly small, in range 9–22 g, occasionally larger, e.g. young of Grey Plantain-eater *Crinifer piscator*. Takes some weaver nestlings and few eggs. Birds may be more important as breeding season food for young. Preference for lizards probably influences lowland distribution in hot climates; but still unaccountably absent E Africa in ideal habitat with abundant lizards. Adult food requirement probably *c.* 40 g/day.

Breeding Habits. Very well known; both African races studied in detail. Pairs either resident in territories or, in migrant W African race, use temporary territories, abandoned after breeding. Strongly territorial, and much more vocal and obvious in breeding season than any forest accipiter. In N Nigeria (and elsewhere, W Africa) display begins Sept–Oct soon after arrival, or onset of dry weather. Pairs chase one another, calling loudly and continuously; may end in soaring or diving display. In commonest advertisement display, 1 or both soar in circles, often very high, calling; a 3rd or 4th bird may take part, and such displays are often triggered off by intruders. Later, perform undulating flights in which 1 or both flies upward with shallow wing-beats, followed by short dive with wings close. When pair established, ♂ feeds ♀ near future nest-site, calling to her, whereupon she responds with begging calls and flies to him. In W Africa, copulation occurs from mid-Nov on, *c.* 2 months after earliest displays. Occurs many times daily, chiefly early morning or late evening, later at any time, often associated with courtship feeding (Smeenk and Smeenk-Enserink 1977).

NEST: in trees, new one usually built annually, occasionally old one or same fork used again (Tarboton 1978c). Built in fork well below canopy, sometimes on lateral branch, in W Africa 5–15 m above ground, in Transvaal often in plantations of exotic eucalyptus at 8–18 m above ground, av. 13 m. Small, rather frail structures of thin sticks, resembling large doves' nests, 25–30 cm across by 7–15 cm deep. 1 (South Africa) contained 608 pieces of material, mainly twigs and leaf petioles, lined with bark chips (174 pieces); lining of bark chips normally distinctive for this species. In W Africa almost all building done by ♂, but in South Africa ♀ takes major share in observed case. ♂ often flies about, carrying twigs, and calling. Pair may build several nests working on up to 3 at same time, finally using 1. ♀ in W Africa remains near nest, calling excitedly when ♂ brings material (Smeenk and Smeenk-Enserink 1977; Tarboton 1978c).

EGGS: 2–3 eggs, usually 2, laid at 2–3 day intervals; W and South African mean (31 clutches) 2·23; no observed latitudinal difference. Rounded ovals; dull bluish white, sparsely or rather heavily spotted brown, with grey undermarkings. SIZE: (59 eggs, *A. b. poly-*

zonoides) 33·4–40·0 × 28·1–31·3 (36·8 × 29·9); mean (100 African eggs, both races) 36·7 × 29·4; WEIGHT: 16–17 g (Schönwetter 1960).

Laying dates: W Africa Jan–May (late in dry season), varying according to latitude—lat. 5–7°N Jan–Feb, chiefly Jan; lat. 8–10°N Jan–Apr, especially Feb–Mar; north of lat. 10°N Apr–May (Smeenk and Smeenk-Enserink 1977); Ethiopia Mar–May (late dry); E Africa Jan, Feb, May, Nov, no clear peak; Zambia Sept–Dec, mainly Sept–Oct (late dry); Zimbabwe, Botswana, Transvaal, Natal Aug–Jan inclusive, peaking Oct (end dry season). If first clutch lost, may re-lay within 2–3 weeks. Throughout range, except E Africa (where few records indicate no definite preference), lays late in dry season, so that young are in nest in subsequent rains; scarcity in E Africa perhaps associated with bimodal rainfall pattern. Impossible to correlate laying dates with food abundance or availability on present evidence.

Incubation begins 1st egg; in all observed cases mainly by ♀, fed near nest by ♂. Typically, ♂ arrives, calls 'ke-wick' (up to 50 times if ♀ does not answer), and ♀ flies to him to receive prey. ♂ brings 5–9 items daily, av. 7. While she feeds, ♂ may sit on eggs briefly and ♀ may then push him off when returning. ♀ may also leave eggs unattended, mostly when only 1 egg of clutch has been laid (up to 51% of time); later sits very tight, eggs unattended at most 12% of time. ♀ may change position repeatedly and position of eggs also changed often. May leave to obtain twigs, but normally stays within 50 m and apparently does not catch own prey. Food requirement estimated 37 g/day (Tarboton 1978c). Towards end of period ♀ reluctant to leave nest, even to receive food from ♂. Incubation period: 28–29 days (3 good records).

Chicks hatch at intervals, possibly shorter than laying interval. ♀ eats or carries away eggshells. Down white at first, becoming grey later (diagnostic for species). Egg tooth disappears between 5–9 days; at 10 days wing- and tail-feathers emerge; at 12 days first contour feathers appear; chick is largely feathered by *c.* 20 days, fully feathered at 28 days. Climbs out onto branches at 30 days, and makes 1st flight unaided at 32 days (Smeenk and Smeenk-Enserink 1977).

In early fledging period all food brough by ♂, up to 15 small items (including many insects) per day. ♀ remains on nest with chick, brooding for up to 31% of time at day 4, reduced to nil by day 14; when off nest returns to brood in rainstorms. Share of sexes in hunting after day 14 not well known, but only ♀ ever seen to feed chicks, and all prey probably brought by ♂, 8–10 (av. 8·7) items per day, but individual items larger, including more birds; food intake of ♀ and 1 chick estimated 54 g, rising to 65 by day 14 (Tarboton 1978c).

After 1st flight young remain near nest for some time, gradually moving further away. Only ♀ seen to feed flying young, roles of parents now apparently almost reversed, ♀ bringing most or all prey. Young start to hunt for themselves at 35–40 days, but are still mainly dependent on parents up to 63–70 days. Post-fledging period occurs in rains, and successful W African adults do not migrate north until young independent (Smeenk and Smeenk-Enserink 1977; Thiollay 1975b).

Some pairs apparently do not lay annually (Transvaal: Tarboton 1978c) and many broods or eggs, and sometimes adults, lost to predators (harrier hawks and genet cats suspected). 0·8–1·1 young/pair/year recorded several areas (Ivory Coast, Nigeria, Transvaal), av. (29 pairs) 0·93 young/pair/year overall. Young can probably breed in 1st year after fledging, so that, if mortality before sexual maturity were *c.* 50%, adult life need only average *c.* 2 years.

References
Tarboton, W. (1978c).
Thiollay, J.-M. (1975–78).
Smeenk, C. and Smeenk-Enserink, N. (1977).

Accipiter brevipes (Severtsov). **Levant Sparrowhawk. Epervier à pieds courts.**   **Plate 22**

Astur brevipes Severtsov, 1850. Bull. Soc. Imp. Nat. Moscou, 23, No. 3, p. 234, pl. 1–3; Voronezh Province, Russia.   (Opp. p. 355)

Range and Status. Palearctic winter migrant to Africa, breeding Greece and Yugoslavia east to Iran and Caspian Sea area. In Africa Egypt south to S Sudan, possibly W Ethiopia; recorded also Niger, Zaïre and Tanzania. Uncommon to rare as far as known; but perhaps sometimes overlooked, mistaken for Shikra *A. badius* in tropical Africa. Large numbers seen on migration at Bosphorus, but apparently few at Suez, main wintering area apparently unknown (Stresemann and Amadon 1979). Should be looked for in NE tropical Africa.

Description. Full description omitted as apparently scarce even in Egypt; for details see Brown and Amadon (1968).

Field Characters. Forms a superspecies with Shikra, occupying a breeding range between tropical Africa and Asian races of Shikra. Could be confused on migration routes with European Sparrowhawk *A. nisus*, but has longer more pointed wings. Underwing surface of ♂ appears almost plain white, very conspicuous in flight, not strongly barred as in European Sparrowhawk. ♀ is also paler below, finely barred brown on body, less so on underwing-coverts. Black wing-tips always diagnostic (Porter *et al.* 1976). Where occurs in range of African races of Shikra (S Sudan, Ethiopia?), ♂ distinguishable by almost plain white, unbarred undersurface, darker grey upperside, with 6–8, not 4–5, dark bars on outer tail feathers. ♀ more heavily barred than Shikra ♀. Young much more heavily barred and streaked dark brown below than juvenile Shikras. In the hand, 5th primary always much shorter than 4th, in Shikra 5th primary only a little shorter. Averages 15–20% larger (wing ♂ av. 218, ♀ 235) than Eritrean Shikra *A. b. sphenurus* (wing ♂ av. 182, ♀ 188).

Accipiter brevipes

Voice. Not recorded. Said to be distinctive, 'kawaker-kawaker' Mackworth-Praed and Grant (1952); but other descriptions suggest 'kee-wik, kee-wik' very like Shikra.

General Habits. Little known in Africa. In breeding range, apparently kills more birds, and fewer lizards and insects than Shikra. Practically nothing recorded of habits in Africa; but said to resemble those of bird-eating European Sparrowhawk rather than Shikra. Identity of any unusually large pale 'Shikra' should be checked, especially in Sudan or W Ethiopia.

Food. Small birds and mammals; also insects.

Accipiter erythropus (Hartlaub). **Red-thighed Sparrowhawk; Western Little Sparrowhawk. Epervier de Hartlaub.**   **Plates 23 and 31**

Nisus erythropus Temminck = Hartlaub, 1855. Journ. Ornith., 3, p. 354; Rio Bontry, Ghana.   (Opp. pp. 370 and 466)

Range and Status. Resident; two races, inhabiting respectively upper Guinea forests, and forest from Cameroon to W Uganda; not outside forest. Skulking, small, difficult to see, probably commoner than sup- posed; as seen only uncommon, at best frequent. Habitat decreasing through destruction for cultivation, and apparently would not adapt well to such destruction; decreasing, but probably not threatened.

Accipiter erythropus

Description. *A. e. erythropus*: Gambia to Nigeria. ADULT ♂: above, including upperwing-coverts, practically black, some white spots on scapulars; uppertail-coverts, practically black, some white, forming a clear bar. Chin and throat white, contrasting strongly with black cheeks. Rest of underside, including underwing-coverts, grey, almost entirely obscured by fine chestnut vermiculations, thus appearing chestnut; undertail-coverts white. Wing-feathers above blackish, below tipped blackish grey, bases whitish, barred blackish brown. Tail above almost black, with large white spots on inner webs of all but central feathers, forming broken white bar when spread; below grey, with 8 dark bars on outer, 4 on innermost feathers. Eye orange to red; cere and legs orange-yellow. ♀ similar, more distinctly barred on chestnut underside, browner above, larger. SIZE: wing, ♂ 145–152, ♀ 154–169; tail, ♂ 108, ♀ 118; tarsus, 43–45.

IMMATURE: above brown, many feathers edged rufous, especially on nape, uppertail-coverts brown, tipped white. Below buffy white, sparsely spotted and barred dark sepia and black, sides and thighs barred chestnut; underwing-coverts pale rufous, spotted dark brown. Wing-feathers above dark brown, below pinkish buff basally, broadly tipped and barred dark brown. Tail above dark brown, with 2 irregular broken buffy bars; below greyish buff, barred dark brown as in adult. Eye red or orange, cere and legs yellow.

DOWNY YOUNG: unknown; probably white.

A. e. zenkeri Reichenow. Cameroon to E Zaïre, W Uganda south to N Angola, Gabon. Larger: wing ♂ 146–149, ♀ 174–180. WEIGHT: ♂ 78–82, ♀ 132–136 (Brosset 1973), also 1

♂ 94, 1 ♀ 170 (Friedmann and Williams 1971). Darker above, chestnut below, occasionally more clearly barred; less distinct white tail spots.

This species has been amalgamated with the African Little Sparrowhawk *A. minullus* as a subspecies by Wattel (1973); but was considered a good species by Brown and Amadon (1968) and is so considered by Stresemann and Amadon (1979). Grounds for this include occurrence close to range of *A. minullus* in W Uganda without any intermediate types, and strikingly different immature plumage. The case is analogous to the '*tachiro*' and '*tousselenii*' groups of the African Goshawk *A. tachiro*, but apparently more clearly demarcated. Further study needed.

Field Characters. Occurs alongside forest races of African Goshawk and Chestnut-flanked Sparrowhawk *A. castanilius*. Distinguishable by very small size, rather short tail, with 2 irregular white bars composed of spots, and white uppertail-coverts forming in adults a clear, in immatures an indistinct bar. Adults are much blacker above than the African Little Sparrowhawk, somewhat larger, and not strongly barred below. Immatures quite different, whitish below, not strongly barred, or with the large dark roundish spots of the African Little Sparrowhawk.

Voice. Recorded (2a, 27). Shrill, reedy 'kew-kew-kew', resembling that of African Little Sparrowhawk.

General Habits. Little known; a retiring skulking species of dense forest country, seldom emerging into open. When once seen, said to be fairly tame, often allowing close approach. Flies low below canopy, rarely, or never emerging above it. Individuals trained for falconry in France attacked both birds and small mice, and took birds in weight range 8–40 g (Brosset 1973). Sedentary where found.

Food. Small birds, including waxbills, small weavers; also many insects, e.g. large butterflies, dragonflies.

Breeding Habits. Scarcely known. In Sierra Leone, a subadult ♀ paired with an adult ♂ observed building in tall tree, inaccessible, not further described. Eggs would thus have been laid May (rains). 2 eggs of *A. e. erythropus* are bluish white. SIZE: 37·8–38·8 × 30·6–31·6; WEIGHT: estimated 20·5 g.

Reference
Brosset, A. (1973).

Plates 23 and 31
(Opp. pp. 370 and 466)

Accipiter minullus **(Daudin). African Little Sparrowhawk. Epervier minulle.**

Falco minullus Daudin, 1800. Traité d'Orn. 2, p. 88; (ex Levaillant) Gamtoos River, Cape Province.

Range and Status. Resident savannas and thornbush areas of E, NE and southern Africa from Uganda, S Sudan, Ethiopia, south to Angola south of the forest, thence south to Cape Province; inexplicably absent from suitable habitat, W Africa. Probably commoner than supposed, but at best seen frequently, usually uncommon. Not at present threatened, and can probably adapt to habitat changes if trees not completely denuded.

Description. ADULT ♂: above, slate grey to nearly black, including upperwing-coverts; uppertail-coverts white, forming conspicuous white bar. Throat white, sharply defined from blackish sides of face. Breast to mid-belly greyish white, washed rufous, narrowly barred brown, barring less distinct on undertail-coverts; underwing-coverts pale rufous, barred blackish. Wing-feathers above brown, barred black, notched white; below grey, washed rufous, barred darker grey. Tail above blackish, tipped white, with 2 conspicuous white spots on inner webs, forming a broken white bar when spread; below whitish, washed rufous with 4 dark bars on inner and 7–8 on outer feathers. Eye yellow-orange; cere, legs, yellow. ADULT ♀: similar, browner, more heavily barred. SIZE: wing ♂ 136–145 (141), ♀ 156–164 (159); tail, 105–130; tarsus, 38–46. WEIGHT: ♂ (3) 75–85 (80·9); unsexed (prob. ♀) 82–105.

IMMATURE: crown blackish, rest of upperside dark brown, edged buff; uppertail-coverts brown, tipped white. Underside white, sparsely streaked on throat, and on breast and belly with numerous large round dark brown spots, fewer on undertail-coverts; underwing-coverts pale rufous spotted blackish. Wing-feathers above dark brown, becoming whitish basally on inner webs, paler on secondaries, barred dark brown, below pinkish grey, barred dark grey-brown. Tail above dark brown, tipped buff with 3–4 broad dark bars, below whitish, washed rufous with 3–4 broad dark bars on inner, 7–8 on outer feathers. Eye brown, then turns yellow; cere greenish yellow, legs yellow. Moults into approximately adult plumage within 3 months; birds in residual immature plumage sometimes breed at less than 1 year old.

DOWNY YOUNG: white, becoming more buff later. Eye brown, cere greyish cream, legs fleshy orange.

Field Characters.

A tiny, plump-looking, rather short-tailed, short-legged sparrowhawk, almost unmistakable because of very small size (that of a small dove). Adults recognizable by 2 broken white bars on tail, and white uppertail-coverts. Immatures in 1st plumage normally distinguishable from any other by small size, large blackish round (not streaky or drop-shaped) spots on breast and belly. Appears to be not much more than half the size of Shikra *A. badius*, darker above, with barred, not plain-looking tail. Much smaller and stumpier-looking than Ovampo Sparrowhawk *A. ovampensis*. Rarely occurs within dense forest, but if so, distinguishable from closely allied Red-thighed Sparrowhawk *A. erythropus* by lack of chestnut on underside, paler upperparts; barring on wings and tail similar in pattern.

Voice.

Recorded (6, 27). Generally very silent, except near nest. A rapid, high-pitched, reedy 'kew-kew-kew-kew-kew' uttered in series of 5–6 calls. Voice of ♂ higher-pitched than ♀, a rapid 'whit-whit-wheet'. Also a chipping call, 'tsik, tsik'. Begging call, a longer-drawn 'kyak' or 'ki-ack' at intervals of 1–3 s. High-pitched 'kweeek-kweeek' by ♀ when mating. Small begging young give feeble cheeping calls.

General Habits.

Well known. Not shy, but little seen, as normally remains within dense cover. In E, NE and southern Africa, frequents woodlands, *Acacia* thornbush, and may breed in highland forests, Kenya. In semi-arid thornbush (e.g. *Acacia–Commiphora*) mainly along riverine strips and thickets; and in Transvaal preferring eucalyptus groves for breeding. Absence from apparently suitable habitat W Africa inexplicable, either on grounds of food supply or possible competition.

Diurnal behaviour not well known. Roosts in trees, but hard to observe by day. Once located, can be easily watched as confiding and tame. Spends most of day perched in cover, seldom flying far. Usually perches well inside canopy, making short flights to catch birds or insects, when very agile, twirling and jinking almost like

Accipiter minullus

flycatcher. Catches most bird prey by short swift dash from cover, but also recorded to jump upwards, seizing fast-flying prey as it passes (Jackson and Sclater 1938). Bold and aggressive for its size, with surprisingly powerful grip. Apparently resident where it occurs, no movements recorded.

Food.

Mainly small birds in weight range 10–40 g, a few larger birds up to own weight, *c.* 80 g. Occasionally small mammals, lizards, and many large insects (especially by immatures soon after 1st flight).

Breeding Habits.

Very well known; one nest studied throughout cycle (Liversidge 1962). Regularly territorial, pairs occurring in same areas successive years, but always breeding therein. Aggressive near nest-site, attacking much larger birds up to size of Hooded Vulture *Necrosyrtes monachus*. Density, Transvaal, 1 pair/100 km² , perhaps higher elsewhere (Tarboton 1978b). Same general site used for breeding many years (at least 20, Kenya).

Courtship begins, South Africa, up to 6 weeks before egg-laying. No spectacular displays, but increased calling early morning followed by both sexes carrying twigs, with fluttering wings; twigs not always taken to nest, often dropped. In pre-copulation display ♂ fluffs feathers, exposing especially white uppertail-coverts and white tail-spots; raises tail, droops wings, sways head from side to side; ♀ assumes exaggerated begging posture, crouching, with quivering wings. Copulation frequent, on tree near nest, or on nest itself, frequency decreasing just before egg-laying (Liversidge 1962).

NEST: usually small, slight structure of sticks, sometimes stout at base; at most 30 cm across by 15 cm deep, often smaller, semi-transparent, with shallow central cavity 13–18 cm across by 5 cm deep. Cavity lined with finer sticks, and green leaves added after onset of incubation. Lining of leaves with no bark chips diagnostic, and distinguishes nests from those of Shikra or

Gabar Goshawk *Micronisus gabar*. Built at any height from 5–25 m above ground, in a high main fork or large fork on lateral limb, shaded, below canopy; in Transvaal *Eucalyptus* plantations selected in *Acacia* woodlands. Both sexes build; in observed cases most twigs brought by ♀, who also initiates collection. Much material dropped, or carelessly placed, and ♂ interrupts building to catch prey, to feed ♀ before egg-laying. New nests normally built annually, in same general area, sometimes re-used (Tarboton 1978b).

EGGS: 1–3, usually 2, laid at 48-h intervals; mean (23 authenticated clutches) 1·91; any reported clutch of 4, and all marked eggs considered doubtful (Colebrook-Robjent and Steyn 1975). Round ovals, unmarked white or greenish-white. SIZE: (43) 32·6–37·8 × 26·9–28·4 (34·8 × 28·1); WEIGHT: *c*. 18 (clutch of 2), 35–40% of ♀ bodyweight.

Laying dates: South Africa Sept–Dec, peaking strongly Oct (early rains, perhaps triggered by first rain); Zambia Aug–Oct (late dry season); Kenya Mar and Oct–Nov (late dry–early rains); Ethiopia Mar, Apr (late dry). Apparently prefers to breed everywhere late in dry season or early rains, with young in nest in rains.

Incubation begins 1st egg; at first intermittent, later sitting tight. Carried out by both sexes, ♀ more than ♂, *c*. 80% daylight and most nights; 1 ♂ has been known to sit all night. ♂ feeds ♀ near nest, several times daily, calling her off to receive food, chiefly early morning and near midday. ♀ apparently kills no prey in incubation; incubation spells by ♂ often associated with feeding ♀. Incubation period: 31–32 days, longer than for some larger species.

Eggs hatch within 24 h. Days 1–5 chicks wholly downy, 1st feather show at 6 days, fully feathered by 16 days; weight increase very rapid to this stage, thereafter slower. No sibling aggression recorded. Young exercise, move to branches, practise wing-flapping frequently 17–21 days; at this stage develop voice like adult, and threaten siblings and adults with food. Can feed themselves after 20–23 days, make 1st flight independent of parent at 25–26 days.

Days 1–10 of fledging period, ♀ broods chicks; continuous brooding days 1–5 then decreases by day, ceasing by day 13; but chicks may still be shaded from sun. ♂ broods chicks sometimes in days 1–10, thereafter not recorded. He brings all prey throughout fledging period, up to 7 kills daily. ♀ is called off nest by ♂; flies and snatches prey, often without stopping, returns to nest and feeds chicks; ♂ does not feed chicks.

Flying young remain near nest for up to 2 weeks, in that time learning to feed themselves; first prey, insects. Precocious, beginning adult display calling while still dependent on parents, especially young ♂♂. Probably independent within 1 month, moult into adult plumage within *c*. 3 months and can breed within 1 year of fledging. No good available data on breeding success, but 1–2 young reared per successful nest.

References

Colebrook-Robjent, J. R. and Steyn, P. (1975).
Liversidge, R. (1962).
Tarboton (1978b).

Plates
22 and 31
(Opp. pp. 355
and 466)

Accipiter ovampensis Gurney. Ovampo Sparrowhawk. Epervier de l'Ovampo.

Accipiter ovampensis Gurney, 1875. Ibis, p. 367, pl. 6; Okavango River, South West Africa.

Range and Status. Resident Ghana and Togo east to Ethiopia, south to eastern Transvaal and Namibia; in open savanna and bushveld. Apparently regular resident only in southern African range, where breeds; may be a transequatorial intra-African migrant to W Africa, not breeding there. At best frequent, usually uncommon, in most of Africa uncommon to rare.

Description. ADULT ♂: (normal phase) above, including upperwing-coverts, slate grey, paler on sides of head sometimes with white on nape. Uppertail-coverts clearly barred white. Chin and throat grey, freckled with white; rest of underparts, including underwing-coverts, white, barred dark grey or brown, but almost unbarred on thighs and undertail-coverts. Primaries and secondaries dark brown above, below grey, barred dark grey or blackish. Tail above brown, tipped white, with 4 triangular white marks in centre of each feather, including the shafts, and 4 darker bars; below white, barred dark grey to blackish. Eye brown; cere orange; legs dull orange or yellow; bill basally orange, ♀ larger, browner, more heavily barred. SIZE: wing, ♂ 210–225, ♀ 245–253; tail, ♂ 145–150, ♀ 160–190; tarsus, 43–53. WEIGHT: 119–305 (194·5); ♂ probably 105–190 (av. *c*. 140), ♀ 180–305 (av. *c*. 260) (Biggs *et al.* 1979)). ADULT ♂: (melanistic phase) almost entirely dull black, showing some dark barring on greyish flight- and tail-feathers below, some white on uppertail-

coverts, white spots on tail shafts; eye red, legs and cere orange-yellow.

IMMATURE: crown streaked brown and blackish; head sometimes all buff, crown darker, surrounded by white eyebrow. Rest of upperparts dark brown, edged and tipped rufous; feathers of nape basally white, and uppertail-coverts spotted white. Below, chin and throat pale rufous, breast richer rufous, streaked dark brown; rest of underside white, washed rufous, barred brown or rufous, paler on undertail-coverts and thighs. Underwing-coverts whitish barred dark brown. Primaries above dark brown, barred black, secondaries dark brown, paler, spotted white on inner webs; below terminally grey, basally whitish, barred black. Tail above dark grey, broadly banded black, white shaft-spots on grey parts; below grey towards tip, basally white, tipped black with 5 black bars. Eye brown, cere and legs dull yellow.

DOWNY YOUNG: white; eye dark brown, cere and legs pinkish orange.

Field Characters. In all plumages, if seen well, rather small head and, from rear, white spots on tail-shafts distinctive. Resembles Gabar Goshawk *Micronisus gabar* most, but distinguished by yellow-orange, not red, legs, barred breast and less white on uppertail-coverts. Melanistic adults are duller, more slaty black than melanistic Gabar Goshawks, have orange, not bright red, legs, faintly barred tail and wings. Immatures distinguishable by lack of white on uppertail-coverts, less heavily streaked breast and white tail spots; white eyebrow often obvious and distinctive. Distinguishable from Shikra *A. badius* (in similar habitat) by barred, not plain-looking, tail and white or white-marked uppertail-coverts; also considerably larger.

Voice. Not recorded. Distinctive, generally unlike that of any similar-sized sparrowhawk. A high-pitched whistling 'weeeet-weeet', and a repeated, short, high-pitched whistle 'kee-kee, kee-kee', somewhat like some calls of the Rufous-chested Sparrowhawk *A. rufiventris*, ♀ a loud, fast-repeated 'kwee-kwee-kwee' on seeing ♂ with food; a harsh, low 'krr-krr-krr' in threat. Chicks at first utter weak cheeping; later 'kee-kee-kee-kee' like adults. Decidedly more vocal and bold near nest than most accipiters.

General Habits. Little known, especially outside southern Africa. Inhabits semi-arid broad-leaved savannas, and especially *Acacia* bushveld, also mopane *Colophospermum mopane* woodlands, sometimes *Brachystegia* or *Baikaeia* woodland. Often remains within thick cover, but may also perch right in the open. In South Africa has adapted to mixed farmland and plantations, locally more common than other accipiters, breeding in eucalyptus groves. Density varies from 1 pair/30–35 km² to 1/350 km², and population in Transvaal has increased through exotic plantations (Tarboton, 1978b).

Hunts from within cover, but also often perches on open tree-tops, attacking prey in swift short dash. Flushes and pursues flocks of, for example, weavers, and catches birds in flight. May perch above waterholes, awaiting possible prey coming to drink. Gives the impression of being very swift, active species, unusually graceful for an accipiter on the wing, in this way also resembling Gabar Goshawk.

Believed to be migratory, but not well documented; in Transvaal probably resident. Little observed north of equator, or in E Africa, but breeds rarely in Kenya; no W African breeding records, suggesting it is entirely migrant to W Africa.

Food. Mainly birds, perhaps some insects. ♂ apparently kills small passerines in weight range 10–60 g, ♀ may kill larger doves, *Streptopelia* spp. Recorded prey includes bee-eaters, woodpeckers, hoopoes, pipits, weaver birds; smallest a prinia, largest small doves, up to 120 g.

Breeding Habits. Well known; several Transvaal nests studied (Kemp and Kemp 1975b). Some pairs are very strongly territorial, attacking other much larger birds and raptors (e.g. Long-crested Eagle *Lophaetus occipitalis* and Augur Buzzard *Buteo rufofuscus*, Kenya). Will nest in same plantation with other small *Accipiter* spp., e.g. African Little Sparrowhawk *A. minullus* or Shikra, but not with powerful Black Sparrowhawk *A. melanoleucus* (W. Tarboton, pers. comm.).

NEST: in trees; in Transvaal, plantations of eucalyptus selected, and have probably resulted in increase of the species. All known Transvaal nests in exotic plantations.

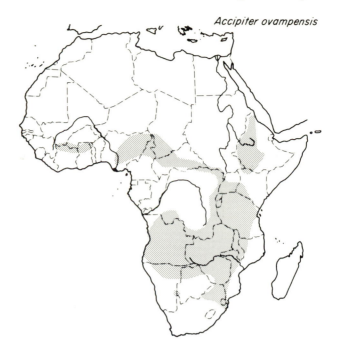

Accipiter ovampensis

1 Kenya nest in mixed olive and *Croton* forest. New nests built annually, but in same general area, usually 10–15 m above ground, sometimes higher. Recognizably larger than nests of Shikra or African Little Sparrowhawk, of sticks, *c.* 50 cm across by 20 cm deep, with central cup 15 cm across by 5 cm deep. Normally unlined, except for a few bark flakes, but sticks used in construction often have green leaves, probably not collected from ground. Both sexes build, ♀ apparently most. ♀ remains near nest before laying, and is fed there by ♂. Copulation frequent, just before egg-laying, near nest, often associated with feeding.

EGGS: normally 3, probably laid at intervals of 2 days. Rounded ovals, whitish, more or less heavily blotched and spotted light and dark brown with slaty or purplish undermarkings. Normally 1 egg in each clutch is heavily marked, other 2 less heavily, but not related to laying date. SIZE: (26) 37·8–45·4 × 32·2–36·5 (42·23 × 33·15).

Incubation begins 1st egg, by ♀ only, fed by ♂ (up to 3 kills/day). Period: 33 days (Kemp and Kemp 1975b).

Chicks hatch at intervals corresponding to laying intervals; can barely lift heads. At 12 days down is thicker, greyer, tips of primaries just emerging. By day 18 primaries well developed, some contour and feathers of crown showing; day 24, well-feathered back and wings, still downy on breast and head. Make 1st flight at 33 days; are then free of down, but wing- and tail-feathers not yet full grown.

Only ♀ broods young; ♂ brings all prey up to day 18 of fledging period after which ♀ probably helps. Full details not recorded, but ♀ stands on nest much of time after days 4–5, and may leave it to perch near for up to 30 min. ♂ hunting rate increases to up to 7 kills per day, and at end of fledging period ♀ probably helps, killing larger birds (doves). In few recorded cases, only 2 out of 3 chicks reared as 3rd died (Kemp and Kemp 1975b). Nothing recorded of post-fledging behaviour.

References
Brown, L.H. (1970).
Kemp, A. C. and Kemp, M. I. (1975b).

Plate 22

(Opp. p. 355)

Accipiter nisus (Linnaeus). European Sparrowhawk. Epervier d'Europe.

Falco Nisus Linnaeus, 1758. Syst. Nat. (10th ed.), p. 92; Europe = Sweden.

Range and Status. Resident and Palearctic migrant; *A. n. punicus* breeds Morocco east to Tunisia, north and west of Atlas Mountains. Nominate *A. n. nisus* is scarce winter migrant to tropical Africa, straggling as far south as Kenya and Tanzania. *A. n. punicus*, frequent to common in wooded areas; migrant *A. n. nisus* uncommon to rare tropical Africa, perhaps overlooked. Formerly common winter migrant to parts of N Africa, reduction observed in recent years reflecting reduction of species in European breeding range through agricultural pesticides (Brosset 1971).

Accipiter nisus

▨ Breeding area
▧ Non-breeding areas

Description. *A. n. nisus* (Linnaeus): Europe, migrating to Africa. ADULT ♂: above dark slate, including upperwing-coverts; some white on nape, forehead tipped rufous, scapulars white, barred rufous, longer uppertail-coverts tipped white. Sides of head rufous; chin and throat white to buff, streaked dark brown. Rest of underside, including underwing-coverts white, tinged more or less rufous, barred rufous and brown. Wing-feathers above dark brown, outer webs and tips greyish, inner grey basally white, barred dark brown; below grey, paler basally, barred dark brown. Tail above dark brown, washed slate, tipped white, with broad subterminal and 4–5 narrower dark bars; below grey, barred dark brown. Eye bright yellow; cere and feet yellow. ♀ much larger, browner generally, more heavily barred darker brown below than ♂ and much heavier. SIZE: wing, ♂ (96) 186–208 (198·3); ♀ (120) 223–248 (236·4); tail, ♂ 135–154, ♀ 166–176; tarsus, 50–56. WEIGHT: ♂ (102) 117–186 (137·6); ♀ (79) 210–305 (256·2).

IMMATURE: above, dark brown, feathers edged rufous; below white to pale buff, streaked dark brown on chin and throat; breast, belly, underwing-coverts and scapulars barred dark brown; undertail-coverts paler, tipped buff. ♀ has narrower buff edgings above, underparts usually white, more strongly streaked and barred with darker brown than ♂. Eye greenish grey, becoming yellow; cere and legs greenish yellow. Immatures moult into adult plumage in first summer, and may breed in immature plumage.

DOWNY YOUNG: white; 2nd down with buff tinge; eye dull, dark, becoming greenish grey; legs, cere yellowish.

A. n. punicus Erlanger. Resident NW Africa; similar, averaging slightly paler, slightly larger; wing ♂ 203–214 (209); ♀ 237–243 (242).

Field Characters. Migrants entering Africa via Bosphorus-Suez route can be distinguished from Levant Sparrowhawk *A. brevipes* by rufous cheeks, and heavy barring below on wings and tail in adults; adult ♂ Levant Sparrowhawk much paler generally, with black wing-tips, also diagnostic in ♀ and immatures. European Sparrowhawk has 4–5 visible tail bars, Levant Sparrowhawk 5–6. Within Africa proper could scarcely be confused with much smaller Shikra *A. badius* or normal Gabar Goshawk *Micronisus gabar* (occurring in same range); Gabar Goshawk has white rump, Shikra much paler grey and has plain unbarred tail above when flying away. In Ethiopia might occur with similar-sized Rufous-chested Sparrowhawk *A. rufiventris*, but this has plain unbarred rufous underside, including underwing-coverts, and white throat; barring on wings and tail in flight similar. In NW Africa large ♀ *A. n. punicus* could be found with small ♂ Northern Goshawk *A. gentilis*; very similar, but Northern Goshawk has proportionately longer wing, relatively shorter tail, usually a marked white eyebrow; care required in this case.

Voice. Recorded (not Africa) (2a). Normal call a sharp, rapidly repeated 'kew-kew-kew-kew', higher-pitched in ♂ than ♀; also rendered 'kek-kek-kek-kek-kek', 'kiv-kiv-kiv-kiv'. With food, low 'kew-kew-kew' or 'keoo-keoo-keoo' in alarm; excitement or display 'kirrr-kirrr' or 'tirrr-tirrr'. Young emit long-drawn, begging mews. Voice is not diagnostic, except from Shikra or Levant Sparrowhawk, but higher-pitched and calls much more rapidly uttered than of Northern Goshawk. Migrants in Africa generally silent but some collected first attracted attention by calling (Jackson and Sclater 1938); mainly vocal near breeding localities.

General Habits. Little known in Africa, intimately known in Europe. European migrants entering Africa follow well-known routes through Bosphorus-Suez, and via Gibraltar; autumn passage mainly Oct. Many also cross Mediterranean, especially in spring when they are caught by falconers at Cape Bon, Tunisia, and other places; used to hunt quail, and later released unharmed; usually only ♀♀ used (Brosset 1971). Migration via Cape Bon in spring suggests that those entering Africa via

Middle East first move westward, returning north in spring.

Habits of migrants in rest of Africa little recorded; presumably similar to those of species elsewhere, frequenting woodlands, forests, but also hunting over open country. NW African resident race evidently behaves like European frequenting wooded areas, hunting also in open country. Typically hunts by flying along or behind cover, suddenly slipping over to surprise small birds, especially flocking species such as sparrows and finches. Most prey caught by surprise, rather than speed. Often very bold, pursuing prey into farmyards, for example, but like others of the genus is generally retiring, normally hard to see considering its numbers.

In tropical Africa practically nothing recorded on habits; but occurs in savannas and thornbush rather than forest, behaving in such surroundings much like any other small accipiter. Those seen or collected in Kenya were in semi-arid *Acacia* woodland, not frequented by resident Rufous-chested Sparrowhawk.

Food. In Africa little recorded. In Europe, a very wide variety of small birds, av. 39 g, with 82% of prey less than 50 g (Tinbergen 1946). House Sparrows *Passer domesticus* and finches are favoured prey, both in Europe and NW Africa. Largest prey killed (by ♀♀ only) woodpigeons, 500–600 g. In NW Africa kills mainly small birds, occasionally jackdaws, partridges (Etchécopar and Hüe 1967).

Breeding Habits. In Europe, intimately known, perhaps best studied of any raptor (e.g. Tinbergen 1946; Newton 1973); in NW Africa little detail described, but presumably similar. In Europe is territorial, pairs frequenting the same areas from year to year, but also hunting up to 12 km outside territory, or within territories of pairs which fail early in breeding season. Display consists of soaring with spread tail; slow flapping flight; and diving with half-closed wings. In slow flapping flight 1 or both birds fly to and fro over same area, with slow deliberate wing-beats, rising sharply at each turn, analogous to undulating display flights of many other raptors. Birds may then spiral upwards, increasing speed of wing-beats, and finally plunge in steep dive, sometimes swinging up again to repeat. ♂♂ seen performing thus may be diving at ♀♀ perched near nest-site. Most display occurs early morning, in sunny weather.

NEST: in trees, in Europe at any height from 1·5–25 m above ground. Conifers preferred, also often in NW Africa (Etchécopar and Hüe 1967). Some nesting site used for years, but new nest constructed annually; site often near clearing or track in forest. Most nests built close to main trunk in conifers, in forks well below canopy in deciduous trees. New nests slight structures of sticks, not more than 35 cm across, semi-transparent; later are lined with green leaves and chips of bark. Built almost entirely by ♂, feeds ♀ near nest while building.

EGGS: (NW Africa) 2–5 recorded; NW Africa mean (53 clutches) 4·0; much lower than in Europe (4·9–5·0 Britain; 4·7 Denmark); in Europe laid at 2–3 day intervals. Broad ovals, pale bluish green, rarely unmarked, usually heavily spotted and blotched, mainly round broad end, with dark brown and chocolate, much more heavily marked than in any tropical African species. SIZE: (15 eggs, *A. n. punicus*) 39·7–43·8 × 28·0–34·0 (41·0 × 31·7) (Schönwetter 1960); mean (60) 36–46 × 29–35 (Etchécopar and Hüe 1967); WEIGHT: *c.* 23; clutch of 4, 36% of ♀ bodyweight.

Laying dates: NW Africa mid Apr–mid June (late spring).

Incubation begins 2nd or 3rd egg; by ♀ only, fed near nest by ♂, who calls her off to receive food, av. *c.* 3 items daily. In later stages she seldom leaves and is fed on nest. Period: 32–36 days. av. 35 each egg (Newton 1973).

Chicks hatch at intervals over up to 4 days but, as ♀ does not start to incubate with 1st egg, little size difference at hatching; no sibling aggression observed. 1st feathers show at *c.* 13 days, largely feathered by day 21, and can then feed themselves on prey brought to nest. Almost completely feathered day 28, then climb out on branches and make 1st flights, independent of parents at 24–30 days. Can be sexed early in fledging period by smaller size and thinner tarsi of ♂♂. Also ♂♂ fly earlier than ♀♀ and are generally more active.

In first 20 days of fledging period ♀ remains at or on nest, ♂ brings all prey. Rate of killing increases immediately after hatch, av. 6 items/day in 1st week, up to 8 or more by day 20; ♀ also feeds on these. ♀ broods young almost continuously days 1–5, regularly to days 8–10, thereafter reduced, standing on nest, or perched beside it till young partly feathered at 20–21 days. Thereafter ♀ also kills prey, often larger items, helping to increase food supply in late fledging period. ♂ not known to feed young, and if ♀ is lost before they can feed themselves they die.

Fledged young remain near nest, dependent on parents for 21–28 days after 1st flight; this period probably correlated with hardening of flight feathers. Await arrival of parents with food, usually ♀ at this stage, and in last stages fly to meet her, taking food foot-to-foot in air, or on perch near. Then become independent and disperse from area. NW African race does not migrate, remaining in breeding range in winter.

Breeding success in NW African race not known, but elsewhere normally *c.* 1 young fewer than av. clutch size; in *A. n. punicus* may be *c.* 3·0, much higher than in tropical species. In Europe broods in recent years adversely affected by pesticides; not known how severe such effects may be in NW Africa.

References
Etchécopar, R. D. and Hüe, F. (1967).
Heim de Balsac, H. and Mayaud, N. (1962).
Newton, I. (1973).
Tinbergen, L. (1946).

Plates
22 and 31

(Opp. pp. 355
and 466)

Accipiter rufiventris Smith. Rufous-chested Sparrowhawk; Red-breasted Sparrowhawk. Epervier menu.

Accipiter rufiventris A. Smith, 1830. South Afr. Quart. Journ., (1), p. 231; no locality, South Africa.

Range and Status. Resident from South Africa north to Angola, Katanga District (S Zaïre), Kenya and Ethiopia; normally in forests or plantations, local in highland forests in E and NE Africa. Near sea level at Cape, up to 3700 m Ethiopia. Uncommon to frequent; threatened in some E African and Ethiopian localities by habitat destruction, but perhaps increasing South Africa in plantations.

Accipiter rufiventris

Description. *A. r. rufiventris* Smith: S Africa north to Zaïre and Kenya. ADULT ♂: above, dark slate, including upperwing-coverts; some concealed white on nape and scapulars. Below, chin and throat white or pale rufous, rest of underside, including underwing-coverts, rufous, faintly barred on undertail-coverts. Wings above dark brown, with white on inner webs, and indistinct paler bars; below whitish, broadly barred blackish brown. Tail above brown, tipped whitish, with 4 paler crossbars; below whitish, broadly barred blackish brown. Eye yellow; cere and feet yellow. ♀ similar; larger, generally browner above, richer rufous below. SIZE: wing, ♂ 200–225 (214), ♀ 230–245 (235); tail, ♂ 155–162, ♀ 180–195; tarsus, ♂♀ 49–57. WEIGHT: unsexed 185, 210.

IMMATURE: dark brown above, many feathers edged rufous. Below white, streaked on breast, barred on belly and thighs pale rufous, sometimes appearing all pale rufous like adult. Tail- and wing-feathers barred dark and lighter brown, pattern similar to adult. Eye yellow, cere and legs yellow.

DOWNY YOUNG: white; 2nd down greyer; soft parts not described.

A. r. perspicillaris (Rüppell). Highlands of Ethiopia; darker, somewhat larger, wing ♂ 192.

Wattel (1973) and several others have considered this species a race of the European Sparrowhawk *A. nisus*. However, it is separated from any breeding race of *A. nisus* by

at least 3000 km; is nearly plain rufous, not clearly barred below; and its distribution is analogous to that of the African Marsh Harrier *Circus ranivorus* and Mountain Buzzard *Buteo oreophilus*, in highlands of E and NE Africa. As it is little known, we retain it as a species pending further study.

Field Characters. Adults within range could hardly be confused with any other *Accipiter* sp. as whole undersurface of body and underwing-coverts almost plain rufous, with little barring; lack of obvious bars would also distinguish it from European Sparrowhawk. Immature is more barred below, but bars not so distinct as in European Sparrowhawk. Somewhat resembles immature Gabar Goshawk *Micronisus gabar*, but not heavily streaked on breast, or as heavily barred on belly and underwing-coverts. Also frequents quite different habitat.

Voice. Not recorded. Resembles European and several other sparrowhawks. A sharp, staccato 'kew-kew-kew' possibly by ♂. Long-drawn mew, 'weeeeuw', possibly by begging ♀ or young. Other described calls include a wheezy 'weeeee'; in alarm a harsh 'chek-chek-chek'; and a call of 3 long-drawn out whistles. Not diagnostic, especially from many calls of African Goshawk *A. tachiro*.

General Habits. Little known. In South Africa occurs in thick woods and forests, not in open country. Frequents both natural forests and exotic plantations; probably has benefited from establishment of the latter and occurs in towns (e.g. Cape Town, Kirstenbosch gardens). Requires such forests or woodlands to breed, but hunts also in adjacent open country, and quite a small plantation of 1–2 ha may harbour a pair. Further north, in Zambia–Zimbabwe–Malawi, mainly in evergreen montane forests, but also in denser *Brachystegia* woodlands, and along riverine forest strips. In Kenya, almost entirely in mountain forests at 2000 m or over, up to 3000 m; and in Ethiopia in highland forests from 2000–3700 m, from *Juniperus* (cedar) forests at lower forest edge to dense thickets of Giant Heath *Erica arborea* at upper limit of trees in, for example, Semien Mountains. This type of distribution, with altitude range increasing from Cape Province to Ethiopia, is shown by several other species, e.g. Mountain Eagle Owl *Bubo capensis*.

Habits not well described, but apparently resemble those of European Sparrowhawk, flying along or through cover, surprising small birds. In Ethiopia readily flies across large tracts of open country to hunt, provided any small areas of forest available (e.g. round churches). Swift, bold and aggressive wherever it occurs. Sedentary throughout range year-round.

Food. Birds, not well detailed. Said to take young poultry. A few small mammals, some insects, e.g. flying termites.

Breeding Habits. Little known. In display 1 or both birds circle high above nesting wood, calling frequently, but no spectacular displays noted.

NEST: in trees, often exotic conifers, or eucalyptus. Small structures of sticks, lined with green leaves; no data on share of sexes, duration of occupation, but thought to build new nest annually, like several other accipiters.

EGGS: 2–4 eggs; Natal mean (14 clutches) 2·93 (Dean 1971). White, heavily blotched at broad end with brown, variable. SIZE: (38 eggs, South Africa) 36·3–44·5 × 27·5–36·1 (41·0 × 32·5); WEIGHT: *c.* 23.

Laying dates: South Africa Oct, Nov (spring) in Cape; Aug–Dec, peaking Oct–Nov, early rains in Natal; Zambia Oct (early rains); Kenya, no definite records,

possibly Nov–Dec., after main rains (Mau Narok), on evidence of displaying birds. Ethiopia, no records.

Incubation period: unknown, no details.

Young hatch over several days. 2nd down develops at 4–6 days, primaries emerge at *c.* 10 days, contour feathers on back and breast at *c.* 15 days; can stand at 16–18 days, shortly after feed themselves. 1st flight at *c.* 25 days, thereafter remain at least 7 days in area of nest. Both parents said to bring prey to young; but probably ♂ only in early stages. Cycle poorly described, but probably similar to other small *Accipiter* spp.

Breeding success not recorded; but said to be good in E. Transvaal, 2–3 young reared per nest (D. Allan, pers. comm.).

Accipiter melanoleucus Smith. Black Sparrowhawk; Great Sparrowhawk. Autour noir.

Accipiter melanoleueus [sic] A. Smith, 1830. South Afr. Quart. Journ., (1) p. 229–230; no locality = South Africa.

Plates 23 and 31
(Opp. pp. 370 and 466)

Range and Status. 2 subspecies; forested areas of Africa south of the Sahara from Senegal east to Ethiopia, thence south to Cape Province from near sea level to 3000 m. Generally in natural forests, but adapts well to exotic plantations, and occurs in small isolated forests and along riverine forests in woodlands. Probably decreasing through destruction of habitat in parts of tropical Africa, but increasing in South Africa through establishment of plantations in previously open plains (Tarboton *et al.* 1978).

Description. *A. m. melanoleucus* Smith: South and E Africa west to Gabon. ADULT ♂: crown to tail, including upperwing-coverts, black, concealed white spots on nape and scapulars. Cheeks black; chin, throat, breast, centre of belly and undertail-coverts white. Sides of breast, flanks and thighs black, blotched white; axillaries and underwing-coverts white, spotted and barred black. Wing-feathers above dark brown, almost black, becoming basally white on inner webs; below, white, barred black. Tail above dark brown, broadly tipped black with 4 indistinct darker bars; below white, broadly barred blackish. Eye red; cere and legs yellow. ♀ usually considerably larger, browner or more slaty above, and with heavier black markings on sides, thighs and underwing-coverts. Although no overlap apparent in recorded measurements small ♀♀ may overlap large ♂♂. SIZE: wing, ♂ 287–295, ♀ 333–342; tail, ♂♀ 210–267; tarsus, ♂♀ 73–90. WEIGHT: (19) unsexed 476–980 (699·3); ♂ probably 450–650; ♀ 750–980 (Biggs *et al.* 1979).

Completely black melanistic adults are known to nominate *A. m. melanoleucus*, not recorded in *A. m. temminckii*.

IMMATURE: above, head brown, streaked blackish; rest of upperside blackish brown, many feathers edged rufous. Below, buff to pale rufous, variably streaked black, ♂♂ generally more rufous with narrow streaks, ♀♀ paler, almost white, with larger drop-shaped black streaks. Wings above blackish brown, barred darker; below dark rufous, broadly barred dark brown. Tail above dark grey-brown, broadly barred blackish; below greyish rufous, barred blackish. When leaving nest eyes are brown, becoming grey shortly after. Cere dark greenish grey; legs pale yellow. More rufous colour of ♂♂ below appears sex-linked, but this not invariable (Hartley 1976).

DOWNY YOUNG: white; eye brown, cere greenish, legs pale yellow.

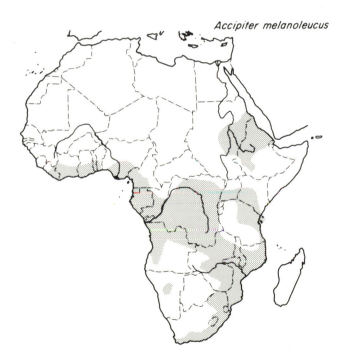

Accipiter melanoleucus

A. m. temminckii (Hartlaub). Africa from Senegal to Central African Republic, south to Gabon and Congo. Similar, rather blacker above; somewhat smaller: wing ♂ 251–273, ♀ 290–310; WEIGHT: ♂ 430–490, ♀ 650–790 (Brosset 1973).

Field Characters. The largest resident accipiter in most of Africa. In normal adult plumage almost unmistakable, black above, white below, with conspicuous black-barred patches on thighs, flanks and sides. Dark red eye is almost invisible within black cheeks. Could not normally be mistaken for any other resident accipiter in adult plumage. Immatures browner, rufous or almost chestnut below, streaked black; might be confused with immatures of African Goshawk *A. tachiro* (especially small ♂♂ with large ♀♀ of latter), but these normally whiter below, more heavily spotted with drop-shaped black markings. Melanistic adult is blacker than that of

African Goshawk, with less evident paler tail-bars. Long tail and pure white underside of body normally diagnostic from any small forest eagle (such as Ayres' Hawk Eagle *Hieraaetus dubius* or Cassin's Hawk Eagle *Spizaetus africanus*), together with habits.

Voice. Recorded (2a, 6, 18). ♂♂, ♀♀ and young distinct. Usually silent except near nest. ♂ normally utters single, sharp high-pitched 'kyip' or 'chip', sometimes disyllabic 'ker-chip', 1st syllable audible only at close range. ♀, normally a loud, rather harsh 'kew-kew-kew-kew-kew' repeated 5–6 times; sometimes a single short 'chep', duetting with ♂ 'kyip'. Both utter long-drawn mew 'keeeeee-uw' or 'weeeeee-u'. Young utter more sibilant harsher versions of adults' call; begging 'schreeeee-uw', and low whistles with prey. In copulation, a distinctive trilling 'trrrrueeee-trrrueeee' probably by ♀. Voice of ♂ always higher-pitched than that of ♀; that of young harsher, less whistling and musical.

General Habits. Well known. Very difficult to observe, as normally remains inside forest canopy, seldom soaring above it, though perhaps does so more often in W Africa. Flies silently from perch to perch, and may allow close approach, remaining absolutely motionless, regarding observer fixedly in 'snaky' posture, head held low, feathers compressed. Although retiring and difficult to see, is not shy, and can be extremely bold in human presence. Such wary behaviour unconnected with persecution. Despite preference for dense shade and cover individuals emerge to sunbathe on open lawns (O'Keefe, pers. comm.).

Hunts both inside and outside forest. Locates prey either by sight or by ear (e.g. calling Scaly Francolins *Francolinus squamatus*). Within forest, hunting methods little observed, but recorded attending swarms of driver ants, presumably to catch birds themselves intent on securing disturbed insects (Brosset 1973). Attacks pigeons and doves in the open, pursuing active fast-flying doves for up to 1·5 km, forcing them to ground

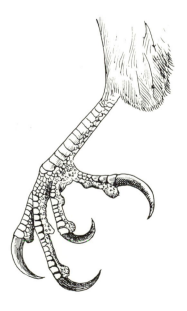

and catching them after spectacular series of jinks and twists (I. S. C. Parker, pers. comm.). Also attacks poultry, especially free-ranging in African village compounds, and is then extremely bold. Despite observed attacks on poultry, very few poultry remains recorded.

Is active dawn to dark, hunting at any time of day; but perhaps most early morning, late afternoon. Roosts in trees, often near nest-site, but outside breeding season very difficult to locate. Migratory southern Nigeria May–Aug (K. Curry-Lindahl, pers. comm.). Elsewhere apparently sedentary in home range year-round, but also capable of extraordinary wanderings; one taken out at sea near Dakar (Murphy 1924), others seen migrating through arid thornbush N Kenya, or setting out to fly across wide freshwater lake (Brown and Brown 1979).

Food. Mainly birds, especially doves, pigeons. 385 recorded items (Brown and Brown 1979; Tarboton *et al.* 1978) included 380 birds (98·7%). Of these, 230 doves (*Streptopelia*, *Aplopelia* spp.), 37 larger pigeons (*Columba*, *Treron*) and 41 francolins (*Francolinus*). Av. weight of prey estimated (Kenya) 220 g (range 25–1500, most 80–300). Other birds include African Goshawks, hornbills (*Tockus*, *Tropicranus*), turacos, Crowned Lapwings *Vanellus coronatus* and various passerines, smallest being Forest Greenbuls *Andropadus* spp. Range of prey clearly incidates hunting in open country as well as forest, with most prey perhaps caught in open. In Transvaal open-country francolins and smaller doves relatively important (Tarboton *et al.* 1978). In dense tropical forest attacked hornbills *Tropicranus* and large Afep Pigeon *Columba unicincta* (Brosset 1973). Only 7/385 identified items were domestic poultry, despite ready availability of poultry to 1 pair studied Kenya for 8 years (Brown and Brown 1979). Largest item naturally attacked is guineafowl; ♀ hawk probably takes larger prey on average than ♂.

Has been trained for falconry (Brosset 1973) and in controlled experiments ♀♀ attacked prey of 180–1100 g (quail to cock pheasant), ♂♂ 150–900 g (thrush to young pheasant). ♀ also killed rabbit (2500 g) and domestic cat. Normal wild prey is half adult weight or less; but can kill prey up to 3–4 times own weight in favourable conditions. Food requirement not accurately known; estimated perhaps 15% of mean bodyweight, 65–127 g according to sex and subspecies; at times certainly less (e.g. incubating ♀♀).

Breeding Habits. Intimately known, all aspects studied at 1 nest. Pairs are resident in territories year-round; home range not accurately established, estimated 12·5 km² of mixed forest and open country (Kenya), but certainly also hunts outside home range. In Transvaal, *c.* 1 pair/65 km², but not uniformly distributed (Tarboton *et al.* 1978). Nearest neighbour distance, Kenya, *c.* 1·5 km between pairs, sometimes less.

Neither vocal nor aerial displays obvious; means of establishing territory or home range in dense forest obscure. Rarely, soars above forest, but normally does not call (cf. very vocal African Goshawk). W African birds perhaps more active in this way, soaring singly or in pairs above forest, calling at intervals. No spectacular aerial or undulating displays known, but slow, deliberate 'harrier-like' wing-flaps rarely observed, similar to other accipiters. Generally extraordinarily unobtrusive in display. Near nest, vocal duets with ♂ and ♀ alternating, 'kyip-chep-kyip-chep', heard rarely. Copulation occurs near nest, ♀ soliciting ♂ by crouching; he flies to her and mounts. Act accompanied by distinctive loud trilling call, probably by ♀.

NEST: in trees in tall forest, often very high up; 8–36 m recorded, av. (Transvaal) 17 m. In Transvaal exotic trees selected (99/103 nest-sites), but in most of Africa indigenous species used. Eucalyptus often preferred to other exotics; and readily breeds in towns in eucalyptus. Nest normally in a main fork, built close to trunk, less often on lateral branch; of sticks, mostly copiously lined with green leaves (individuals vary). New nest is *c.* 0·5–0·6 m across by 0·3 m deep, with deep central cup; with successive years' use becomes larger, up to 1 m across and 0·8 m deep. Species is unique among accipiters in regular use of same nest for long periods, 8–22 years recorded. If nest collapses new one built in same fork. Pairs normally have 1 nest, rarely 2 (again unusual for genus).

Share of sexes in building unknown; nest repair may be protracted near equator, 40–135 days, shorter elsewhere; nests sometimes repaired and not used. ♀ is fed by ♂ near nest-site for up to 70 days before laying, but may also kill for herself in that time.

EGGS: 1–4, normally 2–3; Transvaal mean (31 clutches) 2·8; Kenya clutch of 2 commoner than 3. Laying interval not known, perhaps 2–3 days. Rounded ovals; plain pale blue or blue-green, sometimes with sparse brown spots or lilac undermarkings; inside shell deep green against light. SIZE: (22, *A. m. melanoleucus*) 49·6–59·8 × 39·6–44·5; (*A. m. temminckii*, slightly smaller) 51·2–52·4 × 39·8–40·8; WEIGHT: estimated 47–52 g; mean clutch 2·8 thus *c.* 16% ♀ bodyweight.

Laying dates: S Africa (Transvaal), Namibia, Botswana, Zimbabwe June–Dec, peaking Sept, Oct (62% of records) (late dry season); Zambia July–Nov, peak Sept–Oct (late dry season); E Kenya, Mar–June, also Oct, Dec; W Kenya, Uganda Oct, Apr; coastal Kenya July–Oct; W Africa, Aug, Oct (late rains). In southern Africa laying peaks just before break of rains, in E Africa most records show laying in heavy rains, with peak Apr–May in E Kenya producing young in nest in subsequent cool dry season; in southern Africa young in nest in heavy rains.

Incubation begins 1st egg; almost entirely by ♀, but ♂ sometimes sits briefly when he feeds ♀ at nest; once recorded to sit for 50 min (Brown and Brown 1979). ♂ feeds ♀ at or near nest once a day (based on dawn-dark watches) on small remnant of his own kill. ♀ stands up frequently (15–20 times/day) for spells of 2–11 min; preens, stretches, settles again, usually facing other way; does this mainly in warmer hours of day, sitting tight morning and evening. Sits very tight, generally hard to disturb; usually only tip of tail visible. When ♂ arrives with food, he calls, ♀ leaves, receives food, feeds away from nest and returns. ♂ may visit nest briefly at other times, ♀ usually taking no

notice. Incubation period: 37–38 days (3 good records).

Young hatch at intervals, estimated 1–2 days. At first invisible, inactive; become active and can just stand at *c.* 12–13 days. Wing-feathers visible 14 days; can now stand to defaecate over nest rim. Contour feathers appear 18–19 days, mainly feathered on body and wings 22–23 days, feathering almost complete 26–28 days. Earliest wing-flapping at 14 days, just able to feed themselves on prey at 19–20 days. Days 20–37 or later young more active, standing up and walking about, preening and, towards end of period, running round or across nest raising and flapping wings. Make 1st flight at 37–43 days, individuals varying, possibly according to food availability.

In captive-bred birds violent sibling aggression observed (A. Brosset, pers. comm.), but in all wild nests observed none seen (6 broods, 3 different ♀♀). Young first gaining possession feeds first, other or others later.

1st flight is usually short hop to a nearby tree, a few metres only. ♂♂ recognizable early by relatively thin tarsi, greater activity, earlier feathering of body, and make 1st flights earlier than larger ♀♀. Sex ratio at fledging about equal.

Roles of adults in fledging period clear-cut. ♀ remains on or near nest entire fledging period, ♂ feeds himself, mate and brood of 2–4. Killing rate normally increased from 1 item/day in incubation to 2–3, but sometimes only 1/day in fledging period. ♀ broods young by day days 1–5, reducing; thereafter, at least in shaded forest sites, does not brood by day, but stands on nest, brooding at night. After 14 days usually perches near, leaving young alone in nest, but may return to repel, e.g. Sykes monkey *Cercopithecus mitis*. Extremely inactive, remains perched in same position for hours. Feeds young on prey brought by ♂ up to day 19–20, thereafter does not feed them, but still remains near, and visits nest to obtain prey after they finish; some ♀♀ carry prey remains far from nest, others leave them below favoured perches. Behaviour variable, some ♀♀ spending long periods on nest, especially in evening, even with large young. ♀ regularly roosts on branch near nest to end of fledging period, sometimes thereafter.

Post-fledging period 45–50 days, occasionally longer. For first 5–6 days young cannot fly far and permit close approach; roost in nest. Thereafter increasingly active, roosting in trees, not in nest, becoming shy and hard to approach towards end of period (estimated when young not seen 2 consecutive days). Fed by both adults in this period, ♀ taking active share as soon as first young leaves nest (3 different ♀♀, 6 observed broods). Prey at first taken to nest, young feeding there. Later, adults arrive, call, and young fly to them, feeding on branches away from nest; prey remains accumulate below favoured feeding perches. Young at this stage noisy, uttering loud begging mews, soliciting either parent or whichever young has prey. ♀ roosts near nest for first few days, young then left alone.

Breeding success: Transvaal, 42 pair-years, 36 (86%) laid, reared 69 young, i.e. 1·64/pair overall, 1·91 per breeding pair, 0·7 young per egg laid; Kenya, 10 pair-years, 7 (70%) laid, reared 13 young, i.e. 1·3 pair overall, 1·85/pair which laid. 1 pair reared 5 successive broods totalling 11 young to independence, perhaps 100% success from laying to independence. Such success probably unusual, but this large species apparently more regularly successful than some smaller species, e.g. Shikra *A. badius* (1·1/ successful nest).

No data available on survival thereafter. Young probably cannot breed in 1st year after leaving nest, but may do so in 3rd year; as in other accipiters some ♀♀ breed when not in full mature plumage.

References
Brosset, A. (1973).
Brown, L. H. and Brown, B. E. (1979).
Tarboton, W. R. *et al.* (1978).

Plate 22

(Opp. p. 355)

Accipiter gentilis (Linnaeus). Northern Goshawk. Autour des palombes.

Falco gentilis Linnaeus, 1758. Syst. Nat. (10th ed.), p. 89; (Swedish) Alps.

Range and Status. Holarctic, Europe, N Asia, N America and, in Africa, N Morocco. In Africa, resident *A. g. arrigonii* remains year-round, perhaps augmented by migrant (race unknown) in winter (Etchécopar and Hüe 1967). Uncommon to rare; only recently proved to breed Morocco (Maes 1978).

Accipiter gentilis

Description. *A. g. arrigonii* (Kleinschmidt), ADULT ♂: crown blackish brown, with a white streaked eyebrow and black cheeks and ear-coverts extending to nape. Rest of upperparts, including upperwing- and tail-coverts dark slaty grey; some white bars on bases of scapulars and uppertail-coverts. Chin white, sometimes barred brown; rest of underparts, including underwing-coverts, white, finely barred dark brown, least on undertail-coverts. Wing-feathers above dark brown, washed grey, inner webs mottled white and brown, tipped whitish and broadly barred blackish; below grey, broadly barred dark brown. Tail above dark brown to dark grey, tipped white, 1 broad subterminal and 3–4 other broad dark bars; below greyish, broadly tipped and barred black-brown. ♀ similar, markedly larger (especially heavier in most races), usually browner generally, more heavily barred below than ♂. Eye orange to red; cere and feet yellow. SIZE: (N African birds) wing, ♂ 293–330, ♀ 335–375; tail, ♂ av. 199, ♂ 242; tarsus, ♂ av. 70, ♀ 77 (Etchéopar and Hüe 1967). WEIGHT. ♂ *c.* 800, ♀ *c.* 1200.

IMMATURE: crown dark brown, edged rufous. Rest of upperside brown, tipped buff or rufous; scapulars and uppertail-coverts buff, barred brown. Below dull pale rufous, boldly marked with blackish drop-shaped spots, broader on underwing-coverts, fewer on thighs and undertail-coverts. Wing-

and tail-feathers above brown, tipped rufous, broadly and clearly barred dark brown; below pale rufous, barred dark brown. Eye greenish grey becoming yellow; cere and feet yellow.

DOWNY YOUNG: not described for *A. g. arrigonii*; in other races at first white, 2nd down greyer; eye grey, cere and feet pale yellow.

Immatures of nominate race assume full adult plumage at *c.* 15 months and can breed in 3rd year.

Field Characters. Normally unmistakable, a very large accipiter as big as a buzzard, with longer, narrower wings, and much longer, heavily barred tail. Large ♀ European Sparrowhawks *A. nisus* could be confused with small ♂ Northern Goshawks; but are browner, wings relatively broader and shorter, tail relatively longer. Rufous underside of immature, longitudinally streaked blackish, distinctive. Size normally diagnostic; but if in doubt assume European Sparrowhawk.

Voice. Not recorded. Much deeper, harsher than that of European Sparrowhawk, but of similar quality. Variously described as 'ga-ga-ga-ga', 'kak-kak-kak', 'gi-ak, gi-ak, gi-ak, gi-ak'; a deeper harsher version of the European Sparrowhawk 'kew-kew-kew', delivered more slowly. Begging young and ♀♀ a long-drawn mew 'wueeeeeh-wueeeeeh' lasting *c.* 1 s, with similar pauses. Voices would be distinctive from sparrowhawk, if in doubt, near a nest-site, as much deeper, more rasping, notes delivered more slowly.

General Habits. Little known in NW Africa; evidently rare, seldom seen. Inhabits cork oak woods and perhaps cedar (*Cedrus atlanticus*) and conifer forests in N Moroccan mountains. Remains generally within cover, and in N Africa evidently hard to locate, seldom emerging into open.

Much more powerful than any other accipiter (adult ♀♀ can kill mammals to size of a hare); nevertheless mainly hunt birds in cover. Hunts by short flights, taking prey by surprise, or perches and watches intently. Nothing in detail known in NW Africa, but assumed to behave like other members of the species. Despite size, extremely manoeuvrable in and out of tree trunks among dense woodland.

Adults are apparently entirely sedentary in NW African range, but immatures may leave breeding territories and wander; and in NE Morocco, Algeria and Tunisia vagrants, possibly not of resident race, occur in winter (Etchécopar and Hüe 1967).

Food. Little recorded in NW Africa. In Europe, mainly birds and squirrels, but takes more large mammals than most *Accipiter* spp. Both sexes can kill prey in range 20–1500 g, but only ♀♀ can kill larger mammals. Analysis of over 15,000 items (Europe) shows birds make up *c.* 90%, mammals 10%. Birds preferred are in weight range 300–600 g, including especially wood-pigeons, domestic pigeons, some partridges and corvids, notably jays *Garrulus* spp.; smallest items buntings and finches, largest European brown hare *Lepus europaeus*. Food requirement, probably 100–125 g/day/adult.

Breeding Habits. Intimately known in Europe; in NW Africa not proven to breed until 1974–5, but evidently has bred for many years as nests long-established. Pairs remain in home range year-round, becoming more obvious in spring when displaying. Display occurs late winter Jan–Feb, mainly soaring and diving over breeding area, with characteristic, slow, deliberate 'harrier-like' wing-flaps. ♂ may also perform undulating display, shallow dives alternating with upward swoops. Display accompanied by calling. 2 NW African nesting areas were 15 km apart.

NEST: N Moroccan nests were in oak trees 10–15 m above ground; large, solid structures typical of the species, 0·8–1 m or more across by 30–50 cm deep. Elsewhere, Goshawks occupy a nest for several years, but may also build new nests frequently, but not annually like most smaller accipiters. ♂ said to build most, but accounts vary. Mating frequent in nest-building period, up to 10 times daily, continuing for 50–60 days (Holstein 1942).

EGGS: (Europe) 1–5, usually 3, clutch and brood size related to food supply (Sulkava 1964); 1 clutch of 3 recorded Morocco (Mars 1978). Laid at 3-day intervals, clutch of 3 taking 7 days to deposit. Unmarked pale bluish white. SIZE: (10, *A. g. arrigonii*) 53·0–58·0 × 41·0–43·7 (55·4 × 42·7) (Schönwetter 1960); WEIGHT: *c.* 57 g, clutch of 3 thus *c.* 15% of ♀ bodyweight.

Laying dates: Morocco, late Mar-early Apr (clutch of 3 laid 24 Apr, partly feathered young 10 June, feathered young 18 June: Mars 1978).

Incubation mainly by ♀, 36–38 days per egg in other races. ♀ is fed near nest by ♂, who may sit briefly while ♀ is off feeding, sometimes for longer periods in early incubation.

Young when hatched, feeble, helpless; feathers emerge *c.* day 18, almost completely feathered day 38. Can feed themselves from day 28 on, thereafter more active. Climb out onto branches days 35–41, make 1st flights at 43–45 days. Record of feathered young N Morocco 18 June, thus suggests hatching very early May from eggs laid late Mar.

♀ broods young days 1–10, perches near nest up to day 16; young then left alone more. ♂ brings all prey, increasing killing rate, apparently at will, from 1–2/day to 5–6/day; food requirement for 2 young estimated at 13 kg (Holstein 1942), equivalent to 20–30 pigeon-sized birds or corvids. Broods of 1–2 so far recorded Morocco.

Young after leaving nest are dependent on adults for *c.* 50 days; then possibly leave parental territory. Better details needed Morocco, but young are said to wander (Etchécopar and Hüe 1967).

References
Etchécopar, R. D. and Hüe, F. (1967).
Maes, J.-P. (1978).

Genus *Urotriorchis* Sharpe

Medium-sized accipiter-like hawks of dense forest. Differ from *Accipiter* spp. in having a round nostril with central tubercle; tail very long, graduated, longer than head and body combined; tarsi and talons strong, rather thick, tarsi partially feathered in front. Without exceptionally long tail would be regarded as belonging to genus *Accipiter* (D. Amadon, pers. comm.).

Urotriorchis macrourus (Hartlaub). **Long-tailed Hawk. Autour à longue queue.**

Plates 23 and 31 (Opp. pp. 370 and 466)

Astur macrourus Temminck = Hartlaub, 1855. Journ. Ornith., 3, p. 353; Dabocrom, Ghana.

Range and Status. Resident dense tropical forests from Liberia eastwards, including the Congo River basin, to W Uganda. Apparently uncommon to rare, but probably commoner than supposed as very difficult to observe. Must be decreasing with destruction of primary forest habitat.

Description. ADULT ♂: above, dark slate grey, paler on cheeks, darkest on wings; rump sometimes spotted white, uppertail-coverts pure white, forming clear white bar. Chin and lower throat grey; rest of underparts, including under-wing-coverts, deep chestnut, almost maroon; undertail-coverts white. Primaries and secondaries above dark brown, barred black, notched white on inner webs; below white, barred black. Tail above blackish, tipped white, with 4 irregular white bars on each feather; below white, barred black. Eye reddish yellow; cere and feet yellow, ♀♀ similar, averaging larger. SIZE: wing, ♂♀ 266–310; tail, 305–370; tarsus, 72–78. WEIGHT: 1 ♂ 491·5 (Friedmann and Williams 1971).

IMMATURE: above, blackish brown, including uppertail-coverts, edged and marked tawny-rufous. Below, white, sometimes almost unmarked, with large blackish spots on breast and sides. Wings above banded black and brown, below whitish, banded black. Tail above brown, broadly banded black, below white, banded black. In young birds tail is normally shorter than adult's; a captive at 15 months had not developed a full tail. In possible subadult plumage chestnut feathers of underside are narrowly barred white.

DOWNY YOUNG: unknown.

Field Characters. Unmistakable if seen; a large, very long-tailed hawk, black above, chestnut below, with conspicuous white spots on long graduated tail. Rarely occurs in open areas; appears like gigantic long-tailed cuckoo, white tail spots and rump very conspicuous.

Urotriorchis macrourus

Could not be confused with any other bird of prey, but does vaguely resemble White-crested Hornbill *Tropicranus albocristatus*, which has similar long tail. Is easily distinguished from this species by other habits, however.

Voice. Recorded (2a). Normally silent, but captive young apparently vocal (Cockburn 1946). A long, high, scream, 'weeeeee-eh', uttered from high up in trees.

General Habits. Little known; apparently mainly inhabits dense tall canopy, where hard to locate. Rarely emerges into open, but occasionally flies across clearings and roads, and said to take poultry in African villages. Resident and sedentary wherever it occurs. A young bird kept in an aviary was aggressive, killing other young raptors kept with it.

Food. Little known. Arboreal mammals, including scale-tailed squirrels, rodents; forest birds. Stout tarsus and foot suggest preference for mammal prey.

Breeding Habits. Unknown; but a recently fledged young bird kept in captivity suggested breeding in W African forests July–Aug (height of rains).

References
Cockburn, T. A. (1946).

Genus *Butastur* Hodgson

A mainly eastern genus of 4 spp., 1 in Africa. Medium-sized; wings long, slightly pointed; tail moderately long, folded wings reach tip. Bill rather small, weak; eyes white or pale yellow; nostril circular without tubercle. Tarsus rather long, with frontal transverse scutes. Toes short, weak; adapted to taking small prey. One of many 'subbuteonine' genera, intermediate between *Accipiter* and *Buteo*.

Plates 24 and 30
(Opp. pp. 371 and 451)

Butastur rufipennis (Sundevall). Grasshopper Buzzard. Buse des sauterelles.

Poliornis rufipennis Sundevall, 1851. Öfv. K. Vet.—Akad. Förh., 7, (1850), p. 131; Khartoum, Sudan.

Range and Status. Resident from Senegal and Gambia east to Somalia, Kenya and N Tanzania, south of Sahara. Regular intra-African migrant, moving north to breed in drier parts of range in wet season (Apr–Sept), south to southern woodlands in dry season (Oct–Mar); in E Africa moves south in wet season (Nov–Dec). Locally common to abundant especially near grass fires and burned ground. Numbers probably stable.

Description. ADULT♂: above, grey-brown, darker on head, with dark shaft streaks. Mantle and lesser upperwing-coverts narrowly edged rufous. Greater coverts and primaries light rufous, primaries tipped blackish, forming conspicuous pale rufous patch in open wing. Secondaries basally rufous, terminally dark brown, tipped white. Chin and throat white or buff, with 1 median and 2 other dark streaks either side of throat. Underside of body rufous, breast with dark shaft streaks; axillaries grey-brown, spotted buff, underwing-coverts white. Tail above and below grey, with darker subterminal and other faint darker bars. Cere and base of bill yellow; eye pale yellow; legs pale yellow. ♀ similar, only slightly larger. SIZE: wing, ♂ 274–311 (286), ♀ 295–330 (307); tail, ♂ 160–175, ♀ 172–182; tarsus, ♂ 55–58, ♀ 57–61; span, 890–990. WEIGHT: ♂ 310–342 (326), ♀ 300–383 (344) (Thiollay 1978b).

IMMATURES: bright rufous head and nape, streaked dark brown; broader rufous tips to mantle and covert feathers; conspicuous white tips to primaries and secondaries; tail unbarred; bill blacker. Generally more rufous above than adult, but readily recognizable.

DOWNY YOUNG: undescribed.

Field Characters. A slim, medium-sized, rather long-legged hawk. When perched, a little like Black Kite *Milvus migrans*, but immediately distinguishable from it by square tail. In flight unmistakable through large pale rufous patch on wing. Very prominent yellow cere, base of bill and eye, black wing-tips and tail are obvious in the field. Not easy to confuse with any other species; field habits assist.

Voice. Recorded (1e, 2a). Normally very silent in non-breeding season; but in breeding areas a loud, repeated 'ki-ki-ki-ki-keee', varied. Far from being completely mute, as sometimes reported, is very vocal in breeding quarters (where little observed).

General Habits. Little known in northern breeding range; observed in detail in southern dry-season range (Thiollay 1975–78). Is regular intra-tropical migrant from breeding areas in semi-arid *Acacia* steppe at 9–15°N, Apr–Sept, to near southern fringes of Guinea woodlands and edge of forest in dry season Oct–Feb. Apparently does not breed through whole of possible wet-season range and in dry-season range local, tending to be nomadic, large numbers appearing in certain localities one year, none the next (N Nigeria 7–8°N). May be more regular migrant in western part of tropical range, Ivory Coast – Gambia; but this general migration pattern persists as far east as S Sudan, N Uganda, extreme western Kenya, in northern tropical monomodal rainfall regime.

Southward movement begins after breeding Sept, when rains cease at 12–15°N. Progress southwards probably associated with increasing severity of dry season and onset of grass fires. Reaches 10°N *c.* end-Oct; 8°N (Nigeria) *c.* mid-Nov; 5°N in Ivory Coast 5–15 Dec. In Nigeria does not normally migrate further south than 7°N, often not reaching that far; but may appear in relatively open country caused by cultivation further south than elsewhere in general range. Exact extent of southward movement probably more affected by local ecology and seasonal conditions than latitude.

Gregarious both on southward migration and in dry-season range, in flocks or small groups, sometimes in large numbers (50–100 or more) near grass fires. May also be seen singly, especially in E Africa, where rarer. Preferred habitat open savanna with some trees, but also frequents cultivated territories, open grassland and sometimes dense broad-leaved woodlands. Does not normally proceed south beyond or even to northern fringe of forest belt. Remains in southern range only until rains begin, leaving soon after first heavy rains fall. This varies with latitude, period of residence longer at 10°N than at 8° or 5°N.

Within dry-season range, individuals may be spread out over wide area, or be semi-gregarious, collecting at abundant food supplies (fires, termite swarms) and largely ignoring other species. Individuals may take up temporary territory, same bird seen repeatedly in same locality. Often quite tame, easy to approach and observe. Prefers to perch on low bare trees, 4–8 m above ground. Perches in same spot for long periods, then moves some distance to another perch. In flight buoyant, easy, a little like harrier *Circus* spp., but with longer glides, fewer flaps, erratic upward swoops, finally swinging up to perch on tree from low flight.

In Ivory Coast, at peak numbers (Feb), may outnumber any resident species and all migrants except Black Kites, forming 25–30% of biomass of intra-tropical migrants (which in Feb exceeds that of all residents combined: Thiollay 1975b). Captures most prey on ground (85–90%), some (5–10%) in low herbage, and

Butastur rufipennis

5% in air, latter being mainly small swarming insects (alate termites and ants). Hunts where most likely to be successful, taking advantage of any local abundance caused by grass fires or recent burn. Captures 0·2–1·6 small items/h, most successful on bare burned ground (Thiollay 1977a). Peak numbers in Ivory Coast coincide with maximum abundance or availability of grasshoppers.

In NE and E Africa is irregular transequatorial migrant south to E Kenya and NE Tanzania, reaching, at most, *c.* 4–5°S. Frequents dense semi-arid *Acacia-Commiphora* thornbush with little long grass, habitat quite different to that in W Africa; never as numerous. Passes south through N Somalia Oct (Archer and Godman 1937), arrives near southward limits of migratory range Nov, remaining Dec, period of residence corresponding here not with dry season and fires but most regular heavy rains; however, may also be affected by maximum or abundant food supplies.

Leaves W African dry-season range almost as soon as rains fall, Feb, and has gone from southern parts of range by Mar–Apr. May then be breeding at southern fringe of breeding range, *c.* 10°N. Breeding birds may leave earlier, or not migrate so far southward. Departs entirely when grass cover 90%, after good rains. Northward movement is much less obvious than southward, possibly with pre-breeding dispersal into pairs; but is little observed. Reaches northern fringe of range May–June, sometimes even later, July (Chad: Salvan 1968), but such late migrants may not breed.

Food. Mainly insects, especially grasshoppers and mantids, caught at grass fires and on burned ground. Quantitative analysis (Ivory Coast) of 1520 recorded items states 1498 insects, 1120 of which were small spp. (alate termites and ants); 276 grasshoppers, mantids, stick insects relatively more important by weight. Some spiders, millipedes, crabs; a few small birds, snakes, small mammals. Grasshoppers and locusts probably most important food. In E Africa perhaps takes more birds, e.g. *Quelea* near watering places. Food in breeding areas not described.

Breeding Habits. Although relatively common, little known. Presumably dispersed in pairs, certainly not gregarious. No published details of territorial or aerial display, but apparently is then vocal, advertising presence in certain areas.

NEST: in trees, rather resembling that of Black Kite; constructed of sticks, solid and deep, *c.* 35 cm across by up to 40 cm deep, with central cup *c.* 15 cm across, lined with green leaves (which immediately distinguishes it from that of Black Kite). Sites are often low trees; but have been recorded at up to 10–12 m above ground, varying locally. Not known to be used repeatedly.

EGGS: 1–3; laying interval unknown. Bluish white, speckled, spotted and streaked rufous, with obscure lilac undermarkings. SIZE: (7) 42·2–50·1 × 35·8–37·4 (46·1 × 36·3) (Schönwetter 1960).

Laying dates: Sudan, N Nigeria Mar; Somalia Apr (reported by Erlanger, no recent records; Archer and Godman 1937).

Incubating bird said to sit tight; otherwise no recorded details.

References
Thiollay, J.-M. (1975–78).

Genus *Kaupifalco* Bonaparte

Small hawks, resembling *Accipiter* more than *Buteo*, but intermediate. Wings rather short, pointed rather than rounded; tail long, folded wings do not reach half length. Head rather large; bill short, accipiter-like. Tarsus short, upper half feathered, rest scutellated in front and reticulated behind. 1 sp., endemic to Africa.

Plates 24 and 31
(Opp. pp. 371 and 466)

Kaupifalco monogrammicus (Temminck). Lizard Buzzard. Buse unibande.

Falco monogrammicus Temminck, 1824. Pl. Col., livr. 53, pl 314; Senegal.

Range and Status. Resident woodlands and thornbush south of Sahara from Senegal east to Ethiopia, south through Kenya, Uganda to Transvaal, Natal, and Angola. Frequent, locally common; numbers probably stable, perhaps decreasing locally.

Description. *K. m. monogrammicus* (Temminck): Senegal east to Ethiopia and Kenya. ADULT ♂: above, slate grey, paler on sides of face and upperwing-coverts, blackish on lower back and rump; uppertail-coverts pure white, forming conspicuous

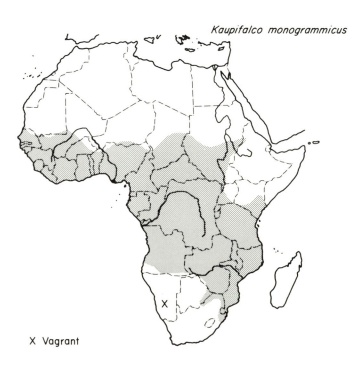

Kaupifalco monogrammicus

X Vagrant

band. Throat white, with a central black streak; neck, sides and chest grey. Lower breast, belly flanks and axillaries closely barred white and dark brown; underwing- and undertail-coverts white. Wing-feathers blackish, greyer on secondaries, tipped white, outermost primaries edged white. Tail blackish, broadly tipped white with 1, rarely 2, broad white crossbands. Eye dark red-brown; cere and ring round eye orange-red; feet orange. Sexes alike, ♀ only slightly larger. SIZE: wing, ♂ 201–228, ♀ 222–240; tail, ♂ 130–136, ♀ 141–155; tarsus, ♂ 50–54, ♀ 53–55. WEIGHT: ♂ 220–275 (241), ♀ 282–340 (310) (Thiollay 1977a).

IMMATURE: differ in having buff edges on mantle and coverts, belly and undertail-coverts buff, breast browner, median black throat streak less developed. Eye brown, becoming paler and yellower, cere and feet orange-yellow. Assume adult plumage within 1 year, but probably not then sexually mature.

DOWNY YOUNG: above, grey, paler on crown, with dark hair-like tips. Below, pale grey, whitish on thighs. Eye blackish brown, feet and cere dull pale orange.

K. m. meridionalis (Hartlaub). Scarcely distinct; Tanzania south to South Africa. Slightly large: wing ♂ 210–225, ♀ 222–248; WEIGHT: 77 unsexed 223–338 (294·2), ♂ (1) 275, ♀ (5) 248–374 (306). Rather heavily barred below, especially on thighs.

Field Characters. Could only be confused with several small *Accipiter* spp. Appears stouter-bodied, more thick-set than any, with relatively large head, perching very upright. From front, uniform grey upperbreast with black median throat streak distinctive at close range. From rear, especially in flight, white uppertail-coverts and single broad white tail-band diagnostic. Has distinctive thrush or woodpecker-like undulating flight when moving from perch to perch, rapid ascending flaps alternating descending glide with closed wings.

Voice. Recorded (2a, 8, 9, 14, 18, 19, 22a, 26). A clear, melodious whistling 'kli-oo, klu-klu-klu-klu-klu' uttered at regular intervals from perch. Also, clear *Buteo*-like 'peee-oh' uttered from perch, or nest, at intervals of *c.* 15 s. Normally rather silent except in breeding season, but sometimes betrays presence in thick cover by calling. Voice has contact function between pair members and display function (Thiollay 1976b). Does not call in flight as far as known. Voice regularly mimicked by robin chats *Cossypha* spp., even in areas where Lizard Buzzard does not often occur.

General Habits. Very well known; studied in detail in Ivory Coast (Thiollay 1975–1978). Preferred habitat is well watered deciduous broad-leaved tall grass woodland, with, for example, *Combretum, Terminalia, Brachystegia* and various tall grasses. Less common in cultivation on forest edges and in *Acacia–Commiphora* thornbush, E Africa, often there along riverine strips with taller *Acacias* spp. Prefers warm moist lowlands, but found E Africa to 1800 m. Adapts readily to cultivated country and often perches on dead trees in farm clearings; but would disappear if all woodland destroyed. Not found in open grasslands, must have arboreal cover.

Rarely flies above canopy except in nuptial display. In woodland, perches either in cover or on bare branch staring mainly downward; and prefers areas with long grass to burned or bare ground. Stiff plumage and relatively long legs considered adaptations for catching prey in long grass (Thiollay 1978a). Uses a series of perches, flying from one to another on av. 3–4 times/h. Catches most prey (70%) in tall dense cover, mainly long grass, unlike most other spp. Most caught by quick short swoop to ground, seldom in flight. Birds normally unafraid of this hawk, do not mob it, and pay little attention to it even when in flight, but this not invariable.

Resident wherever it occurs, performing no migrations. Local changes of individual territories may occur, but different birds often found in same localities for many successive years, continuously inhabiting preferred places.

Food. Mainly insects, lizards, small snakes, some frogs and small mammals (usually rodents). Of 374 recorded items, Ivory Coast, 237 insects (mainly grasshoppers); 89 snakes (mainly small, non-venomous) and lizards, especially skinks; and 23 mammals, probably more important by weight. Occasional molluscs and arachnids. Elsewhere, mainly lizards and grasshoppers, occasionally small birds, including e.g. chick of another raptor (possibly African Little Sparrowhawk *Accipiter minullus*). Most food taken in low vegetation (43% in tall grass), little on ground; but may be more successful on burned or bare ground, taking 1·2 items/h (cf. 0·3–0·8/h in cover); evidently such habits vary.

Breeding Habits. Well known; not intensively studied. In optimum habitat, pairs distributed regularly through woodland at *c.* 80 ha/pair, of which only 30–50 ha regularly used. Very much rarer E Africa and southern Africa generally. Complete counts difficult because of preference for dense woodland, except when vocal early in breeding season.

Display mostly vocal, birds uttering either single clear mewing calls or multi-noted 'song' when perched. Voice advertises adults in territory, and being audible, they then appear more common. Adults react by calling to others within 100 m in dense cover, or up to 200 m if area more open. Early in breeding season very vocal, falling silent later. No aerial displays noted anywhere.

NEST: built in trees, not usually large, at (Ivory Coast) 11–18 (av. 13) m above ground; elsewhere recorded at 3–25 m. Usually well below canopy in a main fork, also often on lateral branches. Small but rather solid structures up to 30–35 cm across, built of sticks and lined with pieces of debris, sometimes moss; not usually green leaves. Usually used only once (Thiollay 1976b). Both sexes build, shares not detailed; one may bring material which the other (perhaps ♀) arranges.

EGGS: 1–3, usually 2 recorded; Ivory Coast mean (23 clutches) 1·91, Natal (17) 2·0 (Thiollay 1976b; Dean 1971). Greenish white to pale blue; usually unmarked, occasionally with a few red streaks and spots. SIZE: (80, *K. m. meridionalis*) 40·2–47 × 33–37·5 (43·9 × 35·2); (18, *K. m. monogrammicus*, similar) 40·4–46·5 × 33·1–36·5 (44·0 × 33·9) (Schönwetter 1960); WEIGHT: *c.* 28–29.

Laying dates: W Africa Feb, Mar, especially 15 Feb–15 Mar (Thiollay 1976); Sudan Mar–Apr; E Africa recorded Jan, Feb, Aug, Oct (all dry months, both dry seasons); Zambia Aug–Dec, peaking strongly Oct (11/17 records: Benson *et al.* 1971); Zimbabwe, Transvaal, Natal Sept–Feb, especially Oct. Throughout range lays late in dry season, with young in nest early rains.

Incubation by ♀ alone in few observations; may be fed near nest by ♂, or leave to kill own prey. ♂ spends much of day perched near nest, and pair call to each other frequently. ♂♂ aggressive to other much larger birds, e.g. Hooded Vulture *Necrosyrtes monachus*, near nest; and 1 ♀ recorded to leave nest, returning with chick of another raptor, probably Little Sparrowhawk. Prey may be cached near nest, on a branch, and eaten later. 2–3 small items suffice pair per day. Incubation period: estimated 30 days (Thiollay 1976b); 1 exact record 33 days (Chittenden 1979).

No details recorded of fledging period, but ♀ remains on or near nest in early stages; both sexes bring prey to larger young. Period *c.* 40 days (Chittenden 1979). Young leave nest in W Africa in May, in heavy rains. Young begin to catch prey *c.* 1 month after fledging; probably independent 7 weeks after fledging (Chittenden 1979).

Breeding success: in optimum habitat in W Africa, of 32 pairs in 2700 ha, 23 laid (28% non-breeding), resulting in 1·91 eggs/occupied nest, 1·37/pair overall. 1·52 eggs hatched/occupied nest (80% of eggs laid), 0·91 young fledged/breeding pair (60%), 0·66 young reared/pair overall; success in neighbouring areas apparently similar (Thiollay 1976b). Young probably do not breed until more than 2 years old.

References
Thiollay, J.-M. (1975–78).

Genus *Buteo* Lacépède

Medium-sized to rather large soaring hawks, unspecialized, versatile. Beaks usually rather short, nostril normally lacking tubercle, cere large. Heads rather large, rounded. Wings moderately long, broad, 3–4 primaries emarginated, adapted for soaring; tails moderately long to short. Tarsi usually bare, but in *B. lagopus* feathered to toes. Plumage of many species highly variable with light and dark morphs; immatures different from adults. The 2nd largest genus of Accipitridae, with 25 accepted spp., cosmopolitan except in Australasia, most varied in N and S America. Of 6 African spp., 1 purely a Palearctic winter migrant, 1 a Palearctic vagrant, 4 resident. Usually only 1–2 spp. resident in any part of Africa, and if more than 1, ecologically separated.

Plates
24 and 30
(Opp. pp. 371
and 451)

Buteo buteo (Linnaeus). Common Buzzard; Steppe Buzzard. Buse variable.

Falco Buteo Linnaeus, 1758. Syst. Nat. (10th ed.), p. 90; Europe (restricted to Sweden).

Range and Status. *B. b. vulpinus* (Steppe Buzzard) Palearctic migrant from N and E Europe, south to Cape Province. Common, locally abundant on migration, in winter quarters frequent to common. No obvious decline in numbers recent years. *B. b. buteo* (Common Buzzard) mainly sedentary in Europe or scarce winter migrant to NW Africa, a few passing Gibraltar reaching Liberia in extreme south of range.

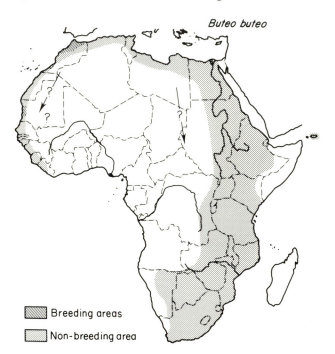

Buteo buteo

▨ Breeding areas
▢ Non-breeding area

Description. *B. b. vulpinus* (Gloger): breeding N and E Europe, wintering mainly E and southern Africa to Cape Province. ADULT ♂: very variable, with dark and pale phases. Pale phase—crown brown; faintly streaked whitish. Neck, back and upperwing-coverts brown or reddish brown, barred brown and whitish on uppertail-coverts. Below, buff or white, streaked on throat, blotched on breast, spotted and barred red-brown on belly and underwing-coverts. Thighs dark rufous, undertail-coverts barred rufous and white. Wing-feathers above dark brown, primaries tipped blackish; below, white, tipped blackish, forming a blackish trailing edge on secondaries; outer primaries basally black forming a conspicuous black carpal patch. Tail above rufous, broadly barred subterminally darker brown, variously barred dark brown; below grey, tinged rufous, with darker tip; sometimes plain unbarred rufous. Eye brown; cere and legs yellow. SIZE: wing, ♂ 338–387 (359), ♀ 352–400 (374); tail, ♂ 170–207 (185), ♀ 175–209 (191); tarsus, ♂♀ 69–82; wing-span, ♂ 1018–1200,

♀ 1176–1277 (1277). WEIGHT: adult South African migrants, unsexed, 560–1000 (739·1); European adults, ♂ 600–675 (627), ♀ 710–1175 (851) (Broekhuysen and Siegfried 1971; Brown and Amadon 1968; Glutz von Blotzheim *et al.* 1971).

Pale phase can vary below through a more heavily barred type with broad rufous chest-band, blotched darker, to pale rufous, streaked darker brown, with blackish shaft streaks or, in darkest form, rich dark chestnut, with broad blackish shaft streaks. In darkest forms, inner secondaries mainly rufous brown, barred; black patch at base of primaries larger, more conspicuous. Tail above dark rufous, broadly tipped subterminally blackish, with some narrow dark bars; below grey, obscurely barred darker.

IMMATURE: generally paler than adult, streaked rather than barred below. Crown more whitish, many feathers of upperparts broadly edged rufous. Below, throat whitish, streaked brown; breast and belly whitish, broadly streaked dark brown; underwing-coverts whitish, streaked and barred brown; thighs and undertail-coverts barred brown and white. Eye grey to grey-brown, cere and legs pale yellow.

B. b. buteo (Limmaeus). NW Africa south to Liberia. Much less rufous; tail-feathers much less rufous and barred.

Field Characters. A small buzzard, with noticeably longer, more slender wings than in large resident species, moderately long tail; much smaller than either Long-legged *B. rufinus* or Jackal *B. rufofuscus* Buzzards, same size as Mountain Buzzard *B. oreophilus*. Adults normally distinguished from Mountain Buzzard by generally less heavily barred underside; immatures by streaky markings, rather than large, round, dark blotches. In some plumages extremely hard to distinguish from Mountain Buzzard, but any plain dark or pale chestnut form is Steppe Buzzard.

Voice. Recorded (2a). In winter normally silent. If it calls, a sharp, high-pitched mew, 'peee-oo'; like that of Mountain Buzzard, but somewhat lower-pitched, less clear and ringing; not diagnostic.

General Habits. Well known. Winter migrant late Sept – early Apr to tropical and southern Africa. Migrant streams of Steppe Buzzards move both southeast and southwest in Europe, the much more numerous eastern stream entering Africa via Suez. Western migrants may leapfrog over normally resident Common Buzzards *B. b. buteo*, but only a few enter Africa via Gibraltar. The main eastern population enters E Africa and proceeds south, mainly east of the Nile Valley, through Ethiopia and the E African highlands. Migrates by day only, usually in flocks, sometimes large ones (hundreds together). Follows mountain ranges, ridges, escarpments when available, using slopes of high mountains (e.g. Mount Elgon, 4500 m) to gain height, then glides on. Crossing large areas of plains, mounts in circling flocks on thermals, then glides to another, mounting again. Travels round large freshwater lakes, e.g. Lake Victoria, not even crossing quite narrow gulfs 20 km wide. Most migrants pass Suez mid–late Sept; reach Kenya (equator) early-mid Oct; Cape Province late Oct–Nov, taking *c.* 1 month to travel 9000–10,000 km in straight line (further as bird flies). Earliest arrivals E and South Africa early Sept. Flocks normally migrate without feeding, but individuals may remain a few days in same area, feeding *en route*.

Within tropical Africa prefers woodlands, forests and mountain forests to open plains; but must sometimes cross these. Most pass on through E Africa to South Africa, but a few winter near equator. Individuals may then take up temporary winter territory for 2–3 weeks, observed in same area almost daily, then disappearing. In main winter range in South Africa from Transvaal–Cape Province is much the most numerous buzzard, one of the commonest raptors. In Transvaal commonest in

open country of mixed cultivation and grassland, dispersed at *c.* 1/13 km². Individuals spend most of southern summer in same area, and 1 known to return to same area in successive years (Tarboton 1978b). In Cape Province may be abundant, perching on road-side telegraph poles, feeding in open semi-arid country and light scrub. Immatures arrive slightly later than adults, and remain longer before departure. Av. weight of immatures lower than adults, but weight of both increases slightly from mean 654 g 11 Oct to mean 714 g 30 Mar (Broekhuysen and Siegfried 1971).

Return northward migration begins Feb, accelerating Mar, continuing to early Apr. Readily observed in South Africa, 760 counted Transvaal 13 Feb–18 Mar (Newman 1978), individuals are dispersed near equator. Northward moving migrants delayed by cloud in Transvaal hunt actively. All have left Africa by mid-Apr.

Food. In Africa, mainly small rodents. Some small ground birds, reptiles and large insects. Does not often take swarming alate termites. All prey taken on ground by short swoop from elevated perch.

References
Broekhuysen, G. J. and Siegfried, W. R. (1971).

Buteo oreophilus Hartert and Neumann. Mountain Buzzard. Buse montagnarde.

Buteo oreophilus Hartert and Neumann, 1914. Orn. Monatsb., 22, p. 31; Koritscha, Ethiopia.

**Plates
24 and 30**
(Opp. pp. 371
and 451)

Range and Status. Resident, with scattered distribution in montane forests of NE and E Africa from SE Ethiopia – N Tanzania; then a large gap to Malawi, reappearing Transvaal south to Cape Province. Usually frequent, sometimes common. Numbers reduced some areas by destruction of forest; but in South Africa may be increasing following planting of large areas of pines;

considered threatened South Africa (Red Data Book) but numbers probably stable.

Description. *B. o. oreophilus* Hartert and Neumann: S Ethiopia south to N Tanzania. ADULT ♂: crown, back, upperwing- and uppertail-coverts brown to dark brown, crown feathers basally white, of back basally barred brown and white. Chin and throat white, streaked or spotted dark brown. Breast and belly white, tinged rufous, with large round dark brown blotches; thighs and undertail-coverts white, barred rufous, underwing-coverts brown to dark brown, marked rufous and white on inner webs, especially below, forming conspicuous pale carpal patch broadly tipped and barred blackish. Tail grey-brown to brown above, below grey to grey-brown, largely white on inner webs of outer feathers, broadly tipped dark grey-brown and with 6–7 dark bars. Eye, cere and feet yellow. ♀ similar, larger, usually more heavily barred and blotched. SIZE: wing, ♂ 332–336, ♀ 345–356; tail, ♂ 174–183, ♀ 180–196; tarsus, 61–72.

IMMATURE: like adult, but less heavily blotched below, more streaky; feathers of upperside edged rufous. Eye brown, cere and feet yellow.

DOWNY YOUNG: greyish white; eye brown, cere and feet pale yellow.

B. o. trizonatus Rudebeck. South Africa from Cape Province north to Natal and E Transvaal. Similar in size: wing ♂ 318–352 (335), ♀ 330–362 (349); WEIGHT: (1) unsexed, 700. Much more rufous edging to feathers of upperside, underparts less heavily spotted, more streaked, with broad pale band across breast; underwing-coverts white, sparsely spotted brown.

This species often regarded as a race of the Common Buzzard *B. b. buteo* and is certainly marginally distinct, but Vaurie (1961) regards it as a good species and this is also accepted by Stresemann and Amadon (1979), who also discard

Buteo oreophilus

the name *B. tachardus* Smith proposed by Brooke (1974) on grounds of priority. We therefore continue to use the long-accepted scientific name for this species.

Field Characters. Cannot be confused with any race of the Jackal Buzzard *B. rufofuscus* anywhere in range; much smaller, with entirely different voice. Easily confused, however, especially in South Africa, with migrant Steppe Buzzards *B. b. vulpinus* from Oct–Apr as similar-sized and much alike. In E Africa, the resident race is much more heavily marked with large round blotches below in adults; in South Africa the resident race is paler below, both in flight and when perched, than most Steppe Buzzards, with almost plain pale tail below, and broad whitish band across chest. Immatures are almost white below, sparsely streaked dark brown and much paler than most immature Steppe Buzzards. Confusion could occur, however, between individuals unless handled and measured.

Voice. Recorded (18). Calls often, a loud clear mew, 'peee-oo' or 'peeeew', alternatively rendered 'keeee-oo', 'keeeer' or 'keeee'; sometimes 'keeee-hehehe' (South Africa). Resembles voice of Steppe Buzzard, but seems more piercing and higher-pitched. Any small *Buteo* sp. calling thus in African highland forests is almost certainly Mountain Buzzard.

General Habits. Little known. Inhabits forests, thus ecologically separated in most of range from Jackal Buzzard in same general area, but they sometimes (e.g. SE Ethiopia) occur together. In South Africa occurs in remnant natural forests and exotic plantations in mountainous areas from Cape Mountains north to escarpments of E Transvaal. In E Africa is confined to montane forests, between 2200–3500 m, and seldom occurs in open montane moorlands at higher altitudes, or on adjacent grassy plateaus. In SE Ethiopia mainly confined to montane forests at 2500–3600 m, especially in *Hagenia* and *Hypericum* woodlands. In Zaïre in and above *Hagenia* and *Hypericum* zones between 3000–3600 m; in Guinea, Liberia and Ivory Coast between 900–1300 m (K. Curry-Lindahl, pers. comm.). Alti-

tude range increases northwards from near sea level in Cape Province (Knysna), to 1000–2000 m in Transvaal, further north only at high altitudes.

Apparently sedentary wherever it occurs, pairs found in same areas annually. Normally seen flying, as inconspicuous when perched; attracts attention by frequent calling. Alternatively, seen perched on conspicuous tree-top, often overlooking a glade, where may be hunting. Hunts also within forest cover, especially (E Africa–Ethiopia) relatively open woods of *Hagenia* and *Hypericum*. Catches most prey on ground or on trees, but can probably catch some flying birds. Solitary, or in pairs; any records of flocks almost certainly indicate confusion with Steppe Buzzard.

Food. Few definite records. Mainly small mammals, but also chameleons, other lizards, frogs, some birds.

Breeding Habits. Little known. Pairs have regular territories, defended as in Common Buzzard *B. b. buteo* by soaring and frequent calling. Display flights spectacular, vertical plunging dives at great speed for up to 300–350 m from high soaring flight, with wings half closed, turning up at bottom of dive to repeat, or plunging into forest. Also performs undulating displays, with shorter dives followed by upward swoops, repeated. Mutual soaring and calling above forest is frequent; sometimes ♂ then dives at ♀, who rolls and presents claws; displays very like those of Common Buzzard.

NEST: in trees, large structure of sticks, lined with green leaves; probably used repeatedly for several years, but no details.

EGGS: normally 2; round ovals, dull white, unmarked or indistinctly blotched brown. SIZE: 51·0–58·2 × 39·8–45·0.

Laying dates: W Kenya Mar (dry); E Kenya Sept, Oct (dry); South Africa, Cape, Aug–Nov, peak Sept–Oct (spring). In tropical areas lays late in dry season, but young may then be in nest in rains. Little other detail recorded.

Incubation said to be by ♀ only; period estimated 30 days. Fledging period *c.* 40 days (McLachlan and Liversidge 1978).

Plates
24 and 30
(Opp. pp. 371
and 451)

Buteo rufinus (Cretschmar). Long-legged Buzzard. Buse féroce.

Falco rufinus Cretschmar, 1827. Rüppell, Atlas Reise Nördl. Afrika, Vögel, p. 40, pl. 27; upper Nubia, Shendi, Sennar and Ethiopia.

Range and Status. Palearctic migrant and resident. Nominate *B. r. rufinius* breeds Central Europe east to Central Asia; scarce winter migrant to N and NE Africa, recorded once, Zambia. *B. r. cirtensis* resident, non-migratory, breeds N Morocco east to Egypt. Numbers not recorded to have varied much in recent years.

Description. *B. r. rufinus* (Cretschmar): N and NE Africa. ADULT ♂: highly variable, several rather distinct phrases, as follows:

(i) Dark phase: all dark brown, some are blackish, feathers of head edged rufous. Primaries blackish, becoming white on inner webs, with white shafts, mottled and edged brown innermost tipped brown, edged blackish forming clear white patch in spread wing. Tail plain cinnamon brown, with broad subterminal blackish bar.

(ii) Rufous phase: lighter brown above, feathers of back and wing-coverts broadly edged rufous, mainly rufous on head and neck. Below, generally bright rufous, paler on chin, blotched and barred brown. Tail uniform pale rufous. Wing-feathers blackish, becoming whitish basally, innermost tipped brown, edged blackish.

(iii) Paler head and neck yellowish brown, feathers with broad pale edges. Below, pale yellowish brown, streaked and mottled brown on abdomen, thighs and undertail- and wing-coverts. Tail pale rufous, almost white in some, broadly tipped darker brown.

(iv) Pale phase: as (iii) but browner, less rufous, markings almost white. Head and shoulders very pale brown; underside white, streaked light brown.

In all, eye golden or yellow; cere greenish yellow; legs bright yellow. SIZE: wing, ♂ 418–447 (436·6), ♀ 450–487 (462·1); tail, ♂ 224–240 (231·7), ♀ 240–289 (261·2); tarsus, ♂ 83–92 (85·9), ♀ 86–95 (89·8); wing-span, ♂ 1262–1430 (1355), ♀ 1405–1480 (1445). WEIGHT: ♂ 1100–1281 (1179), ♀ 1147–1760 (1218) (Glutz von Blotzheim *et al.* 1971).

IMMATURE: generally like adult, but more rufous edgings above, and tail feathers with numerous dark bars.

B. r. cirtensis (Levaillant). Breeds N Africa; generally paler, most like phases (iii) or (iv) above. Much smaller: wing ♂ 345–384, ♀ 380–425.

Field Characters. Nominate *B. r. rufinus* normally unmistakable because of large size (similar to that of a small eagle and 10–20% larger than Augur Buzzard *B. rufofuscus augur*) in Ethiopia and E Africa. Almost plain pale rufous tail also distinctive in adult, and, when perched, long yellow legs noticeable. Very much larger than any Steppe Buzzard *B. buteo vulpinus*. *B. r. cirtensis* only breeding buzzard in NW Africa; considerably larger and paler than migrant Steppe Buzzards. Immatures with barred tails sometimes scarcely distinguishable from Steppe or Common Buzzard *B. b. buteo*, scarcely, if at all, larger, but have noticeably longer legs when perched. In flight, whitish patch at base of primaries, generally pale underside and tail normally distinctive.

Voice. Recorded (2a). *B. r. cirtensis*: a sharp mew, like that of Common Buzzard, perhaps higher-pitched, and more squealing or wheezy. *B. r. rufinus*: silent in winter quarters.

General Habits. Little known in Africa; *B. r. cirtensis* in N Africa little known; here occupies ecological niche of Common Buzzard, occurring in oak and conifer woods, mixed woodland and cultivation, maccia, and in subdesert steppes. Generally seen perched on trees, rocks, fenceposts, telegraph poles, awaiting opportunity to catch prey. Sluggish, not as inclined to fly as smaller buzzards. In Ethiopia–Kenya rare migrant individuals of *B. r. rufinus* usually solitary, but may associate with Tawny and Steppe Eagles *Aquila rapax*, for instance when all are attracted to rat plagues. May then settle on ground freely.

Migrant *B. r. rufinus* leaves northern breeding areas Aug, passes through Middle East Sept, and may reach equator (Kenya) by 10 Sept; however, most E and NE African records Nov–Jan. A few migrants also reach N Africa, mainly Egypt, but occur as far west as Algeria, and recorded south to Hoggar in Sahara (Etchécopar and Hüe 1967). Most of the migrant Asia population does not enter Africa, wintering further north or east.

Food. Mainly small mammals, especially rodents, maximum size that of young hare. Some lizards and

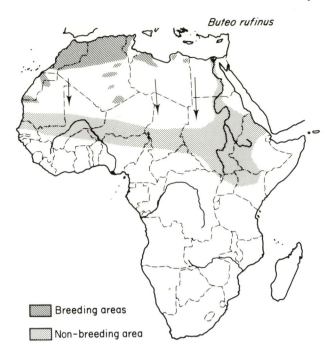

Buteo rufinus

▨ Breeding areas

☐ Non-breeding area

small snakes. In N Africa stated to live mainly on poultry, wounded birds and carrion (Etchécopar and Hüe 1967); may eat these, but is not wholly dependent on them. In E Africa–Ethiopia feeds on grass rats *Arvicanthis*, gorging at rat plagues, and mole rats *Tachyroyctes*; perches on ground and easily catches either.

Breeding Habits. Little known (*B. r. cirtensis* little detail recorded; *B. r. rufinus* little better known). Pairs have regularly established breeding sites used annually. Display virtually undescribed, but apparently performs undulating displays similar to other *Buteo* spp. *B. r. cirtensis* soars and calls over breeding site.

NEST: mainly on cliffs, sometimes in trees; in N Morocco perhaps prefers cliffs, even in wooded areas where large trees available. Structure at first small, a mere circle of sticks, becoming larger with repeated use, 80–100 cm across by *c.* 30–50 cm thick. Made of sticks and lined with green leaves, very like that of Common Buzzard. Pairs may have more than one nest on same cliff, close together.

EGGS: 2–4, laying interval unknown; N Africa mean (34 clutches) 2·5 (Heim de Balsac and Mayaud 1962). White to greenish white, blotched brown, with grey under-markings. SIZE: (42, *B. r. cirtensis*) 47·5–60·1 × 40·5–46·5 (55·0 × 44·0) (Schönwetter 1960); WEIGHT: *c.* 59.

Laying dates: N Africa 2nd half Mar–early May, 1 brood of 6 downy chicks reported (Heim de Balsac and Mayaud 1962). No other good details available; but whole breeding cycle from egg-laying to departure of young probably *c.* 75 days.

References

Etchécopar, R. D. and Hüe, F. (1967).
Heim de Balsac, H. and Mayaud, N. (1962).

Plate 24

(Opp. p. 371)

Buteo lagopus (Pontoppidan). Rough-legged Buzzard. Buse pattue.

Falco Lagopus Pontoppidan, 1763. Danske Atlas, 1, p. 616; no locality = Denmark.

Range and Status. Palearctic winter migrant straggling south to N Africa at Cape Bon (Mayaud 1970) and Libya (K. Curry-Lindahl, pers. comm.). Full description omitted as only vagrant.

Field Characters. About same size as Common Buzzard *B. b. buteo*, larger than Steppe Buzzard *B. b. vulpinus*, smaller than Long-legged Buzzard *B. rufinus*. Readily distinguished by broad dark brown band across lower breast, contrasting with white, streaked throat, pale streaked upperbreast. Pale phase individuals much paler, more greyish than Common Buzzards. In flight, underwing generally pale, including underwing-coverts, with black tips to all feathers, prominent black spot at carpal joint. Tail basally white, unbarred, with conspicuous broad blackish subterminal band, diagnostic from any other buzzard. At close quarters feathered tarsi distinguish it from all but pale phase Booted Eagle *Hieraaetus pennatus*, which lacks black tail bar and has dark wing-feathers contrasting with whitish underwing-coverts.

Plates 24 and 30

(Opp. pp. 371 and 451)

Buteo auguralis Salvadori. Red-necked Bussard; Red-tailed Buzzard. Buse d'Afrique.

Buteo auguralis Salvadori, 1865. Atti. Soc. Ital. Sci. Nat., Milan, 8, p. 377; Ethiopia.

Range and Status. Resident; intra-tropical migrant, from Sierra Leone east to W Ethiopia, south through Zaïre and Uganda to Angola. Mainly in lowlands, Cameroon to 2500 m (Young 1946). Frequent, locally common, occasionally abundant in migrant flocks.

Buteo auguralis

Description. ADULT ♂: crown red-brown, sides of head, neck and mantle chestnut, feathers with black centres; back and upperwing-coverts dark brown. Throat white, feathers tipped dark brown; upper breast dark brown, clearly defined from white lower breast, belly, undertail- and underwing-coverts, with large blackish heart-shaped spots on breast, some chestnut mottling on underwing-coverts and axillaries. Primaries and secondaries brown above, tipped black; secondaries barred darker brown, primaries basally white. Tail rufous-chestnut, subterminally banded black. Eye brown, cere and feet yellow. Sexes alike ♀ slightly larger; SIZE: wing, ♂ 225–361 (341), ♀ 339–395 (367); tail, 178–205; tarsus, 77–82. WEIGHT: (8) ♂ 560–620 (580), ♀ 660–890 (760) (Thiollay 1978a).

IMMATURE: above brown, feathers edged rufous; breast, belly and thighs rich tawny, some dark spots on breast and flanks. Wing-feathers rufous-brown, barred darker towards tip, tail rufous, irregularly barred darker. Eye brown; cere and feet yellow. May moult to adult plumage by first becoming white below, losing rufous edges above, then acquiring dark brown upper breast and spots on white lower breast.

DOWNY YOUNG: white, grey on crown and round eye, tinged cinnamon on back rump and wings; eye brown, cere and feet pale yellow.

Field Characters. A small buzzard, normally not found with any other. Easily distinguished from Steppe Buzzard *B. b. vulpinus* by white dark-spotted underside contrasting strongly with dark breast, chestnut head and neck. Much smaller than Augur Buzzard *B. rufofuscus augur*, distinguished at once by dark upper breast and chestnut head and neck. Rufous tail not diagnostic. Might perhaps be confused with Beaudouin's Snake Eagle *Circaetus gallicus beaudouini*, but much smaller, with chestnut head, neck and tail, and yellow legs.

Voice. Not recorded. Loud clear mewing scream, 'peeee-ah', shriller than similar calls of Steppe or Common Buzzard *B. b. buteo*; also 'pee-pee-pee-peeah'. Vocal in display and when soaring, otherwise silent. Call also diagnostic from Augur Buzzard.

General Habits. Well known. Inhabits broad-leaved woodlands from Sierra Leone east to W Ethiopia, and in south edges of forest, not dense primary forest. Habitat in northern part of range at northern limit 10–12°N much more open than in southern breeding range, but never very arid; avoids very dry seasons in north by migrating south to breed.

Habits in non-breeding range little observed. Migrates south at end of rains, beginning late Sept, passing 7–8°S in Nigeria mainly late Oct-early Nov. In Ivory Coast first arrivals 5°N late Sept, most arriving Oct, remaining till early May. Breeds in southern heavily wooded parts of range, then moves north again, after onset of main rains. Southward migration obvious, in small groups or singly, often soaring above mountain tops to gain height and glide on. Northward movement occurs singly, breeding birds and immatures probably remaining later than non-breeding or unsuccessful birds; little observed, moving singly and unobtrusively.

Within southern breeding range prefers areas with mixed forest and open spaces, plantations, small farms, open areas in savanna, forest edges and burned ground. Often perches on dead trees in cultivation, watching for prey. In Ivory Coast hunts most in cultivation and plantations, especially in secondary forest (62% of time); 32% of time in natural open savanna and degraded savanna (Thiollay 1977a). 99% of kills made on ground, 1% in low herbage, apparently none in flight. Rather unobtrusive by day, flying little.

Food. 1 analysis, Ivory Coast, recorded 57 insects (mainly alate termites, grasshoppers, mantids); 4 spiders, millipedes, crabs; 9 reptiles, including a large venomous viper; 7 amphibians; 2 small mammals; 5 birds, of which 2 adult. Generally subsists on small animals, largest a mouse or snake; reptiles and mammals relatively important by weight, vertebrates 61% by weight (Thiollay 1977a). Elsewhere, similar—frogs, lizards, including chameleons, small snakes, small mammals, insects.

Breeding Habits. Little known. Pairs occupy temporary territories, but extent not studied; same area may be used repeatedly. Display mainly mutual soaring and calling, excited screaming. ♂ also performs undulating display, with steep dives and upward swoops. Also

'rocking aerobatics', weaving from side to side in flight (Holman 1947). Pairs soaring together often trail feet (as in Jackal Buzzard), but rolling and presenting claws not recorded.

NEST: in trees, usually high up, inaccessible, often in *Borassus* palms. In Cameroon highlands sometimes on cliffs (Serle 1950). May be used repeatedly successive years, nest repair brief. New nests take many weeks to construct, may not be used that year (Holman 1947); of sticks, lined with green leaves. May be small, or after several years' use measure up to 1 m across. Situation in woodlands, in *Borassus* palms 10–15 m above ground, but in forests normally higher, up to 30 m or more. No data on role of sexes in building.

EGGS: 2–3; blunt ovals, bluish white, variously, usually sparsely, streaked and spotted brown. SIZE: 49·3–58·5 × 42·6–47·3.

Laying dates: W Africa Jan–Feb; Zaire Oct, Jan; S Sudan Feb. Thought to breed Darfur, Sudan, July, but most improbable. Scanty records all indicate laying late in dry season, with young in nest early in subsequent heavy rains.

Incubation reported to be carried out by both sexes, mainly ♀; if ♀ shot may immediately be replaced (next day). Combined incubation and fledging periods probably *c.* 50–60 days, young leaving nest Mar–Apr (early rains), migrating north *c.* 1 month later.

References
Holman, F. C. (1947).
Thiollay, J.-M. (1977–78).
Serle, W. M. (1950).

Buteo rufofuscus (J. R. Forster). Jackal Buzzard; Augur Buzzard. Buse rounoir; Buse augure.

Falco rufofuscus J. R. Forster, 1798. In Levaillant's Naturg. Afr. Vög., p. 59, pl 16; South Africa (ex Levaillant).

Plates 24 and 30
(Opp. pp. 371 and 451)

Range and Status. Resident; 3 races (possibly 2 good species), throughout more mountainous regions of southern and E Africa from Cape Province to N Somalia; western limit is western Ethiopian escarpment, W Uganda, parts of highland Zaïre and Angola. In most of range the commonest buzzard; common, locally abundant, at least frequent. Occurs in South Africa from sea level to highest peaks, lower altitude limit increasing northwards, not below 1000 m Kenya, 1500 m Ethiopia, but occurring on Afro-alpine moorlands to summits of very high peaks at 5000 m or over (Mount Kenya, Semien Mountains, Ethiopia). Numbers probably stable, nowhere threatened; adapts well to cultivated land and dense human habitation, probably benefiting therefrom, and from, for example, planted eucalyptus trees on otherwise treeless plateaus (Ethiopia).

Description. *B. r. rufofuscus* (J. R. Forster): South Africa south of Limpopo River and Damaraland, Namibia. ADULT ♂: above, almost black, flecked white; uppertail-coverts and tail (above and below) chestnut, sometimes with a dark subterminal bar. Below, chin and throat white, spotted black on sides of breast and throat. Rest of underside, including

Buteo rufofuscus

▦ *B r rufofuscus*
▨ *B r augur*
▤ *B r archeri*

underwing-coverts pale to rich rufous or chestnut, mottled black. Primaries above black, externally ashy grey, secondaries whitish, both barred black; wing-feathers below white, tipped black, forming dark trailing edge, barred black on inner webs of secondaries. Eye red-brown; cere and feet yellow. SIZE: wing, ♂ 393–410 (401), ♀ 423–444 (432); tail, 180–220; tarsus, 76–85. WEIGHT: 55 unsexed 790–1370 (1064); ♂♂ probably 790–1100, ♀♀ 1000–1370; 1 ♀ recorded 1530 (Biggs *et al.* 1979).

IMMATURE: browner above, black on forehead, nape, mantle. Below, including underwing-coverts, pale chestnut, with dark shaft streaks, some black spots. Wing-feathers terminally black, basally white, externally washed grey; secondaries browner, barred darker brown towards tip. Tail brown, with 11–12 dark bars. Eye brown; cere and feet yellow.

Adult plumage acquired by series of moults, beginning with wing- and tail-feathers at 9 months, then contour feathers. 1st moult complete at 18–20 months but full adult plumage not acquired until 2·5–3 years; upperside darkens, tail loses bars, underside becomes more chestnut. Probably can breed at 3 years old.

DOWNY YOUNG: white; eye brown, cere and feet pale yellow. Of *B. r. augur* darker, dull pale grey; eye grey-brown, cere and feet yellow.

B. r. augur Rüppell (Augur Buzzard). Central Africa north of Limpopo River north to Ethiopian highlands. Above, slaty black, tail and uppertail-coverts chestnut. Below, including underwing-coverts, white, with dark spots (heavier in ♀♀) on sides of throat. Immatures browner above, pale brownish below; tail brown, barred darker brown. Slightly larger: wing ♂ 384–405 (413), ♀ 435–446 (439) (Lendrum 1979); wing-loading, (1) 45 N/m². WEIGHT: ♂ 880–1160, ♀ 1097–1303; ♂ (5) av. 988, ♀ (7) av. 1130 (Lendrum 1979).

A melanistic form of this race occurs; all black except grey and black barred wing-feathers, and chestnut tail. Rare in southern part of range, in Kenya averaging *c.* 10% of individuals, reaching maximum of 50–55% in wet cold forests of Bale Mountains, SE Ethiopia; commoner in wet forested areas.

B. r. archeri Sclater. Highlands of N Somalia; slightly smaller: wing 379–436. Has more chestnut on feathers of upperside; adults have throat white with black on sides of neck; rest of underparts rich chestnut. Immatures have white undersides, barred tails; plain chestnut tail is acquired before chestnut of underside of body (Archer and Godman 1937).

The last 2 races *B. r. augur* and *B. r. archeri* may form a separate species *B. augur* Rüppell, as suggested by, for example, Brooke (1975). Reasons include: (i) very strikingly different plumage in *B. r. rufofuscus* and *B. r. augur* with no intermediates; (ii) no melanistic morphs in *B. r. rufofuscus*; (iii) some differences in bodily proportions, notably length of inner secondaries (Brooke 1975); and (iv) different voice (undescribed in *B. r. archeri*). These may be adequate reasons for recognizing 2 spp., but *B. r. rufofuscus* has never been thoroughly studied in the field, and the differences in bodily proportions are slight, while most habits are very similar. We therefore consider it best to leave this as 1 sp., with the strong possibility that 2 distinct spp. may be demonstrated by further detailed study, especially in South Africa.

Field Characters. In most of range, much the commonest and most obvious buzzard, scarcely possible to confuse with others. Much larger than Mountain Buzzard *B. oreophilus*, with very different voice; also ecologically separated in most areas. Adult *B. r. augur* immediately distinguished from migrant Long-legged Buzzard *B. r. rufinus* by pure white underside. In flight, *B. rufinus augur* vaguely resembles Bateleur *Terathopius ecaudatus* (especially melanistic morph), flying with wings held at marked dihedral and characteristic rocking motion from side to side; however, easily distinguished from this species by very broad wings, when spread almost touching spread tail. Much larger than Red-necked Buzzard *B. auguralis*, without chestnut neck and head, dark breast and spots on underside; also ecologically separated (W Ethiopia).

Voice. Recorded (2a, 6, 8, 18, 19, 26, 28). Jackal Buzzard *B. r. rufofuscus*: a sharp, high-pitched bark, 'kweh' or 'bweh', resembling bark of jackal *Canis mesomelas*. Also, a mewing 'kip-kweeeu, kweeeu, kweeeu'; 'peee-ee-eew'; 'wheee-uw, wheeee-uw' or 'kreeee-uw', slightly rasping, and lower-pitched than mew of Mountain Buzzard. Augur Buzzard *B. r. augur*: a distinctive, crowing bark 'ah-aow-ah-aow' or 'o-waa-o-waa', that of ♂ higher-pitched than of ♀. In display repeated 'ah-waaa-ah-waaaa', higher-pitched, longer than normal call. No mewing calls at all. Voice difference is strongest argument for recognizing 2 different species. Augur Buzzard is noisy, calling frequently; Jackal Buzzard relatively silent. Voice of Somali Buzzard *B. r. archeri* not described; if markedly different this may be yet a 3rd species.

General Habits. Well known. Throughout range, mainly found in mountains or hilly country, avoiding lowland plains, but occurring where a small hill or escarpment breaks large areas of plains. In South Africa Jackal Buzzard occurs from sea level to summits of Cape and Natal/Drakensberg mountain ranges (to 3500 m, Lesotho), but also in broken Karoo subdesert scrub, anywhere with small hills and rocky escarpments. In Central Africa, Augur Buzzard frequents any hilly country, from 1000 m upwards; and in E Africa–Ethiopia occurs from isolated hills in semi-arid plains of thornbush at 1000 m to high moorlands of Mounts Kenya and Kilimanjaro, Semien and Bale Mountains. Here is normally ecologically separated from Mountain Buzzard, occurring in grasslands below forest edge and in moorlands above forest; but in SE Ethiopia is also found in open *Hagenia–Hypericum* forests, hunting both within forest and in glades or open moorlands.

Habits of E and Central African Augur Buzzard much more fully described than of South African Jackal Buzzard. Pairs frequent same areas regularly, roosting on trees or, less often, cliff ledges (more on cliffs at very high altitudes). Can fly very soon after dawn, and then either flies from one hunting perch to another, or soars or hovers over open country. Perches on dead or live trees, or on flower spikes of giant lobeleas on Afro-alpine moorlands. Perches especially (where available) on pylons, telegraph posts, fence posts, waiting for prey, very often along roadsides. In Zimbabwe, perched 58% of time, soaring 29%, hovering 13% (Lendrum 1979). Prey commonly caught crossing bare open spaces such as roads; and buzzard does not hesitate to snatch prey even from between fast-moving vehicles (E Africa). Towards midday, either rests in shade of tree foliage, or soars much higher than at other times. In mountainous country with strong winds and updraughts, rides these with exquisite grace, poising almost motionless in violent gusty winds, constantly adjusting wing-tips, using strong upcurrents to maintain stationary position while watching for prey. Individuals often frequent same area daily, using same perches repeatedly; but may move preferred hunting ground temporarily to, for example, recently burned area where prey such as rats freshly exposed. Frequently perches on ground, or low mounds, especially in Ethiopian–Kenyan highlands when hunting mole rats (*Tachyroyctes* spp.). Then may detect mole rat from air, alight silently near; when rat moves again in burrow, seizes it underground with sudden short pounce. Hunts mainly in morning, but also may hunt in afternoon and evening, returning to roost normally just before dark, sometimes 1–2 h before. Pairs frequently hunt close together, either feeding on the other's kills if large enough.

Sedentary wherever it occurs, performing no migrations; apparently not even driven to lower altitudes from very high mountains with nightly frost (Ethiopia–Kenya) in cold wet rainy seasons. Immatures wander more than adults, which remain in territories throughout life of an individual (very easily observed in melanistic morphs).

Food. Variable; highly adaptable, taking any available prey from small grasshoppers to large powerful snakes such as cobras, puff-adders. Mammals to size of rock hyrax, hare; some ground birds, frogs. In E Africa–Ethiopia preferred food is rats, mole rats, other small mammals and a few ground birds, such as larks, pipits. In Zimbabwe, detailed recent studies show preference for reptiles, 32/54 items (mammals 20/54; birds 2/54); but mammals perhaps proportionately more important by weight (Lendrum 1979). Up to 83% reptiles recorded at another nest (Weaving 1972). Takes carrion in form of road kills, but seldom seen at or near large carcasses with other carrion birds (vultures, marabous). In Lesotho Jackal Buzzard feeds on placentae of sheep when lambing. Preferred food where available undoubtedly rodents, especially field rats *Arvicanthis*, and mole rats; highest population density found where such prey abundant (Kenya–Ethiopia).

Probably cannot catch birds in flight; almost all prey caught from perches by short downward swoop, often when exposed in open ground, e.g. on road; but can detect small green grasshopper among tall weeds at over 100 m, flying straight to it. Often hovers in open country, like other buzzards, poising head to wind with gently fanning wings; then descends in graceful 'parachuting' pose, controlling speed of descent by angle of wings, finally raising them vertically above back to drop on prey at short range.

Breeding Habits. Very well known. Intensely territorial, maintaining discrete territories regularly used by long succession of different adults for up to 30 years or more. Territory consists of inner core used in breeding season, and larger outer range used when not breeding (Lendrum 1979). Territory size, Zimbabwe, estimated *c.* 20 km², but in E Africa often much smaller; nearest neighbour distance between nests, Kenya Rift Valley, less than 1 km, suggesting territories of only 1

km² or less. Overall average, Matopos hills, 17 km² pair; in Kenya–Ethiopia often much less. Pairs remain year-round in territory, defending it not only against other Augur Buzzards, but against much larger, more powerful raptors such as Verreaux's Eagle *Aquila verreauxi*, Lammergeier *Gypaetus barbatus*; in turn may be attacked by smaller species, such as Black-shouldered Kite *Elanus caeruleus*, kestrels.

Display spectacular and beautiful, typically aerial. ♂ soars above ♀ with dangling feet, calling, then descends gracefully with wings upraised (parachuting); ♀ responds by calling, lowering feet and, when ♂ approaches, sometimes gently touching her back, rolls sideways and touches his feet; pair repeats this performance many times, gradually descending. ♂ may also stoop at perched ♀, forcing her to squat flat on perch. One or both may also soar to height, then dive and swoop up again over nest-site, most often during incubation (Lendrum 1979). Similar displays not described in Jackal Buzzard. Copulation occurs on tree perches or on tops of boulders, cliff ledges; may occur up to 4 times in 25 min, averaging *c.* 2 h between acts, at any time of day (Lendrum 1979). 2 ♂♂ known to copulate with same ♀, and polyandry during part of breeding cycle once recorded. Polygyny, 1 ♂ with 2 ♀♀, also recorded (Lendrum 1979); 1 of the 2 ♀♀ bred, the other built nest but did not lay.

NEST: either on cliffs or trees, depending on locality. In Jackal Buzzard more nests on cliffs than trees. In Augur Buzzard, Zimbabwe, most nests on cliffs or at base of trees growing on cliffs (Lendrum 1979), but in E Africa–Ethiopia most nests in trees, except at very high altitudes, where cliffs usually preferred. Nests recorded in Giant Groundsel (*Senecio barbatipes*) at 4000 m in Mount Elgon crater and on cliff at 4000 m in Arussi Mountains, Ethiopia. Most nests in trees are 7–15 m above ground, sometimes higher (e.g. in tall eucalyptus). Normally shaded, within canopy, often on lateral branch, but sometimes entirely open to sun on top of tree. In E Africa and Somalia thorny *Acacia* or *Euphorbia* spp. often preferred. In Ethiopia species has benefited and increased through plantation of eucalyptus in otherwise treeless plateaus (by order of Emperor Menelik II). Nests are large structures, normally used for several years; pairs may have 2–3, usually preferring 1. Made of sticks, lined with green leaves, 56–64 cm across by 15–19 cm deep (18, Matopos: Lendrum 1979); sometimes larger and deeper, 1 m by 30 cm E Africa. Both sexes build, ♂♂ especially bringing green material. Sticks broken off trees, or picked up from ground. Most building occurs from soon after dawn to 08.00 h, occasionally later. Material is added until late in fledging period (Lendrum 1979). ♀ spends much time in nest, shaping bowl etc. just before laying, but apparently is not fed by ♂ at that time.

EGGS: 1–3, laid at 2–3 day intervals. Means: (28 clutches, *B. r. rufofuscus*) 1·93 (Dean 1971); (34, Matopos, Zimbabwe) 2·03; (*B. r. augur*, E Africa–Ethiopia) 1–3, no marked difference; (*B. r. archeri*, Somalia) 1–2, no clutch of 3 known, 1 frequent, averaging smaller (Archer and Godman 1937). Round ovals; white or bluish white, usually sparingly marked brown, sometimes unmarked. SIZE: (*B. r. rufofuscus*) 54·4–64·8 × 44·0–50·6 (59·7 × 47·4); (53, *B. r. augur*) 55·1–59·3 × 43·5–47·2 (Lendrum 1979); (3, *B. r. archeri*) 54·7–59·2 × 42·8–57·7 (56·8 × 45·1) (Schönwetter 1960); WEIGHT: 65–74.

Laying dates: *B. r. rufofuscus*, South Africa (Cape area) July–Nov, peaking Aug–Sept (late winter–early spring); Transvaal, Natal June–Dec, peak July–Sept (dry season). *B. r. augur*, Zimbabwe July–Oct, peak Aug–Sept (dry season) (Lendrum 1979); Zambia July–Oct (dry); E Africa extended seasons; Uganda–W Kenya 1 record in each of 7/12 months; E Kenya records 10/12 months, especially June–Sept (33/55 records), cool mid-year dry season (but at very high altitudes main dry season Jan–Mar preferred); Ethiopia Jan, Mar, Sept, Nov (dry season preferred at high altitudes); Zaïre May. *B. r. archeri*, end Mar–early Apr (late dry season) (Archer and Godman 1937). Eggs often laid late in dry season, young sometimes in nest subsequent rains.

Incubation begins 1st egg. Carried out by both sexes (*B. r. augur*), ♀ most in early stages, ♂'s share increasing in 3rd week to 40%, decreasing to 26% in last week (Lendrum 1979); only ♀ at night. Incubation period: 39–40 days (Lendrum 1979). Hatching time: (1 record) 39 h.

Chicks hatch at intervals, resulting in violent inter-sibling strife beginning 24–48 h after hatching of 2nd chick, continuing for 5–8 days until younger chick eliminated; movement by younger chick appears to stimulate aggression by elder, and more likely to occur when parent off nest. Younger normally eliminated, but occasionally reared (E Africa). Weight increases from *c*. 30 g at hatching to 200–250 g at 14 days; then rapidly to 850–900 at 25 days, more slowly thereafter to 1000–1100 at 42 days. Tarsus development complete by 28 days. 1st feathers (primaries) appear at 7 days, contour back feathers by 21 days. Mainly feathered day 35, with adherent down; fully feathered, little visible down day 42. Thereafter development mainly in wing-feathers. Fledging period not exactly known, but estimated 48–55 days, maximum 59 days (Weaving 1972).

♀ broods young up to 10 days old much of the time; thereafter spends much of time off nest, remaining nearby. ♂ brings all prey at this stage. Full details not available, but young continue to be fed by adults till 40–45 days old, when well feathered (Van Someren 1956). After 1st flight remain near nest for some time, until 70 days after hatching; many have left area 2–3 weeks after 1st flight when 65–70 days old, but some remain near until 90–100 days from hatch (Lendrum 1979; Van Someren 1956).

Some pairs do not breed annually. In 78 observed pair-years, 59 chicks reared from 63 definite attempts, i.e. 0·75/pair/year overall, 0·93/breeding pair, 1·00/successful nest. Most common cause of loss, egg predation, possibly by ravens or monkeys. At estimated 75% mortality before sexual maturity at 3 years, adults would require a breeding life of 10 years; observations suggest this is longer than normal.

References
Lendrum, A. L. (1979).
Van Someren, V. G. L. (1956).
Weaving, A. J. S. (1972).

Genus *Aquila* Brisson

The most widespread and generally best-known of several genera of eagles with feathered tarsi. Cosmopolitan, except South America. Medium-sized to large eagles, mainly brown, 1 African sp. (*A. verreauxi*) black and white; immatures not normally very different from adults. Most powerful and predatory, beak and feet strong, beak arched, hind talon long, strong. Heads and necks with lanceolate feathers. Wings long, sometimes broad, with 6–7 outer primaries emarginated on both webs, adapted for soaring. Tail moderately long to long, rounded or wedge-shaped. Feed mainly on mammals, some birds, some carrion.

7 of 9 spp. are found in Africa. 3, *A. pomarina*, *A. clanga* and *A. heliaca*, are purely Palearctic winter migrants. 2, *A. rapax* and *A. chrysaetos*, breed in Africa and in Eurasia, *A. chrysaetos* only in NW Africa; *A. rapax* subspecies also migrate in winter from Palearctic. *A. verreauxi* is resident, sedentary in mountains, mainly E and South Africa west to Sudan. Smallest, *A. wahlbergi*, is transequatorial intra-tropical migrant, breeding mainly in southern Africa. All African species well known to intimately known, except the migrants, *A. pomarina*, *A. clanga* and *A. heliaca*, little known in Africa, well known in Europe.

Most lay 1–3 eggs, usually 2; have clucking, yelping or barking (not whistling or screaming) voices. *A. chrysaetos* and *A. verreauxi* are ecological counterparts, forming a superspecies with 2 Australasian species. *A. wahlbergi* is unique in being small, slightly crested, laying only 1 egg, and having whistling voice. It may not therefore be correctly placed in this genus, but 'fits' no better elsewhere.

3 medium-sized; all-brown species, *A. pomarina*, *A. clanga* and *A. rapax*, are notoriously difficult to identify in the field. Their distribution and habits in Africa in the Palearctic winter are thus imperfectly known, as the migrants *A. pomarina* and *A. clanga* are often overlooked among more numerous resident and migrant *A. rapax* subspecies. For full details on this subject see Porter *et al.* (1976).

Aquila pomarina Brehm. Lesser Spotted Eagle. Aigle pomarin.

Aquila Pomarina C. L. Brehm, 1831. Handb. Naturg. Vög. Deutschl. p. 27; Pomerania.

Range and Status. Palearctic winter migrant to southern Africa, mainly Oct–Apr, south to E Transvaal, Zimbabwe, Botswana and Namibia. Probably commonest eagle in mid-east migrant concentrations, but rarely noticed in Africa, where range and status ill-defined.

Description. *A. p. pomarina* Brehm, ADULT ♂: all dull brown with (often) whitish uppertail-coverts and nape. Wing-feathers dark brown, contrasting with paler underwing-coverts, often with white or pale bases to 3 outermost primaries, forming a pale spot at carpal joint. Tail-feathers plain brown, unbarred. Eye, feet and cere yellow. SIZE: wing, ♂ 444–493 (470), ♀ 475–505 (492); tail, ♂ 198–237 (217), ♀ 216–234 (225·7); tarsus, ♂ 82–97 (90·6), ♀ 81–99 (91·1); wingspan, ♂ 1340–1455, ♀ (1) 1593. WEIGHT: ♂ (16) 1053–1509 (1197), ♀ (21) 1195–2160 (1499); unsexed (7) Africa 1256–1835 (1542), apparently averaging heavier in winter range. (Glutz von Blotzheim *et al.* 1971; Biggs *et al.* 1979).

IMMATURE: usually darker brown, with larger pale nape patch, and much more white on uppertail-coverts, visible at long range. Secondaries irregularly tipped and spotted buff-white; lesser and greater upperwing-coverts tipped with small white spots. Eye brown, cere and feet yellow.

Rarely, a pale phase occurs, creamy white, with contrasting dark wing- and tail-feathers. Moults to adult plumage in 3–4 years, some spots still show at 3 years.

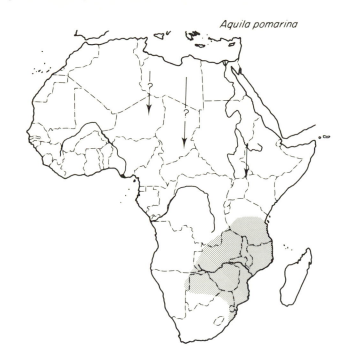

Aquila pomarina

Field Characters. Easily confused with Greater Spotted and Tawny Eagles (*A. clanga* and *A. rapax*); many recent reported sightings E Africa may in fact be Tawny Eagles. Adults usually paler, duller brown than those of Greater Spotted Eagle, but some indistinguishable. In flight, wings held well forward, slightly below horizontal, with normally 6 or 7, separated primaries visible at wing-tip, and usually with marked whitish patch at base of innermost primaries. Wings relatively longer, slimmer, with deeper notch between secondaries and tail than in Greater Spotted Eagle; tail relatively longer, more wedge-shaped. Much less rufous than adult Tawny Eagle in southern African winter range, but some northern Tawny Eagles indistinguishable in colour. Immatures readily recognized by small oval white spots on upperwing-coverts, but whitish crescent-shaped patch above base of tail is not reliable distinction, either from Greater Spotted or Tawny Eagle. At close range, round nostril distinguishes it from Tawny Eagle, not from Greater Spotted Eagle. Relatively long legs, with short feathers forming tight-fitting 'trousers', as opposed to loose 'flags', useful field distinction from Tawny Eagle. Wahlberg's Eagle *A. wahlbergi* is much smaller and slimmer than this species, but also relatively long-legged.

Voice. Recorded (2a). In Africa, silent; in Europe a high-pitched bark or yelp 'kyek-kyek', or cluck 'tyuck'. Also, rapid 'jib-jib-jib' and high-pitched whistling calls. Bark or yelp is much higher-pitched than in Tawny Eagle.

General Habits. Little known in Africa. Most enter via Bosphorus and Suez, a few crossing Mediterranean. Southward migration peaks mid-Sept, when is much the commonest migrant eagle, reduced to a few by early Oct. Once within Africa, scarcely observed north of equator on way to winter quarters; very few definite records E Africa until recently. May often be overlooked in company with migrant Steppe Eagles *A. rapax orientalis*; but some recent records questionable. Perhaps moves south rapidly in large flocks, rarely descending to ground. Winters mainly in southern *Brachystegia* woodland in rainy season Nov–Mar. Fairly common also *Acacia* woodland, Kruger Park, Transvaal. Migrant flocks reported Kenya, Nov, going south, and Tanzania, Mar, going north (Bowles 1967; N. R. Fuggles-Couchman, pers. comm.). Peak northward migration occurs at Suez *c.* 20–25 Apr, not observed E and NE Africa. In main wintering area apparently solitary or in small groups, habits little known. More detailed information needed.

Food. In Europe, mainly small mammals up to 400 g, especially rodents; some lizards, frogs, young birds, carrion. In Africa little known; insects probably relatively important, e.g. grasshoppers caught at grass fires, alate termites.

References
Glutz von Blotzheim, U. N. *et al.* (1971).

Plate 25

(Opp. p. 418)

Aquila clanga Pallas. Greater Spotted Eagle. Aigle criard.

Aquila Clanga Pallas, 1811. Zoogr. Rosso-Asiat., 1, p. 351; Russia and Siberia.

Range and Status. Palearctic winter migrant to Africa Oct–Apr, chiefly NE Africa, unknown south of equator. Earlier records suggest common on migration Bosphorus-Suez late Sept, early Oct, but recent observations suggest frequent confusion with other spp. In Africa formerly recorded quite common Ethiopia (Eritrea), associated with locust swarms (Smith 1957), but recently status obscure. Accurate records scarce and many doubtful as often confused with Tawny Eagle *A. rapax*.

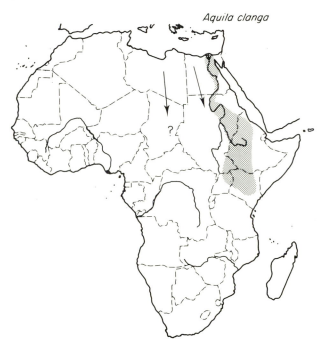

Aquila clanga

Description. ADULT: all dark brown, fresh plumage strongly glossed purplish above; below, duller, paler. Crown, nape, upper and undertail-coverts often edged buff or whitish. Tail- and wing-feathers blackish to purple-brown, tail unbarred in full adults. Eye brown; cere and feet yellow. SIZE: wing, ♂ 490–520 (504), ♀ 520–545 (529); tail, ♂ 218–253, ♀ 237–262; tarsus, 91·5–106; wing-span, ♂ 1585–1770 (1664), ♀ 1670–1820 (1747). WEIGHT: ♂ 1537–2000 (1702), ♀ 2150–3200 (2586).

IMMATURE: very dark brown; scapulars, back, rump with broad central whitish or buff streaks, forming large oval spots on scapulars and upperwing-coverts, often almost obscuring dark ground. Uppertail-coverts broadly tipped white; secondaries tipped whitish, forming whitish trailing edge; tail-feathers barred. Eye brown; cere and feet yellow.

Adult plumage assumed in 4–6 years by reduction of white spots, bars and feather tips till all dark brown. An albinistic creamy buff phase, with blackish wing-feathers occurs.

Field Characters. Easily confused with Lesser Spotted *A. pomarina* and especially Tawny Eagle; probably often overlooked. Usually much darker brown than Lesser Spotted Eagle, glossed purplish. In flight, broader-winged, shorter-tailed, heavier-bodied, wings held well forward, slightly below horizontal, showing 7 emarginated primaries, more obviously bent and spread than in Lesser Spotted Eagle. Immatures readily distinguished by much larger white spots. Some Tawny Eagles are as dark, but lack gloss and are larger. On ground Greater Spotted Eagle is longer-legged, less heavily 'trousered' than Tawny Eagle. Round, not oval nostril diagnostic at close range.

Voice. Recorded (2a). In Africa, silent; in Europe, barking cluck, 'kluck-kluck' or 'tyuck-tyuck', resembling barking of small hound, pitch between shriller Lesser Spotted and deeper Tawny Eagle.

General Habits. Little known in Africa, often confused with other species; status may recently have changed. Formerly said to enter Africa via Bosphorus-Suez, common to abundant end Sept–early Oct, later than Lesser Spotted Eagle peak, moving in small flocks of 2–6. Records suggest reduction by 50–75% 1900–1950; may now be much rarer, only a few passing yearly, perhaps not accurately identified. Return migration more diffuse, commencing Feb, entering Europe late Mar–mid Apr.

In Europe habitat moist wooded areas. African range said to be mainly on semi-arid plateaus and lowland grasslands, NE Sudan, Ethiopia (Eritrea). Distribution of desert locust swarms may have been important before control effective after 1950. Recent good records scarce, but suggest similar northeast distribution, not south of 5° N, in semi-arid *Acacia* grasslands. Formerly, often seen with Tawny Eagle races at locust swarms in numbers (Smith 1957); now possibly nomadic, solitary, easily overlooked.

Food. Europe, especially small ground mammals, frogs; occasionally larger mammals (to 500 g) some water birds, snakes, lizards, fish. Africa, insects probably important, especially locusts, termites, grasshoppers. Apparently not an active, powerfully predacious eagle.

References

Glutz von Blotzheim, U. N. et al. (1971).
Smith, K. D. (1957).

Plates 25 and 29

(Opp. pp. 418 and 450)

Aquila rapax (Temminck). Tawny Eagle; Steppe Eagle. Aigle ravisseur.

Falco rapax Temminck, 1828. Pl. Col. livr. 76, pl. 455; South Africa.

Range and Status. Resident and Palearctic migrant. 2 resident races throughout Africa south of Morocco east to N Ethiopia, in semi-arid grasslands, thornbush, sub-desert scrub. 2 Palearctic migrant races *A. r. nipalensis* and *A. r. orientalis* (Steppe Eagles) occur mainly E and NE Africa in open plains, south to Transvaal, Namibia, most not passing equator. By far the commonest resident or migrant large brown eagle, normally common, locally abundant (groups of 50–100). The only resident large brown eagle Apr–Sept. Total numbers may exceed 250,000; not threatened, as often commensal with man, except in South Africa, where has recently disappeared from some former habitat (Tarboton 1978b).

Description. *A. r. rapax* (Temminck): South Africa north to N Kenya and S Ethiopia, west to Uganda, eastern Zaïre, Rwanda and Burundi. ADULT ♂: very variable. Generally all rufous-brown, varying pale to very dark, almost black; more regularly rufous in south. Tail-coverts often paler, forming whitish patch at base of tail. Wing-feathers blackish, contrasting with brown body and underwing-coverts. Tail-feathers brown, indistinctly barred blackish. Eye pale brown to yellow; cere and feet yellow. ♀ larger, darker, sometimes streaky brown on underside. SIZE: wing, ♂ 485–513 (501), ♀ 525–560 (545); tail, 245–295; tarsus, 79–92. WEIGHT: 27 unsexed 1696–3100 (2351); ♂ 1850–1950, ♀ 1500–2400 (Biggs *et al.* 1979).

IMMATURE: paler, sometimes more streaky than adult, but dark brown immatures known. Usually have more white on uppertail-coverts. Pale tips to secondaries, upper and underwing-coverts form broad whitish bars above and below on wing, and pale trailing edge. In dark plumage more streaky, blotchy look. Within 1 year may become much paler, creamy buff, sometimes white ('blondes'); blackish wing-quills contrast stongly. Eye dark brown, cere and feet yellow.

DOWNY YOUNG: white to pale grey; eye dark brown, cere and feet pale yellow.

Very pale individuals ('blondes') are normally immatures in faded plumage; but almost white and almost black adults known E Africa.

A. r. belisarius (Levaillant) (including former *A. r. raptor*). Ranges Morocco south to Nigeria east to Ethiopia, grading into *A. r. rapax* N. Kenya. Darker, usually more streaky brown, not rufous; Moroccan specimens paler, some whitish. Larger: wing ♂ 495–535 (515), ♀ 500–555 (525); wing-span ♂ 1750, ♀ 1720–1850; WEIGHT: ♂ *c.* 2000, ♀ 1950–2550 (R. Meinertzhagen, pers. comm.).

A. r. orientalis Cabanis. Breeds E Europe and Asia east to S Siberia; winters mainly E and NE Africa, some south to Transvaal, SE Africa, but most not passing far south of equator. Larger, sometimes much larger than resident subspecies. Adults usually darker, more uniform brown. Immatures distinctive, body brown to dark brown, uppertail-coverts largely white. Secondaries, median and greater coverts broadly tipped cream or whitish, forming several broad pale bars above and below wing; at rest have barred, scaled appearance. SIZE: wing ♂ 510–560 (527), ♀ 525–605 (575). WEIGHT: ♂ 2260–2700, ♀ 2270–4850; ♂♀ 4 (S Africa), 2300–3300 (R. Meinertzhagen, pers. comm.; Biggs *et al.* 1979).

A. r. nipalensis Hodgson. Breeds Mongolia-Transbaikalia; winters N India. Once recorded Zaïre (Prigogine 1976) and very large Steppe Eagles seen in Ethiopian highlands may be this race. Still larger: wing ♂ av. 577, ♀ 632; weight: ♂ *c.* 3000, ♀ to 4850 (almost as large as Golden Eagle *A. chrysaetos*).

These 2 migrant races sometimes regarded as a full species, *Aquila nipalensis* Steppe Eagle (e.g. Brooke *et al.* 1972), but the consensus of opinion is that they are conspecific.

Field Characters. Often confused with other medium–large brown migrant African eagles in winter Sept–Apr, but always much commoner; any doubt suggests Tawny Eagle and many 'spotted' eagles prove to be immature Tawny Eagles. Usually a heavily built, loosely plumaged, ragged-looking eagle in flight; broad wings show 7 emarginated wing-tip primaries, deep secondaries near body; broad, rounded tail is usually spread. On ground, relatively short, heavily 'trousered' legs useful distinction from both spotted eagles. Faint

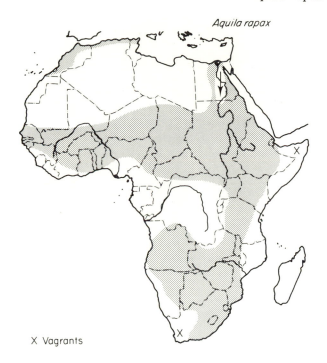

Aquila rapax

X Vagrants

bars in tail fewer, more wavy than in Greater Spotted Eagle *A. clanga*, but hard to see. Migrant Eurasian Steppe Eagles larger to much larger than resident forms, some almost as large as Imperial *A. heliaca* or Golden Eagle, but uniform dark brown in adult, broadly barred pale in immatures. Broad pale wing-bars of immatures diagnostic. Migrant Steppe Eagles more inclined than resident Tawny Eagles to perch on ground or rocks. Oval nostril at close range, yellow gape of Steppe Eagle, extending behind eye, useful in field. All races Tawny Eagle piratical, robbing other eagles and raptors of prey; this habit unknown in spotted eagles.

Voice. Recorded (18, 26). Sharp clear bark, 'kioh' or 'kowk', varying in pitch; uttered especially in display or during piracy. At nest ♀ utters sibilant, high-pitched 'schree-eep', probably soliciting food. Voice pitch intermediate between smaller spotted eagles and larger Golden and Imperial Eagles. Never very vocal, but if large brown eagle in tropical Africa calls, is probably Tawny Eagle.

General Habits. Very well known. Resident races prefer semi-arid *Acacia* savanna, open plains, thornbush, semi-desert, usually with less than 700 mm annual rainfall. Normally avoid, but may wander into denser woodlands, especially in dry season. Normal habitat open, usually dry lowlands, or plateaus to 2500 m. Migrant Eurasian races found both in lowlands and on high plateaus and mountains to 4500 m, e.g. high Ethiopian moorlands, where feed especially on mole rats. Tend to perch more on ground or rocks; resident races normally perch on trees, pylons, telegraph poles; no fixed preference, however, and several races may mingle in suitable habitat from lowlands to high moorlands.

Migrant Eurasian races rarely recorded entering Africa through Suez; must either do so unobserved, or be misidentified as spotted eagles. Within E and NE Africa outnumber residents by 4–6:1 and spotted eagles

by perhaps 50–100:1. Main migration route may follow Rift Valley through Ethiopian highlands to Lake Turkana, then down Eastern Rift to Mau highlands, and on to open plains S Kenya–N Tanzania. Some, chiefly immature, reach Zimbabwe, Namibia, Transvaal (Brooke *et al.* 1972; Jensen 1973). Migrants enter Africa mainly Oct, earliest reaching equator late that month. Move in groups or flocks, in Ethiopia sometimes 50–100 or even more together. Return migration more dispersed, in singles or pairs, migrating at height, Mar, Apr. A few may oversummer (perhaps immatures). Resident races tend to be nomadic in E and NE Africa, concentrating near sources of abundant food (e.g. *Quelea* colonies), but wandering widely; in southern Africa more permanently resident. In W Africa, perform more or less regular southward movement into denser woodlands Oct–Nov, returning north to more arid areas in wet season Apr–Sept.

Both resident and migrant forms usually roost from *c.* 2 h before sundown till 2 h after dawn; usually fly only when thermals assist soaring. Roost on trees, sometimes on ground, in ploughed fields (Ethiopia, associated with rat plague). Heavy rain enforces perching on trees, fences or telegraph posts; reluctant to fly when soaking wet, but may then feed on swarming alate termites on ground.

When hunting, most often perches on trees, posts, rocks, hummocks, termite hills, watching for possible prey. Steppe Eagles more likely to perch on ground. Both migrant and resident races often gregarious, in mixed flocks, associated with abundant food, e.g. rat plagues, locust swarms, *Quelea* colonies, breeding colonies of flamingoes. Although most prey taken on ground with ease, can also catch active strong flying birds (e.g. Speckled Pigeon *Columba guinea*) in full flight, with spectacular swift swoop, and kills flying flamingoes at height by day, striking them in air. May actually inhibit movements of flamingo from lake to lake by day, forcing nocturnal movements. When feeding on termites, several surround entrance to termitarium as alates emerge, gobbling them rapidly on ground.

Resident N African race *belisarius* is commensal with man in W, N and NE Africa frequenting villages, camps and cattle kraals, picking up any available scraps, carrion. Commensal habits less common N Kenya, rare south of equator, unknown southern Africa in nominate *rapax*, suggesting habit may be associated with older densely populated areas (as in Indian *A. r. vindhiana*). Migrant races common in densely inhabited regions, Ethiopia, but not actually commensal with man, though may feed in cultivated country. In E Africa prefer uninhabited plains, e.g. Serengeti, but also cultivated farmlands, feeding on rats, mole rats.

Food. Eats anything from alate termites to dead elephants. Much more rapacious, powerful predator than normally stated. Kills live mammals to size of dik-dik (4 kg), hare, gazelle calf, or as small as grass mice (40 g). In E Africa–Ethiopia, favoured food is semiblind mole rat *Tachyoryctes* spp., *c.* 200 g. Birds taken from size of small doves to medium-sized bustards (2000 g), especially game birds (francolins, guineafowl); domestic poultry taken, especially N and NE Africa. Reptiles from small lizard to cobra 1·8 m long, some probably picked up dead. Occasional amphibians, and, when available, feeds on locust swarms, swarming alate termites, gobbling these on ground. Preys heavily on *Quelea* breeding colonies, eating both adults and young. Kills some smaller carnivorous mammals, e.g. mongooses; but adult jackals, for example, probably taken as carrion. Regularly collects road kills, and some odd items, e.g. Secretary Bird *Sagittarius serpentarius*, and nocturnal spring hare *Pedetes* probably taken so. Feeds, especially E and N Africa, on carrion and can repel any vulture species at will. Haunts breeding colonies of Lesser and Greater Flamingoes (*Phoeniconaias minor* and *Phoenicopterus ruber*), e.g. in centre of Lake Natron; but then is mainly scavenger. In 2 large samples of 538 and 208 recorded items, mammals 37–39·5%; birds 35·4–49·5%; reptiles 12·5–25·1%; mammals probably most important by weight, birds by number. Birds more important in South Africa (Smeenk 1974; Steyn 1980b).

Besides killing own prey, is regularly and compulsively piratical, attacking any other species with prey, even much larger more powerful eagles such as Martial Eagle *Polemaetus bellicosus*. Robs other raptors from size of kestrel to Lammergeier *Gypaetus barbatus*, vultures, Marabou Stork *Leptoptilos crumeniferus*. May, for example, watch White Stork *Ciconia ciconia* or Marabou following plough, then rob them of dead mole rats they collect (P. Sessions, pers. comm.). Migrant Steppe Eagles also piratical, habit helping distinction from spotted eagles in mixed groups, and supporting close relationship with Tawny Eagle.

Breeding Habits. Very well known. Resident races regularly occupy territories, used sometimes for many years (up to 50 years: W. Tarboton, pers. comm.). In optimum habitat (E African plains, Kruger National Park) pairs occupy ranges of 35–55 km², sometimes even less, 25 km², not all regularly used. Lower densities probably reduced by human persecution, or destruction of nest trees by elephants, e.g. Tsavo National Park. Recent nests on pylons, Transvaal, spaced 20 km apart, suggesting ranges of 100 km² (Tarboton 1978b). Aggressive, piratical nature probably ensures wide espacement.

At av. 100 km² (locally exceeded) probable total habitat of 12 million km² would support 120,000 pairs plus immatures, i.e. at least 250,000.

Display not spectacular, ♂ or both birds soaring over site. ♂ may dive and swoop up again, descending gradually in a series of 'pot-hooks'. Pair may soar together, calling; and ♂ may then swoop at ♀ who may roll and present claws. Occasionally, whirling descent with locked claws observed. Migrant races sometimes display in winter quarters, suggesting early pair formation, or maintenance of existing bond.

NEST: normally in trees, thorny preferred, usually *Acacia* or spiny *Terminalia* spp. Also *Bombax*, baobabs, large figs, other broad-leaved trees, even native conifers (*Juniperus*, Kenya–Ethiopia) or exotic pines. In Kruger–Timbavati 95% of nests in *Acacias*, especially *A. nigrescens* (W. Tarboton, pers. comm.). A few Transvaal nests on electricity pylons, habit perhaps increasing (Tarboton 1978b). In E Africa especially *A. xanthophloaea*, *A. seyal*, *A. tortilis*. Nest very characteristic, broad shallow, basin-shaped, placed right on top of tree or at tip of large lateral branch, at any height from 3·5 m above ground, usually 10–20 m. Made of sticks, *c.* 1–1·5 m across by 30–50 cm deep, occasionally deeper (sticks mainly thorny, 1–2·5 cm thick), lined mainly with dry grass, some green leaves. Usually used for 1–3 years then abandoned, new one built some distance away or nearby. Growth of long thorny *Acacia* shoots round nest probable cause of earlier abandonment than normal in large eagles (Steyn 1973). Nests often collapse quickly once abandoned, but site may be re-occupied some years later.

EGGS: 1–3, usually 2, laid at 3-day intervals; mean (18 E and southern African clutches) 1·72. White, sometimes unmarked, sometimes boldly marked brown, red-brown and grey undermarkings. SIZE: (71, *A. r. rapax*) 62·5–75·5 × 50·0–60·0 (70·2 × 56·3); (27, *A. r. belisarius*) 64·0–74·0 × 51·5–55·3 (69·0 × 53·75) (Schönwetter 1960); WEIGHT: 112–118.

Laying dates: W Africa–Ethiopia Nov–Dec, Mar (dry season); Somalia Oct–Feb, peaking Jan (dry); NW Kenya–Uganda Sept, Oct (early dry); E Kenya Mar–Oct, especially May–July (mid-year cool dry season); Zambia, Tanzania Apr–Sept (throughout dry season); Zimbabwe, Botswana, Namibia, Transvaal Apr–Oct, peak May–July (dry season). In most areas lays late rains or early dry season, in E Africa cool mid-year season preferred; young sometimes in nest in rains.

Incubation begins 1st egg; mainly by ♀, sometimes by ♂; ♀ at night, ♀ not normally fed near nest by ♂, but leaves to feed. Sits very tight, often invisible; if disturbed, more liable than most eagles to predation by crows (possibly because of carrion in nest and very open site). Incubation period: 4 records vary 39–45 days, most 43–45 days.

Chicks hatch at intervals of 2–3 days; younger then weighs *c.* 85–100 g, elder 143. Violent sibling aggression then usually eliminates younger quickly; one case each of 2 young reared recorded in South Africa and Kenya. Eaglet increases from hatching weight to 115 g day 1; 215 day 5; 780 day 14; 1000 day 21; 1430 day 28; 1500 day 35; 1680 day 42; 2150 day 49; 2525 day 56 (heavier than parents). 1st down at 10 days replaced by denser, greyer 2nd down. Feathers emerge on upper surface at 20 days, developing faster above (resembling snake eagle), probably an adaptation due to open nest-site. Fully feathered above at 35 days, but downy on head and underside; feathered all over at 50 days. Can feed itself at 40 days, but solicits parent and may still be fed by them up to 70 days. Bill full grown at 56 days, tarsus by 42 days, coinciding with ability to feed itself. Remains long thereafter in nest, making 1st flight, in absence of parents at 76–85 days, av. 7 records 84 days (unusually long for an eagle this size).

Days 1–10 ♀ remains on nest, brooding or shading young by day, brooding by night; ♂ may also shade and brood small chicks. After day 7 often leaves chick exposed for hours, perching near; but returns to shelter it from rain or very strong sun. ♀ continues perching near for up to 40 days, thereafter leaving eaglet mainly alone; after 50 days neither parent normally near by day, but one or both may roost near till 70 days. Up to 40 days ♂ brings most or all prey; may feed eaglet if ♀ absent. After 50 days ♀ also brings prey.

After 1st flight young remains near nest, feeding, roosting, perching for *c.* 40 days; often spends some time in the nest. Thereafter becomes independent of nest area, perhaps accompanying parents in home range, or finding own prey, especially carrion, scraps in N Africa.

Breeding success: Zimbabwe, in 26 pair-years, 19 young reared, 0·73/pair/year, 1·00/successful nest; some non-breeding. In E Africa (Tsavo Park) in 18 pair-years, estimated 0·5 young/pair/year, more non-breeding; overall estimated 0·64/pair/year. Assuming 75% mortality before sexual maturity in *c.* 4 years, adult life must be *c.* 12 years, 16 altogether.

References
Smeenk, C. (1974).
Steyn, P. (1973, 1980b).

Aquila heliaca Savigny. Imperial Eagle. Aigle impérial.

Aquila heliaca Savigny, 1809. Descr. Egypte, Hist. Nat., 1, p. 82, pl. 12; Upper Egypt.

Plate 25

(Opp. p. 418)

Range and Status. Palearctic winter migrant Egypt, Sudan, Ethiopia (Eritrea), straggling south to Kenya, in open lowland grasslands. Perhaps formerly bred Morocco, no recent records; now rare winter migrant.

Description. *A. h. heliaca* Savigny: of all range excluding Spain. ADULT: dark brown to blackish brown, with conspicuous contrasting whitish nape and white 'epaulette' on scapulars. Wing-feathers blackish, darker than coverts. Tail basally grey, mottled dark brown, subterminally broadly

Aquila heliaca

The pale juvenile plumage develops to the very dark adult by becoming still paler at 1st moult, with fewer streaks below, then becoming patchy or streaky, dark and light as dark adult body feathers grow in; late subadult is all dark with paler, faintly barred wing-feathers. Full adult plumage acquired in c. 7 years, but birds may breed in subadult plumage.

A. h. adalberti Brehm. Spain, possibly Morocco; darker, with larger white shoulder patches; smaller, wing 570–640. Immatures more reddish above than *A. h. heliaca*, streaked below only on breast.

Field Characters. Large to very large, heavily built, but very long-winged eagles with powerful deeply hooked bills. In adult plumage, white 'epaulettes' and very pale nape contrasting with dark brown body and grey tail, broadly tipped blackish, contrasting with pale brown undertail-coverts are diagnostic. 1st immature plumage, strongly streaked below, diagnostic. Pale bars at feather tips on upperwing could cause confusion with large Steppe Eagle; but immature Imperial Eagle usually paler, bands or bars narrower, less conspicuous than in Steppe Eagle. Larger, heavier-billed than largest Steppe Eagles and in flight pale wedge on inner primaries and relatively longer wings diagnostic.

Voice. Not recorded. In Africa unknown; in Europe a deep sonorous bark 'owk-owk'.

General Habits. Little known in Africa; perhaps overlooked among more numerous Steppe Eagles. Migrates into Africa via Suez in small numbers, less than 1:100 spotted eagles, in late Sept–mid Oct. Further north migrates in flocks, in Africa apparently solitary. Main wintering area, so far as known, Egypt and grasslands of Sudan (*A. h. heliaca*); any seen Morocco probably *A. h. adalberti*. Habits appear similar to Steppe Eagles, but recorded only in lowlands.

Food. Mammals in weight range 500–2000 g (rabbits, hares); snakes, lizards, some birds, some carrion. Scarcely recorded in Africa.

banded blackish, tipped whitish; undertail-coverts contrasting pale brown. Eye pale brown; feet and cere yellow. SIZE: wing, ♂ 562–597 (577), ♀ 610–643 (626); tail, ♂ 244–285 (266), ♀ 276–296 (287); tarsus, ♂ 90–110 (100·3), ♀ 97–116 (105·7); wing-span, ♂ 1900–2100 (1954), ♀ 2040–2110 (2070). WEIGHT: ♂ 2600–3950, ♀ 2800–4250.

IMMATURE: above, tawny buff, rump and uppertail-coverts almost plain, elsewhere feathers broadly edged brown, appearing streaky. Below, sandy to rufous-buff, feathers of breast and abdomen broadly edged brown, producing strongly streaked appearance. Outer primaries blackish, contrasting with paler coverts; inner primaries pale brown, producing marked pale wedge in spread wing. Secondaries paler, buffy brown on inner pairs, most feathers tipped paler, producing narrow pale bars across upperwing (like Steppe Eagle *A. rapax orientalis*, but narrower). Tail brown, tipped pale. Eye brown, cere and feet yellow.

Plates 26 and 29
(Opp. pp. 419 and 450)

Aquila wahlbergi Sundevall. Wahlberg's Eagle. Aigle de Wahlberg.

Aquila Wahlbergi Sundevall, 1851. Öfv. K. Vet. Akad. Förh. p. 109; Mohapvani, Botswana.

Range and Status. Resident; intra-African transequatorial migrant, breeding mainly south of equator, more rarely to 14°N, in savannas, grass plains, thornbush and woodland, usually in rainfall 600–1000 mm/year. Frequent, sometimes common in breeding areas, locally abundant on migration. Non-breeding areas still obscure, but probably in north tropical savannas of Sudan, Chad, west to Gambia, from Mar–Aug, in rains.

Description. ADULT ♂ (normal phase): dark sepia brown, paler on wing-coverts, abdomen and sides of head; a distinct occipital crest. Primaries blackish, basally, becoming paler on inner webs. Secondaries blackish. Tail above blackish brown, sometimes obscurely barred. Underwing-coverts dark brown, contrasting with underside of flight-feathers and tail silvery grey. Eye brown, cere and feet yellow. ♀ larger. SIZE: wing, ♂ 400–435, ♀ 435–445; tail, ♂ 215–230, ♀ 235–250; tarsus, 71–82. WEIGHT: ♂ 437–845; 42 unsexed 670–1400 (1147) (Biggs *et al.* 1979).

IMMATURE: very like adult, even in first plumage. Rather paler below, streakier on head and neck, feathers and upperside often edged paler.

DOWNY YOUNG: dark grey-brown to pale greyish white. Eye brown, cere, legs, yellow.

Individuals vary greatly, from very dark to pale brown, or cream, nearly white; c. 80% are medium brown; 14% dark brown; and 5% cream or white (Kemp and Mendelsohn 1975; W. Tarboton, pers. comm.). In cream phase, whole body is creamy white, some blackish shaft streaks or spots, contrasting strongly with blackish wing- and tail-feathers. Very dark birds often have buff-brown cap on head. Dark birds produce dark young, and pale birds pale young.

Field Characters. A small, very slim, relatively long-legged eagle, usually appearing dark brown, little larger than Black Kite *Milvus migrans*, smaller than some *Buteo* spp. In flight, body very slim, long wings held straight out, with wing-tip primaries barely separated, quick wing-beats, resembling Northern Goshawk *Accipiter gentilis*. Tail rather long, square, not usually spread when soaring. Much smaller and slimmer than Tawny Eagle *Aquila rapax* or even Lesser Spotted Eagle *Aquila pomarina* (with which it could be confused in winter). Unlikely to occur with Greater Spotted Eagle *Aquila clanga*. Dark, usually barred tail distinguishes it from smaller, much stockier, dark phase Booted Eagle *Hieraaetus pennatus*.

Voice. Recorded (27). Distinctive, whistling; the only *Aquila* sp. which does not cluck or bark. In display, clear shrill double wail 'kleeeee-ay'; near nest, rapid repeated 'kyip-kyip-kyip', greeting or recognition; a loud, long-drawn, gull-like yelp by ♀, answered by ♂; and high-pitched, rat-like squealing by young or adults, associated with, for example, food or nesting material, uttered with head thrown back. Normally rather silent, even in breeding quarters.

General Habits. Well known in breeding areas, little known in non-breeding areas; observed sporadically on migration between these. Non-breeding area of most of population includes Sudan (Darfur, June), Chad, N Nigeria, Guinea, Gambia; but some may also breed in these areas. Migrates south into Kenya–Tanzania July–Aug, more than 1000 seen daily N Uganda (Thiollay 1975c); usually migrates in smaller groups or singly, often following escarpments. Few connected observations of migration, but some remain year-round in breeding quarters near equator.

In breeding range frequents both uninhabited and cultivated areas, possibly commoner in the latter. Perches much in trees, where inconspicuous, seldom seen except in flight, usually soaring *c.* 100–200 m above woodlands. May hunt much from flight; 1♂ spent 32% of day in flight in 4 periods of 31–77 min (Tarboton 1977). Also hunts from perches, and catches some prey by low flight among trees at speed, possibly having seen it earlier. Not normally shy of man, but unobtrusive, difficult to observe for long in thick cover. Attends grass fires to catch disturbed insects, especially on migration, when is often semi-gregarious. Rarely, makes spectacular, fast, long, slanting stoops at prey from high flight. Smaller, slimmer ♂ is apparently a more agile hunter than ♀.

After breeding in southern Africa Sept–Jan again departs northwards; some, perhaps immatures, remain year-round near equator. Unknown whether northern breeding population (probably small) migrates south across equator in non-breeding season. Completely absent south tropical Africa Mar–late Aug. Northward migration diffused, little observed, birds probably moving singly, over longer period than southward movement. Successful breeders and young may leave later than others.

Food. Varies according to locality, but particularly lizards, small mammals, some gamebirds. Takes mammals to size of young hare, gamebirds up to 300 g. Some young poultry taken. In Kenya, 50% reptiles, 30% mammals, 20% birds; Transvaal, 30% reptiles and

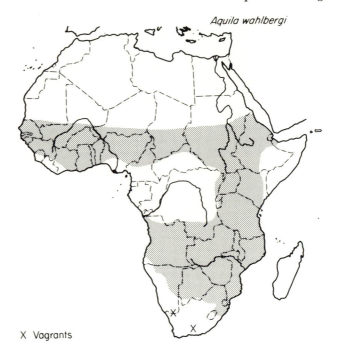

Aquila wahlbergi

X Vagrants

large amphibians, 39% mammals, 31% birds. Birds and mammals probably more important by weight (50%, Kenya). Most birds are ground species, from *Cisticola* and waxbills to Cattle Egret *Bubulcus ibis*, gamebirds and doves. Prey normally caught on ground (Brown 1952–3; Steyn 1962; Tarboton 1977).

Breeding Habits. Well known. On arrival, pair displays over nest-site with whistling calls, soaring at 200 m or over, higher than normal flight. Several adjacent pairs may display together. ♂ occasionally dives at ♀ who turns over and presents claws. Display not usually prolonged, and nest building or repair begins soon after arrival.

NEST: pair roosts near or in nest tree; mating occurs on tree branch near nest, or on nest. A new nest may take only 14 days to complete, of sticks, fully lined with green leaves, 45 cm across by 25 cm thick. Older nests after repeated use may be 75–80 cm across by 50–60 cm thick. Trees larger than most in area selected, often baobabs, thorny acacias, large *Terminalia* or, in southern Africa, *Faurea saligna*. Uses eucalyptus trees and often prefers to site nest in river valley where slippery barked fig trees often selected. In Ethiopia, nests in eucalyptus trees in Addis-Ababa, abnormal habitat at 2500–2800 m. Nest repair usually takes less than 1 month, eggs laid within a month of arrival. Pairs normally have 1–3 alternative nests close together, but many only 1. Nest normally used 3–4 years, then new one built, perhaps moving 1–2 km over a decade; rarely, nest used annually for 9–15 years.

EGGS: almost invariably 1; a few genuine clutches of 2 recorded South Africa. apparently associated with above average rainfall (Tarboton 1977). Dull white, usually with a few small clear brown markings at broad end, sometimes heavily clouded and blotched red-brown, with grey undermarkings. SIZE: (100 eggs) 52·7–62·0 × 45·5–52·0 (61·6 × 48·6); WEIGHT: *c.* 73.

Laying dates: Uganda Aug–Nov, mainly Sept–Oct; Zimbabwe, Zambia, Transvaal Aug–Oct, mainly Sept–

Oct, perhaps peaking slightly later than nearer equator. Only reliable records, Ethiopia, from range north of equator, also in Sept–Oct; a Nigerian record, June, may be unreliable (P. Ward, pers. comm.). In most of breeding range lays late in dry season, with young in nest in rains; but in Ethiopia lays end rains.

Incubation usually by ♀ only, fed at nest by ♂. ♂ sometimes takes share of up to 30% by day, often after bringing food; may incubate for nearly 2 h. ♀ usually sits tight, squatting low in nest, nearly invisible on close approach. Incubation period: 45–46 days. ♂ roosts near nest, and often perches on roost tree during day.

Young hatch in 24 h from chipping. At first brooded continuously, but can endure long absences by parent within 5 days of hatch. Feathers emerge on body at c. 25 days, cover down by 45 days; nearly fully feathered by 50 days. Young can swallow small prey (lizards) whole at 25 days, stand and walk about at 28, but still dependent on parental assistance with larger prey up to 42 days, when partly-feathered; culmen and tarsus by then fully developed (Steyn 1962). Wing-flapping from 40 days on; 1st flight at 62–80 days, usually 70–75. Food requirement of feathered young estimated 170 g daily.

♀ remains on nest 50–60% of daylight in days 1–15, broods at night, in rain; ♂ brings food and, rarely, broods for short periods. Up to 40–45 days ♀ roosts in nest with young, brooding if needed; thereafter joins ♂ on roost perch near nest. Up to 45 days entire family

depends on ♂; after 45 days, when chick partly-feathered and able to feed itself, ♀ brings most prey. Parental time on nest gradually reduced to less than 1% of daylight by 65–70 days.

After 1st flight eaglet leaves nest area by day, but returns to roost for up to 2 weeks in nest or tree. Parents leave nest area almost at once. Rarely, eaglet remains more than 2 months near nest, but often kills prey within a few days of 1st flight, and soon becomes independent. Av. fledging date for 1 Oct eggs, c. 15 Feb; northward migration out of breeding area begins late Feb and Mar.

Breeding success: Kenya, c. 0·65 young/pair/year; Zimbabwe lower, av. 0·56, reduced by some human interference. In 130 recorded nest-years (Kenya, Zimbabwe, Transvaal), 111 pairs laid (85%) and 71 young were reared, equivalent to 0·55/pair overall, 0·64/breeding pair and 1·00/successful nest; 2 young from rare clutches of 2 never reared. At estimated 75% mortality before sexual maturity at 3 years (period not known), adults would need to live for av. 14 years as adults to maintain stable population. Observations suggest this is too long and mortality must be lower; but individuals 6 years old as adults known.

References
Brown, L. H. (1952–3, 1955).
Steyn, P. (1962).
Tarboton, W. (1977).

Plates 25 and 29
(Opp. pp. 418 and 450)

Aquila chrysaetos (Linnaeus). Golden Eagle. Aigle royal.

Falco Chrysäetos Linnaeus, 1758. Syst. Nat. (10th ed.), p. 88; Sweden.

Range and Status. Scarce resident in mountains, Rio de Oro, north to Morocco and Algeria; Sinai; occurs Hoggar ranges; some migrate south in winter across northern Sahara.

Aquila chrysaetos

Description. *A. c. homeyeri* Severtzov, ADULT: above, dark brown; lanceolate feathers of head and nape tipped pale golden. Below, paler brown, still paler on thighs, tarsi almost white. Primaries basally greyish, banded and mottled blackish; tail-feathers irregularly banded dark grey and blackish, broadly tipped blackish. Eye pale brown, cere and feet yellow. SIZE: wing, ♂ 570–615 (593), ♀ 615–705 (653); tail, 280–310; tarsus, 80–105; wing-span, ♂ c. 2000, ♀ c. 2200. WEIGHT: ♂ c. 3200–4000, ♀ heavier.

IMMATURE: darker brown than adult, lacking the pale nape, but with large white patch, barred darker, at base of primaries; tail basally white, broadly tipped blackish. Eye dark brown; cere and feet yellow.

DOWNY YOUNG: pure white; eye brown, cere and feet pale yellow.

Adult plumage acquired over 4–5 years in 2-stage continuous moult, with successive reduction of white patches on wings and tail base, and development of pale nape.

Field Characters. The only large eagle likely to be seen in NW African mountains. A very large and powerful, but, in flight, slim and graceful eagle. At rest, adults all dark brown, appearing almost black, except for nape. In flight slim body, long tail, relatively short inner secondaries help to distinguish from much rarer Imperial Eagle *A. heliaca*, and very large Steppe Eagles *A. rapax orientalis* and *A. r. nipalensis*, which would not normally occur in same range. Immatures easily distinguished by large white patch at carpal joint of wing in flight and broad whitish tail base.

Voice. Not recorded. Usually silent. Commonest call a loud cluck, 'tsyewk' or 'tsyuch', repeated by ♀ and young. ♂ utters sharp 'pleek'. Rarely, a loud clear repeated yelp, 'weooo-hyo-hyo-hyo'; mewing cries in display.

General Habits. Little known in Africa. Inhabits mountains and rocky areas, but also visits plains, especially in winter, when snow covers mountains. Northern populations of some other races migrate, but *A. c. homeyeri* normally resident. Some, probably immatures, migrate south across Sahara, adults remaining year-round in breeding areas.

Normally seen soaring in mountains, or perching on cliffs and rocks; sometimes trees, posts. Mountain upcurrents permit soaring early morning to late evening. May hunt any time of day, either on wing or from perch. More active, spends more time soaring and on wing hunting than Imperial Eagle or Steppe Eagle. When soaring high, is not hunting, but advertising presence in territory. Roosts on cliffs or large trees. Active for up to 16/24 h in summer, 8/24 h in winter.

Hunts mainly mammals, caught on ground by short diving stoop, or merely dropped on from low soaring flight. Can catch large birds on wing, especially game birds, ducks, storks, other raptors. In winter in Europe feeds much on carrion and several may gather near a carcass.

Food. Adaptable, will feed on wide range of prey, but prefers medium-sized mammals of 500–2000 g; also many large birds, some reptiles, frogs. Can occasionally kill larger mammals (e.g. young deer) up to 40 kg, especially when handicapped by e.g. snow. Hares, ground squirrels, small carnivores (e.g. foxes), young gazelles probably important N Africa, but little recorded. Takes gamebirds (e.g. partridges) and larger birds to size of White Stork *Ciconia ciconia*; in W Sahara, large *Uromastix* lizards (Valverde 1957). Carrion taken, especially in winter, but not fed to nestlings. Food requirement 230–270 g/day/adult.

Breeding Habits. Little known in Africa, elsewhere intimately studied. Adult pairs remain in mountain breeding territories year-round except when forced to move by hard winter or heavy snow. Remain mated for life of any individual, but bereaved bird at once obtains alternate mate if possible.

Display flights spectacular, especially on fine winter days, or in early spring. Mainly by ♂, in steep undulating dives and upward swoops, usually silent often over ridges, perhaps at edge of territory. Mutual spectacular soaring and diving displays by pair, ♂ uppermost diving at ♀, who sometimes rolls and presents claws; may repeat such manoeuvres several times. In early spring several pairs may soar close together, perhaps defining territories by aerial encounter without combat. Mating occurs on ground, not always near nest, up to 3 months before laying. Some traditional breeding sites occupied by successive pairs for centuries.

NEST: on cliffs, sometimes trees (not recorded N Africa); semi-permanent, often used for 50 years or more by different adults. Pairs have 1–12 nests, usually 2–3, sometimes only one, with 1 preferred. Disturbance by humans stimulates repeated shifting of nest-site. Regular espacement normal in mountain ranges, but several pairs may nest on one mountain in desert country, with 'radical' hunting territories. New nest is small, a scrape on ledge surrounded by sticks, lined with softer material. Later becomes huge, up to 4 m deep by 1·5 m across in trees, 2–3 m deep on ledges. On cliffs usually broader and flatter than in trees, up to 3 m across, with central cup *c.* 1 m across and 15 cm deep. Made of any available material, larger when abundant timber available. Built by both sexes of dry and living sticks up to 2 m long and 5 cm thick; lined with rushes, moss, green sprays of trees; sprigs of conifers preferred if available. Continue adding material until late in fledging period. Nest-building occurs any time of year, especially if non-breeding, or unsuccessful; normally mainly late winter-early spring. In Europe 15–25% of pairs do not breed each year; in Africa no data.

EGGS: 1–3, usually 2, laid at 3-day intervals; N Africa mean (41 clutches) 1·90 (Heim de Balsac and Mayaud 1962). Rounded ovals; dull white, usually sparingly, sometimes heavily marked red-brown, brown, with purplish under markings; 1 of clutch of 2 usually larger, more heavily marked than the other. SIZE: (58, *A. c. homeyeri*) 70·3–83·1 × 53·5–63·0 (74·6 × 58·8) (Schönwetter 1960); WEIGHT: *c.* 145.

Laying dates: N Africa late Jan–early Apr (perhaps later in high mountains) (Heim de Balsac and Mayaud 1962).

Incubation begins 1st egg. Normally by ♀ only, but ♂ may take some share, up to 40% by day; including nights, 90–95% by ♀. ♀ not normally fed on nest by ♂, but leaves to feed (perhaps on carrion). Period: estimated 41–44 days in various parts of range, not recorded N Africa.

Young hatch at 2–3 day intervals; weigh 90–105 g at hatch. Elder, weighing *c.* 250 g when younger hatches, dominates or kills younger in *c.* 80% of cases; 2 young recorded reared S Sahara (Heim de Balsac and Mayaud 1962). Parents ignore sibling strife; dead chick falls from nest, or is eaten by parents or sibling.

Young requires continuous brooding 1–7 days; 7–20 days, brooding reduced by day and by 21 days can stand long exposure, especially if nest north-facing, or shaded. Resistant to cold but rapidly killed by exposure to strong hot sun. 1st feathers emerge at 21–25 days; by 45–50 days body largely feathered, head downy. By 50 days can feed itself, may eat small prey or tear at large prey earlier. Fly at 65–80 days in temperate climates; in N Africa period unknown, but estimated 70–80 days (Heim de Balsac and Mayaud 1962).

♀ remains mainly on nest first 20 days of fledging period, brooding or shading chicks, but leaving for long periods after 15 days; from 21–40 days usually perches near nest. Feeds chicks and herself on prey brought by ♂. ♂ may brood chicks for periods soon after hatch, enabling ♀ to leave area, though apparently does not kill or bring prey to nest after such absences. ♂ rarely feeds young, usually in absence of ♀, but is recording feeding with ♀ present. Family depends on ♂ for food up to 50 days, after which ♀ also hunts. ♂ sometimes roosts near nest, but after 50 days neither parent may roost near.

After 1st flight young remain 2–3 weeks near nest, probably till wing- and tail-feathers harden, enabling strong flight. Thereafter follow parents to distant parts of range. May remain loosely attached to parents till following spring, apparently not always repelled from home range. More often, leave home range in autumn; may then move to lower ground, wander widely and migrate more than adults.

Breeding success in Africa not recorded: broods usually 1, occasionally 2 successfully reared. May be c. 0·6–0·7/pair overall; 0·8/breeding pair; and 1·1/successful nest. Expected adult life span c. 12 years, 16–17 altogether.

References
Etchécopar, R. D. and Hüe, F. (1967).
Heim de Balsac, H. and Mayaud, N. (1962).
Valverde, J. A. (1957).

Plates 25 and 29
(Opp. pp. 418 and 450)

Aquila verreauxi Lesson. Verreaux's Eagle; Black Eagle. Aigle de Verreaux.

Aquila Verreauxi Lesson, 1830. Cent. Zool. p. 105, pl 38; interior of Cape of Good Hope.

Range and Status. Resident, mountainous areas of S, E and NE Africa to W Sudan and N Chad; occurs Sinai. Sea level – 5000 m, mainly absent wooded Central Africa. Frequent, locally common in optimum habitat. Numbers probably stable.

Aquila verreauxi

Description. ADULT ♂: wholly black, except white centre of black, rump, uppertail-coverts, and some scapulars, forming a white 'V' on shoulders. Primaries basally whitish, barred, forming large, pale carpal patch. Eye brown, cere, eyelids and feet yellow-orange. SIZE: wing, ♂ 565–595, ♀ 590–640; tail, 315–360; tarsus, 105–110. WEIGHT: ♀ (4) 3100–5779 (4069); unsexed 3792–4300.

IMMATURE: crown and mantle rich rufous, forehead streaked white; cheeks black. Uppertail- and upperwing-coverts blackish, edged pale brown, producing scaled appearance. Rump and lower back white, streaked brown. Wing- and tail-feathers nearly black, primaries paler basally, barred darker forming pale carpal patch. Lower throat and beast pale brown, becoming black on chest, again brown on belly and thighs. Eye brown, cere and feet yellow.

DOWNY YOUNG: pure white; eye dark brown, cere and feet pale yellow.

Adult plumage assumed in moult of 2 main stages. In 1st stage most brown feathers are replaced by black, so that sub-adult resembles adult rather than immature. Full maturity, c. 5 years (W. R. Spofford, pers. comm.).

Field Characters. Adult unmistakable, about size of Golden Eagle *A. chrysaetos*, but slimmer, more graceful, with very short inner secondaries so that wing appears leaf-shaped in flight. All black except white back and white patch at carpal joint. 1st immature, a striking mixture of rufous and black, unlike any other large eagle, except perhaps some adult Golden Eagles (unlikely to occur in same area).

Voice. Recorded (2a). Usually silent. Normal call a cluck resembling that of turkey, 'pyuck' or 'tsyuck', by adult and young; rarely a savage harsh alarm bark 'chyow'; a ringing 'whaeee-whaeee-whaeee', associated with excitement; mewing or whistling 'heeeeee-oh' or 'weeeee-o' in display; wheezy chittering with prey.

General Habits. Very well known. Inhabits rocky mountains, gorges, isolated kopjes and inselbergs from near sea level in Cape Province to 5000 m in Kenya–Ethiopia; breeds Ethiopia to 4200 m. Adult pairs normally reside permanently in home ranges, do not migrate or wander far; immatures usually leave areas with full adult populations. Prefers drier areas with less than 750 mm annual rainfall, absent from heavily wooded or forested areas even if suitable rocky hill breeding sites exist; found in subdesert N Kenya and Sudan.

Home ranges vary from less than 10 km² pair (Zimbabwe) to 25 km² pair (E Africa), and 60 km² pair parts of South Africa (Siegfried 1968; Gargett 1975). Total hunting area within home range varies according to abundance of hyrax colonies; if scattered, separated, range is larger. Also affected by availability of cliff nesting sites, e.g. in Karoo, South Africa. Suitable sites with abundant hyrax exist, but lack these eagles; reason unknown. Densest eagle populations occur where food abundant, with unlimited rocky cliffs. Territory is maintained year-round by soaring display flights, perching on prominent rocks and trees where visible to neighbouring pairs. Is in form of inverted truncated cone of air, with ground areas not overlapping, but overlap in air at upper limits of territory (Gargett 1975).

Roosts regularly on or near nest cliff, pair often together, usually settling to roost 30–60 min before dark, sometimes only at dusk. Take wing soon after dawn, may soar along cliff faces, probably not seriously hunting till later. In heat of day may perch in shade of tree on rock face or shaded ledge, preening for hours. Usually on wing again in late afternoon–evening. Most hunting probably between 07.00–10.00 and 16.00–18.00 h. In well stocked areas can catch hyrax at almost any time, within a few minutes.

Flight very distinctive, soaring magnificently without wing-flaps along or over ridges and cliffs; wing held with marked dihedral. Periods of soaring flight interspersed with periods of perching and preening. Pairs feed on each other's kills, and are seldom far apart for long. Does not normally soar high except in display over home range.

Food. Where hyrax plentiful, apparently 98% *Procavia* and *Heterohyrax*, weighing up to 3500 g. In Somalia, Ethiopia, also dik-dik, young and adult klipspringers, hares; largest normal prey *c.* 10 kg. Rarely birds (guineafowl, francolins) and carnivorous mammals (mongoose); exceptionally, carrion. Food requirements apparently high, estimated in captives to be *c.* 400 g/day/adult, 360 kg/pair/year. Proportionately more than Golden Eagle, otherwise ecologically comparable. Can gorge 1200 g at 1 meal in several hours.

Breeding Habits. Intimately known; probably the world's most intensively studied eagle (Tanzania: Rowe 1947; Zimbabwe: Gargett 1971, 1975, 1978). Breeding ranges apparently defined by territorial, non-combative flights and perching in clear view of neighbours. Neighbours recognized and tolerated; intruders, young or old, repelled. Where common, as in Matopos hills, Zimbabwe, several pairs often soar near each other without obvious territorial aggression or other behaviour.

Display, extremely spectacular. ♂ and also ♀ perform very swift, undulating displays, deep, steep dives followed by upward swoop of up to 300 m traversing 400–500 m, sometimes rolling or somersaulting at top of swoop, repeated 1–7 times. Series of swoops may resemble pendulum, ♂ swinging back and forth; on curving or twisting course, or up and down along straight line, sometimes near border of territory. Also, often, mutual soaring, with ♂ occasionally diving at ♀, who turns over and presents claws; rarely, whirling with feet locked (but actual fighting suspected in such cases). Display stimulated by good soaring weather, presence of mate, food, departure from nest, presence of humans; not aggressive to humans. Mating occurs on rocky perches near nest up to 30 days before egg laying; lasts 5–10 s.

NEST: normally on cliffs, rarely (4 authentic records) on trees, when euphorbias preferred (Brown 1955; Perrett 1976). Pairs have 1–5 nests, usually 1–2, with 1 preferred; av. per pair *c.* 1·3. Made of sticks, lined with green leaves, usually broad, flattish structures 1·5–

2·5 m across by 0·5–1 m deep; sometimes (in high cold mountain climates) tower-like, up to 3 m deep. Central cup *c.* 1 m across by 15–20 cm deep. Built by both sexes; nest repair sporadic; may occur almost any season, intensifying just before egg-laying. ♂ may bring most material, ♀ remaining in nest and working sticks into structure. Most small sticks or green leaves brought in bill, large sticks in feet.

EGGS: 1–3, usually 2, laid at 3-day intervals; mean (167 South and E African clutches) 1·92. Laid most often in morning, some in afternoon. May be left exposed by ♀, not immediately incubated; then predated by ravens, baboons, possibly pythons; after natural loss pairs rarely re-lay (*c.* 1%). Elongated ovals, bluish white, sparsely marked reddish brown, or unmarked. SIZE: (30) 71·0–86·0 × 56·0–62·0 (76·9 × 58·6); WEIGHT: (actual) 115–158.

Laying dates: South Africa, Cape area, May–Sept, most July–Aug (late winter); Transvaal, Zimbabwe, Zambia, S Tanzania, Mar–Oct peaking May–July (end rains–early dry; in Zimbabwe dates varying according to rainfall); Kenya, N Tanzania Feb–Sept, peak June–July (mid-year cool dry season); Ethiopia–Somalia Oct–Dec (dry); Sudan possibly Dec–Mar. Most eggs laid early in long dry seasons, but near equator (with 2 short dry seasons) often in heavy rains.

Both sexes incubate by day, ♀ only at night. Incubation may not begin at once, or be continuous days 1–2; incubation temperature 40°C. Some ♂♂ take large day-time share, up to 50%, but most less than 30%. ♀ normally incubates 80–85% of 24 h. ♂ feeds sitting ♀, and may sit while she feeds; all prey in incubation period killed by ♂. 1 egg often infertile. Incubation period: 43–47 days, varying with eggs and individual birds (Gargett 1971).

Young hatch in 48–65 h at *c.* 3-day intervals. Weigh 90–100 g at hatch; 200 day 4; 1000 day 20; 2000 day 33; 3000 day 55; and *c.* 3500 at 1st flight. Elder chick normally kills or dominates younger; observed in detail (Gargett 1978), elder killed younger in 72 h, during which it pecked younger 1569 times in 38 bouts totalling 187 min, in 34 daylight h. Parents do not intervene. If younger is removed, hand-fed, later replaced, fighting continues while chicks downy; but when feathered tolerate each other. Hand-reared eaglets may grow faster than nest-reared (Gargett 1970). In over 650 records only 1 known case of 2 chicks reared (Brown 1974b).

1st feathers, primaries 30–32 days, contours 35 days; down covered with feathers 60 days. 1st flight 90–99 days Kenya, Tanzania, Zimbabwe; shorter periods suspected South Africa. Can stand weakly at 35 days, attempts to tear at prey 35–40 days, but usually requires parental assistance with prey up to 60 days, when partly feathered; thereafter independent of parental feeding.

♀ broods young up to 97% of time in first 48 h; ♂ may also brood for short spells. Brooding reduced to 30% of daylight by 20 days; usually thereafter parent only stands with or shades chick on nest, but brooding renewed in cold wet weather or hot sun. ♀ roosts regularly in nest up to 60 days, sporadically to 70 days, thereafter near; ♂ roosts away from the nest, sometimes on cliffs near. Up to 30 days, 80% of prey killed by ♂; thereafter ♀ takes greater share, killing and bringing 50% of prey in days 60–90.

Young sometimes fed shortly after hatching (up to 5 small meals in first 24 h), sometimes given nothing 1st day. Appetite increases rapidly until, at 90–95 days probably needs 500 g/day. Av. 1·2 hyrax brought per day in early fledging period, rising to 1·5/day at end; ♀ feeds herself and young on these. Total: c. 1·4/day, or c. 115 killed for ♀ and young. Some additional kills by ♂ not brought to nest.

Young fly without parental stimulus or starvation. Post-fledging period, 100–125 days, young becoming gradually more active. Days 1–30, mainly in or perching near nest, roosting in nest at night, making only short uncertain flights. Days 30–60, longer flights (4–15 min), flying c. 20% of day-time, up to 0·8 km from nest. Follows parents some distance, but still roosts in or near nest at night, sometimes returning in dusk. Days 60–120, longer flights, following parents, or out of sight, ceasing to roost in nest, but on perches near. Calls

noisily throughout the post-fledging period. Is apparently dependent on parents throughout for food, not known to kill for itself, and may be brought more prey than needed, with prior claim to feed. Is apparently finally repelled from nesting territory by adults 100–125 days after 1st flight.

Breeding success: 652 records include 442 layings, rearing 339 young; 0·52 young/pair/year, 0·77 young/breeding pair. About 66% pairs breed annually and 50% rear young. Breeding is perhaps inhibited by successful breeding in previous year, or too close proximity to another pair (Gargett 1969). At 75% mortality rate before sexual maturity, expected adult life span in 15–16 years, 19–20 years altogether.

References

Brown, L. H. (1952–3).
Brown, L. H. et al. (1977).
Gargett, V. (1969, 1970, 1971, 1972, 1975, 1978).
Rowe, E. G. (1947).
Siegfried, W. R. (1968).

Genus *Hieraaetus* Kaup

Medium-sized to rather small, slender eagles; 6 Old World spp. Active swift predators, with whistling or fluting voices. Heads sometimes slightly crested; wings rather long, pointed or rounded; tail relatively longer than in *Aquila*; legs long, toes and talons long and strong; hind claw longer than culmen. Immature plumages markedly different from adult. Inhabit woodlands, forest edges, sometimes forest, rather than very open mountainsides or plains. Feed mainly on birds, some mammals, all caught alive, not or very seldom carrion. Habits somewhat resemble those of large *Accipiter* spp., hence English name 'hawk eagle'.

4 spp. occur in Africa, 2 are endemic. All are breeding residents, one also a Palearctic winter migrant. Recently, the genus has sometimes been merged with *Aquila* (e.g. Smithers 1964); but the most modern view (Benson *et al.* 1971; Stresemann and Amadon 1979) is that it is distinct. The aberrant *Aquila wahlbergi* has recently been placed in this genus by Smeenk (1974), but is not typical of *Hieraaetus* either.

Plate 26

(Opp. p. 419)

Hieraaetus fasciatus (Vieillot). Bonelli's Eagle. Aigle de Bonelli.

Aquila fasciata Vieillot, 1822. Mém. Soc. Linn. Paris, 2. pt., 2, p. 152; Fontainebleau, France, and Sardinia.

Range and Status. Resident in wooded rocky hills, Mediterranean basin, including Morocco, Algeria, Tunisia, usually at low altitudes. Frequent to uncommon; probably reduced recent years by direct persecution (as in France).

Description. *H. f. fasciatus* (Vieillot), ADULT ♂: above, blackish to sooty brown, some white mottlings. Cheeks, throat white, streaked brown. Body below white, broadly streaked, or with drop-shaped blackish spots. Undertail-coverts streaked and barred; underwing-coverts mottled blackish on white; median and greater coverts usually black forming conspicuous transverse black underwing bar. Primaries above dark brownish to black, outer webs greyish forming grey carpal patch above, wing-feathers below white to grey-brown, tipped blackish forming dark trailing edge, primaries basally greyish, forming conspicuous pale carpal patch. Tail above greyish, broadly tipped blackish, with 5–6 other indistinct darker bars; below white or greyish, broadly tipped blackish. Eye, cere and feet yellow. ♀ usually browner, more heavily streaked than ♂, and larger. SIZE: wing, ♂ (8) 465–542 (483),

♀ (7) 486–522 (509), maximum 560; tail, ♂ 240–260 (251), ♀ 253–268 (261); tarsus, ♂ 93–109 (102), ♀ 99–106 (103); wingspan, 1735. WEIGHT: ♂ juveniles (3) 1500–2160; ♀ (2) 2000–2500; unsexed 1712–2386 (Glutz von Blotzheim *et al.* 1971; Brown and Amadon 1968).

IMMATURE: paler, browner than adult. Head pale brown, streaked blackish; back and wings above brown to dark brown; below pale chestnut, narrowly streaked blackish, thighs paler buff. Wing-feathers above dark brown, secondaries tipped paler, primaries whitish on inner webs forming pale carpal patch. Tail above grey-brown, below buffy grey, barred brown. Eye brown, cere and feet yellow.

DOWNY YOUNG: greyish white; eye brown, cere and feet pale yellow.

Immature plumage develops to adult over 3–4 years by darkening above, becoming paler below, streaks forming larger dark spots.

Field Characters. The largest typical hawk eagles, appearing dark brown or blackish above, mainly white, streaked darker below. In flight, black underwing-coverts conspicuous and diagnostic; grey patch above and below wing at carpal joint also useful. Appears much larger, much paler below on body than Booted Eagle *H. pennatus* and has barred tail. Feathered tarsi distinguish from any *Buteo* sp. at close range, and black underwing-bar also diagnostic. In flight, rather rounded wings with short secondaries, forming deep 'notch' between base of wing and spread tail helpful. Immatures more difficult to distinguish but are more rufous, more streaked blackish below than those of Booted Eagles.

Voice. Not recorded. Normally silent away from breeding areas, where vocal; calls distinctive when heard. Mellow, fluting whistles, e.g. 'heee-o, heee-o', 'wheee-uw, wheee-uw', 'huiii-hi-hi-hi-hi', sharper 'kip-kip-kip', or low-pitched, fluting 'klu-klu-klu'. All quite unlike any *Aquila* sp., much less shrill and piercing than mewing calls of buzzards; and lower-pitched than sharp calls of Booted Eagle, longer drawn-out. Begging calls of young, long-drawn, rather sibilant whistling, but resemble those of adult.

General Habits. Little known in Africa, very well known Europe. Habits in N Africa probably similar to more arid parts of European range. Adult pairs reside in home range year-round, do not migrate; but immatures wander. Adults roost regularly near nest-site, arriving 1–2 h before dark, leaving 1–3 h after dawn, usually flying in full daylight only. Forage in home range for 4–5/10–11 daylight hours midwinter, at most 11–12/18–20 h midsummer, probably less. In spring spend more time near nest and may then forage for short periods only. Are certainly not hunting whole of possible foraging time, as often seen perched on cliffs or trees, resting, preening, often in shade (Cheylan 1972).

Normally seen in flight, soaring round cliffs or steep hill-sides, hunting over open lowlands, including cultivated areas; in Morocco may be seen in almost naked desert, with cliffs. Demeanour generally bold, but not aggressive to other species, even near nest area, where may breed among European Griffons *Gyps fulvus*; not shy of man, except in areas where severely persecuted (France). Rather seldom seen perching, as often chooses inconspicuous perch on shaded ledge, bushy cliff-face, or in shady trees. May forage as far as 10–12 km, occasionally up to 25 km, away from nest site (Thiollay 1968).

Hunts mainly on the wing, also from perches. Very swift and active, can catch flying birds such as jackdaws by swift stoop below them, then turning up to catch them in flight (Rivoire and Hüe 1949); alternatively attacks from perch on cliff, or tree on slope, surprising prey by swift diving attack. Very powerful and active for size, often killing prey as heavy as, or heavier than itself.

Food. Birds, varying from size of thrush to Houbara Bustard *Chlamydotis undulata*, especially gamebirds (partridges). Occasionally geese, other raptors (such as Long-legged Buzzard *Buteo rufinus*), herons, storks. Mammals from mice to rabbits; rabbits most important food, S France (54% by number, 80% by weight: Blondel *et al.* 1969); some lizards including, in N Africa, spiny-tailed *Uromastix* spp. In N Africa probably more

Hieraaetus fasciatus

dependent on gamebirds, notably Barbary Partridge *Alectoris barbara*. Most prey taken on ground, but some birds on wing.

Breeding Habits. Little known N Africa; very well known Europe. Normal home range not easily measured as populations recently severely reduced by persecution, S Europe; but perhaps *c.* 100 km²/pair where no severe persecution. Nothing known N Africa.

Pairs frequent breeding site year-round, roosting normally in neighbourhood of nest. Display occurs commonly autumn (Oct–Nov) then decreases in midwinter, increasing again in spring, especially Feb–Apr (Cheylan 1972). Spectacular, ♂ performing steep undulating dives and upward swoops; much mutual soaring, diving and swooping together near breeding site. ♂ may dive at ♀, who may roll and touch his feet with hers. Mutual displays continue late into fledging period, and after young have left nest area intensify again. Pairbond probably life-long; definite data lacking.

NEST: on cliffs 15–150 m high, usually very inaccessible near middle or upper part of cliff; often based on or behind bush, or in deep niche or ledge. Very large for size of bird, almost as large as that of Golden Eagle *Aquila chrysaetos*, used repeatedly. Pairs have 1–5 nests, usually 1–3. New nest *c.* 1 m across by 50 cm deep, may become 2 m across and 2 m deep after many years' use. Made of sticks, lined with green leaves. Both sexes build, especially ♀ who may remain in nest while ♂ brings twigs. Nest repair may occur in autumn, intensifying early spring; material continually added late into fledging period.

EGGS: 1–3, laid at intervals of *c.* 3 days; N Africa mean (40 clutches) 2·07. Rather broad ovals, white, lightly streaked and spotted brown, some greyish undermarkings. SIZE: (80, N Africa and Europe) 63·5–73·5 × 49·4–57·3 (68·76 × 53·79) (Glutz von Blotzheim *et al.* 1971). WEIGHT: *c.* 112.

Laying dates: N Africa, Tunisia, Algeria, early Feb–

Mar; in Morocco rarely Jan, usually Feb (Heim de Balsac and Mayaud 1962).

Incubation begins 1st egg. Mainly or entirely by ♀ fed by ♂ on or near nest. ♂ occasionally incubates briefly, usually when ♀ off feeding; his main function is to catch prey and guard nest area (Blondel *et al.* 1969). ♀ incubates steadily, leaving to defaecate, then often bringing back green branch. Period: 37–39 days (several days shorter than smaller tropical African Hawk Eagle *H. spilogaster*).

Young entirely downy days 1–20; can shuffle on tarsi at 7 days. Wing-feathers emerge at 20 days, tail-feathers and wing-coverts by 25 days; can then stand unsteadily. Stand easily by day 28, part-feathered day 30; day 37 body almost completely feathered, still downy on head and neck; days 40–43 down covered by head feathers, downy only on centre of breast. Days 50–52 almost wholly feathered, begin wing-flapping; day 59, often bounding about with frequent wing-flapping. 1st flight made at 61 days, independent of parents. Thereafter disperse from nest within a few days (Blondel *et al.* 1969).

Roles of adults clear-cut; ♂ brings most prey (85–90%) and ♀ feeds young, almost until 1st flight. Young still dependent on adult for food at 45 days, when largely feathered. ♀ remains on nest brooding young, or standing with them, up to day 15; absent for longer periods thereafter, but remains near. Small chicks brooded constantly in cold weather, but in warm weather ♀ stands over them or beside them. After 21 days ♀ leaves nest for longer periods, but remains near; much spectacular mutual display with ♂ when he brings prey then resumed. In hot sun ♀ returns to nest and shades chicks with spread wings, sometimes for several hours, up to day 45, when chicks feathered; thereafter shading not needed, but chicks seek shade if ♀ spreads wings. ♂ hunts for himself, ♀ and brood. Kills increase from 1/day early in period to maximum 3–4 in late fledging period. ♀ feeds on kills, but ♂ has usually decapitated and part-eaten them before arriving. Feeds given *c.* once every 4·5 h (3–4 times daily); may last for 30 min or more. Food requirement estimated at 32 kg for adults and brood during fledging period, in 1 well observed case 83% rabbits by weight. ♀ and young solicit ♂ for food with loud calling.

Breeding success not documented; but although no sibling aggression observed (Blondel *et al.* 1969), 2 young not often reared. No data on survival or longevity, even in France where best known.

References

Blondel, J. *et al.* (1969).
Cheylan, C. (1972).

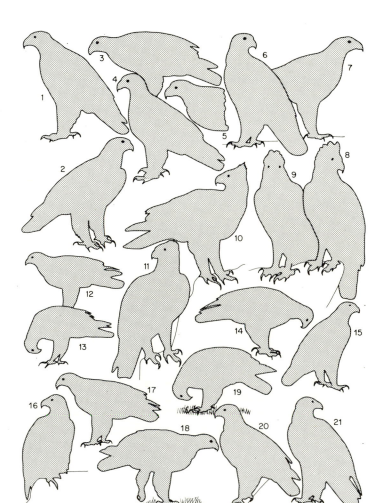

Plate 25

Aquila chrysaetos Golden Eagle (p. 412)
1. ADULT, 2. IMMATURE.

Aquila heliaca Imperial Eagle (p. 409)
Race *heliaca*: 3. IMMATURE, 4. ADULT.
Race *adalberti*: 5. ADULT.

Aquila verreauxi Verreaux's Eagle (p. 414)
6. ADULT, 7. IMMATURE.

Stephanoaetus coronatus Crowned Eagle (p. 429)
8. ADULT ♀, 9. IMMATURE.

Polemaetus bellicosus Martial Eagle (p. 433)
10. ADULT, 11. IMMATURE.

Aquila pomarina Lesser Spotted Eagle (p. 405)
12. ADULT, 13. IMMATURE.

Aquila clanga Greater Spotted Eagle (p. 406)
14. IMMATURE, 15. ADULT.

Aquila rapax Tawny Eagle (p. 406)
Race *rapax*: 16. IMMATURE, 17. ADULT ♂,
18. ADULT ♀.
Race *belisarius*: 19. ADULT.
Race *orientalis* (Steppe Eagle): 20. IMMATURE,
21. ADULT.

Hieraaetus spilogaster **(Bonaparte). African Hawk Eagle. Aigle autour Fascié.**

Spizäetus spilogaster De Bus de Gisignies = Bonaparte, 1850. Rev. Mag. Zool., Paris, ser. 2, 2, p. 487; Ethiopia.

Range and Status. Resident savannas, woodlands, thornbush, and forest edges in Africa south of Sahara, from Senegal east to Somalia, south to E Cape Province. Normally in rainfall 500–1200 mm/year, commonest in semi-arid deciduous woodland; much rarer in apparently ideal habitat in W than in E and southern Africa. Normally frequent to uncommon; sparse in arid areas, avoids dense forest. Numbers probably decreasing everywhere through destruction of large nesting trees by cultivation and direct persecution, including some by Africans.

Description: ADULT ♂: above, nearly black, some white flecks; base of spread primaries grey, forming conspicuous grey patch. Tail dark grey, subterminally banded and broadly barred black. Cheeks, throat, underside of body white, with sparse clear drop-shaped blackish spots; thighs white. Median and greater underwing-coverts largely or wholly black, forming conspicuous transverse bar. Primaries and secondaries below white, becoming rufous on inner secondaries, all tipped black, forming dark trailing edge. Tail below pale grey, subterminally banded blackish, indistinctly barred darker grey. Shafts of wing and tail-feathers white. ♀ usually rather browner

Hieraaetus spilogaster

Plate 26

Hieraaetus fasciatus Bonelli's Eagle (p. 416)
Race *fasciatus*: 1. IMMATURE ♂, 2. ADULT ♀.

Lophaetus occipitalis Long-crested Eagle (p. 426)
3. IMMATURE, 4. ADULT.

Hieraaetus dubius Ayres' Hawk Eagle (p. 424)
5. ADULT ♂, 6. ADULT ♀, 7. ADULT ♀ (melanistic form), 8. IMMATURE ♂.

Hieraaetus spilogaster African Hawk Eagle (p. 419)
9. ADULT ♂, 10. IMMATURE ♀.

Hieraaetus pennatus Booted Eagle (p. 422)
11. IMMATURE ♂, 12. ADULT ♂ (dark phase), 13. ADULT ♀ (pale phase).

Spizaetus africanus Cassin's Hawk Eagle (p. 428)
14. IMMATURE, 15. ADULT.

Aquila wahlbergi Wahlberg's Eagle (p. 410)
16. ADULT (dark phase), 17. ADULT (normal phase), 18. IMMATURE.

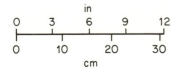

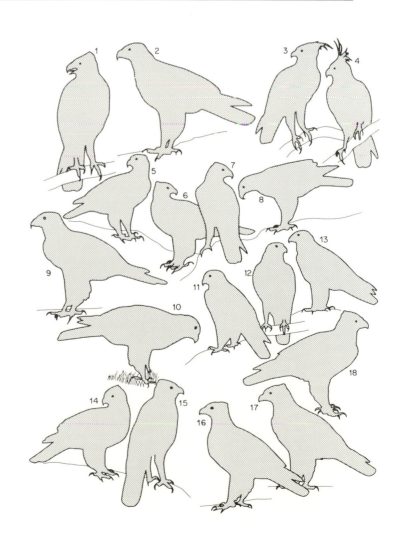

above, markedly larger, more heavily spotted below. Eye pale yellow; cere and feet yellow. SIZE: wing, ♂ 412–446, ♀ 435–465; tail, 225–290; tarsus, 90–100. WEIGHT: unsexed (56) 1150–1750 (1420); ♂ probably 1150–1400, ♀ 1400–1750, with little overlap (Biggs *et al.* 1979); actual, ♂ (2) 1221, 1300; ♀ (4) 1444–1640.

IMMATURE: above, dark brown, crown streaked blackish, some feathers edged rufous, greyer on upperwing-coverts. Below, rich dark rufous, including underwing-coverts, which lack black transverse bar; thighs and tarsi paler, buff. Primaries and secondaries above dark brown, indistinctly barred blackish, greyer at base of primaries forming paler carpal patch. Below, buff to pale rufous, tipped and inconspicuously barred darker brown. Tail above dark brown, broadly tipped blackish with more numerous dark bars than in adult; below buff, indistinctly barred darker brown. Eye brown at first, becoming yellow; cere and feet yellow.

DOWNY YOUNG: 1st down grey-brown above, whitish on abdomen; 2nd down (14 days) white except on brown head; eye brown, cere and feet pale yellow.

This species has in the past been regarded as a race of Bonelli's Eagle *H. fasciatus spilogaster*; but recent detailed research on breeding and other habits indicates that, although very closely related, it is a good species.

Field Characters. Medium-sized eagle with rounded wing-tips, spread wings almost long ovals, with short inner secondaries forming deep notch between long spread tail and wing. Perched, adults unmistakable, black above, almost pure white below with a few small drop-shaped black spots. In flight wings and tail white with dark tips, but not obviously or heavily barred, no white spot at base of wing on leading edge. Ayres' Hawk Eagle *H. dubius*, often said to be similar, is much smaller, has less rounded wings and is heavily barred on wing- and tail-feathers. At close range or in hand white primary and tail shafts diagnostic. Pale grey carpal patch both above and below wing clear and distinctive in flight. Immatures brown above, with plain rich rufous underwing-coverts, and faint bars; general shape also distinctive.

Voice. Not recorded. Distinctive when heard, but usually silent except when breeding. Mellow, fluting whistles, 'klu-klu-klu-kluee' or 'klueee-kluee', normal; also harsher 'kweee-oo-kweee-oo', 'ko-ko-ko-kwee-oo', 'kweee-oo' by ♂ and ♀ during nest repair; squealing 'squeee-ya-squee-ya' by ♀ soliciting ♂ with prey, becoming a more clucking 'schree-chok', 'shreee-chok' when ♂ approaches; sibilant 'hseee-o-hseeeeo' by ♂; shorter, more conversational 'kwi-kwi-kwi', 'kwip-kwip-kwip' and 'ko-wee-ko-weee' by both at nest. Voice of ♂ more melodious, that of ♀ harsher, deeper. Begging calls of young, shrill 'weee-yik', 'weee-yik' (Brown 1952; Steyn 1975).

General Habits. Very well known. Preferred habitat is broad-leaved, tall-grass, deciduous woodland, fairly open, and often mixed with cultivation; also denser *Brachystegia* woodland and *Acacia* grass veld, or dense thornbush; in more arid areas usually along riverine strips of tall *Acacia* woodland. Frequents forest edges, but not within dense forest, and often likes isolated forested mountains rising from open country.

Pairs reside permanently within home range; extent difficult to establish as often irregularly distributed; E Africa, 56–84 km²/pair, not all used; Transvaal lowveld, usually 55–110 km²/pair; optimum (Kruger Park) 15–23 km²/pair; Zimbabwe (Matopos) 30 km²/pair (Brown 1952 and unpub.; Tuer 1973; Steyn 1975; Smeenk 1974; Tarboton 1978b). Where widely and irregularly dispersed, probably uses only part of available area, rarely hunting more than 5 km from nest. Minimum nearest neighbour distance, Zimbabwe, 3 km (Tuer 1973).

Not often seen except on wing, but sometimes perches on conspicuous trees, e.g. to roost. Often soars round mountain-tops in heat of day, if available. Otherwise usually seen flying 100–200 m above ground, often over woodland or riverine strips. May often be soaring very high, out of sight. Pair very often together, or rejoin to feed on each other's prey. Comes to water holes where guineafowl or doves may water, and waits in tall trees for chance of kill. Generally bold, unafraid of man, even under moderate persecution. Pays little attention to other raptors or other birds, unless intending to kill; but regularly attacks some large eagles, e.g. Verreaux's *Aquila verreauxi* and Tawny Eagles *A. r. rapax*, especially if near nest-sites.

Hunts both from flight and from perches. Often makes quick dash from dense cover, like giant *Accipiter*, or flies low among trees, surprising possible prey. May also stoop from soaring position, observing prey 0·5–1 km away, and catching it unawares. Near water holes, perches on tall trees, and attacks guineafowl coming to drink, frequently pursuing right into dense vegetation in determined manner. Swifter birds, e.g. doves, may be taken on wing, by swift swoop from elevated perch, or surprise attack along river valley. Go-away-birds (*Corythaixoides*) and small hornbills probably caught on wing when crossing open spaces.

Food. Exceptionally powerful for its size, often killing animals much heavier than itself. Probably prefers large birds, especially gamebirds, but food varied according to habitat and availability. In E Kenya, Tsavo Park, 54 items comprised 29 mammals, of which 19 were dik-diks (4 kg), and 25 birds, including bustards, francolins, hornbills (Smeenk 1974). Elsewhere, mainly gamebirds (francolins, guineafowl), and some poultry in African cultivated areas (Brown 1952). 104 items recorded Zimbabwe included 77 birds, mainly francolins (49) (Steyn 1975). Where hyrax available (E Africa, Zimbabwe) takes young individuals. Often kills small carnivores, such as mongooses; rarely other raptors, e.g. Barn Owl *Tyto alba*; a few lizards, including chameleons, and snakes; immatures occasionally take insects. Most prey weighs more than 300 g; maximum weight, mammals 4 kg (dik-dik, 2·8 times av. adult weight); birds up to 2 kg (bustards). Trained captives regularly kill European hares over 4 kg; 1 killed an adult tomcat of 4300 g, after a struggle.

Breeding Habits. Intimately known Zimbabwe, E Africa; almost unknown W Africa; little detail South Africa. Same breeding sites used by same pairs for many years; pair-bond probably life-long for individuals (in one case estimated 10 years for both: Steyn 1975). In E Africa, long-used site may suddenly be abandoned for no obvious reason, reoccupied many (up to 23) years later.

Nuptial display not usually spectacular, mainly mutual soaring over nest-site, with some calling; occasionally pair soars up to height, where ♂ may perform undulating display near ♀; then perhaps stoops at her, whereupon she rolls and presents claws. Mating occurs on trees near nest, or on nest itself; ♀ crouches, ♂ perched beside her mounts, ♀ twists long tail to side, ♂ fluffs belly feathers; little obvious wing-flapping; silent; may occur twice within 2 h in nest repair period (Steyn 1975).

NESTS: usually in trees, sometimes on cliffs, often then shaded, at base of tree or bush. Tall trees preferred, often thorny acacias, but in E Africa also often large figs, *Terminalia*, baobabs. Usually high up, under canopy, in high main fork; sometimes lower, well within canopy, and often far out on large lateral branch at any height from 4·25–36 m above ground, most 9–15 m, depending on trees. Often situated on hill-side, or in tall tree growing along water course; if in open woodland, in solitary tree much larger than others around. Very large for size of bird, usually basin-shaped, much wider than it is deep. New nest may be 1–1·3 m across by 0·5 m deep; with repeated use reaches 2 m across and up to 1 m thick centrally. Made of large sticks, usually copiously lined with green leaves, from selected trees in near vicinity. Both sexes build, especially ♀, who continues bringing much green material through mid-late fledging period; ♂ may spend periods in nest in incubating or brooding posture, making kicking motions with feet (Steyn 1975). Pairs usually have 1–2 nests, sometimes 3, often only 1; alternatives may not be regularly used, 1 often preferred. Human interference probably stimulates frequent moves (Steyn 1975), but regularly successful pairs also move without human interference.

EGGS: 1–3, usually 2, laid at at least 2-day intervals; mean (127 E, Central and southern African clutches) 1·74; true mean probably higher, as some incomplete clutches of 1 probably included. Rounded ovals; dull chalky white, sparingly or heavily marked with red-brown, and grey or purplish undermarkings; 1 egg of clutch of 2 often more heavily marked than other. SIZE: (75) 59·4–69·6 × 47·6–54·0 (64·8 × 52·4) (Steyn 1975; McLachlan and Liversidge 1978). WEIGHT: (10) 75–100 (87) (Tuer 1972).

Laying dates: southern Africa May–Oct, peaking June–July (cool dry winter); E Africa, E Kenya–S Uganda May–Sept, most June–July (mid-year cool dry season); N Uganda, W Kenya Oct–Nov, early main dry season; no record W Africa.

Incubation begins 1st egg; mainly or entirely by ♀, ♂ taking small share for short periods by day, usually associated with bringing prey for ♀. ♀ sits tight, difficult to disturb, may often allow observer begin climbing tree before leaving. Incubation period: not exactly determined but estimated 41–44 days, probably 43 days (much longer than larger Bonelli's Eagle).

Chicks feeble when hatched, eyes partly open; elder considerably heavier and more active than younger, which hatches 2–3 days later, resulting in violent sibling aggression in which younger normally soon eliminated. 2nd, thicker, whiter down emerges at 14 days; primary quills show at 21 days, head then brown; partly feathered at 35 days, and completely feathered on body, little down visible by 50 days; thereafter main development in wing- and tail-feathers. Weight increases from 80 g at 2 days to 200 at 9; 395 at 14; 740 at 21; 950 at 28; 1135 at 35; 1160 at 42; 1250 at 49. Tarsus and culmen fully developed by 35 days, when eaglet can feed itself. Much wing-flapping and climbing out onto branches after day 65. 1st flight made, independent of parents, at 55–80 days, usually 65–75; mean (11 good records) 69. Smaller lighter ♂♂ fly earlier than heavier ♀♀.

♀ plays major part in brooding, tending and feeding young; but 1 ♂ known to brood and feed young (E Africa: Brown 1955). Newly hatched eaglet is closely brooded by ♀, but by 10 days (2nd down developing) brooding reduced to *c.* 50% by day, thereafter steadily decreasing till little brooding by day after day 21; ♀ may spend much time on nest, however, av. (16–30 days) 56·1% daylight hours, less than 10% after chick feathered. Individuals vary; ♀ may stand beside and shade chick with open wing in sunny nests, or perch on branch in shaded sites. Some ♀♀, less often ♂♂, violently and dangerously aggressive to human intruders, ♂ visits mainly to bring food, part-eating any prey himself first; ♀ brings some prey in last 20 days of fledging period, but usually remains near, and will feed eaglets if solicited right to end of period (70 days). ♂ spends little time in vicinity early stages, and hardly any near end, but rarely may visit nest with ♀ when large feathered eaglets in it (Brown 1952). Some ♂♂ roost near nest, up to *c.* day 40; others never roost near nest. ♀ roosts near nest to near end of fledging period, and between days 15–45, when much off nest but perching near, brings many green branches; most likely to attack humans at that stage.

Young usually do not remain long near nest, at most 14 days after 1st flight; can then presumably accompany parents to foraging grounds. Family remains loosely attached, young flying with parents, for up to 60 days after 1st flight, perhaps longer.

Breeding success very variable, from 1–10 young reared in neighbouring pairs in 12 years (Steyn 1975). Overall, in 50 pair-years, 38 pairs bred (76%) and reared 27 young; i.e. 0·54 young/pair/year overall, 0·71/breeding pair, and 1·08/successful nest. No recorded case of 2 young reared southern and southern central Africa, but 2/15 cases Kenya. At 75% mortality before sexual maturity at 4 years (estimated), adults would need to live for 15 years in stable population; probably too long, so mortality must be lower.

References
Brown, L. H. (1952–3, 1955).
Steyn, P. (1975).

**Plates
26 and 30**
(Opp. pp. 419
and 451)

Hieraaetus pennatus (Gmelin). Booted Eagle. Aigle botté.

Falco pennatus Gmelin, 1788. Syst. Nat. 1, p. 272; no locality = France.

Range and Status. Resident and Palearctic migrant. Breeds southern Europe, N Africa (Morocco, Algeria, Tunisia) and in Cape Province, South Africa. These 2 populations, not racially distinct, both migrate in non-breeding season to other parts of Africa, European birds probably mingling in austral winter with Cape Province breeding birds. In Africa, frequent to uncommon, except at points of entry at migration routes.

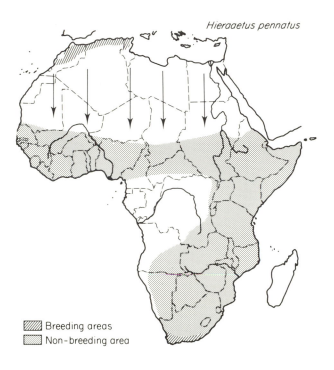

Hieraaetus pennatus

▨ Breeding areas
▧ Non-breeding area

Description. *H. p. pennatus* (Gmelin), ADULT ♂: pale phase—forehead, lores, whitish. Head and neck tawny to rufous-brown, streaked darker. Back and upperwing-coverts dark brown, paler on lesser coverts; a white spot at base of wing on leading edge. Below, including underwing-coverts, pure white to buff, streaked brown on chin, breast, upper flanks. Wing-feathers above blackish, primaries basally barred and mottled white, producing a pale carpal patch; secondaries browner, edged buff; below brown, barred grey, primaries tipped blackish. Tail above pale brown sometimes obscurely barred, below brown, faintly barred grey. Eye, brown; cere and feet yellow. ♀ larger, often darker. Dark phase—resembles pale phase from above or behind, but below all dark brown, streaked blackish; some feathers above edged paler. Tail-feathers and base of primaries usually paler brown; a blackish patch on underwing-coverts at carpal joint. This phase uncommon N Africa, *c.* 20% South Africa, 20–25% overall; ♀♀ more often dark than ♂♂. SIZE: wing ♂ 353–390 (369·1), ♀ 380–428 (409·3); tail, ♂ 187–202 (195·3), ♀ 196–218 (211·2); tarsus, ♂ 59–64 (61·7), ♂ 65–71 (68·8); wing-span, 1140–1310. WEIGHT: ♂ (9) 510–770 (709); ♀ (10) 840–1250 (975).

IMMATURE: like adult, but underside more rufous, streaked blackish; head more rufous, uppertail-coverts paler; dark-phase immatures resemble dark-phase adults. Eye darker brown, cere and feet yellow.

DOWNY YOUNG: white; of dark phase, grey. Eye brown, cere and feet yellow.

Field Characters. A very small eagle, slightly smaller than Common Buzzard *Buteo b. buteo*; rather stockily built, short-winged, but very swift. In pale phase dark wing-feathers contrast strongly with nearly white underwing-coverts and body, somewhat resembling Egyptian Vulture *Neophron percnopterus*; distinguished by short head and bill, square, not wedge-shaped tail. Dark phase somewhat resembles Wahlberg's Eagle *Aquila wahlbergi*, but shorter-winged, stockier in body, and normally soars with tail spread. Both phases from above recall Black Kite *Milvus migrans*, with paler brown upperwing-coverts and U-shaped pale rump-patch, but at once distinguished by square tail, feathered tarsus. White spot at base of wing recalls Ayres' Hawk Eagle *H. dubius*, but immediately distinguishable from this by lack of heavy barring on tail and wings, different habitat and habits; also is much paler generally. Almost plain, unbarred tail in both phases is useful. Immatures of dark phase more difficult to recognize with certainty, but pale-phase immatures resemble adult.

Voice. Recorded (2a). Generally silent except in breeding quarters, when very vocal; sometimes known as 'singing eagle'. In display, shrill whistling calls, 'pi-peee, pi-pi-pi-peeee'; or long series of short, whistled notes in rising and falling cadence 'pipipipipipipi-kikikikikikiki-pipipipipipipipi'. Shorter series of sharp whistles, 'kli-kli-kli' or 'bi-bi-bi'. ♂ with food 'kli-kli-kli-kli-yuck-yuck-yuck', answered excitedly by ♀ with 'kliac-kiac-kiac-kiac'. In South Africa ♀ soliciting ♂ for prey calls 'kyip-kyip-kyip', resembling calls of Wahlberg's Eagle. Small young begging utter cheeping calls, later 'kyip-kyip-kyip' as in adult (Glutz von Blotzheim *et al.* 1971; Irribarren 1975; Steyn and Grobler 1981).

General Habits. Well known Europe; little known N Africa, and well known South Africa. Migrant from both breeding areas, arriving in S European and N African breeding range late Mar–early Apr, departing end Aug–mid Sept. In South Africa breeding birds arrive Aug, depart Mar; but some may remain longer. Position complicated as European birds may migrate to South African breeding range, mingling with indistinguishable South African breeding birds, but perhaps with some ecological separation, those seen in high mountains or near forests not South African breeders. South African breeders probably migrate NW Mar–Aug to NW Cape and Namibia.

In N Africa frequents both wooded country (N Morocco) and open barren hill-sides. Cape Province breeding population frequents intermediate zone between Cape Macchia and Karoo vegetation, low bushes or scrub on mountain-sides, generally more open than Moroccan habitat. On migration may be found anywhere, in deserts, woodlands, high mountains (to 4000 m Ethiopia, Kenya); perhaps commonest in semi-arid woodlands, but can occur over or in forests. Usually seen singly, or at most pairs together; then usually in breeding habitat. 1 record of 50 together moving north Apr (Donnelly 1966) may be misidentification.

Hunts either by flying over open country, soaring *c.* 200–300 m above ground, suddenly stooping at prey with great speed; or alternatively perches in trees, making sudden attacks on prey. Latter method used in European woodlands, but little in NW or South Africa, except by migrants, which may frequent wooded areas. Hunting range normally includes woodland and open country. Most prey is taken on ground, but can probably catch birds on wing. Occasionally performs spectacular swift stoops from much greater height, descending almost vertically with wing-tips folded to tail tip in heart-shaped silhouette, then resembling Ayres' Hawk Eagle.

Food. Mainly birds, some mammals, in Europe varying locally. Mammals from size of small mouse to young rabbit; rabbits important Spain, probably less, N Africa. Birds from size of small warbler to adult partridges, large pigeons (10–400 g). Species typical of open country (plovers, gamebirds) predominate in some European areas over woodland species. No good data N Africa, but in South Africa 55 recorded items comprised 54% birds, 13% mammals, 33% lizards. Birds include Speckled Pigeon *Columba guinea*, gamebirds, doves, plovers and small ground species (larks, buntings). Some reptiles taken, perhaps more important in warm semi-arid areas (e.g. South Africa) than wooded European haunts. Some insects, including swarming alate termites (Steyn and Grobler 1981; Geïlikman 1959; Golodushko 1958). Takes some young poultry if not enclosed and available in home range.

Breeding Habits. Very well known; only recently rediscovered as breeding bird in South Africa (Martin *et al.* 1980). Preliminary estimate of numbers (Brooke and Martin, in press) suggesting minimum of 100 pairs may be too low. Scattered, but probably commonest eagle in Cape Province, pairs in suitable habitat breeding 0·5–1 km apart. No data N Africa, but in Europe pairs may be 0·5–1 km apart in optimum habitat. Hunting range in breeding season includes open country not immediately adjacent to nest-site.

Both in N and South Africa pairs arrive in breeding localities 3–4 weeks before egg-laying, sometimes earlier. Pair-bond is apparently life-long despite migratory habit, as same individuals recognized in same territory 4 successive years (Irribarren 1975). Alternatively, bond may be to site, as migrants are usually solitary in winter quarters. Breeding activity commences immediately after arrival (as in Wahlberg's Eagle).

Nuptial display spectacular. On arrival pairs soar over home range, or may perch (Spain) on conspicuous outlook points, where pale phase birds clearly visible to neighbours (Irribarren 1975). In South Africa, very inconspicuous when perched. ♂♂ also perform swift, vigorous undulating displays, with steep dives of 100–200 m followed by upward swoops, wings folded to tail-tip in dive and re-opened for upward swoop, often

accompanied by long series of 'ki-ki-ki-ki' notes on rising and falling scale. Later, ♂ may soar above ♀, dive at her with wing-tips folded to tail-tip; both may then dive into nest area, perhaps alighting to copulate. Copulation on tree branches, on cliff ledges, or on nest; occurs during 2 weeks before egg-laying. Immatures occupying territories may copulate, but do not lay (Irribarren 1975).

NEST: pairs have 1–3 nests, usually 2, sometimes only 1; used for several successive years, then perhaps moving to another locality. In N and South Africa normally built on cliffs in gorges or ravines; in N Africa sometimes in trees. On cliffs, usually shaded by bush or small tree. May use nests of other large raptors (Black Kite, spotted eagles) or Black Stork *Ciconia nigra* as foundation. Tree nests are solid, rather small structures, varying with site; of sticks, lined with green leaves, 0·4–1 m across by 0·3–0·6 m deep. Nests under bushes, South Africa, small and often difficult to locate, not more than 0·5 m across and shallow. If several alternative sites available, move frequently or annually, but same nest may be used several successive years. Nest repair of old nests short, beginning at once, or soon after arrival, egg-laying *c.* 2 weeks later. If no eggs laid may continue longer (May, Spain: Irribarren 1975). Both sexes build.

EGGS: 1–3, normally 2, laid at 2–3 day intervals (Mošanský and Danko 1969); mean (65 N African clutches) 2·0 (Heim de Balsac and Mayaud 1962); 2 normal, South Africa, judging from few available records (Steyn and Grobler 1981). Rounded ovals; dull bluish or greenish white, normally unmarked South Africa, elsewhere often spotted and blotched red-brown, with pinkish undermarkings. SIZE: (65 eggs, N Africa and Spain) 50·0–60·2 × 39·6–47·5 (54·3 × 44·1) (Glutz von Blotzheim *et al.* 1971); (8, South Africa) 51·5–58·0 × 42·2–45·8 (Europe). WEIGHT: 56·0–58·6.

Laying dates: N Africa mid-late Apr, sometimes to mid-May (Heim de Balsac and Mayaud 1962); South Africa 2nd half Sept; in late spring or early summer both areas.

Incubation begins 1st egg; either wholly or mainly by ♀, who is fed at nest by ♂, but in South Africa ♂ takes some share by day (Steyn and Grobler, in press) and may perch near nest without relieving ♀. Period: at least 37–38 days Spain (Irribarren 1975); 1 exact record South Africa, 40 days.

Young when hatched feeble, helpless. 2nd down emerges at *c.* 10 days; wing- and tail-feathers by 20 days; contour feathers appear at *c.* 25 days; partially feathered 35 days, and by 38 days wing- and tail-feathers half-grown. Body covered with feathers by 45 days, still downy on head and underwing-coverts. Begin to tear at food themselves within 10 days (Steyn and Grobler 1981), regularly by 25 days (Irribarren 1975); and at 38 days mantle over prey, threatening adults (Mošanský and Danko 1969). Weight increases from 46·5 g at hatch to 540–830 by 40 days, and just before 1st flight to 640–642 and 810–884, varying perhaps according to sex (Garzón 1968). Despite hatching interval of 2 or more days, no sibling aggression reported; and in South Africa 1 brood of 2 showed extraordinary size difference, one partly feathered while other still almost entirely downy (Steyn and Grobler 1981). Such size difference not reported by other observers. Much wing-flapping and bounding about on nest before 1st flight at 40–50 days. 1st flight made independently of parents at 51–53 days (Spain: Irribarren 1975); in South Africa 50–54 days (2 exact records); young may fly prematurely at 44 days, surviving thereafter (Irribarren 1975).

In days 1–10 ♀ broods young; thereafter brooding reduced, but ♀ remains standing on or in vicinity of nest, ♂ bringing almost all prey throughout fledging period. In South Africa 1 ♀ brought 1/28 prey seen, late in fledging period; ♂ may bring prey at short intervals (28 min minimum, South Africa). In all observed cases, prey brought plucked, headless, legless and wingless, even mammals being plucked of fur and sometimes partly dismembered. 1–3 items brought/day and food requirement of a captive young estimated at 300 g/day (Golodushko 1958).

Good data on breeding success lacking; but lack of sibling aggression results in 2 young often being reared

(Spain, Europe: Irribarren 1975; Golodushko 1958). 1 egg often infertile, thus reducing brood size; in South Africa, 2 young reared in several recent cases (Steyn and Grobler 1981).

Young remain dependent on parents for at least 60 days after 1st flight. Remain near nest and fed there for 10–14 days, thereafter accompanying parents in foraging range; recorded still with parents up to 47 days after 1st flight (Spain: Irribarren 1975) and 64 days (South Africa: Steyn and Grobler 1981). In Europe, migrate south c. 2 weeks before adults, 135–140 days after egg-laying. Adults may remain up to mid–late Sept, N Africa, Mar, South Africa; may then display again briefly as if re-establishing territorial rights (Irribarren 1975).

References
Glutz von Blotzheim, U. N. et al. (1971).
Irribarren, J. J. (1975).
Martin, J. E. and M. R. (1974, 1976).
Steyn, P. and Grobler, J. H. (1981).

Hieraaetus dubius (Smith). Ayres' Hawk Eagle. Aigle d'Ayres.

Plates 26 and 30

(Opp. pp. 419 and 451)

Morphinus dubius A. Smith, 1830. S. Afr. Quart. Journ., ser. 1, p. 117; Olifants River, Cape Province.

Range and Status. Scarce resident, forested and wooded areas of Africa south of Sahara, avoiding densest forests and semi-arid areas. Intra-continental migrant in South African range, south of Limpopo River. Inexplicably, uncommon to rare throughout range.

Description: ADULT ♂: forehead, and a broad eyebrow white. Back and upperwing-coverts brown, lightly mottled or edged whitish; a conspicuous white spot at base of leading edge of wing. Below, white, with large conspicuous spade-shaped

Hieraaetus dubius

X Vagrants

black spots on breast and belly, broadly barred on thighs; underwing-coverts dark brown, mottled white, undertail-coverts and tarsi pure white. Wing-feathers above blackish, including shafts; below grey-brown, heavily and broadly barred blackish, no obvious paler carpal patch. Tail above grey, broadly tipped blackish, with 3–4 narrower blackish bars; below grey-brown, heavily barred blackish. Eye yellow-orange, cere and feet yellow. ♀ larger, normally much more heavily spotted below, white forehead and eyebrow reduced, eye darker orange. SIZE: wing, ♂ 326–345, ♀ 360–420; tail, ♂ 175, ♀ 205–223; tarsus, 56–78. WEIGHT: ♂ (1) 714, ♀ (2) 879, 940.

IMMATURE: forehead and eyebrow buff, crown and nape rufous, streaked dark brown. Wing-coverts and back dark brown, edged paler, appearing 'scaled'. Below, warm buff, narrowly streaked blackish, paler on flanks, legs and under-tail-coverts unstreaked. Tail above dark grey-brown, below grey, broadly tipped and barred darker, as in adult. Eye pale grey-brown, cere and feet pale yellow. Immatures can usually be sexed by extent of buff on forehead and eyebrow, more in ♂♂. White spot at base of wing not obvious.

DOWNY YOUNG: dull white, 2nd down paler; eye brown, cere and feet pale yellow.

Immatures probably moult to adult plumage in 1 stage by becoming darker above, lighter and more heavily spotted, not streaked, below. Individual adults vary from very white ♂♂ to very dark, heavily spotted and barred ♀♀; melanistic individuals of either sex known, almost entirely black, with a few white spots, white forehead and eyebrow reduced, but white spot at base of wing conspicuous.

This species should correctly be called *Hieraaetus ayresii* (Gurney) (Brooke and Vernon, in prep.), as the name *Morphinus dubius* was applied by A. Smith to what could only have been a Booted Eagle *H. pennatus*, on the description and distributional and ecological grounds.

Field Characters. Descriptions which suggest this species easily confused with African Hawk Eagle *H. spilogaster*, or Booted Eagle *H. pennatus* in adult

plumage, are misleading, as it is virtually unmistakable once known. Differs from African Hawk Eagle in being smaller in size, and having usually conspicuous white forehead and spot at base of wing, and dark, heavily barred wing- and tail-feathers. Distinguishable from pale-phase Booted Eagle by heavily barred tail and wings; much darker, not contrasting underwing-coverts, white forehead; both, however, have basal white spot at leading edge of wing. Immature resembles young Booted Eagle, but darker, more rufous below, always much more heavily barred on wings and tail.

Voice. Recorded (2a). Usually silent except near nest, where very vocal. Distinctive, high-pitched, but melodious whistling 'hueeeep, hueeeep'; or 'hip-hip-hip-hueeep' especially in aerial display. Lower-pitched 'hip-hip-hip' when perched. Young begging utter high-pitched cheeping calls.

General Habits. Little known outside the breeding season. Pairs may frequent breeding site most of year, but probably wander widely outside breeding season. In South Africa evidence indicates northward migration in Austral winter. Inexplicable rarity obscures good estimate of home range; but probably *c.* 25 km²/pair regularly used in breeding season.

Seldom seen, usually suddenly, flying briefly near forest, over dense woodland along rivers, or on isolated mountain tops. Probably spends much of day flying at great height, as often appears in swift descending flight as if from nowhere. If not in flight, appears to spend hours perched within canopy of large leafy trees, not on exposed bare limbs; is then very inconspicuous.

An extremely dashing swift little eagle, with magnificent flying powers, combining speed of large falcon and agility of goshawk. Hunts prey in swift, near-vertical dives, with wing-tips folded to tail-tip in characteristic heart-shaped silhouette, shooting into forest canopy and weaving at speed in and out among branches. Alternatively dives fast into tree-top and pursues prey by extremely quick twisting and jinking among branches. Can dive into forest canopy at speed emerging with prey without stopping, in manner unique to this species. Probably catches many birds in flight. In view of extraordinary flying powers, and abundant, readily available prey, general rarity in range inexplicable.

Food. Mainly birds in weight range 40–200 g; usually unrecognizable when brought to nest, but includes bulbuls, small doves, helmet-shrikes, woodpeckers (recognized by feet); mainly small forest or woodland species. Occasionally larger birds, including gamebirds to size of guineafowl (adult about twice eagle's weight); a few mammals, e.g. olive tree squirrel *Paraxerus ochraceus*. As such food normally abundant, rarity not explained by lack of preferred food supply.

Breeding Habits. Intimately known Kenya, 2 sites observed for 30 and 10 years; elsewhere little known. Pairs frequent breeding site for 60–90 days before laying, perching near, roosting in area, displaying over site. Mate for life of any individual, bereaved bird obtaining another mate. Pair much attached to each other, usually not far apart, but ♀ more inclined to perch near nest.

Magnificent flight fully used in display. Pair soars high above forest near nest, often close together, repeatedly calling, sometimes diving into forest at speed. ♀ may then perch in nest or nest tree, where ♂ repeatedly dives close past her, weaving swiftly between branches. Mutual soaring displays continue throughout breeding season; ♂ may dive at ♀ from more than 500 m above; or pair may soar very high, almost out of sight, in aerial display, with ♂ diving at ♀, or performing swift undulations close to her.

NEST: in trees, usually in shady fork or on lateral branch, 8–20 m above ground. May use foundation of other bird's nest (e.g. harrier hawk) or build own. Apparently very unskilled builders; nests often collapse within year, causing breeding failure, or before next season, forcing fresh building; nest may be abandoned unused. In secure site nest compact, *c.* 80 cm across by 50 cm deep, smaller when first built. Usually used repeatedly but may be abandoned if, for example, fall of branch exposes it to sunlight. All known pairs have only 1 nest. Built by both sexes, mainly ♀. Nest repair of old structure sporadic, in bouts over several months, intensifying shortly before egg-laying. Several green branches added daily late in nest-repair period. New nests may take 3–4 months to build, may then be abandoned unused, or never finished.

EGGS: Kenya, always 1; South Africa, 2 reported, but no good recent records, old records doubtful. White, sparsely blotched brown and purplish. SIZE: (12) 53·9–59·0 × 42·5–47·0 (55·7 × 43·9). Details require confirmation.

Laying dates: Kenya, Mar, May–Sept, peak June–Aug (mid-year cool dry season); Zimbabwe, reported May; South Africa, reported July–Sept, but identity doubtful (Tarboton 1978b). Kenya layings normally in dry season; but 1 re-laying in Mar resulted in successful breeding throughout heaviest rains.

Incubation by ♀ only, fed every 2–3 days at nest by ♂; he brings prey, calls ♀ off to receive it, but does not incubate while she feeds. ♂ often perches near nest when not hunting, or visits nest without food, when ♀ usually leaves and solicits, returning shortly. Incubation period: (3 records) 45 days.

Downy young helpless; 1st feathers show at *c.* 25 days, cover down by 53 days, crest then visible. Can stand at 28 days, may tear at food at 40 days, but usually dependent on parental help to 55 days; self-feeding coincides with full feathering, and development of bill and tarsus. Young usually rather sluggish in nest, wing-flapping only after 60 days. Solicits parent with food up to end of fledging period. 1st flight made at av. 75 days (once at 17.30 h).

♀ remains on or near nest during most of fledging period. ♂ brings most prey up to day 55, when ♀ also hunts; ♀ may hunt earlier if ♂ delays. Food requirement increases to 1–2 kills daily. ♀ broods young continuously days 1–8; thereafter day-time brooding reduced, ceasing after day 28. Up to 25 days, ♀ mainly on nest; days 25–50, ♀ perches in area, attacking intruders, feeding young on prey brought by ♂. After 50 days ♀ spends long periods away, also kills prey, especially if ♂ fails. ♂ never feeds young, is uneasy on nest, usually stays only a few seconds. Throughout fledging period ♀ roosts on nest with young; ♂ does not roost near nest. ♀ readily attacks human intruders, is extremely bold and aggressive; sometimes aided by ♂ if both present.

After making 1st flight independently, young returns to roost in nest, with ♀ for first few days of post-fledging period, thereafter alone, up to 21 days. Then makes longer flights, and leaves nest area within 30 days; presumably then with parents in home range, but details unknown.

Breeding success abnormally low for an eagle of this size. Only good data from Kenya, where 2 sites show similar results over 10 and 30 years. Appears to be adversely affected by inefficient nest-building causing frequent collapse of nest, often containing young or egg; interference from other raptors, e.g. Peregrine Falcon *Falco peregrinus*; some predation of adults or young by arboreal mammals (genet cat suspected) and by large shrikes *Malaconotus* spp. (Brown 1953). Eggs sometimes fall from nests, but may then re-lay after some weeks or months. 40 good Kenya records indicate overall breeding success of 0·30 young/pair/year, and 0·65 per egg laid, much lower than that of related African Hawk Eagle. At an estimated mortality of 75% before sexual maturity, adults would have to live 26–27 years to maintain population. Known ages of recognizable wild adults at 2 sites over 10 and 30 years, 3–12 years in ♂♂, 3–8 in ♀♀; therefore overall range 3–12, av. 6 (Brown and Davey 1978). Accordingly, mortality of young must be negligible, or these sites abnormally unsuccessful.

References
Brown, L. H. (1955, 1966, 1974c).
Brown, L. H. and Davey, P. R. A. (1978).

Genus *Lophaetus* Kaup

A monotypic endemic genus of rather small eagles. Plumage black, that of immature similar to that of adult. Bill rather weak, gape wide; head with a long waving crest. Wings rather short, rounded; tail more than half wing length, broad when spread. Feet rather weak, claws short. The genus is probably most closely allied to *Spizaetus*, having a high screaming voice and long crest, like some eastern *Spizaetus* spp. However, differences in habits, and the fact that the immature plumage is like that of adult make it preferable to retain this as a monotypic genus.

**Plates
26 and 29**
(Opp. pp. 419
and 450)

Lophaetus occipitalis (Daudin). Long-crested Eagle. Aigle huppard.

Falco occipitalis Daudin, 1800. Traité d'Orn., 2, p. 40; Knysna District, Cape Province.

Range and Status. Resident wooded areas and better watered savannas of Africa south of Sahara, from Senegal east to Ethiopia, south to E Cape Province; has apparently declined in extreme southern range in recent years. Elsewhere frequent to common; numbers probably stable, perhaps locally increasing. One of few species that benefits from small-scale African cultivation, often commonest in cultivated areas, breeding readily in introduced eucalyptus or other exotic trees.

Description. ADULT ♂: all black or very dark brown, with conspicuous white patches, barred darker, above and below wing at carpal joint; underwing-coverts mainly white; white tail base, and greyish white tarsi. Tail black, with 3 greyish white bars. A long waving occipital crest of 6–7 feathers. Eye yellow to golden, cere and feet yellow. ♀ larger. SIZE: wing, ♂ 350–376, ♀ 370–408; tail, ♂ 192–200, ♀ 215–250; tarsus, 92–110. WEIGHT: ♂ 912–1363, ♀ 1367–1523.
IMMATURE: resembles adult, with less prominent crest, some white tips to neck feathers and upperwing-coverts; generally browner, more mottled white. Eye grey or brown, cere and feet yellow.

DOWNY YOUNG: greyish white, eye grey, cere and feet pale yellow.
Some individuals, mainly in South Africa, apparently adults, have brown, not white tarsi; reason not clear.

Field Characters. Unmistakable in any plumage. At rest black colour, long, loose crest waving in wind distinctive. In flight, is mainly black above and below with white underwing-coverts, normally white thighs and conspicuous white patches above and below wing at carpal joint. Wings short, rounded, held well forward and flapped rapidly through short arc.

Voice. Recorded (1e, 2a, 8, 18, 22a, 28). Often very vocal, especially in breeding season, but also when soaring and when feeding. Loud clear high-pitched scream, 'keeeee-eh' or 'keeeee-ee-eh'; also often a long series of sharp calls, 'kik-kik-kik-kik-keee-eh', repeated for minutes on end. Sharp, querulous sounding 'kyeh-kyeh'. Other calls variously rendered 'screee-screee'; 'yeep-yeep'. At nest with food for young, adults and young utter sibilant 'sseeee-yuk, sseeeee-yuk' or 'kleeyuk-kleeyuk', somewhat resembling *Aquila* spp.; eaglets also 'kip-kip-kip'. Voice of ♀ always lower-pitched than that of ♂. Varied calls, once known, are distinctive, and diagnostic for species.

General Habits. Well known. Frequents woodlands, mixed cultivation and woodlands, forest edges, plantations, and low-lying swampy grasslands with tall trees. In semi-arid areas of less than 700 mm annual rainfall largely confined to neighbourhood of vleis, swamps and along riverine forest strips. Not found within dense forest. Occurs sea level to at least 3000 m (Ethiopia, Kenya), but commonest in lowlands. Adapts well to cultivated areas with some tall trees, introduced or indigenous. May be locally common, but absent from similar suitable habitat not far away. Normally sedentary, probably to some extent nomadic in non-breeding season, perhaps moving in association with fluctuating rodent abundance. Not regularly migratory anywhere.

Generally seen perched on prominent tree, telegraph pole, fence post, watching for prey, or soaring 100–300 m above ground (seldom flies higher). Spends most of day perched, making frequent flights from perch to perch, and often uses same perches day after day, or visits same feeding area repeatedly. Responds quickly to local grass fires, which expose rodent prey, within main home range, then using such burned areas to hunt daily for long periods. Hunts most actively early morning and evening; 75% of rodents caught before 10·30 h, 21% after 15·00 h. Often soars in mid-morning and rests in shade in heat of day; does kill some prey in midday hours, however (Hall 1979a).

Catches all prey on ground, from perch, not from or in flight. Perched individuals watch ground intently, and on seeing prey crane forward, then drop on prey in short slanting stoop, raising wings above back to make strike at end of swoop. Usually 1 success/3–4 attacks. Large gape assists in the swallowing of whole prey.

Food. Mainly small rodents, especially, in southern Africa, vlei rat *Otomys* (over 95%). Elsewhere *Arvicanthis*, *Praomys*, *Rhabdomys*, *Lemniscomys*. Largest prey normally taken possibly mole rats *Tachyoryctes* (infrequent) and fully grown Red-necked Francolin *Francolinus streptophorus* (Steyn 1978). A few young or disabled ground birds, and some small birds e.g. *Quelea*; apparently cannot regularly catch any very active prey. Guineafowl and mongoose reported, without proof. A few small lizards, some insects; but apparently does not feed on alate termite swarms. Credibly reported to eat fruit occasionally, also crabs and hatchery trout (Steyn 1978). Small prey usually swallowed whole, larger rodents transported in beak. Although common in densely populated African areas, not known to take poultry; basically beneficial in agricultural land.

Breeding Habits. Very well known. In tropical Africa pairs reside in home ranges year-round in some areas, move out of them in non-breeding season in others. Extent of range difficult to ascertain, but probably *c.* 2000–3000 ha/pair. Often not regularly distributed over

Lophaetus occipitalis

X Vagrants

all suitable terrain, as, for example, Wahlbergs' Eagle *Aquila wahlbergi* is in similar habitat.

Display not spectacular, voice more important than aerial evolutions. Mainly by perching and calling, or single birds (rarely pairs) soaring and calling over breeding site. Very vocal in display, but any more spectacular flying displays rare. ♂ occasionally performs brief undulating flights, alternately diving and swooping up again, but not regular. Copulation occurs on trees near nest, normally from 07.00–11.00 h, increasing in frequency before egg-laying; may occur twice within an hour and continue after eggs laid, or may persist even when birds do not breed. ♂ normally perches near ♀, calls and mounts, but sometimes flies straight to ♀ back. Sometimes associated with feeding of ♀ by ♂.

NEST: 1–2/pair, rather small structures usually high in tall trees, but below canopy, at 7–25 m above ground, mainly 12–20 m. Often in eucalyptus, when constructed mainly of leafy eucalyptus twigs, elsewhere of sticks, lined with green leaves. Sometimes placed on clumps of parasitic *Loranthus*, when hard to see. New nest small slight structure 0·5 m wide by 15 cm deep, barely accommodating adult. If used for several years, may reach 0·8 m across by 30 cm deep. Both sexes build, ♀ most. Green branches added before egg-laying and up until mid-fledging period. New nests constructed frequently, even annually, seldom used for more than 3 years; same pair may have nests 2 km apart within home range. Occasionally uses nests of other species.

EGGS: 1–2, 1 about as common as 2; E Africa mean (13 clutches) 1·46; southern Africa (21) 1·62. Laid at at least 2–3 day intervals, possibly sometimes much longer (up to 14 days: Hall 1979b; L. H. Brown, unpub.). Rounded ovals, dull greyish white, clouded with grey, purple and dull brown, rarely with distinct brown spots; easily distinguished from those of similar-sized eagles. SIZE: (18) 57·9–62·3 × 44·7–51·0 (59·8 × 47·5); WEIGHT: *c.* 75.

Laying dates: Nigeria Mar; Sudan Mar–Apr; Ethiopia June–Aug; E Kenya Feb, Mar, June, Aug–Dec, with no obvious peaks. W Kenya–Uganda Jan, Feb, June, Oct–Dec; Zambia–Zimbabwe–Malawi June –Dec, especially Aug–Sept; Natal June–Sept. Lays most often in dry seasons, but near equator often in rains.

Incubation normally begins 1st egg; but may be peculiar, adult brooding in incubation posture for days in empty nest. 1 also known to incubate deserted egg of Wahlberg's Eagle for 44 days (Brown 1952–3). ♀ normally incubates all day and most of night; is fed at or near nest by ♂, who often then incubates for short spells. In most detailed record (504 h continuous daily dawn–dark watch: Steyn 1978), eggs incubated 88·9% of daylight, by ♀ for 414 h (82·1%), ♂ for 34 h (6·75%). ♂ incubated on 17/42 days in spells of a few minutes to 8 h; more regularly in latter half of period. ♂ normally feeds ♀ near nest, but in long absences she may kill prey herself. Incubation period: 42 days.

Young when hatched feeble, cannot stand or move much, brooded continuously. If 2 hatch at normal 2–3 day intervals, little or no sibling aggression. In 2 cases where young apparently hatched 14–15 days apart (Hall 1979b; L. H. Brown, unpub.), no sibling aggression noted despite large size difference. Clutch size thus more closely related to brood size than in some other eagles. By day 15, active, 2nd down developing, crest appearing, wing- and tail-feathers visible; contour feathers appear at 20 days, partly feathered 25 days, fully feathered 40 days. Weight increases from 60 g day 1 to 98 day 5; 340 day 15; 490 day 20; 680 day 25; 900 day 30; 1200 day 40; and 1230 day 80. Wing fully developed by day 80 (i.e. c. 25 days after 1st flight, based on captive: Steyn 1978). Young always rather inactive in nest compared to some other eagles; little wing-flapping, but move onto branches before 1st flight, made independent of parents; before 1st flight may climb further up tree, from branch to branch. Fledging period: 53–58 days, av. 55 (5 good records: Steyn 1978; Hall 1979b).

In early fledging period ♀ broods young continuously most of time; but stands some time on nest-edge. Brooding reduced to c. 70% daylight by day 5, 53% day 8, then steadily decreases to 25–30% day 20; no brooding after day 40, but when not brooding ♀ often spends long periods perched on edge of nest, or near it until chicks partly-feathered; little brooding or shading by day after day 30. ♂ brings most prey up to day 40 when eaglet partly-feathered; thereafter ♀ also brings some prey. ♀ usually leaves nest to receive prey from ♂; when standing idle on or near nest removes cast pellets, and brings many green sprays. Most prey brought in crop and regurgitated into nest.

Most young leave neighbourhood of nest soon after 1st flight, but may return at intervals. Remain in general nest area for at least 2 months; are recorded as still being fed by parents at 122 and 127 days, but will attempt to kill for themselves at 90 days (can then be trapped). May begin to perform adult display flights and calling c. 4 months after leaving nest, and are virtually indistinguishable from adult at 180 days old (Steyn 1978).

No adequate data on breeding success, but many pairs do not breed annually. In Kenya av. brood/ successful nest 1·29 from mean clutch of 1·46; 4 south African nests produced 5 young (1·25/pair overall, 1·67/ successful nest). Lack of sibling aggression results in higher success rate when rearing young; but this may be countered by frequent non-breeding.

References
Hall, D. (1979a, b).
Steyn, P. (1978).

Genus *Spizaetus* Vieillot

World-wide in tropics, especially oriental. 10 spp., 1 African. Small to medium-sized eagles, with short, rounded wings, conspicuously long tails, usually 80–90% of wing length. Heads sometimes crested, bill usually short; legs and feet often powerful. Plumage varied, sometimes with colour phases; immatures strikingly different from adults. All known species have high-pitched, screaming voices. Systematics still obscure, often very little-known birds.

The former monotypic African genus *Cassinaetus* W. L. Sclater is now considered the sole African representative of this genus.

Plates
26 and 30
(Opp. pp. 419
and 451)

Spizaetus africanus (Cassin). Cassin's Hawk Eagle. Spizaète de Cassin.

Limnaetus africanus Cassin, 1865. Proc. Acad. Nat. Sci. Philadelphia, p. 4; Ogabi R., Gabon.

Range and Status. Resident, dense tropical forests from Togo east to Gabon, Cameroon, E Zaïre and W Uganda. Usually thought to be rare, is probably commoner than supposed, but seldom seen. Habitat decreasing through tree-felling and human interference, but not as yet acutely threatened.

Description. ADULT ♂: above, head, back, upperwing-coverts sooty brown, feathers basally white. Below, white, with black patch on sides of breast, blackish axillaries and mainly black underwing-coverts. Legs white, with blackish markings out-side thighs. Primaries above chocolate, tipped blackish, basally whitish on inner webs, with 2 dark bars. Tail brown, broadly tipped black with 3 dark bars, below paler, barred blackish. ♀ similar, larger. Eye brown to brownish cream; cere and feet pale yellow. SIZE: wing, 330–341; tail, ♂ 225–234 (229), (1) ♀ 266; WEIGHT: ♂ (2) 938, 1049; ♀ (1) 1153 (Friedmann and Williams 1970).

IMMATURE: head pale rufous, lores darker, throat and crown streaked black. Back and upperwings grey-brown edged buff, becoming paler on wings, secondaries tipped white. Below, rufous-buff, breast obscurely spotted blackish, becoming paler, more heavily spotted, on flanks, abdomen; undertail-coverts white, spotted brown, tipped cinnamon; thighs buff, tarsi almost white. Underwing-coverts white, tinged buff, spotted blackish. Tail-feathers grey-brown, tipped white, with blackish subterminal and one narrower dark bar 60 mm from tip. Eye grey-brown; cere and feet pale yellow.

DOWNY YOUNG: undescribed, probably white (on basis of body-down: Chapin 1932).

Immature probably attains adult plumage by darkening above, becoming whiter below except on wing coverts which darken with age.

Field Characters. A powerful, heavily built eagle for its size, with long tail and short rounded wings. Larger, heavier, shorter-winged, longer-tailed than Ayres' Hawk Eagle *Hieraaetus dubius*, much whiter below, with black wing-coverts; adults mainly dark above, but not heavily barred except on tail. Immatures much paler, cinnamon-rufous head, spotted not streaked on breast, wings not heavily barred below. In all plumages smaller, relatively much longer-tailed than African Hawk Eagle *H. spilogaster*. Dark patches on sides of breast could cause confusion with Black Sparrowhawk *Accipiter melanoleucus*, but is much larger and has feathered tarsus. White feathered tarsus also distinguishes it from Congo Serpent Eagle *Dryotriorchis spectabilis* in same habitat. A dark grey and white, buzzard-sized, short-winged, long-tailed eagle soaring above dense forest is likely to be this species.

Voice. Recorded (14). A long, high, clear scream, 'weeeee-e' or 'eeeeee-eh', uttered when soaring above forest lasting 1–2 s (Taylor, pers. comm.).

General Habits. Little known. Inhabits the canopy of primary forest, where usually invisible. When seen, usually soaring above forest at no great height, but probably spends most time perched quietly within foliage. On evidence of numbers obtained in small area of Kalinzu forest, Uganda, (3 in 11 days) may be commoner than generally supposed (Friedmann and Williams 1970).

Food. Birds and squirrels, probably caught high up in tall forest trees.

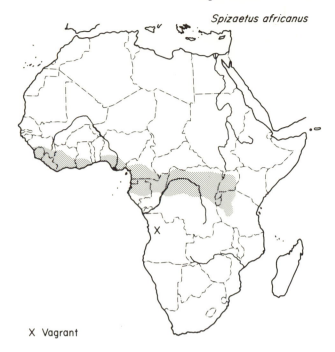

Spizaetus africanus

X Vagrant

Breeding Habits. Scarcely known; only 2 nests ever discovered (Brosset 1971; MacDonald and Taylor 1977). Said to frequent same nest-site for many years (probably correct: Brosset 1971). NEST: large stick structure in tall forest tree, lined with green leaves. EGGS: possibly laid Ghana Oct (early dry). Ghana nest contained a well grown young bird 16 Dec, but observers gave no description. Parent unobtrusive near nest. Young was still present at nest-site 6 months after 1st record, suggesting prolonged post-fledging period, as in Crowned Eagle *Stephanoaetus coronatus*.

References

Brosset, A. (1971).
MacDonald, M. A. and Taylor, I. R. (1977).

Genus *Stephanoaetus* W. Sclater

Large, very powerfully built forest eagles, with short broad rounded wings and long tail. Beak deep strongly arched, powerful; head with long erectile double crest. Legs thick, toes extremely strong, talons thick, long, sharp, adapted for catching and killing large mammals.

This monotypic endemic African genus has sometimes been merged with *Spizaetus*; but is very much larger and more powerful than most *Spizaetus* spp. and is best regarded as a specialized offshoot of that genus.

Stephanoaetus coronatus (Linnaeus). Crowned Eagle. Aigle blanchard.

Falco coronatus, Linnaeus, 1766. Syst. Nat. (12th ed.), 1, p. 124; Coast of Guinea (ex Edwards).

Plates 25 and 29 (Opp. pp. 418 and 450)

Range and Status. Resident forested and heavily wooded areas of tropical Africa from Guinea east to W Ethiopia, thence south to E Cape Province. Frequent to uncommon throughout; reduced through destruction of habitat by agriculture, not yet threatened.

Description. ADULT ♂: crown dark to rufous-brown, with prominent black-tipped double crest. Cheeks, sides of head and neck pale brown to rufous, variable. Rest of upperparts including upperwing-coverts blue-black. Throat brown, rest of underside white to warm buff, heavily barred and blotched black; thighs and legs closely barred and spotted black and

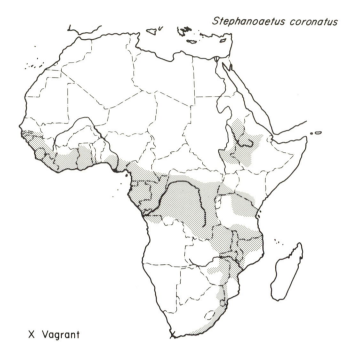

Stephanoaetus coronatus

X Vagrant

white, underwing-coverts chestnut spotted black. Wing-feathers above brown, broadly tipped black, with 2 black bars; below almost white, tipped black, with 2 distinct but broken black bars. Tail above blue-black, with 2 broad greyish bars; below greyer, barred and tipped black. Eye pale yellow-whitish; cere and feet ochre-yellow; gape dull yellow. ♀ larger, usually more heavily barred, with shorter crest, relatively longer-tailed than ♂. SIZE: wing ♂ 445–490, ♀ 500–525; tail, ♂ 300–330, ♀ 325–370; tarsus, 85–103; wing-span, ♂ (1) 2085; aspect-ratio, 6; wing-loading, 67 N/m². WEIGHT: ♂ (2) 3400, 4120; ♀ (2) 3175, 3853 (abnormal, as ♀♀ normally heavier).

IMMATURE: head and entire underparts white, spotted black on thighs and legs; upper breast tinged rufous. Above, light brown or grey, feathers edged paler, appearing scaled, especially on upperwing-coverts. Wing-feathers above grey-brown, tipped blackish, with 2 narrow dark crossbars. Tail black, with a narrow white tip and 3 broad pale bars. Eye grey-brown, becoming yellow; cere greyish; feet dull yellow.

DOWNY YOUNG: pure snowy white; eye and cere grey, feet pale dull yellow.

1st immature retains similar plumage for *c.* 2 years, becoming more rufous and developing a few spots on breast. At *c.* 2·5 years moults in 1 stage into somewhat browner, duller version of adult plumage; at 3 years almost indistinguishable from adult. Can lay eggs at 3·5 years, but possibly not fully mature till 5 years.

Field Characters. A very large, immensely powerful eagle, with short, very broad wings, long tail. Generally dark above; buff, richly barred black below, with heavily barred grey and black wings and tail, chestnut underwing-coverts. Adults virtually unmistakable either perched or in flight; perches very erect, with long tail vertical below perch. Much larger, darker than any other forest eagle. Immatures purer grey and white than young Martial Eagles *Polemaetus bellicosus*, with spotted thighs, heavily barred wings and tail in flight; short wings, long tail distinctive.

Voice. Recorded (2a, 6, 14, 18, 19, 21c, 22a, 26, 28). A very vocal species, heard in display almost daily in tropical habitat. ♂ display call a shrill 'kewick-kewick-kewick' or 'kewee-kewee-kewee' repeated 20–30 times as bird rises and falls in undulating display, ceasing when display flight stops; audible when bird is beyond range of naked eye. Voice of ♀ lower-pitched, more mellow 'kooi-kooi-kooi', in series of 20–30 notes, sometimes given together with ♂ in display. Both sexes can utter either call, but normally call as stated here. Call of adults with food, or of young soliciting food, rapid 'quee-quee-quee-quee-quee-quee' loud and shrill, repeated sometimes by young for up to 2 h with short breaks; rises in pitch and becomes more rapid and excited, 'pi-pi-pi-pi-pi', when food delivered. Sibilant 'sseeeoh' from ♂ soliciting ♀ for food; ♀ solicits with 'quee-quee-quee' call. Calls immediately locate displaying ♂ high above forest and completely diagnostic. Frequently mimicked by, for example, robin-chats *Cossypha* spp., which helps to identify unoccupied nests.

General Habits. Well known but little described except in E Africa. Preferred habitat is forest, but occurs in *Brachystegia* woodland, more open savanna with remnant forest in river valleys, on hills with relict forest patches, and even in *Acacia* forest along rivers in semi-arid areas. Pairs are resident year-round in territory or home range, not migrating. Except in flight, very difficult to locate, as normally perch silently in tall forest trees, either hunting or resting. May sometimes be seen on prominent exposed perch, but normally perches inside leafy forest tree, on high branch under canopy, easily overlooked even at close range. If nest is in small patch of forest (e.g. hill-top), usually roosts near it.

May also soar over forest, not in active display, first mounting to height, then descending again to another part of home range. Mounting, circles on thermals, soaring easily on broad wings. Descending, characteristically glides down, varying angle of glide by raising or lowering tail (raising it increases angle) and folding or spreading wings. May end such flights by almost vertical rapid plunge, neatly landing on tree perch. From ground, can fly almost vertically upwards to tree branch. Is agile and manoeuvres itself with ease among dense leafy tree-tops, despite size.

Hunts mainly from high perches, watching ground intently and dropping on prey on forest floor. Alternately may attack monkeys from flight, perhaps having located them from some distance earlier. Can subdue and kill young antelopes up to size of half-grown bushbuck calf, 18–20 kg in weight (5 times own weight), and full-grown adult forest duiker. Large prey may require a considerable struggle; when killed eagle will dismember it and cache severed limbs in forest trees far from site of kill, feeding on them over several days. Pairs feed on each other's kills, usually present together at the site of a large kill. Will come to struggling animals caught in snares, or in evening may perch close to waterhole waiting for antelopes to come to drink. May swoop at full-grown larger antelopes, e.g. bushbuck (Daneel 1979), but does not kill. Most prey taken on ground, including monkeys, which descend to ground to escape if not taken entirely by surprise. Monkeys and tree hyrax also taken in trees. Leopards reputed to act in concert with eagle, catching monkeys descending to ground. Monkeys also said to be attracted by eagle's soft whistling call, then caught (MacLatchey 1937), but such observations require further authentication. Adult ♂ monkeys often contemptuous of eagle, running up trees and plucking at eagle's legs (Brown 1971), but eagle in flight usually elicits alarm call from monkeys.

Food. Almost entirely mammals, preferring forest antelopes, notably (E Africa) suni *Nesotragus moschatus*. 243 items, Kenya included 141 antelopes, of which 101 were suni; largest, young bushbuck, 18–20 kg, and adult Harvey's duiker *Cephalophus natalensis* 10–12 kg. Tree hyrax *Dendrohyrax arboreus* commonly taken and, in more arid areas, rock hyrax, *Procavia* and *Heterohyrax*, Kills large mongooses (*Ichneumia*, *Herpestes*) and large powerful domestic cats; a few large lizards, *Varanus* sp. Very rarely birds, but in Zimbabwe (*Brachystegia* woodland) 31 items included 13 gamebirds (Read, pers. comm.). Of 548 items recorded South Africa 42% hyrax (Jarvis *et al.*, in prep.). Very rarely takes domestic stock, even when easily available in African smallholder areas. Monkeys, supposedly main prey in dense forest areas, certainly taken less than antelopes in areas where well studied; but may be under-represented in data gathered from bone remains near nests as eaten completely, bones and teeth too in most cases. Bones are completely digested, and only chitinous remains (hair, hooves, horns) appear in castings, which are seldom found. Regularly kills mammalian prey as large as, or heavier than, itself, probably using immensely powerful legs and long hind talons to subdue struggling antelopes, for

example; but also known to strike monkey off branch by violent blow, recovering it dead from ground (Vesey-Fitzgerald, pers. comm.). When striking monkey (or human) passes immediately above animal at speed and delivers violent downward blow with open feet; sensation resembles blow with heavy stick. Prey is then partly eaten and dismembered on ground, then cached in trees and used successive days until finished. May be robbed by large mammals, e.g. leopard, hyena, jackal.

Food requirement of pair (based on 11-year study, Kenya) is 130–135 large mammals/year for adults and young, totalling estimated 436 kg killed/year. Of this, 366 kg (84%) antelopes, only 34 kg (7·8%) monkeys, 9 kg miscellaneous (large mongooses). This would average *c.* 480 g/eagle/day, so may be an overestimate. Can gorge 1200 g in a meal; but can survive for days on av. 110 g/day, *c.* 3% of bodyweight (Brown 1971).

Breeding Habits. Intimately known Kenya; not studied in detail elsewhere. All studies to date not in true dense forest habitat, but in marginal areas, so may not be fully representative. Pairs present year-round in home range, may visit nest or display any time of year near equator, displaying daily in fine soaring weather. In Mount Kenya forests nearest neighbour distance between pairs is 1·5–2 km, so that entire home range may not exceed 10 km², in optimum habitat with abundant prey. Equally, long-term occupation of isolated patches of forest on widely separated mountaintops is common; home range then may be much larger.

Display very spectacular, often repeated, aerial. ♂ soars high, gaining height on thermals, then begins long series of steep, often deep undulations, diving 100–150 m, then swooping up again, flapping wings rapidly at top of swoop, repeating 7–10 times, calling continuously while in display; after 1 such bout regains lost height on thermal, then repeats. May often be too high to locate with naked eye, binoculars required; but calls still clearly audible from ground. Displays most often when thermal activity strongest between 11.00 and 14.00 h, rarely later. ♀ sometimes joins ♂ whereupon he swoops up and down above her, calling, then may dive at her; she turns back and presents claws to his. ♀ may also display alone, with undulations usually not as steep as ♂'s, and less prolonged calling; may thus repel strange ♀♀ from territory. Mating occurs on or near nest, often following presentation of food by ♂. ♀ flies, calling excitedly, into nest; ♂ alights, sometimes runs round and round ♀, with lifted wings exposing barring and chestnut underwing-coverts. Act accomplished by twisting long tail sideways, permitting cloacal union; lasts 5–10 s. May not necessarily be followed by egg-laying in any year.

NEST: enormous, usually built in main shaded fork of large forest tree, very often growing in river valley, at 15–40 m above ground. All known pairs E Africa have only 1 nest, used for up to 50 years. A new nest may be built in 5–6 weeks, and is c. 1·5–1·8 m across by 0·5–0·7 m deep; with repeated use becomes up to 2 m across and 3 m deep. Is usually much deeper, more massive that that of any other African eagle. Made of large sticks, up to 1·5 m long and up to 3 cm thick, collected from ground or neighbouring trees, carried in feet; later lined copiously with broad-leaved green sprays, in E Africa always gathered within 200 m of nest, certain trees preferred. When gathering leafy sprays, bird settles, flops about in foliage, seizes spray in bill, tugs it off and goes to nest. Both sexes build, ♀ more than ♂. ♀ often builds alone, and if both building together ♀ may remain in nest while ♂ goes to and fro collecting material.

EGGS: 1–2, laid at c. 3-day intervals; Kenya mean (9 clutches) 1·32, but probably biased, more probable av. (33 records) 1·7; Zimbabwe and Natal mean (43 clutches) 1·63 (Dean 1971; Tuer and Tuer 1974). Same ♀ may lay 1 or 2 eggs different years. Rounded ovals, small for size of bird, dull white, usually lightly, sometimes more heavily spotted brown with purplish or grey under-markings. SIZE: (23) 60·9–75·5 × 50·8–57·9 (68·2 × 53·6); WEIGHT: 87–100 (Tuer and Tuer 1974).

Laying dates: Nigeria Oct (early dry); E Kenya, N Tanzania Apr, June–Dec inclusive, peaking June–Aug, (mid-year cool dry season); W Kenya, Uganda Jan, June, Dec (all dry months); Zambia–Zimbabwe Aug–Sept, mainly Sept; Natal, Transvaal June–Nov, peaking late Sept–Oct (late dry season). Young often in nest in heavy rains. Same ♀ known to lay June (1), July (2), Aug (1) and Dec (1); laying dates thus often dependent on individuals rather than season. Failure at any stage of long breeding cycle may result in re-laying at unusual date.

♀ roosts in nest tree before egg-laying, and is fed there by ♂. With 2 eggs, incubation begins 1st egg; may be by ♀ alone, or (more often) ♂ takes considerable share by day; ♀ carries out 70–90% overall. ♀ is fed at nest by ♂ or, if she leaves for long periods and kills, she may bring prey to ♂. Av. interval between kills in incubation 3·3 days, but may be up to 10 days; large kills permit feeding at need for several days after kill. Incubation period: 49 days (3 accurate records); 1 record 51 days (Tuer and Tuer 1974).

If 2 chicks hatch elder soon dominates and kills younger, which has never been known to survive long, or be reared. Eaglet unusually active and powerful from early age, regularly feeds itself while still downy. Weigh 95 g at 2 days; 984 at 30 days; 1700 at 57 days; 2025 at 69; 2250 at 77 (Tuer and Tuer 1974). Can stand at 30 days; 1st feathers emerge through down c. 40 days; fully feathered by 60 days. Then mainly left alone in nest by both parents, day and night. Attempts to feed itself at 25–30 days, can feed from large kill at 40–45 days. Thereafter feeds itself on kills brought every 2·5 days on average in late fledging period, at intervals of sometimes up to 13 days. Fledging period very long, and eaglets move out onto branches before 1st flight. ♂♂ more active than ♀♀, fly earlier. Duration, 103–125 days, usually 110–115 days, ♂♂ leaving c. 10 days earlier than ♀♀ (106 cf. 115 days). Make 1st flight independent of parental presence; sex ratio at fledging about equal (9 ♂: 8 ♀ recorded).

Roles of parents clear-cut. ♂ brings all prey up to c. 60 days; rate of killing approximately doubled immediately after hatch to 1 prey/1·55 days; ♀ and young feed on kills brought. ♂ approaches, perching at intervals, calling; answered by ♀ with loud shrill food calls; ♂ then flies into nest and deposits prey, leaving at once; does not feed young, even in absence of ♀. ♀ feeds young up to 40 days, but thereafter it can normally feed itself. ♀ perches within 200 m of nest up to 60 days and roosts near nest; thereafter hunts also, now bringing more kills than ♂. Rate of killing reduced to 1/2·5 days, sometimes longer, late in fledging period. When ♀ perches near but not on nest, brings many green branches. Broods very small young continuously days 1–10, brooding reduced in daylight days 11–20, ceasing by day after day 21, ceasing at night after day 35. Shaded nest-site often reduces need to brood or shade young. ♀ is dangerously aggressive with small or partly-grown young in nest, readily attacking and sometimes striking human intruders; must be treated with caution when investigating nest contents.

Post-fledging period protracted, 9–11 months. Young remains perched all day in shade near nest, usually within 200–300 m, sometimes returning to it. Parent bringing food calls; young flies into nest screaming excitedly; parent then delivers prey at nest and young feeds there. Rate of killing at this stage av. 1/3 days, but intervals often longer. Young learns to kill for itself during this period; earliest known kill 61 days after 1st flight. At end leaves of own accord, is not driven away by parents, who continue to bring prey and call as usual; if they receive no response from young, cease bringing prey and gradually or soon commence new breeding cycle. If fully successful, breeding cycle from nest-repair to independence occupies 20–22 months, and pair can only breed at best every 2nd year; failure triggers a new attempt, even at unusual seasons.

Breeding success: in 54 Kenya cases, 0·39/pair/year overall, 0·78/breeding attempt, 1·0/successful nest. 1 South African case suggests annual successful breeding, with parents repelling previous year's eaglet (Fannin and Webb 1975), but evidence doubtful and most

Transvaal pairs apparently breed every 2nd year as in Kenya (Tarboton 1978b). In marginal habitat (Matopos, Zimbabwe) may be even less regular, breeding success calculated at *c.* 0·18/pair/year (Tuer and Tuer 1974). Most fledged young probably attain independence, as most Kenya pairs breed regularly every 2 years. 1 ♀ laid 5 eggs, all hatched and were reared to fledging stage, and 4 out of 5 to independence. Last daughter of this ♀ much less successful (1 young in 12 years!). At 75% mortality

before sexual maturity, age of adults would need to be at least 20–21 years. Known recognizable individuals have lived for 9–12 years, av. *c.* 11 as adults, or 15 altogether, indicating real juvenile mortality of *c.* 55% before sexual maturity.

References
Brown, L. H. (1952–3, 1955, 1966, 1971, 1972b).
Brown, L. H. *et al.* (1977).

Genus *Polemaetus* Heine

Very large eagles with long, broad wings, relatively short tail. Bill powerful, but not as strong and deeply arched as in *Stephanoaetus*. A short crest. Tarsi and legs long, toes long, talons long and sharp, adapted for catching swift-moving prey in open country.

In proportions this monotypic genus resembles a giant *Hieraaetus* species; but the moult pattern and very marked difference in adult and immature plumages indicate it stands apart from that genus. It is closer to *Stephanoaetus*, but has a very different habitat and mode of life.

Polemaetus bellicosus (Daudin). Martial Eagle. Aigle martial.

Falco bellicosus Daudin, 1800. Traité Orn, 2., p. 38; Great Namaqualand, Cape Province (ex Levaillant).

Plates 25 and 29 (Opp. pp. 418 and 450)

Range and Status. Resident savannas of tropical and southern Africa from Senegal east to Somalia, south to Cape Province. Frequent to uncommon; but much less common in western tropical Africa than in E and southern Africa. Numbers decrease due to destruction of habitat, invasion of woodlands by small-scale cultivators and some direct persecution, but probably not yet threatened except locally; can survived in cultivated areas if human population not too dense.

Description. ADULT ♂: upperparts, including upperwing-coverts, brownish grey, feathers edged paler; a slight occipital crest. Throat, neck and upperbreast grey-brown, rest of underside of body white, sparsely spotted subterminally dark brown. Underwing-coverts mottled brown and white. Primaries and secondaries above blackish to dark brown, below brown, with indistinct narrow paler bars, grey above, whitish below. Tail above dark brown barred grey-brown, below brown barred grey. Eye yellow, cere and feet blue-grey. ♀ similar, usually more heavily spotted, larger. SIZE: wing ♂ 560–610, ♀ 605–675; tail, ♂ 273–280, ♀ 280–320; tarsus, ♂ 97–118, ♀ 114–130; wing-span, 2·1–2·6 m. WEIGHT: 2 captive ♀♀ 5924–6200; 17 unsexed 3012–5657 (3965); 1 ♂ 5100 (Biggs *et al.* 1979).

IMMATURE: above dark grey, edged paler; distinctly crested. Below white, with 2 lines of dark spots down each side of breast. Underwing-coverts mottled grey-brown and white. Wings and tail barred as in adult, but greyer. Eye yellow-brown, cere and feet grey to greenish grey.

DOWNY YOUNG: above dark grey, with pale grey forehead, large pale grey patches on back and flanks. Eye brown, cere and feet pale grey.

The immature retains similar plumage through several moults until *c.* 5 years old, then moults almost at once into full adult plumage, with a brief intermediate stage when breast and throat are spotted, spots coalescing with time; underwing-coverts then heavily marked dark brown. This moult pattern accounts for the few intermediate or subadult birds seen (W. R. Spofford, pers. comm.).

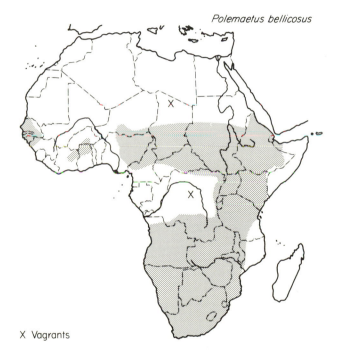

Polemaetus bellicosus

X Vagrants

Field Characters. Very large eagles, the largest in Africa. Normally unmistakable by size, dark grey-brown back, largely white underside with small dark spots. May be mistaken for Black-breasted Snake Eagle *Circaetus gallicus pectoralis*, which lacks brown spots on white breast and belly, is much smaller and has largely white underwing with clearly visible narrow blackish bars. Martial Eagle has dark, mottled underwing-coverts and dark wing-feathers below. Immature can only be confused with immature Crowned Eagle *Stephanoaetus coronatus*; is generally browner above, with unspotted white tarsi and thighs, and lacks heavy dark bars on tail and wings; in flight much longer-winged, shorter-tailed.

Voice. Not recorded. Generally rather silent. In display, a loud clear series of notes, 'klee-klee-klee-klee-klooeee-kloeeee-kuleee', uttered either from perch or in flight. Commonest call a low, mellow, whistling 'hlueeeoh', or 'queeeor', usually uttered when perched. A low, gulping 'quolp', and subdued calls 'kwip, kwip' by young at sight of food. Young recently out of nest but still dependent utter loud clear 'klee-klee-kleee-kuleee-kuleee' like adult display call. Voice diagnostic as unlike any other.

General Habits. Well known. Elusive, difficult to locate in most areas; rather shy of man. Frequents any type of more or less open country from forest edges mixed with cultivation to broad-leaved woodland, *Acacia* savanna, grass plains, thornbush, and semi-desert with low scrub; even true desert along watercourses. Mainly in lowlands, but up to 2400 m. Must have some large trees for breeding. Adults normally sedentary in home range year-round; immatures may wander, but no regular movements.

Spends most of day in flight, often soaring at great height, normally with very steady wings. The most aerial of any large African eagle other than Bateleur, *Terathopius ecaudatus*. Seldom seen perched, but when seen is usually on top of prominent tree, or on large tree on hill-side or escarpment, from whence it can detect and attack prey. More often seen perched in southern Africa than in E Africa, in areas with similar eagle population. Often soars high over hill-tops, and may then be seen by lying on back and scanning sky

in
0   3   6   9   12

0   10   20   30
cm

Plate 27

Falco tinnunculus Common Kestrel (p. 445)
Race *tinnunculus*: 1. ADULT ♀, 2. ADULT ♂,
3. IMMATURE ♀.
Race *rufescens*: 4. ADULT ♂, 5. ADULT ♀.

Falco naumanni Lesser Kestrel (p. 443)
6. ADULT ♀, 7. ADULT ♂, 8. IMMATURE ♂.

Polihierax semitorquatus Pygmy Falcon (p. 441)
9. ADULT ♀, 10. ADULT ♂, 11. IMMATURE ♀,
12. IMMATURE ♂.

Falco rupicoloides Greater Kestrel (p. 448)
13. ADULT ♂, 14. IMMATURE ♀.

Falco amurensis Eastern Red-footed Falcon
(p. 458)
15. ADULT ♂, 16. ADULT ♀, 17. IMMATURE ♂.

Falco vespertinus Red-footed Falcon (p. 457)
18. ADULT ♂, 19. ADULT ♀, 20. IMMATURE ♂.

Falco alopex Fox Kestrel (p. 452)
21. IMMATURE, 22. ADULT.

Falco ardosiaceus Grey Kestrel (p. 453)
23. ADULT, 24. IMMATURE.

Falco dickinsoni Dickinson's Kestrel (p. 454)
25. ADULT, 26. IMMATURE.

Falco chicquera Red-necked Falcon (p. 455)
27. ADULT, 28. IMMATURE.

Falco columbarius Merlin (p. 464)
29. ADULT ♂, 30. IMMATURE ♀.

with binoculars. Probably travels long distances soaring daily, but daily movements scarcely possible to follow.

Hunts from high exposed perch, perhaps more often on wing. May observe prey at great distance (up to 5–6 km) and attack in long slanting stoop, suddenly surprising prey, and braking violently with spread wings and tail to make kill. May also perch, for example, nnear waterhole where guineafowl gather, and attack with short swift stoop, but will not normally crash into vegetation after prey (cf. *Hieraaetus*). Very rarely, hovers, with wings flapped briefly through short arc.

Roosts on trees, often using same tree for several successive nights, sometimes pairs together; may then have a large partly-consumed kill nearby. Does not, as Crowned Eagle *Stephanoaetus coronatus* does, dismember and cache kill in trees safe from ground predators. If prey cannot be lifted to tree-top or perch, is eaten *in situ* on ground, individuals returning for up to 5 days to same kill.

Food. A very wide range of mammals, birds and reptiles, varying according to availability and area. In E Africa, large gamebirds and other birds (guineafowl, smaller bustards, White Stork *Ciconia ciconia*, Egyptian Goose *Alopochen aegyptiacus*) important; some poultry. Mammals from size of ground squirrel *Euxerus* to impala calf and dik-dik (4 kg); in Tsavo Park dik-dik commonest. In South Africa mammals, birds and reptiles, notably *Varanus* lizards. In Transvaal, 24 of 52 items *Varanus* (Tarboton 1976). In Cape Province, 346 items included 99 viverrids (mongooses, genets), 93 hares and rabbits (Leporidae), 26 hyrax, 11 ground squirrels. Sample is biased as based on bone remains only. Prey includes carnivorous mammals as large as caracal *Felis caracal*, and some small adult antelopes. Some young domestic stock taken, but even where eagle is actively persecuted on this account (Cape Province), only 30/346 items domestic stock (less than 8%, mainly from 2/9 sites). Is generally less powerful than Crowned

Plate 28

Falco peregrinus Peregrine Falcon (p. 474)
Race *pelegrinoides*: 1. ADULT, 2. IMMATURE.
Race *peregrinus*: 3. ADULT, 4. IMMATURE.
Race *brookei*: 5. ADULT, 6. IMMATURE.
Race *minor*: 7. ADULT, 8. IMMATURE.

Falco eleonorae Eleanora's Falcon (p. 460)
9. ADULT (dark phase), 10. IMMATURE, 11. ADULT (pale phase).

Falco cuvieri African Hobby (p. 469)
12. IMMATURE, 13. ADULT.

Falco subbuteo Hobby (p. 465)
14. ADULT ♂, 15. IMMATURE ♀.

Falco fasciinucha Teita Falcon (p. 477)
16. ADULT, 17. IMMATURE.

Falco concolor Sooty Falcon (p. 462)
18. IMMATURE, 19. ADULT.

Falco cherrug Saker Falcon (p. 473)
20. ADULT ♀, 21. IMMATURE ♂.

Falco biarmicus Lanner Falcon (p. 470)
Race *tanypterus*: 22. IMMATURE ♀, 23. ADULT ♂.
Race *biarmicus*: 24. IMMATURE ♀, 25. ADULT ♂.

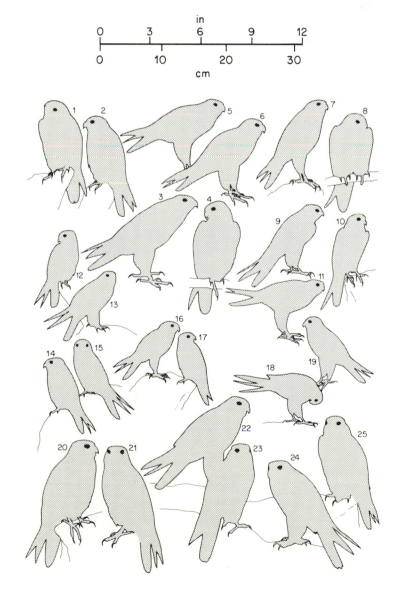

Eagle, less able to kill large mammal prey, largest items young antelopes weighing perhaps 5 kg. Large birds and reptiles more often taken, but mammals of 1–4 kg probably most important by weight (Boshoff and Palmer 1980; Tarboton 1976; Smeenk 1974).

Breeding Habits. Very well known; 1 Kenya site continuously recorded 31 years. Pairs are evenly distributed over suitable habitat, in large home ranges of c. 150–200 km² in optimum habitat; in E Africa same breeding sites continuously occupied more than 30 years, but in South Africa (Kruger Park) some shift of nest-sites occurs over period of time (W. Tarboton and A. C. Kemp, pers. comm.). Nest-sites, E Africa, almost exactly 12 km apart in woodland, but may be further apart where large trees destroyed by elephants (Smeenk 1974).

Display not spectacular; mainly soaring and calling over nest-site, or perching and calling near nest. Rarely, ♂ soars above nest-site or hill-side and performs undulating display in flight, but briefly, with only shallow undulations. Method of establishing and maintaining remarkably regular spatial distribution not known.

NEST: in trees, usually 1 per pair, sometimes 2 or more. Same site used for many years, but pair may often, even annually, build new nests, unlike Crowned Eagle. At 1 site 9 new nests built in 31 years, 5 by 1 pair successive years; some other nests used for up to 15 years without change. Large, basin-shaped structures of thick sticks; at first broad and shallow, c. 1·5 m across by 0·5 m deep, but with repeated use reach 2 m across by 1–1·3 m deep. Normally in tall isolated trees, often situated on escarpment or hill-top, recorded at 5–30 m above ground, usually 10–20. In savannas, trees larger than most are selected, e.g. *Terminalia*, baobabs, large *Acacia* spp., *Faurea saligna*. Nest may be in a high main fork, more rarely on large lateral branch, sometimes shaded, but often completely open to sun. In Transvaal, has recently bred on electricity pylons, habit perhaps increasing (Tarboton 1978b). Nest repair and building mainly by ♀, ♂ sometimes bringing sticks; may occupy 2–6 weeks, and if alternate sites available, more than 1 may be built up, 1 finally chosen. Lined rather sparingly with green leaves, which continue to be brought until late in fledging period.

EGGS: invariably 1; any reported clutches of 2 (South Africa) require confirmation. Rounded or regular ovals, greenish white or pale greenish blue, variously, often heavily marked with brown and grey undermarkings, chiefly at broad end. SIZE: (25) 74·0–86·6 × 57·0–68·7 (80·7 × 64·1); WEIGHT: c. 182 (Schönwetter 1960).

Laying dates: South Africa, Cape Province Apr–July; Transvaal–Natal Mar–Nov, peaking June–Aug (early in winter dry season); Zambia Apr, June–July (dry); E Kenya, N Tanzania Mar–Sept inclusive, peaking Apr–June (late in main rains); NW Kenya May, Aug (rains); Somalia Aug, Oct, Nov (dry); few good records W Africa, Senegal Nov; Sudan (Daifur) Jan (dry). Dry season laying date often results in young leaving nest in rains.

Incubation normally by ♀ only, but ♂ sometimes incubates briefly, especially when ♀ is feeding; individuals vary. ♂ feeds ♀ in incubation period near nest. Period: 51 days ± 1 day (M. Jankowitz, pers. comm.); 53 days (Tarboton 1976).

Newly-hatched young weak and feeble; becomes more active after 20 days. 1st feathers appear 32 days, largely feathered by 50 days, completely by 70 days. Remains long in nest thereafter, main development then in growth of large wing- and tail-feathers. Wing-flapping, varying according to sex and individuals, vigorous and frequent 70 days onwards. 1st flight made without parental presence at 99–104 days, in 1 case at 10.00 h. May be long, up to 1 km, sometimes right across valley, sometimes just to a nearby tall tree.

♀ broods young closely days 1–10; brooding thereafter reduced by day, probably coinciding with development of 2nd down. Brooding ceases by day after day 14, but continues at night. ♀ remains in neighbourhood of nest until c. day 50, either standing on nest or perching near; roosts in nest with chick, or on branch beside it. ♂ brings all prey up to day 50, usually visiting nest briefly; does not feed young. Thereafter ♀ brings most prey, ♂ seldom appears (but individuals vary). ♀ normally continues to roost near nest until late in fledging period, sometimes arriving c. 1 h before dark after absence all day, for up to 90 days after hatch. ♂ visits nest only to bring prey, roosts nowhere near.

Young may return to nest to roost for some days after 1st flight, thereafter roosting near nest for up to 3 months. Is fed in nest, or on trees nearby by ♀ for up to 3 months; thereafter probably follows parents to more distant home range. Soon after 1st flight habits become very aerial, frequently soaring for long periods by day, quite unlike Crowned Eagle. Post-fledging period probably lasts 5–6 months, but exact duration uncertain because of increasingly aerial habits of young, which travels long distances daily away from nest, soaring at great height. Young probably kills for itself well before final independence.

Breeding success variable, some pairs very successful, breeding annually and regularly, others averaging no better than 1 young/3 years. In 64 pair-years (involving 7 different sites, Kenya), 40 eggs produced 32 young, i.e. 0·5 young/pair overall, 0·8/breeding pair. At 1 site, recorded for 31 years, several successive pairs laid 20 eggs, reared 13 young (below average); another, observed 13 years, reared 9 young; and same tree was reoccupied successfully 3 years after nest destroyed by fire. At 75% mortality before sexual maturity, av. adult life would be 16 years, c. 21–22 altogether. Mortality probably lower, as can apparently maintain fairly stable populations even in areas where persecuted (Cape Province). A young ♂, possibly young of previous year, has been known to mate with an adult ♀ successfully rearing young (Tarboton 1976).

References
Brown, L. H. (1952–3, 1966).
Smeenk, C. (1974).
Tarboton, W. (1976).

Suborder SAGITTARII

Family SAGITTARIIDAE: Secretary Bird

Very large, mainly terrestrial birds of prey, with very long legs, and short toes. Beaks relatively weak; sides of face naked, brightly coloured. A long erectile crest of somewhat spatulate, black-tipped feathers on nape. Body plumage grey and black. Wings moderately long, broad, rather rounded, well adapted for soaring flight (but seldom so used). Tail graduated; 2 central tail feathers greatly elongated. Legs long, strong, terminating in short toes with short blunt talons, unable to grasp and carry prey, but adapted for long-distance walking through grassland or on bare ground, and killing prey by impact. The femoral muscles differ from those of other birds of prey; the basipterygoid process is long, and the furculum and crista sterni are ankylosed (K. H. Voous, pers. comm.).

The family has only 1 genus and species, the Secretary Bird *Sagittarius serpentarius*, endemic to Africa. Although generally considered to be an aberrant terrestrial Falconiform, it may be wrongly placed in this order. It was considered to be allied to the S American Cariamidae by Verheyen (1957) and egg-white protein electrophoresis indicates possible Gruiform affinities (W. R. Spofford, pers. comm.). In the absence of full comparative studies both of the Secretary Bird and its possible cariamid relatives, it is preferable to retain it as an aberrant Falconiform. Fuller studies, especially of behaviour, are required to establish its true affinities.

Genus *Sagittarius* Herman

***Sagittarius serpentarius* (Miller). Secretary Bird. Messager serpentaire.**

Falco serpentarius J. F. Miller, 1779. Icon. Anim., pt. 5, pl. 28; Cape of Good Hope.

**Plates
1 and 29**
(Opp. pp. 34
and 450)

Range and Status. Resident throughout semi-arid savannas, grass plains and subdeserts of Africa south of Sahara from Senegal east to Somalia, and south to Cape Province, but much more numerous in South and highland E Africa than in lowland W Africa from W Ethiopia to Senegal. Locally common, occasionally even abundant, but generally uncommon to frequent. Decreasing in most of range through invasion of habitat by African cultivators and pastoralists. Adapts well to large-scale commercial ranching or even large cereal farms, but disappears from areas cultivated by large numbers of smallholders. Possibly decreasing in South Africa, still its main stronghold. Seldom directly persecuted, but is unable to breed successfully in areas of high human population density, as nests very vulnerable to children.

Description. ADULT ♂: crown, mantle, back, lesser and median wing-coverts bluish grey; nape with long erectile crest of black-tipped feathers. Rump black, uppertail-coverts white, sometimes barred black. Below, greyish white to pale grey, including underwing-coverts; belly and thighs black. Primaries, secondaries and long scapulars black, above and below. Tail grey, tipped white, broadly banded black subterminally, with a 2nd black band basally; central feathers projecting, very long, grey, tipped white, subterminally banded black. Eye pale brown; cere bluish grey; bare facial skin orange or yellow; legs greyish flesh. Sexes nearly alike, ♂♂ often paler than ♀♀, with a longer crest and tail, and somewhat larger. SIZE: wing, ♂ 630–670, ♀ 610–660; tail, ♂ 670–854, ♀ 570–705; tarsus, 295–320. WEIGHT: 1 ♂ 3809, 1 ♀ 3405; 6 unsexed 3740–4270 (4052) (Biggs *et al.* 1979).

1ST IMMATURE: resembles adult, but has yellow, not orange, facial skin, is somewhat or much browner in plumage; has shorter central tail feathers, and greyish, not brown eye.

DOWNY YOUNG: at first white to pale grey; at *c.* 14 days down is darker grey; legs and bare facial skin yellow.

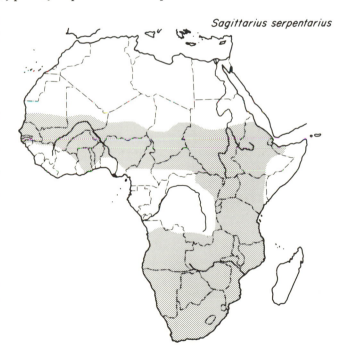

Sagittarius serpentarius

Field Characters. Unmistakable; a large, grey and black terrestrial bird standing *c.* 1·3 m tall, with very long legs, long projecting central tail feathers, and long crest on nape, often waving in wind, especially when bird bows its head or looks downward. Walks with measured gait, head and neck moving back and forth like domestic hen (or goat). In flight (rarely seen soaring at height) grey body plumage contrasts with black wing-quills, and long tail and legs protruding behind create characteristic silhouette, somewhat resembling Lam-

mergeier *Gypaetus barbatus*; but broader-winged than this species with legs and central tail feathers protruding beyond most of wedge-shaped tail.

Voice. Not recorded. Normally silent, but at nest and in nuptial display utters varied hoarse growling, groaning, or croaking calls, rendered 'gorrrr-orrr' or 'korr-korr-korr'; also mewing cries when roosting at night. Young in nest utter penetrating 'chee-uk-chee-uk-chee-uk' up to 30 days old; thereafter groan or growl like adult. Young in nest sometimes throw heads back to call in manner of African Fish Eagle *Haliaeetus vocifer*. Deep hoarse voice and mode of calling generally very different from most Accipitridae, but somewhat reminiscent of snake eagles *Circaetus* spp.

General Habits. Well known; but considering unique interest, still inadequately studied. Frequents open grasslands, semi-desert plains, scrub (Karoo), and open *Acacia* and *Combretum* woodlands, usually avoiding very dense bush. Habitat is probably limited firstly by height of grass (avoids any area with grass more than 1 m tall in rains, preferring grass 0·5 m high or less); and secondly by terrestrial pedestrian hunting habits, as needs to walk long distances to secure adequate prey. Hence not found in true deserts, but can survive in semi-desert scrub, e.g. Kalahari. Is far more numerous in South African grasslands and highland E African grasslands than in apparently ideal short lowland grasslands W Ethiopia, Sudan and W Africa; may be sensitive to high temperature, avoiding hot lowlands, even if otherwise ideal.

Roosts nightly on trees, very often nest tree; otherwise usually flat-topped acacias, or *Balanites* spp. (in South Africa sometimes exotic introduced pines). Pairs often roost together, even if apart for much of day. 1–2 h after dawn (sometimes later in wet weather, when grass is soaked), jumps to ground, and thereafter spends much of day foraging in neighbouring grassland. Walks steadily through grassland; av. 120 paces/min, estimated walking speed 2·5–3 km/h. Normal pace is interspersed with bouts of short quick stamping steps, *c.* 180/min, often stamping repeatedly in small area to disturb prey. Towards midday may rest in shade of trees, but often active in heat of day. During day may take dust bath, and in arid areas drinks. Pairs roosting together usually forage within sight of each other. Towards sunset, both birds move back towards roosting trees, usually used for many successive nights even if not nesting there, and fly up to roost 1–2 h before dark. Invariably move downwind first and fly upwind to roost. Regular roost trees become covered with droppings, insect remains and castings.

Catches all prey on ground, usually in bill, but sometimes kills with feet. Stamping bouts when foraging disturb prey, which is then killed by swift hard downward blows of feet; such prey may be any size from grasshopper to large snake. Most prey small, however (insects, small rodents, small amphibia, lizards), large items only occasionally eaten (Kemp and Kemp 1978). Prey often taken by quick forward thrust of head, sometimes making a quick dart to one side, or running after prey for a few paces with half-spread wings. All prey swallowed whole, then carried in crop. Cannot carry any prey in feet, and may cache a rat, or other larger prey under bush, returning later to collect it.

Not normally gregarious, but pairs often together for long periods and, after breeding, family parties of 3–4 usually forage together. When not breeding, many often frequent certain areas, other adjacent areas (perhaps with less available food) being temporarily deserted. Moves from one area to another mainly on foot, even walking through narrow open spaces between blocks of forest to reach temporarily favoured area. Not known to perform any regular movements, but in most areas highly nomadic, disappearing from apparently suitable localities for months or years, reappearing later. In Transvaal highveld, apparently more sedentary than in E Africa, pairs being regularly found in same ranges year-round (W. Tarboton, A. Kemp, pers. comm.). In arid areas (Kalahari, Namib) still more nomadic, and congregate locally in groups of up to 50 near waterholes. Probably moves from place to place most often on foot; but can also soar well, and has been seen from aircraft at 3800 m above ground (Carr-Hartley, pers. comm.).

Nomadic and terrestrial habits, and mode of feeding resemble more those of a large bustard than a bird of prey; but whether this is due to convergence derived from feeding in specialized habitat, or true relationship with the Gruiformes remains obscure.

Food. Not quantitatively analysed. Insects, small amphibians, lizards and snakes, some young birds and eggs, small ground rodents. Although reputed to feed much on snakes, principal food is probably abundant grasshoppers, small rodents next in importance. Castings at nests or roosts consist largely of rodent fur and insect remains. Largest animals killed are snakes, such as puff-adders or cobras, and young hares. Small antelopes such as steinbuck *Rhaphicerus campestris* and mountain reedbuck *Redunca fulvorufula* flee from foraging Secretary Bird, which could not kill adults, but conceivably could in infancy. Eats no carrion as far as is known; but is attracted to grass fires and recently burned areas, collecting small dead animals on ground, but not near flames.

Breeding Habits. Very well known. In breeding season pairs are dispersed in large home ranges, probably *c.* 5000–6000 ha, defended from other Secretary Birds. Near boundary of range, residents pursue intruders, running fast along ground with wings held above back. When overtaking intruder, resident jumps above it and strikes downwards with feet. Intruder normally withdraws after one or several such attacks, whereupon resident birds rejoin and walk round and round one another, crests erected, evidently excited. Occasionally, groups of 4–6 may be seen running through grassland with wings upheld. Function of such behaviour not clear, but perhaps some form of communal display, vaguely resembling dancing behaviour of cranes.

Aerial nuptial or territorial display consists of soaring high, uttering loud groaning or croaking calls. Pairs may soar together near breeding site, rising to 500 m or more on thermals, then perform undulating displays typical of Accipitridae. Sometimes one (? ♂) dives at other with feet outstretched whereupon lower bird (? ♀) may turn and present claws in typical accipitrine manner. Such aerial displays rare. Probable nuptial display on ground consists of one bird chasing other on twisting course through grass with wings upheld above back, resembling inter-territorial repulsion displays. Mating occurs either on ground or in trees; not described in full detail.

NEST: in trees, normally thorny; those most often selected are *Acacia* spp., e.g. *A. mellifera, A. heteracantha*. In E Africa often *Balanites*, especially if pruned to dense thicket by browsing giraffes making it impenetrable from below. In Cape Province exotic pines; and also often uses dense clumps of thorny *Capparis* or *Carissa* growing on termite mounds. Safe height above ground is less important than dense, thorny nature of tree or bush chosen; thus varies from 2·5–13 m, av. 5 m in southern Africa. Large flat structure of sticks, 1–1·5 m across by 0·3–0·5 m. deep when newly built, sometimes becoming larger with repeated use (up to 2–2·5 m. across but never very deep). Resembles nest of Lappet-faced Vulture *Aegypius tracheliotus*, and may be appropriated by this species. Broad shallow central depression lined with grass, sometimes also pieces of dung, and usually heavily spattered with droppings, bits of insects and castings, helping identification. Pairs have 1–2 nests, and may use them for many years or soon abandon them. Both sexes build, carrying all nesting material in bill (impossible for them to carry it in feet). Just before egg-laying ♀ spends long periods at nest, and may sit in incubation posture on empty nest for some time. Pair often roosts on prospective nest tree for several months, but may not then lay.

EGGS: 1–3, laid at 2–3 day intervals; southern Africa mean (126 clutches), 1·96; East Africa similar. Elongated ovals, pale bluish green or white, with chalky texture, sometimes a few blood smears. SIZE: (62, South Africa) 68·0–87·0 × 51·2–65·0 (78·25 × 56·51); mean (South and E Africa) 78·0 × 57·0 (Schönwetter 1960); WEIGHT: calculated 130.

Laying dates: Cape Province, winter and summer rainfall, Aug–Nov, peaking Sept (early spring); Transvaal and Orange Free State, all months except Mar recorded, no obvious peaks; arid Karoo-Namib areas Feb, May, Aug–Oct, perhaps peaking in dry season; Zimbabwe, Malawi, Zambia, South Africa (Kruger Park and Natal) records all months, but marked peak Aug–Dec, especially Oct–Nov (late dry-early rains); E Africa, E Kenya, N Tanzania, 11/12 months with 2 peaks May–June, Oct–Dec (late long rains and short rains); S Tanzania Jan, July, Aug, Dec (dry and in rains); N Kenya Mar, Apr, May, Sept, Oct (dry and rains); Ethiopia, 10/12 months, no obvious peaks; Somalia Mar, June; Sudan–W Africa, few records, probably mainly in dry season. In areas of low rainfall, season extended, probably favouring late rains or main rains. In southern African summer rainfall areas, laying peaks late dry season, young then in nest in rains.

Incubation begins 1st egg, by ♀ only in cases observed; she may leave nest to feed, or be fed at nest by ♂, who may also visit with dry grass or sticks. ♂ perhaps also incubates (as he shares in brooding of young). Incubation period: at least 42, probably 43–44 days (45 days ± 1: Steyn 1959).

Young hatch at intervals of 2–3 days; in clutches of 3, 1 egg often infertile. Despite hatching interval, little or no sibling aggression observed. 1st white down replaced by thicker greyer down within 14 days. 1st feathers (crest) emerge at *c.* 21 days; body and flight feathers by 28 days; largely feathers at 40–45 days; fully feathered by 60 days (but very variable). Weight increases from 56 g at hatch to *c.* 500 at 20 days; 1100 at 30; 1700 at 40; 2000 at 50; 2500 at 60; and 3000 at 70, just before 1st flight. Weight increase apparently irregular, variable, especially in later stages, when 1 or more young may die, probably through food shortage. Can stand weakly at 40 days to feed themselves, and tarsus is 95% of final length at 45 days; thereafter stand to feed themselves, but are usually fed by parents for some time after they can stand. From day 60 onwards perform vigorous bouts of wing-flapping and, on approach of human intruder, squat flat in nest; such reaction not normally provoked by, for example giraffe browsing on nest tree. Normally leave nest without parental stimulus at 75–85 days, but period very variable, good records ranging from 65–106 days; mean of 10 records South and E Africa, 83 days 2 young in same nest recorded fledging at *c* 90 and 106 days both survived (W. Tarboton, pers. comm.). Young may also survive premature departure at 47–50 days, then remaining on ground below nest until able to walk well. Normally leave nest by jumping or making short glide to ground; may not then return immediately until wings stronger, but may return same night to roost. Unhatched, infertile eggs may be removed by parents and dropped 200 m away (P. Johnson, pers. comm.). Dead young normally left to rot in nest, not eaten by siblings.

Both parents tend and brood young in early fledging period, ♀ most. Days 1–10 brood 90% by day and all night, this thereafter reduced to 50% between days 10–20, possibly connected with development of thicker down. Parental visits then reduced till late in fledging period, either or both visiting nest for only moments daily, and do not roost with young. Roosting at nest by ♂ ceases after 25 days, but ♀ may roost there longer. ♂ brings most prey in 1st half, ♀ most in 2nd half of fledging period; but both bring prey right up to end. In early fledging period young are fed by regurgitation on liquid matter (presumably digested insects). ♂ may visit nest, regurgitate crop load on nest, which is then re-swallowed by ♀, or he may feed young direct. If adult has large solid prey in crop (e.g. rat or snake), this must apparently by regurgitated first before digested liquid matter can be produced. All prey brought is carried in crop, and loads are often large; may consist of large numbers of grasshoppers, a mass of small mice, or a mixture (e.g. 10 lizards, a mouse and a young hare). Foraging parent near nest sometimes caches prey too large to swallow immediately (e.g. rat) under bush, returning to collect it later, then regurgitating it first. Small prey, such as grasshoppers, fed direct to young, but larger, e.g. snakes, held down with foot, torn up with bill, and morsels offered to young, as in, for example, eagles. Once young can feed themselves (after 45 days), mass of food is regurgitated into nest and left for young to collect.

Despite absence of sibling aggression, 2 young seldom reared, and no definite record of 3 having fledged. Mean of 35 partly-feathered or large broods (SAOSNRC) 1·4, probably further reduced to perhaps 1·2–1·3/successful nest. Overall breeding success much lower, as non-breeding frequent; no good long-term continuous records published. After leaving nest, young soon accompany parents to foraging range and can feed themselves on, for example, insects. Age at sexual maturity and first breeding unknown, lack of obvious immatures in population making estimates difficult.

References
Brown, L. H. (1955).
Steyn, P. (1959).
Van Someren, V. G. L. (1956).

Suborder FALCONES

This suborder, considered by some to be a full Order Falconiformes (e.g. Voous 1977), includes the New World caracaras and milvagos, and the cosmopolitan falcons. The Falcones differ from the Accipitres in several anatomical features, e.g. the vomer ends in an oval swelling touching the maxillo-palatine process; the syrinx has large external typani, with the intrinsic syringeal muscles inserted; and the dorsal vertebrae are fused. The eggs of all Falcones appear buff inside when held up to the light; the wing moult is invariably ascendant, whatever the size of the bird, beginning with primary No. 4, and proceeding in both directions; and, in the true falcons at least, the droppings fall below the perch and are not ejected in a powerful liquid stream (a difference recognized by falconers in the term 'mutes' as opposed to the accipitrine 'slice'). Similarities with the suborder Accipitres include many behaviour patterns, notably in nuptial displays; similar sequence of immature and adult plumages; and predatory habits.

Some authorities consider that the Falcones show similarites to owls. The musculature of the head and neck, for example, is more similar to that of owls than of hawks (Starck and Barnikol 1954). Also, no Falcones (excepting the primitive New World caracaras) build their own nests, breeding instead on the ground, on cliff ledges or in the nests of other birds, as do owls. They resemble owls too in that they kill their prey by biting and breaking the neck; hold food in 1 foot; hiss as young in threat to an intruder; and perform some common movements which denote curiosity, such as head-bobbing. However, at least some members of the suborder Accipitres share some of these behaviour patterns. The Falcones are certainly a very distinct suborder, though whether they merit recognition as a full order is still open to question. Here we follow Stresemann and Amadon (1979) in regarding them as a distinct suborder of the large order Falconiformes.

The Falcones has only 1 family, Falconidae, divided into 2 subfamilies: the Polyborinae, including the 'primitive' New World caracaras; and the Falconinae, including all true falcons and falconets. All African species belong to the latter, and belong to 2 genera, *Polihierax*, Pygmy Falcons, and *Falco*, true falcons.

Family FALCONIDAE: pygmy falcons and falcons

Subfamily FALCONINAE

Genus *Polihierax* Kaup

Very small falcons. Sexually dimorphic, ♀♀ having more chestnut plumage. Distinguished from *Falco* mainly by small size and breeding habits. Bill toothed, nostril round to oval without tubercle. Wings rather short, pointed; tail square to graduated. Tarsi covered with round scales, upper part feathered; talons acute. 2 spp., 1 African, *P. semitorquatus*.

Polihierax semitorquatus (Smith). Pygmy Falcon. Fauconnet d'Afrique.

Falco simitorquata [sic] A. Smith, 1836. Rep. Exp. Expl. Centr. Afr., p. 44; Kuruman, Botswana.

Range and Status. Resident semi-arid and arid thorn-bush and scrub in 2 disjunct areas, northeastern Africa (S Sudan, Ethiopia, Somalia, Kenya south to Tanzania); and southwestern Africa (S Angola, Namibia, Botswana south to Cape Province, east to W Transvaal). Range in southern Africa nearly coincides with that of Social Weaver *Philetairus socius*, and in NE Africa largely with that of White-headed Buffalo Weaver *Dinemellia dinemelli*. Dependent on these for breeding, occurs occasionally outside this range as non-breeder. Normally frequent, sometimes common; resident, not normally migratory.

Description. ADULT ♂: forehead white; crown and occiput blue-grey, a white collar on hindneck. Back and upperwing-coverts blue-grey, paler; uppertail-coverts white. Sides of face and underparts, including underwing- and undertail-coverts white. Wing- and tail-feathers black, spotted on outer web, notched and barred on inner web with white. Eye brown; cere red-orange; legs pinkish orange. ADULT ♀: maroon or chestnut back. Little size difference. SIZE: wing, ♂ 110–119 (115), ♀ 110–119 (116); tail, 69–74; tarsus, 24–28. WEIGHT: ♂ (2) 59, 64, ♀ (12) 54–67 (59·6) (Biggs *et al.* 1979).

IMMATURE: feathers of crown, neck and back edged reddish; underside buffy white. ♀ has chestnut back; legs and cere pale orange or yellow, paler than adult's. Adult plumage assumed in 1 year or less.

DOWNY YOUNG: white, blind, eyes open within a few days.

Field Characters. A very small, stocky, short-tailed falcon, more like a large shrike than a small falcon. Normally seen perched on elevated branch or dead tree, when white underside and grey back somewhat resemble White Crowned Shrike *Eurocephalus anguitimens*. Short curved beak and lack of white crown distinguish it from this species. Chestnut back of ♀ always diagnostic. Flight rapid, purposeful, undulating, wing-flaps alternating with short downward swoops also distinctive. In flight, white spots in tail and wing show clearly.

Voice. Recorded (6). Most existing descriptions misleading. Generally silent outside breeding season. Calls described include thin, squeaky 'tsip-tsip'; 'kiki-*kik*' (last syllable accented), or 'twee-twee-twip', used by ♂ calling ♀ from nest; a sharp ringing 'ki-ki-ki-ki-ki-ki-ki-ki' by young in threat; in copulation, purring 'kirrrrr-kirrrr-kirrrr'; begging chicks 'seee-seee-seeee'. All calls high-pitched, penetrating, but not very loud (Maclean 1970).

General Habits. Well known. Frequents open semi-desert scrub, *Acacia* thornbush and, in NE Africa, *Commiphora* thornbush, seldom entering broad-leaved *Combretum* woodland. Normally occurs where rainfall ranges from 200–600 mm/year, but also found in arid desert with less than 100 mm/year (Namib) as long as Social Weavers present. More likely to frequent higher rainfall areas in NE African range than in southern Africa. Prefers a mixture of trees and open ground, but

Polihierax semitorquatus

may be found in very dense bush, or open plains with scattered trees. Generally sedentary, pairs or individuals found regularly in same areas day after day and year after year.

Roosts in nests of buffalo weavers in NE Africa, Social Weavers in southern Africa. Becomes active soon after dawn, emerging and commencing hunting. Then perches on regularly favoured tree-tops, branches, overlooking open ground, preferably nearly bare (e.g. road). Observes keenly, and can turn head almost completely to look backwards over tail. May remain hunting in open situations until sun becomes hot at *c.* 10.00 h in northern range; then usually seeks shade, but is sometimes still active at midday. Becomes active again in evening, and may hunt until close to dusk, when it returns to roost. Full details not available.

Normally hunts from perch, dropping in short swift swoop to catch prey. Bobs head frequently up and down. Perhaps rarely flies down some small birds in open. Most prey taken on ground.

Food. Chiefly large insects and small lizards; some small birds up to 20 g and small rodents. In analysis of 333 pellets, 122 insects only (36·7%); 38 lizards only (11·4%); 123 insects and lizards (36·9%); all others, rodents and birds, usually mixed with insects (15%). Numerical preponderance of insects misleading; lizards, small rodents, birds more important by weight. Lizards estimated 50·5% by weight. All vertebrate bones digested, only chitinous insect remains, feathers, scales found in castings (Maclean 1970).

Breeding Habits. Very well known in southern Africa, little known NE Africa. Breeds invariably in nests of weaver birds, in southern Africa exclusively the communal nests of Social Weavers; *c.* 25% of all such nests in Kalahari occupied by falcons. In NE Africa apparently breeds most in thorny nests of White-headed Buffalo Weaver, but also reported in nests of White-browed Sparrow Weaver *Plocepasser mahali*. Perhaps does not use buffalo weaver nests unless lined by some other bird, e.g. Superb Starling *Spreo superbus* or other weavers.

At onset of breeding season pair re-occupies old, used chambers in nest of Social Weaver or investigates new ones; roost in chosen chambers together. Little obvious display noted. Pre-copulation, ♂ and ♀ sit next to each other on perch; ♂ greets ♀ with silent tail-wagging display, moving tail up and down. ♀ solicits by crouching and sometimes erecting white uppertail-coverts, exposing chestnut back. ♂ mounts and copulates, emitting purring calls; dismounts. ♀ then remains in submissive posture, while ♂ repeatedly bobs head; he may then fly into nest-chamber calling ♀, who may follow, also calling. Copulation frequent before egg-laying. Little detail on NE African race, but ♀ may solicit ♂ from tree-top, ♂ then flies to her and may alight directly on back, copulating sometimes silently. May then preen, but do not preen each other. In Kalahari eggs laid within 3 weeks of mating.

EGGS: 2–4, laid at at least 2-day intervals; mean (17 clutches) 3·06, av. 3·2 in good years, 2·9 in bad years. Pure dull white, rounded. SIZE: (8, southwestern Africa) 28·0–29·5 × 22·0–23·5 (28·8 × 22·8); mean (17) 27·9 × 22·3 (Maclean 1970); NE Africa, no larger, mean (3) 28 × 23·5.

Laying dates: Somalia June (rains); NE Kenya July, Sept, Nov (mainly dry season); Kalahari Aug–Mar (in summer rains). Rains apparently not essential.

Incubation may begin with 1st egg, or after 2nd egg laid. Both sexes incubate, ♀ most. ♂ feeds ♀, mainly with lizards, calling her out to receive prey; may then incubate briefly while she feeds. ♀ incubates at night,

♂ roosts in adjacent chamber. Incubation period: estimated 27–31 days, probably 28–29, similar to much larger falcons.

Young hatch over a period, so are different in size. 1st wing-feathers show through white down at 7 days, completely feathered by 21 days. Leave nest at 27–40 days but return to it thereafter at intervals. Fledging period: *c.* 30 days. Inside nest, young dislike light and clamber up sides of chamber to avoid it.

In early stages ♀ remains brooding young, ♂ brings food, mainly lizards. Calls ♀ out, she receives it, returns to nest and feeds brood. ♀ hunts little until chicks are feathered (after 21 days). Data suggest lizards vital to rear brood, insects alone probably inadequate. In favourable years may be double brooded, 2nd brood following 1st at interval of 2–6 weeks, sometimes longer, 2·5 months. 2nd broods are not smaller than 1st.

After leaving nest young accompany parents for up to 2 months, when can kill for themselves; may be tolerated by parents who have started 2nd brood, but do not then roost with them. Young ♀♀ soon distinguishable from ♂♂; can breed when 1 year old.

Of 64 eggs in 18 nests, 34 hatched (53·1%) and 29 chicks flew, i.e. 1·7 young/pair breeding; no non-breeding pairs recorded. Breeding success may normally be rather higher, as some eggs deserted through human interference. Predation is slight. Parents are aggressive near nest, especially with large young. Advantage to falcon of nesting association with weavers is probably safe secure nest-site (less safe in NE Africa) and to host Social Weaver perhaps some protection against, for example, snakes (though falcons occasionally eat weavers). No clear advantage to larger buffalo weavers, as heavier and more powerful than falcons.

References
Maclean, G. L. (1970).

Genus *Falco* Linnaeus

The original generic name for all birds of prey known to Linnaeus (1758), now reserved for the true falcons. Small or medium-sized raptors, the ♀♀ larger, sometimes much larger than ♂♂; immature plumages often different from adults. Bills short, pointed, with a distinct tomial tooth on the edge of the upper mandible (used for breaking the necks of prey); nostril round, with a central bony tubercle; eyes large, normally dark brown, surrounded by a ring of bright-coloured skin; head often with black 'moustache' streaks; necks short; wings long, pointed, outer primaries sometimes notched; tails long to moderate; legs normally short, feet powerful or rather weak, varying with food taken. Both sexes have brood patches. Body plumage highly variable, rufous, grey or black, Sometimes with colour phases; plumages of immatures usually duller, browner than adult, streaked below.

The 2nd largest genus in the Order Falconiformes, with 36 spp., 18 in Africa. Of these, 7 are endemic residents; 5 purely Palearctic winter migrants; and 7 have breeding populations, augmented by Palearctic migrants in winter. 2 of these breed only in NW Africa and thus are properly Palearctic species, migrating to the Ethiopian region.

The genus is divided into a number of distinct groups, sometimes classified by earlier authorities as separate genera, as follows: kestrels—4 spp. (*naumanni, tinnunculus, rupicoloides, alopex*), all with resident populations; 2 are sexually dimorphic and all are basically rufous. Hobbies and near allies—4 spp., 2 (*subbuteo* and *eleonorae*) breeding only in NW Africa, 1 (*cuvieri*) an endemic resident, and 1 (*concolor*) breeding in the Red Sea and Persian Gulf; *concolor* and *eleonorae* migrate to Madagascar in winter. Gyrfalcon allies—2 spp. (*biarmicus* and *cherrug*), *biarmicus* being the common large resident falcon, and *cherrug* a Palearctic migrant. Peregrines and allies—2 spp. (*peregrinus* and *fasciinucha*), *peregrinus* being cosmopolitan with resident African races augmented by winter migrants, and *fasciinucha* an unaccountably rare endemic resident.

2 other spp. (*ardosiaceus* and *dickinsoni*), both endemic tropical residents, have been called kestrels, but are quite unlike true kestrels in their habits and plumage. *F. chiquera*, with races resident in Africa and India, has been

allied with the Holarctic Merlin *F. columbarius*, a scarce Palearctic migrant to NW Africa, for no sound reason, and 2 others, *vespertinus* and *amurensis* (sometimes regarded as a subspecies of *vespertinus*), share some of the habits of kestrels and hobbies, and perform very remarkable migrations from Europe or Asia in winter.

Several African spp. (*alopex*, *rupicoloides*, *dickinsoni*, *chicquera*) are curiously local in distribution, unaccountably absent from suitable habitat in some parts of the continent; and the Teita Falcon *F. fasciinucha* is quite unaccountably rare in its wide E and Central African range.

Falco naumanni Fleischer. Lesser Kestrel. Faucon crécerellette.

Falco Naumanni Fleischer, 1818. In Laurop and Fischer's 'Sylvan' for 1817/1818, p. 174; 'Southern Germany', error for Sicily.

Plates 27 and 32 (Opp. pp. 434 and 467)

Range and Status. Resident, breeding NW Africa (Morocco, Algeria, Tunisia), where locally abundant near breeding colonies in spring–summer. Migrant to semi-arid savannas and plains of Africa, especially E and South Africa, wintering in large numbers Transvaal, Orange Free State and Cape Province, locally very abundant at winter roosts and commonest small raptor in highveld. No recent decreases documented, either in breeding or wintering quarters; may have been favoured rather than otherwise by increased agriculture in winter range.

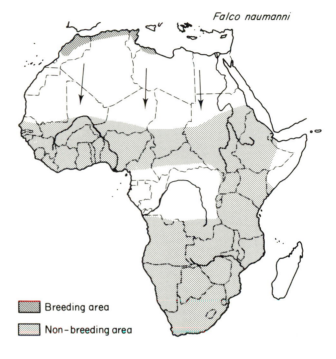

Falco naumanni

▨ Breeding area

☐ Non-breeding area

Description. ADULT ♂: crown, pale blue-grey. Mantle, back, lesser and median upperwing-coverts and scapulars pale chestnut, unspotted, some scapulars subterminally blue-grey. Rump and uppertail-coverts blue-grey, median coverts merging to blue-grey; greater wing-coverts blue-grey. Ear-coverts and sides of neck blue-grey, contrasting sharply with creamy chin and throat; breast and flanks buff, sparsely spotted black, becoming paler, unspotted on belly and under-tail-coverts. Axillaries below pinkish buff to grey, spotted blackish, underwing-coverts white tinged rufous, sparsely spotted dark brown. Primaries and some outer secondaries brownish black, edged and tipped whitish, basally white, mottled brown on inner webs. Tail blue-grey above, tipped whitish, subterminally banded black, outer webs of feathers barred darker; below pale grey, subterminally barred black. Cere and orbital ring yellow; eye dark brown; legs and feet orange-yellow; claws white or pale brown. ADULT ♀: differs in having forehead whitish, with black shaft streaks; black and upperwing-coverts chestnut, narrowly barred black, becoming blue-grey on lower back, rump and uppertail-coverts. Sides of head and throat pale buff; an indistinct moustachial streak. Rest of underside, including underwing-coverts, buff to pale chestnut, sometimes unmarked, usually streaked and spotted dark brown. Primaries blackish brown barred rufous, becoming more rufous on secondaries, innermost chestnut, barred brown, below pinkish brown, banded darker brown. Tail chestnut, tinged grey, tipped buff, with broad sub-terminal and many other blackish bars, sometimes reduced; below pale grey-brown, banded darker brown. Similar in size to ♂. SIZE: wing, ♂ 21 227–247 (233·5); ♀ (11) 226–244 (234·8); tail, ♂ 133–148 (140·4), ♀ 139–155 (144·3); tarsus, ♂ 29·5–33 (31·3), ♀ 30–31·5 (30·4). WEIGHT: ♂ (17) 120–185 (148), ♀ (11) 140–208 (170), ♀ little larger in size to ♂ but markedly heavier (Glutz von Blotzheim *et al.* 1971); in winter range, ♂ (6) 116–162 (138), ♀ (5) 109–148 (134) (Biggs *et al.* 1979).

IMMATURE: resembles adult ♀, rump and uppertail-coverts often tinged grey, moustachial streak indistinct; young ♂ develops blue-grey tail feathers tinged rufous, with some blackish bars. Cere, orbital ring and legs yellow; eye dark brown. Has acquired almost full adult plumage and can breed within 1 year.

DOWNY YOUNG: white; 2nd down thicker, woollier, white; eye brown, cere and feet pale yellow.

Field Characters. A small, slender, graceful, long-winged, long-tailed falcon, often found in company with Common Kestrel *F. tinnunculus* and red-footed falcons. Smaller and generally more slender than Common Kestrel. At close range ♂♂ have unspotted chestnut backs, no moustachial streak on cheeks; and in flight have almost unbarred white or buff underside of wing (barred in Common Kestrel). ♀♀ and immatures more difficult to distinguish, but from below in flight appear much paler, less heavily barred, often with unstreaked breasts; from above, a slate blue patch often visible on secondaries. At very close range, pale brown or whitish talons diagnostic, but very difficult to see clearly. Generally much more gregarious than Common Kestrel. Immatures usually darker, more rufous, less heavily streaked than immature Red-footed Falcon *F. vespertinus*, but care needed in identification. In all plumages, much paler rufous than resident races of Common Kestrel.

Voice. Not recorded. In winter quarters normally silent except at communal roosts, when noisy at night. At breeding colonies in spring a high-pitched, rapidly repeated 'kri-kri-kri-kri-kri', and a slower, more rasping 'kirrri-kirrri'; also rendered 'kik-kik-kik-kik-kik', 'keh-chet-chet-kik', and 'kihik' of 'kitchit'; all calls higher-pitched than those of Common Kestrel. In copulation and in sexual excitement a low chattering 'tscheee-tscheee', later 'tscheef-tscheef'.

General Habits. Well known. Within most of African range prefers open plains, subdesert steppes, open cultivated country, sometimes deserts, avoiding heavily wooded or bushed areas, though it must pass over these on migration. Most favoured natural habitat open short-grass plains, but in breeding quarters cultivated areas and scrub-covered hill-sides. Commonest in highland E Africa and southern Africa in winter, much less common in W Africa, where frequents more arid savannas normally further north than Common Kestrel; rarely, occurs south to 6°N in Nigeria, near edge of forest, and to 5°N in Ivory Coast (Thiollay 1975).

Almost invariably gregarious or highly gregarious, seldom seen singly, normally in small groups or large loose flocks. Both on northward migration in spring and in winter quarters in winter roost communally, often in huge numbers, usually in groves of introduced eucalyptus, sometimes in the centre of towns. At roosts in South Africa 30,000–70,000 recorded; av. (155) 990 (Rudebeck 1963; Siegfried and Skead 1971). In South African winter quarters leave roosts soon after dawn and spread out, hunting over open country at estimated overall density 1/7 km² (Siegfried and Skead 1971). On wing most of the day, returning to roost in evening; even at night usually alert, frequently calling in crowded roosts (Rudebeck 1963). In E Africa large flock seen together is likely to be mostly or all Lesser Kestrels; but in W Africa mingles freely with Common Kestrel, and on passage, especially northward in N Africa in spring, often with Red-footed Falcons.

Foraging on wing, flies low, usually c. 10–20 m above ground, turning repeatedly into wind to poise against strong winds with motionless wings, or hovers in light breezes like Common Kestrel; tends to hover less often and poise with still wings more than Common Kestrel. Swoops from flight to catch insects in flight or on ground, then settling briefly before taking to wing again. Catches more insects in air than Common Kestrel. Attends grass fires and snatches disturbed insects close to flames. Seldom seen perching by day.

Southward migration from breeding areas begins Aug, scattered parties forming into larger flocks before departure. In Mediterranean region southward passage peaks late Sept–mid Oct. Peak passage through NE and E Africa is in late Oct–early Nov, but some reach Zambezi by mid–Oct, and main wintering area in southern Africa is occupied late Oct–Mar, with peak numbers Nov–late Feb. One ringed bird had travelled 8785 km from Kazakhstan. Total wintering population at least 155,000, based on roost counts (Siegfried and Skead 1971). Northward passage begins late Feb, increasing in Mar, and peaking in Apr–early May in E and N Africa. Earliest arrivals reach breeding colonies late Mar, most not till Apr. Height of northward passage out of Africa occurs 1–15 Apr. Most migration into and out of Africa follows main migration routes through Suez and Gibraltar, but many, especially on northward migration, cross Mediterranean on broad front. Main

northward migration follows more westerly course than southward, thus resembling that of Red-footed Falcon (often then in company together). Feeds freely both on southward and northward migration; but in E Africa on passage often passes in large flocks high up, evidently travelling considerable distances without feeding. On migration behaviour generally resembles that of red-footed falcons more than Common Kestrel.

In summer breeding quarters groups centre on breeding colonies, forage singly or in small flocks at some distance, in open fields or low scrub, returning to colony area to roost or feed young. Is then seen singly, or in small groups more often than in winter quarters. Foraging behaviour essentially similar, flying low over ground against wind, repeatedly turning into wind to poise or hover before swooping at prey.

Food. Mainly insects, especially grasshoppers, crickets, mole crickets (*Gryllotalpa*) and large beetles. In summer in Europe grasshoppers and other Orthoptera 50·5%; other insects 40·5%, with rare dragonflies, small lizards and occasional small rodents. May occasionally take small young ground birds, e.g. larks. Insects estimated 98% by weight Austria (Glutz von Blotzheim *et al*. 1971). Food on migrations and in winter quarters not quantatively analysed, but certainly mainly or entirely insects, many caught in flight, e.g. near grass fires, varied with small lizards, occasional small mammals. Feeds upon caterpillars of army worm *Spodoptera exempta*, formerly (before effective control) on locusts. Food requirement per day estimated at c. 40 g (Glutz von Blotzheim *et al*. 1971).

Breeding Habits. Very well known in Europe, not studied in detail N Africa. Arrives at breeding colonies c. 3–4 weeks before egg-laying. Display not spectacular, mainly soaring around colony, in pairs, small flocks or groups, accompanied by loud calling. Copulation takes place on rock cliffs, buildings, or on topmost branches of adjacent trees, both sexes maintaining balance by waving wings. ♂ feeds ♀ before egg-laying, presenting prey in bill after catching and carrying it in feet.

NEST: breeds either on natural rock cliffs, in gorges, or in large old buildings; N African colonies found most often in natural rock sites, as suitable buildings (e.g. cathedrals) scarce. Colonies composed of 2–3 to 100 or more pairs, 15–25 pairs common. ♂ selects nest-site and attracts ♀ to it; Usually in hole, crack, or on overhung ledge, not in open site. No actual nest built, eggs being laid in earth scrapes often lined with fur or insect remains. In Europe, occasionally reported as breeding in holes in trees, or abandoned nests of other birds, not so far in Africa. Abundant suitable rock sites available N Africa. Same site may be used by same birds successive years.

EGGS: 3–6, laid at intervals of 1–2 days; Morocco mean (25 clutches) 4·56 (Heim de Balsac and Mayaud 1962), apparently averaging larger than European (where 233 av. 3·8: Glutz von Blotzheim *et al*. 1971). Rounded ovals, slightly pointed, pale red-brown or buff, variously spotted all over with darker red-brown, sometimes lightly marked, usually heavily, sometimes form-

ing a cap at one end, or a band round centre. SIZE:
(336) 30·4–39·5 × 26·3 – 32·0 (34·63 × 28·58); WEIGHT:
(31) 14·5–19·4 (16·9); av. clutch *c.* 77 g, *c.* 44% of ♀
bodyweight.

Laying dates: NW Africa end Apr–mid May (Heim
de Balsac and Mayaud 1962).

Incubation begins with last egg; by ♀ only, or ♂
may take small share, for instance while ♀ feeding;
estimated 5–10% of daylight (Blondel 1964). Incubation period: 28–29 days.

Details of development of young not fully described;
remain in nest hole, mainly with ♀, till 15 days old,
then emerge and are fed near entrance. Then may weigh
180–190 g, almost adult weight. ♀ broods young in hole
in early stages, and ♂ brings all prey. Later, when young
active, ♀ also kills, but most prey still brought by ♂ to
end of fledging period. Most prey insects, brought
mainly in heat of day when insect activity maximal
(Blondel 1964). Young suffer (in France) from com-

petition from jackdaws, are not adequately defended by
adults. Make 1st flight at 26–28 days, thereafter remaining some time near nest, continuing to be fed by parents.

No data on breeding success in N Africa; but in
Europe, of 327 nestings with 1092 eggs, 721 young
hatched (66%) and 522 young flew in 251 successful
nests (53·3% of eggs, 72·4% of eggs hatched), i.e. 1·59/
breeding pair and 2·87/successful nest. No evidence of
non-breeding pairs reported, so that population in
autumn is *c.* 175% of spring population. Young can
breed in their 1st year, but some do not (Glutz von
Blotzheim *et al.* 1971). Young depart from breeding
colonies in July, commence southward migration *c.* 1
month later in Europe.

References
Blondel, J. (1964).
Glutz von Blotzheim, U. N. *et al.* (1971).
Rudebeck, G. (1963).
Siegfried, W. R. and Skead, D. M. (1971).

Falco tinnunculus Linnaeus. Common Kestrel; Rock Kestrel. Crécerelle des clochers.

**Plates
27 and 32**
(Opp. pp. 434
and 467)

Falco Tinnunculus Linnaeus, 1758. Syst. Nat. (10th ed.), p. 90; Sweden.

Range and Status. Resident and Palearctic migrant.
Nominate *tinnunculus* breeds NW Africa and migrates
to Africa from Palearctic in winter, when frequent to
common, sometimes locally abundant in flocks. 4 resident races (*rupicolaeformis*, *archeri*, *rufescens* and *rupicolus*), all usually frequent to common, but locally
outnumbered north of equator in winter by migrant
tinnunculus. Resident breeding *rufescens* unaccountably
rare in apparently optimum habitat in Kenya–N
Tanzania, in equatorial 2-season rainfall regime. Adapts
well to human habitations and benefits from agriculture,
opening up woodland habits, breeding also in towns.
Not threatened anywhere in known range.

Description. *F. t. tinnunculus* Linnaeus: breeds NW Africa
from S Sahara–Libya. ADULT ♂: forehead cream; crown, nape,
and hindneck blue-grey, with black shaft streaks. Mantle,
scapulars and upperwing-coverts pale chestnut, spotted black,
spots smaller on upper back; primary coverts brownish
black, spotted chestnut. Rump and uppertail-coverts blue-
grey. Sides of face and indistinct eyebrow cream; ear-
coverts grey, contrasting with black moustachial streak. Chin
and throat pale buff; rest of underside, including underwing-
coverts, buff to cream, spotted black on breast, more heavily
on flanks, plain buff on belly and undertail-coverts; underwing-coverts barred and spotted black. Primaries and outer
secondaries above blackish brown, barred whitish on inner
webs, narrowly edged and tipped whitish becoming chestnut on inner secondaries, subterminally spotted black; below,
primaries tipped blackish, largely white barred grey on
inner webs, becoming pale pinkish buff, spotted black on
inner secondaries. Tail above blue-grey, below pale grey,
tipped whitish, banded black subterminally, rest sometimes
unbarred, usually with several narrower blackish bars. Cere
and orbital skin yellow, eye dark brown, legs yellow. ADULT
♀: differs in being much more heavily barred, spotted
and streaked black than ♂. Forehead creamy, becoming
chestnut on crown and neck, streaked black, sometimes
tinged bluish. Upper back, mantle and upperwing-coverts
pale chestnut, spotted on upper back and mantle, more
often heavily barred blackish; primary coverts blackish, barred

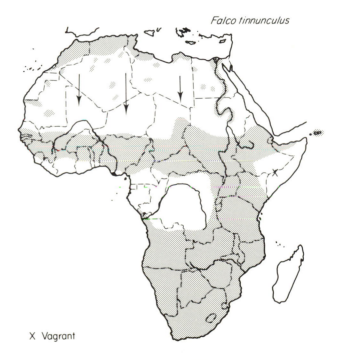

Falco tinnunculus

X Vagrant

rufous. Lower back chestnut, barred black, or blue-grey; rump
and uppertail-coverts blue grey. Lores and eyebrow creamy
white; ear-coverts pale greyish, and indistinct moustachial
streak. Rest of underparts, including underwing-coverts,
pale rufous, buff or cream, streaked, spotted and barred
blackish, always more heavily than ♂. Primaries above and
below blackish, barred rufous on inner pairs, becoming
rufous, barred brown, edged white on secondaries, bars darker
below. Tail above pale chestnut, sometimes tinged grey,
tipped whitish, broad subterminal and many other blackish
bands; below pale grey, tipped white, broadly banded subterminally and barred black. Larger than ♂. SIZE: wing, ♂
230–266 (244), ♀ 235–275 (254·5); tail, ♂ 150–174 (162),
♀ 152–188 (171); tarsus, ♂ 37–43 (40·7), ♀ 37·5–47·2 (41·1).
WEIGHT: ♂(85) 143–252(196); ♀(97) 154–290(221); ♀♀ heavier
in autumn (Brown and Amadon 1968; Glutz von Blotzheim
et al. 1971).

1ST IMMATURE: above, like adult ♀, but more heavily and evenly barred blackish brown; rump and uppertail-coverts chestnut, paler than ♀, seldom tinged grey. Tail rufous, basally tinged grey, generally greyer in young ♂♂, with broad sub-terminal black band and several other blacker bars. Below, like adult ♀, but blackish streaks broader, generally paler. Eye dark brown, cere pale green, feet paler yellow than adult.

DOWNY YOUNG: 1st down thin, short, white; 2nd long, thick, buffish grey above, paler buff below. Eye dark brown, cere pale green, legs pale yellow.

Immature acquires full adult plumage over 2·5–3 years by a gradual moult from Aug–Apr (1st summer—2nd spring), continuing later in 2nd year, completed by a 3rd moult in June–July in 3rd summer. In ♂♂ grey crown, rump and tail are acquired, and barring decreases and becomes darker, clearer, in ♀♀. May breed in subadult plumage, most not till 2nd year.

Of at least 10 subspecies, 4 occur in continental Africa, all darker, more rufous than nominate *tinnunculus*, with sexual dimorphism in tropical and southern African forms reduced.

F. t. rupicolaeformis (Brehm). Egypt; migrant to N Ethiopia in winter. Darker rufous in all plumages than *F. t. tinnunculus*, more richly coloured throughout. Smaller: wing ♂ 223–247 (235), ♀ 230–248 (242).

F. t. archeri Hartert and Neumann. Somalia and Coastal Kenya; Socotra. Paler than *rupicolaeformis*, rather more heavily barred above than *tinnunculus*. Smaller; wing ♂ 218–229, ♀ 233–242.

F. t. rufescens Swainson. Resident in tropical Africa from Upper Guinea east to highland Ethiopia, thence south to S Tanzania and N Angola. Much darker, deeper rufous-chestnut above, more heavily barred, more heavily spotted below. In ♂♂, crown darker slate, grey tail always with some bars; wing ♂ 223–237, ♀ 233–258. Reputed to occur in same range as *archeri* in Somalia; not known if they interbreed. Unaccountably scarce in apparently optimum habitat in Kenya near equator, reappearing commonly in S Tanzania.

F. t. rupicolus Daudin. Resident rest of southern Africa south to Cape of Good Hope. Paler than *F. t. rufescens*, sexual dimorphism reduced, adult ♀♀ with much grey on head and tail, greyer than most larger kestrels. Wing ♂ 217–248 (236), ♀ 240–258 (247); WEIGHT: unsexed (99) 145–247 (192) (Biggs *et al.* 1979).

Field Characters. Small reddish brown falcons, ♂♂ with grey tails and heads, less obvious in tropical and southern races. European and N African *tinnunculus* often gregarious in winter flocks, in company with Lesser Kestrel *F. naumanni*, is larger, heavier-bodied, darker rufous, spotted above in ♂♂, and in flight always much more heavily barred on underwing and tail than Lesser Kestrel; but in mixed flocks confusion can occur, especially with immatures. Resident African races always much darker rufous than Lesser Kestrel, more heavily barred, normally dispersed in pairs, not gregarious. At close range, more heavily spotted and barred upperparts, black claws distinguish from Lesser Kestrel, and dark brown eye from Greater Kestrel *F. rupicoloides*. Characteristically hovers far more than any other kestrel, with spread tail and rapidly fanning wings.

Voice. Recorded (2a, 27). Migrants in tropical Africa normally rather silent. May utter shrill rasping cries, 'kree-kree-kree', lower-pitched, harsher than Lesser Kestrel. Breeding birds are vocal, uttering varied rasping or screeching calls variously rendered; e.g. high-pitched, shrill, reedy 'keeee-keeee-keeee' and a shorter 'kik-kik-kik' singly or repeated; trilling 'krrreeee' or

'wreeee' in excitement or display. Also, e.g. 'wit-wit-wit'; 'kii-kii-kii'; in breeding areas 'zirrr-zirrr', 'wrreee-wrree', or 'trriiit'. Begging young utter rasping 'zirrr, zirrr'. Generally, high-pitched, reedy or rasping screeches, voice of ♀ always lower-pitched than that of ♂. Voices of African races appear similar to those of European and N African races.

General Habits. Very well known; but not observed in detail in African resident races. Generally frequent open country or light woodland, in all habitats from sub-desert to forest edges, and towns, often breeding on buildings. Hunts either over natural grassland or scrub, or in cultivation and open pastures. Enters and hunts in thick woodland or scrub more often than Lesser Kestrel, but prefers open ground with low herbaceous vegetation or grass. Has adapted to a very wide variety of habitats, so that absence from apparently ideal habitat of grassland with abundant breeding cliffs in Kenya and N Tanzania is all the more inexplicable, either on grounds of food supply or possible competition with other species (such as Black-shouldered Kite *Elanus caeruleus*) occurring with it in same range, e.g. in South Africa or Ethiopia.

Normally roosts on cliffs, sometimes in trees; in winter gregarious at roost, but much less so than Lesser Kestrel. Resident African races usually roost singly or in pairs, close to or at nesting site, for much of year, on cliffs or buildings. Leaves roost and is active soon after dawn, then hunting over open ground until has fed. May then rest where it is, or return to perch near nest-site in heat of day. Normally has returned to roost 2–3 h before dark, but occasionally hunts late in evening. European race recorded hunting by moonlight.

Habitually hunts by flying low, 5–20 m above ground, repeatedly turning into wind and hovering with fanning wings, tail spread, body somewhat angled above horizontal, head looking downwards and held motionless while body and wings move. Hovers much more than Lesser Kestrel; but in strong winds also poises almost motionless head to wind, occasionally flicking wing-tips. Alternatively, hunts from perches, on dead trees, rocks, cliffs, telephone wires and posts or electricity pylons (last 2 especially in open treeless country where other perches scarce). From hover, descends to kill prey with wings held above back, raising them vertically close to ground to accelerate final plunge, at impact striking downwards hard with outstretched legs and feet. Mode of attack from perch usually similar, but more slanting and may fly out from perch, hover, attack or fail, and return. Catches many insects in flight, snatching them in feet and transferring to bill while in air. No good data on success rate in Africa; but elsewhere, *c.* 1/8 hovers results in attack. If successful, usually eats prey on ground if small, but if large transports it to perch before feeding.

Resident African populations are greatly augmented in winter by Palearctic migrant *tinnunculus* from Eurasia. N and NW African populations of *tinnunculus* and *rupicolaeformis* also migrate, but are barely distinguishable in winter flocks. *F. t. tinnunculus* occurs alongside *F. t. rupicolaeformis*, *rufescens*, *archeri*; and *rupicolaeformis* with *rufescens* and *archeri*, neither as far south as range of *rupicolus*. Migrants are generally gregarious, local residents (which may be breeding when migrants present) sedentary in pairs. Southward migration begins in Europe Aug, enters Africa in numbers late Sept–early Oct, and reaches equator by 10 Oct. Rather few travel south of equator, but in W Africa regularly travels farther south into heavier woodland than Lesser Kestrel, common at 7–8°N in Nigeria. Migrants attend grass fires prevalent in W African savannas Nov–Jan. Northward return movement begins early Mar, and most have gone by end–Mar, a few straggling into Apr; spring movement is generally earlier than in Lesser Kestrel. On migration, often travels in mixed flocks with Lesser Kestrel, sometimes also Red-footed Falcon *F. vespertinus* and flies higher. Feeds on migration as Lesser Kestrel. Less inclined to cross Mediterranean on broad front than Lesser Kestrel, most entering or leaving Africa through main routes, Gibraltar and Suez, and to lesser extent via Cape Bon, Tunisia, especially in spring.

Food. Staple diet of resident birds is probably small mammals, lizards and some ground birds, caught from hover or perch. Food of migrants in tropical Africa includes more insects, mainly grasshoppers, caught in long grass, in air, near grass fires or on burned ground. Catches swarming alate termites, and (before effective control) locusts. Recent British results suggest insects and other invertebrates more important by weight in diet than usually supposed. Few good data on local African races as scarcely studied, but food includes many insects, small mammals, small birds, and lizards. Small reptiles possibly more important in tropical than temperate haunts, but better data needed. In towns subsists largely on abundant rodents attracted by domestic scraps (e.g. Ethiopia). Most prey taken on ground, but some small birds and many insects caught in flight. Largest recorded prey (Europe) *c.* 600 g, normally under 40 g. Daily food requirement 40–60 g.

Breeding Habits. Of African resident races little known to (at best) well known. In Europe intimately known; habits probably similar in Africa, certainly no obvious differences observed. Resident African races are dispersed in pairs in suitable habitat, usually rather sparse. No good population density estimates anywhere, and may sometimes (W Africa) be limited by lack of available cliff nesting sites, but despite abundant food supply and often abundant nest-sites no tropical or South African resident race at present approaches recorded densities of *F. t. tinnunculus* in Europe.

Display more spectacular than in Lesser Kestrel. Pairs soar over site calling, and ♂ makes series of stoops at ♀, either perched or in flight, swinging up again after each stoop. If on wing, ♀ may turn over and present claws, and ♂ may stoop so close as to almost strike ♀. Some display observed in resident tropical races throughout year, and pair continues to frequent breeding cliff even when not breeding. Copulation occurs on cliffs, trees near nest-site, most often just before egg-laying.

NW African nominate *tinnunculus* breeds singly on cliffs, sometimes in trees in nests of other birds, or on buildings; Egyptian *rupicolaeformis* similar. Tropical African *rufescens* normally breeds on cliffs, in Ethiopia sometimes on buildings (e.g. castles in Gondar), not in trees. Somalian *archeri* mainly on cliffs, sometimes river banks, trees, buildings. Southern African *rupicolus* normally breeds on cliffs, sometimes on buildings, occasionally in nests of other birds including those of Hammerkop (McLachlan and Liversidge 1978). ♂ selects nest-site.

NEST: no actual nest built, eggs laid in earth scrape, often containing some fur, old castings or insect remains. Same site regularly used annually, presumably by different birds.

EGGS: NW Africa 4–6, mean (25 clutches) 4·52 (Heim de Balsac and Mayaud 1962); South Africa 3–5, normally 4, mean (25 Natal clutches) 3·62 (Dean 1971); tropical Africa 3–4, av. perhaps smaller. Normally laid at 2–3 day intervals, occasionally longer. Rounded ovals, yellowish or buff, usually almost covered with dark red and red-brown spots and blotches, rarely pale yellowish with few blotches. SIZE: (N Africa) 37–41·5 × 30–33 (Etchécopar and Hüe 1968); (*F. t. archeri*) 37–42 × 30–32 (38·8 × 31·5); (20, *F. t. rufescens*) 36·3–42·0 × 27·7–31·8 (38·4 × 30·8) (Schönwetter 1960); (100, *F. t. rupicolus*) 35·0–43·3 × 30·3–35·0 (39·9 × 33·3) (McLachlan and Liversidge 1978); little racial or regional difference. WEIGHT: (Europe, *F. t. tinnunculus*) 17·5–22 (av. 19·8–21).

Laying dates: NW Africa late Mar–late May; W Africa (*rufescens*) good data lacking, Oct–Dec (dry season); Ethiopia Dec (dry); Somalia (*archeri*) Apr–June, peaking early May (rains); E Kenya, N Tanzania (*rufescens*) June–Sept (mid-year dry season); S Tanzania Aug (dry); Zambia–Zimbabwe–Malawi, Transvaal–Natal (*rupicolus*) Aug–Dec, peaking Sept–Oct (late dry); Cape, winter rainfall and Sept–Nov (spring). In tropics generally breeds in dry seasons, except in Somalia where peaks in wettest months, and apparently all breeding south of equator is in 2nd half of year.

Incubation begins either with 1st egg or later, near completion of clutch. Mainly by ♀, who is fed near nest by ♂; but ♂ sometimes incubates briefly by day. ♀ may either leave nest to receive food from ♂, or may leave to find prey herself. Incubation period: Europe (*tinnunculus*) 27–29 days each egg, av. 28; South Africa (*rupicolus*) 31 ± 1 day (McLachlan and Liversidge 1978). Food supply does not apparently affect clutch size, but if food short incubating ♀♀ frequently abandon eggs (Holland, not necessarily applicable in tropics: Cavé 1968).

Young may hatch at intervals if eggs incubated early, but if onset of incubation delayed emerge almost simultaneously. Hatching period usually 3–5 days, each egg taking *c.* 24 h to hatch; hatching weight 14–18 g, increasing to 31 g at day 4; 63 at day 8; thereafter rapidly to max 250 g at 20–22 days in ♂♂, 280 g at 26 days in ♀♀, often then exceeding mean adult weight. Can be sexed in nest by weight after 22 days, ♀♀ then averaging heavier (Cavé 1968). Feathers emerge through down at *c.* 12 days and cover body by 20 days; weight then reduced as flight feathers develop. Make 1st flight (Europe) 27–30 days in ♂♂, 27–32 in ♀♀ (Cavé 1968). 33–34 days stated for *rupicolus*, South Africa (McLachlan and Liversidge 1978).

In early fledging period ♀ remains in nest with young, brooding them or standing over them. ♂ brings all prey, and increases rate of killing from that in incubation period. ♀ hunts little; is dependent, with brood, even late in fledging period, on ♂. Appetite of growing young estimated 35% of bodyweight, so that ♂ must catch 4–5 times own requirement to rear brood. Under stress, unusual food items (birds especially) may be taken (Holland: Cavé 1968). No good data from anywhere in Africa.

Breeding success in Africa unknown. In Britain averages about one less than clutch size (3·75 from 4·72: Brown 1976), but allowing for incubation failures and other losses, is probably *c*. 2·5 young/pair breeding. Ringing returns in Britain indicate 60–65% mortality in 1st winter, with only 11% of young surviving to 3rd year. Adult British Common Kestrels must live for 2 years as breeding birds to replace themselves. Comparable data from Africa entirely lacking.

References
Cavé, A. J. (1968).
Glutz von Blotzheim, U. N. *et al.* (1971).
Piechocki, R. (1959).

Plates 27 and 32
(Opp. pp. 434 and 467)

Falco rupicoloides Smith. Greater Kestrel; White-eyed Kestrel. Faucon aux yeux blancs.

Falco Rupicoloides A. Smith, 1829. S. Afr. Commercial Advertiser 4 (30 May); no locality = South Africa.

Range and Status. Resident; nominate *F. r. rupicoloides* frequent to common southern Africa in semi-arid grasslands and open country north to Zambezi, thence local, uncommon to S Tanzania. *F. r. arthuri* local, discontinuous distribution, generally uncommon, at best frequent, plains of E African highlands, Kenya and N Tanzania; *F. r. fieldi* Somalia, NE and SE Ethiopia possibly N Kenya south to Marsabit, usually uncommon, local and discontinuous distribution but locally common Somalia. Nowhere actually threatened; but small local E African populations could be exterminated by spread of African cultivation.

Description. *F. r. rupicoloides*: southern Africa. ADULT ♂: head and neck pale rufous, streaked black. Back, shoulders scapulars and upperwing-coverts darker rufous, boldly barred black. Rump and uppertail-coverts pale slate grey, barred

dark grey; tail slate grey, tipped white, with 5–6 black cross-bars. Below, pale fawn, breast and belly streaked brown, flanks barred dark brown-black, undertail-coverts almost white; underwing-coverts pale fawn to white. Wing-feathers above dark brown, inner webs banded rufous, below pale rufous tipped black. Cere and orbital ring yellow; eye cream or very pale brown; legs yellow. Sexes alike, ♀ somewhat heavier. SIZE: wing, ♂ 259–290 (276), ♀ 265–294 (281); tail, 144–187 (162); tarsus, 44–54 (50). WEIGHT: ♂ (14) 209–285 (260), ♀ (13) 240–295 (272) (A. C. Kemp, pers. comm.); unsexed (333) 181–334 (261) (Biggs *et al.* 1979).

IMMATURE: resembles adult, but flight feathers broadly tipped buff; flanks streaked; rump and tail rufous, barred black (not grey); cere, orbital ring blue-green, eye dark brown.
DOWNY YOUNG: pale pinkish or orange-buff; 2nd down brown; cere blue-green, legs pale yellow, eye dark brown.
F. r. arthuri (Gurney). N Tanzania, Kenya; similar, somewhat smaller: wing ♂ 245–257, ♀ 248–257. WEIGHT: ♂ (4) 165–191 (178), ♀ (2) 193, 207.
F. r. fieldi (Elliot). Somalia, NE and SE Ethiopia, south through semi-desert N Kenya, perhaps to Marsabit, where may intergrade with *arthuri*. Much paler, ground colour almost straw-colour. Smaller: wing ♂ 236–245, ♀ 247–252.

Field Characters. Resembles ♀ and immature of Common and Lesser Kestrels (*F. tinnunculus* and *F. naumanni*) but larger, appears more heavily barred and has larger head; adults immediately distinguishable in flight away by grey tail, heavily barred black. At close range when perched, white eye immediately diagnostic. Does not hover as often as Common or Lesser Kestrels, and in flight is swifter, more like a typical falcon, often speeding along close to ground. The Somali subspecies is much paler than any resident or migrant race of Common Kestrel.

Voice. Recorded (6). A variety of calls associated with different activities not yet described in literature. In 'flicker dive display' utters high-pitched 'kee-ke-rik, kee-ke-rik', or 'kee-ker-rik, keeerrr'. In alarm, a double note 'kwe-kwe'; in threat, a screaming 'waa-waa-wueh-wueeeh-wueeeh' becoming more high-pitched. Calls generally not like those of Common Kestrel in same areas.

Falco rupicoloides

General Habits. In South Africa well known, elsewhere little known. In South Africa found in almost any type of open country from *Acacia* woodland with 800 mm annual rainfall to semi-desert, even full desert in Namib; but prefers open grass plains of highveld, Transvaal and Orange Free State, and Karoo bush scrub where locally common. In E Africa and, as far as known, Ethiopia–Somalia, open grass plains and grassy subdeserts, dotted with acacias, avoiding thick bush. Is associated with distribution of Cape Rook *Corvus capensis*, normally breeding in their abandoned nests; but does not occur in entire range of Cape Rook, and is inexplicably local, occurring, for example, in grasslands south of Mount Longonot in Kenya, but not in similar grasslands 15–20 km to north (rooks occurring in both). Requires mixture of grasslands with some bare ground (Transvaal: A. C. Kemp, pers. comm.). Patches of fairly dense populations alternate with larger tracts where this falcon is altogether absent.

May either be permanent resident (e.g. some parts of Transvaal, Somalia and Kenya Rift Valley) or nomadic, appearing at irregular intervals and in varying numbers, to breed and then move away. In Somalia, NE Ethiopia *F. r. fieldi* frequents open grasslands dotted with acacias at 1000–1200 m, sometimes at lower altitudes, and is apparently regularly resident in same area, as in parts of Kenya Rift Valley. Apparently performs no regular migrations anywhere.

Often hunts from flight, sometimes hovering like Common Kestrel, but most often from perches. Typically seen perched on upper branches of dead tree, telegraph post, or electricity pylon; and probably has benefited from establishment of pylon lines, permitting breeding in areas devoid of tall trees. Catches most prey from perch by short swoop to ground; but also some from hovering flight, and may also fly swiftly close to ground through open bush, perhaps surprising and catching small birds in typical falcon manner. Most prey taken on ground, but some small birds in flight.

Food. Not quantitatively described; mainly invertebrates, but some small mammals, small reptiles (including small snakes) and some small birds (Kemp 1978).

Breeding Habits. Very well known (A. C. Kemp, in prep.). Where regularly resident, pairs are distributed in established defended territories of *c.* 5–6 km² with focal area round nest-site (Kemp 1978). ♂ is responsible for most territory maintenance, principally by perching in prominent positions, clearly visible to neighbours. May also advertise presence in territory by 'high hovering'—when hunting in flight in open country suddenly rises to 50 m or more and hovers. ♂ also soars, possibly with some display function, and near boundary attacks other kestrels which trespass. ♀ takes little part in such activity.

Nuptial displays consist of diving repeatedly with swerving flight (flicker-diving), mutual soaring, and diving towards mate with feet drooping. ♂ performs flicker dives more often than ♀, sometimes towards other kestrels, with aggressive function. ♀ takes part in mutual displays, but these performed by ♂ only once incubation has started. ♂ alighting at nest raises wings vertically above back; ♀ does so occasionally.

NEST: eggs are laid in abandoned or old nests of other birds, normally Cape Rook, sometimes other corvids, e.g. Somali Crow *Corvus ruficollis edithae* (Somalia). Recorded using nest of Secretary Bird *Sagittarius serpentarius* southern and E Africa; also those of Lappet-faced Vulture *Aegypius tracheliotus*. In Kenya, nests of Cape Rooks in low but extremely thorny *Acacia drepanolobium*, with galls also inhabited by ants (*Crematogaster* spp.) usually used. In Transvaal, nests of Cape Rooks either in eucalyptus plantations or on electricity pylons used; both enable breeding in areas formerly devoid of suitable sites. Distribution and breeding apparently related to that of Cape Rook, but does not occur in entire range of that species, varying locally in inexplicable manner, not connected with food supply.

EGGS: 3–5, probably laid on successive days (Hunt 1978); southern Africa mean (12 clutches) 3·83; E Africa 2–4, mean (8) 3·38; Somalia 3–5, usually 4 (Archer and Godman 1937; EANRC). Small for size of bird, rounded ovals, white or pale buff, normally less heavily marked red-brown and brown than those of Common Kestrel, ground colour usually visible, spots sometimes forming a cap at broad end. SIZE: (100, *F. r. rupicoloides*) 40·0–45·6 × 32·0–35·4 (43·3 × 34·5); (20, *F. r. fieldi*) 37·6–40·4 × 30·9–32·7 (39·1 × 31·8); (24, *F. r. arthuri*) av. 39·6 × 31·2; WEIGHT: 21–27; clutch of 4 *c.* 35% of ♀ bodyweight (Schönwetter 1960).

Laying dates: southern Africa Aug–Oct (late dry season); E Kenya, N Tanzania Feb–June, Aug, Nov, with peak Apr, May (main rains); Somalia Apr–mid June, peaking June, (just after main rains). In South Africa lays in dry season, elsewhere apparently in or after main rains, when grass long and insects abundant.

Incubation probably begins when clutch nearly complete, as hatching almost synchronous (Hunt 1978). Mainly by ♀, fed near nest by ♂, but ♂ takes some share by day. Incubation period: 33 days.

Chicks hatch almost together, each taking at least 24 h to break from egg. Weight *c.* 19 g at day 1; 32 day 3; 125–140 day 10, 240–275 day 17, 270–318 day 31, when can just fly if disturbed. Tarsus and bill continue growth up to end of fledging period. Other details of development of feathers not recorded. Would make 1st normal flight at 33–34 days (Hunt 1978).

In early fledging period ♀ remains on or near nest; she and brood then fed by ♂. She leaves nest to receive prey from him, feeding chicks herself. May be essential for her to remain near nest to repel possible predators (e.g. crows) which she vigorously attacks near nest. In later stages she also kills and brings prey to nest. ♂ exploits *c.* 50–65% of total territory when feeding brood, ♀ only immediate neighbourhood of nest (Kemp 1978). No available data on breeding success, but smaller young often die.

References

Hunt, C. (1978).
Kemp, A. C. (1978).

Plate 29

All birds depicted from below.

Aegypius tracheliotus Lappet-faced Vulture (p. 336)
1. ADULT.

Gyps africanus African White-backed Vulture (p. 326)
2. IMMATURE, 3. ADULT.

Sagittarius serpentarius Secretary Bird (p. 437)
4. ADULT.

Neophron percnopterus Egyptian Vulture (p. 322)
5. ADULT, 6. IMMATURE.

Gypaetus barbatus Lammergeier (p. 318)
7. IMMATURE, 8. ADULT.

Necrosyrtes monachus Hooded Vulture (p. 324)
9. ADULT.

Aegypius occipitalis White-headed Vulture (p. 338)
10. IMMATURE, 11. ADULT.

Gyps rueppellii Rüppell's Griffon (p. 329)
12. ADULT, 13. IMMATURE.

Gyps coprotheres Cape Vulture (p. 333)
14. ADULT.

Gypohierax angolensis Vulturine Fish Eagle
(p. 316)
15. ADULT, 16. IMMATURE.

Gyps fulvus European Griffon (p. 331)
17. ADULT, 18. IMMATURE.

Aegypius monachus Cinereous Vulture (p. 335)
19. ADULT.

Aquila verreauxi Verreaux's Eagle (p. 414)
20. ADULT, 21. IMMATURE.

Stephanoaetus coronatus Crowned Eagle (p. 429)
22. ADULT, 23. IMMATURE.

Haliaeetus vocifer African Fish Eagle (p. 312)
24. ADULT, 25. IMMATURE.

Aquila chrysaetos Golden Eagle (p. 412)
26. ADULT, 27. IMMATURE.

Aquila rapax orientalis Steppe Eagle (p. 407)
28. IMMATURE.

Aquila rapax rapax Tawny Eagle (p. 407)
29. ADULT (normal), 30. ADULT (pale).

Lophaetus occipitalis Long-crested Eagle (p. 426)
31. ADULT.

Aquila wahlbergi Wahlberg's Eagle (p. 410)
32. ADULT (dark phase), 33. ADULT (pale phase)

Terathopius ecaudatus Bateleur (p. 347)
34. IMMATURE, 35. ADULT ♀, 36. ADULT ♂.

Polemaetus bellicosus Martial Eagle (p. 433)
37. ADULT, 38. IMMATURE.

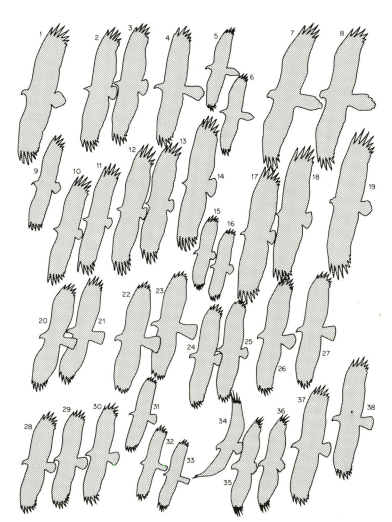

Plate 30

All birds are depicted from below.

Aquila pomarina Lesser Spotted Eagle (p. 405)
1. ADULT, 2. IMMATURE.

Hieraaetus spilogaster African Hawk Eagle (p. 419)
3. ADULT, 4. IMMATURE.

Hieraaetus pennatus Booted Eagle (p. 422)
5. ADULT (dark phase), 6. ADULT (pale phase).

Polyboroides typus African Harrier Hawk (p. 351)
7. ADULT.

Pernis apivorus Honey Buzzard (p. 299)
ADULTS—8. dark phase, 9. pale phase, 10. normal phase.

Spizaetus africanus Cassin's Hawk Eagle (p. 428)
11. IMMATURE, 12. ADULT.

Hieraaetus dubius Ayres' Hawk Eagle (p. 424)
13. ADULT, 14. IMMATURE.

Dryotriorchis spectabilis Congo Serpent Eagle (p. 350)
15. ADULT.

Butastur rufipennis Grasshopper Buzzard (p. 392)
16. ADULT.

Buteo oreophilus Mountain Buzzard (p. 397)
17. ADULT.

Buteo auguralis Red-necked Buzzard (p. 400)
18. ADULT.

Buteo buteo vulpinus Steppe Buzzard (p. 396)
19. ADULT.

Circaetus cinereus Brown Snake Eagle (p. 343)
20. ADULT.

Buteo rufofuscus augur Augur Buzzard (p. 402)
21. ADULT.

Buteo rufofuscus rufofuscus Jackal Buzzard (p. 401)
22. ADULT, 23. IMMATURE.

Milvus migrans Black Kite (p. 307)
24. ADULT.

Buteo rufinus Long-legged Buzzard (p. 398)
25. ADULT.

Circaetus gallicus beaudouini Beaudouin's Snake Eagle (p. 340)
26. ADULT.

Circaetus cinerascens Smaller Banded Snake Eagle (p. 346)
27. ADULT.

Circaetus fasciolatus Southern Banded Snake Eagle (p. 344)
28. ADULT.

Pandion haliaetus Osprey (p. 295)
29. ADULT.

Circaetus gallicus pectoralis Black-breasted Snake Eagle (p. 340)
30. ADULT, 31. IMMATURE.

Milvus milvus Red Kite (p. 310)
32. ADULT.

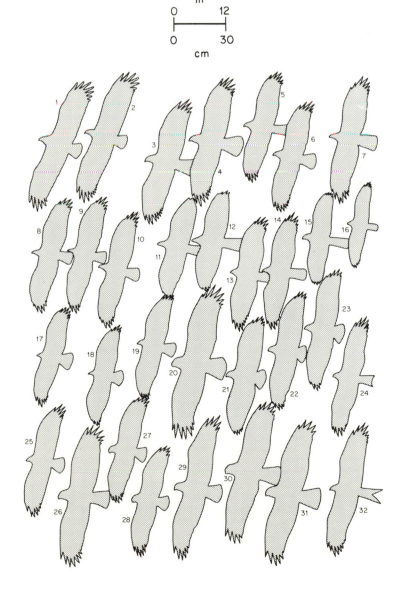

**Plates
27 and 32**
(Opp. pp. 434
and 467)

Falco alopex (Heuglin). Fox Kestrel. Faucon renard.

Tinnunculus alopex Heuglin, 1861. Ibis p. 69, pl. 3; Gallabat, Sudan.

Range and Status. Resident savannas and subdeserts of W tropical Africa from Ivory Coast east to Sudan, extreme W Ethiopia, thence south to NW Kenya west of Lake Turkana and N Uganda; recorded once south of equator at Lobo, Serengeti National Park. Commonest in semi-arid savanna, but breeds in Guinea woodlands at 8°N in Nigeria (Ilorin) and in arid subdesert W Kenya. Normally frequent to uncommon, occasionally common (N Chad, NW Kenya: Salvan 1968; Forbes-Watson 1963; EANRC). Not threatened. Absence from apparently suitable habitat, with no likely competitors south of equator and east of Rift Valley inexplicable.

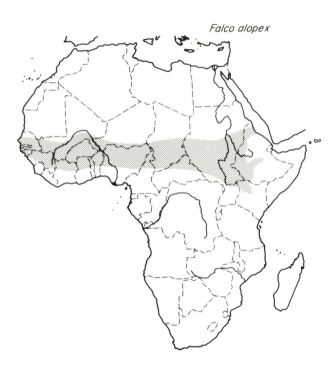

Falco alopex

Description. ADULT ♂: entire body above and below dark foxy red. Head with narrow back shaft streaks, broader on back and upperwing-coverts. Underparts rather pale red, narrowly streaked black except on belly, throat and thighs. Primaries black on outer webs, tipped black on inner; remainder of wing-feathers white with black wedge-shaped bars on inner webs. Tail with *c.* 15–17 narrow black bars. Cere and orbital ring yellow; eye pale brownish yellow; legs ochre-yellow. Sexes alike, ♀ slightly larger. SIZE: wing, ♂ 266–293, ♀ 269–308; tail, ♂ 180–212, ♀ 181–210; tarsus, ♂ 43–44, ♀ 43–45.

IMMATURE: resembles adult, but has heavier and clearer dark marking on wing-coverts and scapulars, and broader black tail bars.

DOWNY YOUNG: no accurate description, but said to be white.

Field Characters. Unmistakable, a slim, long-winged, very long-tailed dark reddish falcon, larger than the Common Kestrel *F. tinnunculus*. In flight, whitish underwing tipped black, and barred black on inner feathers distinctive. Tail long, not usually spread, with many narrow dark bars. Somewhat resembles Grasshopper Buzzard *Butastur rufipennis* in general shape; but immediately distinguished by lack of rufous patch in spread wing, and typical falcon-like flight.

Voice. Recorded (2a). High-pitched, rather rasping screeches, 'kreee-kreee-kreee', not readily distinguished from those of Common Kestrel; normally silent except near breeding sites, where vocal in display.

General Habits. Little known. Generally a rather uncommon solitary bird, found only near isolated rocky hills; in N Chad almost every rocky hill has a pair (Salvan 1968), and in NW Turkana recorded as semi-gregarious, breeding in loose colonies (EANRC). Normally found in lowlands with isolated hills, but in NW Ethiopia to at least 2200m. Sedentary in some areas, in S Nigeria at 8°N and most parts of W African savannas, is dry season migrant, arriving Oct, breeding Mar, and departing north again about June, in rains.

Is misnamed 'kestrel' as has few kestrel-like habits. Normally, in open country perches on trees, and catches prey by short swoop from perch to ground; does not hover. In general behaviour more a long-winged, long-tailed falcon than kestrel. Attends grass fires freely, catching disturbed insects in wing, and movements south to breed in W Africa are possibly connected with annual fires Nov–Feb.

Food. Little described; insects, small mammals, small lizards and possibly some small ground birds.

Breeding Habits. Little known. Breeds in holes and on sheltered ledges on steep rocky hills, usually inaccessible. Same site is used year after year; and in NW Kenya many pairs (20 +) recorded breeding in same locality (EANRC). In nuptial display, pair soar and fly round breeding haunt, screaming to one another, display resembling that of other small falcons.

EGGS: probably 2–3. Resemble those of kestrels, round ovals, buff or reddish, heavily marked with darker red spots. SIZE: (2) 39·6–40·0 × 31·6–32·3 (39·8 × 30·0); WEIGHT: *c.* 22 (Schönwetter 1960).

Laying dates: breeds Darfur and Sennar, Sudan June–Sept (rains); N Nigeria May (rains); NW Kenya (Turkana) May (rains). In Nigeria at 8°N apparently breeds in late dry season laying 6–15 Mar; with young in heavy rains, but eggs not seen, elsewhere apparently in rains. Only ♀ seen to incubate; nests in NW Kenya contained 1–2 small downy young in June (mid-year cool dry season). Better data needed.

References
Brown, L. H. and Amadon, D. (1968).
Serle, W. M. *et al.* (1977).

Falco ardosiaceus Vieillot. Grey Kestrel. Faucon ardoisé.

Falco Ardosiaceus Vieillot, 1823. Encycl. Meth., Orn. livr. 93, p. 1238; Senegal.

Range and Status. Resident lowland tropical savannas of Africa south of *c.* 12°N from Senegal east to Ethiopia (Eritrea), thence south to Angola, Zambia, as far south as Cunene and Okavango rivers, Botswana. Normally uncommon, locally frequent; numbers probably stable.

Description. ADULT ♂: entirely slate grey above and below, palest on throat, feathers with darker shaft streaks, most noticeable on head and neck. Primaries blackish, indistinctly mottled and barred white on inner webs. Tail grey, all but central feathers notched paler grey on inner webs. Cere and bare orbital skin bright yellow or greenish yellow; eye brown; legs bright yellow. Sexes alike, ♀ rather larger. SIZE: wing, ♂ 205–232, ♀ 235–251; tail, ♂ 128–152, ♀ 150–164; tarsus, ♂ 38–45, ♀ 40–47. WEIGHT: ♂ 205–255 (222), ♀ 240–250 (247) (Thiollay 1977a); ♂ (5) 215–250 (232), ♀ (5) 195–300 (248·4) (Biggs *et al.* 1979).

IMMATURE: resembles adult, paler grey on abdomen.

DOWNY CHICK: undescribed; probably buff or fawn becoming grey as feathers grow.

Field Characters. Unmistakable in most areas where it occurs, the only solid grey falcon. Could only be mistaken (and then only in E Africa) for Sooty Falcon *F. concolor* in adult plumage; but is smaller and paler, has short wings when folded not reaching tail tip, rather large conspicuous yellow cere and bare facial skin, obscurely barred wing-feathers and square tail. Mode of flight and habitat entirely different to those of Sooty Falcon, and does not normally occur in E African coastal areas where Sooty Falcon occurs on passage.

Voice. Not recorded. Normally silent. At nest utters a shrill 'keek-keek-keek'; also said to utter a rattling whistle 'like a squeaky bicycle'; and in alarm or when feeding young, a harsh staccato twittering or chattering (Loosemore 1963).

General Habits. Little known. A shy, silent, solitary species, apparently mainly or entirely sedentary where it occurs, not moving seasonally even in W Africa (Thiollay 1975a, b). Each individual requires at least 100–300 ha and the same individuals regularly frequent small parts of total range. The name 'kestrel' is a complete misnomer, as habits in no way resemble those of true kestrels. Seldom flies high above ground; is usually seen perched or flying low at speed over grassland or among trees, sweeping up to alight on another perch. Very swift direct flight entirely unlike that of kestrels.

Hunts either from high perches av. 15 m above ground (Thiollay 1977a), making short swift stoop to ground to catch, for example, grasshoppers and lizards; or alternatively in swift low flight over open grassland, pursuing any bird startled by passage. Never hovers like true kestrel, but occasionally soars up to 300 m above ground. Prefers to hunt over recently burned areas, or in more open patches among denser woodland, often associated with poor drainage. Most prey taken on ground, or in low herbage, but some birds possibly caught in flight (A. Root, in prep.). Aerial swarming

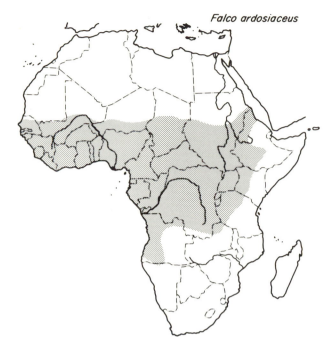

Falco ardosiaceus

alate termites taken but does not come to grass fires (Thiollay 1976a).

Food. E Africa mainly lizards, especially *Agama* spp. up to 25 cm long; some small rodents; birds, including young Temminck's Courser *Cursorius temminckii*, Yellow-throated Long-claw *Macronyx croceus*, *Cisticola* spp., which frequent open grassland; toads and frogs. Of 338 items (Ivory Coast), 287 insects, 20 reptiles, 9 small mammals, 3 birds (Thiollay 1978). Reported to take bats, but observed pairs in nests were always at roost in nests well before dark (A. Root, in prep.). Occasionally takes oil palm fruit. 58% of prey taken in open savanna, 27% in woodland, 15% in clearings in natural areas; and in cultivated areas often hunts in large fields (Thiollay 1977a).

Breeding Habits. Very well known. Pairs appear regularly spaced over available habitat, but are dependent on available Hamerkop nests (*Scopus umbretta*) for breeding, and do not breed in every area where Hamerkops found. In S Kenya 2 nests were 6 km apart, and pairs hunt up to 3 km from nest. In Ivory Coast 3 pairs regular in 2700 ha, suggesting home ranges of *c.* 1000 ha (A. Root, in prep; Thiollay 1975a).

Reputed to breed in holes in trees, and recently reported to do so in Ivory Coast (Thiollay 1976b) without positive proof. All recent proven records have been in Hamerkop nests (Serle 1943; Loosemore 1963; Dean 1974; A. Root, in prep.). Nest may be appropriated containing fertile Hamerkop eggs (Serle 1943) but is normally empty; since Hamerkops repeatedly build new nests, sufficient empty nests usually available (A. Root, in prep.). Very large tree holes might be needed. However, Grey Kestrels do not occur in whole of

Hamerkop's range and are uncommon generally, so association with Hamerkop not universal.

NEST: a scrape at back of chamber of Hamerkop nest, c. 60–75 cm from entrance; scrape is typically made in litter of bark chips, sometimes with Barn Owl *Tyto alba* pellets. To enter, falcon makes swift upward swoop straight into entrance hole, hangs for a moment, walks in. Both birds of pair roost in chamber in breeding season, but no details of courtship observed. Mating occurs inside nest, not observed (A. Root, in prep.).

EGGS: 3–5, probably laid at at least 24 h intervals; all recent Kenya records 4. Despite dark nest-site are not unusually light for falcon eggs; round ovals, pinkish buff, streaked and spotted rusty brown, markings heavier at narrow end in recent records. SIZE: (9) 40·4–43 × 31·6–34 (41 × 33·3) (Serle 1943); 38–40 × 32·33 (A. Root, in prep.).

Laying dates: Nigeria Apr; Sudan reported Mar–Apr; Uganda Apr; S Kenya Aug–Sept; Tanzania Oct; Angola Aug. South of equator lays in or late in dry season, in W Africa apparently in late dry–early rains.

Incubation does not begin with 1st egg, but probably on completion of clutch (as cold incomplete clutches found in Hamerkop nest later incubated: A. Root, in prep.). By ♀ mainly, but ♂ takes a share, sometimes for up to 40 min by day. ♂ feeds ♀, arriving with prey,

calling, whereupon she leaves and receives prey by aerial food pass with much calling; if ♀ then flies away, ♂ may then enter and incubate. ♀, wishing to return after absence, utters short chattering calls; ♂ then rises and leaves. Both sexes roost in nest during incubation period. Duration estimated at least 26, less than 31, days (A. Root, in prep.).

Hatching occurs over several days in some cases, which suggests incubation may begin before clutch complete. Food is offered to chicks within a few minutes of hatch, but one so offered food did not feed until 20 h old. ♀ brood chicks in nest continuously for first 5 days, but then leaves them to hunt by day. May catch grasshoppers within 5 min. Sheltered, secure nest-site probably permits ♀ to leave chicks unusually early. Details of chick development not described, and length of fledging period still unknown (A. Root, in prep.). Has been suggested that clumped or grouped nests in Hamerkop ranges, some occupied by Hamerkops themselves, others by Barn Owls, may limit availability of breeding sites and explain relative rarity of Grey Kestrel.

References
Loosemore, E. (1963).
Serle, W. M. (1943).

Plates 27 and 32
(Opp. pp. 434 and 467)

Falco dickinsoni Sclater. Dickinson's Kestrel. Faucon de Dickinson.

Falco dickinsoni P. L. Sclater, 1864. Proc. Zool. Soc. London, p. 248; Chibasa, Shire River, Malawi.

Range and Status. Resident tropical lowland savannas and cultivated areas from Tanzania south to Mozambique, Zambia, Zimbabwe, N Botswana, Angola, N Transvaal. Normally uncommon to frequent, locally common; partly associated with *Borassus* palms, especially with *Hyphaene*, generally requiring some form of palm tree but inexplicably absent Kenya Coast,

with abundant *Hyphaene* and coconuts. Numbers probably stable, and breeds in some densely populated areas, e.g. Zanzibar and Pemba.

Description. ADULT ♂: head and nape pale grey, tinged brown, finely streaked black, becoming blackish slate on back and upperwing-coverts, uppertail-coverts pale grey. No moustachial streak. Chin, throat pale grey, finely streaked blackish; breast, belly and underwing-coverts brownish grey streaked blackish, thighs plain grey, undertail-coverts paler grey. Primaries above black, barred grey or white, bars mottled on inner webs, secondaries plain slate grey; below primaries dark grey, barred whitish on inner webs, barring reduced on secondaries, innermost plain grey. Tail above pale grey, tipped grey, with broad subterminal and 6 narrower black bars, below pale grey barred blackish. Cere and large orbital ring yellow; eye brown; legs yellow. ♀ similar, little larger than ♂. SIZE: wing, 210–236; tail, 130–150; tarsus, 35–38. WEIGHT: (37) 167–246 (210); ♂ (3) 200, 169, 207; ♀ (2) 235, 207 (Biggs *et al.* 1979).

IMMATURE: like adult, but browner, especially below. Eye brown, cere blue-green, legs yellow.

DOWNY YOUNG: greyish white; bill pale pinkish mauve, paler at tip; legs yellow.

Field Characters. Unmistakable, a grey falcon with dark grey wings, paler head, conspicuously paler uppertail-coverts when flying away, and grey tail barred black.

Voice. Not recorded. Silent away from breeding sites, but then high-pitched 'keee-keee' when soliciting or presenting food and in alarm; subdued whistling from incubating bird; soft, mewing 'ki-ki-ki' when bringing

Falco dickinsoni

food. Said also to utter a whistle-like 'kill-koo' when flying together; chicks utter chirping 'weep-weep' and in distress a trill like that of a cricket. Young also utter a high scream 'keee-ee-ee' (Colebrook-Robjent and Tanner 1978; White 1945).

General Habits. Little known. A bird mainly of low-lying savannas, commonest along swampy flood plains. Prefers the neighbourhood of *Borassus* and especially *Hyphaene* palms, but not strictly confined to these, will also frequent coconut groves. Prefers open country not far from water to thickly wooded areas; very local within wide range.

Hunts almost entirely from perches, usually on dead palm stumps or trees. Makes slanting swoops to collect prey from ground 'with a certain amount of elegance but no great vigour' (White 1945). Occasionally hovers in flight, and may detect and catch prey then, but most prey taken from perches. Can fly fast, like Grey Kestrel *F. ardosiaceus*, but apparently catches few prey in fast flight. Is normally tame, easy to approach and observe. Mainly sedentary wherever it occurs, but individuals, perhaps immatures, may wander far from normal haunts. Post-breeding dispersion into adjacent woodlands occurs, birds attracted, for example, by grass fires or cane fires in sugar plantations.

Food. Insects, lizards, some small birds, small mammals, bats, amphibia, crabs all recorded. In non-breeding season insects probably most important, but in breeding season 46 recorded items included 18 large insects, 5 amphibia, 11 lizards, 1 bat, and 2 small rodents, suggesting breeding depends on capture of larger prey (Colebrook-Robjent and Tanner 1978).

Breeding Habits. Well known (Colebrook-Robjent and Tanner 1978). No marked nuptial display recorded, except probable mutual soaring over site, with greeting calls.

NEST: in hollows in crowns of dead palm trees, coconut trees (Zanzibar and Pemba), *Borassus*, *Hyphaene*, and baobabs (*Adansonia digitata*) from 7·5 to over 18 m above ground; normally inaccessible to humans, difficult to examine. 1 record in Hamerkop *Scopus umbretta* nest (Cook 1971). No actual nest built, eggs laid on

debris inside hollow. Same ♀ recorded laying in same hole 2 successive years.

EGGS: 1–4, laying interval not established; Zambia mean (12 clutches) 2·75. Colour variable, basically white, usually blotched and smeared pinkish brown to brick red, or buff, blotched and smeared purplish brown, sometimes stippled pale pinkish buff. SIZE: (27) 35·8–42·1 × 29·7–33·8 (39·6 × 31·2) (Colebrook-Robjent and Tanner 1978); also (7) 35·3–40·7 × 28·4–32 (38 × 30·8).

Laying dates: southern tropical Africa (Malawi, Zambia, Zimbabwe) July, Sept–Nov, probably peaking Sept (late dry season); Tanzania (Pemba Island) July–Aug (mid-year dry season); all known records suggest cycle completed mainly in dry season, young leaving nest early rains.

Scanty data indicate incubation mainly by ♀, fed by ♂, who may also catch prey and not take it to nest; but sexes hard to distinguish. Period unknown, probably over 30 days (Colebrook-Robjent and Tanner 1978).

Recently hatched chicks 1–2 days old weigh 25–28 g. At 22–23 days when partly-feathered, weigh 190–210 g, wings 121–123 mm long; 1st feathers probably emerge at *c*. 10–12 days. Clamber out of nest hole at 29–30 days; still cannot fly at 30–31 days, but are then active, often preening and flapping wings on edge of nest hole. Fledging period probably *c*. 33–34 days.

Days 1–6 an adult, probably ♀, remains in hole with chicks, fed by ♂. Thereafter little brooding by day (67/280 min, day 7–8); sheltered nest-site and warm climate probably permit early cessation of brooding. ♂ probably brings most prey up to day 20, but ♀ may also catch prey when off the nest, not brooding, and perhaps feed chicks. In last 10 days both sexes feed young; 11 items brought daily in 2 dawn–dark watches, (i) 10 large insects, 1 lizard; (ii) 5 small amphibia, 2 crickets, 1 rat, 2 chameleons, 1 unidentified. Adults then deliver prey to nest and leave at once.

Breeding success and survival rate not determined; eggs frequently infertile (9/33); in 1 nest 2 young reared from clutch of 3.

Reference
Colebrook-Robjent, J. F. R. and Tanner, I. C. (1978).

Falco chicquera **Daudin. Red-necked Falcon. Faucon chicquera.**

Falco chicquera Daudin, 1800. Traité d'Orn., 2, p. 121; Bengal.

Plates 27 and 32 (Opp. pp. 434 and 467)

Range and Status. 2 races *ruficollis* and *horsbrughi* resident from Senegal to Ethiopia (Eritrea), thence south to Cape Province. In most of Africa distribution is inexplicably linked to, and numbers limited by, availability of *Borassus* palms, as species only breeds in these and is not always found even where they occur; but in southern Africa (Zambia and Kalahari desert) locally more numerous, breeding in crows' nests in acacia trees. Thus, uncommon to rare most of Africa, regularly found only near *Borassus* clumps, locally fre-

quent southern Africa. Numbers probably stable or locally decreasing with felling of *Borassus* palms for cultivation. Nominate *chicquera* breeds India.

Description. *F. c. ruficollis* Swainson: Africa south of Sahara, south to Zambezi valley. ADULT ♂: crown, nape, sides of neck and hindneck dark rufous, finely streaked black; a blackish moustachial streak. Back, scapulars, upperwing-coverts blue-grey, barred black on wing-coverts and scapulars. Cheeks white, contrasting strongly with crown, separated by blackish

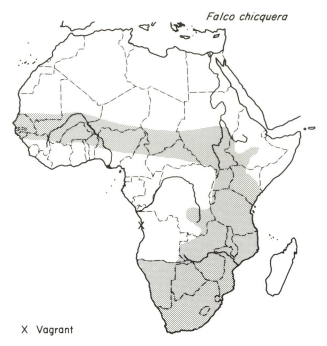

Falco chicquera

X Vagrant

line. Throat and upper breast white, separated from lower breast and belly by rufous band. Lower breast, belly, thighs and underwing-coverts white, barred black, bars finer on thighs. Primaries blackish brown, somewhat barred paler grey on inner webs, secondaries dark grey-brown; rest of wing-feathers below dark grey-brown, some paler mottling. Tail above blue-grey, with a broad subterminal and many narrower black bars, below paler grey, barred black. Cere and orbital ring yellow; eye light brown; legs yellow. Sexes alike, ♀ larger, SIZE: wing, ♂ 190–200 (1 specimen, 218), ♀ 212–236; tail, ♂ 116–125 (1 specimen, 145), ♀ 136–140; tarsus, ♂ (20) 33–39, ♀ (11) 38–40 (Bannerman 1930).

IMMATURE: resembles adult, generally duller and browner. Darker rufous, streaked black on head and neck, throat and breast streaked brown, breast with rufous wash, underparts more heavily barred. Cere and orbital ring yellow, eye brown, legs yellow, duller than adult.

DOWNY YOUNG: white; eye brown, cere and legs pale yellow.

F. c. horsbrughi Gunning and Roberts. South Africa, south of Zambesi to N Cape Province. Similar, rather larger: wing ♂ 203–227, ♀ 230–240. WEIGHT: ♂ (3) 139–160, ♀ (1) 305; unsexed (6) 178–255 (212); ♀ probably 190 or over, ♂ 139–178 (Biggs *et al.* 1979).

Field Characters.
A small, very swift, slim falcon, when perched easily recognized by rufous head and neck contrasting strongly with grey upperparts, barred black, and white underside, barred black, both in adult and immature plumage. Same size as a kestrel, but much swifter, longer-winged; rufous head and white, barred underside would immediately distinguish from African Hobby *F. cuvieri*. Addiction to *Borassus* palms in most areas also helps identification.

Voice.
Recorded (22a). Shrill, rasping, screaming calls 'tiririri, tirrrirrrirreee'; good details not available.

General habits.
Little known Africa, better known India (where also frequents *Borassus* palms). Pairs regularly frequent same clumps of *Borassus* (sometimes only 2–3 palms). Otherwise most often seen singly, flying high and fast, usually at 50–100 m, well above tree level, but may also fly fast and low through woodlands. Flies with quick wing-beats, seldom gliding for long, and seldom soars. Has been allied to Holarctic Merlin *F. columbarius*, as swift, small-sized, bird-killing falcon, but has no other real similarities to this sp. Hunts often in pairs, and is used in falconry to hunt, for example, quail.

In most of Africa, link with *Borassus* palms limits range to well-watered, tall grass savannas, often swampy flood plains. In subdesert Kalahari and N Cape Province habits different, there frequenting strips of *Acacia* woodland along watercourses, hunting in adjacent open country, breeding in abandoned nests of Cape Rook *Corvus capensis*. Similar habits recently suspected NW Kenya. In some tropical areas (Zambia) dependence on *Borassus* palms is less exclusive, pairs also frequenting riverine woodlands of *Acacia albida*, breeding in nests of Pied Crow *Corvus albus*. In such situations hunts over adjacent open floodplains, and in Kalahari often attacks doves drinking at waterholes.

Sedentary wherever it occurs, no migrations or even much local movement noted. A pair may hunt up to 3 km from nest-site, but if one is seen at all a nest-site is probably not distant. Roosts nightly at nest-site or in palm clump close to it, hunts in morning, often or usually returning to rest in palm clump at midday, and hunts again in evening. Sometimes hunts late towards dusk, then probably catching bats. Most prey is caught in air by swift chase in true falcon manner, some taken on ground.

Food.
Mainly small birds caught on wing, but readily attacks birds as big as itself, e.g. *Streptopelia* doves, Pied Kingfisher *Ceryle rudis*. Some lizards, small rodents taken on ground. Occasionally catches bats late in evening on wing (Fry 1964).

Breeding Habits.
Well known. Same favoured site is used annually for many years; pair can usually be located there daily. Early in breeding season pair becomes much more vocal, flying continually from perch to perch, screaming shrilly. Performs no obvious striking aerial manoeuvres, display mainly consisting of much mutual flying about and calling. Much calling occurs at nest-site finally selected, pair then perching there continually. Size of home range normally irrelevant in scattered isolated pairs in *Borassus* clumps; but in relatively high population density along Zambian rivers estimated 5·6 km²/pair (Colebrook-Robjent and Osborne 1974).

NEST: breeds either at base of living *Borassus* palm frond, near centre of tree, among debris or, more often, in old nests of corvids. In W Africa Speckled Pigeon *Columba guinea* (also here associated with *Borassus*) may provide nest structure. In Zambia nests of Pied Crow selected, in Kalahari of Cape Rook; crows' nests are old or abandoned, crows not ejected by falcons. In crows' nests, breeds at any height from 4–10 m above ground, in *Borassus* palms 11 m or over, up to 20 m, normally inaccessible.

EGGS: 2–4 recorded, normally 4, laying interval not established; Zambia mean (7 clutches) 3·6 (including 1 clutch of 2 laid by subadult); may re-lay if fresh eggs taken in same tree within 19 days. Rather elongated ovals, whitish, largely obscured by pinkish or yellowish brown, rather chalky texture, variously spotted, smeared and blotched with dull reddish brown; fade and become paler in incubation; are unlike eggs of Merlin. SIZE: (45, *F. c. ruficollis*, Zambia) 39·4–45·1 × 30·9–33·5 (42·0 × 32·0).

Laying dates: Nigeria Feb (dry); Sudan Mar, Apr (late dry); Kenya coast July, Aug (dry, cool); Zambia May, July–Sept, probably peaking Sept (end-rains, dry,

cool); Kalahari, Sept (dry). Throughout range breeds in dry season.

Incubation probably all or mainly by ♀; is fed at nest by ♂, who calls her off to receive prey. Few other details published, but incubation period (for a replacement clutch) recorded as 33 days, and fledging period for another nest 37 days (Colebrook-Robjent and Osborne 1974).

Reference
Colebrook-Robjent J. F. R. and Osborne, T. O. (1974).

Falco vespertinus Linnaeus. Red-footed Falcon. Faucon kobez.

Falco vespertinus Linnaeus, 1766. Syst. Nat. (12th ed.), 1, p. 129; 'Ingria' = former Gouvernement St Petersburg, Russia.

Plates 27 and 32
(Opp. pp. 434 and 467)

Range and Status. Palearctic winter migrant mainly to western half of Africa from NW Cape Province to Zambia, Zaïre and Angola. Locally common to very abundant, roosting in thousands together, and gregarious on migration, often with Eastern Red-footed Falcon *F. amurensis* and Lesser Kestrel *F. naumanni*. No recent decline noted.

Description. ADULT ♂: above, and sides of head, dark slate grey becoming almost black on uppertail-coverts. Chin throat, breast, flanks and underwing-coverts slate grey, paler, with dark shaft streaks on flanks. Lower belly, thighs and undertail-coverts dark chestnut, undertail-coverts sometimes marked slate grey. Wing-feathers above very dark grey, below grey, silvery on outer webs, shafts black. Tail above and below black. Bill bright orange, tipped blue-grey, cere and orbital ring and legs bright orange, eye blackish brown. ADULT ♀: forehead buff to pale chestnut on crown and nape with dark shaft streaks. Mantle and scapulars slate grey, barred blackish; upper mantle washed rufous. Back, rump and uppertail-coverts paler slate grey, barred blackish. Lores and a narrow band round eye black; a dark brown moustachial streak. Ear-coverts, sides of neck, chin and throat buff, becoming rufous or chestnut-buff, variable, on rest of underparts, including underwing-coverts; flanks finely streaked black, axillaries and underwing-coverts spotted dark brown. Primaries above blackish, tinged silver on outer webs, outer secondaries barred greyish black; on all inner webs comb-like pale grey marking, sometimes washed rufous; innermost secondaries slate, barred blackish; below grey, washed rufous, barred blackish. Tail above pale slate grey, tipped rufous, broadly banded black subterminally with *c.* 6 narrower blackish bars; below pale grey, subterminally banded and barred black. Bill yellowish at base; cere and orbital ring pale orange; eye brown; legs pale orange. Size similar, ♀ averages heavier. SIZE: wing, ♂ (66) 224–255 (239·7), ♀ (68) 232–255 (245·1); tail, ♂ 119–135 (127·3), ♀ 122–138 (129·3); tarsus, ♂ (24) 28–30·5 (29·4), ♀ (17) 28–30·5 (29·1). WEIGHT: ♂ (14) 115–169 (155·6), ♀ (10) 130–197·3 (171·2) (Glutz von Blotzheim *et al.* 1971).

IMMATURE: resembles ♀ but paler, more heavily marked below. Head, nape, ear-coverts and underside pale buff to creamy white, streaked on crown and underside, barred on underwing-coverts dark brown; undertail-coverts plain buff. Round eye and a large moustachial streak, black. Back and upperwing-coverts dark brownish grey, indistinctly barred blackish, edged rufous or buff. Wing-feathers dark brownish grey, edged buff, paler below. Tail blackish, tinged rufous above, more rufous below, basally barred whitish. Bill pale grey, cere, orbital ring and legs orange-red (paler than adults), eye dark brown.

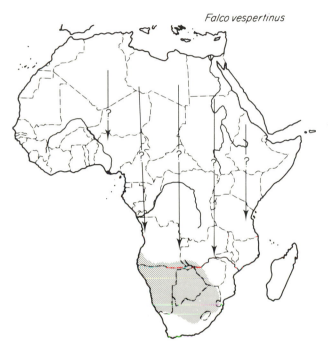

Falco vespertinus

Subadult ♂ has slate grey back, indistinctly barred black; retains some buff edges to wing-feathers; forehead, throat and cheeks whitish, streaked blackish, crown and nape slate grey; breast and belly light chestnut, finely streaked black; tail-quills dark slate, indistinctly barred black.

Field Characters. A small, very graceful falcon, smaller than Lesser Kestrel, often in company with it; flight more like that of Hobby *F. subbuteo*, however, more gliding, less hovering and poising, but often similar to kestrels. ♂♂ distinctive, general colour above and below dark slate grey, with dark chestnut thighs and belly; subadults have chestnut breast and belly. Distinguished from Eastern Red-footed Falcon by grey, not white underwing-coverts. ♀ distinguished from Lesser Kestrel by whitish head and neck, dark grey barred underparts; more rufous below, less heavily spotted than ♀ Eastern Red-footed Falcon. Immatures of both species more easily confused with kestrels, but immature of this species darker, duller, greyer above, especially on tail, than immature of Lesser Kestrel or

Common Kestrel *F. tinnunculus*. Distinctly smaller than Common Kestrel, with heavy black moustachial streak and area round eye, much paler cheeks and underside; rather more rufous than immature Eastern Red-footed Falcon. In mixed flocks presence of adults is helpful; single immatures difficult to identify with certainty.

Voice. Recorded (2a). In winter quarters silent except at communal roosts, where utters a babble of shrill high-pitched cries, rather resembling those of kestrels, but higher-pitched, sometimes more drawn out, 'kee-kee-kee' or 'keewii-keewii-keewii'. Voice not diagnostic without seeing bird as almost exactly the same as that of Eastern Red-footed Falcon.

General Habits. Well known. Enters Africa mainly through Middle East and Suez, many also crossing Mediterranean on broad front concentrated near Greek and Italian peninsulas, as far west as Italy. Having reached Africa travels largely unobserved to southern winter range in western subtropical and tropical savannas and grasslands, eastern limits W Kenya and E Zaïre, moving mainly west of Rift Valley. Southward migration begins in breeding quarters Central Europe late Aug, peaks late Sept, Oct, ending by end-Oct. Earliest arrivals reach E Africa early Oct, possibly moving south on rain fronts of inter-tropical convergence zone (as in Hobby) but less often seen. Reach main southern African winter quarters Nov-early Dec.

In winter quarters form large communal roosts sometimes of thousands, usually in groves of eucalyptus, often in towns or villages. Little specific detail recorded, but apparently leaves roosts at or soon after dawn, foraging in adjacent open country, returning to roost some time before dusk, circling in flocks over roost trees before settling for night. May intermingle to some extent with Eastern Red-footed Falcon, but winter ranges mainly separate; may also occur and roost with Lesser Kestrel. Prefers highveld cool grasslands and arid scrub, but recorded as far south and east as E Cape Province.

When hunting is generally more graceful in flight than Lesser Kestrel, resembling more Hobby, gliding gracefully with outspread wings, turning into wind and hovering less than kestrels. Often perches on dead trees, stumps, telegraph or fence posts. Few good details available on winter habits of either this or Eastern Red-footed Falcon; uncertain, for instance, whether same birds roost for long periods in same places or move from one to another.

Return migration begins late Feb, accelerates and peaks, towards end of rains in southern summer. Northward movement through tropics largely unobserved, flocks perhaps travelling at great height, seldom approaching ground. Reaches Mediterranean coastal areas Apr, where often in company with Lesser Kestrels in N African countries. Northward movement takes more westerly course than southward, crossing Mediterranean commonly as far west as Cyrenaica, rarely west to Morocco and Algeria. Is then less intensely gregarious than in winter quarters, travelling in flocks, often with Lesser Kestrels, roosting in groves of eucalyptus (Stanford 1954). Hunts close to ground, more in manner of Lesser Kestrel, flying head to wind, sometimes hovering, and often perching on telegraph lines and posts. Last stragglers pass Cape Bon June (Payn 1948), but most have left by mid-May, crossing Mediterranean on broad front.

Food. In Africa mainly insects, especially swarming alate termites caught on wing, and grasshoppers caught either on ground or in flight. May feed on alate termites towards dusk, returning to roost in late evening; grasshoppers may be caught more easily in heat of day, when more inclined to fly. In breeding quarters feeds largely on small amphibia, some small birds and mammals, and may take some of these items in winter quarters too. Food in winter quarters is dependent on wet conditions of southern summer rainfall regime.

Reference
Mayaud, N. (1957).

Plates 27 and 32
(Opp. pp. 434 and 467)

Falco amurensis Radde. Eastern Red-footed Falcon. Faucon de l'Amour.

Falco vespertinus var *amurensis* Radde, 1863. Reisen Süden Ost-Siberian, 2, p. 102; Zeya River, Amurland.

Range and Status. Palearctic winter migrant to E tropical Africa south to Cape Province. On migration and at communal roosts abundant or very abundant; otherwise frequent to common in winter quarters. Numbers probably stable.

Description. ADULT ♂: whole head, most of body and upperwing-coverts dark slate grey; underwing-coverts and axillaries white, thighs and undertail-coverts dark chestnut. Wing-feathers above and below blackish slate, tail above and below black. Cere, orbital ring and legs red; eye dark brown. ADULT ♀: forehead whitish, head and nape grey, streaked black; back and upperwing-coverts slate grey, barred black. A marked black moustachial streak, cheeks and throat plain creamy white. Rest of underside, including underwing-

coverts creamy white to pale buff, heavily spotted and barred blackish, undertail-coverts plain buff. Wing-feathers above and below blackish grey. Tail above and below slate grey barred black. Bill whitish; cere, orbital ring and legs orange (paler than ♂); eye dark brown. Slightly larger, averaging heavier than ♂. SIZE: wing, ♂ 218–235 (232), ♀ 225–242 (234·3); tail, ♂ 110–132 (119.8), ♀ 111–132 (123·1); WEIGHT: ♂ 97–155 (136), ♀ 111–188 (148).

IMMATURE: resembles adult ♀, but paler on head and neck; feathers of back and wings edged rufous or buff; cere, orbital ring and feet yellow-orange, rather than red or dark orange.

This species was formerly considered a race of Red-footed Falcon *F. vespertinus*, *F. v. amurensis* (Brown and Amadon 1968). Although the habits of both are very similar, e.g. breeding in abandoned corvid nests and migrating to southern tropical Africa, the very distinct colouration of the adult ♂

and ♀, the former with white underwing-coverts, and the extraordinary and still unexplained migration pattern, with largely separate winter ranges and widely disjunct breeding ranges suggests they should be regarded as a good species, the course adopted by Stresemann and Amadon (1979).

Field Characters. ♂ unmistakable, dark slate plumage contrasting strongly with white underwing-coverts. ♀ darker grey, especially on head and nape than ♀ Red-footed Falcon; paler, whitish, more heavily barred and spotted below. Easily distinguished from ♀ Lesser Kestrel *F. naumanni* by generally dark grey upperparts, white, conspicuously spotted underparts. Immatures have pale heads, very distinct moustachial streaks and heavily spotted undersides. Mode of flight more like Hobby *F. subbuteo* than kestrel, gliding near ground almost like large swift.

Voice. Not recorded. Indistinguishable from that of Red-footed Falcon, mainly silent except at communal roosts where extremely noisy, calling in confused babel of high-pitched cries, 'kiwee-kiwee'; locally called 'Kakuwikuwi', Malawi (Benson 1951).

General Habits. Well known. Performs the most extraordinary migrations of any raptor wintering in Africa. Breeds north of Himalayas; apparently enters Assam in large numbers autumn, thereafter largely disappearing until it reappears S Tanzania, Zambia, Malawi; believed to cross Indian Ocean unseen. A few may enter Africa, N Somalia (Obbia), but no major passage down Indian subcontinent or through Arabia noted autumn. Earliest arrivals reach E Africa Nov, most reaching winter quarters late Nov–early Dec; southward migration through tropical E Africa mainly unobserved, perhaps takes place at height, or even at night. Could not cross Indian Ocean without several nights uninterrupted flight.

Winters mainly Malawi south to Transvaal, foraging by day in savannas and grasslands, and roosting nightly in large numbers in certain favoured clumps of trees. Roosts may contain 4000–5000 birds (Benson 1951). Same clump of trees used year after year for many years, eucalyptus apparently selected in this century (did not exist in areas concerned much before 1900). May share roost with Pied Crow *Corvus albus*, possibly also with Lesser Kestrels and Red-footed Falcons to some extent; but range of these 2 mainly separate. May roost in larger numbers together just before northward migration Feb.

Behaviour described at 1 roost (Benson 1951) shows that falcons leave roost in groups together, almost immediately after dawn, all leaving within 10 min. Thereafter, hunt in groups or flocks over open country, feeding on grasshoppers caught on ground or in air, and especially on flying alate termites. Return to roost shortly before sunset, circling in large flocks over roost for 0·5–1 h before finally settling, when almost dark. 1 tree may harbour at least 100 individuals, and trees not occupied by crows are selected. Extremely noisy at roost, babel of calls almost deafening; continue to be noisy all night, and especially before dawn. Ground beneath roost is carpeted with feathers and droppings.

Falco amurensis

In Transvaal both Eastern Red-footed Falcons and Red-footed Falcons occur together, Eastern perhaps preferring more lowland warmer areas (ratio 100:1 on Springbok Flats cf. 3:1 on highveld: Tarboton 1978). Remains resident in winter for c. 3 months, late Nov–early Mar inclusive. Northward passage begins before end–Feb, intensifying early Mar. Again, movement is largely unobserved, presumably occurring at height and perhaps at night. However, as in Red-footed Falcon, takes more westerly course than southward autumn movement, some passing through N Tanzania and E Kenya, very large flocks sometimes then seen, usually high up. Recent observations Somalia (J. Ash, in prep.) demonstrate passage of flocks up to 100 together in spring, in company with European Rollers *Coracias garrulus*, Lesser and Common Kestrels and Hobbies; but most must leave from further south, probably south of equator, perhaps assisted by prevailing westerly winds. Those passing through Somalia, and thence via Arabia and Afghanistan, perhaps trapped by easterly winds, unable to cross ocean with favourable winds. Migration still largely a mystery, certainly the most remarkable of any raptor known.

Food. In Africa, probably entirely insects, mainly alate swarming termites and grasshoppers. This source of food associated with southern tropical rainfall regime, termites swarming Nov–Feb and grasshoppers then abundant. Both red-footed falcons lay down large quantities of fat prior to migration, and in Malawi are considered good to eat by Africans (confirmed by Benson 1951).

Reference
Benson, C. W. (1951).

Plate 28

Falco eleonorae Géné. Eleonora's Falcon. Faucon d'Eléonore.

(Opp. pp. 435)

Falco Eleonorae Gene, 1839. Rev. Zool., 2, p. 105; Sardinia.

Range and Status. Resident and Palearctic migrant. Breeds islands in Mediterranean and off Algerian and Moroccan coast (Mogador) south to Canaries. 1 inland colony suspected Tunisia, not confirmed (Vaughan 1961). Migrates in winter through Mediterranean and Red Sea to Somalia, and down E African coast, wintering mainly in Madagascar, some possibly inland in S Tanzania, Mozambique. Migration route still largely mysterious. Locally abundant at densely packed breeding colonies, normally uncommon to rare E Africa, but in flocks, Somalia, in migration. Total population estimated minimum 4825–5790; mean (most probable) 11,000–13,000; maximum 17,500–21,000; all figures include immatures (Walter 1979).

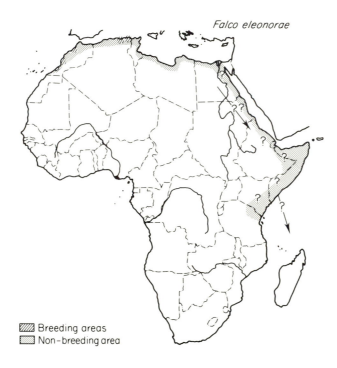

Falco eleonorae

▨ Breeding areas
▨ Non-breeding area

Description. ADULT ♂: normal pale phase—above, from crown to tail-coverts, including upperwing-coverts and wing-feathers, dark slaty or sooty brown, shafts darker. Ear-coverts, chin, throat buff, with broad dark brown moustachial streak. Rest of underside, pale or darker rufous, variable, streaked and sometimes washed black; underwing-coverts dark brown, a few rufous mottlings. Wing-feathers below, plain dark grey. Tail above dark slate grey, below dark grey indistinctly barred rufous. Cere, orbital ring and feet yellow; yellow brighter in ♂♂; eye dark brown. ♀ similar, slightly larger. SIZE: wing, ♂ 300–335 (316), ♀ 310–366 (327); tail, ♂ 175–210 (190), ♀ 175–210 (195); tarsus, ♂♀ 37–39; WEIGHT: ♂ av. 350, ♀ (11) 340–450 (388) (Walter 1979).

Dark phase—wholly dark blackish or dark grey-brown, paler on tail and darkest on crown and upperwing-coverts. About 25% of all birds throughout range are dark phase; on Mogador 28–29%; intermediate phases also occur.

IMMATURE: like adult with some feathers tipped buff, some rufous barring on inner secondaries and scapulars, 12–13 dull rufous bars in tail; below, like adult but, in pale phase, more heavily streaked black, tail and inner secondaries clearly barred rufous, outer wing-feathers indistinctly barred. Dark-phase immatures have barred tails, and some rufous

mottlings and bars above and below on body. Bars on wing and tail almost invisible in field.

DOWNY YOUNG: white to greyish white; chicks of dark phase not normally different. Eye dark brown, cere and orbital ring pale blue, legs pale yellow, becoming brighter with maturity. When partly-feathered, dark-phase young identifiable by barred undertail-coverts.

Field Characters. A large but very slim falcon, with distinctive, very graceful sailing or gliding flight, resembling a huge swift. As long as a Peregrine *F. peregrinus*, but much slimmer and lighter, with exceptionally long wings, when folded reaching tail-tip. From below in flight, very dark underwing-coverts contrasting with grey wing-feathers, appearing much paler against light (pale phase), diagnostic. Most resembles Hobby *F. subbuteo*, but plain unbarred wing-feathers contrasting with dark wing-coverts normally distinguish it from this species; Hobby has barred wing-feathers and bright rufous thighs and undertail-coverts. Immatures have spotted or barred underwing-coverts, but also have nearly plain wing-feathers, as normally seen in flight. Larger, longer-winged, flight more graceful and leisurely than that of Hobby. Dark-phase birds distinguished from ♂ Red-footed Falcon *F. vespertinus* by lack of chestnut thighs and bright red feet and cere, and by mode of flight. Larger, altogether much darker than adult Sooty Falcon *F. concolor*, but may be hard to distinguish it from this in field in winter quarters (Walter 1979; Porter *et al.* 1976).

Voice. Recorded (2a). In winter quarters silent. At breeding islands (where not likely to be mistaken for other species) various harsh strident screeching calls, associated with various activities described as follows (Walter 1979). Recognition or greeting 'kyark-kew-it' uttered in air, 2nd syllable higher-pitched; incubating birds respond to partners greeting call with low chuckle 'uig-uig-uig'. Territorial call 'hey-kyerk' or 'hey-kirk-kerk', last syllable accented, uttered flying near nest-site and in diving display. Display call, excited crowing 'krok-krak-kuuk' by ♂, accompanied by fanned tail in display. In copulation a short, repeated 'kirr, kirr' possibly uttered by both sexes; when transferring prey, loud shrill 'yee-err' 'yee-eet' or 'ky-rir-kyrt', uttered with back hunched, sometimes for several minutes; ♂ utters soft 'dyett-dyett' when arriving with prey. In alarm, intense, harsh 'kak-kek-kek' usually by ♀. Also by chicks more than 17 days old; in distress 'yeeert-yeert' uttered by ♀. When fighting in air, high-pitched, screaming 'tsee-err'. Various other sharp or harsh calls not associated with any particular activity, 'yi-et-yit'; 'did-dad-dad'; 'kyrr'; 'dewi'; 'tro-et' (like crane); a heron-like croak 'raerk'. Young when cold or in discomfort utter 'uip-wuip' in egg and when very small; 'pui-pui' begging when small, becoming higher-pitched, insistent 'pyeep-pyeep' when more than 10 days old; sharp 'pyep-pep, pyep' in alarm or anger; older chicks utter excited 'kyerr-kyerrr'. Illustrated by sonagrams in Walter (1979).

General Habits. Intimately known in breeding quarters, one of the most thoroughly studied raptors; little known on migration to winter quarters and in winter quarters; much still unexplained. Arrives in Mediterranean and N African breeding quarters in late Apr and early May, a few earlier; at Mogador (Morocco), main African breeding colony, may not arrive till mid-May. At first widely dispersed, hunting over adjacent mainland or large island areas (in Mediterranean) feeding mainly on insects. Breeding population concentrates near breeding colonies from late May onwards till breeding completed Oct; non-breeding immatures and subadults may remain more widely dispersed, but all apparently move to Mediterranean or other breeding areas.

During breeding season July–Oct, hunts migrants crossing Mediterranean, catching them over sea by various techniques; behaviour at Mogador somewhat different from most Aegean colonies. Hunting area extends 3–5 km from west to northeast of colony, birds caught either over island itself, or far out over sea. Hunting continues throughout day; ♂♂ leave colony soon after dawn, and most kills made 06·30 h (2·5 h after dawn) to 17·00 h (several hours before sunset). Methods include soaring at height, up to 1000 m above sea, stooping at any migrant seen; alternatively falcon flies head to wind beating wings at 160–200/min, at any height from 300–600 m or more above sea, stooping at prey from above; many falcons may attack same bird, 1 succeeding. Often also chase prey low over sea, even in rough weather. If successful, falcon immediately returns with prey to breeding island, attempting to avoid neighbours, which may try to pirate prey. May catch 1–3 birds/h, and often catch more than can be used at once by ♀ and brood, depositing them in 'larders'. At Mogador, more hunting low over waves seen that in Aegean colonies, *c.* 33% of all pursuits at low level; such variations possibly associated with weather conditions. Some hunting occurs at night, as falcons leave colony late in evening, perhaps catching nocturnal migrants over mainland; also known to hunt in moonlight.

Little known about hunting behaviour in winter quarters, but in Madagascar feeds mainly on insects, often caught late in evening; probably catches beetles attracted by flowering trees and alate termites. No consistent activity pattern recorded, but rain temporarily stops hunting. Immediately after rain catch prey high in air, eating it while still flying, in manner of Hobby.

All members of species apparently winter Madagascar, those from Mogador and Canaries apparently first moving north to northeast into Mediterranean, then through Mediterranean and Red Sea to Somalia. Autumn migration begins late Oct, and all have left by mid-Nov. except odd stragglers. Practically nothing known of route; but believed to travel round through Mediterranean and Red Sea rather than straight across continent from Mogador to Madagascar; none recorded W Africa, and few from mainland Africa. Possibly migrates at great height, unseen, without feeding, but may find aerial plankton (insects) *en route*. 1 caught in mist nets at Ngulia, Tsavo, E Kenya (Backhurst and Pearson 1980) supports this hypothesis. 1 ringed Mogador 11 Sept, 1960 recovered Madagascar mid-Jan, 1962, must have made the journey twice (Terrasse 1963).

Return migration begins late Feb, or Mar, most leaving Madagascar Mar, few remaining till Apr. Has been collected, Somalia 5–17 May (Archer and Godman 1937) and in Gulf of Suez 12 Apr (Meinertzhagen 1954), but otherwise passes unseen. All evidence indicates that migration both in autumn and spring occurs at great height, or over sea, in either case unlikely to be seen unless forced down to low level; however, may be overlooked among migrating flocks of Hobbies.

Food. In breeding colonies, entirely migrant birds, caught over sea or island. 101 species recorded, varying from small warblers to Manx Shearwaters *Puffinus puffinus* and swifts; commonest (Mogador) Woodchat Shrike *Lanius senator* (499), Whitethroat *Sylvia communis* (361), Pied Flycatcher *Ficedula hypoleucos* (138), Redstart *Phoenicurus phoenicurus* (395) and Sprosser *Luscinia megarhynchos* (326), these forming 80% by number of 2139 records (Walter 1968; Vaughan 1961). Others exceeding 50 include Grasshopper Warbler *Locustella naevia* (100), Melodious Warbler *Hippolaia polyglotta* (79), Subalpine Warbler *Sylvia cantillans* (53), European Swift *Apus apus* (88); recorded prey includes 24 quail. 90% of prey weigh 30 g or less, av. 24 g, at Mogador. Hoopoes *Upupa epops* important elsewhere, but seldom taken Mogador. Daily food requirement estimated 51·8 g/adult ♂; 34·5/adult ♀; 43·1/chick; and 129·4–258·8/pair with 1–4 young. Seasonal requirement (75 days, Mogador) 6·47 kg/pair, 8·84 kg–15·95 kg/pair with brood; whole Mogador colony 2153 kg/season. At av. prey weight 24 g, this equals 98,708 birds/season, Mogador.

In winter, apparently entirely insects; seasonal rainfall in Madagascar, with most rain Nov–Mar, results (as with Red-footed Falcons and Hobby) in abundant insects in winter range.

Breeding Habits. Very well known. Breeds in very dense colonies on rocky islands, 1 site also known on Moroccan mainland cliff. Overall breeding density Mogador (360 pairs) 5·6 pairs/ha (178·6 m²/pair) but locally much denser, 68–70 m²/pair with nearest nests less than 2 m apart, av. *c.* 10 m apart. Factors influencing very dense populations include availability of holes and inability to see near neighbours when on nest. Defended territory very small, but may be larger in more open sites than on cliffs with many deep holes, crannies and projections.

Display principally aerial, consists of flying about and screaming; ♂♂ may perform undulating display flights, or dive at ♀ who may roll and present claws. Many birds perform together. ♂ selects nest-site and advertises himself by repeatedly taking off, making short flight, returning, screaming, sometimes with prey which he may eat, hide, or abandon. Perched ♂ bends forward, raises shoulders of wings, and holds tail above back, widely fanned, uttering rooster-like crowing call for several seconds. After pairing, similar display used to repel other ♂♂ from site. Many pairs already formed before arrival, some birds as in other years, but single ♂♂ attract ♀♀, and cement pair-bond by frequent feeding. ♂ also rhythmically bows head and neck to feet, each bow lasting c. 1 s, sometimes up to 100 bows/min.

Later, bowing precedes copulation; bowing probably has appeasement element, also used when ♂ desires prey in possession of ♀. ♀ soliciting copulation approaches ♂ with body horizontal, repeated 'yeerk-yer-yeek' calls; ♂ flies or jumps to her back, balancing with wings; ♀ crouches, lifts tail (usually to left) and ♂ lowers his to achieve union. Copulation lasts 8–12 s., ♂ then dismounts immediately or may remain 10–15 s on back of ♀. Copulation occurs most in morning and evening, 5–6 times in 24 h, sometimes up to 12–17. Pair-bond lasts at least 1 season, sometimes more. Same birds often return to same site in such cases (Ristow 1975).

NEST: on Mogador, most nest-sites in vertical cliffs with numerous holes or crannies, sometimes in deep holes with eggs not visible from exterior. No structure built, eggs laid on bare earth, or collection of small stones. Elsewhere may breed in open site on top of flat island, under bush or ledge of rock. Cliff sites Moroccan mainland similar to those in Mogador, in holes and crannies.

EGGS: 1–4, at intervals of 2 days or more; clutch of 4 takes 7–8 days to lay. Mogador clutches average larger than Aegean, mean (148) 2·98. Rounded ovals, pale reddish ground, more or less obscured by darker red spots, blotches, sometimes forming cap at narrow or broad end; some eggs yellowish or whitish. SIZE: (143) 38·5–45·0 × 30·0–36·0 (42·1 × 33·2). WEIGHT: fresh, calculated 26 g (Schönwetter 1960), near end of incubation 19·5–29·5 (24·2) (Walter 1979).

Laying dates: late July, sometimes early Aug; all between 10 July and 7 Aug, laying largely synchronized.

Incubation begins before completion of clutch. Mainly or entirely by ♀, fed near nest by ♂, who may occasionally incubate by day, associated with feeding ♀. Period: 30–33 days Mogador, av. 31 days (Walter 1979), cf. earlier estimate of 28 days (Vaughan 1961).

Hatching occurs over 24 h each chick, occasionally 2–4 days; clutch hatches in 1–5 days. Most chicks, Mogador, hatch 15–25 Aug, averaging rather earlier than Mediterranean colonies. Newly hatched chicks weigh 15–22 g day 1; av. 42 day 5; 140 day 10; 372 day

20; 450–490 day 30; and reach maximum weight 470–510 days 35–40 (c. 130–135% av. adult weight), then decreasing to 425–500 at 45 days. No sibling aggression observed, any chicks lost dying of starvation, occasionally predation; inter alia, eaten by humans. When first hatched, white, half-blind; 1st feathers emerge c. day 12; partly feathered 22 days, when tarsus and bill almost fully developed; thereafter main growth in wings and tail. Make earliest flights at 37 days, usually somewhat later, especially very overweight young.

♀ remains on nest with young in early stages; she and young dependent on ♂. After day 10 (when 2nd down developed) ♀ does not brood chicks much but remains in vicinity of nest, receiving food from ♂. ♂ must increase rate of killing to 2–4 times that of incubation period to satisfy brood. He visits nest, but not observed to feed chicks. ♀ receives prey and feeds young. ♀ remains near nest, and in presence of intruders calls loudly but is not very aggressive; may swoop low but does not normally strike humans.

Young remain only c. 15 days in colony before leaving for winter quarters. Most have left by end-October, a few remaining until early Nov. Ringing returns suggest random dispersal of young, 1 from Mogador recovered central Spain (Terrasse 1963), and others from Mediterranean colonies also to north-northeast, north-northwest, and west of ringing location; all other recoveries Madagascar.

Breeding success Mogador better than in Mediterranean colonies. From 53 clutches with 160 eggs, 142 young hatched (88·7%), and 134 young flew (83·7% of eggs, 94·4% of young hatched); equivalent to 2·53 young/breeding pair and 2·63/successful nest (51). Success better per egg laid in larger clutches, av. 0.61 young-egg in clutch of 1 and 0·9/egg in clutch of 4, suggesting chicks of older, more experienced birds, laying larger clutches, survive better. No data on longevity or age at 1st breeding, but most probably breed first when 2 years old; at 75% mortality before sexual maturity adults must live av. 3 years as adults to maintain stable population.

References
Vaughan, R. (1961).
Walter, H. (1979).

Plates 28 and 32 (Opp. pp. 435 and 467)

Falco concolor Temminck. Sooty Falcon. Faucon concolore.

Falco concolor Temminck, 1825. Pl. Col. livr. 56, pl. 330 and text—Senegal etc.; (restricted to Barquan Is, Gulf of Aqaba, by Vaurie, 1965, Birds Pal. Fauna, Non-Passeriformes, p. 227).

Range and Status. Resident; breeds Libyan desert on mainland, and on islands in Red Sea and Persian Gulf. In non-breeding season, Nov–Mar, E African coast as far south as Natal, wintering especially Madagascar; sometimes seen also inland in Sudan, Lake Victoria basin and Rift Valley, Kenya. No good estimate of breeding numbers, but in winter quarters outnumbers Eleonora's Falcon *F. eleonorae* by up to 10:1 (Walter 1979), suggesting main breeding habitats of Sooty Falcons still

undiscovered. At 10:1 total population would be 50,000–200,000 (mean c. 120,000); no such breeding numbers known.

Description. ADULT ♂: above and below, slate grey, paler on upperwing-coverts, scapulars, rump and uppertail-coverts, with narrow blackish shaft streaks. Below, a small buff patch on throat and a blackish spot below eye. Wing-feathers above and below black, contrasting with grey coverts; tail dark slate grey above and below, unbarred. Cere and orbital ring lemon yellow; eye dark brown; legs orange-yellow. ♀ similar; slightly larger. SIZE: wing, ♂ 264–283 (274), ♀ 273–297 (285); tail, ♂ 127–135 (131), ♀ 130–141 (136); tarsus, ♂ 32–35·5 (34), ♀ 34–36·5 (34·8).

IMMATURE: browner than adult above, some feathers edged buff or rufous. Below buff, heavily streaked and blotched slate grey or blackish, sometimes obscuring ground colour. Cere and legs yellow, eye brown.

A dark phase occurs, darker slate grey in adult; immatures of this phase perhaps resemble normal adults, generally slate grey.

DOWNY YOUNG: white; legs, cere and bill pinkish.

Field Characters. Resembles Grey Kestrel *F. ardosiaceus*, but distinguished from this species by much longer wings, more slender build, smaller bill and less obvious yellow cere and orbital skin, folded wings reaching tail-tip; wing-feathers plain black, not barred, tail slightly wedge-shaped, not square. Does not normally occur in same habitat. Adults easily confused with dark-phase Eleonora's Falcon but black wing-feathers contrasting with relatively pale underwing-coverts, smaller size and relatively shorter tail useful. Immature resembles pale-phase Eleonora's Falcon or Hobby *F. subbuteo*, but more heavily streaked below; hard to distinguish with certainty at any distance.

Voice. Not recorded, or well described. Sharp, plaintive, kestrel-like calls; a skirling screech not unlike curlew in alarm; and a staccato chatter when disturbed near nest (Clapham 1964).

General Habits. Little known. An active, fast, slim falcon, in many ways resembling Eleonora's Falcon, but apparently less gregarious; occurs in same areas in Madagascar in winter, but commoner on African mainland. Breeds singly in Libyan desert, and colonially on islands in Red Sea and elsewhere. In breeding grounds frequents chiefly rocky areas or old coral cliffs, but also sandy areas with rock outcrops; and in Libya completely barren desert. Winter quarters entirely different, moist savannas, even forest or forest edges with copious rainfall. Here estimated to occur at densities of up to 5/km² (Walter 1979) in W Madagascar, in rainfall of 750–800 mm/year.

Migrates south when breeding complete (late Oct–Nov); most travel south through Somalia–Kenya coastal thornbush, stopping briefly *en route* and feeding. Some, possibly from N Sahara breeding localities, travel down Nile to Sudan and Lake Victoria basin, and perhaps also down Rift Valley through Ethiopia–Kenya; but few definite data. On passage through coastal Kenya moves in small flocks and may be locally common for about a month (I. S. C. Parker, pers. comm.) Feeds freely on migration, especially on birds.

Most winter in Madagascar, but recent records indicate many in coastal Mozambique, some as far south as Natal (A. Vittery and T. Oatley, pers. comm.). In winter quarters hunts mainly from perches, usually on tall baobabs or dead upper branches of tall trees, hawking insects; active soon after first light. Like Eleonora's Falcon, unable to hunt in heavy rain, but soon afterwards hawks insects high in air, eating them in flight.

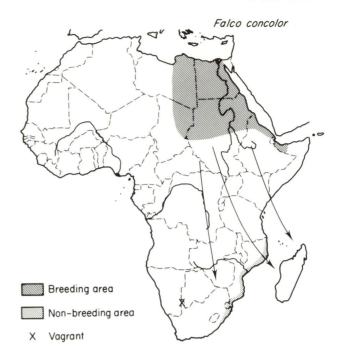

Falco concolor

Breeding area

Non-breeding area

X Vagrant

Normal method of hunting in breeding quarters is not aerial, but from perches on rocks or small trees. Catches birds flying below it with short swift stoop and, if flying high above, leaves perch, gains height till above prey, then attacks; may also sometimes catch prey in direct upward flight from perch (Clapham 1964). Most prey apparently caught over land, not over sea (cf. Eleonora's Falcon). Often hunts in pairs, and when adjacent pairs pursue same prey, waste time and effort repelling each other. Fails to kill more often than it succeeds, but no good quantitative data on hunting success available.

Northward return migration begins late Feb, continuing in Mar; scarcely observed, but perhaps overlooked among, for example, flocks of Hobbies on northward passage. Date of arrival at Red Sea breeding ground unknown.

Food. On breeding islands mainly birds, especially bee-eaters, Hoopoes *Upupa epops*, orioles, some small waders. Also takes small warblers, *Phylloscopus* and *Sylvia* spp., Yellow Wagtails *Motacilla flava* and wheatears, *Oenanthe* spp. Prey probably varies according to availability, but data suggest preference for larger species relative to falcon's weight than in Eleonora's Falcon. On southward migration through Kenya coastal savannas often takes small birds, notably *Quelea* spp. (I. S. C. Parker, pers. comm.). In winter quarters in Madagascar feeds almost exclusively on insects, as in Eleonora's Falcon. Also recorded to take bats and late flying insects, and often hunts in dusk. On breeding islands does not store surplus food in 'larders' as Eleonora's Falcon does, possibly because intense heat would soon render them putrid (Clapham 1964). Taking relatively large prey would also make larders less necessary.

Breeding Habits. Well known. Breeds on islands in Red Sea, preferring rocky and stony areas; not in tight-packed colonies, pairs at least 40–50 m apart. Nothing known about arrival on islands or early courtship.

NEST: usually in clefts or holes in cliffs near sea, but sometimes under euphorbias or rocks up to 120 m from sea, possibly further. A nest in heart of Libyan desert was under low cairn stones; some shelter and shade apparently essential, heat of nest-site normally intense in Aug–Sept (Booth 1961; Clapham 1964).

EGGS: 1–4, usually 2–3; mean (11 clutches) 2·55 (Clapham 1964). Rounded ovals resembling kestrel eggs, but paler buff, sometimes almost white, spotted ochre-brown. SIZE: (9) 38·6–40·9 × 29·7–32·4 (40·1 × 31·2) (Schönwetter 1960); WEIGHT: *c.* 22. Laying interval not known, but chicks of markedly different sizes suggest at least 2 days.

Laying dates: Libya Aug; Dahlac Island, Red Sea, July, Aug.

Adults very aggressive towards humans near nest-site, swooping and striking intruders freely. Incubation apparently begins 1st egg, perhaps because of intense heat. Share of sexes unknown, but both have brood patches (von Heuglin 1869). Normally all eggs hatch (Clapham 1964) and broods of 2–4 small young suggest breeding success probably good; no other details available. Young leave nest early Oct, all soon migrating south.

References

Booth, B. D. McD. (1961).
Clapham, C. S. (1964).

Plate 27

(Opp. p. 434)

Falco columbarius Linnaeus. Merlin. Faucon émerillon.

Falco columbarius Linnaeus, 1758. Syst. Nat. (10th ed.), 1, p. 90; South Carolina (ex Catesby).

Range and Status. Scarce Palearctic winter migrant to NW Africa (*F. c. aesalon*), straggling in winter to Egypt (*F. c. insignis*). Numbers of *F. c. aesalon* much reduced in breeding range in recent years largely because of pesticides; this probably reflected in fewer recent records NW Africa.

Description. *F. c. aesalon* Tunstall: Europe to N Russia, W Siberia. ADULT ♂: crown dark slate finely streaked black; an indistinct eyebrow and frontal band whitish, streaked black; a broad rufous moustachial streak, tipped blackish. Rest of upperparts bluish slate, darkest on mantle, paler on rump and uppertail-coverts, finely streaked black; scapulars greyer, sometimes barred brown. Lores white, tipped black, forming a blackish line in front of eye; cheeks and ear-coverts greyish white, marked rufous, streaked black, ear-coverts tipped slate. Chin and throat buff or greyish white streaked blackish on throat; rest of underparts pale rufous, fading to whitish in

Falco columbarius

old plumage, finely streaked blackish brown, streaks forming drop-shaped spots on flanks; underwing-coverts barred and streaked dark brown and rufous, undertail-coverts plain buff. Primaries greyish black, tipped pale grey, barred greyish on inner webs; secondaries greyer, less barred. Tail basally slate grey, paler on inner webs, tipped whitish, with broad subterminal and incomplete black bars on inner webs; below barred grey and whitish, with broad subterminal blackish band. Cere, orbital skin and legs yellow; eye dark brown. ADULT ♀: generally browner, more heavily marked than ♂. Has more pronounced whitish forehead and eyebrow; rest of upperparts brown rather than slate, streaked black, some feathers tipped rufous, incompletely barred on mantle and scapulars; greyer, sometimes slate, on back and rump; cheeks and ear-coverts whitish streaked brown. A blackish line before eye, and faint dark brown moustachial streak. Underside white to creamy white streaked brown, finely on throat, mid-belly and undertail-coverts, heaviest on breast and upper belly, irregular broad brown bars on flanks; axillaries and underwing-coverts whitish, barred rufous. Primaries, secondaries and primary upperwing-coverts dark brown tipped buff, spotted on outer and barred on inner webs rufous to buff; below barred dark brown and buff. Tail above dark brown, tipped creamy, barred buff to rufous, or ashy grey on central feathers; below grey barred grey-brown to whitish on both webs. Larger than ♂. SIZE: wing, ♂ 193–210, ♀ 210–233; tail, ♂ 116–127, ♀ 133–141 (137); tarsus, 35–39. WEIGHT: ♂ 150–215 (186·5), ♀ 187–255 (231·5).

IMMATURE: like ♀, but lacks grey rump and uppertail-coverts; eye dark brown, cere and orbital skin bluish, feet yellow. Immature ♂ acquires adult plumage in 1 moult, beginning at *c.* 9 months, complete by 17 months; may have bred by then.

F. c. insignis (Clark). Breeds Siberia, Turkestan, N India to Japan, some Egypt in winter; paler. SIZE: wing ♂ 190–208 (199·2), ♀ 220–231 (225·1); WEIGHT: ♂ (2) 164, 190; ♀ (4) 155–205 (178).

Field Characters. Small, stockily built, very swift falcons, ♂♂ appearing scarcely larger than large thrush. Within winter range could only be confused with kestrels; but has slate grey black (dark brown in ♀), is more compact, with swift, sometimes undulating flight. From Hobbies *F. subbuteo* (unlikely to occur in winter

---

in range) easily distinguished by broader, less pointed wings and slaty colour, especially in ♂♂, no red thighs. More likely to be confused with European Sparrowhawk *Accipiter nisus*, but has pointed wings, relatively short tail and swift, direct flight, normally distinctive.

Voice. Recorded (2a). In Africa silent; if heard, commonest call of ♂ is high-pitched rapid 'ki-ki-ki-ki-kee', of ♀, lower-pitched 'kek-ek-ek-ek-ek'.

General Habits and Food. Scarcely known N Africa. Frequents lowlands and coastal marshes in most areas in winter, often perching on ground or low posts. Feeds on birds caught in swift pursuit flight, repeatedly rising above and diving at quarry at great speed; alternatively flies low above ground and, if surprising prey, pursues it swiftly, jinking and twisting with great agility. Most prey caught in flight; young may feed on large insects before learning to catch birds.

Falco subbuteo Linnaeus. Hobby. Faucon hobereau.

Plate 28

Falco Subbuteo Linnaeus, 1758. Syst. Nat. (10th ed.), p. 89; Sweden.

(Opp. p. 435)

Range and Status. Resident and Palearctic migrant. Breeds NW Africa in summer, May–Sept; migrant in winter Oct–Apr, mainly through E and NE Africa to southern tropical Africa, some south to South Africa. Locally common to abundant on passage, common to frequent in winter quarters, sometimes commonest small falcon; no recent declines noted.

Description. *F. s. subbuteo* Linnaeus: Europe and Asia, migrant to Africa. ADULT ♂: narrow eyebrow and forehead white; crown, nape, back and upperwing-coverts dark slaty to blackish brown, with an indistinct collar on nape whitish, edged rufous, some feathers edged rufous. Cheeks and sides of neck white, with a broad black moustachial streak, and another, less regular, behind ear-coverts. Throat, upper breast, upper belly and flanks, underwing-coverts and axillaries buff to pale rufous, boldly streaked or spotted blackish. Lower belly, thighs, undertail-coverts reddish brown, finely streaked black. Wing-feathers above blackish brown, tinged slaty, with tooth-like buff or rufous bars on inner webs; below grey, barred pale rufous. Tail above brownish slate, tipped buff, all but central feathers barred rufous to buff on inner webs; below grey, barred rufous. Cere, gape, orbital skin and legs bright yellow; eye dark brown. ♀ similar, usually rather browner, more heavily streaked below, especially on thighs and undertail coverts; larger. SIZE: wing, ♂ 240–272, usually 247–272 (255·5), ♀ 255–286 (268·7); tail, ♂ 116–140 (130), ♀ 125–142 (134); tarsus, ♂ 32–25·5 (34·3), ♀ 33–37·5 (35·2). WEIGHT: ♂ (11) 131–222 (200), ♀ (10) 141–225 (229) (Brown and Amadon 1968; Glutz von Blotzheim *et al.* 1971).

IMMATURE: resembles adult, but browner, less blackish above, feathers edged rufous, more strongly barred rufous on scapulars. Below, more heavily streaked blackish, thighs, lower belly and undertail-coverts pale rufous. Wing- and tail-feathers darker than in adult, tipped buff to rufous, with more rufous barring and on tail bars on outer as well as inner webs. Cere and orbital ring pale blue-grey, legs yellow, eye dark brown.

DOWNY YOUNG: above pale buff, below pure white; 2nd down coarser, greyer; cere and legs pale yellow, eye brown.

Field Characters. A slim, graceful, long-winged falcon about size of Common Kestrel *F. tinnunculus* or slightly larger, but with shorter tail. Leisurely, swift-like flight, gently stroking air with wings rather than rapidly flapping them. In flight, appears generally dark with whitish streaked underparts; rufous thighs and undertail-coverts only obvious at close range. Distinguished from African Hobby *F. cuvieri* in all plumages by pale streaked upper breast, belly and underwing-coverts; from adult pale-phase Eleonora's Falcon *F. eleonorae* by much smaller size, pale streaked underwing-coverts, not

Falco subbuteo

☒ Breeding areas
▦ Non-breeding area

contrasting strongly with barred wing-feathers. Immatures more difficult to distinguish from immature pale-phase Eleonora's and immature Sooty Falcon *F. concolor*, but smaller, shorter-winged than Eleonora's Falcon, with paler, less contrasting underwing-coverts, and marked (often double) moustachial streaks on face and cheek. Moustachial streak also distinguishes it from Merlin *F. columbarius*. About same size as immature Sooty Falcon, but less slaty above, less heavily streaked below, and with more marked facial and moustachial streaks. Such differences often hard to detect except at close range in immatures, not easily identified.

Voice. Recorded (2a). In Africa apparently completely silent. In breeding quarters (Europe) often vocal; commonest call 'kew-kew-kew-kew-kew' repeated. In display an excited bisyllabic 'kirik-kirik' or 'whitsyoo'; a sharp, incisive 'keek' and a subdued 'wer-wer-wer-wer-wee-wee' with food. Begging young 'wee-wee-wee'. Calls high-pitched, with a petulant timbre, not loud; rather distinct from those of other small falcons breeding in same area.

(*Continued on p. 468.*)

Plate 31

Melierax metabates Dark Chanting Goshawk
(p. 368)
1. ADULT from above, 2. IMMATURE from below.

Micronisus gabar Gabar Goshawk (p. 366)
3. ADULT (normal phase) from above, 4. from
below, 5. ADULT (melanistic phase).

Accipiter rufiventris Rufous-chested Sparrowhawk
(p. 386)
6. ADULT from above, 7. from below.

Accipiter castanilius Chestnut-flanked Sparrowhawk
(p. 376)
8. ADULT from above, 9. from below.

Accipiter badius Shikra (p. 376)
10. ADULT from above, 11. from below.

Accipiter ovampensis Ovampo Sparrowhawk
(p. 382)
12. ADULT from above, 13. from below.

Accipiter minullus African Little Sparrowhawk (p. 380)
14. ADULT from above, 15. from below.

Accipiter erythropus Red-thighed Sparrowhawk
(p. 379)
16. ADULT from above, 17. from below.

Aviceda cuculoides African Cuckoo Falcon (p. 298)
18. ADULT from below, 19. IMMATURE from below.

Accipiter tachiro African Goshawk (p. 373)
20. ADULT from above, 21. from below.

Machaerhamphus alcinus Bat Hawk (p. 301)
22. ADULT from below.

Urotriorchis macrourus Long-tailed Hawk
(p. 391)
23. ADULT from above, 24. IMMATURE from below.

Accipiter melanoleucus Black Sparrowhawk
(p. 387)
25. ADULT from above, 26. from below.

Kaupifalco monogrammicus Lizard Buzzard
(p. 394)
27. ADULT from below.

Plate 32

Falco rupicoloides Greater Kestrel (p. 448)
1. ADULT from above, 2. from below.

Falco tinnunculus Common Kestrel (p. 445)
3. ADULT ♂ from above, 4. from below, 5. ADULT ♀ from below.

Polihierax semitorquatus Pygmy Falcon (p. 441)
6. ADULT ♂ from above, 7. ADULT ♀ from below.

Falco naumanni Lesser Kestrel (p. 443)
8. ADULT ♂ from above, 9. from below, 10. ADULT ♀ from below.

Falco alopex Fox Kestrel (p. 452)
11. ADULT from above, 12. from below.

Falco ardosiaceus Grey Kestrel (p. 453)
13. ADULT from above, 14. from below.

Falco dickinsoni Dickinson's Kestrel (p. 454)
15. ADULT from above, 16. from below.

Falco vespertinus Red-footed Falcon (p. 457)
17. ADULT ♂ from above, 18. from below, 19. ADULT ♀ from below.

Falco amurensis Eastern Red-footed Falcon (p. 458)
20. ADULT ♂ from above, 21. from below, 22. ADULT ♀ from below.

Falco concolor Sooty Falcon (p. 462)
23. ADULT ♂ from above, 24. IMMATURE from below, 25. ADULT ♂ from below.

Falco peregrinus minor Peregrine Falcon (p. 474)
26. ADULT ♂ from above, 27. from below, 28. IMMATURE from below.

Falco biarmicus Lanner Falcon (p. 470)
29. ADULT ♂ from below, 30. IMMATURE from below, 31. ADULT ♂ from above.

Falco chicquera Red-necked Falcon (p. 455)
32. ADULT ♂ from above, 33. ADULT ♀ from below.

Falco cuvieri African Hobby (p. 469)
34. ADULT ♂ from above, 35. IMMATURE from below.

Falco fasciinucha Teita Falcon (p. 477)
36. IMMATURE from below, 37. ADULT ♂ from above.

General Habits. Well known. Migrant to southern tropical Africa, especially *Brachystegia* woodland belt, some further south in winter to E Cape Province Oct–Mar. Very few migrants recorded W Africa but some must winter W Africa as NW African breeding population absent in winter, and is recorded E Morocco in spring moving north (Smith 1968). Recently a few recorded tropical Africa (Senegal, Mali, Ivory Coast) Sept–Apr (Thiollay 1975a). Main wintering population undoubtedly enters Africa via Middle East and Suez, some crossing Mediterranean, passes through Ethiopia, Kenya (probably mainly in highland areas) mid Oct–Nov, and reaches winter quarters in southern tropical Africa in late Oct–Nov. Southward migration is clearly associated with southward-moving rain fronts of Intertropical Convergence Zone (ITCZ), Hobbies appearing, often in abundance, following thunderstorms Ethiopia and Kenya, feeding on alate termites. Give impression of descending from height, then passing on; but sometimes forced down to roost on trees, occasionally many together if caught by thunderstorm near dusk. May regain height by deliberately flying into base of thunderstorm, are then possibly carried upwards to unknown heights.

In winter quarters southern Africa frequents any moist woodland or forest edges, probably preferring *Brachystegia*. Is then dispersed singly, in pairs or in small parties, not roosting gregariously like Lesser Kestrel *F. naumanni* or red-footed falcons, though may associate with these when hunting flying termites. Roosts singly or in small groups in trees, and is on wing much of day. Probably moves locally according to availability of rainstorms and termites, avoiding temporarily dry areas (Moreau 1972). Large rain clouds and, at night, lightning visible from 150 km can probably be reached in at most 2–3 h flight.

Northward passage begins Zambia Jan and Feb, most leaving before Mar, latest date May (K. Curry-Lindahl, pers. comm.). Pass through Kenya late Mar–early Apr in flocks, usually smaller than autumn flocks; scattered individuals often seen. Northward movement also associated with northward shift of rain-bearing ITCZ, producing thunderstorms and associated alate termite swarms. Usually seen in association with thunderstorms and alate termites, possibly travelling at great height, descending to near ground to feed. Most pass through Kenya and Somalia late Mar–Apr depending on rains, and all have gone by end-Apr or early May.

Behaviour in summer quarters, Morocco and Tunisia, not well described; but presumably similar to breeding areas in S Europe, pairs dispersed over country in individual home ranges. No good data on e.g. numbers and size of home range, but any range normally includes nesting wood and adjacent open country in Europe, probably similar N Africa.

Food. In Africa apparently mainly alate termites in winter; these swarm immediately after, sometimes during thunderstorms, and Hobbies apparently descend to catch them in flight, usually 100–200 m above ground, sometimes lower. Falcon catches termite in feet, shifts it to beak, detaches abdomen, and discards hard thorax and head. If raining, repeatedly shakes feathers dry while in flight. Not seen to take small birds or grasshoppers in winter quarters. In summer, may at first feed on insects, but when breeding, dependent mainly on small birds, notably aerial species (larks, swallows, martins, tree pipits). May also rob kestrels of small mammalian prey. Fledged young learn to catch large insects (dragonflies, beetles) before birds (Tinbergen 1932; Schuyl *et al.* 1936). Largest prey taken *c.* 80 g; food requirement estimated 40–45 g, supplied by 1–2 birds; but hundreds of alate termites needed per day.

Breeding Habits. Little known N Africa, very well known Europe; presumably similar NW Africa. Pairs occupy home ranges of *c.* 1200 ha in France (Thiollay 1968) including nesting wood and open country in which to hunt; in parts of Europe prefers heathlands with isolated clumps of trees to solid woodlands.

Pairs usually arrive already paired or pair soon after arrival. Display spectacular, aerial, pair soaring, swooping and circling over breeding site, often in evening. From height ♂ dives at ♀, who may roll and present claws, or both dive at great speed to near ground, then turn up again to repeat. ♂ also reported performing corkscrew-like dive at great speed emitting sound like drumming snipe (Pounds 1948). ♂ feeds ♀ in courtship, sometimes by aerial food pass at speed, sometimes perched; he then sidles along branch towards her, prey in beak, standing high and displaying chestnut thighs and belly; analogous to ritualized bowing displays of Eleonora's Falcon and Peregrine *F. peregrinus*.

NEST: uses old nests of other birds, normally corvids, occasionally herons.

EGGS: 1–4, laid at 2–3 day intervals; 3–4 recorded NW Africa (3 clutches of 3 and 2 clutches of 4: Heim de Balsac and Mayaud 1962; Etchécopar and Hüe 1967). Rounded ovals; yellowish buff, speckled all over red-brown, which fades to yellowish in incubation. SIZE: (150) 36·5–46·5 × 29·6–35·7 (41·8 × 32·6); N Africa mean 41·5 × 32·5 (Etchécopar and Hüe 1967).

Laying dates: NW Africa late May, early June.

Incubation begins with 2nd egg; by ♀ only, fed by ♂ at or near nest. He normally arrives with prey, calls and ♀ leaves nest to receive it in aerial food-pass, or on perch. Incubation period: 28 days.

Young hatch at intervals in large clutches; same day in clutch of 2. No sibling aggression occurs. 1st feathers emerge at *c.* 12 days; are covered with feathers by 21 days. Make 1st flight at 28–32 days, young ♂♂ probably more active, leaving earlier than young ♀♀, but some broods all fly same day.

♀ remains on nest days 1–10, brooding young even in fine weather. Thereafter broods little except at night, but remains near nest until after young are feathered at 21 days. ♂ brings all prey up to this stage; thereafter ♀ may also hunt but most prey brought by ♂ to end of fledging period. Feeding rate is 4–5 small birds daily in early period, rising to *c.* 10 towards end. ♂ plucks prey in early stages, but are brought fully feathered towards end. ♂ hunts from very early dawn to late evening. ♂

can apparently supply demand, as in Europe few losses occur in fledging period from starvation. On available figures (Britain: Brown 1976), from 100 eggs *c.* 80 young would hatch, 52 fly, i.e. *c.* 1.4 young reared/pair/year. No data from NW Africa.

Young recently fledged remain near nest; can fly strongly by day 7. Then fly to meet parents bringing food. ♀ usually remains near nest but sometimes also hunts. Wings and shoulder girdles of avian prey dropped beneath feeding perches, making identification easy. Young begin trying to catch large insects after *c.* 10 days, play at chasing birds or each other, but not known to catch birds while dependent on adults for 33–34 days after 1st flight. Then disappear from nest area and probably become independent of parental assistance Sept, just before migration. Move out of Europe late Sept–early Oct. May not be able to breed until full adult plumage acquired at 2 years old.

References

Schuyl, G. *et al.* (1936).
Tinbergen, N. (1932).

Falco cuvieri Smith. African Hobby. Faucon de Cuvier.

Plates
28 and 32
(Opp. pp. 435
and 467)

Falco Cuvieri A. Smith, 1830. South Afr. Quart. Journ. (1) p. 392; no locality = South Africa.

Range and Status. Resident tropical Africa from Ivory Coast east to Ethiopia, thence south to E Cape Province, in forests and well watered savannas. Normally frequent, but in some areas uncommon, largely restricted to highlands in E Africa–Ethiopia. Numbers possibly decreasing locally through destruction of habitat; but also adapts well to cultivated areas with abundant populations of Pied Crow *Corvus albus*, then breeding even in towns.

Description. ADULT ♂: entire upperside dark slate grey to nearly black, darkest on head and upper back; may show some chestnut on nape. Forecheeks and moustachial streak black. Rest of cheeks and sides of neck rufous-buff, becoming deeper rufous on throat, rich dark rufous on breast, belly and undertail-coverts, breast and sides more or less finely streaked black; underwing-coverts buff, streaked black. Primaries blackish, spotted rufous on inner webs. Tail black, washed greyish above, paler grey below, tipped pale rufous, all but central feathers barred light rufous. Cere, orbital ring and legs yellow to orange; eye dark brown. ♀ similar, but slightly larger, browner. SIZE: wing, ♂ 208–243, ♀ 230–254, (Ivory Coast, 9 specimens) ♂ 218–232 (222), ♀ 233–240 (236); tail, ♂♀ 108–125; tarsus, 30–35. WEIGHT: ♂ 150–178 (166), ♀ 186–224 (200) (Thiollay 1978).

IMMATURE: like adult, but browner and darker above, most feathers edged rufous, more broadly and conspicuously streaked below; cere, orbital ring and feet pale greenish yellow, eye dark brown.

DOWNY YOUNG: 1st down dirty creamy yellow, cere blue-grey, feet yellowish, eye brown. 2nd down denser, grey.

Field Characters. A small, slim, very long-winged and swift falcon, appearing very dark-coloured in field, when often seen late in evening in poor light. Dark rufous underside distinguishes it in any plumage from Hobby *F. subbuteo*. Distinguishable from Teita Falcon *F. fasciinucha* by lack of grey uppertail-coverts and rump, much richer chestnut below, slimmer build.

Voice. Recorded (2a, 24). High-pitched, screaming 'keeeeee-ee' or 'kiki-keeee', or rapidly repeated 'kik-kik-kik'. Also a call 'a little like a gull, but uttered more quickly and shriller' (Forbes-Watson 1963). Often calls in flight near breeding area, otherwise normally silent.

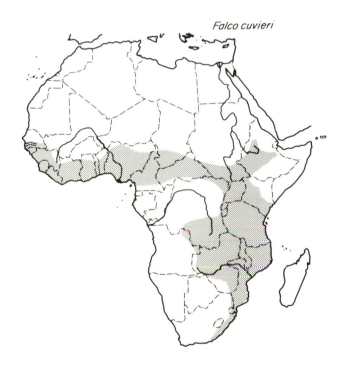

Falco cuvieri

General Habits. Well known Ivory Coast (Thiollay 1975–78), otherwise little known, unaccountably rare in much of range. Resident where it occurs, but may possibly be locally migratory South Africa; any movements not well documented. In W Africa occurs commonly in forest–savanna mosaic Ivory Coast, but scarce elsewhere, said to prefer areas not disturbed by humans. In Uganda, W Kenya, relatively common in formerly forested country with extremely dense human populations; elsewhere in Kenya largely confined to forest edges in highlands, seldom seen, in habitat shared with Rufous-chested Sparrowhawk *Accipiter rufiventris*. No definite rules for habitat generally applicable, but always avoids semi-arid areas, found mostly in rainfall of not less than 1200 mm/year. May be found breeding in centre of large towns (e.g. Kampala, Uganda).

Is little seen by day, normally perching high up in tall trees. Becomes most obvious in evening, when frequently hunts at speed, either close to ground, or at 50–100 m above it, often late into dusk. Attracted to swarms of emerging alate termites, hence (probably) preference for perennially moist areas. Roosts in trees, usually near nest-site, pair remaining there year round.

Hunts exclusively by aerial chase, either of termites or of small birds. Sometimes pursues birds from high perches, catching, for example, swallows at 400 m above ground (Thiollay 1978). More often, flies fast along edges of forest or through open woodland, pursuing any bird it sees small enough to catch. Takes 56% of prey in open savanna, 27% in wooded savanna (Ivory Coast: Thiollay 1977a), but this varies locally. All prey taken in flight, 28% low aerial, 78% high aerial. Success rate high, catches 95% of insects and 72% of birds pursued (Thiollay 1978a).

Food. In non-breeding season insectivorous, but in breeding season depends on birds. 1886 items, Ivory Coast, comprised 1836 insects (1390 small, probably flying termites), 48 adult birds, 1 amphibian, 1 small mammal. Birds relatively much more important by weight; if av. only 30 g could equal entire insect intake. Taking termites, catches them in feet, transfers to bill in flight, bites off body and discards thorax and wings. Birds killed and carried to arboreal perch to eat. Several may congregate at large termite swarm, then feed like Hobby. Normally aggressive, tolerates other species when feeding on termite swarms.

Breeding Habits. Well known. Where studied (Ivory Coast), pairs evenly distributed over available terrain, av. home range in forest-savanna mosaic only *c.* 160–200 ha/pair, to some extent limited by availability of nest-sites (in corvid or other raptor nests). Adult home ranges also used by subadults, apparently without severe conflict. A 3rd adult often present near established sites, takes part in territorial defence. Breeding site vigorously defended, first by calling, then, if that unsuccessful, by attack. In breeding season will not tolerate any other raptor nesting within 100 m, sterilizing some 30 ha round nest-site for others (Thiollay 1975b). Hunting not confined to small breeding range, extends up to at least 2 km away from it (possible area, 12,400 ha).

Display largely vocal, pairs calling to one another constantly near nest-site; perform few aerial displays despite very swift flight.

NEST: always in tall trees, in nest of another large raptor or corvid, sometimes in masses of arboreal epiphytes (Thiollay 1977a). Preferred sites W Kenya–

Uganda nests of Pied Crow *Corvus albus*, also Black Kite *Milvus migrans*. In W Africa prefers nests of Vulturine Fish Eagle *Gypohierax angolensis* in bases of *Borassus* palm fronds, sometimes usurping occupied nests; may even eject egg already in nest. Also known to eject harrier hawks. In E Africa nests of corvids usually abandoned ones, used when crows not breeding.

EGGS: 2–3, laying interval not established; E Africa mean (4 clutches) 2·75; W Africa (7) 2·86. Round ovals; cream, almost entirely obscured by red-brown mottlings. SIZE: 36·0–40·9 × 29·0–31·8 (*c.* 39·8 × 31·8); WEIGHT: *c.* 20·5 (Schönwetter 1960).

Laying dates: Ivory Coast 15 Feb–15 Apr, peaking late Mar (late dry season–early rains); Uganda, W Kenya Dec, Jan–Apr inclusive, possibly peaking Feb; E Kenya, N Tanzania Apr, Aug, Oct (mainly late in dry seasons); Zambia Oct; Zimbabwe Sept; southern Africa Sept–Nov (dry and into rains). Apparently prefers to lay late in dry season, young flying in following heavy rains.

Only ♀ known to incubate, fed by ♂ at or near nest. Incubation period: not accurately determined, but *c.* 30 days.

After young hatch, ♀ broods young in early stages, and later remains near nest. Is very aggressive, attacking any intruder, including humans. ♀ and brood apparently mainly dependent on ♂ for most of fledging period, but ♀ may leave to hunt termites for herself. All prey brought by ♂ to nest are plucked birds. If ♀ absent, he does not feed young, but awaits her return; and may deposit prey in tree-crotch, and leave it there without attempting to feed young himself (Forbes-Watson 1963). Good details of development of young lacking, but by 14 days feathers have emerged, and fledging period estimated at *c.* 30 days (Steyn 1965; Thiollay 1976b).

Breeding success of 14 pairs, Ivory Coast, low. 7/14 pairs bred, laid 20 eggs, hatched 14, reared 7 young; i.e. 0·50/pair overall, 1·0/breeding pair and 1·0/successful nest. Main cause of failure, egg loss (*c.* 30% of all laid) to unknown predators. If this is typical, at 75% mortality before sexual maturity adults must live 16 years to maintain population (unlikely). On evidence of undeveloped gonads in 2nd year, young probably cannot breed until 2 years old (Thiollay 1975b).

References

Forbes-Watson, N. M. (1963).
Steyn, P. (1965).
Thiollay, J.-M. (1975–78).

Plates 28 and 32 (Opp. pp. 435 and 467)

Falco biarmicus Temminck. Lanner Falcon. Faucon lanier.

Falco biarmicus Temminck, 1825. Pl. Col. livr. 55, pl. 324 and text; Caffraria and Cape of Good Hope.

Range and Status. Resident; the dominant large falcon all over Africa, especially south of Sahara; in NW Africa commoner in deserts and subdeserts, absent from a narrow coastal strip of moist wooded country in N Morocco–Tunisia. Generally frequent, often common; probably increasing at present in South Africa through establishment of eucalyptus plantations and pylon lines (with associated crows' nests). Adapts well to heavily populated country in, for example, Kenya, W Africa and Ethiopia. May be threatened locally by demands from falconers (e.g. Sudan), but generally thriving.

Description. *F. b. biarmicus* Temminck: South Africa north to Zaïre, Uganda, Kenya, S Ethiopia. ADULT ♂: narrow frontal band white; forehead blackish, shading to rufous on crown and nape, finely streaked blackish. Upperparts bluish grey, paler on rump and uppertail-coverts, feathers edged paler and obscurely barred darker grey. Cheeks and throat whitish; a black moustachial streak and black band from behind eye to nape. Breast and most of underside pale pinkish, with sparse pear-shaped brown spots on flanks, smaller on thighs, and bars on underwing-coverts. Primaries and secondaries above dark brown, with oblong whitish or pale brown bars on inner webs; below whitish, barred brown. Tail above grey to brownish, tipped whitish, with 10–12 dark grey bands; below paler grey, banded darker. Cere, orbital ring and legs yellow; eye dark brown. ADULT ♀: larger, normally browner above, more heavily spotted and barred below than ♂. SIZE: wing, ♂ 308–332 (317), ♀ 340–360 (350); tail, ♂ 160–178, ♀ 185–210; tarsus, ♂ 46–55, ♀ 45–52. WEIGHT: 48 (unsexed) 430–910 (587), ♂♂ propably 430–600, ♀♀ 600–910 (Biggs *et al.* 1979); 1 pair, ♂ 528, ♀ 756 (W. Tarboton, pers. comm.).

IMMATURE: above, brown, feathers edged buff, crown pale rufous. Below, buff, heavily streaked dark brown or blackish. Cere and orbital ring grey, legs pale yellow, eye dark brown.

DOWNY YOUNG: 1st down greyish white; 2nd woollier, pale grey. Cere greyish white, legs pale yellow, eye brown.

F. b. abyssinicus Neumann. The whole of N tropical Africa, south of Sahara from Somalia and Ethiopia west to Senegal. Larger: wing ♂ 318–333, ♀ 353–387; more heavily barred and spotted below in adults.

F. b. tanypterus Schlegel. N Africa from Cyrenaica to Egypt; paler, crown buff rather than rufous, chest spotted blackish. Wing ♂ 314–338, ♀ 355–375.

F. b. erlangeri Kleinschmidt. NW Africa from Cyrenaica west to Morocco, south to S Sahara and Tadmait plateau. Still paler, smaller: wing ♂ 308–324, ♀ 338–359.

The species has by some (e.g. Meinertzhagen 1954) been considered conspecific with the Saker *F. cherrug*; but in Europe and W Asia subspecies of these 2 species are very distinct within the same area, so both are best regarded as full species.

Field Characters. Only likely to be confused with Peregrine *F. peregrinus* and Saker Falcons. Normally distinguished from Peregrine by pale rufous crown, paler upperparts generally, less pronounced moustachial streak, and almost plain, unbarred underside. Longer-tailed, less stockily built than Peregrine; and in flight wing-tips less neatly pointed. More difficult to distinguish from Saker where ranges overlap (especially the pale desert races *tanypterus* and *erlangeri*), but Lanner is smaller, greyer above, with pale rufous rather than cream or whitish crown. Saker is definitely brown, while Lanner is grey with brownish edges to feathers. Tail of Saker spotted, not barred as in Lanner. Immatures especially hard to distinguish, but immature Lanner is more heavily streaked below, except on belly, darker, more uniform brown above than Saker. Care always needed even at close range in N Africa; but Saker would not occur in most of Lanner's range, except rarely in winter, Oct–Mar inclusive.

Voice. Recorded (2a). Usually silent away from breeding localities. Distinctive from Peregrine, commonest call is shrill, sometimes piercing, keening or screaming 'kirrrr-kirrrr', 'kirrrr-rrreee' or 'schreeeee', higher-pitched than similar whining or keening calls of

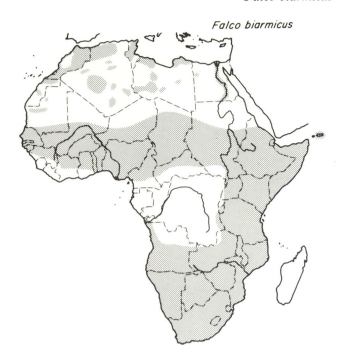

Falco biarmicus

Peregrine. ♂ utters double call, 'whitsyew', similar to ♂ Peregrine's call, but higher-pitched. In anxiety near nest, sharp, rasping 'hek-hek-hek-hek' similar to anger calls of Peregrine but higher-pitched. Incubating ♀ utters clucking calls on seeing ♂ with food, 'kek-kek'. Young begging, a trilling 'kyurrr-kyurrr' (Barbour 1971).

General Habits. Very well known. Inhabits any type of open country from forest edges to deserts, and sea level to summits of highest mountains, up to 5000 m in Ethiopia. Commonest in open savanna and grassland, but occurs in depths of Sahara and Namib deserts, on cliffs in forests (Mount Elgon, W Kenya) and in formerly forested, densely inhabited country in Kenya and Ethiopia. Is not confined to areas with cliffs (as is Peregrine), but breeds in open woodland wherever nests of other raptors or crows are available. In Transvaal often now breeds in crows' nests on pylons in otherwise treeless country, thus benefiting from human activity; also freely uses *Eucalyptus* plantations in same way and breeds in several towns (Addis Ababa, Durban, Salisbury, Pretoria). Adaptability and, probably, less specialized feeding habits leads to its dominance over Peregrine in most of Africa, N African coastal areas excepted.

Normally resident where it occurs, pairs found daily in same haunts roosting regularly on cliffs, usually near breeding site. In W Africa locally migratory, moving south into moister savannas in dry season, probably breeding, then moving north in wet season. At 8°N, in Nigeria (broad-leaved savanna/forest mosaic) is regular Oct–June, stragglers to July, absent only Aug–Sept; further north, present year-round. In southern Africa, arid areas (Kalahari, Namib), often nomadic, appearing in numbers for short periods locally, perhaps in response to rainfall, then moving away. Such nomads may not be territorial breeding birds, but surplus adults,

subadults and juveniles (A. C. Kemp, pers. comm.). In deserts of N Africa apparently permanently resident; but occurrence in any locality not well documented.

Hunts from flight, often killing or seizing bird prey in air by spectacular stoop; but, unlike Peregrine, also freely takes prey on ground. Powers of flight spectacular, capable of extremely fast stoops, killing with very small tolerance margins on ground, e.g. a Stone Partridge *Ptilophachus petrosus* snatched in flight from rock face after swift near-vertical stoop of 300–400 m. In N Ethiopia (Semien and Bale Mountains) feeds much on abundant small rats *Arvicanthis*, often found in plague numbers; then flies low over ground at high speed, snatching rats at mouths of burrows. In NW African deserts takes large, powerful, spiny-tailed *Uromastix* lizards, checking in swift flight over level ground to sieze prey. May occasionally take avian prey 'head on' flying in opposite direction. In inhabited areas takes free-range poultry by swift attacks from sailing or soaring flight, rushing at speed between trees and buildings. Ability to hunt gamebirds has led to extensive use in falconry, but will not generally 'wait-on' above falconer, and may be best flown from fist; opinions vary on suitability for falconry. Certainly is more adaptable than Peregrine, taking greater variety of prey and in more varied situations; hence, possibly, dominance in Africa.

Food. Not quantitatively analysed. Mainly birds, taken either in flight or on ground, from size of Nyanza Swift *Apus niansae* to full-grown guineafowl and small bustards, 1500 g. Small mammals e.g. rats *Arvicanthis*, and, in flight, large fruit bats *Eidolon* spp.; more rarely, other bats. In NW Africa, and probably other arid areas, lizards important. In Sahara sometimes behaves like Eleonora's Falcon *F. eleonorae*, preying on migratory birds, but mainly in spring (Jany 1960). Feeds freely on swarms of alate termites, and when so feeding may snatch in passing swallows feeding on same prey. Preferred food probably birds in size range 50–500 g; but when these scarce will take almost anything available.

Certainly takes young domestic poultry if available and not housed; locally (W Kenya, Nigeria) poultry may be important prey.

Breeding Habits. Very well known, but, surprisingly, never very intensively studied in Africa. Resident breeding pairs are normally distributed over terrain in established ranges; in Transvaal these av. 40–50 km² with pairs at 3·1–4 km apart (Tarboton 1978). Estimated total population Transvaal, 1340 breeding pairs, probably increasing as new pylon sites made available. 2 pairs may breed 150–250 m apart if hunting ranges radiate. Elsewhere, probably similar; but in many very open areas is limited by lack of suitable sites either on cliffs, or in nests of other raptors or crows.

Display spectacular, mainly aerial, pair soaring together above breeding site, breaking off to perform extremely swift aerobatics, diving at speed and suddenly rising again, or one chasing other on weaving, twisting course. ♂, soaring above, may dive at ♀, who may turn over and present claws. On nest cliff, pair often perches, screaming softly, for long periods, or may soar high without aerobatics, screaming. ♂ probably selects nest-site and attracts ♀ to it. Copulation occurs near nest-site, either on topmost branches of tree or on cliff ledge and is recorded to occur after clutch laid (Dalling 1975). ♂ feeds ♀ during display, and before laying.

NEST: either in scrape on cliff ledge or (probably more often) in old nests of other large raptors, or storks, especially corvids (Pied Crow *Corvus albus* and Cape Rook *C. capensis*). Nests of Cape Rooks on pylons have in recent years aided spread of Lanners; may use an old nest with rook in another on same pylon (W. Tarboton, pers. comm.). In Kenya, N Nigeria, Ethiopia, Pied Crows' nests in tall introduced eucalyptus preferred to those of Cape Rook. Also, may nest on buildings in large towns, using any available site, possibly (Addis Ababa, Ethiopia) using small stick nests of Speckled Pigeon *Columba guinea* as foundation. Builds no structure itself, and apparently does not eject rightful owners from occupied nests, using old ones as available. Even recorded, for example, breeding in Cape Rook's nest on windmill, with piston of pump moving up and down through middle of nest (Namaqualand: N. Macgregor, pers. comm.).

EGGS: 2–5, usually 3–4; recorded clutch of 1 probably incomplete; at least 2 recorded clutches of 5 (Barbour 1971; Dalling 1975); South Africa mean (82 clutches) 3·53 (Dean 1971; W. Tarboton, pers. comm.); N Africa (22) 3·0 (Heim de Balsac and Mayaud 1962); E Africa, Somalia, Nigeria av. perhaps smaller, usually 2–3. Laid at 2–3 day intervals (Dalling 1975). Broad ovals; white or pale cream, speckled and blotched all over with reddish yellowish and purplish brown, largely obscuring ground, but usually paler than Peregrine eggs. SIZE: (23, *F. b. biarmicus*) 47·3–55 × 37·7–42·9 (52·3 × 40·7); (13, *F. b. abyssinicus*) 45·8–53 × 37–40 (49·7 × 38·6); mean (50, *F. b. erlangeri*) 51·2 × 40·2; mean (40, *F. b. tanypterus*) 52·7 × 41·1; WEIGHT: 41·47 (Schönwetter 1960).

Laying dates: South Africa, E Cape Province Aug; Transvaal, Natal July–Oct, peaking Sept (dry); Zambia –Zimbabwe–Malawi May–Nov, peaking Aug–Sept (dry); E Kenya, N Tanzania June–July, Dec (in both dry seasons); Somalia Apr, May (early rains); Ethiopia Mar–May (late dry–early rains); Sudan, N Nigeria Jan–Mar (late dry); central Sahara, Mar; Egypt Mar–Apr; Morocco, Algeria, Tunisia Mar–Apr (Heim de Balsac and Mayaud 1962). In N Africa and central Sahara lays in northern spring, in central Sahara timing perhaps related to spring migration of passerines (Jany 1960); in tropical and southern African summer rainfall areas, dry season, except Somalia–Ethiopia where may breed in rains.

Incubation begins 1st or 2nd egg. By both sexes, ♂ often taking large share (up to 30% of daylight), but individuals vary. ♂ feeds ♀ on nest, but she may also be off long enough to kill own prey. ♀ sits by night. Incubation period: various records estimate 28–35 days, usually 30–31; more exact data needed.

Eggs hatch over shorter period than laying, 3–4 days, indicating incubation of first-laid eggs incomplete. When first hatched, young feeble, helpless, require constant brooding. 1st down replaced by 2nd, more copious, woolly down by c. 6 days; 1st flight-feathers emerge at 12–13 days; contour feathers emerge on back and scapulars 20–22 days; by 30 days covered with feathers, still downy on neck and underparts; completely feathered by 36 days. Are able to move about nest and seize food at 22 days and soon after can feed themselves. First wing-flapping observed 15 days, but still unsteady when defaecating over nest rim at 30 days. Weight increases from 46 g soon after hatch to 200 at day 10, 500 day 20, 710 day 30 (Kemp 1975). Fledging period: in various records 33–43 days, most 35–40 (Barbour 1971; Dalling 1975; Sinclair and Walters 1976; W. Tarboton, pers. comm.).

♀ broods or shades chicks in nest up to day 10; ♂ may also brood small chicks (Barbour 1971). ♂ brings most prey, often unplucked, ♀ leaving nest to receive it on nearby ledge, building or tree; if ♂ delays, ♀ may leave and hunt, and may catch prey (poultry) within 5 min (Barbour 1971). ♂ also known to feed chicks of 13 days old or more. Days 10–20, ♀ usually remains near nest attacking other large birds and possible enemies, e.g. dogs, cats, and sometimes humans; but generally less aggressive than Peregrine. When young feathered, ♀ also hunts, but generally remains near nest much of time, even late in fledging period.

Breeding success generally good, broods of 2–4 regularly reared; mean (47 flying broods, Transvaal) 2·51 (71% of mean clutch size); but allowing for some failures and non-breeding pairs true overall success lower. 3 pairs observed over 9 pair-years laid 36 eggs, fledged 17 young, i.e. 1·89/pair/year overall, suggesting true breeding success is c. 50–55% of mean clutch size. Recent Transvaal data from pairs nesting on electricity pylons suggest broods reared there may be above average (W. Tarboton, pers. comm.).

No detailed data available on post-fledging period, but young may remain near nest for up to 3 months after 1st flight (Dalling 1975). Probably do not breed until 3 years old. Assuming 1·8 young/pair/year overall, and 75% mortality before sexual maturity, av. adult life would be c. 4·5 years.

References
Barbour, D. Y. (1971).
Dalling, J. (1975).
Kemp, A. C. (1975).
Sinclair, J. C. and Walters, B. (1976).

Falco cherrug Gray. Saker Falcon. Faucon sacre.

Plate 28

Falco cherrug J. E. Gray, 1834. Illus. Ind. Zool., 2, pts 15–16, pl. 25; India (in winter).

(Opp. p. 435)

Range and Status. Normally scarce Palearctic winter migrant to NW and N tropical Africa (*F. c. cherrug*), south to Sudan, Ethiopia and reaching equator in Kenya. Uncommon to rare, occurring only between Oct and Mar, or, at latest, Apr. Not proven to breed N Africa.

Description. *F. c. cherrug* Gray: breeds Europe east to Altai, Mongolia, Afghanistan. ADULT ♂: crown and nape creamy white to pale buff, finely streaked black. Back, upperwing- and uppertail-coverts brown, edged rufous, appearing generally reddish. A thin blackish moustachial streak and an indistinct dark streak behind eye to nape. Entire underparts, including underwing-coverts, white, the breast lightly, belly and thighs more heavily, spotted dark brown, underwing-coverts streaked dark brown. Wing-feathers above sepia, edged buff, notched and spotted white on inner webs of primaries, secondaries sparingly spotted rufous. Below grey brown, most of inner webs of primaries white, secondaries spotted white. Tail above brown, below grey-brown, with large oval white spots on both webs. Cere, orbital ring and legs dull pale yellow; eye dark brown. ♀ larger, often darker brown. SIZE: wing, ♂ 336–372 (357), ♀ 375–423 (394); tail, ♂ 190–200, ♀ 207–235; tarsus, ♂♀ 50–58. WEIGHT: ♂ 730–890 (c. 816), ♀ 970–1300 (c. 1125) (Glutz von Blotzheim *et al.* 1971).

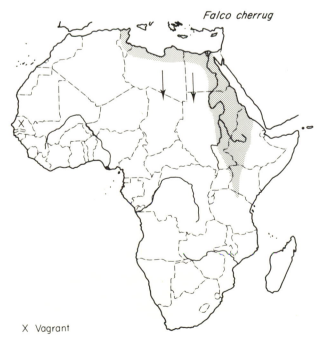

Falco cherrug

X Vagrant

IMMATURE: above, like adult, but crown more heavily streaked, feathers of upperparts darker brown, edged rufous, broadly edged white on tail-coverts. Below, white, each feather broadly streaked dark brown or blackish, sometimes almost obscuring white ground, heaviest on belly, sparse or absent on throat and undertail-coverts. Tail- and wing-feathers brown above, greyish brown below, deeply notched white on primaries, secondaries sparingly spotted rufous, all but central tail feathers with large oval white spots. Cere, orbital ring and feet greyish or bluish, eye brown.

Field Characters. Appears markedly larger than Lanner *F. biarmicus*; a brown bird above with conspicuous creamy crown, below (in adult plumage) largely white, without obvious markings. Immatures more difficult to identify; but smaller moustachial streak, very pale crown, generally brown appearance above, and heavily streaked, sometimes almost wholly black, belly distinguish it. Spots, as opposed to bars, in tail feathers diagnostic in hand, but hard to see in field. Lanner is generally darker brown above, more heavily streaked below, except on belly, than Saker.

Voice. Not recorded. Not well described but similar to other large *Falco* spp., especially Lanner. Usually silent outside breeding season, or gives a loud 'kek-kek-kek-kek' and a single, short, repeated scream, hoarser than that of Peregrine *F. peregrinus*.

General Habits. In winter, often frequents marshy areas and margins of lakes, hunting especially waders and ducks. Normally seen perched on tree, or flying fast and low; main hunting method is fast low flight, surprising prey. More powerful than Lanner, regularly kills larger prey, including sandgrouse, gamebirds, duck and small bustards. Is prized in falconry, and then will hunt Houbara Bustard *Chlamydotis undulata*, and stoop at gazelles (confusing them and helping salukis to catch them).

Food. In breeding quarters takes mainly small ground mammals, some lizards; probably also takes these in Africa, but little detail recorded.

Falco peregrinus Tunstall. Peregrine Falcon. Faucon pèlerin.

Plates
28 and 32
(Opp. pp. 435
and 467)

Falco Peregrinus Tunstall, 1771. Orn. Brit., p. 1; Great Britain.

Range and Status. Resident and Palearctic migrant. 2 races, *F. p. peregrinus* and *F. p. calidus*, are Palearctic winter migrants to parts of Africa; and 3, *F. p. brookei*, *F. p. pelegrinoides* and *F. p. minor*, are resident on the Mediterranean Coast, in N African deserts and in tropical Africa respectively. *F. p. brookei* of the Mediterranean and *F. p. pelegrinoides* of N and NW Africa (including the Atlantic coastline) are apparently less affected than northern European or American subspecies by organochlorine pesticides and are frequent to uncommon in suitable habitat. *F. p. minor* is discontinuously distributed over tropical Africa, occurring in small local pockets, where it is frequent; elsewhere uncommon to rare. Does not appear to be adversely affected by pesticides or human interference, and may breed in towns (Nairobi), but is apparently unable to compete effectively with the slightly larger and more adaptable Lanner *F. biarmicus*. The small population is probably stable.

Description. *F. p. minor* Bonaparte: tropical Africa south of Sahara from Ghana to NW Ethiopia, south to Cape Province. ADULT ♂: a narrow frontal band white. Crown, nape, deep moustachial streak and upper cheeks almost black, becoming dark slate on back and upperwing-coverts, barred blackish. Lower back and uppertail-coverts blue-grey, barred blackish. Sometimes a broken dark rufous collar on hind nape. A patch between moustachial streak and ear-coverts, throat and upper breast white, tinged buff; rest of underside white or buff, more or less heavily spotted and barred blackish, bars heaviest on underwing-coverts and axillaries. Wing-feathers above dark slate-grey, becoming greyer on secondaries, barred grey on inner webs; below grey, barred blackish. Tail, above, basally blue-grey, becoming dark slate terminally, tipped whitish, barred black, bars broader towards tip; below grey, barred blackish. Cere, orbital ring and legs deep yellow–orange; eye dark brown. ♀ larger, usually somewhat browner above, more heavily barred below. SIZE: wing, ♂ 265–311, ♀ 297–318; tail, ♂ 127–148, ♀ 150–155; tarsus, ♂ 45–50, ♀ 53–55. WEIGHT: ♂ c. 500, ♀ 700–750 (Condy 1973).

IMMATURE: above much browner than adult, feathers edged rufous on back and wing-coverts; moustachial streak narrower, browner than in adult; scapulars edged with tooth-like rufous markings. Ear-coverts buff to pale rufous, underside buff or pale rufous, streaked blackish on breast and belly, barred blackish on flanks, thighs and underwing-coverts. Bars narrower, wavy, on undertail-coverts. Wing- and tail-feathers dark brown above, greyer brown below, barred as in adult. Cere, orbital ring and legs yellow; eye dark brown.

DOWNY YOUNG: 1st down sparse, white; 2nd down voluminus, woolly, dull greyish white. Cere, orbital ring and legs pale yellow, eye dark brown.

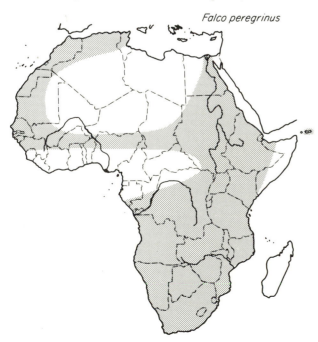

Falco peregrinus

Other resident subspecies are:

F. p. brookei Sharpe. Coast of the Mediterranean from Cape Spartel east to Tunisia, wherever suitable maritime cliffs occur. Larger than *F. p. minor*: wing ♂ 280–300, ♀ 320–340; paler than *minor* but darker than nominate *peregrinus*, more heavily barred below with some rufous on nape.

F. p. pelegrinoides Temminck. Atlantic Coast of Morocco south to Mauritania, and inland deserts to S Atlas, east to Nubia; migrant in winter to N Kenya, probably elsewhere within range of *F. p. minor*. Small: wing, ♂ 262–293, ♀ 282–332; weight: 1 ♀ 610. Very pale, brownish grey above, with rufous nape and ear-crown, below pinkish buff, barred dark brown.

This race and *F. p. babylonicus* are combined by some (e.g. Vaurie 1965) in a separate species *F. pelegrinoides*. They appear, however, analogous to pale desert races of the Merlin *F. columbarius* or Lanner Falcon *F. biarmicus*; and *pelegrinoides* is not known to breed separately within the range of *F. p. brookei* or *F. p. minor*. Accordingly we regard this distinct race (known as the Barbary Falcon by falconers), as a subspecies of *F. peregrinus*, not a full species. Further research in the breeding range is needed to establish the facts.

Migrant Palearctic races are:

F. p. peregrinus Tunstall. Breeds Europe east to N Russia, south to Mediterranean and Caucasus. Larger than resident African races: wing ♂ 292–325, ♀ 344–370; weight: ♂ 550–660 (622), ♀ 740–1120 (1010). Paler slate grey above, less heavily barred below than *F. p. brookei* or *F. p. minor*.

F. p. calidus Latham. Breeding N Russia and Siberia east to Lena River. Migrant in winter principally to E Africa, as far south as Natal. Larger: wing ♂ 305–330, ♀ 350–378; weight: ♂ 678–740, ♀ 825–1300. Paler than *F. p. peregrinus* and much paler slate grey above than *F. p. minor* in same area; much larger than *minor*.

Field Characters. Adult Peregrines of any race are distinguishable from any race of Lanner by smaller size; chunkier, stouter build; more pointed, shorter wings; shorter tail; and barred undersides. Most races have no or little rufous on nape; *F. p. pelegrinoides* has rufous nape, but is barred below, and is much smaller than northern desert races of Lanner *F. b. erlangeri* and *F. b. tanypterus*; much smaller and darker than Saker *F. cherrug*. In flight, from rear, pale slate grey uppertail-coverts and base of tail normally diagnostic from Lanner. Immatures more difficult to distinguish from immature Lanner, but darker above, have much darker heads with much broader moustachial streak, generally more heavily barred below. Yellow cere and legs of immature *F. p. minor* distinguish it from immature Lanner, but immature *peregrinus* has bluish cere. All Peregrines of any race appear neater, more 'finished', with cleaner and sharper lines in flight than any Lanner or Saker. Any Peregrine is very much larger, appearing at least twice the size of the diminutive related Teita Falcon *F. fasciinucha*.

Voice. Recorded (2a). Various calls associated with specific activities. Most often heard, angry, raucous 'hak-hak-hak' of alarm at nest-site, deeper, louder than similar call of Lanner; voice of ♀ (falcon) lower-pitched than that of ♂ (tiercel). ♂ attracting ♀ to nest-site utters bisyllabic 'chick-ik, chick-ik' or 'witchew-witchew'. ♀ soliciting food, sometimes in alarm, a long-drawn 'waaaaik-waaaik'; recognition, a long-drawn 'weeeee-chew', creaking in tone. Also, long-drawn, whining or keening calls 'shreeeee-shreeeee' near nest and in flight.

Short sharp notes 'kik', 'chip', 'chek'. Away from nest normally silent, as are migrants in winter quarters; but near nest-site vocal year-round, especially in flight. Voice normally harsher, deeper than that of Lanner in same areas.

General Habits. Little known in Africa, in any resident race; intimately known in Europe and America. Peregrines have attracted intense interest since 1960 because of decline of northern populations through contamination by organochlorine pesticides. They are indirectly responsible for recognition of this environmental problem and the subsequent steps taken by most governments to ban or reduce the use of organochlorines.

F.p. brookei is apparently still present along N African Mediterranean coast, less affected than some northern races by persecution by falconers. In this area is maritime in habit, living along sea cliffs, resident wherever it occurs, entirely sedentary, pairs found in same haunts daily, year-round. Perches mainly on sea cliff ledges and hunts inland from there; no good details available. *F. p. pelegrinoides* replaces *brookei* along Atlantic coast, and occurs in inland deserts, but not extreme arid part of Sahara. In Morocco–Algeria–Tunisia apparently sedentary, but further east is at least partly migratory, rarely occurring in winter south to N Kenya. *F.p. minor* has extraordinary discontinuous distribution throughout tropical African range, confined to rocky hills and cliffs, otherwise apparently unconnected with habitat, occurring locally in pockets or patches, then absent over large areas. Generally very scarce W African tropics, despite many available cliff nesting sites; absent from most of Ethiopia and Somalia, then found locally in Kenya at quite high densities (2 sites known not more than 3 km apart). In E Kenya, on slopes of Mount Kenya, is dominant large falcon, breeding on forested hill-tops or in formerly forested areas now intensively cultivated. Replaced by Lanner in more arid areas further east, but in Tsavo Park occupies arid thornbush at low altitudes while Lanner inhabits forested and cultivated country in adjacent mountain ranges. Lanner is only large falcon in highland Ethiopia in Afro-alpine moorland, Peregrine the only one in Afro-alpine moorlands and crater highlands of Tanzania. Further south Peregrine occurs sparsely within range of Lanner, invariably associated with rocky hills. Distribution and relations with Lanner inexplicable on ecological grounds, but appears unable to compete with Lanner. However, both may use same breeding cliffs in different years, even same ledge; 1 record of both breeding successfully within 400 m on same rocky hill (Pelchen, EANRC)

Where resident, African Peregrine remains year-round in same breeding haunt, roosting on nest cliff, but not necessarily at nest-site. Pair spends much of day perching on series of cliff perches, occasionally making short flights from perch to perch, and usually repelling other raptors and crows, by violent attack. Usually hunts in morning; either ♂ or ♀ may be absent several hours, normally alone. Usually kills and eats prey away from nest-site, not returning with it except in breeding season. At least 60–70% of daylight spent on or near nesting cliff; short flights may be made out of sight, but not necessarily for hunting purposes.

Kills almost all prey in air by extremely swift, often near vertical stoop; believed sometimes to attain speeds of up to 250 km/h (maximum 300 km/h), but such speed not usually necessary. Prey is overhauled from behind, sometimes after sweeping up from below, and either seized and carried off (small items) or struck dead in air by violent downward blow of powerful feet (Goslow 1971). No data on success rate in Africa, but elsewhere varies from apparent ability to kill almost at will to 1 success/15 attacks (Rudebeck 1950). Attacks are frequently launched from long range, possible prey sighted at 400 m or more, and killed 1–1·5 km or more from point of launching attack, either from soaring flight or perch on high cliff (*F. p. peregrinus*, France: Monneret 1973b). Hunting methods in Africa appear to be similar. Peregrine may dash suddenly at speed among, for example, *Quelea* or doves watering at desert waterhole, skimming low over ground, clearly coming from far off, surprising prey and catching 1. May select and pursue single individual, repeatedly stooping at it until caught or lost. Migrants on Kenya coast (probably *calidus*) may be maritime, roosting on isolated coral islands, feeding on terns caught over sea. Migrants often follow coastlines, but also found inland, e.g. on island in middle of Lake Shala, Ethiopia, or resident some days at Lake Nakuru. Migrants may appear anywhere, racial determination difficult.

Food. Almost entirely birds caught in flight, a few bats. Few definite records, but prey in Kenya of resident *minor* probably mainly doves *Streptopelia* spp., and smaller birds, including mousebirds *Colius* spp., weaver birds, European Bee-eaters *Merops apiaster*, glossy starlings. Perhaps selects high-flying doves or flocking species liable to fly across open spaces. In Nairobi, feeds on domestic pigeons (as in other towns) and Red-winged Starling *Onycognathas morio* caught, for example, in crowded supermarket car park. 1 record domestic poultry, certainly caught on ground. Takes European Bee-eaters on passage, flying high in flocks; this species may be unusually vulnerable. No details on N African races, but *pelegrinoides* probably feeds mainly on small birds, e.g. larks; *brookei*, like other maritime Peregrines, feeds much on feral Rock Pigeons *Columba livia*, or true wild pigeons. Apparent inability to compete with Lanner inexplicable, as Peregrine appears perfectly capable of obtaining prey, and is generally more aggressive than Lanner.

Breeding Habits. Well known in Africa; intimately known in Europe and North America. Resident races breed entirely on rock cliffs, no records known in old nests in trees. *F. p. brookei* and part of population of *F. p. pelegrinoides* breed on sea cliffs, all others inland. Occasionally breeds on tall buildings (Nairobi Law Courts and Hassan's Tower, Rabat), but normally on natural rock ledges, usually very inaccessible. Most known Kenya sites are rock faces on inselbergs; but 1 recorded on overhung ledge behind waterfall.

Pair is present year-round in all known *minor* sites, probably similar in other races. Some mutual display at almost any time of year, increasing in intensity 1–2 months before laying. Pair soar together, frequently calling, and perform spectacular aerobatics, diving for up to 500 m at speed, swinging up again, apparently regaining height effortlessly. ♂ selects nest-site, taking position on 1 or several possible ledges, flying out to meet ♀, then alighting again; in pairs already mated this may be reduced, seldom seen Kenya (in *minor*). ♂ feeds ♀ during courtship, and copulation may occur up to 12 times daily (Condy 1973); occurs on nest ledge, or ledges near it, with much calling.

NEST: a scrape, always on rock ledges, often overhung, or in embrasure or pothole filled with earth. Same actual ledge not usually used annually if many available, but varies. Several Kenya nest-sites continuously occupied 30 years, probably much longer, nesting on different ledges on same cliff; some nest-sites are alternately used by Lanner and Peregrine.

EGGS: 1–4, laid at 2–3 day intervals; N Africa mean (14 clutches, *F. p. pelegrinoides*) 3·42 (Heim de Balsac and Mayaud 1962); Kenya clutches (*minor*) usually 2–3, occasionally 1 or 4, mean (10) 2·6; Zimbabwe 3–4 (Condy 1973). Very round ovals; buff or yellowish ground almost entirely obscured by spots, blotches and smears of dark brick red or red-brown, normally darker than Lanner eggs. SIZE: (5, *F. p. minor*) 44·2–48·1 × 33·0–37·0 (46·0 × 35·0); (30, *pelegrinoides*) 48·4–54·0 × 37·0–41·5 (51·2 × 39·3); (22, *brookei*) 47·4–53·3 × 37·0–42·7 (51·0 × 40·2); WEIGHT: 42·46 (Schönwetter 1960).

Laying dates: NW Africa (*pelegrinoides*) mid Mar–early Apr, mainly Mar; E Kenya, N Tanzania June–Oct, with strong peak Aug (11/16 records) (mid-year dry season); southern Africa July–Oct, mainly Aug, Sept (dry). Tropical African race lays in dry season, cool mid-year season preferred, perhaps also connected with availability of passage migrants, e.g. bee-eaters in fledging period.

Incubation begins with 2nd or last egg Europe; not known Africa. Mainly by ♀, but ♂ takes large share some sites by day (spells of up to 1 h 20 min), sometimes up to 20–25% of daylight. ♀ is off long enough to hunt and may kill own prey. Otherwise fed by ♂ near nest, who calls her off to receive partly eaten prey, either on nearby ledge or by foot to foot pass in air. Incubation period: estimated 31 days (Condy 1973; H. A. Isack, unpub. notes, Kenya).

Chicks hatch at intervals in broods observed Kenya, suggesting incubation may begin with 1st egg. At first helpless, continuously brooded by ♀; when 2nd voluminous down develops are usually left alone. 1st feathers burst through down at *c.* 12 days, largely cover body by 25 days, still downy on head and neck. Main growth then in wing-feathers. Can stand and walk before they are feathered, and in latter stages perform frequent wing-flapping exercises, walk about on ledges if broad enough, retreating into shady caverns, or under overhangs, in heat of day. Make 1st flights independent of adults between 40–45 days, 42 days estimated Zimbabwe (Condy 1973).

♀ broods young in early stages by day and night; returns to brood in wet weather if off. After *c*. 10 days brooding ceases by day, but ♀ remains near nest and is very aggressive, freely attacking and striking humans, dogs or other large birds (e.g. ravens, eagles, buzzards). Calls loudly when attacking and ♂ may then, if present, also attack violently, striking humans without hesitation. When young feathered, parents cease to roost on nest ledge, but roost nearby, and, if present, continue to defend nest. Young normally fed by ♀ only, but after 10–14 days, if ♂ brings prey and finds ♀ absent, he may feed young. Young are fed in turn, hungriest first, feeding rate at least 10–15 morsels/min. Once feathered, tear up food for themselves and are not fed by parents. Daily food requirement appears to be less than in temperate or cold climates—1–3, usually 1–2, items/day Kenya; but sometimes more (up to 12 *Quelea* per day: Condy 1973).

Young cannot fly strongly for 7 days after 1st flight; thereafter become stronger on wing and spend much time in air, flying about nest cliff. Are dependent on ·parents for at least 45 days after 1st flight, probably longer. Breeding success, Kenya, estimated *c*. 1·7/pair overall including non-breeding years, 2·0/breeding pair. No records available in any detail beyond egg stage in NW Africa.

References

Condy, J. B. (1973).

Falco fasciinucha Reichenow and Neumann. Teita Falcon. Faucon taita.

Plates 28 and 32
(Opp. pp. 435 and 467)

Falco fasciinucha Reichenow and Neumann, 1895. Orn. Monatsber., 3, p. 114; Teita, Kenya.

Range and Status. Resident; discontinuous distribu-.ion from S Ethiopia (Yavello) through E African highlands south as far as Zambezi (Livingstone), Matopos Hills and E highlands, Zimbabwe. Incomprehensibly uncommon to rare throughout wide range, but relatively common in Zambezi gorge below Victoria Falls. Apparently prefers highland areas of relatively low rainfall (600–800 mm/year); but may also occur in lowland semi-arid areas, especially outside breeding season.

Description. ADULT ♂: forehead, sides of occiput and nape pale chestnut; crown, moustachial streak, a line behind eye and sides of nape black. Rest of upperparts, including upper-wing-coverts, dark grey, becoming clear pale grey on rump, uppertail-coverts and tail (conspicuous when in flight away). Below, chin and throat buff, rest of underparts pale rufous or cinnamon with narrow dark shaft streaks, darker rufous on thighs; underwing-coverts buff, spotted blackish. Wing-feathers above blackish, below grey, barred darker. Tail above and below paler grey, with indistinct blackish bars, tipped pale buff. Cere orbital ring and legs yellow; eye dark brown. ♀ similar, slightly larger. SIZE: wing, 203–207; tail, *c*. 80; WEIGHT: ♂ (1) 212, ♀ (1) 306 (Ripley and Heinrich 1966; McLachlan and Liversidge 1978).

IMMATURE: resembles adult; generally more rufous above, but lacks the chestnut sides and back of head (or these are reduced); below darker rufous, more heavily streaked and spotted blackish than adult; rump darker grey than in adult. Wing-feathers, scapulars tipped buff. Cere, orbital ring and legs yellow; eye dark brown.

DOWNY YOUNG: 1st down dirty white to pale grey; 2nd down darker, dull grey. Cere and legs pale greyish at first, becoming pale yellow before fledging; eye brown.

Field Characters. Resembles a tiny Peregrine *F. peregrinus*, with short, strong, stoutly built body, rather short wings, and clear grey rump when seen in flight from behind or below. Is only likely to be confused with African Hobby *F. cuvieri*, which is stouter bodied, and in flight has relatively shorter broader wings, flapped rapidly through short arc; flight quite unlike that of Hobby *F. subbuteo*. Adults lack dark chestnut underside of Hobby, but immatures may be more difficult to distinguish. At close range, very white chin,

Falco fasciinucha

upper throat and sides of face distinctive from African Hobby. Owing to rarity, any identifications require careful authentication.

Voice. Not recorded. A high-pitched screaming, like calls of Peregrine, but weaker, thinner; chicks in nest 'kree-kree' (R. Dowsett, in prep.).

General Habits. Little known. General rarity and scattered distribution is the more incomprehensible since in the Zambezi gorge below Victoria Falls it is at least frequent, if not common. Appears to be a perfectly efficient small falcon. Most reported localities are in or near highland massifs, or isolated, relatively high mountains in relatively low rainfall, including the type locality Teita Hills, E Kenya, in which it was not positively reported between the late 19th century and 1976 (Lack 1976). May visit lowlands, usually in semi-arid thornbush or plains, but is not proven to breed there. All breeding records to date are from the southern part of the range (Zimbabwe, Zambia, Malawi); but appears sedentary wherever it occurs. Recorded at altitudes from 800–3800 m.

Political problems have prevented detailed study in Zambezi gorge since 1965, but it here appears a perfectly efficient predator, having no greater difficulty in killing prey than any other falcon (R. Dowsett, in prep.). Appears generally to have the habits of a small Peregrine, i.e. roosts regularly on cliffs near nest-site, less regularly when not breeding, hunts by day, returning to perch near nest-site in afternoon or evening, kills small birds in flight by swift stoop, sometimes among woodland. Pair is very often together, either near, or even away from the nest-site.

Food. Mainly small birds, from size of bulbul (40 g) to perhaps doves *Streptopelia* spp. (80–120 g). Positively identified prey includes bulbuls, Rock Martin *Hirundo rufigula*, and Chestnut-collared Pratincole *Glareola nuchalis* (both found in Zambezi gorge); seen to attack *Quelea*. Most prey observed has been birds, usually unidentifiable, plucked. ♂ is known to catch and cache birds in 'larders' until required at nest. Also takes insects, eating them in flight (cf. Hobby) or on perch if large (Hunter *et al.* 1979).

Breeding Habits. Well known (R. Dowsett, in prep.). In Zambezi gorge pairs are *c.* 5 km apart in straight line, with *c.* 12 km of zigzag cliff face between. Little available detail on display, but pairs soar together above nesting site, screaming (barely audible above roar of river). Mating occurs near nest, on trees growing from cliff face; ♂ may fly direct to land on back of ♀, mating taking 20 s (Colebrook-Robjent 1977).

NEST: most known nests have been in holes in basalt, usually dark and difficult to see into; 1, Malawi, in hole on face of inselberg, such sites probably more common in most of range; apparently prefers shaded, dark sites. No actual structure, eggs laid on scrape in gravel or debris; any reference to stick nests (McLachlan and Liversidge 1970) erroneous.

EGGS: 3–4, laid on at least alternate days, perhaps every 3rd day (R. Dowsett, in prep.). Rounded to rather long ovals; pale yellowish buff, with small yellowish brown spots all over, largely obscuring ground; paler than most Peregrine eggs. SIZE: (4) 41·9–45·2 × 34·1–34·7 (43·0 × 35·5) (Colebrook-Robjent 1977).

Laying dates: Zambia July–Oct; Malawi Sept.

Incubation by both sexes, ♂ for *c.* 10% of daylight, ♀ for 80%, rest uncovered. Incubation period: 26 days for 3rd egg of clutch of 3 (R. Dowsett, in prep.).

Chicks hatch over 3 days (1 nest) indicating incubation of 1st laid eggs incomplete. Require brooding at first, but by day 3 are active, ♀ has difficulty brooding them. By day 10, are only brooded when exhausted and quiescent. Still entirely downy day 10, but can then shuffle on tarsi, and defaecate outside nest-edge; restrained by ♀ from approaching nest-edge by pecks on head. Other details lacking, but fledging period may be *c.* 30–35 days (R. Dowsett, in prep.).

Both sexes brood young, but all prey brought by ♂ in early fledging period. By day 10 ♀ takes some part in feeding. In all-day watch (13·7 h, day 10–11) ♀ brooded 69% of time, ♂ 9·8%, chicks unattended 15·8%; ♀ near nest additional 5%, not brooding; was absent for periods of up to 1 h, apparently killing own prey in that time, not feeding on prey brought to young, ♂ brooded 40 min in absence of ♀. Food brought this day, 9 items, all birds, totalling possibly 300 g, between 06.40 and 18.10 h; thus falcon apparently has no difficulty killing prey. 7 items brought by ♂, 2 by ♀, showing she also hunts for young by day 11. Not all prey freshly caught, some brought from 'larder' nearby. Similar feeding rates (*c.* 1 kill/1·5 h) seen on other days (R. Dowsett, in prep.).

Both parents very aggressive to other birds near nest, attacking much larger species, e.g. Black Kite *Milvus migrans*, African Goshawk *Accipiter tachiro*, Peregrine Falcon, Black Stork *Ciconia nigra*; may attack other species outside nesting season for no apparent reason.

Scanty available data suggest breeding success satisfactory, flying broods of 2–3 recorded in Zambezi gorge, Malawi. Successful breeding, evidently successful, or easy capture of prey (abundant small birds, insects) makes rarity of this falcon completely inexplicable. Conceivably, may suffer from competition with larger falcons (Peregrine or Lanner); but innumerably suitable sites available within range, most areas, lacking any such competition.

References
Colebrook-Robjent, J. F. R. (1977).
Hunter, N. D. *et al.* (1979).

BIBLIOGRAPHY

Our bibliography has been arranged in two parts: (1) a list of general and regional works and check lists concerning African birds which have been consulted for more or less every family. These have not then been repeated in (2), a list of references grouped under family headings containing all the works referred to by the authors for each section. Therefore, if a reference quoted in the text does not appear under the appropriate family heading in list 2, it will be found in list 1.

These two lists cover all the works consulted by the authors whether actually quoted in the text or not (see p. 27), except in the case of Dr L. H. Brown. We regret that, after his death, we were unable to trace any of his sources which were not already specifically mentioned in his text.

1. General and Regional References
(consulted for all families)

Allen, G. M. (1930). The birds of Liberia. *In* 'The African Republic of Liberia'. Vol. 5, pp. 636–748. Contr. Dept. Trop. Med. and Inst. Trop. Biol. Med. Cambridge, Mass.

Archer, G. and Godman, E. M. (1937–1961). 'The Birds of British Somaliland and the Gulf of Aden'. Vols 1–2. Gurney and Jackson, London (1937); Vols 3–4. Oliver and Boyd, Edinburgh (1961).

Bailey, R. S. (1968). The pelagic distribution of sea-birds in the western Indian Ocean. *Ibis* **110**, 493–519.

Bannerman, D. A. (1930–1951). 'The Birds of Tropical West Africa'. Vols 1–8. Crown Agents, London.

Bannerman, D. A. (1953). 'The Birds of West and Equatorial Africa'. 2 vols. Oliver and Boyd, Edinburgh.

Basilio, A. (1963). 'Aves de la isla de Fernando Poo'. Editorial Coculsa, Madrid.

Benson, C. W. (1953). 'A Check List of the Birds of Nyasaland'. Nyasaland Society, Blantyre and Lusaka.

Benson, C. W. (1963). The breeding seasons of birds in the Rhodesias and Nyasaland. Proc. XIII Int. Orn. Cong. 1962, pp. 626–639.

Benson, C. W. and Benson, F. M. (1977). 'The Birds of Malawi'. Montfort Press, Limbe, Malawi.

Benson, C. W. and White, C. M. N. (1957). 'Check List of the Birds of Northern Rhodesia'. Government Printer, Lusaka.

Benson, C. W., Brooke, R. K., Dowsett, R. J. and Irwin, M. P. S. (1971). 'The Birds of Zambia'. Collins, London.

Bouet, G. (1955–1961). 'Oiseaux de l'Afrique Tropicale'. Office de la Recherche Scientific et Technique Outre-Mer, Paris.

Bourne, W. R. P. (1963). Avian breeding seasons in southern Africa. Proc. XIII Int. Orn. Soc. 1962, pp. 831–854.

Britton, P. L. (Ed.) (1980). 'Birds of East Africa'. East African Natural History Society, Nairobi.

Britton, P. L. and Zimmerman, D. A. (1979). The avifauna of Sokoke Forest, Kenya. *J. E. Afr. Nat. Hist. Soc.* **169**, 1–16.

Broekhuysen, G. (1967). Bird migration in the most southern part of the African continent. *Vogelwarte*, **24**, 6–16.

Brooke, R. K. and Sinclair, J. C. (1978). Preliminary list of southern African seabirds. *Cormorant* **4**, 10–17.

Brown, L. H. and Britton P. L. (1980). 'The Breeding Seasons of East African Birds'. East Africa Natural History Society, Nairobi.

Brunel, J. and Thiollay, J. M. (1969–1970). Liste préliminaire des oiseaux de Côte d'Ivoire. *Alauda* **37**, 230–254; **38**, 72–73.

Bundy, G. (1976). 'The Birds of Libya'. Brit. Ornithological Union Check List No. 1. BOU, London.

Cave, F. O. and Macdonald, J. D. (1955). 'Birds of the Sudan'. Oliver and Boyd, Edinburgh.

Chapin, J. P. (1932–1954). The birds of the Belgian Congo. *Bull. Am. Mus. Nat. Hist.* **65, 75, 75A, 75B**.

Chappuis, C. (1980). List of sound-recorded Ethiopian birds. *Malimbus* **2**, 1–15, 82–98.

Clancey, P. A. (1964). 'The Birds of Natal and Zululand'. Oliver and Boyd, Edinburgh.

Clancey, P. A. (1965–1976). A catalogue of the birds of South African subregion. Pts 1–5. *Durban Mus. Novit.* 7(9), 201–304; 7(10), 305–388; 7(11), 389–464; 7(12), 465–544; 7(13), 545–633; Suppl. Pts 1–3, *Durban Mus. Novit.* 8(16), 275–324; 9(2), 25–76; 9(12), 163–200.

Clancey, P. A. (1971). A handlist of the birds of southern Moçambique. Lourenco Marques: *Inst. Invest. Cientifica Moçambique*, Ser. A, **10**, 145–302; **11**, 1–167.

Clancey, P. A. (Ed.) (1980). 'Checklist of Southern African Birds'. Southern African Ornithological Society, Johannesburg.

Cooper, J. (1972). A checklist of the birds of the Zambezi Valley from Kariba to Zumbo. *S. Afr. Avif. Ser. Perc. Fitzp. Inst. Afr. Orn.* **85**, 1–44.

Cramp, S. and Simmons, K. E. L. (Eds) (1977, 1980). 'The Birds of the Western Palearctic', Vols I, II. Oxford University Press, Oxford.

Curry-Lindahl, K. (1960). Ecological studies on mammals, birds, reptiles and amphibians in the eastern Belgian Congo. *Annl. Mus. r. Congo belge* **87**, 1–170.

Cyrus, D. and Robson, N. (1980). 'Bird Atlas of Natal'. University of Natal Press, Pietermaritzburg, South Africa.

Dean, W. R. J. (1971). Breeding data for the birds of Natal and Zululand. *Durban Mus. Novit.* 9(6), 59–61.

Dean, W. R. J. (1974). Breeding and distributional notes on some Angolan birds. *Durban Mus. Novit.* **10**, 109–125.

Dekeyser, P. L. and Derivot, J. H. (1968). Les Oiseaux de l'ouest africain. Fascicule III. Inititations et Études africaines. No. 19. Inst. fon. Afr. noire, Dakar.

Devillers, P. (1976). Project de nomenclature française des oiseaux du monde. *Gerfaut* **66**, 153–168; 391–421.

EANRC East African Natural History Society Nest Record Cards, Nairobi, Kenya.

Eisentraut, M. (1972). Die Wirbeltierfauna von Fernando Poo und Westkamerun. *Boon. zool. Monogr.* no. 3.

Etchécopar, R. D. and Hüe, F. (1967). 'The Birds of North Africa'. Oliver and Boyd, Edinburgh.

Frade, F. (1951). Catálogo das aves de Moçambique. Ministerio das Colónias, Lisbon.

Frade, F. and Bacelar, A. (1955). Catálogo das aves da Guiné Portuguesa. *Annl. Junta. Invest. Ultram.* **10**, 4.

Friedmann, H. (1930, 1937). Birds collected by the Childs

Frick expedition to Ethiopia and Kenya Colony. *Bull. U.S. Nat. Mus.* **153** 1930, 1–516; 1937, 1–506.

Fry, C. H. (1979). Coded bibliography of African ornithology 1975–1978. *Malimbus* Suppl. no. 1.

Fry, C. H. (1980). Coded bibliography of African ornithology, 1979. *Malimbus* Suppl. no. 2.

Germain, M., Dragesco, J., Roux, F. and Garcin, H. (1973). Contribution à l'ornithologie du Sud-Cameroun. *Oiseau* **43**, 119–182, 212–259.

Gill, F. B. (1967). Observations on the pelagic distribution of seabirds in the western Indian Ocean. *Proc. U.S. Nat. Mus.* **132**, 1–33.

Good, A. I. (1952). The birds of French Cameroon. *Mém. Inst. fr. Afr. noire, Sér. Sci. nat.* **2**.

Gore, M. E. J. (1981). 'The Birds of the Gambia'. British Ornithologists' Union Check List No. 3. BOU, London.

Hall, B. P. and Moreau, R. E. (1970). 'An Atlas of Speciation in African Passerine Birds'. British Museum (Natural History), London.

Heim de Balsac, H. and Mayaud, N. (1962). 'Les Oiseaux du Nord-Quest de l'Afrique'. Paul Lechevalier, Paris.

Heinrich, G. (1958): Zur Verbreitung und Lebensweise der Vögel von Angola. *J. Orn.* **99**, 121–141, 322–362, 399–421.

Heinze, J., Krott, N. and Mittendorf, A. (1978). The bird world of Morocco. *Vogelwarte* **99**(4); 132–137.

Heinzel, H., Fitter, R. S. R. and Parslow, J. L. F. (1972). 'Birds of Britain and Europe with North Africa and the Middel East'. Collins, London.

Hoesch, W. and Neithammer, G. (1940). Die Vogelwelt Deutsch-Südwestafrikas. *J. Orn. Sonderheft.*

Irwin, M. P. S. (1978). 'A Bibliography of the Birds of Rhodesia 1873–1977'. Rhodesia Ornithological Society, Salisbury.

Jackson, F. J. and Sclater, W. L. (1938). 'The Birds of Kenya Colony and the Uganda Protectorate'. Gurney and Jackson, London.

Jensen, R. A. C. and Clinning, C. F. (1976). 'Birds of the Etosha National Park'. Nat. Cons. Tourism Div. S.W. Afr. Admin., Windhoek.

Keith, S., Twomey, A., Friedmann, H. and Williams, J. (1969). The avifauna of the Impenetrable Forest, Uganda. *Am. Mus. Novit.* **2389**.

Lamarche, B. (1980). Liste commentée concentrés des Oiseaux du Mali. 1. Non-passereaux. (Typed manuscript.)

Lippens, L. and Wille, H. (1976). 'Les Oiseaux de Zaire'. Lanoo, Tielt.

Mackworth-Praed, C. W. and Grant, C. H. B. (1957, 1960). 'Birds of Eastern and North Eastern Africa'. 2 vols. Longmans, London.

Mackworth-Praed, C. W. and Grant, C. H. B. (1962–1963). 'Birds of the Southern Third of Africa'. 2 vols. Longmans, London.

Mackworth-Praed, C. W. and Grant, C. H. B. (1970, 1973). 'Birds of the West Central and Western Africa'. 2 vols. Longmans, London.

McLachlan, G. R. and Liversidge, R. (1978). 'Roberts Birds of South Africa', (4th edn). Trustees of the John Voelcker Bird Book Fund, Cape Town.

Maclean, G. L. (1971). The breeding seasons of birds of the south-western Kalahari. *Ostrich* Suppl. 8, 179–192.

Malzy, P. (1962). La faune avienne du Mali. *Oiseau et R.F.O.* **32**, no. spécial, pp. 1–81.

Mayr, E. and Cottrell, G. W. (Eds) (1979). 'Peters Check List of Birds of the World'. Vol. 1 (2nd edn), Museum of Comparative Zoology, Cambridge, Mass.

Moltoni, E. (1936). Gli uccelli fino ad oggi notificati per la Somalia italiana. *Atti Soc. ital. Sci. nat.* **75**, 307–389.

Moltoni, E. and Ruscone, G. G. 1940–1944. 'Gli uccelli dell'Africa Orientale Italiana'. Milan.

Moreau, R. E. (1950). The breeding seasons of African birds. *Ibis* **92**, 223–267, 419–433.

Moreau, R. E. (1961). Problems of Mediterranean-Saharan migration. *Ibis* **103a**, 373–427, 580–623.

Moreau, R. E. (1966). 'The Bird Faunas of Africa and its Islands'. Academic Press, London and New York.

Moreau, R. E. (1972). 'The Palaearctic-African Bird Migration Systems'. Academic Press, London and New York.

Morel, G. J. (1972). 'Liste commentée des oiseaux du Sénégal et de la Gambie'. Off. Rech. Scient. Tech. Outre-Mer, Dakar.

Morel, G. J. (1980). Supplement No. 1 to the 'Liste commentée des oiseaux du Sénégal et de la Gambie'. (Mimeographed) Off. Rech. Scient. Tech. Outre-Mer, Dakar.

de Naurois, R. (1969). Peuplements et cycles de reproduction des oiseaux de la côte occidentale d'Afrique. *Mém. Mus. natn. Hist. nat. Paris*, **56**.

Newman, K. (Ed.) (1979). 'Birdlife in Southern Africa'. Macmillan, South Africa.

Newman, K. (1980). 'Birds of Southern Africa' Vol. 1: 'Birds of the Kruger National Park'. Macmillan, South Africa.

Pakenham, R. H. W. (1971). 'The Birds of Zanzibar and Pemba'. British Ornithological Union Check List No. 2. BOU, London.

Priest, C. D. (1933–1936). 'The Birds of Southern Rhodesia', 4 vols. William Clowes, Edinburgh.

Prozesky, O. P. M. (1970). 'A Field Guide to the Birds of Southern Africa'. Collins, London.

Rand, A. L. (1951). Birds from Liberia. *Fieldiana Zool.* **32**(9), 558–653.

Rand, A. L., Friedmann, H. and Traylor, M. A. (1959). Birds from Gabon and Moyen Congo. *Fieldiana Zool.* **41**, 221–411.

Ripley, S. D. and Bond, G. M. (1966). The birds of Socotra and Abd-el-Kuri. *Smithsonian Mis. Coll.* **151**, 1–37.

Rosa Pinto, A. A. (1970). Um catálogo das aves do distrito da Huila [Angola]. Mem. Trab. Inst. Invest. Ci. Angola No. 6. Luanda, Angola.

Salvan, J. (1967–1969). Contribution à l'étude des oiseaux du Tchad. *Oiseau* **37**, 255–284; **38**, 53–85, 127–150; **39**, 38–69.

Schönwetter, M. (1960). 'Handbuch der Oologie', Lieferung 1. (Meise, W. Ed.). Akademic-Verlag, Berlin.

Schouteden, H. (1948–1952). De vogels van Belgisch Congo en van Ruanda-Urundi. *Annls Mus. r. Congo belge* Ser. **4**, **2** and **3**.

Serle, W., Morel, G. J. and Hartwig, W. (1977). 'A Field Guide to the Birds of West Africa'. Collins, London.

Smith, K. D. (1957). An annotated check list of the birds of Eritrea. *Ibis* **99**, 1–26, 307–337.

Smith, K. D. (1965). On the birds of Morocco. *Ibis* **107**, 493–526.

Smithers, R. H. N. (1964). 'A Check List of the Birds of the Bechuanaland Protectorate and the Caprivi Strip'. Trustees of the National Museum of Southern Rhodesia, Salisbury.

Smithers, R. H. N., Irwin, M. P. S. and Paterson, M. L. (1957). 'A Check List of the Birds of Southern Rhodesia'. Rhodesia Ornithological Society, Salisbury.

Snow, D. W. (Ed.) (1978). 'An Atlas of Speciation in African Non-passerine Birds'. British Museum (Natural History), London.

SAOSNRC. Southern African Ornithological Society Nest Record Cards, University of Cape Town.

Tarboton, W. R. (1968). 'Check List of Birds of the South Central Transvaal'. Witwatersrand Bird Club, Johannesburg.

Thomsen, P. and Jacobsen, P. (1979). 'The Birds of Tunisia'. Odenae, Denmark.

Traylor, M. A. (1963). 'Check-list of Angolan birds'. Comp. Diam. Angola, Museo do Dundo, Lisbon.

Urban, E. K. (1970). 'Bibliography of the Avifauna of Ethiopia'. Haile Sellassie I University Press, Addis Ababa.

Urban, E. K. and Brown, L. H. (1971). 'A Checklist of the Birds of Ethiopia'. Haile Sellassie I University Press, Addis Ababa.

Van der Elzen, R. (1975). The avifauna of Cameroon. *Boon. zool. Beitr.* **26**(1–3), 49–75.

Van Someren, V. G. L. (1932). Birds of Kenya and Uganda. *Novit. Zool.* **37**, 252–380.

Van Someren, V. G. L. (1956). Days with birds. *Fieldiana Zool.* **38**.

Van Someren, V. G. L. and Van Someren, G. R. C. (1949). The birds of Bwamba. *Uganda J.* (Spec. Suppl.).

Vaurie, C. (1959, 1965). 'The Birds of the Palearctic Fauna'. 2 vols. Witherby, London.

Voous, K. H. (1973, 1977). List of recent Holarctic bird species. *Ibis* **115**, 612–638, **119**, 223–250, 376–406.

Watson, G. E., Zusi, R. L. and Storer, R. E. (1963). 'Preliminary Field Guide to the Birds of the Indian Ocean'. Smithsonian Institution, Washington.

White, C. M. N. (1960). A check list of the Ethiopian Muscicapidae (Sylviinae). Part 1. *Occ. Pap. Nat. Mus. Sth Rhod.* **24**B, 399–430.

White, C. M. N. (1961). 'A Revised Check List of African Broadbills, Pittas, Larks, Swallows, Wagtails and Pipits'. Government Printer, Lusaka.

White, C. M. N. (1962). A check list of the Ethiopian Muscicapidae (Sylviinae). Part II. *Occ. Pap. Nat. Mus. Sth Rhod.* **26**B, 653–694.

White, C. M. N. (1962). A check list of the Ethiopian Muscicapidae (Sylviinae). Part III. *Occ. Pap. Nat. Mus. Sth Rhod.* **26**B, 695–738.

White, C. M. N. (1962). 'A Revised Check List of African Shrikes, Orioles, Drongos, Starlings, Crows, Waxwings, Cuckoo-shrikes, Bulbus, Accentors, Thrushes and Babblers'. Government Printer, Lusaka.

White, C. M. N. (1963). 'A Revised Check List of African Flycatchers, Tits, Tree creepers, Sunbirds, White-eyes, Honey eaters, Buntings, Finches, Weavers and Waxbills'. Government Printer, Lusaka.

White, C. M. N. (1965). 'A Revised Check List of African Non-passerine Birds'. Government Printer, Lusaka.

Williams, J. G. (1963). 'A Field Guide to the Birds of East and Central Africa'. Collins, London.

Winterbottom, J. M. (1963). Avian breeding seasons in southern Africa. Proc. XIII Int. Orn. Cong. 1962, pp. 640–648.

Winterbottom, J. M. (1968). A check list of the land and fresh water birds of the western Cape Province. *Ann. S. Afr. Mus.* **53**, 1–276.

Winterbottom, J. M. (Ed.) (1969). 'Checklist of the Birds of South Africa'. South African Ornithological Society List Committee.

Winterbottom, J. M. (Ed.) (1971). 'Priest's Eggs of Southern African Birds'. Winchester Press, Johannesburg.

Winterbottom, J. M. (1971). 'A Preliminary Check List of the Birds of South West Africa'. S. W. Afr. Scient. Soc., Windhoek.

Winterbottom, J. M. (1972). The ecological distribution of birds in southern Africa. *Monogr. Perc. Fitzp. Inst. Afr. Orn.* **1**, 1–82.

Witherby, H. F., Jourdain, F. C. R., Ticehurst, N. F. and Tucker, B. W. (1938–1941). 'The Handbook of British Birds'. Witherby, London.

2. References for each family

Order STRUTHIONIFORMES

Suborder STRUTHIONES

Family STRUTHIONIDAE: Ostrich

Amer, M., Boulos, L., Fadell, A. M. A. and Nagati, A. K. (1980). Report of the wild life and endangered species of Elba Mountain from 18/1/1979 to 7/2/1979. *Egyptian J. Wildlife Nat. Res.* **3**, 161–172.

Bertram, B. C. R. (1979). Ostriches recognize their own eggs and discard others. *Nature* **279**, 233–234.

Brunning, D. F. (1974). Social structure and reproductive behavior in the Argentina gray rhea (*Rhea americana albescans*). Thesis, University of Colorado.

Hurxthal, L. M. (1979). Breeding biology of the Ostrich *Struthio camelus massaicus* Neumann in Nairobi Park. Ph.D. thesis, University of Nairobi.

Lamprey, H. F. (1964). Estimation of the large mammal densities, biomass and energy exchange in the Tarangire Game Reserve. *E.A. Wildl. J.* **2**, 1–46.

Leuthold, W. (1977). Notes on the breeding biology of the Ostrich *Struthio camelus* in Tsavo East National Park, Kenya. *Ibis* **119**, 541–544.

Negere, E. (1980). The effect of religious belief on conservation of birds in Ethiopia. Proc. IV Pan-Afr. Orn. Congr. pp. 361–365. South African Ornithological Society, Johannesburg.

Robinson, E. R. and Seely, M. K. (1975). Some food plants of ostriches in the Namib Desert Park, South West Africa. *Madoqua* Ser. 2, **4**(74–80), 99–100.

Sauer, E. G. F. and Sauer, E. M. (1966a). Social behaviour of the South African Ostrich, *Struthio camellus australis*. *Ostrich* Suppl. 6; 183–191.

Sauer, E. G. F. and Sauer, E. M. (1966b). The behaviour and ecology of the South African Ostrich. *Living Bird* **5**, 45–75.

Schmidt-Nielsen, K. S. (1972). 'How Animals Work'. Cambridge University Press, Cambridge.

Schüz, E. (1970). Das Ei des Strausses (*Struthio camelus*) als Gebrauchs- und Kultgegenstand. *Tribus* **19**, 79–90.

Siegfried, W. R. and Frost, P. G. H. (1974). Egg temperature and incubation behaviour of the ostrich. *Madoqua* Ser. I, **8**, 63–66.

Sinclair, A. R. E. (1978). Factors affecting the food supply and breeding season of resident birds and movements of Palaearctic migrants in a tropical African savanna. *Ibis* **120**, 480–497.

Smit, D. J. v. Z. (1973). Ostrich farming in the Little Karoo. Bull. No. 358. Dept Agricultural Technical Services. Government Printer, Pretoria.

Walls, G. L. (1942). The vertebrate eye and its adaptive radiation. Bull. No. 19. Cranbrook Institute of Science, Bloomfield Hills, Michigan.

Order PROCELLARIIFORMES

Family DIOMEDEIDAE: albatrosses

Alexander, W. B. (1963). 'Birds of the Atlantic Ocean'. Putnam's Sons, New York.

Bannerman, D. A. and Bannerman, W. M. (1963–1968). 'Birds of the Atlantic Islands'. Vols I–IV. Oliver and Boyd, Edinburgh.

Bednall, D. K. (1956). The sea-birds of the southeast coast of Arabia. *Ibis* **98**, 138.

Berruti, A. (1976). The Phoebetria albatrosses of Marion Island. *Cormorant* **1**, 12–13.

Bourne, W. R. P. (1977). Albatrosses occurring off South Africa. *Cormorant* **2**, 7–10.

Brooke, R. K. and Sinclair, J. C. (1978). Preliminary list of Southern African seabirds. *Cormorant* **4**, 10–17.

Brooke, R. K., Sinclair, J. C. and Berruti, A. (1980). Geographical variation in *Diomedea chlororhynchos* (Aves: Diomedeidae). *Durban Mus. Novit.* **12**, 171–180.

Clancey, P. A. (1968). The low latitude race of the Wandering Albatross, *Diomedea exulans dabbenena* Mathews in South African water. *Ostrich* **39**, 267–268.

Clancey, P. A. (1978a). On the nominate race of the Wandering Albatross *Diomedea exulans* Linnaeus 1758. *Durban Mus. Novit.* **11**, 309–11.

Clancey, P. A. (1978b). Greyheaded Albatross in Natal. *Ostrich* **49**, 51.

Clancey, P. A. (1978c). On Shy Albatrosses from Natal. *Cormorant* **5**, 30.

Cooper, J. (1974a). Lightmantled Sooty Albatross *Phoebetria palbebrata*. *Ostrich* **45**, 133.

Cooper, J. (1974b). Albatross displays off the southwest coast of South Africa. *Notornis* **21**, 234–238.

Elliott, H. (1969). The Wandering Albatross. *In* 'Birds of the World'. (Gooders, J. Ed.) Vol. I, pp. 29–31. IPC, London.

Gooders, J. (Ed.) (1971). 'Birds of the World'. Vols I–IX. IPC, London.

Harper, C. and Kinsky, F. C. (1978). 'Southern Albatrosses and Petrels: an identification guide'. Victoria University Press.

Harrison, P. (1979). Identification of Royal and Wandering Albatrosses. *Cormorant* **6**, 13–20.

Landsborough-Thomson. A. (Ed.) (1964). 'A New Dictionary of Birds'. Nelson, London.

Nicholls, G. H. (1979). Underwater swimming by albatrosses. *Cormorant* **6**, 38.

Oatley, T. B. (1979). Underwater swimming by albatrosses. *Cormorant* **7**, 31.

Penny, M. (1974). 'The Birds of Seychelles and the Outlying Islands'. Collins, London.

Ross, G. J. B. (1972). Immature Grey-headed Albatross *Diomedia chrysostoma* at Maitland River, Eastern Cape. *Ostrich* **43**, 136.

Samuels, R. (1979). More observations by Ronnie Samuels on sea-birds. *Diaz. Diary* **73**, 6.

Serventy, D. L., Serventy, V. and Warham, J. (1971). 'The Handbook of Australian Sea-Birds'. A. H. & A. W. Reed, Sydney.

Shaughnessy, P. D. and Frost, P. G. H. (1976). An observation of the nominate race of the Shy Albatross in South African waters. *Cormorant* **1**, 4.

Sinclair, J. C. (1978). The seabirds of a trawling voyage. *Bokmakierie* **30**, 12–16.

Summerhayes, C. P. (1976). Seabird observations between Dakar and Cape Town, December 1973–January 1974. *Ostrich* **47**, 55.

Swales, M. K. (1965). The Seabirds of Gough Island. *Ibis* **107**, 17–42, 215–227.

Tuck, T. and Heinzel, H. (1979). 'A Field Guide to the Seabirds of Southern Africa and the World'. Collins, London.

Watson, G. E. (1966). 'Seabirds of the Tropical Atlantic Ocean'. Smithsonian Press, Washington.

White, C. M. N. (1973). *Diomedea cauta* in South African waters. *Bull. Br. Orn. Club* **93**, 56.

Family PROCELLARIIDAE: fulmars, shearwaters, petrels, prions

Alexander, W. B. (1954). Notes on *Pterodroma aterrima* Bonaparte. *Ibis* **96**, 489–491.

Alexander, W. B. (1963). 'Birds of the Atlantic Ocean'. Putnam's Sons, New York.

Bailey, R. S. (1964). Cruise of the R. R. S. *Discovery* in the Indian Ocean. *Sea Swall.* **17**, 52–56.

Bailey, R. (1966). The sea birds of the south-east coast of Arabia. *Ibis* **108**, 224–264.

Bannerman, D. A. and Bannerman, W. M. (1963–1968). 'Birds of the Atlantic Islands'. Vols I–IV. Oliver and Boyd, Edinburgh.

Bourne, W. R. P. (1955). On the status and appearance of the races of Cory's Shearwater *Procellaria diomedea*. *Ibis* **97**, 145–149.

Bourne, W. R. P. and Warham, J. (1966). Geographical variation in the Giant Petrels of the genus *Macronectes*. *Ardea* **54**, 45–67.

Brooke, R. K. and Sinclair, J. C. (1978). Preliminary list of South African seabirds. *Cormorant* **4**, 10–17.

Brown, L. H. (1974). Probable Wedge-tailed Shearwater *Puffinus pacificus* off Watamu. *Bull. E. Afr. Nat. Hist. Soc.* Feb. 1974, 23.

Brown, R. G. B., Bourne, W. R. P. and Whal, T. R. (1978). Diving by Shearwaters. *Condor* **80**, 123–125.

Clancey, P. A. (1955a). On an occurrence of the Fairy Prion in Natal *Pachyptila turtur* (Kuhl). *Ostrich* **26**, 167.

Clancey, P. A. (1955b). The Slender-billed Dove-Petrel in Natal; a new South African species (*Pachyptila belcheri* (Matthews). *Ostrich* **26**, 167.

Clancey, P. A. (1966). The Flesh-footed Shearwater, *Procellaria carneipes* (Gould), in Natal. *Ostrich* **37**, 197.

Clancey, P. A. (1971). The Fairy Prion in Zululand. *Ostrich* **42**, 301.

Conroy, J. W. H., Bruce, G. and Furse, J. R. (1975). A guide to the plumages and iris colours of the Giant Petrels. *Ardea* **63**, 87–92.

Cooper, J. (1976). Both species of Giant Petrels at Quoin Rock, Bredasdorp district. *Cormorant* **1**, 8.

Cooper, J. (1979). Seasonal and spatial distribution of the Antarctic Fulmar in South African waters. *Cormorant* **7**, 15–19.

Cooper, J. and Elliott, C. C. H. (1974). The status of the Antarctic Fulmar in South African waters. *Ostrich* **45**, 254–255.

Cooper, J. and Sinclair, J. C. (1979). Kerguelen Petrel, a species new to southern Africa (*Pterodroma brevirostris* Lesson). *Ostrich* **50**, 117.

Gibson-Hill, C. A. (1949). Notes on the Cape Hen *Procellaria aequinoctialis*. *Ibis* **91**, 442–426.

Gooders, J. (Ed.) (1969–1971). 'Birds of the World'. Vols I–IX. IPC, London.

Harper, C. and Kinsky, F. C. (1978). 'Southern Albatrosses and Petrels: an identification guide.' Victoria University Press.

Harris, M. P. (1966a). Breeding biology of the Manx Shearwater *Puffinus puffinus*. *Ibis* **108**, 17–33.

Harris, M. P. (1966b). Age of return to' the colony, age of breeding and adult survival of Manx Shearwaters. *Bird Study* **13**, 84–95.

Harris, M. P. (1969). Food as a factor controlling the breeding of *Puffinus l'herminieri*. *Ibis* **111**, 139–156.

Harrison, P. (1978). Cory's Shearwaters in the Indian Ocean. *Cormorant* **5**, 19–20.

Imber, M. J. (1973). The food of Grey-faced Petrels (*Pterodroma macroptera gouldi* (Hutton)) with special reference to diurnal vertical migration of their prey. *Anim. Ecol.* **42**, 645–662.

Jarry, G. (1969). *Oiseau et R.F.O.* **39**, 112–120.

Jensen, R. A. C. and Jensen, M. K. (1967). The Flesh-footed Shearwater in South Africa. *Ostrich* **38**, 289.

Johnstone, G. W. (1974). Field characters and behaviour at sea of Giant Petrels in relation to their oceanic distribution. *Emu* **74**, 209–218.

Jouanin, C. and Gill, F. B. (1967). Recherche du Petrel de Barau, *Pterodroma baraui*. *Oiseau et R.F.O.* **37**, 1–19.

King, W. B. (1974). Wedge-tailed Shearwater (*Puffinus pacificus*). *Smithsonian Contrib. Zool.* **158**, 53–95.

Kuroda, N. (1954). 'On the Classification and Phylogeny of the Order Tubinares, particularly the shearwaters (*Puffinus*)'. Privately published, Tokyo.

Landsborough-Thomson, A. (Ed.) (1964). 'A New Dictionary of Birds'. Nelson, London.

Lawson, W. (1963). On the occurrence of the Soft-plumaged Petrel *Pterodroma mollis* (Gould) in Mozambique. *Ostrich* **34**, 176.

Lockley, R. M. (1942). 'Shearwaters'. J. M. Dent & Son, London.

Lockley, R. M. (1959). *In* 'The Birds of the British Isles' (Bannerman, D. A. Ed.) pp. 92–100. Oliver and Boyd, Edinburgh.

Lockley, R. M. (1971). The life history of *Puffinus puffinus*: a review. *Oiseau et R.F.O.* **41**, 163–175.

Mallet, G. E. and Coghlan, L. T. (1964). Cory's Shearwater *Procellaria diomedea* breeding in the Azores. *Ibis* **106**, 123–125.

Mougin, J. L. (1967). Étude écologique des deux espèces de Fulmars. *Oiseau et R.F.O.* **37**, 57–103.

Murphy, R. C. (1936). 'Oceanic Birds of South America' pp. 329–471. American Museum of Natural History, New York.

Murphy, R. C. (1951). The populations of Wedge-tailed Shearwater (*Puffinus pacificus*). *Am. Mus. Novit.* **1512**, 1–21.

Murphy, R. C. (1952). The Manx Shearwater, *Puffinus puffinus*, as a species of World-wide distribution. *Am. Mus. Novit.* **1586**, 1–21.

Nicholls, G. H. (1978). Postcranial partial albinism in the Whitechinned Petrel. *Cormorant* **5**, 29.

Olson, S. L. (1975). Remarks on the generic characters of *Bulweria*. *Ibis* **117**, 111–113.

Penny, M. (1974). 'The Birds of Seychelles and the Outlying Islands'. Collins, London.

Palmer, R. S. (1962). 'Handbook of North American Birds'. Vol. 1. Yale University Press, New Haven, USA.

Phillips, J. H. (1963). The pelagic distribution of the Sooty Shearwater *Procellaria grisea*. *Ibis* **105**, 340–353.

Randall, R. M. (1978). The Little Shearwater on St. Croix Island. *Safring* **7**, 15–16.

Ross, G. J. B. (1971). Antarctic Fulmar *Fulmaris glacialoides*. *Ostrich* **42**, 137.

Round, P. D. and Swann, R. L. (1977). Aspects of the breeding of Cory's Shearwater *Calonectris diomedea* in Crete. *Ibis* **119**, 350–353.

Rowan, M. K. (1951). The Greater Shearwater *Puffinus gravis* at its breeding grounds. *Ibis* **94**, 97–121.

Rowan. A. N., Elliott, H. F. and Rowan, M. K. (1951). The 'spectacled' form of the Shoemaker *Procellaria aequinoctialis* in the Tristan da Cunha group. *Ibis* **93**, 169–179.

Samuels, R. (1979). More observations by Ronnie Samuels on sea-birds. *Diaz. Diary* **73**, 6.

Serventy, D. L., Serventy, V. and Warham, J. (1971). 'The Handbook of Australian Sea-Birds'. A. H. & A. W. Reed, Sydney.

Shaughnessy, P. D. and Sinclair, J. C. (1979). White phase Southern Giant Petrels in southern Africa. *Cormorant* **7**, 11–14.

Sinclair, J. C. (1978a). The Kerguelen Petrel in South Africa and its comparison with Soft-Plumaged Petrel. *Bokmakierie* **30**, 99–101.

Sinclair, J. C. (1978b). Sight records of the Wedge-tailed Shearwater off Southern Africa. *Ostrich* **49**, 46.

Sinclair, J. C. (1978c). The seabirds of a trawling voyage. *Bokmakierie* **30**, 12–16.

Sinclair, J. C. (1979). Birds observed at sea in the Indian Ocean. *Cormorant* **7**, 7–10.

Swales, M. K. (1965). The seabirds of Gough Island. *Ibis* **107**, 17–42 and 215–227.

Tuck, T. and Heinzel, H. (1979). 'A Field Guide to the Seabirds of Southern Africa and the World.' Collins, London.

Voisin, J. F., Shaughnessy, P. D. and Williams, A. J. (1977). Catching Nellies in South West Africa. *Cormorant* **3**, 19–20.

Van Oordt, G. J. and Kruijt, J. P. (1953). On the pelagic distribution of some Procellariiformes in the Atlantic and Southern Oceans. *Ibis* **95**, 615–637.

Voous, K. H. (1970). Blue Petrels (*Halobaena caerulea*) in Cape Seas. *Ardea* **58**, 266–267.

Voous, K. H. and Wattel, J. (1963). Distribution and migration of the Greater Shearwater. *Ardea* **51**, 143–157.

Warham, J. (1956). The breeding of the Great-winged Petrel *Pterodroma macroptera*. *Ibis* **98**, 171–185.

Warham, J. (1962). The biology of the Giant Petrel *Macronectes giganteus*. *Auk* **79**, 139–160.

Watson, G. E. (1966). 'Seabirds of the Tropical Atlantic Ocean'. Smithsonian Press, Washington.

Watson, G. E. (1974). The correct gender of *Daption* Stephens 1826. *Auk* **91**, 419–421.

White, C. M. N. (1953). Petrels in East African waters. *Ibis* **95**, 549.

Family HYDROBATIDAE: storm-petrels

Alexander, W. B. (1963). 'Birds of the Atlantic Ocean'. Putnam's Sons, New York.

Allan, R. G. (1960–1963). The Madeiran Storm Petrel *Oceanodroma castro*. *Ibis* **103b**, 274–295.

Bailey, R. S., Pocklington, R. and Willis, P. R. (1968). Storm-petrels *Oceanodroma* spp. in the Indian Ocean. *Ibis* **110**, 27–34.

Bannerman, D. A. and Bannerman W. M. (1963–1968). 'Birds of the Atlantic Islands'. Vols I–IV. Oliver and Boyd, Edinburgh.

Clancey, P. A. (1965). The races of *Oceanites oceanicus* (Kuhl) occurring in South African waters. *Ostrich* **36**, 142–143.

Feare, C. J. and Bourne, W. R. P. (1978). The occurrence of 'Portlandica' Little Terns and absence of Damara Terns and British Storm Petrels in the Indian Ocean. *Ostrich* **49**, 64.

Gooders, J. (Ed.) (1969–1971). 'Birds of the World'. Vols I–IX. IPC, London.

Harper, C. and Kinsky, F. C. (1978). 'Southern Albatrosses and Petrels: an Identification Guide'. Victoria University Press.

Harris, M. P. (1966). Breeding biology of the Manx Shearwater *Puffinus puffinus*. *Ibis* **108**, 17–33.

Landsborough-Thomson, A. (Ed.) (1964). 'A New Dictionary of Birds'. Nelson, London.

Mackworth-Praed, C. W. and Grant, C. H. B. (1953). On a

new petrel to the East African list (*Oceanites marina*). *Bull. Br. Orn. Club* **73**, 82.

Penny, M. (1974). 'The Birds of Seychelles and the Outlying Islands'. Collins, London.

Robins, C. R. (1966). Observations on seabirds of Annobon and other parts of the Gulf of Guinea. *Stud. Trop. Oceanogr. Miami* **4** (Part 1), 128–133.

Serventy, D. L., Serventy, V. and Warham, J. (1971). 'The Handbook of Australian Sea-Birds'. A. H. & A. W. Reed, Sydney.

Tuck, T. and Heinzel, H. (1979). 'A Field Guide to the Seabirds of Southern Africa and the World'. Collins, London.

Watson G. E. (1966). 'Seabirds of the Tropical Atlantic Ocean'. Smithsonian Press, Washington.

Watson, G. E. (1975). 'Birds of the Antarctic and Sub-Antarctic.' American Geographical Union, Washington, D.C.

Order SPHENISCIFORMES

Family SPHENISCIDAE: penguins

Alexander, W. B. (1963). 'Birds of the Ocean'. Putnam's Sons, New York.

Bannerman, D. A. and Bannerman, W. M. (1963–1968). 'Birds of the Atlantic Islands'. Vols I–IV. Oliver and Boyd, Edinburgh.

Berry, H. H., Seely, M. K. and Fryer, R. E. (1974). The status of the Jackass Penguin *Spheniscus demersus* on Halifax Island off South West Africa. *Madoqua* **3**, 27–28.

Cooper, J. (1972). Sexing the Jackass Penguin. *Safring News* **1**, 23–25.

Cooper, J. (1976). Breeding biology of the Jackass Penguin with special reference to its conservation. Proc. IV Pan-Afr. Orn. Congr. pp. 227–231. Southern African Ornithological Society, Johannesburg.

Cooper, J. (1977a). Energetic requirements for growth of the Jackass Penguin. *Zool. Afr.* **12**, 201–213.

Cooper, J. (1977b). Census of the Jackass Penguin on Dyer Island. *Cormorant* **2**, 15–17.

Cooper, J. (1977c). Jackass Penguins sunning at sea. *Auk* **94**, 586–587.

Cooper, J. (1978a). Moult of the Black-footed Penguin. *Int. Zoo. Yb.* **18**, 22–27.

Cooper, J. (1978b). First definite record of King Penguin for Continental Africa. *Ostrich* **49**, 45.

Cooper, J. (1979a). More Rockhopper Penguins ashore in South Africa. *Cormorant* **6**, 35–36.

Cooper, J. (1979b). Second record of Macaroni Penguin ashore in South Africa. *Cormorant* **6**, 36.

Cooper, J. (1980). Rockhopper Penguin *Eudyptes chrysocome* in: new data on rarely recorded seabirds in Southern Africa. *Cormorant* **8**, 101.

Cooper, J., Ross, G. J. B. and Shaughnessy, P. D. (1978). Seasonal and spatial distribution of Rockhopper Penguins ashore in South Africa. *Ostrich* **49**, 40–44.

Crawford, R. J. M. and Shelton, P. A. (1978). Pelagic fish and seabird interractions off the coasts of South West and South Africa. *Biol. Conser.* **14**, 85–109.

Davies, D. H. (1955). The South African pilchard (*Sardinops ocellata*). Bird predators, 1953–1954. *Invest. Rep. Div. Fish. Un. S. Afr.* **18**, 1–32.

Davies, D. H. (1956). The South African pilchard (*Sardinops ocellata*) and maasbanker (*Trachurus trachurus*): bird predators, 1954–1955. *Invest. Rep. Div. Fish. Un. S. Afr.* **23**, 1–40.

Eggleton, P. and Siegfried, W. R. (1979). Displays of the Jackass Penguin. *Ostrich* **50**, 139–167.

Falla, R. A. (1937). British Australian and New Zealand Antarctic Research Expedition Report. Series B, Vol. 2, Birds.

Frost, P. G. H., Siegfried, W. R. and Burger, A. E. (1976a). Behavioural adaptations of the Jackass Penguin *Spheniscus demersus* to a hot, arid environment. *J. Zool.* **179**, 165–187.

Frost, P. G. H., Siegfried, W. R. and Cooper, J. (1976b). Conservation of the Jackass Penguin. *Biol. Conser.* **9**, 79–99.

Gooders, J. (Ed.) (1969–1971). 'Birds of the World'. Vols I–IX. IPC, London.

Landsborough-Thomson, A. (Ed.) (1964). 'A New Dictionary of Birds'. Nelson, London.

Liversidge, R. and Thomas, A. (1972). Seabirds off the south-western Cape of South Africa. Proc. XV Int. Orn. Cong. pp. 665–666.

Penny, M. (1974). 'The Birds of Seychelles and the Outlying Islands'. Collins, London.

Rand, R. W. (1960). The biology of guano-producing seabirds. The distribution, abundance and feeding habits of the Cape Penguin, *Spheniscus demersus*, off the south-western coast of the Cape Province. *Invest. Rep. Div. Fish. Un. S. Afr.* **41**, 1–28.

Rand, R. W. (1963). The biology of guano-producing seabirds, 4. *Invest. Rep. Div. Fish. Un. S. Afr.* **43**, 1–32.

Ross, G. J. B., van der Elst, R. and de Villiers, A. F. (1978). First record of Macaroni Penguin in South Africa. *Ostrich* **49**, 47.

Serventy, D. L. and V. and Warham, J. (1971). 'The Handbook of Australian Sea-Birds'. A. H. & A. W. Reed, Sydney.

Siegfried, W. R. (1977). Packing of Jackass Penguin nests. *S. Afr. J. Sci.* **73**, 186.

Siegfried, W. R. and Crawford, R. J. M. (1978). Jackass Penguins, eggs and guano: diminishing resources at Dassen Island. *S. Afr. J. Sci.* **74**, 389–390.

Siegfried, W. R., Frost, P. G. H., Kinahan, J. B. and Cooper, J. (1975). Social behaviour of Jackass Penguins at sea. *Zool. Afr.* **10**, 87–100.

Tuck, T. and Heinzel, H. (1979). 'A Field Guide to the Seabirds of Southern Africa and the World'. Collins, London.

Watson, G. E. (1966). 'Seabirds of the Tropical Atlantic Ocean'. Smithsonian Press, Washington.

Westphal, A. and Rowan, M. K. (1970). Some observations on the effects of oil pollution on the Jackass Penguin. *Ostrich* Suppl. 8, 521–526.

Order GAVIIFORMES (*see Cramp and Simmons (1977) in List I*)

Order PODICIPEDIFORMES

Family PODICIPEDIDAE: grebes

Benson, C. W. and Irwin, M. P. S. (1964). The African subspecies of the Great Crested Grebe. *Bull. Br. Orn. Club* **84**(8), 134–137.

Broekhuysen, G. J. and Frost, P. G. H. (1968a). Nesting behaviour of the Black-necked Grebe *Podiceps nigricollis* (Brehm) in Southern Africa. I. The reaction of disturbed incubating birds. *Bonn. zool. Beitr.* **19**(3–4), 350–361.

Broekhuysen, G. J. and Frost, P. G. H. (1968b). Nesting behaviour of the Black-necked Grebe, *Podiceps nigricollis* in Southern Africa. II. Laying, clutch size, egg size, incubation and nesting success. *Ostrich* **39**(4), 242–252.

Brown, A. R. and Morris, A. (1960). Breeding of Black-necked Grebe *Podiceps nigricollis* in South West Cape. *Ostrich* **31**(4), 175.

Burger, A. E. and Berruti, A. (1977). Dabchicks *Podiceps ruficollis* feeding in association with Maccoa Ducks *Oxyura maccoa*. *Ostrich* **48**(1–2), 47.

Clark, A. (1977). Courtship behaviour in the Blacknecked Grebe *Podiceps nigricollis*. *Ostrich* **48**(1–2), 47.

Dean, W. R. J. (1977). Breeding of the Great Crested Grebe at Barberspan. *Ostrich* Suppl. 12, 43–48.

Heim de Balasc, H. (1952). Rythme sexual et fecondité chez les oiseaux du nord-ouest de l'Afrique. *Alauda* **20**(4), 213–242.

Morel, G. and Morel, M.-Y. (1962). La reproduction des oiseaux dans une région semi-arid: la valée du Sénégal. *Alauda* **30**, 161–203, 241–269.

Ruwet, J. C. (1963). Notes écologiques et éthologiques sur les oiseaux des plaines de la Lufira superieure (Katanga). Pt. I. *Rev. Zool. Bot. afr.* **68**, 1–60.

Siegfried, W. R. (1971). Feeding association between *Podiceps ruficollis* and *Anas smithii*. *Ibis* **113**(2) 236–238.

Simmons, K. E. L. (1975). Further studies on Great Crested Grebes. 1. Courtship. *Bristol. Orn.* **8**, 89–107.

Skead, D. M. (1977a). Feeding association between Dabchicks and four *Anas* species. *Ostrich* Suppl. 12, 132–133.

Skead, D. M. (1977b). Weights of birds handled at Barberspan. *Ostrich* Suppl. 12, 117–131.

Steyn, P. (1964). Cape Dabchicks eating flying termites. *Ostrich* **35**(1), 65.

Storer, R. W. (1963).Courtship and mating behavior and the phylogeny of the grebes. Proc. XIII Int. Orn. Cong. 1962, pp. 562–569.

Storer, R. W. (1979). Order Podicipediformes. *In* 'Peters Check List of Birds of the World'. Vol. 1, 2nd edn (Mayr, E. and Cottrell, G. W. Eds) Museum of Comparative Zoology, Cambridge, Mass.

Storer, R. W., Siegfried, W. R. and Kinahan, J. (1975). Sunbathing in grebes. *Living Bird* **14**, 45–57.

Wood, M. G. (1949). A Little Grebe's nest in Kano. *Nigerian Field* **14**, 54–64.

Order PELECANIFORMES

Dorst, J. and Mougin, J.-L. (1979). Order Pelecaniformes. *In* 'Peters Check List of Birds of the Word', Vol 1, 2nd edn (Mayr, E. and Cottrell, G. W. Eds) Museum of Comparative Zoology, Cambridge, Mass.

Sibley, C. G. (1960). The electrophoretic patterns of avian egg-white proteins as taxonomic characters. *Ibis* **102**, 215–284.

Suborder PHAETHONTES

Family PHAETHONTIDAE: tropicbirds

Diamond, A. W. (1975). The biology of tropic birds of Aldabra Atoll, Indian Ocean. *Auk* **92**(1), 16–39.

North, M. E. W. (1946). Mait Island—a bird rock in the Gulf of Aden. *Ibis* **88**, 478–501.

Randall, R. M., Randall, B. M., Batchelor, A. L. and Ross, G. J. B. (1981). The status of seabirds associated with islands in Algoa Bay, South Africa, 1973–1981. *Cormorant* **9**, 85–104.

Stonehouse, B. (1962). The tropic birds (genus *Phaethon*)—of Ascension Island. *Ibis* **103b**, 124–161.

Suborder PELECANI

Family SULIDAE: gannets, boobies

Alexander, W. B. (1963). 'Birds of the Ocean'. Putnam's Sons, New York.

Bannerman, D. A. and Bannerman, W. M. (1963–1968). 'Birds of the Atlantic Islands'. Vols I–IV. Oliver and Boyd, Edinburgh.

Britton, P. L. (1977). Red-footed Booby *Sula sula*. *Bull. Br. Orn. Club* **97**, 54–56.

Broekhuysen, G. J., Liversidge, R. and Rand, R. W. (1961). The South African Gannet *Morus capensis* 1. Distribution and movements. *Ostrich* **32**, 1–19.

Davies, D. H. (1955). The South African pilchard (*Sardinops ocellata*). Bird predators, 1953–1954. *Invest. Div. Fish. Un. S. Afr.* **18**, 1–32.

Dorward, D. F. (1962a). Comparative biology of the White Booby and the Brown Booby *Sula* spp. at Ascension. *Ibis* **103b**, 174–220.

Dorward, D. F. (1962b). Behaviour of Brown Boobies *Sula* spp. *Ibis* **103b**, 221–234.

Gerhart, J. G. and Turner, D. A. (1978). Birds of Latham Island. *Scopus* **2**, 1–6.

Gibson-Hill, C. A. (1947). Notes on the birds of Christmas Island. *Bull. Raffles Mus.* **18**, 87–165.

Gibson-Hill, C. A. (1948). Display and posturing in the Cape Gannet *Morus capensis*. *Ibis* **90**, 568–572.

Gooders, J. (Ed.) (1969–1971). 'Birds of the World'. Vols I–IX. IPC, London.

Gurney, J. H. (1913). 'The Gannet, a Bird with a History'. London.

Jarvis, M. J. F. (1969). Interactions between man and the South African Gannet *Sula capensis*. *Ostrich* Suppl. 8, 497–513.

Jarvis, M. J. F. (1971a). Ethology and Ecology of the South African Gannet, *Sula capensis*. Unpublished Ph.D. thesis, University of Cape Town.

Jarvis, M. J. F. (1971b). The South African Gannet (*Sula capensis*). Printed extract from unpublished Ph.D. thesis, University of Cape Town.

Jarvis, M. J. F. (1971c). The systematic position of the South African Gannet. *Ostrich* **43**, 211–215.

Jarvis, M. J. F. (1972). A comparison of methods in a behaviour study of the South African Gannet. *Zool. Afr.* **7**, 75–83.

Jarvis, M. J. F. (1974). The ecological significance of clutch size in the South African Gannet (*Sula capensis* (Lichtenstein)). *J. Anim. Ecol.* **43**, 1–17.

Jarvis, M. J. F. (1977). A comparison of methods in a behaviour study of the South African Gannet. *Zool. Afr.* **7**(1), 75–83.

Landsborough-Thomson, A. (Ed.) (1964). 'A New Dictionary of Birds'. Nelson, London.

Murphy, R. C. (1924). Observations on birds of the South Atlantic. *Auk* **31**, 439–455.

Nelson, J. B. (1964). *Ibis* **106**, 63–77.

Nelson, J. B. (1978). 'The Sulidae: Gannets and Boobies'. Oxford University Press, Oxford.

Penny, M. (1974). 'The Birds of Seychelles and the Outlying Islands'. Collins, London.

Rand, R. W. (1959). The biology of guano-producing seabirds. The distribution, abundance and feeding habits of the Cape Gannet, *Morus capensis*, off the southwestern coast of the Cape Province. *Ostrich* Suppl. 3, 31–33.

Rand, R. W. (1963a). The biology of guano-producing seabirds: composition of colonies on the Cape Islands. *Invest. Rep. Div. Fish. S. Afr.* **43**.

Rand, R. W. (1963b). The biology of guano-producing seabirds: composition of colonies on the south-west African islands. *Invest. Rep. Div. Fish. S. Afr.* **46**.

Randall, R. and Ross, G. J. B. (1978). Increasing population of Cape Gannets on Bird Island, Algoa Bay, and observations on breeding success. *Ostrich* **50**, 168–175.

Reinsch, H. (1969). 'Der Basstölpel. Die Neue Brehm-Bücherei'. 111 pp.

Robins, C. R. (1966). Observations of the seabirds of Annobon and other parts of the Gulf of Guinea. *Stud. Trop. Oceangr. Miami* **4** (Part 1), 128–133.

Ross, G. J. B. (1978). Historical status of gannets and other seabirds on Bird Island, Algoa Bay. *Cormorant* **4**, 18–21.

Serventy, D. L., Serventy, V. and Warham, J. (1971). 'The Handbook of Australian Sea-Birds'. A. H. & A. W. Reed, Sydney.

Siegfried, W. R. (1976). Cape Gannets and other seabirds off the Transkei coast. *Cormorant* **1**, 5.

Simmons, K. E. L. (1967a). The role of food supply in the biology of the brown booby at Ascension Island. Unpublished M.Sc. thesis, Bristol.

Simmons, K. E. L. (1967b). Ecological adaptations in the life history of the brown booby at Ascension Island. *Living Bird* **6**, 187–212.

Simmons, K. E. L. (1970). Ecological determinants of breeding adaptations and social behaviour in two fish-eating birds. *In* 'Social Behaviour in Birds and Mammals'. (Crook, J. H. Ed.) Academic Press, London, and New York.

Sinclair, J. C. (1978). The seabirds of a trawling voyage. *Bokmakierie* **30**, 12–16.

Stonehouse, B. (1962). Ascension Island and the British Ornithologist's Union Centenary Expedition 1957–59. *Ibis* **103b**, 107–123.

Tuck, T. and Heinzel, H. (1979). 'A Field Guide to the Seabirds of Southern Africa and the World'. Collins, London.

Watson, G. E. (1966). 'Seabirds of the Tropical Atlantic Ocean'. Smithsonian Press, Washington.

Family PHALACROCORACIDAE: cormorants, shags

Bailey, R. (1966). The sea-birds of the southeast coast of Arabia. *Ibis* **108**, 224–264.

Bell-Cross, G. (1973). Observations on fish-eating birds in central Africa. *Honeyguide* **76**, 23–31.

Benson, C. W. and Pitman, C. (1958). Further breeding records from Northern Rhodesia. *Bull Br. Orn. Club* **78**(9), 164–166.

Berry, H. H. (1974). The Crowned raced of Reed Cormorant *Phalacrocorax africanus coronatus* breeding underneath Walvis Bay guano platform, South West Africa. *Madoqua* **8**, 59–62.

Berry, H. H. (1975). History of the guano platform on Bird Rock, Walvis Bay, South West Africa. *Bokmakierie* **27**(3), 60–64.

Berry, H. H. (1976a). Physiological and behavioural ecology of the Cape Cormorant *Phalacrocorax capensis*. *Madoqua* **9**, 5–55.

Berry, H. H. (1976b). Mass mortality of Cape Cormorants, caused by fish oil in the Walvis Bay region of South West Africa. *Madoqua* **9**, 57–62.

Berry, H. H. (1976c). The wind that makes the birds breed. *Afr. Wildl.* **30**(6), 16–21.

Berry, H. H. (1977). Seasonal fidelity of Cape Cormorants to nesting areas. *Cormorant* **2**, 5–6.

Berry, H. H. and Berry, C. U. (1975). A check list and notes on the birds of Sandvis, South West Africa. *Madoqua* **9**(2), 5–18.

Berry, H. H., Millar, R. P. and Louw, G. N. (1979). Environmental cues influencing the breeding biology and circulating levels of various hormones and tri glycerides in the Cape Cormorant. *Comp. Biochem. Physiol. Comp. Physiol.* **62**(A), 879–884.

Birkhead, M. E. (1978). Some aspects of the feeding ecology of the Reed Cormorant and Darter in Lake Kariba, Rhodesia. *Ostrich* **49**, 1–7.

Bowen, W., Gardiner, N., Harris, B. J. and Thomas, J. D. (1962). Communal nesting of *Phalacrocorax africanus*, *Bubulcus ibis*, and *Anhinga rufa* in southern Ghana. *Ibis* **104**, 246–247.

Bowmaker, A. P. (1963). Cormorant predation on two central African lakes. *Ostrich* **34**, 3–26.

Britton, P. L. (1970). Some non-passerine bird weights from East Africa. *Bull. Br. Orn. Club* **90**, 142–144.

Brooke, R. K. (1979). A fish catching technique of the Reed Cormorant. *Cormorant* **7**, 26.

Brosset, A. (1966). Les oiseaux du Maroc oriental de la Mediterranée à Berguent. *Alauda* **34**(3), 161–205.

Brunel, J. and Thiollay, J. M. (1969–1970). Liste preliminaire des oiseaux de Cote d'Ivoire. *Alauda* **37**, 230–254; **38**, 72–73.

Burger, A. E. (1978). Functional anatomy of the feeding apparatus of four South African cormorants. *Zool. Afr.* **13**(1), 81–102.

Calburn, S. (1969). 'Calburn's Birds of Southern Africa'. Purnell, Cape Town.

Cooper, J. (1969). Egg size of the Reed Cormorant. *Ostrich* **40**, 215.

Crawford, R. J. M. and Shelton, P. A. (1978). Pelagic fish and seabird interrelationships off the coasts of South West and South Africa. *Biol. Conser.* **14**, 85–109.

Curry-Lindhal, K. (1970). Spread-wing postures in Pelecaniformes and Ciconiiformes. *Auk* **87**, 371–372.

Davies, D. H. (1955). The South African Pilchard (*Sardinops ocellata*). Bird predators, 1953–4. *Invest. Rep. Div. Fish. Un. S. Afr.* **18**, 1–32.

Davies, D. H. (1958). The South African pilchard (*Sardinops ocellata*) and Maasbanker (*Trachurus trachurus*). The predation of sea-birds in the commercial fishery. *Invest. Rep. Div. Fish Un. S. Afr.* **31**, 1–16.

Dekeyser, P. L. (1955). Notes d'Ornithologie ouest africaine. *Bull. Inst. fr. Afr. noire* **17**, 1214–1218.

Donnelly, B. G. (1966). An invasion of Cape Cormorants *Phalacrocorax capensis* into Algoa Bay with a note on mortality. *Ostrich* **37**, 228.

Dupuy, A. R. (1973). Premier inventaire des oiseaux du Parc nationale de basse Casamance (Senegal). *Bull. Inst. fr. Afr. noire* Ser. A, **35**(3), 723–740.

Dupuy, A. R. (1975). Nidification de Hérons pourprés (*Ardea purpurea*) au Parc National des oiseaux du Djoudj, Senegal. *Oiseau et R.F.O.* **45**, 289–290.

Dupuy, A. R. (1976). Données nouvelles concernant la reproduction de quelques especes aviennes au Senegal. *Oiseaux et R.F.O.* **46**, 47–62.

Dutton, T. P. (1972). Large mixed colony of herons, Reed Cormorant, and Openbill on the Pongolo River floodplain. *Lammergeyer* **17**, 66.

Duxbury, W. R. (1963). Food of nestling Cattle Egret and Reed Cormorant. *Ostrich* **34**, 110.

Elgood, J. H., Fry, C. H. and Dowsett, R. J. (1973). African migrants in Nigeria. *Ibis* **115**, 1–45; 375–411.

Fraser, W. (1974). Feeding association between Little Egret and Reed Cormorants. *Ostrich* **45**, 262.

Gandrille, G. and Trotignon, J. (1973). Prospection post-estivale au Banc d'Arguin (Mauritanie). *Alauda* **41**(1–2), 129–159.

Germain, M., Dragesco, J., Roux, F. and Garcin, H. (1973). Contributés à l'ornithologie du Sud-Cameron. 1. Non Pass. *Oiseau et R.F.O.* **43**, 119–182.

Gooders, J. (Ed.) (1969). 'Birds of the World,' Vol. I. IPC, London.

Haydock, E. L. (1956). Breeding record of *Phalacrocorax carbo lucidus* in Central Province of Northern Rhodesia. *Ostrich* **27**, 87–88.

Hopson, J. (1966). Notes on a mixed cormorant and heron breeding colony near Malamfatori (Lake Chad). *Bull. Niger. Orn. Soc.* **3**, 21–34.

Jarvis, M. J. F. (1970). The White-breasted Cormorant in South Africa. *Ostrich* **41**, 118–119.

Jefford, T. G. and Urban, E. K. (1972). Behavioral responses to temperature in the Cormorant, *Phalacrocorax carbo lucidus*, from Lake Shala, Ethiopia. Proc. XV Int. Orn. Cong. pp. 656–657.

Jones, P. J. (1978). A possible function of the 'wing-drying' posture in the Reed Cormorant *Phalacrocorax africanus*. *Ibis* **120**, 540–542.

Junor, F. J. R. (1972). Estimation of the daily food intake of piscivorous birds. *Ostrich* **43**, 193–205.

Klug, S. and Boswall, J. (1970). Observations from a water bird colony, Lake Tana, Ethiopia. *Bull Br. Orn. Club* **90**(4), 97–105.

Liversidge, R. (1968). Bird weights. *Ostrich* **39**(4) 223–277.

Lockhart, P. S. (1968). White-breasted Cormorant *Phalacrocorax carbo*. *Ostrich* **39**, 271.

Marshall, A. J. and Roberts, J. D. (1959). The breeding biology of equatorial vertebrates: reproduction of cormorants (Phalacrocoracidae) at latitude 0°20′N *Proc. Zool. Soc. Lond.* **132**(4), 617–625.

Matthews, J. P. (1961). The pilchard of South Africa (*Sardinops ocellata*) and the Marsbanker (*Trachurus trachurus*). Bird predators. *S. W. Afr. Mar. Res. Lab. Invest. Rep.* **3**, 1–35.

Meinertzhagen, R. (1954). 'Birds of Arabia'. Oliver and Boyd, Edinburgh.

Milstein, P. le S. and Jacka, R. D. (1970). Establishment of a large heronry. *Ostrich* **41**, 208–210.

Morel, G. J. and Morel, M.-Y. (1961). Une héronnière mixte sur le Bas-Senegal. *Alauda* **29**(2), 99–117.

Mundy, P. J. and Cook, A. W. (1974). The birds of Sokota.

Part 3: Breeding Data. *Bull. Nig. Orn. Soc.* **10**(37), 1–28.

Mwenya, A. N. (1973). Ornithological notes from south east of Lake Bangweulu. *Puku* **7**, 151–161.

de Naurois, R. (1961). Recherches sur l'avifauna de la Côte Atlantique du Maroc. Du Détooit de Gibraltar aux Iles de Mogador. *Alauda* **29**, 241–259.

Olver, M. D. and Kuyper, M. A. (1978). Breeding biology of the Whitebreasted Cormorant in Natal. *Ostrich* **49**, 25–30.

Pain, H., Tyler, S. J. and Vittery, A. (1975). A checklist of the birds of Addis Ababa. (Cyclostyled.) Addis Ababa Ethiopian Wildf. and Nat. Hist. Soc., 20 pp.

Penzhorn, B. L. and van Straaten, P. F. (1976). Attentions to the checklist of birds of the Addo Elephant National Park, South Africa. *Koedoe* **19**, 177–178.

du Plessis, S. S. (1957). Growth and daily intake of the Whitebreasted Cormorant in captivity. *Ostrich* **28**(4), 197–201.

Rand, R. W. (1951). The guano platforms of South West Africa. *Ibis* **93**(2), 309–310.

Rand, R. W. (1960). The biology of guano-producing sea-birds. 3. The distribution, abundance and feeding habits of the cormorants *Phalacrocoracidae* off the South West coast of the Cape Province. *Invest. Rep. Div. Fish. Un. S. Afr.* **42**, 5–32.

Rand, R. W. (1963). The biology of guano-producing sea-birds. 4. Composition of colonies on the Cape Islands. *Invest. Rep. Div. Fish. Un. S. Afr.* **43**.

Reynolds, J. F. (1977). Thermo-regulatory problems of birds nesting in arid areas in East Africa: a review. *Scopus* **1**, 57–68.

Rijke, A. M. (1968). The water repellency and feather structure of cormorants, Phalacrocoracidae. *Ostrich* **38**, 163–165.

Ripley, S. D. and Bond, G. (1966). The birds of Socotra and Abd-el-Kuri. *Smithsonian Mis. Coll.* **151**(7), 1–37.

Schouteden, H. (1966). La fauna ornithologique du Rwanda. Musée Royal de l'Afrique Centrale—Tervuren, Belgique; Documentation Zoologique No. 10.

Schüz, E. (1968). Ornithologischer Oktober-Besuch am Tana-See (und bei Addis Abeba), Äthiopien. *Stuttgarter Beitr. Naturkunde* **189**, 43 pp.

Shaughnessy, P. D. (1979). Further notes on Crowned Cormorants on the mainland of South West Africa/Namibia. *Cormorant* **6**, 37–38.

Shaughnessy, P. D. and Shaughnessy, G. L. (1978). Crowned Cormorants on the coast of South West Africa/Namibia. *Cormorant* **5**, 21–25.

Siegfried, W. R., Williams, A. J., Frost, P. G. H. and Kinahan, J. B. (1975). Plumage and ecology of cormorants. *Zool. Afr.* **16**, 183–192.

Siegfried, W. R., Frost, P. G. H., Cooper, J. and Kemp, A. C. (1976). South African Red Data book—Aves. *S. Afr. Natn. Sci. Progr. Rep.* **7**.

Stronach, B. W. H. (1968). The Chagana heronry in western Tanzania. *Ibis* **110**, 345–348.

Tarboton, W. R. (1977). The status of communal herons, ibis and cormorants on the Witwatersrand. *S. Afr. J. Wildl. Res.* **7**, 19–25.

van Tets, G. F. (1965). A comparative study of some social communication patterns in the Pelecaniformes. *Orn. Monogr.* No. 2.

Tomlinson, D. N. S. (1979). Interspecific relations in a mixed heronry. *Ostrich* **50**, 193–198.

Tree, A. J. (1972). Further records of albinism and lutinism in the Eastern Cape. *Ostrich* **43**(3), 184.

Tree, A. J. (1978). A visit to Makgadikgadi Pan in April 1974. *Honeyguide* **95**, 39–41.

Turner, D. A. (1978). The heronry at Lake Jipe. *Scopus* **2**(2), 47–48.

Urban, E. K. (1979). Observations on the nesting biology of

the Great Cormorant in Ethiopia. *Wilson Bull.* **91**, 461–463.

Urban, E. K. and Jefford, T. G. (1974). The status of the cormorants *Phalacrocorax carbo lucidus* and *Phalacrocorax carbo patricki*. *Bull. Br. Orn. Club* **94**, 104–107.

Vincent, A. A. (1945). The breeding habits of some African birds. *Ibis* **87**, 82–84.

Wallace, D. I. M. (1973). Sea birds at Lagos and in the Gulf of Guinea. *Ibis* **115**(4) 559–571.

von Westernhagen, W. (1970). Über du Brütvogel der Banc d'Arguin (Mauretaninen). *J. Orn.* **111**, 206–226.

Whitfield, A. K. and Blaber, S. J. M. (1979). Feeding ecology of piscivorous birds at Lake St. Lucia, Part 3: Swimming birds. *Ostrich* **50**; 10–20.

Williams, A. J. (1978). Nests and cormorant biology. *Cormorant* No. 4, 22–27.

Williams, A. J. and Burger, A. E. (1978). The ecology of the prey of Cape and Bank Cormorants. *Cormorant* No. 4, 28–29.

Williams, J. G. (1966). A new cormorant from Uganda. *Bull. Br. Orn. Club* **86**. 48–50.

Winterbottom, J. M. (1969). Waterbirds in Ovamboland. *Ostrich* **40**(1) 27–28.

Family ANHINGIDAE: darters

Allen, T. T. (1961). Notes on the breeding behaviour of the Anhinga. *Wilson Bull.* **73**, 115–125.

Beesley, J. S. S. (1976). Darter *Anhinga rufa*. *Ostrich* **47**(4), 214.

Birkhead, M. E. (1978). Some aspects of the feeding ecology of the Reed Cormorant and Darter in Lake Kariba, Rhodesia. *Ostrich* **49**, 1–7.

Bowen, W., Gardiner, N., Harris, B. J. and Thomas, J. D. (1962). Communal nesting of *Phalacrocorax africanus*, *Bubulcus ibis*, and *Anhinga rufa* in southern Ghana. *Ibis* **104**, 246–247.

Burger, J., Miller, L. M. and Hahn, D. L. (1978). Behaviour and sex roles of nesting Anhingas at San Blas, Mexico. *Wilson Bull.* **90**, 359–375.

Cott, H. B. (1961). Scientific results of an inquiry into the ecology and economic status of the Nile Crocodile (*Crocodilus niloticus*) in Uganda and Northern Rhodesia. *Trans. Zool. Soc. London* **91**, 211–350.

Dorst, J. and Mougin, J.-L. (1979). Order Pelecaniformes. *In* 'Peters Check List of Birds of the World', Vol. 1, 2nd edn (Mayr, E. and Cottrell, G. W. Eds) Museum of Comparative Zoology, Cambridge, Mass.

Duhart, F. and Deschamps, M. (1964). Notes sur l'avifaune du delta central nigerien. *Oiseau et R.F.O.* 33, 1–99.

Dupuy, A. R. (1973). Premier inventaire des Oiseaux du Parc nationale de Basse Casamance (Senegal). *Bull Inst. fr. Afr. noire* Ser A, **35**(3), 723–740.

Dupuy, A. R. (1975). Nidification de Hérons pourprés (*Ardea purpurea*) au Parc national des Oiseaux du Djoudj, Senegal. *Oiseau et R.F.O.* **45** 289–290.

Dupuy, A. R. (1976). Données nouvelles concernant la reproduction de quelques espèces aviennes au Senegal. *Oiseaux et R.F.O.* **46**, 47–62.

Fraser, W. (1971). Birds at Lake Ngami, Botswana. *Ostrich* **42**, 128–130.

Friedmann, H. (1930). Birds collected by the Childs Frick Expedition to Ethiopia and Kenya Colony, Pt. 1. *Bull. U.S. Nat. Mus. Washington* 153.

Good, A. I. (1952). The birds of French Cameroon. *Mem. Inst. fr. Afr. noire* 14.

Jensen, J. V. and Kirkeby, J. (1980). 'The Birds of The Gambia'. Aros Nature Guide, Aathus, Denmark.

Junor, F. J. R. (1972). Estimation of the daily food intake of piscivorous birds. *Ostrich* **43**, 193–205.

Klug, S. and Boswall, J. (1970). Observations from a water bird colony, Lake Tana, Ethiopia. *Bull. Br. Orn. Club* **90**(4), 97–105.

Lockhart, P. S. (1968). African Darter *Anhinga rufa*. *Ostrich* **39**, 271.

Malzy, P. (1962). La fauna avienne du Mali. *Oiseau et R.F.O.* **32**, 1–81.

Manson, A. J. (1969). Breeding of the Darter. *Honeyguide* **59**, 34–35.

Marshall, B. (1972). Gymnogene feeding on Darter eggs. *Honeyguide* **72**, 34.

Milstein, P. le S. (1975). The biology of Barberspan, with special reference to the avifauna. *Ostrich* Suppl. 10.

Milstein, P. le S. and Jacka, R. D. (1970). Establishment of a large heronry. *Ostrich* **41**, 208–210.

Morel, G. J. and Morel, M-Y. (1959). Dates de reproduction de quelques oiseaux du Sahel Senegalais. *Ostrich* Suppl. 3, 260–263.

Morel, G. J. and Morel, M.-Y. (1961). Une heronniere mixte sur le Bas-Senegal. *Alauda* **29**(2), 99–117.

Mwenya, A. N. (1973). Ornithological notes from south east of Lake Bangweulu. *Puku* **7**, 151–161.

North, M. E. W. (1959). The great heronry of Garsen on the River Tana. *J. E. Afr. Nat. Hist. Soc.* **23**(4), 159–160.

Owre, O. T. (1967). Adaptations for locomotion and feeding in the Anhinga and the Double-crested Cormorant. *Orn. Monogr.* No. 6.

Ruwet, J. C. (1963). Notes écologiques et éthologiques sur les oiseaux des plaines de la Lufira superieure (Katanga). I. Podicipedes, Steganopodes, Gressores, Anseres. *Rev. Zool. Bot. afr.* **58**, 1–60.

Ruwet, J. C. (1965). 'Les Oiseaux des Plaines et du Lac-Barrage de la Lufira Superieure (Katanga maridional)'. Editions FULREAC, Université de Liège.

Stronach, B. W. H. (1968). The Chagana heronry in western Tanzania. *Ibis* **110**, 345–348.

Tarboton, W. R. (1975). Breeding notes on the Darter, *Anhinga rufa*. Witwatersrand Bird Club *News* **88**, 8–9.

Tarboton, W. R. (1977). The status of communal herons, ibis and cormorants on the Witwatersrand. *S. Afr. J. Wildl. Res.* **7**, 19–25.

Taylor, J. S. (1957). Notes on the birds of inland waters in the Eastern Cape Province with special reference to the Karoo. *Ostrich* **28**, 1–80.

van Tets, G. F. (1965). A comparative study of some social communication patterns in the Pelecaniformes. *Orn. Monogr.* No. 2.

Tree, A. J. (1978). A visit to Makgadikgadi Pan in April 1974. *Honeyguide* **95**, 39–41.

Van Someren, V. G. L. (1956). Days with birds. *Fieldiana Zool.* **38**.

Vernon, C. J. (1976). Heronries in Rhodesia in 1973/74. *Honeyguide* **86**, 25–29.

Vestjens, W. J. M. (1975). Breeding behaviour of the Darter at Lake Cowal, NSW. *Emu* **75**(3), 121–131.

Vincent, A. A. (1945). The breeding habits of some African birds. *Ibis* **87**, 82–84.

Family PELECANIDAE: pelicans

Baxter, R. M. and Urban, E. K. (1970). On the nature and origin of the feather colouration in the Great White Pelican *Pelecanus onocrotalus roseus* in Ethiopia. *Ibis* **112**(3), 336–339.

Brown, L. H. and Urban, E. K. (1969). The breeding biology of the Great White Pelican *Pelecanus onocrotalus roseus* at Lake Shala, Ethiopia. *Ibis* **111**(2), 199–237.

Burke, V. E. M. and Brown, L. H. (1970). Observations on the breeding of the Pink-backed *Pelican Pelecanus rufescens. Ibis* 112(4), 499–512.

Cooper, J. (1980). Fatal sibling aggression in pelicans—a review. *Ostrich* 51, 183–186.

Din, N. A. and Eltringham, S. K. (1974a). Ecological separation between White and Pink-backed Pelicans in the Ruwenzori National Park, Uganda. *Ibis* 116, 28–43.

Din, N. A. and Eltringham, S. K. (1974b). Breeding of the Pink-backed Pelican *Pelecanus rufescens* in Ruwenzori National Park, Uganda with notes on Marabou Storks *Leptopilus crumeniferus. Ibis* 116, 477–493.

Din, N. A. and Eltringham, S. K. (1977). Weights and measures of Uganda pelicans with some seasonal variations. *E. Afr. Wildl. J.* 15(4), 317–326.

Feely, J. M. (1962). Observations on the breeding of the White Pelican, *Pelecanus onocrotalus*, at Lake St. Lucia, Zululand, during 1957 and 1958. *Lammergeyer* 2(2), 10–20.

Jensen, J. V. and Kirkeby, J. (1980). 'The Birds of The Gambia'. Aros Nature Guide, Aathus, Denmark.

Mundy, P. J. and Cook, A. W. (1974). The birds of Sokoto. Part 3: Breeding data. *Bull. Niger. Orn. Soc.* 10(37), 1–28.

Portmann, A. (1937). Beobachtungen über die post-embryonale Entwicklung des Rosenpelicans. *Rev. Suisse Zool.* 44(21), 363–370.

Serle, W. (1943). Further observations on northern Nigerian birds. *Ibis* 1943, 264–300.

Urban, E. K. (in press). Time of nesting and number of nesting Great White Pelicans at Lake Shala, Ethiopia, and elsewhere in Africa. Proc. V Pan-Afr. Orn. Congr.

Vareschi, E. (1979). The ecology of Lake Nakuru (Kenya). II. Biomass and spatial distribution of fish (*Tilapia grahami* Boulenger = *Sarotherodon alcalicum grahami* Boulenger). *Oecologia* 37, 321–335.

Vesey-Fitzgerald, D. (1957). The breeding of the White Pelican *Pelicanus* (sic) *onocrotalus* in the Rukwa Valley, Tanyanyika. *Bull. Br. Orn. Club* 77(8), 127–128.

Family FREGATIDAE: frigatebirds

Diamond, A. W. (1975). Biology and behaviour of frigate birds *Fregata* spp. on Aldabra Atoll. *Ibis* 117, 302–333.

Nelson, J. B. (1975). The breeding biology of frigatebirds—a comparative review. *Living Bird* 14, 113–155.

Order CICONIIFORMES

Suborder ARDEAE

Family ARDEIDAE: herons, egrets, bitterns

Amadon, D. (1953). Avian systematics and evolution in the Gulf of Guinea. *Bull. Am. Mus. Nat. Hist.* 100(3), 395–451.

Archibald, E. (1949). Note on a White-backed Night Heron. *Ostrich* 20(3), 170.

Audin, H. (1963). Goliath Heron breeding in the Sebakwe National Park. *Honeyguide* 40, 4–5.

Ayres, T. (1878). Additional notes on the ornithology of the Transvaal. *Ibis*, Ser. 4. 2, 281–301.

Backhurst, G. C. and Pearson, D. J. (1977). Ethiopian region birds attracted to the lights of Ngulia Safari Lodge, Kenya. *Scopus* 1, 98–103.

Baird, D. A. (1979). Twenty-eight additions to Archer and Godman's 'Birds of British Somaliland and the Gulf of Aden'. *Bull. Br. Orn. Club* 99, 6–9.

Beasley, A. J. (1975). Feeding behaviour of Yellow-billed Egret. *Ostrich* 46, 189–190.

Beesley, J. S. S. (1971). A waterbird colony in Tanzania. *Bull. E. Afr. Nat. Hist. Soc.* 5, 73.

Beesley, J. S. S. (1972). A nesting colony of Black-headed Herons *Ardea melanocephala* in Arusha, Tanzania. *Bull. E. Afr. Nat. Hist. Soc.* 1972, 47–48.

Beesley, J. S. S. (1976a) Cattle Egret *Ardeola ibis. Ostrich* 47(4), 215.

Beesley, J. S. S. (1976b). Great White Egret *Egretta alba. Ostrich* 47(4), 215.

Beesley, J. S. S. (1976c). Little Bittern *Ixobrychus minutus. Ostrich* 47(4), 214.

Bell-Cross, G. (1973). Observations on fish-eating birds in central Africa. *Honeyguide* 76, 23–31.

Benson, C. W. (1964). Birds associating the ungulates. *Auk* 81, 436.

Benson, C. W. and Dowsett, R. J. (1969). The Madagascar Squacco Heron, *Ardeola idea*, in Zambia. *Puku* 5, 217.

Benson, C. W. and Irwin, M. P. S. (1966). Some intra-African migratory birds. III. *Puku* 4, 49–56.

Benson, C. W. and Penny, M. J. (1971). Land birds of Aldabra. *Phil. Trans. Roy. Soc. London*, Ser. B. 260, 417–527.

Benson, C. W. and Pitman, C. (1958). Further breeding records from Northern Rhodesia. *Bull. Br. Orn. Club* 78(9), 164–166.

Benson, C. W. and Pitman, C. (1961). Further breeding records from Northern Rhodesia (No. 2). *Bull Br. Orn. Club* 81, 156–163.

Benson, C. W. and Pitman, C. (1963). Further breeding records of Northern Rhodesia/Zambia. *Bull. Br. Orn. Club* 83, 32–36.

Benson, C. W. and Pitman, C. R. S. (1964). Further breeding records from Northern Rhodesia (No. 4). *Bull. Brit. Orn. Club* 84, 54–60.

Benson, C. W. and Pitman, C. (1966). Further breeding records from Northern Rhodesia/Zambia. *Bull, Br. Orn. Club* 86, 22.

Benson, C. W. and Serventy, D. L. (1956). Breeding data from Katema Island, Northern Rhodesia. *Ostrich* 27(4), 171–172.

Benson, C. W., Brooke, R. K., Dowsett, R. J. and Irwin, M. P. S. (1971a). 'The Birds of Zambia. Collins, London.

Benson, C. W., Brooke, R. K. and Irwin, M. P. S. (1971b). The Slaty Egret is a good species. *Bull. Br. Orn. Club* 91, 131–133.

Berlioz, J. (1949). L'albinisme du plumage chez les ardéidés. *Oiseau et R.F.O.* 19(1), 11–30.

Berlioz, J. (1959). Notes sur les Aigrettes dimorphiques en Afrique. Proc. I Pan-Afr. Orn. Congr. *Ostrich* Suppl. 3, 415–417.

Berlioz, J. (1961). Le polymorphisme-mutationnel chez les Ardeides de l'ancien Monde. *C. r. Somm.-Séanc-Soc.* 37, 3–7.

Berry, H. H. and Berry, C. U. (1975). A checklist, and notes on the birds of Sandvis, South West Africa. *Madoqua* 9(2), 5–18.

Berthet, G. (1948). Les quartiers d'hiver des hérons pour pres *Ardea purpurea* L. 1766 de la Dombes. *Alauda* 16, 237–238.

Beven, G. (1946). Does the Buff-backed Heron really remove ticks from the bodies of animals? *Ibis* **88**, 133.

Binford, L. C. and Zimmerman, D. A. (1974). Rufous-bellied Heron in Kenya. *Bull. Br. Orn. Club* **94**, 101–102.

Blaker, D. (1965). Flies in Cattle Egret diet. *Ostrich* **36**, 147.

Blaker, D. (1969a). Behaviour of the Cattle Egret *Ardeola ibis*. *Ostrich* **40**, 75–129.

Blaker, D. (1969b). The behaviour of *Egretta garzetta* and *E. intermedia*. *Ostrich* **40**, 150–155.

Blaker, D. (1971). Range expansion of the Cattle Egret. *Ostrich* Suppl. 9, 27–30.

Bock, W. J. (1956). A generic review of the family Ardeidae (Aves). *Amer. Mus. Nov.* **1779**, 49 pp.

Bodenham, R. (1945). Notes on migrants and resident birds in the North Suez Canal areas from March 1 to December 5 1944. *Zool. Soc. Egypt* 7, 21–47.

de Bont, A. F. (1960). Observations sur les oiseaux d'eau au Katanga (Congo Belge). *Gerfaut* **50**(1), 73–85.

Boswall, J. (1971). Notes from coastal Eritrea on selected species. *Bull. Br. Orn. Club* **91**, 81–84.

Bowen, W., Gardiner, N., Harris, B. J. and Thomas, J. D. (1962). Communal nesting of *Phalacrocorax africanus*, *Bubulcus ibis*, and *Anhinga rufa* in southern Ghana. *Ibis* **104**, 246–247.

Brelsford, W. V. (1942). Further field notes on Northern Rhodesian birds. *Ibis* **6**, 83–90.

Brelsford, W. V. (1947). Notes on birds of Lake Bangweulu area in Northern Rhodesia. *Ibis* **89**, 57–77.

Britton, P. L. (1967). Some records from Mozambique. *Ostrich* **38**, 46.

Britton, P. L. (1970a). Birds of the Balovale district of Zambia. *Ostrich* **41**, 145–190.

Britton, P. L. (1970b). Some non-passerine bird weights from East Africa. *Bull. Br. Orn. Club* **90**, 142–144.

Britton, P. L. (1975). Dark-coloured egrets on the Kenya coast. *Bull. E. Afr. Nat. Hist. Soc.* **1975**, 64–65.

Broekhuysen, G. J. and Broekhuysen, M. H. (1961). Feeding behaviour of the Black Heron *Melanophoyx ardesiaca*. *Ostrich* **32**, 185.

Brooke, R. K. (1967). Further breeding records from Zambia (No. 6). *Bull. Br. Orn. Club* **87**, 120–122.

Brooke, R. K. (1970). Cattle Egrets at Glendale. *Honeyguide* **61**, 33.

Brooke, R. K. (1971a). Avian scavengers in Luanda Harbor. *Bull Br. Orn Club*, **91**, 46.

Brooke, R. K. (1971b). Check the Slaty Egret. *Bokmakierie* **23**, 91–92.

Brosset, A. (1971). Premières observations sur la reproduction de six oiseaux africains. *Alauda* **39**, 112–126.

Browder, J. A. (1973). Long-distance movements of Cattle Egrets. *Bird Banding* **44**(3), 158–170.

Cackett, K. (1970). Cattle Egrets breeding in the Rhodesian Lowveld. *Honeyguide* **61**, 33–34.

Cackett, K. (1974). News from the Lowveld. *Honeyguide* **78**, 21–23.

Calder, D. R. (1971). A Green-backed Heron with red soft parts. *Bull. Br. Orn. Club* **91**(4), 108.

Cannell, I. C. (1968). Notes from Angola. *Ostrich* **39**, 264–265.

Cantoni, J. and Castan, R. (1961). Nidification d'*Egretta garzetta* (L.) sur l'Ile de Chikli, Lac de Tunis. *Alauda* **28**(1), 34–37.

Cawkell, E. M. and Moreau, R. (1963). Notes on birds in the Gambia. *Ibis* **105**, 156–178.

Chapin, J. P. (1956). The Cattle Egret in Africa. *Audubon Mag.* **58**, 75, 88.

Cheylan, G. (1979). A propos du héron mélanocephale dans Paléarctique. *Alauda* **42**(2), 111–112.

Child, G. (1972). A survey of mixed 'heronries' in the Okavango Delta, Botswana. *Ostrich* **43**(1), 60–62.

Clancey, P. A. (1959a). On the race of Cattle Egret *Ardeola ibis* (Linnaeus) occurring in the Ethiopian zoogeographic region. *Bull. Brit. Orn. Club* **79**, 13–14.

Clancey, P. A. (1959b). The Cattle Egret of the Ethiopian Region. *Bull Br. Orn. Club* **79**, 79–80.

Clancey, P. A. (1968a). On variation in the Cattle Egret, *Bubulcus ibis*. *Ostrich* **39**(3), 193–194.

Clancey, P. A. (1968b). Variation in *Ardeola ralloides* (Scopoli) (Aves: Ardeidae). *Arnoldia* (*Rhodesia*) 3(37), 1–5.

Clancey, P. A. (1969). Racial variation in the Cattle Egret. *Ostrich* **40**, 217–218.

Clancey, P. A. (1971). A handlist of the birds of southern Moçambique. *Inst. Invest. Cientifica Moçambique* 10, Serie A.

Clancey, P. A. (1976). Interesting feeding behaviour in the Little Egret and Brownhooded Kingfisher. *Ostrich* **47**(2), 131.

Cockburn, T. H. (1946). Ticks and the diet of the Buff-backed Heron. *Ibis* **88**, 127.

Connor, M. A. (1979). Feeding association between Little Egret and African Spoonbill. *Ostrich* **50**, 118.

Cooper, J. (1970). Canopy-formation in the Black Heron. *Ostrich* **41**, 212–214.

Cooper, J. (1971). Wing-beat rate in the genus *Ardea*. *Honeyguide* **67**, 23–25.

Cooper, J. and Marshall, B. E. (1970). Observations on the nestlings of the Goliath Heron, *Ardea goliath*, in Rhodesia. *Bull. Br. Orn. Club* **90**, 148–152.

Cott, H. B. (1961). Scientific results of an inquiry into the ecology and economic status of the Nile Crocodile (*Crocodilus niloticus*) in Uganda and Northern Rhodesia. *Trans. Zool. Soc. London* **91**, 211–350.

Cowles, R. B. (1930). Notes on the nesting of the African Green Heron (*Butorides atricapilla*) in Natal. *Auk* **47**, 465–470.

Cowper, S. G. (1977). Dry season birds at Enugu and Nsukka. *Bull. Niger. Orn. Soc.* **13**(43), 57–63.

Craib, C. L. (1975). Breeding and roosting of Green-backed Heron, *Butorides striatus*. Witwatersrand Bird Club *News* **89**, 6–7.

Craufurd, R. Q. (1966). Notes on the ecology of the Cattle Egret *Ardeola ibis* at Rokupr, Sierra Leone. *Ibis* **108**, 411–418.

Cronje, P. H. (1966). Black Heron *Melanophoyx ardesiaca* breeding at Potchefstroom. *Ostrich* **37**, 238.

Curry-Lindahl, K. (1968). Taxonomy of the herons (Ardeidae) illustrated by ethological studies. A preliminary account. *Vår Fågelvärld* **27**, 289–308.

Curry-Lindahl, K. (1971). Systematic relationships in herons (Ardeidae), based on comparative studies of behaviour and ecology. *Ostrich* Suppl. 9, 53–70.

Day, D. H. (1978). Letter to the editor. *Bokmakierie* **30**, 108.

Dean, G. J. W. (1964). Stork and egret as predators of the red locust in the Rukwa Valley outbreak area. *Ostrich* **35** 95–100.

Dekeyser, P. L. (1947). Notes d'ornithologie ouest-africaine. No. 3. A propos des Aigrettes grises de l'Afrique Occidental. *Bull. Inst. fr. Afr. noire* **9**, 363–372.

Dekeyser, P. L. and Villiers, A. (1951). Nidification d'Aigrettes blanches au Senegal. *Bull. Inst. fr. Afr. noire* **13**(1), 151–154.

Delacour, J. (1946). Under-wing fishing of the Black Heron, *Melanophoyx ardesiaca*. *Auk* **63**, 441–442.

Dowsett, R. J. (1979). Recent additions to the Zambian list *Bull. Br. Orn. Club* **99**, 94–98.

Dowsett, R. J. and de Vos, A. (1963/1964). The ecology and numbers of aquatic birds in the Kafue flats, Zambia. *Wildf. Trust Ann. Rep.* **16**, 67–73.

Dragesco, J. (1960). Notes biologiques sur quelques Oiseaux d'Afrique equatoriale. *Alauda* **28**(2), 81–92.

Dragesco, J. (1961). Monographies des oiseaux du Banc

d'Arguin. L'Aigrette Dimorpha. *Science et Nature* **47**, 1–4.

Duhart, F. and Deschamps, M. (1964). Notes sur l'avifaune du delta central nigerien. *Oiseau et R.F.O.* **33**, 1–99.

Dupuy, A. (1970). Données sur les migrations transsahariennes du printemps 1966. *Alauda* **38**, 278–285.

Dupuy, A. R. (1975). Nidification de Hérons pourprés (*Ardea purpurea*) au Parc National des Oiseaux du Djoudj, Senegal. *Oiseau et R.F.O.* **45**, 289–290.

Dupuy, A. R. (1976). Données nouvelles concernant la reproduction de quelques espèces aviennes au Senegal. *Oiseaux et R.F.O.* **46**, 47–62.

Dutton, T. P. (1972). Large mixed colony of herons, Reed Cormorant, and openbill on the Pongolo River floodplain. *Lammergeyer* **17**, 66.

Elgood, J. H., Sharland, R. E. and Ward, P. (1966). Palaearctic migrants in Nigeria. *Ibis* **108**, 84–116.

Elgood, J. H., Fry, C. H. and Dowsett, R. J. (1973). African migrants in Nigeria. *Ibis* **115** 1–45, 375–411.

Elliott, C. C. H. (1978). Night Heron and Lesser Black-backed Gull recoveries in Chad. *Bull. Niger. Orn. Soc.* **14**, 26–27.

Elliott, H. F. I. and Monk, J. F. (1952). Land-bird migration on the Suez route to East Africa. *Ibis* **94**, 528–530.

Farkas, T. (1962). Contribution to the bird fauna of Barberspan. *Ostrich* Suppl. 4.

Feely, J. M. (1964). Heron and stork breeding colonies in the Luangwa Valley. *Puku*, 2, 76–77.

Ferguson, J. W. H. and Jensen, R. A. C. (1973). Little Bittern *Ixobrychus minutus minutus*. *Ostrich* **44**(2), 126.

Field, G. D. (1975). The Yellow-billed Egret *Egretta intermedia* in Sierra Leone. *Bull. Niger. Orn. Soc.* **11**, 53–55.

Field, G. D. (1978). Status of Ciconiiformes in Sierra Leone. *Bull. Niger. Orn. Soc.* **14**, 42–46.

Forbes-Watson, A. (1966). A further note on reef herons in East Africa. *J. E. Afr. Nat. Hist. Soc.* **25**(3), No. 112, 233.

Fourie, L. I. K. (1968). Goliath Heron and pelicans. *Lammergeyer* **8**, 50–51.

Frade, F. (1959). New records of non-resident birds, and notes on some resident ones, in Sao Tome and Principe Islands. *Ostrich* Suppl. 3, 317–320.

Fraser, W. (1971). Breeding herons and storks in Botswana. *Ostrich* **42**, 123–127.

Fraser, W. (1974). Feeding association between Little Egret and Reed Cormorant. *Ostrich* **45**, 262.

Friedmann, H. and Loveridge, A. (1937). Notes on the ornithology of tropical East Africa. *Bull. Mus. Comp. Zool. Harvard* **81**.

Fuggles-Couchman, N. R. (1939). Notes on some birds of the Eastern Province, Tanganyika Territory. *Ibis*, Ser. 14. 3(1), 76–106.

Gill, E. L. (1952). Some first records for the Cape. *Bokmakierie* 4(2), 27–29.

Gooders, J. (Ed.) (1969). 'Birds of the World', Vol. I. IPC, London.

Goodfellow, C. F. (1966). Some additions to Jacot-Guillarmod's 'Catalogue of the birds of Basutoland' (1963). *Ostrich* **37**(1), 62–63.

Grant, C. H. B. and Mackworth-Praed, C. W. (1933a). On the relationship, status, and range of *Egretta garzetta*, *Demigretta gularis*, *D. schistacea*, *D. asha*, and *D. dimorpha*, a new subspecies and the correct type-locality of *Egretta garzetta*. *Bull. Br. Orn. Club* **53**, 189–195.

Grant, C. H. B. and Mackworth-Praed, C. W. (1933b). Further notes on *Demigretta schistacea*, *Egretta garzetta garzetta*, *Egretta garzetta dimorpha* and some corrections. *Bull. Br. Orn. Club* **53**, 245–247.

Grieg-Smith, P. W. (1977). Breeding dates of birds in Mole National Park, Ghana. *Bull. Niger. Orn. Soc.* **13**(44), 89–93.

Grieg-Smith, P. W. and Davidson, N. C. (1977). Weights of West African savanna birds. *Bull. Br. Orn. Club* **97**, 96–99.

Grimes, L. G. (1967). Breeding of the Black Heron in Ghana. *Bull. Br. Orn. Club* **87**, 1–2.

Guichard, K. M. (1947). Birds of the inundation zones of the river Niger, French Soudan. *Ibis* **89**, 450–489.

Hachisuka, M. (1926). A revision of the genus *Gorsachius*. *Ibis* **12**(2), 585–592.

Hafner, H. (1975). Sur l'evolution récente des effectif reproducteurs de quatre espèces de hérons en Camargue. *Ardeola* **21**, 819–825.

Hamilton, K. (1944). Common Grey Heron nesting and other birds at Grasmere Farm, Pretoria. *Ostrich* **15**(1), 71–72.

Hamling, H. H. (1953). Observations on the behaviour of birds in Southern Rhodesia. *Ostrich* **24**(1), 9–16.

Hancock, J. and Elliott, H. (1978). 'The Herons of the World'. Harper and Row, New York.

Harvey, W. G. (1975). The habitat preferences of different colour morphs of *Egretta garzetta* on the Tanzanian coast. *Bull. Br. Orn. Club* **95**, 171–172.

Heatwole, H. (1965). Some aspects of the association of Cattle Egrets with Cattle. *Anim. Beh.* **13**, 79–83.

Helbig, L. (1968). Ethologische Beobachtungum an gefangengehaltenen *Egretta garzetta*, *Leucophoyx thula* und *Ardeola ibis* ausserhalb der Brutzeit. *Beitr. Vogelk.* 13(6), 397–454.

Holman, F. C. (1946). Does the Buff-backed Heron really remove ticks from the bodies of animals? *Ibis* **88**, 232–233.

Hopson, J. (1966). Notes on a mixed cormorant and heron breeding colony near Malamfatori (Lake Chad). *Bull. Niger. Orn. Soc.* **3**, 21–34.

Hornby, H. E. (1975). Occurrence of Rufous-bellied Heron in Hartley District. *Honeyguide* **82**, 35–36.

Irwin, M. P. S. (1969). *Ardeola idae* Hartlaub in Rhodesia. *Bull. Br. Orn. Club* **89**, 3–4.

Irwin, M. P. S. (1975). Adaptive morphology in the Black and Slaty egrets *Egretta ardesiaca* and *Egretta vinaceigula* and relationships within the genus *Egretta* (Aves: Ardeidae). *Bonn. zool. Beitr.* **26**, 155–163.

Irwin, M. P. S. and Benson, C. W. (1967). Notes on the birds of Zambia; Part III. *Arnoldia (Rhodesia)* 3(4), 1–30.

Jeffery, E. B. and Laycock, H. T. (1965). The Grey Heron (*Ardea cinerea*) nesting in Nyasaland. *Nyasaland J.* **18**, 20–21.

Jenni, D. A. (1973). Regional variations in the food of nestling Cattle Egrets. *Auk* **90**(4), 821–826.

Jensen, J. V. and Kirkeby, J. (1980). 'The Birds of The Gambia'. Aros Nature Guide, Aathus, Denmark.

Junor, F. J. R. (1972). Estimation of the daily food intake of piscivorous birds. *Ostrich* **43**, 193–205.

Keep, M. E. (1971). Inexplicable egret movements. *Lammergeyer* **13**, 57.

Keep, M. E. (1973). A breeding record of the White-backed Night Heron. *Afr. Wildl.* **27**, 182–183.

Keve, A. and E. Patkai. (1959). Hungarian ringed birds in Africa. *Ostrich* Suppl. 3, 321–330.

Kinnear, N. B. (1942). Common Bittern from Nigeria. *Bull. Br. Orn. Club* **42**(442), 56.

Klug, S. and Boswall, J. (1970). Observations from a water bird colony, Lake Tana, Ethiopia. *Bull. Br. Orn. Club* **90**(4), 97–105.

Kushlan, J. A. (1978). Feeding ecology of wading birds. *Nat. Aud. Res. Rap.* 7, 249–297.

Lack, P. (1977). A small heronry at Lake Jipe, Tsavo. *Scopus*, 1, 82.

Langley, C. H. (1978). Dwarf Bittern in the Cape Peninsula. *Ostrich* **49**(1), 47.

Lawson, W. J. (1964). Breeding of the Black Heron in southern Africa. *Ostrich* **35**, 58–59.

Leveque, R. and Winkler, R. (1977). Observation d'une aigrette 'melanique' au Maroc. *Alauda* **45**, 125.

Lockhart, P. S. (1976). Yellowbilled Egret *Egretta intermedius*. *Ostrich* **47**(4), 215.

Lynes, H. (1925). On the birds of north and central Darfur with notes on the West-Central Kordofan and North Nuba Provinces of British Sudan. *Ibis* **112**(1), 71–131, 344–416, 541–590, 757–797.

Macdonald, M. A. (1976). Field identification of the Yellow-billed Egret. *Bull. Niger. Orn. Soc.* **12**, 73–75.

Macdonald, M. A. (1977). Notes on Ciconiiformes at Cape Coast, Ghana. *Bull Niger. Orn. Soc.* **13**, 139–144.

Macdonald, M. A. (1978a). Records of Palaearctic migrants in Ghana. *Bull. Niger. Orn. Soc.* **14**, 64–68.

Macdonald, M. A. (1978b). The Yellow-billed Egret in West Africa (Aves:Ardeidae). *Rev. Zool. Afr.* **92**, 191–200.

Macleod, J. G. R. and Norris, A. (1966). New records for the Kalahari Gemsbok Park. *Ostrich* **37**, 229.

Malherbe, A. P. (1963). Notes on birds of prey and some others at Boshoek, North of Rustenburg during a rodent plague. *Ostrich* **34**, 95–96.

Malzy, P. (1962). La fauna avienne du Mali Oiseau. *Oiseau et R.F.O.* **32**, 1–81.

Mann, C. F. (1976). The birds of Teso District, Uganda. *J. E. Afr. Nat. Hist. Soc.* **156**, 16 pp.

Marais, J. (1968). Great White Heron in Bontebok National Park. *Ostrich* **39**, 41.

Markus, M. B. (1963). The Black Heron. *Bokmakierie* **15**, 21–22.

Marshall, B. (1977). Goliath Heron attempting to attract fish. *Honeyguide* **91**, 35–36.

Masterson, A. and Borrett, R. (1968). A guide to the Ardeidae in Rhodesia. *Honeyguide* **58**, 15–26.

Mathiasson, S. (1963). Visible diurnal migration in the Sudan. 1962, pp. 430–435. Proc. XIII Int. Orn. Congr. Amer. Ornith. Union.

Meinertzhagen, R. (1930). 'Nicoll's Birds of Egypt', Vol. 2. Hugh Rees Ltd., London.

Meyerriecks, A. J. (1959). Foot-stirring feeding behaviour in herons. *Wilson Bull.* **71**(2), 153–158.

Meyerriecks, A. J. (1960). Comparative breeding behaviour of four species of North American herons. *Publ. Nuttall Orn. Club* **2**, 1–158.

Meyerriecks, A. J. (1966). Additional observations on 'foot-stirring' feeding behaviour in herons. *Auk* **83**, 471–472.

Meyerriecks, A. J. (1971). Further observations in use of the feet by foraging herons. *Wilson Bull.* **83**(4), 435–438.

Middlemiss, E. H. J. (1955). Food of juvenile egrets. *Ostrich* **26**, 159.

Miles, M. J. (1977). Observations of Little Bitterns at Lusaka. *Bull. Zambian Orn. Soc.* **9**, 16–20.

Milewski, A. V. (1976). Feeding ecology of the Slaty Egret *Egretta vinaceigula*. *Ostrich* **47**, 132–134.

Mills, M. G. L. (1976a). Great White Egret *Egretta alba*. *Ostrich* **47**, 215.

Mills, M. G. L. (1976b). Night Heron *Nycticorax nycticorax*. *Ostrich* **47**, 215.

Milon, P. (1959). Observations biologiques sur *Egretta garzetta dimorpha* Hartert à Madagascar. *Ostrich* Suppl. 3, 250–259.

Milon, P., Petter, J. J. and Randrianasolo, G. (1973). Faune de Madagascar. XXXV. Oiseaux. OSTROM, Tananarive.

Milstein, P. le S. (1969). Moult in the Goliath Heron. *Ostrich* **40**(4), 215.

Milstein, P. le S. and Hunter, H. C. (1974). The spectacular Black Heron. *Bokmakierie* **26**, 93–97.

Milstein, P. le S. and Jacka, R. D. (1970). Establishment of a large heronry. *Ostrich* **41**, 208–210.

Milstein, P. le S., Prestt, I. and Bell, A. A. (1970). The breeding cycle of the Grey Heron. *Ardea* **58**, 171–257.

Mock, D. W. (1978). Pair-formation displays of the Great Egret. *Condor* **80**, 159–172.

Mock, D. W. and Mock, K. C. (1980). Feeding behavior and ecology of the Goliath Heron. *Auk* **97**, 433–448.

Molesworth, A. E. N. (1968). White-backed Night Heron *Gorsachius leuconotus*. *Ostrich* **39**(4), 271.

Morant, P. D. (1980). Twenty-first ringing report for Southern Africa. *Ostrich* **51**(4), 204–214.

Moreau, R. E. (1967). Water-birds over the Sahara. *Ibis* **109**, 232–259.

Morel, G. J. and Morel, M.-Y. (1959). Dates de reproduction de quelques oiseaux du Sahel Senegalais. *Ostrich* Suppl. 3, 260–263.

Morel, G. J. and Morel, M.-Y. (1961). Une héronnière mixte sur le Bas-Senegal. *Alauda*, **29**(2), 99–117.

Morel, G. J., Morel, M.-Y., and Roux, F. (1962). Données nouvelles sur l'avifaune du Senegal. *Oiseau et R.F.O.* **32**, 28–56.

Mundy, P. J. and Cook, A. W. (1974). The birds of Sokota. Part 3: Breeding data. *Bull. Niger. Orn. Soc.* **10**(37), 1–28.

Mungure, S. A. (1973). Sight record of nest making by Green-backed Herons, *Butorides striatus*. *Bull. East Afr. Nat. Hist. Soc.* **1973**, 159.

Murton, R. K. (1971). Polymorphism in Ardeidae. *Ibis* **113**, 97–99.

Mwenya, A. N. (1973). Ornithological notes from south east of Lake Bangweulu. *Puku* **7**, 151–161.

Myburgh, N. (1969). Little Bittern nestling in the South-west Cape. *Ostrich* **40**(1), 25.

de Naurois, R. (1966). Le héron pourpre de l'archipel du Cape Vert, *Ardea purpurea bournei*, esp. nov. *Oiseau et R.F.O.* **36**, 89–94.

de Naurois, R. (1975). The Grey Heron of the Banc d'Arguin (Mauritania). *Bull. Br. Orn. Club* **95**, 135–140.

Niven, C. K. (1939). White-backed Night Heron. *Ostrich* **10**(2), 129–130.

Niven, P. (1952). White-backed Night Heron at Amazi. *Bokmakierie* **4**(2), 29–31.

North, M. E. W. (1945). Does the Buff-backed Heron really remove ticks from the bodies of animals? *Ibis* **87**, 469–470.

North, M. E. W. (1959). The great heronry of Garsen on the River Tana. *J. E. Afr. Nat. Hist. Soc.* **23**(4), 159–160.

North, M. E. W. (1963). Breeding of the Black-headed Heron at Nairobi, Kenya, 1958–62. *J. E. Afr. Nat. Hist. Soc.* **24**, 33–63.

North, M. E. W. (1966). A reef heron at Lake Nakuru, Kenya. *J. E. Afr. Nat. Hist. Soc.* **25**, 231–232.

Oreel, G. J. (1978). On the field identification of the Yellow-billed Egret. *Bull. Niger. Orn. Soc.* **14**(46), 89.

Owen, D. F. (1955). The food of the Heron *Ardea cinerea* in the breeding season. *Ibis* **97**(2), 276–295.

Owen, D. F. (1959). Some aspects of the behaviour of immature Herons, *Ardea cinerea*, in the breeding season. *Ardea* **47**, 187–191.

Owen, D. F. (1960). The nesting success of the Heron *Ardea cinerea* in relation to the availability of food. *Proc. Zool. Soc. Lond.* **133**, 597–617.

Owre, O. T. (1967). The Reef Heron, *Egretta schistacea* Ehrenb., in interior East Africa. *J. E. Afr. Nat. Hist. Soc.* **26**, No. 2 (114), 61–63.

Palmer, R. S. (Ed.) (1962). 'Handbook of North American Birds', Vol. I. Yale University Press, New Haven.

Parsons, J. (1976). Counts of Ciconiiform nesting in three colonies near Kisumu heronry—27 April 1976. *Bull East Afr. Nat. Hist. Soc.* **1976**, 61–62.

Parsons, J. (1977). The effect of predation by Fish Eagles on the breeding success of various Ciconiiformes nesting near Kisumu, Kenya. *J. Nat. Hist.* **11**, 337–353.

Payne, R. B. (1979). Family Ardeidae. *In* 'Peters Check List of Birds of the World', Vol. 1, 2nd edn (Mayr, E. and Cottrell, G. W. Eds) Museum of Comparative Zoology, Cambridge, Mass.

Payne, R. B. and Risley, C. J. (1976). Systematics and evolutionary relationships among the herons (Ardeidae). *Miscel. Pub. Mus. Zool. Univ. Mich.* **150**, 115 pp.

Peakall, D. B. and Kemp, A. C. (1976). Organochlorine residue levels in herons and raptors in the Transvaal. *Ostrich* **47**, 139–141.

Penry, E. H. (1976). Grey phase Cattle Egret in Kitwe. *Zambian Orn. Soc.* **8**, 70–71.

Pike, E. (1950). Notes on the nesting of the White-backed Night Heron *Nycticorax leuconotus*. *Ostrich* **21**(1), 36.

Pineau, J. and Giraud-Audine, M. (1977). Notes sur les oiseaux nicheurs de l'extreme nord-ouest du Maroc: reproduction et movements. *Alauda* **45**, 75–103.

Pitman, C. R. S. (1927). Some notes on the breeding and other habits of *Ardea melanocephala*. *Ool. Rec.* 7, 26–34.

Pitman, C. R. S. (1962). Further notes on some bird/other animal association in Africa. *Bull. Br. Orn. Club* **82**, 100–101.

du Plessis, S. S. (1963). The feeding behaviour of the Black Heron *Melanophoyx ardesiaca*. *Ostrich* **34**, 111–112.

Polson, A. and Gitay, H. (1972). A possible role of the Cattle Egret in the dissemination of the granulosis virus of the bollworm *Ostrich* **43**, 231–232.

Pooley, A. G. (1967). Some miscellaneous ornithological observations from the Ndumu Game Reserve. *Ostrich* **38**, 31–32.

Prigogine, A. (1975). Les populations du héron crabier *Ardeola ralloides* au Zaire, au Rwanda, et au Burundi. *Gerfaut* **65**, 59–94.

Prigogine, A. (1976). Occurrence of the Madagascar Squacco Heron *Ardeola idae* in Central Africa. *Bull. Br. Orn. Club* **96**, 96–97.

Recher, H. F. (1972a). Colour dimorphism and the ecology of herons. *Ibis* **114**, 552–555.

Recher, H. F. (1972b). Territorial and agonistic behaviour of the Reef Heron. *Emu* **72**, 126–130.

Recher, H. F. and Recher, J. A. (1972a). The foraging behaviour of the Reef Heron. *Emu* **72**, 85–90.

Recher, H. F. and Recher, J. A. (1972b). Herons leaving the water to defecate. *Auk* **89**, 896–897.

Rencurel, P. (1972). Observations sur la nidification du Héron Garde-Boeufs *Ardeola ibis* (L) dans l'Ile du Bou-Regreg. *Alauda* **41**, 278–286.

Reynolds, J. F. (1965). Association between Little Egrets and African Spoonbill. *British Birds* **58**, 468.

Rice, D. W. (1963). Birds associating with elephants and hippopotamuses. *Auk* **80**, 196–197.

Rowan, M. K. (1961). Breeding of Purple Heron at Verloren Vlei. *Ostrich* **32**, 145–146.

Ruwet, J. C. (1963). Notes écologiques et éthologiques sur les oiseaux des plaines de la Lufira superieure (Katanga). I. Podicipedes, Steganopodes, Gressores, Anseres. *Rev. Zool. Bot. afr.* **58**, 1–60.

Ruwet, J. C. (1965). 'Les Oiseaux des Plaines et du Lac-Barrage de la Lufira Superieure (Katanga méridional)'. Editions FULREAC, Université de Liège.

Rydzewski, W. (1956). The nomadic movements and migrations of the European Common, *Ardea cinerea* L. *Ardea* **44**, 71–188.

Salvan, J. (1963). Le héron garde-boeuf nicheur à Brazzaville. *Oiseau et R.F.O.* **33**(1), 78–79.

Salvan, J. (1972). Notes ornithologiques du Congo-Brazzaville. *Oiseau et R.F.O.* **42**, 241–252.

Scheven, J. (1957). Zum Beuteerwerb der Reiher. *Orn. Mitteil.* **9**, 230–231.

Schouteden, H. (1953). Le Héron crabier de Madagascar (*Ardeola idae*) au Congo belge. *Rev. Zool. Bot. afr.* **48**, 294–296.

Schouteden, H. (1966). La fauna ornithologique du Rwanda. Musée Royal de l'Afrique Centrale—Tervuren, Belgique; Documentation Zoologique No. 10.

Schuttee, G. W. (1969). Goliath Heron observations. *Lammergeyer* **10**, 100.

Schüz, E. (1968). Ornithologischer Oktober-Besuch am Tana-See (und bei Addis Abeba), Äthiopien. *Stutt. Beitr. Naturk.* **189**, 43 pp.

Serle, W. (1943). Further observations on northern Nigerian birds. *Ibis* **1943**, 264–300.

Sharland, R. E. (1978). Ringing in Nigeria 1977, 20th annual report. *Bull. Niger. Orn. Soc.* **14**, 24–26.

Sibley, F. C. (1962). The Yellow-billed Egret *Mesophoyx intermedius* in Nigeria. *Ibis* **104**, 250.

Siegfried, W. R. (1965). The status of the Cattle Egret in the Cape Province. *Ostrich* **36**, 109–115.

Siegfried, W. R. (1966a). Age at which Cattle Egrets first breed. *Ostrich* **37**, 198–199.

Siegfried, W. R. (1966b). On the food of nestling Cattle Egrets. *Ostrich* **37**, 219–220.

Siegfried, W. R. (1966c). Time of departure from the roost in the Night Heron. *Ostrich* **37**, 235–236.

Siegfried, W. R. (1966d). The status of the Cattle Egret in South Africa with notes on the neighbouring territories. *Ostrich* **37**, 157–169.

Siegfried, W. R. (1968). Temperature variation in the Cattle Egret. *Ostrich* **39**, 150–154.

Siegfried, W. R. (1969). Energy metabolism of the Cattle Egret. *Zool. Afr.* **4**, 265–273.

Siegfried, W. R. (1970). Mortality and dispersal of ringed Cattle Egrets. *Ostrich* **41**, 122–135.

Siegfried, W. R. (1971a). Communal roosting in the Cattle Egret. *Trans. Roy. Soc. S. Afr.* **39**, 419–443.

Siegfried, W. R. (1971b). Feeding activity of the Cattle Egret. *Ardea* **59**, 38–46.

Siegfried, W. R. (1971c). Plumage and molt of the Cattle Egret. *Ostrich Suppl.* 9, 154–164.

Siegfried, W. R. (1971d). Population dynamics of the Cattle Egret. *Zool. Afr.* **6**, 289–292.

Siegfried, W. R. (1971e). The food of the Cattle Egret. *J. Appl. Ecol.* **8**, 447–468.

Siegfried, W. R. (1971f). The nest of the Cattle Egret. *Ostrich* **42**, 193–197.

Siegfried, W. R. (1972a). Aspects of the feeding ecology of Cattle Egrets, *Ardeola ibis*, in South Africa. *J. Anim. Ecol.* **41**, 71–78.

Siegfried, W. R. (1972b). Breeding success and reproductive output of the Cattle Egret. *Ostrich* **43**, 43–55.

Siegfried, W. R. (1972c). Food requirements and growth of Cattle Egrets in South Africa. *Living Bird* **11**, 193–206.

Siegfried, W. R. (1978). Habitat and the modern range expansion of the Cattle Egret. *Nat. Aud. Soc. Res. Rep.* **7**, 315–324.

Skead, C. J. (1952). The status of the Cattle Egret, *Ardeola ibis*, in the eastern Cape Province. *Ostrich* **23**, 186–218.

Skead, C. J. (1956). The Cattle Egret in South Africa. *Audubon Mag.* **58**, 206–209, 224–225.

Skead, C. J. (1964). Black-headed Herons (*Ardea melanocephala* (Vigors and Children)), nesting on a krans. *Ostrich* **35**(3), 236.

Skead, C. J. (1966). The study of the Cattle Egret, *Ardeola ibis* Linnaeus. *Ostrich Suppl.* **6**, 109–139.

Skead, D. M. (1963). Cattle Egret *Bubulcus ibis* feeding on flies off the Cape eland *Taurotragus oryx*. *Ostrich* **34**, 166.

Skinner, J. D. and Skinner, C. P. (1974). Predation on the Cattle Egret, *Bubulcus ibis*, and Masked Weaver, *Ploceus velatus*, by the Vervet Monkey, *Cercopithecus aethiops*. *S. Afr. J. Sci.* **70**(5), 157–158.

Smalley, M. E. (1979). Cattle Egrets feeding on flies attracted to mangoes. *Malimbus* **1**(2), 114–117.

Smith, K. D. (1965). On the birds of Morocco. *Ibis* **107**, 493–526.

Stronach, B. W. H. (1968). The Chagana heronry in western Tanzania. *Ibis* **110**, 345–348.

Stuart, C. T. and Stuart, P. (1976). Little Bittern *Ixobrychus minutus. Ostrich* **47**(4), 214.

Symmes, T. C. L. (1951). Display of the Black-headed Heron. *Ostrich* **22**(1), 38.

Tarboton, W. R. (1967). Rufous Heron *Ardeola rufiventris* breeding in the Transvaal. *Ostrich* **38**, 207.

Tarboton, W. R. (1977). The status of communal herons, ibis and cormorants on the Witwatersrand. *S. Afr. J. Wildl. Res.* **7**, 19–25.

Tarboton, W. R. (1979). The Nyl floodplains and its birds. *Bokmakierie* **31**, 26–31.

Tarboton, W. R. Notes on the Dwarf Bittern, in prep.

Taylor, J. S. (1948). Notes on the nesting and feeding habits of *Ardea melanocephala. Ostrich* **19**, 203–210.

Taylor, J. S. (1957). Notes on the birds of inland waters in the Eastern Cape Province with special reference to the Karoo. *Ostrich* **28**, 1–80.

Taylor, J. S. (1972). The Black-headed Heron. *Animals* **13**, 688–689.

Theiler, G. (1959). African ticks and birds. *Ostrich* Suppl. 3, 353–378.

Ticehurst, C. B. (1931). Notes on Egyptian birds. *Ibis* **73**, 575–578.

Tomlinson, D. N. S. (1974a). Studies of the Purple Heron. Part 1: Heronry structure, nesting habits and reproductive success. *Ostrich* **45**, 175–181.

Tomlinson, D. N. S. (1974b). Studies of the Purple Heron. Part 2: Behaviour patterns. *Ostrich* **45**, 209–223.

Tomlinson, D. N. S. (1975). Studies of the Purple Heron. Part 3: Egg and chick development. *Ostrich* **46**, 157–165.

Tomlinson, D. N. S. (1976). Breeding behaviour of the Great White Egret. *Ostrich* **47**, 161–178.

Tomlinson, D. N. S. (1979). Interspecific relations in a mixed heronry. *Ostrich* **50**, 193–198.

Traylor, M. A. and Parelius, D. (1967). A collection of birds from the Ivory Coast. *Fieldiana Zool.* **51**(7), 91–117.

Tree, A. J. (1966). Some recent bird observations from the North Kafue basin. *Ostrich* **37**(1), 30–36.

Tree, A. J. (1973). Yellow-billed Egret *Egretta intermedia. Ostrich* **44**(2), 126.

Tree, A. J. (1978). A visit to Makgadikgadi Pan in April 1974. *Honeyguide* **95**, 39–41.

Tucker, J. J. (1975). The wintering of Black-headed Herons in Zambia. *Bull. Zambian Orn. Soc.* **7**, 35–36.

Turner, D. A. (1978). The heronry at Lake Jipe. *Scopus* **2**(2), 47–48.

Turner, D. A. (1980). The Madagascar Squacco Heron *Ardeola idae* in East Africa, with notes on its field identification. *Scopus* **4**(2), 42–43.

Uÿs, J. M. and Clutton-Brock, T. H. (1966). The breeding of the Rufous-bellied Heron (*Butorides rufiventris*) in Zambia. *Puku* **4**, 171–180.

Van Ee, C. A. (1973). Cattle Egrets prey on breeding Queleas. *Ostrich* **44**, 136.

Van Someren, V. G. L. (1956). Days with birds. *Fieldiana Zool.* **38**.

Vaurie, C. (1963). Systematic notes on the Cattle Egret (*Bubulcus ibis*). *Bull. Br. Orn. Club* **83**(9), 164–166.

Vernon, C. J. (1971). Observations on *Egretta vinaceigula. Bull. Br. Orn. Club* **91**, 157–159.

Vernon, C. J. (1976). Heronries in Rhodesia in 1973/74. *Honeyguide* **86**, 25–29.

Vernon, J. D. R. (1973). Observations sur quelques oiseaux nicheurs du Maroc. *Alauda* **41**(1–2), 101–109.

Verschurren, J. (1977). Note sur la faune ornithologique du Burundi, principalement près du Bujumbura. *Gerfaut* **67**, 3–21.

Vincent, A. A. (1945). The breeding habits of some African birds. *Ibis* **87**, 82–84.

Vincent, J. (1947). Habits of *Bubulcus ibis*, the Cattle Egret, in Natal. *Ibis* **89**, 489–491.

Voisin, C. (1970). Observations sur le comportement du Héron Bihoreau *Nycticorax n. nycticorax* en periode de reproduction. *Oiseau et R.F.O.* **40**, 307–339.

Voisin, C. (1976). Etude du compartement de l'Aigrette Garzetta (*Egretta garzetta*) en periode de reproduction. *Oiseau et R.F.O.* **46**, 387–425.

Voisin, C. (1977). Etude du compartement de l'Aigrette Garzetta (*Egretta garzetta*) en periode de reproduction. *Oiseau et R.F.O.* **47**, 65–103.

Voisin, C. (1978). Utilization des zones humides du Delta Rhodaniern par les Ardeides. *Oiseau et R.F.O.* **48**(3), 217–380.

Walsh, F. (1971). Further notes on Borgu birds. *Bull. Niger. Orn. Soc.* **8**(30), 25–27.

Watmough, B. R. (1978). Observations on nocturnal feeding by Night Heron *Nycticorax nycticorax. Ibis* **120**, 356–358.

Westernhagen, von. W. (1970). Über du Brütvogel der Banc d'Arguin (Mauretainen). *J. Orn.* **111**, 206–226.

White, C. A. (1947). Night-heron alighting on water and swimming. *British Birds* **40**, 314.

White, C. M. N. (1949). Systematic notes on African birds. *Bull. Br. Orn. Club* **69**, 112–113.

Whitfield, A. K. and Blaber, S. J. M. (1979). Feeding ecology of piscivorous birds at Lake St. Lucia. Part 2: Wading birds. *Ostrich* **50**, 1–9.

Wiese, J. H. (1976). Courtship and pair formation in the Great Egret. *Auk* **93**, 709–724.

Winterbottom, J. M. (1969). Waterbirds in Ovamboland. *Ostrich* **40**(1), 27–28.

Wood, T. D. (1970). Unusual heron meal. *Lammergeyer* **12**, 80.

Wood, D. (1974). A bittern at Lake Naivasha. *Bull. E. Afr. Nat. Hist. Soc.* **1974**, 104.

Suborder SCOPI

Family SCOPIDAE: Hamerkop

Cowles, R. B. (1930). The life history of *Scopus umbretta bannermani* in Natal. *Auk* **47**, 159–176.

Gentis, S. (1976). Co-operative nest building by Hamerkops. *Honeyguide* **88**, 48.

Jackson, F. J. and Sclater, P. (1938). 'The Birds of Kenya Colony and the Uganda Protectorate', Vol. 1. Gurney and Jackson, London.

Jensen, J. V. and Kirkeby, J. (1980). 'The Birds of The Gambia'. Aros Nature Guide, Aathus, Denmark.

Kahl, M. P. (1967). Observations on the behaviour of the Hamerkop *Scopus umbretta* in Uganda. *Ibis* **109**, 25–32.

Liversidge, R. (1963). The nesting of the Hamerkop, *Scopus umbretta. Ostrich* **34**(2), 55–62.

Serle, W. (1943). Further observations on northern Nigerian birds. *Ibis* **1943**, 264–300.

Siegfried, W. R. (1975). On the nest of the Hamerkop. *Ostrich* **46**(3, 4), 267.

Wilson, R. T. and Wilson, M. P. (in press). Breeding biology of the Hamerkop *Scopus umbretta* in Central Mali. Proc. V Pan-Afr. Orn. Congr.

Suborder CICONIAE

Family CICONIIDAE: storks

Anderson, A. B. (1949). Marabou nesting colonies of the southern Sudan. *Sudan Notes Rec.* **30**, 114–118.

Anthony, A. J. (1977). A further breeding record of the Woolly-necked Stork. *Honeyguide* **89**, 36–40.

Bigalke, R. (1948). A note on the breeding of the White-bellied Stork (*Sphenorynchus abdimii*) in the National Zoological Gardens, Pretoria. *Ostrich* **19**(3), 200–202.

Blancou, L. (1960). Notes sur des Oiseaux de l'Afrique Centrale. *Oiseau et R.F.O.* **30**, 276–278.

Brown, L. H., Powell-Cotton, D. and Hopcraft. J. B. D. (1973). The biology of the Greater Flamingo and Great White Pelican in East Africa. *Ibis* **115**, 352–374.

Fincham, J. E. (1971). Black Storks breeding near Lalapanzi. *Honeyguide* **65**, 25–27.

van der Heiden, J. T. (1974). Openbill Storks nesting near Salisbury colony at Prince Edward Dam. *Honeyguide* **76**, 33–36.

Jensen, J. V. and Kirkeby, J. (1980). 'The Birds of The Gambia'. Aros Nature Guide, Aathus, Denmark.

Kahl, M. P. (1966a). A contribution to the ecology and reproductive biology of the Marabou stork (*Leptoptilos crumeniferus*) in East Africa. *J. Zool. Lond.* **148**(3), 289–311.

Kahl, M. P. (1966b). Comparative ethology of the Ciconiidae. Pt. 1. The Marabou Stork, *Leptoptilos crumeniferus* (Lesson). *Behaviour* **27**, 76–106.

Kahl, M. P. (1968). Recent breeding records of storks in Eastern Africa. *J. E. Afr. Nat. Hist. Soc. Nat. Mus.* **27**(1)(116), 67–72.

Kahl, M. P. (1971a). Social behaviour and taxonomic relationships of the storks. *Living Bird* **10**, 151–170.

Kahl, M. P. (1971b). Food and feeding behaviour of Openbill Storks. *J. Orn.* **112**(1), 21–35.

Kahl, M. P. (1972a). Comparative ethology of the Ciconiidae. Part 4. The 'typical' storks (genera *Ciconia*, *Sphenorhynchus*, *Dissoura* and *Euxenura*). *Z. Tierpsychol.* **30**(3), 225–252.

Kahl, M. P. (1972b). Comparative ethology of the Ciconiidae. Pt. 5. The Openbill Storks (Genus *Anastomus*). *J. Orn.* **113**(2), 121–137.

Kahl, M. P. (1972c). Comparative ethology of the Ciconiidae. The Wood Storks genera *Mycteria* and *Ibis*). *Ibis* **114**, 15–29.

Kahl, M. P. (1973). Comparative ethology of the Ciconiidae. Part 6. The Blacknecked, Saddlebill, and Jabiru Storks (genera *Xenorhynchus*, *Ephippiorhynchus*, and *Jabiru*). *Condor* **75**(1), 17–27.

Kahl, M. P. (1979). Family Ciconiidae. *In* 'Peters Check List of Birds of the World'. Vol. 2, 2nd edn (Mayr, E. and Cottrell, G. W. Eds) Museum of Comparative Zoology, Cambridge, Mass.

McLachlan, G. R. (1963). European Stork *Ciconia ciconia* ringed as nestling in South Africa recovered in Northern Rhodesia. *Ostrich* **34**(1), 48.

Morris, A. (1979). Saddlebill fishing methods. *Honeyguide* **98**, 33.

Mundy, P. J. and Cook, A. W. (1974). The birds of Sokoto. Part 3: Breeding data. *Bull. Niger. Orn. Soc.* **10**(37), 1–28.

Parsons, P. F. (1974). Openbill Storks nesting. *Honeyguide* **78**, 41–43.

Pomeroy, D. E. (1975). Birds as scavengers of refuse in Uganda. *Ibis* **117**, 69–81.

Pomeroy, D. E. (1977). The biology of Marabou Storks in Uganda. 1. Some characteristics of the species, and the population structure. *Ardea* **65**(1/2), 1–24.

Pomeroy, D. E. (1978a). The biology of Marabou Storks in Uganda. II. Breeding biology and general review. *Ardea* **66**(1/2), 1–23.

Pomeroy, D. E. (1978b). Seasonality of Marabou Storks *Leptoptilos crumeniferus* in Eastern Africa. *Ibis* **120**(3), 313–321.

Scott, J. A. (1975). Observations on the breeding of the Woolly-necked Stork. *Ostrich* **46**(3/4), 201–207.

Vernon, C. J. (1975). Saddlebill Stork breeding at Rainham. *Honeyguide* **83**, 40.

Family BALAENICIPITIDAE: Shoebill

Buxton, L., Slater, J. and Brown, L. H. (1978). The breeding behaviour of the Shoebill or Whale-headed Stork *Balaeniceps rex* in the Bangweulu Swamps, Zambia. *E. Afr. Wildl. J.* **16**, 201–220.

Cottam, P. A. (1957). The pelecaniform characters of the skeleton of the Shoe-billed Stork, *Balaeniceps rex. Bull. Br. Mus. (Nat. Hist.) Zool.* **5**, 51–71.

Fischer, W. (1970). 'Der Schuhschnabel'. Die Neue Brehm-Bücherei, A. Ziemsen Verlag, Wittenberg Lutherstadt.

Guillet, A. (1978). Distribution and conservation of the Shoebill, *Balaeniceps rex*, in the southern Sudan. *Biol. Conser.* **13**(1), 39–50.

Guillet, A. (1979). Aspects of the foraging behaviour of the Shoebill. *Ostrich* **50**, 252–255.

Kahl, M. P. (1979). Family Balaenicipitidae. *In* 'Peters Check List of Birds of the World'. Vol. 1, 2nd edn (Mayr, E. and Cottrell, G. W. Eds) Museum of Comparative Zoology, Cambridge, Mass.

Mathews, N. J. C. (1979). Observations of the Shoebill in the Okavango Swamp. *Ostrich* **50**, 185.

Family THRESKIORNITHIDAE: ibises, spoonbills

Amadon, D. (1953). Avian systematics and evolution in the Gulf of Guinea. *Bull. Am. Mus. Nat. Hist.* **100**(3), 395–451.

Anonymous. (1951). A breeding record of the Glossy Ibis. *Ostrich* **22**, 108–110.

Anthony, A. J. (1978). Hadedah nesting at Chipinda Pools, Conarezhou National Park. *Honeyguide* **95**, 33–34.

Ash, J. S. and Howell, T. R. (1977). The Bald Ibis or Waldrapp *Geronticus eremita* in Ethiopia. *Bull. Br. Orn. Club* **97**, 104.

Barbour, D. J. (1968). Glossy Ibis *Plegadis falcinellus. Ostrich* **39**(4), 271

Bauer, K. N. and Glutz von Blotzheim, V. N. S. (1966). 'Handbuch der Vögel Mitteleuropas'. Vol. 1. Akademische Verlagsgesellschaft, Frankfurt am Main.

Beesley, J. S. S. (1971). A waterbird colony in Tanzania. *Bull. East Afr. Nat. Hist. Soc.* **1971**, 73.

Benson, C. W. and Pitman, C. (1961). Further breeding records from Northern Rhodesia (No. 2). *Bull. Br. Orn. Club* **81**, 156–163.

Benson, C. W. and Pitman, C. R. S. (1964). Further breeding records from Northern Rhodesia (No. 4). *Bull. Br. Orn. Club* **84**, 54–60.

Blaker, D. (1967). Spoonbills in the Western Cape. *Ostrich* **38**, 157–158.

Bodenham, R. (1945). Notes on migrants and resident birds in the North Suez Canal areas from March 1 to December 5 1944. *Zool. Soc. Egypt* **7**, 21–47.

Boswall, J. (1971). Notes from coastal Eritrean on selected species. *Bull. Br. Orn. Club* **91**, 81–84.

Britton, P. L. (1970). Some non-passerine bird weights from East Africa. *Bull. Br. Orn. Club* **90**, 142–144.

Britton, P. L. (1971). Must the Kisumu Heronry be condemned a second time? *Africana* **4**(7), 20–22, 32–33.

Brosset, A. and Erard, C. (1976). Première descriptions de

la nidification de quatre espèces en fôret Gabonaise. *Alauda* **44**, 205–235.

Brossett, A. and Dragesco, J. (1967). Oiseaux collectés et observés dans le Haut-Ivindo. *Biol. Gabon.* **3**(2), 59–88.

Brouwer, G. A. (1964). Some data on the status of the Spoonbill, *Platalea leucorodia* L., in Europe, especially in the Netherlands. *Zool. Meded. Leiden* **39**, 481–521.

Burger, J. and Miller, L. M. (1977). Colony and nest site selection in White-faced and Glossy Ibises. *Auk* **94**, 664–676.

Cawkell, E. M. and Moreau, R. (1963). Notes on birds in the Gambia. *Ibis* **105**, 156–178.

Chapin, J. P. (1923). The Olive Ibis of Dubus and its representative on São Thomé. *Am. Mus. Nov.* (84), 9 pp.

Chapman, E. A. (1969). Gambian observations, winter 1946–47. *Bull. Br. Orn. Club* **89**, 96.

Clark, R. A. (1979a). DDT contamination of the Sacred Ibis. *Ostrich* **50**, 134–138.

Clark, R. A. (1979b). Seasonal levels of body fat, protein, ash and moisture in the Sacred Ibis. *Ostrich* **50**, 129–134.

Clark, R. A. (1979c). The food of the Sacred Ibis at Pretoria, Transvaal. *Ostrich* **50**, 104–111.

Clark, R. A. and Clark, A. (1979). Daily and seasonal movements of the Sacred Ibis at Pretoria, Transvaal. *Ostrich* **50**, 94–103.

Colston, P. R. (1971). Additional non-passerine bird weights from East Africa. *Bull. Br. Orn. Club* **91**(4), 110–111.

Connor, M. A. (1979). Feeding association between Little Egret and African Spoonbill. *Ostrich* **50**, 118.

Cooke, P., Grobler, J. H. and Irwin, M. P. S. (1978). Notes on Sacred Ibis breeding and other birds at a dam on Aisleby Municipal Sewage Farm, Bulawayo. *Honeyguide* **96**, 5–11.

Cooper, K. H. and Edwards, K. Z. (1969). A survey of Bald Ibis in Natal. *Bokmakierie* **21**, 4–9.

Cunningham-van Someren, G. R. (1976). Bird notes from Karen. *Bull. E. Afr. Nat. Hist. Soc.* **1976**, 134–136.

Currie, M. H. (1974). Hadeda Ibis *Bostrychia hagedash*. *Ostrich* **45**(2), 133.

Curry-Lindahl, K. (1978). Conservation and management problems of wading birds and their habitats: a global overview. *Nat. Aud. Soc. Res. Rep.* No. 7, pp. 83–97.

Dorst, J. and Roux, F. (1972). Esquisse écologique sur l'avifaune des Monts du Balé, Ethiopie. *Oiseaux et R.F.O.* **42**, 203–240.

Dowsett, R. J. (1969). Ringed Sacred Ibis *Threskiornis aethiopica* recovered in Zambia. *Puku* **5**, 59–63.

Dragesco, J. (1961). Observations éthologiques sur les oiseaux du Banc d'Arguin. *Alauda* **29**, 81–98.

Duhart, F. and Deschamps, M. (1964). Notes sur l'avifaune du delta central nigerien. *Oiseau et R.F.O.* **33**, 1–99.

Dupuy, A. R. (1975). Nidification de Hérons pourprés (*Ardea purpurea*) au Parc National des Oiseaux du Djoudj, Senegal. *Oiseau et R.F.O.* **45**, 289–290.

Dupuy, A. R. (1976). Données nouvelles concernant la reproduction de quelques espèces aviennes au Senegal. *Oiseau et R.F.O.* **46**, 47–62.

Elgood, J. H., Sharland, R. E. and Ward, P. (1966). Palaearctic migrants in Nigeria. *Ibis* **108**, 84–116.

Elgood, J. H., Fry, C. H. and Dowsett, R. J. (1973). African migrants in Nigeria. *Ibis* **115**, 1–45, 375–411.

Feely, J. M. (1964). Heron and stork breeding colonies in the Luangwa Valley. *Puku* **2**, 76–77.

Field, G. D. (1978). Status of Ciconiiformes in Sierra Leone. *Bull. Niger. Orn. Soc.* **14**, 42–46.

Friedmann, H. and Loveridge, A. (1937). Notes on the ornithology of tropical East Africa. *Bull. Mus. Comp. Zool. Harvard*, **81**.

Friedmann, H. and Williams, J. G. (1969). The birds of the Sango Bay forests, Buddu County, Masaka District, Uganda. *Contr. Sci. Los Angeles County Mus.*, No. 162.

Gooders, J. (Ed.) (1969). 'Birds of the World', Vol. I. IPC, London.

Grieg-Smith, P. W. (1977). Breeding dates of birds in Mole National Park, Ghana. *Bull. Niger. Orn. Soc.* **13**(44), 89–93.

Hamel, H. D. (1975). Ein Beitrag zur Populationsdynamik des Waldrapps *Geronticus eremita*. *Vogelwelt* **96**, 213–221.

Hartley, A., Tongue, P., van Zinderen Bakker, E. M., Winterbottom, J. M. and Winterbottom, M. G. (1968). Breeding of Glossy Ibis on Berg River, Cape Province. *Ostrich* **39**, 39–40.

Hirsch, U. (1976). Beobachtungen am Waldrapp *Geronticus eremita* in Marokko und Versuch zur Bestimmung der Alterszusammensetzug von Brutkolonien. *Orn. Beob.* **73**, 225–235.

Hirsch, U. (1977). Co-operation invited on the protection of the Bald Ibis *Geronticus eremita*. *Bull. Br. Orn. Club* **97**(2), 72.

Hirsch, U. (1978a). Artificial nest ledges for Bald Ibises. *In* 'Endangered Birds: Management Techniques for Preserving Threatened Species'. (Temple, S. A. Ed.) pp. 61–69. University of Wisconsin Press, Madison.

Hirsch, U. (1978b). Zum Schutz des Waldrapp (*Geronticus eremita*). *J. Orn.* **119**, 467–468.

Hirsch, U. (1979a). Protection of *Geronticus eremita*. *Bull. Br. Orn. Club* **99**, 39.

Hirsch, U. (1979b). Studies of West Palearctic birds. 183: Bald Ibis. *British Birds* **72**, 313–325.

Holman, F. C. (1946). Does the Buff-backed Heron really remove ticks from the bodies of animals? *Ibis* **88**, 232–233.

Holyoak, D. (1970). Comments on the classification of Old World ibises. *Bull. Br. Orn. Club* **90**, 67–73.

Hopson, J. (1966). Notes on a mixed cormorant and heron breeding colony near Malamfatori (Lake Chad). *Bull. Niger. Orn. Soc.* **3**, 21–34.

Huntley, B. J. and Huntley, M. A. (1974). Hadeda Ibis *Bostrychia hagedash*. *Ostrich* **45**(2), 133.

Jensen, J. V. and Kirkeby, J. (1980). 'The Birds of The Gambia'. Aros Nature Guide, Aathus, Denmark.

Jourdain, F. C. R. (1934). The Bald Ibis (*Gomatibis eremita*). *Ool. Rec.* **14**, 1–5.

Keith, S. (1971). Birds of the African Rain Forest No. 9. Sounds of Nature L.P. 33 (recording). Federation of Ontario Naturalists and American Museum of Natural History.

Keve, A. and Patkai, E. (1959). Hungarian ringed birds in Africa. *Ostrich* Suppl. 3, 321–330.

Kieser, G. A. and Kieser, J. A. (1977). Spoonbills breeding in the northern Karoo. *Bokmakierie* **29**(2), 53.

Klug, S. and Boswall, J. (1970). Observations from a water bird colony, Lake Tana, Ethiopia. *Bull. Br. Orn. Club* **90**(4), 97–105.

Kumerloeve, H. (1978). Waldrapp, *Geronticus eremita* (Linnaeus, 1758) und Glattnackenrapp, *Geronticus calvus* (Boddaert, 1783): Zur Geschichte ihrer Erforschung und zur gegenwartigen Bestandssituation. *Ann. Naturhistor. Mus. Wien* **81**, 319–349.

Line, L. J. (1941). Nesting of the Hadada Ibis (*Hagedashia hagedash hagdash*). *Ostrich* **11**, 137–139.

Lockhart, P. S. (1975). Glossy Ibis fishing technique. *Bokmakierie* **27**, 84.

Lynes, H. (1925). On the birds of north and central Darfur with notes on the West-Central Kordofan and North Nuba Provinces of British Sudan. *Ibis* (112): 1, 71–131, 344–416, 541–590, 757–797.

Macleod, J. G. R., Martin, J. and Uys, C. J. (1960). Grey-headed Gulls and Spoonbills in the Bredasdorp area. *Ostrich* **31**, 80.

Manry, D. (1978). Life with Schaapen Island's Sacred Ibises —A personal account. *Safring News* **7**, 13–15.

Manry, D. (1979). Ecoethology of a colonial, cliff-nesting ibis: the Bald Ibis *Geronticus calvus*—a progress report. Mimeo Rpt., 37 pp.

Martin, R. J. (1971). Hadedah *Bostrychia hagedash*. *Ostrich* **42**, 137.

Martin, R. J. (1972). Hadeda nesting in the southern entrance of the Seven-Weeks Poort. *Ostrich* **44**, 185–186.

Mathiasson, S. (1963). Visible diurnal migration in the Sudan. pp. 430–435. Proc. XIII Int. Orn. Congr., 1962.

Meinertzhagen, R. (1930). 'Nicoll's Birds of Egypt', Vol. 2. Hugh Rees Ltd., London.

Meinertzhagen, R. (1937). Some notes on the birds of Kenya Colony, with especial reference to Mount Kenya. *Ibis* **1937**, 731–760.

Miller, L. M. and Burger, J. (1978). Factors affecting nesting success of the Glossy Ibis. *Auk* **95**, 353–361.

Mills, M. G. L. (1976). Glossy Ibis *Plegadis falcinellus*. *Ostrich* **47**, 216.

Milstein, P. le S. (1973). Buttons and Bald Ibises. *Bokmakierie* **25**(3), 57–60.

Milstein, P. le S. (1974). More Bald Ibis buttons. *Bokmakierie* **26**, 88.

Milstein, P. le S. and Jacka, R. D. (1970). Establishment of a large heronry. *Ostrich* **41**, 208–210.

Milstein, P. le S. and Siegfried, W. R. (1970). Transvaal status of the Bald Ibis. *Bokmakierie* **22**, 36–39.

Milstein, P. le S. and Wolff, S. W. (1973). Status and conservation of the Bald Ibis in the Transvaal. *J. S. Afr. Wildl. Mgmt Ass.* **3**, 79–83.

Moreau, R. E. (1967). Water-birds over the Sahara. *Ibis* **109**, 232–259.

Morel, G. J. and Morel, M.-Y. (1961). Une héronnière mixte sur le Bas-Senegal. *Alauda* **29**,(2), 99–117.

de Naurois, R. (1973). Les ibis des iles de S. Tome et du Prince: Leur place dans le groupe des *Bostrychia* (= *Lampribis*). *Arq. Mus. Bocage* **4**(5), 157–173.

de Naurois, R. and Roux, F. (1974). Précisions concernant la morphologie, les affinités et la position systematique de quelques oiseaux du Banc d'Arguin (Mauritania). *Oiseau et R.F.O.* **44**, 72–84.

Neame, G. B. (1968a). Glossy Ibis, *Plegadis falcinellus*, distribution. *Ostrich* **39**, 271.

Neame, G. B. (1968b). Spoonbill breeding in the Eastern Cape. *Ostrich* **39**, 265.

Neumann, O. (1928). Neue Formen von Nordost- und Ost-Afrika. *J. Orn.* **76**, 783–787.

North, M. E. W. (1959). The great heronry of Garsen on the River Tana. *J. E. Afr. Nat. Hist.* **23**(4), 159–160.

Ossowski, L. L. J. (1952). The Hagedan Ibis, *Hagedashia hagedash hagedash* (Latham) and its relation to pest control in wattle plantations. *Ann. Natal Mus.* **12**, 279–290.

Palmer, R. S. (Ed.) (1962). 'Handbook of North American Birds', Vol. I. Yale University Press, New Haven.

Parnell, F. I. (1942). The Bald Ibis in Basutoland. *Ostrich* **13**, 100–101.

Parsons, J. (1976). Counts of Ciconiiform nesting in three colonies near Kisumu heronry—27 April 1976. *Bull. E. Afr. Nat. Hist. Soc.* **1976**, 61–62.

Parsons, J. (1977). The effect of predation by fish eagles on the breeding success of various Ciconiiformes nesting near Kisumu, Kenya. *J. Nat. Hist.* **11**, 337–353.

Pienkowski, M. W. (Ed.) (1975). Studies on coastal birds and wetlands in Morocco, 1972. University of East Anglia Expeditions to Morocco 1971–72, special report, 97 pp.

Pitman, C. R. S. (1928). The nesting of *Hagedashia hagedash nilotica*—the Nile Valley Hadada, in Uganda. *Ool. Rec.* **8**, 44–46.

Pitman, C. R. S. (1931). Further notes on the breeding of *Hagedasha hagedash nilotica*—the Nile Valley Hadada in Uganda. *Ool. Rec.* **11**, 48.

Pocock, T. N. and Uys, C. J. (1967). The Bald Ibis in the North-Eastern Orange Free State. *Bokmakierie* **19**, 28–31.

Quickelberge, C. D. (1972). Spoonbills in the Eastern Cape Province. *Ostrich* **43**(1), 67.

Raseroka, B. H. (1975a). Breeding of the Hadadah Ibis. *Ostrich* **46**, 208–212.

Raseroka, B. H. (1975b). Diet of Hadadah Ibis. *Ostrich* **46**, 51–54.

Rencurel, P. (1974). L'Ibis chauve *Geronticus eremita* dans le Moyen-Atlas. *Alauda* **42**, 143–158.

Reynolds, J. F. (1965). Association between Little Egrets and African Spoonbill. *British Birds* **58**, 468.

Reynolds, J. F. (1972). Some new records for Tanzania National Parks. *Bull. E. Afr. Nat. Hist. Soc.* **1972**, 141.

Reynolds, J. F. (1977). Thermo-regulatory problems of birds nesting in arid areas in East Africa: a review. *Scopus* **1**, 57–68.

Roberts, A. (1905). A visit to a breeding colony of *Ibis aethiopica* (Sacred Ibis). *J. S. Afr. Orn. Union* **5**(3), 32–33.

Robin, P. (1973). Comportement des colonies de *Geronticus eremita* dans le sud marocain, lors des periodes de secheresse. *Bonn. zool. Beitr.* **24**(3), 317–322.

Roux, F. (1974). West African survey. *IWRB Bul.* **38**, 69–71.

Rüppell, G. (1977). Quantitative Unterschiede bei Landemanövern von alten und jungen Ibissen (*Threskiornis aethiopicus*). *J. Orn.* **118**, 282–289.

Schüz, E. (1967). Ornithologischer April-Besuch in Äthiopien, besonders am Tanasee. *Stuttgarter Beitr. Naturk.* **171**, 22 pp.

Serle, W. (1943). Further observations on northern Nigerian birds. *Ibis* **1943**, 264–300.

Siegfried, W. R. (1966a). The Bald Ibis. *Bokmakierie* **18**, 54–57.

Siegfried, W. R. (1966b). The present and past distribution of the Bald Ibis in the Province of the Cape of Good Hope *Ostrich* **37**, 216–218.

Siegfried, W. R. (1968). Spoonbills breeding at Stellenbosch, Cape Province, South Africa. *Ostrich* **39**, 199.

Siegfried, W. R. (1971). The status of the Bald Ibis in southern Africa. *Biol. Conser.* **3**, 88–91.

Siegfried, W. R. (1972). Discrete breeding and wintering areas of the Waldrapp *Geronticus eremita* (L.). *Bull. Br. Orn. Club* **92**, 102–103.

Skead, C. J. (1951). A study of the Hadadah Ibis *Hagedashia h. hagedash*. *Ibis* **93**, 360–382.

Skead, C. J. (1966). Hadedah Ibis *Hagedashia hagedashia* (Latham) in the Eastern Cape Province. *Ostrich* **37**, 103–108.

Smith, G. H. (1943). Parachute action when settling of Sacred Ibis and Spoonbill. *Ostrich* **14**(3), 192–194.

Smith, K. D. (1970). The Waldrapp *Geronticus eremita* (L.) *Bull. Br. Orn. Club* **90**, 18–24.

Stronach, B. W. H. (1968). The Chagana heronry in western Tanzania. *Ibis* **110**, 345–348.

Symons, R. E. (1924). The nesting of the Green Ibis, *Theristicus hagedash* in South Africa. *Comp. Ool.* (1), 10–13.

Tarboton, W. R. (1977). The status of communal herons, ibis and cormorants on the Witwatersrand. *S. Afr. J. Wildl. Res.* **7**, 19–25.

Taylor, J. S. (1957). Notes on the birds of inland waters in the Eastern Cape Province with special reference to the Karoo. *Ostrich* **28**, 1–80.

Tree, A. J. (1978). A visit to Makgadikgadi Pan in April 1974. *Honeyguide* **95**, 39–41.

Turner, D. A. (1978). The heronry at Lake Jipe. *Scopus* **2**(2), 47–48.

Urban, E. K. (1974a). Breeding of Sacred Ibis *Threskiornis aethiopica* at Lake Shala, Ethiopia. *Ibis* **116**, 263–277.

Urban, E. K. (1974b). Flight speed and wingflapping rate of Sacred Ibis. *Auk* **91**, 423.

Urban, E. K. (1978). 'Ethiopia's Endemic Birds'. Ethiopian Tourist Organization, Addis Ababa. 30 pp.

Uys, C. J. and Broekheysen, C. J. (1966). Hadedah *Hagedashia hagedash* nesting on telegraph pole. *Ostrich* 37, 239–240.

Vincent, A. A. (1945). The breeding habits of some African birds. *Ibis* 87, 82–84.

Vincent, J. and Symons, G. (1948). Some notes on the Bald Ibis, *Geronticus calvus* (Boddaert). *Ostrich* 19, 58–62.

Wackernagel, H. (1964). Brutbiologische Beobachtungen am Waldrapp, *Geronticus eremita* (L.), im Zoologischen Garten Basel. *Orn. Beob.* 61, 49–60.

von Westernhagen, W. (1970). Über du Brütvogel der Banc d'Arguin (Mauretanien). *J. Orn.* 111, 206–226.

Whitelaw, D. (1968). Notes on the breeding biology of the African Spoonbill *Platalea alba*. *Ostrich* 39, 236–241.

Wilson, P. J. (1957). Breeding of African Spoonbill *Platalea alba* (Scop.) in the South Western Cape. *Ostrich* 28, 236.

Winterbottom, J. M. (1958). African Spoonbill nesting colony in the Karoo. *Ostrich* 29(2), 89.

Winterbottom, J. M. (1972). Range of the Hadeda. *Ostrich* 43, 186.

Order PHOENICOPTERIFORMES

Jenkins, P. M. (1957). The filter-feeding and food of flamingoes (Phoenicopteri). *Phil. Trans. Roy. Soc. London.* Ser. B. No. 674, 240, 401–493.

Kear, J. and Düplaix-Hall, N. (Eds) (1975). 'Flamingos'. T. & A. D. Poyser, Berkhamsted.

Sibley, C. G., Corbin, K. W. and Haavie, J. H. (1969). The relationships of the flamingos as indicated by the egg-white proteins and hemoglobins. *Condor* 71, 155–179.

Family PHOENICOPTERIDAE: flamingoes

Berry, H. H. (1972). Flamingo breeding on the Etosha Pan, South West Africa, during 1971. *Madoqua* Ser. I, 5, 5–27.

Berry, H. H., Stark, H. P. and van Vuuren, A. S. (1973). White Pelicans *Pelecanus onocrotalus* breeding on the Etosha Pan, South West Africa, during 1971. *Madoqua* 7, 17–31.

Brown, L. H. (1958). The breeding of the Greater Flamingo *Phoenicopterus ruber* at Lake Elmenteita, Kenya Colony. *Ibis* 100, 388–420.

Brown, L. H. (1971). Flamingo. *World of Birds* 1, 13–18.

Brown, L. H. (1973). 'The Mystery of the Flamingos'. East African Publishing House, Nairobi.

Brown, L. H. and Root, A. (1971). The breeding behaviour of the Lesser Flamingo, *Phoeniconaias minor*. *Ibis* 113, 147–172.

Brown, L. H., Powell-Cotton, D. and Hopcraft, J. B. D.

(1973). The breeding of the Greater Flamingo and Great White Pelican in East Africa. *Ibis* 115, 352–374.

Gallet, E. (1950). 'The Flamingos of the Camargue'. Blackwells, Oxford.

de Naurois, R. (1965). Une colonie reproductrice du petit flamant rose, *Phoeniconaias minor* (Geoffroy) dans l'Aftout es Sahel (sud-ouest Mauritanien). *Alauda* 33, 166–176.

Porter, R. N. and Forrest, G. W. (1974). First successful breeding of Greater Flamingo in Natal, South Africa. *Lammergeyer* 21, 26–33.

Ridley, M. W., Moss, B. L. and Percy, R. C. (1955). The food of flamingoes in Kenya Colony. *J. E. Afr. Nat. Hist. Soc.* 22(5), 147–158.

Robertson, H. G. and Johnson, P. G. First record of Greater and Lesser Flamingos breeding in Botswana, in prep.

Scott, D. A. (1975). Iran. In 'Flamingos'. (Kear, J. and Düplaix-Hall, N. Eds), pp. 28–32. T. & A. D. Poyser, Berkhamsted.

Studer-Thiersch, A. (1966). Altes und Neues über das Fütterungssekret der Flamingos *Phoenicopterus ruber*. *Orn. Beob.* 63, 85–89.

Tuite, C. (1981). Flamingoes in East Africa. *Swara* 4(4), 36–38.

Uys, C. J., Broekhuysen, G. J., Martin, J. and MacLeod, J. G. (1963). Observations on the breeding of the Greater Flamingo *Phoenicopterus ruber* Linnaeus in the Bredasdorp district, South Africa. *Ostrich* 34(3), 129–154.

Vareschi, E. (1978). The ecology of Lake Nakuru (Kenya). 1. Abundance and feeding of the Lesser Flamingo. *Oecologia (Bul.)* 32, 11–35.

Order ANSERIFORMES

Suborder ANSERES

Family Anatidae: swans, geese, ducks

Alder, P. (1963). The calls and displays of African and Indian Pygmy Geese. *Wildf. Trust Ann. Rep.* 14, 174–175.

Ash, J. S. (1977a). First known breeding of the Ruddy Shelduck *Tadorna ferruginea* south of the Sahara. *Bull. Brit. Orn. Club* 97, 56–59.

Ash, J. (1977b). Birds seen at Lake Deemtu, Ethiopia. *Bull. Brit. Orn. Club* 97, 59.

Backhurst, G. C., Britton, P. L. and Mann, C. F. (1973). The less common Palaearctic migrant birds of Kenya and Tanzania. *J. E. Afr. Nat. Hist. Soc.* 140, 1–29.

Ball, I. J., Frost, P. G. H., Siegfried, W. R. and McKinney, F. M. (1978). Territories and local movements of African Black Ducks. *Wildfowl* 29, 61–79.

Bannerman, D. A. (1938). Nesting of *Dendrocygna viduata* in Nigeria. *Ibis* 2, 767–768.

Blaauw, F. E. (1917). On the breeding of the South African Black Duck (*Anas sparsa*). *Ibis* 5, 69–71.

Blaauw, F. E. (1927). On the breeding of the Blue-winged Goose of Abyssinia (*Cyanochen cyanopterus*). *Ibis* 3, 422–424.

Boswall, J. (1973). Additional voice recordings of the Anatidae. *Wildf. Trust Ann. Rep.* 14, 137–140.

Roulton, R. and Woodall, P. (1974). The breeding seasons of waterfowl in Rhodesia. *Honeyguide* 78, 36–38.

Brand, D. J. (1961). A comparative study of the Cape Teal (*Anas capensis* Gmelin) and the Cape Shoveller (*Spatula capensis* (Eyton) with special reference to breeding biology, development and food requirements. Unpublished Ph.D. thesis, University of South Africa.

Brand, D. J. (1964). Nesting studies of the Cape Shoveller *Spatula capensis* and the Cape Teal *Anas capensis* in the Western Cape Province 1957–1959. *Ostrich* Suppl. 6, 217–221.

Britton, P. L. (1970). *Bull. Br. Orn. Club* **90**, 147.

Broekhuysen, G. J. (1955). Breeding record of Whistling Duck for the neighbourhood of Cape Town. *Ostrich* **26** (3), 169.

Brown, L. H. (1966). Blue-winged Goose. *In* Report on Nat. Geogr. Soc. W. W. F. Exp. to study Mountain Nyala *Trogelophus buxtoni*. Special Mimeo. Report, 89 pp.

Brown, L. H. and Seely, M. (1973). Abundance of the Pygmy Goose *Nettapus auritus* in the Okavango Swamps, Botswana. *Ostrich* **44**, 84.

Browne, P. W. D. (1979). 'Bird Observations in Southwest Mauritania during 1978 and 1979.' Off. Rech. Scient. Tech. Outre-Mer., Senegal.

Brush, A. H. (1976). Waterfowl feather proteins: analysis of use in taxonomic studies. *J. Zool* **179**, 467–498.

Clancey, P. A. (1967). 'Gamebirds of Southern Africa.' Purnell, South Africa.

Clancey, P. A. (1976). The Shelduck *T. tadorna* in South Africa. *Ostrich* **47**, 145.

Clark, A. (1964). The Maccoa Duck (*Oxyura maccoa* (Eyton)). *Ostrich* **35**, 264–276.

Clark, A. (1965). Identification of the sexes of the Hottentot Teal. *Ostrich* **36**, 50.

Clark, A. (1966). The Social Behaviour patterns of the Southern Pochard *Netta erythrophthalma brunnea*. *Ostrich* **37**, 45–46.

Clark, A. (1969b). The breeding of the Hottentot Teal. *Ostrich* **40**, 33–36.

Clark, A. (1969a). The behaviour of White-backed Duck. *Wildfowl* **20**, 71–74.

Clark, A. (1971). The behaviour of the Hottentot Teal. *Ostrich* **42**, 131–136.

Clark, A. (1973). Hybrid *Anas undulata* and *Netta erythrophthalma*. *Ostrich* **44**, 265.

Clark, A. (1974a). The status of the Whistling Ducks in South Africa. *Ostrich* **45**, 1–4.

Clark, A. (1974b). Facial discolouration in the Whitefaced Whistling Duck. *Ostrich* **45**, 261.

Clark, A. (1974c). The breeding of Hottentot Teal. *Bokmakierie* **26**, 31–32.

Clark, A. (1974d). Plumage changes in the male Maccoa Duck. *Ostrich* **45**, 33–38: 251–253.

Clark, A. (1976). Observations on the breeding of Whistling Ducks in Southern Africa. *Ostrich* **47**, 59–64.

Clark, A. (1977). Review of the records of three Palaearctic ducks in Southern Africa. *A. querquedula*, *A. acuta*, *A. clypeata*. *Bull. Br. Orn. Club* **97**, 107–114.

Clark, A. (1978a). Some aspects of the behaviour of Whistling Ducks in South Africa. *Ostrich* **49**, 31–39.

Clark, A. (1978b). Notes on Maccoa Duck displays. *Ostrich* **49**, 86.

Clark, A. (1979). The breeding of the Whitebacked Duck on the Witwatersrand. *Ostrich* **50**, 59–60.

Clark, A. (1980a). Notes on the breeding biology of the Spur-winged Goose. *Ostrich* **51**, 179–182.

Clark, A. (1980b). Breeding seasons of Southern Pochard in Southern Africa. *Ostrich* **51**, 122–124.

Clarke, J. E. (1972). Annual report for the year 1971. 40 pp. Department of Wildlife, Fisheries and National Parks. Lusaka, Zambia.

Cooper, J. (1960). Notes on Wildfowl in Natal. *Natal Bird Club News Sheet* **70**.

Cramp, S. and Conder, P. J. (1970). A visit to the oasis of Kufra, spring 1969. *Ibis* **112**, 261–263.

Curry-Lindahl, K. (1975). 'Fåglar över Land och Hav. En global översikt av Fåglarnas Flyttning' (Birds over Land and Sea. A global Survey of the Migration of Birds). 243 pp. Stockholm.

Day, D. H. (1977). A morphological study of Yellowbilled Duck and Redbilled Teal. *Ostrich* Suppl. **12**, 86–96.

Dean, W. R. J. (1970). *Anas hottentota* and *Oxyura maccoa* eggs in one nest. *Ostrich* **41**, 216.

Dean, W. R. J. (1977). Long distance migrants. *Fauna and Flora* **30**, 9–11.

Dean, W. R. J. (1978). Moult seasons of some Anatidae in the Western Transvaal. *Ostrich* **49**, 76–84.

Dean, W. R. J. and Skead, D. M. (1977). The sex ratio in Yellowbilled Duck, Redbilled Teal and Southern Pochard. *Ostrich* Suppl. **12**, 82–85.

Dean, W. R. J. and Skead, D. M. (1979). The weights of some southern African Anatidae. *Wildfowl* **30**, 114–117.

D'Eath, J. O. (1967). The Comb Duck (*Sarkidiornis melanotus melanotus*) in captivity. *Avicult. Mag.* **73**, 197–198.

Delacour, J. (1954–1964). 'The Waterfowl of the World.' Vols 1–4. Country Life, London.

Delacour, J. and Mayr, E. (1945). The Family Anatidae. *Wild. Bull.* **57**, 3–55.

Dewar, J. M. (1924). 'The Bird as Diver.' Witherby, London.

Douthwaite, R. J. (1976). Weight changes and wing moult in the Red-billed Teal. *Wildfowl* **27**, 123–127.

Douthwaite, R. J. (1977). Filter-feeding ducks of the Kafue Flats, Zambia. *Ibis* **119**, 44–65.

Douthwaite, R. J. (1978). Geese and Red-knobbed Coot on the Kafue Flats in Zambia 1970–1974. *E. Afr. Wildl. J.* **16**, 29–47.

Douthwaite, R. J. (1980). Seasonal changes in the food supply, numbers and male plumages of Pygmy Geese on the Thamalcakane river in Northern Botswana. *Wildfowl* **31**, 94–98.

Dowsett, R. J. (1966). The status and distribution of the Hottentot Teal *Anas punctata* in Zambia. *Puku* **4**, 125–127.

Dowsett, R. J. and de Vos, A. (1965). The ecology and numbers of aquatic birds in the Kafue Flats, Zambia. *Wildfowl* **16**, 67–73.

Duff, A. G. (1979). Sauchets du Cap *Anas smithii* au Maroc. *Alauda* **47**, 216–217.

Dupuy, A. R. and Fournier, D. (1981). Resultats du denombrement aerien des oiseaux d'eau dans le Parc National des Oiseaux du Djoudj. I.W.R.B., unpublished.

Edelstein, G. (1932). Note on the nest of the South African Shelduck. *Ostrich* **3**, 61.

Elgood, J. H., Fry, C. H. and Dowsett, R. J. (1973). African migrants in Nigeria. *Ibis* **115**, 1–45.

Eltringham, S. K. (1973). Fluctuations in the numbers of wildfowl on an equatorial hippo wallow. *Wildfowl* **24**, 81–87.

Eltringham, S. K. (1974). The survival of broods of Egyptian Goose in Uganda. *Wildfowl* **25**, 41–48.

Elwell, N. H. and McIlleron, W. G. (1978). A wild place on the Witwatersrand: Summervlei. *Afr. Wildl. Mag.* **32**, 36–38.

Friedmann, H. (1947). Measurements of birds from Africa. *Condor* **49**, 189–195.

Frost, P. G. H., Ball, I. J., Siegfried, W. R. and McKinney, D. F. (1979). Sex ratios, morphology and growth of the African Black Duck. *Ostrich* **50**, 220–233.

Geldenhuys, J. G. (1975). Waterfowl (Anatidae) on irrigation lakes in the Orange Free State. *Ostrich* **46**, 219–235.

Geldenhuys, J. N. (1976a). Relative abundance of waterfowl in the Orange Free State. *Ostrich* **47**, 27–54.

Geldenhuys, J. N. (1976b). Breeding status of waterfowl in the Orange Free State. *Ostrich* **47**, 137–139.

Geldenhuys, J. N. (1976c). Physiognomic characteristics of wetland vegetation in South African Shelduck habitat. *S. Afr. J. Wildl. Res.* **6**, 75–78.

Geldenhuys, J. N. (1977). Feeding habits of South African Shelduck. *S. Afr. J. Wild. Res.* **7**, 5–9.

Geldenhuys, J. N. (1979). The population ecology of the South African Shelduck *Tadorna cana* (Gmelin 1789) in the Orange Free State. Unpub. D.Sc. thesis (Wildlife Management), University of Pretoria.

Geldenhuys, J. N. (1980). Breeding seasons of Egyptian Geese and South African Shelducks in Central South Africa. Proc. IV Pan-Afr. Orn. Cong., pp. 267–275, Southern African Ornithological Society, Johannesburg.

Geldenhuys, J. N. (1981a). Moults and moult localities of the South African Shelduck. *Ostrich* **52**, 129–133.

Geldenhuys, J. N. (1981b). Breeding ecology of the South African Shelduck. *S. Afr. J. Wildl. Res.* **10**.

Gooders, J. (Ed.) (1969–1971). 'Birds of the World'. Vols I–IX. IPC, London.

Hall, P. (1976). The status of Cape Wigeon *Anas capensis*, Three-banded Plover *Charadrius tricollaris* and Avocet *Recurvirostra avosetta* in Nigeria. *Bull. Niger. Orn. Soc.* **12**, 43.

Hall, P. (1977). Black Duck *Anas sparsa* on Mambilla Plateau, first record for Nigeria. *Bull. Niger. Orn. Soc.* **13**, 80–81.

Harwin, R. M. (1971). Movements of the Knob-billed Duck. *Honeyguide* **68**, 35–37.

Jacobs, P. and Ochando, B. (1979). Repartition geographique et importance numerique des Anatidés hivernantes en Algèrie. *Gerfaut* **69**, 239–251.

Jarry, G. (1969). Notes sur les oiseaux nicheurs de Tunisie. *Oiseau et R.F.O.* **39**, 112–120.

Johnsgard, P. A. (1961a). The taxonomy of the Anatidae – a behavioural analysis. *Ibis* **103a**, 71–85.

Johnsgard, P. A. (1961b). Tracheal anatomy of the Anatidae and its taxonomic significance. *Wildfowl* **12**, 59–69.

Johnsgard, P. A. (1962). Evolutionary trends in the behaviour and morphology of the Anatidae. *Wildfowl* **13**, 130–148.

Johnsgard, P. A. (1965). 'Handbook of Waterfowl behaviour'. Cornell University Press, Ithaca, New York.

Johnsgard, P. A. (1967). Observations on the behaviour and relationships of the White-backed Duck and the Stiff-tailed Ducks. *Wildf. Trust Ann. Rep.* **18**, 98–107.

Johnsgard, P. A. (1968a). 'Waterfowl: their Biology and Natural History'. University of Nebraska Press, Lincoln.

Johnsgard, P. A. (1968b). Some observations on Maccoa Duck behaviour. *Ostrich* **39**, 219–222.

Johnsgard, P. A. (1978). 'Ducks, Geese and Swans of the World'. University of Nebraska Press, Lincoln.

Johnsgard, P. A. and Kear, J. (1968). A review of parental carrying of young by waterfowl. *Living Bird* **7**, 89–102.

Johnson, A. R. and Hafner, H. (1972). Dénombrement de la sauvagine en automne 1971 sur les zones humides de Tunisie et Algérie. *Bull. Int. Wtrfwl Res. Bur.* **33**, 51–62.

Johnstone, G. T. (1960). Notes from the New Grounds. *Avic. Mag.* **1960**, 67–71.

Jones, T. (1972). 1971 Breeding season at Leckford. *Avic. Mag.* **78**, 22–24.

Jones, M. A. (1978). White-faced Whistling Duck *Dendrocygnae viduata* (Linnaeus, 1766) carrying their young. *Honeyguide* **94**, 19–21.

Kear, J. (1967). Notes on the eggs and downy young of *Thalassornis leuconotus*. *Ostrich* **38**, 227–229.

Kellogg, P. P. (1962). 'Sound-recording expedition'. Newsletter to Members. Cornell University, Ithaca, New York.

Kolbe, H. (1972). 'Die Entenvögel der Welt'. Neudamm.

Lack, D. (1968). 'Ecological Adaptations for Breeding in Birds'. Methuen, London.

Landsborough-Thomson, A. (Ed.) (1964). 'A New Dictionary of Birds'. Nelson, London.

Langley, C. H. (1979). A further breeding record .for the Fulvous Whistling Duck from the Cape Peninsula. *Ostrich* **50**, 62.

Lees-May, N. (1974). Egg of Maccoa Duck in the nest of the Redknobbed Coot. *Ostrich* **45**, 39–40.

Lockley, R. M. (1942). 'Shearwaters'. J. M. Dent & Son, London.

Loeffler, H. von (1977). Observations on the Anatidae fauna of the Bale Mountains, Ethiopia. *Egretta* **20**, 36–44.

Lorenz, K. (1951–1953). Comparative studies on the behaviour of Anatidae. *Avic. Mag.* **57**, 157–182; **58**, 86–96, 172–184; **59**, 24–34, 80–91.

Macdonald, M. A. and Taylor, I. R. (1976). First occurrence of the Cape Wigeon *Anas capensis* in Ghana. *Bull. Niger. Orn. Soc.* **12**, 44.

McKinney, D. F. (1970). Displays of four species of Blue-winged ducks. *Living Bird* **29**, 64.

McKinney, D. F. (1965a). The comfort movements of Anatidae. *Behaviour* **25**, 120–220.

McKinney, D. F. (1965b). The comfort movements of Anatidae. *Behaviour* **25**, 120–220.

McKinney, D. F., Siegfried, W. R., Ball, I. J. and Frost, P. G. H. (1978). Behavioural specializations for river life in the African Black Duck (*Anas sparsa* Eyton). *Zool. Tierp.* **48**, 349–400.

Macnae, W. (1959). Notes on the biology of the Maccoa Duck. *Bokmakierie* **11**, 49–52.

Meadows, B. S. (1978). *Anas penelope* in Kenya. *Scopus* **2**, 97.

Meadows, B. S. (in press). Numbers and seasonality of filter-feeding ducks in Kenya. Proc. V Pan-Afr. Orn. Congr.

Meanley, B. and A. G. (1958). Post-copulatory display in Fulvous and Black-headed Tree Ducks. *Auk* **75**, 96.

Meanley, B. and A. G. (1959). Observations on the Fulvous Tree Duck in Louisiana. *Wilson Bulletin* **71**(1), 33–45.

Middlemiss, E. (1958a). Stages in development of *Anas undulata*. *Ostrich* **29**, 126–127.

Middlemiss, E. (1958b). The Southern Pochard *Netta erythrophthalma brunnea*. *Ostrich* Suppl. 2, 1–34.

Milstein, P. le S. (1973). Maccoa Duck *Oxyura punctata* parasitizing Fulvous Duck *Dendrocygna bicolor* nest. *Bokmakierie* **25**, 74.

Milstein, P. le S. (1975a). The biology of Barberspan with special reference to the avifauna. *Ostrich*. Suppl. 10, 1–74.

Milstein, P. le S. (1975b). How baby Egyptian Geese leave a high nest. *Bokmakierie* **27**, 49–51.

Milstein, P. le S. (1977). 'A Guide to the Waterfowl of the Transvaal'. Tvl. Prov. Admin. (Nat. Cons Div.), Pretoria.

Milstein, P. le S. (1977a) Black River Duck eating minnow and trout. *Bokmakierie* **29**, 19.

Milstein, P. le S. (1979). The evolutionary significance of wild hybridization in South African highveld ducks. *Ostrich* Suppl. 13, 1–48.

Morel, G. J. and Roux, F. (1966). Les migrateurs paléarctiques au Sénégal. *Terre et Vie* **113**, 19–72, 143–176.

Morel, G. J. and Roux, F. (1973). *Terre et Vie* **27**, 523–550.

Muffett, D. J. (1948). White-backed Duck *Thalassornis leuconotus* in Northern Nigeria. *Ibis* **90**, 604.

Newman, K. B. (1964). Whistling Duck (*Dendrocygna bicolor* (Viellot)) nesting in the Transvaal. *Ostrich* **35**, 121.

Owen, M. (1977). 'Wildfowl of Europe'. Macmillan, London.

Pitman, C. R. S. (1965). The nesting and some other habits of *Alopochen*, *Nettapus*, *Plectropterus* and *Sarkidiornis*. *Wildfowl Trust Ann. Rep.* **16**, 115–121.

Prozesky, O. P. M. (1959). Preliminary observations on clutch laying, incubation and fledging period of Spur-winged Goose. *Bull. S. Afr. Mus. Ass.* **7**, 52–54.

Raikow, R. J. (1971). The osteology and taxonomic position of the White-backed Duck, *Thalassornis leuconotus*. *Wilson Bull.* **83**, 270–277.

Reardon, J. (1977). Flight speed of Egyptian Goose. *Honeyguide* **89**, 47.

Rooth, J. (1971). The occurrence of the Greylag Goose *Anser anser* in the western part of its distribution area. *Ardea* **59**, 17–27.

Roux, F. (1970). Palearctic waterfowl in tropical West Africa. Proc. Int. Reg. Meet. Cons. Wildf. Res. Lenningrad, 1968, pp. 265–273.

Roux, F. (1973). Census of Anatidae in the central delta of the Niger and Senegal delta—January 1972. *Wildfowl* **24**, 63–80.

Roux, F. (1976). 'The status of Wetlands in the West African Sahel: their value for waterfowl and their future'. Proc. Inst. Conf. Cons. Wetlands and Waterfowl 1974, pp. 272–287. Inst. Waterfowl Res. Bur.

Roux, F., Jarry, G., Maheo, R. and Tamisier, A. (1976). Importance, structure et origine des populations d'Anatidés hivernant dans le delta du Sénégal. Oiseau et R.F.O. 46, 299–336.

Roux, F., Jarry, G., Maheo, R. and Tamisier, A. (1977). Importance, structure et origine des populations d'Anatidés hivernant du Sénégal. Oiseau et R.F.O. 47, 1–24.

Rowan, M. K. (1963). The Yellowbill Duck Anas undulata Dubois in Southern Africa. Ostrich Suppl. 5, 1–56.

Sanigho, N. (1978). Rapport National du Delta de la Republique du Mali. I.W.R.B., unpublished.

Scott, P. and The Wildfowl Trust. (1972) 'The Swans'. Michael Joseph, London.

Siegfried, W. R. (1962a). Observations on the post-embryonic development of Egyptian Goose Alopochen aegyptiacus (L.) and the Redbill Teal Anas erythrorhyncha Gmelin. Invest. Rep. Dept. Nat. Cons. (Cape) 2, 9–17.

Siegfried, W. R. (1962b). Nesting behaviour of the Redbill Teal Anas erythrorhyncha Gmelin. Invest. Rep. Dept. Nat. Cons. (Cape) 2, 19–24.

Siegfried, W. R. (1964a). The number of feathers in the nests of South African Anatidae. Ostrich 35, 61.

Siegfried, W. R. (1964b). Parasitic egg laying in South African Anatidae. Ostrich 35, 61–62.

Siegfried, W. R. (1965). Duck nesting in the Cape Peninsula area. Ostrich 36, 82–83.

Siegfried, W. R. (1966). On the post-embryonic development of the South African Shelduck Tadorna cana (Gmel.). Ostrich 37, 149–151.

Siegfried, W. R. (1967). Trapping and ringing of Egyptian Geese and African Shelduck at Vogelvlei, Cape. Ostrich 38, 173–178.

Siegfried, W. R. (1968a). The Black Duck in the South-West Cape. Ostrich 40, 213–214.

Siegfried, W. R. (1968b). Non-breeding plumage in the adult male Maccoa Duck. Ostrich 39, 91–93.

Siegfried, W. R. (1969). Breeding season of the Maccoa Duck in the South-Western Cape. Ostrich 40, 213.

Siegfried, W. R. (1970a). Wildfowl distribution, conservation and research in Southern Africa. Wildfowl 21, 89–98.

Siegfried, W. R. (1970b). Double wing-moult in the Maccoa Duck. Wildfowl 21, 122.

Siegfried, W. R. (1971). Our ducks and geese. In 'Birdlife in Southern Africa' (Newman, K. B. Ed.) pp. 83–92. Purnell, South Africa.

Siegfried, W. R. (1973a). Morphology and ecology of the southern African whistling ducks (Dendrocygna). Auk 90, 198–201.

Siegfried, W. R. (1973b). Post-embryonic development of the Ruddy Duck and some other diving ducks. Int. Zoo. Yr. Bk. 13, 10 pp.

Siegfried, W. R. (1974). Brood care, pair bonds and plumage in southern African Anatini. Wildfowl 25, 33–40.

Siegfried, W. R. (1976). Social Organization in Ruddy and Maccoa Ducks. Auk 93, 560–570.

Siegfried, W. R. (1979). Social Behaviour of the African Comb Duck. The Living Bird 17, 85–104.

Siegfried, W. R. and Van der Merwe, F. J. (1975). A description and inventory of the displays of the Maccoa Duck Oxyura maccoa. Zool. Tierp. 37, 1–23.

Siegfried, W. R., Ball, I. J., Frost, P. G. H. and McKinney, D. F. (1975). Waterfowl populations in the Eerste River Valley, South Africa. J. S. Afr. Wildl. Mangt. Ass. 5, 69–73.

Siegfried, W. R., Burger, A. E. and Van der Merwe, E. J. (1976a). Activity budgets of male Maccoa Duck Oxyura maccoa. Zool. Tierp. 37, 23.

Siegfried, W. R., Burger, A. E. and Frost, P. G. H. (1976b).

Energy requirements for breeding in the Maccoa Duck. Ardea 64, 171–191.

Siegfried, W. R., Burger, A. E. and Caldwell, P. J. (1976c). Incubation behaviour of Ruddy and Maccoa Ducks. Condor 78, 512–517.

Siegfried, W. R., Frost, P. G. H., Ball, I. J. and McKinney, F. (1977). Evening gatherings and night roosting of African Black Ducks. Ostrich 48, 5–16.

Skead, D. M. (1976). Social behaviour of the Yellow-billed Duck and Red-billed Teal in relation to breeding. Unpublished M.Sc. thesis, University of Natal.

Skead, D. M. (1977a). Pair-forming and breeding behaviour of the Cape Shoveller at Barberspan. Ostrich Suppl. 12, 75–81.

Skead, D. M. (1977b). Diurnal activity budgets of Anatini during winter. Ostrich Suppl. 12, 65–74.

Skead, D. M. (1977c). Pair-bond of the Cape Shoveller. Ostrich Suppl. 12, 135–136.

Skead, D. M. (1977d). Weights of birds handled at Barberspan. Ostrich Suppl. 12, 117–131.

Skead, D. M. (1980). The ecological relationship of the Yellow-billed Duck to its habitat at Barberspan and vicinity. Unpublished D.Sc. thesis Potchefstroom University.

Skead, D. M. and Dean, W. R. J. (1977a). Seasonal abundance of Anatidae at Barberspan. Ostrich Suppl. 12, 49–64.

Skead, D. M. and Dean, W. R. J. (1977b). Status of the Barberspan avifauna, 1971–1975. Ostrich Suppl. 12, 3–42.

Sugden, L. G. (1973). Canadian Wildlife Service Report No. 24.

Thomas, D. D. and Condy, J. B. (1965). Breeding of Hottentot Teal Anas punctata Burchell in Southern Rhodesia. Ostrich et R.F.O. 36, 88–89.

Todd, F. S. (1979). 'Waterfowl: Ducks, Geese and Swans of the World'. Sea World Press, San Diego.

Treca, B. (1976). Les oiseaux d'eau et la riziculture dans le delta du Sénégal. Oiseau et R.F.O. 45, 259–265.

Treca, B. (1979). Note sur la reproduction du Canard Arme Plectropterus gambensis au Sénégal. Malimbus 1, 29–31.

Treca, B. (1980). Nouvelles données sur la reproduction du Canard Arme Plectropterus gambensis au Sénégal. Malimbus 2, 25–28.

Treca, B. (1981). Régime alimentaire de la Sarcelle d'été (Anas querquedula L.) dans le delta du Sénégal. Oiseau et R.F.O. 51, 33–58.

Urban, E. K. (1969). A guide to the birds of Lake Abiata. Walia 1, 24–37.

Urban, E. K. (1970). Status of the Palearctic Wildfowl occurring in Ethiopia. Proc. Int. Reg. Meet. Cons. Wildl. Res. pp. 318–320.

Urban, E. K. (1978). 'Ethiopia's Endemic Birds'. Addis Ababa. 30 pp.

Van Ee, C. A. (1971). Variations in the head pattern of the female South African Shelduck. Ostrich 42, 149–150.

Van Someren, V. G. L. (1943). Short note: Anas strepera. Ibis 85, 345.

Vernon, C. J. (1971). Report on the status of Rhodesian waterfowl. Rhod. Nat. Cons. Dept. 229/1971.

Viellard, J. (1972). Recensement et statut des populations d'Anatidés du bassin tchadien. Cah. O.R.S.T.O.M., Ser. Hydrobiol. 6(1), 85–100.

Williams, J. G. (1956). On the downy young of Aythya erythrophthalma. Bull. Br. Orn. Club 76, 140–141.

Wilson, R. T. and Wilson, M. P. (1980). Notes sur la nidification du Canard casqué (Sarkidiornis melanotos) en zone soudano-sahélienne. L'Oiseau et R.F.O. 50, 117–124.

Winterbottom, J. M. (1974). The Cape Teal. Ostrich 45, 110–132.

Wintle, C. C. (1981). Notes on the breeding behaviour of the White-backed Duck. Honeyguide 105, 13–20.

Woodall, P. F. (1974). Status of Anatidae in Rhodesia. Unpublished M.Sc. thesis, University of Rhodesia.

Woolfenden, G. E. (1961). Post cranial osteology of the waterfowl. *Bull. Florida State Mus. Biol. Sci.* **6**, 1–129.

Zaloumis, E. A. (1976). Incubation period of the African Pygmy Goose. *Ostrich* **47**, 231.

Order FALCONIFORMES

Suborder ACCIPITRES

Family ACCIPITRIDAE: Osprey, cuckoo falcons, honey buzzards, fish eagles, Old World vultures, snake eagles, harriers, goshawks, sparrowhawks, buzzards, eagles

Anthony, A. J. (1976). Lappet-faced Vultures of the Gonarezhou. *Bokmakierie* **28**, 54–57.

Bernis, F. (1975). Migracion de Falconiformes y *Ciconia* spp. por Gibralter. II. Analisis descriptivo del verano-otono. *Ardeola* **21**, 498–594.

Biggs, H. C., Kemp, A. C., Mendelsohn, H. P. and Mendelsohn, J. M. (1979). Weights of southern African raptors and owls. *Durban Mus. Novit.* **12**, 73–81.

Black, R. A. R. and Ross, G. J. B. (1970). Aspects of adaptive radiation in Southern African Accipiters. *Ann. Cape Prov. Mus. (Nat. Hist.)* **8**, 57–65.

Black, H. L., Howard, G. and Stjernstedt, R. (1979). Observations on the feeding behaviour of the Bat Hawk (*Machaerhamphus alcinus*). *Biotropica* **11**, 18–21.

Blondel, J., Coulon, L., Girerd, B. and Hortigue, M. (1969). Deux cents heures d'observation auprès de l'aire de l'Aigle de Bonelli. *Nos Oiseaux* **30**, 37–60.

Boshoff, A. F. and Palmer, N. G. (1980). Macro-analysis of prey remains from Martial Eagle nests in the Cape Province. *Ostrich* **51**, 7–13.

Boswall, J. (1977). Notes on tool-using by Egyptian Vultures *Neophron percnopterus*. *Bull. Br. Orn. Club* **97**, 77–78.

Boudoint, Y. (1953). Etude de la biologie du Circaëte Jean le Blanc. *Alauda* **21**, 86–112.

Boughton-Leigh, P. W. T. (1932). Observations on nesting and breeding habits of birds near Ilorin, Nigeria. *Ibis* **13**(II), 457–470.

Bowles, R. N. (1967). Lesser Spotted Eagle on migration. *J. E. Afr. Nat. Hist. Soc.* **26**, 87.

Broekhuysen, G. J. and Siegfried, W. R. (1971). Dimensions and weight of the Steppe Buzzard in Southern Africa. *Ostrich* Suppl. 9, 31–39.

Brooke, R. K. (1974). *Buteo tachardus* Andrew Smith 1830. *Bull. Br. Orn. Club* **94**, 59–62.

Brooke, R. K. (1975). The taxonomic relationship of *Buteo rufofuscus* and *Buteo augur*. *Bull. Br. Orn. Club* **95**, 152–154.

Brooke, R. K., Grobler, J. H., Irwin, M. P. S. and Steyn, P. (1972). A study of the migratory eagles *Aquila nipalensis* and *A. pomarina* (Aves: Accipitridae) in Southern Africa. *Occ. Pap. Natn. Mus. Sth. Rhod.* **85**(2), 61–144.

Brooke, R. K., Martin, R., Martin, J. and Martin, E. (1980). The Booted Eagle, *Hieraaetus pennatus*, as a breeding species in South Africa. *Gerfaut* **70**, 297–304.

Brosset, A. (1961). Ecologie des oiseaux du Maroc oriental. *Trav. Inst. Sci. chérif. (Zool.)* **22**, 1–55.

Brosset, A. (1969). Le comportement prédateur de l'épervier tropical *Accipiter tousseneli*. *Biol. Gabon.* **5**, 275–282.

Brosset, A. (1971). Premières observations sur la reproduction de six oiseaux Africaines. *Alauda* **39**(2), 112–126.

Brosset, A. (1973). Evolution des *Accipiters* forestiers de l'est du Gabon. *Alauda* **41**, 185–201.

Brown, L. H. (1952). On the biology of the large birds of prey of the Embu District, Kenya Colony. *Ibis* **94**, 577–620.

Brown, L. H. (1953). On the biology of the large birds of prey of the Embu District, Kenya Colony. *Ibis* **95**, 74–114.

Brown, L. H. (1955). Supplementary notes on the biology of the large birds of prey of Embu District, Kenya Colony. *Ibis* **97**, 38–64, 183–221.

Brown, L. H. (1966). Observations on some Kenya Eagles. *Ibis* **108**, 531–572.

Brown, L. H. (1969). A first breeding record for the Southern Banded Snake Eagle *Circaetus fasciolatus* in Kenya. *Ibis* **111**, 391–392.

Brown, L. H. (1970). Recent breeding records for Kenya. *Bull Br. Orn. Club* **90**, 2–6.

Brown, L. H. (1971). The relations of the Crowned Eagle *Stephanoaetus coronatus* and some of its prey animals. *Ibis* **113**, 240–243.

Brown, L. H. (1972a). The breeding behaviour of the African Harrier Hawk *Polyboroides typus* in Kenya. *Ostrich* **43**, 169–175.

Brown, L. H. (1972b). Natural longevity in wild Crowned Eagles *Stephanoaetus coronatus*. *Ibis* **114**, 263–265.

Brown, L. H. (1974a). The races of the European Snake Eagle *Circaetus gallicus*. *Bull. Br. Orn. Club* **94**, 126–128.

Brown, L. H. (1974b). A record of two young reared by Verreaux's Eagle. *Ostrich* **45**, 146.

Brown, L. H. (1974c). Is poor breeding success a reason for the rarity of Ayres' Hawk Eagle? *Ostrich* **45**, 145.

Brown, L. H. (1977). The status, population structure and breeding dates of the African Lammergeier *Gypaetus barbatus meridionalis*. *Raptor Res.* **11**, 49–58.

Brown, L. H. (1980). 'The African Fish Eagle'. Purnell, Cape Town.

Brown, L. H. and Amadon, D. (1968). 'Eagles, Hawks and Falcons of the World'. Vols 1, 2. Hamlyn, Middlesex.

Brown, L. H. and Brown, B. E. (1979). The behaviour of the Black Sparrowhawk *Accipiter melanoleucus*. *Ardea* **67**, 77–95.

Brown, L. H. and Bursell, G. (1968). A first breeding record of the Cuckoo Falcon in Kenya. *J. E. Afr. Nat. Hist. Soc.* **27**, 49–51.

Brown, L. H. and Cade, T. J. (1972). Age classes and population dynamics of the Bateleur and African Fish Eagle. *Ostrich* **43**, 1–16.

Brown, L. H. and Davey, P. R. A. (1978). Natural longevity in Ayres' Eagle. *Bokmakierie* **30**, 27–31.

Brown, L. H. and Hopcraft, J. B. D. (1973). Population structure and dynamics of the African Fish Eagle *Haliaeetus vocifer* at Lake Naivasha, Kenya. *E. Afr. Wildl. J.* **11**, 255–269.

Brown, L. H. and Root, A. (1971). The breeding behaviour of the Lesser Flamingo *Phoeniconaias minor*. *Ibis* **113**, 147–172.

Brown, L. H., Gargett, V. and Steyn, P. (1977). Breeding success in some African eagles related to theories about sibling aggression and its effects. *Ostrich* **48**, 65–71.

Burton, P. J. K. (1978). The inter-tarsal joint of the Harrier Hawks *Polyboroides* spp. and the Crane Hawk *Geranospiza caerulescens*. *Ibis* **120**, 171–177.

Cheylan, G. (1972). The yearly cycle of a pair of Bonelli Eagles *Hieraaetus fasciatus*. *Alauda* **40**, 214–234.

Chittenden, H. N. (1979). The incubation, nestling and postnestling periods of the Lizard Buzzard. *Ostrich* **50**, 186–187.

Cockburn, T. A. (1946). Some birds of the Gold Coast, with

observations on their virus and parasite infections. *Ibis* **88**, 387–394.

Colebrook-Robjent, J. F. R. and Steyn, P. (1975). On the nest and eggs of the Little Sparrowhawk *Accipiter minullus*. *Bull. Br. Orn. Club* **95**, 142–147.

Cooper, J. (1970). Birds of prey and their food: African Marsh Harrier feeding on ad. *Anas erythrorhyncha* which it had apparently killed. *Honeyguide* **64**, 28.

Daneel, A. B. C. (1979). Prey size and hunting methods of the Crowned Eagle. *Ostrich* **50**, 120.

Davey, P. and Davey, G. (1980). Swallow-tailed Kites breeding at Porr, Lake Turkana. *Bull. E. Afr. Nat. Hist. Soc.* **1980**, 47–48.

Donnelly, B. G. (1966). The range of the Booted Eagle, *Aquila pennata* (Gmelin), in Southern Africa with a note on field identification. *Ann. Cape Prov. Mus.* **5**, 109–115.

Dupuy, A. (1972). Le Balbuzard fluviatile, *Pandion haliaetus*, au Sénégal. *Oiseau et R.F.O.* **42**(4), 289–290.

Elgood, J. H., Fry, C. H. and Dowsett, R. J. (1973). African migrants in Nigeria. *Ibis* **115**, 1–45; 375–411.

Evans, P. R. and Lathbury, G. W. (1973). Raptor migration across the Straits of Gibraltar. *Ibis* **115**, 572–585.

Fannin, A. and Webb, D. (1975). Notes on the breeding of the Crowned Eagle. *Honeyguide* **82**, 36.

Fenton, M. B., Cumming, D. H. M. and Oxley, D. J. (1978). Prey of Bat Hawks and availability of bats. *Condor* **79**, 495–497.

Fernandez, J. A. (1975). Consideraciones sobre el regimen alimenticio de *Gyps fulvus*. *Ardeola* **21**, 209–217.

Friedmann, H. and Williams, J. G. (1970). The birds of the Kalinzu Forest, Southwestern Ankole, Uganda. *Los Angeles County Mus. Contr. Sci.* **195**, 27 pp.

Friedmann, H. and Williams, J. G. (1971). The birds of the lowlands of Bwamba, Toro Province, Uganda. *Los Angeles County Mus. Contr. Sci.* **211**, 70 pp.

Gargett, V. (1969). A Black Eagle's survival trek. *Bokmakierie* **21**, 78.

Gargett, V. (1970). Black Eagle survey, Rhodes Matopos National Park. A population study 1964–1968. *Ostrich* Suppl. 8, 397–414.

Gargett, V. (1971). Some observations on Black Eagles *Aquila verreauxi* in the Matopos, Rhodesia. *Ostrich* Suppl. 9, 91–124.

Gargett, V. (1972). Black Eagle *Aquila verreauxi* population dynamics. *Ostrich* **43**, 177–178.

Gargett, V. (1975). The spacing of Black Eagles in the Matopos, Rhodesia. *Ostrich* **46**, 1–44.

Gargett, V. (1978). Sibling aggression in the Black Eagle in the Matopos, Rhodesia. *Ostrich* **49**, 57–63.

Garzón, J. (1968). Las rapaces y otras aves de la sierra de Gata. *Ardeola* **14**, 97–130.

Geïlikman, B. O. (1959). Ökologie einiger breitvögel des Chosrowsker Waldes. *Zool. Sborn. Zool. Inst. Akad. Nauk. Armen. SSR.* **11**, 5–64.

Glutz von Blotzheim, U. N., Bauer, K. M. and Bezzel, E. (1971). 'Handbuch der Vögel Mitteleuropas'. Vol. 4. Akademische Verlagsgesellschaft, Frankfurt am Main.

Golodushko, B. Z. (1958). *Trudy Zapoved. Khoz. Belovezh. Pushka* **1**, 100–109.

Goodwin, D. (1949). Notes on migration of birds of prey over Suez. *Ibis* **91**, 59–63.

Hall, D. (1979a). Food of the Longcrested Eagle. *Ostrich* **50**, 256.

Hall, D. (1979b). Records of Longcrested Eagles rearing two young. *Ostrich* **50**, 187.

Hartley, R. (1976). Some notes on the plumage of Black Sparrowhawks. *Bokmakierie* **28**, 61–63.

Heim de Balsac, H. (1954). De l'Oued sous au fleuve Sénégal. Oiseaux reproducteurs. Particularités écologiques, distribution. *Alauda* **22**, 10–205.

Heim de Balsac, H. and Heim de Balsac, T. (1949–50). Les migrations des oiseaux dans l'ouest du Continent africain. *Alauda*, **27–28**, 129–143; 206–221.

Hiraldo, F., Delibes, M. and Calderon, J. (1979). El Quebrantahuesas *Gypaetus barbatus* (L.). Sistemática, taxonomia, biologia, distribucion y proteccion.

Holman, F. C. (1947). Birds of the Gold Coast. *Ibis* **89**, 623–650.

Holstein, V. D. (1942). *Astur gentilis dubius* (Sparrman). *Biol. Stud. Danske Rovfugle* **1**, 129–140.

Houston, D. C. (1974). Food searching in griffon vultures. *E. Afr. Wildl. J.* **12**, 63–77.

Houston, D. C. (1975). The moult of the White-backed and Rüppell's Griffon Vultures *Gyps africanus* and *Gyps rueppellii*. *Ibis* **117**, 474–488.

Houston, D. C. (1976). Breeding of the White-backed Vulture and Rüppell's Griffon Vulture *Gyps africanus* and *Gyps rueppellii*. *Ibis* **118**, 14–40.

Hustler, K. (1976). Notes on the Black Harrier. *Bokmakierie* **28**, 73.

Irribarren, J. J. (1975). Biologiá del Aquila Calzada (*Hieraaetus pennatus*) durante eliperiódo ne nidification en Navarra. *Ardeola* **21**, 305–320.

Jeffrey, R. D. (1977). Three nests of the Cuckoo Falcon in Rhodesia. *Honeyguide* **90**, 33–34.

Jensen, R. A. C. (1972). The Steppe Eagle *Aquila nipalensis* and other termite eating raptors in South West Africa. *Madoqua* **1**, 73–76.

Kemp, A. C. and Kemp, M. I. (1975a). Observations on the White-backed Vulture *Gyps africanus* in the Kruger National Park, South Africa, with notes on other avian scavengers. *Koedoe* **18**, 51–68.

Kemp, A. C. and Kemp, M. I. (1975b). Observations on the breeding biology of the Ovambo Sparrowhawk, *Accipiter ovampensis* Gurney (Aves: Accipitridae). *Ann. Trans. Mus.* **29**, 185–190.

Kemp, A. C. and Kemp, M. I. (1976). Nesting cycle of the Gabar Goshawk. *Ostrich* **47**, 127–129.

Kemp, A. C. and Mendelsohn, J. (1975). What colour is Wahlberg's Eagle? *Bokmakierie* **27**, 72–74.

Kemp, A. C. and Snelling, J. C. (1973). Ecology of the Gabar Goshawk in southern Africa. *Ostrich* **44**, 154–162.

Kruuk, H. (1967). Competition for food between vultures in East Africa. *Ardea* **55**, 172–193.

Laszlo, S. (1939). *Aquila* **46–51**, 247.

Lathbury, G. (1970). A review of the birds of Gibraltar and its surrounding waters. *Ibis* **112**, 25–43.

Laybourne, R. C. (1974). Collision between a vulture and an aircraft at an altitude of 37,000 feet. *Wildl. Bull.* **86**(4), 461–462.

Ledger, J. A. and Annegan, H. J. (1980). Electrocution hazards to the Cape Vulture (*Gyps coprotheres*) in South Africa. *Biol. Conser.*

Lendrum, A. J. (1976). Brown Snake Eagles breeding in the Matopos. *Bokmakierie* **28**, 92–93.

Lendrum, A. J. (1979). The Augur Buzzard in the Matopos, Rhodesia. *Ostrich* **50**, 203–214.

Lévêque, R. (1964). A propos d'un nid provençal du Percnoptère. *Nos Oiseaux* **27**, 329–332.

Liversidge, R. (1962). Breeding biology of the Little Sparrowhawk *Accipiter minullus*. *Ibis* **104**, 399–406.

Lorber, P. (1971). Roosting of Black-breasted Snake Eagles communal roost in June. *Honeyguide* **67**, 32.

MacDonald, M. A. and Taylor, I. R. (1977). Notes on some uncommon forest birds in Ghana. *Bull. Br. Orn. Club* **97**, 116–120.

MacLatchey, A. R. (1937). Contribution à l'étude des oiseaux du Gabon méridional. *Oiseau et R.F.O.* **7**, 71–76.

Mackworth-Praed, C. W. and Grant, C. H. B. (1952). 'Birds of Eastern and North-eastern Africa'. Vol. 1. Longmans, Green and Co., London.

Malherbe, E. (1970). Observations on the breeding of the African Marsh Harrier. Witwatersrand Bird Club News Sheet No. 70, 1–8.

Mares, J.-P. (1978) La reproduction de l'autour des palombes dans la nord-ouestmarocain. *Alauda* **46**, 358–359.

Martin, J. E. and Martin, M. R. (1974). Booted Eagles breeding in the South-Western Cape Province. *Bokmakierie* **26**, 21–22.

Martin, J. E. and Martin, M. R. (1976). Booted Eagles breeding in the Cape Midlands. *Bokmakierie* **28**, 70–74.

Mayaud, N. (1970). Additions et contribution à l'avifaune du nord-ouest de l'Afrique. *Alauda* **38**, 27–43.

Meinertzhagen, R. (1956). Roost of wintering harriers. *Ibis* **98**, 535.

Meyer, F. (1958). Der Rotmilan. *Beitr. Vogelkde* **6**, 203–234.

Moreau, R. E. (1945). On the Bateleur, especially at the nest. *Ibis* **87**, 224–249.

Morel, G.-J. and Poulet, A.-C. (1976). Notes et faits divers. Un important dortoir *d'Elanus caeruleus*, Accipitridae, au Sénégal. *Oiseau et R.F.O.* **46**(4), 429–430.

Morgan, A. D. (1979). Observations on immature fish eagles. *E. Afr. Nat. Hist. Soc. Bull.* **1979**, 65–66.

Mošanský, A. and Danko, S. (1969). Verbreitung und Bionomie des Zwergadlers in den Westkarpaten (Slowakei). *Zool. Listy* **18**, 369–380.

Mundy, P. J. (1978). The Egyptian Vulture *Neophron percnopterus* in southern Africa. *Biol. Conser.* **14**, 307–316.

Mundy, P. J. and Cook, A. W. (1972). Vultures. *Bull. Niger. Orn. Soc.* **9**, 8–9.

Mundy, P. L. and Ledger, J. A. (1975). Notes on the Cape Vulture. *Honeyguide* **83**, 22–28.

Mundy, P. J. and Ledger, J. A. (1976). Griffon vultures, carnivores and bone. *S. Afr. J. Sci.* **72**, 106–110.

Mundy, P. L. and Ledger, J. A. (1977). Cape Vulture Research report for 1976. *Bokmakierie* **29**, 72–75.

Mundy, P. J. and Ledger, J. A. (1978). Cape Vulture recovery data. *Safring News* **7**, 21–31.

Mundy, P. J., Ledger, J. and Friedman, R. (1980). The Cape Vulture Project in 1977 and 1978. *Bokmakierie* **32**, 208.

Murphy, R. C. (1924). The marine ornithology of the Cape Verde Islands. *Bull. Am. Mus. Nat. Hist.* **50**, 211–228.

Newman, K. B. (1978). Raptor and stork migration report. *Bokmakierie* **30**, 61–64.

Newton, I. (1973). Studies of sparrowhawks. *Brit. Birds* **66**, 271–278.

Nieboer, E. (1973). Geographical and ecological differentiation in the genus *Circus*. Ph.D. Thesis, Free University, Amsterdam.

North, M. E. W. (1944). Some East African birds of prey. *Ibis* **86**, 134–137.

Parsons, J. (1977). The effect of predation by fish eagles on the breeding success of various Ciconiiformes nesting near Kisumu, Kenya. *Kenya J. Nat. Hist.* **11**, 337–353.

Pennycuick, C. J. (1971a). Gliding flight of the White-backed Vulture *Gyps africanus*. *J. Exp. Biol.* **55**, 13–38.

Pennycuick, C. J. (1971b). Control of gliding angle in Rüppell's Griffon Vulture *Gyps rueppelli*. *J. Exp. Biol.* **55**, 39–46.

Pennycuick, C. J. (1972). Soaring behaviour and performance of some East African birds observed from a motor glider. *Ibis* **114**, 178–218.

Pennycuick, C. J. (1976). Breeding of the Lappet-faced and White-headed Vultures *Torgos tracheliotus* and *Trigonoceps occipitalis* on Serengeti plains, Tanzania. *E. Afr. Wildl. J.* **14**, 67–84.

Penzhorn, B. (1976). Grootwitvalke, Ratels en jakkalse. *Laniarius* **4**, 18–19.

Perret, A. (1976). The avifauna of Waza National Park, Cameroon in December. *Bull. Niger. Orn. Soc.* **12**, 18–24.

Pineau, J. and Girard-Audine, M. (1974). Notes sur les migrateurs travesant l'extreme nord-ouest du Maroc. *Alauda* **42**, 159–188.

Plug, I. (1978). Collecting patterns of six species of vultures (Aves: Accipitridae). *Ann. Trans. Mus.* **31**, 51–63.

Porter, R. F., Willis, I., Christensen, S. and Nielsen, B. P. (1976). 'Flight Identification of European Raptors'. T. & D. Poyser, Berkhamstead.

Prigogine, A. (1976). Additions à l'avifaune du Zaire. *Gerfaut* **66**, 307–308.

Rivoire, A. and Hüe, F. (1949). L'Aigle de Bonelli *Hieraaetus fasciatus* (Vieillot) 1822. *Oiseau et R.F.O.* **19**(2), 116–149.

Rodriguez-Jiménez, F. L. and Balcélls, R. (1968). Notas biológicas sobre el alimoche en el Alto Aragón. *Publ. Cent. pir. Biol. exp.* **2**, 159–187.

Rowe, E. G. (1947). Breeding biology of *Aquila verreauxi* Lesson. I,II. *Ibis* **89**, 387–410, 576–606.

Rudebeck, G. (1957). 'South African Animal Life', Vol. 4. Almqvist and Wiksell, Stockholm.

Rudebeck, G. (1961). Observations on the Bearded Vulture (*Gypaetus barbatus*) in South Africa, with notes on behaviour and field characters. *In* 'South African Animal Life'. pp. 406–414. Almqvist and Wiksell, Stockholm.

Safriel, U. (1968). Migration at Elat, Israel. *Ibis* **110**, 283–320.

Salvan, J. (1968). Contribution à l'étude des oiseaux du Tchad. *Oiseau et R.F.O.* **38**, 53–85.

Schipper, W. J. A. (1973). A comparison in prey selection in sympatric harriers *Circus* in Western Europe. *Gerfaut* **63**, 17–120.

Schipper, W. J. A. (1977). Hunting in three European harriers (*Circus*) during the breeding season. *Ardea* **65**, 53–72.

Schipper, W. J. A., Buurma, L. S. and Bossenbroek, Pr. (1975). Comparative study of the hunting behaviour of wintering Hen Harriers *Circus cyaneus* and Marsh Harrier *Circus aeruginosus*. *Ardea* **63**, 1–29.

Serle, W. (1943). Further field observations on northern Nigerian birds. *Ibis* **85**, 264–300.

Serle, W. (1950). A contribution to the ornithology of the British Cameroons. *Ibis* **92**, 343–376.

Serle, W. (1954). A second contribution to the ornithology of the British Cameroons. *Ibis* **96**, 47–90.

Siegfried, W. R. (1968). Breeding season, clutch and brood sizes in Verreaux's Eagle *Aquila verreauxii*. *Ostrich* **39**, 139–149.

Siegfried, W. R., Frost, P. G. H., Cooper, J. and Kemp, A. C. (1976). South African Red Data Book—Aves. *S. Afr. Natn Sci. Progr. Rep.* **7**.

Smeenk, C. (1974). Comparative ecological studies of some East African birds of prey. *Ardea* **62**, 1–97.

Smeenk, C. and Smeenk-Enserink, N. (1975). Observations on the Pale Chanting Goshawk *Melierax poliopterus* with comparative notes on the Gabar Goshawk *Micronisus gabar*. *Ardea* **63**, 93–115.

Smeenk, C. and Smeenk-Enserink, N. (1977). Observations on the Shikra *Accipiter badius* in Nigeria. *Ardea* **65**, 148–164.

Snelling, J. C. (1971). Some information obtained from marking large raptors in Kruger National Park, Republic of South Africa. *Ostrich* Suppl. **8**, 415–427.

Steyn, P. (1960). Observations on the African Fish Eagle. *Bokmakierie* **12**, 21–28.

Steyn, P. (1962). Observations on Wahlberg's Eagle. *Bokmakierie* **14**, 7–14.

Steyn, P. (1964). Observations on the Brown Snake Eagle. *Ostrich* **35**, 22–31.

Steyn, P. (1965). Some observations on the Bateleur. *Ostrich* **36**, 203–213.

Steyn, P. (1966). Observations on the Black-breasted Snake Eagle. *Ostrich* Suppl. **6**, 141–154.

Steyn, P. (1972a). African Fish Eagle: a record of breeding success. *Ostrich* **43**, 181–183.

Steyn, P. (1972b). Further observations on the Brown Snake Eagle. *Ostrich* **43**, 149–164.

Steyn, P. (1973). Observations on the Tawny Eagle. *Ostrich* **41**, 1–22.

Steyn, P. (1974). 'Eagle Days'. Purnell, Cape Town.

Steyn, P. (1975). Supplementary notes on the nesting of the Brown Snake Eagle. *Ostrich* **46**, 118.

Steyn, P. (1975). Observations on the African Hawk Eagle. *Ostrich* **46**, 87–105.

Steyn, P. (1978). Observations on the Longcrested Eagle. *Bokmakierie* **30**, 3–10.

Steyn, P. (1980a). Breeding and food of the Bateleur in Zimbabwe (Rhodesia), *Ostrich* **51**, 168–178.

Steyn, P. (1980b). Further observations on the Tawny Eagle. *Ostrich* **51**, 54–55.

Steyn, P. and Barbour, D. Y. (1973). Observations at a Little Banded Goshawk's nest. *Ostrich* **44**, 140–141.

Steyn, P. and Grobler, J. H. (1981). Breeding biology of the Booted Eagle in South Africa. *Ostrich* **52**(2), 108–118.

Stresemann, E. and Amadon, D. (1979). Order Falconiformes. *In* 'Peters Check List of Birds of the World'. Vol. 1, 2nd edn (Mayr, E. and Cottrell, G. W. Eds). Museum of Comparative Zoology, Cambridge, Mass.

Suetens, W. and van Groenendaal, P. (1967). La nidification du Vautour Moine, *Aegypius monachus* (L.). *Gerfaut* **57**, 93–118.

Sulkava, J. (1964). Zur Nährungsbiologie des Habichts *Accipter g. gentilis* (L.). *Aquila* **3**, 1–103.

Tarboton, W. R. (1976). Martial Eagles: an unusual breeding episode. *Bokmakierie* **28**, 29–32.

Tarboton, W. R. (1977). Nesting, territoriality and food habits of Wahlberg's Eagle. *Bokmakierie* **29**, 46–50.

Tarboton, W. R. (1978a). Hunting and energy budget of the Black-shouldered Kite. *Condor* **80**, 88–91.

Tarboton, W. R. (1978b). A survey of birds of prey in the Transvaal. *Transvaal Nat. Cons. Div. Progr. Rep.* TN 6/4/4/9.

Tarboton, W. R. (1978c). Breeding of the Little Banded Goshawk. *Ostrich* **49**, 132–143.

Tarboton, W. R., Lewis, M. and Kemp, A. C. (1978). The status of the Black Sparrowhawk in the Transvaal. *Bokmakierie* **30**, 56–59.

Terrasse, J. F. and Boudoint, Y. (1960). Observations sur la reproduction du Vautour fauve, du Percnoptère et du Gypaëte barbu dans les Basses-Pyrénées. *Alauda* **28**, 241–257.

Thiollay, J. M. (1968). Essai sur les rapaces du midi de la France. Distribution—écologie—tentative de dénombrement. *Alauda* **35**, 140–150.

Thiollay, J.-M. (1972). Le peuplement avien d'uns région de contact savane-forêt en moyenne Côte-d'Ivoire. *Ann. Univ. abidijan, sér. Ecologie* **4**(1), 5–132.

Thiollay, J. M. (1975a). Les rapaces des parcs nationaux de Côte d'Ivoire. Analyse de peuplement. *Oiseaux et R.F.O.* **45**, 241–257.

Thiollay, J. M. (1975b). Les rapaces d'une zone de contact savane-forêt en Côte d'Ivoire. 1. Présentation du peuplement. *Alauda* **43**, 75–102. 2. Densité, dynamique et structure du peuplement. *Alauda* **43**, 387–416.

Thiollay, J. M. (1975c). Migrations de rapaces africaines en Ouganda et au Rwanda. *L'Oiseau et R.F.O.* **45**, 192–194.

Thiollay, J. M. (1976a). Besoins alimentaires quantitatifs de quelques oiseaux tropicaux. *Terre et Vie* **30**, 229–245.

Thiollay, J. M. (1976b). Les rapaces d'une zone de contact savane-forêt en Côte d'Ivoire. 3. Modalités et success de la reproduction. *Alauda* **44**, 275–300.

Thiollay, J. M. (1977a). Les rapaces d'une zone de contact savane-forêt en Côte d'Ivoire. 4. Modes d'exploitation du milieu. *Alauda* **45**, 197–218.

Thiollay, J. M. (1977b). Distribution saisonnière des rapaces diurnes en Afrique occidentale. *Oiseau et R.F.O.* **47**, 253–294.

Thiollay, J. M. (1978a). Les rapaces d'une zone de contact savane-forêt en Côte d'Ivoire. 5. Spécialisations alimentaires. *Alauda* **46**, 147–170.

Thiollay, J. M. (1978b). Les migrations de rapaces en Afrique occidentale: adaptions écologiques aux fluctuations saisonnières de production des écosystèmes. *Terre et Vie* **32**, 89–133.

Thiollay, J. M. and Meyer, J. A. (1978). Densité, taille des territoires, et production dans une population d'Aigles pêcheurs *Haliaeetus vocifer* (Daudin). *Terre et Vie* **32**, 203–219.

Thompson, A. L. and Moreau, R. E. (1957). Feeding habits of the Palm-nut Vulture *Gypohierax*. *Ibis* **99**, 608–613.

Thurow, T. L. and Black, H. L. (1980). Ecology and behaviour of the Gymnogene. *Ostrich* **52**, 25–35.

Tinbergen, L. (1946). De Sperwer als roofvijand van Zangvogels. *Ardea* **34**, 1–213.

Tomkinson, D. J. (1975). Notes on the mass-carrying ability of the African Fish Eagle. *Lammergeyer* **22**, 19–22.

Tuer, F. V. (1973). Notes on the African Hawk Eagle and Wahlberg's Eagle in the Matopos. *Honeyguide* **75**, 19–21.

Tuer, V. and Tuer, J. (1974). Crowned Eagles of the Matopos. *Honeyguide* **80**, 32–39.

Valverde, J. A. (1957). 'Aves del Sahara Español'. Madrid.

Valverde, J. A. (1959). Moyens d'expression et hiérarchie sociale chez le Vautour fauve *Gyps fulvus* (Hablizl). *Alauda* **27**, 1–15.

Van Lawick-Goodall, J. and Van Lawick-Goodall, H. (1966). Use of tools by the Egyptian Vulture *Neophron percnopterus*. *Nature* **212**, 1468–1469.

Van Someren, V. G. L. (1956). Days with birds. *Fieldiana Zool.* **38**.

Vaurie, C. (1961). Systematic notes on Palaearctic birds: 47. Accipitridae: the genus *Buteo*. *Am. Mus. Novit.* **2042**.

Wattel, J. (1973). Geographical differentiation in the genus *Accipiter*. *Publ. Nuttall Orn. Club* 1–231. Cambridge, Massachusetts.

Weaving, A. J. S. (1972). Augur Buzzards. Observations at a nest. *Honeyguide* **70**, 19–20.

Weaving, A. (1977). Observations on a breeding pair of Cuckoo Falcons. *Honeyguide* **90**, 28–31.

Whitfield, A. K. and Blaber, S. J. M. (1978). Feeding ecology of piscivorous birds at Lake St. Lucia, South Africa. Part 1. Diving birds. *Ostrich* **49**, 185–198.

Wilson, R. T. (in press). Environmental changes in Western Darfur, Sudan over half a century and their effects on selected bird species. *Malimbus*.

Young, C. G. (1946). Notes on some birds of the Cameroon Mountain District. *Ibis* **88**, 348–382.

Zimmerman, D. A. (1970). An earlier nesting record of *Circaetus fasciolatus* in Kenya. *Ibis* **112**, 264.

Suborder SAGITTARII

Family SAGITTARIIDAE: Secretary Bird

Biggs, H. C., Kemp, A. C., Mendelsohn, H. P. and Mendelsohn, J. M. (1979). Weights of southern African raptors and owls. *Durban Mus. Novit.* **12**, 73–81.

Brown, L. H. (1955). Supplementary notes on the biology of the large birds of prey of Embu District, Kenya Colony. *Ibis* **97**, 38–64, 183–221.

Glutz von Blotzheim, U. N., Bauer, K. M. and Bezzel, E. (1971). 'Handbuch der Vögel Mitteleuropas', Vol. 4. Akademische Verlagsgesellschaft, Frankfurt am Main.

Kemp, M. I. and Kemp, A. C. (1978). *Bucorvus* and *Sagittarius*: two modes of terrestrial predation. Proc. Symp. Afr. Predatory Birds, pp. 13–16.

Steyn, P. (1959). A peep at the Kalahari. *Bokmakierie* **11**, 11–13.

Stresemann, E. and Amadon, D. (1979). Order Falconiformes. *In* 'Peters Check List of Birds of the World'. Vol. 1, 2nd edn. (Mayr, E. and Cottrell, G. W. Eds). Museum of Comparative Zoology, Cambridge, Mass.

Van Someren, V. G. L. (1956). Days with birds. *Fieldiana Zool.* **38**.

Verheyen, R. (1957). Contribution au démembrement de l'ordo artificiel des Gruiformes (Peters 1934). II. Les Cariamiformes. *Inst. Roy. Sci. Nat. Belgique Bull.* **33**(39).

Suborder FALCONES

Family FALCONIDAE:
pygmy falcons and falcons

Backhurst, G. C. and Pearson, D. J. (1980). Southward migration at Ngulia, Tsavo, Kenya, 1979/80. *Scopus* **4**, 14–20.

Barbour, D. Y. (1971). Notes on the breeding of the Lanner. *Bokmakierie* **23**, 2–5.

Benson, C. W. (1951). A roosting site of the Eastern Red-footed Falcon *Falco amurensis. Ibis* **93**, 467–468.

Biggs, H. C., Kemp, A. C., Mendelsohn, H. P. and Mendelsohn, J. M. (1979). Weights of southern African raptors and owls. *Durban Mus. Novit.* **12**, 73–81.

Blondel, J. (1964). Notes sur la biologie et le régime alimentaire du Faucon crécerellette. *Nos Oiseaux* **28**, 294–298.

Booth, B. D. McD. (1961). Breeding of the Sooty Falcon in the Libyan Desert. *Ibis* **103a**, 129–130.

Brown, L. H. (1976). 'British Birds of Prey'. Collins, London.

Brown, L. H. and Amadon, D. (1968). 'Eagles, Hawks and Falcons of the World'. Vols 1, 2. Hamlyn, Middlesex.

Cavé, A. J. (1968). The breeding of the Kestrel, *Falco tinnunculus* L., in the reclaimed area Oostelijk Flevoland. *Ned. J. Zool.* **18**, 313–407.

Clapham, C. S. (1964). The birds of the Dahlac Archipelago. *Ibis* **106**, 376–388.

Colebrook-Robjent, J. F. R. (1977). The eggs of the Teita Falcon *Falco fasciinucha. Bull Br. Orn. Club* **97**, 44–46.

Colebrook-Robjent, J. F. R. and Osborne, T. O. (1974). High density breeding of the Red-necked Falcon *Falco chiquera* in Zambia. *Bull. Br. Orn. Club* **94**, 172–176.

Colebrook-Robjent, J. F. R. and Tanner, I. C. (1978). Observations at a Dickinson's Kestrel nest in Zambia. *Proc. Symp. Afr. Predatory Birds* 62–70.

Condy, J. B. (1973). Peregrine Falcons in Rhodesia. *Honeyguide* **75**, 11–14.

Cook, G. (1971). Nest record of Dickinson's Kestrel. *Honeyguide* **68**, 33–34.

Dalling, J. (1975). Lanners in central Salisbury. *Honeyguide* **84**, 23–26.

Forbes-Watson, N. M. (1963). Breeding of the African Hobby *Falco cuvieri. J. E. Afr. Nat. Hist. Soc.* **24**, 74.

Fry, C. H. (1964). Red-necked Kestrel *Falco chiquera* hunting bats. *Bull. Niger. Orn. Soc.* **1**(4), 19.

Glutz von Blotzheim, U. N., Bauer, K. M. and Bezzel, E. (1971). 'Handbuch der Vögel Mitteleuropas'. Vol. 4. Akademische Verlagsgesellschaft, Frankfurt am Main.

Goslow, G. E. (1971). The attack and strike of some North American raptors. *Auk* **88**, 815–827.

Hunt, C. (1978). Observations on the Greater Kestrel. *Bokmakierie* **30**, 35.

Hunter, N. D., Douglas, M. G., Stead, D. E., Taylor, V. A., Alder, J. R. and Carter, A. T. (1979). A breeding record and some observations of the Teita Falcon *Falco fasciinucha* in Malawi. *Ibis* **121**, 93–94.

Jany, E. (1960). An Brutplätzen des Lannerfalken (*Falco biarmicus erlangeri* Kleinschmidt) in einer Kieswuste der inneren Sahara (Nordrand des Serir Tibesti) zur Zeit des Frühjahrszugs. Proc. XII Int. Orn. Congr. Helsinki, 1958. pp. 343–352.

Kemp, A. C. (1975). The development of a Lanner Falcon chick, *Falco biarmicus* Temminck (Aves: Falconidae). *Ann. Trans. Mus.* **39**, 191–197.

Kemp, A. C. (1978). Territory maintenance and use by breeding Greater Kestrels. Proc. Symp. Afr. Predatory Birds, pp. 71–76.

Lack, P. C. (1976). The status of the Teita Falcon. *Bull. E. Afr. Nat. Hist. Soc.* Sept/Oct. **1976**, 103–104.

Loosemore, E. (1963). Grey Kestrel in Tanganyika. *J. E. Afr. Nat. Hist. Soc. and Coryndon Mus.* **24**, 67–70.

Maclean, G. L. (1970). The Pygmy Falcon *Polihierax semitorquatus. Koedoe* **13**, 1–21.

Mayaud, N. (1957). La migration 'en boucle' du Faucon kobez *Falco vespertinus* L. en Afrique du Nord et Méditeranée. *Alauda* **25**, 24–29.

Meinertzhagen, R. (1954). 'Birds of Arabia'. Oliver and Boyd, Edinburgh.

Monneret, R.-J. (1973a). Etude d'une population de Faucons pèlerins dans une région de l'Este de la France. Analyse des causes possibles de régression. *Alauda* **41**, 121–128.

Monneret, R.-J. (1973b). Techniques de chasse du Faucon pelerin *Falco peregrinus* dans une region de moyenne montague. *Alauda* **41**(4), 403–412.

Payn, W. H. (1948). Notes from Tunisia and Eastern Algeria: February 1943 to April 1944. *Ibis* **90**, 1–21.

Piechocki, R. (1959). 'Der Turmfalke (*Falco tinnunculus*)'. Die Neue Brehm-Bücherei, No. 116, 71 pp.

Porter, R. F., Willis, L., Christensen, S. and Nielsen, B. P. (1976). 'Flight Identification of European Raptors'. T. and A. D. Poyser, Berkhamsted.

Pounds, H. E. (1948). Wing-drumming of Hobby. *British Birds* **41**, 153–154.

Ripley, S. D. and Heinrich, G. H. (1966). Comments on the avifauna of Tanzania 1. *Postilla* **96**, 45.

Ristow, D. (1975). Neue Ringfunde vom Eleonorenfalken (*Falco eleanorae*). *Vogelwarte* **28**, 150–153.

Rudebeck, G. (1950). The choice of prey and modes of hunting predatory birds with special reference to their selective effect. *Oikos* **2**, 65–88.

Rudebeck, G. (1963). 'South African Animal Life'. Vol. 9. Swedish Natural Sciences Research Council, Stockholm.

Schuyl, G., Tinbergen, L. and Tinbergen, N. (1936). Ethologische Beobachtungen am Baumfalken (*Falco s. subbuteo* L.). *J. Orn.* **84**, 387–433.

Serle, W. (1943). Further field observations on northern Nigerian birds. *Ibis* **85**, 264–300.

Siegfried, W. R. and Skead, D. M. (1971). Status of the Lesser Kestrel in South Africa. *Ostrich* **42**, 1–4.

Sinclair, J. C. and Walters, B. (1976). Lanner Falcons breed in Durban. *Bokmakierie* **28**, 51, 52.

Stanford, J. K. (1954). A survey of the ornithology of northern Libya. *Ibis* **96**, 449–473, 606–624.

Smith, K. D. (1968). Spring migration through southeast Morocco. *Ibis* **110**, 452–492.

Starck, D. and Barnikol, A. (1954). *Morpriol. Jahrb.* **94**, 1–64.

Steyn, P. (1965). A note on the breeding of the African Hobby *Falco cuvieri* Smith. *Ostrich* **36**, 29–31.

Stresemann, E. and Amadon, D. (1979). Order Falconiformes. *In* 'Peters Check List of Birds of the World', Vol. 1, 2nd edn (Mayr, E. and Cotrell, G. W. Eds) Museum of Comparative Zoology, Cambridge, Mass.

Tarboton, W. R. (1978). A survey of birds of prey in the Transvaal. *Transvaal Nat. Cons. Div. Progr. Rep.* TN 6/4/4/9.

Terrasse, J. F. (1963). A propos de deux reprises de *Falco eleanorae*. *Oiseau et R.F.O.* **33**, 56–60.

Tinbergen, N. (1932). Beobachtungen am Baumfalken (*Falco s. subbuteo*). *J. Orn.* **80**, 40–50.

Thiollay, J.-F. (1968). Essai sur les rapaces du midi de la France. Distribution—écologie—tentative de dénombrement *Alauda* **36**(1–2), 52–62.

Thiollay, J. M. (1975a). Les rapaces d'une zone de contact savane-forêt en Côte d'Ivoire. 1. Présentation du peuplement. *Alauda* **43**, 75–102. 2. Densité, dynamique et structure du peuplement. *Alauda* **43**, 387–416.

Thiollay, J. M. (1975b). Les rapaces des parcs nationaux de Côte d'Ivoire. Analyse de peuplement. *Oiseaux et R.F.O.* **45**, 241–257.

Thiollay, J. M. (1976a). Besoins alimentaires quantitatifs de quelques oiseaux tropicaux. *Terre et Vie* **30**, 229–245.

Thiollay, J. M. (1976b). Les rapaces d'une zone de contact savane-forêt en Côte d'Ivoire. 3. Modalités et succès de la reproduction. *Alauda* **44**, 275–300.

Thiollay, J. M. (1977a). Les rapaces d'une zone de contact savane-forêt en Côte d'Ivoire. 4. Modes d'exploitation du milieu. *Alauda* **45**, 197–218.

Thiollay, J. M. (1977b). Distribution saisonnière des rapaces diurnes en Afrique occidentale. *Oiseau et R.F.O.* **47**, 253–294.

Thiollay, J. M. (1978). Les rapaces d'une zone de contact savane-forêt en Côte d'Ivoire. 5. Spécialisations alimentaires. *Alauda* **46**, 147–170.

Vaughan, R. (1961). *Falco eleanorae*. *Ibis* **103a**, 114–128.

Vaurie, C. (1965). Systematic notes on Palaearctic birds. No. 44. Falconidae: the genus *Falco* (Part 1, *Falco peregrinus* and *Falco pelegrinoides*). *Am. Mus. Novit.* **2035**.

Von Heuglin, M. T. (1869). 'Ornithologie Nordost-Afrikas'. T. Fischer, Cassel.

Voous, K. H. (1977). List of recent Holarctic bird species. *Ibis* **119**, 376–406.

Walter, H. (1979). 'Eleonora's Falcon. Adaptations to Prey and Habitat in a Social Raptor'. University of Chicago Press, Chicago.

White, C. M. N. (1945). The ornithology of the Kaonda-Lunda Province, Northern Rhodesia—Part II. Systematic list. *Ibis* **87**, 185–202.

3. Sources of Sound Recordings

The numbers given in the text under Voice refer to these names and sources which, unless otherwise stated, are listed in Chappuis (1980) and are available at the British Library of Wildlife Sounds (BLOWS). There may be other sources unknown to us.

1a. BBC Natural History Recording Library.

1b. Bell, F. (*In* Boswall, J. H. P. and North M. E. W. (1976). A discography of bird sound from the Ethiopian zoogeographical region. *Ibis* **109**(4), 521–533.

1c. Berry, H. H. (1976). Physiological and behavioural ecology of the Cape Cormorant *Phalacrocorax capensis*. *Madoqua* **9**(4), 5–55.

1d. Boswall, J. (1963). Additional voice recordings of the Anatidae. Wildfowl Trust 14th Annual Report, pp. 137–140.

1e. Brunel, J.

2a. Chappuis, C.

2b. Cowles, R. (*In* Boswall and North (1976). See 1b.)

3a. Despin, B.

3b. Downey, S. P. (*In* Boswall and North (1976). See 1b.)

4. Erard, C.

5. Farkas, T.

6. Fitzpatrick Bird Communications Library (available through the Transvaal Museum, Pretoria, South Africa).

7. Gill, F.

8. Gregory, A. R.

9. Grimes, L.

10. Guttinger, H. R.

11. Horne, J. (available through the National Museum, Nairobi, Kenya).

12. Johnson, E. D. H.

13. Jouventin, P.

14. Keith, S.

15. le Maho, Y.

16. Margoschis, R.

17. MacChesney, D. (available through the Library of Natural Sounds, Laboratory of Ornithology, Cornell University).

18. MacVicker, R.

19. M. E. W. North (available through J. Horne).

20a. Payne, R. B.

20b. Queeny, E. M. (*In* Boswall and North (1976). *See* 1b.)

20c. Roché, J. C.

21a. Sellar, P. J.

21b. Smithers, R. H. N. (private collection).

21c. Stannard, J.

22a. Stjernstedt, R.

22b. Sveriges Radio, Stockholm, Sweden.

23. Tollu, B.

24. Vieillard, J.

25. Voisin, J. F.

26. Walker, A.

27. Watts, D. E.

28. Zimmermann, D. and M.

29. Zino, A.

30. Library of Natural Sounds (*see* 17).

INDEXES

Bold page numbers indicate the main species account for a bird; italic, the relevant plate illustration.

Scientific Names

509

English Names

French Names

A

B

C

D

E

F

G